WORDS AND PHRASES
legally defined

Volume 4: R–Z

WORDS AND PHRASES
legally defined

THIRD EDITION

under the General Editorship of
John B Saunders
of Lincoln's Inn, Barrister

Volume 4: R–Z

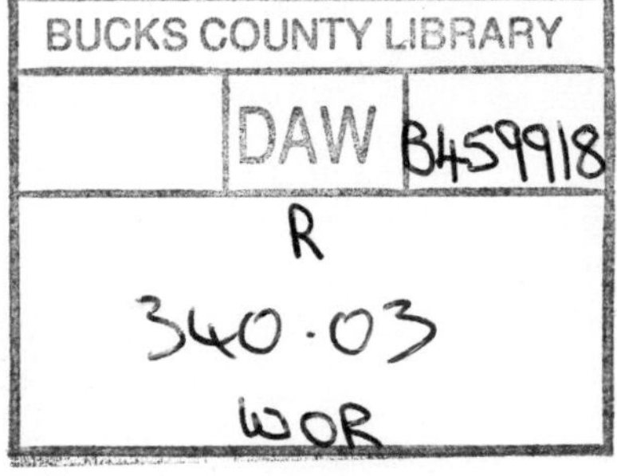

London
Butterworths
1990

United Kingdom	Butterworth & Co (Publishers) Ltd, 88 Kingsway, LONDON WC2B 6AB and 4 Hill Street, EDINBURGH EH2 3JZ
Australia	Butterworths Pty Ltd, SYDNEY, MELBOURNE, BRISBANE, ADELAIDE, PERTH, CANBERRA and HOBART
Canada	Butterworths Canada Ltd, TORONTO and VANCOUVER
Ireland	Butterworth (Ireland) Ltd, DUBLIN
New Zealand	Butterworths of New Zealand Ltd, WELLINGTON and AUCKLAND
Puerto Rico	Equity de Puerto Rico Inc, HATO REY
Singapore	Malayan Law Journal Pte Ltd, SINGAPORE
USA	Butterworth Legal Publishers, AUSTIN, Texas; BOSTON, Massachusetts; CLEARWATER, Florida (D & S Publishers); ORFORD, New Hampshire (Equity Publishing); ST PAUL, Minnesota; and SEATTLE, Washington

First published 1990

British Library Cataloguing in Publication Data

Words and phrases legally defined.—3rd ed/edited by John B Saunders
1. Commonwealth countries. Common law countries. Law—Encyclopaedias
I., Saunders, John B (John Beecroft), *1911—*
342.009171′241

ISBN 0 406 08040 2 (set)
0 406 08041 0 (vol 1)
0 406 08042 9 (vol 2)
0 406 08043 7 (vol 3)
0 406 08044 5 (vol 4)

Typeset by Phoenix Photosetting, Chatham, Kent
Printed and bound in Great Britain by
Mackays of Chatham PLC, Chatham, Kent

OVERSEAS REVISING EDITORS

Australia
Arthur E Garcia LLB(NSW), LLM(Syd)

Canada
Heather Probert LLB
of the Ontario Bar

New Zealand
Hellen Papadopoulos LLB
Barrister and Solicitor of the High Court of New Zealand

USA
Michael G Walsh
Assistant Professor in Business Law at the College of Commerce and Finance, Villanova University, Villanova, Pennsylvania

EDITORIAL MANAGER

Margaret Cherry LLB

The United Kingdom material in this volume states the law as at 30 November 1989. Material from jurisdictions outside the United Kingdom is up-to-date to 30 September 1989.

R

RACE *See also* DOG RACE; HORSE RACE

'One person running alone against time may be properly called a foot-race, as well as one horse starting alone to be a horse-race which has often been the case.' *Lynall v Longbothom* (1756) 2 Wils 36 at 38, per Bathurst J

Canada [A condition in an insurance policy provided that the insured should not drive or operate the insured automobile in any 'race' or speed test.] 'I have been referred to various definitions of the word "race" and am prepared to accept that appearing in the Shorter Oxford Dictionary, namely, that it is a "contest of speed". Coming within such a definition any contest that has been pre-arranged or is for a bet or wager is clearly a race. I am also of the opinion, however, that there may be what can be called contests of speed for short periods on our highways which do not constitute a race as where two vehicles vie to get away first from a stopped position at a stop light. . . . The evidence narrows down to this that for a distance of 200 feet or more during which time the witness . . . had them in view, these vehicles were travelling abreast. This action by the respective drivers for that distance did not, in my opinion, constitute a race particularly in the absence of any evidence as to excessive speed.' *Gore Mutual Insce Co v Rossignoli* [1964] 2 OR 274 at 276, 277, Ont CA, per McGillivray JA

Canada [The statutory conditions of automobile insurance precluded coverage for 'race' or speed test.] 'A chase, according to the Oxford English Dictionary is, among other things, the action of chasing, that is, of pursuing with a view to catching, while a race is the act of running, riding, sailing, etc, in competition with one or more rivals, a contest of speed. On the application of those meanings, it seems obvious that while a chase and a race may on occasion share certain physical similarities, the object is vastly different in each case and it cannot therefore properly be said that by implication or otherwise the word "chase" includes the elements of a test between rivals that is inherent in the word "race" or that they are synonymous.' *McDougal v Wawanesa Mutual Insurance Co* (1969) 2 DLR (3d) 721 at 725, BCSC, per Verchere, J

RACE MEETING *See* MEETING

RACIAL GROUP

'Racial group' means a group of persons defined by reference to colour, race, nationality or ethnic or national origins, and references to a person's racial group refer to any racial group into which he falls. (Race Relations Act 1976, s 3(1))

RACKRENT *See also* RENT

'Rackrent', in relation to property means a rent that is not less than two-thirds of the rent at which the property might reasonably be expected to let from year to year, free from all usual tenants rates and taxes, and deducting from it the probable average annual cost of the repairs, insurance and other expenses (if any) necessary to maintain the property in a state to command such rent. (Building Act 1984, s 126)

'A rack rent in legal language means a rent that represents the full annual value of the holding. The fact that in addition to the rent reserved a substantial premium has been paid by the tenant is clear evidence that the rent is not a rack rent.' *Ex p Connolly to Sheridan & Russell* [1900] 1 IR 1 at 6, per Holmes LJ

'Section 9(4) of the Housing Act 1936 [repealed; see now the Housing Act 1985, s 207] provides that for the purposes there relevant "the person who receives the rackrent of a house . . . or who would so receive it if the house were let at a rackrent, shall be deemed to be the person having control of the house". The term "rackrent" was defined in Blackstone's Commentaries, 4th ed, vol 2, p 43, as "a rent of the full value of the tenement, or near it". Swinfen Eady LJ described it in *Gundry v Dunham* [85 LJKB

422] as "the value at which the premises are worth to be let by the year in the open market—that is to say, what a tenant, taking one year with another, may fairly and reasonably be expected and required to pay".' *Rawlance v Croydon Corpn* [1952] 2 All ER 535 at 543, CA

[*See also* the Highways Act 1980, s 329(1).]

RADIATION HAZARDS

In this Act . . . 'radiation hazards' means the dangers of ionising radiations emitted by radioactive substances or other sources. (Radiological Protection Act 1970, s 1(4))

RADIOACTIVE MATERIAL

'Radioactive material' means a substance produced by a process of nuclear fission or by any other process whereby a substance is subjected to bombardment by neutrons or is otherwise subjected to ionising radiations. (Electricity (Amendment) Act 1961, s 1)

RADIUS

[The appellant was charged that he, on a certain date, being the proprietor of a motor vehicle, unlawfully used motor fuel for a journey outside a particular 'radius' under an order (now revoked) relating to the use of such fuel.] 'There is here no context which suggests any special meaning and no evidence was given that the word "radius" has any special meaning in the motor trade. The word, therefore, should here receive its natural meaning, and in that sense it imputes a circle, so that what is permitted by the Order is a journey within a circle of 15 miles radius having its centre at the place where the vehicle is normally kept. The justices were mistaken in accepting the contentions of the respondent that, the object of the Order being the saving of fuel, the word "radius" was used with an unusual meaning and must be construed as 15 miles by road.' *Langley v Wilson* [1943] 2 All ER 213 at 214, DC, per Lord Caldecote LCJ

RAFFLE

Australia 'The word "raffle" is a well-known word in popular use, and as popularly used it denotes, I think, a scheme under which some article is disposed of by selling to a number of persons for a fraction of its value a chance of obtaining it, and then determining by lot the person who is to have it. According to the common method, numbered tickets are sold, the number of all the tickets sold are placed in a container from which a number is drawn and the purchaser of the ticket bearing that number is the winner of the article. Two or three or more articles may, of course, be disposed of under the one scheme. . . . The difficulty which I feel myself in assigning a precise logical *differentia* to distinguish a raffle from any other form of lottery . . . arises partly, at any rate, from the variety of schemes which may be comprehended by the expression "by lot". But it is not without significance that the word "raffle" is in common use not only as a noun but as a transitive verb, and I think that the essential feature of a raffle is that it involves a disposal of an article as distinct from a competition for a money stake provided by the entrants'. *Forge v Mays* [1946] VLR 423 at 426, per Fullagar J

RAG FLOCK

'Rag flock' means flock which has been produced wholly or partly by tearing up spun or woven or knitted or felted materials, whether old or new, but does not include flock obtained wholly in the processes of the scouring, milling or finishing of newly woven or newly knitted or newly felted fabrics. (Rag Flock and Other Filling Materials Act 1951, s 35)

RAILWAY

'Railway' means any railway used for the purposes of public traffic whether passenger, goods, or other traffic, and includes any works of the railway company connected with the railway. (Railway Employment (Prevention of Accidents) Acts 1900, s 16)

'Railway' includes a light railway other than one which is of the nature of a tramway, that is to say, laid mainly or exclusively along a highway and used mainly or exclusively for the carriage of passengers. (Public Utilities Street Works Act 1950, s 39)

'Independent railway undertaking' means a railway undertaking not forming part of the undertaking of any of the Boards, being an undertaking the carrying on of which is authorised by, or by an order made under, an Act of Parliament. (Transport Act 1962, s 52)

'Railway' does not include—
(a) a light railway laid wholly or mainly along a public carriageway and used wholly or mainly for the carriage of passengers, or
(b) a railway which, under the statutory provisions relating thereto, is to be treated as forming part of a tramway, or
(c) a railway laid wholly or mainly over a beach or wholly along a pier, or
(d) a railway of the nature of a lift providing communication between the top and bottom of a cliff.
(Transport Act 1962, s 52)

'The question is, whether the sidings and turntables come within the meaning of the proviso [to a section of a local Act] as "land used only as a railway". Does the proviso mean land occupied by the rails only on which goods and passengers are carried from place to place; or does it include land used for the purpose of turning carriages from one line to another, by sidings and turntables? I think that it includes both descriptions of land.' *Midland Rly Co v Birmingham Corpn* (1865) 13 LT 404 at 405, per Shee J

Canada 'The question is what is meant by the "railway tracks" for which rails are to be admitted free. . . . The appellants . . . are the owners of what the legislature of their own province calls a single or double track street railway, and the line which they work is called a railway track. These expressions are not conclusive as to the meaning of the term as used by the Dominion Legislature in the Act under discussion [Ontario Street Railway Act 1887]. But they shew that the term is known to draftsmen of statutes in Canada, and is there applied to such a line as that of the appellants. It seems to their Lordships to be good evidence as to the meaning of the term in the mouth of a Canadian Legislature, and to afford prima facie ground for holding that "railway track" includes a line of street railway.' *Toronto Rly Co v R* [1896] AC 551 at 556, PC, per Hobhouse.

Canada [Insurance coverage depended on no railway passing within a specified distance of the insured property.] 'The contention put forward by the plaintiffs in their pleadings and at the trial was that the word "railway" in the warranty necessarily means only a completed railway authorised to be operated for general public traffic, and does not include such a railway as the International Railway here in question which was at the time of the issuance of the policy and also when the fire occurred a railway in course of construction only, and not open for general public traffic. I cannot accept this contention. Although the International Railway Company only began to operate with respect to general *public traffic* a short time after the fire, it had been in operation for all construction purposes and *for freight traffic* for some length of time before the policy issued.' *Guimond v Fidelity-Phenix Fire Insurance Co* (1912) 47 SCR 216 at 220, 221, SCC, per Davies J

Canada 'Now the word "railway" imports locomotion on or over "rails" furnishing a service within fixed and rigid limits: and precise language would be necessary to bring within its scope transportation operations by means of power and vehicles unknown when the legislation was firest enacted, with a service of a high mobile character and involving different considerations of public policy.' *Quebec Railway Light & Power Co v Town of Beauport* [1945] SCR 16 at 40, SCC, per Rand J

Railway company

'Railway company' means any person or body of persons, corporate or unincorporate, being the owner or lessee or owners or lessees of or working any railway worked by steam or otherwise than by animal power in the United Kingdom, constructed or carried on under the powers of any Act of Parliament and used for public traffic, and every building, station, wharf, dock, and place which belong to or are under the control of a railway company, are in the other portions of this Act included in the expression 'railway'. (Explosives Act 1875, s 108)

Railway premises

In this Act 'railway premises' means a building occupied by railway undertakers for the purposes of the railway undertaking carried on by them and situate in the immediate vicinity of the permanent way or a part (so occupied) of a building so situate, but does not include—
(a) office or shop premises;
(b) premises used for the provision of living accommodation for persons employed in the undertaking, or hotels; or
(c) premises wherein are carried on such processes or operations as are mentioned in s 123(1) (electrical stations) of the Factories Act 1961 and for such supply as is therein mentioned.
(Offices, Shops and Railway Premises Act 1963, s 1)

Railway station

'The terms "railway" and "railway station" are not mere legal terms; they are the descriptions in ordinary phraseology of well-understood things of an ordinary kind. . . . As to a "station" the term is not in ordinary sense used as a description merely of the actual existing structures at a station; but as the description of a space actually set apart for, and generally used as, a resting-place for traffic, or a place for dealing with it in a particular way, although every part of the space is not covered with structures or used for passing along or for deposit.' *South Eastern Rly Co v Railway Comrs* (1881) 50 LJQB 201 at 211, CA, per Brett LJ

RAINFALL

'Rainfall' includes any fall of snow, hail or sleet. (Water Resources Act 1963, s 135)

RAISE *See also* ARISE

[The Railways Act 1921, s 58(1)(b) (repealed) enacted that the charges to be fixed for an amalgamated company should be such as would yield a certain revenue, and in addition (inter alia) such allowance as might be necessary to remunerate adequately any additional capital which might have been 'raised' or provided in respect of expenditure on capital account, etc.] 'There is no difficulty about the meaning of the word "raised". Capital is "raised" when it is offered to and subscribed for by the public.' *Re Standard Charges Schedule* (1925) 94 LJKB 364 at 367, CA, per Pollock MR

[The Factories Act 1961, s 26(1) makes provisions with regard to every chain, rope or lifting tackle used for the purpose of "raising" or lowering persons, goods or materials.] 'It is perhaps not without interest and not without relevance to the construction of the section, which uses the words "lifting tackle" and "raising", that in common parlance anyone would refer to the operation on which the plaintiff was engaged as raising or lifting. It was not only raising or only lifting or only hoisting, of course. There was going to be only a slight lift in order to enable the plaintiff to get something underneath the scab [hardened metal overspill from a furnace]. Though I do not place too much reliance on this, it is not uninteresting to observe that counsel for the defendants, in the course of his cross-examination of the plaintiff, in many instances used the word "lifting", and . . . the crane driver, in describing what he was doing on the instructions of the plaintiff, uses both "raise" and "lift". Moreover in the pleaded defence of the defendants, they use, what is perhaps another synonym, the word "hoisted". It is, as I have said, a point within a very small compass; but I have come to the conclusion without any sort of doubt whatever that this was an operation of raising. If I might put it perhaps in a frivolous way for a moment, it seems to me that in effect what the defendants are saying here is that: "It is a raising or a lifting: but it is only a little one." But the operation appears to me to fall four square within the term "raising".' *Ball v Richard Thomas and Baldwins Ltd* [1968] 1 All ER 389 at 394, CA, per Davies LJ

Raising portions

[The Accumulations Act 1800, s 2 (repealed; see now the Law of Property Act 1925, s 164(2)) enacted that nothing in the Act should extend to any provision for 'raising' portions for any child or children of any grantor, settlor, or devisor, or to any child or children of any person taking any interest under any such conveyance, settlement, or devise.] 'The question which I have to determine is whether this direction for accumulation after the widow's death and during the lifetime of the daughter is a provision for "raising" a portion for the grandchild within the meaning of the proviso in s 2. . . . The phrase "raising portions" in itself suggests . . . raising a fund out of a larger fund.' *Re Elliott, Public Trustee v Pinder* [1918] 2 Ch 150 at 153, 154, 157, per Sargant J

'The relevant section of the Law of Property Act 1925, is s 164. . . . The words of sub-s (2) on which counsel for the beneficiaries relies are these: "This section does not extend to any provision . . . (ii) for raising portions for (a) any child, children or remoter issue of any grantor, settlor or testator." That language has been criticised as not being very clear, but it has to a certain extent been clarified by judicial decision. The section does not say: "Any provision for the benefit of any child." Something more must be found before the exception operates. The provision must be one "for raising portions". The phrase "raising portions" is a technical phrase in conveyancing. A more accurate way to express the intention of the legislature might possibly have been to use the phrase "for creating portions".'

Re Bourne's Settlement Trusts, Bourne v Mackay [1946] 1 All ER 411 at 414, CA, per Lord Greene MR

RANSOM

Ransom is a contract entered into between the captors and the commander of a captured ship, by which the captors permit the captured ship to proceed under safe conduct in consideration of a sum of money paid or promised by the commander in his own name and that of the owners of the captured ship. The practice of payment of ransom is largely obsolete and is prohibited by law in many countries. (37 Halsbury's Laws (4th edn) para 1341)

'The word "ransom" is synonymous with "redeem".' *Havelock v Rockwood* (1799) 8 Term Rep 268 at 276, per Lord Kenyon CJ

RAPE *See also* CONSENT

For the purposes of section 1 of the Sexual Offences Act 1956 (which relates to rape) a man commits rape if—

(a) he has unlawful sexual intercourse with a woman who at the time of the intercourse does not consent to it; and
(b) at the time he knows that she does not consent to the intercourse or he is reckless as to whether she consents to it;

and references to rape in other enactments . . . shall be construed accordingly. (Sexual Offences (Amendment) Act 1976, s 1(1))

'Rape is unlawful carnal knowledge of a woman without her consent by force, fear or fraud, and it is an essential ingredient of that particular offence that it must be without the woman's consent.' *R v Miller* [1954] 2 All ER 520 at 530, per Lynskey J

'Rape is not a word in the use of which lawyers have a monopoly and the question to be answered in this case, as I see it, is whether according to the ordinary use of the English language a man can be said to have committed rape if he believed that the woman was consenting to the intercourse and would not have attempted to have it but for his belief, whatever his grounds for so believing. I do not think that he can. Rape, to my mind, imports at least indifference as to the woman's consent.' *Director of Public Prosecutions v Morgan* [1975] 2 All ER 347 at 352, HL, per Lord Cross of Chelsea

RASH

Rash and hazardous speculation

'All commerce is, in its nature, in some degree speculative, and speculation is hazardous. The offence in the 159th section [of the Bankruptcy Act 1861 (repealed; see now the Insolvency Act 1986, s 362(1))] cannot consist merely of "hazardous speculation". It is obvious that "rash speculation" is of the essence of the case.' *Re Heyn, ex p Heyn* (1867) 2 Ch App 650 at 653, per Rolt LJ

'The argument here comes to this, that the section [Bankruptcy Act 1883, s 28 (repealed; see now the Insolvency Act 1986, s 362(1))] is only applicable to rash and hazardous speculation in trade. It is admitted that speculations on the Stock Exchange would come within the words. It is clear also that gambling, whether at gambling-houses or elsewhere, and betting are rash and hazardous speculations. The Bankruptcy Act applies to non-traders as well as to traders, and the section refers to speculations generally.' *Re Barlow, ex p Thornber* (1886) 3 TLR 218 at 218, CA, per Lord Esher MR

'There is the question whether, if it be a speculation, was it rash and hazardous [within the Bankruptcy Act 1890, s 8(3) (repealed; see now the Insolvency Act 1986, s 362(1))]? Without attempting to define exhaustively what is a rash and hazardous speculation, I may say that in my opinion a speculation which no reasonably careful man would enter into having regard to all the circumstances of the case is a rash and hazardous speculation.' *Re Keays, ex p Keays* (1891) 9 Morr 18 at 23, CA, per Lopes LJ

'The county court judge bases his decision upon the ground that it is more risky and more hazardous to buy for a client who is intending to pay or receive the differences, as the case may be, than it is to buy for a client who is intending to take up the shares and pay for them. I cannot see how that can be made out. Whether it is risky at all depends entirely upon whether the client has the means to pay the difference which may be expected to result or has not. . . . I think he [the bankrupt] has not sufficiently explained the fact that he entered into transactions which might not unnaturally eventuate in his becoming liable for a sum larger than he was able to pay; and when a man does enter into a transaction which may have such a result as that, it seems to me that he is indulging in a rash and hazardous speculation [within the Bankruptcy Act 1883, s 28 (repealed; see supra)].' *Re Jenkins, ex p Jenkins* (1891) 39 WR 430 at 431, DC, per Cave J

RATE

[Domestic rates have been abolished in Scotland, with effect from the financial year beginning 1 April 1988, have been replaced by a system of community charges: see the Abolition of Domestic Rates etc (Scotland) Act 1987. Similar provisions will come into force in England and Wales from the financial year beginning 1 April 1990: see the Local Government Finance Act 1988. Non-domestic subjects continue to be liable to pay rates.]

RATE OF EXCHANGE

Australia 'I think the phrase "rate of exchange" when used in an Act of Parliament prima facie means, as it does in ordinary parlance, the commercial rate of exchange, that is to say, the rate at which drafts for payment in a foreign country in the currency of that country can be purchased for sterling at the relevant date. Where a debt is payable in foreign currency the amount of English currency required to pay it "must be arrived at by taking the real value in English currency of the foreign currency where payable as a purchasable commodity—ie, in practice, according to the rate of exchange existing at the particular time between the currencies" (see per Vaughan Williams LJ in *Manners v Pearson & Son* (1898) 1 Ch 581 at 592)." *Alexander Stewart & Sons Ltd v Robinson* (1920) 29 CLR 55 at 59, per Knox CJ

RATIFICATION

Under certain conditions an act which, at the time it was entered into or done by an agent, lacked the authority, express or implied, of a principal, may by the subsequent conduct of the principal become ratified by him and made as effectively his own as if he had previously authorised it. . . . A ratification may be of one act or a series of acts; and as a general rule every act, other than one which is void at its inception, may be ratified, whether legal or illegal, provided that it was capable of being done by the principal himself. (1 Halsbury's Laws (4th edn) para 756)

'Ratifying properly and so as to involve personal liability is adopting a contract purported to be made . . . when in fact there was no authority to make it; subsequent ratification will make it your contract, so as to make you personally liable.' *Jones v Hope* (1880) 3 TLR 247 n at 249 n, CA, per Cotton LJ

'In ordinary parlance "ratification" is used to express the giving of consent by one without whose consent a transaction entered into by others would be incomplete or invalid; and also the confirmation of a provisional agreement or of an imperfect obligation by the same parties who made the one or were not legally bound by the other. Ratification by a court of law may, in my opinion, signify that the court is to examine the transaction submitted to it, and to decide according to its discretion whether the terms of the transaction are such that the parties ought or ought not to be bound by the agreement which they have made; or it may mean that the court is to give its formal approval, without reference to the terms of the transaction, on being satisfied that due provision has been made for protecting and securing the legal interests of third parties which would be prejudicially affected if no such provision were made.' *Stewart v Kennedy* (1890) 15 App Cas 75 at 99, HL, Lord Watson

'To constitute a valid ratification three conditions must be satisfied: first, the agent whose act is sought to be ratified must have purported to act for the principal; secondly, at the time the act was done the agent must have had a competent principal; and, thirdly, at the time of the ratification the principal must be legally capable of doing the act himself.' *Firth v Staines* [1897] 2 QB 70 at 78, per Wright J

'Doubtless a person can confirm and ratify a contract which was in fact made on his behalf. But an undisclosed principal must exist at the time of the contract. He cannot be brought into life as a principal after the contract has been made without any recognition of his existence. No doubt a third person, by agreement with one of the principals, may, as between those two persons, take an interest in the contract; but that subsidiary contract does not create any privity between the third person and the other principal to the original contract. To establish that a man's thoughts, unexpressed and unrecorded, can form the basis of a contract so as to bind other persons and make them liable on a contract they never made with persons they never heard of, seems a somewhat difficult task.' *Keighley, Maxsted & Co v Durant* [1901] AC 240 at 251, HL, per Lord James of Hereford

RATING (Naval)

In this Act 'rating' means a member of Her Majesty's naval forces of or below the rate of chief petty officer; and any reference in this Act to a rating, or to a rating of any particular rate, shall include a reference to a warrant officer, non-commissioned officer, marine, soldier or airman who is subject to this Act, or to any such warrant officer or non-commissioned officer of rank corresponding with that rate, as the case may be. (Naval Discipline Act 1957, s 133(2))

RATIO DECIDENDI

The enunciation of the reason or principle upon which a question before a court has been decided is alone binding as a precedent. This underlying principle is often called the ratio decidendi, namely the general reasons given for the decision or the general grounds upon which it is based, detached or abstracted from the specific peculiarities of the particular case which gives rise to the decision. (26 Halsbury's Laws (4th edn) para 573)

RATIONAL

Australia 'Now, what does the word "rational" [within the Criminal Code Act 1924–1986 (Tas), s 1] mean? I'm the first to admit that it is not a term of art, it is not a legal term, it has no fixed or certain meaning in law, as far as I know—indeed, it is very difficult to say that it has a fixed or certain meaning in the science of knowledge or metaphysics or psychology or anything else; one has only to pick up any book on the subject to find out the difficulties there are in arriving at a certain definition. But the Oxford English Dictionary has been referred to and that says that a rational person is a person who has the faculty of reasoning—endowed with reason. Later in the same work it says that reason is "that intellectual power or faculty ordinarily employed in adopting thought or action to some end". Perhaps another way of putting it is that the ability to reason means the ability to arrive at conclusions independently of direct perception, for instance, to proceed from facts or concepts, learned, remembered or perceived, to conclusions which are not directly perceived or implanted. If you like, it implies an ability to proceed from premises to conclusions by methods, of course, which are within the normal range of acceptation and experience.' *R v Schell* [1964] Tas SR 184 at 188, per Crisp J

RAW MATERIAL

New Zealand 'The objects for which the company was established are thus set out in the memorandum of association: "A The manufacture and sale of butter, cheese, and preserved milk, and of ham, bacon, pork, and all other products which can be derived from or made out of cows and pigs, the raw material for which products shall be supplied by members." . . . "Raw material" is not an apt word to include live-stock; in my opinion it means milk, not cows, and in reference to ham, bacon, pork, etc, it does not mean living pigs, but the carcases.' *McGregor v Pihama Co-operative Dairy Co* (1907) 26 NZLR 933 at 934, 938, per Cooper J; also reported 9 GLR 373 at 376

REACH

'I think it may be laid down that a vessel has reached the place of loading, as distinguished from the spot of loading, when she has entered that port from which her voyage is to commence.' *Davies v McVeagh* (1879) 4 Ex D 265 at 268, CA, per Bramwell LJ

REACTOR *See* NUCLEAR

READY

Ready and willing *See also* ABLE AND WILLING

'The words "ready and willing" imply not only the disposition, but the capacity to do the act.' *De Medina v Norman* (1842) 11 LJ Ex 320 at 322, per Lord Abinger CB

'In common sense the meaning of . . . an averment of readiness and willingness must be that the noncompletion of the contract was not the fault of the plaintiffs, and that they were disposed and able to complete it if it had not been renounced by the defendants.' *Cort v Ambergate etc, Rly Co* (1851) 17 QB 127 at 144, per cur

Ready to load

[A charterparty provided that if the ship should not be 'ready to load' on or before a specified day, the charterers should have the option of cancelling the charter.] 'The only question is whether the ship was ready to load on May 31. The meaning of the stipulation is that if she was not ready to load within working hours on that day the charterers might cancel the charter-party. In ordinary English a ship cannot be said to be "ready to load" when she is only partially ready to load a cargo. . . . The stipulation is to be construed according to the ordinary meaning of the words, so that in such a case the ship must, so far as the incoming cargo is concerned, be empty so as to be ready for the whole cargo to be put on board. But the plaintiffs' ship was not ready in that sense on May 31, and therefore the charterers had a right to cancel.' *Groves, Maclean & Co v Volkart Brothers* (1885) 1 TLR 454 at 455, CA, per Brett MR

'If the whole of the carrying part of the vessel was at the disposal of the charterers she was "ready" within the meaning of the charterparty. . . . It has been . . . argued that the ship was not fully "lined", but the charter-party said nothing about lining, and to give effect to such an argument would be to hold that the ship must not only be "ready", but also "fit" to load. I am not prepared to import that word into the charter-party. There is, therefore, nothing to justify the defendants in throwing up the charter-party.' *Vaughan v Campbell, Heatley & Co* (1885) 2 TLR 33 at 33, CA, per Lord Esher MR

[A charterparty gave to the charterers an option of cancellation if the ship was not 'ready for loading' on a certain date.] 'A vessel is not ready to load unless she is discharged and ready in all her holds so as to give the charterers complete control of every portion of the ship available for cargo, except so much as is reasonably required for ballast to keep her upright.' *Lyderhorn Sailing Ship Co Ltd v Duncan Fox & Co* [1909] 2 KB 929 at 938, 939, CA, per Cozens Hardy MR

Ready to sail

'The question turns upon this—whether we are to read the expression "if such should happen, and the vessel not be ready to sail on the 4th of December, buyers to have the option of cancelling the contract," looking at it with reference to all the facts and circumstances at the time the contract was entered into, to mean "if such should happen, and the vessel should not sail", etc. I think we cannot do this violence to the language of the parties, consistently either with the words themselves or those in connexion with which they used. The meaning of the parties appears to me to be this—the vessel is to sail on the 1st of December, "accidents excepted"; that is, if by the occurrence of an accident she is unable to sail that day, she is to sail as soon thereafter as possible; and if the accident is of so serious a nature that she is not ready to sail on the 4th, then it is open to the buyer to cancel the contract. If the ship is ready to sail on the 4th of December, provided an accident prevented her sailing on the 1st, the buyer cannot rescind the contract. If she is ready to sail on the 4th, but is prevented by stress of weather, she is bound to sail on the 5th, or any other, being the first day that she has an opportunity. Then there can be no doubt that she was ready to sail on the 4th. Readiness to sail, is a specific act; and at six o'clock on the evening of that day she was ready to sail.' *Smyth v Schilizzi* (1856) 4 WR 460 at 460, per Pollock CB

READY MONEY *See also* CASH

'It is true that, in strict legal language, what is called money deposited at a banker's is nothing more than a debt, and cannot be called ready money; but, in the ordinary language of mankind, money at a banker's is called ready money, and we must construe a will according to the ordinary language of mankind.' *Taylor v Taylor* (1837) 1 Jur 401 at 402, per Lord Langdale MR

[A testator by his will left his 'ready money' at his bankers, in his dwelling-house, or elsewhere, to his wife, stating that by the expression 'ready money' he meant money not invested in securities or otherwise, but which he had in hand for current expenses.] 'The balances in the hands of the testator's bankers and of his agent, and the dividends due on the stock, which he might have received on applying for them, pass by the bequest: but . . . the rent of the house, and the interest on the mortgage which at the testator's death had not been transferred to the credit of his account with Ranken, who, therefore, then held it as agent for the mortgagor, do not pass.' *Fryer v Ranken* (1840) 11 Sim 55 at 57, per Shadwell V-C

'The next question made is as to the meaning of the term "ready money". That the will refers to such ready money as there might be at the testator's death, and not merely to such ready money as he had at the date of the will, is, I think, plain from the nature of the subject, and agreed on all hands. The contention has been, whether certain sums mentioned in the Master's report do or do not from their nature fall under the description of "ready money". Upon the £116 12*s* cash in the house, there has been and can be no question. Clearly, it is ready money. It is, I think, on the other hand equally clear that the debts due to the testator at his death from his agents and other persons, however safe, and with whatsoever facility obtainable, were not included under that description, with the exception only of the two sums of £6,024 0*s* 11*d* and £16,615 15*s* 1*d*. The former of these is described in the report as the balance at the testator's death in the hands of Messrs Hobhouse & Co, the testator's bankers at Bath. The latter is described in the report as the balance due to the testator at his death from Messrs Child & Co, his bankers in London. The argument has proceeded on the basis that these two sums were ordinary bankers' balances on banking accounts of the usual description, kept in the usual manner, that neither of them bore interest, and that in the customary mode it was competent to the testator at any moment to have drawn cheques payable to the bearer on demand for the whole. He had a residence at Bath, but it seems, none in London or its vicinity. The main dispute on this part of the case has been whether these two sums are to be considered as "ready money". According to the decision in *Carr v Carr* [(1811) 1 Mer 541 n], they would have passed, or might have passed, under a bequest of debts due to the testator. That I think is not conclusive against their capacity of passing under a bequest of ready money. . . . I consider, therefore, these two balances as ready money.' *Parker v Marchant* (1842) 1 Y & C Ch Cas 290 at 305, 306, 308, per Knight Bruce V-C; affd 1 Ph 356

'The dividends in question were due on stock belonging to the testator, for which he had not received or demanded the dividend warrants. The testator going himself, or any person acting for him under a power of attorney, might have obtained the dividend warrants, and might have converted them into cash; but my opinion is, that dividends, in that situation, are not "ready money", unless there is something in the context to give the words some other than their ordinary meaning.' *May v Grave* (1849) 3 De G & Sm 462 at 463, per Knight Bruce V-C

'The sum of money or balance due to the testator, upon which the question in this case arises, is the sum of £900, which had been in the hands of Mr Chambers to be invested on security. Mr Chambers having died in the testator's lifetime, this particular sum of money thus deposited with Chambers remained uninvested, and to be accounted for by Chambers' executors. Under these circumstances the sum in question is the testator's money in the hands of Chambers' executors. It has, however, been contended, that it passed as "ready money"; but it is impossible to hold that it passed by such a bequest.' *Cooke v Wagster* (1854) 2 Sm & G 296 at 299, 300, per Stuart V-C

'It is contended that the direction to pay money after payment of debts, has been held in many cases, to pass the whole residuary estate, as that is the fund out of which the debts would be payable, but this cannot extend to the case of a bequest of ready money. In *Parker v Marchant* [supra], it was held that "ready money" extended to money actually in the house, and any balance at the bankers; as according to the usages of society, it would refer to a balance at the bankers rather than to money actually in the house. I have no hesitation, therefore, in concluding that the sum at the Savings' Bank, as to which notice has been given, passes together with the cash in the house. As to the promissory notes, they cannot be considered as ready money. The petitioners will be declared entitled to the balance at the Savings' Bank, and to the cash in the house.' *Re Powell* (1859) 7 WR 138 at 139, per Wood V-C

'I think the question as to the money at the private bankers' clear beyond all possibility of doubt. It is said that it did not pass by the gift of the ready money, because the trustees are afterwards directed to get in all debts and other money due and owing or otherwise payable to the testator at the time of his decease. But the will must be read so as to make every part of it agree, and the moneys which the trustees are to get in must mean other money than that which is given to the daughter. On authority, therefore, as well as on principle, I think the £104 at the private bankers' passed under the description of "ready money". The only question is whether there is any difference between that sum and the £750 on deposit. But it seems that no notice was necessary before drawing it out, and being liable to the testator's cheques whenever they might be presented, I think that also clearly passes under the description of "ready money". But if there were any doubt on the point, it is so settled in *Manning v Purcell*

[(1855) 7 De G M & G 55]. The interest due upon the mortgage is a debt, and cannot be called ready money, and it has never been held to be so. The dividends on shares or stocks fall under the same head, and likewise the two pensions. I must declare, therefore, that the daughter is entitled to the two sums at the bankers', but not to what was due to the testator in respect of the pensions, or the interest on mortgages, or the dividends on shares and stocks.' *Stein v Ritherdon* (1868) 37 LJ Ch 369 at 373, per Malins V-C

'I am of opinion that there is nothing in the terms of the general devise and bequest of the residue to the executors and trustees of the testator's will which can be considered to have had the effect of cutting down the evident intention of the testator by his use of the words "ready money" in the gift to the widow, which in common parlance would be understood to include money lying at a banker's; and that there is nothing in the terms of the principal gift to impose any actual locality upon the money. I shall, therefore, hold that the moneys at the bankers—the whole balance of £1,448 16*s*—passed by the specific bequest to the widow, and must be paid to her.' *Tallent v Scott* (1868) 18 LT 900 at 901, per Giffard V-C

'In my opinion it is not so important to consider under what circumstances the deposits were made as to consider the actual course of business between the parties. In this case the actual course of business between the parties seems to have been that the testator used her deposit account in precisely the same manner as if it had been another current account. I am accordingly of opinion that in this case the gift of the testatrix's ready money belonging to her or standing in her name or to her credit at her bank passes the money on deposit at her bankers at her death.' *Re Rodmell, Safford v Safford* (1913) 108 LT 184 at 185, per Farwell LJ

REAL ESTATE *See also* ESTATE

'Real estate' includes—

(i) Chattels real, and land in possession, remainder, or reversion, and every interest in or over land to which a deceased person was entitled at the time of his death; and
(ii) Real estate held on trust (including settled land) or by way of mortgage or security, but not money to arise under a trust for sale of land, nor money secured or charged on land.

(Administration of Estates Act 1925, s 3(1))

'Estate' means real and personal estate and 'real estate' includes—

(a) chattels real and land in possession, remainder or reversion and every interest in or over land to which the deceased person was entitled at the time of his death; and
(b) real estate held on trust or by way of mortgage, or security, but not money to arise under a trust for sale of land, nor money secured or charged on land.

(Supreme Court Act 1981, s 128)

Canada '[W]hen the testator herein directed his executor to sell his real estate and to invest the proceeds thereof and to pay the income therefrom to his two daughters, etc, the testator intended to direct, and did direct, his executor to sell his land and to invest and pay the proceeds as above. Such a direction by the testator included the land in question, . . . the surface rights therein, the mineral rights therein in situ and . . . not only corporate inheritances as the surface rights and mineral rights in situ, but also all inheritances issued out of them or concerning or exercisable within them, as rent, estovers, common, or other profits whatever, granted out of land.' *Re Montreal Trust Co's Application (Cleveland Estate)* (1962) 41 WWR 193 at 202, Sask QB, per McKercher J

Real and personal estate

'Real and personal estate' means every beneficial interest (including rights of entry and reverter) of the intestate in real and personal estate which (otherwise than in right of a power of appointment or of the testamentary power conferred by statute to dispose of entailed interests) he could, if of full age and capacity, have disposed of by his will. (Administration of Estates Act 1925, s 52)

REAL PROPERTY

The term 'property' is used to denote either rights in the nature of ownership or the corporeal things, whether lands or goods, which are the subjects of such rights. 'Real' denotes that the thing itself, or a particular right in the thing, may be specifically recovered; and, since originally specific recovery was only allowed in cases where the claimant was entitled to a freehold interest, that is, an estate for life or a greater estate, 'real property' denotes (1) land and things attached to land so as to become part of it, and (2) rights in the land which endure for a life or were, under the law before 1926, inheritable, whether these involve full ownership or only some partial enjoyment of the land or the profits. On the other hand, rights in land which endured for a term of years only were not originally specifically recoverable and were described as 'chattels real'. (39 Halsbury's Laws (4th edn) para 301)

REALISE

'Having listened with attention to all the arguments addressed to me on the meaning of the word "realised" in article 121 [of the articles of association] which provides that "no dividends shall be paid except out of the realised profits arising from the business of the company", I must say that my opinion has never wavered for a moment. If there were nothing else than what I have read I should hold without hesitation that "realised" must there have its ordinary commercial meaning, which, if not equivalent to "reduced to actual cash in hand", must at least be "rendered tangible for the purpose of division". The article is in a negative form. It is a prohibition against payment, and against the payment of dividends except out of realised profits arising from the business of the company. The precise thing intended to be prohibited is the payment of dividends in respect of "estimated" profits as distinguished from "realised".' *Re Oxford Benefit Building & Investment Society* (1886) 35 Ch D 502 at 510, per Kay J

'If you speak of realising stocks or securities or give your broker instructions to do so, what is meant by realising? Nothing more than their sale and conversion into money at the highest price that can reasonably be obtained.' *Board of Trade v Block* (1888) 13 App Cas 570 at 579, per Lord Fitzgerald

' "The costs of realisation" means, to use Pearson J's words [in *Batten v Wedgwood Coal & Iron Co* (1884) 28 Ch D 317] "the costs of the actual sale". Those are to be paid in priority to the general expenses of the liquidation.' *Lathom v Greenwich Ferry Co* (1895) 72 LT 790 at 793, per Kekewich J

'On April 21, 1922, the Treasury made an offer to the holders of . . . bonds entitling them to surrender their holdings in exchange for £134, 3½ per cent Conversion Loan for each £100, 5 per cent National War Bonds. In response to this offer, the appellants surrendered their holdings of four million of the first series, and £2,205,000 of the second series, and subsequently, in exercise of their rights under the terms of the original issue, exchanged their remaining holdings into the 5 per cent War Loan. If such transactions be accepted as the equivalent of the realisation of the original holdings, it is agreed that the profit or excess value would amount to £141,750. . . . The Bank contended that there had in fact been no realisation of profit. . . . The exchange effected in the present case was in fact the exact equivalent of what would have taken place had instructions been given to sell the original stock and invest the proceeds in the new security . . . and the fact that this "transformation" took place by the process of exchange does not in my opinion avoid the conclusion that there has been what is described as a realisation of the security.' *Westminster Bank Ltd v Osler* [1933] AC 139 at 146–148, per Lord Buckmaster

[The Theft Act 1968, s 22(1), provides that a person handles stolen goods if (inter alia) he dishonestly undertakes or assists in their 'realisation' by or for the benefit of another person.] 'Realisation merely involves the exchange of the goods for money. It seems to the court that he who pays is just as much involved in the realisation as he who receives the payment and since the former pays the latter the realisation is clearly for the benefit of the latter, albeit it may also benefit the former.' *R v Deakin* [1972] 3 All ER 803 at 808, CA, per cur.

REALM

'When it is used as synonymous with territory, I take the true meaning of the term "realm of England" to be the territory to and over which the common law of England extends—in other words, all that is within the body of any county—to the exclusion of the high seas, which come under a different jurisdiction only because they are not within any of those territorial divisions, into which, among other things for the administration of the law, the kingdom is parcelled out.' *R v Keyn* (1876) 2 Ex D 63 at 197, per Cockburn CJ

REASON TO BELIEVE

[The Matrimonial Causes Act 1950, s 16(2) (repealed; see now the Matrimonial Causes Act 1973, s 19(3)) provided that in any proceedings for divorce on the ground of presumption of death, the fact that for seven years or upwards the other party to the marriage had been continually absent from the petitioner, and the petitioner had no 'reason to believe' that the other party had been living within that time, should be evidence that he or she was dead until the contrary was proved.] 'The test whether or not there is "reason to believe that the other party has been living" must relate to the standards of belief of a reasonable man and not to those of the particular petitioner. The Legislature could hardly have intended that on the same set of facts the right to relief might vary according to whether the petitioner happened to be a moron or a senior wrangler—with their differing approaches to what constitutes such "reason".' *Thompson v Thompson* [1956] 1 All ER 603 at 605, 606, per Sachs J

REASONABLE

'The Lord Chief Justice told the jury, that . . . if "reasonably" meant any thing else than "in good faith", it meant, "according to his reason", as contra-distinguished from "caprice". . . . The direction of the Lord Chief Justice was right.' *Booth v Clive* (1851) 10 CB 827 at 834, 837, per cur.

'The word "reasonable" has in law the prima facie meaning of reasonable in regard to those existing circumstances of which the actor, called on to act reasonably, knows or ought to know.' *Re A Solicitor* [1945] KB 368 at 371, per cur.

'My only doubt concerns the use of the expression "a reasonable man", since this to lawyers connotes the man on the Clapham omnibus by reference to whom a standard of care in civil cases is ascertained. In judging of intent, however, it really denotes an ordinary man capable of reasoning who is responsible and accountable for his actions, and this would be the sense in which it would be understood by a jury.' *Director of Public Prosecutions v Smith* [1960] 3 All ER 161 at 169, HL, per Viscount Kilmuir, LC; also reported [1961] AC 290 at 331

[A condition in an insurance policy stipulated that the insured should take 'reasonable' precautions to prevent accidents and disease.] 'The . . . word to be construed in this context is "reasonable". "The insured shall take reasonable precautions to prevent accidents." "Reasonable" does not mean reasonable as between the employer and the employee. It means reasonable as between the insured and the insurer having regard to the commercial purpose of the contract, which is inter alia to indemnify the insured against liability for his (the insured's) personal negligence. Obviously the condition cannot mean that the insured must take measures to avert dangers which he does not himself foresee, although the hypothetical reasonably careful employer would have foreseen them. That would be repugnant to the commercial purpose of the contract, for failure to foresee dangers is one of the commonest grounds of liability in negligence. What in my view is "reasonable" as between the insured and the insurer, without being repugnant to the commercial object of the contract, is that the insured should not deliberately court a danger, the existence of which he recognised, by refraining from taking any measures to avert it. Equally the condition cannot mean that, where the insured recognises that there is a danger, the measures which he takes to avert it must be such as the hypothetical reasonable employer, exercising due care and observing all the relevant provisions of the Factories Act 1961, would have taken. That too, would be repugnant to the commercial purpose of the contract, for failure to take such measures is another ground of liability in negligence for breach of statutory duty. What in my judgment is reasonable as between the insured and the insurer, without being repugnant to the commercial purpose of the contract, is that the insured, where he does recognise a danger, should not deliberately court it by taking measures which he himself knows are inadequate to avert it. In other words, it is not enough that the employer's omission to take any particular precautions to avoid accidents should be negligent; it must be at least reckless, i.e., made with actual recognition by the insured himself that a danger exists, not caring whether or not it is averted. The purpose of the condition is to ensure that the insured will not refrain from taking precautions which he knows ought to be taken because he is covered against loss by the policy.' *Fraser v Furman (B N) (Productions) Ltd* [1967] 3 All ER 57 at 62, 63, CA, per Diplock LJ

Australia 'The word "reasonable" has often been declared to mean "reasonable in all the circumstances of the case". The real question, in my opinion, is to determine what circumstances are relevant. In determining this question regard must be paid to the nature of the transaction. A circumstance which had no relation to the property which was the subject matter of the transaction but which depended entirely upon the personal position or personal desires of the owner of the property, would not, in my opinion, be a relevant circumstance in determining what was reasonable.' *Opera House Investment Pty Ltd v Devon Buildings Pty Ltd* (1936) 55 CLR 110 at 116, per Latham CJ

'"Reasonable" is a relative term, and the facts of the case must be considered before what constitutes a reasonable contract can be determined.' Ibid at 117, per Starke J

Reasonable acts of trustees

[The Judicial Trustees Act 1896, s 3(1) (re-enacted in the Trustee Act 1925, s 61) empowers the Court to relieve a trustee of personal liability for breaches of trust, where the trustee has acted honestly and 'reasonably', and ought fairly to be excused.] 'The legislature has made the absence of all dishonesty a condition precedent to the relief of the trustee from liability. But that is not the grit of the section. The grit is in the words "reasonably and ought fairly to be excused for the breach of trust". . . . I suppose . . . that in the view of the legislature there might be cases in which a trustee, though he had acted reasonably, ought not fairly to be excused. . . . The copulative "and" is used, and it may well be argued that in order to bring a case within the section it must be shown not merely that the trustee has acted "reasonably" but also that he ought "fairly" to be excused for the breach of trust. I venture, however, to think that, in general and in the absence of special circumstances, a trustee who has acted "reasonably" ought to be relieved and that it is not incumbent on the Court to consider whether he ought "fairly" to be excused, unless there is evidence of a special character showing that the provision of the section ought not to be applied in his favour.' *Perrins v Bellamy* [1898] 2 Ch 521 at 527, 528, per Kekewich J

'Trustees not infrequently, either by nature or lack of education, fall short of the standard of reasonableness attributed by Courts of Equity to persons of ordinary intelligence and diligence. It is their misfortune and not their fault, but so far as I know no trustee has ever been held not liable for a breach of trust by reason of his natural deficiencies or his lack of educational advantages. He may have acted perfectly honestly and to the best of his ability, but if he has not come up to the Court's standard of prudence he is still held liable. . . . It appears, however, . . . that in considering whether a trustee has acted reasonably . . . the terms of the instrument creating the trust ought to be taken into consideration. If an ordinary business man might reasonably entertain a particular view of the construction of the instrument, and the action of the trustee would have been justified if that view had been the true one, that trustee cannot be said to have acted unreasonably merely because this view of the construction of the instrument is wrong.' *Re Mackay, Griessemann v Carr* [1911] 1 Ch 300 at 306, 307, per Parker J

Reasonable and probable cause

'This is an action on the case, for falsely, and without reasonable or probable cause, preferring a charge of felony against the plaintiff; and the question is, whether the learned judge was correct in directing the jury that the defendant's disbelief of the truth of the charge was some evidence of want of probable cause. . . . In order to justify a defendant, there must be a reasonable cause,—such as would operate on the mind of a discreet man: there must also be a probable cause,—such as would operate on the mind of a reasonable man; at all events such as would operate on the mind of the party making the charge; otherwise there is no probable cause for him.' *Broad v Ham* (1839) 5 Bing NC 722 at 724, 725, per Tindal CJ

'To succeed in an action for malicious prosecution the plaintiff must allege and establish two things—absence of reasonable and probable cause and malice. . . . Now I should define reasonable and probable cause to be, an honest belief in the guilt of the accused based upon a full conviction, founded upon reasonable grounds, of the existence of a state of circumstances, which, assuming them to be true, would reasonably lead any ordinarily prudent and cautious man, placed in the position of the accuser, to the conclusion that the person charged was probably guilty of the crime imputed. There must be: first, an honest belief of the accuser in the guilt of the accused; secondly, such belief must be based on an honest conviction of the existence of the circumstances which led the accuser to that conclusion; thirdly, such secondly mentioned belief must be based upon reasonable grounds; by this I mean such grounds as would lead any fairly cautious man in the defendant's situation so to believe; fourthly, the circumstances so believed and relied on by the accuser must be such as amount to reasonable ground for belief in the guilt of the accused.' *Hicks v Faulkner* (1881) 8 QBD 167 at 171, 172, DC, per cur.

'It is not a wrongful act for any person who honestly believes that he has reasonable and probable cause, though he has it not in fact, to put the criminal law in motion against another; but if to the absence of such reasonable and probable cause a malicious motive operating upon the mind of such prosecutor is added, that which would have been a rightful (in the sense of a justifiable) act if done without malice becomes with malice wrongful and actionable.' *Quinn v Leathem* [1901] AC 495 at 524, per Lord Brampton

'The ultimate fact, which is to be inferred from the constituent facts, is whether the defendant had reasonable and probable cause for instituting the proceedings or actively forwarding them. The crucial questions for consideration are stated along with that for malice by Lord Atkinson in *Corea v Peiris* [[1909] AC 549, PC]. The ascertainment of this ultimate fact depends—as one would naturally expect in view of the object and policy of the law in protecting persons reasonably and bona fide pursuing their duty or their right—not on the actual guilt of the plaintiff, but "upon the reasonable bona fide belief in the existence of such a state of things as would amount to a justification of the course pursued in making the accusation complained of. . . . It is not essential in any case that facts should be established proper and fit and admissible as evidence to be submitted to the jury upon an issue as to the actual guilt of the accused [*Hicks v Faulkner* (1878) 8 QBD 167 at 173]".' *Davis v Gell* (1924) 35 CLR 275 at 287, 288, per Isaacs ACJ

'In proving the existence of reasonable and probable cause, the defendant is confined to information of which he was aware at the time of the prosecution. He cannot justify a prosecution that failed by showing that facts of which he did not know made it reasonable.' *Commonwealth Life Assurance Society Ltd v Smith* (1938) 59 CLR 527 at 542, per cur.

Reasonable care *See also* DUE DILIGENCE

[During a cricket match a batsman hit a ball which struck and injured the respondent who was standing on a highway adjoining the ground.] 'A breach of duty has taken place if they show the appellants guilty of a failure to take reasonable care to prevent the accident. One may phrase it as "reasonable care" or "ordinary care" or "proper care"—all these phrases are to be found in decisions of authority—but the fact remains that, unless there has been something which a reasonable man would blame as falling beneath the standard of conduct that he would set for himself and require of his neighbour, there has been no breach of legal duty.' *Bolton v Stone* [1951] 1 All ER 1078 at 1087, HL, per Lord Radcliffe (also reported in [1951] AC 850 at 868, 869)

Australia 'Reasonable care does not connote the observance in its exercise of an unqualified duty to protect other members of the community, and to avoid harm to oneself. Persons are entitled to conduct themselves on the supposition that others will to a reasonable extent behave prudently and look out for themselves; that is to say, that those others will take proper steps to avoid known risks, that they will act in a non-negligent manner.' *Perry v Ellis* [1946] SASR 282 at 293, per Mayo J

Reasonable cause

[A clause in a deed of settlement of a company provided that an extraordinary general meeting specially called for the purpose might remove from his office any director or auditor for negligence, misconduct in office, or any other 'reasonable cause'.] 'The question is . . . whether the expression "reasonable cause" contained in such a deed of a trading partnership can be held to be such a cause, as upon investigation in a court of justice must be held to be bona fide founded on sufficient evidence and just; or whether it ought not to be held to mean such cause as in the opinion of the shareholders duly assembled shall be deemed reasonable. We think the latter is the true construction and effect of the deed.' *Inderwick v Snell* (1850) 2 Mac & G 216 at 221, 222, per cur.

'The Court of Queen's Bench has always considered that it has been open to that Court . . . to correct any Court, or tribunal, or body of men who may have a power . . . of removing from office, if it should be found that such persons have disregarded any of the essentials of justice in the course of their inquiry, before making that removal, or if it should be found that in the place of reasonable cause those persons have acted obviously upon mere individual caprice. There is a power in the Courts of Law . . . to examine whether reasonable cause has been assigned; and . . . by "reasonable" must be meant "just cause".' *Osgood v Nelson* (1872) LR 5 HL 636 at 649, per Lord Hatherley LC

'The proviso to the Criminal Law Amendment Act 1922, s 2, as amended by the Criminal Law

Amendment Act 1928, s 1 [both repealed by the Sexual Offences Act 1956], which says: "Reasonable cause to believe that a girl was of or above the age of 16 years shall not be a defence to a charge under the Criminal Law Amendment Act 1885, ss 5, 6 [also repealed by the Act of 1956] . . . provided that in the case of a man of 23 years of age or under the presence of reasonable cause to believe that the girl was over the age of 16 years shall be a valid defence on the first occasion on which he is charged with an offence under this section" [cf now the similar but differently worded provisions of s 6(3) of the Act of 1956]. These youths were under the age of 23 years, and sought to bring themselves within that proviso. The evidence which they gave, however, made it quite clear that, though in fact there might have been evidence that they had a reasonable cause to believe that the girl was over the age of 16 years, none of them had in fact directed his mind to the question at all, and none of them in fact could say that he believed the girl was over 16 years of age. What has been decided in *R v Banks* [[1916] 2 KB 621] does not help the accused. Avory J in the judgment of the court in that case said at p 622: ". . . the phrase 'had reasonable cause to believe' means 'had reasonable cause to believe, and did in fact believe', i.e., that the person charged believed on reasonable grounds that the girl was at least 16 years of age." . . . In our opinion, not only are we bound by the decision of *R v Banks* [[1916] 2 KB 621], but we all think with all respect to our predecessors, that that decision was correct.' *R v Harrison, R v Wallis, R v Ward, R v Gooding* [1938] 3 All ER 134 at 135, CCA, per cur.

'I am not disposed to deny that, in the absence of a context, the prima facie meaning of such a phrase as "if A B has reasonable cause to believe" a certain circumstance or thing, it should be construed as meaning "if there is in fact reasonable cause for believing" that thing and if A B believes it. But I am quite unable to take the view that the words can only have that meaning. It seems to me reasonably clear that, if the thing to be believed is something which is essentially one within the knowledge of A B or one for the exercise of his exclusive discretion, the words might well mean if A B acting on what he thinks is reasonable cause (and, of course, acting in good faith) believes the thing in question.' *Liversidge v Anderson* [1941] AC 206 at 219, 220, per Lord Maugham

Reasonable diligence *See also* DUE DILIGENCE

'The question I have to decide is, whether what has been done constitutes reasonable diligence? The meaning of this expression is, not the doing of everything possible, but the doing of that which, under ordinary circumstances, and having regard to expense and difficulty, can be reasonable required.' *The Europa* (1863) 2 New Rep 194 at 196, per Dr Lushington; on appeal sub nom *Dean v Richards, The Europa* (1863) 2 Moo PCCNS 1

[The Limitation Act 1980, s 32(1)(c) provides that, in the case of an action for relief from the consequences of a mistake, the period of limitation shall not begin to run until the plaintiff has discovered the mistake, or could with 'reasonable diligence' have discovered it.] 'In the context to which I have to apply them, in my judgment, I conclude that reasonable diligence means not the doing of everything possible, not necessarily the using of any means at the plaintiff's disposal, not even necessarily the doing of anything at all, but that it means the doing of that which an ordinarily prudent buyer and possessor of a valuable work of art would do having regard to all the circumstances, including the circumstances of the purchase.' *Peco Arts Inc v Hazlitt Gallery Ltd* [1983] 3 All ER 193 at 199, per Webster J

Reasonable doubt

'What is a real and substantial doubt? It is only another way of saying a reasonable doubt, and a "reasonable doubt" is simply that degree of doubt which would prevent a reasonable and just man from coming to a conclusion.' *Bater v Bater* [1950] 2 All ER 458 at 459, CA, per Denning LJ

'I have never yet heard any court give a real definition of what is a "reasonable doubt", and it would be very much better if that expression was not used. Whenever a court attempts to explain what is meant by it, the explanation tends to result in confusion rather than clarity. It is far better, instead of using the words "reasonable doubt" and then trying to say what is a reasonable doubt, to say to a jury: "You must not convict unless you are satisfied by the evidence given by the prosecution that the offence has been committed." The jury should be told that it is not for the prisoner to prove his innocence, but for the prosecution to prove his guilt, and that it is their duty to regard the evidence and see if it satisfies them so that they can feel sure, when they give their verdict, that it is a right one.' *R v Summers* [1952] 1 All ER 1059 at 1060, CCA, per cur.

'To practitioners of English law the expression

"reasonable doubt" is a well-known and time-honoured phrase. Since the case of *R v White* [(1865) 4 F & F 383], at any rate, judges have been accustomed to direct juries that in order to be justified in convicting in a criminal case they must not act on a mere balance of probabilities but must be satisfied of the accused's guilt beyond reasonable doubt. And it has become usual to instruct juries that a reasonable doubt is such a doubt as would cause them hesitation in grave and important concerns of their own, but that a mere fanciful doubt is not to be considered a reasonable doubt.' *Ministry of Pensions v Greer* [1958] NI 156 at 162, per Black LJ

Canada 'By reasonable doubt as to a person's guilt is meant that real doubt—real as distinguished from illusory—which an honest juror has after considering all the circumstances of the case and as a result of which he is unable to say: "I am morally certain of his guilt".' *R v Sears* [1948] OR 9 at 14, Ont CA, per Roach JA

Canada 'Reasonable doubt was defined by the learned trial judge as "a doubt such as would influence a man in his ordinary daily affairs". That definition has often been used but, with respect, it is not correct. The doubt which can be regarded as "reasonable" in testing sufficiency of evidence in criminal cases must have regard to the gravity of the crime charged and to all the circumstances attending its commission. These considerations are far different from those which might "influence" a man in "ordinary affairs of daily life" where very slight probabilities may be sufficient to create or overcome doubt." *R v Hrynyk* [1949] 1 WWR 129 at 134, Man CA, per Dysart JA

Reasonable excuse

Canada 'The refusal of the police constable to permit the appellant to speak to his lawyer, in the circumstances of this case, deprived him of the right to retain and instruct counsel without delay, and constituted a reasonable excuse for his refusal to comply with the demand of the police constable that he take a breath test. Having regard to the provisions of the Bill of Rights, s 223(2) of the Criminal Code [RSC 1970, c C-34] is required to be construed and applied in this sense, so that, unless it is apparent that an accused person is not asserting his right to counsel bona fide, but is asserting such right for the purpose of delay or for some other improper reason, the denial of that right affords a "reasonable excuse" for failing to provide a sample of his breath as required by the section.' *Brownridge v R* [1972] SCR 926 at 932, SCC, per Ritchie J

Reasonable man

'For the purposes of the law of provocation the "reasonable man" has never been confined to the adult male. It means an ordinary person of either sex, not exceptionally excitable or pugnacious, but possessed of such powers of self-control as everyone is entitled to expect that his fellow citizens will exercise in society as it is today.' *Director of Public Prosecutions v Campbell* [1978] 2 All ER 168 at 173, 174, HL, per Lord Diplock

Reasonable precautions

Canada 'Nor do I think there is any room for controversy as to what "reasonable precautions" [for the safety of employees] means . . . I think one must put oneself in the position of an employer assumed to be both prudent and competent and to have applied his mind seriously to the risks of harm to which his employees might be exposed in the course of their employment. Then, I think, one must ask oneself whether the facts in evidence, in themselves or in the inferences properly arising from them, establish that the occurrences which caused the damage complained of would not fall within the risks reasonably foreseeable by such an employer so applying himself to the matter of the safety of his employees, under a proper sense of his duty in that respect.' *Colpron v Canadian National Rly Co* [1934] SCR 189 at 192, SCC, per Duff CJ

Reasonable price

[The Landlord and Tenant (Rent Control) Act 1949, s 3(1)(b) (repealed; see now the Rent Act 1977, s 123) provided that where the price charged for furniture, fittings, etc, which a tenant had been made to buy exceeded the 'reasonable price' of the articles, the excess should be treated as a premium.] '"The reasonable price" within s 3(1)(b) of the Landlord and Tenant (Rent Control) Act 1949 means, I think, the price which is reasonable between the parties for the articles as they are, fitted and situate in the premises, without regard to extraneous circumstances such as the desire of the tenant to obtain a tenancy. It is not the price which would be realised if the articles were removed from the premises and sold in an auction room. It is the price which one would reasonably expect to be agreed between an incoming tenant who was ready to take over the articles and an outgoing tenant who was ready to leave them there. The incoming tenant would, no doubt, have regard to the expense to which he would be put if he had to buy the articles and fix them himself, making, of course, an allowance for depreciation. The outgoing tenant would have regard to the fact that, if he had to take them out, they would fetch very little. It is obvious that, as between a willing outgoing tenant and a willing incoming tenant, there is room for a good deal of latitude in the ascertainment of the figure, but, if a price were put on the articles which was more than the replacement cost, that could not be a "reasonable" price. In the present case the parties together made an inventory of the articles. They based their figures on the cost prices, presumably with some allowance for depreciation. I do not think that anyone could say that that was not the reasonable price as between them.' *Eales v Dale* [1954] 1 All ER 717 at 720, CA, per Denning LJ; see also [1954] 1 QB 539

Reasonable rental

Australia 'The parties provided for a "reasonable rental". This, in our opinion, means a rental which is reasonable in the light of all the relevant circumstances.' *Email v Robert Bray (Langwarrin) Pty Ltd* [1984] VR 16 at 21, per cur.

Reasonable time

Where anything is limited to be done within a 'reasonable time' or at a 'reasonable hour', the question what is a reasonable time or reasonable hour must necessarily depend on the circumstances, and is therefore a question of fact. If a contract is silent as to time for performance of an act, the law implies that it is to be done within a reasonable time, and what period is reasonable is a question of fact. (45 Halsbury's Laws (4th edn) para 1147)

[The question was what was a 'reasonable time' within which notice that a promissory note or bill of exchange had been dishonoured should be given by the holder to the indorser.] 'It is of dangerous consequence to lay it down as a general rule, that the jury should judge of the reasonableness of time. It ought to be settled as a question of law. If the jury were to determine this question in all cases, it would be productive of endless uncertainty. The next day at the most is as long as is necessary in a case circumstanced like this. If the parties live at a small distance, this is sufficient time; if at a greater, they should write by the next post.' *Tindal v Brown* (1786) 1 Term Rep 167 at 169, per Ashurst J

'Notice [of abandonment of ship] must be given in reasonable time; the Court being the judge of what is reasonable; and cases have been urged, in which they have decided what is and what is not reasonable. But what is the reasonable time within which notice should be given, must, in every case, depend on the circumstances of that individual case. Here there is no evidence of any communication to the owner, of the circumstances of the loss, previously to the arrival of the captain; and the notice having been given on the day but one after the owner was furnished with the full means of knowing all the facts of the case, must be deemed sufficient.' *Read v Bonham* (1821) 3 Brod & Bing 147 at 154, per Dallas CJ

'There is no doubt that, on charges of felony, a magistrate has a power to commit for further examination, but that can only be for a reasonable time; and as to what is a reasonable time, that must greatly depend upon the circumstances of each particular case. The question of reasonable time is a mixed question of law and fact.' *Davis v Capper* (1829) 4 C & P 134 at 138, per Vaughan B

'The term "reasonable time" in the declaration means a space of time within which the ship may, with proper speed, be unloaded, whenever she is in a condition for that process; not a reasonable period to be dated from a given time.' *Taylor v Clay* (1846) 9 QB 713 at 724, per Lord Denman CJ

'Under ordinary circumstances, when a man is called upon by a contract to do an act, and no time is specified, he is allowed a reasonable time for doing it; and what is a reasonable time may depend on all the circumstances of the case.' *Alexiadi v Robinson* (1861) 2 F & F 679 at 684, per Cockburn CJ

'The charterparty contained no statement as to the number of days, which should be allowed to the charterers for discharging the cargo; they were therefore bound to unload the vessel within a reasonable time. In my judgment a reasonable time for doing an act is a time within which it can be done by a person working reasonably; but the time which he spends in making his preparations for doing the act is not to be taken into account.' *Wright v New Zealand Shipping Co Ltd* (1878) 4 Ex D 165 n at 168 n, CA, per Bramwell LJ

'The contract between the parties to this action was that which the law implies, namely, that the ship should be unloaded at her port of discharge within a reasonable time. A reasonable time means a reasonable time under ordinary circumstances, and in the absence of some stipulation altering the implied contract between the parties and charterers would not be relieved from the consequences of fortuitous or unforeseen impediments affecting only the due performance by them of their part of the contract.' Ibid at 170 n, per Thesiger LJ

'There is no doubt that the duty of providing, and making proper use of, sufficient means for the discharge of cargo, when a ship which has been chartered, arrives at its destination and is ready to discharge, lies (generally) upon the charterer. If, by the terms of the charterparty, he has agreed to discharge it within a fixed period of time, that is an absolute and unconditional engagement, for the non-performance of which he is answerable, whatever may be the nature of the impediments which prevent him from performing it, and which cause the ship to be detained in his service beyond the time stipulated. If, on the other hand, there is no fixed time, the law implies an agreement on his part to discharge the cargo within a reasonable time; that is (as was said by Mr. Justice Blackburn, in *Ford v Cotesworth* [(1868) LR 4 QB 127]) "a reasonable time under the circumstances". Difficult questions may sometimes arise as to the circumstances which ought to be taken into consideration in determining what time is reasonable. If (as in the present case), an obligation, indefinite as to time, is qualified or partially defined by express or implied reference to the custom of practice of a particular port, every impediment arising from or out of that custom or practice, which the charterer could not have overcome by the use of any reasonable diligence, ought (I think) to be taken into consideration.' *Postlethwaite v Freeland* (1880) 5 App Cas 599 at 608, per Lord Selborne LC

'There is of course no such thing as a reasonable time in the abstract. It must always depend upon circumstances. . . . The only sound principle is that the "reasonable time" should depend on the circumstances which actually exist.' *Hick v Raymond & Reid* [1893] AC 22 at 28, 29, per Lord Herschell LC

Reasonable user

Australia 'The words "reasonable user" in the context of s 129c [of the Transfer of Land Act 1893–1986 (WA)] mean use for any purpose for which a reasonable neighbour might reasonably use his land after taking into account all the circumstances and the existing character of the neighbourhood and the extent to which the user may interfere with the adjoining owners' comfortable enjoyment of their properties or reduce the value of those properties.' *Smith v Australian Real Estate and Investment Co Ltd* [1964] WAR 163 at 166, per Negus J

REASONABLY

[A lease contained a proviso which enabled the tenant, if he had 'reasonably' fulfilled the covenants of the lease, to continue the tenancy for a further seven or fourteen years.] 'The proviso is not that the tenant must have fulfilled the covenants to the lease, but that the tenant must have reasonably fulfilled the covenants to the lease. Two interpretations of the word "reasonably" have been put before me. Counsel for the defendants says that the word governs "fulfilled" and, therefore, one starts with the fact that the tenant must fulfil his obligations under the lease. The result is, says counsel, that before the tenant can extend his lease he must show that he has done that work which would be necessary to fulfil the covenant. If he has done that work, the word "reasonably" comes into play and the landlord may not be able to complain if the work is not quite up to the standard necessary strictly to fulfil the covenant. . . . Counsel for the plaintiff, on the other hand, says that that is not the right way of looking at the matter. The insertion of the word "reasonably" means that the parties have agreed that the tenant may exercise his option provided he has behaved as a reasonable tenant might have behaved in relation to his covenants. The difference between the two points of view may best be illustrated in this way. It may well be necessary, in order to keep the premises in good and substantial repair, to re-paint the premises each three years, or indeed at even shorter intervals, but a reasonably minded tenant might well come to the conclusion that the premises will come to no harm if the repainting is left over for a further year. In those circumstances, could a tenant exercise his option half way through the fourth year? Counsel for the plaintiff would say "Yes"; counsel for the defendants would say "No". I have come to the conclusion that counsel for the plaintiff is right, and that by inserting the word "reasonably" the parties not only intended to mean, but must be deemed to have meant, that the tenant can exercise his option provided he behaves during his tenancy in a way in which a reasonably minded tenant might well behave.' *Gardner v Blaxill* [1960] 2 All ER 457 at 461, 462, per Paull J

Reasonably accessible *See* ACCESSIBLE

Reasonably necessary

'The words "reasonably necessary", used as a phrase in which the adverb is designed to qualify the adjective, are meaningless. A thing is necessary or it is not necessary. It may be regarded or treated as necessary in one context and not in another, but the context cannot be provided by merely preceding the word "necessary" with an adverb such as "reasonably". As it stands, the phrase, to me, is a contradiction in terms.' *Re Naylor Benzon Mining Co Ltd* [1950] Ch 567 at 575, per Wynn-Parry J

Reasonably practicable

[The Coal Mines Act 1911, s 102(8) (repealed; see now the Mines and Quarries Act 1954, s 157) provided that the owner of a mine should not be liable to an action for damages as for breach of statutory duty in respect of any contravention of or non-compliance with any of the provisions of the Act if it was shown that it was not 'reasonably practicable' to avoid or prevent the breach.] ' "Reasonably practicable" is a narrower term than "physically possible" and seems to me to imply that a computation must be made by the owner, in which the quantum of risk is placed on one scale and the sacrifice involved in the measures necessary for averting the risk (whether in money, time or trouble) is placed in the other; and that if it be shown that there is a gross disproportion between them—the risk being insignificant in relation to the sacrifice—the defendants discharge the onus on them. Moreover, this computation falls to be made by the owner at a point of time anterior to the accident.' *Edwards v National Coal Board* [1949] 1 KB 704 at 712, CA, per Asquith LJ

REBUILD

[A tenant for life was authorised by the testator's will to lease property for a certain time for the purpose of effectually 'rebuilding' and repairing any messuage.] 'To rebuild might mean to pull down entirely, and re-edify in the same shape as before; or it might signify rebuilding some parts and repairing the rest: but taking it in either way, rebuilding and repairing must be something different from repairing merely.' *Doe d Dymoke v Withers* (1831) 2 B & Ad 896 at 902, per Parke J

[A lease contained a covenant on the part of the lessee to 'rebuild' within a specified time, a new house and premises.] 'The first covenant, that on the subject of rebuilding, is, that the appellants will within a specified time "rebuild" on the site of the messuage, in a substantial and workmanlike manner, a new house and premises suitable for merchants and dealers' counting-houses and salerooms. It was argued before the Vice Chancellor, and the argument has been renewed before me, that this word "rebuild" involved the obligation of erecting the new house not only on the same site, but in the same manner and in the same style and shape and with the same elevation as the old building. It is clear that no such conclusion can be derived from the use of the word "rebuild"; and even were it possible to construe the word as containing any such implication, the implication would be rebutted by the words which follow, to the effect that the house and premises shall be suitable for merchants and dealers' counting-houses and salerooms. That is a new purpose to which the old building was not applied, and it was the purpose therefore which must be considered as regulating and determining the shape and character of the new building to be erected.' *Low v Innes* (1864) 4 De G J & Sm 286 at 288, 289, per Lord Westbury LC

[The Settled Land Act 1890, s 13(4) (repealed; see now the Settled Land Act 1925, s 83, Sch III) provided for the payment out of capital monies of sums for the 'rebuilding' of the principal mansion-house on settled land.] 'Structural alterations and repairs, however extensive, do not, in my opinion, amount to a "rebuilding" of the principal mansion-house. It was not intended that alterations and improvements, much less repairs, should be paid for out of capital money, except in the special instances provided for by the Acts. I observe in the "improvements" added by the Act of 1890, s 13, that sub-s 2 speaks of "additions to or alterations" in buildings; and then sub-s 4 deals with "rebuilding", and I think this last sub-section means only what it says, and must be construed strictly, and confined to the actual rebuilding of the mansion-house.' *Re De Teissier's Settled Estates, Re De*

Teissier's Trusts, De Teissier v De Teissier [1893] 1 Ch 153 at 158, per Chitty J

'What is the scope of sub-s iv [of the Settled Land Act 1890, s 13 (repealed; see supra)]? It is the rebuilding of the principal mansion-house. Could you justify the expenditure of capital moneys in rebuilding the principal mansion which is pulled down simply because it is ugly and rebuilt to suit the tenant for life? I think not. That is really the case with regard to these stables. These stables are old stables. They are very good except that they want better ventilation and better draining. They are not out of repair. They are not destroyed, but the tenant for life wants to make a magnificent house, and does not want to have ugly stables, and this necessity for pulling down these stables is a piece of artistic fancy. I cannot bring myself to hold that that is a rebuilding of the principal mansion-house within the true meaning of this sub-section.' *Re Gerard's (Lord) Settled Estate* [1893] 3 Ch 252 at 261, CA, per Lindley LJ

'Supposing most of the house front were pulled down and a small part left, and the rest of the house was rebuilt, it could not be said that there was not a rebuilding; again, if the house was burnt and the walls were left standing and made use of in erecting the new house, there would none the less be a rebuilding. Nor would the introduction of alterations and enlargements make any difference in that respect. And I do not think it would make any difference if the site were slightly shifted. If the house were built at a distance that would be another matter. That is one view of the case. I do not think, however, it follows that every rebuilding would be a rebuilding authorised by the section [the Settled Land Act 1890, s 13 (repealed; see supra)]. For example, supposing a tenant for life of a large estate, or his predecessor, had been content to live in some mere farmhouse or a small villa residence, if he were to erect a large mansion with all the requirements suited to his position as the owner of such an estate, I do not think that that ought to be considered a rebuilding within the meaning of the enactment. I think there must be really a substantial rebuilding, and not merely alterations and enlargements. . . . I come to the conclusion that there has been a rebuilding on a somewhat enlarged scale, so as to make the mansion-house, as it exists at present, more suited to modern requirements and the size and value of the estate to which it is now attached. I do not see anything in the section [the Settled Land Act 1890, s 13 (repealed; see supra)] to say that the rebuilding must be for a particular purpose. The purpose of rebuilding is left very much to the discretion of the tenant for life, subject to the assumption that he is acting bona fide. . . . In this case I come to the conclusion that the whole expenditure has been made upon a rebuilding within the Act.' *Re Walker's Settled Estate* [1894] 1 Ch 189 at 192, per North J

[It was proposed to pull down part of a house consisting of old and inconvenient rooms, and to erect on the site thereof certain new rooms, the old external and internal walls being used as far as possible.] 'This is an application by the tenant for life, the first tenant in tail (being an infant, and appearing by his next friend) and the trustees of certain settled estates to obtain leave to make an expenditure out of the capital moneys under sub-s iv of s 13 of the Settled Land Act 1890 [repealed; see supra]. . . . Now, in the present case I have the purchase by the trustees of a mansion-house, which is not suited for modern requirements. The tenant for life and the architect say that the proposed changes are necessary for the proper enjoyment of the mansion-house. . . . Now, the question I must ask is, "Is this a rebuilding as distinct from an alteration of a building?" For reasons best known to the legislature they have drawn a distinction. I cannot bring my mind to think this is a building. It is true that in *Re Walker's Settled Estate* [supra], North J found that particular changes were in his view, a rebuilding. But as he says: "I think it is a question of fact in each particular case", his judgment does not assist me. I have the Act of Parliament and the lucid judgment of Chitty J; and I cannot say that this is a rebuilding.' *Re Wright's Settled Estates* (1900) 83 LT 159 at 159, 160, per Farwell J

'The first part of the summons relates to the application of a sum of £12,700 in rebuilding the principal mansion-house. The application to sanction the payment of this sum out of capital moneys was made under s 13, sub-s (iv), of the Settled Land Act 1890 [repealed; see supra], which provides that improvements authorised by the Settled Land Act 1882 [repealed], shall include "the rebuilding of the principal mansion-house on the settled land, provided that the sum to be applied under this subsection shall not exceed one-half of the annual rental of the settled land". . . . It is quite clear that in order to bring the case within sub-s (iv) it is not necessary that every brick and stone shall be rebuilt. The question is whether the house is to be substantially rebuilt.' *Re*

Kensington Settled Estates (1905) 21 TLR 351 at 351, per Swinfen Eady J

'By s 13, sub-s (iv), of the Settled Land Act 1890 [repealed; see supra], the rebuilding of the principal mansion-house on the settled land is included as one of the improvements authorised, but that is subject to this proviso "that the sum to be applied under this sub-section shall not exceed one-half of the annual rental of the settled land".' In the first place, I have to consider whether the moneys said to have been expended in rebuilding the hall have been really so expended, or whether they have been expended merely in making alterations and additions to it. Now the hall, as it existed prior to the work done by the present tenant for life, and as it exists now, is described in paragraph 3 of Mr Coatsworth's affidavit, and the conclusion to which I have come on reading that paragraph is that although the external walls of the old hall appear to remain standing and a great part of the work done by the present tenant for life consists merely of additions to that, yet so much has been done to the interior of the old hall in the way of reconstruction and rearrangement, that in substance I am able to say that the money expended has been expended in rebuilding the hall.' *Re Windham's Settled Estate* [1912] 2 Ch 75 at 79, 80, per Warrington J

See, generally, 42 Halsbury's Laws (4th edn) para 815.

RECEIPT

For the purposes of this Act the expression 'receipt' includes any note, memorandum, or writing whereby any money amounting to two pounds or upwards or any bill of exchange or promissory note for money amounting to two pounds or upwards, is acknowledged or expressed to have been received or deposited or paid, or whereby any debt or demand, or any part of a debt or demand, of the amount of two pounds or upwards, is acknowledged to have been settled, satisfied, or discharged, or which signifies or imports any such acknowledgment, and whether the same is or is not signed with the name of any person. (Stamp Act 1891, s 101(1))

'The distinction between a receipt and a release is, the release extinguishes the claim, and when given, in itself annihilates the debt; but a receipt is only evidence of payment, and if the proof be that no payment was made, it cannot operate as evidence of payment against such proof.' *Bowes v Foster* (1858) 27 LJ Ex 262 at 266, per Martin B

'To constitute a receipt of anything there must be a person to receive and a person from whom he receives, and something received by the former from the latter, and in this case that something must be a sum of money. A mere entry in an account which does not represent such a transaction does not prove any receipt, whatever else it may be worth.' *Gresham Life Assurance Society v Bishop* [1902] AC 287 at 296, HL, per Lord Lindley

[An instrument in writing was presented on behalf of a company and was indorsed on a deed executed by the company, which deed had created redeemable debenture stock redeemable at any time. The instrument was an acknowledgment that the debenture stock secured by the trust deed, and interest, had been 'redeemed, paid off, and satisfied'. It was held that such instrument came under the heading 'Receipt' in the Schedule to the Stamp Act 1891.] 'The document in question, I think, has not any force as an instrument putting an end either to any obligation or to any security. It is merely evidence that the obligation or security no longer is in effective existence, and it comes, therefore, quite clearly under the heading "Receipt". . . . I think that this document does not come within the term "discharge" in the schedule, and that it can only be stamped as a receipt.' *Firth & Sons Ltd v Inland Revenue Comrs* [1904] 2 KB 205 at 207, 208, per Channell J

'The question raised in this case may be stated very shortly. It is whether when counsel, after payment of a fee of £2 or upwards, places his initials or name against the fee on his brief or at the foot of a statement of fees the document is liable to stamp duty as a receipt. . . . The schedule to the Stamp Act 1891, specifies the instruments on which duties are payable, and in that schedule are to be found these words "Receipt given for or upon the payment of money amounting to £2 or upwards". The expression "receipt" is defined by s 101, sub-s 1, as including any note, memorandum or writing, whereby any money amounting to £2 or upwards . . . is acknowledged or expressed to have been received or deposited or paid. The schedule says "receipt given". That means it must be a document given by the person receiving the money to some other person presumably to the person who has paid.' *General Council of the Bar (England) v Inland*

Revenue Comrs [1907] 1 KB 462 at 471, 472, 476, 478, per Bray J

'Unquestionably, if you say a person has given you a receipt for something, what you mean is he has given you something which you can keep as your own and produce on all occasions that it is required, particularly in a court of law. . . . To be a receipt, it must be a document whereby the receipt or deposit or payment of money is acknowledged or expressed.' *A-G v Northwood Electric Light and Power Co Ltd* [1947] KB 511 at 517, 518, CA, per Lord Greene MR

Australia 'A document is not a receipt unless it is an acknowledgment to "somebody" presumably the payer, for money received or paid. . . . It is sufficient if the acknowledgment is express or tacit.' *Comr of Stamp Duties v Small* (1950) 80 CLR 177 at 184, per McTiernan J

Australia 'It is, we think, of no consequence that, in New South Wales, a barrister has no legal right to sue at law for his fees, for a barrister who, in the course of his practice, is earning and receiving fees is, in the language of the section [the Bankruptcy Act 1924–1960 (Cth), s 101 (repealed; see now the Bankruptcy Act 1966–1986 (Cth), s 131(1)], just as much "in receipt" of the resultant income as would be a person who, for his services, is, or will in the ordinary course, become entitled to be remunerated by salary or wages or by a share of business or trading profits. "In receipt of" is, we think, descriptive of an existing and continuing state of affairs and, that being so, it is immaterial that the fees of a barrister are not legally recoverable.' *Falstein v Official Receiver* [1963] ALR 369 at 372, per cur.

RECEIVE *See also* HANDLE

References in any enactment passed before this Act to an offence abolished by this Act shall, subject to any express amendment or repeal made by this Act, have effect as references to the corresponding offence under this Act, and in any such enactment the expression 'receive' (when it relates to an offence of receiving) shall mean handle, and 'receiver' shall be construed accordingly. (Theft Act 1968, s 32(2)(a))

Australia 'Prima facie, as a matter of the ordinary English language, I think "received" means actually get into their hands. A number of cases, however, have been cited which show that the Courts have displayed an inclination to treat the word as meaning "receivable" in order to prevent the accident of whether trustees have or have not paid over money to affect the rights of beneficiaries. In some cases the word received is construed as being equivalent to "vested in possession".' *Pilcher v Logan* (1914) 15 SR(NSW) 24 at 27, per Harvey J

New Zealand [A will made special provisions in case any child of the testator should die before 'receiving' his or her share of the estate.] 'The word "receiving" . . . is not apt to describe a failure to vest. . . . There seems no sufficient reason why the word "receiving" should not be given its more ordinary meaning. That ordinary meaning may be either (a) actually receiving into his possession and control, or (b) becoming entitled to what has been described as the de jure receipt of his share—that is to say, to be credited with a specific appropriation in account of the share and the proceeds therefrom. That means it is *debitum in praesenti solvendum in futuro*—i.e., presently owing but not payable till a later date.' *Re Hill, Hill v Caile* [1948] NZLR 356 at 363, 364, per Fair J

In Betting Acts

[The Betting Act 1853, s 4 (repealed; see now the Betting, Gaming and Lotteries Act 1963, s 8(1)) made it an offence for the owner or occupier of premises to use them for 'receiving' money for betting.] 'The justices were wrong in holding that the mere taking of money and papers into the back room without the knowledge of the persons making the bets was not "receiving" within the meaning of s 4. In my opinion they were wrong on that finding, and I think that there was quite sufficient evidence to bring the case within s 1. In order to bring a case within s 4 there must be a finding that the person charged did either directly or indirectly receive some money or valuable thing as a deposit on a bet.' *Boulton v Hunt* (1913) 109 LT 245 at 249, DC, per Bankes J

'The section in question, s 1(1) of the Street Betting Act 1906 [repealed; see now the Betting, Gaming and Lotteries Act 1963, s 8(1)], reads as follows: "Any person frequenting or loitering in streets or public places, on behalf either of himself or of any other person, for the purpose of bookmaking, or betting, or wagering, or agreeing to bet or wager, or paying or receiving or settling bets shall . . ." be guilty of an offence. As it seems to me, the sole question here is what is meant by receiving bets in that phrase "or paying or receiving or settling bets". There are three possible meanings; the first is the one which I understand to be that which the justices accepted, namely, that the phrase "receiving bets", covered the physical receipt of the slips of paper which evidenced the contracts . . .; the second possible meaning, which is the one advocated by counsel for the appellant, is that receiving bets means accepting bets in the sense of accepting an offer and entering into a contract. . . . The third possible meaning, and the one which I think is correct, is that "receiving bets" in the context of sub-s (1) of s 1 of the Act of 1906 is referring to a financial transaction resulting from the contract which has been entered into. . . . For my part . . . I think that the natural meaning of "receiving bets" in this context is to receive the losses resulting from bets.' *Bland v Cowan* [1963] 2 All ER 184 at 187, per Lord Parker CJ; also reported in [1963] 2 QB 735 at 741

RECEIVER

A receiver is a person appointed for the collection or protection of property. He is appointed either by the court or out of court by individuals or corporations. If he is appointed by the court, he is an officer of the court deriving his authority from the court's order. If he is appointed out of court, he is an agent and has such powers, duties and liabilities as are defined by the instrument or statute under which he is appointed and derive from the general law of agency. (39 Halsbury's Laws (4th edn) para 801)

'A "receiver" is a term which was well known in the Court of Chancery, as meaning a person who receives rents or other income paying ascertained outgoings, but who does not, if I may say so, manage the property in the sense of buying or selling or anything of that kind. If a receiver was appointed of partnership assets, the trade stopped immediately. He collected all the debts, sold the stock-in-trade and other assets, and then under the order of the court the debts of the concern were liquidated and the balance divided. If it was necessary to continue the trade at all, it was necessary to appoint a manager, or a receiver and manager as it was generally called. . . . The receiver merely took the income, and paid necessary outgoings, and the manager carried on the trade or business.' *Re Manchester & Milford Rly Co, ex p Cambrian Rly Co* (1880) 14 Ch D 645 at 653, CA, per Jessel MR

RECEIVING STOLEN GOODS

[Receiving stolen goods was an offence under the Larceny Act 1916, s 33. This Act has been repealed by the Theft Act 1968, s 22(1) of which makes it an offence to 'handle' stolen goods. *See* HANDLE; RECEIVE.]

RECENT INVENTION

Australia 'I do not understand the expression "recent invention" to mean only recent conscious and deliberate falsification of an account. I understand the term to include recent invention in the sense of recent construction of an account, whether the result of deliberate falsification or the result of some suggestion, even though the witness has not been conscious of the fact that the witness was suggestible and was acceding to suggestion.' *Frankcombe v Holloway* [1957] VR 139 at 141, per Sholl J

RECEPTACLE

Receptacle includes a vehicle or stall and any basket, bag, box, vessel, stand, easel, board, tray or other structure or thing which is used (whether or not constructed or adapted for such use) as a container for or for the display of any article or thing; and article or thing includes any living thing. (London County Council (General Powers) Act 1947, s 15)

RECEPTION

[By the National Health Service Act 1946, s 79 (repealed; see now the National Health Service Act 1977, s 128(1)) the word 'hospital' is defined as meaning any institution for the 'reception' and treatment of persons suffering from illness, etc.] 'It was argued that the clinic was a hospital within the meaning of this definition. Was it an institution for the reception and treatment of persons suffering from illness? Certain words are not very clearly defined, but I think "institution" means something which is set up and possibly the clinic was something which was set up. Was it for the reception and treatment of persons suffering from illness? It was plainly for the purpose of treatment of persons suffering from illness. As to "reception", it is said that that merely means that a person shall be received at a particular place and there treated. It has been argued, on the other hand, that "reception" means more than that, that it means taking people into a building and keeping them there, as is normally done at a hospital. In my opinion that is the appropriate meaning to be applied to this definition. It is not satisfied merely by some form of treatment at a dispensary or clinic or out-patients department.' *Re Couchman, Couchman v Eccles* [1952] 1 Ch 391 at 395, 396, per Danckwerts J

RECESS

Australia 'By "an ordinary recess" [within the Workers' Compensation Act 1958–1986 (Vic), s 8(2)(a)(ii)], I take it, is meant a break or interruption of limited duration in the continuity of a normal working day, regularly allowed for meals or rest. The phrase seems to connote a suspension of activity which is to be resumed at the end of a stated period. Recesses, variously called lunch-hours, tea breaks, smokos, stand-downs, etc, are normal features of employment in many industries. They are ordinary recesses. It seems to me a misuse of words to say that the appellant when he was swimming was temporarily absent from his place of employment during an ordinary recess.' *Landers v Dawson* [1964] ALR 1137 at 1141, per Windeyer J; 110 CLR 644 at 654

Canada 'I favour the interpretation which I use in this opinion that the term "recess' [at schools] is restricted to short periods of relaxation or play within the instructional day when students are necessarily under supervision and not permitted to leave the school grounds. I do not think the term includes "midday intermission" or "noon-hour".' *Winnipeg School Division No 1 v Winnipeg Teachers' Association No 1* (1972) 31 DLR (3d) 336 at 341, Man QB, per Hunt J

RECKLESS

[An action was brought for damages in respect of untrue statements in a prospectus inviting subscriptions for shares in a company.] 'The case put for the plaintiff is based upon what Lord Herschell said [in *Derry v Peek* (1889) 14 App Cas 337]. . . . He says, at page 374: 'I think the authorities establish the following propositions. First, in order to sustain an action of deceit, there must be proof of fraud, and nothing short of that will suffice. Secondly, fraud is proved when it is shown that a false representation has been made (1) knowingly, or (2) without belief in its truth, or (3) recklessly, careless whether it be true or false." An action of this kind cannot be supported without proof of fraud, an intention to deceive, and . . . it is not sufficient that there is blundering carelessness, however gross, unless there is wilful recklessness, by which I mean wilfully shutting one's eyes, which is of course fraud.' *Angus v Clifford* [1891] 2 Ch 449 at 464, 469, CA, per Lindley LJ

'The ordinary meaning of the word "reckless" in the English language is "careless", "heedless", "inattentive to duty". Literally, of course, it means "without reck". "Reck" is simply an old English word, now, perhaps, obsolete, meaning "heed", "concern", or "care".' *R v Bates* [1952] 2 All ER 842 at 845, 846, CCC per Donovan J

'The term "recklessly", I think, does not really give rise to much difficulty. It means something more than mere negligence or inadvertence. I think it means deliberately running an unjustifiable risk. There is not anything necessarily criminal, or even morally culpable, about running an unjustifiable risk; it depends in relation to what risk is run; it may be a big matter or it may be a small matter.' *Reed (Albert E) & Co Ltd v London and Rochester Trading Co Ltd* [1954] 2 Lloyd's Rep 463 at 465, per Devlin J

[The Prevention of Fraud (Investments) Act 1958, s 13(1) (see now the Financial Services Act 1986, s 47(1)) makes it an offence to induce or attempt to induce another person to enter into an agreement for the disposal, etc, of shares, by the 'reckless' making of any statement, promise, etc.] '"Reckless" is a word which is in quite common use, and the ordinary citizen when asked whether there was any difficulty in defining the word "reckless", would, I venture to think, say "No". He is accustomed to it in many ways—reckless driving, reckless conduct, and now, in the Act of 1958, a reckless statement or a reckless promise. The first point to note is that the word "reckless", in s 13(1) of the Act of 1958, is not applied to the person who makes the statement or gives the promise. You have not got to consider whether the person was a reckless sort of person. What you have got to consider is whether the statement or the promise has been proved to be a reckless statement or promise.

If you look up the meaning of the word "reckless" in the Oxford English Dictionary . . . you will find with regard to such things as statements or promises that there is only one meaning given and that meaning is "Characterised . . . by heedless rashness". In other words, the statement or promise must be a rash statement or promise and must be made heedless of whether the person making it has any real facts on which to base the statement or the promise. Facts, of course, may include what one has been told by apparently responsible persons, and I do not think that it would be right to import into the word "reckless" a meaning which might include a statement made as a result of an apparently responsible person having given one the information on which one makes the statement or gives the promise. Of course, if one knows facts outside what one has been told, that must be taken into consideration. I want to say something else. A man may honestly and strongly hold an opinion with which others disagree. Provided that he bases that opinion on facts which he has reason honestly to believe exist and makes the statement or gives the promise because of the existence of those facts, then, in my judgment, that statement or promise is not reckless. He has reckoned, although he may have reckoned wrongly or may even have been somewhat careless in the conclusion to which he has come. Carelessness, in my judgment, may not in itself be sufficient to constitute recklessness, although, of course, it is one of the factors which have to be taken into account. Clearly, a statement or promise cannot be both careful and reckless. On the other hand, I do not think that it is necessary to find dishonesty. A statement or promise may be reckless although the person making it, in some somewhat vague way, thinks that the statement is true and the promise is warranted. I would sum it up in this way. Before a jury can convict under s 13(1) of the Prevention of Fraud (Investments) Act 1958, they must be satisfied of three things: (i) that the statement or promise was in fact made; (ii) that it was a rash statement to make or a rash promise to give; and (iii) that the person who made the statement or gave the promise had no real basis of facts on which he could support the statement or the promise. If those three matters are proved to the satisfaction of a jury, then, in my judgment, the jury may convict. If any one of those three matters is not proved, then the jury must find a verdict of not guilty. In considering the matter, bases of fact may, and indeed must, include that which has been told to the person charged by apparently respectable and responsible persons.' *R v Grunwald* [1960] 3 All ER 380 at 384, per Paull J

'In my view, "recklessly" means grossly careless. Recklessness is gross carelessness—the doing of something which in fact involves a risk, whether the doer realises it or not; and the risk being such having regard to all the circumstances, that the taking of that risk would be described as "reckless". The likelihood or otherwise that damage will follow is one element to be considered, not whether the doer of the act actually realised the likelihood. The extent of the damage which is likely to follow is another element, not the extent which the doer of the act, in his wisdom or folly, happens to foresee. If the risk is slight and the damage which will follow if things go wrong is small, it may not be reckless, however, unjustified the doing of the act may be. If the risk is great, and the probable damage great, recklessness may readily be a fair description, however much the doer may regard the action as justified and reasonable. Each case has to be reviewed on its own particular facts and not by reference to any formula. The only test, in my view, is an objective one. Would a reasonable man, knowing all the facts and circumstances which the doer of the act knew or ought to have known, describe the act as "reckless" in the ordinary meaning of that word in ordinary speech? As I have said, my understanding of the ordinary meaning of that word is high degree of carelessness. I do not say "negligence", because "negligence" connotes a legal duty.' *Shawinigan Ltd v Vokins & Co Ltd* [1961] 3 All ER 396 at 403, per Megaw J

'Recklessness has, in my opinion, a subjective meaning; it implies culpability. An action which would be reckless if done by a man with adequate knowledge, skill or resources might not be reckless if done by a man with less appreciation of or ability to deal with the situation. One would be culpable, the other not.' *British Railways Board v Herrington* [1972] 1 All ER 749 at 758, HL, per Lord Reid

'A driver is guilty of driving recklessly if he deliberately disregards the obligation to drive with due care and attention or is indifferent whether or not he does so and thereby creates a risk of an accident which a driver driving with due care and attention would not create.' *R v Murphy (William)* [1980] 2 All ER 325 at 329, CA, per cur.

[The Criminal Damage Act 1971, s 1(1) makes it an offence without lawful excuse to destroy or damage property belonging to another either intentionally or being 'reckless' as to whether such property would be destroyed or damaged.] '"Reckless" as used in the new statutory definition of the mens rea of these offences is an ordinary English word. It had not by 1971 become a term of legal art with some more limited esoteric meaning than that which it bore in ordinary speech, a meaning which surely includes not only deciding to ignore a risk of harmful consequences resulting from one's acts that one has recognised as existing, but also failing to give any thought to whether or not there is any such risk in circumstances where, if any thought were given to the matter, it would be obvious that there was . . . In my opinion, a person charged with an offence under s 1(1) of the 1971 Act is "reckless as to whether or not any property would be destroyed or damaged" if (1) he does an act which in fact creates an obvious risk that property will be destroyed or damaged and (2) when he does the act he either has not given any thought to the possibility of there being any such risk or has recognised that there was some risk involved and has none the less gone on to do it. That would be a proper direction to the jury; cases in the Court of Appeal which held otherwise should be regarded as overruled.' *R v Caldwell* [1981] 1 All ER 961 at 966, 967, HL, per Lord Diplock

'It only surprises me that there should have been any question regarding the existence of mens rea in relation to the words "reckless", "recklessly" or "recklessness". Unlike most English words it has been in the English language as a word in general use at least since the eight century AD almost always with the same meaning, applied to a person or conduct evincing a state of mind stopping short of deliberate intention, and going beyond mere inadvertence, or, in its modern though not its etymological and original sense, mere carelessness. The Oxford English Dictionary quotes several examples from Old English, many from the Middle English period, and many more from modern English. The word was familiar to the Venerable Bede, to Langland, to Chaucer, to Sir Thomas More and to Shakespeare. In its alternative and possibly older pronunciation, and etymologically incorrect spelling (wretchless, wretchlessly, wretchlessness) it was known to the authors of the Articles of religion printed in the book of Common Prayer. Though its pronunciation has varied, so far as I know its meaning has not. There is no separate legal meaning to the word.' *R v Lawrence* [1981] 1 All ER 974 at 978, HL, per Lord Hailsham of St Marylebone (adopted, *R v Seymour* [1983] 2 All ER 1058, HL)

'Recklessness on the part of the doer of an act does presuppose that there is something in the circumstances that would have drawn the attention of an ordinary prudent individual to the possibility that his act was capable of causing the kind of serious harmful consequences that the section which creates the offence was intended to prevent, and that the risk of those harmful consequences occurring was not so slight that an ordinary prudent individual would feel justified in treating them as negligible. It is only when this is so that the doer of the act is acting "recklessly" if, before doing the act, he either fails to give any thought to the possibility of there being any such risk or, having recognised that there was such risk, he nevertheless goes on to do it.' Ibid at 982, per Lord Diplock

Australia 'The standard test of a man's mind in the commission of an act is the foreseeable consequences. If he applied his mind to the consequences, and without concluding that they would probably happen (which is criminal intent) his state of mind was that he did not care whether they happened or not, that is recklessness.' *R v Stones* [1956] SR (NSW) 25 at 34, per cur.

RECOGNISED

'The word "recognised" is a very common word, particularly in connection with the phrase "recognised holidays" in many industries, and it is to be found in industrial agreements and industrial awards. "Recognised" must, in my opinion, mean that a day is recognised as a holiday in the industry or in the particular occupation of the person carrying on a branch of industry—a day in respect of which a worker in the industry or in the enterprise would say without doubt: "Why, of course we always treat that as a holiday." That could be said of August Bank Holiday. There must be very few industries in which August Bank Holiday is not by common consent treated as a recognised holiday. There is no need to attempt to give an exhaustive definition or place an exhaustive construction on the word. It is quite sufficient for the purposes of this appeal to say that the argument that "recognised" means that the employer can himself decide what day is to be a holiday is quite wrong. The county court judge in his judgment seemed to think that a day which it was agreed by both the employer and employee should be a holiday would be a recognised holiday within the meaning of the definition. I do not propose to express any opinion upon that. It may very well be—I do not express this as an opinion but as a warning—that the matter is not free from doubt. It might be that an employer might agree with his men to take an extra day a week off through the year. It would require to be argued on the facts of any such case as to whether or not an agreement of that kind could convert the day in question into a recognised holiday.' *Cummins v Holloway Brothers (London) Ltd* [1944] 1 All ER 296 at 297–299, CA, per Lord Greene MR

RECOMPENSE

Australia 'That section [the Defence Act 1903–1939 (Cth), s 67] imposes an obligation upon the owner of various things required for naval or military purposes, including a boat or vessel, to furnish them for those purposes when required to do so. . . . The section goes on to say that the owner shall be recompensed therefor in manner prescribed. . . . In the present case, it is probably true that regulations [if] made under s 67 . . . of the Defence Act might have given interest. But can we extract from the word "recompense" in s 67 an authority to award it? If we work out the implications of the word "recompense" according to ordinary legal principles, we have the decision in *Swift's Case* [[1925] AC 520] for our guidance upon the place interest takes in the conception of compensation in English law. . . . Our Constitution, when it refers to "just terms" is placing a qualification on the legislative power it bestows to acquire property compulsorily. But it is, I think, difficult to say that it makes it necessary for the legislature to give more than the full content of "compensation" as compensation is understood in English law, and we know from the House of Lords that a right to interest on the amount payable for the thing is not always or necessarily included. . . . Whatever may be the correct view of compensation forming a replacement of income-producing capital assets, I do not think that we can find in s 67, interpreted in the light of s 51 (xxxi) [of the Commonwealth of Australia Constitution Act 1901], enough to enable us to award interest upon the recompense we now hold to be payable.' *Commonwealth v Huon Transport Pty Ltd* (1945) 70 CLR 293 at 316, 326, per Dixon J

RECONDITION

[A contract for the sale of tractors stipulated that the tractors should be fully 're-conditioned'.] '"Re-condition" is not a word to be found in the dictionary, but it obviously means "to put back into condition"; not, of course, into brand-new condition, but to renew the machine in the sense of giving it a new lease of life. It means more than overhauling or repairing. In any machine there are some parts which are intended to last as long as the machine itself lasts, and other parts which have a shorter life and need to be renewed from time to time. Re-conditioning requires, I think, that the machine should be thoroughly examined—usually that means "stripping down"—to see what renewable parts are worn, and all such parts which are substantially worn should be renewed. To insist that every slightly used part should be scrapped would be absurd. But any part that is left must, I think, have most of its life still in front of it, so that the machine, as a whole is given, as I say, a new lease of life. . . . I do not think that "fully" adds much to "re-conditioned", but it does add something. The reason why "re-conditioned" by itself is distrusted in the trade is, I think, because the word has been seized on by people who smarten up a machine with a new coat of paint and sell it as re-conditioned. "Fully" is thought necessary to exclude that practice. In truth, I think that, if a machine was sold as "re-conditioned" without qualification, it would not be enough to prove that part of it was re-conditioned. I can see, however, that qualifications might be implied. If, for example, a car was sold as "re-conditioned", it might be suggested that the term was intended to apply only to the engine, or something of that sort. The advantage of "fully" is that it expressly excludes qualifications of this sort.' *Minster Trust Ltd v Traps Tractors Ltd* [1954] 3 All ER 136 at 144, per Devlin J

New Zealand [A second-hand car was sold on a representation that the vehicle had been 'reconditioned' throughout.] 'In Webster, 2nd Edn (1938) the definition is: '(1) To restore (something worn) to sound condition by readjustments and replacement of parts; to renovate; as a reconditioned automobile." If that is the meaning of the word—and I accept that as being its meaning—the renovation or restoration required would not, as it seems to me, be to complete as the appellant contended it should be. I am content to treat it as a question of degree.' *Harper v South Island Holdings Ltd* [1959] NZLR 629 at 633, 634, per Hutchison J

RECONSTRUCTION

Of company *See also* AMALGAMATION

Where an undertaking is being carried on by a company and is in substance transferred, not to an outsider, but to another company consisting substantially of the same shareholders with a view to its being continued by the transferee company, there is a reconstruction. It is none the less a reconstruction because all the assets do not pass to the new company, or all the shareholders of the transferor company are not shareholders in the transferee company, or all the liabilities of the transferor company are not taken over by the transferee company. (7 Halsbury's Laws (4th edn) para 2149)

'The question which I have to decide turns upon the true construction of the fourth condition in these debentures, and particularly on the meaning of the words "if the company commences to be wound-up otherwise than for the purposes of reorganisation or reconstruction". . . . What is included in "reconstruction" by persons conversant with company law? There is one mode of reconstruction which may perhaps be said to be within the strict sense of the term. That is when there is a winding-up order, an arrangement with creditors sanctioned by the court under the Joint Stock Companies Arrangement Act 1870 [repealed; see now the Companies Act 1985, Part XIII, ss 425–430], and a stay of the winding-up, upon which the old company, having reconstructed itself according to the arrangement, would recommence business and go on as the old company. That would certainly be reconstruction within the condition. The company would still continue to exist; but that, and that alone, would be too narrow a meaning to give to "reconstruction" here. The usual mode of reconstruction is when a company resolves to wind itself up, and proposes the formation of a new company, which is to consist of the old shareholders, and to take over the old undertaking, the old shareholders receiving shares in the new company. In that case the old company ceases to exist in point of law, and there is in form a sale to the members of a new corporation. But the company is in substance, and may be fairly said to be, reconstructed. . . . The question to be asked is, whether the new company is practically the same as the old, even though in law it is a separate corporation? According to the textwriters reconstruction does not include amalgamation, or a sale by a company of its undertaking to another existing company. . . . Reorganisation, though a less familiar term, can have no wider meaning than reconstruction. Though it is not necessary to express an opinion, I think that the two terms are used as alternative expressions. The present case is that of a comparatively small company joining with a large company, and the transaction might be compared with the case of a large railway company buying up a small railway company on terms that the shareholders of the small company should receive shares in the larger company. Would any reasonable person call that a reconstruction or reorganisation of the small company?' *Hooper v Western Counties & South Wales Telephone Co Ltd* (1892) 68 LT 78 at 79, 80, per Chitty J

'What does "reconstruction" mean? To my mind it means this. An undertaking of some definite kind is being carried on, and the conclusion is arrived at that it is not desirable to kill that undertaking, but that it is desirable to preserve it in some form, and to do so, not by selling it to an outsider who shall carry it on—that would be a mere sale—but in some altered form to continue the undertaking in such a manner as that the persons now carrying it on will substantially continue to carry it on. . . . But it does not involve that all the assets shall pass to the new company or resuscitated company, or that all the shareholders of the old company shall be shareholders in the new company or resuscitated company. Substantially the business and the persons interested must be the same. Does it make any difference that the new company or resuscitated company does or does not take over the liabilities? I think not. I think it is none the less a reconstruction because from the assets taken over some part is expected provided that substantially the business is taken, and it is immaterial whether the liabilities are taken over by the new or resuscitated company or are provided for by excepting from the scheme of reconstruction a sufficient amount to answer them. It is not, therefore, vital that either the whole assets should be taken over or that the liabilities should be taken over. You have to see whether substantially the same persons carry on the same business; and if they do, that, I conceive, is a reconstruction.' *Re South African Supply & Cold Storage Co, Wild v South African Supply & Cold Storage Co* [1904] 2 Ch 268 at 286, per Buckley J

Of premises

[Landlords of business premises gave notice to their tenants under the Landlord and Tenant Act 1954, s 25 that they would oppose the grant of a new tenancy on the ground (provided by s 30(1)(f) of the Act) that they intended to 'reconstruct' the premises.] 'In my judgment, the word "reconstruct" in this sub-section is not satisfied by a change of identity; there must be substantial work of construction. The word "reconstruct" here is best expressed, I think, by the synonym "rebuild". There must be in effect a rebuilding of the premises or (of course) of a "substantial part" of those premises. Whether there is work of that character and to such a degree is primarily a matter for the county court judge.' *Cadle (Percy E) & Co Ltd v Jacmarch Properties Ltd* [1957] 1 All ER 148 at 149, CA, per Denning LJ (also reported in [1957] 1 QB 323 at 328)

'The argument which has been directed to this court by counsel for the landlords is based on this proposition: that the word "reconstruct" must not be read in too literal a sense. He admits that the word "reconstruct" involves physical work, but he says that that does not necessarily cover the whole meaning of the word, which may be satisfied by some physical work coupled with a change of identity or character of the building such as is envisaged here. I notice that the word "reconstruct" follows the word "demolish" in the sub-section. "Demolish" clearly involves the physical act of destruction; and I agree with Denning LJ that the word "reconstruct" seems to be equivalent to "rebuild" and to contemplate a state of affairs where there has been a measure of demolition falling short of a total demolition.' Ibid at 150, per Hodson LJ

Australia 'Now "reconstruction" is given various significations. It may denote constructing anew, rebuilding or remodelling, in the sense of a total alteration of the premises or some part of the premises, and so involving structural changes and transformations. It may include reparations of a particular kind; renovations, viz, that of rebuilding some part of the premises more or less in its previous form; but the word is also used to cover what are simply repairs. I apprehend the true intendment of the regulation is that the last-mentioned meaning is not included: compare *Agar v Nokes* [(1905) 93 LT 605 at 609].' *Returned Sailors, etc, League of Australia v Abbott* [1946] SASR 270 at 272, per Mayo J

Australia 'We have come to the conclusion that the word "reconstruction" in s 62(5)(m) [of the Landlord and Tenant (Amendment) Act 1948–1986 (NSW)] includes the renewal or alteration or remodelling of the premises demised which, in the present case, means Office B itself and not the multi-storeyed building. The uncontradicted evidence discloses that Office B, as a result of the work to be performed in relation to it, is to have its old entrance entirely done away with and a fresh entrance made to it from another part of the building; it is to be provided with a means of ingress and egress to and from Office A which it never had before; it will entirely lose its existing fixture partition walls; upon an area of some 1100 square feet it will have a new floor surface by means of the affixation of vinyl tiles; its walls will be repainted. In these circumstances, having regard to the nature and size of the demised premises and the nature of the work to be performed and the changes in the structural layout thereof resulting from the work proposed, we are of the opinion that it could not be said that there is no evidence of reconstruction. We venture to suggest that no one could regard Office B after the completion of this work and say that it had not been the subject of an extensive measure of alteration or remodelling. From a self-contained office divided in itself it would have become an undivided area and a part of a large office suite. Though the meaning of an ordinary English word used in a statute is a question of fact, not of law, nevertheless a finding by a tribunal of fact can be disturbed if the facts inferred by it or which can only be inferred by it from the evidence are necessarily within the description of the word or phrase in the statute and the tribunal has made a contrary finding. In that situation its decision is wrong in law.' *Williams v Evans* [1966] 1 NSWR 245 at 251, 252, per Asprey and Holmes JJA

RECORD (Disc)

'Record' means any record or similar contrivance for reproducing sound, including the sound-track of a cinematograph film. (Dramatic and

Musical Performers' Protection Act 1958, s 8(1); Theatres Act 1968, s 7(3)).

RECORD (Document)

'It will have been seen that throughout all the cases there is one governing rule—certiorari is only available to quash a decision for error of law if the error appears on the face of the record. What, then, is the record? It has been said to consist of all those documents which are kept by the tribunal for a permanent memorial and testimony of their proceedings: see Blackstone's Commentaries, Vol 3, p 24. But it must be noted that, whenever there was any question as to what would, or should not, be included in the record of any tribunal, the Court of King's Bench used to determine it. It did it in this way. When the tribunal sent their record to the King's Bench in answer to the writ of certiorari this return was examined, and, if it was defective or incomplete, it was quashed: see *R v Apsley* [(1671) Sty 85], *R v Levermore* [(1700) 1 Salk 146], and *Ashley's Case* [(1697) 2 Salk 479]. Alternatively, the tribunal might be ordered to complete it: *Williams v Lord Bagot* [(1824) 2 Dow & Ry KB 315] and *R v Warnford* [(1825), 5 Dow & Ry KB 489]. It appears that the Court of King's Bench always insisted that the record should contain, or recite, the document or information which initiated the proceedings and thus gave the tribunal its jurisdiction and also the document which contained their adjudication. Thus in the old days the record sent up by the justices had, in the case of a conviction, to recite the information in its precise terms, and in the case of an order which had been decided by quarter sessions by way of appeal, the record had to set out the order appealed from: see *Anon* [(1697) 2 Salk 479]. The record had also to set out the adjudication, but it was never necessary to set out the reasons: see *South Cadbury (Inhabitants) v Braddon, Somerset (Inhabitants)* [(1710) 2 Salk 607], nor the evidence, save in the case of convictions. Following these cases, I think the record must contain at least the document which initiates the proceedings, the pleadings, if any, and the adjudications, but not the evidence, nor the reasons, unless the tribunal chooses to incorporate them.' *R v Northumberland Compensation Appeal Tribunal, ex p Shaw* [1952] 1 All ER 122 at 131, 132, CA, per Denning LJ (also reported in [1952] 1 KB 338 at 351, 352)

'My Lords, in the case for the appellants, an order for certiorari is sought on the ground that there is an error of law on the face of the record. When certiorari is sought on such a ground, evidence is not as a rule admissible. The error must appear on the face of the proceedings without the aid of extrinsic evidence. But what is the "record" for this purpose? It is not confined to the formal record of the proceedings such as is kept by a superior court of record, which used to be enrolled on parchment in Blackstone's day and is filed at the Central Office in our day. Certiorari goes to all inferior tribunals, not only to those which are courts of record but also to those which are not; and not only to those which keep a formal record, but also to those which do not. When certiorari issues to any of these tribunals, there must be brought before the Queen's Bench not only the formal order of the tribunal but also, as the old writ said, "all things touching the same": and this includes the reasons for the decision when the tribunal gives them. This goes back as far as the time of Holt CJ. In 1702 in a case [*Ryslip Parish v Hendon Parish* (1698) Holt KB 572] where justices had ordered a poor man to be removed from Ryslip to Hendon, he said: "Where the justices of peace do give a special reason for their settlement, and the conclusion which they make in point of law will not warrant the premises, there we will rectify their judgment: but if they have given no reason at all, then we will not ravel into the fact." The court would not compel a tribunal to give its reasons if it did not wish to do so; but, if it did so, it became part of the record. . . .' *Baldwin and Francis Ltd v Patents Appeal Tribunal* [1959] 2 All ER 433 at 444, HL, per Lord Denning; also reported [1959] AC 663 at 687, 688

[The House of Lords did not determine what documents form part of the record for the purpose of the principle that certiorari may issue for error of law on the face of the record.]

[The question was what constituted the 'record' for the purposes of granting certiorari for error on the face of the record.] 'Although the old authorities do show a stricter approach to what constituted the "record", the modern authorities show that the judges have relaxed the strictness of that rule and taken a broader view of the "record" in order that certiorari may give relief to those against whom a decision has been given which is based on a manifest error of law. We therefore hold that the reasons contained in the transcript of the oral judgment of the Crown Court constitute part of the record for the purposes of certiorari and we are entitled to look at it to see if they contain errors of law.' *R v Crown Court at Knightsbridge, ex p International Sporting Club (London) Ltd* [1981] 3 All ER 417 at 424, per cur.

[The question was whether certain documents were admissible in evidence as 'records' within the Civil Evidence Act 1968, s 4(1).] 'I have come to the conclusion that the documents which form part of the large bundle before me are not records within the meaning of s 4 of the 1968 Act. The intention of that section was, I believe, to admit in evidence records which a historian would regard as original or primary sources, that is documents which either give effect to a transaction itself or which contain a contemporaneous register of information supplied by those with direct knowledge of the facts.' *H v Schering Chemicals Ltd* [1983] 1 All ER 849 at 852, per Bingham J

Australia 'In my view, it could not be said that historical documents written up years after the event, comprising a mixture of information derived from primary records and received orally by persons who may have had personal knowledge of those matters, meets the description of a 'continuous record'. The term, I am satisfied, relates to entries made progressively, and reasonably contemporaneously to the matters which they record in a single document or series of documents comprising part of a system for the recording of information.' *Atra v Farmers & Graziers Co-op Ltd* (1986) 5 NSWLR 281 at 285, per Wood J

New Zealand 'I do not obtain from the regulations any assistance in determining whether the words "adoption records" in s 23 [of the Adoption Act] include records other than those held in court. It would however, I think, be straining the meaning of words to hold that they mean documents other than those on the Court file.' *D v Hall* [1984] 1 NZLR 727 at 733, per Hillyer J

Contract of *See* CONTRACT

Estoppel of *See* ESTOPPEL

RECORDING

'Sound recording' means—

(a) a recording of sounds, from which the sounds may be reproduced, or

(b) a recording of the whole or any part of a literary, dramatic or musical work, from which sounds reproducing the work or part may be produced,

regardless of the medium on which the recording is made or the method by which the sounds are reproduced or produced. (Copyright, Designs and Patents Act 1988, s 5)

RECOVER

[Section 11 of Stat (1850) 13 & 14 Vict c 61 (repealed; see now the County Courts Act 1984, s 20) deprived a plaintiff of costs where he 'recovered' less than a certain amount.] 'It seems to me, that if a man brings an action and declares, and the defendant pleads payment of money into court, and the plaintiff takes it out of court, he "recovers" it in that action; for he obtains by means of that action money which he could not obtain without it. That seems to me the good sense and reason of the matter.' *Parr v Lillicrap (Lillicup)* (1862) 1 H & C 615 at 618, per Martin B

'Property is "recovered", so the authorities seem to show, when the plaintiff has been enriched as the result of the action.' *Wagg v Law Society* [1957] 2 All ER 274 at 278, per Harman J (also reported in [1957] Ch 405 at 412)

'The first point raised by counsel for the plaintiff is that the £100 paid into court is not money "recovered" in the action [within the County Courts Act 1934, s 47(1) (repealed; see now the County Courts Act 1984, s 20)]. In my view, it is. The action was brought; the money was paid into court in the action; the notice of acceptance of the money has been given under the rules in relation to the action: and the money will be paid to the plaintiff as the result of the action having been brought by him. That being so, it seems to me quite clear that this is money "recovered" in the action.' *Parkes v Knowles* [1957] 3 All ER 600 at 602, per Lynskey J

New Zealand [A company's power of attorney authorised the attorney to demand, sue for, and 'recover' all money due.] 'The word "recover" has been held to mean something more than suing. In *Haines v Welch* [(1868) LR 4 CP 91] "recover" was held to mean "to obtain in any legal manner", and hence it was said that it gave the right to distrain for rent in arrear, as well as to recover the rent by action, the learned and eminent judge, Mr Justice Willes, saying "The word 'recover' is now often used in the larger sense of obtaining in any legal manner". And a petition to wind up is a mode of obtaining in a legal manner the payments of debts: see per Richmond J in *Re Extended Wakatu Goldmining Company (Limited) Moore v Cuff and others* [(1894) 13 NZLR 544]. In *Morris v Duncan* [[1899] 1 QB 4 DC] it was held that "recover" did not limit the proceedings that could be taken to an action. A proceeding before Justices was authorised by the word "recover". In *Howard v Baillie* [(1796) 2 Hy Bl 618] it was said, "Thus an authority to receive and recover debts includes a power to arrest". Now, the proceeding by petition is a mode of recovering a debt, for it is often successful without the proceeding to wind up being continued, and the petition may be withdrawn: see, amongst many other cases to this effect, the case of *Re Times Life Assurance and Guarantee Company* [(1869) LR 9 Eq 382].' *Re Gilbert Machinery Co (No 1)* (1906) 26 NZLR 47 at 50, per Stout CJ; also reported 8 GLR 489 at 491

New Zealand [The Workers' Compensation Act 1922 (NZ), s 49(4) (repealed) was as follows: 'When judgment has been recovered by or on behalf of any person for compensation that person shall not be entitled thereafter to recover damages from any person in respect of the same accident unless the court is satisfied that all reasonable steps have been taken to obtain satisfaction of the judgment for compensation, and that the judgment has not been satisfied.'] 'Callan J refers to what was said by Kennedy LJ in *Page v Burtwell* [[1908] 2 KB 758]. What the Lord Justice there said was that it appeared to him to be a narrow and unjustifiable view to hold that "recover" means to "recover in the course of and as the result of some litigious proceedings". It is true that he interpreted the word "recover" as meaning "applied for and received", but he was speaking there of the recovery of compensation where there was no litigation, and in such a case the word "recover" means "applied for and received". To "recover judgment" is a different thing. That means, of course, to recover judgment in a Court of competent jurisdiction and it seems to us that if the Compensation Court had jurisdiction to make the order, then the plaintiff did obtain a judgment. That, in our opinion, is all the word "recover" means in that context.' *Logie v Union Steam Ship Co of New Zealand Ltd* [1945] NZLR 388 at 395, 396, CA, per Northcroft J; also reported [1945] GLR 169 at 172

RECOVERABLE

[An agreement provided that a claim for moneys lent should not be 'recoverable' until the amount of an overdraft should have been paid.] 'In my opinion the words "shall not be recoverable" in the agreement are equivalent to "shall not be receivable" or "shall not be received".' *Berwick v Matthews* (1892) 66 LT 564 at 565, DC, per Day J

New Zealand [The Workers' Compensation Act 1922 (NZ), s 49(3) (repealed) provided that any sum received by a worker by way of compensation should be deducted from the sum 'recoverable' from any person by way of damages in respect of the same accident.] 'The subsection refers to that which is recoverable—i.e., legally enforceable by action because of a civil liability. It does not refer to an amount recovered under an agreement of compromise.' *Charming Creek-Westport Coal Co Ltd v Crawford* [1950] NZLR 835 at 838, per Northcroft J; also reported [1950] GLR 493 at 495

RECOVERY

New Zealand 'The words ["unlikely to recover" in s 10(g) of the Divorce and Matrimonial Causes Act 1928 (NZ) (repealed)] are susceptible of meaning a complete return to mental health with a mind no longer impaired by any unsoundness or disease; they are susceptible, too, of meaning such a degree of recovery as to render confinement in a mental hospital unnecessary and to make practicable the return of the individual to his or her home, with perhaps a resumption of his or her former occupation. Since, under the section, it has been judicially determined that to be "of unsound mind" connotes such a kind and degree of mental unsoundness as to justify committal to a mental hospital, it would be logical and in consonance with this interpretation that recovery should mean the attainment of a state which, while falling short of perfect mental health, was nevertheless such that detention in a mental hospital was no longer warranted.' *W v W* [1952] NZLR 812 at 814, per Gresson J

RECREATION

Australia 'The word "recreation" is a very wide word. The definition of it in the Oxford Dictionary is: "The action of recreating oneself or another, or the fact of being recreated by some pleasant occupation, pastime or amusement." It seems to me that the obtaining of historical, geographical or topographical information by members of the public, whether they be local residents or whether they be tourists, is a recreation of those members of the public. It is not necessary that the information should aid the recreation of the public upon the area or only upon the area. It is sufficient if the obtaining of the information is a recreation. It is true that one tends to think of recreation in terms of physical or sporting activities, to the exclusion of the cultivation of the mind, or the satisfaction of man's desire for knowledge. I do not think that any such limitation can be put upon the words. A public library is a source of public recreation in the same way as a public racecourse, even though it may not be frequented by as large a number of persons. A public art gallery, or a public concert hall, serves the purpose of public recreation in the same way as a public sports field. A man must be whole in mind and body and he requires recreation of his mind, as well as for his body.' *A-G v Cooma Municipal Council* [1962] NSWR 663 at 667, per Jacobs J

RECTIFICATION

Of contract

'The essence of rectification is to bring the document which was expressed and intended to be in pursuance of a prior agreement into harmony with that prior agreement. Indeed, it may be regarded as a branch of the doctrine of specific performance. It presupposes a prior contract, and it requires proof that, by common mistake, the final completed instrument as executed fails to give proper effect to the prior contract.' *Lovell & Christmas Ltd v Wall* [1911] 104 LT 85 at 88, CA, per Cozens-Hardy MR

'In ordering rectification the court does not rectify contracts, but what it rectifies is the erroneous expression of contracts in documents. For rectification it is not enough to set about to find out what one or even both of the parties to the contract intended. What you have got to find out is what intention was communicated by one side to the other, and with what common intention and common agreement they made their bargain.' Ibid at 93, per Buckley LJ

[Cited in *Joscelyne v Nissen* [1970] 1 All ER 1213, CA.]

Of register of members

[Upon an application to the court, an order was made for the register of members of a company to be 'rectified'.] 'The name of Mr Cuthbert has been struck out of the register and the register rectified. The effect of that is exactly the same as if it had never been put in. That is the meaning of "rectified". You strike it out by way of rectification, and the Court has therefore declared that it ought never to have been entered at all. They have struck it out from the beginning.' *Pulbrook v Richmond Consolidated Mining Co* (1878) 9 Ch D 610 at 615, per Jessel MR

'Altering the register so as to make it conformable with a lawful transfer is not to rectify the register under s 35 [of the Companies Act 1862 (repealed; see now The Companies Act 1985, s 359)]. That section only comes into operation when the company improperly puts on the register a name which ought not to be on it, or improperly refuses to put on the register a name that ought to be on it.' *Re National Bank of Wales* (1897) 66 LJ Ch 222 at 226, 227, CA, per Lindley LJ

RECTOR *See* VICAR

REDEEM

'To redeem' means, in relation to any trading stamps, to exchange such stamps (whether by delivering up the stamps or by suffering the same to be cancelled or otherwise howsoever) for money or for goods or for any other benefit, allowance, concession or advantage (but not including the service or repair by the seller or manufacturer of the goods upon or in connection with the purchase of which the stamps are delivered or the replacement of such goods if defective); and the expressions 'redeemable' and 'redemption' shall be construed accordingly. (Trading Stamps Act 1964, s 10)

Australia 'The meanings of "redeem" in the Oxford English Dictionary are instructive. For example, they include "to buy back (a thing formerly possessed)": "to make payment for (a thing held or claimed by another)". The Macquarie Dictionary, to which we should now perhaps make equal reference, is to the same effect. Thus "redeem" is a word which naturally refers to the act of the person who owes the liability which is to be recovered.' *John While & Sons Pty Ltd v Changleng* [1985] 2 NSWLR 163 at 164–165, per Samuels JA

REDEEMABLE

[A prospectus stated that debentures were 'redeemable' within seventeen years.] 'Does "redeemable" mean "liable to redemption", or does it mean that the debentures are to be all, in fact, redeemed within the specified period? In my opinion, it means that they are to be liable to redemption, and there is no obligation on the company to redeem them. . . . In my opinion the word "redeemable" was used for the purpose of informing the debenture-holders that they would not necessarily receive the interest at 6 per cent during the whole of the seventeen years, because the company had an option to redeem the debentures.' *Re Chicago & North West Granaries Co Ltd, Morrison v Chicago & North West Granaries Co Ltd* [1898] 1 Ch 263 at 266–268, per North J

'I agree that, prima facie, the true legal meaning of the word "redeemable" when applied to stock is stock liable to redemption, that is to say, liable to be redeemed at the option of the mortgagor or person who has the right to redeem. . . . If that be the prima facie meaning of the word "redeemable" the prima facie meaning of the word "irredeemable" when applied to stock is stock that the mortgagor has no power to redeem.' *Re Stocks (Joseph) & Co Ltd, Willey v Stocks (Joseph) & Co Ltd* (1909) [1912] 2 Ch 134 n at 140, per Eve J

REDELIVERY

'I agree . . . that it is impossible to construe the word "redelivery" in this charterparty in a literal sense. This is not a contract of demise. It is an ordinary contract whereby the possession of the ship remains in the shipowner. The services of the ship, master, and crew were let to the charterers who could never do more by way of redelivery than restore or give up those services to the owner.' *Italian State Railways v Mavrogordatos* [1919] 2 KB 305 at 314, 315, CA, per A T Lawrence LJ

REDEMPTION

'We are, on the whole, in agreement as to the natural meaning of "redemption" in relation to an obligation such as a land improvement rentcharge, that is to say, that it connotes a compounding of future payments as distinct from the mere payment of the periodical sums as they become due.' *Re Sandbach* [1951] Ch 791 at 803, CA, per cur.

Equity of *See* EQUITY–EQUITABLE

REDUCE

Australia [The question was as to the meaning of the word 'reduce' in the sense of reducing charges for telegrams.] 'The words "shall have power to reduce" do not etymologically include a power to reduce to nothing or abolish.' *Eastern Extension Australasia & China Telegraph Co Ltd v Commonwealth* (1908) 6 CLR 647 at 664, per Griffith CJ

'Primarily, the reduction of a charge means its diminution. When we are offered goods at reduced prices we do not expect to get them for nothing, however cheap they may have been before the reduction. But then it is said that the power may be exercised by successive steps until next to nothing remains, so that when an infinitesimal sum is reached by way of residuum, the charges have been practically abolished. To this there is a plain answer. Assuming the successive exercises of the power, there must be something left, and when that ultimate something is reached, *ex vi termini* there is neither a reduction to nothing nor an abolition. In truth, the power to reduce involves a direction to leave something, and therefore entire abolition is not an exercise of the power granted.' Ibid at 668, per Barton J

'Taking the word in its ordinary meaning "reduce" does not mean "abolish".' Ibid at 678, per O'Connor J

REDUNDANCY PAYMENT

'As this is one of our first cases on the Redundancy Payments Act 1965, [repealed] it is as well to remind ourselves of the policy of this legislation. As I read the Act, a worker of long standing is now recognised as having an accrued right in his job; and his right gains in value with the years. So much so that, if the job is shut down, he is entitled to compensation for loss of the job—just as a director gets compensation for loss of office. The director gets a golden handshake. The worker gets a redundancy payment. It is not unemployment pay. I repeat "not". Even if he gets another job straightaway, he nevertheless is entitled to full redundancy payment. It is, in a real sense, compensation for long service.' *Lloyd v Brassey* [1969] 1 All ER 382 at 383, per Lord Denning MR

[*See* now, as to redundancy payments, the Employment Protection (Consolidation) Act 1978, Part VI.]

REDUNDANT

'Answers should not be redundant. It may not, perhaps, be easy to define the meaning of this term in a short sentence, but the true meaning I take to be this,—the respondent is not to insert in his answer any matter foreign to the articles he is called upon to answer, although such matter may be admissible in plea, but he may, in his answer, plead matter by way of explanation pertinent to the articles, even if such matter shall be solely in his own knowledge, and to such extent incapable of proof; or he may state matter which can be substantiated by witnesses; but, in this latter instance, if such matter be introduced into the answer, and not afterwards put in plea, or proved, the court will give no weight or credence to such part of the answer.' *Dysart v Dysart* (1843) 3 Curt 543 at 545, 546, per Dr Lushington

RE-ENGAGEMENT

'The case turns on the construction of the contract of October 31, 1892, the dispute being as to the meaning of the word "re-engagements" in that contract. I agree that the construction of the contract is for the judge. But the question here is whether another contract—viz, that of November 19, 1894, comes within the terms of the former contract. That is a question which is rightly left to the jury. By the earlier contract the defendant agreed to accept engagements through the firm of Didcott and Co at three music-halls for certain periods during 1893 and the two following years, at a certain salary and on certain conditions, and he agreed to pay 10 per cent commission on those engagements and on all his re-engagements at those establishments. On November 19, 1894, the defendants, without the instrumentality of Didcott and Co, entered into contracts to appear at the same music-halls in 1896. But in these contracts the salary was different, and there were differences in the other terms. The plaintiffs claim that these were re-engagements. In my opinion it is impossible to say as a matter of law that they were re-engagements as distinguished from fresh engagements. Where there were differences in the terms of engagement, the judge could not lay it down that the case in question was a re-engagement; but it was right to leave the matter to the jury. Neither do I think that the learned judge had misdirected the jury in this case. It is, I think, impossible to give an exact definition of "re-engagement". In my opinion the proper thing to do was that which the learned judge had done here—viz, to give the jury instances of what would be a re-engagement and of what would be a fresh engagement, and ask them under which category they thought the present case came. The learned judge pointed out to the jury the differences in the agreements, and they came to the conclusion that this was a fresh engagement, and not a re-engagement.' *Arnold v Stratton* (1898) 14 TLR 537 at 537, 538, CA, per A L Smith LJ

RE-ENTRY

'I do not see how it is possible, on any construction of this proviso for re-entry, to say that the lessors have re-entered, when all that they have done is to give a notice of their intention to re-enter, founded on a statement that the lease had determined, which had not in fact happened, or a demand for possession founded on that notice. I think the only thing here that could be relied upon as equivalent to actual re-entry was the issue of the writ.' *Moore v Ullcoats Mining Co Ltd* [1908] 1 Ch 575 at 588, per Warrington J

REFER TO DRAWER

'I respectfully adopt the language of Scrutton J, as he then was, in *Flach v The London & South Western Bank Ltd* [(1915) 31 TLR 334]. There the learned judge said that the words "Refer to drawer" in his opinion, in their ordinary meaning, amounted to a statement by the bank, "We are not paying; go back to the drawer and ask why", or else, "go back to the drawer and ask him to pay".' *Plunkett v Barclays Bank Ltd* [1936] 2 KB 107 at 120, per du Parcq J

REFINER

United States The term 'refiner' means any person engaged in the refining of crude oil to produce motor fuel, and includes any affiliate of such person. (Petroleum Marketing Practices Act 1978, s 101(5))

United States The term 'refiner' means any person engaged in—
(A) the refining of crude oil to produce automotive gasoline; or
(B) the importation of automotive gasoline.
(Petroleum Marketing Practices Act 1978, s 201(5))

REFRESHMENT

'Beer may be "refreshment", but it is not "entertainment".' *Taylor v Oram* (1862) 1 H & C 370 at 377, per Pollock CB

'I cannot understand how it can be said that a loaf of bread, sold for human consumption, is not a loaf of bread sold for refreshment. "Refreshment" is not a term of art. When one talks about a person taking "refreshments" one means taking some article of food generally different from what I may call a full meal—something light—a refresher. Bread is a refreshment just as much as a bun or a ham sandwich is a refreshment. It may not be so attractive, but it is a refreshment and part of a meal. That, I think, must be conceded. Therefore, you have the position that under Sch I to this Act [Shops (Sunday Trading Restrictions) Act 1936 (repealed; see now the Shops Act 1950, Sch V)] bread can be sold as a refreshment.' *Binns v Wardale* [1946] KB 451 at 455, 456, DC, per Lord Goddard CJ

REFRESHMENT HOUSE

Late night refreshment house

[The original expression 'refreshment house' (under the repealed Refreshment Houses Act 1860) was replaced by the expression 'late night refreshment house' under the Late Night Refreshment Houses Act 1969, s 1, as set out below.]

For the purposes of this Act, a 'late night refreshment house' is a house, room, shop or building kept open for public refreshment, resort and entertainment at any time between the hours of 10 o'clock at night and 5 o'clock of the following morning, other than exempt licensed premises. (Late Night Refreshment Houses Act 1969, s 1, as amended by the Local Government (Miscellaneous Provisions) Act 1982, s 7)

['Exempt licensed premises' means a house, room, shop or building which (i) is licensed for the sale of beer, cider, wine or spirits and (ii) is not kept open for public refreshment, resort and entertainment at any time between normal evening closing time and 5 o'clock of the following morning: Act of 1982, s 7(2).]

REFUSAL *See also* FIRST REFUSAL

[A testatrix by her will provided that any person becoming entitled under her will to the rents of her estate should forfeit his interest if he 'refused' or neglected to live in the mansion house for so many months in the year.] 'The question is, whether the infant plaintiff was bound within . . . three months to enter into occupation of the house, and to continue to reside there for nine months in every year. In my opinion, the plaintiff was not bound to do this, and he is entitled to the estate. . . . The effect of . . . the limitations is not to give him the estate on condition that he resides and occupies the house, but they are expressed as taking away the estate from him if he does not fulfil the condition, and we must see on what precise event the estate is to go over. The only event mentioned is, if the person who becomes entitled to the estate "refuses or neglects" to reside in the house; and an infant cannot "refuse or neglect" to reside in a particular place if the persons to whom his legal custody and care are committed do not choose that he shall do so. The words are not if he "omit" to reside, or if he "does not reside" but if he "refuse or neglect" to reside; and, in my opinion, an infant, who cannot control or fix the place where he is to reside, cannot within the terms of this clause be said to "refuse or neglect" to reside at the place mentioned: and for this reason also the clause does not apply to the infant plaintiff during his infancy.' *Partridge v Partridge* [1894] 1 Ch 351 at 359, per North J

'Where a valuable property is given to an officer in the army or navy, whose duties may require his absence from home for a lengthened period, on condition that, if he refuses or neglects to reside for a certain period in each year at a certain house, the property is to go over, it is surely not reasonable to suppose that the settlor intended that necessary absence from home, during part of the required period of residence, for the purpose of discharging his official duty, should amount to a refusal or neglect to reside within the meaning of the condition.' *Re Adair* [1909] 1 IR 311 at 317, per Wylie J

[A will contained a clause which provided that the interest of any tenant for life should cease if within a certain period he 'refused' or neglected to take the name and arms of the testator.] 'What . . . is the true construction and effect of this clause, which is that 'in case any such person shall refuse or neglect within the said calendar months to take use and bear such surname and arms' and so on? Supposing this infant had . . . become entitled to the estates as tenant in tail in possession a few days after his birth, could it by any possibility be said that an infant of that age had "refused or neglected" to do the act in question? The expression "refuse or neglect" involves the idea of some exercise of discretion, some exercise of will, on his part. . . . I think, therefore, that when the testator in this case refers to "refusal or neglect" by a person he must be taken not to include an infant in the class of persons who in his view can "refuse or neglect".' *Re Edwards, Lloyd v Boyes* [1910] 1 Ch 541 at 550, 551, per Warrington J

'The question that I have to determine is whether a person of the name of Barrett, who is alleged to have become entitled in the year 1923 to the possession of the settled property as tenant in tail male, in complete ignorance not only of the fact that he had so become entitled, but even of the very existence of the will and its contents, and who remained in such ignorance for a year or two thereafter, can be said to have "refused or neglected" to take the name and arms of Dick. . . . "The expression 'refuse or neglect' involves the idea of some exercise of discretion, some exercise of will, on his part" [per Warrington J in *Re Edwards* (supra)]. If the word "neglect" connotes the exercise of the will it cannot include a failure or omission which is due to ignorance of the provisions of the document, and which therefore does not result from any operation of the mind.' *Re Quintin Dick, Cloncurry (Lord) v Fenton* [1926] Ch 992 at 999, 1000, 1006, per Romer J

'A petitioner who only succeeds in proving a refusal in which he has acquiesced does not, in our opinion, establish that non-consummation is due to a wilful refusal by the respondent within the meaning of the statute [Matrimonial Causes Act 1937 s 7(1)(a) (repealed; see now the Matrimonial Causes Act 1973, s 12(b))].' *Baxter v Baxter* [1947] 1 All ER 387 at 389, CA, per Lord Greene MR; affd [1948] AC 274

REFUSE (Rubbish) *See also* RUBBISH

In this section [provision of refuse dumps and control of dumping of abandoned vehicles, etc] . . . 'refuse' includes any matter whatsoever, whether inorganic or organic. (Civic Amenities Act 1967, s 18(6))

[The Mersey Dock Acts Consolidation Act 1858, s 85, provided that no ballast, rubbish, dust, ashes, shingle, stones or other 'refuse' or things should be thrown or emptied into any dock.] 'The justices have found that the yellow oil in the dock, and the traces of oil and water on the side of the ship, and the mixture of oil and water, were in fact refuse, i.e., waste or used oil, or waste or used oil and water, within the ordinarily accepted meaning of the word refuse. We must consider what genus or class of refuse was aimed at by the statute. I have no doubt that the liquid class of refuse was equally aimed at with refuse of a solid order, and that so long as it tended to be prejudical to the works, the section was intended to apply to both liquid and solid refuse.' *Gray v Heathcote* (1918) 16 LGR 557 at 560, DC, per Shearman J

House refuse

'House refuse' means dust, ashes, cinders, breeze, rubbish, or filth but does not include trade refuse. (City of London (Various Powers) Act 1961, s 29)

[The question was whether waste paper emanating from a converted dwelling-house used as an office was 'house refuse' (and therefore removable without charge) or 'trade refuse' for the purposes of the Public Health Act 1936. Neither expression is defined in the Act, though an earlier repealed statute defined 'house refuse' as meaning 'ashes, cinders, breeze, rubbish, night-soil, and filth, but . . . not . . . trade refuse'.] 'It is only necessary for the purposes of the present case to decide whether or not the waste paper refuse produced by the appellant company in their office premises was house refuse within s 72 of the 1936 Act [prospectively repealed by the Control of Pollution Act 1974]. For my part I think that house refuse within s 72 is refuse produced by a house, and of the kind which one would ordinarily expect a house to produce occupied as a house. If that is the correct approach, it follows that the justices were right in deciding that the waste paper refuse was not house refuse, it did not emanate from a house and in these circumstances I would dismiss his appeal.' *Iron Trades Mutual Employers Insurance Association Ltd v Sheffield Corpn* [1974] 1 All ER 182 at 186, per May J

Street refuse

'Street refuse' means dust, dirt, rubbish, mud, road scrapings, ice, snow or filth. (City of London (Various Powers) Act 1961, s 29)

Trade refuse

'Trade refuse' means the refuse of any trade, manufacture or business or of any building materials. (City of London (Various Powers) Act 1961, s 29)

REFUSE OR NEGLECT *See* REFUSAL

REGARD

New Zealand [The Costs in Criminal Cases Act 1967, s 5(2), provides that, without limiting or affecting the court's discretion under s 5(1), the court, in deciding whether to grant costs and the amount of any costs granted, shall have 'regard' to all relevant circumstances and in particular (where appropriate) to seven considerations.] 'The first question . . . is what is meant by the words "shall have regard to". I do not think they are synonymous with "shall take into account". If the appropriate matters had to be taken into account, they must necessarily in my view affect the discretion under s 5(1) and it is clear from s 5(2) that the matters to be regarded are not to limit or affect that discretion. I think the legislative intent is that the court has a complete discretion but that the seven matters, or as many as are appropriate, are to be considered. In any particular case, all or any of the appropriate matters may be rejected or given such weight as the case suggests is suitable. I propose to examine the matter on that footing.' *R v CD* [1976] 1 NZLR 436 at 437, per Somers J

REGISTER

Of members of company

'The Act of Parliament [Companies Act 1862 (repealed; see now the Companies Act 1985, s 22)] says in the 23rd section that the subscribers shall be members, and "every other person who has agreed to become a member of a company under this Act and whose name is entered on the register of members shall be deemed to be a member of the company". Did these gentlemen agree to become members of the company? In my opinion it is clearly made out that they did agree to become members of the company. . . . It appears to me that the first proposition is made out that they have agreed to become members of the company under the Act. Then are their names entered on the "register of members"? It is said that they are not entered on the "register of members", in which their names do not appear, that being, in fact, equally true of every person in this company except the original members to whom the shares were originally allotted. Then on the part of the company it is said: True it is they are not inserted in that list which has got on its outside the title "Register of Members", because we have inserted no names in that except the names of the original shareholders. But in that very list itself there is a plain unmistakeable reference to another book, which other book the company says—and I agree with what the company says on that subject—is, in fact and in truth, a second volume of the register of shareholders. It does in truth and in substance, and it appears to me also in form, give the whole information which it was intended by the Act of Parliament should be given by the register, and the only thing in fact, from which a person having occasion to ascertain anything with regard to the state of the company could get the information which he desired to have. First of all it is a book called the "Members' Ledger". It begins with an index, upon which the name of every person who ever has been a member of this company appears. Then when you turn to the name of each person you find his exact position from the beginning to the end, what shares he originally held, what shares he had parted with, what shares he had acquired, and what shares he had lost by re-transfer. It appears to me impossible to conceive any book which could more completely give the information which the Act of Parliament requires to be given to any person having occasion to inspect the books of the company than that, and I am satisfied that it was intended to be the register of members subsequent to the original list of the original members.' *Re Land Credit Co of Ireland (Weikersheim's Case)* (1873) 28 LT 653 at 655, per James LJ

[The Companies Act 1862, s 25 (repealed; see now the Companies Act 1985, s 352) enacted that every company should keep a 'register of members'.] 'The authorities which have been cited shew that a book or document intended to be a register may be admitted as a register, although the requirements of the Act of Parliament as to the keeping of a register have not been regularly complied with; but I am not aware of any authority for saying that rough memoranda or sheets of paper not intended as a register at all, but intended as materials from which a register may be prepared, can be a register. It is clear from the evidence that these allotment sheets were never intended to be the register. They were allotment sheets giving certain details respecting the allottees, and containing a column referring to the register, and were intended as materials from which the register was to be formed as distinguished from the register itself. We should be straining the language of the Act of Parliament, and straining the evidence if we were to hold that these sheets constituted the register.' *Re Printing Telegraph & Construction Co of Agence Havas, ex p Cammell* [1894] 2 Ch 392 at 398, CA, per Lindley LJ

See, generally, 7 Halsbury's Laws (4th edn) paras 357 et seq.

Of mortgages

[The Companies Act 1862, s 43 (repealed; see now the Companies Act 1985, Part XII (ss 395–409)) enacted that a limited company should keep a 'register of mortgages' and charges specifically affecting property of the company.] 'It is plain to me that the secretary of the company made the entries in the book which was called a Register of Transfers of Shares, intending thereby to comply with the requirements of s 43, and this was done the day after the agreement was come to for extending the term for the payment of the mortgage debt. It is now said by the liquidators that this book was not a register of mortgages, because on the outside of the book there was not a word to show that it was a register of mortgages. On the outside of the book there was printed the name of the company, and the words "Register of Transfers". . . . I think I should be going not only beyond the Act, but beyond what the most ordinary common sense would suggest, if I were to say that the registration could not be valid unless it was made in a separate volume, although it was a separate register of mortgages in the same volume with the register of transfers of shares. To my mind the Act does not require that the registration of mortgages shall be made in a separate volume.' *Re Underbank Mills Cotton Spinning & Manufacturing Co* (1885) 31 Ch D 226 at 231, per Pearson J

Registered mark

'Registered trade mark' means a trade mark that is actually on the register. (Trade Marks Act 1938, s 68)

United States The term 'registered mark' means a mark registered in the United States Patent and Trademark Office under this chapter or under the Act of March 3, 1881, or the Act of February 20, 1905, or the Act of March 19, 1920. (Lanham Act 1946, s 45)

REGISTRANT

Trademarks and tradenames

United States The [term] . . . 'registrant' embrace[s] the legal representatives, predecessors, successors and assigns of such . . . registrant. (Lanham Act 1946, s 45)

REGISTRATION

'Seeing that the convention [Warsaw Convention as to carriage by air] contains no explanation of "register" or "registration", I will say what I think it means. In ordinary speech a "register" is a book which contains a list of persons or things of which it is important to keep a record. Entries in it are made by a person who is authorised to keep the list. The Shorter Oxford English Dictionary says that a register is "a book in which regular entry is made of any details sufficiently important to be exactly recorded", and that "to register" is "to make formal entry in a particular register", and that "registration" is "the act of registering". The earliest use that I know of is the "register of writs" (*registrum brevium*). But I remember well the school "register" which was kept by the master, and you had to answer to your name. Nowadays we all speak of a "registered letter", or sending it by "registered post". You can take the letter to the post office. The lady behind the counter has a book in front of her. She enters in it the name and address on the letter and hands you the counterpart. It is then dispatched as a "registered letter". In such case the register is the book in which she enters the details. The registration is made when she makes the entry.' *Collins v British Airways Board* [1982] 1 All ER 302 at 305, CA, per Lord Denning MR

REGISTRATION STATEMENT

United States The term 'registration statement' means the statement provided for in s 77f of this title, and includes any amendment thereto and any report, document, or memorandum filed as part of such statement or incorporated therein by reference. (Securities Act of 1933, s 2(8))

REGULAR

'Regularity depends on the nature and requirements of the route and exigencies of the traffic; and a car [in this case, a tramcar] is none the less a regular running car because it is sometimes withdrawn for the purpose of being repainted or repaired.' *Griffiths & Millington Ltd v Southampton Corpn* (1906) 70 JP 179 at 180, 181, per Buckley J

'In my judgment, the particulars state quite plainly that between the times mentioned these particular firms were regularly manufacturing, that is to say were in the ordinary course of their business during the whole of that period manufacturing, these particular goods. By that I do not mean that they were making them every day, but as they required them in the course of their regular business they made these particular goods in accordance with one or other of the processes which they have set out in their particulars.' *British Thomson-Houston Co Ltd v Crompton Parkinson Ltd* (1935) 52 RPC 409 at 411, 412, per Farwell J

Canada 'I conclude that "regularly" in the present context [a clause in a lease as to renewal where payments regular] means only uniformly, orderly, and systematically observing the stipulated times for payment or performance as opposed to casually, spasmodically, or intermittently—a meaning which requires substantial, but not punctual or exact compliance with the provisions of time.' *McLaughlin v Bodnarchuk* (1957) 8 DLR (2d) 596 at 599, BCCA, per Davey JA

REGULAR FORCES *See* ROYAL FORCES

REGULATE

[By the Matrimonial Homes Act 1967, s 1(2), either spouse may apply to the court for an order (inter alia) 'regulating' his or her right to occupy the dwelling house.] 'In the Oxford English Dictionary under the word "regulate" there is not given any meaning which could possibly include prohibition. Thus, the word "regulating" in itself is not apt to include a power to prohibit.' *Tarr v Tarr* [1972] 2 All ER 295 at 302, HL, per Lord Pearson

REHEARING

Australia 'In my opinion, a rehearing ordered under s 106 of the Western Australian Marine Act 1982–1986 (WA) should be construed as being in the nature of a new trial. . . . This accords not only with the natural and primary meaning of the word but also with what I conceive to be the legislative intent.' *R v Syme* [1970] WAR 153 at 157, per Jackson CJ

REINSTATE

'The condition in the policy [of fire insurance] gave the defendants the option of reinstating or repairing the machinery instead of paying the amount of the loss or damage. The word "reinstate" applies to property which is damaged, and the word "replace" to that which is destroyed.' *Anderson v Commercial Union Assurance Co* (1885) 55 LJQB 146 at 149, CA, per Cotton LJ

'From the collocation of the words it would seem that "reinstate" is used with reference to property which has been damaged, and "replace" to property which has been destroyed. In construing the word "reinstate" it must be remembered that it is a general word used in a policy which may refer to the insurance both of buildings and also of chattels. . . . When one is dealing with property in the nature of chattels, the term "reinstate" means to replace the chattels not in situ but in statu; and all that the defendants are bound to do is to make the chattels as good as they were before the fire.' Ibid at 149, per Bowen LJ

'It appears to me that reinstatement involves

putting the specified person back, in law and in fact, in the same position as he occupied in the undertaking before the employer terminated his employment.' *Hodge v Ultra Electric Ltd* [1943] 1 KB 462 at 466, per Tucker J

'The natural and primary meaning of to "reinstate" as applied to a man who has been dismissed (*ex hypothesi* without justification) is to replace him in the position from which he was dismissed, and so to restore the status quo ante the dismissal.' *William Dixon Ltd v Patterson* 1943 SC(J) 78 at 85, per the Lord Justice-Clerk (Lord Cooper)

REINSURANCE *See* INSURANCE

RELATE

Australia [The City of Brisbane Town Planning Act 1964–1986 (Qld), s 22(2) (see now s 22(1)(d)) requires a copy of an advertisement of an application for a permit to be posted 'on the land to which the application relates or applies'.] 'Reliance was placed on the ordinary meaning of the word "relate"—a word capable of wide meaning, and certainly wider than the word "applies". It was said that the natural meaning of the words of the expression would include any parcel of land part of which was the subject of the application, because if an application is made in respect of land which forms part of a larger parcel, it can rightly be said that the application relates to the parcel as a whole. The expression "relates or applies" is a curious one in this context, where obviously it is not intended to refer to two different classes of land, but perhaps it was chosen because it was thought that where the application was to erect a building, rather than to use land, a simpler expression, such as "the land in respect of which the application was made" would not suffice. However that may be, the relationship or connexion between an application and the land which is contained within the same boundaries as that which is the subject of the application, but which is not in itself of the application, may be remote. To construe the expression as referring to the land the subject of the application does not involve any departure from the natural meaning of the words.' *Pioneer Concrete (Qld) Pty Ltd v Brisbane City Council* (1983) 44 LGRA 346 at 355–356 (High Court of Australia) per Gibbs J

RELATED COMPANY

Trademarks and tradenames

United States The term 'related company' means any person who legitimately controls or is controlled by the registrant or applicant for registration in respect to the nature and quality of the goods or services in connection with which the mark is used. (Lanham Act 1946, s 45)

RELATING TO

'The submission [to arbitration] . . . is of all existing differences, and "anything in anywise relating thereto". These last words were relied on, as extending the power of the arbitrators to matters arising after the submission; but they clearly have no such effect, the matters relating to the existing differences must themselves exist at the same time with the existing differences.' *Re Morphett* (1845) 2 Dow & L 967 at 978, per Coleridge J

RELATIONS *See also* FRIEND; RELATIVE

For the purposes of this section [registration of street traders] a person shall be treated as being related to another if the latter is the wife, husband, father, mother, grandfather, grandmother, stepfather, stepmother, son, daughter, grandson, granddaughter, stepson, stepdaughter, brother, sister, half-brother or half-sister of the former and shall be deemed to be so related notwithstanding that he is so related only through an illegitimacy or in consequence of an adoption. (London County Council (General Powers) Act 1957, s 66(2))

'Where one devises the rest of his personal estate to his relations, or to be divided among his relations, without saying what relations, it shall go among all such relations as are capable of taking within the statute of distribution [see now the Administration of Estates Act 1925]; else it would be uncertain; for the relation may be infinite.' *Anon* (1716) 1 P Wms 326 at 326, 327, per Jekyll MR

[A testator by his will desired his wife, either at or before her death, to give certain leases to such of his 'relations' as she should think most deserving.] 'Here the word relation is a legal description, and this is a devise to such relations, and operates as a trust in the wife, by way of power of naming and apportioning, and her non-performance of the power shall not make the devise void, but the power shall devolve on the court; and though this is not to pass by virtue of the statute of distributions, yet that is a good rule for the court to go by. And therefore I think it ought to be divided among such of the relations of the testator, Nicholas Harding, who were his next of kin at her death.' *Harding v Glyn* (1739) 1 Atk 469 at 470, per Verney MR

'Relation is a very general word, and takes in any kind of connection; but the most common use of it is to express some sort of kindred either by blood or affinity; though properly by blood. The testator certainly does not use it in the general sense, nor in the vulgar sense; because he refers it to the statute of distribution; which has nothing to do with affinity, but blood only. Then does it take in the wife? It cannot be said there is no relation between husband and wife; but the question is, whether it be such relation, as is here meant? He mentioned the statute of distribution; it certainly means relations included in the statute by *next of kin*, which words are in both the clauses thereof used in opposition to a wife, *kindred* meaning of the same family and kind with the intestate.' *Davies v Baily* (1747) 1 Ves Sen 84 at 84, per Lord Hardwicke LC

[A testator devised lands to his wife for her life, and after her decease to his kinsman R B and to the heirs of his body, and for the want of such issue, to be sold, and divided amongst his relations, according to the Statute of Distributions 1670 (see now the Administration of Estates Act 1925) where no will is made.] 'What is the sense to be put on the word relation? In the will it is used in an improper manner; it signifies, in grammar, an abstract quality, any relation that arises in social life; but, in vulgar acceptation, it is transferred to a personal sense, and is so used in this will, as if he had said *kindred*, which is the word in the statute, and where the will refers to the statute, it must be taken as the statute takes it. Strictly, the wife is no relation to the husband; relation, in dictionaries, means *consanguinei* and *affinis*, but by the statute it means kindred by blood only. . . . I think, if the strict sense of the word does not take in the wife, it falls in with the intention, for he gives his wife the rents of the estate for life, and then to his nephew in tail. Nothing can be more improbable, than to imagine he had in view his wife's being alive at the determination of the entail, to share in the distribution of the money at that time. . . . Suppose he had ordered a division between my own relations, as the statute directs, this plainly would have included relations in blood only, and can never in common parlance mean his wife; and the words my relations mean the same as my own.' *Worseley v Johnson* (1753) 3 Atk 758 at 761, 762, per Lord Hardwicke LC

'The question here turns upon the expression "relations on my side": the testator has not in this passage said "my nearest relations". In another part he gives five pounds to his nearest relation. The state of the family does not throw much light upon this latter clause; but we may guess that he meant Aynsworth Thwaites, who was his nearest male relation. If in the latter he meant him, the word "nearest" equally applies to the other maternal cousin in the same degree, who is one of the lessors of the plaintiff, which is an argument against rejecting the maternal line. Now although relation is a word of very vague and general import, yet it has obtained a certain degree of ascertained meaning in the courts where questions of this sort have arisen with respect to personal property; that is, it means those who are entitled to take as relations under the statute of distributions. This rule of interpretation has been adopted to control the more extensive and lax sense of the word. The term then having obtained this construction in courts of equity, I do not see why it should not obtain the same construction in courts of law; and if so, the consequence is clear, that the three first cousins who were living at the time of the testator's death, are entitled to take.' *Doe d Thwaites v Over* (1808) 1 Taunt 263 at 269, per cur.

'The expression in the will, of "relations unprovided for", is too ambiguous for the court to take notice of; and the only inquiry the court will make is, who are the persons whom the court is accustomed to regard as being intended by "relations"? namely, who are the next-of-kin? and, as it happens that the five nieces are the sole next-of-kin, they must in one way or other be entitled to the testatrix's estate.' *Cracklow v Norie* (1838) 7 LJ Ch 278 at 279, per Lord Langdale MR

'It is contended that the word "relations" in the will of Thomas Deakin means prima facie legitimate relations; that although Lydia Deakin [his wife] had not at the date of Thomas Deakin's will any such relations, she might have had issue by a subsequent marriage who would have been legitimate relations of hers, and that under these circumstances Thomas Deakin cannot be taken to have authorised her to make an appointment in favour of persons who are not legally her relations. . . . Now, among a "wife's relations" may be included her children or issue if she has any; but the word "relations" is a much wider term than issue, and certainly, according to its ordinary meaning, includes other persons than children or issue. . . . I think, therefore, that the appointments made by the will of Lydia Deakin are good, except that in favour of John Oscar Wilkinson, whom she describes as "the natural son of my sister Phoebe Williams". There is nothing either in the will or the external circumstances (so far as I am entitled to look at them) which would entitle me to draw the inference that the testator included him among the persons whom he designated as his wife's relations.' *Re Deakin, Starkey v Eyres* [1894] 3 Ch 565 at 568, 569, 572, 573, per Stirling J

'If the court were to read a gift to "relations" as covering everybody between whom and the testator or testatrix there was a nexus of blood, the result would be to embark upon an inquiry which, at all events in the vast majority of cases, would . . . be infinite. . . . In my judgment, whereas before the alteration in the law I should have had to seek the persons who would take under the Statute of Distributions, I must now apply the same principle as before and seek the persons who would take under the Administration of Estates Act 1925. . . . The rule of convenience which was adopted was that "relations" should be construed as meaning those who would have taken under the Statute of Distributions had there been an intestacy. . . . I do not see my way to adopt a new rule of convenience—namely that the term "relations" should be construed as referring to the persons within the degrees of consanguinity indicated in the Act as constituting them possible beneficiaries in the case of intestacy.' *Re Bridgen, Chaytor v Edwin* [1938] Ch 205 at 208–210, per Clauson J

United States 'Person related to' with respect to an individual means (a) the spouse of the individual, (b) a brother, brother-in-law, sister, sister-in-law of the individual, (c) an ancestor or lineal descendant of the individual or his spouse, and (d) any other relative, by blood or marriage, of the individual or his spouse who shares the same home with the individual. 'Person related to' with respect to an organisation means (a) a person directly or indirectly controlling, controlled by or under common control with the organisation, (b) an officer or director of the organisation or a person performing similar functions with respect to the organisation or to a person related to the organisation, (c) the spouse of a person related to the organisation, and (d) a relative by blood or marriage of a person related to the organisation who shares the same home with him. (Uniform Consumer Credit Code 1969, s 1.301(14))

See, generally, 50 Halsbury's Laws (4th edn) para 531.

Blood relations

'The meaning of blood relationship seems clear enough. It cannot here [in a proviso for forfeiture on marrying a blood relation] refer to statutory next of kin. In my opinion it describes the relationship existing between two or more persons who stand in lawful descent from a common ancestor. The claim of descent may be broken by illegitimacy, but with that qualification all persons descended from a common ancestor, however remote, are blood relations.' *Re Lanyon, Lanyon v Lanyon* [1927] 2 Ch 264 at 267, per Russell J

Near relations *See* NEAR RELATIONS; NEAREST

Poor relations

[A testator by his will directed that a certain sum of money should be equally distributed among such of his mother's 'poor relations' as the defendant, his heirs, executors, and administrators for the time being should think objects of charity.] 'The word "relation" is a vague term, and, by several uniform resolutions, the meaning of it has been confined to those who would take under the statute of distribution. Q Whether the word poor will make any difference? I am of opinion, the true construction of the words is, "such of my mother's relations as are poor, and proper objects".' *Brunsden v Woolredge* (1765) Amb 507 at 507, per Sewell MR

'Although I am inclined to regard the class "poor relations" as a social description and stated relatively and as a matter of degree when used by a very wealthy man, and not necessarily a term connoting charity and so entitling the words to a benignant construction, nevertheless the class is, on the authorities, one of sufficient definition. The class is composed of traceable family connections who are in need of financial help.' *Salvesens Trustees v Wye* 1954 SLT 299 at 301, per Lord Carmont

RELATIONSHIP

[A testator by his will directed that his daughter should forfeit half of an annuity if she should have any social or other 'relationship' with a certain person to whom the testator objected.] 'I find some difficulty in knowing exactly what the words "social or other relationship" mean. From the Oxford Dictionary it appears that the word "relationship" may have a number of meanings. In the present case it obviously does not mean any connection by blood or marriage between the two persons in question. It seems to me that there may be a difference between the word "relationship" and "association", as referring merely to the existence of a state of affairs, and the word "associate" which connotes some active steps. In the present case I think that "relationship" means simply the existence of a relative state of facts between the two persons named, or, at any rate, that that situation may be included in the word. It seems to me that it may include, for instance, such things as being members of the same congregation, members of the same omnibus queue, citizens of the same state, and all kinds of things, which merely are a passive existence of facts.' [The clause was accordingly held void for uncertainty.] *Re Jones, Midland Bank Executor and Trustee Co Ltd v Jones* [1953] 1 All ER 357 at 360, per Danckwerts J (also reported in [1953] Ch 125 at 128)

RELATIVE *See also* FAMILY; RELATIONS

'Relative' includes a relative by marriage. (Births and Deaths Registration Act 1953, s 41)

'Relative' in relation to a child means a grandparent, brother, sister, uncle or aunt, whether of the full blood or half-blood or by affinity and includes, where the child is illegitimate, the father of the child and any person who would be a relative within the meaning of this definition if the child were the legitimate child of his mother and father. (Adoption Act 1976, s 72(1))

'Relative', in relation to any person, means any of the following—
(a) his spouse;
(b) any lineal ancestor, lineal descendant, brother, sister, aunt, uncle, nephew, niece or first cousin of his or his spouse; and
(c) the spouse of any relative within paragraph (b) above;
and for the purpose of deducing any such relationship an illegitimate child or step-child shall be treated as a child born in wedlock. (Credit Unions Act 1979, s 31(1))

'Relative', in relation to a child, means a grand-parent, brother, sister, uncle or aunt, whether of the full blood, the half blood, or by affinity. (Child Care Act 1980, s 87(1) as amended by the Family Law Reform Act 1987, s 33(1), (4), Sch 2, para 79(2), Sch 4; Foster Children Act 1980, s 22)

In this Part of this Act [Part II: compulsory admission to hospital and guardianship] 'relative' means any of the following persons:—(a) husband or wife; (b) son or daughter; (c) father or mother; (d) brother or sister; (e) grandparent; (f) grandchild; (g) uncle or aunt; (h) nephew or niece. (Mental Health Act 1983, s 26(1))

In this Part of this Act [Part I: residential care homes] 'relative' means any of the following—(a) husband or wife; (b) son or daughter; (c) father or mother; (d) brother or sister; (e) grandparent or other ascendant; (f) grandchild or other descendant; (g) uncle or aunt; (h) nephew or niece. (Registered Homes Act 1984, s 19(1))

Dependent relative

In this section 'dependent relative' means in relation to an individual—
(a) any relative of his or of his wife who is incapacitated by old age or infirmity from maintaining himself, or
(b) his or his wife's mother who, whether or not incapacitated, is either widowed, or living apart from her husband, or a single woman in consequence of dissolution or annulment of marriage.
(Capital Gains Tax Act 1979, s 105(5))

[A similar definition is to be found in the Inheritance Tax Act 1984, s 11(6).]

In will

'It is settled that under a gift of this description the class is to be ascertained at the testator's death; also that "relatives" mean the persons who would take under the Statutes of Distribution. It is true that when there is an express reference to the statutes, they would take as tenants in common in the shares in which they would have taken on an intestacy. But when there is no express reference to the statutes the case is different. There is nothing then to prevent the ordinary rule from applying, that under a gift to a class without words of severance, all the members of the class take as joint tenants. That being so, and some having died without severing, the survivors will take the whole.' *Eagles v Le Breton* (1873) 42 LJ Ch 362 at 362, 363, per Lord Romilly MR

'The gift is to "the nearest relatives". Whose nearest relatives are meant? As the testator has not made any reference to those of anyone else, I suppose he must mean his own. Then follow the words "then living", which clearly mean living at the death of the widow, the tenant for life. Then we have "to be hereafter named in a codicil"; but the testator has left no codicil, so we cannot give effect to that phrase. What then is the law applicable in this state of circumstances? In the case of *Bullock v Downes* [(1860) 9 HL Cas 1], it was held that, under a gift, after a life interest, to such next of kin by blood of the testator as would under the Statutes of Distribution "have become and been then entitled thereto in case" the testator "had died intestate", the persons entitled were to be ascertained at the death of the testator. We must give some effect to the words in the will "then living", which, as I have said, in my opinion mean living at the death of the testator's widow. As regards the words "nearest relatives", they mean something different from those who would be entitled under the Statutes of Distribution; they must mean relatives by blood.' *Re Nash, Prall v Bevan* (1894) 71 LT 5 at 6, CA, per Lindley LJ

Australia [A testatrix referred, in her will to her 'relatives'.] 'The word "relatives" means here what it naturally and primarily means: those related by blood to the testatrix.' *Re Griffiths, Griffiths v Griffiths* [1926] VLR 212 at 217, per Mann J

RELEASE *See* RECEIPT

RELEVANT

'When I say "relevant" I mean this, so nearly touching the matter in issue as to be such that a judicial mind ought to regard it as a proper thing to be taken into consideration.' *Tomkins v Tomkins* [1948] P 170 at 175, CA, per Lord Greene MR

'The main general rule governing the entire subject [of admissibility of evidence] is that evidence which is sufficiently relevant to an issue before the court is admissible and all that is irrelevant or insufficiently relevant should be excluded. The word "relevant" is used in the sense in which it is defined in art 1 of Stephen's Digest of the Law of Evidence (12th edn). It is there stated that the word "means that any two facts to which it is applied are so related to each other that according to the common course of events one either taken by itself or in connexion with other facts proves or renders probable the past . . . existence . . . of the other." Thus the word "relevant" is to all intents and purposes synonymous with the phrase "of probative value". It must be noted that this basic rule has to be applied to differing circumstances. The words "sufficiently", "insufficiently", "common course of events" and "probable" have to be used, and these are matters of degree and opinion.' *R v Harz, R v Power* [1966] 3 All ER 433 at 449, CCA, per Thesiger J

RELIEF

'The words "relief" and "relieve" are the appropriate terms to describe the remedial action of the Court of Equity in cases where a penalty or forfeiture has been incurred, which the court thinks it equitable that the plaintiff should not lie under or suffer.' *Nind v Nineteenth Century Building Society* [1894] 2 QB 226 at 233, CA, per Davey LJ

'There may be a good charity for the relief of persons who are not in grinding need or utter destitution . . . [but] relief connotes need of some sort, either need for a home, or for the means to provide for some necessity or quasi-necessity, and not merely an amusement, however healthy.' *Inland Revenue Comrs v Baddeley* [1955] 1 All ER 525 at 529, HL, per Lord Simonds; also reported [1955] AC 572 at 585

RELIGION

'What is "religion"? Is it not what a man honestly believes in and approves of and thinks it his duty to inculcate on others, whether with regard to this world or the next? A belief in any system of retribution by an overruling power? It must, I think, include the principle of gratitude to an active power who can confer blessings.' *Baxter v Langley* (1868) 38 LJMC 1 arg. at 5, per Willes J

'It seems to me that "religion" and "faith" are interchangeable words.' *Re Tarnpolsk, Barclays Bank Ltd v Hyer* [1958] 3 All ER 479 at 481, per Danckwerts J

'Religion, as I see it, is concerned with man's relations with God, and ethics are concerned with man's relations with man. The two are not the same, and are not made the same by sincere inquiry into the question, what is God. If reason leads people not to accept Christianity or any known religion, but they do believe in the excellence of qualities such as truth, beauty and love, or believe in the Platonic concept of the ideal, their beliefs may be to them the equivalent of a religion, but viewed objectively they are not religion. . . . It seems to me that two of the essential attributes of religion are faith and worship; faith in a god and worship of that god.' *Barralet v A-G* [1980] 3 All ER 918 at 924, per Dillon J

Australia [The Constitution (Commonwealth of Australia Constitution Act 1901), s 116, provides that 'the Commonwealth shall not make any law for establishing any religion . . . or for prohibiting the free exercise of any religion. . . .'] 'It would be difficult, if not impossible, to devise a definition of religion which would satisfy the adherents of all the many and various religions which exist, or have existed, in the world. There are those who regard religion as consisting principally in a system of beliefs or statement of doctrine. So viewed religion may be either true or false. Others are more inclined to regard religion as prescribing a code of conduct. So viewed, a religion may be good or bad. There are others who pay greater attention to religion as involving some prescribed form of ritual or religious observance. Many religious conflicts have been concerned with matters of ritual and observance. Section 116 must be regarded as operating in relation to all these aspects of religion, irrespective of varying opinions in the community as to the truth of particular religious doctrines, as to the goodness of conduct prescribed by a particular religion, or as to the propriety of any particular religious observance. What is religion to one is superstition to another. Some religions are regarded as morally evil by adherents of other creeds. At all times there are many who agree with the reflective comment of the Roman poet—'*Tantum religio potuit suadere malorum*'. The prohibition in s 116 operates not only to protect the freedom of religion, but also to protect the right of a man to have no religion. . . . Section 116 proclaims not only the principle of toleration of all religions, but also the principle of toleration of absence of religion.' *Adelaide Company of Jehovah's Witnesses Inc v Commonwealth* (1943) 67 CLR 116 at 123, per Latham CJ

Australia 'For the purposes of the law, the criteria of religion are twofold: belief in a supernatural Being, Thing or Principle: and second, the acceptance of canons of conduct in order to give effect to that belief, though canons of conduct which offend against the ordinary laws are outside the area of any immunity, privilege or right conferred on the grounds of religion. Those criteria may vary in their comparative importance, and there may be a different intensity of belief or of acceptance of canons of conduct among religions or among the adherents to a religion. The tenets of a religion may give primacy to one particular belief or to one particular canon of conduct. Variations in emphasis may distinguish one religion from other religions, but they are irrelevant to the determination of an individual's or a group's freedom to profess and exercise the religion of his, or their, choice.' *Church of the New Faith v Commissioner of Pay-Roll Tax* (Vic) (1983) 154 CLR 120 at 136, per Mason ACJ and Brennan J

Advancement of *See* ADVANCEMENT

RELIGIOUS PURPOSES *See also* CHARITY–CHARITABLE PURPOSES

'The two questions to be considered are, first, whether the purpose indicated by the words "having regard to the glory of God, in the spiritual welfare of His creatures", is a religious purpose. . . . For the purpose of answering the first question, I think the will must be read as if the testator had directed the property to be applied in promoting "the spiritual welfare of God's creatures", and I think that a purpose so expressed would be a religious and therefore a charitable purpose.' *Townsend v Carus* (1844) 3 Hare 257 at 261, per Wigram V-C

'It is said, in some of the cases, that religious purposes are charitable, but that can only be true as to religious services tending directly or indirectly towards the instruction or the edification of the public.' *Cocks v Manners* (1871) LR 12 Eq 574 at 585, per Wickens V-C

'What is the meaning to be attached to the words "religious purposes"? There is no doubt that acting on the principle that the law desires *ut res magis valeat quam pereat*, it has been held that into the word "religious" must be previously imported the word "charitable", i.e.

that they must be religious purposes which are charitable, and that, prima facie, they must be so restricted.' *Arnott v Arnott* [1906] 1 IR 127 at 134, per Porter MR

[A testator bequeathed the residue of his estate to the Archbishop of Westminster on trust that he should forthwith in his absolute discretion devote the same to the furtherance of educational or charitable or 'religious purposes' for Roman Catholics in the British Empire in such manner in all respects as he might think fit.] 'The view of Farwell J that the gift is uncertain in that no one can enforce it depends on the proposition that, according to the true meaning of the will, the Archbishop is empowered to apply the fund bequeathed to him, not only for educational and charitable purposes, but also (under the words "for religious purposes") for purposes which do not fall within the ambit of charitable purposes as that phrase is used in this court. In my judgment, that is not the true effect of the phrase "religious purposes" as used in this will. It must be taken to be settled law, at all events in this Court, since *Re White* [[1893] 2 Ch 41], that, in the absence of a context enabling the Court to place some more extended meaning on the words "religious purposes", the phrase must be taken to mean "purposes conducive to the advancement of religion", and, accordingly, purposes which, as stated by Lord Macnaghten in *Income Tax Commissioners v Pemsel* [[1891] AC 531], the law recognises as charitable. No doubt, with a proper context, it might be found that a testator used the phrase in a special wider sense so as to cover a purpose which, though connected with religion or based on religious convictions, is not conducive to the advancement of religion. In *Cocks v Manners* [supra] it was held that the purpose of self sanctification by the observance of various religious practices and rules, though, no doubt, connected with religious conviction, was not a purpose conducive to the advancement of religion. Farwell J appears to find an indication of the use of the phrase "religious purposes" in that extended sense in the words "for Roman Catholics in the British Empire". I fear that I cannot agree that those words supply the necessary context. They seem to me to indicate merely that the beneficiaries of the particular charitable purposes (which include educational and religious and other charitable purposes) for the advancement of which the fund is to be applicable are to be members of the Roman Catholic community. Farwell J further finds support for his view in the collocation of the phrase "religious purposes" with the phrase "charitable purposes". It is true that the phrase "religious purposes" points to a type of purpose which is comprised in the phrase "charitable purposes" as construed in this court, and, accordingly, it is true to say that the words "religious purposes" are superfluous in that, if they were omitted, the fund would (by reason of the word "charitable") be nevertheless available for religious purposes. But superfluous words are not uncommon in wills, and the mere fact that the words are superfluous seems to me to be quite insufficient to justify the court in putting an extended meaning on words which have, as the authorities stand, a well defined meaning.' *Re Ward, Public Trustee v Ward* [1941] Ch 308 at 311, 312, CA, per Clauson J

'Is there any context in the will before the court in the present case which compels the court to hold that the words "religious purposes" are used in some restricted sense? The only context from which any argument to support this view can possibly be drawn must be found in the use of the word "charitable" and the disjunctive "or" in the phrase in which the words "religious purposes" appear. Farwell J accepted the argument that, because the word "charitable" by itself includes religious purposes, and the words "or religious purposes" follow after the word "charitable", the latter words would be redundant unless they were construed as embracing only such religious purposes as are not within the strict legal sense charitable. It is to be observed that the main part of this argument applies with equal force to the meaning to be attributed to the word "educational" which is to be found in the earlier part of the gift, but Farwell J held that "educational" must be given its ordinary meaning. I can see no sufficient reason for adopting the restricted construction. . . . There is no canon of construction which denies to a testator the privilege of indulging, to some extent, in tautology.' Ibid at 317, 318, per Luxmoore LJ

See, generally 5 Halsbury's Laws (4th edn) paras 528 et seq.

Australia [The Estate Duty Assessment Act 1914–1986 (Cth), s 8(5), provides that estate duty shall not be assessed or payable upon inter alia) any estate devised or bequeathed for 'religious scientific, charitable or public educational purposes'.] 'Take . . . the first word "religious". It is not all religious purposes that are charitable. Religious purposes are charitable only if they tend directly or indirectly towards the instruction or the edification of the public [*Cocks v Manners* (supra)]. The word "charitable" in the Elizabethan sense covers a wider field than the word "religious". To express the point in a few words, the word "charitable" in the Elizabethan sense is larger and more comprehensive than the other words in the context. It includes, no doubt, the subject matters expressed by those other words, and in that sense may be said to be redundant if understood in the technical sense in that it is repetition. But it adds something to those words. There is overlapping, no doubt; but if it be read in its popular sense there is also overlapping. The four words are not mutually exclusive. As Lord Herschell said in *Inland Revenue Comrs v Scott* [[1892] 2 QB 152 at 165], little weight is to be attached to the mere fact that specific exemptions are found which would be covered by the wider general word. Take, for instance, the word "religious". If the purpose were religious but not charitable, it would, under this Act, be exempt. If it were charitable but not religious, it would equally be exempt.' *Chesterman v Federal Taxation Comr* (1925) 37 CLR 317 at 320, PC, per cur.

RELIGIOUS WORSHIP *See* WORSHIP

RELOCATION

Of population or industry

'Relocation of population or industry' in relation to any area means the rendering available elsewhere than in that area (whether in an existing community or a community to be newly established) of accommodation for residential purposes or for the carrying on of business or other activities, together with all appropriate public services, facilities for public worship, recreation and amenity, and other requirements, being accommodation to be rendered available for persons or undertakings who are living or carrying on business or other activities in that area or who were doing so but by reason of war circumstances are no longer for the time being doing so, and whose continued or resumed location in that area would be inconsistent with the proper planning thereof. (Town and Country Planning Act 1971, s 290(2)).

REMAINDER *See also* PART

[A testatrix by a holograph will gave pecuniary legacies to her brother, her nieces A and B, and her fiancé. She next bequeathed specific articles of jewellery to her nieces A, B, C and D. The will then concluded with the words 'remainder to be divided between them'. The testatrix left heritable and moveable estate.] 'It appears to me that the word "remainder", in its ordinary meaning, denotes prima facie all that is left of something from which a part has been subtracted. In the context in which the word "remainder" is used in the will under consideration various alternative submissions have been advanced in argument as to the sense in which the testatrix used that word. . . . It appears to me that, where in a holograph document such as the present the form of wording used by the testatrix is to "certify" that she leaves to members of her family circle various sums of money and specific articles, and where it concludes with a direction to divide the "remainder" among a class, that word is to be construed as denoting, in the absence of a context which indicates the contrary, the remainder of the whole estate of which she might die possessed. I infer from the simple and very concise form of words used by the testatrix to express her intention that she did not distinguish in her own mind or in the language she was using between her moveable property and her heritable property. . . . I have come to the conclusion that the word "remainder" ought in the present holograph will to be read as meaning "all that is left of my whole estate", and that it comprises both the moveable and the heritable estate of the testatrix.' *Guthrie's Executor v Guthrie* 1945 SC 138 at 142, 143, per Lord Russell

'The words "with remainder" have always, I think, been construed as showing that the subsequent estate arises on the cesser of the prior estate, which, although expressed as "an estate for life", may fail before the death of the life tenant for various reasons, for instance, by forfeiture, whether under the terms of the will or outside it, because a spouse has witnessed the document, or, as here, by disclaimer.' *Re Hatfeild (deceased), Hatfeild v Hatfeild* [1957] 2 All ER 261 at 265, per Harman J

REMAINING

[A testator by his will, after making specific bequests to certain of his children, devised the proceeds of sale of a house in trust for his 'remaining children'.] 'In my opinion the words "remaining children" must be construed to mean "the others" and cannot be narrowed down to mean "surviving children", although it is possible that, in some cases, on the reading of the whole will the words "remaining children" might be held to mean "surviving children".' *Re Speak, Speak v Speak* (1912) 56 Sol Jo 273 at 273, per Parker J

REMAINS

In this section [interpretation] 'remains' includes any trace or sign of the previous existence of the thing in question. (Ancient Monuments and Archaeological Areas Act 1979, s 61(13))

REMARRIAGE

'The whole scheme of the will is that a certain state of affairs is to go on until an event described as "the death or remarriage of my said wife" should take place. What did that mean in this will? The "said wife" is identified; her death, of course, could happen. What is meant by 'remarriage' in those circumstances? It can only mean marriage. Remarriage in that sense is obviously, on the scheme of the will, to coincide with the termination of the interest expressly given to "my said wife during her widowhood".' *Re Lynch, Lynch v Lynch* [1943] 1 All ER 168 at 169, per Uthwatt J

REMEDY *See also* HERBAL REMEDY

[Rule D of the York-Antwerp Rules 1950 (see now the York-Antwerp Rules 1974) provided that rights to contribution in general average should not be affected though the event that gave rise to the sacrifice or expenditure might have been due to the fault of one of the parties to the adventure; but this was not to prejudice any 'remedies' which might be open against that party for such fault.] 'The question which is disputed at this stage of the argument is whether the word "remedies" in Rule D is wide enough to cover the so-called "equitable" defence, that the casualty was caused by the claimants' own fault. Counsel for the claimants argued that the word "remedies" refers only to positive legal steps which may be taken to assert and enforce a claim, and does not include a mere defence to a claim. Using a very familiar metaphor, one can say that according to his argument a remedy is in the nature of a spear, which a man uses to attack somebody else, and is not in the nature of a shield, with which he seeks to repel somebody else's attack on him. On this point counsel for the respondents referred to the Oxford Dictionary to which I have referred and I find that the first three meanings given to the word "remedies" are: "(1) A cure for a disease or other disorder of body or mind: any medicine or treatment which alleviates pain and promotes restoration to health. (2) A means of counteracting or removing an outward evil of any kind; reparation, redress, relief. (3) Legal redress", and then other meanings are given. . . . Then there was cited, also by counsel for the claimants, Webster's English Dictionary, which I believe was published in the United States, and I think that the material extract which he read was: "(3) The legal means to recover a right or to obtain redress for a wrong". Counsel for the respondents also referred to the derivation of the word "remedy" from the Latin *remedium* and *remedior* and said that the word fundamentally means something healing or curative. He said that an antidote is a remedy and a plea to a claim is an antidote to an ill. Mainly, I am influenced by the evident objects of Rule D of the York-Antwerp Rules, which are to keep the whole question of alleged fault outside the average adjustment and to leave the legal "remedies" in respect of fault unimpaired. There is no reason to suppose an intention to destroy defences while keeping alive cross-claims. The intention which may reasonably be inferred is an intention to preserve the legal position intact at the stage of enforcement. Suitable effect is given to that intention by construing the word "remedies" in Rule D as wide enough to cover defences as well as cross-claims, shields as well as spears, pleas as well as counts.' *Goulandris Bros Ltd v Goldman (B) & Sons Ltd* [1957] 3 All ER 100 at 111, 112, per Pearson J (also reported in [1958] 1 QB 74 at 99, 100)

Australia 'To "remedy" a breach is not to perform the impossible task of wiping it out—of producing the same condition of affairs as if the breach had never occurred. It is to set things right for the future, and that may be done even though they have for some period not been right.' *Batson v de Carvalho* (1948) 48 SR(NSW) 417 at 427, per Sugerman J

REMIT

[The defendant abroad contracted to sell goods sent to him and to 'remit' the proceeds to England by first-class bank bills.] 'I cannot doubt that the word "remit" there means this and nothing but this—that the bank post bills, when obtained in favour of the plaintiffs, should be sent in the ordinary course and the ordinary manner in which such documents are sent by commercial men, namely, by mail, and that as soon as that had been done all obligation and all liability of the defendant ceased.' *Comber v Leyland* [1898] AC 524 at 530, HL, per Lord Herschell

REMOTE

[The Marriage Act 1836, s 26 (repealed by the Marriage Act 1949) provided that, whereas it was expedient that provision should be made for relieving the inhabitants of populous districts 'remote' from the parish church from the inconvenience to which they might be thereby subjected in the solemnisation of their marriages, the Bishop of the diocese might, subject to certain conditions, authorise by a licence the solemnisation of marriage in a chapel for persons residing within a district specified in the licence.] 'I think . . . "remote" should be interpreted not as having a narrow but a wide signification, and that when a district . . . is so situated that the transit from the district to the parish church, from whatever cause, may occupy an inconvenient length of time, the Bishop . . . might properly grant a licence. . . . In the present case the word "remote" should not be interpreted as having reference to distance of mileage only, but to the time that may, from the blocks in the streets during the London season, be occupied in the transit from the district to the parish church.' *Re St George's, Albemarle Street, Petition* (1890) Trist 134 at 142, 143, per the Bishop of London

REMOVE

[The Harbours, Docks, and Piers Clauses Act 1847, s 56, enacts that the harbour-master may 'remove' any wreck or other obstruction to a harbour, dock, or pier, or the approaches to the same, and also any floating timber which impedes the navigation thereof, and the expense of removing any such wreck, obstruction, or floating timber shall be repaid by the owner of the same.] 'Apart from the provisions of s 56 of the Harbours, Docks, and Piers Clauses Act 1847, it seems to be clear that, according to English law, the owner of a ship-wrecked and sunken vessel which has become an obstruction to navigation through no fault on his part, and of which he has lost or relinquished the possession, management, and control, is not under any obligation to remove it or under any liability to pay or contribute to the payment of the expenses of its removal. . . . It seems to me that the removal contemplated by s 56 is removal in the interest and on behalf of the owner as well as in the interest and for the benefit of the public. To entitle the harbour-master to repayment under s 56, it is I think incumbent upon him to remove the obstruction in such a manner that at the conclusion of the operation it is substantially in the same plight and condition as it was at the commencement, or at any rate with some regard to the interest of the owner whose interest I think the enactment meant to be regarded. What has the harbour-master done here? He has "dispersed the wreck by explosives". That no doubt is a very complete and effectual sort of removal, but it is not, I think, the sort of removal which is contemplated by the section. It is to be observed that under this section the harbour-master is not given power to destroy. Another statute was passed to give that power. Here there was not removal, but total destruction. Not one scrap or atom of the wreck was salved; not a single penny is brought into the account as the produce of the sale of any part of the wreck. It sounds to me like a grim joke to ask the owner, where there is an owner, to pay for the expense of annihilating his property because he is chargeable by statute—and fairly chargeable—with the cost of its removal.' *Arrow Shipping Co Ltd v Tyne Improvement Comrs, The Crystal* [1894] AC 508 at 527, 528, 531, 532, per Lord Macnaghten

REMUNERATION *See also* EARNINGS

In this Act 'remuneration', in relation to any person, includes any benefit, facility or advantage, whether in money or otherwise, provided by the employer or by some other person under arrangements with the employer, whether for the first-mentioned person or otherwise, by reason of the fact that the employer employs him, and any reference to the payment of remuneration shall be construed accordingly. (Remuneration, Charges and Grants Act 1975, s 7)

'I think the word "remuneration" . . . means a quid pro quo. If a man gives his services, whatever consideration he gets for giving his services seems to me a remuneration for them. Consequently, I think if a person was in the receipt of payment, or in receipt of a percentage, or any kind of payment which would not be an actual money payment, the amount he would receive annually in respect of this would be "remuneration".' *R v Postmaster-General*

(1876) 1 QBD 658 at 663, 664, per Blackburn J; on appeal (1878) 3 QBD 428, CA

[The question was whether the claimant, who was in full-time business on her own account, was engaged in 'remunerative work' within the Supplementary Benefits Act 1976, s 6(1) (now substituted by the Social Security Act 1980, s 6 Sch 2) and so disentitled to claim benefit although her activities had resulted in a loss.] 'I do not think any material distinction could be drawn between remunerative, remunerating and remunerated work. The first two seem to mean the same and the third could be used if you regarded the work as remunerated (or paid) rather than the person who does it as remunerated (or paid) for it. But what I find an impracticable distinction is that between a job which makes a net profit of £1 and a job which makes a net loss of £1 at any particular time. To call the first remunerative and the second not is difficult enough; to suppose that the legislature meant to exclude the first from entitlement to supplementary benefit but the second not is to my mind impossible. Both are, in my opinion, remunerative, regardless of the question whether the weekly, monthly or yearly balance sheet shows a credit or a debit balance, just as the paid worker is engaged in remunerative work regardless of what he would get if he went out of work or into retirement. What the remunerated worker, whether self-employed or employed by others, does with his or her remuneration, whether by choice or under compulsion or by choice determined by the compulsion of economic necessity, is irrelevant to the remunerative character of the work and the commission's statutory duty under s 6(1).' [Held: the claimant was engaged in remunerative full-time work and so not entitled to claim benefit.] *Perrot v Supplementary Benefits Commission* [1980] 3 All ER 110 at 116, CA, per Stephenson LJ

Australia 'The ordinary meaning of "rate of remuneration" covers rates of remuneration for overtime.' *Chalmers v Commonwealth* (1946) 73 CLR 19 at 34, per McTiernan J

'The ordinary meaning of remuneration is pay for services rendered.' Ibid at 37, per Williams J

RENEW *See also* REPAIR

'What is the meaning of applying for a renewal of a licence? It can only mean that the licence holder is applying to renew that which is in existence and is on the point of expiring.' *R v Crewkerne Licensing JJ* (1888) 21 QBD 85 at 87, CA, per Lindley LJ

'Renewing a bill means as a rule that the new bill shall be between the same parties, and that the amount etc, shall be the same.' *Barber v Mackrell* (1892) 68 LT 29 at 31, CA, per Smith LJ

New Zealand 'A promissory note is by s 84 of "The Bills of Exchange Act 1908", an unconditional promise in writing made by one person to another, signed by the maker, engaging to pay on demand or at fixed or determinable future time a sum certain in money to the holder as defined. I have to determine whether this is an unconditional promise, and whether it promises payment of a sum certain in money. . . . I think it at least doubtful whether this contains a promise to pay in money. If the words "to be renewed if required" mean, as they appear to mean, that the promisor has the privilege of tendering a promissory note in payment, then the first obligation is not to pay in money, but in money or a promissory note according to the election of the maker. Such an instrument is not a promissory note: *ex parte Imeson, Re Seaton* [(1815) 2 Rose 225]. In that case the note was substantially in the same form as in this. I think that those words must have that meaning. They express a privilege or condition conferring a right on the promisor, and the word "renewed" not "postponed" is used. This carries with it the right to three days' grace on renewal, whilst a mere right to postpone would not.' *Lamb v Somerville* (1909) 29 NZLR 138 at 139, 140, per Chapman J; also reported 12 GLR 171 at 172

New Zealand 'The defendant relies upon the right to renew for "yearly periods", and argues that such renewals cannot be for "yearly periods" if in the course of any one of these periods it can be brought to a close upon a month's notice. I think this view is not sustainable. The parties agreed in the first instance to a lease for a period of one year but provided for its earlier termination upon notice from the lessor. "The right to renew" given by the typewritten addition must mean "the right to renew the foregoing lease". It does not suggest that the renewal is subject to some, only, of the terms of the lease. That which the lessee has the right to renew for yearly periods is the lease, with all its incidents as for the initial yearly period. If it be not this which is to be renewed, then I am at a loss to know what it is the lessee may renew.' If, as I understand it, the lease for one year may be renewed for succeeding "yearly periods", then each successive renewal thus acquired is of the lease originally granted with all its provisions including the one about termination upon notice. Upon the assumption that the continuance of the defendant's tenancy has proceeded from successive renewals for yearly periods of the original term, then I am of opinion that the defendant throughout has held subject to the right of the plaintiff to terminate each of these periods by giving the appropriate notice.' *Victoria Mansions Ltd* [1941] GLR 223 at 224, per Northcroft J

RENOUNCE

'Counsel for the Attorney-General asked us to construe the word "renounce" in the phrase [in a will] "or renounce it at any future date" as having the technical significance of the word when used in reference, say, to a legacy, meaning, renounce it altogether before ever it has been in any respect enjoyed. I do not take that view of the meaning of the word in this context. The phrase is: "Should the government of the Commonwealth of Australia refuse this bequest at the time of my death or renounce it at any future date . . .", and it is to be borne in mind that the opportunity of enjoying this gift may arise immediately (if, for example, the prior life tenants surrendered) or at some distant date after the death of one or both of them. In such a context, and having regard to the dictionary use of the word "renounce", it seems to be that the testator was saying "Should the Commonwealth at any time, and whether it has in the meantime taken under the benefit or not, give up or surrender its beneficial interest".' *Re Spensley's Will Trusts* [1954] 1 All ER 178 at 187, CA, per Evershed MR

RENT

Generally

Rent is the recompense paid by the tenant to the landlord for the exclusive possession of corporeal hereditaments. It need not consist of the payment of money. It may consist in the render of chattels, or the performance of services, but rent of this nature constitutes rent within the meaning of the Rent Act 1977 only if the parties to a tenancy otherwise subject to that Act have quantified its value in terms of money. The possibility of distraining is the mark of rent, and so it cannot be reserved out of incorporeal hereditaments, inasmuch as the landlord cannot distrain upon these; but it may be reserved out of a remainder or reversion, as the landlord can distrain when the property falls into possession. The modern conception of rent is a payment which a tenant is bound by his contract to make to his landlord for the use of the property let. (27 Halsbury's Laws (4th edn) para 211)

Rent is either rent service or rentcharge. In either case it is a periodical payment made in respect of land, but the two forms of rent are fundamentally different. Rent service is incident to the relationship of the landlord and tenant. It is a payment made by the tenant as a recompense for the use of the land, and the receipt of it constitutes the chief beneficial right of ownership. The landlord enjoys his ownership by virtue of the receipt of rent. A rentcharge, on the other hand, is a burden on the ownership. The owner of the rentcharge is entitled to a fixed periodical sum as against the owner of the land, and, in effect, this is paid out of the rent service which the owner of the land receives. (39 Halsbury's Laws (4th edn) para 384)

Rent includes yearly or other rent, toll, duty, royalty, or other reservation, by the acre, the ton, or otherwise. (Conveyancing Act 1881, s 2)

'Rent' includes a rent service or a rentcharge, or other rent, toll, duty, royalty, or annual or periodical payment in money or money's worth, reserved or issuing out of or charged upon land, but does not include mortgage interest. (Law of Property Act 1925, s 205; cf Administration of Estates Act 1925, s 55(1), and Land Registration Act 1925, s 3)

'Rent' includes yearly or other rent, and toll, duty, royalty, or other reservation, by the acre, or the ton, or otherwise; and in relation to rent, 'payment' includes delivery; and 'fine' includes premium or fore-gift, and any payment, consideration, or benefit in the nature of a fine, premium, or fore-gift. (Settled Land Act 1925, s 117)

'Rent' includes any periodical sum payable by the tenant to the landlord in connection with his tenancy (whether under the lease or otherwise) in respect of lighting, heating, board, furniture or other services; and any reference to the rent payable under a lease shall be construed as including a reference to any such sum as aforesaid. (Landlord and Tenant (Requisitioned Land) Act 1942, s 13)

'The lease contains a reddendum, and whatever services or suits are thereby reserved partake of the character of rent. Now, one of the services to be rendered to the lessor in this case is, that the lessee shall grind all the corn grown upon the demised premises at the lessor's mill. It is true that rent goes with the reversion of the land in respect of which it is reserved. But in this case, at the time of granting the lease, the lessor was seised in fee of the mill, as well as of the reversion of the premises demised; and, therefore, so long as the property in the mill and the reversion of the demised premises continued to be in the same person, the suit to the mill would continue to be a suit due to the owner of the reversion of the demised premises, and would, therefore, in that respect, be in the nature of a rent. It is by no means unusual for the owner of a mansion and estate to stipulate with his tenants that they should carry coals to his mansion, and perform other similar services, and as long as the ownership of the mansion and the estate continues in the same person, those services are in the nature of rent, to be rendered to the reversioner of the lands demised.' *Vyvyan v Arthur* (1823) 1 B & C 410 at 414, per Bayley J

'Looking to the reddendum, the most important part of the deed for this purpose, I find that the rent to be reserved, "therefor", that is, for the demise of the residence, is £15, clearly a rent reserved in respect of the enjoyment and issuing out of the residence. Then there is a marked difference in the covenant as to what is to be paid for the enjoyment of the easement in the garden. That is done by a covenant in a subsequent part of the deed, whereby, after covenanting to pay the real rent, there is a further covenant to pay a further rent or sum for and in respect of the easement. Here, then, we have a marked distinction between the reservation of what really is a rent and a covenant to pay a sum in respect of an easement.' *Robins v Evans* (1863) 2 H & C 410 at 420, per cur.

'In speaking of coal . . . we talk constantly about the "rent" and "royalty" of coal. The phrases are figurative: you pay rent in one sense it is true; but rent generally has been understood to be a return from the soil, and not to be a consumption or taking away of the soil; whereas of course where the soil consists of coal and other minerals you are actually taking it away.' *Greville-Nugent v Mackenzie* [1900] AC 83 at 87, 88, per Lord Halsbury LC

[The Landlord and Tenant Act 1709, s 1, enacts that goods taken in execution must not be removed from the premises unless the party taking them pays the 'rent' for the said premises.] 'The public-house was expressed to be let "at the rent of £150 a year for the said premises". Now be it observed that those words "the rent for the said premises" are the very words used in the statute. . . . When you find this £150 defined as being the rent for the said premises I cannot see why we should fail to adopt the definition. Then there are these very peculiar words: "and the additional yearly sum"—it is not called rent—of £1,250 in lieu of premiums for the goodwill of the business and for the use of the fixtures and fittings upon the premises. . . . This sum is not described as rent. . . . But when I find that a clear distinction is drawn between rent and yearly sum I am not disposed to give to those words any other than their natural meaning. Therefore I think that the landlord had no right to distrain for this additional yearly sum.' *Cox v Harper* [1910] 1 Ch 480 at 487, CA, per Cozens-Hardy MR

[The Housing Act 1936, s 2(1) (repealed; see now the Landlord and Tenant Act 1985, s 8) provided (inter alia) that there should be implied in any contract to let a house situate in the administrative county of London at a 'rent' not exceeding a certain sum a condition that the house was, and an undertaking that the house would be kept, reasonably fit for human habitation.] 'Atkinson J took the view that the word "rent" in the section does not mean what it says, namely rent, but annual value. Accordingly, he held that, where a tenant pays what is sometimes called an inclusive rent—that is to say, paying rent and leaving the landlord to bear the rates—the sum paid by the tenant is not to be the test, but some other sum to be ascertained by deduction from that of whatever is the fair and just apportionment in respect of rates for the part of the premises which he occupies, if he has indeed occupied only part. With all respect to the learned judge, I cannot accept the view which he took of the construction of the section. The section requires the existence of a contract. The rent referred to in the section appears to me to mean, and to mean only, the rent payable by virtue of that contract by the tenant to the landlord. I can see no justification for dissecting that contractual payment and attributing part of it to something which is called the annual value of the house, or of part of the house, and attributing the rest of it to rates or an apportioned sum in respect of rates. It seems to me that the legislature has taken, for reasons no doubt thought good by it, a simple and clear test about which nobody could be confused, namely, the actual contractual rent paid by the tenant to the landlord. . . . In my opinion, "rent" in this section means contractual rent, and no deduction falls to be made in respect of rates and taxes, or anything else.' *Rousou v Photi* [1940] 2 KB 379 at 383–385, CA, per Greene MR

'The expressions "rent", "tenant", and "landlord" when used in conjunction can, I think, only connote the existence of a tenancy, and none the less so when there is express reference to rent payable for the land.' *Mellows v Buxton Palace Hotel Ltd* (1943) 113 LJKB 170 at 173, CA, per Luxmoore LJ

'"Rent service" has been defined as "an annual return made by the tenant in labour, money or provisions in retribution for the land that passes" (see Gilbert on Rents (1758), p 9, Co Litt 142a). No technical words are needed in order to create a rent service, but in regard to that it is a return of something that was not in the grantor before the words "reddendo", "reservando", "solvendo" and "inveniendo" were treated as proper words (see Gilbert, p 30). Of these words "reservando" seems to have captured the ear, with the result that it has become usual to refer to the rent agreed to be paid by a lease as the "rent reserved by a lease". But, in my view, "rent" and "rent reserved" do not differ in meaning.' *Samuel v Salmon & Gluckstein Ltd* [1946] Ch 8 at 12, per Uthwatt J

Australia 'I can see no good reason why the word "rent" used by the parties should not be given its ordinary meaning of a sum issuing out of the land demised payable by the lessee to the lessor for the right to occupy that land and all that went with it and to use it for the purpose for which it was demised.' *Junghenn v Wood* [1958] SR (NSW) 327 at 330, per Owen J

Australia 'This [rent] is a word which in its strict and technical legal sense denotes a consideration to be rendered by a lessee to his lessor, but it is a word commonly used by laymen to denote a payment being made in respect of occupation of premises, even though the occupation be that of a licensee.' *Metcalfe & Morris Pty Ltd v Reekie* [1963] NSWR 459 at 462, per Maguire J

Canada 'The word "rent" [used in the Income Tax Act RSC 1952, c 148, s 106(1)(d), providing for a withholding tax on rent paid to non-residents; see now RSC 1970, c I–5, s 158] has a fixed legal meaning and does not include all payments which a tenant is bound to make under the terms of a lease. Normally money expended for taxes is not rent because it is not usually reserved or payable to the landlord.' *CI Burland Properties Ltd v Minister of National Revenue* [1967] CTC 432 at 436, Ex Ct, per Cattanach J; affd 68 DTC 5220, SCC

Of small holding

'Full fair rent' in relation to a small holding means the rent which a tenant might reasonably be expected to pay for the holding if let as such and the landlord undertook to bear the cost of structural repairs. (Small Holdings and Allotments Act 1926, s 2(6))

Quit rent

'A quit rent is not necessarily a rent payable to the Crown, and strictly speaking, means a rent payable to the lord, when the tenant goes quit and free of all other services; but in Ireland this term is usually applied to those acreable rents which were reserved in Crown grants in fee-simple of lands forfeited in the rebellion of 1641.' *Re Maxwell's Estate* (1891) 28 LR Ir 356 at 358, per Bewley J

Rentcharge *See* RENTCHARGE

Rents and profits

'It is true that where there is no direction for a sale, the court has gone by several gradations. When any particular time is mentioned, within which the estate would not afford the charge, the court directed a sale: and then went further, till a sale was directed on the words rents and profits alone, when there was nothing to exclude or express a sale. . . . As to the intention, there is not one case in ten, where the court had decreed a sale on the words rents and profits, that it has been agreeable to the testator's intention; yet the court has, in aid of a creditor directed a sale, by a kind of discretionary power, on the ground of law, that rents and profits in a will, mean to pass the land itself.' *Baines v Dixon* (1747) 1 Ves Sen 41 at 42, per Lord Hardwicke LC

'In construing the words "rents and profits" in a will upon such a subject to amount to a power to raise a gross sum of money, the occasion, on which the necessity of providing that sum would arise, must be observed. The time cannot be known with certainty; depending on a contingency. Neither can the exact amount be specified: that also depending on contingencies; the value of the estate; the contract with the lessor; the event, whether one life has dropped; or more, as in this instance. This however is clear; that, whenever the occasion for renewal arises, and a given sum can be agreed upon for it, it is absolutely necessary, that it should be paid immediately; as those, who are to grant the renewal upon that payment, cannot be expected to wait for a gradual payment out of the annual rents and profits, as they arise; but are to receive a gross sum, to be paid immediately: that necessarily arising from the intention to preserve the whole property entire; which would be endangered by suffering another life to drop. It was fairly argued, that, though the natural interpretation of these words is annual rents and profits, and such a direction to raise money by rents and profits seems to be put in contradistinction to sale or mortgage, the word "profits" *ex vi termini* includes the whole interest; as a devise of the profits would pass the land itself. A direction of this sort, however, to raise money out of the rents and profits, is not exactly the same as a devise of the estate under that description by giving the profits. The construction cannot depend on the effect of the word "profits" *per se*: which would include all the land produces: but that word "profits"is to be taken, as it stands here, coupled with rents. Whatever might have been the interpretation of these words, had the case been new, whatever doubt might have arisen upon them, as denoting annual, or permanent, profits, it is now too late to speculate; this court having by a technical, artificial, but liberal, construction, in a series of authorities, admitting it not to be the natural meaning, extended those words, when applied to the object of raising a gross sum at a fixed time, when it must be raised, and paid, without delay, to a power to raise by sale or mortgage; unless restrained by other words.' *Allan v Backhouse* (1813) 2 Ves & B 65 at 74, 75, per Plumer V-C

'A direction to raise and pay legacies out of land, without any other direction whatever upon the subject, would make them raisable and payable one year after the death of the testator; and, in my opinion, it is not varied by the fact, that they are to be levied and raised out of the rents of the estate, because, in a great many cases (and this I think is one of them) the Court would hold that the words "rents and profits" were used as equivalent to "the estate", unless the testator had expressly directed that an accumulation should take place, and that the legacy should not be paid until the accumulation of rents had amounted to the sum required for that purpose.' *Londesborough (Lord) v Somerville* (1854) 19 Beav 295 at 303, per Romilly MR

'Rents and profits must mean ordinary rents and profits, and not merely nominal rents reserved upon leases for lives, and if the vendors meant these words "rents and profits" to have any other than their ordinary meaning, it was upon them to have expressed upon the face of the conditions of sale the meaning which they intended the words to import.' *Hughes v Jones* (1861) 3 De G F & J 307 at 314, per Turner LJ

'The question is, in what sense the testator used the terms "rents and profits". Those words may have different meanings, and they have been held to extend to the proceeds of the sale of an estate. But the most usual and proper meaning is annual rents and profits.' *Lovat (Lord) v Leeds (Duchess) (No 2)* (1862) 2 Drew & Sm 75 at 77, per Kindersley V-C

RENTAL *See also* ANNUAL RENTAL

'I think "rental" means the total amount of the rents payable by the several tenants to the landlord or his agent, that is to say, the total amount appearing in the rent-book which I suppose most landowners would keep, shewing the rents paid by their several tenants.' *Re Windham's Settled Estate* [1912] 2 Ch 75 at 80, per Warrington J

RENTAL VALUE

'Rental value' means the annual rent which a tenant might reasonably be expected to pay for the land if the land had continued in the same condition as at the date when entry [of unoccupied land by a local authority for the purpose of providing allotment gardens] was made under this section, or at the date when possession thereof was so first taken as aforesaid as the case may be. (Allotments Act 1922, s 10)

RENTCHARGE *See also* RENT

A rentcharge is an annual sum issuing out of land, but not as an incident of tenure, the due payment of which is secured by a right of distress. It is called a rentcharge because the land in respect of which it is paid is charged with a distress. Where there was no power of distress the rent was called a rent seck.

In some cases the power to distrain for a rentcharge could arise at common law, apart from any express reservation. In 1731 the like remedy by distress and sale as in the case of rent reserved upon lease was extended to rents seck, and rents and annuities charged on land were in effect converted into rentcharges. A person entitled under an instrument which came into operation after 1881 to receive an annual sum out of any land or out of the income of any land, whether charged by way of rentcharge or otherwise, not being rent incident to a reversion, has a statutory power of distress and certain other statutory remedies.

Since 1925 a rentcharge at law can only subsist as an estate in fee simple or as a term of years absolute and must be in possession, issuing out of or charged on land, being either perpetual or for a term of years absolute. (32 Halsbury's Laws (4th edn) paras 1203, 1204)

For the purposes of this Act 'rentcharge' means any annual or other periodic sum charged on or issuing out of land, except—
(a) rent reserved by a lease or tenancy, or
(b) any sum payable by way of interest.
(Rentcharges Act 1977, s 1)

[The Act of 1977 prohibits the creation of ordinary rentcharges, provides for the compulsory extinguishment of existing rentcharges, and provides improved procedures for redemption and appointments, etc.]

RENTED PREMISES

Canada 'In my opinion a sound construction would be that the words "rented premises" have a broader connotation than a mere physical space, and encompass not only that physical space but what the tenant is entitled to either under the terms of the written lease or the implied tenancy agreement, and I point out that counsel for the appellant in its factum referred to such matters as air-conditioning and use of the sauna bath and swimming pool as "imposed by collateral agreement". Therefore, I have come to the conclusion that the words "rented premises" in s 96(1) [Landlord and Tenant Act, RSO 1970, c 236; see now RSO 1980, c 232] include the duty of the landlord to provide the tenant with proper ingress and egress to the apartment and to provide the tenant with air-conditioning for the apartment and the use of the sauna bath and swimming pool.' *Pajelle Investments Ltd v Herbold* (1975) 62 DLR (3d) 749 at 754, 755, SCC, per Spence J

REPAIR *See also* MAINTAIN–MAINTENANCE

'Repairs' includes any work of maintenance, decoration or restoration, and references to repairing, to keeping or yielding up in repair and to state of repair shall be construed accordingly. (Landlord and Tenant Act 1954, s 69)

'"Repaired", I think, means patching where patching is reasonably practicable, and where it is not you must put in a new piece.' *Inglis v Buttery* (1878) 3 App Cas 552 at 579, per Lord Blackburn

'However large the words of the covenant may be, a covenant to repair a house is not a covenant to give a different thing from that which the tenant took when he entered into the covenant. He has to repair that thing which he took; he is not obliged to make a new and different thing.' *Lister v Lane* [1893] 2 QB 212 at 216, 217, per Lord Esher MR

'"Repair" and "renew" are not words expressive of a clear contrast. Repair always involves renewal; renewal of a part; of a subordinate part. . . . Repair is restoration by renewal or replacement of subsidiary parts of a whole. Renewal, as distinguished from repair, is reconstruction of the entirety, meaning by the entirety not necessarily the whole but substantially the whole subject-matter under discussion.' *Lurcott v Wakely* [1911] 1 KB 905 at 923, CA, per Buckley LJ

'I do not think there is any substantial difference in construction between "repair", which must mean "repair reasonably or properly" and "keep in good repair" or "sufficient repair" or "tenantable repair". . . . The tenant must when necessary restore by reparation or renewal of subsidiary parts the subject matter demised to a condition in which it is reasonably fit for the purposes for which such a subject matter would ordinarily be used.' *Anstruther-Gough-Calthorpe v McOscar* [1924] 1 KB 716 at 728–731, CA, per Scrutton LJ

'I take the word "repair" as meaning, in the language of Lord Blackburn in *Inglis v Buttery & Co* [supra], the making good defects, including renewal where that is necessary.' *Greg v Planque* [1936] 1 KB 669 at 677, CA, per Slesser LJ

'Very broadly speaking, I think that to repair is to remedy defects, but it can also properly include an element of the "stitch in time which saves nine". Work does not cease to be repair work because it is done to a large extent in anticipation of forthcoming defects or in rectification of merely incipient defects, rather than the rectification of defects which have already become serious. Some element of anticipation is included.' *Day v Harland and Wolff Ltd* [1953] 2 All ER 387 at 388, per Pearson J

'I agree with counsel for the plaintiff that the word "repair" in its ordinary context indicates the putting back into good condition of something that, having been in good condition, has fallen into bad condition. That is undoubtedly the ordinary sense of it when the word "repair" is applied to a travelling road. This, however, was not a travelling road, but a working place, and when the word "repair" is applied to a working place, it seems to me certainly no extravagant distortion of its meaning to say that it would include such an operation [making the roof and sides secure after firing] as was here being performed.' Ibid at 640, per Evershed MR

'Unfortunately, the terms "repair", "maintenance" and "adjustment" are not mutually exclusive. One cannot, therefore, by describing some operation as "maintenance" or "adjustment", exclude the possibility that it is also a "repair". Furthermore, in considering whether any particular work may properly be called a repair, one must, I think, remember that our language abounds in instances of particular operations or activities which acquire distinctive names or descriptions but still remain species of one genus of operations or activities bearing a comprehensive name. The particular name, however, becomes so much used that the comprehensive term fades into the background, until the precise question has to be answered: "It it applicable?" For example, there are a whole host of operations which can be properly described as "cutting", but each of which has its own distinctive name: chopping, sawing, scything, mowing—even shaving. The Divisional Court recently heard much argument on the question whether drilling was cutting, and decided that it was. So it is, I think, with the word "repair". It covers a host of things, many of which are given distinctive names which become so popular that it becomes very easy to think of them as something different from repairs.' *Reilly v British Transport Commission* [1956] 3 All ER 857 at 859, per Donovan J

' "Repair" means restoration to a sound condition after injury or decay, and in the case of a composite subject, such as a motor vehicle, includes the replacement of worn-out or injured parts in order to restore the vehicle to a serviceable condition.' *Perth Assessor v Shields Motor Car Co Ltd* 1956 SLT 264 at 267, per Lord Patrick

'Applying this conception that "repair" involves putting right that which has gone wrong, I believe that tightening a nut which has come loose is within it.' *Cade v British Transport Commission* [1958] 2 All ER 615 at 618, HL, per Viscount Kilmuir LC; also reported [1959] AC 256 at 265

'It is true that the primary meaning of the word "repair" is to restore to sound condition that which has previously been sound, but the word is also properly used in the sense of "to make good". Moreover, the word is commonly used to describe the operation of making an article good or sound, irrespective of whether the article has been good or sound before. Few people, seeing a hole in a piece of cloth being darned, would inquire whether the hole was left in the process of weaving or developed afterwards, in order that they might choose whether to describe the process of darning as one of completing the process of manufacture or as repair of the cloth. The normal person would simply say that the cloth was being repaired.' *Burns v National Coal Board* 1958 SLT 34 at 39, per Lord Patrick

'Where the covenant is to keep and deliver up in repair there is no substantial difference in construction if there are additional words such as "repair reasonably and properly" or "keep in good repair", or "sufficient repair" or "tenantable repair" or other phrases often used. . . . The test generally is that the premises should be kept and delivered up in that state of repair in which they ought to be found, if they had been managed by a reasonably minded owner, having regard to the age of the premises, and to their character and ordinary uses, or the requirements of the tenants of the class likely to take them at the time of their demise or at the commencement of the term.' Ibid at 112, per Davidson J

'In my opinion the word "repair" has to be considered as an ordinary English word whose meaning depends on the context in which it is used. I do not doubt the correctness of the statement of the Lord Porter in *London & Northern Eastern Railway Co v Berriman* [[1946] 1 All ER 255], that the word contains "some suggestion of putting right that which is wrong". But that does not mean that every putting right of that which is wrong is a repair: if clothes were too dirty to be fit to wear the cleaning of them would not be called repair; if the oil in the sump of a car were at a dangerously low level, putting in oil would not be called repair. With regard to the judgment of Du Parcq J in *Bishop v Consolidated London Properties Ltd* [[1933] All ER Rep 963], I express no opinion as to the correctness of the decision that the presence of a pigeon in a downfall pipe constitutes a breach of a landlord's duty of repair, but I would respectfully suggest that when Du Parcq said "to repair after all merely means to prepare or make fit again to perform its function: it means to put in order" he was giving an unduly extended meaning to the word "repair". To wind up a watch that has stopped and to adjust its hands to the right time is to make it fit again to perform its function, to put it in order. Nobody would describe such an operation as repairing the watch. In relation to a highway I am of opinion that in ordinary speech nobody would speak of the mere removal of an obstruction from the highway as being in itself a repair. . . . I consider that a highway can only be said to be out of repair if the surface of it is defective or disturbed in some way. Not every defect in the surface would constitute being out of repair—e.g. an icy road would not in my view be out of repair. But if the surface is in a proper condition I do not think it can ever be said that the highway is out of repair.' *Hereford & Worcester County Council v Newman* [1975] 2 All ER 673 at 681, CA, per Cairns LJ

[The plaintiff brought an action against a local authority seeking specific performance of the statutory covenant to 'repair' implied by the Housing Act 1961, s 32(1).] 'I find helpful the observation of Atkin LJ in *Anstruther-Gough-Calthorpe v McOscar* [[1924] 1 KB 716 at 734] that repair "connotes the idea of making good damage so as to leave the subject so far as possible as though it had not been damaged". Where decorative repair is in question one must look for damage to the decorations but where, as here, the obligation is merely to keep the structure and exterior of the house in repair, the covenant will only come into operation where there has been damage to the structure and exterior which requires to be made good.' *Quick v Taff-Ely Borough Council* [1985] 3 All ER 321 at 325, CA, per Dillon LJ

Australia 'It is now well established that the repair of a structure may involve renewal or rebuilding of part of it, and that all repairs involve renewal to some extent. . . . It is a question of degree whether rebuilding part of a house does or does not fall within the category of repairing a house. A covenant to repair does not involve the covenantee in an obligation to make improvements, but if he cannot perform his covenant to repair without making improvements, then the expense of making the improvements falls upon him. This is the case whether the necessity arises from physical causes, or from legal causes.' *Graham v Markets Hotel Pty Ltd* (1943) 67 CLR 567 at 579, per Latham CJ

Australia 'As applied to a building . . . "repair" means to renew what is decayed or has deteriorated, and again presupposes an existing building which has fallen into disrepair.' *Re Church of St Jude* [1956] SASR 46 at 53, per Hannan J

Australia 'Repair involves a restoration of a thing to a condition it formerly had without changing its character. But in the case of a thing considered from the point of view of its use as distinct from its appearance, it is restoration of efficiency in function rather than exact repetition of form or material that is significant. Whether or not work done upon a thing is aptly described as a repair of that thing is thus a question of fact and degree.' *W Thomas & Co Pty Ltd v Federal Comr of Taxation* [1966] ALR 915 at 924, per Windeyer J

Highway repair

'"Repair" means making good defects in the surface of the highway itself so as to make it reasonably passable for the ordinary traffic of the neighbourhood at all seasons of the year without danger caused by its physical condition. . . . Thus deep ruts in cart roads, potholes in carriage roads, broken bridges on footpaths or bushes rooted in the surface, make all these highways "out of repair".' *Haydon v Kent County Council* [1978] 2 All ER 97 at 102, CA, per Lord Denning MR

Keep in repair

[The tenant under a lease of a farm and outbuildings agreed to keep and deliver up the demised premises in good repair.] 'If, at the time of demise, the premises were old and in bad repair, the lessee was bound to put them in good repair as old premises; for he cannot "keep" them in good repair without putting them into it. He might have contracted to keep them in the state in which they were at the time of the demise. This is a contract to keep the premises in good repair, as old premises; but that cannot justify the keeping them in bad repair because they happened to be in that state when the defendant took them.' *Payne v Haine* (1847) 16 M & W 541 at 545, per Parke B

'The term "good repair" is to be construed with reference to the subject-matter, and must differ, as that may be a palace or a cottage; but to "keep in good repair" presupposes the putting into it, and means that during the whole term the premises shall be in good repair.' Ibid at 546, per Rolfe B

[A testator gave property to his trustees to receive the rents, issues, and profits and thereout keep the houses, etc, in good, substantial, and tenantable repair.] 'As to repairs, "keeping in repair" means to expend money in putting the leaseholds in repair, assuming them to be out of repair. They must be put in repair, from time to time, out of the income, that is, in ordinary repair; but the income is not to be applied in such extraordinary repairs as would be equivalent to rebuilding the house.' *Crowe v Crisford* (1853) 17 Beav 507 at 510, per Romilly MR

'The testator was the owner of a mansion-house, admitted to be an old house and of considerable dimensions; he was also owner of considerable real estates, comprising farm houses and farm buildings, and he has directed them to be kept in good repair. It is clear the mansion-house and other messuages, except farming buildings, are not to be rebuilt unless all parties consent; but they are to be kept in good repair. Now it is contended that as at the time when the testator died, the premises were in bad condition, they are only to be kept in that condition. But can I say, on the language of the will, that they are to be kept, not in good, but in bad repair? for that is really the argument. What, then, is meant by good repair? that is the true question. I must give some explanation to the expression, so as not to do anything not necessary for upholding the buildings in such a state that they may be fit for fair use and enjoyment. They must be put in such a state of repair as will satisfy a respectable occupant using them fairly.' *Cooke v Cholmondeley* (1858) 4 Drew 326 at 327, 328, per Kindersley V-C

'There is . . . an express covenant by the lessor that he will during the term "keep the main walls and main timbers of the warehouse in good repair and condition". Upon that I make two observations. The first is that, in my judgment, the covenant obliges the lessor to put the main walls and main timbers into good repair and condition, if they were in bad condition, when the lessee took the warehouse. The second is this, that the question, what is "good repair and condition", is to be viewed having regard to the class to which the demised tenement belongs, and not with regard to that tenement itself alone.' *Saner v Bilton* (1878) 7 Ch D 815 at 821, per Fry J

'What is the true construction of a tenant's contract to keep and deliver up premises in "tenantable repair"? Now, it is not an express term of that contract that the premises should be put into tenantable repair, and it may therefore be argued that, where it is conceded, as it is in this case, that the premises were out of tenantable repair when the tenancy began, the tenant is not bound to put them into tenantable repair, but is only bound to keep them in the same repair as they were in when he became the tenant of them. But it has been decided—and, I think, rightly decided—that, where the premises are not in repair when the tenant takes them, he must put them into repair in order to discharge his obligation under a contract to keep and deliver them up in repair. If the premises are out of repair at any time during the tenancy the landlord is entitled to say to the tenant, "you have now broken your contract to keep them in repair"; and if they were out of repair at the end of the tenancy he is entitled to say, "you have broken your contract to deliver them up in repair". I am of opinion that under a contract to keep the premises in tenantable repair and leave them in tenantable repair, the obligation of the tenant, if the premises are not in tenantable repair when the tenancy begins, is to put them into, keep them in, and deliver them up in tenantable repair.' *Proudfoot v Hart* (1890) 25 QBD 42 at 50, CA, per Lord Esher MR

'I think that to keep in thorough repair does not in any way confine the duty of the person who is liable under the covenant to the doing of what are ordinarily called repairs. A house is spoken of as being in thorough repair when it is a house to which no repairs have to be done. But it is a description of a state and not of a mode by which that state has been arrived at, and, therefore in my own mind I draw no wide distinction between keeping in thorough repair and keeping in good condition; they both appear to me to describe the condition of the house. What a surveyor would call in good condition and what a surveyor would call in thorough repair may differ somewhat, but they would be something very like, the one to the other. As I have said, the legal obligation is to keep the house in that state and I confess that I do not think that from the legal point of view there is much difference between the nature of the two obligations.' *Lurcott v Wakely & Wheeler* [1911] 1 KB 905 at 918, CA, per Fletcher Moulton LJ

'The question which has been argued relates to the form of reference. Is it to be framed on the footing that the obligation imposed by the words "will keep . . . in good and tenantable repair" involves a liability to put the premises into good and tenantable repair, or a liability of a less burdensome description? It has been determined by the Court of Appeal that in contracts between landlord and tenant a covenant in these terms by the tenant imposes on him an obligation to put the premises into a good and tenantable state, if they fell short of that condition when he took them. Ought the same construction to be applied to this particular contract? . . . I think . . . the form of the covenant in the present case does impose on the defendant the obligation to put the premises in good and tenantable repair.' *Evans v Shotton* (1918) 87 LJ Ch 527 at 528, per Eve J

Running repairs *See* RUNNING REPAIRS

Tenantable repair

'What is "tenantable repair"? Definitions have been given at different times by the courts. In *Belcher v Mackintosh* [(1839) 2 Mood & R 186] Alderson B directed a jury as to the law with respect to a covenant by a lessee to put premises into "habitable repair", and so to deliver up the same. He says (I am reading from Moody and Robinson's Report): "It is difficult to suggest any material difference between the term 'habitable repair' used in this agreement, and the more common expression 'tenantable repair'; they must both import such a state as to repair that the premises might be used and dwelt in not only with safety, but with reasonable comfort, by the class of persons by whom, and for the sort of purposes for which, they were to be occupied." That is the whole definition, and, so far as it goes, it is a good one. . . . The result of the cases seems to be this: the question whether the house was, or was not, in tenantable repair when the tenancy began is immaterial; but the age of the house is very material with respect to the obligation both to keep and to leave it in tenantable repair. It is obvious that the obligation is very different when the house is fifty years older than it was when the tenancy began. Lopes LJ has drawn up a definition of the term "tenantable repair" with which I entirely agree. It is this: "'Good tenantable repair' is such repair as, having regard to the age, character, and locality of the house, would make it reasonably fit for the occupation of a reasonably-minded tenant of the class who would be likely to take it." The age of the house must be taken into account, because nobody could reasonably expect that a house 200 years old should be in the same condition of repair as a house lately built; the character of the house must be taken into account because the same class of repairs as would be necessary to a palace would be wholly unnecessary to a cottage; and the locality of the house must be taken into account, because the state of repair necessary for a house in Grosvenor Square would be wholly different from the state of repair necessary for a house in Spitalfields. The house need not be put into the same condition as when the tenant took it; it need not be put into perfect repair; it need only be put into such a state of repair as renders it reasonably fit for the occupation of a reasonably-minded tenant of the class who would be likely to take it.' *Proudfoot v Hart* (1890) 25 QBD 42 at 50–53, CA, per Lord Esher MR

REPAIRING COVENANT *See* COVENANT; REPAIR

REPAIRING LEASE *See* LEASE; REPAIR

REPAYMENT

'Repayment is not, nor indeed is payment, a term of art. It can be effected in any way which puts an end to the indebtedness between one person and another. Set off is payment as much as the tender of cash.' *Inland Revenue Comrs v John Dow Stuart Ltd* [1950] AC 149 at 164, per Lord Porter

REPLEVIN

Replevin is a process to obtain a redelivery to the owner of chattels which have been wrongfully distrained or taken from him, upon his finding sufficient security for the rent and costs of action and undertaking that he will pursue an action against the distrainor to determine the right to distrain. The term 'replevin' is applied both to the redelivery of the goods and the action in which the right is tried. Wherever the object of proceedings is to procure the restitution of the specific chattels taken instead of compensation in damages, the proper course is an action of replevin; as an alternative, damages can be recovered in an action of trespass. (13 Halsbury's Laws (4th edn) para 373)

REPORT *See also* FAIR REPORT

Australia [In an application for leave to televise a video tape concerning custody and access proceedings, the question raised was whether the video tape was a 'report'.] 'One of the meanings of the word "report" contained in the Shorter Oxford Dictionary is: "An account brought by one person to another especially of some matter specially investigated". Another meaning is expressed in terms of accounts of statements of speakers or of any occurrence or event especially with a view to publication in the newspaper press. The Macquarie Dictionary contains a meaning of the word "report" as: "An account of a speech, debate, meeting, et cetera, especially as taken down for publication". I am satisfied that the introduction and the video tape do come within the normal meaning of the word "report".' *In the Marriage of RL and DC Bau and Herald-Sun TV Pty Ltd* (1986) 10 Fam LR 897 at 900, per Hase J

REPOSITORY

[Class X in the Town and Country Planning (Use Classes) Order 1950 concerned use as a wholesale warehouse or 'repository' for any purpose. The word 'repository' was not defined in the order.] 'The question is not simply what the word "repository" means in ordinary speech, but what it means as used in class X of the schedule to the 1950 order. The two meanings are not necessarily identical. In ordinary speech the word is seldom used, but when used it is applied mainly to two things, a furniture repository and a repository for documents. In the latter sense it may be applied either to a building such as the Public Record Office or to places such as a safe or a desk in which a person's will or codicils are likely to be found after his death; in neither case is the storage "as part of a storage business". But the Shorter Oxford English Dictionary gives the word a much more general meaning. It gives the first meaning of "repository" as "a vessel, receptacle, chamber, etc. in which things are, or may be, placed, deposited or stored". In this order the meaning is not restricted, because class X includes repository "for any purpose". It seems to me that buildings used for the long-term storage of vehicles fall clearly within that description. The reason why the draftsman preferred the word repository to the commoner word "store" may be that "store" is sometimes used to include a retail shop such as a "department store".' *Newbury District Council v Secretary of State for the Environment* [1980] 1 All ER 731 at 743, HL, per Lord Fraser of Tullybelton

REPRESENT

[The Dramatic Copyright Act 1833, s 2 (repealed; cf now the Copyright, Designs and Patents Act 1988, s 119) forbade persons to 'represent' the dramatic works of others.] 'The word "represent", in this case, must be taken to mean the bringing forward on a stage or place of theatrical representation; and I am of opinion, that if either one song, or more than one song, be taken from a piece, and be performed on a stage, or any place of theatrical entertainment, that would be a "representing" within the Act of Parliament.' *Planche v Braham* (1837) 8 C & P 68 at 74, per Tindal CJ; affd, 4 Bing NC 17

'The question is, whether the defendant represented or caused to be represented [within the Dramatic Copyright Act 1833, s 2 (repealed; see supra)] these pieces because they were represented at his theatre, with the assistance of servants, lights, etc., furnished by him. Even apart from authority, I do not think that, by furnishing servants to another, a man can be said to do all that is done by those servants while under the command of the other. A familiar example may be found in the case of a man letting a ready furnished house, leaving an old servant in it. Suppose the tenant gave a dinner, which was cooked by that servant, who also attend on him at it, and for which the plates and furniture of the landlord were used, no one could say that in any sense of the words the landlord gave that dinner.' *Lyon v Knowles* (1863) 3 B & S 556 at 564, 565, per Blackburn J; affd (1864) 5 B & S 751

New Zealand '"Legally represented" means

assistance in the court by way of representation in the usual way by counsel or by a solicitor where permissible appearing on behalf of the defendant. Whether the defendant has had such representation is a question of fact.' *R v Long* [1977] 1 NZLR 169 at 173, CA, per Cooke J

REPRESENTATION

A representation [in an insurance proposal] is an oral or written statement made by the assured or his agent before or at the time of the making of the contract, and it generally consists of oral communication made, or written instructions shown, by the broker to the insurer. The main distinction in form between a representation and an express warranty is that a representation may be made either orally or in writing and need not be included in the policy, whereas an express warranty must always be included in or written upon the policy, or must be contained in some document incorporated by reference into it. (25 Halsbury's Laws (4th edn) para 237)

A representation is a statement made by a representor to a representee and relating by way of affirmation, denial, description or otherwise to a matter of fact. The statement may be oral or in writing or arise by implication from words or conduct. The representor and the representee must be distinct from one another in substance as well as in name; where the persons claiming to have been deceived by a statement are in effect the same as those who are alleged to have made it, there is no representation which the law can recognise.

Mere praise by a man of his own goods, inventions, projects, undertakings, or other marketable commodities or rights, if confined to indiscriminate puffing and pushing, and not related to particulars, is not representation.

Where instead of basing the exaggeration or puffing upon facts separately stated (in which case each of the two things stands on its own footing, and whereas the one is not a representation at all, the other is wholly so), the representor intermingles it with facts, punctuates it by details or quantifies it by figures, the whole of the compound statement is deemed a representation. Thus, if the statement gives rise to an action where the facts are proved to have been mis-stated, it is no defence to allege that the facts were buried under a mass of indefinite and flattering generalities.

The usual permanent symbols by which a representation is conveyed are words and figures written or printed or produced by any other equivalent means; but plans and drawings, maps, pictures and photographs and the like, may effectively serve the same purpose. Speech is the most common method for the communication of a statement not in writing, but gestures and demeanour may be used in addition to or as an alternative to spoken language. (31 Halsbury's Laws (4th edn) paras 1005, 1017–1020)

In this Part [Part VI: promotion of sales of medicinal products] of this Act 'representation' means any statement or undertaking (whether constituting a condition or a warranty or not) which consists of spoken words other than words falling within para (a) or para (b) of sub-s (2) of this section [which define 'advertisement'], and any reference to making a representation shall be construed accordingly. (Medicines Act 1968, s 92(5))

'Properly speaking a representation is a statement, or assertion, made by one party to the other, before or at the time of the contract, of some matter or circumstance relating to it. Though it is sometimes contained in the written instrument, it is not an integral part of the contract.' *Behn v Burness* (1863) 3 B & S 751 at 753, per Williams J

'Mere silence cannot amount to a representation, but when there is a duty to disclose, deliberate silence may become significant and amount to a representation.' *Greenwood v Martins Bank Ltd* [1933] AC 51 at 57, HL, per Lord Tomlin

Australia 'The word "representation" is one which has been the subject of considerable judicial consideration. Without wishing to express a concluded view on what is embraced in the word it seems to me that in addition to including statements orally or in writing, associated with any pictorial material, conduct may also be added in an appropriate case, at least to the extent of what is embraced in the ordinary meaning of that word.' *Given v Pryor* (1979) 39 FLR 437 at 440, per Franki J

Estoppel by *See* ESTOPPEL

Of deceased person

'Representation' means the probate of a will and administration, and the expression "taking out representation" refers to the obtaining of the probate of a will or of the grant of administration. (Administration of Estates Act 1925, s 55(1))

REPRESENTATIVE

Commercial law

United States 'Representative' includes an agent, an officer of a corporation or association, and a trustee, executor or administrator of an estate, or any other person empowered to act for another. (Uniform Commercial Code 1978, s 1–201(35))

REPRESENTATIVES

In bond

[A bond provided that the obligors or any one or more of them or their respective 'representatives' might at any time determine their or his liability by one calendar month's notice in writing.] 'I must first consider what is the meaning of the word "representatives". Looking at the proviso as a whole, I think that the word includes the legal personal representatives of the obligors. The clause means that the liability of the representatives of a deceased obligor, including his executors and administrators, is to be determined, like the liability of the obligor in his lifetime, only by one calendar month's notice in writing being given.' *Re Silvester, Midland Rly Co v Silvester* [1895] 1 Ch 573 at 576, per Romer J

In will

[A testator by his will made provision for a gift over if there should be no children or 'representatives' of children of A.] 'The word "representatives" is ambiguous, and the meaning of it is to be sought in the context of the will. The testator could not have meant legal personal representatives, as technically designated executors or administrators; for there would be, as a matter of course, persons to fill that character. So he could not have meant next of kin, for such also there must have been. I am of opinion, that the context is to be taken as construing the word "representatives" to mean children.' *Herbert v Forbes* (1831) 1 LJ Ch 118 at 120, per Leach MR

[A testator by his will provided that certain property should be equally divided among all his cousins german then existing, or their 'representatives'.] 'The question is, in what sense has the testator here used the term "representatives". There is no doubt that this term is capable of being interpreted in any sense in which the Court may be satisfied, from the whole context of the will, that the testator intended to use it; and the cases are numerous in which it has been held to mean one thing or another according to the indications, collected from the whole will, of the testator's intention in using it. There is, however, one rule of construction, of universal application, which admits of no exception, and which ought never, under any circumstances, to be parted from, viz. that if any term is used by a testator which has a primary or ordinary legal meaning, that is the sense in which it ought to be construed, unless the Court is reasonably satisfied, by evidence to be collected from the will itself, of the testator's intention to use it, not in that sense, but in some different sense. . . . What, then, is the ordinary and legal meaning of the term "representatives"? Whom does the law regard as properly representing a deceased person with reference to personal property? Certainly his executors or administrators. They represent his person; they represent him in respect of his personal estate. The doctrine of the executor properly representing his testator is as old as the law itself. . . . As I cannot discover in the will any other evidence of such intention, I must construe the term "representatives" in its ordinary legal sense of executors and administrators.' *Re Crawford's Trusts* (1854) 2 Drew 230 at 233, 234, 247, per Kindersley V-C

'The Court will hold the word "representatives", to mean "descendants", where the context and obvious meaning of the expressions employed in the will make that the best construction that can be given to it, and . . . there is no rule of law or construction against construing the word "representatives" to mean "descendants".' *Atherton v Crowther, Deudon v De Massals* (1854) 19 Beav 448 at 453, per Romilly MR

[A testator by his will bequeathed property to his brothers and sisters or their 'representatives'.] 'I am of opinion that the word "representatives" means legal personal representatives.' *Re Henderson* (1860) 28 Beav 656 at 658, per Romilly MR

'The prima facie meaning of the word representative, so far as relates to real estate, is the heir, and, so far as it refers to personal estate, is the executors, if any have been appointed, or if not, the administrators. The burthen of proof lies on anybody contending the contrary.' *Chapman v Chapman* (1864) 33 Beav 556 at 556, 557, per Romilly MR

'The words "representatives" or "legal representatives", or "personal representatives", primarily mean executors or administrators; and in order to put any other meaning on them, you must find in the context some special reason for so doing.' *Re Turner* (1865) 2 Drew & Sm 501 at 508, per Kindersley V-C

[A testatrix by her will devised freehold property to her trustees upon trust to divide the rents and profits thereof equally among her children and their families so long as any of her children should live, and from and after the death of the longest liver of her children upon trust to sell the said property and to divide the proceeds equally among the personal 'representatives' of her several children *per stirpes*.] 'The Master of the Rolls [Romilly MR in *Atherton v Crowther* (supra)] said . . . that *Styth v Monro* [(1834) 6 Sim 49] was a sufficient authority to shew that the court would hold the word "representatives" to mean "descendants" where the context and obvious meaning of the expressions employed in the will made that the best construction that could be given to it, and that there was no rule of law or construction against construing the word "representatives" to mean "descendants". I think that that is the most reasonable view of the words of the will which I have to construe here. The testatrix, in the codicil, has spoken of issue who are to stand in the place of their parents. The gift in the will is of the income for the equal benefit and advantage of all her children; and afterwards the capital is to go to the "personal representatives" of her several children "*per stirpes*". Therefore, when I come to the gift after the death of the survivor of the testatrix's children, it seems to me that I shall be adopting the construction which best carries out the intention of the testatrix if I hold that those words mean descendants of the testatrix's children, viz descendants of all *per stirpes*. If there were only one child, the descendants of that one child would take the whole. I therefore make a declaration that the issue living at the testatrix's death, and born before the death of the last surviving child of the testatrix, are entitled to share *per stirpes*.' *Re Knowles, Rainford v Knowles* (1888) 59 LT 359 at 361, per Kay J

See, generally, 50 Halsbury's Laws (4th edn) para 541

Australia 'The general rule is that the term "representatives" when used in a will means, in the absence of context to the contrary, executors or administrators of the person represented.' *Mocatta v Mocatta* (1915) 19 CLR 515 at 517, per Griffith CJ

REPROBATION *See* APPROBATE AND REPROBATE; ESTOPPEL

See, generally, 9 Halsbury's Laws (4th edn) para 912.

REPRODUCTIVE MATERIAL

References in this Part [Part I: plant breeders' rights] of this Act to reproductive material are references to reproductive material of plant varieties, and include references—

(a) to seeds for sowing,
(b) to seed potatoes and other vegetative propagating material,
(c) to whole plants, as well as parts of plants, where whole plants may be used as reproductive material, and
(d) to ornamental plants and parts of ornamental plants when used commercially as propagating material in the production of ornamental plants and cut flowers.

(Plant Varieties and Seeds Act 1964, s 15)

REPUDIATION

'Repudiation of a contract may mean that, having admittedly made a contract, you decide to break it and break it in such a way that you intend not to proceed with it. Another use of the word "repudiation" is where you say: "There never was a contract at all between us." If it turns out there was a contract, the act of one party denying the existence of it is to repudiate it; but supposing it turns out he was right and there never was a contract, then "repudiation" is used in a different sense from that in which it would be used when an existing contract is broken by a refusal to perform.' *Toller v Law Accident Insurance Society Ltd* [1936] 2 All ER 952 at 956, CA, per Greene LJ

'The word "repudiation" has . . . led to difficulties because it is an ambiguous word constantly used without precise definition in contract law. I do not attempt an exhaustive list of the senses in which the word has been used, but I may give some instances. Repudiation of a contract is sometimes used as meaning that the defendant denies that there ever was a contract in the sense of an actual *consensus ad idem*. . . . Short of this, one party, though not denying that there was the appearance of assent, might claim that the consent was vitiated by fraud or duress or mistake or illegality, and in that sense it is often said that he repudiates the contract. . . . There is, however, a form of repudiation where the party who repudiates does not deny that a contract was intended between the parties, but claims that it is not binding because of the failure of some condition or the infringement of some duty fundamental to the enforceability of the contract, it being expressly provided by the contract that the failure of condition or the breach of duty should invalidate the contract. . . . Another case to which the word repudiation is applied is when the party, though not disputing the contract, declares unequivocally that he will not perform it and, admitting the breach, leaves the other party to claim damages. . . . But perhaps the commonest application of the word "repudiation" is to what is often called the anticipatory breach of a contract where the party by words or conduct evinces an intention no longer to be bound and the other party accepts the repudiation and rescinds the contract. In such a case, if the repudiation is wrongful and the rescission is rightful, the contract is ended by the rescission but only as far as concerns future performance. It remains alive for the awarding of damages either for previous breaches or for the breach which constitutes the repudiation. . . . The difference between repudiating a contract and repudiating liability under it must not be overlooked. It is thus necessary in every case in which the word repudiation is used to be clear in what sense it is being used.' *Heyman v Darwins Ltd* [1942] AC 356 at 378, 379, per Lord Wright

'The meaning of the words "to repudiate" are, according to the Oxford Dictionary "to refuse to discharge or acknowledge a debt or other obligation". Repudiation, it seems to me, for this purpose [repudiation of a contract] must be a conscious act in relation to the contract in question. That distinguishes it from the frustration of a contract.' *William Cory & Son Ltd v City of London Corpn* [1950] 2 All ER 584 at 586, per Lord Goddard CJ; [1951] 2 KB 476

'Repudiation of a contract is nothing but a breach of contract. Except where it is accepted as an anticipatory breach and as a ground for a claim of damages, a repudiation can never be said to be accepted by the other party except in the sense that he acquiesces in it and does not propose to take any action. Otherwise he founds on it as a cause of action.' *White and Carter (Councils) Ltd v McGregor* 1962 SLR 9 at 14, HL, per Lord Keith of Avonholme

REPUGNANT

[The Tramways Act 1870, s 46, provides that the promoters of a tramway may make by-laws that are not 'repugnant' to the laws of the United Kingdom.] 'A by-law is not repugnant to the general law merely because it creates a new offence, and says that something shall be unlawful which the law does not say is unlawful. It is repugnant if it makes unlawful that which the general law says is lawful. It is repugnant if it expressly or by necessary implication professes to alter the general law of the land. I say "by necessary implication" because I have in mind the cases with respect to by-laws prohibiting persons from travelling on railways without a ticket. In those cases by-laws which impose the same penalty as the general law without making a fraudulent intention part of the description of the offence have been held to be bad, because the statute creating the offence say that there must be a fraudulent intention on the part of the person charged with travelling without a ticket, and the by-law, therefore, by implication alters the general law. Again, a by-law is repugnant if it adds something inconsistent with the provisions of a statute creating the same offence; but if it adds something not inconsistent, that is not sufficient to make the by-law bad as repugnant.' *Gentel v Rapps* [1902] 1 KB 160 at 166, per Channell J

Australia 'According to the Oxford Dictionary, it [the word 'repugnant'] has this meaning—as its primary meaning: "contrary or contradictory to, inconsistent or incompatible with, divergent from, standing against, something else"; but the meaning "divergent from, standing against, something else" is marked as obsolete. No doubt the word "repugnant" is often used loosely and rhetorically; but in considering Acts of Parliament, the strict meaning should prima facie be applied.' *Union SS Co of New Zealand Ltd v The Commonwealth* (1925) 36 CLR 130 at 157, per Higgins J

REPUTATION *See also* CHARACTER

Australia 'Reputation is a fact. A person who has the reputation of being a thief is a reputed thief. His repute depends upon the qualities of depravity attributed to him by the community, or by such portion of the community as is aware of his existence and is sufficiently interested to ascribe the characteristics to him and to accept the same as true. Reputation is the popular belief of the nature of a man's character. Theoretically it will be the summation of all that is circulated for, or against, the individual in the community. It might be of slow and imperceptible formation (graduating through stages of rumour). But in some cases the general opinion may be more or less acquired "overnight". Except in the case of eminent or notorious people a reputation may be known only in a small district or to few members of the public.' *Dias v O'Sullivan* [1949] ALR 586 at 591, per Mayo J

REPUTED OWNER

'There is no inflexible rule of law that because a man who was once the owner of goods and has sold them remains in possession of them he must therefore be held to be the reputed owner. . . . If he remains in possession with the reputation of ownership, and in those circumstances which create a reputation of ownership, then the property will pass to his assignees [in bankruptcy]; but it is always a question of fact whether or no the circumstances are such as to create that reputation. What then, are the principles applicable to the determination of that question? Much of the argument seems to me to have proceeded on a fallacious application of the expressions "knowledge of the world" and "known to the public". The doctrine of reputed ownership does not require any investigation into the actual state of knowledge or belief, either of all creditors, or of particular creditors, and still less of the outside world, who are no creditors at all, as to the position of particular goods. It is enough for the doctrine if those goods are in such a situation as to convey to the minds of those who know their situation the reputation of ownership, that reputation arising by the legitimate exercise of reason and judgment on the knowledge of those facts which are capable of being generally known to those who choose to make inquiry on the subject. It is not at all necessary to examine into the degree of actual knowledge which is possessed, but the Court must judge from the situation of the goods what inference as to the ownership might be legitimately drawn by those who knew the facts. I do not mean the facts that are only known to the parties dealing with the goods, but such facts as are capable of being, and naturally would be, the subject of general knowledge to those who take any means to inform themselves on the subject. So, on the other hand, it is not at all necessary, in order to exclude the doctrine of reputed ownership, to shew that every creditor, or any particular creditor, or the outside world who are not creditors, knew anything whatever about particular goods, one way or the other. It is quite enough, in my judgment, if the situation of the goods was such as to exclude all legitimate ground from which those who knew anything about the situation could infer the ownership to be in the person having actual possession.' *Re Couston, ex p Watkins* (1873) 8 Ch App 520 at 528, 529, per Lord Selborne LC

[The Private Street Works Act 1892, s 6 and Sch (repealed; cf now the Highways Act 1980, s 212) provided that provisional apportionments should state the amounts charged on the respective premises and the names of the respective owners, or 'reputed owners'.] 'It is clear that an objection to a provisional apportionment under the Act of 1892 on the ground that it does not contain the correct name of the owner is not necessarily a fatal objective, for by s 6 it is to contain the particulars prescribed in Part I of the schedule, among which are the names of the respective owners "or reputed owners". I feel some doubt whether the learned county court judge gave a proper interpretation to the phrase "reputed owner"; it must mean the person whom the local authority really believes to be the owner, and a person who has been the owner, and whom the local authority has dealt with as such, is certainly a reputed owner.' *Wirral Rural District Council v Carter* [1903] 1 KB 646 at 651, per Channell J

REPUTED THIEF

'A man is not a reputed thief merely because a constable thinks he is a thief, and I cannot see how a man can be said to be a suspected person merely because a constable suspects him. The phrase "a suspected person" in this context, particularly when it is placed in juxtaposition to the words "reputed thief", is, in my judgment, apt to describe and to describe only a person who, quite apart from the particular occasion and antecedently thereto, has become the object of suspicion, just as a "reputed thief" is a person who already has the reputation of a thief.' *Ledwith v Roberts* [1937] 1 KB 232 at 252–254, CA, per Greene LJ

REQUIRE

[A settlement reserved a power to the tenant for life to sell any part of the land which should by virtue of any Act of Parliament be wanted or 'required' for the purposes of any undertaking.] 'The question is, whether the power reserved by the settlement to the plaintiff is such a power as entitles him to deal with the cemetery company in respect of the settled lands, for the purposes of making a cemetery. . . . The lands in question were absolutely required to enable the cemetery company to carry into effect their object. . . . It is then said, that the word "required" has another construction, and does not merely mean lands which are "wanted", but lands which a company can compel the owner to sell; but this is not, in my opinion, the obvious meaning of that word. It is the land that is "required" that the company is entitled to contract for; the words in the settlement are, "such part of the hereditaments wanted or required"; the word "required", meaning what may be necessary and wanted for the purposes of the act; and I do not consider myself at liberty to inquire what is the meaning of the word "required", according to parliamentary usage.' *Kensington (Lord) v West London Cemetery Co* (1838) 8 LJ Ch 81 at 81, 82, per Lord Cottenham LC

[The Settled Land Act 1890, s 11 (repealed; see now the Settled Land Act 1925, s 71) enacted that where money was 'required' for the purpose of discharging an incumbrance on the settled land or part thereof, the tenant for life might raise the money so 'required'.] 'What is the meaning of the word "required"? Where the mortgagee gives notice to call in his money the word is clearly satisfied; the money is "required for the purpose of discharging an incumbrance". But is the section confined to that? I think that it is not. The section must be read as if it meant "where money is reasonably required having regard to the circumstances of the settled land".' *Re Clifford, Scott v Clifford* [1902] 1 Ch 87 at 89, 90, per Buckley J

[The Settled Land Act 1882, s 18 (repealed; see now the Settled Land Act 1925, s 71) empowered the tenant for life to raise money on mortgage of the settled land where money was 'required' for certain purposes.] 'The question really turns upon the construction of s 18. That section allows money to be raised by mortgage of the settled land under certain circumstances and for certain purposes. It says "where money is required for enfranchisement, or for equality of exchange or partition". "Required" does not mean absolutely necessary. It only means this—that where something is proposed to be done which ought to be done and the money is not forthcoming then the money is required.' *Re Bruce, Halsey v Bruce* [1905] 2 Ch 372 at 376, per Kekewich J

'The question is whether a person entitled to exercise the power conferred by the Law of Property Act 1925, s 89(3) is a person entitled to require a legal estate to be vested in him under Sch I, Part II, para 3 of the Act. I feel bound to come to the conclusion that it would be straining the meaning of the words of the paragraph to hold that they include a person who had the power himself, without requiring or doing anything at all except executing a deed, to cause the legal estate to be vested in him. The words "entitled to require any legal estate to be conveyed" mean to require some other person to convey that legal estate. I find a difficulty in seeing how the word "require" can apply to a case where a person can do the act of his own volition.' *St Germans (Earl) v Barker* [1936] 1 All ER 849 at 850, 851, per Crossman J

[The Housing Act 1936, s 75 (repealed; cf now the Compulsory Purchase Act 1965, s 8) provided that nothing in the Act should authorise the compulsory acquisition of any land which (inter alia) formed part of any park, garden or pleasure ground, or was otherwise 'required' for the amenity or convenience of any house.] 'One has to remember that it is pleasant, and, one may say, both an amenity and a convenience to have a good deal of open space round one's house, but it does not follow that the open space is required for the amenity or the convenience of the house. "Required", I think, in this section does not mean merely that the occupiers of the house would like to have it, or that they would miss it if they lost it, or that anyone proposing to buy the house would think less of the house without it than he would if it was preserved to it. "Required" means, I suppose, that without it there will be such a substantial deprivation of amenities or convenience that a real injury will be done to the property owner, and a question like that is obviously a question of fact.' *Re Newhill Compulsory Purchase Order* 1937, *Payne's Application* [1938] 2 All ER 163 at 167, per Du Parcq J

'The section [s 75 of the Housing Act 1936 (repealed; see supra)] should in my judgment be read in the same way as if it had been expanded as follows: "any land which is part of a park, garden, or pleasure ground or any land which is otherwise required for the amenity or convenience of any house". . . . Apart from any question of grammar, this construction appears to me to be the sensible one, for it recognises that once it is established that land sought to be taken is part of a man's park, garden or pleasure ground it ought not to be necessary for its owner to show that he requires it for the amenity or convenience of his house.' *Re Ripon (Highfield) Housing Confirmation Order* 1938, *White & Collins v Minister of Health* [1939] 2 KB 838 at 851, CA, per Luxmoore LJ

[The Patents and Designs Act 1907, s 38(1) (repealed; see now the Patents Act 1977, s 44(1)(c)) made it unlawful to 'require' the purchaser, lessee or licensee of a patent to acquire from the seller, lessor or licensor any article or class of article not protected by the patent.] 'I take first the word "require" in sub-s (1)(b). The effect of a particular condition may be to offer so great an advantage to the licensee if he buys from the licensor that it would be extremely foolish of him not to do that, but I do not think that, in the ordinary use of language, it could properly be said that the effect of such a condition will be to "require" the licensee to do it. I feel bound to hold that sub-s (1)(b) only applies if the effect of the condition is that, whenever certain circumstances occur, the licensee, if he wishes to buy the article, is obliged to buy it from the licensor.' *Tool Metal Manufacturing Co Ltd v Tungsten Electric Co Ltd* [1955] 2 All ER 657 at 671, HL, per Lord Oaksey

[The Road Safety Act 1967, s 2(1) (repealed; see now the Road Traffic Act 1988, s 6) provided that in certain circumstances a constable in uniform might 'require' a person to provide a specimen of breath for a breath test.] 'A request in words which it is clear to the defendant are being made as of right is sufficient to amount to a requirement.' *R v Clarke* [1969] 2 All ER 1008 at 1010, CA, per cur.

[The Road Safety Act 1967, s 3(2) (repealed; see now the Road Traffic Act 1988, s 9) provided that a person while in hospital as a patient might be 'required' to provide a specimen for a laboratory test. 'Can a person properly be said to have been "required" to do something if in fact he has not heard or has not understood the words spoken to him by another person, although the other person has spoken the words in the honest and reasonable belief that they would be, and were being, heard and understood by the person to whom they were addressed? In our judgment, the answer is Yes. The person concerned has been "required". The fact that his brain has not absorbed the sound of the words spoken, or has not processed them into full understanding, does not prevent that which would otherwise be a requirement from being a requirement.' *R v Nicholls* [1972] 2 All ER 186 at 188, CA, per Megaw LJ

Canada [A landlord was entitled to terminate a tenancy where he bona fide 'required' residential premises for the purposes of converting it into a unit in a co-operative corporation as defined in the Real Estate Act.] 'Counsel were agreed that the word "required" contained in s 18(1)(c) [of the Residential Tenancy Act 1977 (BC); see now RSBC 1979, c 365, s 17(1)(c)] is capable, standing alone, of implying either actual "need" or mere "wish", that is to say, that it may, depending on the context, imply a pressing necessity to acquire something or simply a desire to have it . . . But I cannot discover in the Act, taken as a whole, any basis for interpreting the expression "requires" in s 18(1)(c) as implying that there must be a need, pressing or otherwise, for the premises on the part of the landlord in order to warrant the giving of notice to terminate, nor unfortunately, does the Act authorise a distinction to be drawn between termination of mobile home pad tenancies and other residential tenancies. While the expression "bona fide requires" is used in several other sections, particularly in setting period of notice and contribution towards moving costs, s 24, which authorises the rentalsman to set aside notice of termination, does not use the word. It says in sub-s (2)(f) that a notice to terminate is not to be set aside if the rentalsman determines that the landlord "intends to . . . convert [the residential premises] into a . . . unit in a co-operative corporation". This is the key section governing loss of security of tenure, and here intention alone is the criterion. The ambiguity inherent in the word "require" as used in other sections is thus decisively resolved against the contention advanced on behalf of the tenants.' *Walker v Carlill and Carbolic Smoke Ball Corpn* (1979) 11 BCLR 199 at 202–204, BCSC, per Taylor J

Canada [A separation agreement provided for a wife to retain occupancy of the matrimonial home so long as she 'required' it] 'Whichever meaning is given to the word "requires" the agreement clearly contemplates that . . . a sale and division might occur and makes specific provision for it. It would not be reasonable for the parties to agree upon the sale and division only in circumstances of remote possibility. In 1964 they agreed that Mrs

Winrob should occupy the property. That was because she obviously needed it. She was not employed and had three children to look after. Giving her the right of occupancy based upon need, it is difficult to see why the parties would change the basis and allow her in the future to continue occupancy at her desire, after she no longer needed it. If it were just a matter of her wishes why would she ever agree to sale and division of the proceeds? Wives usually outlive their husbands. By acquiescing in sale Mrs Winrob would be giving up the chance of obtaining the whole interest by survivorship. Obtaining the whole interest would offer the prospect to the appellant of other accommodation smaller and perhaps more appropriate to her desires and needs and having money left over for other purposes. Upon a sale and division she would only receive half of the proceeds with which to go out seeking other accommodation. Upon the whole, I think the learned trial Judge was right in finding that the word "requires" was used in the sense of "needs" and that the appellant no longer requires the premises as a home.' *Winrob v Winrob* (1982) 133 DLR (3d) 760 at 763, BCCA, per Macdonald JA

New Zealand [The Wages Protection and Contractors' Liens Act 1939 (NZ), s 34(2) provides: 'In addition to the person to whom the notice of lien or charge is given there shall be joined as a defendant in the action every person to whom the claimant is required by this Part of this Act to give notice of having made the claim of lien or charge. . . .'] 'The word "required" has at least two meanings. The first is necessarily and absolutely required. The other is as a matter of convenience and practical operation required: see *Pitcaithly and Co v John McLean and Son* [(1912) 31 NZLR 648]. In this case the context and the circumstances make it possible for the Court to adopt either meaning, and there is a real doubt which is the right meaning to attach to it here. . . . In my view, prima facie the meaning to be adopted for a word used in any statute is its primary meaning. In this subsection the word "required" is used in the sense that it is "mandatory". If this meaning is adopted it harmonises with s 28(2) of the Act. For under that subsection, as a mortgagee is not included in the definition of "owner", notice is not required to be given to the mortgagee; and the plaintiff is not entitled to join the mortgagee. It seems to me after hearing the respective contentions of counsel that that is the proper construction to be adopted. . . . From a business point of view in certain circumstances, notice may be "required" (in the broader meaning of that word) to protect the lien. It was argued that because the provisions of s 25(3) closely approach the mandatory meaning and may be held to have that meaning if we read the Act as a whole, then it should be given to it in s 34(2). But I do not think that that circumstance is sufficient to justify the Court in departing from what appears to me to be the prima facie meaning of "required" in s 34(2).' *Edyvane v Donnelly* [1946] NZLR 263 at 264, per Fair J; also reported [1946] GLR 120

REQUIRED FOR OCCUPATION

Australia [A notice to quit was given pursuant to the Landlord and Tenant Act 1948, s 37(5)(g) (see now the Landlord and Tenant Act 1958–1986 (Vic), s 82(6)(n)(i)), on the ground that the premises were reasonably 'required' by the lessor for his own 'occupation'.] 'Even if the expression "required for occupation by the lessor" is interpreted merely as "demanded and desired for occupation by the lessor" . . . the demand postulated by the legislature must be a "reasonable" demand, and it must be "for occupation"—for which I take to mean "for the purposes of occupation"—by the lessor or someone else. A reasonable demand for the purpose of personal occupation by a person must have some relation to the actual need of that person for such personal occupation, and so the notion of "need", even if rejected in the interpretation of the word "required", is re-imported in another way by the rest of the phrase.' *Brown v Lusk* [1956] VLR 285 at 289, 290, per Sholl J

REQUIREMENT

'Although the interpretation section, s 35, of the Act [Supplementary Benefits Act 1976] does not interpret or define the meaning of the words "requirements" or "resources", para 3 of Sch 1 does however, in my view, make the meaning of these words reasonably plain. "Requirements" for persons claiming supplementary benefits means, for example, a home, food, clothes and the like. . . . "Resources" means the money available to pay for the requirements. If the persons concerned have not sufficient resources to provide the necessary requirements, the supplementary benefits will bridge that financial gap.' *Supplementary Benefits Commission v Jull, Y v Supplementary*

Benefits Commission [1980] 3 All ER 65 at 71, HL, per Lord Salmon

New Zealand [A clause in a lease provided that the lessor should comply with all 'requirements' and notices received by him and/or the lessee from the government, city council, fire board, or other authority within their respective jurisdictions. A bye-law of the local city council provided that all means of egress should at all times be maintained in good and usable condition.] 'I put upon the word "requirement" a wider meaning than the court was invited to do by counsel for the third party. Departments and local bodies to whom control over such a matter as is here in question is entrusted may exercise their powers in either or both of two different ways—namely (a) they may make a general rule, regulation, or by-law to be obeyed by everybody from the time of its promulgation; or (b) they may give a specific direction to an individual who thereby comes under an obligation which did not previously exist. I think both these exercises of power come fairly within the ordinary and natural meaning of the word "requirements".' *Kersey v Thomson* [1947] NZLR 392 at 398, per Callan J; also reported [1942] GLR 123 at 124

REQUISITION

'Requisition' means, in relation to any property, take possession of the property or require the property to be placed at the disposal of the requisitioning authority. (Compensation (Defence) Act 1939, s 17)

'It should be remembered that the word "requisition" is not a term of art, and, as Pickford LJ explained in *The Broadmayne* [[1916] P 64 at 73], does not connote the same state of things in every particular case. Requisitioning may be, and usually is, nothing more than a hiring of [a] ship which does not take the property in the ship out of the owner, though the owner has no alternative whether he will accept the proposition of hiring or not, or it may involve a taking over of the absolute dominion of the vessel, though this may not be ascertained in any given case until the terms are finally settled.' *The Steaua Romana, The Oltenia* [1944] P 43 at 48, per Lord Merriman P

Australia '"Requisition" is not a technical legal term. The word is used to include the taking of property in full ownership, the taking of the possession of property, and the acquisition of a right to have property used in a particular manner without any taking of possession.' *Australasian United Steam Navigation Co Ltd v Shipping Control Board* [1945] CLR 508 at 521, per Latham CJ

RES GESTAE

Items of evidence are sometimes said to be part of the res gestae, owing to the nature and strength of their connection with the matters in issue, and as such are admissible. 'Res gestae' is an expression mainly of utility in the criminal law concerning the contemporaneity of statements to incidents but, in so far as contemporaneous statements are relevant and accompany and explain matters in issue, they will be admissible. (17 Halsbury's Laws (4th edn) para 6)

'The expression res gestae, like many Latin phrases, is often used to cover situations insufficiently analysed in clear English terms. In the context of the law of evidence it may be used in at least three different ways: (1) When a situation of fact (e.g. a killing) is being considered, the question may arise when does the situation begin and when does it end. It may be arbitrary and artificial to confine the evidence to the firing of the gun or the insertion of the knife without knowing, in a broader sense, what was happening. . . . (2) The evidence may be concerned with spoken words as such (apart from the truth of what they convey). The words are then themselves the res gestae or part of the res gestae, i.e. are the relevant facts or part of them. (3) A hearsay statement is made either by the victim of an attack or by a bystander—indicating directly or indirectly the identity of the attacker. The admissibility of the statement is then said to depend on whether it was made as part of the res gestae. . . . As regards statements made after the event it must be for the judge, by preliminary ruling, to satisfy himself that the statement was so clearly made in circumstances of spontaneity or involvement in the event that the possibility of concoction can be disregarded. Conversely, if he considers that the statement was made by way of narrative of a detached prior event so that the speaker was so disengaged from it as to be able to construct or adapt his account, he should exclude it. And the same must in principle be true of statements made before the event. The test should be not the uncertain one, whether the making of the statement should be regarded as part of the event or transaction. This may often be difficult to show. But if the drama, leading up to the climax, has commenced and assumed such intensity and pressure that the utterance can safely be regarded as a true reflection of what was unrolling or actually happening, it ought to be received. The expression res gestae may conveniently sum up these criteria, but the reality of them must always be kept in mind: it is this that lies behind the best reasoned of the judges' rulings.' *Ratten v R* [1971] 3 All ER 801 at 806, 807, PC, per Lord Wilberforce

RES IPSA LOQUITUR

Under the doctrine res ipsa loquitur a plaintiff establishes a prima facie case of negligence where (1) it is not possible for him to prove precisely what was the relevant act or omission which set in train the events leading to the accident, and (2) on the evidence as it stands at the relevant time it is more likely than not that the effective cause of the accident was some act or omission of the defendant or of someone for whom the defendant is responsible, which act or omission constituted a failure to take proper care for the plaintiff's safety. There must be reasonable evidence of negligence. However, where the thing which causes the accident is shown to be under the management of the defendant or his employees, and the accident is such as in the ordinary course of things does not happen if those who have the management use proper care, it affords reasonable evidence, in the absence of explanation by the defendant, that the accident arose from want of care. (34 Halsbury's Laws (4th edn) para 57)

'In all cases where an action is based on negligence a plaintiff has to prove that there was negligence on the part of the defendant, and that by reason of that negligence he has suffered damage. A good deal has been said, quite properly, about the doctrine of res ipsa loquitur, but when it is invoked it is necessary to be sure what precisely the doctrine is. The words res ipsa loquitur are hardly themselves a proposition of law though they allude to one. They are a figure of speech. What this figure of speech sometimes means is that certain facts are so inconsistent with any view except but that the defendant has been negligent, that any jury which, on proof of those facts, found that negligence was not proved would be giving a perverse verdict. Sometimes the proposition does not go so far as that but may be stated thus: that on proof of certain facts an inference of negligence may be drawn by a reasonable jury although the precise circumstances are not fully known. In *Cole v de Trafford* ([1918] 2 KB 523 at 528), Lord Justice Pickford stated his view of the meaning of the expression in this way: "I take that well-known expression to mean that an accident may by its nature be more consistent with its being caused by negligence for which the defendant is responsible than by other causes, and that in such a case the mere fact of the accident is prima facie evidence of such negligence".' *Easson v London & North Eastern Rly Co* (1944) 60 TLR 280 at 283, CA, per Du Parcq LJ

'I doubt whether it is right to describe res ipsa loquitur as a doctrine. I think it is no more than an exotic, though convenient, phrase to describe what is in essence no more than a common sense approach, not limited by technical rules, to the assessment of the effect of evidence in certain circumstances. It means that a plaintiff prima facie establishes negligence where: (i) it is not possible for him to prove precisely what was the relevant act or omission which set in train the events leading to the accident; but (ii) on the evidence as it stands at the relevant time it is more likely than not that the effective cause of the accident was *some* act or omission of the defendant or of someone for whom the defendant is responsible, which act or omission constitutes a failure to take proper care for the plaintiff's safety.' *Lloyde v West Midlands Gas Board* [1971] 2 All ER 1240 at 1246, CA, per Megaw LJ

Australia 'The doctrine of res ipsa loquitur does not alter the general principle of law that the onus of proving or establishing his case always rests upon the plaintiff. . . . The doctrine means that, at a given point of a trial, the res or circumstances proved by the plaintiff are of themselves sufficient evidence from which negligence may reasonably be inferred. In Lord Dunedin's phrase, the res is "relevant to infer negligence" [*Ballard v North British Rly Co* 1923 SC (HL) 53].' *Davis v Bunn* (1936) 56 CLR 246 at 267, per Evatt J

Canada 'Res ipsa loquitur is a circumstantial rule of evidence based on the concept that, when an accident occurs under circumstances where it is so improbable that it could have happened without the negligence of the defendant, the mere happening of the accident gives rise to an inference that the defendant was negligent.' *Macdonald v York County Hospital Corpn* [1972] 3 OR 469 at 486, 487, Ont SC, per Addy J

RES JUDICATA

The most usual manner in which questions of estoppel have arisen on judgments inter partes has been where the defendant in an action raised a defence of res judicata, which he could do where former proceedings for the same cause of action by the same plaintiff had resulted in the defendant's favour, by pleading the former judgment by way of estoppel. In order to support that defence it was necessary to show that the subject matter in dispute was the same (namely that everything that was in controversy in the second suit as the foundation of the claim for relief was also in controversy or open to controversy in the first suit), that it came in question before a court of competent jurisdiction, and that the result was conclusive so as to bind every other court. . . . Where res judicata is pleaded by way of estoppel to an entire cause of action, rather than to a single matter in issue, it amounts to an allegation that the whole legal rights and obligations of the parties are concluded by the earlier judgment, which may have involved the determination of questions of law as well as findings of fact. To decide what questions of law and fact were determined in the earlier judgment the court is entitled to look at the judge's reasons for his decision and his notes of the evidence, and is not restricted to the record, but, as a general rule, the judge's reasons cannot be looked at for the purpose of excluding from the scope of his formal order any matter which, according to the issues raised on the pleadings and the terms of the order itself, is included in it. (16 Halsbury's Laws (4th edn) paras 1526, 1527).

'There is no difficulty in seeing what, in its strict and proper sense, the plea of res judicata means. The words, "res judicata" explain themselves. If the res—the thing actually and directly in dispute—has been already adjudicated upon, of course by a competent court, it cannot be litigated again.' *Ord v Ord* [1923] 2 KB 432 at 439, per Lush J

'It has been contended on behalf of the wife that it is no longer open to the husband to raise the issue of her adultery because it is res judicata. That phrase is used to include two separate states of things. One is where a judgment has been pronounced between parties and findings of fact are involved as a basis for that judgment. All the parties affected by the judgment are then precluded from disputing those facts, as facts, in any subsequent litigation between them. The other aspect of the term arises where a party seeks to set up facts which, if they had been set up in the first suit, would or might have affected the decision. That is not strictly raising any issue which has already been adjudicated, but it is convenient to use the phrase res judicata as relating to that position.' *Robinson v Robinson* [1943] P 43 at 44, per Henn Collins J

'The doctrine of estoppel per rem judicatam is reflected in two Latin maxims, (i) *interest rei publicae ut sit finis litium* and (ii) *nemo debet bis vexare pro una et eadem causa*. The former is public policy and the latter is private justice. The rule of estoppel by res judicata, which is a rule of evidence, is that where a final decision has been pronounced by a judicial tribunal of competent jurisdiction over the parties to and the subject-matter of the litigation, any party or privy to such litigation as against any other party or privy is estopped in any subsequent litigation from disputing or questioning such decision on the merits. As originally categorised, res judicata was known as "estoppel by record". But as it is now quite immaterial whether the judicial decision is pronounced by a tribunal which is required to keep a written record of its decisions, this nomenclature has disappeared and it may be convenient to describe res judicata in its true and original form as "cause of action estoppel". This has long been recognised as operating as a complete bar if the necessary conditions are present. Within recent years the principle has developed so as to extend to what is now described as "issue estoppel", that is to say where in a judicial decision between the same parties some issue which was in controversy between the parties and was incidental to the main decision has been decided, then that may create an estoppel per rem judicatam.' *Carl-Zeiss-Stiftung v Rayner & Keeler Ltd (No 2)* [1966] 2 All ER 536 at 564, 565, HL, per Lord Guest

'All adjudication, like every piece of social engineering, is a compromise between a number of desiderata, not all of which are easily made consistent. There should, first, be the fullest and truest assessment of all relevant facts. There must, however, secondly, be some protection of individual privacy and liberty. Thirdly, and most relevant of all to this application, it is desirable that disputes within society should be brought to an end as soon as is reasonably practical and should not be allowed to drag festeringly on for an indefinite period. That last principle finds expression in a maxim which English law took over from the Roman law: it is in the public interest that there should be some end to litigation. The principle, for example, applies in the doctrine which is known to lawyers as res judicata; in other words, once there is a decision on a matter by a competent court, it is binding on all courts of similar jurisdiction.' *Edwards v Edwards* [1967] 2 All ER 1032 at 1033, per Sir Jocelyn Simon P

RESALE PRICE *See* PRICE

RESCIND

'Although the word "rescind" has a fairly precise meaning, I readily accept that the word is not invariably used with the same meaning. Thus in a contract it may be used with whatever meaning the contract gives it. If, for instance, the parties to the contract agree to "rescind" it on certain terms, I see no reason why those terms should not contain an agreement for the payment of some sums by one to the other, which may or may not be called "damages". Again, a contract may contain provisions which confer a unilateral power of "rescission" on certain terms in certain events; and if that unilateral power is properly exercised, the consequences of doing so will be as stated in the contract, including the payment of any "damages" for which it provides. In truth, the meaning of the term "rescission" in a contract, like that of any other term, is whatever the contract gives it. . . . In the case before me, however, nobody has relied on, or even mentioned, any provision of the contract relating to rescission; and when the word "rescind" is used otherwise than in a contract, and particularly in a formal document such as a writ or order of the court, I think it will usually, at all events, bear its normal meaning, related to restitutio in integrum and so on.' *Horsler v Zorro* [1975] 1 All ER 584 at 591, per Megarry J

Australia 'As a general proposition it is no doubt true that a person cannot rescind a contract and at the same time in effect affirm it by claiming damages for the breach thereof; but as was pointed out by Harvey CJ in Eq in *Shenstone v Hewson (No 2)* [(1929) 29 SR(NSW) 39], it is at least open to doubt whether the term "rescind" in such a clause [i.e. giving power to rescind on default] is a strict use of language, and whether it may not merely mean put an end to, or determine, the contract, and not rescind *ab initio*; and the dictum of Lord Dunedin in *Mayson v Clouet* [[1924] AC 980, PC] . . . at least suggests that in a case where the vendor does determine the contract under such a clause . . . he still retains a right to sue the purchaser for damages for breach of contract.' *Pitt v Curotta* (1931) 31 SR(NSW) 477 at 482, per Long Innes J

RESCUE

Rescue at common law consists in the forcible freeing of a person from lawful arrest or custody, whether that of a constable or other officer or that of a private person; but where a person is freed from private custody, the rescuer incurs criminal liability only if he knew the person freed was in custody on a criminal charge. In general, rescue is punishable on indictment by a fine and imprisonment at the discretion of the court; but a person who rescues a prisoner he knew to be guilty of treason is himself guilty of treason. (11 Halsbury's Laws (4th edn) para 968)

Goods distrained are regarded from the seizure as being taken by a process of law, and not merely by an assertion of a private right of the distrainor, and the taking of them out of the custody of the distrainor before they are impounded is regarded in the light of a resistance of lawful authority, and is termed a rescue or rescous. To prevent a distress being made is not a rescue, but to prevent it being impounded is. There may be a rescue without any act of the owner in bringing about the escape of cattle, if he resists their recapture; for example when a distress has been taken and the cattle distrained, as they are being driven to the pound, go into the house of the owner who refuses to deliver them to the distrainor when he demands them, there is a rescue in law. There can be no rescue until the thing is actually distrained; and in any case in which the distrainor abandons or quits possession of the chattels, the retaking by the owner is not a rescue. (13 Halsbury's Laws (4th edn) para 362)

RESEARCH *See* SCIENTIFIC RESEARCH

RESERVATION

Strictly the term 'reservation' implies a right of the nature of rent reserved to a landlord or lord of a manor; thus rent, heriots, suit of mill, and suit of court are reservations, and have been described as the only things which, according to the legal meaning of the word, are reservations. It is essential to a reservation that it should issue out of the thing granted. The term is frequently used, however, to denote some incorporeal right over the thing granted of which the grantor intends to have the benefit, such as a fishing right or sporting right or a right of way. (12 Halsbury's Laws (4th edn) para 1531)

If used in its strict legal sense, 'reservation' refers to the payment of rent or rendering of other services by the tenant. The term may, however, be used in a wide sense as meaning any benefit in respect of the subject matter of the grant which is kept by the grantor for himself. Thus, it may imply a keeping back of a physical part of the thing, in which case it is equivalent to an exception, and, accordingly, where the context requires it 'reserving' is construed as making an exception.

'Reserving' may also imply that the grantor is keeping for himself some right of user or of taking the profits of the land, and in conveyancing practice the words 'except and reserving' usually introduce the creation in favour of the landlord of an easement, or of a profit à prendre, such as the free running of water and soil coming from adjacent buildings, the right to make and maintain sewer under the demised premises, rights of way and other easements over the demised premises, or rights of sporting. (27 Halsbury's Laws (4th edn) para 138)

'We are of opinion, that what relates to the privilege of hawking, hunting, fishing, and fowling, is not either a reservation or an exception in point of law; and it is only a privilege or right granted to the lessor, though words of reservation and exception are used. And we think, that what relates to the wood and the underground produce is not a reservation, but an exception. Lord Coke, in his Commentary on Littleton, 47a, says, "Note a diversity between an exception (which is ever of part of the thing granted, and of a thing *in esse*), for which, *exceptis, salvo, praeter*, and the like, be apt words; and a reservation which is always of a thing not *in esse*, but newly created or reserved out of the land or tenement demised." In Sheppard's Touchstone, p 80, "A reservation is a clause of a deed whereby the feoffer, donor, lessor, grantor, etc, doth reserve some new thing to himself out of that which he granted before": and, afterwards, "This doth differ from an exception, which is ever of part of the thing granted, and of a thing *in esse* at the time; but this is of a thing newly created or reserved out of a thing demised that was not *in esse* before; so that this doth always reserve that which was not before, or abridge the tenure of that which was before." And afterwards, "It must be of some other thing issuing, or coming out of the thing granted, and not a part of the thing itself, nor of something issuing out of another thing". And afterwards, "If one grant land, yielding for rent, money, corn, or horse, spurs, a rose, or any such like thing; this is a good reservation: but if the reservation be of the grass, or of the vesture of the land or of a common, or other profit to be taken out of the land; these reservations are void". In Brooke's Abridgement, title Reservacion, pl 46, it is said, that if a man leases land, reserving common out of it, or the herbage, grass, or profits of the land demised, this is a void reservation, for it is parcel of the thing granted, and is not like where a man leases his manor and the like, except White Acre, for there the acre is not leased; but here the land is leased; therefore the reservation of the herbage, vesture, or the like, is void. It must be observed, however, that, though in Co Litt 47a the distinction between a reservation and an exception is pointed out, yet in page 143a, speaking of the word reservation, Lord Coke says, "Sometimes it hath the force of saving or excepting. So as sometime it serveth to reserve a new thing, viz. a rent, and sometime to except part of the thing *in esse* that is granted".' *Doe d Douglas v Lock* (1835) 2 Ad & El 705 at 743–745, per cur.

'The agreement was an ordinary letting of pasture land, but the landlord reserved to himself "(subject to the provisions of the Ground Game Act 1880) all the game, rabbits, wild fowl and fish with liberty for himself and all other persons authorised by him, to preserve, hunt, course, kill and carry away the same", and the tenant agreed (subject to the provisions of the Ground Game Act) "not to shoot or otherwise sport on the land". Although the landlord purported to "reserve" the game, rabbits, etc, this was not in strictness a reservation. It was long settled at common law that an "exception" is only properly allowed of things *in esse*, such as trees or minerals; a "reservation" is only properly admitted of services to be rendered by the tenant, such as paying rent or providing a beast (heriot), whereas a right to come and kill and carry away wild animals is only a liberty or licence—a profit à prendre—which can take effect only by grant and not by exception or reservation. Words of reservation of sporting rights, operate, therefore, not by way of reservation proper, but by way of re-grant by the tenant.' *Mason v Clarke* [1954] 1 All ER 189 at 191, CA, per Denning LJ

RESERVE *See also* WITHOUT RESERVE

Australia 'To reserve a thing, real or personal, is to set it aside, to appropriate it, or to give it up to some special purpose.' *Jones v Commonwealth (No 2)* (1964–65) 112 CLR 206 at 221, per McTiernan J

RESERVE CAPITAL *See* CAPITAL

RESERVE OR AUXILIARY FORCE *See* ROYAL FORCES

RESIDE—RESIDENCE *See also* ABODE; ADDRESS; DOMICILE; DWELLING—DWELLING HOUSE; LIVE; PRIVATE DWELLING

It seems that the word 'resides' refers to a place of permanent and not merely temporary abode, even though one individual may have more than one residence at the same time for the purpose of being sued. A mere place of temporary and compulsory detention such as a prison, or a temporary residence such as lodgings occupied by a person who has a permanent residence elsewhere, is not sufficient. However, a person may 'reside' at a lodging which he occupies permanently, and if a person who has no permanent abode at all, he may be taken to 'reside' at the place where he is temporarily staying. (10 Halsbury's Laws (4th edn) para 107)

The residence of a person is by implication that person's home, where at least he or she has a sleeping apartment or shares one, although merely sleeping on the premises is not conclusive of residence. A person may reside on premises as a guest, or even as a trespasser, and it is not necessary that they should be the only premises where the person resides. (15 Halsbury's Laws (4th edn) para 415)

'It is no uncommon thing for a gentleman to have two permanent residences at the same time, in either of which he may establish his abode at any period, and for any length of time.' *A-G v Coote* (1817) 4 Price 183 at 188, per Wood B

'We must consider the residence to be where the voter sleeps habitually.' *Oldham Election Petition, Baxter's Case* (1869) 20 LT 302 at 308, per Blackburn J

'The place of residence of a person is the place where he eats, drinks, and sleeps.' *Stoke-on-Trent Borough Council v Cheshire County Council* [1913] 3 KB 699 at 706, per Ridley J

'The contrast [in the section of a repealed Act] is not between "absence" and "presence", but between "absence" and "residence", which need not imply actual physical presence.' *Webster v Minister of Health* (1926) 43 TLR 36 at 37, DC, per Lord Hewart CJ

[The question was whether a wife, whilst on trial leave from a mental hospital, was receiving treatment for mental illness as a 'resident' in a hospital within the Divorce (Insanity and Desertion) Act 1958, s 1(1) (repealed; see now the Matrimonial Causes Act 1973, s 1).] 'In the *Swymer* case [*Swymer v Swymer* [1954] 3 All ER 502] the patient remained "continuously" under care and treatment for his mental illness notwithstanding a four-week temporary absence from the mental hospital. Similarly, though the patient in the *Safford* case [*Safford v Safford* [1944] 1 All ER 704] was absent on trial leave periods lasting from four days to about seven weeks, it was held nevertheless that the patient was throughout "detained" in the mental hospital under care and treatment. I conclude as a matter of construction, and in the light of these authorities, that a patient may be still "resident" in a mental hospital notwithstanding temporary absence therefrom.' *Head v Head* [1963] 3 All ER 640 at 642 per Rees J; also reported in [1963] P 357 at 362

'The word "resides" has been given varying meanings according to its context; the same may occur with the phrase "residing with". It seems to me that in this particular context [Rent Act 1977, Sch 1(7)] it imports, as indeed counsel for the defendant rightly conceded, a quality of residence that would not normally obtain, for instance, when a relative is living at premises merely as a caretaker of part or the whole, or living there merely as a salaried hospital nurse detailed for duty there by a welfare service. "Residing with" is something more than "living at", even when the premises become a person's normal postal address.' *Foreman v Beagley* [1969] 3 All ER 838 at 841, 842, CA, per Sachs LJ

[Two students, at the Universities of Bristol and Cambridge respectively, appealed against decisions of the electoral registration officers concerned that they were not entitled to be registered on the 1970 register of electors for their university towns, since they were not resident there on the qualifying date, 10 October 1969.] 'I reject altogether the test of whether the students had a right to their rooms throughout the year. I prefer to go by the ordinary meaning of the word "resident". I follow Viscount Cave LC, in *Levene v Inland Revenue Comrs* [[1928] AC 217], where he said: ". . . the word 'reside' is a familiar English word and is defined in the Oxford English Dictionary as meaning 'to dwell permanently or for a considerable time, to have one's settled or usual abode, to live in or at a particular place'." I would also take into account, as the Act [Representation of the People Act 1949 (repealed; see now Representation of the People Act 1983)] says, the general principles formerly applied and have regard to the purpose and other circumstances of a man's presence at or absence from the address. Hence I derive three principles. The first principle is that a man can have two residences. He can have a flat in London and a house in the country. He is resident in both. The second principle is that temporary presence at an address does not make a man a resident there. A guest who comes for the weekend is not resident. A short-stay visitor is not resident. The third principle is that temporary absence does not deprive a person of his residence. If he happens to be away for a holiday or away for the weekend or in hospital, he does not lose his residence on that account. Applying these principles, I do not think these students are disqualified simply because their parental home is in England. They may be resident at their homes, but they may also be resident in Bristol or Cambridge. I would deplore any test by which a student is disqualified according to whether his parental home was in England or overseas. People who have houses or flats in London and houses in the country can be on the register for both, because they are resident in both, but they can only vote in one. So also with students; they can be on the register for their homes and for their university towns, but they can only vote in one. I think that a person may properly be said to be "resident" in a place when his stay there has a considerable degree of permanence. So I would apply the simple test: was there on 10th of October 1969, a considerable degree of permanence in the stay of the appellants in Bristol or Cambridge? I think there was. They were living there and sleeping there. They were there for at least half the year—as a minimum. Many of them were there for much more, especially the science students, because they have to work in the vacations in the laboratories. There was certainly a sufficient degree of permanence to make them "resident" in Bristol or Cambridge, as the case may be.' *Fox v Stirk, Ricketts v Registration Officer for the City of Cambridge* [1970] 3 All ER 7 at 11, 12, CA, per Lord Denning MR

Australia 'Now the Act [Licensing Act 1928 (Vic) (repealed; see now the Liquor Control Act 1968–1986, s 5(1))] says, "179. No person shall be a bona fide traveller within the meaning of that expression in this Act unless he—(a) resides at least twenty miles [30kms]. . . ." It is where he resides at the moment he is served with the drink that is important. Apart from any authority at all, I should have thought it plain enough that when a person goes to a house or an hotel to spend the night, and leaves in the morning with his bags, having paid his bill, and having finally severed his connection with the house and its inhabitants, he no longer resides there. On the other hand if he has some sort of a home, whether it be a home in a ship, a home in a training camp, a home in a house or a flat which he keeps for the purpose of a residence, even if he is not always there, he is residing there in the true sense of the word, even though absent from it, and even though he has been absent from it for some time. It could only be in an artificial sense that a man, who had spent last night in an hotel on the road, and in the afternoon had come into another hotel and asked for a drink, could be said to be then residing in the hotel which he left in the morning. It may be that a man who spends a couple of days' holiday in the house of a friend can properly be said to be "residing" there, but it certainly is not his residence when he has left it. . . . If I have a house in Melbourne where my wife lives and which I continue to keep up when I am away for a holiday in Sydney, in the ordinary sense of the word my place of residence is in Melbourne. Whether it can also be properly said that I am residing in the hotel I stay at in Sydney, while I stay there, or not, it plainly cannot be said that I am residing in a place which I have temporarily occupied, but have now vacated.' *West v Coombes* [1941] VLR 134 at 137, 138, per Gavan Duffy J

Australia 'Any person who resides in Australia is, by definition, a resident within the meaning of the [Income Tax Assessment Act 1936 (Cth)]. The word "reside" has a very wide meaning, see *FC of T v Miller* (1946) 73 CLR

93; 3 AITR 333 per Latham CJ at 99–100; 337. One of the dictionary meanings of the word "reside" is "to dwell permanently or for a considerable time, to have one's settled or usual abode, to live, in or at a particular place". A person may reside in more than one country at any one time, see *Robertson v FC of T* (1937) 57 CLR 147; 1 AITR 152 per Dixon J at 163; 164 and *Gregory v DFC of T (WA)* (1937) 57 CLR 774; 1 AITR 201 per Dixon J at 777–8; 202.' *Federal Commissioner of Taxation v Applegate* (1979) 9 ATR 899 at 905 per Northrop J

Canada 'Residence alone does not make one a "resident" so as to impose on the municipality in respect of an indigent. There must be an application for relief from which a period of time of residence may be reckoned to ascertain the status of a "resident".' *Daysland v Melrose Municipal District* [1940] 2 WWR 583 at 586, Alta SC, per Harvey CJA.

Canada 'In my opinion a person is resident in Canada within the meaning of the Canadian Citizenship Act [RSC 1970, C-19] only if he is physically present (at least usually) on Canadian territory. I feel that this interpretation is in keeping with the spirit of the Act, which seems to require of the foreigner wishing to acquire Canadian citizenship, not only that he possess certain civic and moral qualifications, and intends to reside in Canada on a permanent basis, but also that he has actually lived in Canada for an appreciable time. Parliament wishes by this means to ensure that Canadian citizenship is granted only to persons who have shown they are capable of becoming a part of our society.' *Blaha v Minister of Citizenship & Immigration* [1971] 1 FC 521 at 524, 525, Cit App Ct, per Pratte J

Canada 'If a person had a reasonable area about his home landscaped or improved with gardens, these additions would add to the enjoyment and pleasure of his surroundings. That portion of his property which so adds to the amenities of his place of abode could quite properly be included as part of his residence for the purpose of deciding how much of his land should be included in this term. On the other hand, the fact that the claimants often rode their horses over the balance of the property or occasionally hunted rabbits or some other form of lesser game thereon, does not, in my opinion, cause that area to be any part of his residence because it is an activity that is not necessarily confined to his property but may be enjoyed in other places.' *Daues v R* (1977) 13 LCR 10 at 17, 18, FCTD, per Grant DJ

New Zealand 'Although the defendants were a foreign corporation it may be properly said as they carry on business in New Zealand that they resided in the colony.' *McCaul v New Zealand Loan & Mercantile Agency Co Ltd* (1883) 1 NZLR 297 at 299, per Williams J

New Zealand 'I think . . . that a bank with a head office at one place and branches at a number of other places would be properly said to have its residence at the place where the head office is, and not at any of the places where the branches are.' *Young v Bain, Re Young* (1902) 21 NZLR 503 at 504, per Williams J; also reported 4 GLR 484 at 485

New Zealand 'The word "reside" is a word of flexible meaning. In its usual meaning, a person is said to reside where he sleeps. The fact that he may be away at work somewhere else in the daytime does not mean that he is not residing at the home to which he returns at night.' *Egmont National Park Board v Blake* [1949] NZLR 177 at 181, per Hutchinson J

Constructive residence

'Where a person goes away from a parish for a temporary purpose, leaving a house or lodging behind him, he is still in effect residing in the parish. On the other hand, if he goes away, even leaving wife and children behind him, and establishes himself elsewhere, there is no residence [*Wellington Overseers v Whitchurch Overseers* (1863) 4 B & S 100]. There must be both a place which he has a right to return to and an intention to return, to constitute a constructive residence; and where a man has gone away and left no residence, though he means to return at a future time, the *animus revertendi* is immaterial.' *R v Glossop Union* (1866) LR 1 QB 227 at 229, per Blackburn J

In Bankruptcy Acts

[The Bankruptcy Act 1883, s 6(1)(d) (repealed; see now the Insolvency Act 1986, s 265(1)(c)) enacted that a creditor should not be entitled to present a bankruptcy petition against a debtor, unless the debtor was domiciled in England, or, within a year (now three years) before the date of the presentation of the petition, had 'ordinarily resided' or had a place of business in England.] 'It is for the petitioning creditor to shew that the case comes within s 6 sub-s 1(a). It is admitted that the debtor is not domiciled in England. The petitioning creditor desires to shew that within a year before the presentation of the petition the debtor had "ordinarily resided" in England. If a young man comes to stay with a relative in London for some weeks it cannot be said that he resides in London. If a person goes to a hotel and stays there a month he cannot be said from that to reside there. This young man came to London, for what purpose we do not know. All we know is that when he was in London he had a bedroom at a lodging-house in Half Moon-street, and he slept there at the intermittent times stated in the affidavits. It is perfectly consistent with that state of things that he was a mere visitor there. There is really no evidence that the debtor "resided" in England. But, further than that, the section requires that he should have "ordinarily resided" in England. He merely came to London on a visit. Even, however, if we assume that he resided here, he did not "ordinarily reside" in London.' *Re Erskine, ex p Erksine* (1893) 10 TLR 32 at 32, CA, per Lord Esher MR

'The learned registrar has . . . held that the debtor had "ordinarily resided" and had "a place of business" in accordance with the section [Bankruptcy Act 1883, s 6(1)(a) (repealed; see supra)]. In dealing with the decision of the registrar, unless we can see that he has applied some wrong principle of law, we ought not to interfere with his decision on a question of fact. The facts shew that for only three months during the year in question was the debtor continuously absent from London. During the rest of the time he was in London for a definite purpose, and though he made occasional visits to the continent, yet London was his central place of dwelling. It has been argued that in point of law the debtor cannot have "resided", because his place of dwelling was not a lodging-house but simply one or more hotels, and that, unless it is shewn that he paid for his rooms, whether he occupied them or not, he cannot be said to have resided in them. It is important to bear in mind that the "residence" of the section is not residence at large, but residence within a particular year. A long sojourn is not a *sine quâ non*. The residence may be a temporary residence for a particular purpose. There must, of course, be some duration—for instance, two or three days would not be sufficient. The purposes for which the debtor was here is one of the elements to be taken into consideration. If he was here for a particular purpose which could not be conveniently disposed of without his presence, and was here for a substantial time, then it becomes a question of fact whether he was ordinarily resident or not. In my opinion there is abundant evidence to support the learned registrar's conclusion.' *Re Bright, ex p Bright* (1903) 51 WR 342 at 343, CA, per Collins MR

In Bills of Sale Act

[The Bills of Sale Act 1854, s 1 (repealed; see now the Bills of Sale Act 1878, s 10), enacted that a bill of sale should be void, unless filed within a certain period with an affidavit of the time when the bill was made or given, and a description of the 'residence' and occupation of the grantor and of every attesting witness to such bill.] 'There may be occasions when we ought to construe the word "residence" as meaning the place where a man sleeps, but the word does not necessarily have that meaning. The object of the enactment was that information should be given where the witness was to be found, in order that he might answer any inquiries respecting the bill of sale. I must guard against being supposed to decide that the place where a person sleeps would not suffice, it is enough for the present purpose to say that the description in this case is sufficient.' *Attenborough v Thompson* (1857) 2 H & N 559 at 563, DC, per Pollock CB

In Copyright Act

[The Copyright Act 1956, s 12(7) (repealed), afforded protection from infringement of copyright in cases, inter alia, where sound recordings were caused to be heard in public at any premises where persons 'reside' or sleep, as part of the amenities provided for them.] 'What the plaintiffs say is that the word "reside" in this subsection implies some degree of permanence and that the subsection does not apply to establishments where there is a constantly fluctuating population of persons who do not normally stay for above a week. If and so far as it applies to hotels it only applies to residential hotels, that is to say where the hotel is substantially the home of the persons who are living there. Of course, the word "reside" may mean very different things in different contexts. Undoubtedly in some contexts one has to draw a distinction between residing in a place and staying for a short time. I was referred to an adoption case before Harman J, *Re Adoption Application* 52/1951 [[1951] 2 All ER 931], where the judge did draw such a distinction and held that the word "reside" in the section in question implied a certain degree of permanence. I find, however, great difficulty in drawing such a distinction here, because, in any given establishment one may find people who are there for very different periods of time. Take a prison or a mental hospital, for example. Some people are sent to live there for long periods, others, on the other hand, are sent there or stay there for quite short periods. Similarly, with hotels. In some hotels one may find old ladies who have lived there for years and are allowed to have their own furniture in their rooms, while other guests stay only for a night or so. Yet all are called "hotel residents" in contra-distinction to members of the public who are not sleeping in the hotel but who merely go in for a drink or to have dinner in the restaurant. So in this context I cannot put the limitation on the word "reside" which the plaintiffs invite me to do. To my mind the visitors in this camp [a holiday camp] are residents residing in the premises for the purpose of this subsection.' *Phonographic Performance Ltd v Pontin's Ltd* [1957] 3 All ER 736 at 739, per Cross J

In Income Tax Acts

'A company cannot eat or sleep, but it can keep house and do business. We ought, therefore, to see where it really keeps house and does business. An individual may be of foreign nationality, and yet reside in the United Kingdom. So may a company. . . . The decision of Kelly CB and Huddleston B in the *Calcutta Jute Mills v Nicholson* [(1876) 1 Ex D 428] and *Cesena Sulphur Co v Nicholson* [(1876) 1 Ex D 428] . . . involved the principle that a company resides for purposes of income tax where its real business is carried on. Those decisions have been acted upon ever since. I regard that as the true rule, and the real business is carried on where the central management and control actually abides.' *De Beers Consolidated Mines Ltd v Howe* [1906] AC 455 at 457, 458, per Lord Loreburn LC

'The appellant in this case is a citizen of the United States of America, and he has been charged under Sch D [of the Income Tax Act 1853 (repealed; see now the Income and Corporation Taxes Act 1988, s 18)] with income tax on a large income which is remitted to him from abroad and received by him in this country. He can only be chargeable if he is a person residing in the United Kingdom. He has been to use a neutral term, sojourning in the United Kingdom, according to the facts found by the commissioners against him, for about twenty years past, and he has lived on board a yacht which is moored at a place in the river Colne, which is found to be within the port of Colchester, in the county of Essex. . . . The point argued in this case is that fixity is so much of the essence of residence that one cannot have a residence except in some structure that is incapable of being moved. Hence it is said that as long as this vessel floats and can be shifted about it cannot be a residence. No authority, no literary reference, and no reason has been adduced for this construction. I am myself unable to understand why a man who personally lives on board a yacht for twenty years a few hundred yards off the shore at Brightlingsea does not reside there.' *Brown v Burt* (1911) 105 LT 420 at 420, 421, CA, per Hamilton J

'Of course it is perfectly right to say that a man has not got to have a residence in the shape of a building to be resident in this country. That is quite clear. But I think that one has to consider not only the time that he is in this country but the nature of his visit and his connection with the country.' *Inland Revenue Comrs v Zorab* (1926) 11 Tax Cas 289 at 291, per Rowlatt J

'I do not attempt to give any definition of the word "resident". In my opinion it has no technical or special meaning for the purposes of the Income Tax Act [now the Income and Corporation Taxes Act 1988]. "Ordinarily resident" also seems to me to have no such technical or special meaning. In particular it is in my opinion impossible to restrict its connotation to its duration. A member of this House may well be said to be ordinarily resident in London during the Parliamentary session and in the country during the recess. If it has any definite meaning I should say it means according to the way in which a man's life is usually ordered.' *Levene v Inland Revenue Comrs* [1928] AC 217 at 232, per Lord Warrington of Clyffe

'The word "resident", it is laid down, has to be applied to artificial persons by analogy from natural persons. With these, residence depends on personal facts. Place of birth, nationality and allegiance are not the tests, nor is domicile, except in a sense that makes it barely distinguishable from residence. Voluntary choice and habitual and repeated action are mainly material, such as making a home, keeping an establishment, pursuing a settled object in or at a particular place. A man can change his residence at will, except that a certain duration of time or fixity of decision is requisite, and, but for the peculiar cases of a convict in gaol or a lunatic lawfully detained in a madhouse, I do not think that residence is ever determined for a natural person simply by the law. Accordingly, under the decisions as well as in principle, "resident" is a term exceedingly unsuited to describe a "statutory person", which can never be non-resident because, by the law of its being, it is a fixture. . . . A company must have a registered office in the United Kingdom, though it can move it about. Then it must keep certain lists and registers, and allow inquirers to inspect them and, although failure in any of these respects does not ipso facto work its dissolution nor is performance of these essential and important obligations a condition concurrent to its continuing to be incorporated, heavy fines may be inflicted for non-performance and, if not paid, may, I assume, lead to winding-up. My Lords, between these requirements and the case of a natural person there is no analogy at all. . . . If the respondent company has no place of trade here and does nothing at its head office but the minimum and occasional formalities required by the Act, it is surely an impossible straining of plain words to call that its "ordinary residence". . . . The office is its English address but its business may be elsewhere. If this is "residence", I think it is "residence" not by analogy to that of a natural person but by an independent metaphor. At any rate, if it is to be called "residence", only the legislature can do it.' *Egyptian Delta Land & Investment Co Ltd v Todd* [1929] AC 1 at 13, 15, per Lord Sumner

Australia 'A company may be a "resident" for the purpose of Income Tax Acts and it may have more than one residence for the purpose of these Acts. A company resides "wherever it keeps house and does business". Accordingly the ascertainment of the residence of a company is mainly a question of fact. If its central management and control abide in a particular place, the company resides there for the purposes of income tax, but it does not follow that it has not a residence elsewhere.' *Koitaki Para Rubber Estates Ltd v Federal Comr of Taxation* (1941) 64 CLR 241 at 246, per Starke J

'The place of residence of an individual is determined not by the situation of some business or property which he is carrying on or owns, but by reference to where he eats and sleeps and has his settled or usual abode. If he maintains a home or homes, he resides in the locality or localities where it or they are situate, but he may also reside where he habitually lives even if this is in hotels or on a yacht or some other place of abode: see Halsbury's Laws of England [4th edn, Vol 23, para 866]. In *Inland Revenue Commissioners v Lysaght* [1928] AC 234 at 244] Viscount Sumner said: "Grammatically the word 'resident' indicates a *quality of the person charged* and is not descriptive of his property real or personal".' Ibid at 249, per Williams J

In proposal for insurance

'It was stated in the form of proposals for the policy of assurance on which the action is brought, that the assured resided at 191 Great Ancots-street, Manchester, and the point raised on behalf of the defendants is whether they can successfully defend an action on the policy, on the ground that the assured was merely temporarily staying at that address and really resided in Ireland. In my opinion the proposition is not tenable. It is not necessary for us to decide the point which would have arisen if the assured had been actually living in Ireland at the time the proposal was made and the policy effected, for the facts here are that the assured was de facto living at the address given at the time in question and for three months after. This brings us to the question as to what is the meaning of the term "residence" in the document of proposal. That document, after the heading, asks, first, the name of the person proposing to effect an assurance, secondly, his profession or occupation, then his residence. Now that, in my opinion, means the place where he is living or residing at the time of making the proposal, and not where he has been residing before or where he is going to reside afterwards.' *Grogan v London & Manchester Industrial Assurance Co* (1885) 53 LT 761 at 763, DC, per Smith J

In Public Health Acts

[The Public Health Act 1875, s 267 (repealed with savings; see now the Public Health Act 1936, s 285), provided that notices, orders and any other documents required to be served under the Act might be served by delivering the same to or at the 'residence' of the person to whom they were respectively addressed.] 'In my opinion, . . . the validity of the service of this summons should be regulated by s 267 of the Public Health Act. Under that section, was it validly served? It was served on a clerk in charge at the appellant's place of business, and the section requires it to be served "at the residence of the person" summoned. . . . In ordinary language, I do not think one would speak of a place of business as a man's place of abode or residence—phrases which, I think, ordinarily mean the same thing; but when the words are used in a statute one must consider the purpose of the statute and the object to be effected by requiring the place of abode or residence to be described or visited. . . . What, then, is the purpose of the provisions by which a summons need not be personally served, but may be left at the "place of residence"? Obviously that it shall get to the person summoned by being left at a place where it is likely to reach him. His place of business will usually be at least as suitable a place for that purpose as the place where he sleeps; frequently more so, as more care is usually taken of business than of private documents. On principle, therefore, I see no reason why the place of business should not be the place of residence for the purposes of serving this summons.' *R v Braithwaite* [1918] 2 KB 319 at 330–332, CA, per Scrutton LJ

In Representation of the People Acts

[The Representation of the People Act 1832 (the Reform Act), s 27 (repealed), provided that a person should not be registered as a borough voter unless he should have 'resided' for six months in the borough, or within seven miles thereof.] 'It is stated that the claimant in this case paid 9d a week for the use of a bedroom. It does not follow from that fact that he had the exclusive right to that room. It is also stated that he slept there twelve times during a period of six months. That is a very small number of times. The fact of sleeping at a place, indeed, by no means constitutes a residence—though, on the other hand, it may not be necessary for the purpose of constituting a residence in any place to sleep there at all. If a man's family are living in a borough, and he is absent for six months, but with the intention of returning, he will still be considered as residing there. But there is nothing of that kind in this case. And the other facts stated, such as the occupation of a closet by keeping wine-samples in it, certainly will not establish a residence.' *Tewkesbury Case, Whithorn v Thomas* (1844) 7 Man & G 1 at 10, per Erle J

'The Act [Representation of the People Act 1832, s 27 (repealed)] distinguishes between occupation and residence, and requires that the person who occupies must also reside in the borough or within seven miles of it. The party may occupy and yet not "reside" there. . . . Residence . . . under this enactment is different from occupation and means where the man lives and where he has his home. It has always been held that a man resides where he lives and has his home, and the old doctrine should be adhered to.' *Barlow v Smith* (1892) 9 TLR 57 at 58, per Lord Coleridge CJ

[See now, as to a person's residence on the qualifying date for an election, the Representation of the People Act 1983, ss 5–7.]

In will

[A testator by his will bequeathed to his trustees certain leasehold premises, to hold upon trust to permit and suffer a legatee to hold and occupy the same during her lifetime, but subject to her 'residing' upon the premises during that lifetime.] 'In the first place, I will take this will and read it as if there was only the trust to suffer the lady to hold and occupy this house on condition of her residing in the said messuage during her lifetime. The lady occupied this house for some time as her natural home, and there married, and after some years, her husband having taken another house, she followed him there. What she has done with No 33 Turner Road, is to let all the rooms but one; there was some rather vague arrangement that she might use the drawing-room or dining-room and the kitchen; she can go in and out as she pleases, and she has the key of the front door. The room which she retained and called "her den" and of which she has the key, is one in which she keeps her writing materials, some clothes, and certain trifles, and there is a bed which she always keeps ready for use. She goes there about two or three times a week, and occasionally has meals and sleeps there. Can this be said to be residence? . . . No doubt a man or a woman may have two residences under certain circumstances. Here I have to consider this particular will. . . . Although I am unwilling to deprive this lady of this house without urgent cause, I cannot bring myself to think that what she has been doing is "residing" in the house. It seems to me that she has been using it for a place of rest and amusement, and not for a residence.' *Re Wright, Mott v Issott* [1907] 1 Ch 231 at 235, 236, per Kekewich J

'The will . . . after bequeathing the testator's furniture and effects to the appellant, continued as follows: "I give, devise and bequeath all other property real and personal to my executors upon the following trusts namely: To manage the corpus of the estate . . . and to pay to or for my said daughter a sum sufficient in their judgment to maintain her suitably until she is forty years of age, after which the whole income of the estate shall be paid to her annually". But the will then proceeded as follows: "The payments to my said daughter shall be made only so long as she shall continue to reside in Canada". . . . No one can suppose that the testator intended either that his daughter should never leave Canada, or that so long as she maintained a residence in Canada she might spend the whole of her time abroad. He must have intended that, though Canada was to be her home in genreal, yet she was to be at liberty to leave Canada for some purposes and for some periods of time. Unfortunately, he omitted to define either the purposes or the periods.' *Sifton v Sifton* [1938] AC 656 at 663, 664, 676, 677, PC, per cur.

Ordinarily resident *See* ORDINARILY RESIDENT

Private residence

'In my opinion, a large building which is to be used as thirty or forty separate residential flats does not answer the description of a messuage to be used as and for a private residence.' *Rogers v Hosegood* [1900] 2 Ch 388 at 394, CA, per Farwell J

'Reside together'

'"Residing together as man and wife", in the language of the Divorce Court, is sometimes called cohabiting, and I should find a great deal of difficulty in distinguishing between residing together as man and wife and cohabiting. I do not think one carries the matter any further by paraphrasing it, but I suppose the words "last ordinarily resided together as man and wife in England" [within the Maintenance Orders Act 1950, s 1(1) (repealed; see now Domestic Proceedings and Magistrates Court Act 1978, s 30(3))] could be paraphrased by saying that the matrimonial home at which the parties last cohabited was in England.' *Lowry v Lowry* [1952] 2 All ER 61 at 62, per Lord Merriman P (also reported in [1952] P 252 at 255, 256)

Royal residence *See* ROYAL RESIDENCE

RESIDENTIAL HOTEL *See* HOTEL

RESIDENTIAL LICENCE

In this Act 'residential licence' means a Part IV licence [justice's on-licence granted under Part IV of the Act] which—

(a) is granted for premises bona fide used, or intended to be used, for the purpose of habitually providing for reward board and lodging, including breakfast and one other at least of the customary main meals; and
(b) is subject to the condition that intoxicating liquor shall not be sold or supplied on the premises otherwise than to persons residing there or their private friends bona fide entertained by them at their own expense, and for consumption by such a person or his private friend so entertained by him either on the premises or with a meal supplied at but to be consumed off the premises.

(Licensing Act 1964, s 94(2))

[See also s 94(3) as to the meaning of 'residential and restaurant licence'.]

RESIDUAL INTEREST

Canada 'It would seem that the use of the term "residual interest" embraces that of "reversionary interest". In other words a general rule-of-thumb distinction for purposes of cases such as this [i.e. partial expropriation] would be: reversionary interest is merely the interest the owner possesses when the easement is at an end, while residual interest is that which the owner possesses not only then but also during the currency of the easement.' *Re Chieftain Development Co Ltd* (1981) 129 DLR (3d) 285 at 297, Alta QB, per Cormack J

RESIDUARY LEGATEE

'The words "legacy" and "residuary legatee" prima facie have reference to personal estate only. There is indeed no magic in the words themselves, and if they are so used by a testator they may no doubt be construed as referring to real estate. Any man may use his own nomenclature if he only expresses what he means. I have not however been able to discover any case which satisfies my mind that independently of context you can understand "legacy" or "legatee" or "residuary legatee" as applying to anything but personal estate. I think that in that case in the House of Lords of *Kellett v Kellett* [(1815) 3 Dow 248] we must understand Lord Eldon and Lord Redesdale to have been of opinion that, if there is nothing to qualify them, the words "legatee" or "residuary legatee" have reference to personal property only. I need not refer to the words used by Lord Eldon (they were very characteristic of his mode of expression) from which I think we may come to the conclusion that that was his opinion, and that the only question he had there was whether there were or were not circumstances that would enable him to put a construction, or rather to say that the testator had put a construction, on those words different from that which they ordinarily import; and he thought there were not. The general rule therefore I take to be, that if you constitute a person residuary legatee or if you speak of him in reference to his character of legatee, you refer only to a gift of personalty or are speaking of him only with reference to some gift of personal property.' *Windus v Windus* (1856) 6 De GM & G 549 at 557, 558, per Lord Cranworth LC

'There is no doubt that if you found the term "residuary legatee" standing alone, above all, if you found it in a will which appeared to make a division between real property and personal property, the prima facie meaning of "residuary legatee" would be the person taking what the law calls the residue of the personal property; but it is a term which must be fashioned and moulded by the context, and if you have a context in which the testator is found looking at his landed property, not as land, but, as something which is all to be sold and turned into money, then the term "residuary legatee" becomes a term as applicable to the proceeds of landed property as it would have been in the first instance to personal property.' *Singleton v Tomlinson* (1878) 3 App Cas 404 at 417, 418, per Lord Cairns LC

'It is well settled that the words "residuary legatee" by themselves prima facie do not apply to real estate, though their application may be extended so as to do so when the context requires it, and when a testator directs his real estate to be sold and disposes of part of the proceeds, it may be taken, I think, that the appointment of a residuary legatee will pass the rest.' *Re Gibbs, Martin v Harding* [1907] 1 Ch 465 at 468, per Joyce J

[A testator, who died possessed of real and personal property, did not, in his will, specifically devise his real estate. His will contained the following appointments: 'I appoint my sister Mrs Rebecca Tronton residuary legatee of this my will and in the event of her predeceasing me I appoint her children any residuary legatees and devisees.' The point at issue was whether the residuary gift to the testator's sister carried the undisposed of real estate.] 'It seems to me that the contrast is too pointed as between Mrs Tronton as "residuary legatee" and the children as "residuary legatees and devisees". If the expression occurred in different portions of the will some attempt might be made to explain the matter. . . . If words mean anything, having regard to the structure of the clause, some meaning must be given to the word "devisees", and the testator must be presumed to have meant something by adding that word in the gift to the children and omitting it in the gift to Mrs Tronton. Normally, the appointment of a person as residuary legatee means that the residual personal estate is given to that person and the appointment of a person as residuary devisee means that the residuary real estate is given to him. In my opinion the effect of the clause is the same as if the testator had said: "I give my residuary personal estate to my sister Mrs Rebecca Tronton in the event of her surviving me and, in the event of her predeceasing me, I give my residuary personal and real estate to her children." If the residuary gift were in that form I do not think the appellant's case would be arguable and in my opinion, that is precisely the effect of the words used by the testator.' *Re Hogg, Pim v Tronton* [1944] IR 244 at 256, per O'Byrne J

[By his will, a testator gave certain pecuniary legacies and then devised and bequeathed one of several holdings of freehold registered land whereto he was beneficially entitled. His will concluded by the appointment of two persons as 'residuary legatees'. The issue before the court was whether the testator's interest in the registered land, other than the holding specifically disposed of, passed to the residuary legatees by virtue of such appointment.] 'The expression "residuary legatees", now quite common and on the face of it quite plain, stands alone in the will of a man whose land was all registered land, and who speaks not at all of "residuary devisees", and the Act of 1891 [Local Registration of Title (Ir) Act 1891], no simple, homely document, is his magna charta for that land. That Act assigned Irish registered land to a peculiar category of its own, unique in our jurisprudence, a category newly invented ad hoc for a tenure that defies the tradition of centuries by treating a fee simple very much like a chattel interest; but the case law for reading "residuary legatee" narrowly dates back to an epoch when the line of demarcation between real property and chattels real held good for all land in this country and the bounds between the succession for the heir or residuary devisee and that taken by a personal representative for the next-of-kin or residuary legatee were generally as notorious as the foreshore between land and sea. In my opinion, the foundations of the distinction have been so deeply and so effectively undermined by statute, in the region of registered land, that a farmer cannot reasonably be assumed to have appreciated and adverted to the difference, unless there be something in his will (and there is nothing here), to suggest that he did. I think this novel freehold tenure exhibits the characteristics of personal property so prominently that an expression so equivocal in fact as "residuary legatees" cannot fairly claim here a preferential reading as a term of art, with a patent risk of consequent misconstruction, and I therefore hold myself free, indeed bound, to turn to the broad, popular meaning, which, if open to me, is decidedly the more probable here, despite the use in the will of "give, devise and bequeath" for the farm at Lislea. . . . I think the context of the will, properly understood (and I include in the context the admissible extrinsic evidence), "fashions and moulds" the phrase containing the controversial words into an intelligible and rational provision of the kind that one would expect from the testator. I have no doubt that to the ordinary man, the expression "residuary legatees" conveys the universal gift of all that is left, and a gratuitous assumption that it conveyed something less to this particular farmer would be inexcusable.' *McInerney v Liddy* [1945] IR 100 at 112–114, per Gavan Duffy J

RESIDUE *See also* BALANCE; REST

'On the one hand, it is true, that "residue" is not a "legacy" in the ordinary sense of the term; and it was justly observed, that "residue" is what remains after payment of legacies.' *Ward v Grey* (1859) 26 Beav 485 at 492, per Romilly MR

'The ordinary sense in which the term residue is used as applied to personal estate is the residue after payment of debts, funeral and testamentary expenses and legacies.' *Re Brooks' Will* (1865) 2 Drew & Sm 362 at 364, per Kindersley V-C

'It appears to have been long-settled law that there is no residue of personal estate until after payment of the debts, funeral and testamentary expenses, and all costs of the administration of the estate of the testator. Therefore, until you have paid the costs, you do not arrive at the net residue at all, and when you do arrive at it, it is distributed according to law. That is the principle.' *Trethewy v Helyar* (1876) 4 Ch D 53 at 56, per Jessel MR

[A testatrix by her will bequeathed to her niece the 'residue of money' at the time of her death. At the time of her death she had no money in the bank and only a negligible sum in the house.] 'I see no reason why, because the law has said the real estate is chargeable with debts and legacies, that should give a meaning to the word "money" different from that which I should otherwise have attributed to it. I am disposed to think that the phrase "residue of money at the time of my death" does mean money, but it means money in this sense, that particular personal property which is left after there has been paid all those things which are properly payable is respect of debts, legacies and funeral and testamentary expenses. I therefore come to the conclusion that on the true construction of this will and codicil, the property which passes is the residuary personal estate.' *Re Emerson, Morrill v Nutty* [1929] 1 Ch 128 at 131, 133, per Tomlin J

' "The residue of my estate" means the residue of what is converted into money remaining over after the payment of the debts, funeral and testamentary expenses and pecuniary legacies. . . . The expression "the residue of my estate" is not used in two different senses in a will simply because in two different connections it may denote different residues. In each case the expression naturally means "that which remains after what has been previously given is withdrawn".' *Re Kelly, Cleary v Dillon* [1932] IR 255 at 259, 260, per Meredith J

Australia 'Speaking generally, the words "the residue" mean what lawyers would in ordinary parlance call the residue, that where the testator for instance, having given different portions of his estate to different people, winds up by saying the rest of my property I give to "A" and "B", they would probably be called his residuary legatees and what was given to them would probably be called the residue.' *Re Madder* [1945] VLR 250 at 257, per Gavan Duffy J

RESIST

Australia [The applicant was convicted of wounding with intent to 'resist' lawful detainer.] 'The word "resist" can be aptly applied to a state of affairs. The word itself means nothing more than "to oppose" or "strive against" or "put a stop to".' *R v Hansford* [1974] VR 251 at 254, per Adam J

RESOLUTION

Ordinary resolution

'It seems to me that the words "ordinary resolution", which are found nowhere in the Act [Companies Act 1948] except in s 184 [see now the Companies Act 1985, s 303] merely connote a resolution depending for its passing on a simple majority of votes validly cast in conformity with the articles.' *Bushell v Faith* [1969] 1 All ER 1002 at 1003, CA, per Harman LJ

RESORT *See also* PLACE OF PUBLIC RESORT

In Betting Acts

[The Betting Act 1853 (repealed; cf now the Betting, Gaming and Lotteries Act 1963, s 1) prohibited the keeping of a house for the purpose of betting with persons 'resorting' thereto.] 'The word used in the section is "resort" and we must assume that the legislature was not putting a special meaning on the word, but was using it in its ordinary, usual, and accustomed sense of "go to", "frequent", go in and out. . . . Supposing that a man in Paris wanted to bet, and sent by the same post three letters to three different persons in Liverpool, Manchester, and Birmingham, instructing them to bet with him, the letters would not improbably be delivered about the same time. Could it be said that he was resorting at one and the same time to three different betting-houses, though he had never set foot in one of them? It was contended by counsel for the prosecution that to confine the meaning of the word "resort" to a physical resorting would be to place a narrow construction upon the Act; but even if that be so, we must put what we believe to be the right construction upon it. They further contended that upon this construction a case would not fall within the Act where a man did not come to the house himself, but sent messengers or representatives to make bets for him, but I should be sorry to suppose for an instant that such a case would not be within the statute as it stands, and would not be consistent with the construction I have put upon the section.' *R v Brown* [1895] 1 QB 119 at 130, per Lord Russell CJ

'To establish the offence it was necessary to prove two things; first that the appellant was using the house in question for a particular purpose, and secondly that the purpose was for betting with persons resorting thereto [contrary to the Betting Act 1853, s 1 (repealed; see supra)]. . . . There must be a physical resorting by persons. Merely writing letters to an address is not sufficient to constitute resorting. On the other hand it is not necessary that the person resorting should actually effect an entrance into the house. If he knocks at the door and an inmate of the house comes and answers the summons; or if he gives a signal and the inmate appears in response to the signal; or if he appears at intervals and the inmate on the look out for him simultaneously appears at the door; in all these cases there would be evidence of resorting although the person did not actually enter the house.' *Taylor v Monk* [1914] 2 KB 817 at 820, 821, per Channell J

RESORT TO

Canada [A wiretap authorisation provided that electronic interception of a private communication might be made at named premises or other locations as might be 'resorted' to by named persons.] 'The appellants argue that the term resort connotes frequent or repeated use and refer to cases such as *Rockert v The Queen* (1978) 38 CCC (2d) 438, 81 DLR (3d) 759, [1978] 2 SCR 704, and *Patterson v The Queen* [1968] 2 CCC 247, 67 DLR (2d) 82, [1968] SCR 157. These cases, however, deal with the meaning of resort as it is used in the definition of a common bawdy-house and common gaming-house. The meaning of the word resort arrived at in these cases depends largely on the concept of a gaming-house or bawdy-house as a public nuisance. I can find no warrant for the acceptance of this meaning of the word resort in other cases. Within the context of the authorisation in this case there is no reason why resort should not receive its plain and ordinary meaning, i.e. go.' *R v Vrany* (1979) 46 CCC (2d) 14 at 23, 24, Ont CA, per Zuber JA

Canada [Interception of private communications was authorised at any place the accused 'resorted to'.] It seems to me the words mean no more and no less than 'go', as Mr Justice Zuber put in in the *Vrany* case [supra]. That being the case, I think the Crown has shown that the authorisation was complied with. The authorities intercepted a conversation at a public telephone resorted to by the respondent.' *R v Leclerc* (1985) 20 CCC (3d) 173 at 178, BCCA, per Taggart JA

RESOURCE

New Zealand 'In a context of land use planning [see the Town and Country Planning Act 1977], it seems to me that resource is meant to describe an actual or potential benefit to the people of New Zealand associated with or arising out of land or other physical features of the environment affected by the planning process. I see no reason to limit the word by reference only to what the land physically contains or supports; in many situations it has to be used before any benefit can arise. It seems to be a legitimate use of "resources" in such a context to regard the land as being a recreational resource if it is or can be used for that purpose, in the same way as one could regard it as being a tourist resource or a food resource.' *EDS v Circular Quay Holdings Ltd* (1985) 10 NZTPA 257 at 260, per Casey J

RESOURCES *See also* REQUIREMENT

'It seems to me that it is perfectly competent for a council, without having specific figures, with the assistance of its experts, to say: this quite clearly from our own knowledge is a matter which plainly comes within the resources of this council, and "the resources" there clearly means not merely cash resources, but their credit in the world, their ability to borrow, and all the rest of it.' *Goddard v Ministry of Housing and Local Government* [1958] 3 All ER 482 at 486, per Lord Parker CJ

RESPECTABLE

Australia [The Children's Court Act 1973 (Vic), s 22, provides that in certain circumstances a child admitted to bail could be placed with some 'respectable person' or persons or in the dwelling house of the member of the police force by whom such child or young person was apprehended.] 'I would judge a respectable person as one who, in the eyes of a majority of ordinary decent members of the community had a good social status, a good reputation, and was decent, honest and proper. I have little doubt the Registrar of the Royal Children's Hospital possessed those qualifications.' *Webb v Johns* [1983] 1 VR 739 at 748, per Beach J

RESPECTIVE

Australia 'The meaning of the word "respective" in legal and statutory language generally is "pertaining to each group or class of those in question".' *R v Licensing Court, ex p Ive, Botterill, Royal Melbourne Golf Club* [1921] VLR 266 at 273, per Cussen J

RESPONDENTIA *See* BOTTOMRY

RESPONSIBLE

[A furrier took out a policy of insurance against burglary in respect of goods belonging to him, and also for goods on his premises on trust or for commission and for which he was 'responsible'.] 'The main point in the case was the position with regard to the goods which had been in the possession of the claimant as a bailee in the course of his trade as a working furrier. The company undertook to pay for the loss of goods which the claimant held in trust and for which he was responsible, and the case turns on the meaning to be given to the word "responsible". The umpire has found that the claimant has not been guilty of any negligence as a bailee, so he would not be liable in law to the true owners of the goods. But the claimant contends that the word "responsibility" must be held to cover the general responsibility of a bailee for goods entrusted to him and was not limited to legal liability in case of loss. The company, on the other hand, contends that responsibility must be limited to legal liability. . . . It appears to be the general opinion of the Judges that responsibility in this connection means legal liability only, and I therefore adopt that view.' *Engel v Lancashire & General Assurance Co Ltd* (1925) 41 TLR 408 at 409, per Roche J

REST *See also* RESIDUE

'The words rest and residue must be taken by all rules of grammar, as well as law, to relate to something that went before.' *Beauclerk v Mead* (1741) 2 Atk 167 at 170, per Hardwicke LC

'Inasmuch as the testator followed the gift of certain pecuniary legacies with the words "The rest of my property in the Three per Cent Consols, etc", it was a reasonable construction to suppose that by the word "rest" the testator intended what should remain after paying the legacies before given; and this view would make the legacies effectual, while a contrary view would defeat them, since there was no other fund able to defray them.' *Foxen v Foxen* (1864) 5 New Rep 1 at 1, per Lord Westbury LC

'It seems to have been conceded on all sides as a general rule, that, with the view of giving effect to all the words of a will, you must give the words "all the rest of my estate" the effect of passing the real estate, if there be other words sufficient to pass the general personal estate.' *Dobson v Bowness* (1868) LR 5 Eq 404 at 407, per Page Wood VC

Canada 'The issue before me is to determine whether that paragraph [in a mortgage] requires the plaintiff to compute the interest upon arrears semi-annually on June and December 1st in each year or whether it is entitled to compute and compound interest on arrears monthly. It appears to me that the interpretation of this paragraph depends upon the meaning of the phrase "with rests". Counsel advised me that they have been unable to locate any case which deals with the meaning of those words. In my opinion, the words must mean the dates upon which the account between the parties to the mortgage would be altered. The mortgage provided for monthly payments, including principal and interest, which were due on the first of each and every month. It appears to me that the account between the parties would change on the first of each month. It is my opinion, therefore, that the arrears of interest should be computed and compounded on the first of each month although they need to be paid only on June 1st and December 1st in each year.' *Montreal Trust Co v Hounslow Holdings Ltd* [1972] 1 OR 179 at 182, Ont SC, per Galligan J

RESTAURANT

Canada 'While primarily the term "restaurant" [in a zoning by-law] suggests a public eating place, at this stage in the development of such establishments I am not prepared to confine the operation of the word in such a manner as would bar the defendant from engaging in anything beyond the serving of meals to be consumed at table on the premises. Once admitting the sale of other foodstuffs, either as a normal incident to the conduct of a restaurant per se or as a related activity commonly associated with or ancillary to such business, I am not prepared to venture upon a catalogue of the types or amounts of such foodstuffs the defendant may sell.' *Singer v Town N'Country Holding Co Ltd* (1966) 56 DLR (2d) 339 at 348, 349, Man QB, per Wilson J

RESTAURANT LICENCE

In this Act 'restaurant licence' means a Part IV licence [justices' on-licence granted under Part IV of the Act] which—

(a) is granted for premises structurally adapted and bona fide used, or intended to be used, for the purpose of habitually providing the customary main meal at midday or in the evening, or both, for the accommodation of persons frequenting the premises; and
(b) is subject to the condition that intoxicating liquor shall not be sold or supplied on the premises otherwise than to persons taking table meals there and for consumption by such a person as an ancillary to his meal.

(Licensing Act 1964, s 94(1).

[See also s 94(3) as to the meaning of 'residential and restaurant licence'.]

RESTITUTIO IN INTEGRUM

The general rule is that of restitutio in integrum: so far as money can do it, the injured person should be put in the same position as he would have been if he had not sustained the wrong, namely if the tort had not been committed or the contract had been performed. This principle, whilst general, is subject to . . . particular principles, and . . . limitations of remoteness. (12 Halsbury's Laws (4th edn) para 1129)

RESTORATION

'Restoration' includes building or partial rebuilding. (Pastoral Measure 1983, s 87(1))

RESTRAINT OF PRINCES *See also* ARRESTS, RESTRAINTS AND DETAINMENTS

[In the normal form of charterparty, and in policies of marine insurance, the excepted perils include 'arrests, restraints and detainments of kings, princes and peoples'.] 'The word "enemies" at least includes enemies of the carrier, if those are not the parties to whom it is specially directed. "King's enemies" means enemies of the sovereign of the carrier, whether that sovereign be an Emperor, a Queen, or a reigning Duke. Lest there should be any left out, it is usual in charterparties to add the words "restraints of princes and rulers". These include all cases of restraint or interruption by lawful authority; leaving the case of pirates to be ranked with other dangers of the seas, within which, according to the authority of the case of *Pickering v Barkley* [(1648)] Sty 132], it falls.' *Russell v Niemann* (1864) 17 CBNS 163 at 174, 175, per Byles J

'Is a blockade a restraint of princes? I think it is. It is an act of a sovereign state or prince; and it is a restraint, provided the blockade is effective. . . . In such a case the obstacle arises from an act of state of one of the belligerent sovereigns, and consequently constitutes a restraint of princes.' *Geipel v Smith* (1872) LR 7 QB 404 at 409, 410, per Cockburn CJ

[British goods were shipped in German vessels, which were scuttled on the high seas by their masters on the outbreak of war, on the instructions of the German government.] 'It is clear that a restraint may operate without any display of force. . . . The restraint which was operating on the master was the compelling force of the German State to which he was subject. In one sense it was a moral compulsion, but in another sense it was more because it may be assumed that he was aware that, if he disobeyed the order, his government had means of vindicating its authority if not at the moment, at least subsequently. . . . Thus the seizure or restraint effected in obedience to that order becomes, in a case like the present, the belligerent act of the German Government though it is committed by the master of a German merchantman, on the high seas, or in neutral territory.' *Rickards v Forestal Land, Timber & Rlys Co Ltd, Robertson v Midows Ltd, Khan v Howard (WH) Brothers & Co Ltd* [1942] AC 50 at 80, 82, per Lord Wright

See, generally, 25 Halsbury's Laws (4th edn) para 161.

RESTRAINT OF TRADE

Restraints upon the general freedom to trade may be roughly divided into restraints imposed on a person by statute, and restraints imposed by virtue of his own agreement. In addition, restraints may be imposed by the rules or practices of professional or other bodies controlling particular activities. A further restraint on freedom to trade arises by operation of law when one trader is given confidential information by another; apart from any contract he is not entitled to use the information for the purposes of trade by way of competition with the other trader.

Restraints of trade by statute include all those cases in which certain trades have been absolutely forbidden by Parliament, or in which restrictions have been imposed by Parliament on the carrying on of particular trades and professions with a view to the maintenance of a proper standard of competence in, and a proper control over, those engaged in them, or with a view to the protection of employees and the public or public order, or the public health and safety, or for purposes of revenue. . . .

A person may be restrained from carrying on his trade by reason of an agreement voluntarily entered into by him with that object. In such a case the general principle of freedom of trade must be applied with due regard to the principles that public policy requires for persons of full age and understanding the utmost freedom to contract, and that it is public policy to allow a trader to dispose of his business to a successor by whom it may be efficiently carried on, and to afford to an employer an unrestricted choice of able assistants and the opportunity to instruct them in his trade and its secrets without fear of their becoming his competitors.

Agreements in restraint of trade are generally made (1) between vendors and purchasers of businesses; (2) between partners; (3) between employers and employees; (4) between independent traders or groups of traders with a view to eliminating or reducing competition, regulating output and the like; (5) between employers with a view to united action in relation to those whom they employ; and (6) between employees with a view to united action in relation to their employers. But the categories of agreements in restraint of trade are not closed. (47 Halsbury's Laws (4th edn) paras 10, 13, 14)

'I think that a covenant entered into in connection with the sale of the goodwill of a business must be valid where the full benefit of the purchase cannot be otherwise secured to the purchaser. It has been recognised in more than one case that it is to the advantage of the public that there should be free scope for the sale of the goodwill of a business or calling. These were cases of partial restraint. But it seems to me that if there be occupations where a sale of the goodwill would be greatly impeded, if not prevented, unless a general covenant could be obtained by the purchaser, there are no grounds of public policy which countervail the disadvantage which would arise if the goodwill were in such cases rendered unsaleable. I would adopt in these cases the test which in a case of partial restraint was applied by the

Court of Common Pleas in *Horner v Graves* [(1831) 7 Bing 735 at 743], in considering whether the agreement was reasonable. Tindal CJ said: "We do not see how a better test can be applied to the question, whether reasonable or not, than by considering whether the restraint is such only as to afford a fair protection to the interests of the party in favour of whom it is given, and not so large as to interfere with the interests of the public. Whatever restraint is larger than the necessary protection of the party can be of no benefit to either; it can only be oppressive, and, if oppressive, it is, in the eye of the law, unreasonable." The tendency in later cases has certainly been to allow a restriction in point of space which formerly would have been thought unreasonable, manifestly because of the improved means of communication. A radius of 150 or even 200 miles has not been held too much in some cases. For the same reason I think a restriction applying to the entire kingdom may in other cases be requisite and justifiable.' *Nordenfelt v Maxim Nordenfelt Guns & Ammunition Co Ltd* [1894] AC 535 at 548, 549, per Lord Herschell LC

'All interference with the individual liberty of action in trading, and all restraints of trade of themselves, if there is nothing more, are contrary to public policy, and, therefore, void. That is the general rule. But there are exceptions. Restraints of trade and interference with individual liberty of action, may be justified by the special circumstances of a particular case. It is a sufficient justification, and indeed, it is the only justification, if the restriction is reasonable—reasonable, that is, in reference to the interests of the parties concerned and reasonable in reference to the interests of the public, so framed and so guarded as to afford adequate protection to the party in whose favour it is imposed, while at the same time it is in no way injurious to the public.' Ibid at 565, per Lord Macnaghten

'Every member of the community is entitled to carry on any trade or business he chooses and in such manner as he thinks most desirable in his own interests, so long as he does nothing unlawful; with the consequence that any contract which interferes with the free exercise of his trade or business, by restricting him in the work he may do for others, or the arrangements which he may make with others, is a contract in restraint of trade. It is invalid unless it is reasonable as between the parties and not injurious to the public interest.' *Petrofina (Great Britain) Ltd v Martin* [1966] 1 All ER 126 at 131, CA, per Lord Denning MR

'A contract in restraint of trade is one in which a party (the covenantor) agrees with any other party (the covenantee) to restrict his liberty in the future to carry on trade with other persons not parties to the contract in such manner as he chooses.' Ibid at 138, per Diplock LJ

'When Lord Macnaghten said in the *Nordenfelt* case [supra] that "in the age of Queen Elizabeth all restraints of trade, whatever they were, general or partial, were thought to be contrary to public policy and, therefore, void", he was clearly not intending the words "restraints of trade" to cover any contract whose terms, by absorbing a man's services or custom or output, in fact prevented him from trading with others; so, too, the wide remarks of Lord Parker of Waddington in the *Adelaide* case [*A-G of Commonwealth of Australia v Adelaide Steamship Co Ltd* [1913] AC 781]. It was the sterilising of a man's capacity for work and not its absorption that underlay the objection to restraint of trade. This is the rationale of *Young v Timmins* [(1831) 1 G & J 331], where a brass foundry was during the contract sterilised so that it could work only for a party who might choose not to absorb its output at all but to go to other foundries, with the result that the foundry was completely at the mercy of the other party and might remain idle and unsupported. The doctrine does not apply to ordinary commercial contracts for the regulation and promotion of trade during the existence of the contract, provided that any prevention of work outside the contract viewed as a whole is directed towards the absorption of the parties' services and not their sterilisation.' *Esso Petroleum v Harper's Garage (Stourport) Ltd* [1967] 1 All ER 699 at 726, 727, HL, per Lord Pearce

RESTRICT

[The Patents and Designs Act 1907, s 38(1) (repealed; see now the Patents Act 1977, s 44(1)(c)) made it unlawful to 'restrict' a purchaser, lessee or licensee of a patent from using any articles, whether patented or not, supplied or owned by a person other than the seller, lessor or licensor or his nominees.] 'I come to the word "restrict". A person though not prohibited, is restricted from using something if he is permitted to use it to a certain extent or subject to certain conditions, but otherwise obliged not to use it, but I do not think that a person is properly said to be restricted from using something by a condition the effect of which is to offer him some inducement not to use it, or in some other way to influence his choice. To my mind, the more natural meaning here is restriction of the licensee's right to use the article.' *Tool Metal Manufacturing Co Ltd v Tungsten Electric Co Ltd* [1955] 2 All ER 657 at 671, HL, per Lord Oaksey

RESTRICTION

'It is, in my judgment, important to bear in mind that it is not strictly accurate to speak of restrictions affecting or imposed on property. It is the owner of the hereditament who is restricted—restricted, that is, in his freedom to use it as he likes. Some of the restrictions on him are of a perfectly general character. For instance, the owner of a house may not use it for an immoral purpose, nor so as to create a public or private nuisance; he may not contravene local by-laws in regard to building operations; he may not use it for harbouring the King's enemies or fugitive criminals. That is the first class of restrictions, and no vendor need call a purchaser's attention to their existence. The other class of restrictions consists of particular restrictions. This class . . . would include a prescribed building line, a requisitioning order, and similar statutory or departmental restrictions directed against the property itself or the owner of it in particular.' *Re City of London Property Co Ltd's Appeal* [1949] Ch 581 at 586, per Vaisey J

RESTRICTIVE COVENANT

See COVENANT

RESULT

'An existing incapacity "results from" the original injury [within the Workmen's Compensation Act 1925, s 9 (repealed)] if it follows, and is caused by, that injury, and may properly be held so to result even if some supervening cause has aggravated the effects of the original injury and prolonged the period of incapacity. If, however, the existing incapacity ought fairly to be attributed to a new cause which has intervened and ought no longer to be attributed to the original injury, it may properly be held to result from the new cause and not from the original injury, even though, but for the original injury, there would have been no incapacity.' *Rothwell v Caverswall Stone Co Ltd* [1944] 2 All ER 350 at 365, CA, per du Parcq LJ

Canada 'This machine [a slot machine] is one which yields different results to the operator as a consequence of any number of successive operations. There is no definite or mathematical certainty as to what the result of successive operations will be. I see no reason to restrict the meaning of the word "result" [in the Criminal Code, RSC, 1927, s 986(4) (now RSC 1970, c C-34, s 180)] to something tangible such as goods, wares or merchandise. The machine may be said to yield different results to the operator within the meaning of the definition whenever different scores are obtained as a result of the play.' *R v North* [1940] 2 WWR 179 at 181, Alta Dist Ct, per Macdonald DCJ

RESULTING TRUST *See* TRUST

RETAIL

'Retail trade or business' includes the business of a barber or hairdresser, the sale of refreshments or intoxicating liquors, the business of lending books or periodicals when carried on for purposes of gain, and retail sales by auction, but does not include the sale of programmes and catalogues and other similar sales at theatres and places of amusement. (Shops Act 1950, s 74)

'Retail trade or business' includes the sale to members of the public food or drink for immediate consumption, retail sales by auction and the business of lending books or periodicals for the purpose of gain. (Offices, Shops and Railway Premises Act 1963, s 1)

Australia 'I think that the natural meaning of "retail" is "sale of commodities in small quantities". From time to time, a retailer may, no doubt, enter into executory contracts to sell, but, in the natural meaning of the word I think that it imports "sale and delivery".' *Wright v Edwards* [1961] SASR 267 at 282, per Napier CJ

New Zealand 'In our opinion the term "at retail" presupposes a trading or a commercial transaction and is used in contradistinction to the term "wholesale". There is, we think, no doubt that a wholesaler is a person who, by way of business, deals only with persons who buy to sell again, whilst a retailer is one who deals with consumers. It would be, we think, a misuse of language to speak of a sale between two private persons as being a sale either at wholesale or at retail.' *Provident Life Assurance Co Ltd v Official Assignee* [1963] NZLR 961 at 965, per North P and Turner J

New Zealand 'The Act [Hire Purchase Act 1971, s 2] is clearly aimed at the buyer's protection, which is more widely and effectively achieved if "retail" is not confined to small-scale dispositions. There is no reason to suppose a large-scale buyer was not intended to benefit, if he is the ultimate user of the goods. He can suffer serious losses from the vendor's uncontrolled exercise of his rights on default, just as easily as the "little man". The regulations made under the Economic Stabilisations Act 1948 have the different purpose of ensuring the economic stability of New Zealand by controlling credit. Again, there seems to be no reason to exclude large-scale deals from their effect; indeed the aim of the regulations would obviously be more effectively achieved by their inclusion. Accordingly I believe the purpose and context of this legislation calls for that meaning to be given to "retail" which commended itself to the Court in . . . *Provident Life Assurance Co Ltd v Official Assignee* [supra]. The scale of the transaction becomes irrelevant, save as a factor in deciding whether it is a sale to an ultimate consumer.' *NatWest Finance v South Pacific Rent-a-Car* [1985] 1 NZLR 651 at 651, per Casey J

Retail shop

'Harley Street is not a shopping centre. I take it that an old fashioned country mill, if such now exists, where people take their grain to be ground, is not a retail shop. Here there is neither purchase nor repair. Again, the public can and do resort to a printer's works to get manuscripts printed and give various instructions. But a printing works is not a retail shop. There is no sale or repair; except indeed in a way of the paper, but this is a negligible factor.' *Aberdeen Assessor v Lumsdens Heirs* 1932 SC 379 at 381, per Lord Sands

Sale of milk

'Selling milk by retail' means selling it—

(a) to any person other than a milk dealer (that is, a person who carries on a business which consists of or comprises the selling of milk) or a manufacturer of milk products (that is a person who carries on a business which consists of or comprises the making of things made from milk or of which milk is an ingredient), or
(b) to such a dealer or manufacturer otherwise than for the purposes of his business as such.

(Food Act 1984, s 47)

RETAIN

'The words are "I desire applied for charitable purposes as I may in writing direct or to be retained by my executor for such objects and such purposes as he may in his discretion select and to be at his own disposal". That does not seem to me to be a direct gift to him beneficially. If the property does not go to charitable purposes in consequence of the testatrix not having given her directions in writing—it was her view that it would be valid for her to direct in writing—then it is "to be retained by my executor". It has been laid down, and I do not wish to controvert it in the least, that, in the construction of a document, a gift to an executor must be construed in the same way as a gift to anybody else, but when the word "retained" is used it seems to me not to be an apt word to convey a direct gift to the executor, it looks very much more like "to be retained by my executor, in his character of executor", and it is to be retained "for such objects and such purposes as he may in his discretion select and to be at his own disposal"; and I read those last words as if they were "and to be at his own disposal for such purposes".' *Re Chapman, Hales v A-G* [1922] 2 Ch 479 at 483, 484, CA, per Lord Sterndale MR

Australia [The Health Acts 1937–1986 (Qld), s 134, provide that an officer taking any sample of food shall divide the sample into three parts and shall 'retain' one part.] 'To "retain" the sample within the meaning of the section does not mean to keep it exclusively in his personal custody, but it does mean that it shall be kept separate and apart from the other parts of the sample and under the control of the person taking the sample or under the control of his agent, so that it can be positively identified as the part of the sample other than the part which had been given to the defendant and the part which had been sent to the analyst.' *Dalton v Hunter* [1953] St R Qd 59 at 65, per Mansfield SPJ

Australia [The Pure Food Act 1908–1986 (NSW), s 24(2), provides that an officer obtaining a sample shall divide it into three parts, one of which he is to 'retain' for examination or analysis.] 'I do not think it is necessary to make a complete examination of everything which might be involved in the word "retain" or to provide an exhaustive definition. It obviously contemplates . . . that there is to be some keeping of this particular third sample separate, apart from the other samples, but it is not necessary that the officer taking the sample should keep it exclusively in his own personal custody, and provided that it was kept by himself or by someone on his behalf under such circumstances that it could be produced and identified as part of the sample originally taken, that is a sufficient compliance with the obligations contained in the section.' *Ex p Archer, Re Bowry* [1957] SR (NSW) 1 at 4, per Street CJ

RETAINER

The act of authorising or employing a solicitor to act on behalf of a client constitutes the solicitor's retainer by that client. Thus, the giving of a retainer is equivalent to the making of a contract for the solicitor's employment, and the rights and liabilities of the parties under that contract will depend partly on any terms which they have expressly agreed, partly on the terms which the law will infer or imply in the particular circumstances with regard to matters on which nothing has been expressly agreed, and partly on such statutory provisions as are applicable to the particular contract. As a general rule, a person has the right to retain the solicitor of his choice, provided the solicitor is willing to act and is not precluded by law or by professional rules from so doing. By the giving and acceptance of the retainer the solicitor acquires his authority to act for and bind the client, and the client becomes bound both personally as between himself and his solicitor, and as between himself and third persons with whom the solicitor deals within the limits of his authority on behalf of his client. (44 Halsbury's Laws (4th edn) para 83)

RE-TRIAL

[The Courts of Justice Act 1928 (Ireland), s 5(1)(b) empowered the court to order, in certain circumstances, a 're-trial'.] 'This court is satisfied that when that sub-section speaks of a "re-trial" it contemplates a proceeding in which the guilt or innocence of the accused is determined. There is no such determination where a jury is unable to agree on a verdict. The word "re-trial" in its legal acceptation in such a context means, in the opinion of this court, a complete and finished trial, and "when there is no verdict there has been in law no trial".' *A-G v Kelly (No 2)* [1938] IR 109 at 113, 114, per Sullivan CJ

RETRIBUTION

Canada 'Reference was made before us to "retribution" as being one of the considerations involved in sentencing. I am of the opinion, with respect, that in those cases where the term "retribution" is used it is loosely equated with the word "punishment", for I cannot believe that "vengeance", a common meaning of the term "retribution", was ever intended. The application of such a meaning involves a loss of that objectivity which is essential to the exercise of the judicial process.' *R v Hinch* (1967) 62 WWR 205 at 209, BCCA, per Norris JA

RETROSPECTIVE

It has been said that 'retrospective' is somewhat ambiguous and that a good deal of confusion has been caused by the fact that it is used in more senses than one. In general, however, the courts regard as retrospective any statute which operates on cases or facts coming into existence before its commencement in the sense that it affects, even if for the future only, the character or consequences of transactions previously entered into or of other past conduct. Thus a statute is not retrospective merely because it affects existing rights; nor is it retrospective merely because a part of the requisites for its action is drawn from a time antecedent to its passing.

The general rule is that all statutes, other than those which are merely declaratory, or which relate only to matters of procedure or of evidence, are prima facie prospective, and retrospective effect is not to be given to them unless, by express words or necessary implication, it appears that this was the intention of the legislature. Similarly, the courts will construe a provision as conferring power to act restrospectively only when clear words are used. (44 Halsbury's Laws (4th edn) paras 921, 922)

'An act may be called retrospective because it affects existing contracts as from the date of its coming into operation. . . . It may more properly be described as retrospective, because it applies to actual transactions which have been completed, or to rights and remedies which have already accrued; or it may apply again to such matters as procedure and evidence; and in each of those matters retrospective legislation has a different effect.' *Gardner & Co v Cone* [1928] Ch 955 at 966, per Maugham J

'Although "retrospective" is an ugly word in the context of construing a statute, it is often misapplied. Thus, in *West v Gwynne* [[1911] 2 Ch 1] this court had to consider a statute which outlawed the right to demand payments, in relation to "all leases", for the landlord's consent to assignment, etc, and it was argued that the statute should not be construed so as to apply to existing, but only future, leases in order to avoid any retrospective construction. This argument was rejected unanimously. Buckley LJ said: "To my mind the word 'retrospective' is inappropriate, and the question is not whether the section is retrospective. Retrospective operation is one matter. Interference with existing rights is another. If an Act provides that as at a past date the law shall be taken to have been that which it was not, that Act I understand to be retrospective. That is not this case . . . There is, so to speak, a presumption that it speaks only as to the future. But there is no like presumption that an Act is not intended to interfere with existing rights. Most Acts of Parliament, in fact, do interfere with existing rights."' *Kuwait Minister of Public Works v Sir Frederick Snow & Partners (a firm)* [1983] 2 All ER 754 at 761, CA, per Kerr LJ

Australia 'There has been some ambiguity in the use of the word "retrospective". In some cases, it has been said that it would give a retrospective operation to a statute to treat it as impairing an existing right or obligation or creating a new right or obligation: *Re School Board Election for Parish of Pulborough* [[1894] 1 QB 725], at p 737; *Re Athlumney* [[1898] 2 QB 547], at pp 551, 552. On the other hand, it was said by Buckley LJ, in *West v Gwynne* [[1911] 2 Ch 1], at pp 11, 12, that an Act is retrospective if it provides that as at a past date the law shall be taken to have been that which it was not. It is not retrospective because it interferes with existing rights—most Acts do. There is no presumption that interference with existing rights is not intended; but there is a presumption that an Act speaks only as to the future. Similarly, it has been said that an amendment of a section in an Act makes it retrospective in its original form but not retrospective so far as it is new: *ex parte Todd* [(1887) 19 QBD 186 at 195]. Upon a consideration of the authorities, I think that, as regards any matter or transaction, if events have occurred prior to the passing of the Act which have brought into existence particular rights or liabilities in respect of that matter or transaction, it would be giving a retrospective operation to the Act to treat it as intended to alter those rights or liabilities, but it would not be giving it a retrospective operation to treat it as governing the future operation of the matter or transaction as regards the creation of further particular rights or liabilities.' *Coleman v Shell Co of Australia Ltd* 45 SR(NSW) 27 at 30, per Jordan CJ

RETURN

In will

'The co-trusteeship was devised to F G Bucknall, "if and when he shall return to England". I take the words in their ordinary sense. I do not say that if he merely came within three miles of the English coast, or if he came on shore for half-an-hour, that would be sufficient to comply with the condition. Perhaps it would not. But here he stayed in England for six months. In that time he might have done all that was necessary to wind up the trust. I think, therefore, the condition was sufficiently complied with.' *Re Arbib & Class's Contract* [1891] 1 Ch 601 at 613, CA, per Lindley LJ

Of capital

Australia 'A return of paid-up capital or a payment off of share capital—whichever form of words be used—is, of course, a distribution by a company to its shareholders but, whether or not what is distributed exceeds the nominal amount by which the capital is reduced, there is always but a single distribution and all that is distributed has the one character, viz a return of paid-up capital or a payment off of share capital. When the capital of a company is divided into shares, the nominal value of a member's shareholding measures, but does not state, his interest in the capital of the company so that, upon a return of capital, that member is entitled to receive his proportionate share of the capital being reduced and not merely a sum equivalent to the nominal value of the reduction being effected.' *Comr of Taxation v Uther* (1965) 112 CLR 630 at 644, per Menzies J

Of writ

'The word "filing", in reference to matters of practice, is very commonly used to express the duty of bringing to the proper office, as the case may be, writs, pleadings, affidavits and other such matters for safe custody, or enrolment. The duty of filing in this sense may be properly considered as included under the word "returning"; for an attorney merely to write "*non est inventus*" on the back of a writ, and put it in his desk, is not to complete the act of returning it, which properly means, in this case, to make such answer, touching the execution of the writ, as shall authorise the issuing of another in continuation of it, and connect the two together on the same record; and for this purpose a necessary step is the bringing to the office.' *Hunter v Caldwell* (1847) 10 QB 69 at 79–81, per cur; affd, sub nom *Caldwell v Hunter* (1848) 10 QB 83

RETURN OF POST *See* POST

RETURNING OFFICER

In England and Wales, the returning officer for a parliamentary election is—

(a) in the case of a county constituency which is coterminous with or wholly contained in a county, the sheriff of the county;
(b) in the case of a borough constituency which is coterminous with or wholly contained in a district, the chairman of the district council;
(c) in the case of any other constituency wholly outside Greater London, such sheriff or chairmen of a district council as may be designated in an order by the Secretary of State made by statutory instrument;
(d) in the case of a constituency which is coterminous with or wholly contained in a London borough, the mayor of the borough;
(e) in the case of a constituency wholly or partly in Greater London which is situated partly in one London borough and partly in a district of any other London borough, the mayor of such London borough or the chairman of such district council as may be designated in an order by the Secretary of State made by statutory instrument.

The City, the Inner Temple and the Middle Temple shall be treated for the purposes of this section as if together they formed a London borough. (Representation of the People Act 1983, s 24(1))

[As to returning officers at local elections, see s 35 of the Act of 1983.]

REVALUATION

Australia 'The question is, what is meant by a revaluation? A revaluation connotes an existing valuation. The ordinary meaning of a valuation is an estimation of the worth of a thing. The ordinary meaning of a revaluation is a fresh estimation of the worth of the same thing.' *Commissioner of Taxation (NSW) v Hardie Investments Pty Ltd* (1946) 73 CLR 490 at 505, per Williams J

REVENUE

'The word "revenue" is a word of somewhat indefinite import, but in its ordinary sense in relation to a business undertaking I think it connotes those incomings of the undertaking which are the products of or are incidental to the normal working of the undertaking.' *London, Midland & Scottish Rly Co v Anglo-Scottish Railways Assessment Authority, London & North-Eastern Rly Co v Anglo-Scottish Railways Assessment Authority* (1933) 150 LT 361 at 365, 367, HL, per Lord Tomlin

Australia 'I take "revenue" to be moneys which belong to the Crown, or moneys to which the Crown has a right, or which are due to the Crown.' *Stephens v Abrahams* (1902) 27 VLR 753 at 767, per Hodges J

Public revenue

In this Part [Part IV: Sch C] of this Act . . . 'public revenue', except where the context otherwise requires; includes the public revenue of any Government whatsoever and the revenue of any public authority or institution in any country outside the United Kingdom. (Income and Corporation Taxes Act 1988, s 45)

' "The public revenue" is an ancient term of art dating at least from the year 1816 when by the Consolidated Fund Act 1816 all the public revenues of Great Britain and Ireland "were consolidated into one Consolidated Fund of the United Kingdom". The expression "public revenue" then became the natural way of describing all the public revenues, and my attention has been directed to the Public Revenue and Consolidated Fund Charges Act 1854, whereby certain charges and payments therein referred to were described as "charged on or made payable out of the several branches of the public revenue". The expression "the public revenue" is also used by text-book writers to describe, and in my judgment signifies, the public revenues of the kingdom, and not the receipts or revenues of a local authority. Money which is payable by a local authority out of its funds cannot in my judgment be appropriately described as "payable out of the public revenue" [within the Income Tax Act 1952 (repealed)], and it can in my judgment make no difference that the local authority receives reimbursement of the money either in whole or in part out of the public revenue.' *Lush v Coles* [1967] 2 All ER 585 at 588, per Stamp J

REVEREND

'The word "reverend" is not a title of honour or of dignity. It is an epithet, an adjective used as a laudatory or complimentary epithet, a mark of respect and of reverence, as the name imports, but nothing more. It has been used for a considerable length of time, not by any means for a very great length of time by the clergy of the Church of England; for the time has been when that title was not commonly borne by them. It has been used in ancient times by persons who were not clergymen at all. It has been used for a considerable time, and it is used at the present day, in common parlance and in social intercourse, by ministers of denominations separate from the Church of England, by ministers of the Wesleyan Church, by ministers of bodies holding a congregational form of government, and by Presbyterian ministers. It is a title which in ordinary life is conceded to them, and which, as among such other, they use. Under those circumstances, it appears to their Lordships impossible to treat this word as a title of honour exclusively possessed by the clergy of the Church of England, so that the minister of another denomination claiming to place it upon a public inscription should be refused permission so to do.' *Keet v Smith* (1876) 1 PD 73 at 79, per cur.

REVERSION

An estate in *reversion* is the residue of an estate left in the grantor, to commence in possession after the determination of some particular estate granted out by him. Sir Edward Coke describes a reversion to be the returning of land to the grantor or his heirs after the grant is over. As, if there be a gift in tail, the reversion of the fee is, without any special reservation, vested in the donor by act of law: and so also the reversion, after an estate for life years, or at will, continues in the lessor. For the fee-simple of all lands must abide somewhere; and if he, who was before possessed of the whole, carves out of it any smaller estate, and grants it away, whatever is not so granted remains in him. A reversion is therfore never created by deed or writing, but arises from construction of law; a remainder can never be limited, unless by either deed or devise. But both are equally transferable, when actually vested, being both estates in *praesenti*, though taking effect *in futuro*. (2 Bl Com 175)

'The action is for trespass on the plaintiffs' lands, and the defendants justify the trespasses as having been committed in the exercise of a right of way over the land in question. . . . The question really turns upon the construction of s 8 of the Prescription Act [1832] 2 & 3 Wm 4, c 71. Under s 2, where a right of way has been uninterruptedly enjoyed in the manner described for the full period of forty years, the right is to be absolute and indefeasible, and in s 8 it is provided that where the land over which the way is claimed has been held under a term of life or years exceeding three, the enjoyment during the continuance of such term is to be excluded from the computation of the period of forty years' enjoyment in case the claim is resisted within three years after the expiration of the term "by any person entitled to any reversion expectant on the determination thereof". It is argued that the plaintiffs are not persons entitled to a reversion expectant on the determination of a term, inasmuch as the female plaintiff is entitled only to a remainder. . . . Now, the words here are, "term of life or term of years" and "reversion expectant upon the determination thereof" is the exact legal description of it. A reversion in law is not a remainder, the difference being that the reversion is what is left, and the remainder is that which is created by the grant after the existing possession.' *Symons v Leaker* (1885) 15 QBD 629 at 631, 632, per Field J

'Section 18 of the Landlord and Tenant Act 1927 . . . provided in sub-s(1) that damages for breach of a repairing covenant should not exceed the amount by which the value of the reversion was diminished through the breach. . . . I understand by "reversion" the property leased which the tenant has handed back.' *Portman v Latta* (1942) 86 Sol Jo 119 at 119, per Croom-Johnson J

REVERT

Australia [A testator bequeathed to his wife all his property in trust for his children, and at her death to 'revert' to the sole use of his children in equal proportions.] 'This word properly means "to come back to a previous state". But here there are only two states, during life, and after her death, so that revert must mean "change" only.' *Stevenson v McIntyre* (1879) 5 VLR 142 at 146, per Molesworth J

Australia 'The word "revert" may be variously considered, as by Lord Cairns LC and by Lord Hatherley in the same case [*O'Mahoney v Burdett* (1874) LR 7 HL 388]. "Revert" rather conveys the notion of coming back to the testator, and thence, when followed by such words as "to A B", passing through the testator as a new gift to A B. That was apparently Lord Hatherley's view.' *National Trustees, Executors & Agency Co of Australasia Ltd v O'Connor* (1919) 27 CLR 60 at 67, per Isaacs J

REVIEW

Australia 'In the Shorter Oxford English Dictionary the first meaning given of the word "review" is "the act of looking over something (again), with a view to correction or improvement", but the meaning in law is also given: "Revision of a sentence, etc, by some other court or authority". It is the latter meaning, suggesting an independent tribunal with power to alter the result, which is significant. . . . That the Shorter Oxford English Dictionary correctly defines the legal meaning of "review" is confirmed by the cases: see *Builders Licensing Board v Sperway Constructions (Syd) Pty Ltd* (1976) 135 CLR 616 at 620 citing *Philips v Commonwealth* (1964) 110 CLR 347 at 350, where the High Court chose the word "review" to describe a rehearing which led to the pronouncement anew of the rights of the parties. . . . It may be conceded that, in an appropriate context, the word "review" could have a quite amorphous meaning; but the word is here used in [telecommunication regulations under] an Act to describe a challenge, to be brought by "application", to administrative action, provision for which is to be made by regulations.' *Colpitts v Australian Telecommunications* (1986) 9 FCR 52 at 63, per Burchett J

REVISE

Australia [The rules of an incorporated club empowered the committee to 'revise' the list of members.] 'I conclude that "to revise the list" has not the limited and strict primary meaning of re-examine the list, but means to alter the list.' *Pettitt v South Australian Tattersall's Club* [1930] SASR 258 at 263, per Piper J

REVOCATION *See also* DEPENDENT RELATIVE REVOCATION; DESTRUCTION

'The word revocation has two meanings—the one, if I may use such an expression, in the probate sense, that is, where one instrument revokes another originally entitled to probate—the other I will call the chancery sense, that is, where a subsequent paper renders an earlier paper inoperative wholly or partly, though both papers may have received probate.' *Brenchley v Lynn* (1852) 2 Rob Eccl 441 at 462, per Dr Lushington

'I may summarise what I consider to be the law thus; If when a subject has been disposed of in a will and the same subject is again disposed of, either in a subsequent will or in a codicil, then if you can find, apart from the description of the subject, words expressly or impliedly effecting revocation, that revocation will stand, whatever the fate of the subsequent disposition; but if the only revocation is that which is to be gathered from the inconsistency of the subsequent disposition with the earlier one, then if the second disposition fails from any reason to be efficacious there will be no revocation.' *Ward v Van der Loeff, Burnyeat v Van der Loeff* [1924] AC 653 at 671, per Lord Dunedin

REVOLT

'The prisoners are charged with an act of piracy, either by exciting a revolt, or endeavouring to do so. The Act of Parliament contains these words, "make or endeavour to make a revolt", and you will have to say, whether the prisoners are brought within the meaning of those words. The statute [Piracy Act 1698], which is the 11 & 12 Will III, c 7, s 8, enacts, that, if any person shall lay violent hands on his commander, etc, or make or endeavour to make a revolt in the ship, he shall be deemed a pirate and a robber. This particular offence was not piracy at common law. Piracy at common law involved a charge of robbery; but this Act of Parliament, perhaps the better to preserve order and discipline on board a ship, makes it piracy to revolt, or to endeavour to excite a revolt. By revolt I understand something like rebellion or resistance to lawful authority. Persons who rebel against and resist the constituted authorities, if they are subjects, are said to be in a state of revolt; and if the crew of a ship combine together to resist the captain, especially if the object be to deprive him of his authority altogether, it will, in my opinion, amount to making a revolt. I think, upon the construction of this Act of Parliament, that the resistance of one person to the authority of the captain would not be a revolt. Revolt means something more than the disobedience of one man.' *R v M'Gregor* (1844) 1 Car & Kir 429 at 431, 432, per Lord Abinger CB

REWARD *See also* HIRE OR REWARD

'Reward', in relation to a flight includes any form of consideration received or to be received wholly or partly in connection with flight, irrespective of the person by whom or to whom the consideration has been or is to be given. (Civil Aviation Act 1982, s 105(1))

New Zealand 'The ordinary definition of reward is a return or recompense made to or received by a person for some service or merit: (2 Shorter Oxford English Dictionary (2nd edn) 1730). It seems to me that the offer of credit for an indefinite period subject to a maximum limit was here, and was so intended by the appellant to be, a recompense or benefit to the retailers if they exclusively purchased the appellant's motor spirits for the purposes of their trade. Further, s 18A(4) [of the Motor Spirits Distribution Act 1953 (repealed)] must be regarded as an interpretative clause and "reward" is expressed to include (inter alia) any concession or allowance, direct or indirect. This seems to me to be an enlargement of the ordinary meaning of the term "reward".' *Europa Oil (NZ) Ltd v Campbell* [1966] NZLR 602 at 603, per McGregor J

New Zealand 'Carriage may be for reward although no one is legally bound to pay for it.' *Transport Ministry v Keith Hay Ltd* [1974] 1 NZLR 103 at 106, per Cooke J

REX

'The word Rex comprehends all the attributes and dignities of the King. . . . The name King surmounts all additions. In the King's grants, his christian name with the word King, is sufficient.' *Anon* (1555) Jenk 209 at 209, per cur.

RIDE

'I remember a case where an action was brought against a magistrate who had seized a horse and cart, on the ground that the driver was riding on the shafts in the king's highway. It turned out, however, that the cart was standing still at the time he was on the shafts; and the court were of opinion that he could not be considered as riding on the shafts within the meaning of the Act of Parliament.' *Parton v Williams* (1820) 3 B & Ald 330 at 336, 337, per Bayley J

'The old established rule is that you must construe a statute grammatically except when such construction leads to a manifest absurdity. I think the result would be an absurdity if we were to treat the conviction of a furious rider as a *casus omissus*. The section [the Highway Act 1835, s 78] creates various offences, amongst them, "if any person riding on any horse or beast, or driving any sort of carriage shall ride or drive the same furiously so as to endanger the life or limb of any passenger". The appellant is found to have committed this offence, but he says although convicted of riding on horseback furiously he must go in peace and cannot be fined because a penalty is imposed only upon persons driving who commit any of these offences. The words immediately following those I have quoted relate to the whole of the previous part of the section,—"every person so offending in any of the cases aforesaid and being convicted of any such offence shall for every such offence forfeit any sum not exceeding £5, in case such driver shall not be the owner of such waggon, cart, or other carriage, and in case the offender be the owner of such waggon, cart, or other carriage then any sum not exceeding £10" [now level 1 on the standard scale]. I cannot think that the word "such" limits the application of penalties only to persons driving their own or other persons' carriages. The expression is somewhat elliptical, but I read the words "in case the offender be the owner of such waggon, cart, or other carriage" to be a mere proviso that such an offender shall suffer a heavier penalty. All other offenders, including drivers, who are not owners of carriages are to forfeit sums within the lower limit of £5, by force of the earlier part of the sentence. Another view which may be adopted is that the word "driver" is used in a wider sense than that generally given to it, and that it includes a person who rides on the back of a horse and may be said to conduct or drive it. I do not think any very great strain would be necessarily put upon the word if it were made to include every person in charge of a horse or carriage, and upon that interpretation also this conviction might be sustained.' *Williams v Evans* (1876) 41 JP 151 at 151, 152, DC, per Grove J

[The reference to level 1 on the standard scale was substituted by virtue of the Criminal Justice Act 1982, ss 38, 46.]

RIFLE *See* FIREARM

RIGHT

Enjoyment as of right

The enjoyment of a right claimed to exist under an alleged custom must be enjoyment 'as of right' in order that the enjoyment may support the claim; that is to say, all acts which it is alleged were committed under and by virtue of the custom in order to establish the custom must have been done without violence, without stealth or secrecy, and without leave or licence asked for and given, either expressly or impliedly from time to time. (12 Halsbury's Laws (4th edn) para 423)

'It is plain that the words "enjoyment as of right" cannot be confined to enjoyment under a strict legal right. . . . The "enjoyment as of right" must mean an enjoyment had, not secretly or by stealth, or by tacit sufferance, or by permission asked from time to time, on each occasion or even on many occasions of using it; but an enjoyment had openly, notoriously, without particular leave at a time, by a person claiming to use it without danger of being treated as a trespasser, as a matter of right, whether strictly legal by prescription and adverse user or by deed conferring the right, or, though not strictly legal, yet lawful to the extent of excusing a trespass, as by a consent or agreement in writing not under seal, in case of a plea for forty years, or by such writing or parol consent or agreement, contract or licence, in case of a plea for twenty years.' *Tickle v Brown* (1836) 4 Ad & El 369 at 382, per cur.

'Those who drafted the Prescription Act [1832] knew well what they were about when, in dealing with the consequences which have to follow from long-continued user, they used the words "as of right". . . . That right means a right to exercise the right claimed against the will of the person over whose property it is sought to be exercised. It does not and cannot mean a user enjoyed from time to time at the will and pleasure of the owner of the property over which the user is sought.' *Gardner v Hodgson's Kingston Brewery Co* [1903] AC 229 at 231, per Lord Halsbury LC

[In the above case a small annual payment was evidence that the right was enjoyed only as of grace.]

'There is only one way in which the public can enjoy a footway, and that is by walking over it. . . . Members of the public enjoy it "as of right", when, as Tomlin J said in *Hue v Whiteley* [[1929] 1 Ch 440 at 445], they use it: believing themselves to be exercising a public right to pass from one highway to another. This seems to me the simplest and truest interpretation of the three words "as of right", as applied to public rights of way. It is doubtless correct to say that negatively they import the absence of any of the three characteristics of compulsion, secrecy or licence.' *Jones v Bates* [1938] 2 All ER 237 at 245, CA, per Scott LJ

New Zealand 'I do not think a way on private property used with the consent of, or at least without objection from, the owner or owners by such members of the public as desire to use it as a passage from saleyards to a hotel and a main road can properly be described as open to or used by the public "as of right".' *Taylor v Seymour* (1915) 34 NZLR 919 at 921, per Denniston J; also reported 17 GLR 382 at 383.

Own right

'I am not prepared to dissent from the view taken by the Master of the Rolls in *Pulbrook v Richmond Consolidated Mining Company* [(1878) 9 Ch D 610]. If we had now to consider for the first time what the meaning of the phrase "holding shares in his own right" is, I am not sure that I should take the view which I understand the Master of the Rolls did take; but it is one thing to say that, and another thing to overrule the construction then put upon the phrase, and to overthrow the practice acknowledged and acted upon ever since that decision. The words in question have acquired . . . a conventional meaning which I for one am not prepared at present to disturb. I think that conventional meaning is this, that a person "holding shares in his own right" means holding in his own right as distinguished from holding in the right of somebody else. I do not think the test is beneficial interest, the test is being on or not being on the register as a member, i.e. with power to vote, and with those rights which are incidental to full membership. It means that a person shall hold shares in such a way that the company can safely deal with him in respect of his shares whatever his interest may be in the shares. I think that is the conventional meaning which that expression has acquired.' *Bainbridge v Smith* (1889) 41 Ch D 462 at 474, 475, CA, per Lindley LJ

[The Bills of Exchange Act 1882, s 61, provides that when the acceptor of a bill is or becomes the holder of it at or after its maturity, 'in his own right', the bill is discharged.] '"In his own right" must mean something more than "not in a representative capacity", as executor for instance. It could not possibly mean that if a thief stole the note from the holder and placed it in the possession of the maker, at or after maturity, the note should ipso facto be satisfied; and yet this would be the result if the words "in his own right" are to bear the limited meaning suggested. I think "in his own right" must mean having a right not subject to that of any one else but his own—good against all the world.' *Nash v De Freville* [1900] 2 QB 72 at 89, CA, per Collins LJ

RIGHT HEIRS

Australia 'I am clearly of the opinion that the words "right heirs" mean neither "children" nor "issue", but are words of purchase, and that the right heirs of the tenant for life take by purchase, and take as *personae designatae*.' *Re Goodwin* (1904) 4 SR(NSW) 682 at 695, per Darley CJ

Australia 'The word "heir" or "heirs" "right heir" or "right heirs" and other equivalent expressions employed as words of purchase in a devise or settlement of land prima facie signify the common law heir.' *Re McIlrath, Union Trustee Co of Australia v McIlrath* [1959] VR 720 at 729 per cur

RIGHT OF COMMON *See* COMMON

RIGHT OF PASSAGE *See* PASSAGE

RIGHT OF WAY

A right of way may exist over the land of another by virtue of a custom. Rights of way existing by custom are to be distinguished both from public rights of way, or highways, which arise either by statute or from the dedication of the soil by its owners to the use of the public, and from private rights of way which are easements properly so called. A customary right of way is one which may be enjoyed by any member of a fluctuating body or class of persons provided that body or class is itself certain. It is regarded as a private right of way in so much as it exists only for the benefit of a limited section of the public, and it cannot be used under a claim of right by any person who is not a member of that body or class in whose favour it exists. Rights of way of this kind may exist in favour of the inhabitants of a parish or a town, or probably of any other district sufficiently well defined to be the local area of any customary right. (12 Halsbury's Laws (4th edn) para 436)

A private right of way may be defined as a right to utilise the servient tenement as a means of access to or egress from the dominant tenement for some purpose connected with the enjoyment of the dominant tenement, according to the nature of that tenement. . . . The classification of private rights of way which was formerly regarded as of importance is now of no practical utility. There are no exact categories under one or other of which every private right of way must fall, as was formerly supposed. The nature and extent of the right depends upon all the circumstances of each particular case, and the former rigid classifications no longer suit the various kinds of ways as they are now regarded by our law. (14 Halsbury's Laws (4th edn) paras 144, 145)

'The question for you is, has the defendant proved a public right of footway over the plaintiff's close, by shewing a constant use and enjoyment on the part of the public, with the acquiescence of the parties interested? All the acts of user seem to have taken place during the occupation of tenants, and their submitting to them cannot bind the owner of the land without proof of his also being aware of it; but still, if you think that such acts of user went on for a great length of time, you may presume that the owner had been made aware of them. The user proved rather goes to support a carriage way than a footway; but, if you think the former has been established, you may find in favour of the latter, as a carriage way always includes a footway. The fact of no repairs having been ever known to be done to the road by the parish, is a circumstance from which you may infer that it is not a public road, inasmuch as the parish is bound to repair all public roads. A gate being kept across it is also a circumstance tending to shew that it is no public road, but not a conclusive one; for a road may have originally been granted to the public, reserving the right of keeping a gate across it to prevent cattle straying.' *Davies v Stephens* (1836) 7 C & P 570 at 571, per Lord Denman CJ

'There is, as it appears to me, a distinction between the user of a way which has been made by the owner of adjoining closes, and a right of way which, previously to such unity of possession, existed from one close to another, and which has become merged by the fact of the same person having become the owner of both properties. . . . It does not appear that there ever was any user of this road or way except by the owners of High Trees Farm, and that only for their owners' convenience. Such user does not, in my opinion, constitute a right of way.' *Thomson v Waterlow* (1868) LR 6 Eq 36 at 41, 43, per Lord Romilly MR

'A contract to grant a right of way with the concurrence of all necessary parties is a contract for the sale of real estate. It is a contract which cannot be performed if the contracting party has not the title to the real estate, or does not acquire a title. It is just as essential to the grant of a right of way as it is to the conveyance of an estate in fee simple, that the vendor should have a title to the land over which the right of way is to be given.' *Rowe v London School Board* (1887) 36 Ch D 619 at 623, 624, per Kekewich J

Way of necessity

A way of necessity is a right of way which the law implies in favour of a grantee of land over the land of the grantor, where there is no other way by which the grantee can get to the land so granted him, or over the land of the grantee where the land retained by the grantor is land-locked. Such a way cannot exist over the land of a stranger. (14 Halsbury's Laws (4th edn) para 153)

'A way of necessity is not a defined way. A way of necessity is a way which is the most convenient access to a land-locked tenement over other property belonging to the grantor; and it is quite clear that the grantor has a right himself to elect in which line, in which course, the way of necessity should go. Here, there is no case of election. The claim is to a way over this particular road, without any right of election at all on the part of the grantor. That of itself would be enough to shew it is not a way of necessity.' *Brown v Alabaster* (1887) 37 Ch D 490 at 500, per Kay J

'I venture to doubt the soundness of this ruling [in *Brown v Alabaster* (supra)] which, if accepted, would be fatal to the purchasers' claim here. It may hold good in a large majority of instances; but if there be only one possible mode of access—one line, that is, or one course—it would, I think, be going too far to say that this alone excludes a way of necessity when the other circumstances of the case are strong to establish it.' *Tichmarsh v Royston Water Co Ltd* (1899) 81 LT 673 at 675, per Kekewich J

Within traffic laws

Canada [For the purpose of traffic laws] 'What is the meaning and scope of this "right-of-way"? It means only that when the pathway of a car and that of a pedestrian cross each other, the car driver has the duty to avoid colliding with the pedestrian. But the duty is not absolute. By circumstances over which the driver may or may not have control, he may justifiably interrupt the pedestrian's free progress, and then it may be the duty of the pedestrian to avoid a collision, if he can. Even when a car has wrongfully interfered with the pedestrian's right-of-way and is moving across his path, or standing upon it, the pedestrian, although wrongfully interrupted, has no right to walk into or against the obstructing car. The "right-of-way" does not carry with it the privilege of exercising that right with one's eyes shut, or without some guard against interfering dangers.' *Rhind v Irvine* [1940] 2 WWR 333 at 335, 336, Man KB, per Dysart J

RIGHT TO LIGHT *See* LIGHT

RIOT *See also* AFFRAY; CIVIL COMMOTION; ROUT; UNLAWFUL ASSEMBLY

A riot is a tumultuous disturbance of the peace by three or more persons assembled together with an intent mutually to assist one another by force if necessary against anyone who opposes them in the execution of a common purpose and who execute or begin to execute that purpose in a violent manner so as to alarm at least one person of reasonable firmness and courage. (11 Halsbury's Laws (4th edn) para 861)

'Does not the word "riotously" in the indictment imply a force? I think it is a force; for how can there be a riotous assembly and breaking down pales without an act of force?' *R v Wind* (1728) 2 Sess Cas KB 13 at 16, per Raymond CJ

'The word "riotously" signifies the manner of doing the act, and does not relate to the intention of doing a thing without going farther.' Ibid at 17, per Reynolds J

'A riot is where three or more are unlawfully collected together to do an unlawful act; as, if they are removing a nuisance in a violent manner, and beat a man, that may constitute a riot. Persons may be riotously assembling together, yet, unless they do some act of violence, it would not go so far as to constitute, actually, a riot. But if they come armed, or meet in such a way as to overawe and terrify other persons, that, of itself, may, perhaps, under such circumstances, be an unlawful assembly. A rout [q.v.] or routous assembly is where they come for some unlawful purpose, intenting to do something in violence, but do not go to the full extent, or take any actual step for accomplishing their purpose.' *Redford v Birley* (1822) 3 Stark 76 at 102, per Holroyd J

'I shall state from the highest authority what in point of law constitutes a riot. It is a tumultuous disturbance of the peace, by three persons or more assembling together of their own authority with an intent mutually to assist one another against any who shall oppose them in the execution of some enterprise of a private nature, and afterwards actually executing the same in a violent and turbulent manner to the terror of the people whether the act intended were of itself lawful or unlawful. It is the effectuating it by force, and in an unlawful manner, that makes a riot. In every riot there must be circumstances either of actual force or violence, or at least of an apparent tendency thereto, such as are naturally apt to strike a terror into the people, as the shew of armour, threatening speeches, or turbulent gestures, for every such offence must be said to be done to the terror of the people; but it is not necessary in order to constitute this crime that personal violence should be committed. . . . But to return to the subject of riot; whenever three or more persons use force or violence, in the execution of any design where the law does not admit or allow the use of such force, all persons concerned therein are rioters. And the law is, that if one person encourages, promotes, or takes a part in a riot by signs, by gestures, or by wearing any badge or ensign of the rioters, he is himself a rioter. If he in any way encourages the rioters he is guilty.' *R v Forbes* (1823) 2 State Tr NS App 939 at 959, per Bushe CJ

'There can be no doubt that if persons create riotous disturbances, then they are guilty of riot, however lawful may be their enterprise.' *R v Graham & Burns* (1888) 4 TLR 212 at 226, per Charles J

'There are five necessary elements of a riot: (1) number of persons, three at least; (2) common purpose; (3) execution or inception of the common purpose; (4) an intent to help one another by force if necessary against any person who may oppose them in the execution of their common purpose; (5) force or violence not merely used in demolishing, but displayed in such a manner as to alarm at least one person of reasonable firmness and courage.' *Field v Metropolitan Police Receiver* [1907] 2 KB 853 at 860, DC, per cur.

'It appears that some one hundred and fifty or two hundred persons, some armed with crowbars and pickaxes, went to the house in question, which was empty . . . and took from it all the inflammable material they could lay their hands on. It was Peace night and they wanted to make a bonfire. Now, no doubt, that constituted a malicious injuring of the plaintiff's property and there was a common purpose to do an unlawful act. But it is said that that is not sufficient to constitute a riot, and the case of *Field v Receiver of Metropolitan Police* [supra] was referred to. . . . The Divisional Court [in that case] . . . laid down the following five elements as constituting a riot. First, that there should be not less than three persons concerned. That, of course, is satisfied here. Secondly, that there should be a common purpose. I think that is satisfied. Thirdly, execution of the common purpose. That is also satisfied. Fourthly, an intent on the part of the above persons to help one another, by force if necessary, against any person who may oppose them in the execution of the common purpose. I think again that that is satisfied. . . . Fifthly, there must be force or violence, not merely used in and about the common purpose, but displayed in such a manner as to alarm at least one person of reasonable firmness and courage. . . . I think that in the present case it is enough to say that these people went to this house with a common purpose in good humour, but armed with crowbars and pick-axes. They did not interfere with anybody because nobody interfered with them, but the man living next door said that although they did not interfere with him he did not dare to interpose, because he believed he would have been injured had he done so. It seems to me that there were all the elements of a riot present in this case.' *Ford v Metropolitan Police District Receiver* [1921] 2 KB 344 at 349–351, per Bailhache J

[A theft was committed by a number of persons with considerable violence and threats of greater violence. It was held that the insurers were not liable under a policy of insurance which excepted them from liability for loss by (inter alia) 'riots'.] 'That there was a riot here in the circumstances in which this money was taken I think it is perfectly impossible to doubt. Force was used, and it is clear that those who were conducting the operation felt that they had force behind them and that they could control the situation—and that amounted to a riot.' *London & Lancashire Fire Insurance Co Ltd v Bolands Ltd* [1924] AC 836 at 844, Lord Finlay

'The word "riot" is a term of art and, contrary to popular belief, a riot may involve no noise or disturbance of the neighbours though there must be some force or violence.' *R v Sharp* [1957] 1 All ER 577 at 579, CCA, per cur. (also reported [1957] 1 QB 522 at 560)

Canada 'The term "riot" involves a tumultuous disturbance of the peace by three or more persons . . .' *Reliable Distributors Ltd v Royal Insurance Co of Canada* [1984] 6 WWR 83 at 87, BCSC, per Wood J

Riotous or tumultuous *See also* UNLAWFUL ASSEMBLY

[The Riot (Damages) Act 1886, s 2(1), makes compensation payable where a house, shop, or building in any police district has been injured or destroyed, or the property therein has been injured, stolen, or destroyed, by persons 'riotously and tumultuously assembled together'; but in fixing the amount of compensation regard shall be had to the claimant's own conduct with regard to such 'riotous or tumultuous' assembly.] '"A house, shop or building in any police district has been injured or destroyed and property injured, stolen or destroyed." Has it been so injured or destroyed by persons riotously or tumultuously assembled together? It seems to me only necessary to state the question to answer it. Counsel for the appellants put a case that might possibly raise some difficulty—namely, where soldiers are on the march from one point to another and in passing through some town they create a riot. What a gross injustice it would, he said, be if the inhabitants of that police district had to pay. That case can be dealt with when it arises. It is not this case. These soldiers were not marching under military discipline; they collected from various parts of the camp, not under military discipline at all, but breaking military discipline in order that they might assemble tumultuously and riotously, and they did it. . . . I believe some of the rioters were dealt with as mutineers. It does not make them any the less persons riotously and tumultuously assembling together within the meaning of the Act.' *Pitchers v Surrey County Council* [1923] 2 KB 57 at 70, 71, per Lord Sterndale MR

'Was this disturbance a riot? That it would have been a riot if committed by persons other than soldiers there can on the findings of the learned judge be no doubt. The only question is whether it ceased to be a riot because it was committed by soldiers in an area which . . . was occupied by the military authorities for the time as a military camp. I think there is no foundation for the suggestion that it is not a riot. . . . I think there can be no doubt whatever that these persons could be indicted in a criminal court in this country for riot. . . . The possibility of a disturbance by three or four soldiers, which is enough to constitute a riot, must have been well within the contemplation of the legislature at the time they made this provision, and if in fact a riot took place within a camp or within barracks and damage is done, I see no reason why a person so damaged should not recover compensation.' Ibid at 74, 75, per Atkin LJ

'The disjunctive use of "riotous or tumultuous" can be explained by the fact that an assembly may well start by being tumultuous and only after a time become riotous, as well. Parliament, I think, may well have had in mind that if one joined a group which was a tumult, and so swelled it, one might be thought (for it is only a matter to be taken into account) to be encouraging or making more probable the conversion of what was merely a tumultuous assembly into an assembly that became riotous, and to that extent it might be a factor to be taken into account in considering how much compensation the plaintiffs should be entitled to receive. . . . In my judgment, the word "tumultuously" was added to "riotously" for the specific reason that it was intended to limit the liability of compensation to cases where the rioters were in such numbers and in such state of agitated commotion, and were generally so acting, that the forces of law and order should have been well aware of the threat which existed, and, if they had done their duty, should have taken steps to prevent the rioters from causing damage.' *Dwyer (J W) Ltd v Receiver for Metropolitan Police District* [1967] 2 All ER 1051 at 1054, 1055, per Lyell J

RIPARIAN TENEMENT

'The proposition that every piece of land in the same occupation which includes a portion of the river bank and therefore affords access to the river is a riparian tenement is, in my opinion, far too wide. In order to test it, let me take an extreme case: nobody in their senses would seriously suggest that the site of Paddington Station and Hotel is a riparian tenement, although it is connected with the river Thames by a strip of land many miles long, nor could it reasonably be suggested that the whole of a large estate of, say, 2,000 acres was a riparian tenement, because a small portion of it was bounded by a stream. Yet, if the argument submitted in the present case on behalf of the defendant company were carried to its logical conclusion, both Paddington Station and Hotel and the hypothetical estate would be riparian tenements. In the present case the site of the defendants' works is, in my opinion, too far away from the river bank to sustain the character of a riparian tenement, and I find as a fact that it is not such a tenement.' *Attwood v Llay Main Collieries Ltd* [1926] Ch 444 at 459, 460, per Lawrence J

RISK *See also* ALL RISKS

'The fallacy in the defendant's argument arises from the double meaning of the word risk. That means both the voyage commenced with necessary conditions to make the underwriters liable, and also the chance of loss during its performance.' *Bradford v Symondson* (1881) 7 QBD 456 at 464, CA, per Bramwell LJ

'I have to read the present policy as I think it would be reasonably understood by any merchant or insurance broker, and doing so I come to the conclusion that the words "all risks by land and water", etc must be read literally as meaning all risks whatsoever. I think they were intended to cover all losses by any accidental cause of any kind.' *Schloss Brothers v Stevens* (1906) 22 TLR 774 at 776, CA, per Walton J

At ship's risk

[Under a charterparty the shipowner undertook the transit of the cargo from the shore to the ship by the ship's boats and crew at ship's risk.] 'The expression "at ship's risk" cannot be strictly correct, because the ship has no risk, but I cannot doubt that the meaning is that the shipowner will take the goods and, when once they are in his possession, treat them as to risks as if they were on board the ship.' *Nottebohn v Richter* (1886) 18 QBD 63 at 65, CA, per Lord Esher MR

[The cargo of a ship, by the terms of a charterparty, was to be 'at ship's risk' when signed for until shipped on board: 'in all other respects' the act of God and perils of the sea were mutually excepted. Some cargo was lost after it was signed for and before it was loaded, and the defendants had deducted the amount from the freight.] 'The charterparty provides that the cargo when signed for is "to be at ship's risk" until shipped . . . when I find that the clause goes on to provide "but in all other respects the act of God, the perils of the seas . . . are always mutually excepted", then I am obliged to come to the conclusion that the earlier part of the clause does mean that the goods, when signed for, are "to be at ship's risk" until shipped in the sense that the ship is to be responsible for anything which may happen during the period between the time when the goods are signed for and when they are shipped.' *Dampskebsselskabet Skjoldborg & Hansen v Calder (Charles) & Co* (1911) 106 LT 263 at 264, per Bray J

Risk of collision

[The Thames By-laws 1898, art 46, provided that where two steam vessels or two steam launches proceeding in opposite directions, the one up and the other down the river, approached each other so as to involve the 'risk of collision', they should pass port side to port side.] 'So far as the question arises on the construction of art 46, that of course is law and not fact; and if risk of collision means, as I think it does, not that an accident presumably will happen, but that the circumstances are such as that precautions ought to be taken to avoid the possibility of danger, then I doubt whether the learned judge has properly applied the rule to the facts with that meaning in mind. Another point is this: that if risk of collision means what I think it means, it involves really what is a question of opinion rather than a question of fact. It is not a mere question of fact whether such circumstances have arisen as that precautions ought to be taken. It is a question of nautical opinion, the opinion of persons skilled in these matters, as to whether the facts are such that in their judgment that state of circumstances has arisen.' *The Guildhall* [1908] P 29 at 41, CA, per Buckley LJ; on appeal sub nom *Guildhall (Owners) v General Steam Navigation Co Ltd* [1908] AC 159

Risk of contamination

'Section 13 of the Food and Drugs Act 1955 [repealed; see now the Food Act 1984, s 13] makes it clear that all these regulations [Food Hygiene Regulations 1955 (revoked; see now the Food Hygiene (General) Regulations 1970)] are made for the purpose of protecting public health. Accordingly, the words "risk of contamination" in reg 8 . . . ought, in my view, to be construed as risk of such contamination as might be injurious to public health. I agree that the question is not whether it is a risk which has in fact damaged someone's health, since that would be locking the stable door after the horse had bolted, and the regulations have in mind . . . prevention rather than cure.' *Macfisheries (Wholesale & Retail) Ltd v Coventry Corpn* [1957] 3 All ER 299 at 303, per Donovan J

RITE *See also* CEREMONY

There is a legal distinction between a rite and a ceremony; a rite consists in services expressed in words; a ceremony in gestures or acts preceding, accompanying, or following the utterance of those words. (14 Halsbury's Laws (4th edn) para 953 *n*)

'No authority has been cited, nor do I believe any can be, to shew that preaching is part of ministering the Sacrament of the Lord's Supper, and, in my judgment, it is not. Neither can preaching be regarded as one of the "other rites of the Church" which are the words in the Advertisements of Queen Elizabeth and in Canon 58 of 1603–4. What the exact meaning of the word "rite" is has not been decided; but the usage of 300 years is enough to shew that, whatever the word means, preaching in a black gown, which seems to have been the ordinary clerical dress, cannot be an infringement of the regulations requiring the use of the surplice in "ministering the Sacraments and other rites of the Church".' *Re Robinson, Wright v Tugwell* [1897] 1 Ch 85 at 96, 97, CA, per cur.

RIVER *See also* ALTERATION (of river bank); BANK; BED (of river); NAVIGABLE RIVER; TIDAL RIVER

In this section [which deals with access to rivers, canals and woodlands] 'river' includes a stream and the tidal part of a river or stream. (Countryside Act 1969, s 16(9))

'The question turns on the construction of the Salmon Fishery Act 1865 [repealed; see now the Salmon and Freshwater Fisheries Act 1975], which is not so express in its terms as to be perfectly clear, though I do not think there can be much doubt in the matter. Section 1 explains the terms used, and "'river' shall include such portion of any stream or lake, with its tributaries, and such portion of any estuary, sea, or sea coast, as may from time to time be declared, in manner hereinafter provided, to belong to such river". Therefore "river" is used in its popular sense, and "river" may also be used so as to include the neighbouring sea coast.' *R v Grey* (1866) LR 1 QB 469 at 472, DC, per Blackburn J

[By s 41 of the Act of 1975 'river' includes a stream. The previous definition in the earlier Act has not been re-enacted.]

Australia 'The definition of "river" contained in reg 3 of the Fish and Fisheries Regulations (NT) (1986) is as follows: "'river' includes creek, stream, billabong, lake and any other watercourse or body of water that flows, directly or indirectly, into the sea, whether seasonally or consistently throughout the year".' *Errington v Jessop* (1982) 59 FLR 99 at 100, 101, per Forster J

ROAD

The term 'road' shall mean any carriageway being a public highway, and the carriageway of any bridge forming part of or leading to the same. (Tramways Act 1870, s 3)

'Road.' [in the sections dealing with the provision of parking places by parish or community councils] means a highway (including a public path) and any other road, lane, footway, square, court, alley or passage (whether a thoroughfare or not) to which the public has access, but does not include a road provided or to be provided in pursuance of a scheme made, or having effect as if made, under s 16 of the Highways Act 1980 (which relates to special roads). (Road Traffic Regulation Act 1984, s 60(4))

'Road' means any length of highway or of any other road to which the public has access, and includes bridges over which a road passes. (Road Traffic Regulation Act 1984, s 142(1))

[See also the Road Traffic Act 1988, s 192(1).]

'Although a car park is, in my opinion, a line of communication, I do not think that anybody in the ordinary acceptance of the word "road" would think of a car park as a road. If we were to hold that this was a road, a piece of waste land by the side of the road to which the public could resort for picnics would have also to be a road, and nobody would call that a road.' *Griffin v Squires* [1958] 3 All ER 468 at 471, per Streatfield J

Australia [The Local Government Act 1919–1986 (NSW), s 224(3), is concerned with cases where any 'road' has been left in the subdivision of private lands.] 'I think it is a mistake to construe the provision as applying only in respect of a road in the sense of a formed way, or even of a tract of land in a physical condition admitting of use for purposes of traffic. . . . The point to observe is that since a subdivision in the sense of the Act is not the result of physical actions, but is the result of transactions dividing up land in point of title, it is necessary to give the word "road" in s 224(3) a meaning such that a division of private land into parts by dealings affecting title may, without more, leave a "road".' *Permanent Trustee Co of New South Wales Ltd v Council of the Municipality of Campbelltown* (1960) 105 CLR 401 at 410, per Kitto J

New Zealand ['Road' is defined in the Transport Act 1962 as including 'any place to which the public have access, whether as of right or not'. The question arose whether a drive on private land leading to a building where a social function was being conducted was a road.] 'The essence of this appeal is the meaning of "any place to which the public have access, whether as of right or not". It is clear that those places to which the public—that is, the general public—have access, as of right or not, constitute "roads". The evidence in this case is clear and unequivocal that it is private land—there is no evidence that any member of the public is entitled to go on it or does go on it, whether or not by any right except for business or social purposes. It is not, in other words, a place to which the public in general resort as a matter of course, though not necessarily of right. It seems to me that this clearly brings it within the test laid down in the case of *Harrison v Hill* [1932 SC (J) 13] where that very distinction was clearly made. It is not enough that premises or a place may be physically open for the public to wander on. It must be that they are so open and so well known to be open that in fact the public do, either continually, or from time to time, without asking anybody's permission, enter upon them. If they do that, it is a place to which the public have access whether as of right or not, and it is a road.' *Police v Smith* [1976] 2 NZLR 412 at 413, SC, per Wilson J

New Zealand 'I am afraid I am unable to accept that any . . . limitations are warranted by the definition of "road" in s 2(1) of the Act [Transport Act 1962]. The words used are simple and in their natural meaning give rise to no apparent difficulty or absurdity. All that is needed is proof that the place in question is one to which the public have access whether as of right or unlawfully. Whether that is the case is a question of fact and the place is no less one to which the public have access because vehicles are not ordinarily found there or that it has none of the external appearances of a road in the ordinary sense of the word.' *McBreen v Ministry of Transport* [1985] 2 NZLR 495 at 499, per Somers J

In bill of lading

'In this case the plaintiffs sought to recover from the defendants the value of two boxes of gold dust, part of eleven received by them at Panama to be carried to the Bank of England. The defendants carried the goods from Panama across the Isthmus by land, shipped them at Chagres, and brought them by steam vessels to Southampton, and thence carried them by the London and South Western Railway to London. The bill of lading was given for them at Panama, acknowledging the receipt of eleven packages . . . to be carried to the Bank of England—"The act of God, the Queen's enemies, robbers, . . . dangers of the sea, roads, and rivers, of whatever nature or kind, excepted". All the packages arrived safely at Southampton and were placed on the rail road to be carried to London, but one of them was stolen secretly from the railway truck before their arrival there. . . . The question is, whether the theft committed on the South

Western Railway was, first, an act of robbers; secondly, was it a danger of roads within the true meaning of the bill of lading? and we are of opinion that it was neither. . . . We do not feel any difficulty as to the meaning of the term "dangers of the roads". We think the word "roads" may be explained by the context to mean maritime roads, in which vessels be at anchor; or suppose it means roads on land, the dangers of the roads are those which are immediately caused by roads, as the overturning of carriages in rough and precipitous places.' *De Rothschild v Royal Mail Steam Packet Co* (1852) 21 LJ Ex 273 at 275, 276, per Pollock CB

In by-law

[A by-law provided that it should be a reasonable excuse for a child not attending school if there was no elementary school within three miles, measured according to the nearest 'road' from the child's residence.] 'The Justices . . . have found that for the last seventeen years the routes coloured blue and green on the map have formed the approaches to the appellant's house, and that the distance by either of these routes to the nearest school is under three miles. It is true that these routes are not public highways, but that is immaterial, for in my opinion the word "road" in this by-law is not confined to highways or to roads constructed for the purpose of carrying every class of traffic. It does not mean a road of any particular class, but simply a route from the residence of a child to the nearest school.' *Hares v Curtin* [1913] 2 KB 328 at 331, DC, per Lord Alverstone CJ

In mine

'Road' does not include an unwalkable outlet. (Mines and Quarries Act 1954, s 182)

In Town Police Clauses Act

[The Town Police Clauses Act 1847, s 38, defines a hackney carriage as a wheeled carriage standing or plying for hire in any street within a prescribed distance, and s 3 defines the word 'street' as including (inter alia) any 'road'. A carriage stood and plied for hire on a piece of ground belonging to a railway company, situated between the public highway and the station. It was held that the carriage was not a hackney carriage because the piece of ground was not a 'road'.] 'A road as used in the Act of Parliament must manifestly mean a public road, a road which the public have a right to use for passage. This is so with all the places mentioned. They are all places of passage, and are all meant to be public. Otherwise, a square which was not public, that is, the inclosure of a square, would be within the Act. I cannot think this is so; and am of opinion that the road spoken of must be a road over which the public have rights; and when we consider that the effect of affirming this conviction would be to make the Act apply to one platform and not to the other; and that the railway company might frustrate its effect by putting up a fence between their private property and the highway, it seems impossible to hold that the case is within the statute.' *Curtis v Embery* (1872) LR 7 Exch 369 at 372, per Bramwell B

Private road

[The Settled Land Act 1882, s 25(viii) (repealed; see now the Settled Land Act 1925, s 83, Sch III) authorised the expenditure of capital money on various improvements, amongst them the making of 'private roads'.] 'With regard to the roads, the tenant for life has spent a considerable sum of money on making a new carriage drive and a new footpath which runs round the new gardens. With regard to the new carriage drive, it seems to me that that does come under the head of "private roads" in s 25, sub-s (viii) of the Act of 1882. It is a road and it is private. The mere fact that it leads from the lodge entrance through the garden to the hall does not make it any the less a road. But with regard to the footpath and what one may call the ordinary paths made in laying out a graden, I do not think they can, under any interpretation, come under the heading of "private roads".' *Re Windham's Settled Estate* [1912] 2 Ch 75 at 81, per Warrington J

ROAD-FERRY *See* FERRY

ROAD VEHICLE *See* VEHICLE

ROADSTEAD

'I can by no means agree to the position that has been laid down, that wherever a ship can find anchorage-ground, there is a road or roadstead within the meaning of this grant. . . . Every anchorage-ground is not a roadstead—a roadstead is a known general station for ships, *statio tutissima nautis*, notoriously used as such, and distinguished by the name, and not every spot where an anchor will find bottom and fix itself. The very expression of coming into a road shews, that by a road is meant something much beyond mere anchorage-ground on an open coast.' *The Rebeckah* (1799) 1 Ch Rob 227 at 232, per William Scott

ROBBERY

A person is guilty of robbery if he steals, and immediately before or at the time of doing so, and in order to do so, he uses force on any person or puts or seeks to put any person in fear of being then and there subjected to force. (Theft Act 1968, s 8(1))

'It is not a robbery if the person be not put in fear, as by assault and violence.' *Anon* (1562) 2 Dyer 224 b at 224 b, per cur.

'Robbery is a felonious taking from the person, putting him in fear, 3 Inst 68, and therefore all the indictments lay a taking *a personâ*, but then the law construes a taking in a man's presence to be taking from the person.' *R v Francis* (1735) Lee temp Hard 113 at 113, per Lord Hardwicke CJ

'The definition of robbery, as it is given by Sir William Staundforde, Sir Matthew Hale, and Mr Serjeant Hawkins, is "a felonious and violent taking of any money or goods from the person of another, putting him in fear"; from which it is evident, that to constitute the crime of robbery, three ingredients are necessary: First, a felonious intent, or *animus furandi*: Secondly, some degree of violence, or putting in fear: and Thirdly, a taking from the person of another.' *R v Donnally* (1779) 1 Leach 193 at 195, per cur.

'In order to constitute robbery, there must be either force or menaces. If several persons so surround another as to take away the power of resistance, this is force.' *R v Hughes & Wellings* (1825) 1 Lew CC 301 at 301, per Bayley J

'In this case the plaintiffs sought to recover from the defendants the value of two boxes of gold dust, part of eleven received by them at Panama, to be carried to the Bank of England. . . . The defendants pleaded the exceptions in the bill of lading in two different pleas: one stating that the loss was occasioned by robbers; the other, by dangers of the roads. . . . It was argued for the defendants, that the word "robbers" ought not to be construed in the technical sense given to the word "rob" by the English law writers, and by some of the English statutes, . . . where it means the felonious taking from the person or in the presence of another, of money or goods, against his will, by force, as putting him in fear, for it was not likely that robbery in that sense would occur, as the packages would not usually be in the personal presence of the defendants or their servants, still less on their persons; and other statutes were cited, where its meaning is much more comprehensive, and includes a taking without force; and besides, in construing such instrument, it was contended that the ordinary meaning of the words used must be followed. We think that position is correct, but we must also look at the circumstances under which the contract was made, and the peculiar subject to which it applied; and taking these into consideration, we cannot doubt that the meaning of the contract was, that the defendants were not to be liable for the loss of the gold dust, where it was taken by force by a *vis major*, which the defendants could not resist, but that they were to be liable where it was pilfered from them. . . . The nature of the transaction shews clearly, therefore, that the word "robbers" means, not "thieves", but robbers by force, to whom the term is more reasonably applied, though in common parlance it is often applied to every description of theft. We have no doubt, therefore, that in this bill of lading this is the proper meaning of the word "robbers"; and this being so, the loss in this case was not by robbers: and that plea, in which the loss is so stated, ought to be found for the plaintiffs.' *De Rothschild v Royal Mail Steam Packet Co* (1852) 7 Exch 734 at 741–743, per cur.

'Though there are statutory enactments in regard to the punishments for robbery and for robbery in its varied forms there is not, and there never has been, any statutory definition of robbery [but see now the definition in the Theft Act 1968, supra]. In Russell on Crime (12th edn, Vol 2, p 851) it is said that robbery is an aggravated species of larceny defined as "felonious taking of money or goods of any value from the person of another or in his presence, against his will, by violence, or putting him in fear" and certain cases and certain of the institutional writers are cited. . . . There is little doubt that the writings and the decisions in regard to robbery reveal a continuous and progressive process of definition. In earlier times the offence was probably limited to cases where there was actual violence to the person and a forcible taking from the person. Gradually the conceptions as to what constituted robbery were extended. Actual violence was not necessary. There might be a putting in fear of violence as by a threat of violence. That could be called constructive violence. So there might be a putting in fear by other means. There could be fear induced by the threat of a charge of an infamous crime. Furthermore, the taking need not have been literally a taking from the person. It could be a taking of goods (against the will) either from the person of another or in his presence.' *Smith v Desmond* [1965] 1 All ER 976 at 979, HL, per Lord Morris of Borth-y-Gest

'Robbery is an aggravated form of theft. It adds an offence against the person to the offence of stealing since the theft is carried out by using violence to the person from whose possession the goods are stolen or by putting him in fear of violence. . . . Where the sequence of events is not planned, but there is an assault which happens to be followed by a theft, there may be room for niceties of argument. Where, however, the whole sequence appears to be one planned transaction one must regard the events as a whole to see if together they amount to robbery. A thief cannot escape the charge of robbery by merely planning his crime in two stages, namely, first violently removing the owner or custodian of the property from its vicinity to a distance at which he cannot see or hear the actual stealing of the property and then, secondly, stealing the property. For that reason, I do not think that it is of any relevance how great the distance to which the custodian of the property is removed (if he is removed by force or fear for the purpose of the theft) whether he be forcibly transported or driven away or rendered insensible. It has no relevance whether in such circumstances he is aware of the actual act of stealing if his lack of awareness has been forcibly produced by the thieves for the purpose of the theft. Although in the old cases there constantly appears the limitation that it must be "in his presence" yet it was accepted that robbery may consist in the driving off of sheep or cattle. This shews that some latitude was given to the words "in his presence". For one would not expect a man who is robbed of his cattle to be standing within fifty yards of them. I do not find it possible to accept the limit of individual perception as the test. It would be absurd that the same acts would constitute a robbery in the case of a young victim in full possession of his faculties, who could perceive the driving off of his cattle, and yet would *not* constitute a robbery if the victim were an old man, who is too short-sighted and hard of hearing to perceive it, though he may know that it is going on. The only relevance of the victim's awareness is this. Is he aware of the theft or intended theft and is he compelled by force or fear to submit to it? Or has he been prevented by violence or threat from becoming aware of the theft and has that enabled the thieves to steal? If the answer to either of these questions is yes, the offence against the person and the theft are combined and the offence of robbery is constituted.' Ibid at 989, 992, per Lord Pearce

Highway robbery

'To constitute the crime of highway robbery, the force used must be either before, or at the time of the taking, and must be of such a nature, as to shew that it was intended to overpower the party robbed, and prevent his resisting and not merely to get possession of the property stolen.' *R v Gnosil* (1824) 1 C & P 304 at 304, per Garrow B

ROGUE AND VAGABOND

Every person pretending or professing to tell fortunes, or using any subtle craft, means, or device, by palmistry or otherwise, to deceive and impose on any of his Majesty's subjects; every person wandering abroad and lodging in any barn or outhouse, or in any deserted or unoccupied building, or in the open air, or under a tent, or in any cart or waggon, . . . and not giving a good account of himself or herself; . . . every person, wilfully, openly, lewdly, and obscenely exposing his person . . . , with intent to insult any female; every person wandering abroad, and endeavouring by the exposure of wounds or deformities to obtain or gather alms; every person going about as a gatherer or collector of alms, or endeavouring to procure charitable contributions of any nature or kind, under any false or fraudulent pretence; . . . every person being found in or upon any dwelling house, warehouse, coach-house, stable, or outhouse, or in any inclosed yard, garden, or area, for any unlawful purpose; . . . and every person apprehended as an idle and disorderly person, and violently resisting any constable, or other peace officer so apprehending him or her, and being subsequently convicted of the offence for which he or she shall have been so apprehended; shall be deemed a rogue and vagabond, within the true intent and meaning of this Act. (Vagrancy Act 1824, s 4, as amended by the Prevention of Crimes Act 1871, the Criminal Law Act 1967, the Theft Act 1968 and the Public Order Act 1986)

ROLLED-UP PLEA *See* FAIR COMMENT

ROLLER SKATING RINK

In this section [under which a local authority may make byelaws as to roller skating rinks] . . . 'roller skating rink' means any place which is for the time being used wholly or mainly for roller skating and for admission to which a charge is made. (Public Health Act 1961, s 75(2))

ROLLING STOCK

'Rolling stock' includes waggons, trucks, carriages of all kinds, and locomotive engines used on railways. (Railway Rolling Stock Protection Act 1872, s 2)

ROOM *See* LIVING ROOM

ROPE

'Rope' includes chain. (Mines and Quarries Act 1954, s 182)

ROUND

'The first thing to be considered is, what is the meaning of rule 23 of the rules and bye-laws for the regulation of the navigation of the River Thames? That rule is, "Steam vessels navigating against the tide shall, before rounding the following points" (including Blackwall Point) "ease their engines and wait until any other vessels rounding the point with the tide have passed clear". . . . I cannot bring myself to think that the judge of the Admiralty Court is right in the opinion which he seems to have expressed (I do not say whether he entertained it or not), that the meaning of the rule was that the vessels which were in the straight, or nearly straight reach, before they began to turn at all, were to wait there until all vessels that might be seen across the land coming in the opposite direction had passed. The effect of that, I think, would be very inconvenient, and would be to hamper the navigation very much, because all the vessels going down the river would remain gathered together in one spot until all that were coming up had passed by; and it is not the meaning which I should have attributed to the words. I think the fair meaning would be pretty nearly . . . that you begin to round when there is so much curving and rounding of the river that the vessels going down the river begin to turn round the land, they then begin to round, and when they have come so far down that the curving of the river ceases and they go straight, they then cease to round.' *Cayzer v Carron Co* (1884) 9 App Cas 873 at 876, 878, 879, per Lord Blackburn

ROUT *See also* CIVIL COMMOTION, RIOT

A rout is a disturbance of the peace by persons, assembled together with an intention to do anything which, if executed, will make them rioters, who move towards the execution of their common purpose but do not take any actual steps for accomplishing it. A rout constitutes a common law offence which is punishable by fine or imprisonment at the discretion of the court. (11 Halsbury's Laws (4th edn) para 860)

ROUTE *See also* HIGHWAY

'In their Lordships' opinion it is impossible to say that "route" and "highway" . . . are synonymous terms. . . . A "highway" is the physical track along which an omnibus runs, whilst a "route" appears to their Lordships to be an abstract conception of a line of travel between one terminus and another, and to be something distinct from the highway traversed.' *Kelani Valley Motor Transit Co Ltd v Colombo-Ranapura Omnibus Co Ltd* [1946] AC 338 at 345, 346, per cur.

[The Town Police Clauses Act 1847, s 21, empowers certain local authorities to make orders for the 'route' to be observed by all carts, carriages, horses and persons, etc.] 'It was the contention of counsel for the plaintiffs . . . that the corporation's order [making two roads into a one-way street] was outside the scope of the section since . . . the order did not amount to an order for "the route to be observed" by vehicles as that phrase in the section ought properly to be interpreted. The argument of counsel for the plaintiffs was to the effect that the word "route" in the section was used, and used exclusively, in the same sense as that in which it is used in phrases like "a bus route" or "a tram route" and signified the course or the street or streets used (or to be used) by vehicles in proceeding from one point to another, regardless of direction; that the phrase was not apt to mean or include merely a direction to be followed; and, more particularly, that an order "for the route to be observed" was never intended to mean or cover, and should not be taken to mean or cover, an order designed to give a particular street or streets a special quality or characteristic, namely, such that any vehicle in the street or streets, whatever might be its point of entry or its destination, must move in the street in one direction only. In support of the argument, it was said, and said with some force, that the idea of "one-way streets" as a means of dealing with day-to-day traffic congestion was something not dreamt of in 1847. . . . I have felt unable to give to the essential words "the route to be observed" so strict and confined a meaning. Although it is, no doubt, true that the words may have been primarily intended—particularly having regard to their context and to the immediately following words "by *all* carts, carriages, horses, *and persons*"—to provide for such expedients as the temporary closing of certain streets or parts of streets and the total diversion of all traffic, including pedestrian, it does not seem to me that the words according to their ordinary and proper usage can be interpreted so as to exclude the ordering of traffic in a thoroughfare to observe one "direction" or "route" therein only. The word "route" is, after all, defined in the Shorter Oxford English Dictionary as: "A way, road, or course; a certain direction taken in travelling from one place to another". . . . Moreover, if a total diversion of all traffic from a particular street or part of a street is comprehended, I do not see why, on the principle that the greater includes the less, there is not also included the diversion of that part only of the traffic that would otherwise go in one direction along it.' *Brownsea Haven Properties Ltd v Poole Corpn* [1958] 1 All ER 205 at 210, 211, CA, per Lord Evershed MR; also reported [1958] Ch 574 at 594, 595

Available route *See* AVAILABLE

ROYAL ASSENT

When a bill has been passed by both Houses of Parliament, or has been passed by the House of Commons under the Parliament Acts, and when a Measure has been approved by both Houses, it is ready to receive the royal assent. Royal assent has not been given by the Sovereign in person since 1854; it is now given either by notification or commission. In either case commissions, sometimes known as letters patent, are prepared in the Crown Office by the Clerk of the Crown in Chancery and are then submitted by the Lord Chancellor to the Sovereign to receive her approval and signature. As soon as the commission has been signed by the Sovereign, it is returned to the Lord Chancellor. The wafer Great Seal is then attached to it, and it is placed on the table of the House of Lords. The authority for the bills which are to receive the royal assent is supplied to the Crown Office by the Clerk of the Parliaments, who sends to the Clerk of the Crown a list of the bills which are to appear in the commission. Bills which are to receive the royal assent are arranged in the following order: public bills, provisional order confirmation bills and private bills. Private bills which have been certified as personal bills are put last of the private bills. Measures are placed after bills.

Royal assent is usually notified to each House of Parliament sitting separately by the Speaker of that House. Notification may take place at any convenient time during a sitting. The Speaker of each House uses the following words: 'I have to notify the House in accordance with the Royal Assent Act 1967 that the Queen has signified her royal assent to the following Acts [and Measures] . . .'.

Between 1854 and 1967 royal assent was invariably signified by Lords Commissioners appointed for the purpose in accordance with a procedure authorised by the Royal Assent by Commission Act 1541. While this procedure remains available for use at any time it has, since the Royal Assent Act 1967, been used only when royal assent has coincided with prorogation. (34 Halsbury's Laws (4th edn) paras 1301–1303)

ROYAL FORCES

Regular air force

'Regular air force' means all of Her Majesty's air forces other than the air force reserve and the Royal Auxiliary Air Force, and other than forces raised under the law of a colony, so however that an officer who is retired within the meaning of any order under s 2 of the Air

Force (Constitution) Act 1917, shall not be treated for the purposes of this Act as a member of the regular air force save in so far as is expressly provided by this Act. (Air Force Act 1955, s 223(1))

Regular forces

'Regular forces' means the Royal Navy, the Royal Marines, the regular army and the regular air force or any reserve or auxiliary force which has been called out on permanent service or which has been embodied. (Reserve Forces (Safeguard of Employment) Act 1985, s 20(1))

'Regular forces' means any of Her Majesty's military forces other than the army reserve, the Territorial Army and the Home Guard, and other than forces raised under the law of a colony, so however that an officer of any reserve of officers, or an officer who is retired within the meaning of any Royal Warrant, shall not be treated for the purposes of this Act as a member of the regular forces save in so far as is expressly provided by this Act. (Army Act 1955, s 225(1))

Reserve force

In this section 'reserve force' means any of the following bodies,
(a) the Army Reserve;
(b) the Territorial Army;
(c) the Air Force Reserve;
(d) the Royal Auxiliary Air Force;
(e) the Royal Naval Reserve including the Royal Fleet Reserve and the special class of the Royal Fleet Reserve; and
(f) the Royal Marines Reserve.
(Reserve Forces Act 1980, s 10(4))

Reserve or auxiliary force

'Reserve or auxiliary force' means the whole or any part of the Royal Naval Reserve (including the Royal Fleet Reserve), the Royal Marines Reserve, the Territorial Army, the Army Reserve, the Air Force Reserve, the Royal Air Force Volunteer Reserve, or the Royal Auxiliary Air Force. (Reserve Forces (Safeguard of Employment) Act 1985, s 20(1))

ROYAL RESIDENCE

'The distinction must be constantly kept in view between a palace and a royal residence. A palace may once have been the residence of the Sovereign, but may have ceased to be so, and yet may continue a palace, though without the privilege which the Sovereign's personal or virtual absence imparts to it. The possibility of residence cannot be the test of this privilege, otherwise it must attach for ever upon a palace once occupied as a royal residence, and which is capable of being fitted up for immediate use, although the Sovereign has never shewn the slightest intention of residing in it. The privilege of immunity from the intrusion of civil process into a palace is not one which attaches to the building itself, but belongs to it only as long as it is actually or virtually the residence of the Sovereign. By the term "virtually" I mean where the palace is occupied by the royal servants, and where it is kept up in such a condition that the Sovereign might, at any time, be able to take up her residence there without disturbing or interfering with the persons or the objects to which it might have been appropriated. This is entirely a question of fact, and one which must be determined by the actual state of things at the time the question arises. It is what may be called a fluctuating question, meaning by the expression one which depends upon changing facts and circumstances. A royal palace may be quitted in such a manner, and so thoroughly dismantled, as to indicate an entire relinquishment of it as a residence from the very day on which it is left. It may have been disused as the actual residence of the Sovereign for a great length of time, and yet have been kept up so as to be ready for immediate occupation if any future wish to reside in it should occur. In the supposed cases there would probably be no difficulty in holding that in the former case the residence of the Sovereign had altogether ceased for the time, and in the latter that there never had been a discontinuance of residence. I cannot think that the criterion is, whether the Sovereign has abandoned the intention of ever returning to a palace which has been discontinued to be the royal residence, because this could not be known at any time, and it would decide the question at once, as the privilege once annexed to the palace could never afterwards be proved to have been lost. It must be remembered that it is not the palace itself which is privileged; the actual or virtual residence of the Sovereign in it alone confers the privilege. So long as such residence continues it imparts the privilege; the moment the residence is not withdrawn merely but altogether abandoned, the privilege ceases.' *A-G v Dakin* (1870) LR 4 HL 338 at 370, 371, per Lord Chelmsford

ROYALTY

A royalty, in the sense in which the word is used in connection with mining leases, is a payment to the lessor proportionate to the amount of the demised mineral worked within a specified period. (31 Halsbury's Laws (4th edn) para 236)

'The reason given by the Commissioners for holding that the sum received was of a revenue nature is that it was paid and received "on account of royalties". A clue to the meaning which the Commissioners attached to the word "royalties" is to be found by referring to *Beare v Carter* [[1940] 2 KB 187] to which they refer. The word "royalty" in connection with a literary or dramatic work is defined in the Shorter Oxford English Dictionary as: "a payment made to an author, editor or composer for each copy of a book, piece of music, etc, or for the representation of a play". It is in the sense of so much per copy that the word "royalty" is used in the Copyright Act 1911 [repealed; see now the Copyright, Designs and Patents Act 1988] itself—see e.g. ss 3 and 19(3)—and this, in our opinion, is the ordinary meaning of the word. A sum paid "on account of royalties" would naturally mean one of two things—either (a) an advance against royalties to become payable in the future, or (b) a sum agreed upon as covering or as estimated to cover a defined or estimated number of copies, in the case of a book, or performances, in the case of a musical or dramatic work. In *Beare v Carter* the word "royalties" is used in the sense above mentioned. . . . The use of the word to signify a percentage of box office receipts is to be found, for example, in the agreement dealt with in *Messager v British Broadcasting Co Ltd* [[1929] AC 151].' *Nethersole v Withers* [1946] 1 All ER 711 at 713, CA, per Lord Greene MR

Australia 'The word "royalty" is most commonly used in connection with agreements for the use of patents or copyrights and in relation to minerals. In the case of patents a royalty is usually a fixed sum paid in respect of each article manufactured under a licence to manufacture a patented article. Similarly the publisher of a work may agree to pay the author royalties in respect of each copy of the work sold. . . . Use of the term "royalty" is not, however, limited to patents, copyrights and minerals. The term has been used to describe payments for removing furnace slag from land (*Shingler v P Williams & Sons* [(1933) 17 Tax Cas 574]) and to payment for flax cut (*Akers v Commissioner of Taxes (NZ)* [[1926] NZGLR 259]) the person paying the royalties becoming the owner of the slag or of the flax. . . . In Australia payments for the right to cut and take away timber are commonly described as royalties in the statutes of the States which relate to this matter. . . . The provisions in these statutes relate to the payments made to the Crown or to some public authority, but the word "royalties" is obviously not used in its primary sense of *jura regalia*, which exist independently of any agreement or dealing between the Crown and its subjects. The royalties referred to in the statutes are simply payments under licences to cut and remove timber. In my opinion the word "royalty" is properly used for the purpose of describing payments made by a person for the right to enter upon land for the purpose of cutting timber of which he becomes the owner, where those payments are made in relation to the quantity of timber cut or removed. Thus I am of opinion that the moneys received by [the appellant] were royalties and accordingly were part of his assessable income.' *McCauley v Federal Comr of Taxation* (1944) 69 CLR 235 at 240, 241, per Latham CJ

Australia [The Income Tax Assessment Act 1936–1986 (Cth), s 26(f), provided that the assessable income of a taxpayer should include any amount received as or by way of 'royalty'. The word 'royalty' is not defined by the Act. (See now s 6 for definition.)] 'Little assistance is to be obtained from the history of the word. For, as Lord Selborne said in *A-G of Ontario v Mercer* [[1885] 8 AC 767 at 778], "in its primary and natural sense 'royalties' is merely the English translation or equivalent of *regalitates, jura regalia, jura regia*". To say that the uses of the word are now figurative and represent analogies to the revenues which some *jura regalia* were seen to yield to the Crown does not help much to ascertain the scope of present usage. It may be noted, however, that the modern applications of the term seem to fall under two heads, namely the payments which the grantees of monopolies such as patents and copyrights receive under licences and payments which the owner of the soil obtains in respect of the taking of some special thing forming part of it or attached to it which he suffers to be taken. It is not fanciful to trace the extension of the word by analogy from the kind of payments which some of the *jura regia* enabled the Crown to obtain. We are not concerned with that application of the word which relates to payments to a patentee owner of a copyright or even of a secret process in respect of articles produced or sold, or books printed or sold or works performed or exhibited under his licence. What matters here is the parallel though distinct development of the meaning of the word which seems to arise from payments made to the Crown in respect of metals and the like won or taken from the soil. Similar payments to the owners of mines are regarded as royalties and by an extension not difficult to follow payments made in respect of the taking under the agreement or licence of the owner of the land of anything which may be considered part of or naturally attached to the soil such as coal, stone, sand, shells, oil and standing timber came to be spoken of as royalties. Warren and piscary and such rights are not heard of amongst us but conceivably there may be things made the subject of royalty which belong to ownership of land that cannot be considered actually to be part of the soil. In the case of monopolies and the like the essential idea seems to be payment for each thing produced or sold or each performance or exhibition in pursuance of the licence. In the same way in the case of things taken from the land the essential notion seems to be that the payment is made in respect of the taking of something which otherwise might be considered to belong to the owner of the land in virtue of his ownership. In other words it is inherent in the conception expressed by the word that the payments should be made in respect of the particular exercise of the right to take the substance and therefore should be calculated either in respect of the quantity or value taken or the occasions upon which the right is exercised.' *Stanton v Federal Comr of Taxation* [1956] St R Qd 421 at 431, per cur.

Canada 'A lease of oil lands ordinarily stipulates the duration of the same, the terms of its renewal, the period within which drilling must be commenced by the lessee, and the percentage of production, called a "gross royalty", to be received by the original landowner or lessor, when and after production begins. The anticipated production of an oil-well is divided by the lessee into one hundred units, each unit being 1 per cent of the production or yield, and, after making provision for any "gross royalties", these units of production, or some of them, are sold to the public, and are usually referred to as "royalties" or "net royalties". The term "royalty", I think, more properly applies to the interest in production reserved by the original lessor by way of rent for the right or privilege of taking oil or gas out of a designated tract of land, and such interest is not subject to deductions for operation, maintenance, and management charges, by the lessee, and it is for that reason that such an interest is usually referred to as "a gross royalty". The remaining interests in production which are sold to the public in order to obtain capital, only participate in production after operating and management expenses, and other charges, are deducted and hence are usually referred to as "net royalties".' *B & B Royalties v National Revenue Minister* [1940] Ex CR 90 at 92, per Maclean J

ROYALTY VALUE

In this section [which deals with writing-down allowances for mineral depletion] . . . 'royalty value', in relation to any output from a source, means the amount of the royalties that would be payable on that output if the person working the source were a lessee under a lease, for a term expiring immediately after that output was produced, granted to him at the date when the expenditure in question was incurred and providing for the payment of such royalties on output from the source as might reasonably have been expected to be provided for by such a lease, but reduced by the amount of any royalties actually payable in respect of that output. (Capital Allowances Act 1968, s 60(11))

RUBBISH *See also* REFUSE

In this section 'rubbish' means rubble, waste paper, crockery and metal, and any other kind of refuse (including organic matter), but does not include any material accumulated for, or in the course of, any business. (Public Health Act 1961, s 34)

'Do the words "rubbish resulting from the demolition", [in the Public Health Act 1936, s 58(1), (2) (repealed; see now the Building Act 1984, s 77(1)) on their true construction, include these machines [boilers, gas engines, dynamo, etc]? It is to be noted that nothing can come within these words unless it is rubbish, and is rubbish which results from the demolition. The Oxford English Dictionary defines "rubbish" as "Waste or refuse material, in early use especially such as results from the decay or repair of buildings; debris, litter, refuse". Other meanings are then added, but to my mind these are the meanings which the word covers in this section. I can see no reason for giving it a more extended meaning in the context in which it occurs, and I think the reason why the section makes no reference to the removal of anything other than rubbish is that it never occurred to the framers of the section that anyone would be so foolish, or so unreasonable, as to desire to leave articles of any value on the site, or to object to their removal. If this is the true construction of the section, I do not think that the machines in question were "rubbish". If, however, they can fairly be described as rubbish, I entirely fail to see how they can fairly be described as "rubbish resulting from the demolition". After any demolition of a structure, it is inevitable that there will be certain things upon the site, for example, fragments of plaster or stucco, pieces of brick and other pieces of matter which were part of the structure when it was standing, and which became rubbish as a result of its demolition. Such things would clearly be "rubbish resulting from the demolition". On the other hand, a house already damaged by fire, or by enemy action, may have in it such articles as a safe or a mantelpiece, each of them complete in itself but built into the wall of the house. If the house is subsequently demolished under the section, and the demolition is carried out with due care, the safe and mantelpiece will still be in existence in their original condition, but each of them will be a wholly separate article instead of being part of a house. This is a result of the demolition, but can it be said that the safe or the mantelpiece is "rubbish resulting from the demolition" within the section? I cannot so construe the section. There may be borderline cases in which it is difficult to say whether the article in question is rubbish, and, if so, whether it results from the demolition. For instance, opinions might differ on the question whether such things as blocks of stone or undamaged bricks, which formed part of the structure demolished, and could be used in other building operations, were "rubbish" within the section, though it would seem clear that, if they are rubbish, they resulted from the demolition. In the present case, while opinions may differ whether the machines in question are "rubbish", I cannot see in what sense they resulted from the demolition.' *McVittie v Bolton Corpn* [1945] KB 281 at 288, 289, CA, per Morton LJ

RULE OF THE ROAD

'The principle upon which all the rules for driving are found, is this: that the driver must bear to the left-hand. Hence the known rules, that, in meeting, you must go to the left, and that, when two carriages are coming the same way, the foremost should move to the left side. These rules of driving are of course not rules of law, but evidence of custom.' *Wayte v Carr* (1823) 1 LJOSKB 63 at 64, per cur.

RULES OF COURT

'Rules of Court' in relation to any court means rules made by the authority having power to make rules or orders regulating the practice and procedure of that court . . . and the power of the authority to make rules of court (as above defined) includes power to make such rules for the purpose of any Act which directs or authorises anything to be done by rules of court. (Interpretation Act 1978, Sch 1)

RUN AWAY

'Section 41(2) [of the Mines and Quarries Act 1954] in its material parts, provides: "In addition to the provision . . . of such safety devices . . . there shall be taken, as respects a person . . . at work at a place in a mine . . . such steps as are necessary to protect him from bodily injury in the event of a vehicle's running away while he is at work at that place." Those words, and in particular "in the event of a vehicle's running away", I would think postulate some undesigned movement of the vehicle. A consideration . . . brings me to the conclusion that the phrase "running away" means that the movement of the vehicle is an unintended movement, and, it follows, is an uncontrolled movement; it means that the vehicles are runaway vehicles.' *Jones v National Coal Board* [1965] 1 All ER 221 at 223, per Nield J

RUNNING DAYS

'The meaning of "running days" is, that the freighter shall not waste time in loading and unloading.' *Pringle v Mollett* (1840) 6 M & W 80 at 83, per Lord Abinger CB

'My opinion is, that the lay days under this charterparty commenced from the time the vessel entered the dock, as she had then arrived at the usual place of discharge. They certainly did not commence at the time of her entering the port, as that might be very extensive; for instance, Gravesend is part of the port of London: and with respect to the days, I think "days" and "running days" means the same thing, namely, consecutive days, unless there be some particular custom. If you wish to exclude any days from the computation they must be expressed.' *Brown v Johnson* (1842) Car & M 440 at 448, per Lord Abinger CB

[A charterparty provided for a certain number of 'running days' for unloading the ship.] 'Merchants and shipowners have invented this nautical term, about which there can be no dispute. They have invented the phrase "running days". It can be seen what it means. What is the run of the ship? How many days does it take a ship to run from the West Indies to England? that is the running of the ship. The run of a ship is a phrase well known. What are "running days"? It is a nautical phrase. "Running days" are those days, on which a ship in the ordinary course is running. . . . "Running days" therefore, mean the whole of every day when a ship is running. What is that? That is every day, day and night. There it is as plain as possible. They are the days, during which, if the ship were at sea, she would be running. That means every day. . . . Therefore, "running days" comprehend every day, including Sundays and holidays, and "running days" and "days" are the same thing.' *Nielsen v Wait* (1885) 16 QBD 67 at 72, per Lord Esher MR

'A dispute arose between shipowners and charterers on a charterparty . . . in regard to the carriage of a cargo of grain from the Argentine. . . . This dispute arises as to the amount of the dispatch money. That is because the shipowner says the time saved was fifteen days seven-and-a-half hours, and the charterers say that it was eighteen days three-and-a-half hours. That difference arises in this way. The clause runs: "The steamer shall be loaded at the rate of (so many tons per running day) Sundays and holidays excepted. . . . Time for loading shall commence to count twelve hours after written notice has been given to the master or agents." Now a "running day" prima facie, as was pointed out by Lord Esher in the case of *Nielsen v Wait* [supra] means a consecutive day, and, as he points out, a "running day" is a nautical phrase. "Running days" in those days were days on which the ship in the ordinary course was running. It therefore means the whole of every day when a ship is running and prima facie means every calendar day, including Sundays. In this case they are clearly not calendar days. They are periods of twenty-four hours, because time is to begin twelve hours after a certain notice, and from that moment when time begins you take your consecutive periods of twenty-four hours as "running days". But the contract provides that you shall not take all consecutive periods of twenty-four hours; because Sundays and holidays are to be excepted. Therefore, when you have started at any particular hour, counting your consecutive twenty-four hours, if a Sunday or a holiday intervenes, you cut that out and omit from the calculation the twenty-four hours of the Sunday or the holiday.' *Hain SS Co Ltd v Sociedad Anónima Comercial de Exportacion y Importación* (1934) 151 LT 305 at 306, 307, per MacKinnon J

RUNNING REPAIRS

[By the Factories Act 1937, s 151(1) (repealed; see now the Factories Act 1961, s 175(10)) the expression 'factory' included certain premises for the construction, reconstruction or repair of locomotives, vehicles, etc, not being premises where only 'running repairs' or minor adjustments were carried out.] 'Repairs which are the result of collision cannot, by any fair construction, be called running repairs. A private chauffeur commonly advertises that he is capable of doing running repairs, but that does not mean that he holds himself out as being capable of effecting repairs which are the result of a collision. A fair definition of running repairs would be repairs of defects which arise in a vehicle in the course of its ordinary running. Minor adjustments are the adjustments which have to be carried out from time to time, when nuts work loose, electrical equipment requires small corrections, small parts, or fuses and so forth. I think those are the sort of running repairs and minor adjustments envisaged by the Factories Act.' *Griffin v London Transport Executive* [1950] 1 All ER 716 at 717, per Lord Goddard CJ

RUST

[Among the excepted perils in a bill of lading was loss or damage arising from 'rust'.] 'With regard to the interpretation of the word "rust" in the exceptions, I think that it means rust inherent or arising in the article itself.' *Barrow v Williams & Co* (1890) 7 TLR 37 at 38, per Charles J

RYLANDS v FLETCHER RULE *See also* ESCAPE

'We think that the true rule of law is, that the person who for his own purposes brings on his lands and collects and keeps there anything likely to do mischief if it escapes, must keep it in at his peril, and, if he does not do so, is prima facie answerable for all the damage which is the natural consequence of its escape. He can excuse himself by shewing that the escape was owing to the plaintiff's default; or perhaps that the escape was the consequence of *vis major*, or the act of God; but as nothing of this sort exists here, it is unnecessary to inquire what excuse would be sufficient. The general rule, as above stated, seems on principle just. The person whose grass or corn is eaten down by the escaping cattle of his neighbour, or whose mine is flooded by the water from his neighbour's reservoir, or whose cellar is invaded by the filth of his neighbour's privy, or whose habitation is made unhealthy by the fumes and noisome vapours of his neighbour's alkali works, is damnified without any fault of his own; and it seems but reasonable and just that the neighbour, who has brought something on his own property which was not naturally there, harmless to others so long as it is confined to his own property, but which he knows to be mischievous if it gets on his neighbour's should be obliged to make good the damage which ensues if he does not succeed in confining it to his own property. But for his act in bringing it there no mischief could have accrued, and it seems but just that he should at his peril keep it there so that no mischief may accrue, or answer for the natural and anticipated consequences. And upon authority, this we think is established to be the law whether the things so brought be beasts, or water, or filth, or stenches.' *Fletcher v Rylands* (1866) LR 1 Ex 265 at 279, 280, per Blackburn J; affd sub nom *Rylands v Fletcher* (1868) LR 3 HL 330

S

SACRILEGE

[This is no longer a statutory offence in England. Under the Brawling Act 1553 it was an offence to break down or deface any altar, crucifix or cross in any church, churchyard or chapel. This Act was repealed by the Criminal Law Act 1967.

Under the Larceny Act 1916 it was the offence of sacrilege to break and enter any place of divine worship and to commit an arrestable offence therein, or similarly to break out of such a place after committing such an offence. This Act too has been repealed, by the Theft Act 1968, under which there is now no separate offence of sacrilege.]

SAFE

[The Factory and Workshop Act 1901, s 10(1) (repealed; see now the Factories Act 1961, s 14) enacted that all dangerous parts of machinery in a factory must either be securely fenced, or be in such position or of such construction as to be equally 'safe' to every person employed or working in the factory as it would be if it were securely fenced.] 'It is true—indeed, it is quite obvious—that the legislature is dealing with dangerous parts of machinery, but its object is not to leave them dangerous. On the contrary, its object is, under stringent penalties, to make them safe. And it is to be observed that the words are "securely fenced", not "somewhat securely fenced", and a little later the word employed is "safe", not "moderately safe". "Safe" means "actually safe", and this actual safety is to be procured (a) by secure fencing, or (b) by safe position, or (c) by safe construction.' *Sowter v Steel Barrel Co Ltd* (1935) 154 LT 85 at 87, DC, per Lord Hewart CJ

[By the terms of a charterparty, the charterers had the right to order a ship to load at two 'safe' berths or loading places.] 'There can, I think, be no question as to the meaning of the word "safe" when used in the contexts now being considered. A place will not be safe unless in the relevant period of time the particular ship can reach it, remain in it, and return from it, without, in the absence of some abnormal occurrence, being exposed to danger.' *Compania Naviera Maropan SA v Bowaters Lloyd Pulp & Paper Mills Ltd* [1955] 2 All ER 241 at 255, per Morris LJ; see also [1955] 2 QB 68

Australia 'By virtue of the contract of employment, an employer owes to his employees an implied contractual duty to have the premises, the appliances, and the system of working used for the purposes of the business in which they are employed as safe for them as the exercise of reasonable care can make them. . . . It is conceived that "safe" in this connection means safe from all dangers so far as protection from such dangers is reasonably practicable and to be expected having regard to the nature of the employment . . . but that the employee is taken to accept the risk of all dangers which are obvious and inherent in the employment, and against which protection is impracticable and unnecessary.' *Key v Comr for Railways* [1941] SR(NSW) 60 at 66, per Jordan CJ

SAFE MEANS OF ACCESS

[The Factories Act 1937, s 26(1) (repealed; see now the Factories Act 1961, s 29) provided that there should be 'safe means of access' to every place at which any person had at any time to work.] 'I have no doubt that this ladder was a "means of access" from the floor of the paint shop to the top of the booth. Was it a "safe" means of access? I agree . . . that "safe" is the converse of "dangerous". It means safe for all contingencies that may reasonably be foreseen, unlikely as well as likely, possible as well as probable.' *McCarthy v Coldair* [1951] 2 TLR 1226 at 1228, CA, per Denning LJ

[The question was the meaning of the words 'safe means of access' in the Building (Safety, Health and Welfare) Regulations 1948, reg 5 (revoked; see now the Construction (Working Places) Regulations 1966).] 'What . . . is the true meaning of the word "safe"? It cannot mean "absolutely safe" in the sense that it must be such means of access that no accident can occur. Indeed, that was not suggested by the plaintiff in this action. Mr Martin Jukes for the defendants, has referred me to two cases, unreported, where the words "reasonably safe" were expressly or implicitly used by the judge in giving his judgment. The first of those was the Scottish case . . . where Lord Mackintosh in two passages refers to the duty there as a duty to provide reasonably safe means of access. In *Collins & Bailiss v Western Aircraft*, heard on assize, Mr Justice Oliver, at the end of his judgment, said: "I think that the duckboard was a safe means of access. I cannot think that 'safe' means 'entirely safe'. It must mean 'safe for a man who is acting reasonably'. I hold that the duckboard was a safe means of access so far as reasonably practicable." It is urged upon me on behalf of the defendants that "safe" means "reasonably safe", bearing in mind the type of man who is going to use it, and it is pointed out, as is perfectly true, that steel erectors are used to heights far greater than the height in this case—that they climb, as one witness said, like cats about steelwork at great heights, often with no hand hold, and walk along the girders or sit astride of them and work their way along them regardless of the height at which the work is done. The evidence of the views of those people working in the business was all one way, that from a steel erector's point of view the job was being done in a perfectly safe way. As I have said, reference has been made to passages in decided cases where the duty is said to be one to provide reasonably safe means of access. For myself, with great deference. I get little help from adding the word "reasonably". It is not in the regulations. If it is used merely in contradistinction to "absolutely safe", I can understand it; but if it is intended to mean "safe for anybody acting reasonably", in the sense of taking full precautions for their own safety, I cannot agree with it. It seems to me that, as is well-known, these regulations are intended among other things, to safeguard workmen against acts which, owing to the frailty of human nature, continually occur of carelessness or inadvertance, and whatever epithet one applies here to the word "safe" I think it must mean a degree of safety which to some extent, at any rate, foresees the fact that human beings, being what they are, will from time to time, whether from tiredness, illness or any other reason, not exercise a very high degree of care for their own safety.' *Sheppey v Matthew T Shaw & Co Ltd* [1952] 1 TLR 1272 at 1274, per Parker J

'I agree that the word "safe" in the regulation [the Building (Safety, Health and Welfare) Regulations 1948, reg 5 (revoked; see supra)] cannot mean absolutely safe, since it is seldom, if ever, possible, let alone reasonably practicable, to attain absolute safety. I concede further that, in determining what is safe within the meaning of the regulation, some regard must be had to the capabilities of the person by whom the means of access is to be used. But the extent to which the statutory requirement of safety can be qualified on this account has its limits.' *Trent v W E Smith (Erectors) Ltd* [1957] 3 All ER 500 at 502, per Jenkins LJ

SAFE PORT

'The charterparty states that the ship shall forthwith proceed (wind and weather permitting) to a safe port in Chili (with leave to call at Valparaiso), or so near thereunto as she may safely get, and deliver the cargo, on freight being paid for the same. Carrisal Bajo was a port in Chili, safe so far as the ordinary incidents of ports are concerned, but a port into which the master could not take the ship without confiscation, unless he or the charterers could obtain a permit from the Government for the time being for her to enter. Neither the master nor the charterers were able to obtain such an order, and therefore the vessel, unless she ran the risk of confiscation, could not enter that port. The charterers named the port of Carrisal Bajo as the port to which the ship was to be taken. Was such a port safe within the meaning of the charterparty? Did it come within the terms of a safe port in Chili? I do not know what force can be given to the word "safe" when added to the word "port". As Carrisal Bajo was a port into which the vessel could not enter without confiscation, it seems to me clearly not within the term contemplated by the parties. It may be that the charterers were perfectly innocent on this occasion as regards any knowledge of the danger that might be incurred by the vessel, but at the same time here is a contract that she is to go into a safe port in Chili, which the charterers shall name. The contention on behalf of the charterers is, that when they named that port, and it was safe in the sense of navigation, they had done all that was necessary, and that, although the vessel could not go to Carrisal Bajo without being confiscated the moment she arrived there, that port was a safe port within the meaning of the charterparty. I think that would be an unreasonable construction.' *Ogden v Graham* (1861) 1 B & S 773 at 779, 780, per Wightman J

[A port is not a 'safe port' unless it is politically safe as well as physically safe.] 'In the absence of all authority, I think that, on the construction of this charterparty, the charterers are bound to name a port which, at the time they name it, is in such a condition that the master can safely take his ship into it; but, if a certain port be in such a state that, although the ship can readily enough, so far as natural causes are concerned, sail into it, yet, by reason of political or other causes, she cannot enter it without being confiscated by the Government of the place, that is not a safe port within the meaning of the charterparty.' Ibid at 780, per Blackburn J

[The above case was approved in *Kodros Shipping Corpn v Empresa Cubano de Fletes, The Evia* [1982] 3 All ER 350, HL]

'I am of opinion that the question in this case depends really upon the construction of the words used in the charterparty. The owner of the freight, that is the person chartering the ship, had a right to order the ship to proceed to any safe port to deliver there, or to go as near thereto as the ship could safely get, and there to "always lay and discharge afloat". Upon the construction of the charterparty, independent of the evidence that the experts gave as to what is meant by a safe port, I am of opinion that the plain meaning of the expression a safe port is a port in which the condition of safety was to be got which is referred to afterwards, that is to say, a port into which she could "safely get and always lay and discharge afloat".' *The Alhambra* (1881) 6 PD 68 at 71, CA, per James LJ

'The charterparty provides that the port to which the ship is ordered to go must be a safe port. The port to which she was in fact ordered to go was Gloucester, and that was in my opinion not a safe port for this ship, for she could not get safely there with her cargo. She drew far too much to get beyond Sharpness with all her cargo on board. . . . In *The Alhambra* [supra] . . . a master, whose ship was chartered to go to a safe port in the United Kingdom, was ordered to go to Lowestoft. It was found that the vessel drew too much water to allow of his getting into the harbour. He refused to lighten the ship in Lowestoft Roads as requested, and went on to Harwich, where he discharged. The Court held that he was justified in so doing on the ground that Lowestoft was not a safe port.' *Reynolds & Co v Tomlinson* [1896] 1 QB 586 at 589–591, DC, per Day J

'The *Saxon Queen* . . . was to be employed, according to the charterparty, in such lawful trades between such safe ports between Hamburg and Brest and the United Kingdom as the charterers should direct. . . . A port may be unsafe at the moment of any order and yet it may be really a safe port under different circumstances. You have to look undoubtedly to see whether it is a safe port at the moment, but I do not think it follows from that that the converse is true, that any port which is safe at the moment, but which is liable to become dangerous at short notice, is necessarily a safe port within the meaning of a charterparty like this.' *Johnston Brothers v Saxon Queen SS Co* (1913) 108 LT 564 at 565, per Rowlatt J

'By the . . . charterparty the vessel was "to call at Teneriffe for orders to discharge at a safe port in the United Kingdom, or so near thereto as she can safely get, always afloat, and deliver such cargo in accordance with the custom of the port for steamers". The *Peerless* duly called at Teneriffe and received orders to discharge at King's Lynn. She proceeded on her voyage, but her draught was such that it was impossible for her at any time, on any tide, to enter the dock at King's Lynn, and she accordingly lightened at a spot known as the Bar Flat Light Buoy, which is about eleven miles off down the Wash. She then went on and discharged the remainder of the cargo in the dock. . . . Was King's Lynn a safe port within the meaning of the charterparty? In my view it was not. A safe port means a port to which a vessel can get laden as she is and at which she can lay and discharge, always afloat.' *Hall Brothers SS Co Ltd v Paul (R & W) Ltd* (1914) 111 LT 811 at 811, 812, per Sankey J

'In my view the word "safe" when used in connection with the word "port" implies that the port must be both physically and politically safe, and I think that the action either of nature or man may render a port unsafe.' *Palace Shipping Co Ltd v Gans SS Line* [1916] 1 KB 138 at 141, per Sankey J

' "Safety" must always be a question of fact and a question of degree, and it involves a consideration of the character of the port itself, the mode of access to it, the dangers of the particular voyage, and the character of the particular vessel concerned.' *Dollar & Co v Blood holman & Co* (1920) 36 TLR 843 at 843 per McCardie J

'A port will not be safe unless, in the relevant period of time, the particular ship can reach it, use it and return from it without, in the absence of some abnormal occurrence, being exposed to danger which cannot be avoided by good navigation and seamanship.' *Leeds Shipping Co Ltd v Société Française Bunge, The Eastern City* [1958] 2 Lloyd's Rep 127 at 131, CA, per Sellers LJ

See, generally, 43 Halsbury's Laws (4th edn) para 647.

SAFEGUARD

New Zealand 'The test of an efficient safeguard is the same as the test which I have explained for the meaning of the word "securely"—that the purpose . . . is to protect both the careful and the inadvertent or inefficient employee from foreseeable—that is, reasonably foreseeable—risk of injury.' *Ralph v Henderson & Pollard Ltd* [1968] NZLR 760 at 761, per Richmond J

SAFELY

[A charterparty provided that a ship should proceed to Riga via Bolderas, or as near thereto as she could 'safely' get, and there load a full cargo of timber.] 'It is perfectly clear what the meaning of this contract is—that the vessel cannot be said to get safely to that place from which she cannot safely get away with a full cargo. The word "safely" means safely as a loaded vessel. Suppose the place to have been such that she could not have taken in with safety to herself a single deal, that would not have been a place whereto she could safely get; and, consequently, as she could not safely get away from within the bar with a full cargo, that was not such a place within the terms of this charterparty.' *Shield v Wilkins* (1850) 5 Exch 304, at 305, per Rolfe B

'I think it may be taken as settled law, that when, by the terms of a charterparty, a loaded ship is destined to a particular dock, or as near thereto as she may safely get, the first of these alternatives constitutes a primary obligation; and, in order to complete her voyage, the vessel must proceed to and into the dock named, unless it has become in some sense "impossible" to do so. It is only in the case of her entrance into the dock being barred by such "impossibility" that the owners can require the charterers to take delivery of her cargo to a place outside the dock. When a vessel in the course of her voyage is stopped, by an impediment occurring at a distance from the primary place of discharge, it has been decided that she cannot be held to have got "as near thereunto as she could safely get", and therefore cannot claim to have completed the voyage in terms of the second alternative.' *Dahl v Nelson, Donkin & Co* (1881) 6 App Cas 38 at 57, per Lord Watson

Safely and securely

[The plaintiff by his declaration alleged that at the request of the defendant he hired the hackney carriage of the defendant, who promised the plaintiff to carry and convey him and his luggage in the hackney carriage 'safely and securely' from Paddington Station to Basing Lane. The defendant contended that the words 'safely and securely' in the declaration imported a promise of absolutely safe conveyance.] 'Apart from authority, the words "safely and securely" are undoubtedly open to the observations addressed to us on the part of the defendant. But it seems to me that a long course of authorities has put a construction upon those words, limiting and restricting them to the particular promise or duty the breach of which is charged. . . . The precedents cited, as well antient as modern, shew that it has been usual, in all cases of bailment, to allege the undertaking to be "safely and securely" to keep or convey the goods, without regard to the particular degree of care resulting in law from the nature of the bailment; and, in the breach, to impute a neglect of that duty. I therefore think we are warranted in saying that the undertaking alleged here is an undertaking to carry the plaintiff and his luggage with that degree of safety and security which in law results from the relation of the parties.' *Ross v Hill* (1846) 2 CB 877 at 891, per Coltman J

Safely landed

Where the risk on goods or other moveables continues until they are 'safely landed', they must be landed in the customary manner and within a reasonable time after arrival at the port of discharge, and if they are not so landed the risk ceases. (Marine Insurance Act 1906, Sch 1(5))

[A policy of insurance on goods from London to Archangel insured them until they should be there discharged and 'safely landed'.] 'The question here is, whether these goods were seized and detained by the Russian government before they were discharged and safely landed. I see no evidence of such seizure or detention. The goods were landed according to the usual course of trade at the port of Archangel. This is all the underwriters undertook for. . . . If the goods are once landed in the usual course of business, the underwriters, on such a policy as the present, are not liable for any subsequent loss. It was meant to indemnify against marine not terrene perils.' *Brown v Carstairs* (1811) 3 Camp 161 at 162, 163, per Lord Ellenborough, CJ

SAFETY

New Zealand [The Transport Act 1962, s 30 (as substituted by the Transport Amendment Act 1988) authorises the court to disqualify an offender from holding a driver's licence if in the opinion of the court the offence relates to road 'safety'.] 'Anything that makes the roads less safe either actually or potentially relates to road safety. This is not to require the existence of danger or risk or the potentiality of it. It is the taking of steps to see that neither will arise. A "safe" incursion into an area where safety reasonably requires no such incursion is not justified. The precaution ought to be observed whether or not in the event anything in the nature of a risk might or did not arise. Therefore in each case the facts ought to be considered and weighed to see whether or not what happened did relate to a breach of what safety reasonably requires and not whether or not the act or omission could be safely indulged in on the particular occasion. It is safety which is being enforced and not simply that lack of safety on the occasion is being punished. The breadth of the concept of safety must not be restricted by necessarily excluding situations which, in the event, turn out to be safe.' *Auckland City Council v Tubman* [1973] 2 NZLR 133 at 135, per Henry J

Place of safety

'Place of safety' means a community home provided by a local authority or a controlled community home, any police station, or any hospital, surgery, or any other suitable place, the occupier of which is willing temporarily to receive a child or young person. (Children and Young Persons Act 1933, s 107(1), as amended by the Children and Young Persons Act 1969)

'Place of safety' means a community home provided by a local authority, a controlled community home, a police station, or any hospital, surgery or other suitable place whose occupier is willing temporarily to receive a child. (Foster Children Act 1980, s 22)

'Place of safety', in relation to a person who is not a child or young person, means any police station, prison or remand centre, or any hospital the managers of which are willing temporarily to receive him, and in relation to a child or young person has the same meaning as in the Children and Young Persons Act 1933. (Mental Health Act 1983, s 55(1))

SAFETY, MOORED IN *See* MOORING

SAFETY CARTRIDGE *See* CARTRIDGE

SAID

'The testator . . . makes the residuary bequest in the following words: "In trust for all and every the children and child of my body living at the time of the decease of my dear wife, equally to be divided between or amongst such children (if more than one) share and share alike as tenants in common" . . . "and if any such children or child shall be deceased before my dear wife" . . . "and such children or child shall leave issue of their, his or her body lawfully begotten, then the children or child of such my son or daughter shall be entitled to the portion of such my son and daughter who may be deceased before the deceased of my dear wife, upon their attaining the age of twenty-one years: provided always that, until the portions hereinbefore provided for any of the said children of my said sons or daughters" . . . "who may have died before their mother, shall become vested, it shall be lawful for my trustees or trustee for the time being to apply the interest and dividends of the portion or portions to which any such child or children may be entitled in expectancy, for the maintenance and education of such child or children." . . . I have looked through the will from the beginning, in order to see whether there had been any mention previously made of sons and daughters so as to account for the testator's making use of the words such and said, when he here speaks of them: and I find that there is no mention made of any son or daughter, except the son Edward. The consequence therefore is that no other meaning can be affixed to the words "said sons or daughters", but that meaning which is before expressed, namely, children or child; and, if that is the case, and you find that he had four sons and two daughters, and that one daughter was dead (though it is very true that these words may be taken to refer to a future daughter that might be born), yet it is obvious that the testator must have had more in his mind the remembrance of the child that had been born and died, than the anticipation of a future child to be born and be a daughter.' *Giles v Giles* (1837) 8 Sim 360 at 364, 365, per Shadwell V-C

[A testator bequeathed a sum of money to his executors upon trust for his four grandchildren, A, B, C, and D, children of his late son X, and the residue, upon the happening of certain contingencies, to his 'said' four grandchildren, and devised his real estate, subject to a life interest to A, charged and chargeable with the payment thereout of £1,500 apiece to B, C, and D, and he directed that if any of the children of his late son X, being a son or sons, should die under the age of twenty-one, or being a daughter or daughters, should die under that age without being or having married, then as well the original share or shares of the children so dying, as the share or shares which by virtue of that present proviso should have survived or accrued to him, her, or them, and in the said several last-mentioned sums of £1,500 apiece of and in the rest of his personal estate and effects thereinbefore bequeathed to them, should go, remain and be to the other or others of the 'said' children, and, if more than one, in equal shares as tenants in common.] 'The construction depends on the meaning to be given to the words "said children" occurring in two clauses of the will, whether they necessarily mean all the children mentioned in the former part of the will, i.e. the four children; or whether they mean the three children to whom the legacies were given when speaking of the legacies, and the four children when speaking of the residue. I think that the words are sufficiently clear and have reference to the four children.' *Dickason v Foster* (1861) 4 LT 628 at 630, CA, per Lord Westbury LC

'In following as you read it any document, when you come upon a word such as the "said" or "such" containing a reference to an earlier part of the document and to some person or thing already mentioned, you do not begin by re-reading the document from the beginning; you look backwards, and you take the nearest sensible antecedent as the appropriate antecedent for the word of reference. It was not denied that that was the natural and ordinary way of reading a document, whether it be a will or anything else, but there was some demur to its being called a rule of interpretation or a rule of law, and it was suggested that it might preferably be called a rule of grammar. I think the name does not matter. What matters is that we should follow, in construing the document, the ordinary natural sequence of thought which the testatrix followed in writing it and which the reader follows automatically as he reads it currently.' *Shepherd's Trustees v Shepherd* 1945 SC 60 at 65, per the Lord President (Normand)

SAIL

'It is clear that a warranty to sail, without the word *from*, is not complied with by the vessel's raising her anchor, getting under sail, and moving onwards, unless at the time of the performance of these acts she has every thing ready for the performance of the voyage, and such acts are done as the commencement of it, nothing remaining to be done afterwards.' *Lang v Anderdon* (1824) 3 B & C 495 at 499, per Abbott CJ

' "Sail" is certainly a very strong expression. In insurance cases it is almost a technical word: it means "start on the voyage".' *Barker v M'Andrew* (1865) 18 CBNS 759 at 774, per Byles J

'If a ship, being perfectly ready to start, having completed her loading and having all her crew on board, leaves the wharf where she has been loading, and proceeds ever so short a distance upon her voyage, and then some physical reason prevents her proceeding further, I think that the proper inference in such a case would generally be that she sailed within the meaning of the word "sail" as used in policies of marine insurance. But I agree that the sailing must be a sailing which is a commencement of the voyage; and, therefore, if a ship, when she leaves the wharf, is not ready for the voyage by reason of not having all her crew on board or some other reason, that may be evidence that she did not then commence her voyage.' *Sea Insurance Co v Blogg* [1898] 2 QB 398 at 401, CA, per Vaughan Williams LJ

'Final sailing' in charterparty

[A charterparty contained the words 'final sailing of the vessel from the port of loading'.] 'We all think, upon reading this charterparty, that something more is meant than the sailing of the vessel, because they use the term "the final sailing of the vessel", and we are not at liberty to reject that term, and we must consider that it is adopted with reference to the particular port of Cardiff where the vessel is to take on board her cargo, and that it means something more than merely having the clearances on board and being ready, and that it means her final departure from that port, and being out of the limits of that artificial port, and being at sea ready to proceed upon her voyage.' *Roelandts v Harrison* (1854) 23 LJ Ex 169 at 173, per Parke B

'The question is, whether this vessel had finally sailed from her last port in the United Kingdom. Final sailing, I apprehend, means getting clear of the port for the purpose of proceeding on the voyage. Here the vessel left the port of Cardiff with no intention of going back. If a vessel goes seven or eight miles from Penarth Dock she is out of port, for she is fairly at sea.' *Price v Livingstone* (1882) 9 QBD 679 at 682, CA, per Lindley LJ

'Sailed or about to sail'

[A clause in a contract described a ship as now 'sailed or about to sail'.] 'To say that a ship "has sailed" is obviously to represent that she has done so. To say that she is "about to sail" is to represent that she is loaded and just about to sail, or that, if she is not already loaded, she will be loaded in a day or two, and will then sail. Taken in connection with the first words "now sailed" it seems to me that the words "or about to sail" amount to a representation that the ship is just ready to sail.' *Bentsen v Taylor, Sons & Co* (2) [1893] 2 QB 274 at 278, per Lord Esher MR

SAILING VESSEL

[The Sea Regulations 1896 (revoked; see now the Merchant Shipping (Distress Signals and Prevention of Collisions) Regulations 1983, SI 1983/708) provided that every vessel under steam, whether under sail or not, should be considered a steam vessel, and, by art 26, that 'sailing vessels' under way should keep out of the way of 'sailing vessels' fishing with nets, or lines, or trawls.] 'The *Pitagaveney* is a Scotch screw steam drift-net fishing vessel of eighty-nine tons gross and twenty-nine tons net register. . . . Giving the best consideration I can to the rules and to the various decisions upon them, the conclusions at which I have arrived upon the various points raised are as follows. The *Pitagaveney* was a "steam vessel", and not a "sailing vessel" fishing with nets within the meaning of art 26. She was a "steam vessel under steam" notwithstanding that she might not, without fouling it, work her propeller by steam.' *The Pitagaveney* [1910] P 215 at 217, 218, 221, per Evans P

See, generally, 43 Halsbury's Laws (4th edn) para 937.

SALARY *See also* ANNUAL SALARY; REMUNERATION

[A testator by his will gave to each of his employees a sum equivalent to two months of their respective current 'salaries or wages' at his decease.] 'Although the words "salary or wages" may be used so as to express the whole of the remuneration payable for the services rendered or the work done, what I have to determine here is the sense in which this testator has used the words. The legacies have reference to a period of two months prior to the testator's death, and it may be difficult to ascertain the extra remuneration by commission during that time. On the whole, I think the testator contemplated something which could be easily calculated, namely a sum equivalent to salaries or wages as distinct from commission or from any profits earned as additional remuneration. The employees are therefore only entitled to two months' actual salary apart from commission.' *Re Smith, Phillips v Smith* [1915] WN 12 at 12, per Eve J

[The Liverpool City Council passed a resolution in September 1914 that any member of the corporation staff who should join the armed forces should (inter alia) be paid such sum as, with the pay and allowances received from the Government, would make up his full salary or wages.] 'It seems to me, and I think I am entitled, after the decision in the House of Lords in *Railway Clearing House v Druce* [(1926) 135 LT 417], to say that when the resolution speaks of a man's full salary or wages it is not speaking of something that somebody also in the same grade may be entitled to, but it is speaking of his full salary or wages, and I think *Druce's* case does establish that where the word used is "salary" or "pay" or "wages" you are entitled to interpret that language as meaning something to which a person is contractually entitled.' *Adams v Liverpool Corpn* (1927) 137 LT 396 at 397, CA, per Bankes LJ

Australia 'Where the engagement is for a period, is permanent or substantially permanent in character, and is for other than manual or relatively unskilled labour, the remuneration is generally called a salary.' *Federal Comr of Taxation v Thompson (J Walter) (Aus) Pty Ltd* (1944) 69 CLR 227 at 233, per Latham CJ

New Zealand 'The term "salary" is ordinarily used to signify the periodical remuneration paid to professional men, clerks, or persons whose duty it is to superintend, and who have in every case an appointment of some permanency. It is never ordinarily used as signifying the remuneration of manual labour, or of any labour when the element of permanency of employment is absent.' *Re Industrial Conciliation & Arbitration Act* 1908 (1909) 28 NZLR 933 at 940, CA, per cur.; also reported 11 GLR 750 at 754

Fee distinguished

'Whenever a sum of money has these four characteristics—first, that it is paid for services rendered; secondly, that it is paid under some contract or appointment; thirdly, that it is computed by time; and fourthly, that it is payable at a fixed time—I am inclined to think that it is a salary, and not the less so because it is liable to determination at the will of the payer, or that it is liable to deductions. I do not mean to say that that is a complete definition of "salary", or that it includes every kind of salary; but I think that, whenever these four circumstances concur, the payment is a salary.' *Re Shine, ex p Shine* [1892] 1 QB 522 at 531, CA, per Fry LJ

'Where . . . the unit of time is a short period of three hours actually worked, there must, I think, be added to Fry LJ's four characteristics [in *Re Shine, ex p Shine*, supra] a fifth, that the contract should provide for the recurrence of the sessions of work throughout the contract period, whether that period is fixed or indefinite. A salary is, as the dictionary definition states, a payment made for "regular work". If the contract provided only for a single session of three hours' work, the payment, though computed with reference to time, would not be described as "salary". It would be more aptly described as a "fee".' *Greater London Council v Minister of Social Security* [1971] 2 All ER 285 at 288, per MacKenna J

SALE

See also ADAPT FOR SALE; AUCTION; BAILMENT; CONDITIONAL SALE AGREEMENT; SALE OF GOODS; SELL

'Sale' includes barter and exchange and 'sell' and 'purchase' shall be construed accordingly. (Deer Act 1980, s 2(4))

'The action is brought upon a guarantee given by the defendants, whereby they undertook, that, if after any sale of certain property referred to, the purchase-money should not be sufficient to satisfy a sum of £1200 which had been advanced on mortgage, thereof, and all interest, costs, charges, and expenses which might be due in respect of the mortgage, they would immediately thereafter make good and pay to the plaintiff such deficiency. The question turns upon the construction of the word "sale" in that instrument. I am clearly of opinion, that, taken in conjunction with the rest of the document, it means a completed sale.' *Moor v Roberts* (1858) 3 CBNS 830 at 841, per Cockburn CJ

[The Stamp Act 1870, s 71 (repealed; see now the Stamp Act 1891, s 55), enacted that where the consideration, or any part of it, for a conveyance on 'sale' consisted of any stock or marketable security, such conveyance was to be charged with ad valorem duty in respect of the value of such stock or security.] 'I do not know what is necessary to constitute a sale, except a transfer of property from one person to another for money, or for the purposes of the Stamp Act, for stock or marketable securities.' *Foster (John) & Sons v Inland Revenue Comrs* [1894] 1 QB 516 at 528, CA, per Lindley LJ

'"Sale" undoubtedly in our law generally imports the exchange of some commodity or some article of property for money, and it will be found so defined in Mr Benjamin's book on Sale, and I think in Lord Blackburn's book also. That is obviously the general meaning of the word; and therefore, if that section [Stamp Act 1891, s 54, which defines a 'conveyance on sale'] stood alone and was not qualified by the subsequent section, it would be necessary to see whether the transaction in question was a sale for money. But then there comes s 55, which says (I omit words which are immaterial and do not help one for this purpose): "Where the consideration for a conveyance on sale consists of any stock", and by the definition that includes any shares, "the conveyance is to be charged with the ad valorem duty in respect of the value of the stock or security". That is a clear indication that there may be, within the meaning of these sections, a conveyance on sale when the transaction is not properly a sale in the ordinary understanding of the word, because it is not for money.' *Coats (J & P) Ltd v Inland Revenue Comrs* [1897] 1 QB 778 at 783, per Wills J; affd on appeal, [1897] 2 QB 423, CA

'A sale prima facie means a sale effectual in point of law, including the execution of a contract where the law requires a contract in writing.' *Rosenbaum v Belson* [1900] 2 Ch 267 at 269, per Buckly J

'I was referred to s 205(1)(xxiv) of the Law of Property Act 1925 which says: "'Sale' includes an extinguishment of manorial incidents, but in other respects means a sale properly so called." It is argued for the plaintiff that a sale means in the case of land, as in the case of goods, an exchange of land (or goods) for money. It is laid down quite clearly in the books which deal with sale of personal chattels that a sale or a contract of sale is an agreement to exchange goods for money, although it is possible that part of the consideration might be something other than money, as, for example, when a person buys a new car for an agreed price, part of which he pays in money and part of which he satisfies by means of surrendering another car. But the general principle of English law is that a sale means the exchanging of property for money. That applies—and I think both counsel agree with this—to a sale of land and a sale of chattels equally. The real problem is: Is it still a sale if no money passes, but one person says to another, as in this case: If you give me a piece of land, I will excuse you the debt which you owe me. Is the agreement one for the discharge of a debt conditional upon the handing over of land, or is it for the sale of land, i.e. for the transfer of land in return for money? In my view, it is a fine point, but, doing the best I can in the absence of authority, on the principles so far as I understand them, I come to the view that it is not properly so called a contract for the sale of land, because it is not really an agreement to hand over land in return for money. It is an agreement to extinguish an existing debt if land is transferred.' *Simpson v Connolly* [1953] 2 All ER 474 at 476, 477, per Finnemore J

'To say of a man who has had his property taken from him against his will and been awarded compensation in the settlement of which he has had no voice, to say of such a man that he has sold his property appears to me to be as far from the truth as to say of a man who has been deprived of his property without compensation that he has given it away. Alike in the ordinary use of language and in its legal concept, a sale connotes the mutual assent of two parties.' *Kirkness (Inspector of Taxes) v Hudson (John) & Co Ltd* [1955] 2 All ER 345 at 348, HL, per Viscount Simonds; see also [1955] AC 696

'The word is unambiguous and denotes a transfer of property in the chattel in question by one person to another for a price in money as the result of a contract express or implied. This is, in substance, the definition of sale given in Benjamin's Sale of Personal Property (2nd Edn, p 1), but for present purposes it is sufficient to emphasise that mutual assent is an essential element in the transaction. It is, no doubt, true that the contract or agreement to sell may precede the formal instrument or act of delivery under which the property passes, but to describe a transfer of property in a chattel which takes place without the consent of transferor and transferee as a sale would seem to me a misuse of language.' Ibid at 366, 367, per Lord Tucker

Australia 'The word "sale" is used in various metaphorical senses. When a man enters into a contract of employment he is sometimes said to "sell his labour", but really there is no transaction of sale; the contract is a contract of employment, not a contract of sale. Similarly, when a banker "deals in credit" he makes loan contracts and does not sell anything.' *Bank of New South Wales v Commonwealth* (1948) 76 CLR 1 at 234, per Latham CJ

Australia [The question was whether the supply of prints from a customer's own negatives was a 'sale'.] 'In addition to developing film for its owner positive prints or transparencies are made for him from the negative and delivered to him for a price to be paid by him. The prints or transparencies are then in my opinion properly said to be sold to him. They were made by the use of his negative certainly; but they are new chattels. The contract pursuant to which they were produced was I think "a contract for the sale of future goods by description" within the meaning of the Sale of Goods Act 1923–1986 (NSW), s 6. Presumably the property in them passed when they were made and were in a deliverable state and appropriated to the contract by their maker. However, we do not have to say when the property passed. The question propounded by the stated case is simply, is the supply of prints and transparencies in such circumstances a sale within the meaning of s 17 of the Sales Tax Assessment Act (No 1) 1930–1986 (Cth) [see now s 17(1)]? . . . In my opinion it is.' *Pacific Film Laboratories v FCT* (1970) 121 CLR 154 at 165, per Windeyer J

Australia 'It was common ground that a sale is constituted by an agreement wherein there is exchange of goods for money or other consideration. One begins with the proposition that the charging of money in exchange for liquor is prima facie inconsistent with a private party. Certain situations, however, do not normally point to a sale, even if money passes in exchange for liquor. Obviously, a private party at home where a person entertains his guests, ordinarily involves no sale. It is the intervention of money or like consideration that raises the possibility of a sale. But the mere intervention of money is not decisive of a sale although it tends to erode somewhat the ordinary inference to be drawn from a private party. Some situations that illustrate the intervention of money without necessarily taking one to a sale would be as follows: There might, for example, be a private function arranged for a particular purpose upon the basis that a group of persons agree to buy liquor and join in the covering of the expenses of the function. If the money passes hands to give effect to that arrangement, it is not a matter, it seems to me, which takes one into the area of sale. Again, where there is a private function for a particular purpose, those invited may be expressly or impliedly requested to make an equitable contribution to the total cost of the function. These examples are of course only examples and are not intended to be exhaustive. They illustrate a situation where, plainly, no legal contract for transfer of property or arrangement enforceable in law is intended.' *More v Lamb* [1981] VR 559 at 561 Supreme Court of Victoria, per Gobbo J

New Zealand 'In *Joel v Barlow* [(1903) 22 NZLR 900] it was held by His Honour the Chief Justice that, where a person enters into possession of a property under an agreement that he shall give up possession when the property is "sold", the term "sold" must be construed in its ordinary popular meaning, and means that the property is "sold" when a binding bargain is made by the vendor to convey the property and by the purchaser to accept a conveyance. In the present case I am of opinion that the agreement between Matthews Bros and the plaintiff was that the plaintiff was to retain possession up to the time the property was "sold" in the ordinary meaning of the term, and that his right to possession determined when he knew that a binding agreement of sale and of purchase was made between Matthews Bros and Corringham.' *Schollum v Barrip* [1916] NZLR 1050 at 1055, per Cooper J; also reported [1916] GLR 683 at 685.

New Zealand 'In general a "sale" in law means a sale for a price in money. Where goods are the subject-matter of a contract this definition of a "sale" was well settled before the passing of the Sale of Goods Act, and that Act defines a contract for the sale of goods as being one whereby the seller agrees to transfer the property in goods to the buyer for a money consideration called the "price". In Williams on Vendor and Purchaser [2nd Edn, Vol I, pp 226–227] the learned author refers to the meaning put by conveyancers upon the term "sale", He states: "It is important to note, with regard to the exercise of a trust for or power of sale, that the term 'sale' is, as a rule, taken in the strict sense of conveyance in consideration of a price paid in money. Trustees acting under a trust for or power of sale are not, therefore, at liberty to accept any other consideration for their conveyance than the payment for money." . . . I think that if a person agrees to sell his property at a particular price, and to take as payment in lieu of money an equivalent for a money consideration, and the transaction is carried out on that basis, it may well be called a "sale" of the property.' *Hamill & Co v Loughlin* [1917] NZLR 784 at 788–790, per Cooper J; also reported [1917] GLR 453 at 455

United States A 'sale' consists in the passing of title from the seller to the buyer for a price (Section 2–401). (Uniform Commercial Code 1978, s 2–106(1))

SALE MADE

New Zealand 'The expression "sale made", contrasted with "contract of sale entered into" has a clear connotation of finality, of a concluded, final and complete transaction. If, as counsel, in my view correctly and consistently with *Beetham v CIR*, agreed, that is not the date when legal title passes, it must I consider be the date when the vendor becomes finally bound, in the sense that the purchaser, provided of course that he is able and willing to perform his part of the bargain, is entitled to call for the legal estate, and to obtain a decree of specific performance if the vendor fails to deliver it. And this, in my opinion, cannot occur until the contract is unconditional' *Mills v Inland Revenue Comr* (1985) 8 TRNZ 404 at 406, per Hardie Boys J

SALE OF FOOD *See* SELL

SALE OF GOODS

Sale is the transfer, by mutual assent, of the ownership of a thing from one person to another for a money price. Where the consideration for the transfer consists of other goods or some other valuable consideration (not being money), the transaction is called exchange or barter, although in certain circumstances [e.g. where payment is made partly by money and partly by other goods] it may be treated as one of sale. (41 Halsbury's Laws (4th edn) para 601)

(1) A contract of sale of goods is a contract by which the seller transfers or agrees to transfer the property in goods to the buyer for a money consideration, called the price.

(2) There may be a contract of sale between one part owner and another.

(3) A contract of sale may be absolute or conditional.

(4) Where under a contract of sale the property in the goods is transferred from the seller to the buyer the contract is called a sale.

(5) Where under a contract of sale the transfer of the property in the goods is to take place at a future time or subject to some condition later to be fulfilled the contract is called an agreement to sell.

(6) An agreement to sell becomes a sale when the time elapses or the conditions are fulfilled subject to which the property in the goods is to be transferred.
(Sale of Goods Act 1979, s 1)

'Contract of sale' includes an agreement to sell as well as a sale. (Sale of Goods Act 1979, s 61(1))

'Sale' includes a bargain and sale as well as a sale and delivery. (Sale of Goods Act 1979, s 61(1))

United States 'Sale of goods' includes any agreement in the form of a bailment or lease of goods if the bailee or lessee agrees to pay as compensation for use a sum substantially equivalent to or in excess of the aggregate value of the goods involved and it is agreed that the bailee or lessee will become, or for no other or a nominal consideration has the option to become, the owner of the goods upon full compliance with his obligations under the agreement. (Uniform Consumer Credit Code 1969, s 2.105(4))

By description

Goods are sold by description where the buyer enters into the contract of sale in reliance on the description of the goods given by or on behalf of the seller. There may be a sale by description although the goods are specific, and goods may be sold by description although sold across the counter. (41 Halsbury's Laws (4th edn) para 688)

(1) Where there is a contract for the sale of goods by description, there is an implied condition that the goods will correspond with the description.

(2) If the sale is by sample as well as by description it is not sufficient that the bulk of the goods corresponds with the sample if the

goods do not also correspond with the description.

(3) A sale of goods is not prevented from being a sale by description by reason only that, being exposed for sale or hire, they are selected by the buyer.
(Sale of Goods Act 1979, s 13)

'The term "sale of goods by description" must apply in all cases where the purchaser has not seen the goods, but is relying on the description alone. It applies in a case like the present, where the buyer has never seen the article sold, but has bought by the description. In that case, by the Sale of Goods Act [1979], s 13, there is an implied condition that the goods shall correspond with the description, which is a different thing from a warranty.' *Varley v Whipp* [1900] 1 QB 513 at 516, per Channell J

By sample

A contract of sale is a contract for sale by sample where there is an express or implied term to that effect in the contract. The mere exhibition of a sample during the negotiation of the contract does not by itself constitute the contract one for sale by sample. (41 Halsbury's Laws (4th edn) para 697)

(1) A contract of sale is a contract for sale by sample where there is an express or implied term to that effect in the contract.

(2) In the case of a contract for sale by sample there is an implied condition—
(a) that the bulk will correspond with the sample in quality;
(b) that the buyer will have a reasonable opportunity of comparing the bulk with the sample;
(c) that the goods will be free from any defect, rendering them unmerchantable, which would not be apparent on reasonable examination of the sample.
(Sale of Goods Act 1979, s 15)

On sale or return

'What is the position of a man who has goods sent to him on sale or return? The owner sends the goods to him with the option of keeping them, and that option the person to whom they are sent may exercise in one of three ways—he may say that he accepts them at the price named, or he may sell them, or he may keep them so long that it would be unreasonable that he should afterwards return them to sender.' *Re Florence, ex p Wingfield* (1879) 40 LT 15 at 16, per Jessel MR

[The Sale of Goods Act 1979, s 18 (re-enacting s 18 of the Act of 1893) lays down (inter alia) the rule (r 4) for ascertaining the intention of the parties as to the time at which the property in the goods is to pass to the buyer, when goods are delivered to the buyer on 'sale or return'.]
'The case raises a nice point of law under s 18 of the Sale of Goods Act. The true view of the contract is that the defendants were only to have the benefit of the right of rejection contained in the contract on the terms that they should actually return the goods. Lord Coleridge observed in *Moss v Sweet* [(1851) 16 QB 493]:—"When goods are sold under a contract of sale or return they pass to the purchaser, subject to an option in him to return them within a reasonable time, and if he fails to exercise that option within a reasonable time the price of the goods may be recovered as upon an absolute sale." That is the true effect of the contract in the present case, and s 18 does not overrule that statement of the law, for it begins with the limitation "unless a different intention appears".' *Ornstein v Alexandra Furnishing Co* (1895) 12 TLR 128 at 128, per Collins J

'The position of a person who has received goods on sale or return is that he has the option of becoming the purchaser of them, and may become so in three different ways. He may pay the price, or he may retain the goods beyond a reasonable time for their return, or he may do an act inconsistent with his being other than a purchaser. The words of the Act [Sale of Goods Act 1979, s 18 (see supra)], are difficult to construe; but it seems to me that if the recipient of the goods retains them for an unreasonable time he does something inconsistent with the exercise of his option to return them, and thereby adopts the transaction. So if he does any other act inconsistent with their return, as if he sells them or pledges them, because if he pledges them he no longer has the free control over them so as to be in a position to return them. In all these cases he brings himself within the words of the section by adopting the transaction, and the property in the goods passes to him.' *Kirkham v Attenborough* [1897] 1 QB 201 at 204, per Lopes LJ

'"Sale or return" are technical words, but they are only so when used in reference to a buyer. . . . There are, of course, different sorts of dealings on sale or return. If a tradesman sends me goods on sale or return he intends that I shall buy them myself, not that I shall sell them either for him or for myself so as to enable me to pay him. But if he sends them to a retail dealer or the like on sale or return for the purpose of his selling them to other people as if they were his own goods, I think that the ordinary doctrine of holding out would apply.' *Weiner v Harris* [1910] 1 KB 285 at 294, 295, CA, per Farwell LJ

United States Unless otherwise agreed, if delivered goods may be returned by the buyer even though they conform to the contract, the transaction is . . . a 'sale or return' if the goods are delivered primarily for resale. (Uniform Commercial Code 1978, s 2–326(1))

SALEABLE UNDERWOODS

See UNDERWOODS

SALMON

'Salmon' includes any fish of the salmon species. (Sea Fish (Conservation) Act 1967, s 22(1))

'Salmon' means all fish of the salmon species and includes part of a salmon. (Salmon and Freshwater Fisheries Act 1975, s 41)

'Salmon' includes all migratory fish of the species Salmo salar and Salmo trutta commonly known as salmon and sea trout respectively. (Import of Live Fish (England and Wales) Act 1980, s 4)

SALVAGE

'Salvage' may signify either the service rendered by a salvor or the reward payable to him for his service.

'Salvage service' in the present sense means that service which saves or contributes to the ultimate safety of a vessel, her apparel, cargo, or wreck, or to the lives of persons belonging to a vessel when in danger at sea, or in tidal waters, or on the shore of the sea or tidal waters, provided that the service is rendered voluntarily and not in the performance of any legal or official duty or merely in the interests of self-preservation. The person who renders the service, that is the salvor, becomes entitled to remuneration known as 'salvage reward'.

Any services rendered in assisting, or in saving life from, or in saving the cargo or apparel of, an aircraft in, on or over the sea or any tidal water, or on or over the shores of the sea or any tidal water, are deemed to be salvage services in all cases in which they would have been salvage services if they had been rendered in relation to a vessel; and where salvage services are rendered by an aircraft to any property or person, the owner of the aircraft is entitled to the same reward for those services as he would have been entitled to if the aircraft had been a vessel. (43 Halsbury's Laws (4th edn) para 1027)

The expression 'salvage' includes all expenses, properly incurred by the salvor in the performance of the salvage services. (Merchant Shipping Act 1894, s 510)

'Salvage' means the preservation or recovery of vessels wrecked, stranded or in distress, or their cargo or apparel, or the recovery of any other property from the water and includes the removal of wrecks, and 'salvage operations' and 'salvage purposes' shall be construed accordingly. (Pensions (Mercantile Marine) Act 1942, s 10)

'The taking care of goods left by the tide upon the banks of a navigable river, communicating with the sea, may in a vulgar sense be said to be salvage; but it has none of the qualities of salvage, in respect of which the laws of all civilized nations, the laws of *Oleron*, and our own laws in particular, have provided that a recompence is due for the saving, and that our law has also provided that this recompence should be a lien upon the goods which have been saved.' *Nicholson v Chapman* (1793) 2 H Bl 254 at 257, per Eyre LCJ

'Salvage, in its simple character, is the service which those who recover property from loss or danger at sea, render to the owners, with the responsibility of making restitution, and with a lien for their reward. It is personal in its primary character, at least; and those who are so employed in the service are those whom the law considers as standing in the first degree of relation to the property and to the proprietors. This is necessary for the protection of the owner, who ought not to be burthened with artificial claims, and it is the natural mode of tracing effects to their efficient causes; for by whom can the service be said to be ostensibly performed, but by those who recover the thing, and on whom can the duty of restoring it lie, but on those who actually regain the possession? These are the principles on which the court proceeds in compelling restitution, when necessary, or in assigning a reward. It looks primarily to the actual salvor, and has uniformly rejected all claims founded on prerogative rights, as of the Lord High Admiral in former times, of lords of manors, of magistrates, and of flag officers, except with reference to assistance substantially and beneficially afforded.' *The Thetis* (1833) 3 Hagg Adm 14 at 48, 49, per Robinson J

'The right to salvage may arise out of an actual contract, but it does not necessarily do so. It is a legal liability arising out of the fact that property has been saved, that the owner of the property who has had the benefit of it shall make remuneration to those who have conferred the benefit upon him, notwithstanding that he has not entered into any contract on the subject.' *The Port Victor (Cargo Ex)* [1901] P 243 at 247, CA, per Jeune P

'When a ship, which is in risk, accepts a service, it is none the less an acceptance, and none the less a salvage service, because someone else whose orders the ship must obey has ordered the ship to accept or because the acceptance is under protest.' *The Kangaroo*, [1918] P 327 at 331, 332, per Hill J

'It is said . . . that even if no benefit was conferred, the services were rendered at request and the res was ultimately saved, and therefore the services must be rewarded. But as I understand the rule as to the rewarding of services rendered at request it is that if a salvor is employed to do a thing and does it, and the property is ultimately saved, he may claim a salvage award, although the thing he does has produced no good result.' *The Tarbert* [1921] P 372 at 376, 377, per Hill J

Canada 'In its popular sense the word "salvage" is used either as a verb, a noun or as in this case [regarding licensing of salvage yards] an adjective. As a verb, it means to rescue or save from wreckage, not necessarily marine wreckage; as a noun it means that which is so rescued or saved. It is used as an adjective in this by-law to qualify the "shop" or "yard" in which salvaged material is kept on hand either for storage or for sale or both.' *R v Greenspoon Bros Ltd* [1965] 2 OR 528 at 529, 530, Ont CA, per Roach JA

Salvage charges

'Salvage charges' means the charges recoverable under maritime law by a salvor independently of contract. They do not include the expenses of services in the nature of salvage rendered by the assured or his agents, or any person employed for hire by them, for the purpose of averting a peril insured against. Such expenses, where properly incurred, may be recovered as particular charges or as a general average loss, according to the circumstances under which they were incurred. (Marine Insurance Act 1906, s 65)

'Salvage charges may, no doubt, in some connection mean claims for volunteer salvage services. But it is quite common to use the words for the purpose of describing those expenses which come within the scope of suing and labouring expenditure; and several witnesses of great experience were called before me to say, and they did say very plainly, that used in a policy such as this they were always understood to bear that meaning.' *Western Assurance Co of Toronto v Poole* [1903] 1 KB 376 at 389, per Bigham J

See, generally, 25 Halsbury's Laws (4th edn) para 263.

SALVOR

'Salvor' means, in the case of salvage services rendered by the officers or crew or part of the crew of any ship belonging to Her Majesty, the person in command of that ship. (Merchant Shipping Act 1894, s 742)

'What is a salvor? A person who, without any particular relation to a ship, in distress, proffers useful service, and gives it as a volunteer adventurer, without any pre-existing covenant that connected him with the duty of employing himself for the preservation of that ship: not so the crew, whose stipulated duty it is (to be compensated by payment of wages) to protect that ship through all perils, and whose entire possible service for this purpose is pledged to that extent.' *The Portreath* [1923] P 155 at 159, per Hill J

SAME

Australia 'That the word "same" can have that meaning [i.e. 'similar' or 'analogous'] is clear not only from decided cases but also from the definition of the word as given in Webster's Dictionary.' *Kingsbury v Martin* (1901) 1 SR(NSW) 272 at 278, per Stephen J

'The word "same" has two meanings. One meaning no doubt is "identical", but the other meaning is "corresponding to", "similar to".' Ibid at 279, per Owen J

Australia 'There is no doubt that the word "same" is capable of meaning "similar" or "of like kind", as the authorities, as well as the dictionaries, show. According to the Oxford

English Dictionary, "same as" usually expresses identity of kind and "same that" absolute identity, except in contracted sentences where "same as" alone is found. The taxpayer accordingly submits that in s 80E(1)(c) [of the Income Tax Assessment Act 1936–1986 (Cth)] the phrase, in its natural and grammatical meaning, refers merely to identity of kind and that if it is not used in this sense it adds nothing to the words of the subsection, since if it had been intended to require absolute identity that could have been achieved by omitting the words "same" and "as", and by simply using the expression "the business it carried on". The meaning of the phrase "same as", like that of any other ambiguous expression, depends on the context in which it appears. In my opinion in the context of the section the words "same as" import identity and not merely similarity and this is so even though the legislature might have expressed the same meaning by a different form of words.' *Avondale Motors (Parts) Pty Ltd v Federal Taxation Comr* (1971) 124 CLR 97 at 105, per Gibbs J

Same offence

[The Criminal Evidence Act 1898, s 1(f)(iii) (amended by the Criminal Evidence Act 1979 by the substitution of the words 'in the same proceedings') permits a witness to be cross-examined as to character if he has given evidence against any other person charged with the 'same offence'.] 'If a house is burgled by a burglar and an hour later it is burgled by another burglar, it would be wrong in my opinion to hold that each burglar was charged with the same offence. In my view, for the offences charged to be regarded as the same for the purposes of s 1(f)(iii), they must be the same in all material respects including the time at which the offence is alleged to have been committed, and a distinct and separate offence similar in all material respects to an offence committed later, no matter how short the interval between the two, cannot properly be regarded as "the same offence".' *Comr of Police for the Metropolis v Hills* [1978] 2 All ER 1105 at 1109, HL, per Viscount Dilhorne

SAMPLE *See also* SALE OF GOODS

Australia 'I understand the word "sample", whether as a matter of law or as a matter of popular speech, to mean a part of a fluid or substance taken from some larger quantity because it is a fair representation of the whole.' *Lawry v West* (1947) 73 CLR 289 at 299, per Dixon J

SANCTION

[The Companies Act 1862, s 131 (repealed; cf now the Companies Act 1985, s 576) empowered a liquidator to 'sanction' share transfers after the commencement of a voluntary winding-up.] 'It was contended in argument that s 131 only contemplated the sanction of the liquidator in order to relieve him from difficulty in ascertaining who was to receive the surplus assets if any should be distributable. But notice to him would suffice for this purpose. Sanction by him means approval and implies a power of disapproval.' *Re National Bank of Wales* (1897) 66 LJ Ch 222 at 227, CA, per Lindley LJ

SANITARY CONVENIENCE

'Sanitary conveniences' includes urinals, water-closets, earth-closets, ash-pits, privies and any similar convenience. (Mines and Quarries Act 1954, s 182; cf Factories Act 1961, s 176)

'Sanitary convenience' means a closet, privy or urinal. (Food Act 1984, s 132(1))

SANITY

Australia 'It is I think undesirable to attempt to frame a definition of the word sanity or to give a complete account of when it may be said that the matter in dispute is the sanity of the patient. Assistance may be found in the definition of insanity and the discussion of that term in *Pope on Lunacy* [2nd ed, 1890, pp 1–3]. That definition of insanity is "a defect of reason consisting either in its total or partial absence or in its perturbation".' *Hare v Riley and AMP Society* [1974] VR 577 at 583, per Norris J

SATISFACTION *See also* ACCORD AND SATISFACTION

Satisfaction is the gift of a thing with the intention that it shall be taken either wholly or partly in extinguishment of some prior claim of the donee. Satisfaction may occur (1) when a covenant to settle property is followed by a gift by will or settlement in favour of the person entitled beneficially under the covenant; (2) when a testamentary disposition is followed during the testator's lifetime by a gift or settlement in favour of the devisee or legatee; and (3) when a legacy is given to a creditor.

Ademption is the term which correctly describes, among other matters, the second category of instances in which the doctrine of satisfaction applies; and where a testamentary gift is wholly or partly extinguished by a subsequent gift or disposition made by the testator in his lifetime the testamentary gift is said to be adeemed in whole or part. (16 Halsbury's Laws (4th edn) para 1407)

'The distinction between ademption and satisfaction lies in this: in ademption the former benefit is given by a will, which is a revocable instrument, and which the testator can alter as he pleases, and consequently when he gives benefits by a deed subsequently to the will, he may, either by express words, or by implication of law, substitute a second gift for the former, which he has the power of altering at his pleasure. Consequently, in this case the law uses the word *ademption*, because the bequest or devise contained in the will is thereby *adeemed*, that is, taken out of the will. But when a father, on the marriage of a child, enters into a covenant to settle either land or money, he is unable to adeem or alter that covenant, and if he give benefits by his will to the same objects, and states that this is to be in satisfaction of the covenant, he necessarily gives the objects of the covenants the right to elect whether they will take under the covenant, or whether they will take under the will. Therefore this distinction is manifest. In cases of satisfaction the persons intended to be benefited by the covenant, who, for shortness, may be called the objects of the covenant, and the persons intended to be benefited by the bequest or devise, in other words, the objects of the bequest, must be the same. In cases of ademption they may be, and frequently are, different.' *Chichester (Lord) v Coventry* (1867) LR 2 HL 71 at 90, 91, per Lord Romilly

'When a testator gives a direction that a particular thing shall be taken by any one in or towards satisfaction of his share, and the thing spoken of exists and belongs to the testator, I cannot doubt that, according to the plain and obvious meaning of the words, he gives that thing to the legatee, and this plain meaning is not controlled or varied, but is rather corroborated, by the addition of such words as 'and shall be brought into hotchpot and accounted for accordingly".' *Re Cosier, Humphreys v Jadsden* [1897] 1 Ch 325 at 333, CA, per Rigby LJ; affd sub nom *Wheeler v Humphreys* [1898] AC 506

SATISFIED

'I hold . . . that in this statute [Matrimonial Causes Act 1950 (repealed; see now the Matrimonial Causes Act 1973, under which the sole ground of divorce is 'breakdown of marriage')] the word "satisfied" does not mean "satisfied beyond reasonable doubt". The legislature is quite capable of putting in the words "beyond reasonable doubt" if it meant it. It did not do so. It simply said *on whom* the burden of proof rested, leaving it to the court itself to decide what standard of proof was required in order to be "satisfied".' *Blyth v Blyth* [1966] 1 All ER 524 at 536, HL, per Lord Denning

'The phrase used in s 4(2) of the Act of 1950 is simply "is satisfied", with no adverbial qualification. The formula "satisfied beyond reasonable doubt" has been a very familiar one for a great many years, and if that meaning had been intended the formula could and should have been used. The phrase "is satisfied" means, in my view simply "makes up its mind"; the court on the evidence comes to a conclusion which, in conjunction with other conclusions, will lead to the judicial decision. There is no need or justification for adding any adverbial qualification to "is satisfied".' Ibid at 541, per Lord Pearson

New Zealand [The Marriage Act 1955, s 15(2) provides (in relation to applications for leave to marry within the degrees of affinity) that the court must be 'satisfied' of certain circumstances.] 'The best opinion I can form is that on such an application as this the evidence must enable the judge to feel what Dixon J [in *Briginshaw v Briginshaw* (1938) 60 CLR 336] defined as "an actual persuasion". That means a mind not troubled by doubt or, to adapt the language used by Smith J in *Angland v Payne* [1944] NZLR 610 at 626, CA], "a mind which has reached a clear conclusion". If a formula has to be phrased, I would adopt one analogous to that expressed in *Edwards v Edwards* [[1947] SASR 258 at 271], and would say that the judge must be "satisfied with the preponderance of probability arrived at by due caution in the light of the seriousness of the charge".' *Re Woodcock* [1957] NZLR 960 at 963, 964, CA, per Finlay ACJ

New Zealand [Under the Licensing Act 1908 (NZ), s 194(1) (repealed) every person found on licensed premises at any time when such premises were required by the Act to be closed was liable to a fine, unless he 'satisfied' the court that he was an inmate, servant, lodger, bona fide traveller, etc.] 'The mind of the court must be "satisfied"—that is to say, it must arrive at the required affirmative conclusion—but the decision may rest on the reasonable probabilities of the case, which may satisfy the court that the fact was as alleged, even though some reasonable doubt may remain. If the probabilities, when considered in the light of all such doubts as may arise with regard to them, do in fact persuade the court, that is, in my opinion, all that is necessary in order to entitle the court to say that it is "satisfied" of the fact. This is what the statute expressly requires on the natural interpretation of its words, and the court is not at liberty to uphold the defence unless the evidence produces in its mind the required acceptance of the truth of the allegation.' *Robertson v Police* [1957] NZLR 1193 at 1195, per F B Adams J

SAVINGS

[An ante-nuptial settlement provided that all 'savings' arising from the income of the wife should be held by the trustees subject to her appointment.] 'Savings may well bear the sense of being something which, at the time of her [the wife's] death, is to be in the hands of the trustees. Two senses may be given to the word: either it will mean money which has been paid to her, and from her not wanting to spend it, handed back to the trustees; or money which has never passed from the hands of the trustees and is a "saving" in this sense, that she has never wanted it and never applied to the trustees for it, as she might have done. With respect to the fund in question, not having applied to the trustees for it, she must be assumed not to have required it and in this sense it may well be said to be savings.' *Re Rosenthall's Settlement* (1857) 6 WR 139 at 140, per Page Wood V-C

SAVINGS BANK *See* BANK—BANKING

SCAFFOLD

'By reg 3(2) [of the Building (Safety, Health and Welfare) Regulations 1948 (revoked; see now the Construction (Working Places) Regulations 1966)] a scaffold is defined as meaning a "temporary structure". I do not think, for my part, that the subsequent words, whereby a scaffold is made to include "any working platform, gangway, run, ladder or step-ladder", have the effect of extending the meaning of "scaffold" to anything other than temporary structures. It seems to me that their effect is merely to show that a temporary structure, in order to be a scaffold, may take one of several forms.' *Curran v William Neill & Son (St Helens) Ltd* [1961] 3 All ER 108 at 115, CA, per Willmer LJ

SCALES

In this section [penalty for using false scales, etc] 'scales' includes weights, measures and weighing or measuring machines or instruments. (Customs and Excise Management Act 1979, s 169(4))

SCHEME

Australia '"Scheme" is a vague and elastic word. Doubtless it connotes a plan or purpose which is coherent and has some unity of conception.' *Australian Consolidated Press, Ltd v Australian Newsprint Mills Holdings Ltd* (1960) 105 CLR 473 at 479, per Dixon CJ

Australia 'In *XCO Pty Ltd v FC of T* (1971) 124 CLR 343; 2 ATR 353, I expressed the effect of some of the authorities which have explained the meaning of the second limb of s 26(a) [Income Tax Assessment Act 1936 (now repealed) (Cth)] as follows (124 CLR at 349; 2 ATR at 357–359): "The word 'scheme' simply means plan, design or programme of action . . . It is not necessary, to constitute a scheme within s 26(a), that the action planned should involve a series of repetition of acts. The alternative 'carrying on or carrying out' appears to cover, on the one hand, the habitual pursuit of a course of conduct, and, on the other, the carrying into execution of a plan or venture which does not involve repetition or system." . . . The scheme must, however, be one which is carried out by the taxpayer himself or on his behalf; it is not enough that the taxpayer derives a receipt from somebody else who has obtained it by carrying out a scheme of profit-making . . . I do not understand the correctness of that statement to be disputed.' *Federal Comr of Taxation v Bidencope* (1978) 8 ATR 639 at 647, per Gibbs J

SCHOLARSHIP

'There are a number of points to be noticed in the language of the bequest which I will set out *seriatim*. (1) The trust is to last for ever, and accordingly is obnoxious to the rule against perpetuities unless it is a valid charitable trust; (2) the persons to benefit are the descendants, rich and poor, of three named individuals; (3) the pecuniary benefits are to take the form of "scholarships", a word which is not, I think, used in any technical sense but merely means that yearly sums are to be provided for the education of the beneficiaries, for so long as the trustees may think proper in each case.' *Re Compton, Powell v Compton* [1945] Ch 123 at 126, 127, CA, per Lord Greene MR

Australia 'Although, no doubt, particular scholarships are frequently established for special purposes—scholarships for research; travelling scholarships; scholarships entitling scholars to free places, at schools, etc, or at a University—I am not prepared to hold that according to common usages of speech or by reason of any authoritative definition, the word "scholarship" in the absence of expressed purposes or conditions attached to it, connotes anything more than the grant of an emolument, normally in a sum of money, to a scholar selected on merit upon some other rational criterion.' *Re Leitch, deceased* [1965] VR 204 at 206, per Adam J

Industrial scholarship

In this section 'industrial scholarships' means scholarships (however described) tenable by persons undertaking full-time courses of higher education provided by a university, college or other institution in the United Kingdom, being courses which appear to the Secretary of State [for Education and Science] or, as the case may be, the person awarding the scholarships to be relevant to a career in industry. (Education Act 1980, s 20(2))

SCHOOL *See also* EDUCATION

'School' includes a Sunday school or a Sabbath school. (Public Health Act 1936, s 343)

'School' means an institution for providing primary or secondary education or both primary and secondary education, being a school maintained by a local education authority, an independent school, or a special school not maintained by a local education authority, and the expression 'school' where used without qualification includes any such school or all such schools as the context may require. (Education Act 1944, s 114(1), as amended by the Education Act 1980, s 34(1))

[A testator by his will directed that the income of his residuary estate should be devoted to the upkeep of the King's Heath Baptist Chapel and 'school' and for the provision of prizes for the scholars of both sexes.] 'There was a suggestion . . . that as the evidence showed that the only school connected with the King's Heath Baptist Chapel was a Sunday-school, the prizes in which had hitherto been in the nature of books, that was not a school of the kind which the testator had in mind when he referred to "school" in his will. I see no reason why I should conclude that the testator did not intend to benefit the Sunday-school, which on the evidence was clearly carried on in connection with the King's Heath Baptist Chapel.' *Re Strickland's Will Trusts, National Guarantee & Suretyship Assocn Ltd v Maidment* [1936] 3 All ER 1027 at 1031, 1032, per Bennett J

[A restrictive covenant prohibited the carrying on of any trade or business except (inter alia) that of a 'school or seminary'.] 'The first question . . . resolves itself into one which can be shortly stated—namely, whether the carrying on of a school of music on the premises is the carrying on of any "trade or business whatsoever excepting only that of a school or seminary, surgeon, or apothecary", or, more shortly, is the carrying on of a school of music the carrying on of a school within the meaning of this covenant? . . . There is some ground for thinking that in a document of the first half of last century the word "seminary" may in the collocation of "school or seminary" have been intended to mean a school for girls, "school" being confined to school for boys. I do not, however, rest my decision on this, but rather upon what appears to be the ordinary meaning of the word, and on the fact that the addition of the word "school" or further words of description—"of music", "of dancing", or as the case may be—indicates that the ordinary meaning is in some way being qualified or extended. There appears to me to be no sufficient reason for admitting any such qualification or extension in what are after all words of exception, and therefore words which must be strictly construed.' *Lawrence v South County Freeholds Ltd* [1939] Ch 656 at 671, 672, per Simonds J

'It appears to me that a "school" is an institution which exists independently of the buildings in which it is housed for the time being. Many a school retained its identity during the war even though it was evacuated to a place two hundred miles away. A school is an institution with a character of its own. If an education authority is under a duty to "maintain" a school, it must see that it retains its fundamental character.' *Bradbury v London Borough of Enfield* [1967] 3 All ER 434 at 438, per Lord Denning MR

Australia 'It seems to me that a "school" is a place where people, whether young, adolescent or adult, assemble for the purpose of being instructed in some area of knowledge or of activity. Thus there are drama schools, ballet schools, technical schools, trade schools, agricultural schools and so on.' *Cromer Golf Club Ltd v Downs* [1972–73] ALR 1295 at 1299, per Barwick CJ

New Zealand 'A building is used as a school if subjects which ordinarily form part of the recognised curriculum of education are taught there. . . . A building is none the less a building used as a school from the mere fact that the teachers live in it.' *Christchurch Corpn v Boland* (1910) 30 NZLR 57 at 61, 62, per Williams J

Aided school

[One of the three categories of voluntary schools under the Education Act 1944, s 15. The governors of these schools continue to appoint their own teachers and to have the teachers' salaries and other maintenance charges paid by the local education authority. They also receive a grant which is now at the rate of 85 per cent from the Secretary of State for Education and Science towards the cost of any alteration which may be required to the school buildings. See the Education Act 1944, s 15.]

Army school

'Army school' means a school established for the purpose of affording education to children of non-commissioned officers and men of Her Majesty's regular land forces, and conducted under the authority of a Secretary of State, and a certificate of the Director General of Military Education or of the Inspector of Naval Schools, as the case may require, shall be sufficient evidence that a school is an army school within the meaning of this Act. (Army Schools Act 1891, s 1(2))

Church school

'Church school' means a voluntary school within the meaning of sub-s (2) of s 9 of the Education Act 1944, including the site and buildings thereof, which by virtue of a statute, or charter, or scheme order or other instrument made by virtue of a statute or other authority, or any trust, or usage, or repute, or any combination thereof is for the time being held on trust for the purposes of primary or secondary education as defined in the Education Acts 1944 to 1953 [now 1944 to 1989], together with instruction (either as part thereof or in addition thereto) in religious knowledge according to the faith and practice of the Church of England. (Diocesan Education Committees Measure 1955, s 3)

Comprehensive school

'Soon after its creation the council, as local education authority, put forward a scheme for bringing all the schools in the area under the comprehensive principle—"comprehensive" in this context not bearing its normal meaning in English, or the meaning it bore in the Education Act 1944, but its meaning in modern political jargon of a system which, in theory, lets everyone into any school without selection by aptitude or ability. Grammar schools, by contrast, allocate places by selection.' *Secretary of State for Education and Science v Metropolitan Borough of Tameside* [1976] 3 All ER 679 at 679, HL, per Lord Wilberforce

Controlled school

[One of the three categories of voluntary schools under the Education Act 1944, s 15. In the case of these schools all financial responsibility . . . is borne by the local education authority. With these financial obligations there also pass to the authority the powers of appointing and dismissing teachers, subject to the right of the governors to be consulted as to the appointment of the head teacher. See the Education Act 1944, s 15.]

County school

Primary and secondary schools maintained by a local education authority, not being nursery schools or special schools, shall, if established by a local education authority or by a former authority, be known as county schools. (Education Act 1944, s 9(2))

Independent school

'Independent school' means any school at which full-time education is provided for five or more pupils of compulsory school age (whether or not such education is also provided for pupils under or over that age) not being a school maintained by a local education authority or a special school not maintained by a local education authority. (Education Act 1944, s 114(1), as amended by the Education Act 1980, s 34(1))

Nursery school

Primary schools which are used mainly for the purpose of providing education for children who have attained the age of two years but have not attained the age of five years shall be known as nursery schools. (Education Act 1944, s 9(4))

Primary school

'Primary school' means . . . a school for providing primary education. (Education Act 1944, s 114(1))

Public school

'Public school' is nowhere defined in law. The name is commonly given to schools represented on the Headmaster's Conference, the Association of Governing Bodies of Public Schools or the Association of Governing Bodies of Girls' Public Schools, but the Public Schools Acts 1868 to 1873 apply to seven schools only, namely Eton, Winchester, Westminster, Charterhouse, Harrow, Rugby and Shrewsbury.

Other bodies associated with public schools are the Society of Headmasters of Independent Schools, the Association of Head Mistresses and the Direct Grant Joint Committee. (15 Halsbury's Laws (4th edn) para 296)

Registered school

'Registered school' means an independent school registered in the register of independent schools, whereof the registration is final. (Education Act 1944, s 114(1))

Secondary school

'Secondary school' means . . . a school for providing secondary education. (Education Act 1944, s 114(1))

Special agreement school

[One of the three categories of voluntary schools under the Education Act 1944, s 15. See that Act, s 15, Sch 3.]

Special school

Schools which are specially organised to make special educational provision for pupils with special educational needs and which are for the time being specially approved by the Secretary of State as special schools shall be known as special schools. (Education Act 1944, s 9(5), as substituted by the Education Act 1981, s 11)

[As to approval of special schools see s 12 of the Act of 1981.]

Voluntary school

Primary and secondary schools maintained by a local education authority, not being nursery schools or special schools, shall . . . if established otherwise than by such an authority [or by a former authority] be known as voluntary schools. (Education Act 1944, s 9(2))

Voluntary schools shall be of three categories, that is to say, controlled schools, aided schools and special agreement schools. (Ibid, s 15(1))

See, generally, 15 Halsbury's Laws (4th edn) paras 70 et seq.

SCHOOL BUILDINGS

'School buildings', in relation to any school, means any building or part of a building forming part of the school premises, except that it does not include any building or part of a building required only—

(a) as a caretaker's dwelling;
(b) for use in connection with playing fields;
(c) for affording facilities for enabling the Secretary of State to carry out the functions conferred on him by paragraph (a) of section 5(1) of the National Health Service Act 1977 and Schedule 1 to that Act; or
(d) for affording facilities for providing milk, meals or other refreshment for pupils in attendance at the school;

and in the principal Act [Education Act 1944] the said expression shall be deemed always to have had the meaning assigned to it by this section. (Education Act 1946, s 4(2), as amended by the National Health Service Act 1977)

SCHOOL LEAVING AGE *See* COMPULSORY SCHOOL AGE

SCIENTIFIC INSTITUTION

Australia 'Thc College [i.e. the Royal Australasian College of Surgeons] would not be the less a scientific institution because it does not confine its activities to abstract or speculative science, but applies scientific knowledge and practice to the advancement of surgery. . . . The activities of the College may benefit its fellows, but the facts related speak for themselves and establish that the College is doing "something higher and larger" than the mere promotion of professional interests. It is actively engaged in the promotion and advancement of science and in the advancement of surgical knowledge and practice. And that, I think, is the main and prevailing and the characteristic nature of the activities of the College.' *Royal Australasian College of Surgeons v Federal Comr of Taxation* (1943) 68 CLR 436 at 447, 449, per Starke J

SCIENTIFIC RESEARCH

'Scientific research' means research and development in any of the sciences (including the social sciences) or in technology. (Science and Technology Act 1965, s 6)

'Scientific research' means any activities in the fields of natural or applied science for the extension of knowledge;

'Scientific research expenditure' means expenditure incurred on scientific research;

references to expenditure incurred on scientific research do not include any expenditure incurred in the acquisition of rights in, or arising out of, scientific research, but, subject to that, include all expenditure incurred for the prosecution of, or the provision of facilities for the prosecution of, scientific research;

references to scientific research related to a trade or class of trades include—

(a) any scientific research which may lead to or facilitate an extension of that trade or, as the case may be, of trades of that class;
(b) any scientific research of a medical nature which has a special relation to the welfare of workers employed in that trade or, as the case may be, trades of that class.

(Capital Allowances Act 1968, s 94)

SCIRE FACIAS

Scire facias on the Crown side of the Queen's Bench Division is a proceeding for the purpose of rescinding or repealing Crown grants, charters and franchises. (11 Halsbury's Laws (4th edn) para 1578)

SCOTCH WHISKY *See* WHISKY

SCRIPT

In this Act 'script' in relation to a performance of a play, means the text of the play (whether expressed in words or in musical or other notation) together with any stage or other directions for its performance, whether contained in a single document or not. (Theatres Act 1968, s 9(2))

SCULPTURE

'Sculpture' includes any cast or model made for purposes of sculpture. (Copyright, Designs and Patents Act 1988, s 4)

'Having heard the evidence in this case, I am clearly of opinion that the productions in question come within the words "any subject being matter of invention in sculpture" of s 1 of [Stat (1814)] 54 Geo 3, c 56 [repealed; see now the Copyright, Designs and Patents Act 1988, s 4 (supra)], and that the plaintiffs are, therefore, entitled to protection in respect of them. . . . Further, having heard the description given by the gentleman from the Science and Art Department, which I am satisfied was a perfectly accurate one, I am clearly of opinion that such productions required ingenuity, artistic taste, judgment, and arrangement. The object of the artist was to produce as perfect a model as possible of certain natural fruits, and the process adopted by him was first to form in his mind a design, the reproductions of which would, he thought, be suitable for the purposes for which they were ultimately destined, viz as drawing models for the various art schools throughout the kingdom. Having, as I suppose, transferred the design to paper, he proceeded to supply himself with the necessary materials, such as fruit, leaves, and branches, with which he experimented until he was able to carry out his design, arranging each portion of the model in such a manner as to make it best answer the purposes for which it was intended. The carving which was needful in order to reproduce the fine lines, which the plaster cast would not alone have given back, having been supplied by artistic skill, and the various parts of the model having been modelled one by one, and put together again by the artist, and the finishing touches added, the model was then complete, and was sent to be moulded. The casts of the models thus made were then sent to the Science and Art Department for approval, and received the sanction of that department if they were considered proper productions for use in the various schools in the country, receiving the usual grant. As I have before said, the history of the mode in which these productions were made seems to me to establish clearly that they were such as were contemplated by this Act.' *Caproni v Alberti* (1891) 65 LT 785 at 786, per Mathew J

SEA *See also* AT SEA; HIGH SEAS; PERILS OF THE SEAS; UNITED KINGDOM WATERS

'The sea' includes any estuary or area of the sea; and references to the sea bed include any area submerged at high water or ordinary spring tides. (Protection of Wrecks Act 1973, s 3(1))

'Sea' includes any area submerged at mean high water springs, and also includes, so far as the tide flows at mean high water springs, an estuary or an arm of the sea and the waters of any channel, creek, bay or river. (Dumping at Sea Act 1974, s 12(1))

'That the public have a right to the free use of the sea for the purposes of navigation has been unchallenged law from the earliest times. It has frequently been enunciated in the form that the sea is a public highway, and that ships have the right *eundi, redeundi, et morandi* over every part of it, no matter to whom the soil lying thereunder may belong. This method of formulating the right is valuable inasmuch as the legal associations which the conception of a highway calls up are strikingly applicable. In some respects, perhaps, the public rights of user of the sea for navigation are from the nature of the case more extensive than in the analogous case of a highway. For instance, it is essential to navigation that there should be a free right of anchoring or otherwise securing in position the navigating vessel, and there is nothing strictly analogous to this in the case of a highway. But these and the like differences arise from differences in the circumstances of the case, and not from fundamental differences in the nature of the right. In both cases there is the free right of passage which cannot be limited otherwise than by Act of Parliament, or (in particular cases) by proof of immemorial user.' *Denaby and Cadeby Main Collieries Ltd v Anson* [1911] 1 KB 171 at 198, 199, per Fletcher Moulton LJ

High seas

'Without investigating the early history of the Admiralty jurisdiction in civil cases, it is sufficient to start from the doctrine well settled in the time of Blackstone, namely: 1 That the Court of Admiralty had no jurisdiction to entertain any causes of action arising within the precincts or body of a county: 2 That the Court had jurisdiction over some causes of action arising on the high seas. I say "some", because their number was limited to what are commonly called maritime causes. It must also be borne in mind that the Court of Admiralty had no jurisdiction over any causes of action arising in foreign countries beyond the seas, but not on the high seas. In 1840 an Act was passed to extend the jurisdiction in certain causes of action [Admiralty Court Act 1840 (repealed)]. . . . The Act was held to define the jurisdiction of the Court of Admiralty on the high seas as well as within the body of a county. The expression "high seas", when used with reference to the jurisdiction of the Court of Admiralty, included all oceans, seas, bays, channels, rivers, creeks, and waters below low-water mark, and where great ships could go, with the exception only of such parts of such oceans, etc., as were within the body of some county. . . . A foreign or colonial port, if it was part of the high seas in the above sense, would be as much within the jurisdiction of the Admiralty as any other part of the high seas. The jurisdiction, however, is necessarily limited in its application. It can only be exercised over persons or ships when they come to this country. An artificial basin or dock excavated out of land, but into which water from the high seas could be made to flow, would not, I apprehend, be in any sense part of the high seas, whether such basin or dock were in this country or in any other.' *The Mecca* [1895] P 95 at 106–108, CA, per Lindley LJ

SEA COAST *See* COAST

SEA FISH *See* FISH

SEA FISHING BOAT *See also* FISHING BOAT; FISHING VESSEL

'Sea fishing boat' means a vessel of whatever size, and in whatever way propelled, which is used by any person fishing for sea fish. (Sea Fisheries (Shellfish) Act 1967, s 22(2))

SEAL *See also* DEED; UNDER HAND AND SEAL

'The sealing of a deed need not be by means of a seal; it may be done with the end of a ruler or anything else. Nor is it necessary that wax should be used. The attestation clause says that the deed was signed, sealed, and delivered by the several parties; and the certificate of the two special commissioners says that the deed was produced before them, and that the married women "acknowledged the same to be their respective acts and deeds". I think there was prima facie evidence that the deed was sealed.' *Re Sandilands* (1871) LR 6 CP 411 at 413, per Byles J

'To constitute a seal, neither wax, nor wafer, nor a piece of paper, nor even an impression is necessary.' Ibid, per Bovill CJ

'Meticulous persons executing a deed may still place their finger on the wax seal or wafer on the document, but it appears to me that, at the present day, if a party signs a document bearing wax or wafer or other indication of a seal, with the intention of executing the document as a deed, that is sufficient adoption or recognition of the seal to amount to due execution as a deed.' *Stromdale & Ball Ltd v Burden* [1952] Ch 223 at 230, per Danckwerts J

Contract under *See* CONTRACT

SEAM

'Seam' in relation to minerals includes bed, lode and vein. (Railways Clauses Consolidation Act 1845, s 85D added by the Mines (Working Facilities and Support) Act 1923, s 15)

SEAMAN *See also* AT SEA

In Merchant Shipping Acts

'Seaman' includes every person (except masters and pilots), employed or engaged in any capacity on board any ship. (Merchant Shipping Act 1894, s 742, as amended by the Merchant Shipping Act 1970, s 100(1), Sch 3, para 4)

'"Seaman" includes every person . . . employed or engaged in any capacity on board any ship. First of all, is a man in control of the bar a "seaman" within the meaning of the Act? It seems to me that he is a seaman just as the ship's cook or any other person engaged in a similar character on board the ship is a seaman.' *Thompson v Nelson (H & W) Ltd* [1913] 2 KB 523 at 527, 528, per Lord Coleridge J

In Wills Act

[The Wills Act 1837, s 11, provides that a soldier in actual military service, or a mariner or 'seaman' being at sea may dispose of his personal property as he might have done before the passing of the Act.] 'In my opinion, every person employed in any branch of the naval service of His Majesty or of the Merchant Service, from the highest to the lowest, is included, when at sea, in the exceptions contained in the 11th section of the Act. . . . It remains to be considered whether a female typist at sea can be regarded as a "seaman" within the meaning of the exception. If the word "seaman" had been interpreted in its ordinary meaning, as including only persons engaged in seamanship, I think it might have been necessary to read it as importing the masculine gender as none but men are so engaged. But the more extended meaning that has been given to the word seems to exclude a consideration of the difference of sex. . . . If I am right in including in the exception persons serving at sea in such capacities as typists and telegraphists, it seems to me that they are included without distinction of sex.' *In the Goods of Sarah Hale* [1915] 2 IR 362 at 369, per Madden J

'It is not essential that he or she should be actually on the sea; but the contrary principle is not affirmed. It does not necessarily follow that a seaman who is looking forward to a voyage is a "seaman being at sea" [within the Wills Act 1837, s 11 (see supra)]. . . . Applying the legal principles which I accept to the facts of this case, I am of opinion that when Captain Birch was sitting in his own house on the day he made the will he was a seaman on shore, and not a seaman being at sea.' *Barnard v Birch* [1919] 2 IR 404 at 413, per Dodd J

New Zealand 'By our law a will has to be attested unless it is the will of a "soldier being an actual military service" or a "mariner or seaman being at sea". . . . I can find no authority that has gone the length of holding that a seaman living ashore for over five weeks is a seaman at sea. . . . The law was passed so as to allow sailors or soldiers to make wills under circumstances where they could get no advice or assistance in preparing such documents. Here the maker of the will was living on shore, and for a considerable time. He was also not pursuing while on shore any seaman's functions, and had been relieved from duty. . . . There must be something more than being a seaman. The seaman, if not actually at sea, must, in my opinion, be only on temporary leave.' *Re Broadbent* [1916] NZLR 821 at 821–824, per Stout CJ; also reported [1916] GLR 555 at 556

Seaman or marine

The term 'seaman or marine' means a warrant officer, petty officer or seaman, warrant or non-commissioned officer of marines, or marine, or other person forming part, in any capacity, of the complement of any of Her Majesty's vessels, or otherwise belonging to Her Majesty's naval or marine force (not being an officer within the meaning of this Act), or a warrant officer, petty officer or man of the Royal Naval Reserve. (Navy and Marines (Property of Deceased) Act 1965, s 2, as amended by the Armed Forces Act 1971, s 75, Sch 3)

SEAPLANE

'Seaplane' includes a flying boat and any other aircraft designed to manoeuvre on the water but does not include a hovercraft or hydrofoil vessel. (Port of London Act 1968, s 2(1))

'Seaplane' includes a flying boat and any other aircraft designed to manoeuvre on the water. (Civil Aviation Act 1982, s 97(6))

SEASHORE *See also* FORESHORE

The seashore, foreshore or sea beach (for in legal parlance these are generally synonymous terms) is that portion of the realm of England which lies between the high-water mark of medium high tide and low-water mark, but it has been said that all that lies to the landward of high-water mark and is in apparent continuity with the beach at high-water mark will normally form part of the beach, and it has been held on special facts that "foreshore" means the whole of the shore that is from time to time exposed by the receding tide.

The landward limit of the foreshore is the high-water mark of ordinary tides, which is the line of the medium tide between the spring and the neap tides throughout the year, that is, the point on the shore which is, about four days in every week, reached and covered with the tides, although it has been held that it does not matter if from time to time certain areas dry out.

The seaward limit of the foreshore is usually taken to be the low-water mark of such tides.

The modern presumption is that foreshore is a movable freehold and that a grant of foreshore will convey not that which at the time of the grant is between high- and low-water mark, but that which from time to time is between these termini. The application of this presumption is a question of construction, but it will be rebutted only by very strong evidence. Where land is granted with a water boundary, the grantee's title extends to that land as added to or detracted from by accretion or diluvion. (49 Halsbury's Laws (4th edn) paras 287–289)

'Seashore' means the bed and shore of the sea, and of every channel, creek, bay or estuary, and of every river as far up that river as the tide flows, and any cliff, bank, barrier, dune, beach, flat or other land adjacent to the shore [but with the exception of the bed or shore of waters specified in Sch 4 to the Act]. (Coast Protection Act 1949, s 49)

'The deed purports to pass "all that and those, sea-grounds, oyster-layings, shores, and fisheries". If it had conveyed the sea-grounds only, that, prima facie, would have operated as a grant of the soil itself. For, generally speaking, the soil passes by the word ground; as, by the word wood, the soil in which the wood grows passes. If the grantor had intended to pass a limited specific privilege and easement in the soil, and not the soil itself, he ought not to have used such comprehensive words; but words limited and restricted in their sense. It seems to me, therefore, that if the grant had contained only the words sea-grounds, they would have passed the soil. But then, the words oyster-layings are introduced, and it is said, that from these words it is to be inferred that, by the words sea-grounds, it was intended to convey a privilege of laying oysters only. I think, however, that those additional words may have been introduced because the grantor was uncertain as to the nature of the right which he had actually derived from the Crown. Then comes the word shore, which denotes that specific portion of the soil by which the sea is confined to certain limits. That term is wholly inapplicable to the grant of a privilege or easement; it of necessity comprehends the soil itself. . . . The crown by a grant of the seashore would convey, not that which at the time of the grant is between the high and low-water marks, but that which from time to time shall be between these two termini. Where the grantee has a freehold in that which the crown grants, his freehold shifts as the sea recedes or encroaches.' *Scratton v Brown* (1825) 4 B & C 485 at 496, 498, 499, per Bayley J

'The principle which gives the shore to the Crown is that it is land not capable of ordinary cultivation or occupation, and so is in the nature of unappropriated soil. Lord Hale [in *De Jure Maris*, c 4, p 12] gives as his reason for thinking that lands only covered by the high spring tides do not belong to the Crown, that such lands are, for the most part, dry and maniorable; and taking this passage as the only authority at all capable of guiding us, the reasonable conclusion is that the Crown's right is limited to land which is, for the most part, not dry or maniorable. The learned judges whose assistance I had in this very obscure question, point out that the limit indicating such land is the line of the medium high tide between the springs and the neaps. All land below that line is more often than not covered at high water, and so may justly be said, in the language of Lord Hale, to be covered by the ordinary flux of the sea. This cannot be said of any land above that line; I therefore concur with the able opinion of the judges whose valuable assistance I had, in thinking that the medium line must be treated as binding the right of the Crown.' *A-G v Chambers* (1854) 4 De G M & G 206 at 217, 218, per Lord Cranworth LC

'The sands on the seashore are not to be regarded as, in the full sense of the word, a highway.' *Llandudno Urban Council v Woods,* [1899] 2 Ch 705 at 709, per Cozens-Hardy J

'The term "seashore" is a phrase known to the law, and certainly as between the Crown and owners of land adjacent it means that which belongs to the Crown and which is often now described as the foreshore.' *Mellor v Walmesley* [1905] 2 Ch 164 at 177, CA, per Romer LJ

'I agree . . . that prima facie the word "seashore" in the plaintiffs' conveyances means that portion of the land adjacent to the sea which is ordinarily and prima facie vested in the Crown, subject to the rights of the King's subjects of fishing and navigation.' Ibid at 179, per Stirling LJ

'The words "shore" or "beach" as ordinarily used to not mean only the land lying between the lines of medium high and low tide. They cover also land which is, washed by the ordinary spring tides and often land which is only washed, if at all, by exceptionally high tides but which nevertheless is in character more akin to the "foreshore" than to the "hinterland". As ordinarily used neither word has a precise meaning and opinions might well differ whether a particular patch of ground consisting of sand and pebbles interspersed with sparse vegetation should more properly be described as part of the "shore" or "beach" or part of an adjoining field. It is more likely than not that a word used to describe a boundary in a legal document has a precise meaning and it is well settled that the word "seashore" when used to describe the boundary of land comprised in a conveyance means prima facie the foreshore.' *Government of the State of Penang v Beng Hong Oon* [1971] 3 All ER 1163 at 1170, PC, per Lord Cross of Chelsea

'Counsel for the plaintiffs contended that "beach" has the same meaning as "foreshore", and so meant the land between the high and low water marks of ordinary tides. Though this may well have been the usage in Shakespeare's time, I do not think that it can be right today. In the normal use of language I very much doubt whether anyone would now use the term "beach" so as to exclude the sand and shingle which lie immediately above high water mark. The word no doubt includes the foreshore; a child who steps below high water mark to paddle or swim could not, I think, be said to have left the beach. If one begins at the seaward, I would say that the ordinary low water mark (or possibly the low water mark of spring tides) would normally be regarded as the dividing line between the beach and the sea-bed. From low water mark upwards to high water mark and beyond would all fairly be said to be part of the beach: but how far beyond? The *terminus a quo* may be clear, but what of the *terminus ad quem*? In my judgment, all that lies to the landward of high water mark and is in apparent continuity with the beach at high water mark will normally form part of the beach. Discontinuity may be shown in a variety of ways: there may be sand dunes, or a cliff, or greensward, or shrubbery, or trees, or a promenade or roadway, or a dozen other natural or artificial structures or entities which indicate where one leaves the beach for something else. But until one reaches some such indication, I think the beach continues. I may add that I would not regard beaches as being confined to tidal waters. I see no reason why non-tidal waters should not have their beaches, running landwards from the normal water mark.' *Tito v Waddell (No 2)* [1977] 3 All ER 129 at 262, 263, per Megarry V-C

SEASONABLY

United States An action is taken 'seasonably' when it is taken at or within the time agreed or if no time is agreed at or within a reasonable time. (Uniform Commercial Code 1978, s 1–204(3))

SEAWORTHY *See also* UNSEAWORTHY

The vessel must be reasonably fit. 'Seaworthiness' is a relative term and may vary with the class of the ship insured. Thus, a river steamer insured for a sea voyage need not be made as fit for the voyage as an ocean-going vessel. She need only be made as seaworthy as is reasonably practicable by ordinary available means.

Moreover, the standard of seaworthiness varies with the nature of the voyage insured; the vessel may be seaworthy for one voyage but not for another, or for a voyage at one season of the year and not for a voyage at another season; she may be seaworthy when laden with one kind of cargo and not so when laden with another kind.

The ship must be reasonably fit in all respects. She must be competent in hull to encounter the ordinary perils of the seas and properly equipped with the necessary tackle, stores, supplies, provisions, medicines, and other things requisite for the safety of the voyage and those on board her, and she must have her engines and boilers in sound and proper condition, and also an adequate supply of fuel for the voyage.

A temporary defect, however, in the ship's condition, due to some negligence at the time of sailing, does not constitute a breach of the warranty of seaworthiness, provided that the state of the ship is such that, if the master and crew do their duty, the defect can be remedied or any danger from it averted. Thus, a ship is not unseaworthy on account of a porthole being improperly left open at the commencement of the voyage if it can be readily closed at sea whenever necessary.

The vessel must also at the commencement of the voyage be properly manned with a competent master and a competent and adequate crew, and must have a pilot on board at the port of departure in cases where there is an establishment of pilots at that port and the nature of the navigation requires one.

A ship may be seaworthy even if not properly documented at the commencement of the voyage. Lack of proper documentation will, however, discharge an underwriter from liability if the insurance is on the ship and condemnation arose on that ground. (25 Halsbury's Laws (4th edn) paras 66, 67)

A ship is deemed to be seaworthy when she is reasonably fit in all respects to encounter the ordinary perils of the seas of the adventure insured. (Marine Insurance Act 1906, s 39)

'The question depends altogether upon the nature of the implied warranty as to seaworthiness, or mode of navigation, between the assured and the underwriters, on a time policy. In the case of an insurance for a certain voyage, it is clearly established, that there is an implied warranty that the vessel shall be seaworthy; by which it is meant that she shall be in a fit state, as to repairs, equipment, and crew, and in all other respects, to encounter the ordinary perils of the voyage insured, at the time of sailing upon it. If the assurance attaches before the voyage commences, it is enough that the state of the ship be commensurate to the then risk . . .; and if the voyage be such as to require a different complement of men, or state of equipment in different parts of it, as, if it were a voyage down a canal or river, and thence across to the open sea, it would be enough if the vessel were at the commencement of each stage of the navigation properly manned and equipped for it. But the assured makes no warranty to the underwriters that the vessel shall continue seaworthy, or that the master or crew shall do their duty during the voyage; and their negligence or misconduct is no defence to an action on the policy, where the loss has been immediately occasioned by the perils insured against.' *Dixon v Sadler* (1839) 9 LJ Ex 48 at 50, per Parke B

'The term "seaworthy", when used in reference to marine insurance, does not describe absolutely any of the states which a ship may pass through, from the repairs of the hull in a dock till it has reached the end of its voyage, but expresses a relation between the state of the ship and the perils it has to meet in the situation it is in; so that a ship, before setting out on a voyage, is seaworthy, if it is fit in the degree which a prudent owner uninsured would require to meet the perils of the service it is then engaged in, and would continue so during the voyage, unless it met with extraordinary damage. I have not found a definition of the word, but I gather its meaning, as above explained, from the decisions turning upon it.' *Gibson v Small* (1853) 4 HL Cas 353 at 384, per Erle J

'It is now well established as a rule of law that on an insurance for a voyage, either on ship or goods or freight, a warranty of seaworthiness for the voyage of the ship insured, or of the ship in which the goods are carried, is to be implied. Indeed it may be said that a warranty of seaworthiness in voyage policies is the basis of the contract. . . . It was asked, what amount of seaworthiness is required, and to what extent are the assured to go in repairs? Our answer is, that the term "seaworthiness" is a relative term: there is no positive condition of the vessel recognised by the law to satisfy the warranty of seaworthiness. Lord Campbell well observes in *Small v Gibson* [supra]:—"With regard to its (seaworthy) literal or primary meaning, I assume it to be now used and understood that the ship is in a condition in all respects to render it reasonably safe where it happens to be at the time referred to, in a dock, in a harbour, in a river, or traversing the ocean." Seaworthy or not is always a question for the jury, and in all cases the question for the jury will be whether the ship was, at the commencement of the voyage, in such a state as to be reasonably capable of performing it.' *Knill v Hooper* (1857) 2 H & N 277 at 282–284, per cur

'The word "seaworthy" is a well-known term in shipping law, and has a perfectly definite and ascertained meaning. It is used to describe the condition in which a vessel insured under a voyage policy is bound to be on leaving port if the contract of insurance is to be effectual against the underwriter. Baron Parke, in the case of *Dixon v Sadler* [supra], defined the seaworthiness of a vessel thus: "that she shall be in a fit state as to repairs, equipment, and crew, and in all other respects to encounter ordinary perils of the voyage". Other definitions which have been given do not, I think, substantially differ from this.' *Hedley v Pinkney & Sons SS Co Ltd* [1894] AC 222 at 226, 227, per Lord Herschell LC

'The question . . . arises whether insufficient ventilation and an insufficient supply of men constitute a breach of an implied warranty—or, more correctly, the implied condition—of seaworthiness. I think they do. What is the implied warranty in a policy on cargo? It is, in my opinion, exactly the same as the warranty in a policy on ship—that the ship shall be seaworthy for the adventure on which she starts. . . . It cannot be doubted that a ship which put to sea without proper means of providing the necessary ventilation, or without sufficient men to utilise those means, would be unseaworthy for the service required.' *Sleigh v Tyser* [1900] 2 QB 333 at 336, 337, per Bigham J

'As I understand, shipowners have been for a long time endeavouring to limit the general liability cast upon them by law as carriers by sea by inserting special exceptions, without going the length of excepting their liability in respect of the warranty of seaworthiness. . . . I think, however, I am right in saying that as a principle of construction the warranty of seaworthiness will be held not to have been excepted unless it plainly appears that it was intended to except it. . . . Moreover I think that, whatever views may have been entertained in years gone by, the warranty of seaworthiness now includes, and is well known to include, a warranty that the ship and her equipment are fit for the purpose of safely carrying to their destination the goods which the shipowner knows are to be carried on her. I think also that in a bill of lading at the present day the expression "seaworthiness" or "unseaworthiness" would be used, and would be understood as being used, with reference to this well-known extent of the warranty.' *Rathbone, Brothers & Co v MacIver (D) Sons & Co* [1903] 2 KB 378 at 388, 389, CA, per Romer LJ

'With regard to the construction of the words "in seaworthy trim" I think that the arbitrator has taken too narrow a view, and that the true construction is that, when discharge at the first port is finished, the steamer must be left in a condition in which she can safely meet the perils of the sea on her passage to the second port of discharge.' *Britain SS Co Ltd v Louis Dreyfus & Co of New York* (1935) 51 TLR 307 at 308, per MacKinnon J

'As I understand the authorities, there are two aspects of seaworthiness. The first requires that the ship, her crew and her equipment shall be in all respects sound and able to encounter and withstand the ordinary perils of the sea during the contemplated voyage. The second requires that the ship shall be suitable to carry the contract cargo.' *Actis Co Ltd v Sanko Steamship Co Ltd, The Aquacharm* [1982] 1 All ER 390 at 395, CA, per Griffiths LJ

See, also, 43 Halsbury's Laws (4th edn) paras 553 et seq.

Australia 'Seaworthiness has been defined as being in a fit state as to repairs, equipment and crew, and in all other respects, to encounter ordinary perils of the voyage: *Hedley v Pinkney & Sons SS Co* [supra, at 227].' *Cotter v Huddart Parker Ltd* [1942] SR(NSW) 33 at 40, per Jordan CJ

'The expression "seaworthy" may be used in different senses, for instance, it may mean the fitness of the ship to enter on the contemplated adventure of navigation, or fitness to receive the contemplated cargo as a carrying receptacle. A ship unseaworthy in relation to the carriage of a particular cargo may be seaworthy in other respects.' Ibid at 52, per Davidson J

SECOND

[The Offences against the Person Act 1861, s 57, provides that nothing therein contained extends to any person marrying a 'second' time whose husband or wife has been continually absent from such person for the space of seven years, and has not been known to be living within that time.] 'This proviso means precisely what it says, nothing more or less—any second marriage, and not any second or subsequent marriage.' *R v Treanor (or McAvoy)* [1939] 1 All ER 330 at 332, CCA, per Lord Hewart CJ

SECOND COUSIN *See also* COUSIN

'Those only who have either the same great grandfather or the same great grandmother, are second cousins to each other. The testator may have called some persons his cousins who were not so; but that only shews that he made a mistake as to them.' *Bridgnorth Corpn v Collins* (1847) 15 Sim 538 at 541, per Shadwell V-C

'The term "second cousin" has a well-known definite meaning: it means persons having the same great-grandfathers and great-grandmothers.' *Re Parker, Bentham v Wilson* (1880) 15 Ch D 528 at 530, per Jessel MR; affd (1881) 17 Ch D 262

SECOND OFFENCE

'It strikes me .' . . that where the legislature passes a statute and imposes a penalty of £50 for a first offence, it must mean, in the absence of express words to the contrary, that the conviction for the first offence must be under that Act, and the second conviction under the same Act; if it were otherwise, it would be idle to introduce the warning of a lower penalty for the first offence, and to impose a higher penalty for the second." *Re Authers* (1889) 22 QBD 345 at 349, DC, per Hawkins J

SECONDARY EDUCATION

See EDUCATION

SECONDARY EVIDENCE

See EVIDENCE

SECONDARY SCHOOL *See* SCHOOL

SECRET

'In its ordinary connotation, particularly as descriptive of actions, I agree, with the Court of Appeal and the Shorter Oxford Dictionary, "secret" means: "Done with the intention of being concealed; clandestinely". To ascribe to it a meaning wide enough to include actions done "unwittingly", a state of mind which is incompatible with any *intention* to conceal is, in my view, a misuse of the adjective "secret".' *Bristol-Myers Co v Beecham Group Ltd* [1974] 1 All ER 333 at 354, HL, per Lord Diplock

SECRET COMMISSION *See* BRIBERY

SECRET TRUST *See* TRUST

SECRETARY

Club secretary

'Secretary', in relation to a club, includes any officer of the club or other person performing the duties of a secretary and, in relation to a proprietary club where there is no secretary, the proprietor of the club. (Licensing Act 1964, s 201)

Of company

'A secretary is a mere servant; his position is that he is to do what he is told, and no person can assume that he has any authority to represent anything at all.' *Barnett, Hoares & Co v South London Tramways Co* (1887) 18 QBD 815 at 817, per Lord Esher MR

'Times have changed. A company secretary is a much more important person nowadays than he was in 1887 [see supra]. He is an officer of the company with extensive duties and responsibilities. This appears not only in the modern Companies Acts, but also by the role which he plays in the day-to-day business of companies. He is no longer a mere clerk. He regularly makes representations on behalf of the company and enters into contracts on its behalf which come within the day-to-day running of the company's business. So much so that he may be regarded as held out as having authority to do such things on behalf of the company. He is certainly entitled to sign contracts connected with the administrative side of the company's affairs, such as employing staff, and ordering cars, and so forth. All such matters now come within the ostensible authority of a company's secretary.' *Panorama Developments (Guildford) Ltd v Fidelis Furnishing Fabrics Ltd* [1971] 3 All ER 16 at 19, CA, per Lord Denning MR

SECURE

Adjective

'In the present case the word "dangerous" does not appear, but it seems to me that as regards the roof and sides of a travelling road or working place in a pit the word "secure" [in the Coal Mines Act 1911, s 49 (repealed; see now the Mines and Quarries Act 1954, s 48(1))] must mean substantially the same as "not dangerous by reason of liability to fall". A ceiling, for instance, is, I think, secure in ordinary parlance, though an earthquake or a bomb, or even a bath overflowing in a bathroom overhead, may bring it down.' *Jackson v National Coal Board* [1955] 1 All ER 145 at 149, per Hallett J

[The Coal Mines Act 1911, s 49 (repealed; see supra) provided that the roof and sides of every travelling road and working place should be made 'secure'.] 'The purpose of this part of the Act is to prevent accidents, and to my mind "secure" here means in such a state that there will be no danger from accidental falls. The word cannot mean in such a state that the side or roof will stand up against deliberate attack, for no part of a mine can be secure in that sense. I can see nothing inconsistent in saying that a side or roof shall be made secure against accidental falls at a time when steps are being taken to bring it down deliberately.' *Gough v National Coal Board* [1959] 2 All ER 164 at 170, HL, per Lord Reid; also reported [1959] AC 698 at 711

'One must first, I think, be clear what is meant by the word "secure" in this section [Mines and Quarries Act 1954, s 48(1) (see supra)]. It does not mean in my view that the roof is to be impregnable, in the sense that it is to be kept in such a state that there can never be a fall of or from it. When dealing with the same word in the earlier Act [Coal Mines Act] of 1911 and the duty thereby imposed to make a roof secure, the courts have not accepted impregnability as a test. It has generally been recognised that an offence would not occur if a fall was due to certain causes which can be regarded as lying outside ordinary skilled engineering provision, e.g. an earthquake, an atom bomb detonation, an explosion . . . or deliberate operations designed to bring the roof down (see *Gough v National Coal Board* [supra]). I think, therefore, that the meaning of "secure" was correctly stated by McNair J in the *Gough* case, when in the Court of Appeal he said [[1958] 1 All ER 754 at 762]: "secure" means a physical condition of stability which will ordinarily result in safety.' *Brown v National Coal Board*, [1962] 1 All ER 81 at 85, HL, per Lord Radcliffe

'What kind of foreseeable dangers has the manager to guard against? Need he only take steps against those that are a *likely* cause of injury? Or should he go further and take steps against those that are a *possible* cause of injury? The solution to this question is given by the use of the word "secure". It is the self-same word as was used in the Act of 1911 and should, I think, be given the same meaning. The manager must take steps to guard the workmen against those foreseeable dangers which are a possible cause of injury in circumstances which may reasonably be expected to occur.' Ibid at 91, per Lord Denning

Verb

Canada 'The words "to secure" mean to guarantee or make safe against loss, and are not a synonym for the words "to obtain" or "to procure".' *Re Smith* [1952] OR 135 at 147, Ont CA, per Hogg JA

SECURED CREDITOR

'Creditor', in relation to a bankrupt, means a person to whom any of the bankruptcy debts is owed and, in relation to an individual to whom a bankruptcy petition relates, means a person who would be a creditor in the bankruptcy if a bankruptcy order were made on that petition. A debt is secured for the purposes of the Insolvency Act 1986 to the extent that the person to whom the debt is owed holds any security for the debt, whether a mortgage, charge, lien or other security, over any property of the person by whom the debt is owed. (3(2) Halsbury's Laws (4th edn, reissue) para 548)

SECURED PARTY

United States 'Secured party' means a lender, seller or other person in whose favor there is a security interest, including a person to whom accounts or chattel paper have been sold. When the holders of obligations issued under an indenture of trust, equipment trust agreement or the like are represented by a trustee or other person, the representative is the secured party. (Uniform Commercial Code 1978, s 9–105(1)(m))

SECURELY FENCED

'Securely fenced' has the same meaning in each of the statutory provisions requiring machinery to be securely fenced, and means so fenced as to give security to all persons employed or working on the premises against such dangers as may reasonably be expected. Fencing is only secure when it effectively protects the workman from the danger of contact with the exposed part of the machine, but it need not be so constructed that it cannot be climbed over or broken down by an employee determined to get at the machinery. In considering whether secure fencing has been achieved the foreseeable behaviour of persons employed is relevant: secure fencing is that which removes the possibility of injury to anybody acting in a way in which a human being might reasonably be expected to act in circumstances that might reasonably be expected to occur. (20 Halsbury's Laws (4th edn) para 563)

[The Factory and Workshop Act 1901, s 10 (repealed; see now the Factories Act 1961, s 14), enacted that all dangerous parts of machinery in a factory must be 'securely fenced'.] '"Securely fenced"—that is, protected by a fence which was both pervious to sight and removable at will in the course of operation, for these are admittedly conditions of the "secure fencing" of such a part.' *Lauder v Barr & Stroud* 1927 SC(J) 21 at 26, per the Lord Justice-General (Lord Clyde)

'By the Factories Act 1937, s 14 [repealed; see now the Factories Act 1961, s 14] it is provided that: "Every dangerous part of any machinery, other than prime movers and transmission machinery, shall be securely fenced unless it is in such a position or of such construction as to be as safe to every person employed or working on the premises as it would be if securely fenced.". . . The question has been raised as to whether secure fencing must be provided if the result is to make the machine useless either commercially or mechanically for the purpose for which it is designed. . . . Machinery must be securely fenced, and the magistrates, in finding that it was securely fenced for the purposes for which it was used, have, in my opinion, arrived at a decision which is irrelevant for the purposes of the case, or, if it is their decision, it is one for which there was no justification in law upon the material before them. I cannot help observing that this emphasis upon the absolute nature of the provision contained in s 14 may have the effect of hampering the use of machines, used to-day as they are without secure fencing in the sense in which I understand the expression, but that ought not, I think, to weigh with us, and I observe, as has already been mentioned in the course of the argument, that the provisions of s 14(2) give the Secretary of State power . . . to fix and settle the types of fencing which must be provided. . . . I have come to the conclusion that the argument of counsel for the appellant is right and that, if fencing is only secure in so far as it is all that is possible if the machine is to be used at all, that is not securely fencing.' *Dennistoun v Greenhill (Charles E), Ltd* [1944] 2 All ER 434 at 435–437, DC, per Lord Caldecote CJ

'The duty laid upon the occupier in terms by the Factories Act 1937, s 14 [repealed; see supra] is to fence securely: ". . . every dangerous part of any machinery, other than prime movers and transmission machinery . . . unless it is in such a position or of such construction as to be as safe to every person employed or working on the premises as it would be if securely fenced." The obligation imposed is to fence dangerous parts of any machinery—save for such machinery as is expressly excepted—so as to make it secure, and not only secure for the worker at the particular machine which is dangerous, but secure for every person employed or working on the premises.' *Harrison v Metropolitan Plywood Co* [1946] 1 All ER 243 at 245, per Hilbery J

'The word "fence" does not suggest to my mind the massive kind of structure which might be necessary to contain the parts of a large flywheel breaking apart while rotating at high speed. The only express provision in the Act [Factories Act 1937, s 13 (repealed; see now the Factories Act 1961, ss 12–14)] dealing with the kind of fencing required is that it shall be "of substantial construction" (see s 16). But that is scarcely more than an injunction against flimsiness, and it is satisfied by the sort of fence that is sufficient to afford good protection to workmen against contact with the machinery when it is working in situ. Nor does the word "securely" appear to import absolute protection against all possible contingencies, rather than protection against the danger of contact.' *Carroll v Andrew Barclay & Sons Ltd* [1948] AC 477 at 489, per Lord Normand

'The Factory Acts are there, not merely to protect the careful, the vigilant and the conscientious workman, but human nature being what it is, the careless, the indolent, the inadvertent, the weary, and even perhaps in some cases, the disobedient. The duty, as has been said, is not to fence "somewhat securely" but "securely", but there must be some limit placed on the word "securely", and a fence does not necessarily cease to be secure because by some act of perverted and deliberate ingenuity the guard can be forced or circumvented and the safeguards provided thereby rendered nugatory.' *Carr v Mercantile Produce Co Ltd* [1949] 2 KB 601 at 608, per Stable J

'The plaintiff alleged, first, that his injury was due to a breach of s 13(1) of the Factories Act 1937 [repealed; see supra] which provides: "Every part of the transmission machinery shall be securely fenced unless it is in such a position or of such construction as to be as safe to every person employed or working on the premises as it would be if securely fenced." . . . I think that in this group of sections the same test should be applied in deciding whether machinery is "securely fenced" as is applied in deciding whether it is "dangerous". To an allegation that machinery which has, in fact, caused injury is dangerous it is admittedly a good answer to prove that it was not dangerous in any reasonable foreseeable circumstances. I see no difficulty in applying the same test to the question whether machinery is securely fenced.' *Burns v Joseph Terry & Sons Ltd* [1950] 2 All ER 987 at 988, 990, per Somervell LJ; [1951] 1 KB 454, CA

'Section 14 of the Factories Act 1937, and its predecessor s 10 of the Factory and Workshop Act 1901 [both repealed; see now the Factories Act 1961, ss 12–14] have on many occasions been discussed in the courts, and I think that their true construction is not in doubt. In particular, I think it is clear that the obligation imposed by the section to fence securely every dangerous part of any machinery, except as in the section mentioned and subject to its proviso, is an absolute obligation. And by that, I mean that it is not to be qualified by such words as "so far as practicable" or "so long as it can be fenced consistently with its being used for the purpose for which it was intended" or similar words. . . . I think that the obligation to "securely fence" the machinery here in question is unambiguously absolute and will remain absolute unless and until the Minister makes appropriate regulations.' *Summers (John) & Sons Ltd v Frost* [1955] 1 All ER 870 at 872, 873, HL, per Viscount Simonds; see also [1955] AC 740

'To my mind the natural meaning of the word "securely", used in regard to the fencing of a dangerous part of a machine, is that the part must be so fenced that no part of the person or clothing of any person working the machine or passing near it can come into contact with it.' Ibid at 875, per Lord Morton

'I see no escape from the view that, as matters at present stand, the destruction of the machine as a working unit if it is completely fenced, is no answer to the mandatory words of the statute.' Ibid at 889, per Lord Keith

New Zealand 'In essence . . . a machine is not securely fenced . . . unless it is fenced in a way which gives effective protection against reasonably foreseeable risk of injury to workmen from that dangerous machine, bearing in mind that when one considers what is a "reasonably foreseeable risk" one must have regard not only to the foreseeable conduct of a skilled worker intent on his task but also to the foreseeable conduct of careless or inattentive workers. The statutory provisions are designed to protect, to that degree, not only the competent, careful workman but the careless workman. Now, subject to those considerations, of course it must to some extent always be a question of fact and degree for a jury to decide whether in any particular case a particular dangerous part of the machine was securely fenced.' *Ralph v Henderson & Pollard Ltd* [1968] NZLR 759 at 761, per Richmond J

SECURITY—SECURITIES *See also* VALUABLE SECURITY

'Securities' include stocks, funds, and shares. (Settled Land Act 1925, s 117)

'Security' includes shares, bonds, notes, debentures, debenture stock and units under a unit trust scheme. (Borrowing (Control and Guarantees) Act 1946, s 4)

'Securities', in relation to a body corporate, means any shares, stock, debentures, debenture stock, and any other security of a like nature, of the body corporate. (Transport Act 1962, s 92)

'Securities' means shares, stock, debentures, debenture stock, loan stock, bonds, units of a collective investment scheme within the meaning of the Financial Services Act 1986, and other securities of any description. (Stock Transfer Act 1963, s 4, as amended by the Financial Services Act 1986)

(2) 'Securities' does not include shares in a company but, subject to subsection (3) below, includes any loan stock or similar security—

(a) whether of the government of the United Kingdom, any other government, any public or local authority in the United Kingdom or elsewhere, or any company or other body; and
(b) whether or not secured, whether or not carrying a right to interest of a fixed amount or at a fixed rate per cent. of the nominal value of the securities, and whether or not in bearer form.

(3) 'Securities' does not include—

(a) securities on which the whole of the return is a distribution by virtue of section 209(2)(e)(iv) and (v);
(b) national savings certificates (including Ulster Savings Certificates);
(c) war savings certificates;
(d) certificates of deposit (within the meaning of s 56(5));
(e) any security which fulfils the following conditions, namely, it is redeemable, the amount payable to its redemption exceeds its issue price, and no return other than the amount of that excess is payable on it.

(Income and Corporation Taxes Act 1988, s 710)

'The normal meaning of the word "securities" is not open to doubt. The word denotes a debt or claim the payment of which is in some way secured. The security would generally consist of a right to resort to some fund or property for payment; but I am not prepared to say that other forms of security (such as personal guarantee) are excluded. In each case, however, when the word is used in its normal sense, some form of secured liability is postulated.' *Singer v Williams* [1921] AC 41 at 49, HNL, per Viscount Cave

Canada 'I think it undesirable to attempt, in this judgment, any all-encompassing statement as to the meaning of "securities" in this section [s 69(2)(c)] of the Income Tax Act. I am, however, satisfied that Parliament used the word in a popular sense, so as to include instruments for the payment of money with or without some collateral obligation and which are commonly dealt in for the purpose of financing and investment.' *Canadian & Foreign Securities Co Ltd v Minister of National Revenue* 72 DTC 6354 at 6356, Fed Ct, per Collier J

United States The term 'security' means any note, stock, treasury stock, bond, debenture, evidence of indebtedness, certificate of interest or participation in any profit-sharing agreement, collateral-trust certificate, preorganisation certificate or subscription, transferable share, investment contract, voting-trust certificate, certificate of deposit for a security, fractional undivided interest in oil, gas, or other mineral rights, or, in general, any interest or instrument commonly known as a 'security', or any certificate of interest or participation in, temporary or interim certificate for, receipt for, guarantee of, or warrant or right to subscribe to or purchase, any of the foregoing. (Securities Act of 1933, s 2(1))

Floating *See* FLOATING SECURITY

For repayment of money

Australia 'The expression naturally comprehends a right given with a view to securing to the grantee repayment of money outlaid by him in circumstances giving rise to a right of repayment against the payee. Such a security might be granted by the payee in whose favour the grantee made the outlay, in which case the grantee would have the choice of enforcing the security or of simply suing the payee for the debt. Equally, such a security might be granted by a party other than the payee of the outlay, and it would be irrelevant whether the outlay were made in circumstances in which the grantor could be sued for debt or not: so long as proper consideration had been given for it, the security would be enforceable against the grantor as a security for the repayment to the grantee of his outlay, to whomsoever the outlay had been made.' *Ansett Transport Industries (Operations) Pty Ltd v Comptroller of Stamps* [1980] VR 35 at 39, per Tadgell J

In Friendly Societies Act

'The sole point in the appeal is whether the word "security" occurring in the phrase "any other security" in s 44(1)(e) of the [Friendly Societies] Act of 1896 [repealed; see now the Friendly Societies Act 1974, s 46(1)(d)] is meant to include any form of investment of money or must be confined to the stricter or more narrow significance of debts or money claims the payment of which is "secured" or "guaranteed" by a charge on some property or by some document recording the obligation of some person or corporation to pay and so as not to include the holding of shares in limited companies which are of the nature of participations in an enterprise and do not involve the conception of a creditor-debtor relationship. There is no doubt that at the present day the words "security" and "securities" are not uncommonly used as synonymous with "investment" or "investments", and it is tempting in a case such as the present so to stretch the meaning of the words. Several cases were cited in argument to illustrate this popular usage of which *Re Rayner* [*Rayner v Rayner* [1904] 1 Ch 176] is an example. It is necessary for me to refer in detail to the authorities since it was conceded by counsel for the appellants that the prima facie meaning of the words "security" or "securities" is the narrower of the two alternatives already posed and that the meaning will not be extended to the wider alternative in the absence of some context requiring such extension: see, for example, the opinion of Viscount Cave in *Singer v Williams* [[1921] 1 AC 41], followed recently by Crossman J in *Re Smithers* [*Watts v Smithers* [1939] Ch 1015]. I may add that in cases relating to wills, and, particularly, to "home-made" wills, the courts will concede some degree of latitude, in the interpretation of inelegant expressions, which are not to be expected in Acts of Parliament. I am bound, however, to say, as regards drafting elegance, that the language used in the section under review is hardly less delphic than that employed by many an inexpert testator but, applying what I conceive to be proper principles of interpretation to the present case, I do not think that I can, as a judge of first instance, do other than attribute to the word "security" as used in s 44(1)(e) of the Act of 1896 the narrower or stricter interpretation.' *Re United Law Clerks Society* [1946] 2 All ER 674 at 675, per Evershed J

In will

According to its literal meaning, 'securities' includes such money as is secured either on property or on personal security (including even promissory notes and bills of exchange), and any stock or other investment which, by the terms of its creation, is a security for the payment of money; but it does not include money for which a mere acknowledgment of indebtedness has been given, or the ordinary description of stock and shares in a public company. 'Securities' is, however, very commonly used as a synonym for investments, or property dealt with on the Stock Exchange, and this meaning may readily be attributed to the word, and generally other meanings may be given to it, according to the context of the will and the circumstances of the case. (50 Halsbury's Laws (4th edn) para 479)

'A security by promissory note is, in proper interpretation, no security at all—it is merely evidence of the debt; and of so little value does this Court consider such securities, that, if a testator directed his trustees to lay out money in securities approved of by them, and they were to invest such money on the mere security of a promissory note, it would be such a breach of trust as to render the trustees liable for the amount of any loss that might be sustained.' *Stiles v Guy* (1832) 4 Y & C Ex 571 at 574, per Lord Lyndhurst CB

'Mrs Parker defines what she means to appoint, in the first place, as being "all her moneys and securities for money", and that which is not "moneys and securities for money" is to pass by general residuary bequest. I must assume, that, at the time at which her will operated, a person had left her £1,000, but which had not been paid. If so, it was neither "money nor security for money", but a mere debt due to her estate. I know of no case in which the words "moneys and securities for money" have been so extended as to include a debt due to the testator, and I do not think that any such case can be found. No doubt there are very nice distinctions on the subject, thus bills of exchange are securities for money, but I think that an IOU has been held not to be a security for money, which is a singularity. Stock in the funds is considered a security for money, but shares in companies are not. It is unnecessary to go into an examination of the minute distinctions between these cases, but I do not find a single case in which an unsecured debt due to a testator had been held to be either "money or a security for money". A legacy is a mere debt from the estate of the testator, unsecured, except in this sense:—that this Court will enforce the will and secure the legacy; but that is not what is meant by a "security for money".' *Re Mason's Will* (1865) 34 Beav 494 at 498, 499, per Romilly MR

'What is a security for money? One would say that an IOU would be a security for money, and I should have been inclined to think that it was so; but I find it has been held that under the words "securities for money" an IOU will not pass.' *Hopkins v Abbott* (1875) LR 19 Eq 222 at 228, per Malins V-C

[A testator by his will provided that certain monies were to be invested by his executors in such 'securities' as they might think proper.] 'I am of opinion that the word "security" has a definite legal meaning, which it would be highly dangerous to depart from. . . . "Security" means a something which secures money, and not something which may be bought with money. A person purchasing Consols becomes a creditor of the nation, and has his money secured by the national resources. Again, one may have a real security, that is to say, a charge on land, by which the money lent is secured.' *Re Kavanagh, Murphy v Doyle* (1891) 27 LR Ir 495 at 498, per Porter MR

[A testator by his will bequeathed all 'securities' standing in his name.] 'It is well known that "security" really means "something which frees you from care", and where you have invested your money something which with regard to that particular investment enables you, as it were, to be like the gods who live at ease; that primary meaning, however, has now disappeared; language must in course of time change, and in the present case there is evidence to shew that it has changed, that in common parlance and in business matters the word "security" is no longer limited to that which frees a man from care in the sense that his money is known to be safe, and that it must some day be repaid.' *Re Johnson, Greenwood v Greenwood* (1903) 47 Sol Jo 547at 547, per Kekewich J; affd on appeal (1903) 89 LT 520, CA.

'The question . . . is, What is the meaning of the word "security" in this will? In my judgment, in this will the meaning of that word, or rather of the word "securities", is determined . . . by the context of the will. . . . Take this passage in the will: "And I authorise my trustees to continue or leave any moneys invested at my death in or upon the same securities." I think that in this passage "the same securities" obviously means "the same investments"; and I think that the effect of using the words "moneys invested" and the words "securities" to cover the same subject-matter is not to narrow down or limit the natural sense of the words "moneys invested", but to extend what Farwell J considers to be the "strict and primary" meaning of the word "securities", so as to cover anything which, according to the strict and primary meaning of the words "moneys invested", would be covered or connoted by those words.' *Re Rayner, Rayner v Rayner* [1904] 1 Ch 176 at 187, 188, CA per Vaughan Williams LJ

'When any one speaks of "securities" standing in his name he means moneys represented by securities taken in his name and not that the actual paper or parchment happens to be in his own custody or that of another person, under his name.' *Re Mayne, Stoneham v Woods*, [1914] 2 Ch 115 at 117, 118, per Warrington J

'The . . . question which now falls for determination is, What passes under the testatrix's will by the use of the expression "all I possess in money and securities" and "all my estate in money and securities", which I think are synonymously used in this will. . . . It has been rightly contended on behalf of the next-of-kin that the word "securities", when used in an instrument, including a will, has a primary meaning attached to it . . . that is to say, it means securities for money, and not an investment such as stocks or shares other than debenture stock. In the present case the question arises whether in the context of the will there is anything to show tht the testatrix used the word "securities" in other than its primary meaning. There can be no dispute that at the present day the word "securities" has a flexible meaning, and is used frequently, if not universally, in the extended meaning of investments. . . . I think I am entitled to take the word "securities" in the context in which it is used as being used in the extended sense—"all I possess in money and securities" in the mouth of a layman or a laywoman to my mind has a very much more extended meaning than it might have if it were used by a conveyancing counsel in Lincoln's Inn. . . . My impression of the will, reading it as a whole, is this, that she intended by this will to dispose of such part of her estate, including investments, as could be transferred and dealt with readily both by the charity and by her brother and sisters, and for these reasons, possibly quite inadequately expressed, I have come to the conclusion in this case that the strict meaning of "securities" ought not to be given to the expression used in the will, but that it ought to be construed as including all the investments.' *Re Scorer, Burtt v Harrison* (1924) 94 LJ Ch 196 at 199, 200, per P O Lawrence J

[A testator authorised his trustees to invest the trust funds on such 'securities' as they might think fit.] 'I think that "securities" means investments. The term is not confined to secured investments. I am prepared to make a declaration that "securities" includes any stocks or shares or bonds by way of investments.' *Re Douglas's Will Trusts, Lloyd's Bank Ltd v Nelson* [1959] 2 All ER 620 at 623, per Vaisey J; affd [1959] 3 All ER 785, CA

Personal security

'The term personal security is now well understood. It is found in an ordinary textbook, such as Lewin on Trustees. It was used by Lord Kenyon in his judgment in *Holmes v Dring* [(1788) 2 Cox Eq Cas 1], and by Lord Cottenham in *Clough v Bond* [(1838) 3 My & Cr 490]. It occurs in the 16th and 18th sections of the Friendly Societies Act 1875 [repealed]. It includes every case where nothing more is obtained than the personal liability of the borrower, or of the borrower and sureties.' *Grimwade v Mutual Society* (1884) 52 LT 409 at 415, per Chitty J

SEDITION

Sedition in the common law meant acts done, words spoken and published or writings published with a seditious intention, that is an intention (1) to bring into hatred or contempt, or to excite disaffection against, the Sovereign or the government and constitution of the United Kingdom, or either House of Parliament, or the administration of justice; or (2) to excite the Sovereign's subjects to attempt, otherwise than by lawful means, the alteration of any matter in church or state by law established; or (3) to incite persons to commit any crime in general disturbance of the peace; or (4) to raise discontent or disaffection amongst the Sovereign's subjects; or (5) to promote feelings of ill-will and hostility between different classes of those subjects. An intention is not seditious if the object is to show that the Sovereign has been misled or mistaken in her measures, or to point out errors or defects in the government or constitution with a view to their reformation, or to excite the subjects to attempt by lawful means the alteration of any matter in church or state by laws established, or to point out, with a view to their removal, matters which are producing, or have a tendency to produce, feelings of hatred and ill-will between classes of the Sovereign's subjects.

The character of the words used may be good evidence of the nature of the intention. (11 Halsbury's Laws (4th edn) para 827)

'The indictment for sedition must specify the acts—the overt or open acts, by which the seditious intent was evidenced, and in the cases to be specially submitted for your consideration, the acts relied on as indicating the seditious spirit of the accused party are certain newspaper publications, which are alleged to be "seditious libels". It is scarcely necessary to point out that to accomplish treasonable purposes, and to delude the weak, the unwary, and the ignorant, no means can be more effectual than a seditious press. With such machinery the preachers of sedition can sow wide cast those poisonous doctrines which, if unchecked, culminate in insurrection and revolution. Lord Mansfield likened a seditious and licentious press to Pandora's box—the source of every evil. Words may be of a seditious character, but they might arise from sudden heat, be heard only by a few, create no lasting impression, and differ in malignity and permanent effect from writings. Sir Michael Foster said of the latter: "Seditious writings are permanent things, and if published they scatter the poison far and wide. They are acts of deliberation, capable of satisfactory proof, and not ordinarily liable to misconstruction; at least they are submitted to the judgment of the court naked and undisguised, as they came out of the author's hands." I am confident you will concur in the force and justice of the observation of that learned judge.' *R v Sullivan, R v Pigott* (1868) 11 Cox CC 44 at 46, per Fitzgerald J

'The law upon the question of what is seditious and what is not is to be found stated very clearly in a book written by a learned judge—Mr Justice Stephen. . . . That learned judge defines seditious words and libels as meaning words or writing used or written for the purpose of bringing into contempt the Crown or the Constitution of the country, or the administration of justice, or to excite Her Majesty's subjects to alter existing laws otherwise than by lawful and constitutional means. . . . An intention to incite feelings of ill will and hostility between different classes of Her Majesty's subjects may be seditious.' *R v Burns* (1886) 2 TLR 510 at 524, per Cave J

SEE *See also* DIOCESE

'The words "see" and "diocese" seem to be employed as equivalent expressions, although probably the word "see" has strictly a more confined meaning than the word "diocese". The primary reason why a diocese, or, in other words, a limited territorial space, was originally assigned to a bishop, was not, as I apprehend, because his functions or duties were confined to that space, but because, as the superintendence of the bishop was found to be more effectual when exercised principally over a limited extent, a territorial district, termed a diocese, was assigned to him as the limits within which he should principally exercise his authority.' *Natal (Bp) v Gladstone* (1866) LR 3 Eq 1 at 29, 30, per Lord Romilly MR

SEED

'Seeds' includes agricultural and horticultural seeds, vegetable seeds, flower seeds, seeds of grasses, whether used for agricultural purposes or other purposes, and seeds of trees. (Plant Varieties and Seeds Act 1964, s 30)

'The ordinary meaning of "seed barley" is barley which will germinate.' *Carter v Crick* (1859) 4. H & N 412 at 416, per Bramwell B

SEISIN *See* POSSESSION

SEIZURE *See also* CAPTURE

Of goods

For an act of the sheriff or his baliff to constitute a seizure of goods, it is not necessary that there should be any physical contact with the goods seized, nor does such contact necessarily amount to seizure. An entry upon the premises on which the goods are situate, together with an intimation of an intention to seize the goods, will amount to a valid seizure, even where the premises are extensive and the property seized widely scattered, but some act must be done sufficient to intimate to the judgment debtor or his employees that a seizure has been made, and it is not sufficient to enter upon the premises and demand the debt. Any act which, if not done with the court's authority, would amount to a trespass to goods will constitute a seizure of them when done under the writ. Whether or not there has been a seizure is a question of fact. The sheriff should clearly specify which of the debtor's goods have been seized as he must not over-levy. (17 Halsbury's Laws (4th edn) para 489)

Of ship

Seizure includes takings otherwise than by capture, as by revenue or sanitary officers of a foreign State. Seizures and takings at sea include deprivation of possession, whether the seizure or taking was lawful or unlawful and whether by enemies or pirates (25 Halsbury's Laws (4th edn) para 157)

[A vessel was insured by a policy of marine insurance which contained a clause excepting the underwriters from liability for loss or damage through capture and 'seizure'.] 'What is the meaning of the words "capture and seizure"? . . . I am disposed to agree that if the word "capture" had stood alone it might have appeared to point to a belligerent capture, but the addition of the word "seizure" is only officious, as I read the warranty, by supposing that it is to exclude that narrow construction of the word "capture" and to let in other "seizures" . . . by means of the revenue laws of a foreign state. The facts of this case shew what the nature and effect of such a seizure is. The ship was seized in every sense we can put upon the word "seize". It was taken forcible possession of, and that not for a temporary purpose, not as incident to a civil remedy or the enforcement of a civil right, not as security for the performance of some duty or obligation by the owners of the ship, but it was carried into effect in order to obtain a sentence of condemnation and confiscation of the ship. And the case states that that would have been the result of the seizure which took place in the present instance if money had not been paid to redeem the ship from that confiscation and total loss. To my mind those facts are properly described by the word "seizure" in its natural sense.' *Cory v Burr* (1883) 8 App Cas 393 at 395, 396, per Lord Selborne LC

'In the construction of this warranty it is observable that "capture" and "seizure" do not mean the same thing. "Capture" would seem properly to include every act of seizing or taking by an enemy or belligerent. "Seizure" seems to be a larger term than "capture" and goes beyond it, and may reasonably be interpreted to embrace every act of taking forcible possession either by a lawful authority or by overpowering force.' Ibid at 405, per Lord FitzGerald

'The plaintiffs in this case were the owners of a vessel called the *Cypriot*; and they sued the defendants, underwriters at Lloyds, on a policy of insurance effected on that vessel, alleging that she had been lost by perils insured against. The plaintiffs had in the policy warranted the vessel free from capture and seizure, and the consequences of any attempt thereat. The defence was that the loss was a loss by seizure within the meaning of that warranty. . . . From the examination of the master it appeared that on the 7th of October, 1879, the *Cypriot* got ashore while going down the Brass River. On the following day the natives took forcible possession of the ship; drove away the master and crew, and plundered the vessel in the manner there described. The consequence was, as stated in the admissions, that the ship became a constructive total loss. The jury found that the natives seized the vessel for the purpose of plundering the cargo, and not for the purpose of keeping her. It was contended for the plaintiffs that to constitute the seizure of a vessel there must be a taking possession with intent to keep it as one's own, and not merely for purposes of plunder. . . . In my opinion the word "seizure" must be taken in its ordinary and natural meaning, and is not a term of art. . . . I have no doubt that the word "seizure", like many other words, is sometimes used with more general and sometimes with more restricted meaning, and whether it is used in a particular case with the one meaning or the other depends not on any general rule but on the context and the circumstances of the case. This brings us to the consideration of the policy sued on, and after reading it carefully I cannot find any indication that the word "seizure" is used in any but its ordinary and general signification. Indeed, the words "free from capture and seizure and the consequences of any attempt thereat" point to the more general meaning of the word "seizure", since in the case of an unsuccessful attempt at seizure it must obviously be difficult to say what the intention was of those who made the attempt. . . . In truth the natives neither intended to keep possession of the vessel as their own nor to return it to the owners. Their object was plunder, and to facilitate that object they seized the vessel, not caring what became of it after their main object, that of plunder, was effected.' *Johnston v Hogg* (1883) 10 QBD 432 at 432–435, per Cave J

[By a policy of insurance gold was warranted free from 'capture, seizure and detention'.] 'Was this taking a capture, seizure, or detention within the terms of the clause of exception? It has been suggested that these words point to hostile taking, and to hostile taking only. That is probably true of capture. But seizure . . . means more than capture. . . . It has been contended that seizure implies force. So it does. . . . Seizure signifies "the taking of a ship by the act of Governments or other public authority for a violation of the laws of trade, or some rule or regulation instituted as a matter of municipal police, or in consequence of an existing state of war." . . . Seizure is not confined to hostile acts. Nor is the word detention.' *Robinson Gold Mining Co v Alliance, Marine & General Assurance Co* (1901) 70 LJ KB 892 at 896, per Phillimore J

'The policy contains the warranty against "capture, seizure, or detention,', commonly called at Lloyd's the f.c.s. clause. . . . The warranty goes beyond the words "arrest" and "restraint". "Capture" and "seizure" are stronger expressions. It was suggested that what was meant were acts of warfare; but it is clearly settled that the words have no such restricted meaning: *Cory v Burr* [supra]. . . . The word "detention" in the warranty cannot be distinguished from the word "detainment".' *Miller v Law Accident Insurance Co* [1903] 1 KB 712 at 722, CA, per Mathew LJ

'In arguing that there was a seizure, the plaintiffs rely on the decision of the Court of Appeal in *Netherlands American Steam Navigation Co v HM Procurator General* [1926] 1 KB 84. In that case a neutral ship was stopped on the high seas by one of HM Naval Patrol boats under the belligerent right of visit and search, an armed guard was put on board and she was ordered to proceed to a British port for better examination. No formal notice of seizure was given on arrival at the port; she was searched and, no contraband being found, she was released. It was held that those facts sufficiently amounted to a seizure or capture of the ship to give jurisdiction to the Prize Court to entertain a claim for compensation for her compulsory diversion and detention. The jurisdiction of the Prize Court is defined in the commission [issued by the Crown at the outbreak of war] where the court is "authorised and required to take cognisance of and judicially to proceed upon all and all manner of captures, seizures, prizes and reprisals of all ships, vessels and goods that are, or shall be, taken and to hear and determine the same". The decision of the Court of Appeal was directed to that question and rejected the argument that a mere temporary detention in exercise of the right of visit and search was, for the purpose of the definition, inconsistent with capture. This use of the word "seizure" is, no doubt, in a sense wider than that normally used by international lawyers who speak of the centuries-old right of belligerent warships to visit and search merchant ships, whether enemy or neutral, as a right existing before capture or seizure, the words "capture" and "seizure" being treated as synonymous.' *The Mim* [1947] P 115 at 119, per Hodson J

SELF-CONTAINED *See also* FLAT

'In my view, the expression "self-contained", as applied to a flat, only means that it is a complete residence, containing all that is reasonably necessary for the person who resides there. It is not necessary that all the rooms should be within one outer door, or cut off from other parts of the house. The mere presence or absence of a partition is not the test.' *Darrall v Whitaker* (1923) 92 LJ KB 882 at 884, per Lush J

'If "self-contained" means, as presumably it does, something more than separate, I think . . . that a flat or tenement to be self-contained must be within a circle or ambit and must not be scattered, and that no one could make a dwelling-house into self-contained flats by making provision for two occupiers to use rooms scattered about the house, which, although they might be separate from each other, do not constitute self-contained flats in the sense that each of them was confined within its own area.' *Smith v Prime* (1923) 129 LT 441 at 442, per Roche J

SELF-DEFENCE

Every person is justified in using reasonable force to defend himself and those under his care, but the force justifiable is such only as is reasonably necessary. (45 Halsbury's Laws (4th edn) para 1257)

The defence of one's self, or the mutual and reciprocal defence of such as stand in the relations of husband and wife, parent and child, master and servant. In these cases, if the party himself, or any of these his relations, be forcibly attacked in his person or property, it is lawful for him to repel force by force; and the breach of the peace, which happens, is chargeable upon him only who began the affray. For the law, in this case, respects the passions of the human mind; and (when external violence is offered to a man himself, or those to whom he bears a near connection) makes it lawful in him to do himself that immediate justice, to which he is prompted by nature, and which no prudential motives are strong enough to restrain. It considers that the future process of law is by no means an adequate remedy for injuries accompanied with force; since it is impossible to say, to what wanton lengths of rapine or cruelty outrages of this sort might be carried, unless it were permitted a man immediately to oppose one violence with another. Self-defence therefore, as it is justly called the primary law of nature, so it is not, neither can it be in fact, taken away by the law of society. In the English law particularly it is held an excuse for breaches of the peace, nay even for homicide itself: but care must be taken, that the resistance does not exceed the bounds of mere defence and prevention; for then the defender would himself become an aggressor. (3 Bl Com 3, 4)

'It is quite clear that self-defence is a special plea which arises only in the case where a man admits that he did deliver blows; he says they were delivered because the other man attacked him first and if there is no cruel excess, or anything of that type, then it becomes complete exculpation.' *HM Advocate v McGlone* 1955 SLT 79 at 79, per Lord Mackintosh

'The sturdy submission is made that an Englishman is not bound to run away when threatened, but can stand his ground and defend himself where he is. In support of this submission no authority is quoted, save that counsel for the appellant has been at considerable length and diligence to look at the textbooks on the subject, and has demonstrated to us that the textbooks in the main do not say that a preliminary retreat is a necessary prerequisite to the use of force in self-defence. Equally, it must be said that the textbooks do not state the contrary either; and it is, of course, well known to us all that for very many years it has been common form for judges directing juries where the issue of self-defence is raised in any case (be it a homicide case or not) that the duty to retreat arises. It is not, as we understand it, the law that a person threatened must take to his heels and run in the dramatic way suggested by counsel for the appellant; but what is necessary is that he should demonstrate by his actions that he does not want to fight. He must demonstrate that he is prepared to temporise and disengage and perhaps to make some physical withdrawal; and to the extent that that is necessary as a feature of the justification of self-defence, it is true, in our opinion, whether the charge is a homicide charge or something less serious.' *R v Julien* [1969] 2 All ER 856 at 858, per cur

'In their Lordships' view the defence of self-defence is one which can be and will be readily understood by any jury. It is a straightforward conception. It involves no abstruse legal thought. It requires no set words by way of explanation. No formula need be employed in references to it. Only common sense is needed for its understanding. It is both good law and good sense that a man who is attacked may defend himself. It is both good law and good sense that he may do, but may only do, what is reasonably necessary. But everything will depend on the particular facts and circumstances. Of these a jury can decide. It may in some cases be only sensible and clearly possible to take some simple avoiding action. Some attacks may be serious and dangerous. Others may not be. If there is some relatively minor attack it would not be common sense to permit some action of retaliation which was wholly out of proportion to the necessities of the situation. If an attack is serious so that it puts someone in immediate peril then immediate defensive action may be necessary. If the moment is one of crisis for someone in imminent danger he may have to avert the danger by some instant reaction. If the attack is all over and no sort of peril remains then the employment of force may be by way of revenge or punishment or by way of paying off an old score or may be pure aggression. There may no longer be any link with a necessity of defence. Of all these matters the good sense of a jury will be the arbiter.' *Palmer v R* [1971] 1 All ER 1077 at 1088, PC, per Lord Morris of Borth-y-Gest

SELF-EMPLOYED

'Self-employed person' means an individual who works for gain or reward otherwise than under a contract of employment, whether or not he himself employs others. (Health and Safety at Work etc Act 1974, s 53(1))

'Self-employed earner' means a person who is gainfully employed in Great Britain otherwise than in employed earners' employment (whether or not he is also employed in such employment). (Social Security Act 1975, Sch 20)

SELL *See also* SALE

'Now a power to sell means, in the absence of any context, a power to sell for money, and a person who exercises such a power is bound to sell for money.' *Paine v Cork Co* (1900), 69 LJ Ch 156 at 158, per Sterling J

'I have been unable to find any case in which it has been held that instructions given by A B to sell for him his house, and an agreement to pay so much on the purchase price accepted, are not an authority to make a binding contract, including an authority to sign an agreement. If a power of attorney were given to A B to sell an estate, he would, in my opinion, be entitled, in the absence of anything narrowing the meaning of the word "sell", not only to negotiate for but to sign an agreement for sale; and that would give to the word "sell" its full meaning—namely, to conclude a binding agreement for sale.' *Rosenbaum v Belson* [1900] 2 Ch 267 at 271, per Buckley J

Australia 'We think it sufficiently plain that where an owner requests a professional agent to sell his property for him, if there is nothing more the agent becomes entitled to his commission when he sells the property or the property is sold through his intervention, but "sell" and "sold" are ambiguous words and may refer either to the execution of the contract of sale or to the completion of the sale by payment and conveyance. However, in *Rosenbaum v Belson* [supra, at 271] Buckley J described the "full" meaning of sale as being "the conclusion of a binding agreement for sale" and that "sell" should mean "contract to sell" and not "complete the sale" gains some support from the fact that an employment to sell gives authority to the agent to sign a contract on behalf of his principal, but not, we should think, an authority to complete the conveyance. We think "contract to sell" is the primary meaning and the one that should be given to the word "sell" in such a contract.' *Scott v Willmore* [1949] VLR 113 at 115, per Herring CJ and Gavan Duffy J

'"Sell the property" does not, in my opinion, in the circumstances of this case, mean to do all things up to and including the completion of the contract of sale, i.e. including conveyance and payment of the full purchase price. A property is sold, in the ordinarily accepted meaning of that phrase, when a binding and enforceable contract of sale has been made. When that has been done, the matter, generally speaking, does, and would here, pass out of the hands of the agent. The agent is not interested in the matter thereafter except as to deposit received and commission payable.' Ibid at 125, per O'Bryan J

New Zealand 'The word "sell", as ordinarily used, does not, in my opinion, mean "convey". There never could be a vendor and purchaser, as ordinarily understood in law text-books, if there was no sale till a conveyance; and the term "resale" used in our text-books would be inapt if there was no sale till there was a conveyance. The word "sell" means only a binding bargain to convey on the part of the vendor, and to take a conveyance and complete on the part of the purchaser.' *Joel v Barlow* (1903) 22 NZLR 900 at 901, per Stout CJ; also reported 5 GLR 450 at 451

In Markets and Fairs Clauses Act

'The 13th section of the Markets and Fairs Clauses Act [1847] makes it a penal offence to sell tollable goods within the prescribed limits of a market town elsewhere than in the seller's dwelling-house or shop. There is a market at Ilfracombe, and the appellant, a farmer, at his dwelling-house within the prescribed limits made an agreement to sell two pigs then alive, which he was to kill and deliver at the buyer's shop within those limits, where they were to be weighed to ascertain the price, and they were to be at the seller's risk until delivery. . . . What, for the guidance of Justices in future cases, are we to lay down that sale means in the Act before us? All I propose to say is this: I think the cases at present decide that such an agreement for sale, as would popularly be called a sale, although the property does not pass by it and although the acts passing in property occur elsewhere, is to be treated as a sale for the purposes of this Act.' *Lambert v Rowe* [1914] 1 KB 38 at 46, 48, 49, per Ridley J

Sale of food

'We have to deal with [s 6 of] the Sale of Food and Drugs Act 1875 [repealed; see now the Food Act 1984, s 2]. . . . The statute deals with, and is for the prevention of, the adulteration of food and drugs, and it points at particular acts done by particular persons; one of these acts is, under s 6, the act of selling the adulterated article. . . . It provides that no person shall sell to the prejudice of the purchaser any article of food which is not of the nature, substance, and quality demanded by such purchaser. In my opinion, a person who takes the article in his hand, and performs the physical act of transferring the adulterated thing to the purchaser, is a person who sells within this section.' *Hotchin v Hindmarsh* [1891] 2 QB 181 at 186, 187, DC, per Lord Coleridge CJ

SELLER

In this Part of this Act [Part V: rights of an unpaid seller against the goods] 'seller' includes any person who is in the position of a seller, as, for instance, an agent of the seller to whom the bill of lading has been indorsed, or a consignor or agent who has himself paid (or is directly responsible for) the price. (Sale of Goods Act 1979, s 38(2))

'Seller' means a person who sells or agrees to sell goods. (Sale of Goods Act 1979, s 61(1))

[The Pharmacy Act 1868, s 17 (repealed; see now the Poisons Act 1972, s 3) enacted (inter alia) that it should be unlawful to sell any poison unless the article containing the poison bore the name and address of the 'seller'.] 'The case depends on the true meaning of the word "seller" in s 17. It seems clear that the word "seller" as used in that section means the person keeping or controlling the shop or place or carrying on the business where the poison is sold. This construction is consistent with the general policy of the Act, which is to protect the public against the sale of poisons by unqualified persons.' *Templeman v Trafford* (1881) 8 QBD 397 at 402, DC, per Lopes J

'Section 17 [repealed; see supra] of the Pharmacy Act 1868, says that a vessel containing poison must be distinctly labelled . . . with the name and address of the seller, but the section does not specify what particular name and what particular address are to be given. . . . Who is the seller? The seller is not the person who happens to be in the shop, but the person on whose behalf the thing is sold and may be a corporation; the seller is the person who is carrying on the business.' *Edwards v Pharmaceutical Society of Great Britain* [1910] 2 KB 766 at 774, DC, per Bray J

[An employee can apparently commit the offence of selling poison: see *Preston v Albuery* [1963] 3 All ER 897.]

Unpaid seller

The seller of goods is an 'unpaid seller' within the meaning of this Act—

(a) when the whole of the price has not been paid or tendered;

(b) when a bill of exchange or other negotiable instrument has been received as conditional payment, and the condition on which it was received has not been fulfilled by reason of the dishonour of the instrument or otherwise.

(Sale of Goods Act 1979, s 38(1))

SELLING COSTS

New Zealand [The Layby Sales Act 1971, s 9(1)(*a*) uses the phrase 'selling costs in respect of the layby sale'.] 'Although different textbook writers appear to use the expressions 'selling costs' and 'selling expenses' I see no reason to differentiate between the two. They both have the same meaning and are both limited to costs or expenses directly associated with selling. . . . I do not think that the phrase as used in s 9(1)(a) of the Act limits the selling costs to those involving only the layby element of the sale.' *Wood v Universal Fur Co Ltd*, [1985] 1 NZLR 640 at 644, per Davison CJ

SEMINARY *See also* SCHOOL

Canada '"Seminary" is derived from the Latin word "seminarium" meaning "seed"—"plot"—a place where seed is sown and cultivated. Its application to an institution where seeds of learning are disseminated and developed to full flower was an early transition and the word now denotes in its most generally accepted sense a place of education, a school, a college, university or the like.' *Worldwide Evangelization Crusade (Canada) v Beamsville* [1957] OR 80 at 89, Ont CA, per Schroeder JA; revd on other grounds (1959) 21 DLR (2d) 8 (SCC)

Canada 'The word "seminary", standing by itself, has not acquired any fixed legal meaning. It is not, in my opinion, a term of art and its primary meaning is simply a place of education.' *Worldwide Evangelization Crusade (Canada) v Corportion of Village of Beamsville* [1960] SCR 49 at 52, SCC, per Cartwright J

SEND

Where an Act authorises or requires any document to be served by post (whether the expression 'serve' or the expression 'give' or 'send' or any other expression is used) then, unless the contrary intention appears, the service is deemed to be effected by properly addressing, prepaying and posting a letter containing the document and, unless the contrary is proved, to have been effected at the time at which the letter would be delivered in the ordinary course of post. (Interpretation Act 1978, s 7)

'Send' includes deliver, and 'sender' shall be construed accordingly. (Unsolicited Goods and Services Act 1971, s 6(1)

[See further, as to the meaning of 'sender', s 1(4) of the 1971 Act.]

[Statute 1753–4 27 Geo 2, c 15 (repealed) enacted that if any person should knowingly 'send' any letter without any name subscribed thereto, or signed with a fictitious name, threatening to kill or murder any of His Majesty's subjects, or to burn their homes, etc, he should be judged guilty of felony.] 'A letter dropped near the prosecutor with intent that it might reach him, was a sending of it to him.' *R v Wagstaff* (1819) Russ & Ry 398 at 401, CCR per cur

[The Sale of Food and Drugs Act 1899, s 20 (repealed; see now the Food Act 1984, s 102(2)(a)) enacted that a warranty should not be available as a defence to any proceedings under the Act unless the defendant had, within seven days after service of the summons (now three days before the date of the hearing) 'sent' to the prosecutor a copy of such warranty with a written notice stating that he intended to rely on it.] 'The question is whether . . . the document was "sent" by the appellants within seven days of the service of the summons. . . . The summons was served on the appellants on 12th of August, 1911, and on 19th August, 1911, the appellants through their solicitors sent by post from Bristol to the respondent at his address at Chiswick a written notice in the terms of the subsection in question, and they sent at the same time a copy of the warranty to the respondent, and also a like notice by post to the person from whom they received the warranty. . . . In my judgment s 20, sub-s 1, of the Sale of Food and Drugs Act 1899 was complied with by posting the documents within the prescribed time. . . . I think that putting in the post on the afternoon of 19th August, 1911, the copy of the warranty and the notice was a sufficient compliance with the section.' *Retail Dairy Co Ltd v Clarke* [1912] 2 KB 388 at 392, 393, 395, DC per Ridley J

[The Road Traffic Act 1930, s 21 (repealed; see now the Road Traffic Offenders Act 1988, s 1(1)) provided (inter alia) that no person should be convicted of certain offences unless within fourteen days a notice of intended prosecution was served or sent by registered post to him.] 'It is to be observed that the words are "sent . . . to him" not "sent . . . to him and received by him" and a passage in the judgment of A T Lawrence J in *Retail Dairy Co Ltd v Clarke* [supra] seems to be apposite. In that case it was held, with reference to a warranty or invoice under the Sale of Food and Drugs Act 1899, that: "In the absence of any words in the subsection indicating that the word 'sent' is used with any other than its ordinary meaning of 'dispatched' it must be construed as bearing that meaning, and that if a copy of the warranty with the written notice is posted to the purchaser within seven days from the issue of the summons it is 'sent' in compliance with the requirement of the subsection although it does not reach him till after the expiration of the seven days." . . . That case seems to be a clear and relevant authority on the meaning of the words "sent . . . to him". . . . In the present case, by a combination of accidental circumstances, including the fact that the respondent, when he was well enough to be moved from the cottage hospital, did not go home, but went to see some friends in Birmingham and stayed there for some time, the document did not in fact reach his hands within the time contemplated by the statute. On the other hand, it was posted at a time when it might well have been expected that before the expiration of the period named in the statute it would in the ordinary course reach him. Other considerations no doubt would apply if it appeared that the sender of the notice deliberately sent it to a place where he knew that the intended recipient was not or was not likely to be, or in any other way deliberately defeated the intention of this statute, which undoubtedly is to give proper notice. But I see no ingredient in this case which suggests any such conclusion. At the time when the letter was posted by registered post to the address of the respondent, the sender had reason to believe that the letter would reach him before the termination of the allotted time, and I think that the fair inference is that the document was posted with the intention that it should reach him within the allotted time. In those circumstances it seems to me that the act prescribed by the statute was duly performed inasmuch as notice was sent by registered post to the respondent at a time when, in the ordinary course, it might properly have been expected to reach him.' *Stanley v Thomas* [1939] 2 KB 462 at 465–467, per Lord Hewart CJ

'The verb "to send" has various meanings. It may mean to despatch, or to despatch so that in the ordinary course of post the missive would arrive, or to dispatch so that it is received. . . . Though these various meanings are possible, there is no doubt that the ordinary meaning, and therefore in the absence of special circumstances the appropriate meaning, is to despatch. . . . So we are here dealing with a provision which requires a question to be referred within a particular period by a written application being sent. It seems to us that time requirement is satisfied if within that period the application is sent albeit it is not received. Counsel has told us that so far as the Secretary of State can tell such a view would not produce practical inconvenience, and it seems to us that there are advantages in it. It is a view which has received the support of an industrial tribunal in another case, *McCutcheon v Sykes-Marfarland Ltd*, and of Professor Grunfield, though in neither case with any supporting argument. For the reasons given, we think that view is correct and we therefore allow the appeal and remit the case to be heard.' *Nash v Ryan Plant International Ltd* [1978] 1 All ER 492 at 496, per cur

By post

Australia 'The words "sent by post" are ambiguous. A document may be sent by post within the meaning of those words either when it is posted or when it would, in the ordinary course of post, reach its destination: it all depends on the context, as may be seen from such cases as *R v Recorder of Richmond* (1958) 27 LJMC 197, and *Browne v Black* [1912] 1 KB 316. In the present agreement, the words "if sent by post shall be deemed to be delivered in due course of post" indicate that the notice is "sent" within the meaning of cl 3, not when it is posted but when it is deemed to be delivered. The words must be given some effect—they cannot have been intended to be merely nugatory—and they can only mean that a notice, if sent by post, is deemed to have been delivered in due course of post, and that if the notice is not in fact received on or before the expiry date, it must have been posted in sufficient time for the deemed delivery to take place on or before the expiry date if it is to be effective.' *Lewes Nominees v Strang* (1983) 49 ALR 328 at 330, per Gibbs CJ

United States 'Send' in connection with any writing or notice means to deposit in the mail or deliver for transmission by any other usual means of communication with postage or cost of transmission provided for and properly addressed and in the case of an instrument to an address specified thereon or otherwise agreed, or if there be none to any address reasonable under the circumstances. The receipt of any writing or notice within the time at which it would have arrived if properly sent has the effect of a proper sending. (Uniform Commercial Code 1978, s 1–201(38))

SENTENCE

'Sentence' includes an order for detention in a detention centre . . . but does not include a committal in default of payment of any sum of money or failing to do or abstain from doing anything required to be done or left undone. (Criminal Justice Act 1948, s 80, as amended by the Children and Young Persons Act 1969)

'Sentence of imprisonment' does not include a committal in default of payment of any sum of money, or for want of sufficient distress to satisfy any sume of money, or for failure to do or abstain from doing anything required to be done or left undone. (Criminal Justice Act 1967, s 104(1); see also the Magistrates' Courts Act 1980, s 150(1))

(1) In this Act, 'sentence', in relation to an offence, includes any order made by a court when dealing with an offender (including a hospital order under Part III of the Mental Health Act 1983, with or without a restriction order, and an interim hospital order under that Part) and also includes a recommendation for deportation.

(1A) Section 13 of the Powers of Criminal Courts Act 1973 (under which a conviction for an offence for which a probation order or an order for conditional or absolute discharge is made is deemed not to be a conviction except for certain purposes) shall not prevent an appeal under this Act, whether against conviction or otherwise.

(2) Any power of the criminal division of the Court of Appeal to pass a sentence includes a power to make a recommendation for deportation in cases where the court from which the appeal lies had power to make such a recommendation. (Criminal Appeal Act 1968, s 50, as amended by the Criminal Justice Act 1982 and the Mental Health Act 1983))

[The Criminal Appeal Act 1968, s 9 describes the circumstances in which a person can appeal against his 'sentence'.] 'The essential key to the meaning of "sentence" in this context in our opinion is that it is an order, and it is an order made by a court when dealing with an offender, and we think that means when dealing with someone who has offended in respect of his offence.' *R v Hayden* [1975] 2 All ER 558 at 559, CA, per cur

Australia 'The word "sentence" connotes a judicial judgment or pronouncement fixing a term of imprisonment. A term of imprisonment is the period fixed by the judgment as the punishment for the offence.' *Winsor v Boaden* (1953) 90 CLR 345 at 347, per Dixon CJ

Australia '"Sentence", in its ordinary meaning, denotes a judicial judgment or pronouncement made by a court in a criminal or penal context. It is normally inappropriate to judgments or pronouncements made in a purely civil context. But, in my opinion, it is not limited to judgments or pronouncements whereby a person is directed to be imprisoned. "Sentence" properly describes what a court does when for example, it imposes a fine rather than imprisonment. . . . Thus, in my opinion, if a defendant be adjudged liable to pay a fine, that is a sentence, whether or not he be, as ordinarily is the case, ordered to be imprisoned in default.' *Botany Municipal Council v Jackson* [1985] 2 NSWLR 1 at 13, per Mahoney JA

Suspended sentence

A court which passes a sentence of imprisonment for a term of not more than two years for an offence may order that the sentence shall not take effect unless, during a period specified in the order, being not less than one year or more than two years from the date of the order, the offender commits in Great Britain another offence punishable with imprisonment and thereafter a court having power to do so orders . . . that the original sentence shall take effect. (Powers of Criminal Courts Act 1973, s 22(1))

SEPARATE

Australia [The Dividing Fences Act 1951–1986 (NSW), s 5, provides that dividing fence means a fence 'separating' the lands of different owners whether on the common boundary of adjoining lands or on a line other than a common boundary.] 'In my opinion the word "separating" in the definition of "dividing fence" has a functional connotation, which renders it necessary to examine the physical characteristics and function of the fence in question in relation to the physical characteristics of the rest of the land on either side thereof in order to determine whether the statutory criteria is satisfied. The concluding words of the definition of "dividing fence" which contemplate a dividing fence otherwise than on the common boundary seem to me to support such a connotation in the present case. The retaining wall (in question) provides structural support for other materials on and below the surface of (the land on one side of the wall) and thus assists to maintain the surface of (that land) at its present level, but it seems to me that it does not "separate" the two parcels of land in what I consider to be the relevant sense of impending egress or ingress to or from either property.' *Carter v Murray* (1981) 2 NSWLR 77 at 79, per McLelland J

SEPARATE AND APART

Canada [Divorce was available where the parties had lived 'separate and apart' for a specified period.] 'The words "separate and apart" are disjunctive. They mean, in my view, that there must be a withdrawal from the matrimonial obligation with the intent of destroying the matrimonial consortium, as well as physical separation. The two conditions must be met. I hold that they are met here. The mere fact that the parties are under one roof does not mean that they are not living separate and apart within the meaning of the Act. There can be, and I hold that here there has been, a physical separation within . . . one suite of rooms. To hold otherwise would be to deprive the petitioner here of any remedy . . . simply because she is precluded, or was for a period of time precluded, by economic circumstances from acquiring a different suite in which to live.' *Rushton v Rushton* (1968) 2 DLR (3d) 25 at 27, BCSC, per McIntyre J

Canada 'The physical separation of husband and wife is one of the factors which must be taken into consideration in cases of this kind, but there may be physical separation of the parties without there being a finding that the parties are living "separate and apart". For instance, a serviceman may be posted overseas and be away from his wife for over three years without the parties living "separate and apart" within the meaning of the Act.' *Dorchester v Dorchester* [1971] 2 WWR 634 at 636, BCSC, per Macfarlane J

SEPARATE DWELLING

[The Customs and Inland Revenue Act 1891, s 4 (repealed) provided for the assessment to inhabited house duty of houses originally built, or adapted by additions or alterations, and used for the sole purpose of providing 'separate dwellings'.] 'The houses in question have been found . . . to be occupied in separate flats, there being a complete dwelling for all purposes within the confines of each flat, save in so far as the occupants have a common entrance or staircase and also the use in common on certain days of a scullery or wash-house in the backyard. . . . What has been found, I think, entitles the appellant's counsel to say that the houses were originally built for the sole purpose of providing separate dwellings.' *Seaman v Lee* (1899) 68 LJQB 593 at 596, per Kennedy J

'I think that the true test, where the tenant has the exclusive use of some rooms and shares certain accommodation with others, is as follows: there is a letting of part of a house as a separate dwelling, within the meaning of the relevant Acts [see now the Rent Act 1977, s 1] if, and only if, the accommodation which is shared with others does not comprise any of the rooms which may fairly be described as "living rooms" or "dwelling rooms". To my mind a kitchen is fairly described as a "living room", and thus nobody who shares a kitchen can be said to be tenant of a part of a house let as a separate dwelling. In many households the kitchen is the principal living room, where the occupants spend the greater part of the day. Very often it is the warmest part of the house and the family tend to congregate there for that reason. On the other hand, both the bathroom and the WC are rooms which are only visited on occasions for a specific purpose, and I think they may fairly be classed with such a room as a box-room, though no doubt it is not visited so often. I think that this test gives a reasonable construction to the Acts, and one which is in accordance with their general scheme and intention.' *Cole v Harris* [1945] KB 474 at 484, 485, CA, per Morton LJ

SEPARATION

'A man may leave his wife in order to go on public duty, or for business purposes. Before the means of communication were so common and so efficient as they now are husbands employed in distant countries had sometimes to leave their wives for long periods. A husband may leave his wife for a time even for pleasure, if he wants to do something which she does not want to do; or she may leave him for the same reason. In none of these cases, however, are they separated from each other. They have still their common home, or common homes if they are rich people and have more than one house. They will act from the same base, if I may use that expression, and the physical separation, therefore, is immaterial.' *Eadie v Inland Revenue Comrs* [1924] 2 KB 198 at 207, per Rowlatt J

Australia 'The word "separate" is defined in the Oxford English Dictionary as—to put apart, set asunder, to disunite, disconnect, make a division between, to quit the company or society of another or others; to go away, secede or withdraw. "Separation" is defined as—the action of separating or parting, of setting or keeping apart; the state of being separated or parted. The word "separate" used in its dictionary meaning, when referring to persons who have been legally married and who have thereby immediately acquired the rights and assumed the obligations of that conjugal relationship, in my view, applies equally to those who have parted after cohabitation has commenced as to those who have kept apart or withdrawn from each other from the moment they became man and wife. So a husband and wife who part at the church door as the result of an agreement, express or implied, for separation, have "separated". They have withdrawn from each other; they have gone their separate ways; they have commenced to live separate and apart. In other words, they have achieved a "separation"—they have taken the action of keeping apart; they have achieved a state of being separate or apart. It matters not for this purpose whether the agreement for keeping apart be permanent or temporary, nor whether the agreement be made before or after marriage. An agreement for permanent separation, however, made prior to marriage would be illegal as contrary to public policy. See *Brodie v Brodie* [1917] P 271; [1916–17] All ER Rep 237, and the cases there cited. Nor, in my view, does it matter whether a temporary parting results from considerations of the convenience of the parties, or because circumstances beyond their control dictate such a course.' *Mradakovic v Mradakovic* [1966] ALR 1007 at 1008, per Jenkyn J

SEQUESTRATION

'The term "sequestration" has no particular technical meaning; it simply means the detention of property by a court of justice for the purpose of answering a demand which is made.' *Re Australian Direct Steam Navigation Co* (1875) LR 20 Eq 325 at 326, per Jessel MR

Of benefice

Sequestration is the legal means by which the creditors of an incumbent can obtain satisfaction of their debts out of the profits of his benefice. It is obtained by a writ of *fieri facias de bonis ecclesiasticis* or a writ of *sequestrari facias de bonis ecclesiasticis* sued out of the court in which a judgment or order has been obtained for payment of the debt, after a writ of execution has been issued to the sheriff and the sheriff has made a return that the debtor has no goods or chattels out of which the debt can be satisfied, but that he is incumbent of a benefice named in the return. The writ can be issued in an action in the Chancery Division of the High Court where the defendant has been attached for non-payment of a sum which he has been ordered by the Court to pay, and *non est inventus* has been returned to the attachment, and the ordinary writ of sequestration has been thereupon issued, and the return has been made to it that the defendant has no lay property, but is incumbent of a benefice named in the return. The writ is admissible in evidence, even if the judgment roll contains no entry of its having been awarded. It must not be issued for a sum exceeding the amount of the debt due. (14 Halsbury's Laws (4th edn) para 894)

'It seems plain that during the sequestration, unless the bishop makes such inhibition, the incumbent may still perform the services of the Church; and, consequently, it appears to follow that sequestration is very different from suspension. In fact, sequestration is this, that the proceeds of the benefice are taken by an officer appointed by the bishop for the purpose, but in other respects the position of the incumbent, except so far as it may be expressly altered by the statute, remains the same.' *Lawrence v Edwards* [1891] 1 Ch 144 at 149, 150, per Chitty J

Writ of sequestration

The writ of sequestration is a process of contempt by proceeding against the property of the contemnor, and is available as a mode of enforcement of judgments or orders only where the person against whom it is sought to be issued is in contempt of court by disobedience to an order of the court. Before the writ of sequestration will be allowed to issue, therefore, the court must be satisfied, beyond reasonable doubt, that a contempt of court has been committed. The writ of sequestration is a remedy of last resort to enforce a judgment or order which requires a person to do an act within a specified time or which requires a person to abstain from doing a specified act. In the case of a judgment or order in positive terms it is not enough that it requires a person to do a specified act; it must also specify the time within which the required act must be done. A judgment or order for the payment of money to a person, for the payment of money into court, for giving of possession of land, or for the delivery of goods which does not give the defendant the alternative of paying the assessed value of the goods, may be enforced by writ of sequestration, provided, in each case, the time within which the act is required to be done has been expressly specified by the original judgment or order or by a subsequent order obtained for that purpose. (17 Halsbury's Laws (4th edn) para 505)

SERIES

[By the Indictments Act 1915, Sch 1, rule 3 (revoked; see now the Indictment Rules 1971) charges for any offences might be joined in the same indictment if those charges were founded on the same facts, or formed part of a 'series' of offences of the same or a similar character.] 'Were the two offences a series? Could two make a series? This point was decided by the Court of Appeal in *R v Kray* [[1969] 3 All ER 941], and the application for leave to appeal from their decision to this House was refused both by the Court of Appeal and by this House. Widgery LJ, reading the judgment of the court, said: "It may be true that the word 'series' is not wholly apt to describe less than three components, but so to limit its meaning in the present context would produce the perverse result that whereas three murders could be charged in the same indictment two could not. The construction of the rule has not been restricted in this way in practice during the fifty years which have followed the passage of the Act and it is too late now to take a different view." For these reasons the Court of Appeal decided that two offences could constitute a "series" within the meaning of the rule, and I agree with their decision and reasons.' *Ludlow v Metropolitan Police Comr* [1970] 1 All ER 567 at 573, HL, per Lord Pearson

SERMON

[By a deed of 1580 land was assured to trustees to the intent that the rents should be employed for or towards the charges of a 'sermon' once every year to be made in the parish church of West Ham.] 'I find in the Injunctions of Edward 6 and of Elizabeth that the preaching of sermons is directed as part of the ordinary duty of ecclesiastical persons having the cure of souls. In the Book of Common Prayer in use in 1580 the sponsors of a child are exhorted to see that he hears sermons. At the present time the word "sermon" has a distinctly religious meaning, and no one would think of applying the term to a lecture on a scientific or literary subject. That it had such a special meaning in 1580 is I think shewn by the documents which I have already mentioned. A sermon then in my opinion was in 1580 and is now a religious discourse; the preaching of sermons and the hearing them was and is now regarded as a religious exercise. I do not mean to say that a sermon did not then or does not now sometimes deal with matters not in themselves directly connected with religion, but I think that such matters in a sermon properly so called are only relevant so far as they illustrate or enforce the religious instruction or exhortation which is the proper object of a sermon. The result is that in my judgment the object of the settlor was distinctly a religious object, and the scheme ought to preserve the religious character of the charity, and no part of the income ought to be applied to any non-religious purpose.' *Re Avenon's Charity, A-G v Pelly* [1913] 2 Ch 261 at 276, per Warrington J

SERVANT *See also* CIVIL SERVANT; DOMESTIC SERVANT; MENIAL SERVANT

[A testator, Sir Robert Henley, left, by his will, £100 apiece to all his 'servants'.] 'None of the said plaintiffs, but such as were servants to the said Sir Robert before the making of the said will, and did so continue to be servants to him, until the time of his death, can have any pretence to the said legacy and such only as were menial servants, and lived all along in the house with him.' *Jones v Henley* (1685) 2 Rep Ch 361 at 363, per cur.

'I do not know of any actual case of a seaman

being held to be a servant . . . but, as he is hired to render his services for certain wages, and is bound to obey the orders of the master of the vessel who hired him, I think that he is as much a servant as the clerk or shopman of any merchant or tradesman.' *Re Hudson, ex p Homborg* (1842) 2 Mont D & De G 642 at 643, per Sir John Cross

'What is a test as to the relationship of master and servant? A test used in many cases is, to ascertain whether the prisoner is bound to obey the *orders* of his employer so as to be under the employer's *control*; and, on the case stated there does not seem sufficient to show that he was subject to the employers' orders and bound to devote his time as they should direct. Although under this engagement with them, it appears that he was still at liberty to take orders, or to abstain from doing so and the masters had no power to control him in that respect. Where there is a salary that raises a presumption that the person receiving it is bound to devote his time to the service, but when money is paid by commission a difficulty arises, although the relationship may still exist where commission is paid, as in ordinary cases of a traveller and in *R v Tite* [(1861) 30 LJMC 142, CCR]. But in either case there may be no such control and then the relationship does not exist.' *R v Negus* (1873) LR 2 CCR 34 at 36, per Bovill CJ

'I think there was evidence on which the jury might well find that the prisoner either was a clerk or a servant, or was employed as a clerk or a servant. The father held various offices and the prisoner, his son, in consequence of his father's illness, or for other reasons, did the duties which the father would otherwise have had to do himself or to employ a clerk to do. It is true there was no contract binding him to go on doing his duties. But the relation of master and servant may well be terminable at will and while the prisoner did act he was a clerk or servant.' *R v Foulkes* (1875) LR 2 CCR 150 at 152, per Cockburn CJ

'A servant is a person subject to the command of his master as to the manner in which he shall do his work.' *Yewens v Noakes* (1880) 6 QBD 530 at 532–533, per Bramwell LJ

'It is clear that the captain is the servant of the shipowners. He is appointed and paid by them; they can dismiss him, and he is subject to their orders. The seaman is a servant of the owners also. The captain, no doubt, is a superior servant, and the seaman is an inferior servant, bound to obey the orders of the captain; but they are both servants of the same master, employed in the same operation.' *Hedley v Pinkney & Sons SS Co* [1892] 1 QB 58 at 62, CA, per Lord Esher MR

'There is no better working rule for determining the question than that laid down many years ago by Blackburn J in *R v Negus* [supra], where he said that the test is whether the alleged servant is under the control and bound to obey the orders of the alleged master; if he is, then the relationship of master and servant exists.' *Hill v Beckett* [1915] 1 KB 578 at 582, per Avory J

[The Copyright Act 1911, s 5 (repealed; see now the Copyright, Designs and Patents Act 1988, s 11) dealt with the position where the author of a work was in the employment of some other person under a contract of service. The question was whether an examiner who prepared examination papers was a 'servant' of a university within that section.] 'A servant is a person who is subject to the commands of his master as to the manner in which he shall do his work. A person who is employed by a company at a fixed annual salary to supply weekly articles for a periodical is not a servant within s 209 of the Companies Consolidation Act 1908 [repealed; see now the Companies Act 1985, Sch 19, para 9]: *Re Beeton & Co* [[1913] 2 Ch 279]; nor can a visiting physician of a hospital who, for an annual salary, undertakes to exercise his judgment, skill, and knowledge in determining whether a patient can safely be discharged be properly described as a servant: *Evans v Liverpool Corporation* [[1906] 1 KB 160]. . . . In the present case the examiner was employed to prepare the papers. . . . He was to be paid a lump sum. He was free to prepare his questions at his convenience so long as they were ready by the time appointed . . . and it was left to his skill and judgment to decide what questions should be asked. . . . It is impossible to say that the examiner in such circumstances can be appropriately described as the servant of the University.' *University of London Press Ltd v University Tutorial Press Ltd* [1916] 2 Ch 601 at 611, 612, per Peterson J

'I must consider whether the main indications of service are present here or not; and having done so I have come to the conclusion that neither of these persons [outside contributors to a newspaper] was a servant of the company. I particularly note four circumstances. In the first place, they were working entirely away from the company, and not in the office of the company at all. Secondly, they were not exclusively employed in the service of the company, but they might have taken up any amount of other work for other persons, and I think it is highly probable that they did so. Thirdly, they were not bound to render services generally, but only a particular class of service. Fourthly, and most important of all, they might perform the service in question practically as they pleased; they were not working under the control of the company or subject to the command of the master under whom they worked. I do not say that any one of those four circumstances which I have mentioned, except possibly the last, would be entirely conclusive; but I do think that, when all those four circumstances are taken together, it is impossible to say that either of those persons was a servant of the company.' *Re Ashley & Smith Ltd, Ashley v The Company* [1918] 2 Ch 378 at 381, 383, 384, per Sargant J

[A testator by his will left money to every 'servant' in his employ at his death, and who had been so employed for a certain length of time. The question was whether the manager of a stud farm, an estate agent, a stable manager and a trainer took under the bequest.] 'It has been suggested that Boggis and Melville are entitled to take under the testator's will as clerks, but it is really quite clear that the claim is unfounded, although they had considerable clerical duties to perform. On the question whether they were servants, I take a different view. I do not think that the testator's intention was first to give to clerks and then to domestic servants, leaving out a considerable intervening class of persons who were serving the needs and hobbies of the testator. The testator desired to benefit all persons who had ministered to his service, and in the case of a man of the extraordinary wealth of the testator many persons might be in the position of servants whose social position was entirely different from that of those usually ranking in the servant class. So, for example, the captain of a private steam yacht might, although a highly trained navigator, be for the purpose of such a bequest as this a servant. In my judgment, all four persons come within the designation "servants" as used in the testator's will.' *Re Cassel, Public Trustee v Ashley* (1922) 39 TLR 75 at 76, per Sargant J

'The relation of master and servant exists only between persons of whom the one has the order and control of the work done by the other. A master is one who not only prescribes to the workman the end of his work, but directs or at any moment may direct the means also, or, as it has been put, "retains the power of controlling".' *Compania Mexicana de Petroles el Aguila SA v Essex Trading Co* (1928) 32 Ll L Rep 182 at 194, per Bateson J

'Ministers are pre-eminently Her Majesty's servants: a purist might find some anomaly in that because, by constitutional practice, the Sovereign can only act on the advice of a Minister. But no one denies that Ministers come within the category of servants of the Crown for the present purpose. And with regard to others I can see no difficulty at all. The Crown (through or with the advice of a Minister) controls them and directs their activities in a way which, to my mind, makes the term "servant" quite appropriate.' *Bank Voor Handel en Scheepvaart NV v Administration of Hungarian Property* [1954] 1 All ER 969 at 982, HL, per Lord Reid; see also [1954] AC 584

Australia 'It is a mistake to think that only unskilled people can properly be described as servants. If they are subject to detailed control in the manner in which they do their work, they may be servants. The fact that the remuneration is described as a fee rather than as wages is not decisive. The real character of the relation between the parties must be determined, whether the payment made is described as wages, fee, salary, commission, or by any other term.' *Federal Comr of Taxation v Thompson (J Walter) (Aust) Pty Ltd* (1944) 69 CLR 227 at 232, per Latham CJ

New Zealand [While a person retains his status as a lodger in a hotel, he is entitled to entertain his bona fide guests with liquor in that hotel during hours when the premises are required by law to be closed. A person was charged under the Licensing Act 1908 (NZ), s 194 (repealed; see now the Sale of Liquor Act 1989, s 170(2)(b)) with supplying M with liquor during hours when the premises were required to be closed; it was proved that M was a lodger and paid for his board, and, later, agreed to become barman-cellarman at the hotel at a weekly wage of £8 7*s*, on condition that he retained his position as a lodger and had his meals as a guest, and continued to pay board as heretofore.] 'I am not impressed by the suggestion made by counsel for the respondent that the terms "servant" and "lodger" used in s 194 of the Licensing Act 1908 are mutually exclusive. I know that in *Hopper v Cahill* [1925] GLR, Ostler J said that in that section the term "lodger" is contrasted with the terms "inmate" and "servant", but I hardly think that that is necessarily so. Section 194 provides for a penalty against any person found on licensed premises at any time when such premises are required to be closed unless he satisfies the court that he was an inmate, servant, or lodger on such premises. It was necessary to exempt servants, because it is necessary for certain of the servants to be on duty during the hours when the premises are required to be closed; and I agree that in all but an exceptional case, such as the present, a servant cannot be regarded as a lodger. But I cannot see that the words "servant" and "lodger" are . . . necessarily mutually exclusive. . . . MacDonald was on the premises later during the evening, but he was there not as a servant but as a lodger.' *MacDonald v Graham* [1944] NZLR 21 at 23, 24, per Myers CJ; also reported [1944] GLR at 50

Clerk or servant

'I do not propose to attempt to give a general definition of what constitutes a "clerk or servant" within the meaning of head (b) of s 264(1) [of the Companies Act 1929 (repealed; see now the Companies Act 1985, Sch 19, para 9)] or what constitutes a "workman or labourer" within the meaning of head (c) of that subsection. It appears to me that one has to look at the facts of every particular case, including the nature of the business carried on by the employer, and as completing the story, the actual services which are being performed by the member of the staff in question. But there are certain general considerations which do occur to one upon looking at the distinction drawn between head (b) and head (c) by sub-s (1). In the first place, head (b) talks about the "wages or salary . . . of any clerk or servant". Head (c) talks about "the wages of any workman or labourer", and it refers to his wages being possibly payable "for time or for piece work", while the wages or salary referred to in head (b) are referred to as being possibly payable "wholly or in part by way of commission". I think that one general broad distinction is that head (c) is primarily directed to persons who are engaged in what is known as manual labour, while head (b) is directed, in the case of businesses, to the black-coated staff and also to persons who would be called servants, although they would not be denominated clerks and who, in the ordinary way, one would not think of as being engaged in manual labour. That, I think, is the broad distinction. Then, of course, you get this class of distinction, that your workman or labourer is usually engaged on some production job, while the clerk or servant is generally not directly engaged on production work. Therefore, to a certain extent, the contrast is between manual labour and service other than manual labour, but one has to look in each particular case at all the circumstances.' *Re London Casino Ltd, National Provincial Bank's Application* (1942) 167 LT 66 at 67, per Uthwatt J

Household servant

'The words [in the testator's will] are simply these: I give to each of my household servants . . . six months wages. . . . I cannot see that any distinction can be drawn between "domestic" servants and "household" servants. Consequently I think I ought to follow *Ogle v Morgan* [(1852) 1 De G M & G 359] and, holding that "household" servants has the same meaning as "domestic" servants, decide that the testator's gift only applies to those of the testator's servants who formed part of his household—that is to say, who boarded in the mansion-house and took their meals there at the expense of the testator. I must hold, therefore, that the coachman and grooms, who did not board in the house, are not included in the gift.' *Re Drax, Savile v Yeatman* (1887) 57 LT 475 at 475, per Kay J

See, generally, 50 Halsbury's Laws (4th edn) para 543.

Private servant

A 'private servant' is a person who is in the domestic service of a member of the mission and who is not an employee of the sending State. (Diplomatic Privileges Act 1964, Sch I)

SERVICE *See also* ATTENDANCE

Contract of service

'The greater the amount of direct control exercised over the person rendering the services by the person contracting for them the stronger the grounds for holding it to be a contract of service, and similarly the greater the degree of independence of such control the greater the probability that the services rendered are of the nature of professional services and that the contract is not one of service.' *Simmons v Heath Laundry Co* [1910] 1 KB 543 at 549, 550, CA, per Fletcher Moulton LJ

'In *Simmons v Heath Laundry Co* [supra] . . . Fletcher Moulton LJ pointed out that a contract of service was not the same thing as a contract for service, and that the existence of direct control by the employer, the degree of independence on the part of the person who renders services, the place where the service is rendered, are all matters to be considered in determining whether there is a contract of service. As Buckley LJ indicated in the same case, a contract of service involves the existence of a servant, and imports that there exists in the person serving an obligation to obey the orders of the person served.' *University of London Press Ltd v University Tutorial Press Ltd* [1916] 2 Ch 601 at 610–612, per Peterson J

'A contract of service exists if the following three conditions are fulfilled: (i) The servant agrees that in consideration of a wage or other remuneration he will provide his own work and skill in the performance of some service for his master. (ii) He agrees expressly or impliedly, that in the performance of that service he will be subject to the other's control in a sufficient degree to make that other master. (iii) The other provisions of the contract are consistent with its being a contract of service. I need say little about (i) and (ii). As to (i). There must be a wage or other remuneration. Otherwise there will be no consideration, and without consideration no contract of any kind. The servant must be obliged to provide his own work and skill. Freedom to do a job either by one's own hands, or by another's is inconsistent with a contract of service, though a limited or occasional power of delegation may not be. . . . As to (ii). Control includes the power of deciding the thing to be done, the way in which it shall be done, the means to be employed in doing it, the time when, and the place where it shall be done. All these aspects of control must be considered in deciding whether the right exists in a sufficient degree to make one party the master and the other his servant. The right need not be unrestricted. "What matters is lawful authority to command, so far as there is scope for it. And there must always be some room for it, if only in incidental or collateral matters." [*Zuijus v Wirth Brothers Pty Ltd* (1955) 93 CLR 561]. To find where the right resides one must look first to the express terms of the contract, and if they deal fully with the matter one may look no further. If the contract does not expressly provide which party shall have the right, the question must be answered in the ordinary way by implication. The third and negative condition is for my purpose the important one, and I shall try with the help of five examples to explain what I mean by provisions inconsistent with the nature of a contract of service. (i) A contract obliges one party to build for the other, providing at his own expense the necessary plant and materials. This is not a contract of service, even though the builder may be obliged to use his own labour only and to accept a high degree of control; it is a building contract. It is not a contract to serve another for a wage, but a contract to produce a thing (or a result) for a price. (ii) A contract obliges one party to carry another's goods, providing at his own expense everything needed for performance. This is not a contract of service, even though the carrier may be obliged to drive the vehicle himself and to accept the other's control over his performance: it is a contract of carriage. (iii) A contract obliges a labourer to work for a builder, providing some simple tools, and to accept the builder's control. Notwithstanding the obligation to provide the tools, the contract is one of service. That obligation is not inconsistent with the nature of a contract of service. it is not a sufficiently important matter to affect the substance of the contract. (iv) A contract obliges one party to work for the other, accepting his control, and to provide his own transport. This is still a contract of service. The obligation to provide his own transport does not affect the substance. Transport in this example is incidental to the main purpose of the contract. Transport in the second example was the essential part of the performance. (v) The same instrument provides that one party shall work for the other subject to the other's control, and also that he shall sell him his land. The first part of the instrument is no less a contract of service because the second part imposes obligations of a different kind. I can put the point which I am making in other words. An obligation to do work subject to the other party's control is a necessary, though not always a sufficient, condition of a contract of service. If the provisions of the contract as a whole are inconsistent with its being a contract of service, it will be some other kind of contract, and the person doing the work will not be a servant. The judge's task is to classify the contract (a task like that of distinguishing a contract of sale from one of work and labour). He may, in performing it take into account other matters besides control.' *Ready Mixed Concrete (South East) Ltd v Minister of Pensions and National Insurance* [1968] 1 All ER 433 at 439–441, per MacKenna J

Military service *See* ACTIVE SERVICE; MILITARY SERVICE

Serving customers

[The Shops Act 1912, s 4 (repealed see now the Shops Act 1950, s 1) enacted that shops must be closed for the 'serving of customers' not later than 1 pm on one week day in every week.] 'The Shops Act 1912 was passed for the benefit of those who serve as shop assistants. . . . Being intended for the benefit of those serving in shops, the Act is not intended to prevent people buying goods so long as their doing so does not interfere with the object of the Act. I should not assent to any construction of the Act which would prevent shop assistants obtaining their weekly half-holiday; but I do not think that we should so construe it as to make it apply to the supply of articles by automatic machines unless the language of the Act compels us to do so. Section 4 is satisfied by reading the words "for the serving of customers" as meaning "for the personal serving of customers".' *Willesden Urban District Council v Morgan* [1915] 1 KB 349 at 352, 353, DC, per Ridley J

Towage service

[A contract of towage contained the following provision: 'During the towage service . . . the company will not be liable for any damage or loss to or occasioned by the vessel in tow.'] 'In my opinion the words "during the towage service" mean while the service is being conducted—not while it is being interrupted, in the sense that the master of the tug leaves the ship altogether and goes into port and sends out somebody else to do his work. I think the contract contemplates that the tug and tow shall keep together, because it says, "during the towing service the master and crew of the tug boat become the servants of the owners of the vessel in tow." . . . It seems to me that if the master of the tug goes away and asks somebody else to do his work it cannot be said that those words contemplate such a doing of the work as that.' *The Refrigerant* [1952] P 130 at 140, 141, per Bateson J

SERVICE (Of documents)

By post

Where an Act authorises or requires any document to be served by post (whether the expression 'serve' or the expression 'give' or 'send' or any other expression is used) then, unless the contrary intention appears, the service is deemed to be effected by properly addressing pre-paying and posting a letter containing the document and, unless the contrary is proved to have been effected at the time at which the letter would be delivered in the ordinary course of post. (Interpretation Act 1978, s 7)

New Zealand [The Noxious Weeds Act 1950, s 28 (repealed; see now the Noxious Plants Act 1978, s 117) provides that any notice under the Act may be 'served' either by delivering it personally to the person upon whom it is to be served, or by leaving it, or by sending it by post by registered letter addressed to him at his usual or last known place of abode in New Zealand. A notice was sent by registered post to the respondent but was returned unclaimed to the informant. The question was whether it had been 'served' on the respondent.] 'A perusal of the subsection, and consideration of the consequences of service . . . satisfy me that it is the intention of the legislature that, so far as it is within the power of the sender, the notice should come into the hands of the addressee. In this sense the provisions of s 28(1) are permissive only and equate other modes of service with personal service only where the facts proved are such that the proper inference is that the addressee actually received the notice or that the mode adopted is that most likely, in the circumstances, to bring it to his attention. Thus, if it is left at his usual or last known place of abode, or is sent by registered post to that address *and nothing further is known concerning it*, the proper inference is that he received it, just as if it had been placed in his hands by a process server, and if he cannot be located the provision for substituted service by advertisement is a common expedient in law which is recognised as the best practicable means to bring it to his notice, either directly or by friends or acquaintances. But when the address of his home is known and the evidence establishes that the notice was not delivered to that address, the mere proof that the notice was sent "by post in a registered letter addressed to him" there is not proof of service of the notice unless it is also proved that the registered letter was actually delivered at that address. As a registered letter must be signed for (though not necessarily by the addressee), delivery should not be difficult to prove, but it is not necessary to go to that length. So long as it is proved that the registered letter has not been returned undelivered the reasonable inference in most cases will be that delivery was duly made, and s 28(3) appears to sanction that inference.' *Fawcett v Graham* [1973] 1 NZLR 495 at 498, per Wilson J

SERVICE (Verb)

Canada '"Servicing" can mean either rendering all the services for an engine that are specifically requested, or it can mean making periodic tests and inspections, and undertaking to do everything necessary to keep an engine in constant good running order. Similarly, "overhauling" can mean taking an engine down to effect a specific job, or it can mean taking it down to ensure that it will be perfect in all respects. Similarly, both "servicing" and "overhauling" can either refer only to an engine itself, or to all its connections and ancillary equipment.' *Trans-Canada Forest Products Ltd v Heaps Waterous Ltd* (1953) 9 WWR (NS) 179 at 188, BCCA, per S Smith JA; revd on other grounds [1954] SCR 240

SERVICE VOTER *See* VOTER

SERVICES

'Services' includes attendance, the provision of heating or lighting, the supply of hot water and any other privilege or facility connected with the occupancy of a dwelling, other than a privilege or facility requisite for the purposes of access, cold water supply or sanitary accommodation. (Rent Act 1977, s 85(1))

'The contractual services set out are: central heating, constant hot water, passenger and service lifts, lighting and heating of lounge, hall, passages, and staircases. Every one of these seems to me to be a service. If the landlords contracted to provide a lift, the maintenance of it is a service, because the lift has to be worked. It is one of the most important services for the tenants. The non-contractual services provided are: porterage, cleaning common parts, removal of refuse, pest control, floor coverings to common parts. The only questionable item is the floor covering to common parts. That, however, is as much a service as heating and lighting the staircase; it is an amenity which gives a better appearance to the place.' *R v Paddington Rent Tribunal* [1955] 3 All ER 391 at 395, per Lord Goddard CJ; see also [1956] 1 QB 229

New Zealand 'It was submitted that the relationship of hotel-keeper and guest could not be said to entail the selling of goods and the performance of services, and that it was something different. We cannot accept this view. An hotel-keeper does render services, even if that term be regarded in the narrowest way. On arrival, a guest is received and escorted to the room he is to occupy, and his baggage is taken to that room. Thereafter, meals are brought to him, either in the dining-room or in the private room he is to occupy. His shoes may be cleaned and his clothing sent to and received from a laundry. Mail addressed to him is received and delivered. Telephone calls and taxis are obtained as needed. These are only some of the services rendered, but all these are properly described as services. The supply of meals may be considered either as the rendering of services or as the sale and delivery of goods, or it may be something of both. We are unable to regard the supply of meals, as we were invited to do, as something different from either and different from a combination of both. The provision of a bedroom with bed and other furnishings is the rendering of a service. It is not, as we were invited to regard it, solely the conferring of some form of licence. It does involve a licence to occupy the room, though not necessarily even an exclusive occupation, any more than is the temporary occupation of the table at which meals may be taken in the dining-room, but it is none the less the rendering of a service. The provision of chairs in dining-rooms and sitting-rooms is the conferring of a licence to occupy them by a guest, but it is nevertheless a service rendered by the hotel-keeper to the guest.' *Dwyer v Hunter*, [1951] NZLR 177 at 189, 190, CA, per Finlay J; also reported [1951] GLR 20 at 25

New Zealand 'Here the plaintiff, at a stage when his mother was threatened with eviction from the apartment house in Webb Street, agreed to sell to her, at a very moderate price, and on very reasonable terms, the house at 7 Howard Street, in order to enable her to have a home. I do not think that the mere act of selling a house cheaply to the deceased, without more, would constitute the "rendering of services" within the meaning of s 3 [of the Law Reform (Testamentary Promises) Act 1949] but here there was much more than that. He did it in order to provide a home in which his mother could live, a home which she would not be able to buy elsewhere, because of her limited financial resources; a home in which she could and did earn an income through the letting of rooms. Although the subsequent free use of the garage was not part of the consideration for the testamentary promise given, nonetheless I think it may fairly be said to have been given, partly at any rate, in reliance on the carrying out of the testamentary promise. The Act clearly states that the services which may be taken into consideration may be services rendered after the making of the promise. I think, therefore, that the circumstances here do show that the plaintiff rendered a service to his mother by selling the property to her at the price and on the terms he did.' *Re Oliver (deceased)* [1968] NZLR 168 at 170, per Tompkins J

SERVIENT TENEMENT

See EASEMENT

SERVITUDE

An easement is a servitude, but 'servitude' is a wider term and includes both easements and profits à prendre, (14 Halsbury's Laws (4th edn) para 3)

'Servitude' means any liberty, privilege, easement, right or advantage annexed to any land and adversely affecting other land: 'surface servitude' means any servitude annexed to coal or a mine of coal in so far as it adversely affects the surface of any land (with the exception of a right to withdraw support); and 'annexed to' means, in relation to any coal or mine of coal, or to any other land, appertaining or reputed to appertain thereto or to any part thereof, or demised, occupied, or enjoyed therewith or with any part thereof, or reputed or known as part or parcel thereof or appurtenant thereto or to any part thereof. (Coal Act 1938 s 44)

SET ASIDE

Canada '"To set aside" [in a will providing for a sum to be set aside for a contingent legacy] means plainly that the specific sum was to be segregated from the assets of his estate and kept apart for the purpose for which it was intended by the testator to be used. It was not intended by the testator that the sums should continue to be part of the general residue of the estate.' *Re Caplin* (1956) 2 DLR (2d) 314 at 316, Ont CA, per Laidlaw JA

SET-OFF

Where A has a claim for a sum of money against B and B has a cross-claim for a sum of money against A such that B is, to the extent of his cross-claim, entitled to be absolved from payment of A's claim, and to plead his cross-claim as a defence to an action by A for the enforcement of his claim, then B is said to have a right of set-off against A to the extent of his cross-claim. (42 Halsbury's Laws (4th edn) para 406)

'It is said on behalf of the plaintiff that "an admitted set-off" mentioned in s 57 [of the County Courts Act 1888 (repealed; see now the County Courts Act 1984, s 15(3)), which gave the county court jurisdiction to try an action where the debt or demand claimed consisted of a balance not exceeding £50 (now the county court limit) after an admitted set-off of any debt or demand claimed or recoverable by the defendant from the plaintiff] means a set-off which was admitted both by the plaintiff and the defendant before action brought, and that there was no such admitted set-off in the present case. We do not assent to this view of the law. We are of opinion that a person proposing to sue another for a debt, whatever may be its amount, knowing that he is indebted to the person he so proposes to sue in a sum of money which can be set-off against his own claim, may before action admit such set-off, and give the defendant credit for it in reduction of his own demand without any formal assent or admission of the proposed defendant, and sue simply for the true balance alleged to be still due. Such set-off so admitted by the proposed plaintiff is, in our opinion, "an admitted set-off" within the meaning of s 57.' *Lovejoy v Cole* [1894] 2 QB 861 at 864, per cur.

'We have listened to the argument that the defence of a breach of warranty is equivalent to a set-off, and decide against that contention.' *Bright v Rogers* [1917] 1 KB 917 at 921, DC, per Bray J

'With regard to the word "set-off", that is a word well known and established in its meaning; it is something which provides a defence because the nature and quality of the sum so relied upon are such that it is a sum which is proper to be dealt with as diminishing the claim which is made, and against which the sum so demanded can be set-off.' *Re Bankruptcy Notice (No 171 of 1934)* [1934] Ch 431 at 437, CA, per Lord Hanworth MR

SET UP

'The plaintiff in this action, the purchaser of a medical practice, seeks for an injunction to restrain the defendant, the vendor, from committing a breach of a covenant contained in the conveyance. I desire to confine myself to the facts in evidence; and what the defendant has done is this: He has visited two or three old patients, who invited him to attend them professionally without any solicitation on the part of the defendant. I do not think that in itself constitutes a breach of this covenant. I think that a man who visits two or three old patients is not setting up in practice within the prescribed area.' *Robertson v Buchanan* (1904) 73 LJ Ch 408 at 411, CA, per Stirling LJ

'What is alleged to be a setting up of a counterclaim is that the defendants' solicitors have written a letter to the plaintiffs' solicitors saying that the defendants are going to set up a counterclaim. The question is: Is that within the meaning of these rules, "setting up" a counterclaim? . . . By [RSC] Order XIX, r 3 [revoked; see now RSC 1965, Ord 15, r 2] "A defendant in an action may set off, or set up by way of counterclaim against the claims of the plaintiff, any right or claim", and so on. And when one inquires how he is to set up by counterclaim one finds a series of rules beginning with Order XXI, r 10 [see now RSC 1965, Ord 15, r 2]: "Where any defendant seeks to rely upon any grounds as supporting a right of counterclaim, he shall, in his defence, state specifically that he does so by way of counterclaim." . . . It appears to me that setting up a counterclaim must be done by something which is recorded in the Court. I do not think it is necessary to decide in this case whether setting it up in an affidavit under Order XIV [see now RSC 1965, Ord 14] as a defence to a claim, or as a reason why execution should not issue or judgment be given on a claim is "setting up" a counterclaim or not, . . . but it seems to me clear that one cannot extend it to a mere notice from the defendant to the plaintiff.' *The Saxicava* [1924] P 131 at 137, 138, CA, per Scrutton LJ

'The expression "to set up and commence 'a trade'" is a familiar English expression meaning "to start or begin a new trade".' *Fry v Burma Corpn Ltd* [1930] 1 KB 249 at 268, CA, per Lawrence LJ

Canada [A restrictive covenant in an agreement for the sale of assets of a company provided that the vendors would not 'set up business' within the town of L of the same nature as carried out by L E Ltd within five years from date of completion of the agreement.] 'The phrase "set up business" means, certainly in the present context, to establish a place of business, and is entirely distinguishable from "carry on business".' *Chamberlain v Parsons* (1978) 91 DLR (3d) 590 at 591, 592, NSCA, per MacKeigan CJNS

SETLINE

'Setline' means a fishing line left unattended in water and having attached to it one or more lures or baited hooks. (Salmon and Freshwater Fisheries Act 1975, s 1(3))

SETTLE

'I will read the exact words in the policy, as they become of importance: "Being a reinsurance and to pay as per original policy or policies but this insurance is against the risk of the total or constructive loss of the steamer only but to follow hull underwriters in event of a compromised or arranged loss being settled." . . . We have had a good deal of discussion as to the meaning of the word "settled". In my judgment, no importance attaches to that particular word, because, taking it, as was argued, or at least contended, as established by reference to the case of *Beauchamp v Faber* [(1898) 3 Com Cas 302] . . . I am prepared to accept the view that "settled" means adjustment of the loss, or accepting liability for the loss. It does not go so far as to mean payment of the loss, but it means that the loss has been arranged, and that the underwriter is prepared to pay, unless something happens in the meanwhile which will entitle him to refuse; for example, the discovery that it was a fraudulent claim. In any event, that is the view that I take; and I read the word "settled" just as if it were "adjusted" or as if it were "liability being accepted".' *Street v Royal Exchange Assurance* (1914) 111 LT 235 at 235, 237, CA, per Lord Reading CJ

SETTLED ESTATE

'The meaning of a "settled" estate, whether in legal or popular language, as contradistinguished from an estate in fee-simple, is understood to be one in which the power of alienation, of devising, and of transmission according to the ordinary rules of descent, are restrained by the limitations of the settlement; it would be a perversion of language to apply the term "settled" to an estate taken out of settlement, and brought back to the condition of an estate in fee-simple.' *Micklethwait v Micklethwait* (1858) 4 CBNS 790 at 858, per cur.

SETTLED LAND

Land which is or is deemed to be the subject of a settlement is for the purpose of this Act settled land,and is in relation to the settlement referred to in this Act as the settled land. (Settled Land Act 1925, s 2)

'Settled land' includes land which is deemed to be settled land. (Ibid, s 117)

SETTLEMENT

Parliament has from time to time defined 'settlement' for the purposes of particular statutes, but there is no generally accepted definition of the word. However, it may be defined as any disposition of property, of whatever nature, by any instrument or number of instruments, by which trusts are constituted for the purpose of regulating the enjoyment of the settled property successively among the persons or classes of persons nominated by the settlor. 'Settlement' has two different senses in law: it can mean either the documents which express the dispositions that are the settlement, or the state of affairs which the documents bring about. (42 Halsbury's Laws (4th edn) para 601)

'Settlement' means any disposition or dispositions of property, whether effected by instrument, by parol or by operation of law, or partly in one way and partly in another, whereby the property is for the time being—

(a) held in trust for persons in succession or for any person subject to a contingency, or
(b) held by trustees on trust to accumulate the whole or part of any income of the property or with power to make payments out of that income at the discretion of the trustees or some other person, with or without power to accumulate surplus income, or
(c) charged or burdened (otherwise than for full consideration in money or money's worth paid for his own use or benefit to the person making the disposition) with the payment of any annuity or other periodical payment payable for a life or any other limited or terminable period,

or would be so held or charged or burdened if the disposition or dispositions were regulated by the law of any part of the United Kingdom; or whereby, under the law of any other country, the administration of the property is for the time being governed by provisions equivalent in effect to those which would apply if the property were so held, charged or burdened. (Inheritance Tax Act 1984, s 43(2))

[The remainder of the section deals with leases for life or terminating at death, and with settlements in Scotland and Northern Ireland.]

'If there is a gift by a father to a son of money or proceeds of property which can be traced, and the money or proceeds is or are intended to be retained or preserved as the property of the donee, that money or those proceeds will be property in "settlement". On the other hand, if there is a gift of money or proceeds, but it is not intended that the money or the proceeds shall be retained by the donee in the form of money, but shall be expended at once, that will not be a "settlement".' *Re Plummer* [1900] 2 QB 790 at 804, CA, per Lord Alverstone MR

'I find it difficult to reconcile the decisions in *Hubbard v Hubbard* [[1901] P 157] and *Brown v Brown* [[1937] P 7] with the principle that runs through the rest of the cases on this subject. That principle, as I understand it, is that where a husband makes a continuing provision for the future needs of his wife in her character as a wife, which is still continuing when the marriage is dissolved, the provision is a "settlement" which can be brought before the court to see whether the provision should continue now that she has ceased to be a wife. The same applies to a provision by a wife for her husband or by each or either for both. The provision usually takes the form of periodical payments either with the intervention of trustees as in an ordinary marriage settlement, or without them as in a separation deed or a bond; but it may take other forms. The transfer of an investment into a wife's name whether it be a house or shares, or an annuity, seems to me to be in its nature just as much a continuing provision for her future needs as is a periodical payment. The fact that it is made for no consideration other than natural affection and is in that sense a gift does not mean that it is not a 'settlement'. The bond securing the annuity in *Bosworthick's case* [*Bosworthick v Bosworthick*, [1927] P 64] was in that sense a gift. Again, the fact that it is assignable does not mean that it is not a "settlement". A wife is often free to assign her interest under an ordinary marriage settlement or a separation deed, but it is none the less a "settlement". If she should assign her interest, the court might treat the proceeds in her hands as representing the property; and a co-respondent, or indeed any person, who takes an assignment from her with notice that proceedings are pending as to the application of the property, will find that the arm of the court is long enough to reach the property in his hands.' *Smith v Smith* [1945] 1 All ER 584 at 586, per Denning J

'However wide the statutory language in which the term "settlement" is defined, the overriding idea is that of bounty of some description. If there is no bounty, then there is nothing that can even remotely be classed as a settlement with a settlor.' *Inland Revenue Comrs v Plummer* [1977] 3 All ER 1009 at 1026, per Walton J

Compound settlement

The term 'compound settlement' is used to describe a settlement that subsists by virtue of several different instruments, often a series of successive dispositions such as a deed of settlement, a disentailing deed and a deed of resettlement. (42 Halsbury's Laws (4th edn) para 601)

In Bankruptcy Acts

Australia 'The word "settlement" . . . has been considered in many cases in the context of sections in bankruptcy statutes comparable to s 120 [Bankruptcy Act 1966 (Cth)], but generally the word was defined by the relevant statute as including "any conveyance or transfer of property". The Australian Parliament changed the definition of the expression to the form in which it presently appears in the Act as including any "disposition of property"; a wider expression than the previous expression "any conveyance or transfer of property." . . . The construction of the word "settlement" has been settled in England and Australia for an appreciable time and it has acquired an established meaning. But it is very difficult to extract from the decided cases any clear definition of the dispositions of property which will and which will not fall within the operation of s 120. The word was chosen by Parliament to connote a particular kind of disposition of property excluding others. It cannot be said that all dispositions of property are settlements; nor can it be said that a settlement is a settlement simply because it happens to be a disposition of property. The whole of the language of s 120 must be considered to determine the meaning of the expression. . . . In my opinion for there to be a "settlement of property" within the meaning of s 120 there must be a settlement in the ordinary sense of the word, a transaction in the nature of a settlement, though it may be effected by any disposition. The retention of the property in some sense must be contemplated and not its immediate dispersion.' *Barton v Official Receiver* (1984) 58 ALR 328 at 342–343, per Lockhart J

Canada [The Bankruptcy Act, RSC 1952, c 14, s 60 (see now RSC 1970, c B-3, s 69) provides that any settlement of property, if the settlor becomes bankrupt within one year after the date of the settlement, is void against the trustee.] 'The learned trial judge held that the designation of the bankrupt's wife as the beneficiary of his policy of life insurance was a "settlement of property" within the meaning of s 60(1) of the Bankruptcy Act, and I agree with him. I think there emerges from the authorities a definition of the ordinary meaning of "settlement" that it is a disposition of property to be held, either in original form or in such form that it can be traced, for the enjoyment of some other person; and that the designation of a beneficiary of an insurance policy is such a disposition.' *Re Geraci* [1970] 3 OR 49 at 51, Ont CA, per Jessup JA

Canada [A transfer of property by a bankrupt to his wife was attacked as a 'settlement' under the Bankruptcy Act, RSC 1970, c B–3, s 69.] 'A settlement implies an intention that the property shall be retained or preserved for the benefit of the donee in such a form that it can be traced: see *Re Bozanich, A H Boulton Co v Trusts & Guar Co* [1942] SCR 130, 23 CBR 234 at 237, [1942] 2 DLR 145. There was no such intention in the release by the defendant Allan H Shapiro of his interest in the matrimonial home to his wife. It was a compromise or resolution of certain claims exerted against him in the course of matrimonial litigation which compromise or resolution was arrived at in good faith and for substantial valuable consideration. In the circumstances, the defendant Nessa Rose Shapiro was a purchaser within the meaning of s 69 of the Bankruptcy Act: see *Re Pope, ex p Dicksee* [1908] 2 KB 169, CA). The plaintiff therefore fails in its submission that the settlement in question is void under the provisions of s 69 of the Bankruptcy Act.' *Canadian Imperial Bank of Commerce v Shapiro* (1985) 44 RFL (2d) 47 at 53, Ont SC, per Callon J

In conveyancing

Australia 'In various statutes the word has different scope. . . . A conveyancer might be expected to describe a settlement as an instrument providing for the disposition of property, real or personal, for the purpose of ensuring that the same shall be enjoyed by persons in succession.' *Re Symon, Public Trustee v Symon* [1944] SASR 102 at 109, at Mayo J

In Matrimonial Causes Acts

'The word "settlement" [in the phrase "post-nuptial settlement"] in s 25 of the Matrimonial Causes Act 1950 [repealed; see now the Matrimonial Causes Act 1973, s 24(1)(c)], is not used in the conveyancing sense. It includes any provision made by a husband for the future benefit of his wife, if it proceeds on the footing of the then existing marriage. It does not cease to be a settlement on her because the provision is not absolute, but only contingent, nor does it cease to be a settlement on her because it may in its terms also be applicable for the benefit of a wife by a subsequent marriage.' *Lort-Williams v Lort-Williams* [1951] 2 All ER 241 at 245, per Denning LJ; [1951] P 395, CA

In Settled Land Act

'Settlement' includes an instrument or instruments which under this Act or the Acts which it replaces is or are deemed to be or which together constitute a settlement, and a settlement which is deemed to have been made by any person or to be subsisting for the purposes of this Act; 'a settlement subsisting at the commencement of this Act' includes a settlement created by virtue of this Act immediately on the commencement thereof; and 'trustees of the settlement' mean the trustees thereof for the purposes of this Act howsoever appointed or constituted. (Settled Land Act 1925, s 117)

'In some parts of the Act [Settled Land Act 1925] no doubt "settlement" means merely the document or documents creating the settlement: see, for example, ss 1 sub-s 4, 47, and 64. But in general a settlement, for the purposes of the Act, is a state of affairs in relation to certain land, brought about, or deemed to have been brought about by one or more documents, the particular state of affairs being one or more of those specified in sub-ss (i) to (v) of s 1, sub-s 1. A document, may therefore, create more than one settlement. If by means of one and the same document, Blackacre and Whiteacre stand limited in trust for A and his children in strict succession, and for B and his children in strict succession respectively, there are two settlements. In one case the settled land is Blackacre, and A is the tenant for life under the "settlement"; in the other the settled land is Whiteacre, and the tenant for life under the "settlement" is B.' *Re Ogle's Settled Estates* [1927] 1 Ch 229 at 232, 233, per Romer J

'Section 3 of the Act [Settled Land Act 1925] amended by the Law of Property (Amendment) Act 1926, by the addition of the words "not held upon trust for sale", reads as follows: "Land not held upon trust for sale which has been subject to a settlement shall be deemed for the purposes of this Act to remain and be settled land, and the settlement shall be deemed to be a subsisting settlement for the purposes of this Act so long as: (a) any limitation, charge, or power of charging under the settlement subsists, or is capable of being exercised." . . . The words "under the settlement" must mean under the settlement deemed to be existing, that is, in this case, under the compound settlement. In one sense it may be said that where there is a compound settlement, every limitation, charge, or power of charging under any one of the instruments making up the compound settlement is under the compound settlement, but in another sense it is only where it is necessary to resort to the compound settlement for overriding the limitation charge or power that such limitation, charge or power can fairly be said to be a limitation, charge or power under the settlement. Section 3 is a section to facilitate and not to impede dealings with the land, and in my opinion the expression "under the settlement" is used in sub-cl (a) in the second sense which I have indicated.' *Re Draycott Settled Estate*, [1928] Ch 371 at 375, 376, per Tomlin J

Marriage settlement

A marriage settlement is a settlement made in consideration of marriage either before or after the marriage, but after the marriage only if made in pursuance of an ante-nuptial agreement to settle. The form of a marriage settlement has to a large extent become stereotyped although not so stereotyped that any particular provision can be presumed to have been inserted in the settlement. (42 Halsbury's Laws (4th edn) para 603)

[The Bills of Sale Act 1878, s 4, provides that the expression 'bill of sale' shall not include 'marriage settlements'.] 'A post-nuptial settlement executed in pursuance of an ante-nuptial deed falls within the term "marriage settlement" in the Bills of Sale Act.' *Re Reis, ex p Clough* [1904] 2 KB 769 at 778, CA, per Cozens-Hardy LJ

Post-nuptial settlement

A post-nuptial settlement usually contains the same provisions as those contained in an ante-nuptial settlement. It will be considered as a voluntary settlement unless either it is made in pursuance of an agreement made prior to the marriage, in which case it will be deemed to have been made in consideration of the marriage, or it is the result of a bargain made after the marriage between the spouses, or it is made for valuable consideration given by some other person. (42 Halsbury's Laws (4th edn) para 604)

Protective settlement

Protective settlements normally contain a more or less common form set of provisions designed so as to enable the principal beneficiary to enjoy the beneficial interest intended for him without allowing him any power of alienation. Such a settlement, if made by a third person, will be valid against a beneficiary's trustee in bankruptcy, but not if made by the beneficiary himself. (42 Halsbury's Laws (4th edn) para 607)

Strict settlement

Strict settlements of land are of very long standing, their object being to secure that the land should descend from father to son so that the land as a whole could not be alienated unless and until a father and son concurred in so doing. This normally happened on the coming of age of an eldest son or other first tenant in tail in remainder expectant on the death of the tenant for life in possession, when a family arrangement was entered into and a resettlement of the land was executed for the purpose of giving effect to it. It is impossible today to settle land in such a way that it cannot be alienated, since by statute the estate owner in whom the legal estate is vested has an overriding power of disposition. For this reason, and also in consequence of changed economic conditions, the number of these settlements has decreased considerably. (42 Halsbury's Laws (4th edn) para 606)

'I think it is clear that where property is given to be settled upon A and his family in strict settlement, inasmuch as that would be, but for the words in "strict settlement", a gift of an estate of inheritance to A, which would of course give him a right to commit waste, the Court, although it cuts down the estate given to A to a life estate in order to give effect to the words "in strict settlement", gives to A the utmost power over the property consistent with his estate being so cut down, and therefore makes him unimpeachable for waste.' *Stanley v Coulthurst* (1870) LR 10 Eq 259 at 264, per Malins V-C

'Now what did this testator intend by ordering that property, real and personal, was to be put in strict settlement on the marriage of his son? . . . "Strict settlement", in whatever sense the words are used, is meant to protect a wife's property for herself, and, therefore, usually to increase the dominion she would otherwise have over it; but in the case of a husband they can have no such effect or operation. A settlement must diminish and cannot increase a man's rights of ownership over the property settled by him. When, therefore, property belonging (or given) to a man is ordered to be settled, it must be in order to diminish his power of dealing with it, by creating rights in others; and when this is done by a marriage settlement, the persons to be benefited would naturally be the children of the marriage, and, in almost invariable practice, the wife also.' *Wright v Wright* [1904] 1 IR 360 at 365, 366, per Porter MR

SETTLEMENT (Residence)

Canada [A municipality had a duty to support indigent persons having 'settlement' therein. An individual was involuntarily moved to an institution from one municipality to another.] '"Settlement" is not defined in general terms by any statute. Its meaning must be derived from the kind of acts and conduct by which a poor person may acquire or change settlement. It is a concept akin to but different from either "residence" (as used in taxing statutes) or "domicile". A pauper who had settlement in a "poor district", which was a township or small area later made part of a municipality, had the right to receive benefits from the overseers of the poor of the district, usually the doubtful benefit of existing in the county poorhouse. The overseers of a district had no duty to support a pauper whose settlement was elsewhere and they could transport such a person to his district of settlement to be supported by its overseers.' *Re District of Yarmouth and District of Argyle* (1979) 108 DLR (3d) 321 at 322, NSCA, per MacKeigan CJNS

SETTLOR

In this Act 'settlor', in relation to a settlement, includes any person by whom the settlement was made directly or indirectly, and in particular (but without prejudice to the generality of the preceding words) includes any person who has provided funds directly or indirectly for the purpose of or in connection with the settlement or has made with any other person a reciprocal arrangement for that other person to make the settlement. (Inheritance Tax Act 1984, s 44(1))

SEVERAL

'The question is, what is the meaning of the words: "From and after the several deceases of my said daughters?" They mean: "after the deaths of my daughters respectively".' *Woodstock v Shillito* (1833) 6 Sim 416 at 419, per Shadwell V-C

SEVERAL FISHERY *See* FISHERY

SEVERANCE

'It has to be considered whether the contract of sale is severable [within the Sale of Goods Act 1893, s 11(1)(c) (repealed; cf now the Sale of Goods Act 1979, s 31(2))] at the material time in the material respect. In this case the seller had an option to make the contract one transaction or divide it into two or more transactions by his mode of performance. The contract is not severable merely because the seller had that option: you have to see how he has exercised his option in the performance of the contract: if he has by his mode of performance divided the contract into two or more transactions, the contract is "severable" within the meaning of the section. The material time is the time at which the buyer has to decide how he is to treat the seller's breach of condition. Be it assumed that the buyer has accepted part of the goods. If the seller by his mode of performing the contract has made the sale and purchase of that part of the goods a separate transaction, the buyer is entitled to treat the sale and purchase of the remainder of the goods as a separate transaction, and if there has been a breach of condition by the seller the buyer is entitled to reject the remainder of the goods notwithstanding his acceptance of the part. On the other hand, if (as appears to be the case here) the seller has, by his mode of performing the contract, made it an entire contract—not severable—the buyer, having accepted part of the goods, is not entitled to reject the remainder.' *Esmail v Rosenthal (J) & Sons Ltd* [1965] 2 Lloyd's Rep 171 at 182, 183, HL, per Lord Pearson

'As Lord Denning MR said in *Kingsway Investments Ltd v Kent CC* [1969] 1 All ER 601 at 611, [1969] 2 QB 332 at 354: "This question of severance has vexed the law for centuries." He followed the notes to *Pigot's Case* (1614) 77 ER 1177 at 1179: "The general principle is, that if any clause, etc void by statute or by the common law be mixed up with good matter which is entirely independent of it, the good part stands, the rest is void . . . but if the part which is good depends upon that which is bad, the whole instrument is void." . . . The preponderance of [the] authorities seems to me to indicate that, if the valid promises are supported by sufficient consideration, then the invalid promise can be severed from the valid even though the consideration also supports the invalid promise. On the other hand if the invalid promise is substantially the whole or main consideration for the agreement then there will be no severance.' *Alex Lobb (Garages) Ltd v Total Oil GB Ltd* [1985] 1 All ER 303 at 316, 317, CA, per Dunn LJ

SEVERE MENTAL IMPAIRMENT

'Severe mental impairment' means a state of arrested or incomplete development of mind which includes severe impairment of intelligence and social functioning and is associated with abnormally agressive or seriously irresponsible conduct on the part of the person concerned and 'severely mentally impaired' shall be construed accordingly. (Mental Health Act 1983, s 1(2))

SEWER

Apart from statute, the terms 'sewers' and 'drains' have no special technical meanings in law; they are words in popular use of somewhat similar connotation, meaning channels by which liquid is carried off by gravity. In particular they mean artificial channels for draining water from land or for carrying away waste water and feculent and polluted matter from houses and other buildings. . . . In statutes relating to sanitation a distinction is drawn between sewers and drains. Furthermore, 'sewer' sometimes means more than the mere channel and includes the whole apparatus for drawing off and dealing with the water or other liquid. (38 Halsbury's Laws (4th edn) para 339)

'The word "sewer" comes from the word to "sew", i.e. to drain, and has a much more extended signification, embracing works on the largest scale, such as draining the fens of Lincolnshire, by means of canals, etc. In the common sense of the term, it means a large and generally, though not always, underground passage, for fluid and feculent matter, from a house or houses to some other locality; but it does not comprise a cesspool for the purpose of retaining the sewage, whether as a simple deposit or to be converted into manure or other useful purpose.' *Sutton v Norwich Corpn* (1858) 27 LJ Ch 739 at 742, per Kindersley V-C

'At one time this pipe took away the drainage of two houses. . . . It is, therefore, clear that at one time this pipe was a sewer. . . . The owner of No 36 . . . cut off all connection with the pipe which up to then had taken the sewage of his house and of No 42. . . . In my judgment once a sewer . . . always a sewer so long as it is used for the purpose of conveying sewage.' *St Leonard, Shoreditch, Vestry v Phelan* [1896] 1 QB 533 at 537, 538, DC, per Day J

'The question . . . arises, is the culvert a sewer? . . . The mere pollution of a natural stream or watercourse by turning sewage into it does not convert it into a sewer. On the other hand, if the watercourse has become substantially a sewer, the fact that at certain periods of the year clean water flows into it will not in my opinion prevent it from being a sewer. The question is one of fact and degree in each case. See *Falconar v South Shields Corporation* [(1895) 11 TLR 223, CA]. In that case Lindley LJ pointed out that the stream had changed its character completely and had become a sewer in the ordinary sense of the word, i.e. a channel for the reception and carrying away of sewage. It was a dirty, filthy sewer. This description exactly applies to the culvert. . . . It was urged on behalf of the defendants that a stream cannot become a sewer unless all flow of pure or natural water be entirely cut off from it, but in my judgment this argument is not well founded, and the cases of *West Riding of Yorkshire Rivers Board v Reuben Gaunt & Sons Ltd* [(1902) 67 JP 183, DC] and *West Riding of Yorkshire Rivers Board v Preston* [(1904) 69 JP 1 DC] do not establish it.' *A-G v Lewes Corpn* [1911] 2 Ch 495 at 508, per Swinfen Eady J

In Public Health Acts

'Sewer' does not include a drain as defined in this section but, save as aforesaid, includes all sewers and drains used for the drainage of buildings and yards appurtenant to buildings. (Public Health Act 1936, s 343)

['Drain' is defined by the section as meaning a drain used for the drainage of one building or of any buildings or yards appurtenant to buildings within the same curtilage.]

'The definition of sewer [in the Public Health Act 1848, s 2 (repealed; see now the Public Health Act 1936, s 343, supra)] is not precise; but we think the Act ought to be construed with reference to the preamble, and thus giving force to the enactments, we think that the brook, which is formed by the natural drainage of the fields in the neighbourhood, and after receiving the drainage of two houses makes its way into the river Ouse, is not a "sewer" within the meaning of the statute.' *R v Godmanchester Local Board* (1866) LR 1 QB 328 at 336, per cur.

[The Public Health Act 1848, by s 45 (repealed; see now the Public Health Act 1936, s 343, supra) enabled the local Board of Health to cause sewers to be made for effectually draining their district, and by s 2 the word 'sewer' was defined to mean and include sewers and drains of every description, except drains to which the word 'drain', as defined in the section, applied.] 'I think that it [a man-hole] is . . . within s 45. Giving a reasonable construction to the word "sewer", I think that the man-hole is clearly part of the sewer, as being necessary to a sewer properly made, and ought not to be looked upon as a work auxiliary to the use of the sewer.' *Swanston v Twickenham Local Board* (1879) 11 Ch D 838 at 851, CA, per Cotton LJ

[An iron pipe temporarily laid down to carry off the effluent water from sewage works is a 'sewer'.] 'There is nothing compelling the local authority to make the sewer of brick, but they may make it of any convenient material so that objection that an iron pipe is not a sewer [within the Public Health Act 1875, s 4 (repealed; see now the Public Health Act 1936, s 343, supra)] falls to the ground. Effluent water from sewage works is not, in my opinion, pure water, but sewage; and in support of this view there are several sections of the Lea River Act [1886] which speak of conveying effluent water by sewers. The same Act contemplates a sewer being made for temporary purposes; therefore, the objection that this was not a sewer because used for temporary purposes cannot be sustained.' *Tottenham Local Board of Health v Button* (1886) 2 TLR 828 at 828, per Chitty J

'I do think it would be a great stretch of imagination to hold that a large independent building, outside and over the surface, or partly over the surface and partly underneath, meant to be used as an engine-house and works, was part of a sewer,' *King's College, Cambridge v Uxbridge Rural Council* [1901] 2 Ch 768 at 772, 773, per Byrne J

'I . . . am of opinion that the finding of fact by Phillimore J; that the channel in question in this case is a "sewer" within the definition in s 4 [repealed] of the Public Health Act [1875] was correct. It is a well-defined channel to carry and take away the surface water, not only from the road, but also from the roofs and curtilages of the adjacent houses. It is a channel artificially made for this purpose, and, as I gather from the evidence, there are gullies at regular intervals in the channel to allow the water passing along it to descend to a covered sewer below the surface of the road. And, as I understand, there are already about twenty houses draining the surface water from their roofs and curtilages by pipes into the channel. These circumstances to my mind, shew that this is undoubtedly a "sewer" within the definition in s 4.' *Wilkinson v Llandaff & Dinas Powis Rural Council* [1903] 2 Ch 695 at 701, 702, CA, per Romer LJ

'A sewer within this Act of Parliament [Public Health Act 1875, s 4 (repealed)] I conceive must be in some form a line of flow by which sewage or water of some kind, such as would be conveyed through a sewer, should be taken from a point to a point and then discharged. It must have a terminus *a quo* and a terminus *ad quem*. There must be a line of flow from one to the other. It was decided in *Meader v West Cowes Local Board* [[1892] 3 Ch 18], that if you have a thing which conveys sewage, but has no outflow at all, but simply terminates in a pit on the land of the person who lays the pipe, that is not a sewer.' *Pakenham v Ticehurst Rural District Council* (1903) 67 J P 448 at 449, per Buckley J

'The word "sewer" [in the Rivers Pollution Prevention Act 1876, s 7 (repealed; see now the Public Health (Drainage of Trade Premises) Act 1937)] does not necessarily bear the same meaning as in the Public Health Act 1875 [s 4 (repealed; see now the Public Health Act 1936, s 343)], whatever the meaning in that Act may be. I think in the present case it includes the works which are a part of the system through which the sewage flows to the river where it ultimately escapes.' *Brook v Meltham Urban Council* [1909] AC 438 at 440, per Lord Loreburn LC

'It is right . . . to say, in the first instance, that, if I regard the word "sewer" just as a word in ordinary use in the English language, I should understand it to mean a pipe or channel for the conveyance of sewage away from the place where it is produced to some place where it can be got rid of.' *Revenue Comrs v Renfrewshire County Council* (1925) SC 118 at 122, per the Lord President (Lord Clyde)

SEX

See MATTERS OF SEX

SEXUAL INTERCOURSE

Where, on the trial of any offence under this Act, it is necessary to prove sexual intercourse (whether natural or unnatural), it shall not be necessary to prove the completion of the intercourse by the emission of seed, but the intercourse shall be deemed complete upon proof of penetration only. (Sexual Offences Act 1956, s 44)

SHACK

Another class of commonable lands is shack land, which is land over which cattle are allowed to go at shack (that is to go at large to pasture). Such land is open arable or meadow land held in severalty during a portion of the year until the crop or hay has been removed and then becoming commonable to all the parties having severalty rights, but to no others. In this respect may be said to lie the difference between shack lands and Lammas lands (q.v.), which are commonable by others besides the severalty owners. (6 Halsbury's Laws (4th edn) para 520)

SHAFT *See also* MINE; PIT

'Shaft' means a shaft the top of which is, or is intended to be, at the surface. (Mines and Quarries Act 1954, s 182)

SHALL *See also* MAY

'The words shall and may in general acts of parliament, or in private constitutions, are to be construed imperatively.' *A-G v Lock* (1744) 3 Atk 164 at 166, per Lord Hardwicke LC

'The words "it shall and may be lawful", in Acts of Parliament, and other instruments, are obligatory or not, according to the subject matter with respect to which they are used. This is the rule laid down by Chambre J in *Cook v Tower* [(1808) 1 Taunt 372 at 377]. When used in charters, they have generally been construed as giving an option to do or not to do the thing respecting which they are used. In the cases which have been cited, the words were not precisely the same as in the present case. In *Rex v Havering Atte Bower* [(1822) 5 B & Ald 691, 692], the words were, "that the steward and suitors of the manor court should have power and authority to hear and determine all causes arising within the manor, although the same exceeded forty shillings". The holding of such a court was an obvious and undoubted benefit to the suitors of the manor, and therefore in that case, it was held to be obligatory on them to hold the court. Here, however, the words "it shall and may be lawful", occur in a bye-law and relate to the description of persons who may be admitted freemen, the charter itself being silent on that subject. It is impossible to suppose that the corporation, who themselves made this bye-law, should have intended, by using the term "it shall and may be lawful", to make it obligatory upon them to admit to their freedom all the persons therein described. Here the words occur only in a bye-law, and I think they are not obligatory.' *R v Eye Corpn* (1822) 1 B & C 85 at 86, 87, per Abbott CJ

'We must endeavour to construe the words, so that "shall and may" [in an agreement for arbitration] may both stand. "Shall and may" will both stand, by our holding them to be imperative.' *Crump v Adney* (1833) 1 Cr & M 355 at 361, per Lord Lyndhurst CB

'The meaning to be attributed to the phrase "it shall and may be lawful", in a statute, must depend upon the subject matter in every instance. Prima facie these words import a discretion; and they must be construed as discretionary unless there be anything in the subject matter to which they are applied, or in any other part of the statute, to shew that they are meant to be imperative.' *Re Newport Bridge* (1859) 2 E & E 377 at 380, 381, per Crompton J

Australia 'The word "shall" does not always impose an absolute and imperative duty to do or omit the act prescribed. The word is facultative: it confers a faculty or power. . . . The word "shall" cannot be construed without reference to its context.' *Re Davis* (1947) 75 CLR 409 at 418, 419, per Starke J

Shall be binding

Australia 'To say that a determination or award of a tribunal "shall be binding" does not establish an exercise of judicial power. The phrase is devoid of any significance in relation to the exercise of judicial power, for it is as appropriate to the determinations of administrative tribunals as to determinations of tribunals in which judicial power of the Commonwealth is vested.' *Rola Co (Aust) Pty Ltd v Commonwealth* (1944) 69 CLR 185 at 212, per Starke J

Shall die

Australia 'The words "shall die" are . . . vague and constantly used in the sense of shall be dead . . . but this is not their primary meaning. . . . I think . . . that the words "shall die" are not a term of art, but are words which have to be understood, whether in a deed or will, according to their meaning as words in ordinary use.' *Re Halliday, Halliday v Halliday* [1925] SASR 104 at 109, 111, per Napier J

Australia 'As the only way in which they [the beneficiaries] could be participators would be by construing the words "shall die in my lifetime" . . . as equivalent to "shall have died in my lifetime", there is, in my opinion, the plainest possible indication that the testator intended the words to bear that meaning.' *Re Sewell* [1929] SASR 226 at 235, 236, per Murray CJ

SHAM

'As regards the contention of the plaintiff that the transactions between himself, Auto-

Finance Ltd and the defendants were a "sham", it is, I think, necessary to consider what, if any, legal concept is involved in the use of this popular and pejorative word. I apprehend that, if it has any meaning in law, it means acts done or documents executed by the parties to the "sham" which are intended by them to give to third parties or to the court the appearance of creating between the parties legal rights and obligations different from the actual legal rights and obligations (if any) which the parties intend to create.' *Snook v London & West Riding Investments Ltd* [1967] 1 All ER 518 at 528, CA, per Diplock LJ

New Zealand 'The word "sham" is well on the way to becoming a legal shibboleth; on its mere utterance it seems to be expected that contracts will wither like one who encounters the gaze of a basilisk. But by a "sham" is meant, in my opinion, no more or no less than an appearance lent by documents or other evidentiary materials, concealing the true nature of a transaction, and making it seem something other than what it really is. The word "sham" has no applicability to transactions which are intended to take effect, and do take effect, between the parties thereto according to their tenor, even though those transactions may have the effect of fraudulently preferring one creditor to others, and notwithstanding that they are deliberately planned with this in view. If such is their effect, there are statutes and rules of law designed to thwart the intentions of those who enter into them; but the fact that the law discountenances such transactions as these does not render them "shams".' *Paintin & Nottingham Ltd v Miller, Gale & Winter* [1971] NZLR 164 at 175, per Turner J

SHAPE *See* DESIGN

SHARE (Verb)

'Before considering the argument advanced by counsel for the landlord in support of the order for possession, it is necessary to determine the impact on the issues involved of the decision of the House of Lords in *Baker v Turner* [[1950] AC 401]. Until their Lordships decided that case, there was a tendency to assume that if A "shared" a subject-matter with B, B "shared" that subject-matter with A, in a sense of the word "shared" which applied impartially as between them. *Baker v Turner* in the present connection gives the quietus to this facile assumption and decides that where there are two people sharing they need not "share" in the same sense or on an equal basis. They may, if the barbarism can be tolerated, the one be "sharer" and the other "sharee". As between the parties to the sharing, the rights in the thing shared enjoyed by each may be disparate. Both Lord Porter and Lord MacDermott made this clear in relation to the facts before them in that case. A let to B. B sub-let to C, subject to liberty on the part of C to use the kitchen in common with B. Here C is "sharing" with B, and for that reason is unprotected by the Acts, but B is not sharing with C, and he retains protection of the Acts. Why? Because the quality of B's rights in the kitchen differs wholly from the quality of C's rights in it. B can (it may be, must) repair and re-decorate the kitchen. He can hang in it what pictures he likes, can turn on the wireless, and can admit other licensees to use it. C cannot do any of these things. B in this connection is dominant, C is servient. B can say of C: 'You are a mere sharer. I can extrude you. You cannot say I have let to you a separate dwelling." But A cannot say the same to B, for B retains a general exclusive dominion of the kitchen subject only to the licence given by him to C.' *Rogers v Hyde* [1951] 2 All ER 79 at 82, CA, per Lord Asquith of Bishopstone; [1951] 2 KB 923

SHARE (Of estate)

'The plural word "shares" is intended to meet the case of a plurality of children dying without issue, not that of the plurality of shares of any one child. . . . The word share, according to its natural and obvious meaning, includes, or, at all events, if the context requires it, may include, every interest which the child takes under the limitations of the settlement. The word "share" has no technical meaning, and, therefore, in giving effect to the deed in which it occurs, the Court has only to ascertain in what sense it is there used.' *Doe d Clift v Birkhead* (1849) 4 *Exch* 110 at 125, 126, per Pollock CB

'The word "share", unassisted by anything to be found in the context, is to be confined to the original shares, and not extended to accrued shares.' *Dutton v Crowdy* (1863) 33 Beave 272 at 276, per Romilly MR

'No doubt, sometimes, the word "share" will carry an accruing share, sometimes it will not, and that must depend on the whole tenor of the will.' *Edmonstone v Farley* (1868) 18 LT 847 at 848, per Malins V-C

'The material words in the letter are these: "You are of course aware that with my large family Eliza will have little fortune. She will have a share of what I leave after the death of her mother, who I wish to leave in comfortable independence if I should leave her a widow." The plaintiff's contention is that the true meaning and effect of the letter is this: "If you, Mr Farina, will make a settlement on my daughter before her marriage, I will give my assent, and subject only to the rights of my widow, as to which I reserve myself a free hand—I will bind myself to leave her by my will an equal share with all my other surviving children in my property, subject only to debts and testamentary expenses." Upon consideration, I cannot bring myself to believe that this is the true effect of the letter. . . . I regard it as in no sense a proposal or offer, but rather as a representation that the testator was not in a position to make any proposal or to give his daughter anything at the time, but that he intended to give her something at his death. I do not regard it as an offer resulting in a contract by the testator. . . . I think "a share" means "some share" or "some part". The testator has given Mrs Farina £2,000, and has satisfied the obligation, if any, imposed by the letter.' *Re Fickus, Farina v Fickus* [1900] 1 Ch 331 at 335, 336, per Cozens-Hardy J

Australia 'The word "share" may be used in the sense of connoting merely the total interest bequeathed to the person spoken of, as well as part of something to be divided.' *Re Woods (deceased), Woods v Woods* [1941] St R Qd 129 at 136, per Philp J

SHARE AND SHARE ALIKE

'Though the words, "equally to be divided", and, "share and share alike", are, in general, construed, in a will, to create a tenancy in common; yet, where the context shews a joint-tenancy to be intended, the words should be construed accordingly.' *Armstrong v Eldridge* (1791) 3 Bro CC 215 at 215, per Lord Thurlow LC

[Property was devised on trust for sale, the proceeds to be held upon trust for all and every the testator's said sons and daughters 'share and share alike'.] 'Then come the words "share and share alike". What do they mean? Of course, they create a tenancy in common, instead of a joint tenancy. But in whom? In the class described as to which there would have been a joint tenancy, but for the fact that those words follow. . . . Then the words "share and share alike" indicate clearly that the persons who would have taken as joint tenants—that is, the surviving sons and daughters and the family, which is an individual, as it were, for this purpose, are to take share and share alike.' *Re Yates, Bostock v D'Eyncourt* [1891] 3 Ch 53 at 57, per North J

SHAREHOLDER

Every person who shall have subscribed the prescribed sum or upwards to the capital of the company, or shall otherwise have become entitled to a share in the company, and whose name shall be entered on the register of shareholders . . . shall be deemed a shareholder of the Company. (Companies Clauses Consolidation Act 1845, s 8)

SHARES (In company)

A share is a right to a specified amount of the share capital of a company, carrying with it certain rights and liabilities while the company is a going concern and in its winding up. The shares or other interest of any member in a company are personal estate, transferable in the manner provided by its articles but subject to the Stock Transfer Act 1963 (which enables securities of certain descriptions to be transferred by a simplified process) and are not in the nature of real estate. (7 Halsbury's Laws (4th edn) para 415)

'Share' means share in the share capital of a company, and includes stock (except where a distinction between stock and shares is expressed or implied). (Companies Act 1985, s 744)

'What . . . is the character of a share in a company? Is it in its nature a chose in possession, or a chose in action? Such a share is, in my opinion, the right to receive certain benefits from a corporation, and to do certain acts as a member of that corporation; and if those benefits be withheld or those acts be obstructed, the only remedy of the owner of the share is by action. Of the share itself, in my view, there can be no occupation or enjoyment; though of the fruits arising from it there may be occupation, enjoyment, and manual possession. Such a share appears to me to be closely akin to a debt, which is one of the most familiar of choses in action; no action is required to obtain the right to the money in the case of the debt, or the right to the dividends or other accruing benefits in the case of the share; but an action is the only means of obtaining the money itself or the other benefits in specie, the right to which is called in one case a debt and in the other case a share. In the case alike of the debt and of the share, the owner of it has, to use the language of Blackstone, "a bare right without any occupation or enjoyment". A debt, no doubt, differs from a share in one respect, that it confers generally a more limited right than a share and that when once paid it is at an end.' *Colonial Bank v Whinney* (1885) 30 Ch D 261 at 285–287, 290, CA, per Fry LJ (dissenting)

'Where a testator purports by will to dispose of shares in a company, the word "shares" has, in my opinion, a fixed meaning. . . . It means, in my opinion, a proprietary share or portion in the capital stock of the company.' *Dillon v Arkins* (1885) 17 LR Ir 636 at 637, per FitzGibbon LJ

'A share is the interest of a shareholder in the company measured by a sum of money, for the purpose of liability in the first place, and of interest in the second, but also consisting of a series of mutual covenants entered into by all the shareholders inter se in accordance with s 16 of the Companies Act 1862 [repealed; see now the Companies Act 1985, s 14(1)]. The contract contained in the articles of association is one of the original incidents of the share. A share is not a sum of money settled in the way suggested, but is an interest measured by a sum of money and made up of various rights contained in the contract, including the right to a sum of money of a more or less amount.' *Borlands Trustees v Steel Brothers & Co Ltd* [1901] 1 Ch 279 at 288, per Farwell J

'It seems to me that . . . where you have an express power to invest in shares, that is a reference to a form of investment which is not in any material or real respect different from stock, the two things being substantially identical. Accordingly, unless I find a context to the contrary, I ought to interpret this in the sense that the testator intended to include in shares the form of investment which is known as stock.' *Re Boy's Will Trusts, Westminster Bank Ltd v Boys* [1950] 1 All ER 624 at 626, per Romer J

Preference shares

It is not necessary that equal rights and privileges should be attached to all shares; some may be preferential either as to capital or as to dividend, or as to both, or may have peculiar privileges in the matter of voting, or in other respects. . . . These are generally called 'preference' shares, as distinguished from those which are not so privileged, generally called 'ordinary' or 'deferred' shares. There may be preference, ordinary and deferred shares, or shares of more classes than three, each of which has particular rights and conditions attached to it. Founders' shares were sometimes issued to recompense 'founders' or promoters of the company. They were usually shares of small nominal amount, which, although deferred in priority as to dividends, entitled the holders to the whole or a large percentage of the surplus profits remaining after payment of fixed dividends on the shares having priority to the founders' shares. (7 Halsbury's Laws (4th edn) para 176, 176n)

SHEEP

'Sheep' includes any lamb, ewe or ram. (Protection of Animals Act 1911, s 15)

'The word "horse" is a generic term, and includes a gelding, and wherever there is a well-known generic term or name for property, it may be described by that name in an indictment for stealing it. The same objection was made in a case where the indictment described the animal as a sheep, and the proof was the loss of a lamb. It was decided by all the judges, that the word "sheep" was a generic term, and included lambs.' *R v Aldridge* (1849) 4 Cox CC 143 at 143, per Erle J

SHELLFISH *See* FISH

SHELTER *See also* AIR-RAID SHELTER

'A shelter' means any premises, structure or excavation used or intended to be used to provide shelter from any form of hostile attack by a foreign power. (Civil Defence Act 1948, s 9(1))

[A corporation purchased land to be used as a public garden, the deed containing a covenant by the corporation with the vendors to preserve and keep the land to be devoted to pleasure ground purposes as an open space, subject to no building or erections of any kind being put thereupon except such structures as summer houses, a band stand, or 'shelters'.] 'I hold that the word "shelter" in this deed does not include a urinal or a lavatory.' *Stourcliffe Estates Co Ltd v Bournemouth Corpn* [1910] 2 Ch 12 at 21, CA, per Buckley LJ

SHIFT

New Zealand 'In my opinion the words "employed on shift-work" mean work which is done by shifts. If the mill was working continuously for the whole twenty-four hours of the day, three different groups of workers being employed for eight hours each, it would be idle to attempt to deny that the mill was being operated by three shifts. So, where one group of workers work during the day hours and when they leave off another group of workers take up the work of the mill, doing the same work as their predecessors and in the same way, it seems to me that in common parlance the first group of workers constitute a day shift and the second group a night shift. I cannot agree . . . that a shift is limited to a group of workers who work during a period outside what might be called the ordinary working-hours of the day. Nor can I agree . . . that rotation is necessary to constitute as shifts two groups of workers working in the way described. The shifts must exist before there can be any rotation. In considering the interpretation of an expression like "shift" or "shift-work" occurring in an award or other instrument dealing with industrial matters, the Court must have due regard to the meaning which would be placed upon the expression by those concerned in industrial matters, or engaged in industrial employment; and I cannot doubt that groups of workers employed in the manner that I have indicated would in industrial parlance be described as day and night shifts respectively.' *Crombie v Ross & Glendining Ltd* [1941] NZLR 171 at 178, 179, SC, per Myers CJ; also reported [1941] GLR 48 at 50

SHIP *See also* BRITISH SHIP; VESSEL

The term 'ship' includes vessel and boat, with the tackle, furniture, and apparel of the ship, vessel or boat. (Naval Prize Act 1864, s 2)

'Ship' shall include any description of boat, vessel, floating battery, or floating craft; also any description of boat, vessel, or other craft or battery, made to move either on the surface of or under water, or sometimes on the surface of and sometimes under water. (Foreign Enlistment Act 1870, s 30)

'Ship' includes every description of vessel used in sea navigation, whether propelled by oars or otherwise. (Explosives Act 1875, s 108)

'Ship' includes every description of ship, boat, or other floating craft. (Territorial Waters Jurisdiction Act 1878, s 7)

'Ship' includes every description of vessel used in navigation not propelled by oars. (Merchant Shipping Act 1894, s 742)

The term 'ship' includes the hull, materials and outfit, stores and provisions for the officers and crew, and, in the case of vessels engaged in a special trade, the ordinary fittings requisite for the trade, and also, in the case of a steamship, the machinery, boilers, and coals and engine stores, if owned by the assured. (Marine Insurance Act 1906, Sch 1)

'Ship' includes every description of vessel used in navigation, whether propelled by oars or otherwise. (Petroleum (Consolidation) Act 1928, s 23)

'Ship', where used as a noun, includes every description of vessel used in navigation, seaplanes on the surface of the water and hovercraft within the meaning of the Hovercraft Act 1968. (Harbours Act 1964, s 57, as amended by the Hovercraft Act 1968)

'Ship' includes any boat and any other description of vessel used in navigation. (Trade Descriptions Act 1968, s 39(1))

'As the word "ship", in common use, may denote either a mere frame, or a ship with its apparatus ready for sea; so, in marine policies, it may be construed to express either the mere structure of timber, or all that must be combined therewith to make it fit to perform service as a ship; and its meaning in different policies may be made to vary according to the different nature of the services required of the ships insured thereby.' *Gibson v Small* (1853) 4 HL Cas 353 at 383, 384, per Erle J

'The broad distinction between ship and cargo is forcibly put by Lord Stowell in the case of *The Dundee* ([(1823)] 1 Hag Adm 109 at 122). Having to determine the meaning of the phrase "appurtenances to a ship", he says: "A cargo cannot be considered as appurtenances of the ship, being that which is to be disposed of at the foreign port for money, or money's worth vested in a return cargo. Its connection with the ship is merely transitory, and it bears a distinct character of its own. But those accompaniments that are essential to a ship in its present occupation not being cargo, but totally different from cargo, though they are not direct constituents of the ship (if indeed they were, they would not be appurtenances; for the very nature of an appurtenance is, that it is one thing which belongs to another thing); yet if they are indispensable instruments, without which the ship cannot execute its mission and perform its functions, it may, in ordinary loose application, be included under the term ship, being that which may be essential to it, as essential to it as any part of its own immediate machinery."' *The Milan* (1861) Lush 388 at 399, 400, per Dr Lushington

[The owners of a ship agreed to pay to the owners of another ship the amount of the damage caused to that 'ship' by collision therewith.] 'The question is, what is the meaning of the word "ship" in this agreement. Are we to give it its strict and literal meaning? or, are we to construe it as the parties evidently intended it should be construed? The consequence of the former construction would be, that the plaintiffs are to receive the amount of the actual damage done to the frame of the ship, and the costs incurred in the Admiralty court, but are to get nothing for the consequential damage arising from the ship's detention. Looking at the recitals and at the operative part of the agreement, I think we shall best carry out the real intention of the parties by construing "ship" to mean "the owners". The poverty of our language compels us frequently to use expressions which do not with precise accuracy define what we mean. Hence the use of many elliptical phrases: for instance, when we speak of "the Cabinet", we mean the members who sit there: so, when we speak of "the Bar", we mean the members of that body who occupy places whether within or behind the bar. I cannot entertain any doubt.' *Heard v Holman* (1865) 19 CBNS 1 at 11, per Byles J

'Whether a ship is propelled with oars or not, she is still a ship. Most small vessels use something of the kind to propel them. The vessels which came over in the Armada, with perhaps a thousand men on board, were rowed by hundreds of slaves. Yet no one could say they were not ships. I can only suggest that "Every vessel that substantially goes to sea is a ship". I do not mean to say that every little boat that goes a mile or two outside a harbour is a ship, but that where it is really and substantially the business of a vessel to go to sea, it is a ship.' *Ex p Ferguson* (1871) 40 LJQB 105 at 110, per Blackburn J

'By the definition clause of the Merchant Shipping Act 1854 (17 & 18 Vict c 104) [repealed; see now the Merchant Shipping Act 1894, s 742], which is incorporated in the later Act "ship shall include every description of vessel used in navigation not propelled by oars". This definition is copied in the Admiralty Court Act 1861. Taking into consideration the terms in the 3rd subsection of the 30th section of the Merchant Shipping Act Amendment Act 1862 [repealed], "to proceed to sea", and the judgment in *ex p Ferguson* [supra], I am of opinion that the criterion as to whether a vessel falls under the category of "ship" mentioned in the Act, is, whether the vessel be one whose real habitual business is to go to sea; if so, though propelled by oars as well as sails, it is a ship within the meaning of the Act. Upon the evidence before me it does not appear that this vessel does go to sea at all—though it has sails as well as oars. It does not therefore come within the meaning of the term "ship" in the statute.' *The CS Butler* (1874) LR 4 A & E 238 at 240, 241, per Sir Robert Phillimore

'I think it immaterial to consider whether the hopper-barge was "used in navigation" within the meaning of the Merchant Shipping Act 1854, s 2 [repealed; see now the Merchant Shipping Act 1894, s 742] because that enactment directs that the word "ship" shall "include every description of vessel used in navigation not propelled by oars". It does not exclude other meanings of the word. I agree that to hold that a mud-barge is a ship may seem to go very far in the way of interpretation; but we must not overlook the consequences of holding that the hopper-barge is not a "ship". She could take men on board. She falls within the definition cited in Todd's Johnson's Dictionary of the word "ship" from Horne Tooke, namely, "*formatum aliquid*, in contradistinction from a raft for the purposes of conveying merchandise, etc, by water, protected from the water and the weather'. Although this may not be the definition of Johnson, it is the definition of a great master of language; and I think that it applies to the present case. . . . I decide that she is a ship in the common meaning of that term.' *The Mac* (1882) 7 PD 126 at 128, 129, CA, per Lord Coleridge CJ

'I do not want to attempt a definition, but if I had to define "ship or vessel" I should say that it was any hollow structure intended to be used in navigation, i.e. intended to do its real work on the seas or other waters, and capable of free and ordered movement thereon from one place to another.' *Polpen Shipping Co Ltd v Commercial Union Assurance Co Ltd* [1943] 1 KB 161 at 167, per Atkinson J

Canada [The definition of 'ship' in the Federal

Court Act, s 2, provides that it shall include any description of vessel, boat or craft used or capable of being used solely or partly for marine navigation without regard to method or lack of propulsion. The question was whether or not a floating crane was a ship.] 'The definition of ship in the Federal Court Act is not exclusive but inclusive. It, thus, enlarges the term. She [the floating crane] was a barge built for use on water. She was capable of being moved from place to place and was so moved from time to time. . . . She was capable of carrying cargo and had, in fact, done so. She was certainly capable of carrying people and obviously had to do so to enable the crew to carry out their duties. While it appears that she was not capable of navigation herself and was not self-propelled, those facts do not detract from the fact that she was built to do something on water, requiring movement from place to place. Therefore, in my opinion, [she] was a ship.' *National Harbours Board v St John Shipbuilding and Dry Dock Co Ltd* (1981) 43 NR 15 at 26, FCA, per Urie J

See, generally, 43 Halsbury's Laws (4th edn) para 91.

Abandonment of *See* ABANDONMENT

Arrest of *See* ARREST

Arrived *See* ARRIVAL

Building of *See* BUILDING

Course of *See* COURSE OF SHIP

Crossing in navigation *See* CROSS

Home-going ship

'Home-going ship' means a ship plying exclusively in inland waters, or engaged exclusively in coastal excursions; and for the purpose of this definition 'inland waters' means any canal, river, lake, navigation or estuary, and 'coastal excursion' means an excursion lasting not more than one day which starts and ends in Great Britain and does not involve calling at any place outside Great Britain. (Food Act 1984, s 132(1))

New ship

'New ship' means a ship whose keel is laid, or which is at a similar stage of construction, on or after the material date, and 'existing ship' means a ship which is not a new ship; and for the purposes of this subsection the material date—

(a) in relation to a ship whose parent country is a Convention country other than the United Kingdom, is the date as from which it is declared under s 31 of this Act either that the Government of that country has accepted or acceded to the Convention [International Convention on Load Lines] of 1966 or that it is a territory to which that Convention extends, and

(b) in relation to any other ship, is the date of the commencement of this Act.

(Merchant Shipping (Load Lines) Act 1967, s 32)

Part of ship *See* PART

SHIP BROKER

'A broker is only an agent. There may be some brokers who perform somewhat peculiar functions differentiating them in that respect from other agents; but a shipbroker is only an agent to make a charter, just as any one else may be an agent to make a charter.' *Harper & Co v Vigers Brothers* [1900] 2 KB 549 at 562, per Pickford J

SHIP'S DELIVERY ORDER

[A contract for the sale of goods and for their shipment to Liverpool provided that the buyers were to make payment for the goods against documents consisting of invoice, full set of bills of lading, and/or 'ship's delivery order' and a policy or certificate of insurance.] 'A ship's delivery order has never been defined with precision. I will not attempt any general definition, but for the purposes of this contract I take it to mean an order on the ship to deliver goods she was carrying given by a person who has a right to give it. It might be, it is said, an order given by the ship. At least, it must have, in my view, some connection with the ship, or else it is not a ship's delivery order.' *Colin and Shields v Weddel (W) & Co Ltd* [1952] 2 All ER 337 at 342, CA, per Singleton LJ

'I agree with my Lord as to the meaning of "ship's delivery order" in this contract. It means, I think, an order given by the seller directed to the ship, whereby the seller orders the ship to deliver the contract goods to the buyer or his order.' Ibid at 343, per Denning LJ

SHIP'S HUSBAND

'The ship's husband or managing owner is an agent appointed by the other owners to do what is necessary to enable the ship to prosecute her voyage and earn freight.' *Barker v Highley* (1863) 32 LJCP 270 at 272, per cur.

SHIPMENT

Shipment of the goods normally means putting the goods on board a ship. However, where the contract involves an antecedent land transit, it may be the usage and practice of the trade to issue a through bill of lading and to regard shipment as being made in the interior at the time when the goods are put on rail. In such a case the seller performs his duty to ship the goods by putting them on the rail. Where the word 'shipment' appears expressly in the contract and the contract is an English one, it means putting on board a ship, and evidence of usage to the contrary cannot be given to contradict the express terms of the contract. However, the seller may normally perform his contract by purchasing goods afloat which have been shipped during the contract period. (41 Halsbury's Laws (4th edn) para 915)

'"Shipped" means put on something which answers the description of a ship or vessel, no matter what its shape or form may be, for the purpose of being conveyed therein to some destination.' *Clyde Navigation Trustees v Laird* (1883) 8 App Cas 658 at 676, per Lord FitzGerald

'Now, if I give to the word "shipment" the widest meaning of which it is capable, it cannot mean more than bringing the goods to the shipping port and then loading them on board a ship prepared to carry them to their contractual destination.' *Re Comptoir Commercial Anversois and Power, Son & Co* [1920] 1 KB 868 at 878, per Bailache J

'There cannot be the slightest doubt that the words "shipment to be made not later than the end of November next" standing by themselves, mean shipment on the ship which is to carry the goods across the Atlantic. But the plaintiffs say that in this trade [the timber trade], by custom—it is not exactly a custom of the trade, but of the way they use words in this trade—"shipment" means shipment on to the car or loading on to the car at the saw-mills from which the lumber comes. . . . This custom was not admissible to interpret "shipping" as meaning loading on board the cars at the mills.' *Mowbray, Robinson & Co v Rosser* (1922) 91 LJKB 524 at 525, 526, CA, per Lord Sterndale MR

'The matter depends on the proper construction of Clause 5 of the contract. I will read that again. "Each shipment under this contract shall be deemed as a separate contract." It is plain that the seller had the option to ship the goods in separate shipments. The appellants rely on there being two sets of documents, receipts, certificates, bills of lading and insurance contracts. But this does not, in my opinion, decide the matter. The provision of two sets of documents may be purely a matter of convenience, and a simple explanation of this may be that the cloth was exported from Hongkong under two separate quotas, one belonging to the plaintiffs and one belonging to South Textiles Ltd. It has, in my view, no real significance. The real point is the meaning of "shipment". The meaning of "shipment", in my opinion, is putting into a ship, and all the cloth was put into the same ship and on the same day. Accordingly, it was all one single shipment, in my view.' *Esmail v Rosenthal (J) & Sons Ltd* [1964] 2 Lloyd's Rep 447 at 462, CA, per Dankwerts LJ; affd, [1965] 2 Lloyd's Rep 171, HL

In good order and condition

'The words "shipped in good order and condition" [in a bill of lading] are not words of contract in the sense of a promise or undertaking. The words are an affirmation of fact, or perhaps rather in the nature of an assent by the captain to an affirmation of fact which the shipper may be supposed to make as to his own goods.' *Compania Naviera Vasconzada v Churchill & Sim, Compania Naviera Vasconzada v Burton & Co* [1906] 1 KB 237 at 247, per Channell J

'I doubt very much whether the statement "shipped in apparent good order and condition" has any reference to original defects of quality or type. The words seem to me to refer rather to acquired damage or defect in the goods rather than to original defects of quality or type.' *Silver v Ocean SS Co Ltd* [1930] 1 KB 416 at 433, CA, per Greer LJ

'We are here dealing with goods as to which the condition must refer to real condition, and the bills of lading, as they stand, make two completely contradictory statements: (1) "shipped in good order and condition" and (2) "condition unknown". . . . What would those words in a bill of lading convey to anybody who read them? What, in the first place would "shipped in good order and condition" followed by "condition unknown" convey? Speaking for myself, they would have conveyed nothing at all to me. . . . It is true that the words "shipped in good order and condition", as Channell J pointed out [in *Compania Naviera Vasconzada v Churchill & Sim* (supra)] are not words of contract, but they are an affirmation or assent to an affirmation of fact, and in this case they were an affirmation of an untruth. . . . Primarily, however, this is a matter of construction, and I hold that the insertion of the word "condition" in the way it was inserted here, is not such a qualification of the original statement "shipped in good order and condition" as to bring to the mind of anybody reading that document that the goods were or even might be apparently, and to the knowledge of anyone who had seen them, damaged goods.' *The Skarp* [1935] P 134 at 142–144, per Langton J

SHIPOWNER

The expression 'shipowner' includes the master of the ship and every other person authorised to act as agent for the owner or entitled to receive the freight, demurrage, or other charges payable in respect of the ship. (Merchant Shipping Act 1894, s 492)

SHIPPER

[The Harbours, Docks and Piers Clauses Act 1847, s 3, defines owner when used in relation to goods as including any consignor, consignee, 'shipper', or agent for sale or custody of such goods.] 'The shipper is the consignee who has purchased the coals, and has provided the vessel for their transport.' *Ribble Navigation Co v Hargreaves* (1856) 17 CB 385 at 405, per Jervis CJ

SHIPPER'S RISK

'It is a very well known clause that the transhipment of goods is to be "at shipper's risk", and it appears to me only to extend the rights and liabilities of the parties under the bill of lading to the rest of the voyage with this, that any expense that is incurred must be paid by the ship, the risks remaining the same.' *Stuart v British & African Steam Navigation Co* (1875) 32 LT 257 at 262, DC, per Pollock B

SHIPPING *See* COASTAL SHIPPING

SHIPPING PURPOSES

The expression 'shipping purposes' shall include the constructing or doing any work or thing that conduces to the safety or convenience of ships, or that facilitates the shipping or unshipping of goods, and the management and superintending the same, and shall also include the maintenance of any lifeboat or other means of preserving life in case of shipwreck. (Harbours and Passing Tolls, etc Act 1861, s 2)

SHIPWRECK *See also* WRECK

Members of the armed forces and other persons . . . who are at sea and who are wounded, sick or shipwrecked, shall be respected and protected in all circumstances, it being understood that the term 'shipwreck' means shipwreck from any cause and includes forced landings at sea by or from aircraft. (Geneva Conventions Act 1957, Sch 2(12))

SHOP

The expression 'house, shop or building' includes any premises appurtenant to the same. (Riot (Damages) Act 1886, s 9)

'Shop' includes any premises where any retail trade or business is carried on. (Shops Act 1950, s 74)

'Shop' includes any premises, and any vehicle, stall or place other than premises, on or in which any retail trade or business is carried on. (Trading Stamps Act 1964, s 10)

'The true definition of shop, I think, means a place not only for selling but for storing; for instance, a drapery shop is a place for storing drapery goods and such like. But this is not absolutely decisive on the question, for in a fishmonger's shop there may be very perishable articles not meant for storage.' *Pope v Whalley* (1865) 6 B & S 303 at 313, per Mellor J

[The Exmouth Market Act 1867, s 20, made it an offence for an unlicensed person to sell goods in any open place within the limits of the market. Goods having been sold by the defendant in the skittle alley of an inn, the question for the opinion of the court was whether such place was an open place, or the defendant's dwelling-house or 'shop'.] 'This was not a shop belonging to the defendant within the meaning of the Act. The place was an open one to all intents and purposes, so far as the public were concerned, and goods were laid out and offered for sale . . . on a platform or table. I think that in order to constitute a shop there must be some structure of a more or less permanent character. This was not a shop in the popular sense of the term, and I am of opinion, therefore, that the magistrates ought to have convicted.' *Hooper v Kenshole* (1877) 46 LJMC 160 at 162, 163, per Mellor J

'The original grantor intends to lay out his land for particular purposes. He stipulates for certain uses, and only those uses can be made of it. The property is to be wholly used for private houses. Nothing must be done upon any part of it which is a nuisance (e.g. houses of ill-fame, skating-rinks, and the like). One part, however, for general convenience is allowed to be used for shops, which I understand to mean drapers', butchers', and greengrocers' shops, etc, to supply the neighbourhood with their daily wants. A tavern would not come within the definition of shop. It is true that beer is sold there. But a tavern is also a house of entertainment, and travellers have a right to food and refreshment there. I think that upon the estate generally private houses only were to be allowed, but that along this frontage there might be shops of an ordinary character, but not a tavern.' *Coombs v Cook* (1883) Cab & El 75 at 77, per Huddleston B

'Lord Coke says "Every shop in London is a market overt for such things only which by the trade of the owner are put there for sale", [*The Case of Market Overt* (1596) 5 Co Rep 83b]. . . . If, therefore, the sale had been by the defendants and in the shop itself, there could have been no doubt. In the present case, however, the sale was effected in the showroom upstairs . . . and which was as essentially a private place as any convenient room in a private house. It seems to me that by no reasonable stretch of language can the show-room, to be approached only by passing behind the counter in the shop, and with the permission of the defendants or of their servants in the shop and behind the counter, be called a shop. A show-room of this description and so approached is certainly not in ordinary parlance a shop; and I see no reason for such an extension—if I should not more properly say perversion—of the natural and ordinary meaning of the word.' *Hargreave v Spink* [1892] 1 QB 25 at 26, per Wills J

'It is impossible to construe an Act of Parliament otherwise than in accordance with the common use of language; and no person, having regard to the ordinary usage of language, could take the words "shop" and "stall" as meaning the same thing. The persons who are here asserting their claim to the franchise [under the Municipal Corporations (Ireland) Act 1840] describe themselves as stall-holders, not as shop-keepers, thus themselves preserving the distinction.' *Lovell v Callaghan* [1894] 2 IR 346 at 350, per O'Brien J

[The defendant carried on business in a four-storeyed building facing onto Southwark market. The ground floor was used for the sale of fruit and vegetables, the second and third floors for storage, and the top floor for domestic purposes.] 'In my opinion this is a shop as distinct from a warehouse, and it is none the less a shop because there was a warehouse accessory to the shop and used for supplying the shop with the goods which are sold. As was stated in *Pope v Whalley* [supra], the true definition of a shop means a place not only for selling, but for storing. It plainly does; one cannot go into any shop without seeing that. Nor is it any the less a shop because the place where the goods designed for selling in the shop may be in a back yard or anywhere else. But then it is said that this is not a shop because "shop" implies retail sale. It was first said "retail" sale only, and next it was said retail sale at least to some extent. I do not understand how that can be made out. The market, by usage of late years, has been limited, we are told, and I have no doubt accurately, to wholesale dealing, and not to retail dealing, and the shops around have, I gather, followed the same course; but, in my opinion, a shop is none the less a shop because the person keeping the shop elects not to sell small quantities to the chance customers who come in, but to supply other persons who themselves act thereafter as retailers in small quantities to small buyers.' *Haynes v Ford* [1911] 2 Ch 237 at 248, CA, per Cozens-Hardy MR

'The employees in question were waiters in the dining-room and smoking-room in the hotel proper, that is to say, in that part of the hotel which was mainly used by the residents in the hotel, though these rooms were also open to non-residents. It has been contended that the hotel is a shop within the meaning of this Act [Shops Act 1912 (repealed; see now the Shops

Act 1950)]. In my opinion it is not. The Act implies, and states, that it is dealing with shop assistants who are employed to serve customers; but people who are staying in hotels are never spoken of as customers, but as visitors or guests, and it seems to me, therefore, that for the purposes of this Act a shop must necessarily be a place where customers are served. An hotel is not a place of that sort.' *Gordon Hotels Ltd v London County Council, London County Council v Gordon Hotels Ltd* [1916] 2 KB 27 at 36, DC, per Bray J

'Here no member of the public, as such, has any right whatever to enter the premises. In fact, the public do not, and may not, resort there. No goods are on offer to the public or can be bought by the public. The feature of a shop is its appeal to the public, or some section of the public. The feature of these premises is privacy.' *Simmonds Aerocessories (Western) Ltd v Pontypridd Area Assessment Committee* [1944] 1 KB 231 at 238, DC, per cur.

'I . . . have very great sympathy with any shopkeeper who has occasion to consider the Shops Act 1950. Section 1 is extraordinarily difficult to construe. I will not go into it in detail, but clearly the first question is: What is a shop? One gets no assistance from the definition, which merely provides that it includes any premises wherein retail trade or business is carried on. Does "shop" there mean the physical self-contained premises? Can it be construed as applying to a department within those self-contained premises or, indeed, to a counter in a department? It seems to me that, reading the Act as a whole and the regulations, the term "shop" refers to the premises, and although there is no specific finding in this case, I think that it is perfectly clear that where there is a single hereditament consisting of self-contained premises laid out with counters (as is shown on the plan of these premises) the whole of those premises constitutes the shop; it is impossible to say that any particular part of those premises or any particular counter constitutes the shop.' *Fine-Fare Ltd v Brighton County Borough Council* [1959] 1 All ER 476 at 479, per Lord Parker CJ

See, generally, 20 Halsbury's Laws (4th edn) para 419.

Australia 'I think that in the common understanding of the public at large in the commercial and business life of the community a "shop" means a building or structure permanent in its location from which the occupier can at will exclude persons and in which such occupier stores, displays, offers for sale and sells over the counter his goods to persons seeking to purchase such goods on a retail basis by way of comparison with a warehouse in which goods are sold in bulk at wholesale prices to persons requiring the same for resale to consumers in small quantities at retail prices.' *Plummer & Adams v Needham* (1954) 56 WALR 1 at 10, per Walker J

Australia 'The essence of the definition of shop is that a retail business should be carried on, either by actual sales or by exposure of the goods for sale.' *City Motors (1933) Pty Ltd v Tuting* [1964] Tas SR 194 at 198, per Gibson ACJ

Early closing of *See* EARLY CLOSING DAY

Shop premises

'Shop premises' means—

(i) a shop;

(ii) a building or part of a building, being a building or part which is not a shop but of which the sole or principal use is the carrying on there of retail trade or business;

(iii) a building occupied by a wholesale dealer or merchant where goods are kept for sale wholesale or part of a building so occupied where goods are so kept, but not including a warehouse belonging to the owners, trustees or conservators of a dock, wharf or quay;

(iv) a building to which members of the public are invited to resort for the purpose of delivering there goods for repair or other treatment or of themselves there carrying out repairs to, or other treatment of, goods, or a part of a building to which members of the public are invited to resort for that purpose;

(v) any premises (in this Act referred to as 'fuel storage premises') occupied for the purpose of a trade or business which consists of, or includes, the sale of solid fuel, being premises used for the storage of such fuel intended to be sold in the course of that trade or business, but not including dock storage premises or colliery storage premises. (Offices, Shops and Railway Premises Act 1963, s 1)

Wholesale shop

'Wholesale shop' means premises occupied by a wholesale dealer or merchant where goods are kept for sale wholesale to customers resorting to the premises. (Shops Act 1950, s 74)

SHOP ASSISTANT

'Shop assistant' means any person wholly or mainly employed in a shop in connection with the serving of customers or the receipt of orders or the despatch of goods. (Shops Act 1950, s 74)

SHOP CLUB *See* CLUB

SHORE *See also* SEASHORE

Canada 'The word "shore" properly applies only to the sea or other tidal waters but when used with reference to a lake unaffected by the tide it means prima facie the land adjacent to the water and in the absence of any bank of high land to mark the boundary, extends to the water's edge.' *Merriman v Province of New Brunswick* (1974) 45 DLR (3d) 464 at 468, NBCA, per Hughes CJ

SHOTGUN *See* FIREARM

SHOW (Noun)

[The Burgh Police (Scotland) Act 1892, s 397 enacts that 'No public show of any description whatever, whether in open ground or in any house or building, or caravan or tent, and no swings or hobby-horses, and no shooting-gallery, singing or dancing saloon, or bowling or ninepin alley, and no place for playing skittles (all which are hereinafter shortly described or referred to as public shows and other like places of public entertainment), shall be opened or set up within the burgh without the permission of the magistrates'.] 'It appears to me to be abundantly clear that the terms of s 397 are not apt to apply in the case of an entertainment of this nature. This was a concert given in a building which was licensed for the giving of concerts. I do not think that such an entertainment can be aptly described as a public show, even if one adds that the public show may be "of any description whatsoever". I do not think a concert is a public show. But whether or not a concert might fall under such a description if it stood alone, I think the illustrations given immediately afterwards in s 397, under any application of the rule of *ejusdem generis*, exclude an application of the section to such a concert. The enumeration is of events which may take place on open ground, in a house or building, in a caravan or tent; and the enumerated events include only swings or hobby horses, shooting galleries, singing or dancing saloons, bowling or ninepin alleys and a place for playing skittles.' *Benzie v Mickel* 1945 SLT 166 at 167, per Lord Moncrieff

SHOW (Verb)

[The Criminal Evidence Act 1898, s 1(f), provides that a person charged and called as a witness in pursuance of the Act shall not be asked any question tending to 'show' that he has been previously convicted, etc, save in specified circumstances.] 'As to the meaning of the words "tend to show" I see no difficulty. It is not the intention of the question that matters but the effect of the question and presumably the possible answer. Nor is the word "show" in its context ambiguous. Primarily it may mean a visual demonstration but in relation to the giving of oral evidence it can only mean "make known". The issue then is whether the challenged questions made known anything to the jury which they did not know before.' *Jones v Director of Public Prosecutions* [1962] 1 All ER 569 at 572, 573, HL, per Viscount Simonds

'In my judgment "tends to show" means tends to suggest to the jury. . . . If the obvious purpose of this provision is to protect the accused from possible prejudice, as I think it is, then "show" must mean "reveal", because it is only a revelation of something new which could cause such prejudice.' Ibid at 575, per Lord Reid

SHOWMEN'S FAIR *See* FAIR

SICKNESS

[A benefit society provided by its rules that a member should receive benefit during any 'sickness' or accident that might befall him, unless by rioting or drunkeness.] 'I am . . . of opinion that insanity is sickness within the society's rules. The preamble of the rules is wide enough to include it; the words of rule 13, entitling the member to relief, are "during any sickness or accident", except certain excluded cases, insanity not being one. There is nothing to show that temporary illness only was contemplated.' *Burton v Eyden* (1873) LR 8 QB 295 at 298, per Quain J

'The independent chairman of the National Conciliation Board for the co-operative service has made an award in which he has laid down what is to happen with regard to the wages of a workman during sickness. . . . The question is, what is . . . meant by the word "sickness". . . . I come to the conclusion that when the chairman who made the award now under consideration used the word "sickness" he was thinking of a workman who was prevented from doing his work and earning his wages because his body was not in perfect health.' *Maloney v St Helens Industrial Co-operative Society Ltd* [1933] 1 KB 293 at 296–298, CA, per Scrutton LJ

SIDE

'No doubt in a certain context the word "side" might be so used as to be shown by that context to be contra-distinguished from the top, or bottom, or end of a subject of quadrilateral or any other figure. But for this purpose a determining context is necessary. In the absence of such a context it is accurate, both in scientific and in ordinary language, to say that a quadilateral table has four sides.' *Ridsale v Clifton* (1877) 2 PD 276 at 341, PC, per cur.

'The Act [Public Health (Buildings in Streets) Act 1888 (repealed)] forbids the erecting any house or building or any part thereof beyond the front main wall of the house, etc, on either side thereof in the same street. I think that the expressions "house . . . on either side thereof" means a house within some near distance within some degree of proximity, and not one standing some considerable distance away.' *Ravensthorpe Local Board v Hinchcliffe* (1889) 24 QBD 168 at 171, per Fry LJ

SIDECAR

[The appellant was the holder of a provisional driving licence, i.e. was a learner driver. He was riding a motor cycle and carrying a pillion passenger. Attached to the motor cycle was a construction consisting of four planks of wood seven feet long mounted on a steel framework supported by a properly constructed wheel. The platform was about two feet wide. Attached to the platform was additional woodwork adapted to carry a tool box in addition to ladders and buckets for use in a window-cleaning business. The question for the opinion of the High Court was whether justices had been correct in law in deciding that, for the purpose of the Motor Vehicles (Driving Licences) Regulations 1971, reg 6 and the Road Traffic Act 1972, s 88(2) (repealed; see now the Road Traffic Act 1988, s 97(3)), 'sidecar' meant a structure attached to a motor cycle and capable of carrying persons in safety, or whether they should have found that 'sidecar' also included a structure constructed or adapted solely for the carriage of goods.] 'We are dealing with an attachment to a motor bicycle which was properly designed and constructed for the carriage of goods, namely the ladders of a window cleaner and his buckets and sponges and so forth, and the question therefore falls to be decided: is that a sidecar within the meaning of the regulations? It seems to me that it is a sidecar. There is no requirement in any of the statutory provisions to which I have referred laying it down that the sidecar must be one constructed for and fit for the safe carriage of a passenger. It simply is not so defined. Some slight help is to be gained by the fact that in the 1950 regulations [revoked] there is a provision (reg 16(3)(a)) "that for the purposes of this sub-paragraph a motor bicycle shall not be deemed to be constructed or adapted to carry more than one person unless it has a sidecar constructed for the carriage of a passenger attached". That is a completely different piece of legislation, and it is to be noted that it has disappeared from the present regulations, and indeed had done so by 1963. Thus, Parliament has had ample opportunity, if it so wished, to limit the interpretation of the word "sidecar" to an "attachment constructed for and fit for the safe carriage of a passenger" and has not seen fit to do so. In those circumstances it seems to me that a roadworthy attachment to a motor bicycle which is designed for the carriage of goods is just as much a sidecar as a roadworthy attachment constructed for the carriage of a passenger.' *Keen v Parker* [1976] 1 All ER 203 at 207, per O'Connor J

[By the Road Traffic Act 1988, s 186(1), a sidecar is regarded as forming part of the vehicle to which it is attached and not as being a trailer.]

SIDEWALK

Canada 'A sidewalk is that portion of the street set apart for the use of pedestrians.' *Ransome v City of Woodstock* [1969] 1 OR 664 at 665, Ont SC, per Pennell J

Canada 'If "highway" in s 427(1) [of the Municipal Act, RSO 1970, c 284] does not include "sidewalk" then, aside from cases where snow and ice are involved, actions against municipalities for damages with reference to sidewalks would be confined to a common law right of action based on misfeasance; the statutory liability for non-repair would not arise. In my opinion that is clearly not the case; "sidewalk" must be considered as part of a highway as defined in the Municipal Act, s 1, para 10.' *Green v Dixon Road Car Wash Ltd* (1981) 33 OR (2d) 353 at 355, Ont SC, per Craig J

SIGNATURE *See also* UNDER HAND AND SEAL

'Where, by this Act, any instrument or writing is required to be signed by any person it is not necessary that he should sign it with his own hand, but it is sufficient if his signature is written thereon by some other person by or under his authority. (Bills of Exchange Act 1882, s 91)

[A letter beginning 'My dear Robert' and concluding 'believe me the most affectionate of mothers' is not signed within the meaning of the Statute of Frauds 1677, s 4.] 'If I had apprehended at first, that this is the only letter applicable to the purpose of the plaintiff's demand, I should not have suffered the cause to go on; for it was impossible to hold that it could be taken to be sufficiently signed within the statute unless it were by reference to some other instrument having a proper signature. It is a very forced construction of the words of the statute to say that the use of the mere ordinary terms of ceremony constitutes a compliance with the regulations it prescribes. It is not enough that the party may be identified. He is required to sign. And, after you have completely identified, still the question remains, whether he has signed or not. There may be in the instrument a very sufficient description to answer the purpose of identification without a signing; that is, without the party having either put his name to it, or done some other act intended by him to be equivalent to the actual signature of the name—such as a person unable to write making his mark. But it was never said, because you may identify the writer, therefore, there is a signature within the meaning of the statute, if so, the word "I" or "me" would be enough, provided you can prove the handwriting.' *Selby v Selby* (1817) 3 Mer 2 at 6, per Grant MR

'Signature does not necessarily mean writing a person's christian and surname, but any mark which identifies it as the act of the party.' *Morton v Copeland* (1855) 16 CB 517 at 535, per Maule J

'If the name of the party to be charged is printed or written on a document, intended to be a memorandum of the contract, either by himself or his authorised agent, . . . it is his signature, whether it is at the beginning or middle, or foot of the document.' *Durrell v Evans* (1862) 1 H & C 174 at 191, per Blackburn J

'In my judgment . . . it must be taken as established that where an Act of Parliament requires that a document be "signed" by a person, prima facie the requirement of the Act is satisfied if the person himself places on the document an engraved representation of his signature by means of a rubber stamp. Indeed, if reference is made to the Shorter Oxford English Dictionary, 2nd edn, Vol 2, p 1892, it will be found that the primary meaning of the verb "to sign" is not confined to actual writing with a pen or pencil, but appears to have related to marking with the sign of the cross. The later meanings include: "(ii) to place some distinguishing mark upon (a thing or person) . . . (iv) to attest or confirm by adding one's signature; to affix one's name to (a document, etc)". It follows, I think, that the essential requirement of signing is the affixing, either by writing with a pen or pencil or by otherwise impressing on the document one's name or "signature" so as personally to authenticate the document.' *Goodman v Eban (J), Ltd* [1954] 1 All ER 763 at 766, CA, per Evershed MR; see also [1954] 1 QB 550

'In the ordinary way, when a formal document is required to be "signed" by a person, it can only be done by that person himself writing his own name on it, or affixing his own signature on it, with his own hand (see *Goodman v J Eban Ltd* [supra]. But there are some cases where a man is allowed to sign by the hand of another who writes his name for him. Such a signature is called a signature by procuration, by proxy, "per pro", or more shortly "pp". All of these expressions are derived from the Latin *per procurationem*, which means by the action of another. A simple illustration is when a man has broken his arm and cannot write his own name. In that case he can get someone else to write his name for him: but the one who does the writing should add the letters "pp" to show that it is done by proxy, followed by his initials so as to indicate who he is.' *London County*

Council v Vitamins Ltd [1955] 2 All ER 229 at 231, CA, per Denning LJ; see also [1955] 2 QB 218

'It is established, in my judgment, as a general proposition that at common law a person sufficiently "signs" a document if it is signed in his name and with his authority by somebody else, and in such a case the agent's signature is treated as being that of his principal.' Ibid at 232, per Romer LJ

'It has been held in this court that a private person can sign a document by impressing a rubber stamp with his own facsimile signature on it: see *Goodman v J Eban Ltd* [supra], but it has not yet been held that a company can sign by its printed name affixed with a rubber stamp.' *Lazarus Estates Ltd v Beasley* [1956] 1 All ER 341 at 343, 344, CA, per Denning LJ

Australia 'A signature is only a mark, and where a statute merely requires that a document shall be signed, the statute is satisfied by proof of the making of a mark upon the document by or by the authority of the signatory.' *R v Moore, ex p Myers* (1884) 10 VLR 322 at 324, per Higinbotham J

SIGNIFICANT

'Significant', in relation to a change in the character of a school or an enlargement of school premises, implies that there is a substantial change in the function or size of the school. (Education Act 1944, s 114(1) (added by the Education Act 1968, s 1, Sch 1))

['Substantial' is defined by the Oxford English Dictionary as 'of ample or considerable amount, quantity or dimensions'.]

SILVER PLATE *See* PLATE

SIMILAR

Australia [By a building contract it was agreed that a house was to be erected 'similar' to H's house.] 'The word "similar" is an ambiguous word. . . . It would be absurd to hold in such a contract that "similar" means exactly like, because that would involve a slavish copy of all defects latent and patent in the house with which the comparison is made.' *Mays v Roberts* [1928] SASR 217 at 219, per Angas Parsons J

Australia 'I think that what is meant by "similar offences" is offences, generally speaking, of a similar character. For instance in a case of this kind, a case of forgery, I think that all that is necessary is that the other similar offences relied on for the purpose of showing intent should be instances of forgery or of the use of forged documents.' *R v Manning* (1933) 33 SR(NSW) 285 at 289, per Street CJ

SIMONY

Simony, so called from Simon Magus, includes the buying or selling of holy orders or of an ecclesiastical benefice or admission to a benefice. The procuring or acceptance of the presentation, institution, collation, induction or admission to a benefice in consideration of any money, profit or benefit, direct or indirect, or of any promise, agreement or assurance of or for such money, profit or benefit is simoniacal and void. Where it takes place the Queen may present or bestow the benefice for that turn and every person and body giving or taking any such money, profit or benefit, or making or taking any such promise, agreement or assurance is liable, on summary conviction, to a fine not exceeding £100 and the person who so corruptly procures or accepts the benefice becomes thenceforth disabled in law from holding it. (14 Halsbury's Laws (4th edn) para 832)

'I am of opinion that the replication shows neither simony nor ground for equitable relief. Now, in the first place, it does not show that the contract was simoniacal; it in effect alleges that there was a mistake; and this alone is sufficient to establish that there was no simony, for that requires a corrupt intent.' *Wright v Davies* (1876) 46 LJQB 41 at 45, 46, CA, per Lord Coleridge CJ

[The Clergy Discipline Act 1892, s 2 (repealed; but see now the Ecclesiastical Jurisdiction Measure 1963) provided that if a clergyman was alleged to have been guilty of any offence against the laws ecclesiastical, being an offence against morality, and not being a question of doctrine or ritual, he might be prosecuted by the persons and in the manner by the Act prescribed.] 'The first question which their Lordships have to consider is whether the offence of simony, committed by a clerk in order to gain admission to a benefice is . . . "an offence against the laws ecclesiastical being an offence against morality" within the meaning of the above-quoted section of the Act. . . . Their Lordships do not think that simony can fairly be considered as falling within this category.' *Beneficed Clerk v Lee* [1897] AC 226 at 228, 229, PC, per cur.

SIMPLE CONTRACT *See* CONTRACT

SINK

Canada [The contents of a ship's hold were damaged when she filled with water from a leak, but did not sink, and the owner sued the insurers on a policy indemnifying against 'sinking'.] 'I am unable to conclude that the words "This policy insures against loss or damage by . . . sinking . . . while being transported in any . . . motor vessel . . ." were intended to afford indemnity against loss or damage to cargo while being transported in a motor vessel *which was in fact saved from sinking*. . . . In my opinion the word "sinking" . . . can only be meant to apply to the vessel, that it would be extending the language of the policy far beyond its natural and ordinary meaning to construe it as providing insurance against the sinking of the cargo while being transported in a vessel which remains afloat.' *John C Jackson Ltd v Sun Insurance Office Ltd* (1962) 38 WWR 294 at 299, 300, SCC, per Ritchie J

SISTER *See also* MAN

'Sister' includes a sister of the half blood. (Marriage Act 1949, s 78)

[A testator by his will made a bequest to his brothers and 'sisters'. He had one legitimate and one illegitimate sister.] 'It would be impossible to give adequate effect to the use of the plural term "sisters" without including the illegitimate sister as a *persona designata* under the will.' *Re Embury, Bowyer v Page (No 2)* (1914) 111 LT 275 at 276, per Sargant J

SITE

'Site', in relation, to any school, does not include playing fields, but, save as aforesaid, includes any site which is to form part of the school premises. (Education Act 1946, s 16)

Australia '"Site" may perhaps be described as a relative word. The "site" of a house refers no doubt to a defined parcel of land, but the "site" of a battle or of the Federal Capital has a wider meaning, and such a locality may be incapable of definition by metes and bounds.' *Ex p Williams, Re Hobday* (1953) 54 SR (NSW) 54 at 57, per Owen J

Caravan site

In this Part [Part I] of this Act the expression 'caravan site' means land on which a caravan is stationed for the purposes of human habitation and land which is used in conjunction with land on which a caravan is so stationed. (Caravan Sites and Control of Development Act 1960, s 1(4))

'What is being looked for here is a "site" [a caravan site] and that word seems to me to connote a place habitually devoted to some purpose.' *Biss v Smallburgh Rural District Council* [1964] 2 All ER 543 at 554, CA, per Harman LJ; also reported [1965] Ch 335

SITTINGS

Canada 'The word sitting or sittings takes on slightly different meanings dependent upon the context in which it is used. Its meaning is also somewhat different when relating to courts in general than when relating to superior courts of first instance or of appellate jurisdiction; again, "next sittings" of a court has been said to refer to the opening day of a sittings (*R v Tronson* [1932] 1 WWR 537), to a sitting actually held and not to a sitting appointed to be held but adjourned (*McLeod v Waterman* (1903) 9 BCR 370), to the nearest sittings and not just a subsequent sittings (*Hogaboom v Lunt* (1892) 14 PR 480). Generally speaking a sitting of a court is said to refer to a time during which judicial business is transacted before that court; in that sense, it could mean a day, a succession of uninterrupted days or again different days within a given time span for transacting that court's business.' *Paul v R* [1982] 1 SCR 621 at 631, 634, SCC, per Lamer J

SKETCH

The expression 'sketch' includes any photograph, or other mode of representing any place or thing. (Official Secrets Act 1911, s 12)

SKILL

'When a skilled labourer, artisan, or artist is employed, there is on his part an implied warranty that he is of skill reasonably competent to the task he undertakes—*Spondes peritiam artis*. Thus, if an apothecary, a watchmaker, or an attorney be employed for reward, they each impliedly undertake to possess and exercise reasonable skill in their several arts. The public profession of an art is a representation and undertaking to all the world that the professor possesses the requisite ability and skill. An express promise or express representation in the particular case is not necessary. It may be, that, if there is no general and no particular representation of ability and skill, the workman undertakes no responsibility. If a gentleman, for example, should employ a man who is known to have never done anything but sweep a crossing, to clean or mend his watch, the employer probably would be held to have incurred all risks himself. But, in the case under consideration, the correspondence shows, in addition to the implied representation, an express and particular representation by the plaintiff that he did possess the requisite skill.' *Harmer v Cornelius* (1858) 5 CBNS 236 at 246, per Willes J

'Of what advantage to the employer is his servant's undertaking that he possesses skill unless he undertakes also to use it? I have spoken of using skill rather than using care, for "skill" is the word used in the cited case [*Harmer v Cornelius*, supra], but this embraces care. For even in so-called unskilled operations an exercise of care is necessary to the proper performance of duty.' *Lister v Romford Ice and Cold Storage Co Ltd* [1957] 1 All ER 125 at 130, HL, per Viscount Simonds (also reported in [1957] AC 555 at 573)

SLANDER

A slander for which an action will lie is a defamatory statement, made or conveyed by spoken words, sounds, looks, signs, gestures or in some other non-permanent form, published of and concerning the plaintiff, to a person other than the plaintiff, by which the plaintiff has suffered actual damage, often referred to as special damage, which he must allege and prove, or which is actionable per se. (28 Halsbury's Laws (4th edn) para 12)

Slander of goods

An action for slander of goods will lie where the defendant falsely and maliciously publishes words of and concerning the plaintiff's goods and where the publication causes the plaintiff to suffer special damage. (28 Halsbury's Laws (4th edn) para 263)

Slander of title

An action for slander of title lies against anyone who falsely and maliciously disparages the title of an owner of real or personal property, and by doing so, unless the circumstances of the case bring it within the statutory exceptions, causes him special damage. The burden of proving falsity, publication in disparagement of the plaintiff's title, malice and, where essential, special damage is on the plaintiff.

Disparagement of title for this purpose consists in alleging that the owner has no title or a defective or limited title to the property, or has no right or a limited right to deal with it. (28 Halsbury's Laws (4th edn) para 262)

SLATE CLUB *See also* FRIENDLY SOCIETY

'A slate club is generally a small affair formed by placing subscribed money in the hands of some unpaid person who pays sums out of it for the benefit of subscribers in case of sickness, and so on.' *Re One & All Sickness & Accident Assurance Assocn* (1909) 25 TLR 674 at 675, per Parker J

SLAUGHTERHALL

'Slaughterhall' means that part of a slaughterhouse in which the actual slaughtering of any animal or the dressing of carcases takes place. (Slaughterhouses Act 1974, s 34)

SLAUGHTERHOUSE

In this Part of this Act [Part I: slaughterhouses and knackers' yards] . . . 'slaughterhouse' means a place for slaughtering animals whose flesh is intended for sale for human consumption, and includes any place in connection therewith for the confinement of animals awaiting slaughter there or for keeping, or subjecting to any treatment or process, products of the slaughtering of animals there. (Slaughterhouses Act 1974, s 34)

In this Part of this Act [Part II: slaughter of animals] . . . 'slaughterhouse' means any building, premises or place used in connection with the business of killing animals whose flesh is intended for sale for human consumption. (Slaughterhouses Act 1974, s 45)

'Slaughterhouse' means a place for slaughtering animals, the flesh of which is intended for sale for human consumption, and includes any place available in connection with such a place for the confinement of animals while awaiting slaughter there or for keeping, or subjecting to any treatment or process, products of the slaughtering of animals there. (Food Act 1984, s 132(1))

'The appellant's premises had got out of repair, so that they could not be used as a slaughtering-house, but they could be used for one of the purposes in connection with the slaughtering namely, keeping the cattle there for a time without food preparatory to their slaughter; and we are asked whether it can be said, under those circumstances, that the premises were "so used", or "continued to be used", as a slaughterhouse. . . . This place where the cattle were kept for the purpose of being slaughtered was as much a part of the slaughterhouse as the place where they were actually killed.' *Hides v Littlejohn* (1896) 74 LT 24 at 26, per Lawrance J

[A butcher, who was permitted by a farmer to keep his cow in the farm shippon, slaughtered the cow in the shippon, part of the flesh of the cow being intended for sale for human consumption. The farmer was not licensed under s 57 of the Food and Drugs Act 1938 (repealed; see now the Slaughterhouses Act 1974, s 1), to keep the shippon as a slaughterhouse, which latter was defined by s 100 of the Act (see now s 34 of the Act of 1974) as meaning 'any premises used in connection with the business of slaughtering animals, the flesh of which is intended for sale for human consumption'.] 'In my opinion such absurd consequences would follow from our holding that these premises, although it is clear that they do not come within the definition of "slaughterhouses" in the Act, yet were used by the respondent on this occasion as a slaughterhouse, that I am not prepared to differ from the conclusion at which the justices arrived. It has been said with truth . . . that were we to hold otherwise, any person who killed an animal, other than a bird,—if, for example, he shot a rabbit—in his own field he would be guilty of using that field, which comes within the definition of "premises" in s 100 of the Act, as a slaughterhouse. Since no one could ever hope to obtain a licence for the whole of his property, over which he had the right of shooting, as a slaughterhouse, anyone who shot any animal, other than a bird, which was intended for sale for human consumption, would be guilty of an offence under s 57.' *Perrins v Smith* [1946] KB 90 at 92, 93, DC, per Humphreys J

SLAUGHTERING INSTRUMENT

'Slaughtering instrument' means a firearm which is specially designed or adapted for the instantaneous slaughter of animals or for the instantaneous stunning of animals with a view to slaughtering them. (Firearms Act 1968, s 57(4))

SLIGHT

New Zealand 'It is no doubt difficult to define the word "slight". This was pointed out by the Lord Justice Clerk in the Scotch case of *Cruikshank v Northern Accident Insurance Co Ltd* [(1895) 23 R 147]. He said of this word, "That is a word which may be used by different persons according to the variety of views which they are in the habit of taking of things". And again, "One man could truthfully use the word 'slight' where another would use the word 'great' ". The word is therefore indefinite. In fact, to try to define accurately what such an adjective as "slight" means would revive the sophism of Chrysippus, the ancient Greek. When does a deviation become slight, and when does it become large or great? One meaning of "slight" is the phrase "of no importance".' *R v Haynes & Haynes* (1916) 35 NZLR 407 at 413, CA, per Stout CJ; also reported [1916] GLR 297 at 299

SLIP

In Arbitration Act

'In this case a point has arisen relating to the extent of the powers conferred upon arbitrators under s 7(c) of the Arbitration Act 1889 [repealed; see now the Arbitration Act 1950, s 17]. It is an extremely difficult point, and it is an extremely important one. The section reads as follows: "The arbitrators or umpire acting under a submission shall, unless the submission expresses a contrary intention, have power . . . (c) to correct in an award any clerical mistake or error arising from any accidental slip or omission". Upon the construction of those words it seems quite obvious as a matter of grammar that "clerical" belongs to "mistake" only, and that "error arising from any accidental slip or omission" is a second and independent limb of the clause. . . . In the present case the arbitrator made an award including therein certain costs between one of the parties and a third party, and the question arose whether the words he had used included all those costs or only some of them. The award went back to him, and he told Mr Lewis, of the firm of solicitors representing the respondents, that he certainly had made an error in writing his award, and he amended it so that it read, as he said, as he had originally intended it to read. Now that was not the correcting of a clerical mistake within the meaning of s 7(c), which is something almost mechanical—a slip of the pen or something of that kind. But did he correct an error arising from an accidental slip or omission? Here we get upon ground which is almost metaphysical. An accidental slip occurs when something is wrongly put in by accident, and an accidental omission occurs when something is left out by accident. What is an accident in this connection, an accident affecting the expression of a man's thought? It is a very difficult thing to define, but I am of opinion that this was not an accident within the meaning of the clause.' *Sutherland & Co v Hannevig Brothers Ltd* [1921] 1 KB 336 at 340, 341, DC, per Rowlatt J

Underwriting slip

'The slip is, in practice, and according to the understanding of those engaged in marine insurance, the complete and final contract between the parties, fixing the terms of the insurance and the premium, and neither party can, without the assent of the other, deviate from the terms thus agreed on without a breach of faith, for which he would suffer severely in his credit and future business.' *Ionides v Pacific Fire & Marine Insurance Co* (1871) LR 6 QB 674 at 684, 685, per cur.

'The contract which I have to interpret was first reduced into writing in the form of what is called a "slip"—a memorandum of the heads of agreement initialled by the different underwriters who were subsequently to subscribe policies.' *Western Assurance Co of Toronto v Poole* [1903] 1 KB 376 at 389, per Bigham J

SLOW

[A traffic sign consisted of large studs in the road and the word 'Slow'.] 'I do not think that "slow" means any more than "proceed with caution"—"proceed at such a speed that you can stop if, when you get to the crossing, you find somebody, or something, in the process of crossing, or about to cross".' *Buffel v Cardox (Great Britain) Ltd* [1950] 2 All ER 878 n at 878, per Bucknill LJ

'It is not easy to define the word "slow". Its meaning . . . must depend on a variety of circumstances. That which may appear slow to some motorists may strike a pedestrian as fast. I think the fairest way to look on it is that the sign is an indication to the motorist that he is approaching a place of potential danger, and that, therefore, he ought to be driving more slowly than he would drive on a normal open road without any such sign. In other words, his speed ought to be such that he can pull up fairly quickly if someone or something appears from one or other of the cross-roads.' Ibid at 878, per Singleton LJ

SMALLHOLDING

The expression 'smallholding' means an agricultural holding which exceeds one acre and either does not exceed fifty acres, or, if exceeding fifty acres, is at the date of sale or letting of an annual value for the purposes of income tax not exceeding one hundred pounds. (Small Holdings and Allotments Act 1908, s 61, as amended by the Small Holdings and Allotments Act 1926, s 16)

[See generally, as to smallholdings, the Agriculture Act 1970, Part III.]

SMOKE

In this Part of this Act [Part III: nuisances and offensive trades] the expression 'smoke' includes soot, ash, grit and gritty particles. (Public Health Act 1936, s 110)

'Smoke' includes soot, ash, grit and gritty particles emitted in smoke. (Clean Air Act 1956, s 34(1))

Dark smoke

In this Act 'dark smoke' means smoke which, if compared in the appropriate manner with a chart of the type known at the date of the passing of this Act as the Ringelmann Chart, would appear to be as dark as or darker than shade 2 on the chart.

For the avoidance of doubt it is hereby declared that, in proceedings brought under or by virtue of s 1 or s 16 of this Act, the court may be satisfied that smoke is or is not dark smoke as hereinbefore defined notwithstanding that there has been no actual comparison thereof with a chart of the said type; and, in particular, and without prejudice to the generality of the preceding provisions of this subsection, if the Minister by regulations prescribes any method of ascertaining whether smoke is dark smoke as so defined, proof in any such proceedings that that method was properly applied, and that the smoke was thereby ascertained to be or not to be dark smoke as so defined, shall be accepted as sufficient. (Clean Air Act 1956, s 34(2))

SMUGGLE

'This court takes the view that there is no reason to suppose that the jury would associate the word "smugglers" solely with those who seek to evade customs duty. We think that, in the ordinary use of language today, the verb "to smuggle" is used equally to apply to the importation of goods which are prohibited in import and, indeed, one sees the word used quite often in regard to illegal immigrants brought in secretly by night in small boats.' *R v Hussain* [1969] 2 All ER 1117 at 1119, per cur.

SOCIAL WELFARE

'The words "social welfare" [within s 8(1)(a) of the Rating and Valuation (Miscellaneous Provisions) Act 1955 (repealed; see now the General Rate Act 1967, s 40(5)(b))] are almost impossible to define. It would be difficult to conceive an expression which could be wider in its scope; but, for my part, to provide holidays in a seaside camp at cost, arrangements being made to provide varied and healthy recreation in the camp so that people do not walk aimlessly up and down the parade, and have nothing like the same temptation to spend a lot of time in drinking, and where, in addition, mothers can leave their children to be properly looked after during the day and thus get some much needed relaxation themselves, all this to my mind is clearly the advancement of social welfare; and I did not understand counsel for the respondents to contend the contrary.' *Derbyshire Miners' Welfare Committee v Skegness Urban District Council* [1957] 2 All ER 405 at 409, per Donovan J; affd [1957] 3 All ER 692, CA, [1958] 1 QB 298

'The words "social welfare" themselves . . . connote, to my mind, the concept of public benefit. These words comprehend many objects which are beneficial to the community but are not charitable according to the somewhat limited interpretation given in the charity cases. A person is commonly said to be engaged in "social welfare" when he is engaged in doing good for others who are in need—in the sense that he does it, not for personal or private reasons—not because they are relatives or friends of his—but because they are members of the community or of a portion of it who need help. The need may not be due to poverty. It may be due to the conditions of life of the persons concerned. They are usually people who are under a disadvantage compared to others more favourably placed—boys who need a youth club instead of running on the streets—people of small means who are given holidays in a home which they could not otherwise afford—working men who need a club where they can spend their leisure—and so forth. If a person is engaged in improving the conditions of life of others who are so placed as to be in need, he is engaged in "social welfare". But people who are engaged in improving their own conditions of life are not engaged in social welfare. If an organisation is formed by public-spirited folk with the object of providing a boys' club—or a room for a women's institute—it is, no doubt, concerned with the advancement of social welfare; but, if it is formed by a group of persons with the object of providing a social club for their own enjoyment or recreation, it is not. The difference between the two is that the main objects of the one are directed to the public benefit whereas the others are not.' *National Deposit Friendly Society (Trustees) v Skegness Urban District Council* [1958] 2 All ER 601 at 614, HL, per Lord Denning; (also reported [1959] AC 293 at 322, 323)

'I cannot accept public benefit as the test of social welfare, though social welfare may be a public benefit. . . . I would accept the words of the Master of the Rolls [Lord Evershed, in the Court below] where he says: ". . . it is not enough that the objects of the organisation are in some degree related to the advancement of social welfare: they must in a real sense be directed to it".' *General Nursing Council for England and Wales v St Marylebone Corpn* [1959] 1 All ER 325 at 335, HL, per Lord Keith of Avonholme; also reported [1959] AC 540 at 563

SOCIETY *See also* LOTTERY

'Society' includes a club, institution, organisation or association of persons, by whatever name called, and any separate branch or section of such a club, institution, organisation or association. (Pool Competitions Act 1971, s 7(1); Lotteries and Amusements Act 1976, s 23(1))

Australia 'The three words "society, club or association" are words in frequent use in our community and societies, clubs and associations are well-known entities. One knows that many organisations which give themselves the title society or association or club are as often incorporated as they are unincorporated. Small bodies having few members tend perhaps to remain unincorporated whilst the larger groups tend to become incorporated. . . . In *Theosophical Foundation Pty Ltd v Comr of Land Tax (NSW)* [1966] 67 SR (NSW) 70 Sugerman JA stated at 82: "A society, in the relevant sense, is a number of persons associated together by some common interest or purpose, united by a common vow, holding the same belief or opinion, following the same trade or profession, etc: an association (Oxford English Dictionary, 'Society' III 8) (cf the shorter description in Else-Mitchell, Challinor and Greenwood Land Tax Practice 36–37.) A society as thus described, in which the common element pertains to areas concerned with religion, may aptly be described as a religious society." . . . The meaning of "society" as the Oxford English Dictionary definition shows can be the equivalent of "association" and I do not think that any relevant distinction in nature exists between the two. It merely seems to have happened that some organisations are called "associations", others are called "societies" but no meaningful difference can be detected between the two.' *Pro-campo Ltd v Commissioner of Land Tax (NSW)* (1981) 12 ATR 26 at 35–36, per Lee J

SOIL

'The question upon this [local] Inclosure Act arises in this way:—The Act relates to certain interests of the lord of the manor of Canford, by the 58th section it reserves to the lord of the manor all manorial rights, except the right to the soil, and enacts that he may thenceforth hold and enjoy all rents, etc, "and all mines, minerals, quarries", etc, incident to the manor ("except clay and the right to the soil as aforesaid"), as if the Act had not been made. . . . Prima facie it [the word 'soil'] would include everything above or below it, but the word "soil" is throughout this Act used as distinct from the word "land". . . . Now, referring to the dictionaries, I find that Johnson's second definition of the word "soil" is, "earth considered with relation to its vegetative qualities". And in Richardson, the definition of the word is this:—"The earth, land, ground; land with reference to its produce". There is a clear distinction between "soil" and "land". I think the word "soil" throughout the Act is used as equivalent to "surface", though if the question rested on the 27th and 28th sections alone, without the 58th or saving clause, I should have held that the word "soil" included the minerals, and that these sections deprived the lord of his right to them.' *Pretty v Solly* (1859) 26 Beav 606 at 610, 612, 613, per Romilly MR

'The question raised in this case must be determined wholly upon the construction of the General Inclosure Act [1801] 41 Geo 3, c 109 [repealed], and the special [local Inclosure] Act under which the lands in question were inclosed. . . . Now the preamble of the special Act recites that the Duchess of Buccleuch was then the lady of the manor of Plain Furness "and as such was entitled to the soil of all the said moors, commons, and wastes, and to all mines, minerals, and quarries, of what nature or kind soever within or under the same". . . . By the 24th section, it directs that a certain portion of the waste to be inclosed shall be allotted to the lord or lady of the manor as a compensation for his or her right or interest in and to the soil of the said moors, commons, and wastes, which are directed to be inclosed. Then, by the 43rd section, there is reserved to the duchess . . . all mines . . . and minerals. . . . The minerals being thus reserved under all the lands directed to be inclosed, it is clear that the word "soil", in the 24th section, refers to the surface only, and that the allotments thereby directed to be made to the owners of minerals are in satisfaction of the surface rights to the land only.' *Wakefield v Buccleuch (Duke)* (1867) LR 4 Eq 613 at 624, 625, per Malins V-C; affd sub nom *Buccleuch (Duke) v Wakefield* (1870) LR 4 HL 377

'The sections [in the Norton Inclosure Act 1814] first to be looked at are those which say what is to be given to the allottees of parcels of the former wastes. Section 28—the Norton section—will serve as an example. It begins with words which in themselves would transfer the whole parcel awarded and would include in the transfer the mines and minerals, unless they are followed by some exception or reservation; the words are "shall award unto" the College "as Lords of the Manor aforesaid such part and parcel of the remainder of the waste grounds . . . as shall be equal to one full eighteenth part in value thereof". The residue of the section states for what this allotment is to be compensation; it is "in lieu of and as a full and sufficient recompense for their right to the soil of the said common and waste grounds in the manor". In itself "soil" is said to be a "flexible" word, and nowhere are "flexible" words so out of place as in a statute, but we must do what we can with it. In this Act "soil" occurs nine times: thrice in the allotting sections, 18, 21 and 28; once in the quarry section, where it refers to the surface, the subject of grazing or tillage; twice in connection with the value of the surface divested of its actual vesture of trees and shrubs, and thrice in the preamble, where the word obviously means more than the bare surface and less than the entire subject of property, surface and all below it included; it means everything except mines and minerals. I see no reason why in ss 18, 21 and 28 "soil" should be given a third meaning, namely, the whole prism *usque ad inferos*, mines and minerals included, and, if so, it matters little to the argument which of the other two meanings is adopted. . . . Can s 66 cut down the words of transfer in s 28 "shall award such parcel of the remainder of the waste" by means of the later words "as a sufficient recompense for their right to the soil of the said common and waste grounds" so as impliedly to reserve mines and minerals as not being "property for which such allotment or compensation shall be made". My Lords, I do not think this can be done.' *Thomson v St Catharine's College, Cambridge (Masters and Fellows)* [1919] AC 468 at 499–501, per Lord Sumner

SOJOURN

See ORDINARILY RESIDENT

SOLATIUM

'It is true that in Scots law the Latin term solatium is used without distinction both to indicate a claim for compensation for the grief and suffering sustained by the death of a near relative and also for the pain and suffering occasioned to an injured party. But in my view the term solatium may connote different rights. Solatium properly so called denotes a separate right of action given only to near relatives whereas solatium for pain and suffering of an injured party—a term not known apparently to English law—connotes an element in the ascertainment of damages for the injuries suffered by a plaintiff.' *Chaplin v Boys* [1969] 2 All ER 1085 at 1096, per Lord Guest

SOLD

See SALE; SELL

SOLEMNISATION OF MARRIAGE

'The first trust in this settlement was for the settlor, his executors, administrators or assigns, until the then intended marriage should be solemnised between himself and the lady therein mentioned. The first question is, what is the meaning to be ascribed to the word "solemnised" as used in that instrument. As used in that instrument it must, in my judgment, mean validly and effectually solemnised. The ceremony of marriage was indeed gone through afterwards, but the lady and gentleman were domiciled in England, and their domicil had not been changed; and the lady was the gentleman's deceased wife's niece. Therefore the marriage ceremony, although it took place at Neufchatel, was as ineffectual as if there had never been any such ceremony at all.' *Chapman v Bradley* (1863) 4 De G J & Sm 71 at 76, per Knight Bruce LJ

'As to the question upon the construction of the settlement, the point is very short and simple. Where a settlement contains the words "solemnisation of marriage", followed by limitations to take effect thereafter, the plain meaning is a legal marriage, unless it can be shown that the language used is capable of being interpreted in the way in which the respondent seeks to interpret it.' *Neale v Neale* (1898) 79 LT 629 at 631, CA, per Rigby LJ

[A marriage settlement contained a covenant to pay money if a certain marriage were 'solemnised'. Held, that a marriage declared void for impotence did not fall within this phrase.] 'The form of decree nisi in the Divorce Court in the present case is that the marriage in fact had and solemnised at a certain date was pronounced and declared "to have been and to be absolutely null and void to all intents and purposes in the law whatsoever, by reason of the impotence of the said respondent, and the said petitioner be pronounced to have been and to be free from all bond of marriage with the said respondent". Therefore there never was a marriage, although the ceremony was gone through, and the parties lived together as man and wife after that date. The marriage is pronounced null and void ab initio. Not only are they not now married, but they never were. In other words, as Lord Justice Turner says in *Chapman v Bradley* [supra], "there has never been any valid marriage".' *Re Garnett, Richardson v Greenep* (1905) 74 LJ Ch 570 at 573, 574, per Kekewich J

Canada [Provinces have power under the Constitution Act 1867 to legislate in respect of 'solemnisation of marriage', whereas the federal parliament has power in respect of marriage and divorce.] 'The subject-matter, "the solemnisation of marriage in the province", covers and aptly expresses, in my judgment, every manner or mode in which competent parties, intending to contract marriage with each other, might validly so contract. No limitation was placed upon the power of the legislatures to which that subject-matter was assigned. Their powers are plenary. The legislatures of the several provinces may within their several legislative jurisdictions make religious ceremonies necessary to validate a marriage or may make its solemnisation before a civil functionary of any kind sufficient for the purpose with or without witnesses. It is probable that they would have power to declare the solemnisation of marriage to be complete without the presence of a priest, clergyman, minister, civil functionary, or witness, and by the mere consent of the parties intermarrying evidenced in writing or by mere words.' *Re Marriage Laws* (1912) 46 SCR 132 at 340, SCC, per Davies J

SOLICIT

Attempt to influence

New Zealand 'The word "solicit" is a common English word, and it means, in its simplified form, "to ask". In various English dictionaries this simple meaning is given, but other similar words are also used to explain other meanings it possesses, such as "to call for", "to make request", "to petition", "to entreat", "to persuade", "to prefer a request". When a business man or firm or company advertises his or its wares we say he is soliciting custom. He wants to sell his goods, and he solicits people to buy.' *Sweeney v Astle* [1923] NZLR 1198 at 1202; per Stout CJ; also reported [1923] GLR 483 at 485

'The typical case of soliciting orders is where a trader or his traveller goes to some individual whom he selects to try and induce him to buy. If instead of doing this he sends a letter or circular inviting orders, and addressed individually to those whom it is thought worth while, that also would be to solicit orders. If the invitation were addressed or made, say, to the various occupants of some large establishment, such as an hotel or the like, not individually but as a group, I think that would be to solicit orders from each of those occupants. It involves a selection of the persons to be appealed to. So also if the persons invited to give orders are the residents of some selected place or district. In the cases put it is plain that the trader, by singling out the objects of his solicitation, evidences a specific purpose and intention to obtain orders from them.' Ibid at 1204, 1205, per Hosking J; ibid at 486

By solicitor

[The Solicitors' Practice Rules 1936, r 4(a) (now the Solicitors' Practice Rules 1975 and 1987) provided (inter alia) that a solicitor should not act in association with any organisation or person (not being a practising solicitor) whose business was to make, support or prosecute certain claims in such circumstances that such person or organisation 'solicited' or 'received' any payment, gift or benefit in respect of such claims.] 'It does not matter for the purpose of the prohibition whether such a person or organisation actually obtains such business advantage or merely "solicits" it; and that word there means "asks for" or "seeks".' *Re Solicitor* [1945] KB 368 at 372, CA, per cur.

For immoral purposes

[It is possible to 'solicit' a person who is unaware of the solicitation.] 'The appellant was convicted . . . under s 1, sub-s 1(b), of the Vagrancy Act 1898 [repealed; but see now the Sexual Offences Act 1956, s 32], and the conviction was affirmed by the quarter sessions. That subsection provides that "every male person who in any public place persistently solicits or importunes for immoral purposes shall be deemed a rogue and vagabond within the meaning of the Vagrancy Act 1824, and may be dealt with accordingly". It is found as a fact that while in the lavatories and also while in the street he smiled in the faces of gentlemen, pursed his lips, and wriggled his body. . . . The only point suggested is that, inasmuch as it was not proved that anybody had seen his solicitation, the magistrate could not convict. I should be sorry to lay down any such rule. . . . To say that, because on the particular occasion he does not succeed in attracting the notice of any one, there is no evidence upon which he can be convicted of solicitation is an argument which we cannot adopt. . . . In my opinion there was ample evidence to support the conviction.' *Horton v Mead* [1913] 1 KB 154 at 157, 158, DC, per Lord Alverstone CJ

'For my part, I cannot conceive that anyone, apart from authority, could come to the conclusion that Susan Howard [who had offered her services by displaying a card on a notice board in a street] was soliciting in the sense that that word is used in connection with prostitutes. The Street Offences Act 1959 makes it an offence by s 1(1) for a common prostitute to loiter or solicit in a street or public place for the purpose of prostitution. She clearly was not loitering. The only question is: was she soliciting? For my part, I am quite satisfied that soliciting in that connection involves the physical presence of the prostitute and conduct on her part amounting to an importuning of prospective customers. An advertisement is more in the nature of a notice, and though in one sense it may be said to be soliciting custom, certainly something much more than that is needed in the commission of the offence of soliciting by a prostitute.' *Weisz v Monahan* [1962] 1 All ER 664 at 665, per Lord Parker CJ

'This case is governed by the decision of this court just given in *Weisz v Monahan* [supra]. The only difference is that, whereas that was in connection with the Street Offences Act 1959, s 1(1), this is a case under s 32 of the Sexual Offences Act 1956, where it is provided that, "It is an offence for a man persistently to solicit or importune in a public place for immoral purposes". It seems to me that the meaning of "solicit" there must be exactly the same as the meaning of that word in the Street Offences Act 1959, s 1(1), and that, as stated in the previous case, it must involve the physical presence of the alleged offender.' *Burge v Director of Public Prosecutions* [1962] 1 All ER 666 at 667, per Lord Parker CJ

[The question was whether a woman seated at a window could be said to be 'soliciting' for the purpose of prostitution within the Street Offences Act 1959, s 1(1).] 'This young woman, sitting on a stool scantily clad, in a window bathed in red light and in an area where prostitutes were sought, might just as well have had at her feet an advertisement saying: "I am a prostitute. I am ready and willing to give the services of a prostitute and my premises are now available for that purpose." It is clear, in my judgment, that she was soliciting in the sense of tempting or alluring prospective customers to come in for the purpose of prostitution and projecting her solicitation to passers by.' *Behrendt v Burridge* [1976] 3 All ER 285 at 288, per Boreham J

Canada 'The word "solicit" or "soliciting" [as used in the Criminal Code, s 195(1)] generally would involve [a] woman accosting or importuning men for immoral purposes: Shorter Oxford English Dictionary: 3rd ed. . . . It is also clear that solicitation does not have to be done by word, but may be actively pursued by acts such as smiles, winks, body gestures and general attitudes calculated to attract prospective customers.' *R v Goobie* (1973) 11 CCC (2d) 538 at 540, Ont HCJ, per Lacourciere J

Canada [The Criminal Code, s 195(1) (enacted SC 1972, s 13, s 15) states that every person who 'solicits' any person in a public place for the purpose of prostitution is guilty of an offence punishable on summary conviction.] 'It must be noted, and it has been noted below, that the word "solicit" is not defined in the Criminal Code, therefore the courts below have taken what, in my opinion, was a proper course and have turned to established English dictionaries for the purpose of defining the word. The natural choice, of course, is the Shorter Oxford English Dictionary. There, as has been said, the definition is exact and I quote it: "c. Of women: To accost and importune (men) for immoral purposes". Of course, that definition requires, in turn, the definition of the words "accost" and "importune" and it is noted that the definition used those two verbs conjunctively and not alternatively. "Accost", in the same dictionary, is defined as: "3. *trans.* To approach for any purpose; to face; to make up to . . . 4. To address . . . 5. To solicit in the street for an improper purpose." I think I might summarise those definitions by saying, "to confront". "Importune", again in the Shorter Oxford English Dictionary, is variously defined and I choose the following: "3. To solicit pressingly or persistently; to beset with petitions". It was the view of the courts below that the definition of "importune" as "to burden; to trouble; worry, pester, annoy" was obsolete and I am quite ready to agree that "importune" does not import the element of pestering or annoying, but I am of the opinion that it still maintains the meaning of "pressing or persisting". Robertson JA, in giving his reasons in the Court of Appeal for British Columbia, found that there must be "something more" than the demonstration of intention to make herself available for prostitution but that "something more" did not necessarily have to be conduct that is "pressing, persistent, troublesome, worrying, pestering or annoying". In using those various adjectives, Robertson JA was combining two alternative definitions of "importune" in the Shorter Oxford English Dictionary. As I have said, I agree that as to the adjectives "troublesome, worrying, pestering or annoying" modern usage does not require the conduct to amount to compliance therewith, but I am of the opinion that the "something else" is to be "pressing or persistent" within the definition which I have quoted above.' *Hutt v R* (1978) 1 CR (3d) 164 at 169, 170, SCC, per Spence J

SOLICITOR

'The magistrate in this case states his opinion as follows: "I was of opinion that (a) since the respondent's name was on the roll of solicitors on the said 1st of June, 1937, and (b) since it was not necessary that the charge which the respondent witnessed should be witnessed by a solicitor qualified to practise; therefore the respondent's use of the title or description was not an infringement of the Act [Solicitors' Act 1932, s 46 (repealed; see now the Solicitors' Act 1974, s 21)] notwithstanding that he had not in force a practising certificate." If that means, as I am disposed to think it does mean, that the magistrate came to the conclusion as a matter of law that the use of the word "solicitor" by a person whose name is on the roll of solicitors cannot be an indication that he is qualified, or recognised by law as qualified, to act as a solicitor, then, in my view the magistrate came to a wrong decision in point of law. In truth, I think that the matter is a mixed question of law and fact. I certainly would not myself express the opinion that the use of the word "solicitor" by a person whose name is on the roll of solicitors would necessarily be any indication that that person was qualified to act—that is to say, had a practising certificate. On the other hand, it must be perfectly obvious that there are circumstances in which the mere statement by a person that he is a solicitor is an indication, and is intended as an indication, that he is a solicitor for the purposes for which he is discussing some matter with the other person. In other words, that he has a practising certificate, and is entitled to practise.' *Taylor v Richardson* [1938] 2 All ER 681 at 684, per Humphreys J

See, generally, 44 Halsbury's Laws (4th edn) paras 1 et seq.

Disbursements by *See* DISBURSEMENTS

SOLID FUEL

'Solid fuel' means coal, coke and any solid fuel derived from coal or of which coal or coke is a constituent. (Offices, Shops and Railway Premises Act 1963, s 1)

SOLVENT

[The Companies Act 1929, s 266 (repealed; see now the Companies Act 1985, s 617(1)) enacted that where a company was being wound up, a floating charge on the undertaking or property of the company created within six (now twelve) months of the commencement of the winding up was invalid, unless it was proved that the company immediately after the creation of the charge was 'solvent'.] 'A question has been raised as to what "solvent" means in s 266 of the Companies Act 1929. . . . It is not necessary to say that "solvent" there is limited to one meaning; but in my opinion a company is not solvent within the meaning of s 266 unless it can pay its debts as they become due. It has been urged that "solvent" means "commercially solvent", and that if, upon balance-sheet figures, a company's assets exceed its liabilities, the company is solvent. I do not accept that view.' *Re Patrick & Lyon Ltd* [1933] Ch 786 at 791, per Maugham J

SOME *See* PART

SOUND

'I think the word "sound" [in a warranty] means what it expresses, namely, that the animal is sound and free from disease at the time he is warranted to be sound. If, indeed, the disease were not of a nature to impede the natural usefulness of the animal for the purpose for which he is used, as for instance, if a horse had a slight pimple on his skin, it would not amount to an unsoundness: but even if such a thing as a pimple were on some part of the body where it might have that effect, as for instance, on a part which would prevent the putting a saddle or bridle on the animal, it would be different. An argument has, however, been adduced from the slightness of the disease and facility of cure; but if we once let in considerations of that kind, where are we to draw the line? A horse may have a cold, which may be cured in a day; or a fever, which may be cured in a week or month: and it would be difficult to say where to stop. Of course, if the disease be slight, the unsoundness is proportionably so.' *Kiddell v Burnard* (1842) 9 M & W 668 at 670, 671, per Parke B

SOUND RECORDING *See* RECORD (DISC); RECORDING

SOURCE OF INCOME

Australia 'The legislature in using the word "source" meant, not a legal concept, but something which a practical man would regard as a real source of income. . . . The ascertainment of the actual source of a given income is a practical, hard matter of fact.' *Nathan v Federal Commissioner of Taxation* (1918) 25 CLR 183 at 189, 190, per cur

Canada 'I cannot accept the interpretation put by counsel for the Minister in this case on the words "source of income": that there must be net income before there can be a source. In my view the words are used in the sense of a business, employment, or property from which a net profit might reasonably be expected to come.' *Dorfman v Minister of National Revenue* 72 DTC 6131 at 6134, Fed Ct, per Collier J

SOVEREIGNTY

'By "exercising de facto administrative control" or "exercising effective administrative control", I understand exercising all the functions of a sovereign government, in maintaining law and order, instituting and maintaining courts of justice, adopting or imposing laws regulating the relations of the inhabitants of the territory to one another and to the Government. It necessarily implies the ownership and control of property whether for military or civil purposes, including vessels whether warships or merchant ships. In those circumstances it seems to me that the recognition of a Government as possessing all those attributes in a territory while not subordinate to any other Government in that territory is to recognise it as sovereign, and for the purposes of international law as a foreign sovereign State.' *The Arantzazu Mendi* [1939] AC 256 at 263–265, per Lord Atkin

SPAN

Australia 'The primary meaning of the word "span" is simply "width" or "measurement", and it can only be in a secondary or technical meaning that the word can connote the manner of measuring the width, i.e. either from side to side in the clear, or from centre to centre in the case of wooden supports of a bridge.' *Scottish-Australian Coal Mining Co v Redhead Coal Mining Co* (1891) 12 NSWLR 111 at 118, per Owen CJ in Eq

SPAWN

'The preservation of the spawn, fry, or brood of fish has been for centuries . . . a favourite subject of legislation, and the statutes passed for the purpose are extremely numerous. If the plaintiffs had, in the declaration or in the replication, averred that the oyster spat taken by defendant was the spawn, fry, or brood of fish, the defendant could not have defended himself by stating his immemorial right, as one of the subjects of this realm, to take them in plaintiffs' close, being a navigable river. But the declaration stated that "oyster spat" was taken; and the plea justifies taking it, and only denies the repeated assertion of the same immemorial right; still, however, they have alleged, and defendant has not denied, that the oyster spat is the spawn or young brood of oysters; and though the epithet rather applies to fish than spawn, and all the other circumstances in the description, given in the replication, are as consistent with the idea of fish as of spawn, yet it appears to us that the word "spawn" is sufficient. To remove it is unlawful within the statutes of Richard II, which have never been repealed, but frequently recognised; and the immemorial usage cannot have legal existence.' *Maldon Corpn v Woolvet* (1840) 12 Ad & El 13 at 20, 21, per cur.

SPECIAL AGENT *See* AGENT

SPECIAL CIRCUMSTANCES

In Solicitors Acts

[The Solicitors Act 1843, s 41 (repealed; see now the Solicitors Act 1974, s 70(3)), authorised the court to order taxation of a bill of costs after payment if 'special circumstances' appeared to require it.] 'That misconduct or fraud on the part of solicitors, or pressure accompanied by overcharge or overcharges so gross as to amount to fraud, are special circumstances within the Act has been firmly established. I do not desire to preclude myself from saying that there may be other special circumstances which would justify taxation. . . . Willing as I am for the bill to be taxed, I feel obliged to come to the conclusion that there has been neither pressure, nor proof of overcharge, nor other special circumstance to authorise the Court to send it for taxation.' *Re Boycott* (1885) 29 Ch D 571 at 582, 584, CA, per Fry LJ

[The Solicitors Act 1843, s 37 (repealed; see now the Solicitors Act 1974, s 70(3)), authorised the court to order taxation of a bill of costs more than twelve months after delivery in 'special circumstances'.] 'The statute uses the words "special circumstances". Those are wide, comprehensive, and flexible words, and I think that the legislature intended them to be so, and that no Court can or ought to lay down any exhaustive definition of them. Charges which in one case would be special circumstances, in another would not be such. It is for the discretion of the judge, to say what are special circumstances in a particular case. I cannot express my meaning better than by adopting the words of Bowen LJ in *Re Boycott* [supra] when he said: "Special circumstances, I think, are those which appear to the judge so special and exceptional as to justify taxation. I think no Court has a right to limit the discretion of another Court, though it may lay down principles which are useful as a guide in the exercise of its own discretion. It seems to me to be the true view of the statute, that there must be special circumstances making the payment differ from an ordinary payment, and that the judge thereupon has a discretion as to whether they are sufficient to authorise taxation." That is entirely in accordance with my view, and expresses what I desire to convey.' *Re Norman* (1886) 16 QBD 673 at 677, CA, per Lopes LJ

'I agree that there are in this case special circumstances [within the meaning of Solicitors Act 1843, s 38 (repealed; see supra)] by reason of the fact that the bill includes certain items which so far call for investigation by the taxing officer as to make it right that there should be a taxation of the bill. It is now well settled that special circumstances are not confined to duress, pressure, overcharge, or fraud; and the discretion of a judge as to what facts constitute "special circumstances" ought not to be overruled except where he has not exercised his discretion judicially.' *Re Hirst & Capes* [1908] 1 KB 982 at 996, CA, per Kennedy LJ; affd [1908] AC 416

'After the client has once paid the bill, he or she is not thereafter entitled to have it taxed in the ordinary way, and must [under the Solicitors Act 1932, s 66 (repealed; see now the Solicitors Act 1974, s 70)] show that there are special circumstances which justify the Court in making such an order. . . . Pressure, not necessarily pressure by the solicitor, may in itself be ground for holding that there are special circumstances. If it can be shown that there are in the bill gross overcharges which would in the ordinary way necessarily be taxed, that may be a special ground for taxation. But those are not the only grounds, as I understand the authorities, which may justify the Court in making an order.' *Re Solicitors* (1934) 50 TLR 327 at 328, per Farwell J

New Zealand 'In its context in this legislation, which is directed to the assessment of the fairness and reasonableness of bills of costs in the public interest, the expression "special circumstances" should not be construed narrowly and it would be contrary to the social policies underlying these statutory provisions to impose on an applicant the burden of establishing a serious risk of injustice. . . . A factor or combination of factors which may properly be characterised as not ordinary or common or usual may constitute a "special circumstance" justifying the revision of the bill under s 151 [of the Law Practitioners Act 1982].' *Cortez Investments v Olphert & Collins* [1984] 2 NZLR 434 at 439, per Richardson J

In taxing Acts

[The Finance Act 1965, s 44(3) (repealed; see now the Capital Gains Tax Act 1979, s 150(3)) made provision for the market value of shares or securities to be calculated in a particular manner, except where in consequence of 'special circumstances' prices quoted on the London Stock Exchange were by themselves not a proper measure of such market value.] 'Stock Exchange prices are more liable than most open market prices to large and rapid fluctuations. But the taxpayer must take the risk of that unless there are "special circumstances". "Special" must mean unusual or uncommon—perhaps the nearest word to it in this context is "abnormal".' *Crabtree v Hinchcliffe (Inspector of Taxes)* [1971] 3 All ER 967 at 976, HL, per Lord Reid

'There must be many occasions on which the directors of a company are in possession of information which if made public would affect the prices quoted on the London Stock Exchange and where it could be said that in the absence of such information the London Stock Exchange is "working in blinkers", but the fact that directors have such information and the Stock Exchange has not cannot ordinarily by itself amount, in my opinion, to "special circumstances" within the meaning to be given to those words in s 44(3). For circumstances to be special must be exceptional, abnormal or unsual and the mere fact that directors have knowledge which would affect the prices quoted if made public cannot, in my view, be regarded as an unusual circumstance.' Ibid at 983, per Viscount Dilhorne

In Trade Marks Act

[The Trade Marks Act 1938, s 26(3), provides that no applicant to have a trade mark taken off the register shall rely on any non-use of a trade mark that is shown to have been due to 'special circumstances' in the trade.] 'It seems to me (without attempting any precise definition) that the words must be taken to refer to circumstances which are "special" in the sense of being peculiar or abnormal and which are experienced by persons engaged in a particular trade as the result of the working of some external forces as distinct from the voluntary acts of any individual trader.' *Aktiebolaget Manus v Fullwood (R J) & Bland Ltd* [1949] 1 All ER 205 at 207, CA, per Evershed LJ; [1949] Ch 208

SPECIAL DAMAGES *See* DAMAGES

SPECIAL HOSPITAL *See* HOSPITAL

SPECIAL OCCASION

[Under the Licensing Act 1964, s 74(4), special orders of exemption, extending licensing hours, may be applied for on 'special occasions'.] 'First of all, it must be borne in mind that the question of special occasions or no is primarily a question for the justices. That is because they know their local district, and in many instances what is special and what is not may have to be determined according to local knowledge which would not be possessed by judges sitting in a remote court. Point number one to remember is that the justices are prima facie the best judges of the problems given to them. The second point for them to remember, which is clearly borne out by the authorities, is that an application for such an order should be refused if the so-called occasion is too frequent. . . . It is quite obvious to anyone who stops to think about it for a moment that the more often you do a thing the less special it becomes, and there comes a magic dividing line between those cases which are still to be regarded as special because they are not excessive in number and those which have lost their opportunity of being called special for the very reason that there are too many occasions of the kind in question. Thirdly . . . the special occasion must be special in the local or national sense. It is not open to a licensee to make a special occasion and then go and claim the benefit of s 74. If some national event or some local event makes the day special in the ordinary man's use of that word, then the third condition is satisfied.' *Martin v Spalding* [1979] 2 All ER 1193 at 1195, 1196, per Lord Widgery CJ

'The words "special occasion" [in the Licensing Act 1964, s 74(4)] are ordinary words in the English language which may be given their ordinary meaning, and if this is done, in the majority of cases it will not be necessary to look at previous authorities . . . In borderline cases however, the earlier authorities may be of assistance in giving guidance as to the proper approach to the problem or by laying down markers as to what is or is not capable of being a special occasion. The main guidance which is to be obtained from these authorities can be summarised as follows: (1) The occasion can be special from the national or local point of view. A local occasion can include what might be more aptly described as a personal occasion such as a wedding, but the more local or the more personal the occasion, the more carefully it must be scrutinised . . . (2) The more frequently the occasion occurs the less likely it is that it will be a special occasion . . . (3) If the occasion is one created by the licensee solely for the purposes of his licensed business, it is unlikely to be capable of being a special occasion. Such a situation must be distinguished from the position of a registered club which creates, for example, sporting occasions which are celebrated at the club and are capable of being special occasions because they are not created solely for the purpose of the *licensed* business of the club.' *R v Corwen JJ, ex p Edwards* [1980] 1 All ER 1035 at 1037, 1038, per Woolf J

SPECIAL REASONS

[The Road Traffic Act 1930, s 35(1) (repealed; see now the Road Traffic Offenders Act 1988, s 34) provided that where there were 'special reasons' justices were not bound to disqualify a person from holding a driving licence by reason of the commission of an offence under the section.] 'A "special reason" within the exception is one which is special to the facts of the particular case, that is, special to the facts which constitute the offence. It is, in other words, a mitigating or extenuating circumstance, not amounting in law to a defence to the charge, yet directly connected with the commission of the offence, and one which the court ought properly to take into consideration when imposing punishment.' *R v Crossan* [1939] NI 106 at 112, per Andrews CJ

'What . . . can be said to be a special reason [within the Road Traffic Act 1930, s 15(2) (repealed; see now the Road Traffic Offenders Act 1988, s 34)] beyond saying that it must be one that is not of a general character? This was expressly considered by the King's Bench Division of Northern Ireland in *R v Crossan* [supra]. In that case the court adopted a test that I had ventured to use in an address that I gave to the magistrates assembled at the Summer Assizes for Essex in 1937. I suggested that the reasons must be special to the offence, and not to the offender, and the court in adopting what I had said used these words: "A 'special reason' within the exception is one which is special to the facts of the particular case, that is, special to the facts which constitute the offence. It is, in other words, a mitigating or extenuating circumstance, not amounting in law to a defence to the charge, yet directly connected with the commission of the offence, and one which the court ought properly to take into consideration when imposing punishment. A circumstance peculiar to the offender as distinguished from the offence is not a 'special reason' within the exception." I respectfully and entirely agree with and adopt this passage. While it is impossible to enumerate or define everything that can amount to a special reason, one may give as an illustration a driver exceeding the speed limit because he has suddenly been called to attend a dying relative or a doctor going to an urgent call. It is difficult indeed to visualise any special reason in the case of dangerous driving, except the one actually mentioned in the section itself, namely, the lapse of time from the date of a previous conviction. So, too, it is certainly difficult to visualise what could amount to a special reason in the case of driving under the influence of drink or drugs, though perhaps one might be found if the court was satisfied that a drug had been administered to a driver without his knowledge, as for instance where a driver had taken a dose of medicine which he believed to be an ordinary tonic but which in fact contained a powerful drug.' *Whittall v Kirby* [1946] 2 All ER 552 at 555, 556, per Lord Goddard CJ

[The respondent was convicted of causing a motor bicycle to be used on a road without a policy of insurance being in force, contrary to the Road Traffic Act 1930, s 35 (repealed; see supra), and was disqualified from holding a driving licence for 12 months. His appeal against disqualification was allowed by quarter sessions on the ground that there was a 'special reason' for not imposing disqualification in that the respondent honestly believed that the user of the motor cycle was covered by an insurance policy.] 'Belief, however honest, cannot in our opinion, be regarded as a special reason unless it is based on reasonable grounds. It could hardly be even suggested that forgetfulness to renew a policy could be a special reason, and, indeed, this court said in *Whittall v Kirby* [supra] that it could not. Can then, a man who has forgotten the renewal date of his policy and drives in the honest belief that his policy is still current, be in a worse position than one who, having a current policy, believes it covers him in a particular state of circumstances when it does not? It seems obvious that they are both in exactly the same position. It may be that, if a man who felt he did not understand his policy took the advice of someone who was, apparently, in a position to explain it, such as an insurance agent, and received a wrong opinion, this might be considered a special reason, or, again, if the question turned on some obscure phrase which might lead a person to believe he was covered when a court ultimately decided that he was not. Those are questions which can be decided if and when they arise. We express no opinion on them. Here there is no finding or suggestion that the respondent took any advice or that the policy was one which a person in his position or degree of education could not understand, still less that it contained any obscurity or ambiguity. The plain fact is that, having got the policy, he never troubled to acquaint himself with its terms. We cannot hold that a belief founded on no reasonable ground can constitute a special reason.' *Rennison v Knowler* [1947] 1 All ER 302 at 303, 304, per Lord Goddard CJ; sub nom. *Knowler v Rennison* [1947] KB 488

'As I understand the law, for reasons to be "special" within s 15(2) of the Road Traffic Act 1930 [repealed; see supra], they must be special to the facts constituting the offence. The offence here was that of being under the influence of drink or drugs to such an extent as to affect the respondent's ability to control the car. It is an essential ingredient of the offence that the justices should be satisfied that the defendant was drunk at the material time. If there are facts which show that his drunkenness was induced by the malicious act of some third party, or, as in this case, by ignorance of the effect of certain drugs or alcohol, those are matters which the justices are entitled to consider as special circumstances. Once there are special circumstances, the discretion whether or not the defendant shall be disqualified is that of the justices, and as long as they act within the terms of their discretion and on the facts and not perversely this court cannot interfere.' *Chapman v O'Hagan* [1949] 2 All ER 690 at 691, per Lynskey J

[The appellant pleaded guilty to driving a motor vehicle whilst under the influence of drink. He was unaware, at the time, that he was suffering from diabetes.] 'The first and the most important of the other [cases] . . . to which the learned Recorder referred is *Whittall v Kirby* [supra], in which the test was laid down by the Lord Chief Justice [Lord Goddard] . . . in the following words: "A 'special reason' within the exception is one which is special to the facts of the particular case, that is, in other words, a mitigating or extenuating circumstance, not amounting in law to a defence to the charge, yet directly connected with the commission of the offence, and one which the court ought properly to take into consideration when imposing punishment." If one takes the essence of that definition, there are four conditions there laid down which have to be satisfied. The first is that it must be a mitigating or an extenuating circumstance. The next is that it must not amount in law to a defence to the charge. The third is that it must be directly connected with the commission of the offence. In our judgment, the circumstances here are directly connected with the commission of the offence. If it had not been for the fact that the appellant was suffering from diabetes, the offence would not have been committed at all, because he had not taken sufficient drink to affect the mind of an ordinary man who was not suffering from that disease. The fourth is that the matter is one which the court ought properly to take into consideration when imposing punishment.' *R v Wickins* (1958) 42 Cr App Rep 236 at 239, 240, CCA, per Devlin J

'In my judgment there can be no doubt that in a suitable case a medical emergency could constitute a special reason, if by "medical emergency" one means an unexpected situation arising in which a man who has been drinking but not intending to drive is impelled to drive a motor car by a sudden medical necessity. But of such an emergency there was in my judgment, on the material before the justices in this case, no indication at all. All that was said by the respondent's solicitor, as the case finds—and we are of course limited to the material set out in the case—was that the respondent on the occasion of the offence was driving a sick girl, who was the owner of the motor car, to her home. The court apparently was not told what was the nature of the sickness, when the girl became sick, or what were the circumstances, if any, in which her sickness gave rise to any unexpected or impelling necessity for the respondent to drive her home. In those circumstances, in my judgment, the bare fact that the respondent was driving a sick girl home in her own motor car was hardly even a relevant mitigating circumstance, let alone material which could sustain a finding of special reasons for not disqualifying.' *Brown v Dyerson* [1968] 3 All ER 39 at 41, 42, per Bridge J

'Parliament [by the Road Safety Act 1967, (repealed; see now the Road Traffic Act 1988, s 11(2))] has laid down a statutory limit of alcohol in the blood, 80 milligrammes per 100 millilitres of blood, no more, no less. At the same time it has laid down a mandatory penalty of disqualification. Just as the amount of the excess cannot affect the issue of guilt or innocence so also it is of no consequence in regard to disqualification. As has already been said, there may be facts which constitute special reasons, but the amount of the excess is not one of them: as counsel for the appellants put it, a special reason must be something other than the commission of the offence itself.' *Delaroy-Hall v Tadman* [1969] 1 All ER 25 at 31, per cur.

New Zealand [The Transport Act 1949 (NZ), s 41(2) (repealed; see now the Transport Act 1962, s 31) provided that upon the second or subsequent convictions of a person for certain traffic offences committed by him while in a state of intoxication, unless for 'special' reasons the court thought fit to order otherwise, and without prejudice to the power of the court to order a longer period of disqualification, the court should make an order cancelling his motor-driver's licence and disqualifying him from obtaining any such licence for a period of three years from the date of the conviction.] 'A circumstance cannot be a special reason within the meaning of s 41 unless it is special to the facts which constitute the offence in respect of which the court is adjudicating. That view of the matter—which is the view that I think I should adopt, and do adopt—is in accordance with what was laid down in *Whittall v Kirby* [supra], the leading English decision on the matter, which has been repeatedly followed in England. It is true that in that case the attention of the Divisional Court was directed to the distinction between circumstances special to the offence and circumstances special to the offender; but I think that what was there laid down strongly supports the view that a circumstance cannot be a special reason unless it be special to the facts which constitute the offence in respect of which the court is adjudicating.' *Reedy v Brown* [1951] NZLR 1040 at 1042, per Cooke J

New Zealand [The Transport Act 1949 (NZ), s 41 (repealed; see supra) required, on conviction for driving under the influence of drink, cancellation of a licence and disqualification from driving for twelve months, unless for 'special reasons' the court thought fit to order otherwise.] 'If a particular reason is within an admissible category, the question whether it is or is not in the circumstances a "special reason" is a question of fact for the tribunal that is seised of the facts: *Jowett-Shooter v Franklin* [1949] 2 All ER 730. I do not propose to elaborate on the facts of this present case. Holding, as I do, that reasons affecting the public interest may be accepted as "special reasons", the question that remains is whether the reasons here advanced are of sufficient importance, and sufficiently unusual, to justify one in holding that they are "special".' *Profitt v Police* [1957] NZLR 468 at 470, per F B Adams J

New Zealand 'Section 41 of the Transport Act 1949 (repealed; see supra) required cancellation and disqualification of a licence for twelve months "unless for special reasons the court thinks fit to order otherwise". Various judgments in England and New Zealand construed that unqualified phrase "for special reasons" as applying only to the offence and not to the offender. . . . But now, in the context of mandatory disqualification in terms of s 30(3) [of the Transport Act 1962] the relevant phrase is "special reasons relating to the offence", a choice of words plainly designed to apply a definite qualification. . . . The origin of the present legislative provision is therefore clear, and in my view the word "offence" in s 30(3) means that combination of facts which comprises the offence. In my respectful opinion a "special reason" will relate to this type of offence if it relates to any fact forming one of the specific elements of that offence.' *Reichs v Ministry of Transport* [1979] 1 NZLR 636 at 639, per Mahon J

SPECIAL SCHOOL *See* SCHOOL

SPECIALISE

'I do not know what "specialising in the installation of equipment" means. Junior counsel for the Minister, as I understood it, is content to say that that means employing more than half the total workers on the installation of equipment. "Specialising" is a word which I would have thought, with all respect to counsel, has a rather more precise meaning than that. There are decided cases—I do not propose to refer to them—to the general effect that a specialist is somebody who has more than normal qualifications in the activity in question. A gentleman was convicted once of advertising that he was a "canine specialist" when he held no veterinary qualifications. That is the type of user with which one is more familiar in considering the words "specialised" or "specialising".' *Prestcold (Central) Ltd v Minister of Labour* [1969] 1 All ER 69 at 77, CA, per Winn LJ

SPECIALLY

Specially liable

[The Factories Act 1937, s 25(2) (repealed; see now the Factories Act 1961, s 28(2)) provided that for every staircase in a building or affording a means of exit from a building, a substantial hand-rail should be provided and maintained, which, if the staircase had an open side should be on that side, and, in the case of a staircase having two open sides, or in the case of a staircase which, owing to the nature of the construction thereof or the condition of the surface of the steps or other special circumstances was 'specially liable' to cause accidents, such a hand-rail should be provided and maintained on both sides.] 'The cogent factor to my mind is that, ever since 1938 until this accident in 1953, i.e. fifteen years, there has never been a single accident on these stairs, nor indeed on the fourteen similar stairs in this factory, and, although there is a welfare committee of the men, there has never been any suggestion by anyone that there was anything in these steps making them specially liable to cause accidents. I take it that "specially liable" means more than usually liable, and I do not see how it can be said that the condition of the steps is specially liable to cause accidents when no accident has happened for all these years.' *Harris v Rugby Portland Cement Co Ltd* [1955] 2 All ER 500 at 501, CA, per Denning LJ

Specially named

[A testator gave his residuary estate to his several legatees 'specially named' in his will.] 'No doubt the strict and accurate meaning of the terms specially named, is persons mentioned *nominatim*, if not by all their names, by some at least, either their christian or their surnames. If the words had been specially mentioned, then the word "specially" would have meant, not expressly named, but mentioned as special donees. In *Bromley v Wright* [(1849) 7 Hare 334] the legatees were not named; that is not *nominatim*; yet it was held that the testator giving his residue to the legatees "before-named", that meant before mentioned; and that the legatees mentioned were included, though not expressly named; that is the word named was used as mentioned. The question in this case is, whether in the residuary clause the testator meant to include such of the legatees as he has mentioned *nominatim*; or did he mean such of the legatees as he had before mentioned simply. . . . On the question, then, in what sense the testator used the words specially named, he has himself given the key to the interpretation of his meaning. If he meant to give his residue to those only whom he mentioned *nominatim*, why should he exclude from participating in that gift, a class of persons who are not specially named, and who yet take legacies? Under this clause the testator must have considered that unless he specially excluded the parties to take under it, they would take a share of the residue. He has, by expressly excluding them, himself given a clue to the interpretation, or rather a clear enunciation of the interpretation which he puts on the words specially named. I cannot without disregarding what the testator has himself told us, put any other interpretation on the words than that the testator meant by them, legatees specially mentioned. I do not by this at all decide that generally the word "named" is as strong as "specially named"; but only that here the word specially, is not used for the purpose of describing those who are mentioned *nominatim*, but for the purpose of describing those legatees to whom a special benefit is given.' *Re Holmes' Trusts* (1853) 1 Drew 321 at 323–325, per Kindersley V-C

SPECIALTY *See also* CONTRACT

'The word "specialty" is sometimes used to denote any contract under seal, but it is more often used in the sense of meaning a specialty debt, that is, an obligation under seal securing a debt, or a debt due from the Crown or under statute.' *R v Williams* [1942] AC 541 at 555, PC, per cur.

'The Limitation Act 1623, so far as debts were concerned, applied to debts arising only out of simple contracts. Accordingly, very early in the history of the Act, it was held that it did not apply to a debt recoverable by virtue of a statute: *Talory v Jackson* [(1638) Cro Car 513]; *Jones v Pope* [(1666) 1 Wms Saund 34]. Debts due under any bond or other specialty were first made subject to a period of limitation by the Civil Procedure Act 1833 [repealed]. Thereafter the courts regarded statutory debts as specialty debts and as subject to the same period of limitation. I think the first case in which this was expressly laid down is *Cork and Bandon Rly v Goode* [(1853) 13 CB 826]. The Act of 1939 [Limitation Act 1939 (repealed; see now the Limitation Act 1980, s 8)] has, however, effected a material change in the law in this respect. Debts recoverable by virtue of an enactment are now subject to the same period of limitation as those arising from simple contract, while a different period is prescribed for specialties. In my opinion, therefore, "specialties" must now be confined to deeds or contracts under seal.' *Leivers v*

Barber, Walker & Co Ltd [1943] 1 KB 385 at 398, CA, per Goddard LJ

SPECIES

'Species' includes sub-species and variety. (Animals Act 1971, s 11)

SPECIFIC

'I know of no better statement of what constitutes a specific description for this purpose [within the meaning of the Bills of Sale Act (1878) Amendment Act 1882, s 4] than that which we gave in *Carpenter v Deen* [(1889) 23 QBD 566 CA]. In that case I said "The section requires that the chattels shall be 'specifically described'. According to my view, that means described with such particularity as is used in an ordinary business inventory of such chattels". Fry LJ said in that case "In considering the meaning of the words 'specifically described' we should look at the scope and object of the section. They are in my opinion plain. I think they are to facilitate the identification of the articles enumerated in the schedule with those found in the possession of the grantor—that is to say, to render the identification as easy as possible, and to render any dispute as to the intention of the parties as rare as possible, and to shut the door to fraud and controversy, which almost always arise when general descriptions are used. That is to be done as far as possible; by which I mean, as far as is reasonably possible—so far as a careful man of business trying to carry the object of the Act into execution could and would do without going into unreasonable particulars".' *Davidson v Carlton Bank Ltd* [1893] 1 QB 82 at 86, 87, CA, per Lopes LJ

'The seventeenth of the Rules of Construction [in the Schedule to the Marine Insurance Act 1906] is as follows: "17. The term 'goods' means goods in the nature of merchandise, and does not include personal effects or provisions and stores for use on board. In the absence of any usage to the contrary, deck cargo and living animals must be insured specifically, and not under the general denomination of goods." . . . The rule prescribes that deck cargo and living animals must be insured specifically in the absence of any usage to the contrary. What is the meaning of the provision that deck cargo and living animals "must be insured specifically"? I think "specifically" in this connection means "as such". In the case of deck cargo there must, in addition to the ordinary description of the goods, be an intimation in the policy that the goods are to be carried on deck, by inserting "for carriage on deck", or other similar words. In the case of "living animals" the description must convey an intimation that the animals are alive and not mere carcases, that is, if there is any ambiguity in the description there must be added to it the word "live", or some equivalent expression.' *British & Foreign Marine Insurance Co Ltd v Gaunt* [1921] 2 AC 41 at 53, 54, per Lord Finlay

[The Restrictive Trade Practices Act 1956, s 21(1)(b) (repealed; see now the Restrictive Trade Practices Act 1976, s 10(1)) provided that a restriction accepted in pursuance of any agreement should be deemed to be contrary to the public interest unless the court was satisfied that (inter alia) the removal of the restriction would deny to the public as purchasers, etc, other 'specific' and substantial benefits or advantages.] 'To satisfy the requirements of the subsection the alleged benefit must be "specific". We are content to adopt one of the interpretations of this word suggested by counsel for the registrar, and accepted by counsel for the respondents, that is to say that it means explicit and definable.' *Re Net Book Agreement* 1957 [1962] 3 All ER 751 at 774, per cur.

[The Restrictive Trade Practices Act 1976, s 8(2), deals with the position of members of a trade association where the association has made 'specific' recommendations as to actions to be taken or not taken by them.] 'I think that a "specific" recommendation must be intended to mean one which specifies particular action (or inaction) and recommends members to take it either immediately or in a certain event. This appears to me to be in contrast to a statement of policy by the association or a statement that the association will recommend appropriate action if and when that becomes necessary. There must be an actual recommendation for action though it may be implied if the members know what is meant without the precise action being specified.' *National Federation of Retail Newsagents, Booksellers & Stationers v Registrar of Restrictive Trading Agreements* [1972] 2 All ER 1269 at 1274, HL, per Lord Reid

SPECIFIC DISPOSITION *See* DISPOSITION

SPECIFIC GOODS

'Specific goods' means goods identified and agreed on at the time a contract of sale is made. (Sale of Goods Act 1979, s 61(1))

'In order that goods may be specific [within the Sale of Goods Act 1893, s 62 (see now s 61(1) of the Act of 1979, supra)] they must in my view be identified and not merely identifiable. . . . For the purpose of the passing of the actual property in goods as distinguished from a right to ultimately claim a title to the goods as against the vendor or volunteers under him, a present identification of the goods as specific goods appears to be required by the statute. There must be a transfer of the right in re not merely of the right ad rem.' *Kursell v Timber Operators & Contractors Ltd* [1927] 1 KB 298 at 313, 314, CA, per Sargant LJ

'The problem to be solved comes back to the question: were the 500 tons specific goods? . . . There was no ascertainment or identification of the 500 tons out of the cargo in bulk of the motor vessel *Challenger*. . . . The argument for the respondents depends in no small measure upon the validity of the dictum of Lord Westbury in *Holroyd v Marshall* [(1862) 10 HL Cas 191 at 209, 210] which, if premature at the date of its utterance, is said now to be law by virtue of s 52 of the Code [Sale of Goods Act 1893 (repealed; see now s 61(1) of the Act of 1979, supra)]. . . . The Law Journal report [33 LJ Ch 193] runs as follows "A contract for the sale of goods, as, for example, of 500 chests of tea was not a contract which would be specifically performed, because it did not relate to any chests of tea in particular, but a contract to sell the 500 chests of a particular kind of tea, which 'are now in my warehouse in Gloucester' was a contract relating to specific property, and which would be specifically performed". These words appear to indicate clearly specific goods in a specific place, identified and ascertained as the subject-matter of the contract.' *Re Wait* [1927] 1 Ch 606 at 617, 618, 621, CA, per Lord Hanworth MR

SPECIFIC LEGACY *See* LEGACY

SPECIFIC PERFORMANCE

Specific performance is equitable relief, given by the court to enforce against a defendant the duty of doing what he agreed by contract to do; a plaintiff may, therefore, obtain judgment for specific performance even though there has not, in the strict sense, been any default by the defendant before the issue of the writ.

In early times a court of equity assumed jurisdiction to compel a party to a contract to perform his part of the contract when damages recoverable at law were not an adequate remedy. The remedy of specific performance is thus in contrast with the remedy by way of damages for breach of contract, which gives pecuniary compensation for failure to carry out the terms of the contract. The remedy is special and extraordinary in its character, and the court has a discretion either to grant it, or to leave the parties to their rights at law. However, the discretion is not an arbitrary or capricious discretion; it is to be exercised on fixed principles in accordance with the previous authorities. The judge must exercise his discretion in a judicial manner. If the contract is within the category of contracts of which specific performance will be granted, is valid in form, has been made between competent parties and is unobjectionable in its nature and circumstances, specific performance is in effect granted as a matter of course, even though the judge may think it is very favourable to one party and unfavourable to the other, unless the defendant can rely on one of the recognised equitable defences. Where such a defence is available, the existence of a valid contract is not in itself enough to bring about the interference of the court. The conduct of the plaintiff, such as delay, acquiescence, breach on his part, or some other circumstance outside the contract, may render it inequitable to enforce it, or the contract itself may, for example on the ground of misdescription, be such that the court will refuse to enforce it.

The jurisdiction to grant specific performance, formerly exercisable only by a court of equity, is now vested in all branches of the High Court, but actions for the specific performance of contracts relating to the sale, exchange or partition of land, or the raising of charges on land, are assigned to the Chancery Division. The relief still retains its character as an equitable remedy, and the old principles of equitable relief apply. Specific performance is now also made available in county courts for the specific performance of any agreement for the sale, purchase or lease of any property where, in the case of a sale or purchase, the purchase money, or, in the case of a lease, the value of the property, does not exceed county court limit or where the parties agree that a specified county court is to have jurisdiction. (44 Halsbury's Laws (4th edn) para 401)

(1) In any action for breach of contract to deliver specific or ascertained goods the court may, if it thinks fit, on the plaintiff's application, by its judgment or decree direct that the contract shall be performed specifically, without giving the defendant the option of retaining the goods on payment of damages.

(2) The plaintiff's application may be made at any time before judgment or decree.

(3) The judgment or decree may be unconditional, or on such terms and conditions as to damages, payment of the price and otherwise as seem just to the court. (Sale of Goods Act 1979, s 52)

SPECIFIED

[The proviso to the Agricultural Holdings Act 1948, s 2(1) (repealed; see now the Agricultural Holdings Act 1986, s 2(3)) (which made certain lettings which would otherwise not have done so operate as tenancies from year to year) provided that the subsection should not have effect in relation to an agreement for the letting of land made in contemplation of the use of the land only for grazing or mowing during some 'specified period of the year'.] 'It is said that when the statute spoke of a "specified period of the year" it had in mind a period of the year which had some significance in agriculture such as the hay-making season or the summer grazing or the winter grazing. The difficulty which I feel about that construction is that it is impossible to put it accurately into words whereas the section itself is quite clear. In my judgment, a period of 364 days is a specified period of the year just as much as 200, 250 or 350.' *Reid v Dawson* [1954] 3 All ER 498 at 500, CA, per Denning LJ; see also [1955] 1 QB 214

Canada [By the Bankruptcy Act RSC 1952, s 63(3) (see now RCS 1970, c B-3, s 72) nothing contained in the section is to render void any assignment of debts growing due under 'specified' contracts.] 'It would appear to me . . . that the words "specified contracts" do not mean that the contracts are identifiable from some document recording the transaction. It seems to me that they must be unambiguously identified in the document itself.' *Re Paddle River Construction Ltd* (1961) 35 WWR 605 at 618, Alta SC, per Greschuk J

New Zealand 'In my view persons can be specified without being named, provided they are unambiguously identified.' *A v B* [1969] NZLR 534 at 536, per Roper J

SPIRITS *See also* WHISKY

'Spirits' means, subject to subsections (7) and (8) below, spirits of any description and includes all liquors mixed with spirits and all mixtures, compounds or preparations made with spirits but does not include methylated spirits. (Alcoholic Liquor Duties Act 1979, s 1)

[Subsections (7), (8) of the section exclude from the definition of spirits angostura bitters, methyl alcohol and naphtha.]

SPIRITOUS LIQUOR

The expression 'spiritous liquor' shall include every liquid obtained by distillation and containing more than five per centum of alcohol. (North Sea Fisheries Act 1893, s 9)

SPOIL

'Some reliance was placed in argument on the use of the two words "waste or spoil", but in my opinion they are synonymous, though possibly the one may be more appropriately used for what is in its nature permissive and the other for what is in its nature destructive.' *Rush v Lucas* [1910] 1 Ch 437 at 441, 442, per Eve J

SPOLIATION

Spoliation is an injury done by one clerk or incumbent to another, in taking the fruits of his benefice without any right thereunto, but under a pretended title. (3 Bl Com 91)

SPORTING PAPER

[An agreement contained a covenant by which the vendors undertook not to print or publish or permit their names to be used in connection with any 'sporting paper' within ten miles of Bouverie Street.] 'It remains to consider whether the Athletic News is a "sporting paper" within the meaning of clause 4. The covenant was for the protection of the copyright and goodwill of the papers which were sold, and regard must be had to this circumstance in interpreting the clause. Now the Athletic News contains no racing intelligence and no betting odds, and is merely a record of amateur sports, such as cricket, football, cycling, running, etc. . . . It undoubtedly is devoted to "sports" in one sense of the word; but upon the whole I do not think that a paper which deliberately excludes all racing and betting intelligence is a "sporting paper" within the meaning of clause 4.' *McFarlane v Hulton* [1899] 1 Ch 884 at 889, 890, per Cozens-Hardy J

SPORTS GROUND

'Sports ground' means any place where sports or other competitive activities take place in the open air and where accommodation has been provided for spectators, consisting of artificial structures or of natural structures artificially modified for the purpose. (Safety of Sports Grounds Act 1975, s 17(1))

SPORTS STADIUM

'Sports stadium' means a sports ground where the accommodation provided for spectators wholly or substantially surrounds the area used for activities taking place on the ground. (Safety of Sports Grounds Act 1975, s 17(1))

SPOUSE

New Zealand [Under the Adoption Act 1955, s 8(4), the Court may dispense with the consent of a 'spouse' to an application for an adoption order if it is satisfied that the spouses are living apart and that their separation is likely to be permanent.] 'Before it can make use of this subsection the Court must be satisfied that at the time of the application "the spouses are living apart and that their separation is likely to be permanent". In the first place the natural parents are no longer "spouses" which is a term appropriate to married people in relation to each other as partners in marriage, a husband to his wife or a wife to her husband. . . . In the second place where, as here, the natural parents have been divorced for three years and the mother has re-married they are, I think, outside the language of the subsection altogether.' *Re CCR and DJR (Infants)* [1962] NZLR 561 at 563, per Leicester J

SPRING

'Now what are springs and streams? A spring of water, both in law and ordinary language, is, as I understand it, a definite source of water. When we talk of a spring of water we mean a source of water of a definite or nearly definite area, the word "spring" coming from the water springing or bubbling up. It may be an underground spring which supplies a well, and we say that water "wells up". It may be an ordinary spring from which a small stream or rivulet runs above the ground. But those are definite things. A spring of water means a natural source of water of a definite and well-marked extent.' *Taylor v St Helens Corpn* (1877) 6 Ch D 264 at 272, 273, CA, per Jessel MR

SPYING

If any person for any purpose prejudicial to the safety or interests of the State—

(a) approaches, inspects, passes over, or is in the neighbourhood of, or enters any prohibited place within the meaning of this Act; or
(b) makes any sketch, plan, model, or note which is calculated to be or might be or is intended to be directly or indirectly useful to an enemy; or
(c) obtains, collects, records, or publishes, or communicates to any other person, any secret official code word, or pass word, or any sketch, plan, model, article, or note, or other document or information which is calculated to be or might be or is intended to be directly or indirectly useful to an enemy;

he shall be guilty of felony. (Official Secrets Act 1911, s 1(1), as amended by the Official Secrets Act 1920, s 10, Sch 1)

'The Act [Official Secrets Act 1911, s 1, supra] itself might suggest by its title and one or two side headings that the offences it creates are only those of "spying", in the sense of obtaining by surreptitious means information in the possession of one State for the benefit of another. I am satisfied that no one who reads through the first three sections as a whole could suppose that the Act was ever intended to be so limited. . . . The wrongful communication of official information, for instance, is itself an offence under s 2(1)(a) whatever the purpose of the communication and however innocent the recipient of what he communicates.' *Chandler v DPP* [1962] 3 All ER 142 at 148, per Lord Racliffe

SQUARE

[A tax on glass referred to plate glass 'squared' into plates of a specified superficies.] 'I have no doubt in saying, that the legislature used the word "square", not in the strict, but in the common acceptation, confining it to rectangular, but not to equilateral figures. Had they said, that the plates should be measured by square inches, the interpretation put upon the statute by the defendants would have been just; for any shape may in measurement be reduced to square inches; but they have said that it shall be squared, which cannot be applied to oval or irregular figures. Whether it would have been more beneficial to have allowed the manufacturer to have used all shapes, is not a question for a Court of Law.' *A-G v Cast-Plate Glass Co* (1792) 1 Anst 39 at 44, per Eyre CB

SQUATTER

'What is a squatter? He is one who, without any colour of right, enters on an unoccupied house or land, intending to stay there as long as he can. He may seek to justify or excuse his conduct. He may say that he was homeless and that this house or land was standing empty, doing nothing. But this plea is of no avail in law.' *McPhail v Persons Unknown, Bristol Corpn v Ross* [1973] 3 All ER 393 at 395, per Lord Denning MR

STAFF

Australia [Two tickets in a lottery were sent as presents by a retiring matron of a hospital: one was in the name of 'N M & R' (on the domestic staff) and the other in the name of 'BAFS Staff, c/o Sister P——, BAFS Hospital, Brisbane.' The latter ticket won the first prize.] 'I now come to the construction of the term "staff" and must decide whether this constitutes a clear gift to a body of persons who can be ascertained. . . . The ordinary meaning in this connection of the term "staff" is a body of persons employed under the direction of a manager or chief in the work of an establishment, or the execution of some undertaking (e.g. a newspaper, hospital, government survey)—Murray's Dictionary. In this case only one class of persons, the nursing sisters of the hospital staff, put forward a claim to be the staff named in the ticket. I think the domestic staff can be excluded by virtue of the fact that a ticket was taken for three members of such staff. . . . I think the staff outside the hospital can also be excluded, because the donor had not been associated with them in any way. I am not so clear about the position of the medical staff . . . but I think that the word "staff" can reasonably be held in this connection not to include the medical staff.' *Parker v Westby* [1941] St R Qd 47 at 53, 54, per Douglas J

STAGE

Of proceedings

[RSC Ord XVI, r 11 (revoked; see now RSC 1965, Ord 15, rr 6, 8) empowered the court or a judge at any 'stage' of the proceedings to order that the names of parties improperly joined as plaintiffs or as defendants should be struck out and that the names of any parties, whether plaintiffs or defendants, who ought to have been joined, should be added.] 'The words of Order XVI, rr 2 and 11 are quite ample to justify and require the amendment [substitution of name of co-plaintiff after decree]. . . . I base my decision upon the words "at any stage of the proceedings". It has been argued that the rules do not apply after final judgment. They apply, in my opinion, as long as anything remains to be done in the case.' *The Duke of Buccleuch* [1892] P 201 at 212, CA, per Fry LJ

[The Criminal Evidence Act 1898, s 1, provides that every person charged with an offence, and the wife or husband of such person, shall be a competent witness for the defence at every 'stage' of the proceedings.] 'I do not think I ought to hold that a prisoner may, after he has pleaded guilty, be sworn and give evidence on oath and be cross-examined. I hold that "stage of the proceedings" does not apply to the period between a plea of guilty and sentence.' *R v Hodgkinson & Manning* (1900) 64 JP 808 at 808, per Darling J

'It was argued that the words "at every stage of the proceedings" [in the Criminal Evidence Act 1898, s 1 (see supra)] must be limited to the proceedings in the different Courts, that is, before magistrates or at the trial by a jury. We see no reason for so limiting the meaning of those words. We think that those words are intended to enable an accused person to give evidence at every stage of the proceedings where evidence can properly be given; in other words, that wherever the defence can be heard evidence can be given by the defendant.' *R v Wheeler* [1917] 1 KB 283 at 286, 287, CCA, per cur.

STAGE CARRIAGE

In this Act 'stage carriage' shall mean any carriage for the conveyance of passengers which plies for hire in any public street, road or place within the limits of this Act, and in which the passengers or any of them are charged to pay separate and distinct or at the rate of separate and distinct fares for their respective places or seats therein. (Metropolitan Public Carriage Act 1869, s 4)

It is hereby declared that for the purposes of any Act relating to . . . stage carriages . . . in London, the expressions . . . 'stage carriage' . . . include any such vehicle, whether drawn or propelled by animal or mechanical power. . . . (London Cab and Stage Carriage Act 1907, s 6)

'A stage-carriage means a carriage plying regularly from place to place.' *Comley v Carpenter* (1865) 18 CBNS 378 at 390, 391, per Byles J

'The term "stage carriage" is a perfectly well-known one in the English tongue, and means a carriage which plies from one stage to another for the conveyance of passengers who pay a fare—or hire—for their seat or room in the carriage.' *Smith v Mackintosh* 1926 SC(J) 15 at 19, per the Lord Justice General (Lord Clyde)

'In my opinion, there is no doubt that a vehicle which proceeds from stage to stage at regular, or more or less regular intervals, and carries passengers who pay separate fares, is a stage coach or stage carriage, whichever expression is preferred.' *Chapman v Kirke* [1948] 2 KB 450 at 454, per Lord Goddard CJ

STAGE PLAY *See also* PLAY

In this Act the word 'stage play' shall be taken to include every tragedy, comedy, farce, opera, burletta, interlude, melodrama, pantomime, or other entertainment of the stage, or any part thereof: Provided always, that nothing herein contained shall be construed to apply to any theatrical representation in any booth or show which by the justices of peace, or other persons having authority in that behalf, shall be allowed in any lawful fair, feast, or customary meeting of the like kind. (Theatres Act 1843, s 23)

[This was the definition of a play until the middle of 1968. The Act of 1843 was then repealed by the Theatres Act 1968, which abolished censorship of the theatre and amended the law in respect of theatres and theatrical performances. An entirely new definition of play is given in s 18 of the Act of 1968. *See* PLAY.

The two cases below were decided under the old Act.]

'Nothing can be larger than the words of the 6 & 7 Vict c 68 [Theatres Act 1843 (repealed; see supra]. The 2nd section prohibits the keeping any house or other place of public resort for the public performance of "stage-plays", without authority by virtue of letters-patent from Her Majesty, etc, or without licence from the Lord Chamberlain for the time being, or from the justices of the peace. And the interpretation clause s 23 [supra] defines "stage-play" to mean and include "any tragedy, comedy, farce, opera, burletta, interlude, melodrama, pantomime"; and then follow these still more comprehensive words "or other entertainment of the stage, or any part thereof". I observe two words in this Act which were not in the former Act of Stat (1737) 10 Geo 2, c 28, [repealed], viz "burletta" and "pantomime", which may well have been introduced still further to enlarge the meaning of "stage-play". It seems to me that there are here three distinct infringements of the statute. There was a representation of a storm at sea, with a "double" swimming, and then a character appeared upon the stage, in the costume of a Greek prince. It seems to me that these, at all events, formed part of an entertainment of the stage. Then there is the introduction of dialogue between persons not seen by the audience, with the usual theatrical accessories of music and singing and dancing. My Brother Hayes asked whether a public lecture delivered on a stage, with scenery and foot-lights, would be a dramatic entertainment or stage-play within the Act. I am by no means clear that it would not. I do not say that the reflection of figures on mirrors on a stage, without the accessories of actors, dialogue, scenery, lights, and music would constitute an infringement of the statute: but I am clearly of opinion that an entertainment such as that described in this case is within the prohibition of the statute.' *Day v Simpson* (1865) 18 CBNS 680 at 691, 692, per Byles J

'The question raised by this appeal is, whether he [the respondent] has strictly confined himself to music and dancing according to the terms of that licence, or whether that which he has added to the representation does not constitute such an approximation to a dramatic performance as to make the performance a stage-play within the prohibition of the 6 & 7 Vict c 68, s 2 [Theatres Act 1843 (repealed; see supra)]. . . . Dancing and music in public are lawful without the chamberlain's licence; the performance of stage-plays is not. The matter for the magistrate's determination was, whether the entertainment so minutely described in the case comes within the definition given of a stage-play. A great number of females, it seems, dressed in theatrical costume, descend upon a stage and perform a sort of warlike dance; then comes a *danseuse* of superior order, who performs a *pas seul*. If this had been all, nobody could have called the performance a stage-play. But the magistrate adds that the entrance of the *première danseuse* was preceded by something approaching to pantomimic action. The thing so described certainly approached very nearly to a dramatic performance; and it is extremely difficult to determine where the line is to be drawn. The magistrate uses two terms of art, viz, "*ballet d'action*", and "*ballet divertissement*". The former, it is said has a story; the latter has none. . . . With the highest possible respect for the learned magistrate, if I were called upon to decide, as matter of law, whether or not that, which he has described as a "*ballet divertissement*", and as not coming up to his notion of a "*ballet d'action*", came within the meaning and definition of a stage-play in the statute [supra]. I could not come to the conclusion that it was, even if I had gone to see the performance. But, upon the description here given of the entertainment, I am unable to say that the point at which the authority of the music and dancing licence stops has been overstepped.' *Wigan v Strange* (1865) LR 1 CP 175 at 182, 183, per Erle CJ

STAKE OUT

Canada '"Staking out" does not mean putting in a stake. It means "to mark with stakes".' *McAvoy v Herriman* (1958) 27 WWR 105 at 107, NWT Terr Ct, per Sissons JTC

STALLAGE *See also* PICCAGE; TOLL

Payments made for the enjoyment of the exclusive occupation of any portion of the soil for the purpose of exposing goods for sale in a market or fair are usually known as stallage, piccage, pennage or rent. Stallage is the appropriate term for payment for the liberty of placing a stall on the soil or for standing room for cattle or goods within the market or fair. When the soil is broken, the payment is often called piccage. Pennage is a sum payable for the liberty to erect pens. However, piccage and pennage are merely names for particular varieties of stallage. (29 Halsbury's Laws (4th edn) para 637)

'If . . . a person carried commodities in a basket to the market for sale, merely using the basket to exhibit the commodities to customers, and making no other use of the ground, except when tired to place the basket upon it, intending when rested to go to another part of the market, such a use of the ground would not be stallage. It would be nothing more than using the market for hawking, and it might as well be said that cattle in a market, which it is impossible to keep stationary, have an exclusive occupation of one spot of ground, and therefore stallage is payable in respect of them.' *Yarmouth Corpn v Groom* (1862) 1 H & C 102 at 111, DC, per Martin B

'Stallage is a sum payable by a person to the owner of a market in respect of the exclusive occupation of a portion of the soil. For that proposition I will refer to *Mayor of Yarmouth v Groom* [supra]. . . . In order to justify a charge for stallage you must show that the person charged has a right to the exclusive possession of some portion of the soil. According to that case, if a person comes to the market with a chair and a "ped"—that is, a wooden or wicker basket 4 ft long and 2½ ft wide and 2 ft high, with a lid which, being turned back and supported by pieces of wood not fixed in the soil, forms a table on which he exposes his provisions for sale—that person has exclusive occupation of a portion of the soil and is liable for stallage. Against that is the decision in *Townend v Woodruff* [(1850) 5 Exch 506] that, if a person coming to sell at a public market brings his goods in baskets, etc, in which they can be reasonably brought, and such baskets are capable of being moved about, he cannot be charged with stallage. To enable him to be so charged he must have exclusive occupation of the soil. There is another case, *R v Burdett* [(1697) 1 Lord Raym 148], in which it was decided that, if the owner of a market covers the place so completely with stalls that there is no free space left for the persons using the market to sell their wares, the stallage is excessive. And in *Mayor etc, of Northampton v Ward* [(1745) 1 Wilson 107] stallage is explained, and also "piccage", which is where the soil is broken for the purpose of fixing the stall.' *A-G v Tynemouth Corpn* (1900) 17 TLR 77 at 78, per Buckley J

'A fair toll is payable to the owner of the franchise in respect of goods sold in his fair, or brought into his fair for sale, whether he be the owner of the soil or not, and has nothing to do with the ownership of the soil. Stallage is paid in respect of some user of the soil, and can be exacted only by the owner of the soil. It is sufficient to refer to the case of *Northampton Corporation v Ward* [(1745) 2 Stra 1238] and the *Duke of Bedford v St Paul's Covent Garden* [(1881) 51 LJMC 41].' *Newcastle (Duke) v Worksop Urban Council* [1902] 2 Ch 145 at 160, per Farwell J

STAMP

'Stamp' means as well a stamp impressed by means of a die as an adhesive stamp. (Stamp Act 1891, s 122(1))

'Stamp' means as well a stamp impressed by means of a die as an adhesive stamp for denoting any duty or fee. (Stamp Duties Management Act 1891, s 27)

'Stamp' means a mark for use as evidence of the passing of weighing or measuring equipment as fit for use for trade, whether applied by impressing, casting, engraving, etching, branding, or otherwise, and cognate expressions shall be construed accordingly. (Weights and Measures Act 1985, s 94(1))

'It cannot seriously be contended that an obliterated stamp cannot be a stamp in the ordinary use of the English language.' *R v Lowden* [1914] 1 KB 144 at 145, 146, CCA, per Isaacs CJ

STANDAGE

'The umpire has found that, according to the custom of the country, the outgoing tenant is entitled to the grain of the away-going crop, and that he is also entitled to the straw at manurial value. It is further admitted that, by the custom of the country, when applicable, deductions should be made [inter alia] . . . in respect of the rateable proportion of the rent payable in respect of the land upon which the away-going crop has been grown and called "standage".' *Re Constable & Cranswick* (1899) 80 LT 164 at 166, per Bruce J

STANDARD

Australia 'The word "standard" is used in several senses. The meaning of the word may vary in accordance with the context in which it is used. The primary idea which the word expresses is that of a measure of quantity or quality fixed or approved by some authority, e.g., standard foot, standard pound, standard of behaviour.' *R v Galvin, ex p Metal Trades Employers' Association* (1949) 77 CLR 432 at 444

Australia [The Australian Broadcasting Tribunal attempted to enforce television advertising 'standards' which required television advertisements to have Australian content.] 'The meaning of the word "standard" was discussed in *R v Galvin, ex p Metal Trades Employers' Association* [supra] (per Latham CJ, Dixon, McTiernan, Williams and Webb JJ): "The word 'standard' is used in several senses. The meaning of the word may vary in accordance with the context in which it is used. The primary idea which the word expresses is that of a measure of quantity or quality fixed or approved by some authority, e.g., standard foot, standard pound, standard of behaviour." . . . Although, as was said in *Galvin's* case "standard" may refer either to quality or to quantity, here the plural is used and its meaning in its context is, I think, to be found in the plural definition suggested by the Macquarie Dictionary, that is, behaviour that is regarded as socially desirable or acceptable. In my opinion, the ordinary meaning of "standards" and its context suggest that it is the quality of the product, rather than its quantity, that is the subject matter of the Tribunal's power of determination.' *Saatchi & Saatchi Compton (Vic) Pty Ltd v Australian Broadcasting Tribunal* (1984) 56 ALR 640 at 644–645, per Beaumont J

STANDARD TIME *See* TIME

STANDING

[The London Hackney Carriage Act 1831, s 35, provides that every hackney carriage which shall be found 'standing' in any street or place shall be deemed to be plying for hire.] 'It is necessary in the present case to decide what is meant under s 35 by "standing". In my judgment "standing" in the context of that section means something akin to waiting or parking. It does not mean being stationary.' *Eldridge v British Airports Authority* [1970] 2 All ER 92 at 96, per Donaldson J

START

Australia [It was agreed that the defendant should not 'start' a particular kind of business within a defined radius.] 'In my opinion the word "start" as used in the agreement is synonymous with "set up and carry on".' *Cramond v Greig* (1908) 8 SRNSW 143 at 145, per Street J

STARTING PRICE *See* BET; FIXED ODDS

STATE

'State' means a territory or group of territories having its own law of nationality. (Wills Act 1963, s 6)

[The Official Secrets Act 1911, s 1(1), provides that a person who, for any purpose prejudicial to the safety or interests of the 'state', enters, etc, any prohibited place, shall be guilty of felony.] ' "State" is not an easy word. It does not mean the government or the executive. "L'etat, e'est moi" was a shrewd remark, but can hardly have been intended as a definition even in the France of the time. And I do not think that it means, as counsel argued, the individuals who inhabit these islands. The statute cannot be referring to the interests of all those individuals because they may differ and the interests of the majority are not necessarily the same as the interests of the state. Again we have seem only too clearly in some other countries what can happen if you personify and almost deify the state. Perhaps the country or the realm are as good synonyms as one can find and I would be prepared to accept the organised community as coming as near to a definition as one can get.' *Chandler v Director of Public Prosecutions* [1962] 3 All ER 142 at 146, HL, per Lord Reid

'What is meant by "the state"? Is it the same thing as what I have just called "the country"? Counsel for the appellants submits that it means the inhabitants of a particular geographical area. I doubt if it ever has as wide a meaning as that. I agree that in an appropriate context the safety and interests of the state might mean simply the public or national safety and interests. But the more precise use of the word "state", the use to be expected in a legal context . . . is to denote the organs of government of a national community. In the United Kingdom, in relation at any rate to the armed forces and to the defence of the realm, that organ is the Crown.' Ibid at 156, per Lord Devlin

STATELESS *See* ALIEN

STATEMENT *See also* FACT

'Statement' includes any representation of fact, whether made in words or otherwise. (Civil Evidence Act 1968, s 10(1))

' "Statements made", I apprehend means oral statements. "Statements submitted", I apprehend, means written statements.' *Nicol v Kincaid & Co Ltd* (1933) 26 BWCC Supp 68 at 70, 71, per the Lord Justice-Clerk (Lord Alness)

'It seems to me that a statement in the circumstances of this particular case [a computer print-out by a breath-test machine] is a formal written account of facts providing the subject with information that he is entitled to have. The fact that to some people, or even to most people, it may not be immediately intelligible without explanation does not prevent it being a statement.' *Gaimster v Marlow* [1985] 1 All ER 82 at 86, per Lord Lane CJ

Australia 'It is necessary to examine the meaning of the word "statement". . . . It seems reasonably clear that a statement may be made orally or in writing. One of the definitions in the Oxford English Dictionary (1933 edn), vol 10, in relation to "statement" is: "A written or oral communication setting forth facts, arguments, demands or the like." I also note that, in relation to music, a statement is defined as: "A presentation of a subject or theme in a composition." I consider that for the immediate purpose it is sufficient to consider whether or not pictorial material in [an] advertisement forms part of any statement in it. Looking at the question in a broad way it is difficult to see why pictorial material should not form part of a statement. It seems to me a statement may be in any language, including one made by signs that are known and understood by those deaf and dumb people who use them, and one written in shorthand. In the same way I cannot see why pictorial or diagrammatic material should not be included in a statement. The question of a telecast was considered by the Full Court of this Court in *Universal Telecasters (Qld) Ltd v Guthrie* (1978) 32 FLR 360. It was there held that the words "make a statement" in s 53(e) of the Trade

Practices Act (1974–1986) (Cth) were wide enough to cover the telecasting of spoken words.' *Given v Pryor* (1979) 39 FLR 437 at 439, per Franki J

New Zealand 'The word "statement" [as used in the Social Security Act 1964, s 127, as substituted by the Act of 1972] is sufficiently wide to cover any form of representation whether written or oral, just as the other limb of the section dealing with misleading the officer is wide enough to embrace conduct alone or words and conduct combined . . . I do not think that the word "statement" must be given so narrow a meaning that it is to be treated as synonymous in legal definition with "declaration" appearing in s 131. I think that s 127 is deliberately worded so as to render criminal any representation made for the purpose of obtaining a benefit, if it be made with knowledge of its material falsity.' *Police v McNaughton* [1970] NZLR 889 at 891, per Haslam J

Of case

Australia 'It is absolutely settled law both in England and in Australia that the expression "state a case" involves stating facts, that is, the ultimate facts, requiring only the certainty of some point of law applied to those facts to determine either the whole case or some particular stage of it.' *Australian Commonwealth Shipping Board v Federated Seamen's Union of Australasia* (1925) 36 CLR 442 at 450, per Isaacs J

STATION *See also* RAILWAY STATION

Army station

'Station' shall mean and include any camp, barrack, hospital, or arsenal, and property adjacent thereto, the site whereof is held by or in trust for Her Majesty. (Army Chaplains Act 1868, s 2)

Railway station

'I am of opinion, that, if the platform and stairs were taken away, the company would not be prevented, by the terms of the 7th section [of their private Act], from stopping their engines where they pleased, and that the passengers might then get in or out as they best could. . . . I am also of opinion, that the road, platform, and stairs together constitute a station.' *Petre (Lord) v Eastern Counties Rly Co* (1843) 3 Ry & Can Cas 367 at 373, 374, per Knight Bruce V-C

Standing for caravan

'Caravans I think are not "stationed" on an area where one or two of them have casually stopped for a night or more even though there may have been other caravans which have stopped in the vicinity several years.' *Biss v Smallburgh Rural District Council* [1964] 2 All ER 543 at 554, CA, per Harman LJ; also reported [1965] Ch 335

STATIONARY

[Rules for preventing collisions at sea provided that fishing vessels or open boats when at anchor or attached to their nets and 'stationary' should exhibit certain lights.] 'The question is, whether the trawler was a steamer under way, or whether she was a fishing vessel attached to her nets and stationary. . . . What then is the meaning of the word "stationary"? It has been argued that it must mean mathematically stationary. It seems to me that that cannot be so in a tideway unless the vessel is anchored. A vessel must go with the tide unless she is so managed and with her head turned to tide she exactly counteracts the tide—a thing almost impossible to do for five consecutive minutes. Therefore that cannot be the meaning. Then it was suggested that it means that the vessel must not have any way through the water. . . . If it was meant that she was to have no way through the water, the legislature might just as well have said at once that she must not fish at all. . . . Therefore it seems to me clear that the word "stationary" cannot mean mathematically stationary, that is, going by the land and not by the tide; neither can it mean that the vessel is to have no way on her through the water. . . . The result, therefore, is, that we must so construe this word "stationary" as to mean that the vessel is not in fact stationary, though at the same time I think that we are bound to give the fullest effect to so strong a word as "stationary". . . . Upon the best consideration that we can give to it, I think what we must say is this, that she must not be going faster than is necessary to keep herself under command while attached to her nets.' *The Dunelm* (1884) 51 LT 214 at 218, 219, CA, per Brett MR

STATUS

'Marriage is the fulfilment of a contract satisfied by the solemnization of the marriage, but marriage directly it exists creates by law a relation between the parties and what is called a status of each. The status of an individual, used as a legal term, means the legal position of the individual in or with regard to the rest of a community.' *Niboyet v Niboyet* (1878) 4 PD 1 at 11, CA, per Brett LJ

'Status means the condition of belonging to a class in society to which the law ascribes peculiar rights and duties, capacities and incapacities.' *Ampthill Peerage Case* [1976] 2 All ER 441 at 424, HL (Committee for Privileges), per Lord Simon of Glaisdale

Australia 'Without pretending to give an exhaustive definition, I apprehend that the term "status" means something of this sort: a condition attached by law to a person which confers or affects or limits a legal capacity of exercising some power that under other circumstances he could not or could exercise without restriction. That definition, as I have said, may not be exhaustive, but it indicates, at any rate, the sort of thing that is meant.' *Daniel v Daniel* (1906) 4 CLR 563 at 566, per Griffith CJ

STATUS QUO

New Zealand 'As I understand the judgment of the learned judge in the court below, the sole ground upon which the remedy of rescission was refused to the plaintiff was that restoration of the status quo was not possible. To restore the parties precisely to the position in which they were when the contract was entered into is seldom possible, as was observed by Lord Blackburn in the case which I have cited [*Erlanger v New Sombrero Phosphate Co* (1878) 3 AC 1218]; but this is not necessary to the restoration of the status quo in the meaning in which these words must be understood in this connection. The status quo is considered to be restored if the rights of the parties can be equitably adjusted by taking accounts of profits, making allowances for deterioration, or by taking other similar accounts and making other similar allowances so as to do, as was observed by Lord Blackburn, what is practically just.' *Stanley Stamp Co v Brodie* (1914) 34 NZLR 129 at 168, CA, per Edwards J; also reported 17 GLR 328 at 342

STATUTE

A statute, or Act of Parliament, is a pronouncement by the Sovereign in Parliament, that is to say, made by the Queen by and with the advice and consent of both Houses of Parliament, or, in certain circumstances, the House of Commons alone, the effect of which is either to declare the law, or to change the law (normally for the future only, but sometimes with retrospective effect), or to do both. . . .

The classification of statutes into general, local and personal is a classification based on the extent of their operation. A statute is said to be general if it applies to the whole community, local if it is limited in respect of area and personal if it is limited in respect of individuals. . . .

A statute is said to be public if it is one of which judicial notice is taken, private if it is one required to be pleaded and proved by the party seeking to take advantage of it. Every statute passed since 1850 is public in this sense unless it contains an express provision to the contrary. Such a provision has in recent years been included only in personal statutes dealing with private estates. . . .

All statutes are printed by the Queen's Printer, and are classified by him under three heads: (1) public general Acts, (2) local Acts, and (3) personal Acts. The public general Acts comprise all statutes originating in public Bills, except statutes confirming provisional orders, and their chapter numbers are in Arabic characters. The local Acts comprise all statutes of a local character originating in private Bills, together with statutes confirming provisional orders, and their chapters are indicated by small Roman numerals. The personal Acts comprise all statutes of a personal nature originating in private Bills, and are numbered in italicised Arabic figures.

Statutes are classified not only by reference to their scope and the manner of their enactment, but also by reference to such features as the time at which they were passed, and their purposes, methods and duration. These classifications are neither mutually exclusive, nor in all cases exhaustive. They are mainly of practical significance in relation to the interpretation of statutes and do not on the whole reflect distinctions in form or procedure. (Ancient statutes (antiqua statuta) comprise those enacted before the first year of Edward III (1327), and modern statutes (nova statuta are those passed since that time. Declaratory statutes either resolve doubts on a particular point or restate the law on a particular subject and enacting statutes effect a change in the law. Penal statutes provide for the punishment of offences, while remedial statutes grant relief to persons aggrieved. Enabling statutes increase, whereas restraining statutes limit, the power of action. The classification of obligatory and permissive statutes distinguishes between the imposition of duties and the conferring of powers by statute. Mandatory and directory enactments concern the requirements of particular provisions, the distinction between them being that non-compliance with the requirements of mandatory enactments affects the validity of acts done.

The main classifications are (1) ancient and modern statutes; (2) declaratory and enacting statutes; (3) penal and remedial statutes; (4) enabling and restraining statutes; (5) obligatory and permissive statutes and mandatory and directory enactments: (6) affirmative and negative statutes; and (7) temporary and permanent statutes. (44 Halsbury's Laws (4th edn) paras 801, 804–807)

'An Act of Parliament may be general in part, and particular in other part.' *Ingram v Foot* (1701) 12 Mod Rep 611 at 613, per Holt CJ

'The word "statute" has several meanings. It may mean what is popularly called an Act of Parliament, or a code such as the stat [(1275)] of West 1, or all the Acts passed in one Session, which was the original meaning of the word.' *R v Bakewell* (1857) 7 E & B 848 at 851, 852, per Lord Campbell CJ

'The term by "Act of Parliament" [in the Railway Companies Act 1867, s 3] is not confined to one Act; it embraces any number of Acts. It is not required that the Act or Acts should relate to the particular company exclusively, all that is necessary is that the company should be constituted by some Act or Acts for the purpose mentioned.' *Re East & West India Dock Co* (1888) 38 Ch D 576 at 582, per Chitty J

Canada [A statute of Alberta for 1906 enacted that no tax should be payable thereunder in respect to any portion of a line of railway aided by securities under the provisions of any statute.] 'This railway was aided by a guarantee under the provisions of a Dominion statute, but it is said that the word "statute" . . . is limited to a statute of the Province, and that, as no guarantee has been given under the provisions of a provincial statute, the exemption does not apply. . . . In the Supreme Court of Canada . . . the majority . . . hold that the words "any statute" include a Dominion statute. . . . In their natural ordinary sense the words "any statute" . . . would include a Dominion statute, without raising any implication that it would also include a statute enacted by some outside authority, with no jurisdiction to legislate within the Province. . . . On this point their Lordships agree with the judgment of the majority in the Supreme Court of Canada.' *R & Alberta Provincial Treasurer v Canadian Northern Rly Co* [1923] AC 714 at 716–718, PC, per Lord Parmoor.

Codifying statute

The purpose of a codifying statute is to present an orderly and authoritative statement of the leading rules of law on a given subject, whether those rules are to be found in statute law or common law. Between 1882 and 1906 Parliament enacted four such statutes [viz, Bills of Exchange Act 1882, Partnership Act 1890, Sale of Goods Act 1893 and Marine Insurance Act 1906], but the only codification attempted since that time has been in conjunction with law reform. (44 Halsbury's Laws (4th edn) para 808)

[A body of commissioners known as the Law Commission has been set up to promote the reform of English law, and there is also a Scottish Law Commission: see Law Commission Act 1965. Each Commission must keep the law under review with a view to its systematic development and reform, including its codification.]

Consolidating statute

The purpose of a consolidating statute is to present the whole body of the statutory law on a subject in complete form, repealing the former statutes. Consolidation is not a modern invention, but it was in the latter part of the nineteenth century, and particularly after the establishment in 1868 of the Statute Law Committee, that it became the regular feature of the legislative programme which, with one or two interruptions, it has remained to this day. (44 Halsbury's Laws (4th edn) para 809)

'The respondent maintained this singular proposition, that, in dealing with a consolidating statute, each enactment must be traced to its original source, and, when that is discovered, must be construed according to the state of circumstances which existed when it first became law. The proposition has neither reason nor authority to recommend it. The very object of consolidation is to collect the statutory law bearing upon a particular subject, and to bring it down to date, in order that it may form a useful code applicable to the circumstances existing at the time when the consolidating Act is passed.' *Administrator-General of Bengal v Prem Lal Mullick* (1895) LR 22 Ind App 107 at 116, PC, per Lord Watson

'The presumption with which one starts is that a consolidating Act is not intended to alter the law. . . . It may be, however, that the language of the Act is so clearly different from that of the previous statute as to bring about an alteration of law.' *Gilbert v Gilbert & Boucher* [1928] P 1 at 8, CA, per Scrutton LJ

Construction of *See* CONSTRUCTION (Interpretation)

General Act

'A general Act, prima facie, is that which applies to the whole community. In the natural meaning of the term it means an Act of Parliament which is unlimited both in its area and, as regards the individual, in its effects.' *R v London County Council* [1893] 2 QB 454 at 462, CA, per Bowen LJ

Interpretation of *See* CONSTRUCTION (Interpretation)

Penal statute

A statute must be regarded as penal for purposes of construction if it imposes a fine, penalty or forfeiture, other than a penalty in the nature of liquidated damages, or other penalties which are in the nature of civil remedies. (44 Halsbury's Laws (4th edn) para 909)

Preamble to *See* PREAMBLE

Public and private Acts

'An Act of Parliament concerning the revenue of the king is a public law; but it may be private in respect to some clauses in it relating to a private person.' *Anon* (1698) 12 Mod Rep 249 at 249, per Holt CJ

'By a private Act of Parliament, I do not mean merely private estate Acts, but local and personal, as distinguished from general public Acts. Public Acts, it is said in the books, bind all the Queen's subjects. But of private Acts of Parliament it is said, that they do not bind strangers, unless by express words or necessary implication the intention of the legislature to affect the rights of strangers is apparent in the Act; and whether an Act is public or private does not depend upon any technical considerations (such as having a clause or declaration that the Act shall be deemed a public Act), but upon the nature and substance of the case.' *Dawson v Paver* (1847) 5 Hare 415 at 434, per Wigram V-C

STATUTORY COMPANY

See also COMPANY

The expression 'statutory company' means any company constituted by or under an Act of Parliament to construct, work or carry on any . . . water, electricity, tramway, hydraulic power, dock, canal or railway undertaking. (Landlord and Tenant Act 1927, s 25, as amended by the Gas Act 1986)

STATUTORY DAMAGES

See DAMAGES

STATUTORY INSTRUMENT

For the purpose of determining whether a particular document is a statutory instrument a distinction is drawn between (1) documents made in the exercise of powers conferred either by the Statutory Instruments Act 1946 or by statute passed since its commencement; and (2) documents made in the exercise of powers conferred by earlier statutes.

In relation to documents in head (1), the position is straightforward. Such a document is to be known as a 'statutory instrument' if the power is a power to make, confirm or approve orders, rules, regulations or other subordinate legislation, is conferred either on Her Majesty in Council or on a minister of the Crown, and is expressed to be exercisable by Order in Council in the former case and by statutory instrument in the latter.

So far as documents in head (2) are concerned, the position is more complicated, but the underlying principle is that, save as otherwise provided by regulations, a document is to be known as a 'statutory instrument' if the power which the document exercises was a power to make statutory rules within the meaning of the legislation formerly in force, conferred on a rule-making authority within the meaning of that legislation. (44 Halsbury's Laws (4th edn) para 984)

Where by this Act or any Act passed after the commencement of this Act power to make, confirm or approve orders, rules, regulations or other subordinate legislation is conferred on [Her] Majesty in Council or on any Minister of the Crown then, if the power is expressed (a) in the case of a power conferred on [Her] Majesty, to be exercisable by Order in Council; (b) in the case of a power conferred on a Minister of the Crown, to be exercisable by statutory instrument, any document by which that power is exercised shall be known as a 'statutory instrument' and the provisions of this Act shall apply thereto accordingly. (Statutory Instruments Act 1946, s 1(1))

[Similarly, by ibid, s 1(2), rules subsequently made under powers conferred by earlier Acts are also to be known as 'statutory instruments'.]

STATUTORY NUISANCE

See NUISANCE

STATUTORY OBLIGATION

New Zealand 'The phrase "statutory obligation" as used in s 32 of the Workers' Compensation Act 1956 [repealed], clearly includes any obligation or duty laid down by statute and also includes any obligation or duty laid down by statutory regulation. . . . In my view the phrase also includes any obligation however imposed or in whatever manner assumed or undertaken, the breach of which renders any person committing such a breach liable to a penalty prescribed by Act of Parliament or by statutory regulation made under any such Act. The mere fact that an Act of Parliament provides a procedure for the recovery of moneys payable pursuant to an obligation entered into by a person does not, however, make that obligation a statutory obligation.' *Cowie v A-G* [1962] NZLR 378 at 380, per Dalglish J

STATUTORY OWNER

'Statutory owner' means the trustees of the settlement or other persons who, during a minority, or at any other time when there is no tenant for life, have the powers of a tenant for life under this Act, but does not include the trustees of the settlement, where by virtue of an order of the court or otherwise the trustees have power to convey the settled land in the name of the tenant for life' (Settled Land Act 1925, s 117)

STATUTORY POWER

New Zealand 'The definition of "statutory power" in s 3 of the Judicature Amendment Act 1972 contemplated only exercises of power which have a final determinative effect.' *Daemer v Gilliand* [1979] 2 NZLR 7 at 16, per McMullin J

STATUTORY TENANT *See* TENANT

STATUTORY TRIBUNAL

See TRIBUNAL

STATUTORY UNDERTAKERS

[A great many statutes concerned with the provision of public services, e.g. gas, electricity, transport or water undertakings, authorise certain persons to carry out the necessary works in any particular case. Two examples of paragraphs defining 'statutory undertakers' are given below.]

'Statutory undertakers' means any person authorised by any Act (whether public general or local), or by any order or scheme made under or confirmed by an Act, to construct, work or carry on any railway, light railway, tramway, road transport, water transport, canal, inland navigation, dock, harbour, pier or lighthouse undertaking, or any undertaking for the supply of electricity, gas, hydraulic power or water. (Acquisition of Land (Authorisation Procedure) Act 1946, s 8)

'Statutory undertakers' means any persons authorised by an enactment or by an order, rule or regulation made under an enactment, to construct, work or carry on a railway, canal, inland navigation, dock, harbour, tramway, gas, electricity, water or other public undertaking. (Housing Act 1985, s 611(6)(a))

STAY AND TRADE

'I agree that this policy is not a voyage policy, nor a time policy *simpliciter*. . . . But, whatever the policy be called, the purpose of the voyage is distinctly stated. It is that the ship is to "stay and trade" on the African coast. . . . I think the language used means that the vessel may stay for a trading purpose, but for no other; that is, for any purpose which having regard to the usage of the African trade, may fairly be regarded as a "trade purpose". For example, suppose after the cargo was loaded it became doubtful whether the destination originally fixed for it by the owner should be adhered to or whether that destination might not be changed with advantage, a delay whilst the port of discharge was being fixed would be a delay for a trade purpose. . . . It would be a question for a jury whether the purpose was or was not a trade purpose. But in the present case no attempt was made to show that a delay in order to save a wreck belonging to the same owners was, by the usage of the African trade, in any sense a trade purpose; and we must assume, therefore, that the delay was not for the purpose of trade at all, but foreign to it. This being so, the risk undertaken by the underwriter was varied, and he is therefore discharged.' *Company of African Merchants v British & Foreign Insurance Co* (1873) LR 8 Exch 154 at 156, 157, per Cockburn CJ

STEAL *See* STOLEN GOODS; THEFT

STEAM BOILER

In this Part of this Act 'steam boiler' means any closed vessel in which for any purpose steam is generated under pressure greater than atmospheric pressure, and includes any economiser used to heat water being fed to any such vessel, and any superheater used for heating steam. (Factories Act 1961, s 38)

STEAM CONTAINER

'Steam container' means any vessel (other than a steam pipe or coil) constructed with a permanent outlet into the atmosphere or into a space where the pressure does not exceed atmospheric pressure, and through which steam is passed at atmospheric pressure or at approximately that pressure for the purpose of heating, boiling, drying, evaporating or other similar purpose. (Factories Act 1961, s 35)

STEAM RECEIVER

'Steam receiver' means any vessel or apparatus (other than a steam boiler, steam container, a steam pipe or coil, or a part of a prime mover) used for containing steam under pressure greater than atmospheric pressure. (Factories Act 1961, s 35)

STEP

In proceedings

[The Arbitration Act 1889, s 4, (repealed; see now the Arbitration Act 1950, s 4), provided that if any party to a submission commenced any legal proceedings in any court against any other party to the submission in respect of any matter agreed to be referred, any party to such legal proceedings could at any time after appearance, and before delivering any pleadings or taking any other 'steps in the proceedings', apply to that court to stay the proceedings.] 'The second matter relied on was, that the plaintiff had taken out a summons for particulars of the counterclaim. I am inclined to think that that did amount to a step in the proceedings, notwithstanding that subsequently to the date of that summons the counterclaim was amended. . . . Subsequently to the amendment of the counterclaim, upon the bearing of the defendant's summons for directions, the plaintiff applied for and obtained leave to administer interrogatories to the defendant. That I think clearly amounted to a step by the plaintiff in the proceedings.' *Chappell v North* [1891] 2 QB 252 at 255, 256, DC, per Denman J

'The defendant has done two things which are objected to as being "steps in the proceedings" so as to disentitle him to apply under s 4 of the Arbitration Act [1889 (repealed; see supra)]. The first is, that he has applied for and obtained a statement of claim. It is said that that is really a part of the appearance. However that may be, I think it is quite clear that the other thing which he has done, viz, applied for a stay until security for costs has been given, is a step in the proceedings within the section.' *Adams v Catley* (1892) 66 LT 687 at 688, per Mathew J

'What is relied on as steps taken by the defendant is, that his solicitors wrote on two occasions asking for further time to put in a defence, which applications were acceded to. In my opinion, asking for time by letter is not taking a step in the action [within the Arbitration Act 1889, s 4 (repealed; see supra)]; it is taking a step outside the action altogether.' *Brighton Marine Palace & Pier Ltd v Woodhouse* [1893] 2 Ch 486 at 488, per North J

'The authorities show that a step in the proceedings means something in the nature of an application to the court, and not mere talk between solicitors or solicitors' clerks, nor the writing of letters, but the taking of some step, such as taking out a summons or something of that kind, which is, in the technical sense, a step in the proceedings.' *Ives v Barker* [1894] 2 Ch 478 at 484, CA, per Lindley LJ

'It seems to me that the mere filing of affidavits in defence to a motion for a receiver is not in the nature of an application to the Court, and consequently not a "step in the proceedings" within the meaning of the section [s 4 of the Arbitration Act 1889 (repealed; see supra].' *Zalinoff v Hammond* [1898] 2 Ch 92 at 94, 95, per Stirling J

[See further, as to filing an affidavit, *Turner & Goudy v McConnell* [1985] 2 All ER 34 in which the above case was disapproved.]

'Attending this general summons for directions without objection, and without asking for an adjournment, in order to make an application to stay the action, is taking a step in the proceedings within the meaning of s 4 of the Arbitration Act 1889 [repealed; see supra].' *Richardson v Le Maitre* [1903] 2 Ch 222 at 225, per Swinfen Eady J

'Attending and assenting to an order made by the master in chambers amounts to "taking a step" in the action [within the Arbitration Act 1889, s 4 (repealed; see supra)], and the mere fact of the order being made, as in this case, subject to the production of a document by the other side does not, in my opinion, make any difference.' *Cohen v Arthur, Cohen v Cohen* (1912) 56 Sol Jo 344 at 344, per Neville J

'Two questions have been raised: the first, a general question, whether after the King's fiat has been given to a petition of right there is any jurisdiction in the Court under s 4 of the Arbitration Act [1889 (repealed; see supra)] to stay further proceedings on the petition. . . . The existence of the jurisdiction depends upon s 4 of the Arbitration Act 1889. Before that section applies, certain conditions must be fulfilled. First, there must be a submission; secondly, a party to the submission must commence legal proceedings in a court against another party to the submission; thirdly, that party must not have delivered pleadings or taken any other step in those proceedings. If those conditions are fulfilled then that party to the proceedings may apply to the Court to stay them in order that the question may be referred to arbitration. . . . In my judgment the presentation of the petition to the King is not a legal proceeding at all. It is a petition praying the King to allow legal proceedings to be taken. . . . It follows that the granting of the fiat is not a step in any legal proceedings.' *Anglo-Newfoundland Development Co Ltd v R* [1920] 2 KB 214 at 226, 227, CA, per Warrington LJ

See, generally, 2 Halsbury's Laws (4th edn) para 563.

STEPCHILD

'So far as the history of the definition in dictionaries of the word "stepchild" is concerned, while originally it appears likely that the death of the real parent was an essential element in enabling a child to fall into the category of a "stepchild", it is in my view clear that any such qualification on the definition is obsolete.' *Inland Revenue v Russell* 1955 SLT 255 at 256, per the Lord President (Clyde)

STEPSON

New Zealand 'Generally speaking, I think the term "stepson" has relation only to the man to whom the mother of the son is currently married at the time made crucial by any given circumstances. Be this generalisation right or wrong. I am satisfied, having regard to the purposes sought to be achieved by the Deaths by Accidents Compensation Act 1908 (NZ) [repealed; see now the Deaths by Accident Compensation Act 1952] and to the nature of the relationship to which it was intended to extend, that the term "stepson" in that Act extends only to children who possessed that character by virtue of a subsisting marriage when the cause of action sought to be enforced under the Act arose. Were it otherwise, claims from totally unexpected sources might be presented.' *Mander v O'Toole* [1948] NZLR 909 at 912, 913, per Finlay J; also reported [1948] GLR 445 at 446

STERLING

(1) A description of an article, or of the metal in an article, as 'sterling' or (except in the phrase 'Britannia metal') 'Britannia' is to be presumed to be an indication that the article, or the metal is of silver.

(2) If 'sterling' is the word used, the description is to be presumed to be an indication that the silver is of a standard of fineness of 925.

(3) If the word used is 'Britannia' the description is to be presumed to be an indication that the silver is of a standard of fineness of 958.4. (Hallmarking Act 1973, Sched 1, Part III, para 3)

[Britannia metal—'an alloy, mainly tin with copper, antimony, lead or zinc or a mixture of these, similar to pewter'. (Chambers Twentieth Century Dictionary (1972))]

'The . . . question is, whether the allegation in the affidavit to hold to bail, that the defendant was indebted in so many pounds sterling, is sufficiently certain? My three learned Brothers are of opinion that the word sterling is too uncertain and equivocal in itself to be made the foundation of an order to hold to bail, because in their judgment it is not absolutely certain that the party may not be indebted in so much sterling money of Ireland.' *Pickardo v Machado* (1825) 4 B & C 886 at 888, per cur.

[An agreement made in London provided for the employment of the appellant as a tailor in New Zealand at a remuneration of seven hundred pounds 'sterling' a year.] 'In the agreement here in question, the word "sterling", in their Lordships' judgment, is an express term intended to exclude, and in fact excluding, the prima facie rule according to which New Zealand pounds would be meant, as being the currency of the place of payment. It is impossible, in their judgment, to regard the word as indicating simply legal tender at the place of payment, New Zealand. The agreement is clearly on its face a formal and studied document. It is drawn up and executed in London between the respondents' London house and the appellant, a London resident. The insertion of the word "sterling" is not common form in a service agreement like this. If it is used in any business document in London, it naturally means "British sterling", and nothing else. It is used in this sense habitually in exchange quotations, and in documents dealing with international transactions, in which it is necessary to define the currency intended, including transactions with the Dominions. The contrast between sterling (sc, British sterling or currency) and Dominion or Colonial currency is familiar. . . . It is not to be forgotten that in August, 1932, exchange questions were matters of business moment. The appellant, who was going to New Zealand, might naturally desire to be assured that he would be paid in the currency with which he was familiar.' *De Bueger v Ballantyne (J) & Co Ltd* [1938] AC 452 at 461, PC, per cur.

'"Sterling" is, of course, simply the name of our currency, English pounds, shillings and pence. The origin of the word is uncertain. In the *Case of Mixed Money* [(1605) Davies 48] the word "sterling" is said to be derived from the fact that the early kings employed people from the East to make pure English money. These people were called "Esterlings", and the coins they made were called sterling money. This view is not, I believe, acceptable to antiquarians today. They think the word had its origin in the fact that some of the early coins had a small star on them. Howsoever that may be, the phrase "gold sterling" must mean, I think, gold coins of sterling currency, that is, in modern times sovereigns or half-sovereigns.' *Treseder-Griffin v Co-operative Insurance Society Ltd* [1956] 2 All ER 33 at 37, 38, CA, per Denning LJ; also reported in [1956] 2 QB 127 at 147

Australia '"Sterling" in relation to currency, means, according to the Standard Dictionary "having a standard of value or fineness established by the British Government; said of British money of account". See definition of "sterling" in Webster's Dictionary—"Lawful money of England or later of Great Britain or of those British Possessions having no separate coinage"—i.e. sterling means lawful English currency as distinct from a Dominion or Colonial currency which is established independently of English money. This was held to be the meaning off "sterling" in *De Bueger v J Ballantyne & Co Ltd* [supra] this meaning being said to have obtained from the 17th and 18th centuries.' *Bonython v Commonwealth* (1948) 75 CLR 589 at 603, per Latham CJ

STILL-BORN

'Still-born child' means a child which has issued forth from its mother after the twenty-eighth week of pregnancy and which did not at any time after being completely expelled from its mother breathe or show any other signs of life, and the expression 'still-birth' shall be construed accordingly. (Births and Deaths Registration Act 1953, s 41)

STIPULATE

'In the last sentence of the instrument [an agreement for a lease] come the words, "it is lastly stipulated and conditioned, that Watt shall not assign, transfer, underlet, or part with any part of the lands otherwise than to his wife or children". These words are clearly introduced into the instrument on the part of the lessor, for they are for this benefit. The word conditioned is fairly a word of condition. In pleading, a bond is stated to be conditioned for payment of money. It is said that the word stipulated and the word conditioned, being used together, have the same meaning, and import a covenant, and not a condition; but there are several authorities which show that if words both of covenant and condition are used in the same instrument, they both shall operate. If the word stipulated import a covenant, it will operate as such; and if the word conditioned import a condition, it must also operate.' *Doe d Henniker v Watt* (1828) 8 B & C 308 at 315, 316, per Bayley J

STOCK *See also* FARMING STOCK; LIVESTOCK; TRADING STOCK

In bequest

[This word in a will includes crops of corn growing on the land.] 'The case of *Cox v Godsalve* [(1699) 6 East 604, n] before Lord Holt is in terms so much the same as this, that it must conclude it: though but for that case I should have been more inclined to think that stock on the farm meant moveable stock.' *West v Moore* (1807) 8 East 339 at 343, per Lord Ellenborough CJ

[A testator bequeathed to his wife all his furniture, linen, plate, pictures, carriages, horses, and other live and dead 'stock'.] 'I have no doubt the testator intended his wife to take his house and everything in and about it. In *Porter v Tournay* [(1797 3 Ves 311] the words "live and dead stock" were coupled with carriages and horses only, so as evidently to mean only articles *ejusdem generis*, viz, outdoor stock; and Lord Alvanley carefully guarded himself against deciding on the abstract meaning of the words: the case, therefore, cannot govern the present, where the same words follow a list of in-door as well as out-door articles, and must naturally be referred to the whole. As to the books *Ouseley v Anstruther* [(1847) 10 Beav 453 at 462] is a much stronger case, the library there being of very great value. "Stock" according to Johnson, means "store", and is a more appropriate word for the wine. It must be declared that the testator's books and wine were specifically bequeathed to his wife.' *Hutchinson v Smith* (1863) 1 New Rep 513 at 514, per Wood V-C

'The question which I have to decide is whether the bequest of the stock on the farm covered the oats mentioned. In my opinion the word "stock" is quite wide enough to cover a stock of oats, whether it is large or small, irrespective of the season in which it was reaped. A "stock of oats" and a "stock of hay" are familiar expressions. The stock may be last year's, but it is still stock. It may be for consumption on the lands or for sale, but it is still stock.' *Re Drew, Marry v Drew* [1923] 1 IR 35 at 36, per O'Connor MR

Australia [The Water Act 1912 (NSW), ss 7, 13A, as amended (see now ss 7(1)(a)(ii), 13A(1) provides for the granting of licences to permit farmers to pump water from a watercourse 'for watering stock'.] 'If the phrase were limited to sheep, cattle, horses and other quadrupeds the position would be that a riparian owner conducting a poultry farm (where his stock would be fowls, turkeys, ducks or geese) would not breach the provisions of s 7 of the Water Act if any of the water from or in the watercourses was used to provide drinking water for his poultry. The view I have formed is that the word "stock" is used in a wide, broad sense and extends to all forms of stock bought or bred by a primary producer in the course of his trade or business; they must be live-stock, of course, as the context indicates that they require water for their sustenance.' *Graham v Tongue*, [1969] 1 NSWR 611 at 612, per Hardie J

STOCK (Investment) *See also* SHARES (in company)

'Stock' includes fully paid up shares, and so far as relates to vesting orders made by the court under this Act, includes any fund, annuity, or security transferable in books kept by any company or society, or by instrument of transfer either alone or accompanied by other formalities, and any share or interest therein. (Trustee Act 1925, s 68)

'Stock, when formed, is nothing but an aggregation of shares, carrying with it the peculiarity of being capable of minute division. But while ordinary proprietary stock is in substance identical with shares, debenture stock stands in a different position. The debenture stockholder . . . is in no sense a proprietor. . . . His position is that of a creditor.' *Dillon v Arkins* (1885) 17 LR Ir 636 at 637, 638, per Naish LC

[A testator, by clause 11 of his will, empowered trustees to permit his personal estate invested on his decease in any 'stocks', funds, or securities yielding income, to continue in the same state of investment as long as they thought fit. The testator at his death held shares in Canadian land companies which were valuable and paid good dividends, but which were of a wasting character.] 'The particular shares in this case come within the word "stocks" in clause 11, and I am not prepared to hold that they do not also come within the word "securities" in that clause. I am therefore of opinion that under that clause the trustees can retain these shares and that the tenants for life are entitled to receive in specie the whole of the dividends arising from them.' *Re Inman, Inman v Inman* [1915] 1 Ch 187 at 192, per Neville J

Capital *See* CAPITAL

Public stock

[A testator by his will directed that trust funds should be invested in some or one of the 'public stocks' of the Bank of England.] 'The . . . question is what is the meaning of public stocks of the Bank of England. It is said that it has no definite meaning, and, on the other hand, it is said that it means public stock domiciled at the Bank of England. In my view, "public stock" in the year 1868, when the will was executed, had a definite meaning, and meant public stock of this country which formed part of the national debt. In *Wells v Porter* [(1836) 2 Bing NC 722 at 731], Bosanquet J said: "When we find the expression public stocks we must intend the public stocks of this country", and in *Hewitt v Price* [(1842) 4 Man & Gt 355], Tindal CJ said "that case appears to be decisive". Further, in the Act of 1869 [Stat (1869) 32 & 33 Vict c 104 (repealed), s 6] public stock is defined as meaning "any stock forming part of the National Debt and transferable in the books of the Bank of England". I therefore hold that the expression "public stocks" in this will is confined to public stocks forming part of the National Debt of this country.' *Re Hill, Fettes v Hill* (1914) 58 Sol Jo 399 at 400, per Eve J

'Stocks and shares'

'The term "stock", or "capital stock", which is there used, obviously is derived from the consideration that these were what were called joint stock companies, and that "stock" was the short name for "joint stock", and joint stock, in my opinion, is only another name for "shares", because the owner of part of the capital of a company is an owner of a part or a share of the joint stock. The use of the term "stock" appears to me merely to denote that the company have recognised the fact of the complete payment of the shares, and that the time has come when those shares may be assigned in fragments, which for obvious reasons could not be permitted before, but that stock shall still be the qualification, for example, of directors, who must possess a certain number of shares, and that the meetings shall be of the persons entitled to this stock, who shall meet as shareholders, and vote as shareholders, in the proportion of shares which would entitle them to vote before the consolidation into stock. If ever there was a case in which the substance is that "stock" and "shares" are indentical, it is a case of this kind.' *Morrice v Aylmer* (1874) 10 Ch 148 at 154, 155, per Lord Cairns LC

[A testatrix by her will directed her trustees to sell all her 'stocks and shares'. Some of her investments were stocks and shares in limited companies, others were redeemable debenture stock, holdings in public utility companies, and government securities.] 'The natural meaning of "stocks and shares" is stocks and shares in limited companies, and the only use that I make of circumstances in the present case is to come to the conclusion that I find nothing in them to extend that natural meaning.' *Re Everett, Prince v Hunt* [1944] Ch 176 at 179, per Cohen J

'What is the meaning of the gift of "all my stocks and shares" in this particular will? In every-day language, such as the testator was using in this holograph will, that expression, is, I think, quite commonly used as a convenient, compendious and comprehensive term to denote all forms of investment commonly dealt in on stock exchanges, such as are sometimes also compendiously referred to as "stock exchange investments" without any intention of distinguishing between, or excluding any of, the various kinds of investment falling within this wide and general category. It is in this sense members of stock exchanges commonly describe themselves as "stock and share brokers".' *Re Purnchard's Will Trusts, Public Trustee v Pelly* [1948] Ch 312 at 317, per Jenkins J

Trading stock *See* TRADING STOCK

STOCK EXCHANGE TRANSACTION

'Stock exchange transaction' means a sale and purchase of securities in which each of the parties is a member of a stock exchange acting in the ordinary course of his business as such or is acting through the agency of such a member. (Stock Transfer Act 1963, s 4)

STOCK-IN-TRADE

'Nothing shall be deemed stock-in-trade but the shop goods and utensils in trade, though I think the ready money in the till might come within that construction.' *Seymour v Rapier* (1718) Bunb 28 at 28, per Price B

'This lady, during her widowhood, made a settlement, by which, amongst other things, the stock-in-trade and furniture were assigned to trustees for her separate use, free from the control of any future husband; at a future period the stock-in-trade and the other things were to be sold, and the money was to be appropriated to certain uses and upon certain trusts. . . . I think that this, in substance, was what was meant:—during the time the trade was carried on, the stock-in-trade, of necessity, was known to the parties to consist of fluctuating articles, and in the course of that fluctuation, the stock-in-trade as it ultimately subsisted at the time of the sale, did not consist of the same articles as the stock-in-trade at the time of the marriage, or when the deed was executed, but still it was that stock-in-trade which was contemplated by the deed, and was intended to be the subject of the trusts of the deed.' *England v Downs* (1842) 6 Beav 269 at 273–276, per Lord Langdale MR

STOCK-RAISING

Canada 'Is fox-farming included in the meaning of that term? Ordinarily, stock-raising has to do with horses, cattle, sheep, swine and perhaps goats. Such animals as dogs and poultry, and perhaps rabbits are usually not included. . . . Until recent years the raising of foxes was left to nature in the wilds, but has in the last few decades developed into an important industry in this province and country. The purposes of raising foxes are in general much like the raising of sheep, swine or other animals that are bred for the purposes of revenue. In my opinion fox-farming should be considered as stock-raising for the purposes of this Act.' *Re Winnipeg Silver Fox Assessment Appeal* [1941] 1 WWR 48 at 50, Man KB, per Dysart J

STOLEN GOODS

(1) The provisions of this Act relating to goods which have been stolen shall apply whether the stealing occurred in England or Wales or elsewhere, and whether it occurred before or after the commencement of this Act, provided that the stealing (if not an offence under this Act) amounted to an offence where and at the time when the goods were stolen; and references to stolen goods shall be construed accordingly.

(2) For purposes of those provisions references to stolen goods shall include, in addition to the goods originally stolen and parts of them (whether in their original state or not),—

(a) any other goods which directly or indirectly represent or have at any time represented the stolen goods in the hands of the thief as being the proceeds of any disposal or realisation of the whole or part of the goods stolen or of goods so representing the stolen goods; and

(b) any other goods which directly or indirectly represent or have at any time represented the stolen goods in the hands of a handler of the stolen goods or any part of them as being the proceeds of any disposal or realisation of the whole or part of the stolen goods handled by him or of goods so representing them.

(3) But no goods shall be regarded as having continued to be stolen goods after they have been restored to the person from whom they were stolen or to other lawful possession or custody, or after that person and any other person claiming through him have otherwise ceased as regards those goods to have any right to restitution in respect of the theft.

(4) For purposes of the provisions of this Act relating to goods which have been stolen (including subsections (1) to (3) above) goods obtained in England or Wales or elsewhere either by blackmail or in the circumstances described in section 15(1) of this Act shall be regarded as stolen; and 'steal', 'theft' and 'thief' shall be construed accordingly. (Theft Act 1968, s 24)

[Section 15(1) of the Act makes it an offence to obtain property by deception.]

STOP

[The Road Traffic Act 1960, s 77(1) (repealed; see now the Road Traffic Act 1988, s 170(2)) required that, in case of accident causing damage to another vehicle, the driver of a motor vehicle should 'stop' and, if reasonably required to do so, give his name and address and other particulars.] 'Napier J, in *Noblet v Condon* [[1935] SASR 329], was dealing with a case where the driver of the vehicle involved in the accident had stayed stopped for a period which in the judge's view might have been, or the justices may have inferred that it was, up to three or four minutes. Napier J said: "I should be very sorry to give the impression that a momentary pause will exempt the driver of a motor car which is involved in an accident from the necessity of stopping to give the particulars contemplated by the section. Upon my view of the section, the obligation is to stop for such a period as may be reasonable to enable the questions to be put, if there is anybody in the vicinity who desires to put them", and he goes on to consider the conclusions of the justices. I gratefully and respectfully adopt what was said by Napier J in that decision, and for my own part I too think that in s 77(1) of the Road Traffic act 1960, the phrase "the driver of the motor vehicle shall stop" is properly to be construed as meaning the driver of the motor vehicle shall stop it and remain where he has stopped it for such a period of time as in the prevailing circumstances, having regard in particular to the character of the road or place in which the accident happened, will provide a sufficient period to enable persons who have a right to do so, and reasonable ground for so doing, to require of him direct and personally the information which is provided for in s 77(1). It is the driver's own personal obligation to stay for such a period as I have indicated, and personally to provide the information.' *Lee v Knapp* [1966] 3 All ER 961 at 963, per Winn LJ

New Zealand [The Transport Act 1962, s 65(1), places the obligation on a motor vehicle driver who has been involved in an accident to 'stop' and also to ascertain whether any other person has been injured.] 'Now in the ordinary commonly understood sense "stop" means "to cease to move" and accordingly, if a motorist in the circumstances envisaged in the subsection ceases to move (that is, brings his vehicle to a halt) he, in ordinary parlance, stops. But there is no question on the finding of facts by the magistrate but that . . . the appellant did cease to move. He stopped and he did not proceed again for another 10 to 15 seconds. . . . I find that the learned magistrate was wrong in law in holding that the obligation to stop under s 65(1) entailed an obligation to stop for any period for any other purpose.' *Naughton v Christchurch City* [1970] NZLR 1114 at 1116, 1117, per Wilson J

New Zealand [The Transport Act 1962, s 65(1), requires the driver of a motor vehicle which has been involved in an accident to 'stop' and ascertain whether any person is injured.] 'Wilson J [supra] considered that in the ordinary commonly understood sense, the word "stop" means "to cease to move" and on this premise he decided that "if a motorist in the circumstances envisaged in the subsection ceases to move (that is, brings his vehicle to a halt), he, in ordinary parlance stops". With respect, however, it seems to me that in ordinary parlance the word "stop" is capable of having two different meanings when used as an intransitive verb: the first is the meaning just referred to and the second is that of stopping and remaining stopped. These two ordinary meanings of the word are illustrated by the following sentences: (1) The driver stopped within 30 feet. (2) The driver stopped at the scene of the accident for ten minutes. The question as I see it therefore is to decide from the context in which of the two foregoing senses the word "stop" is used in s 65(1) of the Act. . . . If the duty to stop is so interpreted as to enable a driver to leave the scene of an accident as soon as his wheels have stopped turning then it is a duty which appears to me to serve no sensible purpose whatever. This consideration alone is sufficient to convince me that the word "stop" should be given the second of the two meanings to which I have earlier referred. Going a stage further, I think that the actual purpose of sub-s (1) is to insure that a driver must ascertain whether anyone is injured at a time when his own vehicle is stopped and not merely by observation from a moving vehicle. It follows that the duration of the stop which is required by the Act must be measured at least by the time reasonably necessary in all the prevailing circumstances to enable proper inquiry to be made. Possibly it may also have to be measured by reference to the duty to render assistance, but that question does not arise in the present case as nobody was in fact injured.' *Houten v Police* [1971] NZLR 903 at 906, per Richmond J

New Zealand 'The duration of the duty under s 66(1) [of the Transport Act 1962] to remain stopped is governed by the associated obligation to supply information. Once the driver has stopped and has supplied the information thereafter sought, that obligation to stop (and remain stopped) has been exhausted and there is no authority under that section for the constable or traffic officer to make any further demands on the driver at that time.' *Roper v Police* [1984] 1 NZLR 51 at 51, per Richardson J

Stop any street

New Zealand 'Nothing can amount to the "stopping" of a street or part of a street . . . unless it will destroy, or, possibly interfere with, the legal status of the street as a highway.' *Lower Hutt City Council v A-G ex rel Moulder* [1977] 1 NZLR 184 at 190, CA, per Richmond P

STOPPAGE

[A charterparty provided that time for unloading was not to count in the event of (inter alia) 'stoppages'.] 'Stoppage in the ordinary sense implies something that compels the owner of the colliery to suspend his operations, such as a general strike of the men who are working, or a breakdown of the machinery, or an inrush of water into the pit. All these things cause stoppage of a colliery, but I do not think a colliery is stopped when simply one or more of its pits are purposely kept idle because enough ships are not available to carry away one class of coal they produce.' *Arden SS Co Ltd v Mathwin & Son* 1912 SC 211 at 215, per the Lord President (Lord Dunedin)

'I have to construe the meaning of the words in the policy and the slip attached, which made the risk insured against the breakdown of the refrigerating machinery, involving a stoppage for more than twenty-four consecutive hours. . . . There must be a defect developed in the machinery which was grave enough either to bring it to a standstill or to cause those in charge of it—as the most prudent course—to stop it for repairs. . . . In short, there must be something more than falling below the efficiency point to constitute a stoppage of the machinery within the meaning of the policy. The system was a duplex system, either half of which could be kept going so as to produce the required refrigeration, and where there was so much running as to achieve the object aimed at it is impossible to hold that there was a stoppage of the refrigerating machinery merely because some portion of it, which formed part of the refrigerating system, was stopped.' *Vestey Brothers v Union Insurance Society of Canton* (1917) 33 TLR 438 at 438, per Rowlatt J; affd (1918) 34 TLR 232, CA

Australia 'The word "stoppage" is used in a machinery insurance policy, not "stopping". Stoppage means the condition of being stopped. Secondly, it is not the machine the stoppage of which is referred to, but the functions of the machine. The appropriate meaning of the word "functions" in this context is, from the Shorter Oxford Dictionary, the special kind of activity proper to anything; the mode of action by which it fulfils its purpose.' *Sun Alliance & London Assurance Group v NW Iron Co Ltd* [1974] 2 NSWLR 625 at 629, 630, per Sheppard J

STOPPAGE IN TRANSITU

Subject to this Act, when the buyer of goods becomes insolvent the unpaid seller who has parted with the possession of the goods has the right of stopping them in transit, that is to say, he may resume possession of the goods as long as they are in course of transit, and may retain them until payment or tender of the price. (Sale of Goods Act 1979, s 44)

'We must consider a little what stoppage in transitu really is; it is a right given to an unpaid vendor at any time while the goods are still in transitu—that is to say, while they are in the hands of the shipowner as carrier; and what is it? It is a retaking by the unpaid vendor, either on the cancellation of the contract, as some people say, or, as I should rather say, on resuming possession for the purpose of insisting on his lien for the price at any time while the goods are in the hands of the carrier, and have not reached the hands of the purchaser or consignee, and when they are not in his possession.' *Phelps, Stokes & Co v Comber* (1885) 29 Ch D 813 at 821, CA, per Cotton LJ

STORE

'The statutory condition on which the insurance company relies declares that "The Company is not liable . . . for loss or damage occurring while . . . gasoline . . . is . . . stored or kept in the building insured". . . . The lower part of the building was used by Thompson as a drug store and furniture shop. He had an assistant named Post. . . . In June, 1906, Post procured a gasoline stove for cooking purposes. He used it for a short time and then put it by with the gasoline which happened to be in it. On the day of the fire some syrups were wanted in a hurry. . . . Post bethought him of the disused stove, brought it downstairs with the gasoline in it, and lighted it in a room behind the shop. . . . And then in some way . . . the fire broke out suddenly. It was caused, no doubt, by this gasoline stove. The question is, Did the loss occur while gasoline was "stored or kept in this building"? . . . What is the meaning of the words "stored or kept" in collocation and in the connection in which they are found? . . . Their Lordships think those words must have their ordinary meaning. So construing them their Lordships come to the conclusion that the small quantity of gasoline which was in the stove for the purpose of consumption was not being "stored or kept" within the meaning of the statutory condition at the time when the loss occurred.' *Thompson v Equity Fire Insurance Co* [1910] AC 592 at 595–597, PC, per cur.

'I think the contract was clearly a contract to sell "ex store" at Rotterdam, which in my view, in the absence of special circumstances, affecting the conclusion of the contract, is synonymous with "ex warehouse". The primary meaning of each expression seems to me to be a place for the storage of goods or wares.' *Fisher, Reeves & Co v Armour & Co* [1920] 3 KB 614 at 624, CA, per Eve J

New Zealand [The plaintiffs made a proposal in writing for an insurance of stock-in-trade as general storekeepers whilst contained in a building situated on Main Road, Upper Hutt, occupied as a general store. To a question whether any hazardous goods would be 'stored' the plaintiffs answered in the negative.] 'The cases relied on by the plaintiffs may be referred to. *Renshaw v Missouri Insurance Company* [23 Am SR 904] dealt with three points that are raised in this case. . . . The only part of the judgment that at first sight appears to be of importance in this case is that in which the learned judge dealt with the meaning of the word "storage". . . . He held that there was "an intended distinction between storing an article and keeping it for sale". He quoted Webster's Dictionary as to the meaning of the word "stored", saying it meant "to deposit in a storehouse or other building for preservation". This policy has to be read as a whole, and it is, in my opinion, clear that the word "stored" meant brought into the store, whether for sale or not.' *Benge & Pratt v Guardian Assurance Co Ltd* (1914) 34 NZLR 81 at 88, 89, per Stout CJ; also reported 17 GLR 245 at 247

Goods in store

'The plaintiff . . . was living in Germany, and he wished to remove his furniture to this country. . . . The furniture was in substance packed in two lift vans. The advantage of packing the furniture in lift vans is that they are not disturbed until they arrive at the ultimate destination. . . . The policy . . . insured . . . "household furniture and effects valued £1,200 packed in lift van against all risks of whatsoever nature whilst in transit from door to door" . . . and ended up . . . "and for a period of 3 months . . . after arrival whilst in store at Pall Mall Depositories, London, W 1." . . . When the second van came to be opened [after two months], it was found that there was a very large quantity of water on the floor and walls of the van and on the furniture, and it is not in dispute that damage amounting to about £200 had been caused to the furniture. . . . The underwriters' assessor ascertained that, when the goods were delivered for the purpose of storage to the Pall Mall Depository, the vans were placed in an enclosed yard. . . . I think that the goods were "in store" within the meaning of this policy while they were in the possession of the Pall Mall Depository on their premises for the purpose of storage, and that they were being stored by them. Secondly, if I am wrong about that, and if the words do refer to proper storage in a proper store, or in a place where it is proper to store them, then I have come to the conclusion, as I have said, that in vans of this description the goods were "in store", even giving those words the narrow meaning which counsel for the defendants wants me to give them, and that it is very usual with the Pall Mall Depository, and also with very many other depositories, to store vans in this way. It seems to me that the goods were well within the meaning of the policy at the time when the damage happened.' *Wulfson v Switzerland General Insurance Co Ltd* [1940] 3 All ER 221 at 222, 223, 225, per Atkinson J

STORE OR KEEP

'What is the meaning of the words "stored or kept" in collocation and in the connection in which they are found? They are common English words with no very precise or exact signification. They have a somewhat kindred meaning and cover very much the same ground. The expression as used in the statutory condition seems to point to the presence of a quantity not inconsiderable, or at any rate not trifling in amount and to import a notion of warehousing or depositing for safe custody or keeping in stock for trading purposes. It is difficult, if not impossible, to give an accurate definition of the meaning, but if one takes a concrete case it is not very difficult to say whether a particular thing is "stored or kept" within the meaning of the condition.' *Thompson v Equity Fire Insurance Co* [1910] AC 592 at 596, HL, per Lord MacNaghten

STORES

[A local Act enacted that any ship or vessel putting into the river Humber, for the purpose of obtaining 'stores' or provisions only, should be exempt from compulsory pilotage.] 'The question . . . is whether bunker coals are "stores" within the meaning of s 24 of this Act so as to bring the defendants' vessel within the exemption, and so render the employment of a pilot optional and non-compulsory. The collocation of the word "stores" in the section is as follows: "Any ship or vessel putting into the river Humber for the purpose of shelter, or of obtaining stores or provisions only". . . . In seafaring language "stores" may be ambiguous, but, on the whole, having regard to the words of the section and to the juxtaposition of the words "stores or provisions", I am of opinion that they mean some things which are not cargo, and that it gives the word "stores" a natural and reasonable construction in the section to say that it comprises bunker coal.' *The Nicolay Belozwetow* [1913] P 1 at 4, 5, per Evans P

STOREY

'The learned judge . . . held that the top-most storey of a building must necessarily mean a room enclosed by four vertical walls, and that as a consequence rooms built in the roof could not be considered as forming a storey. It seems to me, however, that the surveyors were justified in deciding that the rooms in the present case [rooms enclosed on three sides by vertical walls and on the fourth by a sloping roof] are a storey, and must be taken into account in calculating the height and necessary thickness of the party wall.' *Foot v Hodgson* (1890) 25 QBD 160 at 163, DC, per Mathew J

STORM *See* FLOOD

STRANDING

A ship is not stranded within the meaning of the memorandum [in a Lloyd's policy of marine insurance] if she merely touches on the obstructing object, whether rock, bank or of whatever other nature, without remaining fixed upon it for some space of time, but if she settles down in a quiescent state this is stranding, and the amount of damage sustained by the ship has nothing to do with the question of stranding or not stranding. There is no stranding where the ship takes the ground in the ordinary course of navigation. Where, however, the taking of the ground does not happen solely from those natural causes which are necessarily incident to the ordinary course of navigation in which the ship is engaged, but, either wholly or in part, from some accidental or extraneous cause, there is a stranding. So where, by temporary circumstances, the bottom of a harbour is in a condition different from its ordinary state, and a vessel takes the ground in a different manner from that which was intended, she is stranded within the meaning of the memorandum. (25 Halsbury's Laws (4th edn) para 277).

'It is not merely touching the ground that constitutes a stranding. If the ship touches and runs, the circumstance is not to be regarded. There she is never in a quiescent state. But if she is forced ashore, or is driven on a bank, and remains for any time upon the ground, this is a stranding, without reference to the degree of damage she thereby sustains. To remove all doubt upon the question, this clause is introduced. The stranding is a condition precedent, and when that is fulfilled the warranty against particular average ceases to have any operation.' *Harman v Vaux* (1813) 3 Camp 429 at 431, per Lord Ellenborough CJ

'It appears that the master was compellable by law to take on board a pilot, that it was in consequence of his misconduct, that the ship, being upon an element to which the insurance extends, was placed in such a situation that when the water left her she fell upon her side; and thus the damage happened. Undoubtedly this amounts to a stranding; because the ship was upon a strand.' *Carruthers v Sydebotham* (1815) 4 M & S 77 at 86, 87, per Le Blanc J

'I am of opinion that this was not a stranding. *Ex vi termini* stranding means lying on the shore, or something analogous to that. To use a vulgar phrase, which has been applied to this subject, if it is "touch and go" with the ship, there is no stranding. It cannot be enough that the ship lay for a few moments on her beam ends. Every striking must necessarily produce a retardation of the ship's motion. If by the force of the elements she is run aground, and becomes stationary, it is immaterial whether this be on piles, on the muddy bank of a river, or on rocks on the sea shore; but a mere striking will not do, wheresoever that may happen.' *M'Dougle v Royal Exchange Assurance Co* (1815) 4 Camp 283 at 284, per Lord Ellenborough CJ

[Grounding in the ordinary course of navigation is not a 'stranding'.] 'In *Carruthers v Sydebotham* [supra], the vessel was moored contrary to the usual way, out of the usual place, and against the express orders of the captain. Here, the vessel was proceeding in the ordinary way, and, if this be held a stranding, all insurance to the port of Cork (where vessels are obliged to take the ground) must cease. Before the port of Bristol was improved, every vessel which arrived there was obliged to take the ground.' *Hearne v Edmunds* (1819) 1 Brod & Bing 388 at 389, per Richardson J

'This was an insurance on a perishable commodity, and the object of the memorandum was to exempt the underwriters from loss, unless there was an adequate cause for it. If, however, the ship was stranded, they were to be liable. The case of *Carruthers v Sydebotham* [supra] is very like this. There, on the ebbing of the tide, the ship fell over and received damage, and the Court held, that it amounted to a stranding, because the ship was upon a strand. In *Hearne v Edmunds* [supra], the ship never was on the strand, within the meaning of the parties; for there, in the ordinary course of the voyage, it was quite certain that the vessel would, by the regular flux and reflux of the tide, be left on the mud. And the fair construction of the words of this memorandum, which reconciles that case with *Carruthers v Sydebotham*, must therefore be, that when, in the ordinary course of the voyage, the ship must go on the strand, the underwriter is exempt; but where it arises from an accident and out of the ordinary course, he is liable.' *Rayner v Godmond* (1821) 5 B & Ald 225 at 227, 228, per Bayley J

'I am of opinion that the ship was stranded within the meaning of this policy. . . . A ship driven into a harbour by stress of weather, on entering that harbour meets with an accident, and being moored in deep water, is in danger of sinking. For this reason she is drawn into another part of the harbour, where she immediately takes the ground, and remains fast for some time. I cannot distinguish this from the case of a ship on the high seas, in danger of being wrecked by a storm, and on that account allowed to be driven by the sails and rudder upon the beach of the main ocean.' *Barrow v Bell* (1825) 4 B & C 736 at 740, 741, per Abbott CJ

'A stranding may be said to take place where a ship takes the ground, not in the ordinary course of the navigation, but by reason of some unforeseen accident.' *Bishop v Pentland* (1827) B & C 219 at 224, per Bayley J

'Upon the question, what constitutes a stranding, there have been many decisions within the last forty years, and the difference of circumstances is so minute in many cases wherein a different conclusion has been drawn, that it is not easy to reconcile them all. This distinction, however, appears to me to be deducible, that in instances where the event happens in the ordinary course of navigation, as for instance, from the regular flux and reflux of the tide, without any external force or violence, it is not a stranding; but where it arises from an accident, and out of the common course of navigation, it is.' *Wells v Hopwood* (1832) 3 B & Ad 20 at 23, 24, per Taunton J

'Where a vessel takes the ground in the ordinary and usual course of navigation and management in a tide river or harbour, upon the ebbing of the tide, or from natural deficiency of water, so that she may float again upon the flow of tide or increase of water, such an event shall not be considered a stranding within the sense of the memorandum. But where the ground is taken under any extraordinary circumstances of time or place, by reason of some unusual or accidental occurrence, such an event shall be considered a stranding within the meaning of the memorandum. According to the construction that has been long put upon the memorandum, the words "unless general, or the ship be stranded", are to be considered as an exception out of the exception as to the amount of an average or partial loss, provided for by the memorandum, and, consequently, to leave the matter at large according to the contents of the policy; and as every average loss becomes a charge upon the underwriters where a stranding has taken place, whether the loss has been in reality occasioned by the stranding or no, the true and legal sense of the word "stranding", is a matter of great importance in policies upon goods.' Ibid at 34, 35, per Lord Tenterden CJ

'The words "if the ship be stranded" are words of condition, and that if such condition happens, it destroys the exception and lets in the general words of the policy . . . it is of very great consequence that the meaning of the word *stranding* should be distinctly understood. Now it is perfectly clear, and has been settled by various decided cases, that the term "stranding", neither of the contracting parties could intend a taking of the ground by the ship in the ordinary course of navigation used in the voyage upon which she was engaged. It is needless, therefore, to say, that when a vessel, in the course of a voyage insured, is sailing in a tide river, or puts into a tide harbour, the taking the ground from the natural cause of the deficiency of water, occasioned by the ebbing of the tide, is no stranding within the meaning of the policy. Otherwise, at every ebb of the tide, there would be a stranding; and the memorandum intended for the security of the underwriter against partial losses upon perishable commodities, would be altogether nugatory, as the smallest injury to the cargo, occasioned at an early part of the voyage, would always be a loss within the policy, by reason of the ship discharging her cargo in a tide harbour. The mere taking of the ground, therefore, in a tide harbour, in the place intended by the master and crew, or the proper officers of the harbour, cannot, upon the principle of construction or common sense, be held to constitute a stranding. What more, then, is necessary? We think a stranding cannot be better defined, than it has often been in several of the decided cases, viz where the taking of the ground does not happen solely from those natural causes which are necessarily incident to the ordinary course of the navigation in which the ship is engaged, either wholly or in part, but from some accidental or extraneous cause.' *Kingsford v Marshall* (1832) 8 Bing 458 at 463, 464, per Tindal CJ

'I am of opinion that in this case there was a *stranding* within the meaning of the memorandum to the policy. We have some excellent guides as to what is and what is not a stranding. On the one hand, Lord Tenterden (in *Wells v Hopwood* [supra]) says that "where a vessel takes the ground in the ordinary and usual course of navigation and management, in a tide-river or harbour, upon the ebbing of the tide or from natural deficiency of water, so that she may float again upon the flow of the tide or increase of water, such an event is not to be considered a stranding within the sense of the memorandum". On the other hand, Tindal CJ (in *Kingsford v Marshall* [supra]), says that "where the taking of the ground does not happen solely from those natural causes, which are necessarily incident to the ordinary course of the navigation in which the ship is engaged, either wholly or in part, *but from some accidental or extraneous cause*", then it is a stranding. Now, was not the taking of the ground in the present case occasioned by some accidental or extraneous cause? The ship was bound from Nantes to Dublin; she encounters a gale of wind, and is in great danger when off a place near Palais. She is dragging her anchor, and for the safety of the cargo and crew, and particularly to prevent her from going on shore, the captain runs her into the harbour of Sanzon, where she took the ground. If she had been run on a bank outside the harbour, it would have been a clear case of stranding; then, does it make any difference that she got within the harbour? If, indeed, she had once been in good safety in the harbour, and afterwards grounded by the fall of the tide, that would not have been a stranding; but she never was in good safety in the harbour. It was from her extraordinary peril that she went there at all; and by reason of the state of the weather she was compelled to take the ground in such a manner that she floated only eight times in a month, and then at the top of spring tides.' *Corcoran v Gurney* (1853) 20 LTOS 221 at 221, per Lord Campbell CJ

'It has been argued that there cannot be a stranding while the vessel is in the ordinary course of navigation, and the counsel for the defendant in effect contended that there can be no stranding whilst the vessel is in the ordinary track: I cannot assent to that, for it would follow that whilst she was in the ordinary track of the voyage, no taking the ground could be deemed a stranding, although it might happen from causes of a most unusual kind. It is sufficient to say that where by temporary circumstances the bottom of the harbour is in a different condition from its ordinary state, and a vessel takes the ground in a different manner from that which was intended, she may be said to be stranded.' *Letchford v Oldham* (1880) 5 QBD 538 at 546, per Brett LJ

STRANGER

'It is my opinion that the occupier of a house or land is liable for the escape of fire which is due to the negligence not only of his servants, but also of his independent contractors and of his guests, and of anyone who is there with his leave or licence. The only circumstances when the occupier is not liable for the negligence is when it is the negligence of a stranger. . . . But who is a stranger for this purpose? . . . I think a "stranger" is anyone who in lighting a fire or allowing it to escape acts contrary to anything which the occupier could anticipate that he would do. . . . Even if it is a man who you have invited or allowed into your house, nevertheless, if his conduct in lighting a fire is so alien to your invitation that he should qua the fire be regarded as a trespasser, he is a "stranger". Such as the man in Scrutton LJ's well-known illustration [in *The Carlgarth*, [1927] P 93]: "When you invite a person into your house to use the staircase you do not invite him to slide down the bannisters".' *Emanuel (H & N) Ltd v Greater London Council* [1971] 2 All ER 835 at 839, CA, per Lord Denning MR

New Zealand 'In determining who is a stranger for the purpose of the rule in *Rylands v Fletcher* . . . the essential question is whether there is a power of control over the person on the property.' *Holderness v Goslin* [1975] 2 NZLR 46 at 54, per Mahon J

STRATUM

Australia [Land belonging to the Commissioner for Railways becomes rateable when leased for private purposes, in which case the Valuer-General determines its value. Under the Valuation of Land Act (NSW) 1916–1986, s 4(1), a 'stratum' is capable of being valued.] 'A "stratum" does not include and is not intended to include for rating purposes a column of air having no connection with an existing structure be it an excavation in the ground or tunnel or a building. Thus a mere column of air intended to be filled later by a girder or concrete pillar in the construction of a building to be erected in the future is not such a stratum. A column of air going upwards *ad coelum* with an (inclined) base consisting of an imaginary line defined on a drawing board is not such a stratum. I accept that "land" in the definition means *usque ad coelum et ad inferos*—but the "part" must consist of a "space" or "layer" which in turn must be defined or definable by reference to "improvements or otherwise". A reference to the space in "room No 14" of a building could be regarded as defined or definable.' *Hurstville Super Centre Ltd v Valuer-General* [1966] 2 NSWR 106 at 113, per Wallace P

STRAY

'Section 25 [of the Highway Act 1864 (repealed; see now the Highways Act 1980, s 155)] says, "if any horse, etc, is found straying on or lying about any highway . . . the owner shall be subject to a penalty". . . . When we look at the language of this section, I think there can be no doubt that the intention of the legislature was that if cattle are found straying on the highway which would imply that they were not in the charge of some one who had control over them, that should be an offence, and then, as the words "lying about" are also in this section, omitting the qualification "without a keeper" [which qualification was contained in the corresponding provisions in Stat (1823) 4 Geo 4, c 95, s 75 (repealed) and the Highway Act 1835, s 74 (repealed)], it is clear the meaning is that if the animals do, in fact, lie about the highway, although there may be a keeper with them, that should also be an offence.' *Lawrence v King* (1868) LR 3 QB 345 at 348, DC, per Blackburn J

'It is true that the mere fact of a keeper being with the sheep is not enough to prevent the liability [under the Highway Act 1864, s 25 (repealed; see supra], for the keeper might be negligent, as we found in a case where the keeper was a boy, and was gathering nuts, or was out of the way at the time, and the sheep had been lying seven hours upon the road. But if cattle are being driven along a road and a poor cow becomes tired, and the keeper lets it rest a little, I do not think that any penalty will be incurred in such a case. The justices here seem to have thought the mere fact of the sheep being found straying for a quarter of an hour was enough to convict the appellant, without considering whether the keeper was bona fide driving them and merely stopped to take breath, and in that we think they were wrong. If the man had, under a pretence of driving the sheep, allowed them to loiter and feed on the grass, the justices might have convicted him, but there is nothing to show that the shepherd was not driving the sheep.' *Horwood v Goodall, Horwood v Hill* (1872) 36 JP 486 at 487, 488, per Blackburn J

STREAM

'Stream' includes any river, watercourse or inland water, whether the river, watercourse or inland water is natural or artificial or above or below ground, except—

(a) subject to subsection (3) of this section, any lake, loch or pond which does not discharge into a stream;
(b) any sewer vested in a water authority; and
(c) any tidal waters;

and any reference to a stream includes a

reference to the channel or bed of a stream which is for the time being dry. (Control of Pollution Act 1974, s 56)

'As regards streams of water, that . . . is a technical term. A stream of water, in law, is water which runs in a defined course, so as to be capable of diversion; and it has been held that the term does not include the percolation of water below ground.' *Taylor v St Helens Corpn* (1877) 6 Ch D 264 at 273, CA, per Jessel MR

'The only words which are used in the lease are to be found on p 39 of the printed case. What is there demised is the distillery as described, and the two ponds specially mentioned, together with "right to the water in the said ponds and in the streams leading thereto". The subjects of the lease appear to me, therefore, to be distinctly defined as being the water in the ponds, and the water in the streams leading thereto. . . . I think that the term "streams" necessarily means flowing water, and not water which oozes from a piece of marshy ground, and that unless water flows more or less in a channel, and continuously, it cannot be described as water that flows in "streams" leading to the ponds.' *M'Nab v Robertson* [1897] AC 129 at 138, per Lord Shand

'According to my apprehension, the word "stream", in its primary and natural sense, denotes a body of water having, as such body, a continuous flow in one direction. It is frequently used to signify running water at places where its flow is rapid, as distinguished from its sluggish current in other places. I see no reason to doubt that a subterraneous flow of water may in some circumstances possess the very same characteristics as a body of water running on the surface; but, in my opinion, water, whether falling from the sky or escaping from a spring, which does not flow onward with any continuity of parts, but becomes dissipated in the earth's strata, and simply percolates through or along those strata, until it issues from them at a lower level, through dislocation of the strata or otherwise, cannot with any propriety be described as a stream. And I may add that the insertion of a common rubble or other agricultural drain in these strata, whilst it tends to accelerate percolation, does not constitute a stream, as I understand that expression.' Ibid at 134, per Lord Watson

'Though it be true that the word "stream" in its more usual application does point to a definite stream within defined banks, I do not think it is confined to that meaning. We speak of a stream of tears flowing from the eyes, and we speak of blood streaming from a vein—I think we may well speak of "streams" in the plural as meaning water passing over the superfices of a plane—we may call such a flow of water a stream. I think that the root idea is water in motion from one place to another as distinguished from stagnant water.' Ibid at 143, per Lord Halsbury LC (dissenting)

STREET

At common law 'street' means a thoroughfare, which is not necessarily a highway, which has on one or both sides a more or less continuous and regular row of houses. It is a question of fact whether the houses are sufficiently regular and continuous to constitute the roadway a street. At the same time the context may show that the term is used as including the houses as well as the roadway.

Under the Highways Act 1980, 'street' includes any highway and any road, lane, footpath, square, court alley or passage, whether a thoroughfare or not, and includes any part of a street. The object of such a statutory definition is not to prevent the word carrying its ordinary common law meaning whenever that would be properly applicable, but to enable the word to be used and applied in some situations in which it would not ordinarily be applicable.

It is not a necessary constituent of a street that the public should have rights over it of a kind enjoyed over a highway. (21 Halsbury's Laws (4th edn) paras 795, 796)

The word 'street' shall extend to and include any road, square court, alley, and thoroughfare, or public passage, within the limits of the special Act. (Town Police Clauses Act 1847, s 3)

The term 'street' means a public way situate within a city, town, or village, or between lands continuously built upon on either side, and repaired at the public expense, or at the expense of any turnpike or other trust, or *ratione tenurae*, including the footpaths of such way, and any bridge forming part thereof. (Telegraph Act 1863, s 3)

In this section [which deals with the prohibition of betting in streets and public places]—

(a) the expression 'street' includes any bridge, road, lane, footway, subway, square, court, alley or passage, whether a thoroughfare or not, which is for the time being open to the public . . .; and

(b) the doorways and entrances of premises abutting upon, and any ground adjoining and open to, a street shall be treated as forming part of the street.

(Betting, Gaming and Lotteries Act 1963, s 8)

For the purposes of this section [which deals with gaming in public places]—

'Street' includes any bridge, road, lane, footway, subway, square court, alley or passage, whether a thoroughfare or not, which is for the time being open to the public, and, in the application of this section to Scotland, includes also any common close or common stair. (Gaming Act 1968, s 5(3))

'Street' includes any highway and any road, lane, footpath, square, court, alley or passage, whether a thoroughfare or not, and includes any part of a street. (Highways Act 1980, s 329(1))

'I am not about to question that which has been laid down by Lord Coke in Co Litt 4a, namely, that where a piece of land is granted or is conveyed in England by a grant from the King or by a conveyance from party to party under the word "land" everything is passed which lies below that portion of land down to what is called the centre of the earth—which is, of course, a mere fanciful phrase—and *usque ad cœlum*—which to my mind is another fanciful phrase. By the common law of England the whole of that is transferred by the grant or the conveyance under the term "land". But . . . it does not follow that in a grant or conveyance the word "street" would produce the same result. . . . If the word "street" comprises merely the area of user below the surface, what is there to show that it can include anything but the area of user above the surface? . . . The word "street" includes . . . only so much of the area which is above the surface, as is the area of the ordinary user of the street as a street.' *Wandsworth Board of Works v United Telephone Co* (1884) 13 QBD 904 at 915, 916, CA, per Brett MR

'In my opinion the word "street" when used in the ordinary sense is satisfied by the existence of houses on one side.' *Richards v Kessick* (1888) 57 LJMC 48 at 51, DC, per Wills J

'There is, no doubt, a difficulty in saying at what precise moment some country lane has become a street, as Jessel MR pointed out . . . before the Court of Appeal. He said: "There are two wasy in which a street may come into existence where there was no street before. A person may take a grass field or a country lane (for, in my opinion, it makes no difference whether or not there was a public highway and lane, or a footpath existing before which is thrown into the street and is utilised or whether there was nothing but a mere plot of grass land out of which a new roadway is made), he may take it and build continuous lines of houses so as to form what is commonly known as a street. When I say continuous lines, I do not mean that there are to be no breaks or intervals, but there must be a certain degree of continuity". Then he points out another way in which a street may arise, "that is, where it is not from the first laid out as a street in a formal manner, but may be considered to grow up, so to say, of itself. This often happens where there is an existing highway, and people build houses along the sides of that highway, so that, without any intention of laying out a street, the street grows. When does it become a street? This question cannot be answered until you know the locality". No doubt there may be great difficulty in saying in the latter case when the highway does become a street. The Master of the Rolls points out that when there are continuous lines of buildings on both sides that is one way in which the highway may become a street. But he says that a "new street" does not necessarily mean that there are houses without any break or interval, though there must be "a certain degree of continuity".' *A-G v Rufford & Co Ltd* [1899] 1 Ch 537 at 539–541, per North J

Private street

'Private street' means a street that is not a highway maintainable at the public expense. It includes any land that is deemed to be a private street by virtue of a declaration made under the Highways Act 1980. For certain purposes in relation to any building, it includes any land shown as a proposed street on plans deposited with respect to that building either under building regulations or on an application for planning permission, and any land which, if work for the erection of that building had been commenced, would have become part of an existing highway.

The fact that a part of a street is a highway maintainable at the public expense does not prevent any other part of it from being a part of a private street. (21 Halsbury's Laws (4th edn) para 797)

STREET PARKING PLACE

See PARKING PLACE

STREET TRADING

The expression 'street trading' includes the hawking of newspapers, matches, flowers and other articles, playing, singing or performing for profit, shoe-blacking and other like occupations carried on in streets or public places. (Children and Young Persons Act 1933, s 30)

'Street trading' means the selling or exposing or offering for sale of any article or thing in a street. (London County Council (General Powers) Act 1947, s 15; City of London (Various Powers) Act 1987, s 6)

'Section 13 [of the Employment of Children Act 1903 (repealed; see now the Children and Young Persons Act 1933 (supra)] defines or interprets the expression "street trading" as including "the hawking of newspapers, matches, flowers and other articles, playing, singing or performing for profit, shoe-blacking or any other like occupation carried on in the streets or public places". I quite agree that that definition of street trading is not exhaustive. Street trading may include similar instances of hawking, and doing things *ejusdem generis* with those that are mentioned in s 13; but the section appears to me to indicate that the trading which is prohibited and called 'street trading' is a real trade in the street in this sense, that it must be a trading and seeking of custom in the street.' *Stratford Co-operative Society Ltd v East Ham Corpn* [1915] 2 KB 70 at 76, DC, per Lush J

STREET WORKS

'Street works' means any works for the sewering, levelling, paving, metalling, flagging, channelling and making good of a street, and includes the provision of proper means for lighting a street. (Highways Act 1980, s 203(3))

STRENGTH *See* ADEQUATE STRENGTH

STRESS OF WEATHER

Canada 'An entry by a foreign vessel into Canadian waters cannot be justified on the ground of "stress of weather" unless the weather is such as to produce in the mind of a reasonably competent and skilful master, possessing courage and firmness, a well grounded bona fide apprehension that if he remains outside the territorial waters he will put in jeopardy his vessel and cargo.' *The Ship 'May' v R* [1931] SCR 374 at 382, SCC, per Lamont J

STRICT

Australia [A plaintiff who has been unable to find the owner or driver of the motor vehicle that injured him after 'strict inquiry and search' may sue the authorised insurer.] 'Now "strict inquiry and search" . . . means that whatever search and inquiry has been made must have been made for the purpose, and with the intention, of finding the person searched for—that is, the owner or driver of the car. . . . The act requires not merely inquiry and search but "strict" inquiry and search. This language does not mean that every conceivable step which you can think of must be taken; but it means that no reasonable step in the search or the inquiry must be omitted.' *Wox v Club Motor Insurance Agency Pty Ltd* [1954] ALR 644 at 644, per Lowe J

STRICT SETTLEMENT
See SETTLEMENT

STRIKE (Hit)

Canada 'The words [in a policy] "struck by the described automobile", if taken to mean only that there must be direct physical contact between the automobile and the person of the claimant, could make the possibility of recovery depend upon minute differences in circumstances, entirely unpredictable, such as, for example, whether the claimant had been able to interpose between himself and the automobile some article he was carrying such as a suitcase, a box of tools or unusually thick clothing. In such cases, the force of the impact is transmitted directly to the person of the injured party, regardless of the fact that he has not been "struck by" the automobile in that there is no direct physical contact between himself and it. Had this been a case of an object dislodged by the automobile or flung from the automobile striking the claimant, the matter might have presented more difficulty. Here, however, without dislodging [a] street sign, the automobile caused it to bend in such a way as to strike the claimant and injure her in such a manner as to bring about her death. Here the force of the impact was transmitted directly to the person of the claimant by an object which was and which remained for the critical period in contact with the automobile. The force was thereby transmitted directly from the automobile to the deceased. This, in my view, amounted to a striking within the meaning of the policy.' *Re Strum and Co-Operators Insurance Association* [1973] 2 OR (2d) 70 at 72, 73, per Osler J

STRIKE (Stoppage of work)

'Strike' has been defined as a concerted stoppage of work by workers done with a view to improving their wages, or conditions, or giving vent to a grievance or making a protest about something or other, or supporting or sympathising with other workers in such endeavour. A strike may involve criminal or tortious liability. A worker may lawfully strike by first giving due notice to terminate his contract. If he does not do so the strike is likely to be in breach of his contract and hence unlawful. (47 Halsbury's Laws (4th edn) para 567)

In this Schedule, unless the context otherwise requires, . . . 'strike' means the cessation of work by a body of persons employed acting in combination, or a concerted refusal or a refusal under a common understanding of any number of persons employed to continue to work for an employer in consequence of a dispute, done as a means of compelling their employer or any person or body of persons employed, or to aid other employees in compelling their employer or any person or body of persons employed, to accept or not to accept terms or conditions of or affecting employment. (Employment Protection (Consolidation) Act 1978, Sch 13, para 24(1))

'A strike is properly defined as "a simultaneous cessation of work on the part of the workmen", and its legality or illegality must depend on the means by which it is enforced, and on its object. It may be criminal, as if it be part of a combination for the purpose of injuring or molesting either masters or men; or it may be simply illegal, as if it be the result of an agreement depriving those engaged in it of their liberty of action. . . . Or it may be perfectly innocent, as if it be the result of the voluntary combination of the men for the purpose only of benefiting themselves by raising their wages, or for the purpose of compelling the fulfilment of an engagement entered into between employers and employed, or any other lawful purpose.' *Farrar v Close* (1869) LR 4 QB 602 at 612, per Hannen J

'There is no authority which gives a legal definition of the word "strike", but I conceive the word means a refusal by the whole body of workmen to work for their employers, in consequence of either a refusal by the employers of the workmen's demand for an increase, or of a refusal by the workmen to accept a diminution of wages when proposed by their employers.' *King v Parker* (1876) 34 LT 887 at 889, per Kelly CB

'In my judgment the words "strikes or stoppages" [in a charterparty containing a mutual exception against "the act of God . . . riots, strikes or stoppages'] must mean a strike against employers in that sense of the word, and not a mere neglect or refusal on the part of the men to work. When one hears of persons striking, it does not mean a refusal to work because the weather happens to be hot, but a standing out for higher wages. Now there was no evidence here that the men struck for higher wages. The evidence, on the contrary, shows that they did not want to abandon their work or get more money for it, but to escape from the neighbourhood. So far as the mutual exception clause is concerned, there is here no evidence of anything like a strike in the ordinary sense of the word. Can it be said that there is a different construction to be placed on the clause "any hands striking work which may hinder loading of vessel"? I think not. To construe these words so as to make the term "striking" include any way of abandoning work or abstaining from work would be absurd. If they cannot be construed strictly, the ordinary and everyday sense of the word "strike" must be fallen back upon, which is that of any number of hands in a given department striking against employers for the sake of higher wages.' *Stephens v Harris* (1887) 56 LJQB 516 at 517, 518, per Lord Coleridge CJ

'A strike is an agreement between persons who are working for a particular employer not to continue working for him.' *Lyons (J) & Sons v Wilkins* [1896] 1 Ch 811 at 829, CA, per Kay LJ

'A strike is a general strike if it is not what I will call a particular strike. By a particular strike I understand a strike either by an individual workman or by a particular body of workmen working for a particular master. But if there is a strike against all the masters, and if that strike is taken part in by the workmen irrespective of the masters for whom they are working, that amounts to a general strike.' *Akt Shakespeare v Ekman & Co* (1902) 18 TLR 605 at 606, CA, per Vaughan Williams LJ

'The only matter I have to consider is that meaning of the word "strike". It is true that in the older cases the definition which has been given by various learned judges as to what constitutes a strike has chiefly turned upon the question of wages. It has been said that workmen's demand for increase of wages, or refusal by workmen to accept diminution of wages, is itself a strike. I think those definitions rather show the danger, if I may be allowed to say so, of attempting to give an exhaustive definition of the word "strike", because it is obvious that since those cases were decided many circumstances have arisen which would constitute, or might be held to constitute, a strike. A strike does not depend merely upon the question of wages. At the same time I do not think it would be possible to say that abstention of a workman from mere fear to do a particular thing or perform a particular contract would necessarily constitute a strike. I think the true definition of the word "strike", which I do not say is exhaustive, is a general concerted refusal by workmen to work in consequence of an alleged grievance.' *Williams Brothers (Hull) Ltd v Naamlooze Vennootschap (W H) Berghuys Kolenhandel* (1915) 86 LJKB 334 at 335, per Sankey J

'There is very little guidance in the books as to the meaning of the word "strike". In 1915 Sankey J in *Williams Brothers (Hull) Ltd v Naamlooze Vennootschap WH Berghuys Kolenhandel* [supra] said: "I think the true definition of the word 'strike', which I do not say is exhaustive, is a general concerted refusal by workmen to work in consequence of an alleged grievance.' He took that from the Concise Oxford Dictionary; and ever since Scrutton on Charterparties [1974 edn, p 231] has quoted those words as authoritative. If I may amplify it a little, I think a strike is a concerted stoppage of work by men done with a view to improving their wages or conditions, or giving vent to a grievance or making a protest about something or other, or supporting or sympathising with other workmen in such endeavour. It is distinct from a stoppage which is brought about by an external event such as a bomb scare or by apprehension of danger.' *Tramp Shipping Corpn v Greenwich Marine Inc* [1975] 2 All ER 988 at 991, 992, CA, per Lord Denning MR

'I have come to the conclusion that participation in a strike must be judged by what the employee does and not by what he thinks or why he does it. If he stops work when his workmates come out on strike and does not say or do anything to make plain his disagreement, or which could amount to a refusal to join them, he takes part in their strike. The line between unwilling participation and not taking part may be difficult to draw, but those who stay away from work with the strikers without protest for whatever reason are to be regarded as having crossed that line to take part in a strike. In the field of industrial action those who are not openly against it are presumably for it.' *Coates v Modern Methods and Materials Ltd* [1982] 3 All ER 946 at 955, CA, per Stephenson LJ

Australia 'Apart from any statutory definition there was undoubtedly a strike in fact, because there was a concerted cessation of work on the part of a number of employees in consequence of an industrial difference between the employers and the union to which the employees belonged.' *Metropolitan Gas Co v Federated Gas Employees' Industrial Union* (1925) 35 CLR 449 at 453, per Isaac and Rich JJ

Australia 'It is noticeable that, in most of the attempts to state what amounts to a strike, prominence is given to the cessation or relinquishment of work, or at least the failure to resume work after a normal interruption or suspension. . . . The ordinary meaning of strike is confined to ceasing work—"downing tools". . . . The word "strike" may have more extensive meanings in commercial instruments, and its application may differ in the case of trades or callings in which the workmen ply for hire as luggage porters do, or work upon a succession of jobs as wharf-labourers do. But in a penal provision it ought not to receive an interpretation wide enough to include the concerted refusal of men to enter into a new employment of long duration, even although that employment is offered according to a regular customary practice by which labour is habitually obtained.' *McKernan v Fraser* (1931) 46 CLR 343 at 360, 361, per Dixon J

Canada 'Notwithstanding the able argument [of counsel] we are all of the view that the word "strike" in the context [of an agreement] need not be given the narrow interpretation assigned to it by him. The learned trial judge said [in the court below]: "It seems to me that it would be making a useless distinction, which would only make for a lot of difficulty in society, to say that a man who will work one hour a day when he has agreed to work eight is not on strike or who appears at a place of work for eight hours a day as agreed but spends the bulk of that time not doing anything—to say that he is not on strike, is to be naïve, is to fail to accept the reality of the situation. I understand that the courts were not born yesterday, and that while this form of work stoppage may be novel it is nevertheless a work stoppage or strike. I can see no valid distinction between a man, for example, who refuses to hammer a nail when it is his obligation to do so, and one who takes a day to hammer the nail when it could be hammered in ten seconds. It seems to me that both men are on strike. They are both refusing to do the work that they have agreed to do in accordance with the contract they have with their employer. With this we agree.' *Dover Corpn (Canada) Ltd v Maison Holdings Ltd* [1977] 5 WWR 190 at 191, Alta CA, per McGillivray CJA

STRUCTURAL ADDITION

'To say that a garage, if built next to and touching a building so as to form a continuation or enlargement of it, would be a structural addition [within the Settled Land Act 1925, Sch 3, Part II], but that if the garage was separated by two or three feet from the structure of the house it would not be a structural addition, appears to me to involve a construction of these words which in its consequence would be narrow and capricious. . . . It seems to me that when once the purely physical test of contiguity is abandoned, some other test, not merely a purely physical test, must be adopted. The question is what that test ought to be. The answer in my opinion is that the whole group of buildings, when completed, must be looked upon and considered, and regard must be had to their relationship to one another, their use and so forth. I am not suggesting for a moment that in that examination the question of physical farness or nearness is not a relevant consideration, it is a relevant consideration, but in my opinion it is not the only consideration.' *Re Insole's Settled Estate* [1938] Ch 812 at 816, 817, CA, per Greene MR

STRUCTURAL REPAIRS

'It appears, rather surprisingly, that the expression "structural repairs" has never been judicially defined. . . . I could myself say that "structural repairs" means repairs of, or to, a structure.' *Granada Theatres Ltd v Freehold Investment (Leytonstone) Ltd* [1958] 2 All ER 551 at 552, 553, per Vaisey J; affd [1959] 2 All ER 176, CA; also reported [1959] Ch 592 at 603

STRUCTURALLY DETACHED

[The Leasehold Reform Act 1967, s 2(2) provides that references in Part I of the Act to a house do not apply to a house which is not 'structurally detached' and of which a material part lies above or below a part of the structure not comprised in the house.] 'As a matter of ordinary English, I should regard the meaning as reasonably plain. "Structurally detached" means detached from any other structure. If it is said that this would be the meaning of "detached" alone, and that "structurally" is, on this view, superfluous, I would reply that the adjective is a natural addition because of the following reference to "the structure". The two words complement each other.' *Parsons v Gage (Viscount) (Trustees of Henry Smith's Charity)* [1974] 1 All ER 1162 at 1164, HL, per Lord Wilberforce

STRUCTURE *See also* BUILDING; INDUSTRIAL BUILDING OR STRUCTURE

'Structure' includes any works providing passage or hard standing for persons, animals, or vehicles, including railway or tramway vehicles and aircraft. (Coal-Mining (Subsidence) Act 1957, s 17(1))

In this section [which deals with the power to remove structures from highways] 'structure' includes any machine, pump, post or other object of such a nature as to be capable of causing obstruction, and a structure may be treated for the purposes of this section as having been erected or set up notwithstanding that it is on wheels. (Highways Act 1980, s 143(4))

'There is nothing to suggest here that the word "structure" is not to be used in its ordinary sense. As used in its ordinary sense I suppose it means something which is constructed in the way of being built up as is a building; it is in the nature of a building. It seems to me it is not in the nature of a building, or a structure analogous to a building, unless it is something which you can say quite fairly has been built up. I do not think that is the only guide or the only test, but, roughly, I think that must be the main guide: how has it got there? Is it something which you can fairly say has been built up? I do not think it depends at all on whether it is fixed to the ground. That may be a relevant consideration.' *South Wales Aluminium Co Ltd v Neath Assessment Committee* [1943] 2 All ER 587 at 592, per Atkinson J

'"Structure" means something which is constructed. It is not everything which is "constructed" that would ordinarily be called a building, but every building is a structure.' *Mills & Rockleys Ltd v Leicester City Council* [1946] 1 All ER 424 at 427, per Lord Goddard CJ

'A structure is something which is constructed, but not everything which is constructed is a structure. A ship, for instance, is constructed, but it is not a structure. A *structure* is something of substantial size which is built up from component parts and intended to remain permanently on a permanent foundation; but it is still a structure even though some of its parts may be movable, as, for instance, about a pivot. Thus, a windmill or a turntable is a structure. A thing which is not permanently in one place is not a *structure*, but it may be "in the nature of a structure" if it has a permanent site and has all the qualities of a structure, save that it is on occasion moved on or from its site. Thus, a floating pontoon, which is permanently in position as a landing stage beside a pier, is "in the nature of a structure", even though it moves up and down with the tide and is occasionally removed for repairs or cleaning. It has, in substance, all the qualities of a landing stage built on piles. So, also, a transporter gantry is "in the nature of a structure", even though it is moved along its site.' *Cardiff Rating Authority v Guest, Keen Baldwin's Iron and Steel Co Ltd* [1949] 1 KB 385 at 396, CA, per Denning LJ

Australia 'The word "structure" in its most natural and ordinary meaning is a building, but the word is capable of having the wider meaning of anything constructed out of material parts, and in that sense undoubtedly would include a machine and a caravan.' *R v Rose* [1965] QWN 42 at 43, per Gibbs J

New Zealand 'Can a road be called a "structure" upon land? A structure has been defined, in its most general terms, as a "construction of related parts". That would justify the description of a road unless such a meaning was inconsistent with the context. A road may fairly be described as constructed. We say, "The Romans constructed roads in Britain which are still in use". If the "structure" in the section is to be read as *ejusdem generis* with "building" it would hardly cover a road, but I do not feel bound so to hold it. I think, therefore, I am justified in holding a road to be the construction of a structure upon land.' *Black v Shaw & Official Assignee* (1913) 33 NZLR 194 at 196, per Denniston J; also reported 16 GLR 303 at 304

STRUCTURE PLAN

The structure plan for any area shall be a written statement—

(a) formulating the local planning authority's policy and general proposals in respect of the development and other use of land in that area (including measures for the improvement of the physical environment and the management of traffic);
(b) containing such other matters as may be prescribed or as the Secretary of State may in any particular case direct.

(Town and Country Planning Act 1971, s 7(1A), as substituted by the Local Government Planning and Land Act 1980))

STUDENT

New Zealand 'Mr Barton [counsel] contends that a restricted meaning is to be given to the terms "students" and "graduates". The first of these terms, he says, is limited to students who are enrolled on the books of the University pursuant to the course regulations, although they may not intend to qualify as barristers or solicitors, or those who are taking the course of study prescribed by the Law Practitioners Act. . . . While the meaning of "student" for which Mr Barton contends is recognised by the Oxford English Dictionary as being one of the meanings which that word bears, I do not think that the word should be construed in this narrow sense. I think that the word "student" may also mean a person who is engaged in study whether he be attached to an institution of learning or pursuing some degree of qualification or merely pursuing a reading of the law so long as it is with some close and continuous attention.' *Re Mason (decd)* [1971] NZLR 714 at 729, per McMullin J

STUDIO

'Studio' . . . means a building or group of buildings constructed or adapted for the purpose of making films therein and includes any land occupied with such a building or group of buildings. (Films Act 1985, Sch 1, para 1(1))

SUBJECT

New Zealand 'In my view, anyone who, for the time being, owes allegiance to the Sovereign and enjoys his protection, is fairly described as a subject of the Sovereign, so long as the duty of allegiance and the right to protection exist.' *Arnerich v R* [1942] NZLR 380 at 390, CA, per Callan J; also reported [1942] GLR 264 at 268

SUBJECT TO

[A vendor agreed to sell an estate 'subject to' agreement stating fully the conditions being prepared and signed.] 'What is the effect of the words "subject to"? They introduce a condition or proviso; the offer is conditional—"if an agreement stating fully the conditions is prepared and signed". The very mention of "conditions" suggests that the agreement is to contain something more than a mere statement of sale and purchase. The offer is conditional upon an agreement as to the conditions of sale being prepared and signed. The stipulation as to the agreement forms a term of the offer. . . . In this case the agreement is to be "prepared and signed". Accordingly, the conclusion I come to in this case is that on the documents themselves the preparation of a full agreement was a condition precedent to the conclusion of the bargain and sale.' *Watson v McAllum* (1902) 87 LT 547 at 548, per Joyce J

[By his marriage settlement a husband settled certain property on trust to pay his widow an annuity and 'subject thereto' on certain trusts.] 'What does "subject thereto" mean? As I read the settlement it means subject to the annuity of £400. If that be the true construction, it is absolutely settled . . . that these words "subject thereto" are not merely referential, but mean subject to the full and complete payment of the annuity, and that the effect of them is to make the annuity a charge on the corpus.' *Re Watkin's Settlement, Wills v Spence* [1911] 1 Ch 1 at 4, CA, per Cozens-Hardy MR

'In this case the will gives certain specific legacies and certain pecuniary legacies, and directs them to be paid free of duty, some being in terms postponed till the death of the tenant for life. Those not so postponed are immediate legacies. All the residue is given upon trust for sale. This residue means the residue of the property not specifically bequeathed. I include in the debts and legacies payable immediately after her death the legacy to the executor. The will continues, "and to invest such residuary estate", not what is left after payment of the legacies, "in investments authorised by law, and to pay the income to my sister during her life". Then to set apart such of the investment as will produce the annuities before mentioned. Here follow the words "and subject thereto". In my opinion these words make it clear that the legacies afterwards given are subject to full provision being made for the annuities. I think grammatically the words mean subject to the provision immediately preceding them, and I hold that the words "subject thereto" do not mean in this case subject to all the provisions of the will, but only subject to the provision immediately preceding them. And "subject thereto" certain charitable legacies are given. In my opinion there is no question of priority between those legacies previously given and those now given. I think they rank pari passu inter se.' *Re Colvile, Colvile v Martin* (1911) 105 LT 622 at 622, 623, per Swinfen Eady J

'There is a document which is called a "memorandum of agreement". It is a formal sort of document, bearing a stamp, and signed by the agents for the vendor and by the plaintiff, but it contains the words "subject to surveyor's report". The whole thing is subject to that; it is perfectly well understood in this business with regard to houses that, when a person says that he will buy "subject to surveyor's report", although he agrees everything else, what it means is that he will not decide whether he will take the house until he has seen what his surveyor says about it.' *Marks v Board* (1930) 46 TLT 424 at 424, per Rowlatt J

'In my view "subject to shipment" means "provided the sellers in fact ship", and that meaning must be read with the phrase "any goods not shipped to be cancelled". Reading the two phrases together, the meaning is not "subject to some shipment taking place", but is "sold subject to these goods being shipped".' *Hollis Brothers & Co Ltd v White Sea Timber Trust Ltd* [1936] 3 All ER 895 at 899, per Porter J

Australia [A testator gave the residue of his estate to trustees, after providing for a life interest, on trust to divide it amongst his children but 'subject to' certain trusts.] 'The words "but subject to" which follow the primary absolute gift are, in my opinion, apt to introduce a postponement or restriction of enjoyment without diminution of the estate conferred but not to denote a substitution or replacement.' *Dally v Dally* (1954) Tas SR 12 at 22, per cur.

Canada '[W]hen a provision in a statute is "subject to" another provision requiring something to be done, the first provision is conditional upon the performance of what is required by the provision referred to.' *Massey-Harris Co v Strasburg* [1941] 4 DLR 620 at 622, per MacDonald JA

New Zealand 'Reliance was placed on the last sentence in the declaration that the proposal was the basis of the contract—"viz the proposal is made subject to the company's conditions as printed", etc. "Subject to" must mean from that point of view "swallowed up" or "negatived by".' *Benge & Pratt v Guardian Assurance Co Ltd* (1914) 34 NZLR 81 at 86, per Stout CJ; also reported 17 GLR 245 at 247

SUBJECT TO AVERAGE *See* AVERAGE

SUBJECT TO CONTRACT

'Where you have a proposal or agreement made in writing expressed to be subject to a formal contract being prepared, it means what it says; it is subject to and is dependent upon a formal contract being prepared.' *Winn v Bull* (1877) 7 Ch D 29 at 32, per Jessel MR

[An offer by letter was expressed to be made 'subject to' the execution of a proper contract.] 'With regard to the second defence, that the offer and acceptance were subject to the execution of a "proper" contract, it is said on behalf of the defendant that that makes the whole contract subject to the execution of a formal contract. It is quite obvious that if the offer had stopped short of that stipulation there would have been all the essential terms of a good contract, but it is said that the offer was conditional, and that it could not be a concluded contract until approved by the solicitors. It seems to me that on the authorities that contention must prevail. It was not a merely supplemental stipulation and was not a mere reference to a formal contract, but the offer was made subject to it, and, therefore, there was no concluded contract until it was complied with. The present case, therefore, seems to fall within *Winn v Bull* [supra], and that class of cases, and I hold that there was no contract and the action fails.' *Bromet v Neville* (1909) 53 Sol Jo 321 at 322, per Eve J

'What is the true construction of the words "subject to contract" in the plaintiff's offer? . . . I think the offer means that it is an offer to purchase subject to the preparation and execution of a formal contract. If it is attempted to give that offer any other meaning, that meaninng must be either "subject to this offer being accepted", which is absurd, or "subject to the parties coming to terms on certain details not yet mentioned". In the latter case it would merely amount to an agreement to enter into a future agreement which would clearly confer no rights on any of the parties to it.' *Coope v Ridout* [1921] 1 Ch 291 at 297, CA, per Warrington LJ

[A purchaser of freehold land paid a deposit and signed a document in which it was expressed to be 'subject to a proper contract to be prepared by the vendor's solicitors'.] 'Is it or is it not a concluded agreement, so that the parties are bound by it, or should it be treated as merely a preliminary document, and full effect given to the words in it "subject to a proper contract being prepared by the vendor's solicitors", with the result that until a formal contract is signed the parties are not bound? . . . I think when you look at the words here used that what was intended was that the whole document should be conditional on the execution of a proper contract, to be prepared by the vendor's solicitors. I think it is not possible to hold that the words were merely the expression of a desire for a further contract. In my opinion the word "proper" must be given its full meaning, and I think that the intention of the parties was that the full conditions should be considered in a further contract, and that until that further contract was executed there should be no binding contract for the purchaser of the property.' *Chillingworth v Esche* [1924] 1 Ch 97 at 103–105, CA, per Pollock MR

'I pause here to state plainly what is now well established, that where a person accepts an offer subject to contract, it means that the matters remains in negotiation until a formal contract is settled and formal contracts are exchanged.' *Keppel v Wheeler* [1927] 1 KB 577 at 584, CA, per Bankes LJ

'The contract is stated to be contained in a document addressed by the vendor to the proposed purchaser which contains a reference to restrictive covenants affecting the property, a copy of which the plaintiff was to supply, but which he had not supplied at the date of the issue of the writ. The defendant was asked to sign at the foot of the offer the words "I accept the above offer" to which the defendant's solicitor added the words "subject to contract" before she signed it. It was conceded by counsel for the plaintiff . . . that that was a conditional acceptance, but he contended that the words must be construed as meaning "subject to the approval by the parties' solicitors of a formal contract". I cannot accept that view. I share the opinion of Lord Justice Sargant, as he then was, in *Chillingworth v Esche* [supra] that the expression "subject to contract" has by now acquired a definite ascertained legal meaning, and though there may be very exceptional cases in which the words do not bear that clear legal meaning of "subject to the execution by the parties of a formal contract" the present is not such a case. There is a statement in the vendor's offer which would have made it very unwise for the purchaser's solicitors to have allowed her to sign an unconditional acceptance.' *Wilson v Balfour* (1929) 45 TLR 625 at 625, 626, per Eve J

'The expression "subject to the terms of a lease" is in my opinion at least as strong as "subject to contract". . . . If this be so, no concluded bargain would be reached until the lease had been executed . . . even although the negotiations as to the terms to be contained in the lease had been brought to a conclusion by agreement between the solicitors of the parties.' *Raingold v Bromley* [1931] 2 Ch 307 at 316, per Lawrence LJ

'It has been well settled that the result of an offer "subject to contract", means that the matter remains in negotiation until a formal contract is executed, that is, if the contract is recorded in two parts, until the formal contracts are exchanged. . . . Taught by experience in these Courts it is every-day practice for intending purchasers of property who are making an offer to make their offer in the form of "subject to contract", with the result that they are not at that time bound and have a *locus pœnetentiae* until the formal contracts are exchanged.' *Trollope (George) & Sons v Martyn Brothers* [1934] 2 KB 436 at 455, CA, per Maugham LJ

'The agreement for sale would no doubt be "subject to contract" as understood in the law of England, which parties are agreed to mean that the matter remains in negotiation as between seller and purchaser until a formal contract is settled and the formal contracts are exchanged.' *Dudley Brothers & Co v Barnet* 1937 SC 632 at 637, per the Lord Justice-Clerk (Lord Aitchison)

'I am quite unable to construe the words "subject to the terms of a formal agreement to be prepared by their solicitors" as meaning that the "formal agreement" referred to is not one which is to be executed by the parties in the usual way. An unexecuted document would not be a formal agreement. If any doubt could remain as to the true construction of the phrase, the matter is entirely settled, in my judgment, by the words referring to the undertaking to vacate when called on if no agreement is entered into. It is manifest that the agreement there referred to is the same as the formal agreement mentioned in the earlier passage, and how a formal agreement is to be entered into unless it is executed and exchanged in the usual way I am unable to discover. The real fact of the matter is that the language used here is equivalent to the common and more concise phrase "subject to contract" and it is well settled that that phrase makes it clear that the intention of the parties is that neither of them is to be contractually bound until a contract is signed in the usual way.' *Spottiswoode, Ballantyne & Co Ltd v Doreen Appliances Ltd* [1942] 2 KB 32 at 34, 35, CA, per Lord Greene MR

'It is well settled that, where there has been a definite acceptance of an offer, the fact that the parties intend that it shall be put into a more formal shape does not relieve either party from his liability under the contract. As Lord Blackburn observed in *Rossiter v Miller* [[1878] 3 App Cas 1124]: "I think the decisions settle that it is a question of construction whether the parties finally agreed to be bound by the terms, though they were subsequently to have a formal agreement drawn up". Where, as in the present case, the agreement was oral, it is a question of finding the facts on the evidence, rather than one of construction. Such a case is entirely different from an agreement "subject to contract", where the use of that expression indicates that the parties do not intend to be immediately bound, or, to put it into Latin, that they have no present *animus contrahendi*. . . . Where parties enter into an agreement, where oral or in writing, which is expressly made "subject to contract", or to a stipulation having the like effect, they demonstrate by this stipulation that they have no immediate intention of contracting.' *Law v Jones* [1973] 2 All ER 437 at 443, 445, CA, per Buckley LJ

[The above case did not decide that a letter written 'subject to contract' or forming part of a correspondence conducted subject to a 'subject to contract' stipulation can constitute a note or memorandum of an oral agreement to which it relates sufficient to satisfy the Statute of Frauds, at any rate so long as the 'subject to contract' stipulation remains operative. What it did decide was that, if the parties subsequently enter into a new and distinct oral agreement, the facts may be such that the earlier letter may form part of a sufficient note or memorandum of the later oral agreement notwithstanding that it was 'subject to contract' in relation to the earlier bargain: see *Daulia v Four Millbank Nominees Ltd* [1978] 2 All ER 557, CA]

'The fundamental rule was stated in *Eccles v Bryant* [[1947] 2 All ER 865] and is that when people sell a house "subject to contract", the contract is not concluded until the two parts are exchanged. Those two parts must be in identical terms. If they differ in any material respect, there is no contract. The reason is plain. Each party must be able to act on the faith of the part which he receives signed by the other. He can only safely do this when they are in the same terms in all material respects.' *Harrison v Battye* [1974] 3 All ER 830 at 832, 833, CA, per Lord Denning MR

'Throughout this correspondence the solicitors and surveyors for the house-owner put into their letters the words "subject to contract". In my opinion those words have a decisive effect. They mean: "Although this figure is there and we agree it, it is not to be regarded as binding. It is only a provisional figure subject to further negotiation. It is not binding".' *Munton v Greater London Council* [1976] 2 All ER 815 at 820, CA, per Lord Denning MR

SUBORDINATE LEGISLATION

Subordinate legislation is legislation made by a person or body other than the Sovereign in Parliament by virtue of powers conferred either by statute or by legislation which is itself made under statutory powers. It is frequently referred to as delegated legislation in the former case, and sub-delegated legislation in the latter. . . .

The names given to instruments of a legislative character made in the exercise of delegated powers are various. Chief amongst them are proclamations, Orders in Council, Orders of Council, orders, regulations, rules, schemes, directions, byelaws and warrants. (44 Halsbury's Laws (4th edn) paras 981, 982)

SUBROGATION

Where one person has a claim against another, in certain circumstances a third person is allowed to have the benefit of the claim and the remedy for enforcing it, even though it has not been assigned to him, and he is then said to be subrogated to the rights of the first person. (16 Halsbury's Laws (4th edn) para 1438)

Where the insurer pays for a total loss, either of the whole, or in the case of goods of any apportionable part, of the subject matter insured, he thereupon becomes entitled to take over the interest of the assured in whatever may remain of the subject matter so paid for, and he is thereby subrogated to all the rights and remedies of the assured in and in respect of that subject matter as from the time of the casualty causing the loss. Subject to these provisions, where the insurer pays for a partial loss, he acquires no title to the subject matter insured, or such part of it as may remain, but he is thereupon subrogated to all rights and remedies of the assured in and in respect of the subject matter insured as from the time of the casualty causing the loss, insofar as the assured has been indemnified by that payment for the loss. (25 Halsbury's Laws (4th edn) para 330)

'In order to apply the doctrine of subrogation, it seems to me that the full and absolute meaning of the word must be used, that is to say, the insurer must be placed in the position of the assured. Now it seems to me that in order to carry out the fundamental rule of insurance law, this doctrine of subrogation must be carried to the extent which I am now about to endeavour to express, namely, that as between the underwriter and the assured the underwriter is entitled to the advantage of every right of the assured, whether such right consists in contract, fulfilled or unfulfilled, or in remedy for tort capable of being insisted on or already insisted on, or in any other right, whether by way of condition or otherwise, legal or equitable, which can be, or has been exercised or has accrued, and whether such right could or could not be enforced by the insurer in the name of the assured by the exercise or acquiring of which right or condition the loss against which the assured is insured, can be, or has been diminished. That seems to me to put this doctrine of subrogation in the largest possible form, and if in that form, large as it is, it is short of fulfilling that which is the fundamental condition, I must have omitted to state something which ought to have been stated. But it will be observed that I use the words "of every right of the assured".' *Castellain v Preston* (1883) 11 QBD 380 at 385–388, CA, per Brett LJ

'What is the basis of the doctrine of subrogation? It is simply that, where A's money is used to pay off the claim of B, who is a secured creditor, A is entitled to be regarded in equity as having had an assignment to him of B's rights as a secured creditor. There are other cases of subrogation where B is not secured, but the ordinary and typical example is as I have stated. It finds one of its chief uses in the situation where one person advances money on the understanding that he is to have certain security for the money he has advanced, and, for one reason or another, he does not receive the promised security. In such a case he is nevertheless to be subrogated to the rights of any other person who at the relevant time had any security over the same property and whose debts have been discharged, in whole or in part, by the money so provided by him, but of course only to the extent to which his money has, in fact, discharged their claims.' *Burston Finance Ltd v Speirway Ltd* [1974] 3 All ER 735 at 738, per Walton J

'The doctrine of subrogation does not . . . rest on contract at all. It is an equitable doctrine. . . . If a person, whom I shall call the lender (although he might for example be a guarantor or fill some other role) makes a payment to another person, whom I will call the creditor, which diminishes the liability of a third person, whom I will call the borrower, or if the lender advances money to the borrower which, in accordance with the common intention of the lender and the borrower, is used by the borrower to make a payment to the creditor in discharge of a liability of his, the borrower's, to the creditor, equity will, subject to any contrary arrangement between the lender and the borrower, allow the lender to stand in the creditor's place against the borrower in respect of that part of the borrower's liability to the creditor. The lender is not in law, or I think in equity, an assignee of the creditor's rights, but is treated in equity as if he were so to the extent necessary to enable the lender to exercise those remedies against the borrower which the creditor could have exercised but for the payment to him, and subject to all equities and set-offs which the borrower might have against the lender.' *Orakpo v Manson Investments Ltd* [1977] 1 All ER 666 at 676, CA, per Buckley LJ. [On appeal, see infra.]

'There is no general doctrine of unjust enrichment recognised in English law. What it does is to provide specific remedies in particular cases of what might be classified as unjust enrichment in a legal system that is based on the civil law. There are some circumstances in which the remedy takes the form of "subrogation", but this expression embraces more than a single concept in English law. It is a convenient way of describing a transfer of rights from one person to another, without assignment or assent of the person from whom the rights are transferred and which takes place by operation of law in a whole variety of widely different circumstances.' *Orakpo v Manson Investments Ltd* [1977] 3 All ER 1 at 7, HL, per Lord Diplock

SUBSCRIBE

In Companies Acts

'The general Act [Companies Clauses Consolidation Act 1845] enables the company to recover, by a more concise form of declaration, the amount due for calls from all persons who are shareholders; and, by the 8th section, "Every person who shall have subscribed the prescribed sum, or upwards, to the capital of the company, or shall otherwise become entitled to a share in the company, and whose name shall have been entered on the register of shareholders thereinafter mentioned, shall be deemed a shareholder of the company". The words "every person who shall have subscribed" mean every person who shall have "contracted to subscribe".' *Newry & Enniskillen Rly Co v Coombe* (1849) 3 Exch 565 at 574, per Parke B

'The difficulty arises from the ambiguous meaning of the word "subscribe", which means, in some phrases the consent to pay a sum of money; in others, the assent to some particular thing, such as an article of faith. This statute [Companies Clauses Consolidation Act 1845, s 8] uses the word "subscribe" in its literal sense, viz putting down a person's name for some interest in the capital of the company.' *Waterford, Wexford, Wicklow & Dublin Rly Co v Pidcock* (1853) 8 Exch 279 at 286, per Pollock CB

'When a man is said to "subscribe" for capital in a company, and there is nothing in the document to qualify the expression, the expression imports that he undertakes to pay his subscription in cash.' *Newburgh & North Fife Rly Co v North British Rly Co* 1913 SC 1166 at 1186, per Lord Johnston

United States 'Subscriber' means a person who subscribes for shares in a corporation, whether before or after incorporation. (Revised Model Business Corporation Act 1984, s 1.40(24))

In Wills Act

'Nothing more is required [by the Statute of Frauds 1677, s 5 (repealed; see now the Wills Act 1837, s 9, as substituted by the Administration of Justice Act 1982, s 17)] than that the will should be attested by the witnesses; i.e. that they should be present as witnesses and see it signed by the testator, and that it should be subscribed by the witnesses in the presence of the testator; i.e. that they should subscribe their names upon the will in his presence. . . . It is powerfully urged that the primary meaning of the word "subscribed" is written under; that it must here mean written under the concluding words of the will, and the signature of the testator; that this meaning is emphatically to be given to the word "subscribed" in this section of the Statute of Frauds, from the words which require only signing by the testator; and that the signature of the names of the witnesses ought to be so affixed to the instrument as effectually to prevent any spurious addition to it after it has been executed. . . . If the legislature in its wisdom should think that the signatures of the witnesses should be put upon the same footing with the signature of the testator, they ought to use express language to indicate this intention. The mere requisition that the will shall be subscribed by the witnesses, we think, is complied with, by the witnesses who saw it executed by the testator immediately signing their names on any part of it at his request, with the intention of attesting it.' *Roberts v Phillips* (1855) 4 E & B 450 at 453, 455, 459, per Lord Campbell CJ

[Although the primary meaning of 'subscribed' is 'written under' it is no longer necessary (as it was under the original s 9) for a will to be signed 'at the foot or end thereof'.]

Australia 'The Wills Act does not require the witnesses' signature to appear at any particular place on the will, the word "subscribe" having been held not to indicate that the witnesses have to sign underneath either the testator's signature or the end of the will. Wills have been admitted to probate in which the attestation has been far removed from the testator's signature.' *Re McNamara* [1944] VLR 17 at 20, per O'Bryan J

SUBSIDENCE

'The perils insured against are two: "subsidence and/or collapse", and I have to construe the meaning of those words. "Subsidence" means sinking, that is to say, movement in a vertical direction as opposed to "settlement", which means movement in a lateral direction, but I am of opinion that the word "subsidence" in this policy covers both subsidence in the sense in which I have defined it, and also settlement.' *Allen (David) & Sons Billposting Ltd v Drysdale* [1939] 4 All ER 113 at 114, per Lewis J

SUBSIDENCE DAMAGE

This Act shall apply in relation to any subsidence damage occurring after the passing of this Act; and in this Act the expression 'subsidence damage' means any damage (including an alteration of the level or gradient of property not otherwise damaged such as to affect the fitness of that property for use for the purposes mentioned in the next following subsection [purposes for which, at the date immediately before the damage occurred, the property was or might in all the circumstances reasonably have been expected to be, used])—

(a) to a building or structure or to any of the following works, that is to say, any sewer or drain situated in a building or structure which it serves and any pipes, wire or other fixed apparatus installed in a building or structure for the purpose of providing gas, electricity, water, heating or telephone services for use in that building or structure, and any fixed apparatus (other than pipes or wires) installed outside, but within the curtilage of a building or structure for the purposes of supplying any such service as aforesaid to that building or structure for use therein; or
(b) to works of the following descriptions, that is to say, sewers, drains, and any pipes or wires for the supply of gas, electricity, water, heating, telephone or other comparable services, being either works situated outside any building or structure or works in the nature of mains situated in a building or structure in which they neither begin nor end; or

(c) to any land, not being damage to that land only as the site of an existing building or structure or of existing works such as are mentioned in the two foregoing paragraphs and being damage such as to affect the fitness of that land for use for the purposes mentioned in the next following subsection,

caused by the withdrawal of support from land in connection with the lawful working and getting of coal, or of coal and other minerals worked therewith or the lawful getting of any product from coal in the course of working it, not being—

(i) damage caused in connection with the working and getting of coal and other minerals where the working and getting of the coal was ancillary to the working of those other minerals; or

(ii) damage caused in connection with the working and getting of coal or of coal and other minerals by virtue of the grant of a gale in the Forest of Dean or any other part of the Hundred of St Briavels in the county of Gloucester.

(Coal-Mining (Subsidence) Act 1957, s 1(1))

SUBSIDIARY *See* COMPANY

SUBSTANCE

'Substance' means any natural or artificial substance, whether in solid or liquid form or in the form of a gas or vapour. (Electricity (Amendment) Act 1961, s 1; Health and Safety at Work etc Act 1974, s 53(1))

'Substance' includes a liquid. (Food Act 1984, s 132(1))

'There has been in the past some suggestion that, when an order is made under RSC Ord 38, r 38(1), that the *substance* of the experts' reports be exchanged, then that order is satisfied by the experts merely setting out factual descriptions of the machine and the alleged circumstances in which the accident happened and leaving out any conclusions as to the defects in the machine, the system of work or other relevant opinion evidence. This seems to me to be a total misconception of the ordinary meaning of the word "substance". It is also a misconception of the function of an expert. An expert, unlike other witnesses, is allowed, because of his special qualifications and/or experience, to give *opinion* evidence. It is for his opinion evidence that he is called, not for a factual description of the machine or the circumstances of the accident, although that is often necessary in order to explain and/or justify his conclusions. When the substance of the expert's report is to be provided, that means precisely what it says, both the substance of the factual description of the machine and/or the circumstances of the accident and his expert opinion in relation to that accident, which is the very justification for calling him.' *Ollet v Bristol Aerojet Ltd* [1979] 3 All ER 544 at 544, per Ackner J

'The word "substance" has a wider meaning than "product". Any kind of matter comes within "substance" whereas "product" envisages the result of some kind of process.' *R v Greensmith* [1983] 3 All ER 444 at 447, per cur.

Australia 'The words "in substance" indicate that in making the necessary comparison form should be disregarded.' *Victorian Chamber of Manufacturers v Commonwealth* (1943) 67 CLR 347 at 377, per Rich J

Of action

New Zealand 'The word "substance" is a philosophical term with a long history, and according to philosophical terminology it means "that which requires for its existence the existence of nothing else". It is the "substrate", the "essence", the "thing in itself". It has to be thought of or inferred apart from its accidents. Viewed in this way "the substance of the action" is the essence of what the plaintiff claims. It is not the "cause" of action, or a statement of the reasons why the claim is well founded or should succeed. The "substance" a plaintiff claims in the ordinary jurisdiction of a magistrate's court is "money", "land", or "chattels". Under the old procedure of the Supreme Court actions were classified according to the relief claimed: that was, the substance of the action—that about which there was a controversy—was money, land, or specific relief. . . . The "substance of the action" is the substance of the claim; for an action, as is said in Coke upon Littleton [285a], is nothing save the lawful claim of one's right—"*Action n'est autre chose que loyal demande de son droit*".' *Hills v Stanford* (1904) 23 NZLR 1061 at 1065, 1066, CA, per Stout CJ

SUBSTANTIAL

'This case under the Rent Restriction Acts [repealed; cf now the Rent Act 1977, s 7] turns on the question whether the dwelling-house was bona fide let at a rent which included payments in respect of the use of furniture, and whether the amount of rent fairly attributable to the furniture, regard being had to the value of the same to the tenant, formed a substantial portion of the whole rent. . . . The fact that the appellant had brought a lot of very valuable furniture into a cottage of that type would not take from the landlord's portion its attribute of "substantial" if in itself that portion was substantial; the Act does not require the landlord's furniture to be a substantial proportion in either value or weight, relatively to the whole, but only that his position should be positively or absolutely in itself substantial. This meaning is corroborated by the history of the provision which was introduced into the legislation to modify the earlier law, judicially ascertained, to the effect that any quantity of furniture, however small, in itself, would satisfy the law as it was previously, unless the quantity was so negligible as to be ignored under the maxim *de minimis non curat lex*.' *Maclay v Dixon* [1944] 1 All ER 22 at 22, 24, CA, per cur.

'What does "substantial portion" mean? It is plain that the phrase requires a comparison with the *whole rent*, and the whole rent means the entire contractual rent payable by the tenant in return for the occupation of the premises together with all the other covenants of the landlord. "Substantial" in this connection is not the same as "not unsubstantial", i.e. just enough to avoid the "*de minimis*" principle. One of the primary meanings of the word is equivalent to considerable, solid, or big. It is in this sense that we speak of a substantial fortune, a substantial meal, a substantial man, a substantial argument or ground of defence. Applying the word in this sense, it must be left to the discretion of the judge of fact to decide as best he can according to the circumstances in each case, the onus being on the landlord.' *Palser v Grinling, Property Holding Co Ltd v Mischeff* [1948] AC 291 at 316, 317, per Viscount Simon

[The correct approach in deciding if there is infringement of copyright in a literary compilation is first to determine whether the work as a whole is entitled to copyright, and, second, to enquire whether the part reproduced by the defendant is a 'substantial' part of the whole.] 'Did the appellants reproduce a substantial part of it? Whether a part is substantial must be decided by its quality rather than its quantity. The reproduction of a part which by itself has no originality will not normally be a substantial part of the copyright and therefore will not be protected. For that which would not attract copyright except by reason of its collocation will, when robbed of that collocation, not be a substantial part of the copyright and therefore the courts will not hold its reproduction to be an infringement. It is this, I think, which is meant by one or two judicial observations that "there is no copyright" in some unoriginal part of a whole that is copyright. They afford no justification, in my view, for holding that one starts the inquiry as to whether copyright exists by dissecting the compilation into component parts instead of starting it by regarding the compilation as a whole and seeing whether the whole has copyright.' *Ladbroke (Football) Ltd v William Hill (Football) Ltd* [1964] 1 All ER 465 at 481, HL, per Lord Pearce

Australia 'What is meant by "a substantial part" and "*the* remaining part" of the premises? "Substantial" is not a word with a fixed meaning in all contexts. In certain associations it can be taken to stress the quality of solidarity or strength. It may be related to the appearance of some physical object. With other concepts it may refer to weight, volume, or area. Again it may be used to indicate worth, or stability. Used in a *comparative* setting, "a substantial part" as against "the remaining part", it suggests a dichotomy into the substantial part, and the not-substantial, a contrast, according to cubic contents, or area, between the greater and the less, as between the essential and the subordinate or incidental. In his satiric view of the modern use of language entitled *What a Word*, A P Herbert treats "substantial" in a quantitative sense, as the modern colloquial equivalent of "much" or even "some". It is an unsatisfactory medium for carrying the idea of some ascertainable proportion of the whole.' *Terry's Motors Ltd v Rinder* [1948] SASR 167 at 180, per Mayo J

Australia 'The word "substantial" is not only susceptible of ambiguity: it is a word calculated to conceal a lack of precision. In the phrase "substantial loss or damage", it can, in an appropriate context, mean real or of substance as distinct from ephemeral or nominal. It can also mean large, weighty or big. It can be used in a relative sense or can indicate an absolute significance, quantity or size. The difficulties and uncertainties which the use of the word is liable to cause are well illustrated by the guidance given by Viscount Simon in *Palser v Grinling* [supra] where, after holding that, in the context there under consideration, the meaning of the word was equivalent to "considerable, solid or big", he said: "Applying the word in this sense, it must be left to the discretion of the judge of fact to decide as best he can according to the circumstances of each case." . . . In the context of s 45D(1) of the [Trade Practices] Act 1974–1986 (Cth), the word "substantial" is used in a relative sense in that, regardless of whether it means large or weighty on the one hand or real or of substance as distinct from ephemeral or nominal in the other, it would be necessary to know something of the nature and scope of the relevant business before one could say that particular, actual or potential loss or damage was substantial. As at present advised, I incline to the view that the phrase, substantial loss or damage, in s 45(D)(1) includes loss or damage that is, in the circumstances, real or of substance and not insubstantial or nominal.' *Tillmanns Butcheries Pty Ltd v Australasian Meat Industry Employees Union* (1979) 42 FLR 331 at 348, per Deane J

Australia [The Town and Country Planning Act 1961–1986 (Vict), s 18B(1), provides the responsible authority with power to refuse to grant a permit to use or develop land where the grant of a permit may cause a 'substantial' detriment to any person other than the applicant.] 'I think the word "substantial" must be given its natural meaning, and I think the term must be taken to mean detriment of a real and not trivial or imaginary kind. I also think that the detriment must be a real detriment in the sense that it cannot mean a detriment purely subjective to the mind of a particular person. It must be a detriment in an objective and reasonable sense. Again, it must be borne in mind that the question for me to determine is not whether I would be of the opinion that substantial detriment might have been caused by the grant of the permit, but whether the Council with its intimate knowledge of the area could reasonably form the view that no such detriment would be caused.' *A-G ex rel Whitten v Shire of Gisborne* (1983) 45 LGRA 1 at 9, per Murray J

Australia 'In my view when considered in the context of a definition that talks of a person who is "wholly or substantially dependent on" another, the term "substantially" connotes "in the main", or "essentially".' *Re Bonny* [1986] 2 Qld R 80 at 82, per Ambrose J

New Zealand 'I agree with the President in this Court that the question whether the alterations in this case are "substantial" must be decided on a broad common sense review of all the circumstances, including, of course, as a primary matter a comparison of the extent and cost of the alterations with the extent and value of the premises to be altered . . . While I agree with the President that the decision is one for the Council, nevertheless I am also in agreement with him that it seems difficult, at this distance from the scene, to find a basis upon which it could bona fide be determined that, having regard to such circumstances as have been canvassed before us, the alterations, when considered as alterations to the whole of the premises, could fairly be regarded as "substantial". If the alterations to premises are "substantial" it seems to me that it must follow that those premises must be seen to be substantially altered.' *Ashburton Borough v Clifford* [1969] NZLR 927 at 941, per Turner J

'The word "substantial" in this connection means, in my view, considerable, solid or big and not merely not unsubstantial. A similar meaning was adopted in *Palser v Grinling* [[1948] AC 291]. It is a term which necessarily invokes a comparison, for what would be substantial in one building would not necessarily be substantial in another.' Ibid at 944, per McCarthy J

SUBSTITUTE

In substitution for

New Zealand [The Acts Interpretation Act 1924, s 21(1), provides that: 'In every unrepealed Act in which reference is made to any repealed Act such reference shall be construed as referring to any subsequent enactment passed in substitution for such repealed Act, unless it is otherwise manifested by the context'.] 'To be "in substititution for" means to be put in the place or stand in the stead of the repealed provision. It follows that the new enactment must be of the same character as its predecessor: it must have the same kind of function and the subject-matter must be essentially the same without necessarily being identical in its scope. But, provided the new provision is directed to the same end, there need not be precise correspondence in the manner of dealing with the subject-matter. . . . The process of evaluation and comparison of the two provisions will ultimately lead to a judgment as to whether, in the particular case, the later provision is in substitution for the repealed section, or amounts to a new and different provision.' *Re Eskay Metalware Ltd* (in liquidation) [1978] 2 NZLR 46 at 49, CA, per Richardson J

SUCCEED

Australia [Articles of partnership provided, inter alia, that if either partner should die during the continuance of the partnership, the other partner should 'succeed' to his or her interest in the capital and assets of the partnership.] 'The expression "to succeed to" in reference to property or rights or interests in property is common and imports the act of becoming entitled to the possession and enjoyment of some legal estate or privilege, e.g. "on the death of his father his son succeeded to his father's estate.' *Re Bubnich, Marian v Bubnich* [1965] WAR 138 at 140, per Wolff CJ

SUCCESSOR *See also* HEIR

[A testator by his will gave legacies to certain named persons holding offices in a charitable association, or their 'successors'.] 'Are the gifts to the several individuals named, "or their successors", . . . legacies given to the individuals for their own benefit, or are they given to the holders of offices for the benefit of the associations in which they hold office? . . . The primary meaning of the word "successors" is persons in succession. The persons named were known to the testator to be holders of offices in the association, and the only succession to which he can refer is the succession to those offices. The persons named are not intended to take any personal benefit, but are designated only as the then holders of office, and the gift to them depended on their continuance in such office.' *Re Delany, Conoley v Quick* [1902] 2 Ch 642 at 645, 646, per Farwell J

SUCH

[A testator by his will gave a power to any of his daughters who should leave issue to appoint her share to 'such' child or children, in such manner or form as she should choose.] 'I do not think that the words "such child or children" refer to such issue as the daughter might leave at her death, but to the persons to be selected by her: she was to appoint to such children as she should choose. If the will had stopped at the words "unto such child or children" the case would have resembled *Goldie v Greaves* [(1844) 14 Sim 348], but it proceeds "in such manner and form as she or they should choose". It is clear, that the words "such" and "manner" refer to the choice and selection of the children.' *Harley v Mitford* (1855) 21 Beav 280 at 282, 283, per Romilly MR

'Under the will of Charles Davids a sum of £3,000, three and a half per cent reduced bank annuities, was given upon trust for testator's daughter Rachael Catharine, for life, and after her death to and among such of testator's children as should be then living, in such shares and proportions as the said Rachael Catharine should by will appoint, and in default of appointment equally. One question which was raised was, whether this was an exclusive or only a distributive power; and I am of opinion that there was clearly no power to exclude any of the objects, and that the donee of the power was bound to appoint in favour of all the children who might be living at her death.' *Re Davids' Trusts* (1859) John 495 at 497, 498, per Page Wood V-C

'What is meant by the words "in such manner amongst such issue as my said granddaughter shall by deed or will appoint"? . . . To what is the word "such" to be attributed as its antecedent?—or is it an antecedent itself to a subsequent word? It is often used, not only popularly and inaccurately but legally and in Acts of Parliament, in this sense. Having described particular persons or things, a passage follows speaking of such persons and such things, meaning "as aforesaid", referring to what has gone before; but it is often used generally. It is inappropriate to leave out the words "as aforesaid", thus "among such children" which would mean "the said children", or "as aforesaid". On the other hand, it is often used thus: "such children as so and so shall appoint", and then it refers to what follows, namely, "as" which is always expressed or implied. . . . Beyond all doubt the word "such" is used in the sense of the "aforesaid children", "such issue" or, what is the same thing, "such issue" as before described, as the granddaughter shall leave.' *Stolworthy v Sancroft* (1864) 33 LJ Ch 708 at 710, 711, per Kindersley V-C

Australia '"Such" refers generally and naturally to its last antecedent.' *Re Ninnes* [1920] SALR 480 at 488, per Poole J

Australia 'The word "such" is a word which must have relation to something else.' *Re Godfrey* [1921] SASR 148 at 152, per Poole J

SUDDEN

Australia 'Its primary meaning no less in the Shorter Oxford Dictionary than in the American dictionaries referred to in *Middleton Lumber Co Case* (1959) 333 Par R (2nd) 938 is in summary "unforeseen and unexpected".' *Sun Alliance & London Insurance Group v NW Iron Co Ltd* [1974] 2 NSWLR 625 at 630, per Sheppard J

SUE AND LABOUR

'I think that general average and salvage do not come within either the words or the object of the suing and labouring clause, and that there is no authority for saying that they do. The words of the clause are that in case of any misfortune it shall be lawful "for the assured, their factors, servants, and assigns, to sue, labour, and travel for, in, and about the defence, safeguard, and recovery of" the subject of insurance, "without prejudice to this insurance, to the charges whereof we the insurers will contribute". And the object of this is to encourage and induce the assured to exert themselves, and therefore the insurers bind themselves to pay in proportion any expenses incurred, whenever such expense is reasonably incurred for the preservation of the thing from loss, in consequence of the efforts of the assured or their agents. It is all one whether the labour is by the assured or their agents themselves, or by persons whom they have hired for the purpose, but the object was to encourage exertion on the part of the assured; not to provide an additional remedy for the recovery, by the assured, of indemnity for a loss which was, by the maritime law, a consequence of the peril.' *Aitchison v Lohre* (1879) 4 App Cas 755 at 764, 765, per Lord Blackburn

SUFFER

'I think it would be almost an absurd distinction to suppose that there is any difference between the words "suffer" and "permit". According to the dictionaries, "suffer" means "permit" and "permit" means "suffer". It would really be straining the meaning of the words to say that there is any substantial difference between "suffer" and "permit". *Ex p Eyston, Re Throckmorton* (1877) 7 Ch D 145 at 149, per James LJ

'Arthur Moore, by his will, after making certain previous dispositions . . . devises all his estate . . . on trust for his sons . . . who were to receive the rents and profits thereof for their lives, or until, amongst other things, they should "become bankrupt, or assign, convey, charge or incumber their respective shares of the same, or any part thereof or do or suffer something whereby the same, or some part thereof, would, by operation of law or otherwise, if belonging absolutely to them, become vested in, or payable to, some other person or persons". . . . The question . . . raised depends upon another, namely, whether a person by allowing a judgment to be obtained against him, and the judgment creditor registering the judgment as a mortgage is "suffering something" within the terms of the will. . . . I am of opinion that the words "suffer something" are intended to meet the very state of facts which have occurred. . . . In my opinion, "suffer" is used in contradistinction to "do", "suffer" is passive; "do" is active. I am unable to follow the argument that "suffer" is here used in an active, and not in a passive sense, and all the authorities are against this construction. . . . The word "suffer" includes an act done *in invitum*, as, in this case, the regisration of a judgment mortgage.' *Re Moore's Estate* (1885) LR 17 Ir 549 at 550, 551, per Flanagan J

'I agree that "suffered" [where persons are accused of having caused or "suffered" sewage to pass into a river within the meaning of a local Act] reasonably imports some act of omission on the part of the person "suffering". It does not mean that a person is entirely passive.' *Southall Norwood Urban District Council v Middlesex County Council* (1901) 83 LT 742 at 745, 746, DC, per Phillimore J

[A lease of licensed premises contained a covenant that the lessee would use the premises as a public-house or beerhouse only and would carry on or 'suffer' on the said premises no other trade, business or manufacture during the term and particularly would not suffer to be done on the premises any act whereby the licence might be forfeited without the previous consent in writing of the lessor.] 'The defendant, who was assignee of the lease, sub-let the premises to another person, during whose term an offence was committed against the licensing laws, by reason of which the renewal of the licence was subsequently refused. The plaintiff alleged that by reason of what had occurred there had been a breach of the covenant by the defendant. Kennedy J decided that, having regarded to the terms of the covenant, and the circumstances under which the act treated as a breach occurred, no breach of the covenant was proved. . . . Here the defendant cannot be said to have done, or suffered to be done, the act relied on as a breach of the covenant, because the relation of sub-lessor and sub-lessee does not involve any connection between them in the nature of that between principal and agent. . . . I should say that, prima facie, the meaning of the words "do or suffer to be done" is that they must involve the doing of some act, or some abstention from action by the covenantor himself, or by some person standing in the relation of agent to him, a relation which does not exist as between lessor and lessee.' *Wilson v Twamley* [1904] 2 KB 99 at 103, 105, CA, per Collins MR

'A man who suffers a thing to happen does not necessarily permit it, as he may not have the physical power or the right to stop it; but if he has that power or right, and does not stop it, he suffers the thing to happen.' *Rochford Rural Council v Port of London Authority* [1914] 2 KB 916 at 922–924, DC, per Darling J

[A testatrix by her will directed that, if either of two beneficiaries should alienate or charge their respective annuities or become bankrupt or do or 'suffer' any act or thing whereby the said annuities or any part thereof would or might but for that provision become vested in or payable to any other person or persons, such annuities should cease to be payable.] 'The word "suffer" is capable of more meanings than one. I have come to the conclusion that it is proper to attribute to the word in this clause the meaning "permit".' *Re Hall, Public Trustee v Montgomery* [1944] Ch 46 at 48, per Uthwatt J

Australia 'The meaning of the verb "suffer" is peculiarly susceptible to its context. It may have an active or a passive signification; and it may be used transitively or intransitively . . .; it may range from "permit" down to "fail to prevent, being lawfully entitled and able to prevent". . . . I think it may also mean simply "sustain" or "undergo": *Roffey v Bent* [(1867) LR 3 Eq 759]. That is what was meant by s 3 of the Crimes Act 1958 [Vic] when it used to provide that "whosoever is convicted of murder shall suffer death as a felon". In a context where "suffer" means "permit" it will usually involve some element of volition: *Brown v Julius, ex parte Julius* [1959] Qd R 385 provides an example. In a context where it means "sustain" it may apply to something done in invitum: *Roffey v Bent*, supra; and one may "suffer" the forfeiture of a right or "suffer" an imposition in an appropriate case whether one has knowledge of the circumstances or not, and whether or not one is able to prevent it.' *Hawkins v Probate Duties Comr* [1981] VR 938 at 947, 948 per Tadgell J

New Zealand 'Penalties are imposed on the licensee who "suffers" certain things to be done on the premises, such as gaming; and Cockburn CJ, in *Bosley v Davies* [(1875) 1 QBD 84], says, as to the word "suffer", "A man may be said to 'suffer' a thing to be done if it is done through his negligence". Matthew J in *Somerset v Wade* [[1894] 1 QB 574, DC], says, "'Suffering' is not to my mind distinguishable from 'permitting'. He does not permit drunkenness if he does not know of its existence, or connive at it, or wilfully shut his eyes to it." It does not appear that Matthew J would extend the word "suffer" to cases of honest negligence or want of vigilance. I incline to think, from the expressions he does use, that he would not so extend the meaning of the word "suffer" or "permit".' *Jull v Treanor* (1896) 14 NZLR 513 at 517, per Prendergast CJ

New Zealand [The words 'did cause or permit or suffer' a dog to go at large in a public place occurred in a by-law.] 'It has been pointed out that the word "suffer" may have different meanings (see, for example, *Re Hall* [[1943] 2 All ER 753], and it is sufficient, I think, in the present case to say that, in my view, when both "permit" and "suffer" appear together in a by-law the natural inference is that they do not have the same meaning. It seems to me that, in this context, "suffer" is less positive than "permit" and that it includes taking no action to prevent the wandering of a dog known to be a wanderer. In *Bosley v Davies* [[1875 1 QBD 84], Cockburn CJ said: "A man may be said to 'suffer' a thing to be done, if it is done through his negligence".' *Beaumont v St Kilda Borough* [1975] 2 NZLR 369, per White J

SUFFERANCE *See* DEFAULT

SUFFICIENT

[The Administration of Estates Act 1925, s 36(7), renders an assent or conveyance by a personal representative of a legal estate 'sufficient evidence' that the person in whose favour the assent or conveyance is made is the person entitled to that estate.] 'It is a truism that the word "sufficient" is not the same word as and has not the same meaning as "conclusive". But before the Administration of Estates Act 1925, the words "sufficient evidence" had found a place in Acts of Parliament and from time to time Parliament has enacted that the certificate of some person shall be sufficient evidence of some fact. . . . The fact is that the proper interpretation of the words depends upon the context in which they are placed, and I think one must find some context of a compelling kind before one can decide that the word "sufficient" has the same meaning as "conclusive". Now I can find no context in the Administration of Estates Act 1925 which affords a foundation for a decision that there ought to be placed upon the word "sufficient" in sub-s 7 of s 36, a meaning which it does not usually bear, still less for a decision that it has the same meaning as "conclusive". In my judgment, the meaning and effect of sub-s 7 of s 36 is that a purchaser when investigating title may safely accept a vesting assent as evidence that the person in whose favour it has been made was entitled to have the legal estate conveyed to him unless and until, upon a proper investigation by a purchaser of his vendor's title, facts come to the purchaser's knowledge which indicate the contrary. When that happens, in my judgment, the vesting cannot be and ought not to be accepted as sufficient evidence of something which the purchaser has reason to believe is contrary to the fact.' *Re Duce & Boots Cash Chemists (Southern) Ltd's Contract* [1937] Ch 642 at 649, 650, per Bennett J

[The Finance Act 1965, s 52(4), provided that payments made under a liability for a valuable and 'sufficient' consideration were deductible from income in assessing corporation tax.] 'There is no problem as to the meaning of the word "sufficient"; it connotes adequacy, an adequate *quid pro quo* of the liability incurred.' *Ball (Inspector of Taxes) v National and Grindlays Bank Ltd* [1971] 3 All ER 485 at 494, CA, per cur.

SUFFRAGAN *See* BISHOP

SUICIDE

Felo de se or *suicide* is, where a man of the age of discretion, and *compos mentis*, voluntarily kills himself by stabbing, poison or any other way. (1 Hale PC 411).

[At common law *felo de se* was a felony, but by the Suicide Act 1961 the common law rule was abrogated, though it is an offence under the statute to aid, abet, counsel or procure the suicide or attempted suicide of another.]

(1) It shall be manslaughter, and shall not be murder, for a person acting in pursuance of a suicide pact between him and another to kill the other or be a party to the other being killed by a third person.

(2) Where it is shown that a person charged with the murder of another killed the other or was a party to his being killed, it shall be for the defence to prove that the person charged was acting in pursuance of a suicide pact between him and the other.

(3) For the purposes of this section 'suicide pact' means a common agreement between two or more persons having for its object the death of all of them, whether or not each is to take his own life, but nothing done by a person who enters into a suicide pact shall be treated as done by him in pursuance of the pact unless it is done while he has the settled intention of dying in pursuance of the pact.
(Homicide Act 1957, s 4, as amended by the Suicide Act 1961)

'The question is, what is the meaning, in the policy on the testator's life, of the words "in case the assured shall die *by his own hands*". . . . The words in question in their largest ordinary sense comprehend all cases of self-destruction . . . but, as it is admitted that in their largest sense they comprehend many cases not within their meaning, as used on the present occasion, it is to be considered whether the case of the testator falls within the object for which they are used in this policy. A policy by which the sum insured is payable on the death of the assured in all events, gives him a pecuniary interest that he should die immediately, rather than at a future time . . . and offers therefore a temptation to self-destruction. . . . To protect the insurers against the increase of risk arising out of this temptation is the object for which the condition in question is inserted. It ought, therefore, to be so construed as to include those cases of self-destruction in which, but for the condition, the act might have been committed in order to accelerate the claim on the policy, and to exclude those in which the circumstances, supposing the policy to have been unconditional, would show that the act could not have been committed with a view to pecuniary interest. This principle of construction requires and accounts for the exclusion from the operation of the condition of those cases falling within the general sense of its words, to which it is admitted not to apply—such as those of accident and delirium.' *Borradaile v Hunter* (1843) 5 Man & G 639 at 652–654, per Maule J

[A policy of life assurance was subject to the condition that every policy effected by a person on his or her own life should be void if such person should commit 'suicide'.] 'I feel no doubt as to the import of the expression "commit suicide". In ordinary parlance, every one would so speak of one who had purposely killed himself, whether from *tædium* of life, or transport of grief, or in a fit of temporary insanity. To die by his own hands, or to commit suicide, seems to me to be all one, and to apply to all cases of voluntary self-homicide; and I do not see any reason why a different sense to the ordinary one should be attributed to these words in this instrument; on the contrary, I see very good ground for believing that they are used in their ordinary sense, in order to avoid the consequence which would have followed the adoption of such words as "committing felony of himself", or "self-murder"; as it may well be supposed that juries would, in favour of the family of the deceased, take the same lax view of the evidence as coroners' juries generally do.' *Clift v Schwabe* (1846) 3 CB 437 at 471, per Parke B

'Suicide is not to be presumed. It must be affirmatively proved to justify the finding. Suicide requires an intention. Every act of self-destruction is, in common language, ". . . described by the word suicide, provided it be the intentional act of a party knowing the probable consequence of what he is about": see per Rolfe B in *Clift v Schwabe* [supra].' *Re Davis* [1967] 1 All ER 688 at 690, CA, per Sellers LJ

[Death from self-inflicted injury is not suicide if the death occurs more than a year and a day after the injury was inflicted: see *R v Inner West London Coroner, ex p De Luca* [1988] 3 All ER 414.]

SUIT

'It was argued that "suit" in the English version of the Hague Rules meant an action in the courts and was distinct from an arbitration and that, if a step had been taken in an arbitration in due time but no writ had been issued in the courts, the plaintiffs' claim could have been defeated, if the requirements of the Hague Rules had been invoked, as no "suit" having been established the defendants would have been discharged from liability. The Hague Rules, or more strictly the Carriage of Goods by Sea Act 1924 [repealed; see now the Carriage of Goods by Sea Act 1971, Schedules], which gives statutory effect to them, in art 3, r 6, in the schedule thereto provide clearly for the discharge of defendant shipowners from liability after a period of twelve months, but I see no reason for assuming that the rule was tying the parties to any particular form of litigation. The Convention referred to in the preamble to the Act of 1924 dealt with responsibilities, liabilities, rights and immunities attaching to carriers under bills of lading and on the face of it the method of settling disputes would not seem to be germane. I can see no good reason for giving the word "suit" in this context the limited meaning which has been advanced. The Hague Rules are of international application, arbitration has long been a method of settling disputes agreed by parties to contracts for carriage by sea, and whilst it was agreed that there should be a period of limitation there is nothing to indicate that a step in an arbitration would not be as effective as a writ in an action unless "suit" can only have the meaning in our courts of an action. I do not find any authority which requires us so to hold. In their context I think that the words mean "unless proceedings are brought within one year", and that the commencement of arbitration proceedings would meet the requirement. It was agreed that the English version of the Hague Rules was the same as the Finnish version, which strictly applied in this case. The fact that the rules may call for application under differing legal systems seems to justify a wide interpretation of the word "suit".' *The Merak, T B & S Batchelor & Co Ltd (Owners of Cargo on the Merak) v Owners of SS Merak* [1965] 1 All ER 230 at 234, CA, per Sellers LJ

Suit brought

Canada [A liability insurance policy provided cover against any 'claims made or suits brought'.] At first reading . . . I was of the view that "suits brought", particularly if the *contra proferentem* rule was applicable, meant more than the issuance of a writ. The expression is principally an American one and has been interpreted in Courts of the United States to mean the initiation of a suit. In Canada the words "action brought" received judicial interpretation in *McGrath v Scriven* (1920) 56 DLR 117,

35 CCC 93, [1921] 1 WWR 1075; affirming 52 DLR 342, 33 CCC 70, 54 NSR 1. The Court held that the words meant the initiation of legal proceedings. I have concluded that "suit brought" equals "action commenced" in this case. Rule 4 of the Ontario Rules of Practice provides that an action is commenced when a writ of summons is issued.' *Re St Paul Fire & Marine Insurance Co and Guardian Insurance Co of Canada* (1982) 132 DLR (3d) 60 at 64, Ont HCJ, per Trainor J; affd 1 DLR (4th) 342, Ont CA

SUITABLE

[The appellant's employment as a headmaster was terminated, prima facie on the grounds of redundancy. He was offered work as a supply teacher in the district, at the same salary as formerly. The appellant claimed redundancy payment as this was not 'suitable employment' within the Redundancy Payments Act 1965, s 2(4) (repealed; see now the Employment Protection (Consolidation) Act 1978, s 82(5)(b))]. 'For my part I feel that the tribunal have here misdirected themselves in law as to the meaning of "suitable employment". I accept, of course, that suitable employment is as is said: suitable employment in relation to the employee in question. But it does seem to me here that by the words "suitable employment", suitability means employment which is substantially equivalent to the employment which has ceased. Subsection (3) . . . is dealing with the case where the fundamental terms are the same, and then no offer in writing is needed, but when they differ, then it has to be put in writing and must be suitable. I for my part think that what is meant by "suitable" in relation to the employee means conditions of employment which are reasonably equivalent to those under the previous employment, not the same, because then sub-s (2) would apply, but it does not seem to me that by "suitable employment" is meant employment of an entirely different nature, but in respect of which the salary is going to be the same.' *Taylor v Kent County Council* [1969] 2 All ER 1080 at 1083, 1084, per Lord Parker CJ

New Zealand 'In my opinion the court can, without in any way transgressing the recognised rules of construction, interpret the words "a suitable building for the purposes of a public morgue" as meaning a building provided with all the necessary equipment to render it suitable, and maintained as such.' *Auckland Corpn v Mount Eden Corpn* (1913) 33 NZLR 97 at 101, per Cooper J; also reported 16 GLR 150 at 151

New Zealand 'The word "suitable" [in the Sale of Liquor Act 1962, s 249(8)] qualifies "room". When the words are read together in their natural and ordinary sense they simply mean a room that is fitted for or appropriate to the purposes already mentioned [e.g. use as a bar]. The issue in this connection is whether the room under consideration has the necessary physical attributes. If a room on the premises is of adequate size, is capable of being adequately furnished, is sufficiently independent of the sleeping accommodation and bathroom and ancillary facilities, and is appropriately sited, then it will be "suitable" within the meaning of sub-s (8).' *McGregor v Police* [1970] NZLR 103 at 106, per Macarthur J

SUITABLE ALTERNATIVE ACCOMMODATION

3. For the purposes of s 98(1)(a) [which deals with grounds for possession of certain dwelling-houses] of this Act, a certificate of the local housing authority for the district in which the dwelling-house in question is situated, certifying that the authority will provide suitable alternative accommodation for the tenant by a date specified in the certificate, shall be conclusive evidence that suitable alternative accommodation will be available for him by that date.

4. Where no such certificate as is mentioned in para 3 above is produced to the court, accommodation shall be deemed to be suitable for the purposes of s 98(1)(a) of this Act if it consists of either—

(a) premises which are to be let as a separate dwelling such that they will then be let on a protected tenancy . . . or
(b) premises to be let as a separate dwelling on terms which will, in the opinion of the court, afford to the tenant security of tenure reasonably equivalent to the security afforded by Part VII of this Act in the case of a protected tenancy of a kind mentioned in para (a) above

and, in the opinion of the court, the accommodation fulfils the relevant conditions as defined in para 5 below.

5.—(1) For the purposes of para 4, above, the relevant conditions are that the accommodation is reasonably suitable to the needs of the tenant and his family as regards proximity to place of work, and either—

(a) similar as regards rental and extent to the accommodation afforded by dwelling-houses provided in the neighbourhood by any local housing authority for persons whose needs as regards extent are, in the opinion of the court, similar to those of the tenant and his family; or
(b) reasonably suitable to the means of the tenant and to the needs of the tenant and his family as regards extent and character . . .

(2) For the purposes of sub-para (1)(a) above a certificate of a local housing authority stating—
(a) the extent of the accommodation afforded by dwelling-houses provided by the authority to meet the needs of tenants with families of such number as may be specified in the certificate, and
(b) the amount of the rent charged by the authority for dwelling-houses affording accommodation of that extent,
shall be conclusive evidence of the facts so stated.

6. Accommodation shall not be deemed to be suitable to the needs of the tenant and his family if the result of their occupation of the accommodation would be that it would be an overcrowded dwelling-house for the purposes of Part X of the Housing Act 1985.

7. Any document purporting to be a certificate of a local housing authority named therein issued for the purposes of this Schedule and to be signed by the proper officer of that authority shall be received in evidence and, unless the contrary is shown shall be deemed to be such a certificate without further proof. (Rent Act 1977, Sch 15, Part IV, as amended by the Housing (Consequential Provisions) Act 1985)

In this Part [Part X: overcrowding] 'suitable alternative accommodation', in relation to the occupier of a dwelling-house, means a dwelling as to which the following conditions are satisfied—
(a) he and his family can live in it without causing it to be overcrowded;
(b) it is certified by the local housing authority to be suitable to his needs and that of his family as respects security of tenure, proximity to place of work and otherwise, and to be suitable in relation to his means; and
(c) where the dwelling belongs to the local housing authority, it is certified by them to be suitable to his needs and those of his family as respects accommodation.
(Housing Act 1985, s 342(1))

[See s 342(2), as to the number of persons to be accommodated per bedroom]

'By s 5 [of the Increase of Rent and Mortgage Interest (Restrictions) Act 1920 (repealed; see now the Rent Act 1977, Sch 15 (supra)] the court is not to make an order for possession unless it is satisfied "that alternative accommodation is available which is reasonably suitable to the means of the tenant and to the needs of the tenant . . . and which consists either of a dwelling-house to which this Act applies, or of premises to be let as a separate dwelling". . . . It is evident . . . that there is nothing in the paragraph now in force which suggests the consideration of the suitability of the alternative premises for the business carried on by the tenant.' *Middlesex County Council v Hall* [1929] 2 KB 110 at 112, 113, 115, per Talbot J

'The essential feature of the case on appeal to us is that the judge held as a fact that the alternative accommodation which was so offered by the landlord was suitable within the meaning of the Act [Rent and Mortgage Interest Restrictions (Amendment) Act 1933 (repealed; see now the Rent Act 1977, Sch 15 (supra)] with one exception, namely, that it had not got a garage for a motor car. In my view, when the judge said: "For a tenant who has a car I hold it (that is the house where the landlord was then living) is not suitable alternative accommodation", he was wrong in coming to that conclusion. . . . I turn in s 3 to the subsection dealing with suitable alternative accommodation which says [sub-s (2)]: "A certificate of the housing authority for the area in which the said dwelling-house is situated, certifying that the authority will provide suitable alternative accommodation for the tenant by a date specified in the certificate, shall be conclusive evidence that suitable alternative accommodation will be available for him." . . . The policy of Parliament there obviously was to treat the housing authority as in a position to settle quite definitely the character of "suitable alternative accommodation". That policy reappeared in sub-s (4) under which the housing authority is empowered to give a certificate of suitability, which is to be conclusive. Subsection (3) says: "Where no such certificate as aforesaid is produced to the court, accommodation shall be deemed to be suitable if it consists either—(a) of a dwelling-house to which the principal Acts apply; or (b) of premises to be let as a separate dwelling on terms which will, in the opinion of the court, afford to the tenant security of tenure reasonably equivalent to the security afforded by the principal Acts in the case of a dwelling-house to which those Acts apply." It is important to realise exactly what is required by what I have read. The accommodation must consist either of a dwelling-house to which the principal Acts apply or of a dwelling-house which is let on terms equivalent to those granted by the Rent Restrictions Acts. That is the first condition. The subsection goes on: ". . . and is, in the opinion of the court, reasonably suitable to the needs of the tenant and his family as regards proximity to place of work. . . ." That is the second condition. The third condition is the only other one; it relates to the tenant's means and his family's needs and is expressed alternatively, namely, that the accommodation must be: ". . . either (i) similar as regards rental and extent to the accommodation afforded by dwelling-houses provided in the neighbourhood by any housing authority for persons whose needs as regards extent are, in the opinion of the court, similar to those of the tenant and his family; or (ii) otherwise reasonably suitable to the means of the tenant and to the needs of the tenant and his family as regards extent and character." The judge has found as a fact that, but for the question of the garage, the alternative house offered was in all those respects reasonably suitable. The only question for this court, therefore, is whether the absence of a garage can properly be taken into consideration on the question of the accommodation being suitable. In my view, quite clearly it cannot, for this simple reason, that it is the dwelling-house itself which is the unit throughout the whole of these Rent Restriction Acts, and especially so under s 3(3), which I am now considering.' *Briddon v George* [1946] 1 All ER 609 at 610, 612, 613, CA, per Scott LJ

'I do not think that the offer of a share in a house is an offer of suitable alternative accommodation [under the Rent and Mortgage Interest Restrictions (Amendment) Act 1933, s 3(1)(b) (repealed; see now the Rent Act 1977, Sch 15 (supra)] to a tenant who under a tenancy has a house of his own. It seems to me that accommodation in a house of one's own differs in kind from sharing a house with someone else. When this section speaks of suitable alternative accommodation it means suitable alternative accommodation of the kind, although it may not be in all respects so good, as that which the tenant is enjoying.' *Barnard v Towers* [1953] 2 All ER 877 at 878, CA, per Somervell LJ

SUMMARILY

[RSC 1965, Ord 17, r 5 provides that on the hearing of an interpleader summons, where the applicant is a sheriff the court may 'summarily' determine the question at issue between the claimants.] 'On the hearing of the summons it was open to the master "summarily" to determine the question; but "summarily" there does not mean that he can determine it straight away out of hand. It means only that he can determine it himself without directing an issue. The usual practice of the master when he "summarily" determines the question, is to give a special appointment at which evidence can be taken orally and the witnesses can be cross-examined; and at which the relevant documents can be produced.' *Davis (PBJ) Manufacturing Co Ltd v Fahn* [1967] 2 All ER 1274 at 1276, CA, per Lord Denning MR

SUMMARY PROCEEDINGS

Australia '"Summary", when applied to proceedings, is a descriptive term without restriction to special tribunals and not in ordinary acceptation exclusively confined to Courts of Petty Sessions. It has been held to apply, for instance, to certain proceedings in County Courts and Courts Martial: and application for summary judgment is a well known special mode of procedure in the Supreme Court itself. The term is in law used as a reference to a mode of dealing with certain matters expeditiously and without ordinary incidental formalities (see Oxford Dictionary); in fact, one of the earliest references to the term there cited is "1798, depriving the subject of trial by jury".' *Dowson v McGrath* (1956) 58 WALR 27 at 32, per Dwyer CJ

SUMMER TIME *See* TIME

SUPERANNUATION SCHEME

'Superannuation scheme' means any enactment, rules, deed or other instrument, providing for the payment of annuities or lump sums to the persons with respect to whom the instrument has effect on their retirement at a specified age or on becoming incapacitated at some earlier age, or to the personal representatives or the widows, relatives or dependants of such persons on their death or otherwise, whether with or without any further or other benefits. (Wages Councils Act 1979, s 28)

SUPERFLUOUS

'There is no doubt that the term "superfluous" used in this section [the Lands Clauses Consolidation Act 1845, s 127] means "more than are wanted for the undertaking". And it seems to import that the works have been commenced, that some land has been applied, and that it has been found that more land than is wanted has been taken. But I think that in the general introduction of these sections the expression "which shall not be required for the purposes thereof" is sufficiently large to embrace the case of an undertaking being abandoned.' *Astley v Manchester, Sheffield & Lincolnshire Rly Co* (1858) 2 De G & J 453 at 463, per Lord Chelmsford LC

'It appears to me that it [land] may become "superfluous land" in one of four different ways. It may be, in the first place, land originally taken under compulsory powers, but taken upon a wrong estimate or calculation of the quantity of land which would be required for a purpose for which it is afterwards found out, by experience, that less land than was originally supposed will be sufficient. Or it may, in the second place, be land which, under the provisions of other clauses with which your Lordships are familiar, the railway company may have been forced to take by reason of wishing to take a part only of premises. There, *ex hypothesi*, that which the directors are forced to take is not land which in any sense they wish to take or want for the purposes of their undertaking—it is thrust upon them for the benefit of the landowners, and obviously is superfluous land. Or, in the third place, it may be land taken originally, and required originally for the permanent works of the line, but which, in the course of subsequent years, turns out to have been occupied by works which are abandoned, and which, by reason of the abandonment of those works originally supposed to be permanent, becomes land no longer required by the company. Or it may, in the fourth place, be land which has been allowed to be taken by the company, or which has been forced to be taken by the company for temporary purposes, and which has been taken by the company with the intention originally of its being used only for temporary purposes, which temporary purposes have come to an end.' *Great Western Rly Co v May* (1874) LR 7 HL 283 at 292, 293, per Lord Cairns LC

'The first point to be decided is what are superfluous lands within the meaning of the 127th and following sections of the Lands Clauses Consolidation Act [1845]. In the case of the *Great Western Railway Company v May* [supra], it was decided that the word "thereof" in the preamble to those sections is to be read as meaning "of the undertaking", and consequently the sections are to be read as dealing with lands "which shall not be required for the purposes of the undertaking". . . . Section 127 enacts that the company must sell the superfluous land, and if unsold it is to vest in the adjoining owners. . . . It appears to me to be plain, on the wording of the Act, that "land" in the 127th section means land properly and ordinarily so called, and does not apply to a mere easement or a slice of land taken horizontally. . . . I am satisfied that the word "land" here is used in its ordinary sense, that the word "superfluous" is used in its ordinary sense.' *Re Metropolitan District Rly Co & Cosh* (1880) 13 Ch D 607 at 615–618, CA, per Jessel MR

'I think the cases of *Great Western Railway Company v May* [supra], *Hooper v Bourne* [(1880) 5 App Cas 1], and *Betts v Great Eastern Railway Company* [(1878) 3 Ex D 182, CA], have now settled beyond all controversy what the meaning of "superfluous land" is, and what land ought, under ordinary circumstances, to be considered superfluous land. The test is whether or not there is bona fide reason to believe that within no very distant time, or within a reasonable time, having regard to the nature of the undertaking, the land acquired by the company will be required for the purposes of the undertaking.' *Hobbs v Midland Rly Co* (1882) 20 Ch D 418 at 431, 432, per Manisty J

SUPERIOR COURTS

'To support the view of Mr Bovill, that the Court of Assizes is an inferior Court, two authorities, and only two, were cited. The first was Bacon's Abridgment, tit. "Courts", letter (D), on referring to which it appears to be an authority directly the other way. Courts of record are there divided into Supreme, Superior, or Inferior. Superior Courts of record are more principal or less principal. The more principal are Parliament, Chancery, King's Bench, Common Pleas and Exchequer with the justices itinerant. The less principal Courts are such as are held by commission of gaol delivery, oyer and terminer, assize, nisi prius, etc, and all these seem to stand upon the same footing. A Court of assize or of nisi prius is therefore a superior Court, though a less principal one, and, as such, has authority to commit for contempt, without setting forth the particulars of the contempt in respect of which the commitment is awarded.' *Re Fernandes* (1861) 6 H & N 717 at 725, 726, per cur.

[*See* now Part I of the Supreme Court Act 1981. All courts of assize were abolished, as from 1 January 1972, by the Courts Act 1971, Part II of which established the Crown Court as part of the Supreme Court.]

SUPERIOR LANDLORD

See LANDLORD

SUPERVISOR

United States The term 'supervisor' means any individual having authority, in the interest of the employer, to hire, transfer, suspend, lay off, recall, promote, discharge, assign, reward, or discipline other employees, or responsibly to direct them, or to adjust their grievances, or effectively to recommend such action, if in connection with the foregoing the exercise of such authority is not of a merely routine or clerical nature, but requires the use of independent judgment. (Labor Management Relations Act of 1947, s 2(11))

SUPPLIER

'Supplier' means a person carrying on a business of selling goods other than a business in which goods are sold only by retail. (Resale Prices Act 1976, s 24(1))

SUPPLY

'Supply' includes supply by way of lease or hire, and 'acquire' shall be construed accordingly. (Restrictive Trade Practices Act 1976, s 43(1))

Of drugs

[The Misuse of Drugs Act 1971, s 5(3), makes it an offence for a person to have a controlled drug in his possession with intent to 'supply' it to another.] 'This court has been referred to the Shorter Oxford English Dictionary which gives a large number of definitions of the word "supply", but they have a common feature, viz that in the word "supply" is inherent the furnishing or providing of something which is wanted. In the judgment of this court, the word "supply" in s 5(3) of the 1971 Act covers a similarly wide range of transactions. A feature common to all of those transactions is a transfer of physical control of a drug from one person to another. In our judgment questions of the transfer of ownership or legal possession of those drugs are irrelevant to the issue whether or not there was intent to supply.' *R v Delgado* [1984] 1 All ER 449 at 452, CA, per cur.

Of electricity

'In my opinion "supply" within the meaning of the Act [Electric Lighting Act 1882] and Order is completed at the consumer's terminals. The installation of electricity and provision of fittings is in my opinion a separate business incidental to the use but not to the supply of energy.' *A-G v Leicester Corpn* [1910] 2 Ch 359 at 373, per Neville J

'On the true interpretation of the statute [Electric Lighting (Clauses) Act 1899], delivery must be made at a consumer's terminals, and those terminals must be placed upon some land or some building upon land for which electrical energy is required, and that land or building must be within the undertakers' area of supply.' *A-G v Gravesend Corpn* [1936] Ch 550 at 555, 557, per Bennett J

Of goods

'Supply', in relation to the supply of goods, includes supply by way of sale, lease, hire or hire-purchase, and, in relation to buildings or other structures, includes the construction of them by a person for another person. (Fair Trading Act 1973, s 137(2))

[A taxpayer who dealt in stolen cars appealed to a tribunal against an assessment to value added tax.] 'If any layman had asked the purchaser of one of the stolen motor cars who had supplied him with the car, he would I think have unhesitatingly answered by giving the name of the taxpayer. The fact that it subsequently turned out that it had been supplied under a contract of sale that was in fact void would be neither here nor there, and I am content to adopt the definition of "supply" for the purposes of this case put forward by counsel for the commissioners. "Supply" is the passing of possession in goods pursuant to an agreement whereunder the supplier agrees to part with and the recipient agrees to take possession. By "possession" is meant in this context control over the goods, in the sense of having the immediate facility for their use. This may or may not involve the physical removal of the goods.' *Customs & Excise Comrs v Oliver* [1980] 1 All ER 353 at 355, per Griffiths J

Australia 'The supply of goods does not necessitate a change in ownership of the goods supplied. In many cases the word "supply" is equivalent to the word "provide" and it often happens that a person is provided by others with what belongs to him. Thus a shop, which has a home delivery service, supplies goods upon delivery notwithstanding that they may have been bought in the shop, or by telephone, or by mail order. A supplier is not merely one who sells. He may be one who delivers.' *Commonwealth v Sterling Nicholas Duty Free Pty Ltd* [1972–73] ALR 23 at 30, per Menzies J

Of intoxicating liquor

[A regulation prohibited the sale or 'supply' of intoxicating liquor to any persons in licensed premises, unless the liquor was ordered and paid for by the person supplied.] 'The magistrate said, and I think correctly, that the word "supply" in its natural and ordinary meaning means "to furnish or serve things", but he proceeded to add the words "required or ordered". It seems to me that the addition of those words is going further than the meaning that ought to be given to the words in this regulation.' *Williams v Pearce* (1916) 85 LJKB 959 at 965, DC, per Lord Reading CJ

'The charge in the complaint is laid on the word "supply"—"you did supply to J S" a nip of port wine which was not paid for . . . and I agree with the Lord Chief Justice [in *Williams v Pearce* (supra)] in thinking that "supply" . . . may quite properly be translated as signifying "furnish" or "serve".' *Brown v M'Kechnie* 1916 SC(J) 20 at 22, 23, per the Lord Justice-Clerk

Australia '"Supply" is a very general word and has a wide application, but I doubt whether, when liquor is already at the disposal of a company of men, the act of one or two of them in pouring it into jugs and setting them where all may more readily help themselves falls with it.' *Bennett v Cooper* (1948) 76 CLR 570 at 582 per Dixon J

New Zealand [The Licensing Act Emergency Regulations 1942 (No 2) (NZ), reg 3(1) (revoked; see now s 249 (and certain other sections) of the Sale of Liquor Act 1962) provided that 'every person who, at any time while licensed premises are required to be closed, sells or supplies any liquor, . . . or allows any liquor, whether purchased before or after the hours of closing, to be consumed in any such premises . . . or to be removed from any such premises . . . commits an offence. . . .'] 'It was contended for the appellant that a "supply" involves delivery consequent upon a purchase or gift, in that it involves the notion that the supply is from the owner of the article, or at least from one having control of it, to some one who is not the owner. As a corollary it was argued that "supply" is inept to describe a transaction wherein the article is handed over to its owner. Lord Reading LCJ said in *Williams v Pearce* [supra]: "The word 'supply' in its ordinary and natural meaning means to furnish or serve." There is a line of cases in which the word "supply" has been held to cover the delivery of liquor consequent upon a sale, of which *Rhodes v Bowden* (1907) 26 NZLR 1097, is one. . . . In my opinion, the supply of beer in this case had occurred during permitted hours and the purchaser put the selected beer in the cupboard. What occurred after that when the porter allowed the purchaser to remove the liquor during prohibited hours was not, in my opinion, a "supply". The liquor had already been supplied. To consider . . . the appropriateness of the word "supply" to the transactions here, I think the following test might be applied: Suppose a man in an hotel five minutes before the closing-hour orders and receives a glass of beer. Were he then to leave it, unconsumed, and go to the other end of the bar to talk to someone whom he had seen, and then, one minute after the closing-hour, the barman at his request were to bring it to him in his new position, could it be said that the barman "supplied" the beer one minute after the closing-hour instead of five minutes before? I think not. If I am right in that view, then here, where the case shows that there was a supply within permitted hours and a permission to remove during prohibited hours, the permission to remove, even assistance in removal, would not, I think, constitute supply during prohibited hours.' *Donnithorne v Quartley* [1943] NZLR 105 at 108, per Northcroft J; also reported [1943] GLR at 103, 104

Of milk

Australia 'The concept of supply in my opinion involves both the element of delivery, which may or may not be in pursuance of a contract, and the acceptance of the delivery. When acceptance has been taken of a delivery then, in my opinion, there has been a supply.' *Andaloro v Wyong Co-operative Dairy Society Ltd* [1965] NSWR 1121 at 1138, per Macfarlan J

Of ships stores

'In my judgment, the important difference between "equip" and "supply" is that "supply" is a word which is appropriate for use in connection with consumable stores, such as fuel oil, whereas "equip" connotes something of a more permanent nature. I can well understand that anchors, cables, hawsers, sails, ropes, and such things, may be said to be part of a ship's equipment, although they may have to be renewed from time to time, but such things as fuel oil, coal, boiler water, and food appear to me to be in quite a different category.' *The D'Vora* [1952] 2 All ER 1127 at 1128, per Collingwood J

SUPPORT

Easement of

In the natural state of land one part of it receives support from another, upper from lower strata, and soil from adjacent soil and therefore if one piece of land is conveyed so as to be divided in point of title from another contiguous to it, or (as in the case of mines) below it, the right to support passes with the land, not as an easement held by a distinct title, but as an essential incident to the land itself. . . .

The easement of support is a right acquired over and above the natural rights of support. It may either involve an enhancement to the dominant owner's natural right of support with a corresponding increase of the servient owner's obligations to refrain from interference, or it may involve a diminution of the dominant owner's obligations to refrain from depriving the servient tenement of the support to which the servient owner would otherwise have been entitled.

The easement of support may be defined as the right of an owner of buildings not to have the support which the dominant tenement receives from the land or buildings of his neighbour removed without replacement. The servient owner may, by doing nothing, allow his building to decay and so remove all support without thereby giving the dominant owner any cause of action; but he must not do acts which remove the support without providing a substitute. It follows that the negative right not to have the support removed cannot accurately be expressed in terms of a positive right to have the support maintained. (14 Halsbury's Laws (4th edn) paras 168, 174)

The right of support is a right to have the surface kept at its ancient and natural level. It is not an easement but a natural right incident to the ownership of the soil. . . .

The right of support is independent of the nature of the strata, or the difficulty of propping up the surface, or the comparative values of the surface and the minerals. It is impossible to measure out degrees to which the right may extend. The surface owner's right is, therefore, not modified by the fact that the obligation not to cause damage by subsidence renders the effectual working of the underlying minerals impossible, as where the extent of pillars necessary to maintain the surface undamaged is such as to make the remaining minerals unprofitable to work. (31 Halsbury's Laws (4th edn) para 47)

'In my opinion, the general right which a man prima facie has at common law to the support of his land, either subjacent or adjacent, is a natural right analogous to the right to flowing water, and not an easement.' *Rowbotham v Wilson* (1857) 8 E & B 123 at 151, per Martin B

'I think it clear that any . . . right of support to a building or part of a building, is an easement; and I agree . . . that it is both scientifically and practically inaccurate to describe it as one of a merely negative kind. What is support? The force of gravity causes the superincumbent land or building to press downward upon what is below it, whether artificial or natural; and it has also a tendency to thrust outwards, laterally, any loose or yielding substance, such as earth or clay, until it meets with adequate resistance. Using the language of the law of easements, I say that, in the case alike of vertical and of lateral support, both to land and to buildings, the dominant tenement imposes upon the servient a positive and a constant burden, the sustenance of which, by the servient tenement, is necessary for the safety and stability of the dominant.' *Dalton v Angus* (1881) 6 App Cas 740 at 793, per Lord Selborne LC

Australia 'The literal meaning of the words "in support of" a named or indicated church building is probably limited to the actual support, by underpinning or shoring up, of the building itself; but the true meaning may be in support of the building and fabric of that church and the services held in it.' *Re MacGregor, Thompson v Ashton* (1932) 32 SR(NSW) 483 at 490, per Long Innes J

Of dependants

Canada [The Succession Law Reform Act 1977 (Ont) (see now RSO 1980, c 488, s 58(1)) provided for the making of an order in favour of a dependant where adequate provision for support had not been made by the deceased.] 'These definitions [extracted from various dictionaries] lead me to the conclusion that "support" as used in the SLRA, includes not only furnishing food and sustenance and supplying the necessaries of life, but also the secondary meaning of giving physical or moral support.' *Re Davies and Davies* (1979) 105 DLR (3d) 537 at 542, Ont Surr Ct, per Dymond Surr Ct J

SURCHARGE

'"Surcharge" is a curiously inappropriate expression—more inappropriate than "charge" —for an operation whereby someone, a stranger to the council whose accounts are being audited, is to be compelled to make good the loss which the council has suffered owing to that stranger's negligence or misconduct. The typical (though not the only) use of the term "surcharge", which is not defined in the Act, is that given in the Oxford English Dictionary under meaning 1(c): "A charge made by an auditor upon a public official in respect of an amount improperly paid by him": a very different thing from a charge or levy made on a member of the outside public who is the wrongful recipient or causative agent of such a payment.' *Re Dickson* [1948] 2 KB 95 at 102, CA, per cur.

Canada [The Petroleum and Natural Gas Regulations 1969 (Sask), reg 63, provides that oil produced from Crown lands shall be subject to a royalty 'surcharge']. 'Here . . . is a word capable of many meanings. It has escaped in this country, insofar as I am aware, a judicial definition. Perhaps the variety of uses to which the word can be put, as evidenced by a review of a number of dictionaries, is some reason why it has not come under the interpretative eyes of the courts. I have resorted to the Oxford English Dictionary as did Asquith LJ in *Re Dickson* [supra], when considering the meaning of this word. Just as the Lord Justice made mention of one meaning of the word, appropriate to the study of the relevant statutory provision then under review by him, so do I lift and adopt from the same dictionary the definition of the word that I consider appropriate to the instant circumstances, viz, "to subject to an additional or extra charge or payment". A consideration of reg 63 indicates to me that this is the sense in which the term has been used.' *Canadian Industrial Gas & Oil Ltd v Government of Saskatchewan & A-G of Saskatchewan* [1975] 2 WWR 481 at 510, per Hughes J

SURETY

There are three different kinds of suretyships, distinguishable as follows:

(1) those in which there is an agreement to constitute, for a particular purpose, the relation of principal debtor and surety, to which agreement the creditor secured by it is a party;
(2) those in which there is a similar agreement between the principal debtor and surety only; to which the creditor is a stranger; and
(3) those in which, without any such contract of suretyship, there is a primary and a secondary liability of two persons for one and the same debt, the debt being, as between the two, that of one of those persons only, and not of both, so that the other, if he should be compelled to pay it, would be entitled to reimbursement from the person by whom (as between the two) it ought to have been paid.

(20 Halsbury's Laws (4th edn) para 105)

SURFACE

'Surface' in relation to land includes any buildings, works or things erected, constructed or growing thereon, and 'right to let down the surface' includes a right to let down superincumbent or adjacent strata up to and including the surface. (Mines (Working Facilities and Support) Act 1966, s 14)

'The surface [in a grant of land] means not the mere plane surface but all the land except the mines.' *Pountney v Clayton* (1883) 11 QBD 820 at 839, 840, CA, per Bowen LJ

See, generally, 31 Halsbury's Laws (4th edn) para 16.

SURFACE DAMAGE

'The words "surface damage" is a term well known in the north of England, in the colliery districts: it is damage to the crops, either by using the surface, or by smoke coming from colliery-works or pit-heaps, injuring the growing crops. It is difficult to say that the injury to the foundations of a house, extending to the walls and roof of the house, or to cause a subsidence of the soil, partially or wholly destroying the future utility of the soil, is a surface damage. It may be damage to the house and land, but it is not surface damage.' *Allaway v Wagstaff* (1859) LJ Exch 51 at 58, per Watson B

SURGEON *See* MEDICAL PRACTITIONER

SURNAME *See* NAME

SURPLUS *See also* BALANCE

'I am not sure that there is much difference between "balance" and "surplus", but each of those words presupposes a primary expenditure which is first to be brought into account before ever a balance or a surplus can be ascertained. While I think there is very little difference between "balance" in the headnote and "surplus", which appears in the words of the will itself, I am equally unable to see any real distinction between "balance", "surplus" and "any part of the . . . income not" in the opinion of the trustee "required".' *Re Herbert, Herbert v Bicester (Lord)* [1946] 1 All ER 421 at 423, per Vaisey J

Surplus assets

'In this case I have to decide what is the meaning of the words "surplus assets" in art 114 [of the articles of association of a company]. It is contended on behalf of the holders of the founders' shares that the words "surplus assets" mean surplus after paying the debts and outstanding liabilities only. It is contended on the part of the ordinary shareholders that the words "surplus assets" mean the surplus left, not only after deducting the amount necessary to pay the debts and outstanding liabilities, but also after recouping the shareholders the amount of capital which they have contributed. In my judgment the words "surplus assets" may mean either that which is contended for by the holders of the founders' shares, or that which is contended for by the holders of the ordinary shares. . . . I cannot help feeling that to hold that "surplus assets" meant in this case surplus after the mere payment of debts and outside liabilities would lead to a result so unfair and inequitable that one ought not to arrive at that conclusion unless one is driven to it by the strong words of the article itself. . . . I cannot refuse to arrive at the conclusion that the term "surplus assets" means surplus profits—that is to say, surplus assets after payment of debts and recoupment of capital.' *Re New Transvaal Co* [1896] 2 Ch 750 at 754–756, per Vaughan Williams J

'Clause 6 of the articles provides what is to happen in the event of the winding-up of the company, namely, that the "surplus assets" are to be distributed between the holders of preference shares and ordinary shares according to the amount paid up thereon. Prima facie, I think "surplus assets" means that which remains after all claims of the creditors of the company and the costs of the winding-up have been paid.' *Re Crichton's Oil Co* [1902] 2 Ch 86 at 96, CA, per Stirling LJ

'The expression "surplus assets" [in the memorandum of association of a company limited by shares] must mean what was left after the payment of debts and the repayment of the whole of the Preference and Ordinary capital.' *Re Dunstable Portland Cement Co Ltd* (1932) 48 TLR 223 at 223, per Eve J

SURPRISE

The fact that a party has acted without due deliberation, or under a misapprehension of his rights or of the effect of the transaction, is not a ground for relief in equity unless the case is one in which relief can be afforded on the ground of mistake; but if by the conduct of the other party he has been taken unawares, and has acted without due deliberation and under confused and sudden impressions, this is a case of surprise against which equity will relieve. (16 Halsbury's Laws (4th edn) para 1226)

SURRENDER *See also* DISPOSITION

A surrender is a voluntary act of the parties whereby, with the landlord's consent, the tenant surrenders his lease to the landlord so that the lease merges with the reversion and is thus brought to an end. It is defined as being the yielding up of the term to the person who has the immediate estate in reversion in order that, by mutual agreement, the term may merge in the reversion. The surrender may be either express, that is by an act of the parties having the expressed intention of effecting a surrender, or by operation of law, that is as an inference from the acts of the parties. The parties to the surrender must be the owner of the term and the owner of the immediate reversion expectant on the term. Consequently an underlessee cannot surrender his underlease to the head lessor. A surrender must be of the entire term in the premises; hence a tenancy held jointly cannot be surrendered by one of two joint tenants. However, a part only of the demised premises may be surrendered. (27 Halsbury's Laws (4th edn) para 444)

'We must consider what is meant by a surrender by operation of law. This term is applied to cases where the owner of a particular estate has been a party to some act, the validity of which he is by law afterwards estopped from disputing, and which would not be valid if his particular estate had continued to exist. There the law treats the doing of such act as amounting to surrender. Thus, if lessee for years accept a new lease from his lessor, he is estopped from saying that his lessor had not power to make the new lease; and, as the lessor could not do this until the prior lease had been surrendered, the law says that the acceptance of such new lease is of itself a surrender of the former.' *Lyon v Reed* (1844) 13 M & W 285 at 305, 306, per cur.

New Zealand [The operative clause in a deed provided that a wife, in consideration of permanent maintenance, should 'surrender' her life interest in a marriage settlement.] 'There appears to be no technical meaning attached to the word "surrender" in circumstances such as these. . . . In relation to lands, there may be such a meaning and it is given in Garrow's Law of Real Property in New Zealand (3rd edn 181). By analogy, "surrender" would be an appropriate word to effect the transfer or assignment of a life interest in personalty to a settlor who had created out of his property that life interest but still retained the reversionary interest in the property. No particular form of words is necessary to transfer or assign a chose in action.' *Re Davis's Settlement Trusts* [1950] NZLR 205 at 209, 210, per Stanton J; also reported [1949] GLR 619 at 620

SURRENDER VALUE

'Surrender value [in a policy of insurance] in general means the value or consideration which a company has contracted or is prepared to pay at any particular time during the currency of the contract in consideration of being relieved as from that time of the liability dependent on the continuance of premiums paid.' *Equitable Life Assurance Society of the United States v Reed* [1914] AC 587 at 597, PC, per cur.

SURVIVE—SURVIVOR

The word 'survive' and its derivatives ordinarily refer to the longest in duration of lives running concurrently; they may, however, refer not to concurrent lives but to the fact of living to and after a named event or death. There is no rule of construction as to the period to which survivorship refers apart from a context. The question must in every case be answered by applying ordinary principles of construction to the particular language used and having regard to any relevant surrounding circumstances. The language used must be construed in its natural sense unless the context shows that this would defeat the testator's intention, and the mere fact that, so construed, the will might in certain possible, or even probable, circumstances produce results which seem fanciful or even harsh is not a sufficient ground for adopting another interpretation. Although this fact may raise doubts whether the construction fulfils the testator's intention, doubts are not enough; it must be possible to discover from the language used what the intention was, that is, that the testator intended to use 'survive' in some secondary sense.

'Survivor' and similar words may be used in other than the strict sense. Thus, in a set of dispositions in favour of several persons and their children or issue, the words may be used in a sense in which the element of survivorship involves not a survivorship between the named persons, but the subsistence of a line of children or issue, or of vested estates and interests. Alternatively they may be used as meaning 'others' but, where it is proper to adopt a secondary meaning, a meaning which imports some kind or element of survivorship (for example survival by issue) is to be preferred to construing 'survivors' as equivalent to 'others'. (50 Halsbury's Laws (4th edn) paras 500, 501)

'It was contended that the words, "survivor and survivors of them", were to be construed "other and others". That is a construction which the court has, in some cases, put upon those or similar words; but it is what Lord

Eldon, in *Davidson v Dallas*, calls a "forced construction of the term survivor" ([(1808)] 14 Ves 576), and he contrasts it with what he calls its "natural meaning". It is a construction which the court may sometimes be compelled to adopt, in order to accomplish the intention which appears on the whole of the will.' *Crowder v Stone* (1827) 3 Russ 217 at 223, 224, per Lyndhurst LC

'The question as to both clauses is, whether the words "survivors or survivor" can be read "others or other"; and I am bound to say, that the later authorities lean more strongly than the earlier ones to the strict construction of words; although, in cases where it is necessary to do so in order to render a will intelligible, or where a clear and necessary inference can be drawn from the terms of the will, the court will not hesitate to construe the words "survivors or survivor" as "others or other".' *Re Corbett's Trusts* (1860) John 591 at 596, per Page Wood V-C

'The decisions on this subject are very conflicting, although the rule as settled by modern authorities is, that the word "survivor" is to be construed strictly, and is not to be read "other", unless the rest of the will should render the more liberal and less literal contruction essential, for the purpose of carrying into execution the objects expressed by the will; the exceptions to the strict construction of the word cannot be reduced to any definite rule, and must depend upon the words of each will itself.' *Hodge v Foot* (1865) 34 Beav 349 at 351, 353, per Romilly MR

'My opinion is, that the meaning of the word "survive" or "survivor" imports, that the person who is to survive must be living at the time of the even which he is to survive. I have consulted Johnson and Richardson and the authorities cited by them, and in all instances survive appears to mean to "outlive", that is, to be alive at the time of a particular event or the death of a particular person, which event or person the other is to survive.' *Gee v Liddell* (1866) LR 2 Eq 341 at 344, per Lord Romilly MR

'The question whether the word "survivor" is to be read as "other" has been the subject of innumerable cases; but there is one never-failing guide to all the authorities, namely, that it is the duty of the court to ascertain what the meaning of the testator is, and if it can satisfy itself that the word ought to be read as "other" it is right to substitute the one word for the other.' *Re Johnson, Hickman v Williamson* (1884) 53 LJ Ch 1116 at 1117, per Bacon V-C

'"Surviving" means living beyond some period. Now the true rule for construing a will is, that if a rule has been laid down fixing in the absence of any expressed intention the meaning of a word, then that meaning is to be given to it unless there is something in the context to vary the meaning, and if no such definite rule has been laid down, then the words are to be taken in their natural sense. There is no canon as to the period to which survivorship is to be referred, except that in an immediate gift it is to be referred to the death of the testator, and if there is a life estate then to the determination of the life estate.' *Re Benn, Benn v Benn* (1885) 29 Ch D 839 at 844, CA, per Cotton LJ

'The term "survivor" after the determination of a previous interest undoubtedly means, as a rule, those who are living at that time.' *Re Hill to Chapman* (1885) 54 LJ Ch 595 at 597, CA, per Cotton LJ

[A clause in a will provided 'that if any of my said daughters . . . shall happen to die without leaving lawful issue, or either or both of my said sons shall happen to die before they or either of them attain the age of twenty-one years, then the share of him or her so dying shall go and be in trust for the survivors or survivor of them'.] 'I am bound to hold that the expression "survivors or survivor" means what it says, viz that those surviving the event of death take.' *Re Robson, Howden v Robson* [1899] WN 260 at 261, per Cozens-Hardy J

'There is not, so it happens, any authority precisely covering the event postulated . . . namely, the death of a parent "leaving any issue him or her surviving". The word "surviving", however, which, in my view, according to its ordinary meaning requires that the person who is to survive shall be living both at and after a particular point of time, ought, as it seems to me, to be governed by the same considerations as those which have been applied to the word "living", where the event postulated has been that there should be a child living at a particular point of time e.g., at its father's death.' *Elliot v Lord Joicey* [1935] AC 209 at 218, 219, per Lord Russell of Killowen

'It must be regarded as settled by the House of Lords decision in *Elliot v Joicey* [supra] that the prima facie and ordinary meaning of "surviving" is "living at and after the event" and requires that the person who is to survive shall be living both at and after a particular point of time. So that prima facie a gift to a class of individuals "surviving" an individual means a gift to persons of that class living at the event in question and does not extend to persons coming into existence after the event. One starts therefore, with that prima facie meaning of the word "surviving" which suggests that no issue of the nephew survived the testator within the meaning of the will unless they were in existence at the death of the testator. But it is to be observed that here the requirement is that issue should survive not a single but a double event, i.e. both the death of the testator and the failure of the prior trust. It seems to me that this makes a material difference to the meaning of the word "survive". I think that while fully accepting the meaning of living at the happening of the specific event, when the requirement is that two events should be survived, the word can be given proper effect by interpreting it as living at the happening of the last of the two events specified; when, therefore, the requirement is to survive both the death of the testator and that of another named person, that requirement is met when a person is living at the date of the last of the events which has happened.' *Re Castle, Public Trustee v Floud* [1949] Ch 46 at 48, per Jenkins J

'What is quite certain is that "survive", when used in relation to an event or point of time, predicates prima facie that the propositus is alive at and after the point of time or the event in question.' *Re Hodgson, Hodgson v Gillett*, [1952] 1 All ER 769 at 771, per Roxburgh J

'There can be no doubt that, according to its proper meaning, the word "survive" means that he who survives the given event must be alive both at, and after, the time of that event.' *Re James's Will Trusts, Peard v James* [1960] 3 All ER 744 at 747, per Buckley J

[*See*, generally, pp 754, 755 of the above last case, as to the propositions to be derived from the authorities on the meaning of 'survive' and 'survivor'.]

'There may be . . . surrounding circumstances, or there may be a context which can put on the word "survive" or "survivor" a different meaning from that which it would normally import. In the absence of such circumstances or context, however, the meaning of the word "survivor" is that indicated by Lord Russell of Killowen in *Elliot's* case [supra]. It means that the survivor must be in existence at and live after the date of the postulated event. The word cannot in my view . . . include a person who comes into existence subsequently.' *Re Alsopp, Cardinal v Warr* [1967] 2 All ER 1056 at 1061, per Davies LJ

Australia 'The primary meaning [of survive] is "outlive" not "live after" and as I can see nothing in the context [of the will under review] to control the primary meaning, I adopt it.' *Re Pears, Union Trustee Co of Australia Ltd v Hives* [1940] St R Qd 296 at 300, per Webb SPJ

Australia 'No one can doubt that according to the correct use of English the word "survive" imports life before and after the event survived. . . . The question in the present case, i.e. of the will under consideration, is whether the testator has not sufficiently shown that he did not attach to the word "survive" its full and precise meaning, even if it amount to a grammatical solecism. I think that there are clear indications that he has misused the word "survive" and that all he meant was that the children should not predecease him.' *Brennan v Permanent Trustee Co of New South Wales* (1945) 73 CLR 404 at 409, 411, per Rich J

Australia 'No one doubts that the natural meaning of the word "survive" is to remain alive after the termination of some other continuing thing or after the occurrence of some event. In short it means to outlive. Accordingly, if the word "survive" (in the will under consideration) receives its natural meaning, only those children who were born to nieces before the testator died could survive him and take under the limitation. . . . In the present case, I think the context raises a strong presumption that the testator did not use the word "survive" in its correct sense, and did not intend that the gift of corpus should be confined to the children of his nieces who had been born before his will took effect.' Ibid at 414, 415, per Dixon J

Australia 'The primary meaning of the word "survive" is "outlives" . . . but whether that word is to be given in any particular instrument its primary meaning or the meaning "lives after", so as not to exclude those persons born after the death of the testator . . . will depend upon the true construction of the word in the context in which it appears.' *Wilson v Harris* (1964) 65 SR(NSW) 329 at 338, per Asprey J

New Zealand 'If the testator in his will uses certain words, it must be taken that he uses them in the ordinary and natural sense, unless there is something in the will from which it can be gathered that he used them in some other sense. No doubt, in some of the earlier cases the courts were very ready, when the word "survivors" was used, to find any excuse for reading the word in the non-natural sense of "others". Later cases show, however, that the word "survivors" will be read in its ordinary or natural sense unless there is something to indicate an intention that it is not so used. I do not think there is anything in this will to indicate an intention that it should be read in any other way than the ordinary sense. There are . . . two classes of cases in which the word "survivors" is to be read as "others"—(a) where there is a gift over after the death of all the beneficiaries in order to avoid intestacy; (b) the other, where the terms of the will indicate an intention that the beneficiaries should take *per stirpes*.' *Re Wilson* (1900) 19 NZLR 406 at 408, per Williams J

SUSPECT

'"Good cause to suspect" [within the Poaching Prevention Act 1862] means a reasonable ground of suspicion upon which a reasonable man may act.' *R v Spencer* (1863) 3 F & F 857 at 857, 858, per Martin B

[The question was whether a constable was justified in searching a man as being a person whom he had good cause to 'suspect' of coming from land where he had been unlawfully searching for game, under s 2 of the Poaching Prevention Act 1862, when he had actually seen the respondent upon land and searching for game.] 'I think this point scarcely required a case to be stated in order to settle it. Common sense would at once suggest that after a man has been seen actually poaching he may well be suspected of poaching.' *Hall v Robinson* (1889) 53 JP 310 at 311, DC, per Cave J

Australia 'The word "suspect" requires a degree of satisfaction, not necessarily amounting to belief, but at least extending beyond speculation as to whether an event has occurred or not.' *Commissioner for Corporate Affairs v Guardian Investments Pty Ltd* [1984] VR 1019 at 1025, per Ormiston J

SUSPECTED PERSON

[It was formerly provided, by the Vagrancy Act 1824, s 4, that 'suspected persons' or reported thieves should be deemed to be rogues and vagabonds, and thus subject to arrest. This particular provision of s 4 was repealed by the Criminal Attempts Act 1981, s 8 thus abolishing the offence of 'loitering with intent'.

See now, as to police powers to stop and search persons on suspicion, and to arrest without warrant, the Police and Criminal Evidence Act 1984.]

Australia 'The language used by the Chief Justice in a judgment [*Ex p King* 38 NSWR 483] in which the other members of the Court concurred may be read as giving some support to the appellant's contention. He said suspected person means a person of whom people who know him suspect that when he gets the chance he commits crimes of dishonesty or dishonesty and violence of the kind which are within the reach of rogues and vagabonds.' *Easton v Johnstone* [1947] ALR 115 at 116, per Gavan Duffy J

Australia [The respondent was charged under the Vagrants, Gaming and Other Offences Act 1931–1986 (Qld), s 4(1)(ix)(c), with being a vagrant in that, being a 'suspected person', he was found in a place adjacent to a public place.] 'I hold that in order to be a suspected person within the meaning of the section, the accused must be shown to have become reasonably suspected of dishonesty or criminality at a time prior to the commencement of the occasion which results in his arrest. During that occasion, one or more incidents must occur which establish the criminal intent of the accused, but the suspicion engendered by that incident or those incidents is not by itself enough to put the accused into the category of suspected persons within the meaning of the section.' *Hoppner v Boyland* [1956] St R Qd 531 at 539, per Philip J

New Zealand 'To be a suspect, it is not obligatory that the person be generally suspected, nor that those who suspect need be in any special relationship to the suspected person.' *R v Nakhla (No 1)* [1974] 1 NZLR 441 at 449, CA, per McCarthy P

SUSPENDED SENTENCE

(1) Subject to subsection (2) below, a court which passes a sentence of imprisonment for a

term of not more than two years for an offence may order that the sentence shall not take effect unless, during a period specified in the order, being not less than one year or more than two years from the date of the order, the offender commits in Great Britain another offence punishable with imprisonment and thereafter a court having power to do so orders under section 23 of this Act that the original sentence shall take effect; and in this Part of this Act 'operational period', in relation to a suspended sentence, means the period so specified.

(2) A court shall not deal with an offender by means of a suspended sentence unless the case appears to the court to be one in which a sentence of imprisonment would have been appropriate in the absence of any power to suspend such a sentence by an order under subsection (1) above. (Powers of Criminal Courts Act 1973, s 22(1), (2))

[The remainder of the section makes further provisions and stipulations as to the passing of suspended sentences. Section 23 empowers a court on conviction of a further offence during the operational period of a suspended sentence, to deal with that suspended sentence, e.g. by ordering that the sentence shall take effect, or by varying the original order.

For additional powers of a court to suspend part of a sentence see the Criminal Law Act 1977, s 47(1A) as inserted by the Criminal Justice Act 1982, s 30(4).]

SUSPENSION

Clerical

A censure of suspension is disqualification of a person for a specified time for exercising or performing without the bishop's leave any right or duty of or incidental to his preferment or from residing in the house of residence of his preferment or within such distance of it as is specified in the censure. It may not be imposed in respect of an offence involving matter of doctrine, ritual or ceremonial unless the court is satisfied that the accused has already been admonished on a previous occasion in respect of another offence of the same or substantially the same nature. (14 Halsbury's Laws (4th edn) para 1378)

The censures to which a person found guilty of an offence under this Measure renders himself liable are the following, namely . . . (c) suspension, that is to say, disqualification for a specified time from exercising or performing without leave of the bishop any right or duty of or incidental to his preferment or from residing in the house of residence of his preferment or within such distance thereof as shall be specified in the censure. (Ecclesiastical Jurisdiction Measure 1963 (No 1), s 49)

Of payment

United States 'Suspends payments' with respect to a bank means that it has been closed by order of the supervisory authorities, that a public officer has been appointed to take it over, or that it ceases or refuses to make payments in the ordinary course of business. (Uniform Commercial Code 1978, s 4–104(1)(k))

SUSPICION *See also* BELIEVE

'Suspicion in its ordinary meaning is a state of conjecture or surmise where proof is lacking: "I suspect but I cannot prove". Suspicion arises at or near the starting-point of an investigation of which the obtaining of prima facie proof is the end. When such proof has been obtained, the police case is complete; it is ready for trial and passes on to its next stage. It is indeed desirable as a general rule that an arrest should not be made until the case is complete. But if arrest before that were forbidden, it could seriously hamper the police. To give power to arrest on reasonable suspicion does not mean that it is always or even ordinarily to be exercised. It means that there is an executive discretion. In the exercise of it many factors have to be considered besides the strength of the case. The possibility of escape, the prevention of further crime and the obstruction of police inquiries are examples of those factors . . . There is another distinction between reasonable suspicion and prima facie proof. Prima facie proof consists of admissible evidence. Suspicion can take into account matters that could not be put in evidence at all. There is a discussion about the relevance of previous convictions in the judgment of Lord Wright in *McArdle v Egan* [(1934) 150 LT 412]. Suspicion can take into account also matters which, though admissible, could not form part of a prima facie case. Thus, the fact that the accused has given a false alibi does not obviate the need for prima facie proof of his presence at the scene of the crime; it will become of considerable importance in the trial when such proof as there is is being weighed perhaps against a second alibi; it would undoubtedly be a very suspicious circumstance.' *Hussein v*

Chong Fook Kam [1969] 3 All ER 1626 at 1630, PC, per Lord Devlin

SUSTAIN

New Zealand '"Sustain" [in the Matrimonial Property Act 1976, s 17(1)(d)] means something more than merely to render assistance and to play a role in the running of a farm. It imports the concept of preservation.' *Mitchell v Mitchell* [1983] 2 NZFLR 182 at 188, per Prichard J

SWEAR *See also* BLASPHEMY; OATH

'Swear' includes affirm, declare, and protest. (Commissioners for Oaths Act 1889, s 11)

Australia 'To the definition of "swear" mentioned to the jury by the trial judge . . . as being a religious asseveration by which the party calls his God witness that what he says is the truth or that what he promises to do he will do . . . we also add to it the definition in the Dictionary of English Law by Jowitt, namely "to put on oath, to administer an oath". A justice of the peace taking an affidavit administers an oath but the deponent swears an oath when he says or acknowledges the words of the oath. At common law the form of oath is immaterial provided it is binding on the witness's conscience: Halsbury's Laws of England (4th edn), vol 17, par 264.' *R v Sossi* (1985) 17 A Crim R 405 at 408, per cur.

Canada [A person who used offensive and obscene language in a public place was charged with causing a disturbance in a public place by swearing, contrary to the Criminal Code, 1953–1954 (Can) c 51, s 160(a) (see now RSC 1970, c 34, s 171).] 'The essence of swearing appears to be a reference to God and in the form of an oath. Often used in legal proceedings and in legal documents as an appeal to the truth by invoking the deity the word also includes the use of language which is contemptuous or irreverent of God or the deity.' *R v Enns* (1968) 66 WWR 318 at 320, per Maher DCJ

SWEAT

'Then comes the word "sweating" [in a bill of lading] "loss, damage, or injury arising from sweating". . . . I think the correct view of that word is that expressed by counsel for the plaintiffs—namely, of moisture dropping on to the bags from condensation, which arises if there is moisture which evaporates and then condenses in the hold.' *The Pearlmoor* [1904] P 286 at 299, per Gorell Barnes J

SWING BRIDGE

'Swing bridge' includes any opening bridge operated by mechanical means. (Highways Act 1980, s 329(1))

SYMBOL *See also* TRADE MARK

[The Town and Country Planning (Control of Advertisements) Regulations 1969, reg 14(2), prohibited the display, in advertisements, of letters, figures, 'symbols', emblems or devices above a certain size.] 'The objects in question [pictures of cigarettes and beer] are obviously not letters or figures (which here clearly means numerical figures). Are they symbols, emblems or devices? We have been referred to the dictionary definitions of those terms which do not greatly help save as showing a substantial overlap between their meanings (one finds each defined in terms of one or more of the others) and indicating a common denominator in that a symbol, emblem or device suggests in each case something which points to a meaning beyond itself.' *McDonald v Howard Cook Advertising Ltd* [1971] 3 All ER 1249 at 1252, per cur.

SYSTEM

Safe system of working

'What exactly is meant by "a safe system of working" has never, so far as I know, been precisely defined. I do not venture to suggest a definition of what is meant by system, but it includes, in my opinion, or may include according to circumstances, such matters as the physical lay-out of the job—the setting of the stage, so to speak—the sequence in which the work is to be carried out, the provision in proper cases of warnings and notices, and the issue of special instructions. A system may be adequate for the whole course of the job or it may have to be modified or improved to meet circumstances which arise. Such modifications or improvements appear to me equally to fall under the head of system.' *Speed v Thomas Swift & Co Ltd* [1943] 1 KB 557 at 562–564, CA, per Lord Greene MR

T

TABLE MEAL

'Table meal' means a meal eaten by a person seated at a table, or at a counter or other structure which serves the purpose of a table and is not used for the service of refreshments for consumption by persons not seated at a table or structure serving the purpose of a table. (Licensing Act 1964, s 201)

TAKE

In Game Act

[The Game Act 1831, s 3, makes it unlawful to 'take' any game during the close season.] 'The case must go back, with our intimation that the original capture being by accident does not prevent the subsequent taking being against the statute.' *Watkins v Price* (1877) 47 LJMC 1 DC, per Cockburn CJ

In Lands Clauses Consolidation Act

'During the argument I asked whether it had ever been held that the 68th section of the Lands Clauses [Consolidation] Act [1845] applies to the case where compensation is sought in respect of the whole interest in the land. What seems to have been contemplated by the 68th section of the Act is a remedy to persons who have some limited interest in the land where the land has been lawfully taken by the company. I can discover no ground for holding that the word "taken" by the company means taken either rightfully or wrongfully—taken under a proper authority or taken without any authority at all. That construction seems to me in no way warranted, and no authority has been cited to justify the Court in putting such a construction on the word "taken" in the 68th section. If the railway company, as the plaintiffs have proved, are in possession of his land under a mistake as to the authority under which the possession was taken, they are not rightfully in possession of the land. In my opinion the 68th section applies only to cases where the company must be rightfully in possession, and where compensation is sought by persons having a limited interest.' *Perks v Wycombe Rly Co* (1862) 3 Giff 662 at 672, per Stuart V-C

[The Lands Clauses Consolidation Act 1845, s 80, makes it lawful for the Court of Chancery, in certain cases where monies are deposited in the Bank of England under the provisions of the Act, to order certain costs to be paid by the promoters of the undertaking, including the costs of the purchase or 'taking' of the lands. Section 85 enables promoters to enter on lands before purchase, on making a deposit by way of security and giving a bond.] 'In the event contemplated at the commencement of the 80th section, it is provided that it shall be lawful to the court to do certain things, and amongst those things is the power to direct the payment of the costs of the purchase or taking of the land. It appears to me to be perfectly plain that the company acting under the 85th section is taking lands, and it is to be borne in mind that the word "taking" in the 80th section is used in contrast with "purchase". . . . Is there any reason for not including the costs of the taking under the 85th section in the word "taking" in the 80th section? I can find none.' *Charlton v Rolleston* (1884) 28 Ch D 237 at 253, 254, CA, per Fry LJ

'I think that that expression [the word "taken" in the Lands Clauses Consolidation Act 1845, s 68] means actually taken and entered upon.' *R v Manley Smith, Re Church & London School Board* (1892) 67 LT 197 at 200, DC, per Charles J

TAKE AWAY

Australia [The Criminal Code Act 1924–1984 (Tas), s 189, provides that any person who 'takes away' an unmarried girl under the age of eighteen years out of the possession and against the will of her parent is guilty of an offence.] 'Even if it be that the girl had, without any inducement from the prisoner, even unbeknownst to him, formed the inflexible resolve to leave home, and would have done so in any event, nevertheless if being apprised of her purpose, he actively co-operates in its execution, whereby she leaves with him or goes to him pursuant to their mutual arrangement using money or facilities provided by him for the purpose, there would be a taking within the meaning of the Act. . . . The accused is not in my view of the law entitled to take advantage of the girl's folly or her distress; if not having induced or assisted her to leave he passively receives and harbours her, certainly he commits no offence. Similarly if he merely meets her and goes with her, but if—so far from it being a question of any necessary persuasion or inducement on his part—he should, yielding to her forwardness and earnest request, so combine with her so that the leaving may be said to take place pursuant to a joint plan, then he would be guilty of having taken her away.' *R v Mejac* [1954] Tas SR 26 at 31, per Crisp J

TAKE EFFECT

Canada 'It is an everyday occurrence that a person resigns an office, his resignation to "take effect" on a certain day. A government makes an order to "take effect" a month hence. . . . I conclude that the natural meaning of the words "take effect" in this instance is "producing the desired effect", namely, the termination of the lease.' *Dominion Square Corpn v Aluminium Co of Canada* [1942] 2 DLR 189 at 194, SCC, per Hudson J

TAKE FOR VALUE

United States A holder takes an instrument for value

(a) to the extent that the agreed consideration has been performed or that he acquires a security interest in or a lien on the instrument otherwise than by legal process; or

(b) when he takes the instrument in payment of or as security for an antecedent claim against any person whether or not the claim is due; or

(c) when he gives a negotiable instrument for it or makes an irrevocable commitment to a third person.

(Uniform Commercial Code 1978, s 3–303

TAKE FROM

[The appellants bought beer in a hotel, during licensing hours, but did not begin to remove it until after closing time. Two police officers found them in the act of making the removal, but before they had left the entrance hall. They were convicted of 'taking' away liquor outside permitted hours, in contravention of the Licensing Act 1953, s 100(1)(b) (repealed; see now the Licensing Act 1964, s 59(1)(b)).] 'Counsel for the respondent . . . has had to ask us to read "takes from" in s 100 of the Licensing Act 1953 as being equivalent to "found in the process of taking from". One cannot read a penal section in that way. The ordinary and natural meaning of s 100 in this respect is of a completed act being referred to and nothing else.' *Pender v Smith* [1959] 2 All ER 360 at 361, per Donovan J; also reported [1959] 2 QB 84 at 85

TAKE IN EXECUTION

'What is the meaning of "taken in execution"? Read irrespectively of authorities, it means taken by process of law for the enforcement of a judgment creditor's right, and in order to give effect to that right.' *Blackman v Fysh* [1892] 3 Ch 209 at 216, 217, CA, per Kekewich J

TAKE-OVER

'Take-over offer for a company' means an offer made to all the holders (or all the holders other than the person making the offer and his nominees) of the shares in the company to acquire those shares or a specified proportion of them, or to all the holders (or all the holders other than the person making the offer and his nominees) of a particular class of those shares to acquire the shares of that class or a specified proportion of them. (Company Securities (Insider Dealing) Act 1985, s 14)

TAKE PART

[Under the Supreme Court Costs Rules 1959, r 22, para (3) (revoked; see now RSC 1965, Ord 62, r 22), a notice need not have been given to any party who had not entered an appearance or 'taken part' in proceedings giving rise to taxation proceedings.] '"Taken part" is a broad expression. Although a party has not entered an appearance, yet, if he has taken some part in the proceedings, he is entitled to notice. In my judgment it is taking part in the proceedings (and a very vital part) if, when it is impossible for the case to proceed as it is, a party steps forward and assents to the case being heard and the matter proceeding, especially when thereby the party takes away from himself the chance of entering an appearance.' *Roberts v Roberts* [1965] 2 All ER 160 at 161, CA, per Lord Pearce

[The Representation of the People Act 1969, s 9(1) (repealed; see now the Representation of the People Act 1983, s 93) provided that pending a parliamentary or local government election, it should not be lawful for any item about the constituency or electoral area to be broadcast from a television or other wireless transmitting station in the United Kingdom if any of the persons who were for the time being candidates at the election 'took part' in the item and the broadcast was not made with his consent.] 'In my view, prima facie to take part in something does indicate actively doing something and not merely being a part of; and, when one looks at the rest of this very difficult section, there appears a passage which I will quote. It is the second part of sub-s (1) and it includes the passage: ". . . and where an item about a constituency or electoral area is so broadcast pending a parliamentary or local government election there, then if the broadcast either is made before the latest time for delivery of nomination papers, or is made after that time but without the consent of any candidate remaining validly nominated, any person taking part in the item for the purpose of promoting or procuring his election shall be guilty of an illegal practice, unless the broadcast is so made without his consent." As it seems to me, it is quite impossible to take part in an item for the purpose of doing something unless you are taking an active part; and I do not see that it is possible to construe the words "take part in" in the first part of the section and the words "taking part in the item" in the second part of the section so as to give a different meaning to the phrase "takes part" from "taking part". In my view, the only conclusion which can be drawn from that is "takes part in" means "actively participates in", which is more than "co-operates in". It requires active participation.' *James Marshall v British Broadcasting Corpn* [1979] 3 All ER 80 at 82, CA, per Waller LJ

TAKING AT SEA

'I need only refer to three [text books]. First, there is the statement of the law by the late Mr Arthur Cohen, PC, KC in an article in 17 Halsbury's Laws (1st edn) paras 870–871. This article has long been regarded as of the highest authority on this branch of the law. Under the cross-heading, which includes the phrase "Seizure or takings at sea", the learned author stated: "Seizures and takings at sea include deprivation of possession, whether the seizure or taking was lawful or unlawful, and whether by enemies or pirates." Gow *Marine Insurance* (1st edn, 1896) p 114 stated: " 'Taking at sea' is commonly expressed in modern commercial language as 'seizure'." Templeman *Marine Insurance* (1st edn, 1903) p 34 stated: " 'Surprisals and Takings at Sea'. These words require no explanation, being merely another way of expressing 'Capture'." . . . Indeed, I would venture the view that one has only to look at the phrase in its context [a Lloyd's marine insurance policy] in the list of perils insured against and then to construe it in that context to see that the construction adopted in these three works and indeed others [i.e. that the phrase means capture or seizure, by enemies or pirates] is plainly correct.' *Shell International Petroleum Co Ltd v Gibbs, The Salem* [1983] 1 All ER 745 at 750, HL, per Lord Roskill

TALES

[If a jury has been summoned, but sufficient jurors do not appear, or a sufficient number do not remain after challenges, etc, either party may pray a 'tales', asking the court to make up the deficiency. There cannot, however, be a jury composed entirely of talesmen.] 'In our opinion, if there is a defect in the jury, that is to say, if a full jury cannot be empanelled from the names on the panel, a tales can be prayed. Whether the talesmen must be actually present in the precincts of the court or can be brought in from the street, we need not inquire, because we do not want to give a decision on any point that is immaterial. But it seems to the court that there cannot be a jury composed entirely of talesmen because the very fact that it is a tales imples that there must be a quales. Since writs of error were done away with, records are not now drawn up, but, if the record had been drawn up, the jury panel would have had to be set out in the record and also the names of the jurors who actually were empanelled to try the issue. If there were no jurors who were in the original panel, it would have been plain on the record that twelve people tried the prisoner who had not been summoned, and if a tales is to be summoned there must be, as it seems to the court, a jury composed partly of those who have been summoned, the quales, and added to them, if the record had been drawn up, such persons standing by as would make up the full jury. In this case all the persons who tried the case had never been summoned. If there is a complete defect or shortage of jurors, as happened in this case, the court desires to say that in their opinion the proper course is to require the sheriff to return a further panel *instanter*. It may be that at borough quarter sessions that would be impracticable. We have considered that, as the clerk of the peace summons the jurors. At any rate, if this happens again and the trial is to proceed on the same day, it seems to us that the right course instead of praying tales is to require a fresh panel to be empanelled *instanter*.' *R v Solomon* (1958) 42 Cr App Rep 9 CCA, per Lord Goddard CJ

[*See* generally, as to jury service, the Juries Act 1974; especially s 6 thereto (22 Halsbury's Statutes (4th edn) 413).]

TATTOO

For the purposes of this Act 'tattoo' shall mean the insertion into the skin of any colouring material designed to leave a permanent mark. (Tattooing of Minors Act 1969, s 3)

TAVERN

'I think "tavern keeper" never was a technical term. A tavern has been held to be an inn, and the tavern keeper subject to the liabilities and entitled to the rights of an innkeeper; see the case *Thompson v Lacy* [(1820) 3 B & Ald 283]. In this sense the defendants are certainly not tavern keepers. As to the popular sense of the words, I think that "alehouse", "beerhouse" and "tavern" all imply a place where people can go and buy intoxicating drink and consume it without necessarily buying anything else.' *Lorden v Brooke-Hitching* [1927] 2 KB 237 at 250, 251, per Salter J

TAX *See also* INCOME TAX

Australia 'Direct taxation is taxation by way of pecuniary payments directly imposed in respect of persons or things subject to the jurisdiction of the taxing authority, and the burden of which is designed to fall upon the taxpayer himself. . . . I am of opinion that the levying of duties of Customs on importation is not the imposition of a tax upon property.' *A-G of New South Wales v Collector of Customs of New South Wales* (1908) 5 CLR 818 at 830, 832, per Griffith CJ

Australia 'The word "tax" and its plural "taxes" are not words of invariable signification indicating any exercise whatever of the power of taxation; they are not infrequently used to denote a particular species of imposition, in contradistinction to duties, and to duties of various kinds.' Ibid at 848, per Isaascs J

Australia 'The difference between a pecuniary penalty and a tax is that the former is a sum required in respect of an unlawful act, and the latter is a sum required in respect of a lawful act.' *R v Barger* (1908) 6 CLR 41 at 54, per Isaacs J

Australia 'The primary meaning of "taxation" is raising money for the purposes of government by means of contributions from individual persons.' Ibid at 68, per Griffiths CJ and Barton and O'Connor JJ

Australia 'A compulsory contribution, or an impost, may be none the less a tax, though not so called; the distinguishing feature of a tax being in fact that it is a compulsory contribution, imposed by the sovereign authority on, and required from, the general body of subjects or citizens, as distinguished from isolated levies on individuals.' *Leake v Commissioner of Taxation (State)* (1934) 36 WALR 66 at 67, per Dwyer J

Direct and indirect taxes

Canada 'A direct tax is—in the words which are printed here from Mr Mill's book on political economy—"one which is demanded from the very persons who it is intended or desired should pay it". And then the converse definition of indirect taxes is, "those which are demanded from one person in the expectation and intention that he shall indemnify himself at the expense of another".' *A-G for Quebec v Reed* (1884) 10 App Cas 141 at 143, 144, PC, per cur.

Canada 'I cannot assent to the . . . assumption that "direct taxation within the province" necessarily means only taxation in respect of property physically within the province. . . . A man may be domiciled within a province and be made answerable for taxes imposed upon him in respect of property outside the province, but over which the laws of the province may have given him the only foundation he can have for dominion or legal possession.' *R v Cotton* (1911) 45 SCR 469 at 494, SCC, per Idington J

Canada 'Without reviewing afresh the niceties of discrimination between direct and indirect taxation it is enough to point out that an export tax is normally collected on merchantable goods in course of transit in pursuance of commercial transactions. Whether the tax is ultimately borne by the exporting seller at home or by the importing buyer abroad depends on the terms of the contract between them. . . . While it is no doubt true that a tax levied on personal property, no less than a tax levied on real property, may be a direct tax where the taxpayer's personal property is selected as the criterion of his ability to pay, a tax which . . . is levied on a commercial commodity on the occasion of its exportation in pursuance of trading transactions, cannot be described as a tax whose incidence is, by its nature, such that normally it is finally borne by the first payer, and is not susceptible of being passed on.' *A-G for British Columbia v McDonald Murphy Lumber Co Ltd* [1930] AC 357 at 364, 365, PC, per Lord Macmillan.

Canada 'There is an obvious distinction between an indirect tax, like an ordinary customs or excise duty, which enters into the cost of an article at each stage of its subsequent handling or manufacture, and an impost laid upon the final consumer, as "the particular party selected to pay the tax", who produces the money which his agent pays over. This is mere machinery, and resembles the requirement in British income tax that in certain cases A is assessed for tax which B really bears—a circumstance which does not make income tax "indirect". The test for indirect taxation which Mill prescribed is the passing on of the burden of a duty by the person who first pays it through subsequent transactions to future recipients in the process of dealing with the commodity, or at any rate the tendency so to pass on the burden.' *Atlantic Smoke Shops Ltd v Conlon* (1943) 112 LJPC 68 at 73, PC, per Lord Simon LC

TAX ADVANTAGE

In this Chapter [Part XVII, Ch I: cancellation of tax advantages from certain transactions in securities] 'tax advantage' means a relief or increased relief from, or repayment or increased repayment of, tax, or the avoidance or reduction of a charge to tax or an assessment to tax or the avoidance of a possible assessment thereto, whether the avoidance or reduction is effected by receipts accruing in such a way that the recipient does not pay or bear tax on them, or by a deduction in computing profits or gains. (Income and Corporation Taxes Act 1988, s 709(1))

TAXATION

Australia 'The word "taxation", in my opinion, is not—or not yet—a legal word of art. It is a word that has a general fiscal significance, and should be construed by invoking the same sort of historical and public considerations as were invoked by the High Court when they worked out, by a series of decisions, the meaning of the word "excise". It seems to me that . . . the word "taxation" denotes all forms of general impost, however assessed, levied, or collected, in contrast to charges for services. . . . Clearly the levying and collection of rates is a form of taxation.' *Transport Authority v Adelaide* (1980) 24 SASR 481 at 485, per Wells J

Of costs

'The words "taxation as between solicitor and client" have two meanings. The natural and ordinary meaning, which I will refer to as meaning (A), is an inquiry as to the costs which a client ought properly to pay to his own solicitor, as distinct from "taxation between party and party", which is an inquiry as to the costs which he should recover from the opposite side. The distinction is based on common sense, for if a client authorises his solicitor to incur an unusual or unnecessary expense it is only right that the client should reimburse his own solicitor for it, but it does not follow that he should be able to recover it from the opposite side. The other meaning of "taxation as between solicitor and client", a technical meaning, which I will refer to as meaning (B), is an inquiry as to the costs to be paid to the solicitor out of a common fund in which the client and others are interested and is substantially a taxation as between party and party, but on a more generous scale. When meaning (B) is used a different form of words is needed to describe an inquiry as to the costs which a client ought properly to pay his own solicitor and that is then described as a "taxation as between solicitor and own client".' *Goodwin v Storrar* [1947] KB 457 at 458, per Denning J

TAXIMETER

The expression 'taximeter' means any appliance for measuring the time or distance for which a cab is used, or for measuring both time and distance, which is for the time being approved for the purpose by or on behalf of the Secretary of State. (London Cab and Stage Carriage Act 1907, s 6)

'Taximeter' means any device for calculating the fare to be charged in respect of any journey in a hackney carriage or private hire vehicle by reference to the distance travelled or time elapsed since the start of the journey, or a combination of both. (Local Government (Miscellaneous Provisions) Act 1976, s 80(1))

TEA

'The appellant did not acquire drink, but has acquired dried tea-leaves from which a drink can be made. No one sits down to eat tea, and it is not accurate to say that any one drinks tea. What one drinks, is, not the tea, but the water which has passed through the tea-leaves so as to make an infusion which is known as tea.' *Hinde v Allmond* (1918) 87 LJKB 893 at 893, DC, per Darling J

'Tea is not in itself a food in the sense that it is not nutritious, that you cannot live on it, that it will not increase the amount of tissue in a person as the drinking of milk would—food may be solid food or liquid food—it is not simply because it is a drink that tea is not a food; that is an entire mistake—supposing tea were capable of adding to the tissues as milk will do then it would be quite right to call it simply a food. Tea appears to be nothing in the world but a stimulant.' *Sainsbury v Saunders* (1918) 88 LJKB 441 at 445, DC, per Darling J

TECHNICAL

Rule of law

'A technical rule of law is invoked on behalf of the plaintiffs. A technical rule is one which is established by authority and precedent, which does not depend upon reasoning or argument, but is a fixed established rule to be acted upon and only discussed as regards its application—in truth is "the law".' *Chesterfield & Midland Silkstone Colliery Co Ltd v Hawkins* (1865) 3 H & C 677 at 691, per Martin B

TELECOMMUNICATION

Canada 'The word "telecommunication" can be widely defined. In Robert, *Dictionnaire de la langue française*, 1964, T VI, at p 675, it is defined as "L'ensemble des procédés de transmission d'informations à distance". The word "tele" in Greek means "far". Telecommunications systems, in a general sense, are devices and techniques employed for the transmission of signs, signals, writing, images, sounds or data of any nature by wire, radio or other electromagnetic equipment.' *Maltais v R* [1978] 1 SCR 441 at 443, 444, SCC, per Dickson J

TELEGRAPH

Canada 'Their Lordships . . . think broadcasting falls within the description of "telegraphs". No doubt in everyday speech telegraph is almost exclusively used to denote the electrical instrument which by means of a wire connecting that instrument with another instrument makes it possible to communicate signals or words of any kind. But the original meaning of the word "telegraph" as given in the Oxford Dictionary, is: "An apparatus for transmitting messages to a distance, usually by signs of some kind". Now a message to be transmitted must have a recipient as well as a transmitter. . . . Further, the strict reading of the word "telegraph", making it identical with the ordinary use of it, has already been given up in *Toronto Corporation v Bell Telephone Co of Canada* [[1905] AC 52, PC].' *Re Regulation and Control of Radio Communication in Canada* [1932] AC 304 at 315, 316, PC, per cur.

TELEPHONE

Australia 'It has been suggested that a telephone is an instrument which provides communication from point to point only, and that if what is heard at the receiving end is available for all bystanders to hear, the communication is not telephonic in character. This argument does not appear to be sound. . . . The fact that a large number of receiving instruments can pick up the same message does not alter the telephonic nature of the operation.' *R v Brislan, ex p Williams* (1935) 54 CLR 262 at 270, per Latham CJ

TEMPERATE

'I believe it to be useless to attempt a precise definition of what constitutes "temperate habits", or "temperance", in the sense in which these expressions are ordinarily employed. Men differ so much in their capacity for imbibing strong drinks that quantity affords not test: what one man might take without exceeding the bounds of moderation, another could not take without committing excess. . . . It seems to me to be the fair result of the evidence, that the assured was in the habit of taking more drink than was good for him; that he was frequently affected with drink on occasions when all except himself were sober; that his indulgence to excess had become so apparent that several of his friends remonstrated with him on the subject, and that, instead of repudiating the charge, he admitted it and promised amendment. These facts appear to me to be fully proved, and they are, in my opinion, altogether inconsistent with the truth of the assertion that he was . . . of temperate habits and had always been so.' *Thomson v Weems* (1884) 9 Ap Cas 671 at 686, 695, 696, per Lord Watson

TEMPEST *See* FLOOD

TEMPORARY

Australia [The Social Security Act 1947 (Cth), s 103(1)(d) provides that a child endowment is not payable to a person outside Australia unless that person's absence from Australia is 'temporary' only.] 'The shorter Oxford Dictionary defines "temporary" as "lasting for a limited time; existing or valid for a time (only); transient; made to supply a passing need". The Macquarie Dictionary definition is to similar effect, with the addition of "not permanent". In one sense any absence from Australia, which in fact comes to an end, is temporary; it turns out to have lasted for a limited—as distinct from an unlimited—time and to have been not permanent. In this sense everything in human affairs, including life itself, is "temporary". But it is doubtful whether the word "temporary" was used in this wide sense in s 103(1)(d). As I have pointed out, had it been intended to protect the endowment rights of persons absent abroad for lengthy periods, who ultimately return to Australia and who, in the meantime, maintain some association with Australia, it would have been enough to refer to residence in Australia. Plainly it was intended to be more restrictive than that. I think that the adjective "temporary" was used to denote an absence that was, both in intention and in fact, limited to the fulfilment of a passing purpose. The purpose might be of a business or professional nature; it might be for a holiday or for compassionate or family reasons. But, whatever the purpose, it seems to me to be implied in the concept of "temporary" absence that the absence will be relatively short and that its duration will be either defined in advance or be related to the fulfilment of a specific, passing purpose. If, for example, a businessman travels overseas for a period of three months to engage in sales discussions, intending always to return to his usual home in Australia and in fact returning at the end of that period, there is no difficulty about describing his absence as "temporary". If that same person moves himself and his family to an overseas location, intending to remain there indefinitely in pursuit of business orders, his absence would not properly be described as "temporary"; and I think that this is so even if, after two months for family or personal reasons, he decides to abandon his overseas home and return to Australia. Under such circumstances the absence from Australia would have turned out to be of limited duration, but it would not have been in fulfilment of a passing need.' *Hafza v Director-General of Social Security* (1985) 60 ALR 674 at 682–683, per Wilcox J

Temporary cessation of work

[On an appeal from a decision of the Industrial Tribunal, as to entitlement to redundancy payment, it was claimed that breaks in the appellant's service with the respondents were 'temporary cessation' of work within the Contracts of Employment Act 1963, Sch 1 (repealed; see now the Employment Protection (Consolidation) Act 1978, Sch 13, para 9(1)(b)).] 'The court has been referred to a decision of the Industrial Tribunal in *Minards v Courtaulds Ltd* [[1967 ITR 219], where it was held that: "A temporary cessation of work means a cessation of work for a period which at the time it began was regarded by both employer and employee as intended to come to an end within a foreseeable time." For my part I see very great difficulties in construing the word "temporary" in that way. One observes in the first instance that no such words in regard to intention appear in the Contracts of Employment Act 1963 at all. To give it that interpretation is, I think, to add something which is not there. It seems to me that the proper approach is to look at the matter after the event, looking backwards, and say to oneself: when the employee is re-engaged, if he is, has the cessation been a temporary cessation? If there is evidence of an intention when it began that it should be temporary, that will be very relevant, but the absence of such an intention does not conclude the matter. It can, of course, be asked: what are the limits of "temporary"? If an employee is re-engaged after three years or after three weeks, or whatever it may be, what guide is there: what is the test as to what is temporary? For my part, I do not propose to lay down any test. It is a question of fact for the tribunal in all the circumstances of the case, bearing in mind that we are dealing here with working weeks, and that, at any rate in the case of sickness and injury, an absence of twenty-six weeks is permissible. That is, however, not the test, but at any rate it is some guide.' *Hunter v Smith's Dock Co Ltd* [1968] 2 All ER 81 at 84, per Lord Parker CJ

[By the Contracts of Employment Act 1963, Sch 1 (repealed; see supra) if in any week an employee was absent from work on account of a temporary cessation of work, that week counted as a period of employment in the computation of a period of employment e.g., for redundancy payment). An employee who had twice been employed by the respondents claimed redundancy pay as from the date of his first employment.] 'Was the cessation temporary? . . . It will seldom be possible to say at the time when the employee is first dismissed (and the problem before your Lordships must surely always involve two dismissals), that his cessation of work was temporary. The employee may take up other employment and, whatever his original intentions, may never return to his old employer. He may leave for what he hopes will only be temporary employment elsewhere. In this he may be disappointed for, contrary to his expectation and possibly that of his old employer, his old job may never become available. Or he may find that he prefers his new employment and decides to make it permanent. So the question—was the cessation temporary?—of most cases cannot be answered as at the time in dismissal. The First Division applied the test stated in *Singh v Patterson* [1942 SC(J) 89], where the question was whether the residence of an individual in a particular country was temporary; it was held that the true opposite of "temporary" was not "permanent" but "indefinite" or "unlimited". With all respect, that test can have no relevance here, for in most cases when the employee is dismissed his dismissal at that time must be described as indefinite or unlimited. But counsel on both sides agreed that, as in every case where this problem arises there will have been a re-engagement, one must look at the original dismissal with hindsight, that is to say, with knowledge of all that happened since the original dismissal until the second dismissal, and then decide whether in all the circumstances of the case the original dismissal can properly be described as due to a *temporary* cessation of work.' *Fitzgerald v Hall Russell & Co Ltd* [1969] 3 All ER 1140 at 1152, HL, per Lord Upjohn

Temporary purpose

'Regarded as a question of prescription I should have to consider whether the artificial watercourse was made for a temporary purpose or not. . . . The meaning of "temporary purpose" is . . . not confined to a purpose that happens to last in fact a few years only, but includes a purpose which is temporary in the sense that it may within the reasonable contemplation of the parties come to an end. For example, if a man pumps water from his mines for the purpose of draining them, that is a temporary purpose, as it is limited by the duration of the workings. If a man makes a watercourse leading water to a mill-pond for the use of his own mill on his own land, that is a temporary purpose, as it is limited to the period for which he uses the mill. In both cases, in my judgment, it is a temporary purpose within the meaning of the authorities.' *Burrows v Lang* [1901] 2 Ch 502 at 507, 508, per Farwell J

Temporary use

'It is enough to say that by s 105 of the statute [Factory and Workshop Act 1901 (repealed; see now the Factories Act 1961)] the provisions of the Act with respect to regulations for dangerous trades were to have effect, among other matters, "as if any premises which machinery worked by steam, water, or other mechanical power is temporarily used for the purpose of the construction of a building or any structural work in connection with a building, were included in the word 'factory'." The material fact in this case was that on the 28th of September, 1927, the machinery of a certain hoist erected by the respondents was not actually being used for the purpose of hoisting materials by mechanical power; but two workmen of the respondents were handing timber up from the seventh to the eighth floor through the hoist opening. The hoist remained, in the words of the case, "available to be operated and was intended to be further operated by the respondents for hoisting materials". In these circumstances it is obvious that the contention which was urged on the part of the respondents at the police court that the machinery was not being "temporarily" used, in that it was not being used at the moment on the premises, involves a wrong construction of this section. . . . The construction put upon the section and the contention put before the learned magistrate was that the machinery cannot be said to be temporarily used on the premises, although it is there and has been used, and is going to be used, except at the very moment when it is actually in operation. In my opinion that contention is wrong.' *Barnett v Caxton Floors Ltd, Butler v Kleine Patent Fire Resisting Flooring Syndicate Ltd* (1928) 140 LT 138 at 141, DC, per Lord Hewart CJ

TENANCY *See also* TENANT; TERM OF YEARS

The relationship of landlord and tenant arises as a rule when one person, the landlord, with the intent to create a tenancy confers on another, the tenant, the right to the exclusive possession of land, mines or buildings. The grant or demise must be either for a time which is subject to a definite limit originally, as in the case of a lease for a term of years certain, or for a time which, although originally indefinite, can be made subject to a definite limit by either party as of right by that party giving appropriate notice to the other, for example a tenancy from year to year. The interest in the property which remains in the landlord is called the reversion, and, as a rule, there is incident to it the right to receive from the tenant payment of rent for the use of the property.

The relationship of landlord and tenant was originally one of contract only, but from early times the contract conferred an estate in the land on the tenant without losing all its contractual characteristics.

A contract of tenancy may be created by writing or orally by any words which express the intention of giving and taking possession for a certain period of time, or by conduct. (27 Halsbury's Laws (4th edn) paras 1, 2)

'Tenancy' means a tenancy created either immediately or derivatively out of the freehold, whether by a lease or underlease, by an agreement for a lease or underlease or by a tenancy agreement or in pursuance of any enactment (including this Act), but does not include a mortgage term or any interest arising in favour of a mortgagor by his attorning tenant to his mortgagee, and references to the granting of a tenancy and to demised property shall be construed accordingly. (Landlord and Tenant Act 1954, s 69)

'Tenancy' includes sub-tenancy. (Rent Act 1977, s 152(1))

'Long tenancy' means a tenancy granted for a term of years certain exceeding twenty-one years, whether or not subsequently extended by act of the parties or by any enactment. (Rent Act 1977, s 152(1))

'There can be no tenancy unless the occupier enjoys exclusive possession; but an occupier who enjoys exclusive possession is not necessarily a tenant. He may be owner in fee simple, a trespasser, a mortgagee in possession, an object of charity or a service occupier. To constitute a tenancy the occupier must be granted exclusive possession for a fixed or periodic term certain in consideration of a premium or periodical payments. The grant may be express, or may be inferred where the owner accepts weekly or other periodic payments from the occupier. Occupation by service occupier may be eliminated. A service occupier is as a servant who occupies his master's premises in order to perform his duties as servant. In those circumstances the possession and occupation of the servant is treated as the possession and occupation of the master and the relationship of landlord and tenant is not created.' *Street v Mountford* [1985] 2 All ER 289 at 294, HL, per Lord Templeman

Minor tenancy

'Minor tenancy' means a tenancy for a year or from year to year or any lesser interest. (Land Commission Act 1967, s 26)

Periodic tenancy

A weekly or other periodic tenancy is a tenancy by the week or the period, and does not expire without notice at the end of the first week or period or at the end of each succeeding week or period, there being not a reletting at the beginning of every week or period but a springing interest which arises and which is only determined by a proper notice to quit. A weekly or other periodic tenancy arises either by express agreement or presumption of law. (27 Halsbury's Laws (4th edn) para 202)

Tenancy at sufferance

A person who enters on land by a lawful title, and after his title has ended continues in possession without statutory authority and without obtaining the consent of the person then entitled, is said to be a tenant at sufferance, as distinct from a tenant at will who is in possession with the landlord's consent. This is so whatever was the nature of the tenant's original estate, whether he was tenant for years, or the sub-tenant of a tenant for years, or a tenant at will. (27 Halsbury's Laws (4th edn) para 175)

Tenancy at will

A tenancy at will is a tenancy under which the tenant is in possession, and which is determinable at the will of either landlord or tenant. Although on the creation it is expressed to be at the will of the landlord only or at the will of the tenant only, the law implies that it is to be at the will of the other party also, for every lease at will must in law be at the will of both parties. As in other tenancies, a tenancy at will arises by contract binding both landlord and tenant, and the contract may be express or implied. (27 Halsbury's Laws (4th edn) para 167)

Tenancy from year to year

A tenancy from year to year arises either by express agreement or by presumption of law or by statute. It differs from a tenancy at will in that it can only be determined by notice duly given except where there is a stipulation for determination without notice. The appropriate words for the express creation of the tenancy are 'from year to year'. (27 Halsbury's Laws (4th edn) para 177)

'A tenant from year to year is not a tenant for one, two or three or four years, but he is to be considered as a tenant capable of enjoying the property for an indefinite time, having a tenancy which it is expected will continue for more than a year, but which is liable to be put an end to by notice.' *R v South Staffordshire Waterworks Co* (1885) 16 QBD 359 at 370, per Lord Esher MR

'The expression "tenancy from year to year" was used by the draftsman [in the Agricultural Holdings Act 1948, s 2(1) (repealed; see now the Agricultural Holdings Act 1986, s 2(1))] to describe an interest which had certain invariable characteristics which would enable one to say that other interests are greater or less than it. A tenancy from year to year at common law is an interest which does possess certain invariable characteristics without which it is not a tenancy from year to year and which constitute a standard by which the magnitude of other interests may be judged: it must last for one year, and unless determined at the end of the first year by notice (either six months' notice or whatever other length of notice, if any, is expressly provided for in the contract of tenancy), will be renewed by operation of law for successive periods of one year each, until determined at the end of one such yearly period by such a notice.' *Gladstone v Bower* [1959] 3 All ER 475 at 479, per Diplock J; affd [1960] 3 All ER 353 [1960] 2 QB 384, CA

TENANT *See also* LODGER; TENANCY

'The description "tenant" no more negatives agency than would the description "contracting party". As Lord Sumner said about the description "charterer", the description "tenant" means the person "who by this contract becomes liable to the obligations and entitled to the rights, which this contract allots to the" tenant and, as Lord Sumner and the House of Lords held, such a description is not inconsistent with a person so described being an agent.' *Danziger v Thompson* [1944] 1 KB 654 at 657, per Lawrence J

Australia 'What . . . is the fundamental right which a tenant has that distinguishes his position from that of a licensee? It is an interest in land as distinct from a personal permission to enter the land and use it for some stipulated purpose or purposes. And how is it to be ascertained whether such an interest in land has been given? By seeing whether the grantee was given a *legal right of exclusive possession* of the land for a term or from year to year or for a life or lives. If he was, he is a tenant. And he cannot be other than a tenant, because a legal right of exclusive possession is a tenancy and the creation of such a right is a demise. To say that a man who has, by agreement with a landlord, a right of exclusive possession of land for a term is not a tenant is simply to contradict the first proposition by the second. A right of exclusive possession is secured by the right of a lessee to maintain ejectment and, after his entry, trespass. A reservation to the landlord, either by contract or statute, of a limited right of entry, as for example to view or repair, is, of course, not inconsistent with the grant of exclusive possession. Subject to such reservations, a tenant for a term or from year to year or for a life or lives can exclude his landlord as well as strangers from the demised premises.' *Radaich v Smith* (1959) 101 CLR 209 at 222, per Windeyer J

In Agricultural Holdings Act

In this Act, unless the context otherwise requires . . . 'tenant' means the holder of land under a contract of tenancy, and includes the executors, administrators, assigns, or trustee in bankruptcy of a tenant, or other person deriving title from a tenant. (Agricultural Holdings Act 1988, s 96(1))

'Counsel for the sub-tenants . . . says that the sub-tenants are entitled to the protection of the Act [Agricultural Holdings Act 1948] in the same way as the tenants, and he bases that on s 94(1) [see now s 96(1) of the Act of 1988, supra] the definition section of the Act, which defines "tenant" as: "the holder of land under a contract of tenancy, and includes the executors, administrators, assigns, . . . or trustee in bankruptcy of a tenant or other person deriving title from a tenant". Counsel submits that a sub-tenant is clearly within that definition of "tenant", as he is the holder of land under a contract of tenancy, or, alternatively, he is a "person deriving his title from a tenant", and in those circumstances he is entitled to exactly the same protection as a tenant. That is an attractive argument, but, as has been pointed out by counsel for the landlord, the beginning of the definition section, like that of nearly every other definition section, is worded in this way: "In this Act, unless the context otherwise requires, the following expressions have the meanings hereby respectively assigned to them, that is to say . . ." and so on. It may well be that in certain circumstances the word "tenant" in the Agricultural Holdings Act 1948, will include a sub-tenant, and other persons as well, but whether it does so in any particular case must depend on the context. Although a sub-tenant may have the privilege of a tenant in certain circumstances, a tenant is a tenant of an immediate landlord, and he has rights only in relation to that landlord and not in relation to some other person. If the Act is to be read in any intelligible way at all, it would not be possible under s 24 or s 25 to consider a sub-tenant as being in the position of a tenant in relation to the head landlord.' *Sherwood (Baron) v Moody* [1952] 1 All ER 389 at 393, 394, per Ormerod J

In Landlord and Tenant Act

The expression 'tenant' means any person entitled in possession to the holding under any contract of tenancy, whether the interest of such tenant was acquired by original contract, assignment, operation of law or otherwise. (Landlord and Tenant Act 1927, s 25)

In Rent Act

'Tenant' includes statutory tenant and also includes a sub-tenant and any person deriving title under the original tenant or sub-tenant. (Rent Act 1977, s 152(1))

[The Increase of Rent and Mortgage Interest (Restrictions) Act 1920, s 5(1)(c) (repealed; see now the Rent Act 1977, Sch 5, Case 5), prevented the landlord of a house from recovering possession thereof, unless the 'tenant' had given notice to quit and in consequence thereof the landlord had contracted to sell or let the house.] 'In my opinion the term "tenant" in s 5, sub-s 1(c) means the immediate tenant of the landlord, because he is the only person to whom the clause can apply. To explain my meaning with greater fullness and accuracy I may say that, having regard to the definition, I think that the term "tenant" as used in the Act is prima facie a generic term including the original tenant, a person deriving title under him, a sub-tenant, or any one else who comes within the definition, but that it is only used in that wide sense where the context does not otherwise require. It seems to me that in s 5 sub-s 1(c), the context requires that the term should be used in a narrower sense. Inasmuch as that clause contemplates the case where the tenant has given notice to quit, and the only tenant who can give notice to quit is the original and immediate tenant of the landlord, it follows, owing to the limitations imposed by the clause, and the fact which it implies, that "tenant" as there used must mean the original tenant of the landlord.' *Hylton (Lord) v Heal* [1921] 2 KB 438 at 445, 446, DC, per Rowlatt J

TENANT FOR LIFE *See also* LIFE INTEREST

'Tenant for life' includes a person (not being a statutory owner) who has the powers of a tenant for life under this Act, and also (where the context requires) one of two or more persons who together constitute the tenant for life, or have the powers of a tenant for life. (Settled Land Act 1925, s 117)

'The term "tenant for life" incontestably signifies in its primary meaning a man who holds land for his own life or for the life of another. In the original text of "Blackstone" (Oxford edition, 1765–1769) there occurs the following statement: "Estates for life expressly created by deed or grant are where a lease is made of lands or tenements to a man to hold for the term of his own life, or for that of any other person, or for more lives than one, in any of which cases he is styled tenant for life; only where he hold the estate by the life of another he is usually called tenant *pur autre vie*." . . . In my opinion, I am bound to adopt the prima facie meaning of the term (being as it is a technical term) unless I can find in the particular Act some reason for cutting it down.' *Blaydes v Selby* (1891) 7 TLR 567 at 568, per Chitty J

'By cl xxviii [of the Settled Land Act 1925, s 117 (supra)] "life-tenant" includes a person (not being a statutory owner) who has the powers of a life-tenant under this Act. By cl xxvi "statutory owner" means the trustees of the settlement or other persons who, during a minority, or at any other time when there is no life-tenant, have the powers of a life-tenant under this Act. At first sight it is a little difficult to determine exactly what these two clauses mean. There is no doubt that life-tenant under the Act, unless the context otherwise requires, means a life-tenant proper or a person who has the powers of a life-tenant under the Act and is not a statutory owner.' *Re Craven Settled Estates* [1926] Ch 985 at 989, per Astbury J

TENANT RIGHTS

'Tenant right' is a term used to express the right of the tenant to take or receive after the determination of his tenancy the benefit of the labour and capital expended by him in cleaning, tilling, and sowing the land during his tenancy, which he would otherwise lose by the determination of the tenancy. (1 Halsbury's Laws (4th edn) para 1071)

Australia [The Income Tax Assessment Act 1936–1986 (Cth), s 88(2), provides that—'Where a taxpayer who in the year of income is a lessee of land used for the purpose of producing assessable income has . . . incurred expenditure in making improvements not subject to tenant rights on that land . . . a proportionate part of the amount of that expenditure . . . shall be an allowable deduction.'] 'The words "tenant" and "right" are words to which the law attaches a meaning. In s 88(2) the former is used as an adjective, and the two words make a kind of compound noun which suggests, I think, a particular class of rights belonging to tenants generally rather than a particular class of rights of a special class of tenants. . . . The matters comprised by "tenant right" when the term is used in relation to agricultural holdings, and this is its most common application, are set forth in Halsbury's Laws of England [supra]. . . . If the words "tenant rights" in s 88(2) of the Income Tax Assessment Act refer only to the rights of outgoing tenants of agricultural or pastoral lands there would be a difficulty in deciding whether the words denote the rights depending on statute as well as the non-statutory rights. . . . I can see no valid reason for assuming that Parliament intended to use the words "tenant rights" when enacting s 88(2) as the equivalent of the rights which only agricultural and pastoral tenants may enjoy with respect to improvements. The words are, in my opinion, capable in their legal acceptation of applying to the right which any lessee has at the end of the lease to receive compensation for improvements effected by him upon the land; and in s 88(2) they have, I think, a general application, not a limited and specific application to the rights of agricultural and pastoral tenants only.' *Hotel Kingston Ltd v Federal Comr of Taxation* (1944) 69 CLR 221 at 224–226, per McTiernan J

TENANTABLE REPAIR *See* REPAIR

TENDER *See also* LEGAL TENDER

'The acceptance of a cheque involves passing a judgment on the solvency of the person who tenders the cheque. That was what was done here. The managing clerk was prepared to take the plaintiffs' solicitor's cheque, because he knew, or thought he knew, that his cheque was good; but he had no means of satisfying himself that it was. If it had turned out that there were no funds at the bank to meet the cheque, could it have been said that there was a good tender as against the corporation? It seems to me certainly not. A solicitor who has authority to accept a tender accepts anything short of a tender in cash at his own risk. No doubt it is usual for solicitors to trust each other and to accept each other's cheques, and the practice is desirable because it promotes good feeling and facilitates business. But I think it would be going much too far to say that a solicitor has authority to accept a cheque because he has authority to accept a tender according to the law of the land. I must therefore hold that there was not in this case any sufficient tender.' *Blumberg v Life Interests & Reversionary Securities Corpn* [1897] 1 Ch 171 at 173, per Kekewich J

TENEMENT *See also*

RIPARIAN TENEMENT

'Tenements' and 'hereditaments' mean, respectively, whatever can be the subject of tenure, and whatever is capable of devolving upon death, whether as real property or as personal property, to personal representatives; but they are used in a general sense to include both the corporeal things, such as houses and land, and the rights which arise out of them. Where these rights extend to the exclusive possession of the thing which is the subject of property, they are called corporeal hereditaments, a term which is used to denote both the thing itself and the right of property in the thing; where they fall short of this, as for example in the case of profits à prendre, they are called incorporeal hereditaments. (27 Halsbury's Laws (4th edn) para 131)

Strictly the term 'corporeal' applies to the land itself, whereas rights in the land are incorporeal; but this is not in accordance with legal usage, and a right in the land, if accompanied by possession, is regarded as corporeal, whereas partial rights which do not entitle the owner of them to possession are regarded as incorporeal. Rights in land, whether corporeal or incorporeal, are described by the words 'tenements' and 'hereditaments', 'tenements' meaning primarily that they are the subjects of tenure, although the word is not thus restricted, and 'hereditaments' meaning that they were, while rules of inheritance were in force, capable of passing to the heir. 'Tenements' and 'hereditaments' are not the same in scope, and 'land' is not always restricted to land in the physical sense; it may extend to rights in the land. 'Lands, tenements and hereditaments' comprises both real estate and chattels real; thus although it does not include personal chattels, it formerly comprised copyholds, and it comprises chattels real as well as freeholds . . .

The word 'tenement' is not restricted to lands and other matters which are the subject of tenure. Everything in which a man can have an estate of freehold, and which is connected with land or savours of the realty, is a tenement. Thus the word includes not only land, as the corporeal subject formerly of inheritance, but also all rights which before 1926 would have been heritable issuing out of land, or concerning, or annexed to, or exercisable over, land, although they do not lie in tenure, such as rents, commons and other profits à prendre and (formerly) tithes, and offices or dignities which descend to heirs, whether they relate to land or not.

In popular language 'tenement' means a house or part of a house capable of separate occupation, and is sometimes so used in statutes; and, where the language or the purpose of the statute so requires, the expression is restricted to property capable of visible and physical occupation, and does not include incorporeal rights. (39 Halsbury Laws (4th edn) paras 375, 379)

Land comprehends all things of a permanent, substantial nature; being a word of a very extensive signification. . . . *Tenement* is a word of still greater extent; and though in its vulgar acceptation it is only applied to houses and other buildings, yet in its original, proper, and legal sense it signifies everything that may be *holden*, provided it be of a permanent nature; whether it be of a substantial and sensible, or of an unsubstantial ideal kind. (2 Bl Com 16, 17)

'The right granted by the indenture on which the action is brought is a right to dig for and carry away china clay, and to erect buildings and works incidental thereto upon certain defined lands. The nature of this right is clearly established by the cases of *Doe v Wood* [(1819) 2 B & Ald 724] and *Muskett v Hill* [(1839) 5 Bing NC 694]. These cases establish that it is an incorporeal hereditament, a property, and an estate capable of being inherited by the heir, and assigned to a purchaser, or otherwise conveyed away. It is in truth "a tenement" within the definition of Lord Coke in the First Institute, 20a, who says that "the word 'tenement' includeth not only corporate inheritances, but also inheritances issuing out of them, or concerning or annexed to, or exercisable within them, as rent, estovers, common, or other profits whatever, granted out of land".' *Martyn v Williams* (1857) 1 H & N 817 at 826, 827, per cur.

[The Landlord and Tenant Act 1931 (Ireland), s 55, enacted (inter alia) that no damages should be recoverable for breach of a covenant to repair in a lease if it were shown that, having regard to the age and condition of the 'tenement', the repairing of it in accordance with the covenant was physically impossible or would involve expenditure excessive in proportion to the value thereof.] 'Various and discursive arguments were addressed to us as to the meaning of "tenement" . . . in this section, but I am of opinion that the meaning and intendment of the provision is not open to any considerable doubt. . . . It is, to my mind, abundantly clear that "tenement" means the physical entity which is the subject-matter of the demise, and not any interest therein, and, accordingly, that we have to consider, not the value of any particular interest in the land or premises in question, but the value of the entire interest therein—in other words, the value of the property in fee simple unincumbered.' *Jeroome v Fodhla Printing Co Ltd* [1943] IR 380 at 405, per O'Byrne J

'The parcels are described as "all that building or tenement shop and premises". That indicates that the shop is regarded as something distinct from the rest of the building. I think I may also note the expression "tenement". That is an expression which is sometimes used to mean a house and in particular a dwelling-house. That, however, is not its strictly correct meaning in law, its correct meaning extending as I understand, to every kind of hereditament, both corporeal and incorporeal.' *Levermore v Jobey* [1956] 2 All ER 362 at 365, CA, per Jenkins LJ

Australia 'Although in popular language the term "tenement" means a house or a part of a house capable of separate occupation, and although in a statute where such an expression as "houses and tenements" is used, the popular meaning may be assigned to the word, . . . its strict meaning is everything in which a man can have an estate of freehold and which is connected with land. " 'Tenement', though in its vulgar acceptation it is only applied to houses and other buildings, yet in its original, proper and legal sense it signifies everything that may be holden, provided it be of a permanent nature; whether it be of a substantial or sensible or of an unsubstantial ideal kind"; *Beauchamp v Winn* (1873) LR 6 HL 223 at 241, where Lord Chelmsford thus quotes from 2 Blackstone's Commentaries, p 16 [supra].' *Re Lehrer and the Real Property Act 1900* [1960] NSWR 570 at 575, per Jacobs J

TENEMENT FACTORY *See* FACTORY

TENET

[A newspaper article asserted that the plaintiff had made unwarranted attacks on the 'tenets' of faith.] 'The appellant seeks to contend that the context of the word "tenets" in the incriminated article justifies the innuendo that "tenets" means "dogmas". Their lordships, however, are unable to accept the view that, by reason of the context, the word "tenets" can only mean "dogmas". It is common ground between the parties that, while dogmas might properly be described as tenets, the latter word has a much wider range, and includes opinions on religious matters which do not involve the holder of such opinions in the risk of expulsion from his church.' *Strickland v Bonnici* (1934) 78 Sol Jo 820 at 820, PC, per cur.

TENOR

Canada 'I find no warrant in criminal or common law, nor in that laid down by judges, for construing "according to tenor of policy 65996" [words which occurred in an accident insurance renewal receipt], otherwise than as importing the policy and all contained therein or thereon.' *Youlden v London Guarantee and Accident Co* (1913) 28 OLR 161 at 170, CA, per Hodgins JA

TENURE

'Tenure' denotes the holding of land by a tenant under his lord, and is only appropriate where the feudal relation of lord and tenant can exist. Thus, the subject matter of tenure is primarily land in the physical sense. Where by subinfeudation, prior to the Statute Quia Emptores, the tenant became a mesne lord, he retained the seigniory of the land, and this became, as between him and his lord, the subject of tenure in lieu of the land. The seigniory was usually identical with the lordship of a manor, and when it existed over a number of manors was known as a 'land barony' or 'honour'. Thus tenure exists in land, seigniories, and territorial honours, but other incorporeal interests in land, such as rent charges and easements, although they may fall within the extended meaning which has been given to tenements, are not the subject matter of tenure. (39 Halsbury's Laws (4th edn) para 376)

TERM (Period)

'The plaintiff, the lessor, by the deed set out in the declaration, in consideration of £500 paid, bargains and sells the tenements, of which, by reason of the merger apparent on the face of the deed he must be taken to be seised in fee, for all the residue of the term of fifty-five years after the 25th of June preceding the date of that deed. There is no doubt that a valid term might be created de novo by the bargain and sale for money, and the only question is, whether the use of the word "term" is to prevent their operation, by reason that that term had altogether ceased. . . . The word "term", according to the opinion of Anderson CJ in *Green v Edwards* [(1591) Cro Eliz 216], may be taken "not only for the interest but for the time"; and if so, the residue of the term after a particular event, may mean so many years as should be afterwards to come. And the same doctrine was laid down by Lord Mansfield in *Wright v Cartwright* [(1757) 1 Burr 282]. If we construe the word "term" in this case to be the number of years unexpired, and not the interest in the tenements, we give effect to the instrument.' *Cottee v Richardson* (1851) 7 Exch 143 at 150, 151, per cur

'The phrase "for the term of my lease" has been dealt with by Baron Parke in *Cottee v Richardson* [supra] . . . where he pointed out that the word "term" may be taken not only for the interest but for the time, and he construed the "term" to be the number of years unexpired and not the interest in the tenements.' *Slough Picture Hall Co Ltd v Wade, Wilson v Nevile Reid & Co Ltd* (1916) 32 TLR 542 at 544, per Scrutton J

TERM OF YEARS

A tenancy for a term of years arises by express contract or by statute, and it is essential to the contract that the commencement and duration of the term should be so defined as either to be certain in the first instance, or to be capable of being afterwards ascertained with certainty.

The term may commence either immediately, or from a past or future date. Where it is expressed to commence from a past day, the tenant's actual interest commences only on the execution of the deed, and his liability is limited accordingly. Thus the tenant is not liable, for example, for matters arising before the date of execution under the covenant to repair, or under a covenant not to erect buildings of less than a specified value, unless the lease itself imposes such obligations in respect of the period prior to its execution. Where in a provision of the lease there is a reference to a particular year of it, it is a question of construction whether time is to be measured from the execution of the lease or from the date by reference to which the term is measured. For example, in a lease granted to run for a term of years measured from a past date, a break clause to operate at the end of the seventh year was held to mean at the end of the seventh year reckoned from that past date. Where the term is to commence from a future date, the tenant's interest in the land subsists as from the date of the lease but his right to possession will only arise at the future date specified for the commencement of the term. (27 Halsbury's Laws (4th edn) para 204)

Term of years absolute

'Term of years absolute' means a term of years (taking effect either in possession or in reversion whether or not at a rent) with or without impeachment for waste, subject or not to another legal estate, and either certain or liable to determination by notice, re-entry, operation of law, or by a provision for cesser on redemption, or in any other event (other than the dropping of a life, or the determination of a determinable life interest); but does not include any term of years determinable with life or lives or with the cesser of a determinable life interest, nor, if created after the commencement of this Act, a term of years which is not expressed to take effect in possession within twenty-one years after the creation thereof where required by this Act to take effect within that period; and in this definition the expression 'term of years' includes a term for less than a year, or for a year or years and a fraction of a year or from year to year. (Law of Property 1925, s 205; see also Land Registration Act 1925, s 3; Settled Land Act 1925, s 117; etc)

'A tenancy is a term of years absolute. This expression by s 205(1)(xxvii) of the Law of Property Act 1925, reproducing the common law, includes a term from week to week in possession at a rent and liable to determination by notice or re-entry. Originally a term of years was not an estate in land, the lessee having merely a personal action against his lessor. But a legal estate in leaseholds was created by the Statute of Gloucester (6 Edw 1 (1278)) and the Act 21 Hen 8, c 15 (Recoveries (1529)). Now by s 1 of the Law of Property Act 1925 a term of years absolute is an estate in land capable of subsisting as a legal estate.' *Street v Mountford* [1985] 2 All ER 289 at 291, HL, per Lord Templeman

TERMINATION *See also* CANCEL; DETERMINATION

'Termination', in relation to a tenancy, means the cesser of the tenancy, whether by effluxion of time or for any other reason. (Opencast Coal Act 1958, s 51(1))

'Termination', in relation to a tenancy, means the cesser of the contract of tenancy by reason of effluxion of time or from any other cause. (Agricultural Holdings Act 1986, s 96(1))

[The Landlord and Tenant Act 1954, s 24(1), provides that a tenancy to which Part II of the Act applies shall not come to an end unless 'terminated' in accordance with the provisions of that Part of the Act.] 'Counsel for the landlords argues that "terminated" means "giving a notice to quit"; in other words, when the Act uses the word "terminated", it is referring to the instrument or to the act which is the terminating factor and not to the effluxion of time. Counsel for the tenant disputes that, but I think that the first interpretation is the better one, and I shall assume it to be right. The wording of the section which I have read appears to draw a distinction between a tenancy coming to an end and a tenancy being terminated. Accordingly, for "terminated" I shall read "give notice to quit".' *Orman Bros Ltd v Greenbaum* [1954] 3 All ER 731 at 732, per Devlin J

'For the purposes of these [hire-purchase] agreements, there is a distinction between terminating a hiring . . . and terminating the agreement itself. "Terminate" is an ambiguous word, since it may refer to a termination by a right under the agreement or by a condition incorporated in it or by a deliberate breach by one party amounting to a repudiation of the whole contract.' *Bridge v Campbell Discount Co Ltd* [1962] 1 All ER 385 at 394, HL, per Lord Radcliffe

New Zealand 'The word "terminated" connotes the rescission of the contract by the consent or agreement of both parties.' *Willcocks v New Zealand Insurance Co* [1926] NZLR 805 at 810, per Stringer J; also reported [1926] GLR 530 at 533

United States 'Termination' [in a contract for sale of goods] occurs when either party pursuant to a power created by agreement or law puts an end to the contract otherwise than for its breach. On 'termination' all obligations which are still executory on both sides are discharged but any right based on prior breach or performance survives. (Uniform Commercial Code 1978, s 2–106(3))

TERMS (Rights and obligations) *See also* IMPLIED TERM

Terms or conditions

'Terms', in relation to a tenancy, includes conditions. (Landlord and Tenant Act 1954, s 69)

[The Mining Industry Act 1926, s 13(2) (repealed; see now the Mines (Working Facilities and Support) Act 1966, s 1) provided that where the working of any coal, or the working of any coal in the most efficient and economical manner was impeded by any restrictions, 'terms', or conditions contained in a mining lease, a right to work the coal freed wholly or partially from such restrictions or conditions, or to work the coal on other 'terms' and conditions, might be granted.] 'In my judgment s 13, sub-s 2 of the Act of 1926 does not include within its ambit jurisdiction to review or alter, without compensation or at all, royalties and rents. My reasons for this conclusion are as follows: the language of the section itself seems to me . . . to be inapt and insufficient to confer any such jurisdiction. The section seems to deal exclusively with impediments or obstructions to the actual working or carrying away of minerals. The relief of financial burdens is not expressly mentioned and seems to me to be a different subject-matter which, having regard to its importance and universal application, cannot properly be held to be brought thus incidentally, and almost casually, within the operation of this section.' *Consett Iron Co Ltd v Clavering Trustees* [1935] 2 KB 42 at 74–77, 79, CA, per Roche LJ

New Zealand 'The terms and conditions of the lease are to be fixed by a person whom the testator calls a valuator, but who, whether the words "terms and conditions" include the duration of the term or not, is in fact an arbitrator. It is true that the word "conditions" is a word of art, and has a definite legal meaning; but the word "terms" is not a word of art, and has no definite legal meaning. In ordinary language, if the terms of a lease are spoken of, the word would include the duration of the lease. If a person was asked what were the terms of a particular lease, he would, if he wished to give an intelligent answer, certainly mention the duration of the lease.' *Re Gillespie, Gillespie v Gillespie* (1902) 22 NZLR 74 at 81, CA, per Williams J; also reported 4 GLR 487 at 489

Of award

Australia [By the Conciliation and Arbitration Act 1904–1986 (Cth), s 59, the court may vary any of the 'terms of an award'.] 'The expression "terms of an award" means much more than "clauses" and in fact it was conceded that it had a wider signification. The expression in truth appears to refer to the whole contents of the award as those contents prescribe the rights and obligations of the persons governed by the award or affected by it. The word "vary" is one which no doubt in different contexts may have different meanings. . . . Probably it is enough to say that to vary the terms of the award is to change them in part whether by addition, by excision, by modification or by substitution or by qualification or otherwise.' *R v Tonkin, ex p Federated Ship Painters' Union* [1954] ALR 777 at 778, per cur.

TERMS OF ART

'Documents which are intended to give rise to legally enforceable rights and duties contemplate enforcement by due process of law, which involves their being interpreted by courts composed of judges, each one of whom has his personal idiosyncrasies of sentiment and upbringing, not to speak of age. Such documents would fail in their object if the rights and duties which could be enforced depended on the personal idiosyncrasies of the individual judge or judges on whom the task of construing them chanced to fall. It is to avoid this that lawyers, whose profession it is to draft and to construe such documents, have been compelled to evolve an English language, of which the constituent words and phrases are more precise in their meaning than they are in the language of Shakespeare or of any of the passengers on the Clapham omnibus this morning. These words and phrases to which a more precise meaning is so ascribed are called by lawyers "terms of art", but are in popular parlance known as "legal jargon". We lawyers must not allow this denigratory description to obscure the social justification for the use of "terms of art" in legal documents. It is essential to the effective operation of the rule of law. The phrase "legal jargon", however, does contain a reminder that non-lawyers are unfamiliar with the meanings which lawyers attach to particular "terms of art", and that where a word or phrase which is a "term of art" is used by an author who is not a lawyer, particularly in a document which he does not anticipate may have to be construed by a lawyer, he may have meant by it something different from its meaning when used by a lawyer as a term of art.' *Sydall v Castings Ltd* [1966] 3 All ER 770 at 774, CA, per Diplock LJ

'Modern statutes are drafted by professional legal draftsmen and intended to be read and understood by professional lawyers. As they create legal rights and liabilities, their meaning should be unambiguous and precise, and to aid precision certain habits of composition have been acquired by Parliamentary draftsmen which are familiar to professional lawyers and to the courts. These habits obtain recognition in the canons of statutory construction, though many of them are general rules of composition which any writer seeking clarity of expression is likely to follow, such as *expressio unius exclusio alterius, ejusdem generis*, and *noscitur a sociis*, though, unlike lawyers, he does not express them in the arcane obscurity of the Latin tongue. As regards rules of composition of this kind the main difference between a professional legal draftsman and any other kind of writer is that the Parliamentary draftsman is less likely to depart from them. But there are other habits of professional legal draftsmen which are less widely shared by other kinds of writers or not shared by them at all. Some expressions in common use in documents dealing with legal rights or obligations acquire in a legal context a special meaning different from, or more precise than, their meaning in common speech—they become "terms of art".' *Prestcold (Central) Ltd v Minister of Labour* [1969] 1 All ER 69 at 75, CA, per Lord Diplock

TERRACE

Australia 'As the entire building does not consists of a single dwelling but of several dwellings it will fall within the definition of dwelling-house only if it can qualify as a row of two or more dwellings such as are commonly known as terrace buildings. It is, however, not a terrace building in the sense in which architects use that term because Mr Ashton, a highly qualified architect and town planner who is Chairman of the State Planning Authority, stated in the course of his evidence that a terrace house is one in a row of series which has its own frontage too a public road or public place.' *Holmes v Ryde Municipal Council* [1969] 2 NSWR 139 at 140, per Else-Mitchell J

TERRITORIAL WATERS

[The definition of 'territorial waters' in the Territorial Waters Jurisdiction Act 1878, s 7, was repealed by the Territorial Sea Act 1987, s 3, Sch 2. For the extension of the breadth of the territorial sea adjacent to the United Kingdom from three to twelve miles see s 1 of the 1987 Act.

On the passage of what is now the Act through the House of Lords 'territorial sea' was explained to be 'a belt of waters adjacent to the coast within which a coastal state enjoys sovereignty. This sovereignty must be exercised in a manner which respects certain rights for the benefit of other states, notably the right of innocent passage for vessels passing through the territorial sea'.]

Australia 'The expression "Australian waters" in s 51(x) [of the Commonwealth of Australia Constitution Act 1901–1986] does not denote merely "Australian territorial waters" but it means the whole expanse of waters constituting the marine environs of Australia.' *Bonser v La Macchia* (1969) 122 CLR 177 at 198, per McTiernan J

TERRORISM

'Terrorism' means the use of violence for political ends, and includes any use of violence for the purpose of putting the public or any section of the public in fear. (Prevention of Terrorism. (Temporary Provisions) Act 1989, s 20(1))

New Zealand 'Act of terrorism' means—

(a) any act that involves the taking of human life, or threatening to take human life, or the wilful or reckless endangering of human life, carried out for the purpose of furthering an ideological aim; or

(b) any act involving any explosive or incendiary device causing or likely to cause the destruction of, or serious damage to, any premises, building, installation, vehicle, or property of a kind referred to in any of sections 298 to 304, except subsection (3) of section 298, of the Crimes Act 1961, carried out for the purpose of furthering an ideological aim; or

(c) any act that constitutes, or that would if committed in New Zealand, constitute, a crime against section 79 of the Crimes Act 1961, carried out for the purpose of furthering an ideological aim; or

(d) any act that constitutes, or that would, if committed in New Zealand, constitute, an offence against any of the provisions of the Aviation Crimes Act 1972 or the Crimes (Internationally Protected Persons and Hostages) Act 1980;—

and includes the planning of any such act. (Immigration Act 1987, s 2)

TEST

In this section and in Schedule 2 to this Act 'test' [of condition of vehicle] includes 'inspect' or 'inspection', as the case may require, and references to a vehicle include references to a trailer drawn by it. (Road Traffic Act 1988, s 67(10))

[A regulation made under the Factory and Workshop Act 1901 (repealed; but cf Factories Act 1961, s 22 et seq), provided that all machinery and chains and other gear used in hoisting, or lowering, in connection with the processes should have been 'tested', and should be periodically examined.] 'In my opinion the word "test" is not a technical term, but a word of ordinary current speech in the English language, whose meaning in such a connection is absolutely clear to every one; and the judge, in expounding the regulation, was bound to tell the jury that it required such practical examination or trial of the rope to be made as would determine its ability to satisfy the particular requirements of that rope, which unquestionably included tension under a certain weight, bending over a pulley, and twisting or torsion in the nature of its user.' *Bissett v Heiton & Co Ltd* [1930] IR 17 at 23, 24, per Kennedy CJ

TESTAMENT *See also* WILL

'A will is to be considered in two lights, as to the testament and the instrument. The testament is the result and effect in point of law, of what is the will; and that consists of all the parts; and a codicil is then a part of the will, all making but one testament: but it may be made at different times and different circumstances, and therefore there may be a different intention at making one and the other.' *Fuller v Hooper* (1751) 2 Ves Sen 242 at 242, per Lord Hardwicke LC

See, generally, 50 Halsbury's Laws (4th edn) para 201.

TESTAMENTARY

'I have the authority of a dictionary of some weight as to the meaning of "testamentary". The Century Dictionary puts as the first meaning of "testamentary", relating or appertaining to a will or wills; also, "relating to administration of the estates of deceased persons", and it quotes a passage from Blackstone: "This spiritual jurisdiction of testamentary causes is a peculiar constitution of this island; for in almost all other (even in Popish) countries all matters testamentary are under the jurisdiction of the civil magistrate." That is a recognition of what is familiar to us, that the Court of Probate is also the Court concerned with the grant of letters of administration. The word "testamentary" has ceased to have its purely etymological meaning. The existence of a testament does not seem to me now to be essential to the proper use of the word, and I think it may be equally applied to the case where there is no testament, but where the estate is being administered according to the law of the land.' *Re Clemow, Yeo v Clemow* [1900] 2 Ch 182 at 191, 192, per Kekewich J

Testamentary expenses

It is often important to decide whether costs and expenses incurred by a personal representative are properly payable out of the estate as testamentary and administration expenses or should be borne by the legatees or devisees or persons entitled on intestacy out of their respective interests. The general principle is that the estate must bear the expenses incident to the proper performance of the duties of the personal representatives as personal representatives but not the expenses involved in the execution of trusts which arise after the estate has been administered or an assent given, or the expenses of clearing the property comprised in a gift so as to make it available by way of assent in favour of the donee.

The general costs of administering the estate are testamentary expenses, for this term is not confined to expenses connected with the will, and indeed it applies to an intestacy. The estate must therefore bear the cost of obtaining the grant, collecting and preserving the assets, discharging the debts and distributing the balance. (17 Halsbury's Laws (4th edn) paras 1185, 1186)

'I cannot distinguish between "executorship expenses" and "testamentary expenses". It seems to me the words "executorship expenses" amount to this: they are expenses incident to the proper performance of the duty of the executor in the same way as testamentary expenses are, neither more or less.' *Sharp v Lush* (1879) 48 LJ Ch 231 at 232, per Jessel MR

'That the costs of the executors in the probate action were testamentary expenses appears to me to be beyond controversy; they are the costs properly incurred in upholding the will. The costs of the plaintiff, on the other hand, or the bulk of them . . . were incurred in contesting the will—in asserting that it was a will which ought not to be recognised as the will of the testator; and it does not appear to me, however wide the definition may be, that those costs ought to be regarded as testamentary expenses.' *Re Prince, Godwin v Prince* [1898] 2 Ch 225 at 227–229, per Stirling J

'It is well established that the expression "testamentary expenses" in a will does not, in the absence of some supporting context, extend to duties in respect of foreign property specifically devised or bequeathed.' *Re Matthews's Will Trusts, Bristow v Matthews* [1961] 3 All ER 869 at 877, Pennycuick J

Australia 'The settlement directs that funeral and testamentary expenses are to be paid out of the trust property as well as the debts. I have to determine first of all two points: First as to the cost of obtaining probate. I think this is clearly a primary testamentary expense. . . . Then as to the question whether or not the duty paid is a testamentary expense. . . . Here, I am just as clear it is not.' *Trustees, Executors & Agency Co Ltd v Thorpe* (1900) 26 VLR 99 at 107, per Madden CJ

New Zealand 'Testamentary expenses are expenses incident to the proper performance of the duty of an executor: Williams on Executors [10th edn, Vol 1, p 752]; *Sharp v Lush* [supra]. If the law provides that in consideration of the performance of his duties the executor is to be allowed a commission, that is, I think, a testamentary expense, because the very object of the payment of a commission is to secure the proper performance of these duties, and it is therefore incident to such performance. "Testamentary expenses include, beside probate expenses, the costs incurred by executors in obtaining the advice of solicitors or counsel as to the distribution of their testator's estate; also the costs of the executors and other parties in an action, whether instituted by the executors themselves or by a beneficiary, for the administration of the testator's personal estate; also the testator's funeral expenses; also expenses incurred by the executors for the protection of specific legacies—e.g. for warehousing furniture specifically bequeathed, pending the distribution of the assets; and payment by the executors in discharge of debts falling due from the testator's estate after his death"; Williams on Executors and cases there cited.' *Re Ross* (1906) 25 NZLR 189 at 192, 193, per Williams J; also reported 8 GLR 414 at 416

TESTATOR

'A consistent interpretation seems to me to require us to assign to the term "testator" . . . its natural and widest meaning of "a deceased person who has made a will".' *Dowdall v McCartan* (1880) 5 LR Ir 642 at 647, CA, per Fitzgibbon LJ

TESTIMONIAL

'When a man is given a testimonial because of his work in the past, not directly remunerating him for that work, but recognising how high a regard has been held for him in the association of people with him arising out of the performance of those services, and people recognise the good qualities he has and how zealous and kind he has been, and how eager to advance the interests of his employers or his parishioners or his constituents, or whoever they may be, and they say "We would like to give you something as a mark of our esteem and regard", that is a testimonial.' *Mudd v Collins* (1925) 133 LT 186 at 187, per Rowlatt J

TESTIMONY *See* EVIDENCE

TEXTILE FACTORY *See* FACTORY

THEATRE *See also* PLAY; STAGE PLAY

'Theatre' includes any place used for the exhibition of pictures or other optical effects by means of a cinematograph or other suitable apparatus and any music hall or other similar place of entertainment; and 'performance' has a corresponding meaning. (Shops Act 1950, s 74)

'Theatre' means any building or part of a building constructed wholly or mainly for the public performance of plays. (Theatres Trust Act 1976, s 5)

'As a regular theatre may be a lecture room, dining room, ball room and concert room on successive days, so a room used ordinarily for either of those purposes would become for the time being a theatre, if used for the representation of a regular stage play.' *Russell v Smith* (1848) 12 QB 217 at 237, per cur.

'A "theatre" is properly a place in which spectacles of action—dramas in short—are publicly exhibited; but it cannot be disputed that the word has for long been applied to houses used for ballets and variety entertainments in which the display is dramatic only in an illegitimate sense. . . . What is more to the point—I think the word "theatre" has recently begun to be widely applied to places in which films are shown.' *Scottish Cinema & Variety Theatres v Ritchie* 1929 SC 350 at 354, per the Lord President (Lord Clyde)

Australia 'The meaning of a word like "theatre" must be determined according to its context. I agree . . . that in this context [a licence giving exclusive rights of performing a certain play in "theatres"] the word "theatres" means places at which the play is performed.' *Meynell v Pearce* [1906] VLR 447 at 450, per Cussen J

THEFT *See also* STOLEN GOODS; THIEF

(1) A person is guilty of theft if he dishonestly appropriates property belonging to another with the intention of permanently depriving the other of it; and 'thief' and 'steal' shall be construed accordingly.

(2) It is immaterial whether the appropriate action is made with a view to gain, or is made for the thief's own benefit. (Theft Act 1968, s 1).

[The above is described by the Act as the 'basic definition' of theft. Sections 2–6 of the Act supplement and clarify the above definition by defining some of the terms used therein, viz 'dishonestly', 'appropriates', 'property', 'belonging to another' and 'with the intention of permanently depriving the other of it'. This new offence of theft replaces the former offences of larceny, embezzlement and fraudulent conversion, and the Act accordingly repeals the Larceny Acts of 1861 and 1916.]

'The view of this court is that in relation to partnership property and provisions in the Theft Act 1968 have the following result: provided there is the basic ingredient of dishonesty, provided there be no question of there being a claim of right made in good faith, provided there be an intent permanently to deprive, one partner can commit theft of partnership property just as much as one person can commit the theft of the property of another of whom he is a complete stranger.' *R v Bonner* [1970] 2 All ER 97 at 99, CA, per cur.

New Zealand [The Companies Act 1955, s 220(1)(a), provides that 'theft' or stealing is the act of fraudulently and without colour of right taking or fraudulently and without colour of right converting to the use of any person, anything capable of being stolen, with intent to deprive the owner, or any person having any special property or interest therein, permanently of such thing or of such property or interest.] 'There is nothing novel in the concept that there may be theft within the meaning of s 220(1) from someone who does not have possession of the thing stolen. That is likely to be the situation in most cases of conversion as distinct from taking. The person who steals by converting something of which he has started with innocent possession will be stealing from someone who has no possession. What I think is of more significance is that the person from whom the thing is stolen must be one who is capable of having a *right* to possession. The bailee and the lien holder have such a right and it generally happens that they also have actual possession. The mortgagee or debenture holder, depending on the terms of his security, will no doubt also have a right to possession in the event of default. If he has no such right then it is not easy to see how there could be theft. If, however, he does have that right and the offender fraudulently and without colour of right takes or converts the thing so that the right to possession is removed or frustrated, then it seems to me that this would amount to theft so long, of course, as the necessary intent was present. If the special property or interest is a pecuniary one only in the sense that it involves no more than a debt, then I do not see how it can be said that a taking or converting could amount to theft.' *Police Department v Hawthorn* (1981) 1 BCR 363 at 366, per Quillam J

In Marine Insurance Act

The term 'thieves' does not cover clandestine theft or a theft committed by any one of the ship's company, whether crew or passengers. (Marine Insurance Act 1906, Sch 1, para 9)

'I am reminded that the risk of thieves in a policy of marine insurance does not cover the ordinary clandestine theft, but only theft accompanied by violence, and that certainly is so when the policy is a policy of marine insurance pure and simple; and it is said that the same rule must apply when it is a warehouse-to-warehouse policy as when it is a marine policy, because of clause 5 of the Institute Cargo Clauses annexed to the policy; and it is said that the risk of thieves in a warehouse-to-warehouse policy must have the same construction as in a marine insurance policy, as there was no violence in a case like this, where the goods were left unattended by night. I am not sure that in a warehouse-to-warehouse policy the word "theft" ought to be limited to theft by violence in the same way as it is in a purely marine policy. However that may be, this was clearly a theft by violence. There was a smashing of two sets of doors by crowbars, and it seems to me that clearly was a theft by violence. I do not think by violence there must be an assault on some person or other. It seems to me that when a person comes along and by crowbars smashes in doors, he breaks in and steals by violence, and the facts of this case answer the description of a theft by violence.' *Fabrique de Produits Chemiquès SA v Large (F N)* (1922) 13 Ll L Rep 269 at 268, 269, per Bailhache J

'Until the Theft Act 1968 "theft" was a word unknown, as far as my knowledge goes, to the statute law of this country; and in this context reference may usefully be had to the observations of Maugham LJ, in *Algemeene Bankvereeniging v Langton* [(1935) 40 Com Cas 247]. I direct myself that, in considering whether "theft" within the meaning of the policy has here been established, one does not apply the strict technicalities of the criminal law. Nevertheless, one must advert to what the criminal law has to say about the topic of stealing, larceny or theft. Viscount Sumner said in *Lake v Simmons* [[1927] AC 487 at 509]: ". . . reliance has been placed on two arguments, (a) that in a commercial document no legal technicality of the criminal law should be taken into account . . . I dissent from the view that criminal law should be treated as irrelevant merely because a document is commercial. After all, criminal law is still law and so are its definitions and rules." One must certainly import into this civil action the basic conception of theft, which is that it is an offence involving dishonesty. No man—the man on the top of the Clapham omnibus, the man in Lombard Street, the man of ordinary intelligence anywhere—could fail to recognise that, unless dishonesty is shown, no one should be branded as having committed a theft.' *Nishina Trading Co Ltd v Chiyoda Fire & Marine Insurance Co Ltd* [1969] 2 All ER 776 at 780, CA, per Edmund Davies LJ

THEN

'It is contended that instantly is equivalent to then. . . . We think it not equivalent. "Then", "*adtunc*", means the very time at which the other event happened; it therefore involves the same day; and such is the known sense of the term in pleading.' *R v Brownlow* (1839) 11 Ad & El 119 at 127, per Lord Denham CJ

[The testator gave his property to his wife during widowhood and after her decease to her children 'then living'.] 'The word "then" which is used by the testator, refers to the time of his wife's death; and the children who were living at that time are the only children to take under the gift, unless it should appear, that upon the construction of the whole will, and to effectuate a clear intention appearing in other parts of it, the words "then living" ought to be rejected as repugnant, or to be qualified in order to give effect to other words inconsistent with them.' *Tawney v Ward* (1839) 1 Beav 563 at 565, per Lord Langdale MR

[By a marriage settlement it was provided that if the wife should die in the lifetime of the husband the trust funds should on the death of the husband and failure of issue be held in trust for such persons other than the husband as should 'then' be the next of kin to the wife.] 'I think that the only way that I can make this sentence rational is, by construing the word "then" as meaning "in that event".' *Wheeler v Addams* (1853) 17 Beav 417 at 420, per Romilly MR

'The provision [in a will] is "then in that case, the capital is to be divided between the daughter's children". The word "then" has more meanings than one. It may mean "at that time", or "in that case", or, "in consequence". . . . Any one of those meanings may be given to it in its ordinary acceptation, and we may construe it as synonymous with "in that case", or "in consequence of that".' *Abbott v Middleton, Ricketts v Carpenter* (1858) 7 HL Cas 68 at 119, per Lord Wensleydale

'If Susannah Odell should die before the decease of Ann Gillman, then he [the testator] gave the said sum to such of S Odell's children as should be "then living". The period of time contemplated by the testator is the death of S Odell. "Then" in the second instance in which it occurs means a totally different thing from what it means in the first instance. The first time it is used it means "in that case". The second time it points out the particular moment of time intended by the testator—viz the death of S Odell.' *Drew v Drew* (1874) 22 WR 314 at 315, per Bacon V-C

'In Jarman on Wills, 4th edn, vol 1, p 851, the cases on this point are very neatly summed up. It is stated in the note, "Here it may be noticed that where (as often occurs) life interests are bequeathed to several persons in succession, terminating with a gift to children, or any other class of objects then living, the word 'then' is held to point to the period of the death of the person last named (whether he is or is not the survivor of the several legatees for life), and is not construed as referring to the period of determination of the several prior interests." Then he refers to *Archer v Jegon* [(1837) 8 Sim 446] and says, "The construction is the same, though the person last named die in the testator's lifetime." That is the effect of *Olney v Bates* [(1885) 3 Drew 319]. Then he refers to a string of cases, and the note goes on, "Compare *Gaskell v Holmes* [(1844) 3 Hare 438], and other cases, where, if 'then' had been referred to the last antecedent, a life estate just before coming to the widow would have been defeated." That sums up the authorities, and is in accordance with that which would be the conclusions arrived at simply by looking at the words themselves.' *Re Milne, Grant v Heysham* (1887) 57 LT 828 at 830, CA, per Lindley LJ

'Everyone knows that the word "then" may be used as equivalent to "at that time", or as meaning "in that case".' *Valentine v Fitzsimmons* [1894] 1 IR 93 at 106, per Porter MR

Australia 'Though the word "then" may mean "in that case", it may also mean "at that time".' *Re Anders, Public Trustee v Sack* [1924] SASR 33 at 39, per Poole J

THEREABOUTS

'When the plaintiff entered into this agreement, it could not have been in the contemplation of either party that under such loose and vague words as "or thereabouts" it could have been intended to oblige the defendant to accept eight acres instead of eighty-three acres.' *Davis v Shepherd* (1866) 1 Ch App 410 at 416, per Lord Cranworth LC

'The expression "or thereabouts" is very indefinite. It may include a large excess or a small excess, but at all events there is some excess to be allowed if necessary.' *Re Huddersfield Corpn & Jacomb* (1874) LR 17 Eq 476 at 486, 487, per Malins V-C; affd (1874) 10 Ch App 92

'We must turn to the conveyance, and there we find the land described as two parcels, each . . . "containing, by estimation, one-and-a-half acres or thereabouts". It turned out when the lands came to be measured that the two parcels together amounted to only 2 a 1 r 12 p. And the question is, does this amount to a breach of warranty as to quantity? It will be noted that the conveyance does not say "containing by admeasurement so and so", but "containing by estimation so and so, or thereabouts". I am not aware that any exact definition has been judicially given to these words, although there have been several cases illustrating their meaning—for example, it has been held that a discrepancy of five acres out of forty-one was not so serious as to amount to a breach; *Winch v Winchester* [(1812) 1 Ves & B 375]; on the other hand, a difference of 100 acres out of 349 was considered too serious to be covered by the qualifying expression; *Portman v Mill* [(1826) 2 Russ 570]. . . . I come to the conclusion . . . that the land had been actually and in fact estimated at three acres . . . and that there was consequently no breach of any warranty.' *Joliffe v Baker* (1883) 11 QBD 255 at 273, 274, per Watkin Williams J

New Zealand 'The number of cattle stated in the instrument of security is "549 or thereabouts". After the first sale had been made the cattle left unsold were reckoned to number 627. In this total were included the calves, numbering about 70, which were born before the end of October. These were properly included, we think, in the calculation. . . . Then came the sale of the second lot of cattle, to the number of 124. This sale reduced the number unsold to 503 unless the calves born in November be taken into account. The delivery under the second sale was not made until the 11th of November, and it is probable that more calves were born by that date, but there is no definite information on the subject, and there is a difficulty in taking them into consideration. It was contended, however . . . that the mortgagee was entitled only to have the cattle kept up to the number of 549 or thereabouts, and that the words "or thereabouts" were sufficient to cover the difference in number—viz 46. There are cases where these or similar words have been held to cover a greater difference than that. Thus in *Windle v Barker* [(1856) 25 LJQB 349] a charter-party described a ship as "of the measurement of 180 to 200 tons or thereabouts". The ship measured 257 tons. It was held by the Court of Queen's Bench and the Exchequer Chamber that the charterer had got the ship he contracted for, and was bound to load it. In *Cockerell v Aucompte* [(1857) 26 LJCP 194] the words "more or less" were held sufficient to cover an excess of 27 tons in a contract for the supply of 100 tons of coal, more or less. It is in every case a question of fact whether or not in the circumstances the words of the contract cover the excess or deficiency complained of. In the present case the words "or thereabouts" are sufficient, we think to cover a deficiency of 46, and the courts ought to favour this construction in view of the fact that the deficiency, if it existed at all, must have been made up by the birth of calves during the month of November.' *National Bank of New Zealand v Dalgety & Co* [1925] NZLR 250 at 256, 257, per cur.; also reported [1925] GLR 52 at 57

THEREAFTER

'The present appellants obtained a judgment against the respondent, and then applied for leave to issue execution on or otherwise proceed to the enforcement of the judgment under s 1 of the Courts (Emergency Powers) Act 1939 [repealed]. That liberty they obtained, subject to a provision which was inserted in the order to the following effect: "And it is further ordered that execution be suspended provided that £10 be paid on the 1st of February, 1940, and £10 per month thereafter." The respondent duly paid the £10 on 1st February. The next payment of £10 was in fact not paid till 5th of March. . . . The payment not having been made on 1st March . . . a bankruptcy notice was issued on 2nd of March. . . . Mr Registrar Parton . . . set aside the bankruptcy notice. . . . The point is a very short one. We start off with this, that in this order the word "month" has to be construed as meaning "calendar month", pursuant to . . . RSC, Order LXIV, r 1 [revoked; see now RSC 1965, Ord 3, r 1]. Accordingly, the phrase "£10 per month thereafter" must be construed as "£10 per calendar month thereafter". . . . The word "thereafter" points to sometime as from which the subsequent months are to be calculated. . . . The problem, therefore, is to find out what is the latest date in relation to each month that the payment of £10 must be made. If the months thereafter are to be calculated from 1st of February, the second month would begin at midnight on the 1st–2nd of February and would end at midnight on the 1st–2nd March. Accordingly the last day for payment of the second instalment would be 1st of March, and so on in the subsequent months. . . . That appears to be the true meaning which should be given to the word "thereafter".' *Re Debtor (No 266 of 1940), ex p Judgment Creditors v Judgment Debtor* [1940] Ch 470 at 471–474, per Greene MR

THERETOFORE

[The Towns Improvement Clauses Act 1847, s 53, enables a street to be paved, where the street, although a highway at the passing of the special Act, has not 'theretofore' been well and sufficiently paved, flagged, or otherwise made good.] 'The word "theretofore" is no doubt capable of receiving two different constructions; it may be held to refer either to the time when the work is executed by the commissioners, or to the time when the special Act is passed. I prefer the construction adopted by Baggallay LJ. I agree with his Lordship that the words "although a public highway at the passing of the special Act" are parenthetical; and in that view it appears to be more natural as well as more reasonable to connect the word "theretofore" with the period of the commissioners' operations.' *Portsmouth Corpn v Smith* (1885) 10 App Cas 364 at 375, 376, per Lord Watson

THIEF *See also* THEFT

Australia 'The word "thief" has its technical meaning; that is to say, a person who steals and is prepared to steal to commit the crime of larceny, should opportunity offer. Persons who commit frauds of other kinds are not thieves.' *Dias v O'Sullivan* [1949] ALR 586 at 592, per Mayo J

THING

[A partnership agreement provided that if either of the parties should die during the fourteen years intended for the partnership, and after an account passed between them, the surviving partner should take to his own use all the goods, ready money, and 'things' which on the last casting up before such death should happen to be in stock between them.] 'It is insisted on the part of the defendant that the words in these articles do not extend to oblige the surviving partner to take upon himself the outstanding debts contained in the last account, the words being only, "All the Goods, Ready Money, and Things", but the word things does extend to debts, and is as general a word as could well be made use of.' *Gainsborough v Stork* (1740) Barn Ch 312 at 316, per Lord Hardwicke LC

[A testator by his will gave and bequeathed to his wife four leasehold dwellings, his household goods, all his working tools, all moneys, bills, and bonds in his possession at the time of his decease, and all book debts and moneys due to him and all 'things' that he might possess at his decease.] 'Real estate being a thing which the testator did possess at his decease, it should not pass? . . . I am of opinion that realty did pass under these words.' *Re Turner, Arnold v Blades* (1891) 36 Sol Jo 28 at 28, per North J

THINK FIT

[The Companies (Winding-up) Act 1890, s 8(3) (repealed; see now the Companies Act 1985, s 530(2)), enacted that the official receiver of a company might, 'if he thinks fit', make a further report on matters which it was desirable to bring to the notice of the court.] 'The legislature, for very obvious reasons . . . thought that there might be cases in which it would be very desirable to have persons who might be supposed to have some personal interest in the conduct and management of companies brought to the test of a public examination; and accordingly, the legislature . . . imposed upon the official receiver a duty . . . to submit a preliminary report to the court. . . . But then there came what seems to me to be an absolutely independent and separate set of provisions, and that was that if the official receiver thought fit he was to make a further report. The expression "if he thinks fit" must of course mean if he arrives at a judicial conclusion in his own mind that such facts are before him, and in proof, that it becomes his duty. It is left to him to do it if he thinks fit; it is not made necessary for him to do it in every case, but only in such cases as in his judgment demand such a course to be pursued.' *Ex p Barnes* [1896] AC 146 at 150, HL, per Lord Halsbury LC

[A testator by his will directed his trustees to invest the proceeds of the sale of certain property upon such stocks, funds, and securities as they should 'think fit'.] 'What is the meaning of the words "upon such stocks, funds, and securities as they shall think fit"? . . . I have formed a very strong opinion that they mean "shall honestly think fit". It would be futile for a trustee to say that he thought fit to make an investment which he knew to be wrong. The court would say that he ought not to think fit so to do, and would come to the conclusion that he did not in fact think fit.' *Re Smith, Smith v Thompson* [1896] 1 Ch 71 at 75, 76, per Kekewich J

THIRD PARTY

'The first and main subsection [of a policy] is clear enough. It provides for what is ordinarily called, in this connection, third-party insurance. In the Road Traffic Act 1930, s 35 [repealed; see now the Road Traffic Act 1988, Part VI], which provides for compulsory insurance, the expression used is "third-party risks". Whichever phrase is used, I think that the governing conception is that the insurer is one party to the contract and the policyholder another party, and that claims made by others in respect of the negligent use of the car may be naturally described as claims by third parties.' *Digby v General Accident Fire & Life Assurance Corpn Ltd* [1943] AC 121 at 127, per Lord Simon LC

THOROUGHFARE

Australia 'The question in this case is whether a railway enclosure is a "thoroughfare". . . . This railway was open for public traffic. Every person on paying his fare had a right to sit in the train and pass over the line, and therefore it was a thoroughfare. It is said that a member of the public has no right to walk along the railway line, nor has a person the right to drive or ride along the line; but it does not follow that a place is not a thoroughfare because the right to use it is restricted in a certain way. In England there are many places where the public have a right to walk, but where the public cannot drive or ride, and such places are thoroughfares. It does not follow because a place is not open for all purposes that it is not a thoroughfare.' *Ex p Ryan* (1899) 20 NSWLR 274 at 276, per Darley CJ

THOUSAND

'Words denoting weight, or measure, or number, must undoubtedly be understood in their ordinary sense, unless some specific meaning be prescribed to them by statute, or given by custom. Mercantile instruments have long been expounded according to the usage and custom of merchants . . . and I think, on the same principle, the term thousand, which, in this lease, is applied to the subject of rabbits, may be explained, by the custom of the country, to mean twelve hundred.' *Smith v Wilson* (1832) 3 B & Ad 728 at 734, per Taunton J

THREAT *See also* INTIMIDATION

Of industrial action

'After the decisions that have been given upon this statute [a repealed Act which dealt with illegal combinations of workmen] it is too late to say that the word "threat" is limited to the declaration of an intention to do those acts with which it stands in intimate connection, viz acts of violence to the property or person of another. The cases that have been decided show that the word must have a wider sense; namely, a threat by act or words of doing some injury to another person. But I apprehend that it is the very essence of a threat that it should be made for the purpose of intimidating or overcoming the will of the person to whom it is addressed.' *Wood & Barrow v Bowron* (1866) LR 2 QB 21 at 30, per Lush J

'It is undeniable that the terms "threat", "coercion", and even "intimidation", are often applied in popular language to utterances which are quite lawful and which give rise to no liability either civil or criminal. They mean no more than this, that the so-called threat puts pressure, and perhaps extreme pressure, on the person to whom it is addressed to take a particular course. Of this again numberless instances might be given. Even then if it can be said without abuse of language that the employers were "intimidated and coerced" by the appellant, even if this be in a certain sense true, it by no means follows that he committed a wrong or is under any legal liability for his act. Everything depends on the nature of the representation or statement by which the pressure was exercised. The law cannot regard the act differently because you choose to call it a threat or coercion instead of an intimation or warning.' *Allen v Flood* [1898] AC 1 at 129, per Lord Herschell

'A threat is only an intimation by one to another that unless the latter does or does not do something the former will do something which the latter will not like. But it is impossible to say whether such a threat is or is not lawful until it has been ascertained what it is that is threatened to be done. If the threat is to use violence to person or property, it is obviously an intimation that the threatener intends to use unlawful means for the purpose of attaining his end: and no one would doubt that a threat to do that which is unlawful cannot be defended. Where the threat is part and parcel of a conspiracy or unlawful combination, it may be affected by the illegality of the conspiracy. But omitting cases of conspiracy or combination. I do not understand the legal basis for contending that it is unlawful for a man to threaten to do merely that which he is entitled to do. The act itself is immune from attack, yet an intimation that it will be done is to be a ground of liability. It may be that the idea is due to the belief that the threat is a menace or intimidation, and that it is unlawful, because it puts unlawful pressure upon the person who is subjected to it. If a threat amounts to intimidation or a menace of violence it cannot be defended; but assuming that it does not, the question remains whether it does in fact exercise pressure of an unlawful kind. Omitting cases of conspiracy or combination, I venture to doubt whether the pressure of a mere statement that the speaker intends to do something which he is legally entitled to do if the man to whom he is speaking does not adopt a particular course, can be unlawful pressure.' *Hodges v Webb* [1920] 2 Ch 70 at 89, per Paterson J

Of legal proceedings

[By the Patents and Designs Act 1907, s 36 (repealed; see now the Patents Act 1949, s 65), an injunction might be obtained against a person making groundless 'threats' of legal proceedings in respect of a patent.] 'Using language in its ordinary sense, it is difficult to see that an intimation ceases to be a threat because it is addressed to a third person in answer to an inquiry, or because it is addressed to the supposed infringer himself. We are not dealing with libel or questions of publication—we are dealing with threats. If I threaten a man that I will bring an action against him I threaten him none the less because I address that intimation to himself, and I threaten him none the less because I address the intimation to a third person. . . . What is the subject-matter in the first part of this section? It is a threat about a patent action. Now, every person of common sense knows what is involved in patent actions and what the expense of them is, and everybody knows that to be threatened with a patent action is about as disagreeable a thing as can happen to a man in business, and is the thing most calculated to paralyse a man in his business, even if he be innocent of any infringement of patent law. To say that the threat which the legislature intends to stop is only such a threat as is directed generally to the public by circulars and advertisements, would be to make the protection incommensurate with the evil; because a man might, by addressing a threat at a particular moment to a purchaser, do as irretrievable damage to the manufacturer whose manufacture was about to be purchased as if he had put his threat in *The Times* newspaper. Take the language of the section, and see if it does not run in the same direction. First of all an injunction may be obtained against a continuance of such threats, language which seems to indicate that it is the hanging of the threat over the head of the person threatened which the legislature intends to put an end to. Then when we come to the last paragraph, it says: "Provided that this section shall not apply if the person making such threats with due diligence commences and prosecutes an action for infringement of his patent". The whole meaning of the section seems to me to leap into light. The legislature desires that threats of patent actions shall not hang over a man's head—that the sword of Damocles, in such a case, should either not be suspended, or should fall at once; and it is with that view that the section seems to be framed.' *Skinner & Co v*

Shew & Co [1893] 1 Ch 413 at 423–425, CA, per Bowen LJ

[An action was brought to restrain threats by the defendants, the alleged threats being contained in a letter stating that the defendants would take vigorous steps to protect their rights in a registered design.] 'Let me examine it [the letter] a little more closely by asking: What is a threat? Here again there is no difficulty in expressing as a matter of words what constitutes a threat. The use of any language such as would be understood by a normal reader if it was a letter, or hearer if it was a statement, to mean that the writer, or, if an agent had written the letter, his principal, intended to take proceedings in respect of the act complained of must necessarily constitute a threat of proceedings.' *Rosedale Associated Manufacturers Ltd v Airfix Products Ltd* [1956] RPC 360 at 363, per Lloyd-Jacob J; affd [1957] RPC 239, CA

See, generally, 35 Halsbury's Laws (4th edn) para 644.

THRIFT FUND *See* CLUB

THRIFT SCHEME

'Thrift scheme' means any arrangement for savings, for providing money for holidays or for other purposes, under which a worker is entitled to receive in cash sums equal to or greater than the aggregate of any sums deducted from his remuneration or paid by him for the purposes of the scheme. (Wages Councils Act 1979, s 28)

THROAT

[A prisoner was charged with having cut the 'throat' of a certain person.] 'The question is, whether the term "throat" in the indictment is to be confined to that part of the neck which is scientifically called the throat, or whether it means that which is commonly called the throat; I am clearly of opinion it means the latter, and I do not entertain the slightest doubt about it.' *R v Edwards* (1834) 6 C & P 401 at 401, per Patteson J

THROUGH *See also* BY

'Where a contract is made by an agent, the latter purports to bind his principal, but where the contract is made through an agent, the meaning is that the terms of the contract are arranged through the mediation of the agent.' *National Mortgage & Agency Co of New Zealand Ltd v Gosselin & Stordeur* (1922) 38 TLR 832 at 833, CA, per Warrington LJ

'Were the appellants in this case . . . "the person by or through whom any such payment is made"? I imagine that, on the plain meaning of those words, the words would be apt to describe either the principal or the agent—the principal by whom, or the agent through whom, the payment was made. I reserve any question as to whether or not in this particular case the solicitors could be said to be the persons "by whom" the payment was made, but it seems to me obvious that the payment was made either by them or through them. And indeed the only other suggestion that was made in the case was that they are not the persons "through whom" the payment was made, because "through whom" means the person in consequence of whose instructions the payment was made, which seems to me to be entirely contrary to the plain meaning of the words, which appear to me to indicate agency.' *Rye & Eyre v Inland Revenue Comors* [1935] AC 274 at 278, 279, per Lord Atkin

Canada [The Motor Vehicle Transport Act 1953–1954 (Can) c 59, s 3, refers to transport 'through' the province.] 'In my opinion, the words "through the province" may apply to a vehicle entering the province and then later on leaving it, it may equally apply to a vehicle commencing its journey somewhere in a province and proceeding through that province to the provincial border or in the case at bar, the international border of the United States.' *R v Canadian American Transfer Ltd* (1969) 7 CRNS 372 at 378, Ont SC, per Wells CJHC

Canada 'The versatile preposition "through" derives from the now archaic preposition "thorough". It can be used correctly in a number of different ways and with different meanings. The Oxford English Dictionary (1961) defines the preposition "into" in its ordinary use, in relation to motion or direction, as follows: "expressing motion to a position within a space . . . to a point within the limits of". (This suggests why the phrase "into or out of" would present very serious problems of interpretation.) The same dictionary, in the same sense of motion or direction, gives the following definitions for the preposition "through": 1. From one end, side, or surface of (a body or a space) by passing within it; *usually* implying into at one end, side, etc., and out at the other. (Expressing movement (or extension) either so as to penetrate the substance of a thing, or along a passage or opening already existing in it.) 2. Of motion or direction within the limits of; along within; as in (1), i.e., but *not necessarily implying the traversing of the whole extent from end to end*. . . . It appears that that word may imply as well that which begins and ends within an object or a space. You can travel *through* Ontario (making election speeches, for instance) without leaving the Province; and it would seem proper to so speak even though you had not traversed the whole extent of the Province from end to end.' *R v Beaney* (1969) 4 DLR (3d) 369 at 380, Ont Co Ct, per Matheson, Co Ct J

THROUGHOUT

Australia 'It is an ordinary English word with a well-established meaning. The Oxford English Dictionary (1919) gives the following meanings: as a preposition, "completely or right through (a place)", "through the whole of (a region)": and as an adverb, "right through", "through the whole of (a region)", "in every part", "everywhere": and the Shorter Oxford Dictionary (1967) does not suggest that the word has acquired any different or more limited meaning. It is not possible to hold that an unknown number of individual allotments scattered about a district answer the description of "rateable land throughout the whole of" that district.' *Gartland v Kalamunda Shire* [1973] WAR 37 at 39, per Hale J

TICKET

'Ticket', in relation to any lottery or proposed lottery, includes any document evidencing the claim of a person to participate in the chances of the lottery. (Betting, Gaming and Lotteries Act 1963, s 55)

'Ticket', in relation to any lottery, includes any document evidencing the claim of a person to participate in the chances of the lottery. (Lotteries and Amusements Act 1976, s 23(1))

TIDAL LAND

The term 'tidal lands' means such parts of the bed, shore, or banks of a tidal water as are covered and uncovered by the flow and ebb of the tide at ordinary spring tides. (Railways Clauses Act 1863, s 3)

TIDAL RIVER

The term 'tidal river' means any part of a river within the flow and ebb of the tide at ordinary spring tides. (Railways Clauses Act 1863, s 3)

'There is no case which shows that, because at exceptionally high tides some portion of the river is dammed up and prevented from flowing down and so rises and falls with the tide, that portion of the river can be called tidal. It is unnecessary to go through all the authorities on the subject. In Hale, *de Jure Maris*; Hargrave's Law Tracts 12, the public right of fishing in rivers is treated of in connection with the king's interest in arms of the sea. There seems strong ground, from the whole of the passage, for thinking that the public right of fishing was considered by the author as coextensive with the right of the Crown over the river for public purposes. Lord Hale CJ there says: "Herein there will be these things examinable: 1st What shall be said the shore or *littus maris*; 2nd What shall be said an arm or creek of the sea. . . . For the first of these, it is certain that that which the sea overflows either at high spring tides or at extraordinary tides comes not as to this purpose under the denomination *littus maris*, and consequently the king's title is not of that large extent, but to land that is usually overflowed at ordinary tides. . . . For the second, that is called an arm of the sea where the sea flows and reflows; so that the river of Thames above Kingston, and the river of Severn above Tewkesbury, though they are public rivers are not arms of the sea. But it seems that although the water be fresh at high water yet the denomination of an arm of the sea continues if it flow and reflow as in Thames above the bridge". In the present case there is no regular flow and reflow of the tide at the spot in question, but only an occasional damming back of the water. The law on the subject of the right of the public to fish in rivers is laid down in the case of *Mussett v Burch* [(1876) 35 LT 486, DC], by Cleasby B. He says, "The case in the Irish reports, *Murphy v Ryan* [(1868) IR 2 CL 143], is decisive on the point before us. It expressly decides that the public cannot acquire by immemorial usage any right of fishing in a river in which though it be navigable the tide does not ebb and flow". For this purpose, as I have already said, it seems to me that "tidal navigable river" means that part of the river which under ordinary circumstances is tidal and navigable as such, and it is not enough to show that sometimes under unusual circumstances the river at the place in question is affected by the tide.' *Reece v Miller* (1882) 8 QBD 626 at 630, 631, DC, per Grove J

TIDAL WATERS

The term 'tidal water' means any part of the sea or any part of a river within the flow and ebb of the tide at ordinary spring tides. (Railways Clauses Act 1863, s 3)

'Tidal water' means any part of the sea and any part of a river within the ebb and flow of the tide at ordinary spring tides, and not being a harbour. (Merchant Shipping Act 1894, s 742)

'The question arises as to what is meant by the words "tidal waters" as used in this Act [a local Act] concerning the pollution of rivers. The question is not what is the tide, but what are tidal waters, and I have come to the conclusion . . . that tidal waters must be those which rise and fall, not because they have come up from the sea or estuary and must flow down again, but because when flowing down from their source towards the sea they are arrested in their course and compelled to rise by the action of the tide properly so called, and fall when that pressure is withdrawn. I do not think it necessary to inquire whether the pressure applied to these waters is vertical or horizontal pressure. I do not think myself that one can say what it is. It seems very difficult to say of water flowing up that it could produce purely vertical pressure, as though water coming down was pressing against a dam. One would be inclined to think that the water coming up must get underneath the water which is raised, but I do not think it necessary to inquire how in fact it is done. I come to the conclusion that tidal waters include those which I have indicated in words which I have carefully chosen.' *West Riding of Yorkshire Rivers Board v Tadcaster Rural District Council* (1907) 97 LT 436 at 439, DC, per Darling J

'It may be, though I find it quite unnecessary to consider the matter, that "tidal waters" extend to the open sea; it may be that scientifically it can be said that the tide ebbs and flows everywhere in the sea. But it seems to me that all we are considering here is that part of the sea . . . in which there is at any rate a perceptible, a real, ebb and flow of the tide.' *Ingram v Percival* [1968] 3 All ER 657 at 659, per Lord Parker CJ

TIDE

[The Port of London River By-Laws, r 36, provided that a 'ship navigating against the tide' should, if approaching points or bends, ease her speed.] 'There remains a specific and totally independent point relating to r 36 of the Port of London River By-Laws. It raises two questions. The first is whether, as a matter of construction, the expressions in this rule "navigating against the tide" and "navigating with the tide" refer to an actual tidal stream, operating at the time and place sufficiently to differentiate for the purposes of practical navigation between with it and against it, or only to the state of the tide, that is, ebb or flow, which at that place and time should be expected, according to the published anticipations of the local time tables applicable. . . . One must . . . construe the rule as it stands. It is meant, no doubt, as a practical guide for seamen, to tell them their duty in circumstances to be observed from the bridge. It virtually states the reason for itself, namely, that the ship with a working tide with her has the right of way as against the ship coming the other way, because then the ship more likely to go large and less easy to control will be left free, and the other, with little way to take off, can be pulled up without delay or inconvenience, and leave her free water, in which to round the point. The give-way ship can then come on and if, on entering the tide stream from the slack on rounding the point, she takes a slight sheer, it will not matter. This is how I read it. The ship is navigating against the tide, not against the tide table. The pilot, instead of having to keep one eye on the clock and the other on the tide table, can ascertain his duty by a glance from time to time over the ship's side.' *Hontestroom SS (Owners) v Sagaporack SS (Owners), Hontestroom SS (Owners) v Durham Castle SS (Owners)* [1927] AC 37 at 50–53, per Lord Sumner

TILLAGE

Tillages are the expenses and acts of husbandry in general, such as seeds and labour, fallows and unapplied manure; and, if the landlord accepts tillage and manure, an agreement by him to pay for it will be implied. (1 Halsbury's Laws (4th edn) para 1073)

TIMBER

At common law oak, ash and elm are timber if over twenty years old, but not so old as to have no usable wood in them. Other trees may be timber by the custom of the country. Thus beech is timber by the custom of Buckinghamshire and parts of Gloucestershire. Aspen and horse-chestnut are timber in some counties. Trees less than six inches in diameter have been said not to be timber.

Agricultural usages between landlord and tenant also frequently define the species of trees which are regarded as timber in the localities where the usages subsist. In a contract for the sale of standing timber, 'timber' may be synonymous with 'trees', and so include lops and tops as well as trunks. By statute, 'timber', includes all forest products. (19 Halsbury's Laws (4th edn) para 33)

In this section [which deals with regulations respecting forestry leases] the expression 'timber' includes all forest products. (Settled Land Act 1925, s 48(2))

'The court holds that tithes are not payable on beeches, nor decayed oaks since they are not timber by reason of their decay and as they are converted into fire-wood.' *Holliday v Lee* (1598) Moore KB 541 at 541, per cur.

'A grant of "timber trees and other trees" will not pass fruit trees.' *Bullen v Denning* (1826) 5 B & C 842 at 847, per Bayley J

'With respect to the timber and timber-like trees [assigned by the life tenant as then growing upon the estate], the first question is, what it includes. It includes all wood which is considered timber everywhere, as oak, ash and elm. It also includes all that species of wood which is timber by the custom of the county in which the estate is situated, and evidence is given, that what is not ordinarily considered timber in other counties is timber in this.' *Gordon v Woodford* (1859) 27 Beav 603 at 607, per Romilly MR

'The great question is, what is the meaning of the word "timber" as used by the parties? . . . It could scarcely be fairly intended that a tenant for life should strip the estate of every particle of wood; the fair and probable inference, therefore, from the defendant's informing the plaintiff of the fact, that he was tenant for life, is rather that he meant only timber properly so called to be cut.' *Whitty v Dillon (Lord)* (1860) 2 F & F 67 at 70, per Cockburn CJ

'The question of what timber is depends, first, on general law, that is the law of England; and secondly, on the special custom of a locality. By the general law of England, oak, ash, and elm are timber, provided that they are of the age of twenty years and upwards, provided also that they are not so old as not to have a reasonable quantity of useable wood in them, sufficient, according to a text writer, to make a good post. Timber, that is, the kind of tree which may be called timber, may be varied by local custom. There is what is called the custom of the country, that is of a particular county or division of a county, and it varies in two ways. First of all, you may have trees called timber by the custom of the country—beech in some counties, hornbeam in others, and even whitethorn and black-thorn, and many other trees, are considered timber in peculiar localities, in addition to the ordinary timber trees. Then again, in certain localities arising probably from the nature of the soil, trees of even twenty years old are not necessarily timber, but may go to twenty-four years or even to a later period, I suppose, if necessary; and in other places the test of when a tree becomes timber is not its age but its girth. These, however, are special customs.' *Honywood v Honywood* (1874) LR 18 Eq 306 at 309, 310, per Jessel MR

'It has been repeatedly decided in this and other courts that larch trees are not timber. They are not subject to the same rules as timber trees are. We all know that oak and ash are timber everywhere. There are other kinds of trees which are timber trees by custom in some parts of the country, and not in others, such as birch, and I believe, beech.' *Re Harrison's Trusts, Harrison v Harrison* (1884) 28 Ch D 220 at 227, 228, CA, per Baggally LJ

Ornamental timber

'As the court cannot determine what is ornamental timber, it being merely a matter of taste, they therefore say, that what was planted for ornament, must be considered as ornamental.' *Mahon (Lord) v Stanhope (Lord)* (1808) 3 Madd 523 n at 523 n, per Grant MR

Timber estate

'Once arrive at the fact of what is timber, the tenant for life, impeachable for waste, cannot cut it down. That I take to be the clear law, with one single exception, which has been established principally by modern authorities in favour of the owners of timber estates, that is, estates which are cultivated merely for the produce of saleable timber, and where the timber is cut periodically.' *Honywood v Honywood* (1874) LR 18 Eq 306 at 309, 310

'What is a "timber estate"? Counsel for the defendants disclaimed the definition that it means an estate upon which there is a good deal of timber. A timber estate, they say, is an estate upon which timber is cut periodically to allow a succession to grow up. That definition (unless by timber is meant wood of twenty years growth and upwards) would include coppice, which properly speaking, is oak, ash, or other wood cut at intervals of less than twenty years, so that it springs again from the same stool or stub; and the cutting of this at the proper periods by a limited owner is not waste. But the definition is intended to go further and to include such cutting as has taken place here, namely, the cutting of large timber trees which do not grow again and are not individually cut periodically, but each of which is cut down once for all, and is replaced, not by a growth from the same stool, but by saplings springing up from the self-sown seed of the old trees. That is not coppice.' *Dashwood v Magniac* [1891] 3 Ch 306 at 374, CA, per Kay LJ

'The whole essence of a timber estate is that there should be a regular course of cultivation, the main object being that the timber should produce for the tenant for life income at periodical intervals.' *Pardoe v Pardoe* (1900) 82 LT 547 at 549, per Stirling J

TIME *See also* DAY; HOUR; MONTH; TIME IMMEMORIAL; WEEK; YEAR

Apart from statute or special convention, the hour of the day has to be ascertained by reference to the sun in the particular place. At a given moment, therefore, the time is different in different places. The hour at which a court is fixed to sit means prima facie the hour at the locality where the particular court is to sit, and not Greenwich mean time.

For the purpose of statutes, subordinate legislation, deeds or other legal instruments, it is provided by statute [Interpretation Act 1978, s 9] that, unless the contrary is expressed, expressions referring to time are to be taken to refer to Greenwich mean time [but see note, infra] and not to local time. Regard must be had to this rule in applying the numerous statutes in which certain hours of the day are specified within which acts may or may not be done. It is apprehended that Greenwich, and not local, time must be considered in fixing the hour or day of an event with regard to which provision is made in an instrument such as a policy of insurance, and that on the other hand the statutory rule should not be applied in a case where the instrument was executed or the event was expected to happen or did happen in a foreign country.

It has been held that 'sunset' in certain enactments is not such an expression referring to time as previously mentioned, but refers to local time. (45 Halsbury's Laws (4th edn) paras 1115, 1116)

Subject to the Summer Time Act 1972, s 3 [infra] (construction of references to points of time during the period of summer time), whenever an expression of time occurs in an Act, the time referred to shall, unless it is otherwise specifically stated, be held to be Greenwich mean time. (Interpretation Act 1978, s 9)

[The Summer Time Act 1972 consolidated the Summer Time Acts 1922 to 1947 and the British Standard Time Act 1968, and established that, during the period of summer time, the time for general purposes in Great Britain 'is one hour in advance of Greenwich mean time'. The period of summer time for the purposes of the Act is from two o'clock, Greenwich mean time in the morning of the day after the third Saturday in March (or if that is Easter Day, the day after the Second Saturday in March), and ending at two o'clock Greenwich mean time in the morning of the day after the fourth Saturday in October.

Nothing in the Act is to affect the use of Greenwich mean time for the purposes of astronomy, meteorology or navigation, or to affect the construction of any document mentioning or referring to a point of time in connection with any of these purposes.]

TIME CHARTERPARTY

See CHARTERPARTY

TIME IMMEMORIAL

A right claimed by prescription at common law must have been enjoyed from the time of legal memory, which is said to date from 1189, the commencement of the reign of Richard I, but in point of fact the continuance of a usage for many years in modern times is taken as prima facie proof of its continued existence from time immemorial. (6 Halsbury's Laws (4th edn) para 590)

Every custom must have been in existence from a time preceding the memory of man, a date which has long since been fixed at the year 1189, the commencement of the reign of

Richard I. Where, however, it is impossible to show such a continued existence, the courts will support the custom if circumstances are proved which raise a presumption that the custom in fact existed at that date. Evidence showing continuous user as of right as far back as living testimony can go is regarded as raising this presumption. (12 Halsbury's Laws (4th edn) para 407)

TIME POLICY *See* POLICY OF INSURANCE

TIME RATE

'Time rate' means a rate where the amount of the remuneration is to be calculated by reference to the actual number of hours worked. (Wages Councils Act 1979, s 28)

TIP

In this Act, the expression 'tip' means an accumulation or deposit of refuse from a mine or quarry (whether in a solid state or in solution or suspension) other than an accumulation or deposit situated underground, and where any wall or other structure retains or confines a tip then, whether or not that wall or structure is itself composed of refuse, it shall be deemed to form part of the tip for the purposes of this Act. (Mines and Quarries (Tips) Act 1969, s 2(1))

TITHES

Tithes are the tenth part of all fruits, prædial, personal, and mixed, which are due to God and consequently to His church's ministers for their maintenance. Tithes are payable yearly out of all things which with the aid of cultivation yield increase by the act of God, even though the increase is not realised every year.

Tithes which arise merely and immediately from the ground, such as grain of all sorts, hay, wood, fruits and herbs, are called prædial tithes. Tithes which arise from things immediately nourished by the ground, such as colts, calves, lambs, chickens, milk, cheese and eggs, are called mixed tithes. Tithes which arise from the profits of labour and industry, being the tenth part of the clear gain after charges deducted, are called personal tithes.

Where the tithes are divided into great and small tithes, the great tithes, which are ordinarily the rectorial tithes, are those of corn, hay and wood, and the small tithes, which are ordinarily the vicarial tithes, are the remainder of the prædial tithes, and the mixed and personal tithes. . . .

The inconvenience of collecting tithe in kind and the fluctuating nature of the income derived from it has led to the compounding of tithes from very early times, voluntary compositions being called 'moduses' or compositions real and compositions by local or general statutes being called 'corn rents' or tithe rentcharges. In 1836 a procedure was provided for the commutation of all tithes into tithe rentcharges either by agreement or by compulsion, and in fact almost all tithes have been so commuted. Tithe rentcharge has now been extinguished . . . and it is no longer possible to commute tithes into tithe rentcharge.

Instead of tithe rentcharge the landowner now pays to the Crown a redemption annuity, payable for sixty years, from 2nd October 1936, at the end of which (or sooner if the annuity is redeemed) the land formerly subject to tithe will be absolutely freed from tithe, tithe rentcharge or any similar charge. (14 Halsbury's Laws (4th edn) paras 1209, 1210, 1212)

TITLE *See also* ABSTRACT OF TITLE; DOCUMENT OF TITLE

'As to this word (*titulum*) . . . it has two significations, one properly and strictly, as for a title for which no action lies, as for a condition broken, or upon alienation in mortmain, etc. and so it is taken in Plowden's Commentaries in Nichol's case, fol 484. In another signification it is taken largely; and in this sense, *titulus est justa causa possidendi quod nostrum est*, and signifies the title which one has to land, as by fine, feoffment, etc or by descent, etc, and therefore when the plaintiff makes a title in an assize, the tenant may say, let the assize come upon the title, which is as much as to say, upon the particular conveyance, etc which he makes to the land, etc and it is called *titulus a tuendo, quia* thereby he defends his land, *et plerumque constat ex munimentis quae muniant et tuentur causam*. By release of all title to land, etc all his right is extinct, for it shall be taken strongly against him, and in the largest sense. So when a man has title in the proper sense, either by a condition or by alienation in mortmain, the release of all his right will extinguish this title, for he has *jus possidendi*, and therewith agrees 6 Hen 7 8a. And the English poet saith, "For true it is that neither fraud nor might can make a title where there wanteth right".' *Altham's Case* (1610) 8 Co Rep 150b at 153b, per Coke CJ

[The defendant refused to produce certain documents on the ground that he had obtained them for his defence since the institution of the suit and that they did not relate to or evidence the 'title' of the plaintiff or his predecessors.] '"Title" is an ambiguous word; it may mean the title to real estate or property: properly and technically used, it is the title of the plaintiff to get the relief he asks. . . . In order to protect himself a defendant must state, and it must appear, looking at the schedule and the nature of the documents, that they do not relate to or tend to show not only the title of the plaintiff to the property to be recovered, but the title to the relief he asks.' *Felkin v Herbert (Lord)* (1861) 30 LJ Ch 798 at 799, per Kindersley V-C

Good title

'Where a question arises between parties who are about to enter into the relationship of vendor and vendee, as to the meaning of a good or sufficient title, there must be such a title as the Court of Chancery would adopt as a sufficient ground for compelling specific performance, and that by a stipulation for a good title, must be understood, not such a title as would support a verdict for the purchaser in an action of ejectment against a mere stranger, but such a one as would enable the purchaser to hold the property against any person who might probably challenge his right to it.' *Jeakes v White* (1851) 6 Exch 873 at 881, per Pollock CB

'The question whether there is a good title appears to me to mean whether there is a good title according to the contract the specific performance of which is decreed at the hearing, whether those words are in the decree or not; otherwise in every case every stipulation as to evidence, and every stipulation as to the commencement of the title, and matters of that kind, would have to be referred to specially in the decree.' *Upperton v Nickolson* (1871) 6 Ch App 436 at 442, 443, per James LJ

Title to sue

'By the law of Scotland, a litigant, and in particular a pursuer, must always qualify title and interest. Though the phrase "title to sue" has been a heading under which cases have been collected from at least the time of Morrison's Dictionary and Brown's Synopsis, I am not aware that anyone of authority has risked a definition of what constitutes title to sue. I am not disposed to do so but I think it may fairly be said that for a person to have such title he must be a party (using the word in its widest sense) to some legal relation which gives him some right which the person against whom he raises the action either infringes or denies. . . . The question of title to sue in England bristles with difficulties having their origin in the rigid rules of common law actions, with the subsequent modifications of the results of these rules either by statute or by the concomitant working of the equity jurisdiction. This fact makes these authorities of no assistance in Scottish procedure.' *Dundee Harbour Trustees v Nicol* [1915] AC 550 at 561, 562, 568, per Lord Dunedin

TITLE DEEDS

'Title deeds, at any rate since the reign of Elizabeth, have been regarded from a somewhat singular standpoint in courts of law. They have been called the sinews of the land: see Co Litt 6A. . . . The deeds of appointment in question, since they did not assure or affect directly any estate or interest in any part of the land, are not title deeds of the land in the legal sense; for, in my opinion, the old authorities refer only to title deeds by which the lands or some legal interest therein is assured or dealt with.' *Clayton v Clayton* [1930] 2 Ch 12 at 17, 21, per Maugham J

TO

'I think we ought to construe the word "to" [in an insurance policy] as meaning "towards". That is the sense in which the word is always used in all instruments connected with or relating to marine assurance. It has that meaning in a bill of lading; and I do not know why we should adopt a different meaning in this policy of insurance.' *Colledge v Harty* (1851) 6 Exch 205 at 210, per Pollock CB

TOGETHER

'The answer to the question depends on the ascertainment of the true construction of cl 5 of the testator's will. Clause 5 is in the following terms: "I devise free of duty my house at 74 Brook Street together with the contents except such as I have herein specifically bequeathed some of which in the event of my death during the present war will be at Moulton Paddocks except money and securities from money to my sister Eileen Rogerson". There is nothing further in the will to be considered in connection with this question. Apart from authority the bequest appears to constitute one gift, for the bequest is of the house together with its contents. The ordinary meaning of the words "together with" as stated in the Imperial Dictionary is "in union with", "in company with". Apart from any other context when a testator makes a gift of a house and the furniture in it he would seem to be giving the furniture because it is situated in the house and goes to make up one whole which the testator knows as his furnished house.' *Re Joel, Rogerson v Joel* [1943] Ch 311 at 323, 324, CA, per cur.

Canada [The accused was served with a notice of intention and a breathalyzer certificate, but was later served with a corrected certificate to replace the first but no further notice. The Criminal Code, RSC 1970 c C-34, ss 237(5), provided that a certificate could not be received in evidence unless the accused had been given notice of intention 'together with' a copy of the certificate.] 'Manifestly, s 237 relaxes the normal rules of evidence by providing an easy and convenient way by which the Crown may prove the results of a breath test. To avail itself of this method of proof the Crown must strictly comply with the term of the section which requires that an accused be given reasonable notice of the Crown's intention to produce a certificate of analysis at trial together with a copy of the certificate. In the framework of the criminal legislation in question, the words "together with" must, in my opinion, be construed literally and in accordance with their plain and ordinary meaning which is "simultaneously" or "at the same time as". To interpret these words, as the Crown suggests, to mean "as well as" or "in addition to" would fail to give them full effect and would be tantamount to reading the section as though the word "and" had been used instead of "together with". The language of s 237(5), in my view, compels the conclusion that the notice and certificate must be given at the same time. It follows in the instance case that since a copy of the certificate was not given the appellant together with notice of the Crown's intention to use such certificate at trial, the Crown failed to satisfy the prerequisites of s 237(5) and was not entitled to introduce the certificate as evidence against the appellant.' *R v Costa* (1980) 54 CCC (2d) 61 at 63, Ont HCJ, per Robins J

New Zealand [The defendant was charged with aggravated robbery under the Crimes Act 1961, s 235(1)(b), in that he was 'together' with any other person or persons when he committed the robbery. The question was whether an offence under s 235(1)(b) had been committed when an accomplice was physically present at the robbery but there was no common intention that he should participate physically and directly in the robbery.] 'The effect of s 235(1) was to elevate robbery from a crime punishable by 10 years' imprisonment to one punishable by 14 years' imprisonment if: (a) the offender causes grievous bodily harm, or (b) the offender is "together with any other person or persons" when he commits the robbery, or (c) the offender is armed with any offensive weapon or instrument. It was clear enough in relation to (a) and (c) that the legislature had taken as aggravating circumstances matters directly related to the degree of violence, or threats of violence employed by the offender. . . . The expression "being together with any person or persons" should be construed as having a somewhat similar purpose, and therefore as intended to apply only in situations where the presence together is proved of two or more persons having the common intention to use their combined force, either in any event or as circumstances might require, directly in the perpetration of the crime.' *R v Galey* [1985] 1 NZLR 230 at 234, CA

TOLERANCE

Canada [The test for immorality or indecency of a publication involved consideration of whether the material was tolerable according to current Canadian community standards.] 'I start with a consideration of the word "tolerance" which is defined in the Dictionary of Canadian English as "a willingness to be tolerant and patient towards people whose opinions differ from one's own". As I interpret this definition, it implies, firstly, a knowledge of what those opinions of others might be and, secondly, a willingness to put up with or endure them. Applying interpretation to the matter at hand, it is the duty of the court to determine whether or not, if they were aware of the nature of the magazine in question, the Canadian community taken at large would put up with or endure or tolerate it.' *Re Luscher and Deputy Minister, Revenue Canada Customs and Excise* (1983) 149 DLR (3d) 243 at 246, 247, BC Co Ct, per Anderson Co Ct J

TOLL

Market toll

Toll in the more limited sense of franchise toll is a sum payable by the buyer upon sales of tollable articles in a market or fair. By custom or statute there may be dues, in the nature of franchise tolls, payable on goods brought into a market for sale, whether sold or not; and these are in some cases payable in kind. Toll cannot be payable, unless by statute, on goods not actually brought into the market for sale. Accordingly, no toll can be payable by grant or prescription on the bulk of goods sold by sample in a market, when the sample only is actually brought into the market.

The right to toll has been described as a subordinate franchise appurtenant to a franchise of market or fair. It may be acquired by (1) express grant from the Crown; (2) statute; or (3) prescription or long usage from which a lost grant may be presumed. (29 Halsbury's Laws (4th edn) paras 629, 630)

'The question here is whether a grant or exemption of the general word "toll" is sufficient to exempt from market toll and also stallage. The first was considered in *Bennington v Taylor* [(1700) 2 Lut 1517]; and the . . . case of *Heddey v Welhouse* [(1598) Moore KB 474] and the case in Rolle's Abridgement [*Hickman's Case* (1599) 2 Roll Abr 123, tit Market (B), pl 2] were cited; the court held the general word "toll" included in stallage; and we also come to the same conclusion.' *Lockwood v Wood* (1841) 6 QB 31 at 46, per cur.

'The case at common law would stand thus: The market would be a definite place created by the king's grant for the purpose of selling goods or chattels. The market, unless anything else is said in the king's grant, is free from toll. It was in the king's power to grant a reasonable toll to the lord of the market. For what? Why in respect of the convenience he supplied for the witnessing of contracts made in the market. . . . A witness of a sale in market overt was of importance to the public, and to the parties concerned in the transaction. . . . The grant, however, of the toll in the market which refers to the witnessing of the sale must be special, otherwise no toll could be exacted for goods sold. But besides this toll, which my learned brothers have called a franchise toll, there was another kind of toll which might be payable to the lord. It was a toll payable for or in respect not merely of some user of the soil (because it may be said that in one way everybody who goes into a market uses the soil), but in respect of some user of the soil beyond the mere entry to the market, which was enjoyed in common by all the rest of the public. So stallage was one kind of toll which was payable to the lord of the soil, which I take to be a toll in respect of standing room within the market, as defined by a series of cases decided. Then there is pickage, for something different, a toll not payable merely in respect of standing room, but in respect of the privilege of picking a hole in the ground in order to make the stand more convenient by fitting a pole or a rail, or the like, in the soil. All that is set out in Coke's Institutes, which have been referred to. He says, "Toll in a fair or market is a reasonable sum of money due to the owner of the fair or market upon the sale of things tollable within the fair or market". That is the first class of toll, and he further says, "or for stallage, pickage or the like".' *Bedford (Duke) v St Paul, Covent Garden, Overseers* (1881) 51 LJMC 41 at 45, per Bowen J

Toll thorough

A toll thorough is independent of any ownership of the soil by the original grantee, the consideration necessary to support it being usually the liability to repair the particular highway or bridge. (21 Halsbury's Laws (4th edn) para 138)

Toll traverse

A toll traverse is a toll taken in respect of the original ownership of the land crossed by the public (even if now perhaps severed from it), the land having been at the date of the grant the grantee's private property, and having been then dedicated by him to the public in consideration of the toll to be taken. (21 Halsbury's Laws (4th edn) para 138)

'There are two sorts of toll recognised by the law, toll traverse, and toll thorough; and the plaintiff will be entitled to a verdict on the pleadings in this case, if he establishes his title to either. Where a party has the burden of repairing public highways, he may, though those were public ways at the time that the liability to repair commenced, be entitled to take toll in consideration of those repairs; and that is toll thorough. The public however having an antecedent right to the use of the ways, he can only be so entitled by virtue of such consideration; and for that purpose the plaintiff in this case attempted to prove that the corporation of Cambridge repaired the roads and streets there. He has only proved that they repaired a single road: and having failed to prove that they repair all the roads and streets in Cambridge, where they claim the toll, the consideration fails, and they cannot be entitled to toll thorough. They may, however, be entitled to toll traverse. That arises, when the owner of the soil dedicates it to the use of the public; but, at the time of the dedication, reserves to himself toll from those who pass over it. The reservation must be made at the time; and in this case therefore it must have been made before the time of William the Conqueror, for it appears from Domesday Book that there was then a town, and highways of some standing at Cambridge. At that time the town belonged to the king, and if he or his predecessor, at the time when highways were first made there, reserved toll to themselves for passing over them, he would at that time be entitled to toll traverse. Of that you must judge from the expressions in Domesday Book, and from the evidence of later usage, to which you may presume a rightful beginning, if any such can by law be devised. If at that time the king was entitled, not only to the soil of the town, of which there is no doubt, but also to toll traverse within it, I am of opinion that that right to toll would pass to the burgesses, by the grant of the town with its appurtenances in the charter of King John, without any more express words relating to it.' *Brett v Beales* (1829) Mood & M 416 at 427, 428, per Lord Tenterden CJ

TONIC

'A "tonic", said the . . . witness, is a substance which produces a feeling of vigour and tends to disperse the exhaustion which is common during and after illness. The majority of tonics act by increasing the appetite for food, and, in consequence, the secretion of the digestive juices and the efficiency of the absorption of the food. Others act also on the nervous system directly. The British Pharmaceutical Codex defines "tonics" as "substances which assist nutrition and improve the general tone of the system". It gives lists of heart, nerve and stomach tonics, most of which, I imagine, are, without doubt, medicines. In other words, a "tonic" operates in the same way as does a medicine. It aims at restoring healthy functioning. Indeed, the definition in Webster's Dictionary is "Tonic: restoring healthy functions".' *Nairne v Stephen Smith & Co Ltd & Pharmaceutical Society of Great Britain* [1943] 1 KB 17 at 21, per Atkinson J

TONTINE

'Tontine' means an annuity with benefit of survivorship among several persons. (19 Halsbury's Laws (4th edn) para 104 n)

TOOLS OF TRADE

'On looking at the words of the Act [County Courts Act 1888, s 147 (repealed; see now the County Courts Act 1984, s 89)] the words are that the tools and implements protected [from execution] are the tools and implements of his trade—not his tools and implements at all. The tools and implements of his trade are protected. I think that means the tools and implements which he uses in his trade, and they are equally protected, in my opinion, whether they be actually his own personal property or whether they be hired by him for the purposes of his trade and used by him in his trade.' *Masters v Fraser* (1901) 85 LT 611 at 614, DC, per Darling J

Australia [An application was made for a declaration that an electric cake mixer did not form part of the property divisible amongst the creditors of a bankrupt on the ground that it was a 'tool of trade' of the bankrupt.] 'There is . . . one common characteristic present in all definitions and decisions of "tool" and that is manual operation; and when I am asked what real difference can it make, in determining whether a specific article is a tool or not, that in one case it is worked substantially by manual manipulation and in the other operated electrically without manual manipulation, I can only answer that in my opinion that difference is the essential determinant.' *Toledo-Berkel Pty Ltd v Official Receiver in Bankruptcy* (1953) 56 WALR 21 at 24, per Dwyer CJ

TOP

'"Lop" . . . is well known in the country to mean cutting off the branches of a tree; "topping" is the cutting off its top.' *Unwin v Hanson* [1891] 2 QB 115 at 120, CA, per Lord Esher MR

TORT *See also* BREACH OF DUTY

Those civil rights of action which are available for the recovery of unliquidated damages by persons who have sustained injury or loss from acts, statements or omissions of others in breach of duty or contravention of right imposed or conferred by law rather than by agreement are rights of action in tort. (45 Halsbury's Laws (4th edn) para 1201)

Australia 'Hurt to feelings is recognised in many torts (defamation, negligence, malicious prosecution to mention but three) and I see no reason why a tort of discrimination should not allow for that factor. Discrimination in many circumstances is capable of causing injury in a real sense to the feelings of the person discriminated against.' *Allders International Pty Ltd v Anstee* (1986) 5 NSWLR 47 at 65, per Lee J

TORTFEASOR *See also*

JOINT TORTFEASOR

Canada 'In my view the words "tort feasor" in s 3 [of the Negligence Act, RSO 1950, c 252 (now RSO 1980, c 315, s 3), respecting contribution among tort feasors] refer not to a person who is held liable or admits liability at a trial, but to a person who impliedly assumes or admits liability when he enters into a settlement. In other words, the important time is the time of the settlement, not the time of the delivery of a judgment. A person does not pay anything in settlement of a claim or of an action unless he feels he is liable in some degree, and in my opinion when he settles he becomes a "tort feasor" within the meaning of the section.' *Marschler v Masser's Garage* [1956] 2 DLR (2d) 484 at 490, Ont HCJ, per LeBel J

TOTAL INCOME *See* INCOME

TOTAL LOSS (Marine insurance)

A loss may be either total or partial. Any loss other than a total loss is a partial loss. A total loss may be either an actual total loss or a constructive total loss.

Where the subject matter insured is destroyed or so damaged as to cease to be a thing of the kind insured, or where the assured is irretrievably deprived of it, there is an actual total loss.

Subject to any express provision in the policy, where the subject matter insured is reasonably abandoned on account of its actual total loss appearing to be unavoidable, or because it could not be preserved from actual total loss without an expenditure which would exceed its value when the expenditure had been incurred, there is a constructive total loss. (25 Halsbury's Laws (4th edn) para 298)

(1) A loss may be either total or partial. Any loss other than a total loss, as hereinafter defined, is a partial loss.

(2) A total loss may be either an actual total loss, or a constructive total loss. (Marine Insurance Act 1906, s 56)

'It has been laid down that even where a vessel has not gone to pieces, but is in her original form of a ship, although she has received such injury as to render the expense of repairing her more than she is worth, that will amount to a total loss.' *Hanson v Port of London Ship Loan & Insurance Co* (1849) 10 LT 353 at 353, per cur.

'Lord Mansfield, in the first case which I believe is to be found in the books upon this subject, expressed an opinion, that, upon a policy in this form, there could be no total loss, where the goods still physically existed. Some exceptions have, undoubtedly, been engrafted upon the rule so unequivocally laid down. Still, if the goods are in such a state that they are capable of being forwarded, however they may be deteriorated, the loss is not a total loss.' *Navone v Haddon* (1850) 9 CB 30 at 44, per Cresswell J

'The insurance is "against total loss only". The jury have found that there was a total loss: and the evidence was such as to warrant that finding. It has been urged on the part of the underwriters that they only intended to become answerable for one of the two descriptions of "total loss", viz, the actual total destruction of the subject-matter of insurance, and not for that which all persons conversant with insurance business understand as being a total loss. All I can say is that, if they so intended they have failed to express their intention.' *Adams v Mackenzie* (1863) 13 CBNS 442 at 446, per Erle CJ

Actual total loss

Where the subject-matter insured is destroyed, or so damaged as to cease to be a thing of the kind insured, or where the assured is irretrievably deprived thereof, there is an actual total loss. In the case of an actual total loss no notice of abandonment need be given. (Marine Insurance Act 1906, s 57)

Constructive total loss

(1) Subject to any express provision in the policy, there is a constructive total loss where the subject-matter insured is reasonably abandoned on account of its actual total loss appearing to be unavoidable, or because it could not be preserved from actual total loss without an expenditure which would exceed its value when the expenditure had been incurred.

(2) In particular, there is a constructive total loss—

(i) Where the assured is deprived of the possession of his ship or goods by a peril insured against, and (a) it is unlikely that he can recover the ship or goods, as the case may be, or (b) the cost of recovering the ship or goods, as the case may be, would exceed their value when recovered; or

(ii) In the case of damage to a ship, where she is so damaged by a peril insured against that the cost of repairing the damage would exceed the value of the ship when repaired.

In estimating the cost of repairs, no deduction is to be made in respect of general average contributions to those repairs payable by other interests, but account is to be taken of the expense of future salvage operations and of any future general average contributions to which the ship would be liable if repaired; or

(iii) In the case of damage to goods, where the cost of repairing the damage and forwarding the goods to their destination would exceed their value on arrival.

(Marine Insurance Act 1906, s 60)

'The first question is whether there has been any constructive total loss within the meaning of the contract sued on. It is quite a common practice for an insurer against total and partial loss to reinsure the risk of total loss while keeping himself uncovered as to partial loss. Of course he does this at a premium much lower than that which he himself receives for the double risk, and in the event of the insured vessel sustaining damage by the perils insured against it is very much to his interest that the damage should be sufficiently serious to constitute a constructive total loss, for in that event only can he get his loss recouped by his reinsurer, and secure his profit, namely, the difference between the two premiums. So, in the present case, the plaintiffs are anxious to make that which the shipowners treated as a partial loss under the original policy a total loss under the reinsurance policy. But can they? I think not. What the defendant promised by his contract was to indemnify the plaintiffs if they were called upon to pay a constructive total loss. What, then, constitutes a constructive total loss? I think that to constitute a constructive total loss there must be, not only such a damage to the vessel as to make her not worth repairing, but there must also be a notice of abandonment.' *Western Assurance Co of Toronto v Poole* [1903] 1 KB 376 at 383, per Bingham J

'Where a ship is damaged by a peril insured against, if the cost of repairing the damage, including the cost of raising, would exceed the value of the ship when repaired, she is constructively lost within the meaning of s 21 [of the Merchant Shipping Act 1894]. . . . The learned judge below decided that for insurance purposes the ship was undoubtedly "constructively lost" . . . but that it did not follow that the same rules as are applied for insurance purposes were necessarily to be applied in determining whether a ship is constructively lost under s 21. In my opinion the judgment is erroneous on this point. The expression "constructively lost" has no meaning as applied to a ship, except in connection with marine insurance, and a vessel which is a constructive total loss within the meaning of the term in marine insurance is "constructively lost" within the meaning of s 21 of the Merchant Shipping Act 1894.' *Manchester Ship Canal Co v Horlock* [1914] 2 Ch 199 at 206, 208, CA, per Swinfen Eady LJ

'The expression "constructive total loss" . . . is a technical expression relating to the rights and liabilities of assured and underwriters under marine policies and is not proper to be employed in dealing with the position as between owner and charterer under a charterparty. . . . Constructive total loss is a conception with which, as such, the charterparty has nothing to do. . . . The question what facts will constitute constructive total loss under a hull policy where the vessel is damaged by a peril of the sea appears to me to be fundamentally different from the question what facts will discharge the contract contained in the charterparty when the vessel has been damaged by a peril of the sea. In each case the amount of expenditure required to repair the vessel (if she is repairable) is a vital consideration.' *Carras v London & Scottish Insurance Corpn Ltd* [1936] 1 KB 291 at 313, 314, CA, per Greene LJ

'A constructive total loss is a device intended to subserve the purpose of indemnity by enabling the assured, when, by insured perils, the postulated danger of loss or deprivation is caused, to disentangle himself, subject to definite limits and conditions, from the danger and throw the burden on the underwriters. If the assured elects to avail himself of this option, he must do so by giving notice of abandonment within a reasonable time after the receipt of sufficient information. He is not allowed to await events to see how things turn out, or to decide what may best suit his interests. If he duly elects to abandon on good grounds, the risk is ended, because the assured can recover as for a total loss and the salvage vests in the underwriter.' *Rickards v Forestal Land Timber & Rlys Co Ltd, Robertson v Middows Ltd, Kahn v Howard (W H) Brothers & Co Ltd* [1942] AC 50 at 83, 84, 86, 87, per Lord Wright

TOTALISATOR *See also* FIXED ODDS

'Totalisator' means the contrivance for betting known as the totalisator or pari mutuel, or any other machine or instrument of betting of a like nature, whether mechanically operated or not. (Betting, Gaming and Lotteries Act 1963, s 55)

'The ordinary totalisator, the operation of which, of course, is perfectly well known . . . is a method, of procuring betting or enabling betting to be carried out, in such a way that the mathematically correct odds are always given.' *Elderton v United Kingdom Totalisator Co Ltd* [1946] Ch 57 at 63, CA, per Lord Greene MR

TOURIST AMENITIES

In this Part of this Act [Part I: Tourist Authority and Tourist Boards] 'tourist amenities and facilities' means, in relation to any country, amenities and facilities for visitors to that country and for other people travelling within it on business or pleasure. (Development of Tourism Act 1969, s 2(9))

TOWAGE

'Towage as contradistinguished from salvage, is the mere service of towing a vessel for the sake of expedition alone, she being neither in danger nor difficulty; not the towing of a ship off the ground.' *The Leda* (1855) 10 LT 791 at 791, per cur.

'For the purpose of this case I hold that, in fact, the tug was not towing the vessel. It may be a question of mixed law and fact; if so, I hold in law and I hold in fact that the tug was not towing—that the vessel was not being towed. The tug had gone out to sea in order to deliver some message to this vessel, and she accompanied the vessel on her way back, intending to be her tug when it became necessary to tow her along. In these circumstances a rope was passed from the vessel to the tug, the scope of which was about fifteen fathoms, and I find in fact that there was no towing at all by means of that rope during any times material in this case, and that the point of time had not arrived when it was intended that these vessels should become a tug and tow.' *The Sargasso* [1912] P 192 at 198, per Evans P

See, generally, 43 Halsbury's Laws (4th edn) paras 872 et seq.

TOWAGE SERVICE *See* SERVICE

TOWING-PATH

'As to what is to be deemed the towing-path it seems to us that it is impossible to confine it to the mere beaten track which is described to have been made principally by single horses towing down stream, for, in towing up stream, the horses cannot be in a direct line, and there must be space for them as well as for the driver and for the proper use of the towline; and we think the towing-path must be taken to include so much of the bank as is necessary and proper for the purposes of towing barges.' *Winch v Thames Conservators* (1872) LR 7 CP 458 at 468, 469, per cur.

TOWN

'What the walls of towns were in ancient times, that is, a boundary, continuous buildings are now. By continuous buildings I do not mean buildings which touch each other, but buildings so reasonably near that the inhabitants may be considered as dwelling together. Within the ambit surrounded by such houses is town.' *Elliott v South Devon Rly Co* (1848) 2 Exch 725 at 730, per Alderson B

'I think, where you have an Act of Parliament relating to the local management of a town, that must mean not a town which is existing today to the exclusion of houses which may be afterwards added on to the streets, but it must be taken to mean whatever may be there contemplated under the term "town".' *Milton Comrs v Faversham District Highway Board* (1867) 32 JP 37 at 38, per Cockburn CJ

'Where there is such an amount of continuous occupancy of the ground by houses that persons may be said to be living as it were in the same town or place continuously, there . . . according to the popular sense of the word, and not the legal sense of the word, which would not give at all a sensible definition—the place may be said to be a town.' *London & South Western Rly Co v Blackmore* (1870) LR 4 HL 610 at 615, per Lord Hatherley LC

'There are one or two cases in which definitions

are given of what is considered to be a town. One case is that of *R v Cottle* [(1851) 16 QB 412] . . . which was tried before the late Recorder of the City of London [Mr Russell Gurney] at the Somersetshire assizes, in which the question was whether the *locus in quo* was within the town of Taunton or not, and the learned judge left that question to the jury as one of fact, telling them that the word "town" in the Act [a turnpike Act] was to be understood in the popular sense of "a collection of houses where people congregate", and that they were to consider whether the spot in question was "surrounded by houses so reasonably near to each other that the inhabitants might fairly be said to dwell together". In my judgment that was a very concise way of stating what constitutes a town. In the case of *Elliott v The South Devon Railway Company* [supra], Alderson B gave what in substance was his definition of a town as follows: "What the walls of towns were in ancient times, that is, a boundary, continuous buildings are now. By continuous buildings I do not mean buildings which touch each other, but buildings so reasonably near that the inhabitants may be considered as dwelling together. Within the ambit surrounded by such houses in town, and when the railway passes through the ambit it passes through town". That is the definition given by Alderson B. Lord Campbell CJ, in his judgment in the case of *R v Cottle*, approved very much of Mr Russell Gurney's definition, and at p 420 of 16 QB said: "We think there is no misdirection in this case. The learned judge, with much felicity, comprised in a few words all that was material in the language of the Barons of the Exchequer as to the definition of a town in *Elliott v The South Devon Railway Company*"; and he added that, "the jury could not be misled by that definition." . . . I do not think it is necessary, in order to make an inhabitant of a town, that the house in which he resides should be surrounded by other houses; it is quite sufficient if he lives in such proximity to other houses as that his house, with the other houses in its proximity, may be said to form, in point of fact, one congregation of houses.' *Deards v Goldsmith* (1879) 40 LT 328 at 332, 333, DC, per Hawkins J

TOWN DEVELOPMENT

In this Act the expression 'town development' means development in a district (or partly in one such district and partly in another) which will have the effect, and is undertaken primarily for the purpose of providing accommodation for residential purposes (with or without accommodation for the carrying on of industrial or other activities, and with all appropriate public services, facilities for public worship, recreation and amenity, and other requirements) the provision whereof will relieve congestion of over-population elsewhere. (Town Development Act 1952, s 1)

TOWN GREEN *See* GREEN

TOWN PLANNING SCHEME

Australia 'The word "scheme" when used as a noun is defined in the Shorter Oxford English Dictionary in various ways including "diagram", "a map or plan of a town" and "a programme of action". Each of these meanings is appropriate in the context of the phrase "a town planning scheme" when used in the Act. Without in any way trying to provide an exhaustive definition of the term "town planning scheme" and, indeed, without trying to put words into the mouth of the legislature, I think it is fair to say that for the purpose of the Act a town planning scheme is a programme of action with respect to any land, houses, buildings or other works and structures (which may be situated in any city, town, suburb or rural area) which has the general object of improving and developing such land etc to the best possible advantage.' *Costa v Shire of Swan* [1983] WAR 22 at 24, per Olney J

TOWNSHIP *See also* TOWN

Australia 'A township is a collection of houses and buildings which forms the centre of a living community where people are likely to be and may congregate.' *Chambers v Dutton* [1966] SASR 363 at 367, per Walters J

TOY

'I have been asked to say that, inasmuch as a toy is usually something to be found in the possession of people of tender years, an aeroplane constructed from these parts and used by people from at least the ages of 14 to 60 years, cannot be a toy. It is interesting to speculate whether toys cease to be toys if a father likes the look of a Christmas present which he gives to his young son and plays with it himself. I cannot think that that is the test. The meaning of "toy" is well known. The Shorter Oxford Dictionary thus defines it: "applied to small models or imitations, to ordinary objects used as playthings; as toy, a cannon, train, etc." That meaning is apparently as old as 1836. Does an article cease to be a toy because it is used by people of riper years? I cannot think so, and these construction kits may well be toys.' *Customs and Excise Comrs v E Keil & Co Ltd* [1951] 1 KB 469 at 471, per Croom Johnson J

TRACK

'Track' means premises on which races of any description, athletic sports or other sporting events take place. (Betting, Gaming and Lotteries Act 1963, s 55)

TRACTOR *See* MOTOR TRACTOR

TRADE *See also* RESTRAINT OF TRADE

'Trade' in its primary meaning is the exchange of goods for goods or goods for money and in a secondary meaning it is any business carried on with a view to profit, whether manual or mercantile, as distinguished from the liberal arts or learned professions and from agriculture. However, the word is of very general application, and must always be considered in the context in which it is used. As used in various revenue Acts, 'trade' is not limited to buying and selling, but may include manufacture. In the expression 'restraint of trade' the word is used in its loosest sense to cover every kind of trade, business, profession or occupation. (47 Halsbury's Laws (4th edn) para 1)

'The vessel has done no more than it was agreed she should do. As the policy originally stood, she had liberty to sell, barter, and exchange. . . . Under this general liberty, the jury had no doubt that the vessel had liberty to trade; indeed, the very acts specified are descriptive of trading, and of nothing else.' *Sanderson v Symonds* (1819) 1 Brod & Bing 426 at 429–431, per Dallas CJ

'Trade . . . is a word having a technical meaning connected with buying and selling, and is limited to the case of the buying and selling of wares, and so forth.' *Harris v Amory* (1865) 13 LT 504 at 505, 506, per Willes J

'Now, what does one mean by a trade, or the exercise of a trade? Trade in its largest sense is the business of selling, with a view to profit, goods which the trader has either manufactured or himself purchased. I cannot doubt, upon the facts found, that all Mr Roederer's [a wine merchant's] sales to his English customers are made at Reims for delivery in that place, and the goods sold are, in fact, delivered to the customers in Reims. So far as I can see, not a single bottle of wine is ever sold or delivered by Mr Roederer, either personally or through his agents, in this country. . . . Mr Roederer's trade is selling his champagne; and he exercises that trade where he makes his sales and the profits come home to him.' *Grainger & Son v Gough* [1896] AC 325 at 345, 346, per Lord Davey

'To my mind a trading business is one which depends on the buying and selling of goods.' *Higgins v Beauchamp* [1914] 3 KB 1192 at 1195, per Lush J

'No doubt in a great many contexts the word "trade" indicates a process of buying and selling, but that is by no means an exhaustive definition of its meaning. It may also mean a calling or industry or class of skilled labour.' *Skinner v Jack Breach Ltd* [1927] 2 KB 220 at 225–227, DC, per Lord Hewart CJ

'Section 11 of the Act of 1919 [Industrial Courts Act 1919] shows that "trade" is used as including "industry" because it refers to a trade dispute in the industry of agriculture. The same inference appears from the short title. It is described as an Act to provide for the establishment of an industrial court in connection with trade disputes. Trade and industry are thus treated as interchangeable terms. Indeed, "trade" is not only in the etymological or dictionary sense, but in legal usage, a term of the widest scope. It is connected originally with the word "tread" and indicates a way of life or an occupation. In ordinary usage it may mean the occupation of a small shopkeeper equally with that of a commercial magnate. It may also mean a skilled craft. It is true that it is often used in contrast with a profession. A professional worker would not ordinarily be called a tradesman, but the word "trade" is used in the widest application in the appellation "trade unions".' *National Association of Local Government Officers v Bolton Corporation* [1943] AC 166 at 184, 185, per Lord Wright

'A trade is an organised seeking after profits as a rule with the aid of physical assets.' *Aviation & Shipping Co Ltd v Murray (Inspector of*

Taxes) [1961] 2 All ER 805 at 811, CA, per Donovan LJ

'The word "trade" is no doubt capable of bearing a variety of meanings according to the context in which it is used. In its most restricted sense it means the buying and selling of goods; in a slightly wider sense, it includes the buying and selling of land; there is no reason to exclude, in an appropriate context, the buying and selling of choses in action. It is commonly used ". . . to denote operations of a commercial character by which the trader provides to customers for reward some kind of goods or services" (see *Ransom (Inspector of Taxes) v Higgs* [infra] . . . The expression "stock market" is in common use. Stocks and shares are traded in the market. The trading in that market is done by brokers, who are therefore traders.' *Kowloon Stock Exchange Ltd v Inland Revenue Comr* [1985] 1 All ER 205 at 210, PC, per cur

Australia [The Commonwealth Constitution [Commonwealth of Australia Constitution Act 1901–1986, s 51(i)] provides that the Parliament shall have power to make laws with respect to 'trade and commerce with other countries and among the States'; and s 92 provides that 'trade commerce and intercourse among the States, whether by means of internal carriage or ocean navigation, shall be absolutely free'.] 'In construing both s 51(i) and s 92 it should be remembered that the words to be considered are not only "trade and commerce", but "trade and commerce among the States". The conception of trade and commerce among the States is in my opinion quite inseparable from movement of goods and persons. Commerce in itself does not necessarily involve transportation or movement of goods. There may be a sale of goods on the spot by a vendor to a purchaser, the commercial transaction being concluded without any movement of the goods. But when the trade or commerce is interstate there must be either actual or contemplated movement of goods or persons. In my opinion, this view is strongly supported by the words of s 92. Section 92 does not merely refer to trade, commerce and intercourse among the States, but it refers to such trade, commerce and intercourse "whether by means of internal carriage or ocean navigation." Internal carriage and ocean navigation are not only means by which trade and commerce may incidentally be conducted or effectuated. They are means without which *inter-State* trade and commerce cannot possibly take place.' *Australian National Airways Pty Ltd v Commonwealth* (1945) 71 CLR 29 at 56, per Latham CJ

Australia 'Even when broadly understood the word "trade" is not apt to describe the activity of running a private hospital where patients are accomodated for medical care and attention. The activity of the respondent is, without doubt, within the concept of a "business", but I reject the contention of counsel for the appellant council that to run a business it is necessarily to carry on a trade. Although the word "trade" has a wide and flexible meaning, statements in decided cases which would extend its meaning to cover any commercial activity or any non-residential use of land are, in my respectful opinion, too widely expressed.' *Hornsby Shire Council v Salmar Holdings Pty Ltd* [1972–3] ALR 421 at 423, per Menzies J

Canada [The Exemptions Act, RSA 1955, c 104, s 2(ii) (see now RSA 1980, c E-15, s 1(1)(f)), exempts from execution certain property used in a 'trade or calling'.] 'In my view, these words are used in the Act in the sense of an individual following or having a trade. They apply to a tradesman who is skilled in a trade or craft and not for the purpose of denoting a business. Because of the very nature and structure of a corporate entity it cannot have a "trade or calling" in the context contemplated by the statute. A corporate entity, on the other hand, may conduct a business employing individuals who possess a trade or calling. It may carry on trade in the commercial sense of manufacturing, buying and selling, but the use of the word "trade" in s 2(f)(ii) is not intended in the trading context.' *Western Foundation Borings (Alta) Ltd v Walters Construction Ltd* (1966) 57 WWR 178 at 180, Alta Dist Ct, per Haddad DCJ

In Income Tax Acts

'Trade' includes every trade, manufacture, adventure or concern in the nature of trade. (Income and Corporation Taxes Act 1988, s 832(1))

'The word "trade" is given a statutory meaning . . . by the definition in sect 237 [of the Income Tax Act 1918 (repealed; see now the Income and Corporation Taxes Act 1988, s 832(1) (supra))]. As the definition includes the very word "trade" without qualification, that word must be used in its ordinary dictionary sense and the other words must necessarily be intended to enlarge the statutory scope to be given to the word "trade" in Sched D. Whether the word "adventure" is intended to be read like the word "manufacture" as equally independent of the opening word "trade" or like the word "concern" as qualified by the attribute "in the nature of trade" does not, we think, matter in this appeal, though we incline to think it should be read as independent. The Oxford Dictionary gives several meanings of "adventure", but the most appropriate is that numbered 7: "A pecuniary risk, a venture, a speculation, a commercial enterprise". The two most apt quotations are: "1625 Bacon Ess. XXIV, 293. He that puts all upon Adventures, doth often times brake, and come to Poverty. 1668 Child Disc. of Trade (Ed 4) 54, Whilst interest is at 6 per cent no man will run an adventure to sea for the gain of 8 or 9 per cent". To the word "trade" the most appropriate meanings assigned are No 3 (a) and (b), and No 5 (a) and (b): "3 (a) Course, way or manner of life; course of action; mode of procedure, method. (b) A way or method of attaining an end; a contrivance, expedient. 5 (a) the practice of some . . . business . . . habitually carried on, esp when practised as a means of livelihood or gain; a calling; formerly used very widely, including professions; now usually applied to a mercantile occupation and to a skilled handicraft, as distinguished from a profession . . . In earliest use not clearly distinguishable from 3; (b) Anything practised for a livelihood". Of the textual citations under No 5 we select one each of the 17th, 18th and 19th centuries: "1653 Milton Hirelings Wks 1851 V 371. They would not then so many of them, for want of another Trade, make a Trade of their preaching. 1746 Francis tr Horace Epist 11, i. 167 Unfit for War's tumultuous Trade. 1865 Kingsley Herew i Where learnedst thou so suddenly the trade of preaching?' *Barry (Inspector of Taxes) v Cordy* [1946] 2 All ER 396 at 398, 399, CA, per cur.

'The Income Tax Acts have never defined trade or trading farther than to provide that trade includes every trade, manufacture, adventure or concern in the nature of trade. As an ordinary word in the English language "trade" has or has had a variety of meanings or shades of meaning. Leaving aside obsolete or rare usage it is sometimes used to denote any mercantile operation but it is commonly used to denote operations of a commercial character by which the trader provides to customers for reward some kind of goods or services.' *Ransom (Inspector of Taxes) v Higgs* [1974] 3 All ER 949 at 956, HL, per Lord Reid

Australia 'It has been said that "trade" strictly means the buying and selling of goods. That, however, is a specialised meaning of the word. The present primary meaning is much wider, covering as it does the pursuit of a calling or handicraft and its history emphasizes rather use, regularity and course of conduct, than concern with commodities.' *Bank of New South Wales v Commonwealth* (1948) 76 CLR 1 at 381, per Dixon J

Retail *See* RETAIL

Trade or business

'I cannot read the words "trade" and "business" [in a lease] as synonymous. There are a great many businesses which are not trades, and although, in my opinion, receiving payment for what is done, using what you are doing as a means of getting payment with a view to profit—whether profit is actually obtained or not, must of course be immaterial—is certainly material in considering whether what was being done is, or is not, a business, yet, in my opinion, it is not essential that there should be payment in order to constitute a business. And the mere fact that there is payment in certain circumstances, does not necessarily make a thing a business which if there was no payment would not be a business.' *Rolls v Miller* (1884) 27 Ch D 71 at 85, CA, per Cotton LJ

[A lessee covenanted not to use the dwelling house for the purpose of any 'trade or business' whatsoever or otherwise than as a private dwelling house or professional residence only.] 'What is being done is to keep the house permanently available for the accommodation of any approved person who cares to come and stay there and pay for doing so. I think that such a case as this amounts to carrying on a business. . . . For carrying on a business all that is necesssary, I apprehend, is to take the steps required to secure the necessary customers, and I think it is plain from the letter I have read that the defendant takes steps, by the means which she thinks most adequate, to secure customers, when she wants them.' *Thorn v Madden* [1925] Ch 847 at 851, 852, per Tomlin J

Use for trade

(1) In this Act 'use for trade' means, subject to subsection (3) below, use in Great Britain in connection with, or with a view to, a transaction falling within subsection (2) below where—

(a) the transaction is by reference to quantity or is a transaction for the purposes of which there is made or implied a statement of the quantity of goods to which the transaction relates, and
(b) the use is for the purpose of the determination or statement of that quantity.

(2) A transaction falls within this subsection if it is a transaction for—
(a) the transferring or rendering of money or money's worth in consideration of money or money's worth, or
(b) the making of a payment in respect of any toll or duty.

(3) Use for trade does not include use in a case where—
(a) the determination or statement is a determination or statement of the quantity of goods required for despatch to a destination outside Great Britain and any designated country, and
(b) the transaction is not a sale by retail, and
(c) no transfer or rendering of money or money's worth is involved other than the passing of the title to the goods and the consideration for them.

(4) The following equipment, that is to say—
(a) any weighing or measuring equipment which is made available in Great Britain for use by the public, whether on payment or otherwise, and
(b) any equipment which is used in Great Britain for the grading by reference to their weight, for the purpose of trading transactions by reference to that grading of hens' eggs in shell which are intended for human consumption,

shall be treated . . . as weighing or measuring equipment in use for trade, whether or not it would apart from this subsection be so treated.

(5) Where any weighing or measuring equipment is found in the possession of any person carrying on trade or on any premises which are used for trade, that person or, as the case may be, the occupier of those premises, shall be deemed for the purposes of this Act, unless the contrary is proved, to have that equipment in his possession for use for trade. (Weights and Measures Act 1985, s 7)

TRADE ASSOCIATION

['Trade association' does not include an agricultural marketing board; see s 45(1) of the Agriculture (Miscellaneous Provisions) Act 1968.]

'Trade association' means a body of persons (whether incorporated or not) which is formed for the purpose of furthering the trade interests of its members, or of persons represented by its members. (Restrictive Trade Practices Act 1976, s 43(1))

'Trade association' means a body of persons (whether incorporated or not) which is formed for the purpose of furthering the trade interests of its members or the persons represented by its members. (Resale Prices Act 1976, s 24(1))

TRADE DESCRIPTION *See also* FALSE TRADE DESCRIPTION

(1) A trade description is an indication, direct or indirect, and by whatever means given, of any of the following matters with respect to any goods or parts of goods, that is to say—
(a) quantity, size or gauge;
(b) method of manufacture, production, processing or reconditioning;
(c) composition;
(d) fitness for purpose, strength, performance, behaviour or accuracy;
(e) any physical characteristics not included in the preceding paragraphs;
(f) testing by any person and results thereof;
(g) approval by any person or conformity with a type approved by any person;
(h) place or date of manufacture, production, processing or reconditioning;
(i) person by whom manufactured, produced, processed or reconditioned;
(j) other history, including previous ownership or use.

(2) The matters specified in subsection (1) of this section shall be taken—
(a) in relation to any animal, to include sex, breed or cross, fertility and soundness;
(b) in relation to any semen, to include the identity and characteristics of the animal from which it was taken and measure of dilution.

(3) In this section 'quantity' includes length, width, height, area, volume, capacity, weight and number.

(4) Notwithstanding anything in the preceding provisions of this section, the following shall be deemed not to be trade descriptions, that is to say, any description or mark applied in pursuance of—
(a) . . .
(b) section 2 of the Agricultural Produce (Grading and Marking) Act 1928 (as amended by the Agricultural Produce

(Grading and Marking) Amendment Act 1931) or any corresponding enactment of the Parliament of Northern Ireland;
(c) the Plant Varieties and Seeds Act 1964;
(d) the Agriculture and Horticulture Act 1964 or any Community grading rules within the meaning of Part III of that Act;
(e) the Seeds Act (Northern Ireland) 1965;
(f) the Horticulture Act (Northern Ireland) 1966;
(g) the Consumer Safety Act 1978;

any statement made in respect of, or mark applied to, any material in pursuance of Part IV of the Agriculture Act 1970, any name or expressions to which a meaning has been assigned under section 70 of that Act when applied to any material in the circumstances specified in that section . . . any mark prescribed by a system of classification compiled under section 5 of the Agriculture Act 1967 and any designation, mark or description applied in pursuance of a scheme brought into force under section 6(1) or an order made under section 25(1) of the Agriculture Act 1970.

(5) Notwithstanding anything in the preceding provisions of this section, where provision is made under the Food Act 1984, the Food and Drugs (Scotland) Act 1956 or the Food and Drugs Act (Northern Ireland) 1958 or the Consumer Safety Act 1978 prohibiting the application of a description except to goods in the case of which the requirements specified in that provision are complied with, that description, when applied to such goods, shall be deemed not to be a trade description. (Trade Descriptions Act 1968, s 2, as amended)

TRADE DISPUTE *See also* CONTEMPLATION OR FURTHERANCE

In this Act 'trade dispute' means a dispute between workers and their employer which relates wholly or mainly to one or more of the following, that is to say—(a) terms and conditions, of employment, or the physical conditions in which any workers are required to work; (b) engagement or non-engagement, or termination or suspension of employment or the duties of employment, of one or more workers; (c) allocation of work or the duties of employment as between workers or groups of workers; (d) matters of discipline; (e) the membership or non-membership of a trade union on the part of a worker; (f) facilities for officials of trade unions; and (g) machinery for negotiation or consultation, and other procedures, relating to any of the foregoing matters, including the recognition by employers or employers' associations of the right of a trade union to represent workers in any such negotiation or consultation or in the carrying out of such procedures. (Trade Union and Labour Relations Act 1974, s 29(1), as amended by the Employment Act 1982), s 18; applied by the Employment Protection (Consolidation) Act 1978, s 153(1))

'If printers in a newspaper office were to say "We don't like the article which you are going to publish about the Arabs, or the Jews, or on this or that political issue, you must withdraw it. If you do not do so, we are not going to print your paper". That is not a trade dispute. It is coercive action unconnected with a trade dispute. It is an unlawful interference with the freedom of the press. It is a self-created power of censorship. It does not become a trade dispute simply because the men propose to break their contracts of employment in doing it. Even if the men have a strong moral case, saying, "We have a conscientious objection to this article. We do not want to have anything to do with it", that does not turn it into a trade dispute. The dispute is about the publication of the article, not about the terms and conditions of employment.' *British Broadcasting Corpn v Hearn* [1978] 1 All ER 111 at 117, CA, per Lord Denning MR

'"Trade dispute" is defined by s 29(1) of the 1974 [Trade Union and Labour Relations] Act, as amended by s 18 of the Employment Act 1982 [supra]. Prior to the amendment it read: "In this Act 'trade dispute' means a dispute between employers and workers, or between workers and workers, which is connected with one or more of the following, that is to say [and then various subject matters of disputes are set out.]" For present purposes we are only concerned with "termination of employment". As amended, s 29(1) reads: "In this Act 'trade dispute' means a dispute between workers and their employer which relates wholly or mainly to one or more of the following, that is to say . . ." It will be seen that this revision considerably narrows the scope of "trade dispute". Disputes between workers and workers, demarcation disputes, no longer qualify. Nor do disputes between workers and an employer, unless the employer is *their* employer. Finally it is no longer sufficient that the dispute should be "connected with" one of the specified subject matters. It now has to "relate wholly or mainly to" that subject matter.' *Mercury Communications Ltd v Scott-Garner* [1984] 1 All ER 179 at 199, CA, per Sir John Donaldson MR

TRADE EFFLUENT

'Trade effluent' means any liquid, either with or without particles of matter in suspension therein, which is wholly or in part produced in the course of any trade or industry, including agriculture, horticulture and scientific research or experiment, carried on at trade premises and, in relation to any trade premises, means any such liquid as aforesaid which is so produced in the course of any trade or industry carried on at those premises, but does not include domestic sewage. (Public Health (Drainage of Trade Premises) Act 1937, s 14, as amended by the Public Health Act 1961, s 63(1))

'Trade effluent' includes any liquid (either with or without particles of matter in suspension in it) which is discharged from premises used for carrying on any trade or industry, other than surface water and domestic sewage, and for the purposes of this definition any premises wholly or mainly used (whether for profit or not) for agricultural or horticultural purposes or for scientific research or experiment shall be deemed to be premises used for carrying on a trade. (Control of Pollution Act 1974, s 105(1))

'The definition section, s 14(1) [of the Public Health (Drainage of Trade Premises) Act 1937], which has given rise to a good deal of discussion, provides: " 'Trade effluent' means any liquid, either with or without particles of matter in suspension therein, which is wholly or in part produced in the course of any trade or industry carried on at trade premises and, in relation to any trade premises, means any such liquid as aforesaid which is so produced in the course of any trade or industry carried on at those premises, but does not include domestic sewage." I think that the words "wholly or in part" relate to the composition or constitution of the trade effluent, and that "trade effluent" for this purpose means a fluid which is composed partly of the product of the trade or business and partly of something else which in the ordinary course would be water.' *Yorkshire Dyeing and Proofing Co Ltd v Middleton Borough Council* [1953] 1 All ER 540 at 542, per Lord Goddard CJ

TRADE MARK *See also* DISTINCTIVE

'Trade mark' means, except in relation to a certification trade mark, a mark used or proposed to be used in relation to goods for the purpose of indicating, or so as to indicate, a connection in the course of trade between the goods and some person having the right either as proprietor or as registered user to use the mark, whether with or without any indication of the identity of that person, and means, in relation to a certification trade mark, a mark registered or deemed to have been registered under section thirty-seven of this Act. (Trade Marks Act 1938, s 68)

[A certification trade mark is a mark adapted in relation to any goods to distinguish in the course of trade goods certified by any person in respect of origin, material, mode of manufacture, quality, accuracy or other characteristic, from goods not so certified. Certification trade marks are registrable under the provisions of s 37 of the Act.]

'The fundamental rule is, that one man has no right to put off his goods for sale as the goods of a rival trader, and he cannot therefore (in the language of Lord Langdale in the case of *Perry v Truefitt* [(1842) 6 Beav 66]) "be allowed to use names, marks, letters or other *indicia*, by which he may induce purchasers to believe that the goods which he is selling are the manufacture of another person". A man may mark his own manufacture, either by his name, or by using for the purpose any symbol or emblem, however unmeaning in itself, and if such symbol or emblem comes by use to be recognised in trade as the mark of the goods of a particular person, no other trader has a right to stamp it upon his goods of a similar description. This is what I apprehend is usually meant by a trade mark, just as the broad arrow has been adopted to mark Government stores, a mark having no meaning in itself, but adopted by and appropriated to the Government.' *Leather Cloth Co v American Leather Cloth Co* (1865) 11 HL Cas 523 at 538, per Lord Kingsdown

'The Act of 1938 [Trade Marks Act 1938 (see supra)] in s 68, sub-s 1, defines a trade mark as "a mark used or proposed to be used in relation to goods for the purpose of indicating or so as to indicate a connection in the course of trade between the goods" and the person having the right to use the mark. In construing this definition it is essential to bear in mind what is the function of a trade mark. If there is one thing that may be described as fundamental in this breach of law it is that the function of a trade mark is to indicate the origin of the goods to which it is applied. As it was expressed by Bowen LJ, in *Re Powell's Trade Mark* [[1893] 2 Ch 388, 403, 404]: "The function of a trade mark is to give an indication to the purchaser or possible purchaser as to the manufacture or quality of the goods—to give an indication to his eye of the trade source from which the goods come, or the trade hands through which they pass on their way to the market". I could multiply quotations to the same effect. I was merely repeating a commonplace when on a former occasion I said in this House that it is "of the essence of a trade mark that it should indicate origin and be used as indicative of origin": *Bass, Ratcliff & Gretton Ltd v Nicholson & Sons Ltd* [[1932] AC 130, 154, 155]. It is true that these pronouncements were made before the passing of the Act of 1938 and that this statute enacted a new definition of a trade mark in the words which I have quoted, and also in s 4, when defining the right given by registration, used new language, viz, that registration of a person as the proprietor of a trade mark in respect of any goods should give that person "the exclusive right to the use of the trade mark in relation to those goods". But I do not agree that thereby "a radical alteration in the law relating to trade marks" has been effected, or that there has thereby been conferred "a right crucially different in principle from the rights heretofore enjoyed by the owners of trade marks", as Greene MR and Clauson LJ held in *Bismag Ltd v Amblins (Chemists) Ltd* [[1940] Ch 667, 677, 695]. I do not think that the widened language of the Act of 1938 has inferentially altered the essential conception of a trade mark in law, and in this I agree with and prefer the judgments in the *Bismag Case* . . . of my noble and learned friend, then Simonds J, and MacKinnon LJ, whose reasoning I need not repeat. A trade mark must still be registered in respect of goods, it must be used in relation to goods, it must indicate a connection in the course of trade between goods and the user of the trade mark. A trade mark must thus be used in trade. "Trade" is no doubt a wide word but its meaning must vary with and be controlled by its context. A connection with goods in the course of trade in my opinion means, in the definition section, an association with the goods in the course of their production and preparation for the market. After goods have reached the consumer they are no longer in the course of trade. The trading in them has reached its objective and its conclusion in their acquisition by the consumer.' *Aristoc Ltd v Rysta Ltd* [1945] AC 68 at 96, 97, HL, per Lord Macmillan

'Trade marks in their origin were marks that were applied to goods by their maker so that a buyer by visual examination of the goods could tell who made them. Makers' marks on silver and gold plate afford some of the earliest examples. With the growth of advertising, representations of trade marks have become widely used in advertisements so as to familiarise buyers with the mark, but the application of trade marks to the actual goods or to the packages containing them still constitutes their basic function. The mark may be applied by the maker or whatever visible part of the goods he chooses as suitable. If he habitually places it in a particular position on the goods, its distinctiveness in fact as indicating that the goods are of his manufacture may be associated with the position in which it appears on the goods and in the case of markings of a kind which are not intrinsically uncommon their distinctiveness as a trade mark may depend on the position in which the markings appear on the goods; as, for example, bands of colour or a raised moulded pattern round the neck of a bottle containing the manufacturer's product.' *Smith-Kline & French Laboratories Ltd v Sterling-Winthrop Group Ltd* [1975] 2 All ER 578 at 583, HL, per Lord Diplock

United States The term 'trade mark' includes any word, name, symbol, or device or any combination thereof adopted and used by a manufacturer or merchant to identify his goods and distinguish them from those manufactured or sold by others. (Lanham Act 1946, s 45)

TRADE NAME

United States The terms 'trade name' and 'commercial name' include individual names and surnames, firm names and trade names used by manufacturers, industrialists, merchants, agriculturalists, and others to identify their businesses, vocations, or occupations; the names or titles lawfully adopted and used by persons, firms, associations, corporations, companies, unions, and any manufacturing, industrial, commercial, agricultural, or other organisations engaged in trade or commerce and capable of suing and being sued in a court of law. (Lanham Act 1946, s 45)

TRADE OR BUSINESS *See also* BUSINESS; TRADE

Australia 'Speaking generally the word "trade" suggests some form of mercantile enterprise or occupation, while "business" connotes some type of commercial activity generally associated with the production of some person's livelihood. But both clearly exclude in their general application any suggestion of sport, recreation or pastime.' *Coleman v Grafton Greyhound Racing Club* (1954) 55 SR (NSW) 214 at 218, per Street CJ, Maxwell J and Roper CJ in Eq

TRADE UNION

In this Act, except so far as the context otherwise requires, 'trade union' means an organisation (whether permanent or temporary) which either—

(a) consists wholly or mainly of workers of one or more descriptions and is an organisation whose principal purposes include the regulation of relations between workers of that description or those descriptions and employers or employers' associations; or

(b) consists wholly or mainly of—

   (i) constituent or affiliated organisations which fulfil the conditions specified in paragraph (a) above (or themselves consist wholly or mainly of constituent or affiliated organisations which fulfil those conditions), or

   (ii) representatives of such constituent or affiliated organisations;

and in either case is an organisation whose principal purposes include the regulation of relations between workers and employers or between workers and employers' associations, or include the regulation of relations between its constituent or affiliated organisations.

(Trade Union and Labour Relations Act 1974, s 28(1); Employment Protection (Consolidation) Act 1978, s 153(1))

'I think that the decisions of this House show that, in a sense, a registered trade union is a legal entity, but not that it is a legal entity distinguishable at any moment of time from the members of which it is at that time composed. It remains a voluntary association of individuals but it is capable of suing and being sued in its registered name; it holds property, through trustees, against which a creditor holding a decree against it could levy execution, it acts by agents; and it has other rights and is subject to other liabilities set out in the Trade Union Acts. It differs from an unincorporated association in that it is unnecessary to consider who were the members at any particular time. For instance, it is immaterial who were the members at the time that any cause of action arose, or what members have joined the union since the cause of action arose. The registered trade union may be said to assume a collective responsibility for all members past, present and future, in respect of any cause of action for which it may be made liable, irrespective of the date of the cause of action. On the other hand, the judgment creditor can look only to the funds of such a trade union to satisfy his debt and, to the extent to which these may be augmented from time to time by contributions of members, whether new or old, they will still be available for the unsatisfied judgment creditor. These are important attributes, or characteristics, of a registered trade union which, in my opinion, differentiate it from other voluntary associations and may entitle it to be called a legal entity, while at the same time remaining an unincorporated association of individuals. As an association, its membership is constantly changing, but as a registered trade union, it has a permanent identity and represents its members at any moment of time. It would not, I think, be wrong to call it a legal entity.' *Bonsor v Musicians' Union*, [1955] 3 All ER 518 at 538, 539, HL, per Lord Keith of Avonholm; see also [1956] AC 105

See, generally, 47 Halsbury's Laws (4th edn) paras 491 et seq.

Australia 'From this brief survey of the Act [Trade Unions Act 1928–1986 (Vic), s 3(1)] it will be seen that it is primarily concerned with what is popularly known as a trade union, that is to say an association of workmen in any trade for the protection and furtherance of their own interests in regard to matters affecting their employment such as wages, hours and conditions of labour, and for the provision from their common funds of pecuniary assistance to the members during strikes, sickness, unemployment, old age, etc. Such a trade union might be either a combination for regulating the relations between workmen and employers or one for regulating the relations between workmen and workmen. And it has been held also that it may [be] . . . a combination for imposing restrictive conditions on the conduct of any trade or business. Thus the Full Court of New South Wales in *Bank of New South Wales v United Bank Officers Association* [(1921) 21 NSWR 593] held that an association of bank clerks, though not workmen, came under this head.' *Albion Quarrying Co Pty Ltd v Associated Quarries Pty Ltd* [1945] VLR 1 at 21, per Herring CJ

Australia 'An association of traders may be a trade union under the Act, though it has nothing whatever to do with their position as employers. It must appear, however, that the real or true object of the association is the imposition of restrictive conditions; though it will be sufficient if the imposition is to be merely upon the members themselves in the conduct of the trade or business in which they are interested. The imposition, however, must be common to all the members, a common rule for all.' Ibid at 24

TRADER *See also* MERCHANT

'Trader', in relation to an essential commodity, means any person who for the purposes of any trade or business carried on by him (whether as a producer, merchant, broker, warehouseman, or otherwise) holds from time to time a stock of that commodity. (Essential Commodities Reserves Act 1938, s 6)

'It is argued that the term "trader" is defined in s 55 of the Act [Railway and Canal Traffic Act 1888] in terms which do not include carriers, meaning thereby carriers outside the railway. I do not think that is quite accurate because all we find in s 55 is "the term 'trader' includes any person sending, receiving or desiring to send merchandise by railway or canal", from which alone I do not think that one can gather that the word "trader" may not in a proper case include a carrier.' *Master Lightermen & Barge Owners Assocn v Southern Rly Co* (No 2) (1934) 21 Ry & Can Tr Cas 126 at 155, CA, per Maugham LJ

TRADING *See* STREET TRADING

TRADING COMPANY *See* COMPANY

TRADING STAMP

'Trading stamp' means a stamp which is, or is intended to be, delivered to any person upon or in connection with the purchase by that person of any goods (other than a newspaper or other periodical of which the stamp forms part or in which it is contained) and is, or is intended to be, redeemable (whether singly or together with other such stamps) by that or some other person. (Trading Stamps Act 1964, s 10)

TRADING STOCK

For the purposes of this section [valuation of trading stock on discontinuance of trade] 'trading stock', in relation to any trade—

(a) means property of any description, whether real or personal, being either—
  (i) property such as is sold in the ordinary course of the trade, or would be so sold if it were mature or if its manufacture, preparation or construction were complete, or
  (ii) materials such as are used in the manufacture, preparation or construction of any such property as is referred to in para (i) above; and
(b) includes also any services, article or material, which would, if the trade were a profession or vocation be treated, for the purposes of section 101 [valuation of work in progress at discontinuance of profession or vocation] as work in progress of the profession or vocation, and references to the sale or transfer of trading stock shall be construed accordingly.

(Income and Corporation Taxes Act 1988, s 100(2))

TRAFFIC

'Traffic' includes pedestrians and animals. (Highways Act 1980, s 329(1))

[An agreement between a corporation, which owned a dock and dock railways, and two railway companies, with the lines of which the dock railways were connected, provided that the companies would pay certain charges in respect of 'traffic' in excess of the average annual tonnage of 'traffic' worked by the corporation during a stated period.] 'Is the word "traffic" . . . used in any sense more restricted than its general meaning, say, "rolling stock in transit conveying goods"? The appellants contend that it means "ship's side or dock side traffic", or "import or export traffic"; in other words, that it means rolling stock in transit conveying goods of which a particular quality can be predicated—namely, that the goods came from overseas or are going overseas. I see no reason for so restricting its meaning.' *Great Western Rly & Midland Rly v Bristol Corpn* (1918) 87 LJ Ch 414 at 431, per Lord Wrenbury

New Zealand 'The word "traffic", when used as to railways, seems to mean not only the mere passing and repassing of trains, but the business carried on on the railways; and so, with regard to a wharf, "traffic" is not the mere passing and repassing of persons and vehicles, but the business carried on on the wharf.' *Harrington v Wellington Harbour Board* (1895) 14 NZLR 347 at 354, per Prendergast CJ

TRAFFIC SIGN

'Traffic sign' means any object or device (whether fixed or portable) for conveying, to traffic on roads or any specified class of traffic, warnings, information, requirements, restrictions or prohibitions of any description—

(a) specified by regulations made by the Ministers acting jointly, or
(b) authorised by the Secretary of State,
and any line or mark on a road for so conveying such warnings, information, requirements, restrictions or prohibitions.
(Road Traffic Regulation Act 1984, s 64(1))

TRAFFICKING

[By the Trade Marks Act 1938, s 28(6), the registrar of trade marks may refuse an application to be registered as a registered user if it appears that such grant would facilitate 'trafficking' in the trade mark.] 'Trafficking in a trade mark has from the outset been one of the cardinal sins of trade mark law. But there is no statutory definition of trafficking, and one may suspect that, as with usury in the Middle Ages, though it is known to be deadly sin, it has become less and less clear, as economic circumstances have developed, what the sin actually comprehends. Trafficking must involve trading in or dealing with the trade mark for money or money's worth, but it is not all dealing with a trade mark for money that is objectionable, since it has always been accepted that it is permissible to sell a trade mark together with the goodwill of the business in the course of which the trade mark has been used. . . . I would . . . sum up the position as I see it as follows: 1. Subsection (6) of s 28 shows that trafficking in a trade mark is still a sin and the registration of a user is prohibited if it would tend to facilitate trafficking; 2. Trafficking in this sense means . . . disposing of the mark or the reputation in the name, as of itself a marketable commodity; 3. Before 1938 this was shown if the mark was disposed of, or a licence was granted, independently of the goodwill of the relevant business of the registered proprietor; 4. Since the 1938 Act has come into force, this last criterion must be relaxed in that s 22 permits assignments of a mark apart from goodwill; 5. On the scheme of the 1938 Act and as trafficking remains prohibited the criterion now is that there must be a trade connection between the proprietor of the mark and the goods of the licensee on which the mark is to be used.' *Re American Greetings Corp's Application* [1983] 2 All ER 609 at 619, 621, CA, per Dillon LJ; affd [1984] 1 All ER 426, HL

TRAILER

'Trailer' means a vehicle drawn by a motor vehicle. (Road Traffic Regulation Act 1984, s 136(1))

'Many things are trailers for the purposes of this Act [Road Traffic Act 1930 (repealed; but cf the Road Traffic Regulation Act 1984, s 136(1))] and I do not think that it can really be doubted that a trailer for those purposes includes anything which can be drawn on wheels.' *Garner v Burr* [1951] 1 KB 31 at 33, per Lord Goddard CJ

TRAIN

'A train is a train, whether consisting of trucks laden with goods or of carriages filled with passengers. The character of the load makes no difference. Nor do I think that a locomotive engine is essential to the making of a train.' *Cox v Great Western Rly Co* (1882) 9 QBD 106 at 109, DC, per Mathews J

[The Employers' Liability Act 1880, s 1(5) (repealed) dealt with personal injuries caused to a workman through negligence on the part of a person in charge of a 'train'.] 'Now, my Lords, one word upon what construction your Lordships ought to place upon the words "a train". I doubt very much whether the legislature intended these words to be narrowed in the way which . . . has [been] contended for. I should think, speaking in a general way, that the legislature meant that a locomotive engine by itself, or anything that was drawn along a railway, or was in course of being drawn along a railway by that locomotive engine, should be included in "a train". I doubt very much whether it would depend upon the number of carriages or the number of vehicles going upon wheels which the locomotive was taking along the railway. I should think the legislature intended a very wide scope to be given to the use of these words.' *McCord v Cammell & Co Ltd* [1896] AC 57 at 63, 64, per Lord Halsbury LC

TRAINING

'Training' includes any education with a view to employment . . . (Employment and Training Act 1973, s 13(1))

TRAMWAY

'Tramway' includes a light railway being one which is of the nature of a tramway, that is to say, laid mainly or exclusively along a highway and used mainly or exclusively for the carriage of passengers, and includes a trolley vehicle system. (Public Utilities Street Works Act 1950, s 39)

'Section 43 of the Tramways Act 1870 . . .

prescribes the terms upon which the promoters of a tramway . . . are to sell their undertaking to the local authority. The words are as follows: "Upon terms of paying the then value . . . of the tramway, and all lands, buildings, works, materials, and plant of the promoters suitable to and used by them for the purpose of their undertaking". . . . It appears clear that the word "tramway" cannot be read as synonymous with "undertaking". The words which follow "tramway" are, to my mind, conclusive upon this point. What, then, does "tramway" mean as used in the section? I have examined every instance of its use in the statute, and it appears to me in every other case, at all events, to be used to describe the structure laid down on the highway, and nothing more, and I cannot see my way to give any other meaning to it in the section under consideration.' *Edinburgh Street Tramways Co v Edinburgh Corpn* [1894] AC 456 at 462–464, per Lord Herschell LC

TRANSACTION

'In my opinion, "transaction" [within the Finance Act 1927, s 27(1) (repealed; see now the Income and Corporation Taxes Act 1988, s 392)] is a comprehensive word which includes any dealings with property.' *Barron (Inspector of Taxes) v Littman* [1952] 2 All ER 548 at 555, HL, per Lord Normand; also reported [1953] AC 96 at 113

'The word "transaction" is normally used to denote some bilateral activity but it can be used to denote an activity in which only a single person is engaged.' *Greenberg v Inland Revenue Comrs* [1971] 3 All ER 136 at 149, HL, per Lord Reid

Canada [The Criminal Code, 1953–54 (Can) c 51 s 492(1) (see now RSC 1970, c C-34) provides that each count in an indictment shall in general apply to a single 'transaction'.] ' "Transaction" is a word of quite comprehensive import, which, so far as I am aware, has never been the subject of any exact legal definition. The word has been interpreted as the justice of each case demanded rather than by any abstract definition. In its ordinary sense it is understood to mean the doing or performing of some matter of business between two or more persons. "Transaction" in its broadest sense expresses the concept of driving, doing or acting as is denoted by the Latin word *transagere* from which it is derived. A "transaction" may and frequently does include a series of occurrences extending over a length of time.' *R v Canavan and Busby* [1970] 3 OR 353 at 356, Ont CA, per Schroeder JA

TRANSFER

Canada 'The word "transfer" is not a term of art and has not a technical meaning. It is not necessary to a transfer of property from a husband to his wife that it should be made in any particular form or that it should be made directly. All that is required is that the husband should so deal with the property as to divest himself of it and vest it in his wife, that is to say, pass the property from himself to her. The means by which he accomplishes this result, whether direct or circuitous, may properly be called a transfer.' *Fasken v Minister of National Revenue* [1949] 1 DLR 810 at 822, Ex Ct, per Thorson P

In Firearms Act

'Transfer' includes let on hire, give, lend and part with possession, and 'transferee' and 'transferor' shall be construed accordingly. (Firearms Act 1968, s 57(4))

Of promissory note

'The word "transfer" [in relation to a promissory note] means indorsement and delivery.' *Bromage v Lloyd* (1847) 1 Exch 32 at 35, per Rolfe B

Of shares

'Transferring a share involves a series of steps, first an agreement to sell, then the execution of a deed of transfer and finally the registration of the transfer. The word transfer can mean the whole of those steps. Moreover, the ordinary meaning of "transfer" is simply to hand over or part with something, and a shareholder who agrees to sell is parting with something. The context must determine in what sense the word is used.' *Lyle and Scott Ltd v Scott's Trustees* [1959] 2 All ER 661 at 668, HL, per Lord Reid; also reported [1959] AC 763 at 778

On sale of goods

[The Factors Act 1889, s 10, and the Sale of Goods Act 1893, s 47 (repealed; see now the Sale of Goods Act 1979, s 47(2)) enact that where a document of title to goods has been lawfully transferred to a person as buyer or owner of the goods, and that person transfers the document to a person who takes it in good faith and for valuable consideration, the last mentioned 'transfer' defeats any vendor's lien or right of stoppage in transitu.] 'It was . . .

said that these delivery orders were not documents of title within the meaning of the Factors Act 1889, and the Sale of Goods Act 1893, because they were created by the defendants themselves, and that as the documents did not come to them from someone else they could not be "transferred" by the defendants to Finkler and Co. I cannot accept that argument. A delivery order is not the less a document of title because it is created by the owner of the goods. It would be a curious result if the document by which the owner gets a title can, if passed on by him, give a title to someone else, but that a document created by himself cannot give a title when passed on because it is not a "transfer" but is only a delivery or issue. I cannot narrow the meaning of the word "transfer" in the way suggested. It seems to me that the delivery orders in this case were documents created by the defendants, the owners of the goods, for the purpose of transferring the title to the goods, and the handing of these to Finkler and Co was a "transfer" of the documents just as much as if they had come into existence by the act of some one other than the defendants, had been handed to the defendants, and by them handed on.' *Ant Jurgens Margarinefabrieken v Dreyfus (Louis) & Co* [1914] 3 KB 40 at 44, 45, per Pickford J

TRANSHIP

'For the purposes of exemption from port rates, goods imported for transhipment only mean goods imported from beyond the seas or coastwise for the purpose of being conveyed by sea only to any other port, whether beyond the seas or coastwise.' *Port of London Authority v British Oil & Cake Mills Ltd* [1915] AC 993 at 1009, 1010, per Lord Parmoor

[A bill of lading gave the shipowners liberty to 'tranship' or land and re-ship on board the same or any other vessel.] 'Counsel . . . says that the liberty to tranship which is given in the bill of lading does not apply to transhipment into craft, but only to transhipment into another ocean steamer. I see nothing in the language to make it right to so restrict the meaning of the word "tranship". If one pushed the argument to the extreme it would mean that the transhipment would have to be made by laying the two ocean steamers alongside, which, though not impossible, is so unusual a performance that one cannot help thinking that the words were not intended to have this construction. In my view, the expression "liberty to tranship" is sufficiently wide to cover a liberty to put goods into lighters in order to complete the voyage.' *Marcelino Gonzalez y Compania S en C v James Nourse Ltd* [1936] 1 KB 565 at 573, per Branson J

TRANSIT *See also* STOPPAGE IN TRANSIT

Goods are deemed to be in course of transit from the time when they are delivered to a carrier or other bailee for the purpose of transmission to the buyer until the buyer or his agent in that behalf, takes delivery of them from the carrier or other bailee. (41 Halsbury's Laws (4th edn) para 830)

TRANSLATION

'Making a translation is not a mere question of trying to find out in a dictionary the words which are given as the equivalent of the words of the document; a true translation is the putting into English that which is the exact effect of the language used under the circumstances.' *Chatenay v Brazilian Submarine Telegraph Co Ltd* [1891] 1 QB 79 at 82, per Lord Esher MR

TRANSMISSION MACHINERY

See MACHINERY

TRANSMIT

United States To 'transmit' a performance or display is to communicate it by any device or process whereby images or sounds are received beyond the place from which they are sent. (Copyright Act of 1976, s 101)

TRANSPORT

Canada 'When a friendly stranger on the highway finds a traveller in distress and offers to tow him to the next town, and does so, he is transporting him as a gratuitous guest within the meaning of the Highway Traffic Act, RSM 1940, ch 93, s 85(1) (now RSM 1970, c H60, s 145) which provides that a guest who does not pay for his transportation must prove gross negligence. The argument that a gratuitous guest must be a passenger in his host's car before he is "transported" does not appeal to me; if he stands on the running board, or is towed in a car, toboggan, or sled, he is transported just as much as if he had a seat in his host's car. Some other Highway Traffic Acts to which reference has been made clearly set it forth that the guest must be a passenger riding in his host's car. That is not what our Act says.

If the guest is towed, pulled, pushed or carried, he is in all such cases "transported".' *Freeborn v Bewza* [1943] 1 WWR 589 at 591, Man CA, per Dennistoun JA

Canada [The offence of 'trafficking' in narcotics included 'transporting'.] 'The definition of "transport" was dealt with in *R v Harrington and Scosky* [1964] 1 CCC 189, 41 CR 75, 43 WWR 337, sub nom *R v MacDonald et al; R v Harrington and Scosky*. At p 195 CCC, p 342 WWR, Bird JA made the following observation: "These considerations impel me to the view that the word 'transport' in the definition of 'traffic' is not meant in the sense of mere conveying or carrying or moving from one place to another, but in the sense of doing so to promote the distribution of the narcotic to another. In my opinion, there must be something more extensive than mere conveying, or carrying or moving incidental to one's own use of the drug to warrant a conviction under s 4(1) for trafficking." I agree with Bird JA, supra, that the use of the word "transport" as contained in the definition of "traffic" is meant to imply something more extensive than mere conveying. This does not mean, however, that it has to be read in conjunction with one or more of the other words included in the definition in order to ascertain its intended meaning. In my view, the use of the illustrative words found in the definition of traffic are meant, when taken together, to convey Parliament's concept of what should constitute the crime of trafficking, namely, making the drug available to others.' *R v Greene* (1976) 74 DLR (3d) 354 at 360, Nfld CA, per Morgan JA

Air transport

'Air transport services' means services for the carriage by air of passengers or cargo. (Airports Act 1986, s 82(1))

Of passenger *See* PASSENGER

TRANSPORT UNDERTAKING

'Transport undertaking' means a railway, dock, harbour, pier, canal or inland navigation undertaking, being an undertaking the activities of which, or some of the activities of which, are carried on under authorisation conferred by an enactment, and 'transport authority' means the authority, body or person having the control or management of a transport undertaking, in the capacity in which they have the control or management thereof. (Public Utilities Street Works Act 1950, s 39; see also the Highways Act 1980, s 329(1))

TRAP

'A trap is a figure of speech, not a formula. It involves the idea of concealment and surprise, of an appearance of safety under circumstances cloaking a reality of danger. Owners and occupiers alike expose licensees and visitors to traps on their premises at their peril, but a trap is a relative term. In the case of an infant, there are moral as well as physical traps. There may accordingly be a duty towards infants not merely not to dig pitfalls for them, but not to lead them into temptation.' *Latham v Johnson (R) and Nephew Ltd* [1913] 1 KB 398 at 415, CA, per Hamilton LJ

TRAVEL

'The Pedlars Act 1871, s 3 provides: "The term 'pedlar' means any hawker, pedlar, petty chapman, tinker, caster of metals, mender of chairs, or other person who, without any horse or other beast bearing or drawing burden, travels and trades on foot and goes from town to town or to other men's houses, carrying to sell or exposing for sale any goods, wares, or merchandise, or procuring orders for goods, wares, or merchandise immediately to be delivered, or selling or offering for sale his skill in handicraft? . . . It seems to me that it is impossible to say that because a man arrives at a fixed point and there leaves his vehicle and proceeds to walk through the town, it may be for a mile or it may be for six miles, he is not travelling on foot. He is going from house to house and he is travelling from house to house. The word "travelling" cannot be used here as meaning travelling by train or travelling from one town to another. The man travels on foot as soon as he has left his car or his van or a house.' *Sample v Hulme* [1956] 3 All ER 447 at 448, per Lord Goddard CJ

[A pedlar is one who trades as he travels, going to his customers rather than them coming to him, as distinct from one who merely travels to trade: see *Watson v Malloy* [1988] 3 All ER 459.]

'In my judgment a man who has been physically conveyed on a railway does not cease to travel on that railway merely when he alights on the platform.' *Bremme v Dubery* [1964] 1 All ER 193 at 195, per cur.

'So long as the person is in the process of arriving, . . . having come by a railway conveyance, at the exit or terminus from the arrival platform, he is in my judgment still travelling; and applying that to the facts of the present case, it must be equally clear as a matter of logic that a companion, on whose behalf he tenders a sum of money, is still in the process of travelling when that companion has not himself or herself arrived at the point of having left the arrival platform.' *Murphy v Verati* [1967] 1 All ER 861 at 863, per Winn LJ

Canada '"Travelling" was defined in *White v Beazley* (1817) 1 B & Ald 166 (KB) at p 171 as "a going from one place to another". More recently, in *Murphy v Verati*, [supra], Winn LJ held that: "So long as the person is in the process of arriving . . . he is, in my judgment, still travelling". Similarly, in the Australian case *Commonwealth v Wright* (1956) 96 CLR 536, the court, when asked to determine whether an employee was "travelling" to or from his employment at the time of an injury, addressed itself to the terminal points of the employee's journey. Travelling, Kitto J concluded, is "more naturally used to refer to a passing between" the terminal points of the journey. By that definition if the unfortunate employee in *Wright* had been stopped at a street light or awaiting a bus when he was injured, then the Australian court would have had no difficulty in finding that he was injured while travelling. The cases therefore suggest that "travelling in the same line" does not require that all . . . vehicles be moving at all times. Rather it requires only that they be at or passing points along a common line.' *Wigton v Ratke* (1884) 9 DLR (4th) 464 at 465, 466, Alta QB, per Wachowich J

New Zealand 'In my view, the expression "travelling" where used in s 5 [of the Workers' Compensation Act 1956 (NZ)] imports the idea of going from one place to another. I consider that a person who proposes to use a motor car to travel, that is to go from one place to another, cannot be said to have commenced to travel by the car before he is in the car and the car is ready to start in motion. If, for example, the person proposing to travel by car cleans the windscreen, or puts some water in the radiator or petrol in the petrol tank, before he starts the engine, he cannot be said to have commenced travelling while he is carrying out any of those preliminaries. He must start the engine before he commences his journey, and if he finds difficulty in starting the engine with the self-starter and has to use a starting-handle or push the car in order to get the engine started, he still has not commenced to travel by the car while he is doing any of those things.' *McDowall v New Zealand Plywoods Ltd* [1961] NZLR 514 at 515, 516, per Dalglish J

TRAVELLER *See also* COMMERCIAL TRAVELLER

'The authorities gave no definition of what is a traveller; but, looking at the reason of the thing, I should have thought that any person, who was neither an inhabitant of the house nor a private guest of the innkeeper or his family, but who came into the house as a guest to get such accommodation as is afforded and he was willing to pay for, was a traveller. It does not seem to me to make any difference whether his journey was a long or a short one.' *Orchard v Bush & Co* [1898] 2 QB 284 at 289, DC, per Kennedy J

TRAVELLING FAIR *See* FAIR

TRAWL

'The rule [Sea Regulations 1897, art 9 (revoked; but cf Collision Regulations (Ships and Seaplanes on the Water) and Signals of Distress (Ships) Order 1965, r 9)] is clear—that a trawler when trawling must have her fishing lights up, and when not trawling must have steaming lights up. . . . As I read the rule it means this, that you are fishing when you have your trawl down, or are hauling up your trawl, or shooting it; but that if, having hauled your trawl up, you do not shoot it at once, but steam off to some other spot to trawl, then . . . you cease to be fishing, and you must put up your steaming lights. I think a distinction has to be drawn. If a trawler, immediately after hauling her net, without going to any other ground, shoots her trawl, then she is still fishing during the interval, but if she changes her ground, then she must change her lights.' *The Cockatrice* [1908] P 182 at 188, per Bargrave Deane J

TREASON

By statute a person is guilty of treason who:

(1) levies war against the Sovereign in her realm, or is adherent to the Sovereign's enemies in her realm giving them aid and comfort in the realm, or elsewhere;

(2) compasses or imagines the death of the Sovereign;

(3) within the realm or without, compasses, imagines, invents, devises, or intends the death or destruction, or any bodily harm tending to

the death or destruction, maiming or wounding, imprisonment or restraint of the Sovereign, her heirs and successors, and who expresses, utters, or declares any such compassings, imaginations, inventions, devices, or intentions by publishing any printing or writing or by any overt act or deed;

(4) compasses or imagines the death of the King's wife or of the Sovereign's eldest son and heir;

(5) violates the King's wife or the Sovereign's eldest daughter unmarried or the wife of the Sovereign's eldest son and heir;

(6) endeavours to deprive or hinder any person who is next in succession to the Crown for the time being from succeeding after the demise of the Sovereign to the Crown and the dominions and territories belonging to the Crown and attempts the same maliciously, advisedly and directly by overt act or deed; or knowing the said offence to be done, is an abettor, procurer and comforter of the offender;

(7) slays the Chancellor, Treasurer, or the king's justices, being in their places and doing their offices. (11 Halsbury's Laws (4th edn) para 811)

[The principal Acts relating to treason are the Treason Act 1351 and the Treason Act 1795, which together make the above offences treason. The Treason Act 1842 makes it an offence, punishable by imprisonment, to discharge or aim firearms, or to throw or use any offensive matter or weapon, with intent to injure or alarm Her Majesty.]

'By the common law concealment of high treason was treason.' *Scope's Case* (1415) 3 Co Inst 36

'To be at a consult upon a treasonable design, to meet for that purpose to hear the plot laid, and a design to take away the king's life, or to raise arms against him and to say nothing of this, this is downright treason, and is not misprision of treason.' *R v Walcot* (1683) 9 State Tr 519 at 558, 559, per cur.

'It is said in Foster's Crown Cases (3rd edn) p 183—"Local allegiance is founded in the protection a foreigner enjoyeth for his person, his family or effects, during his residence here; and it ceaseth, whenever he withdraweth with his family and effects". And then on p 185 comes the statement of law upon which the passage I have cited is clearly founded "Section 4. And if such alien, seeking the protection of the Crown, and having a family and effects here, should during a war with his native country, go thither, and there adhere to the King's enemies for purposes of hostility, he might be dealt with as a traitor. For he came and settled here under the protection of the Crown; and, though his person was removed for a time, his effects and family continued still under the same protection. This rule was laid down by all the judges assembled at the Queen's command January 12, 1707". . . . In my view therefore it is the law that in the case supposed in the resolution of 1707 an alien may be guilty of treason for an act committed outside the realm. The reason which appears in the resolution is illuminating. The principle governing the rule is established by the exception: "though his person was removed for a time, his family and effects continued under the same protection", that is, the protection of the Crown. The vicarious protection still afforded to the family, which he had left behind in this country, required of him a continuance of his fidelity. . . . The principle which runs through feudal law and what I may perhaps call constitutional law requires on the one hand protection, on the other fidelity: a duty of the sovereign lord to protect, a duty of the liege or subject to be faithful. Treason, "trahison", is the betrayal of a trust: to be faithful to the trust is the counterpart of the duty to protect. It serves to illustrate the principle which I have stated that an open enemy who is an alien, notwithstanding his presence in the realm, is not within the protection nor therefore within the allegiance of the Crown. he does not owe allegiance because although he is within the realm he is not under the sovereign's protection.' *Joyce v Director of Public Prosecutions* [1946] AC 347 at 365–368, HL, per Lord Jowitt LC

Treason felony

A person is guilty of an offence [treason felony] who, (1) within the United Kingdom or without, compasses, imagines, invents, devises or intends (a) to deprive or depose the Sovereign from the style, honour or royal name of the Crown of the United Kingdom or of any other of Her Majesty's dominions and countries, or (b) to levy war against Her Majesty within any part of the United Kingdom in order by force or constraint to compel her to change her measures or counsels or in order to put any force or constraint upon or in order to intimidate or overawe both Houses or either House of Parliament, or (c) to move or stir any foreigner or stranger with force to invade the United Kingdom or any other of Her Majesty's dominions or countries; and (2) such compassings etc, expresses, utters or declares by publishing any printing or writing or by any overt act or deed. (11 Halsbury's Laws (4th edn) para 823

TREASURE TROVE

See also ABANDONMENT

The Crown gains no title [to treasure trove] unless the treasure is actually hidden in the earth with the intention of recovering it. Therefore, where it is scattered in the sea or on the surface of the earth, or lost or abandoned, it belongs to the first finder; but where the circumstances under which the treasure is found raise a prima facie presumption that it was hidden, it will belong to the Crown unless somebody else can show a better title. (8 Halsbury's Laws (4th edn) para 1513)

Treasure trove is any gold or silver in coin, plate, or bullion found concealed in a house, or in the earth or other private place, the owner thereof being unknown; the treasure belongs to the Queen or her grantee having the franchise of treasure trove. (9 Halsbury's Laws (4th edn) para 1177)

'Several definitions of treasure trove have been cited to me, not substantially differing one from another. I will take that cited in Chitty on Prerogatives, p 152: "Treasure trove is where any gold or silver in coin, plate, or bullion, is found concealed in a house, or in the earth, or other private place, the owner thereof being unknown, in which case the treasure belongs to the King or his grantee, having the franchise of treasure trove; but if he that laid it be known or afterwards discovered, the owner and not the King is entitled to it; this prerogative right only applying in the absence of an owner to claim the property. If the owner, instead of hiding the treasure, casually lost it, or purposely parted with it, in such a manner that it is evident he intended to abandon the property altogether, and did not purpose to resume it on another occasion, as if he threw it on the ground, or other public place, or in the sea, the first finder is entitled to the property, as against every one but the owner, and the King's prerogative does not in this respect obtain. So that it is the hiding, and not the abandonment, of the property that entitled the King to it". It is clear from the very terms of the definition that no direct evidence can be given of the intention to hide, or the intention to abandon, by a person who is *ex hypothesi* unknown. The direct evidence must necessarily be confined to the discovery of articles in fact concealed, and the court must presume the intention to hide or to abandon from the relevant surrounding circumstances, and the motives that usually influence persons acting under such circumstances, according to the ordinary dictates of human nature.' *A-G v British Museum Trustees* [1903] 2 Ch 598 at 608, 609, per Farwell J

'It is one of the requirements of the definition of treasure trove that the coin concerned must have been, as Sir Edward Coke put it, "of ancient time hidden", or as Chitty put it, "concealed in a house, or in the earth, or other private place". The evidence is that these coins were found by the use of a metal detector, in or around a broken urn, buried in the earth in a field at a level lower than would ordinarily be reached by a ploughshare. There is, as always in these cases, no satisfactory evidence of what the topography was in the third century or whether there were or were not buildings around. But it is difficult to suppose that anyone would have placed such a large number of coins in an urn in what seems to have been a rural locality rather than a town if he were not hiding them. There is therefore slight evidence that they were hidden and this, in the absence of any more satisfactory explanation, would be sufficient to establish a claim of treasure trove if . . . the coins were silver coins or coins that were not silver coins but were capable of being treasure trove.' *A-G of the Duchy of Lancaster v G E Overton (Farms) Ltd* [1980] 3 All ER 503 at 503, per Dillon J

TREASURY BILL

Treasury bills of the British government are negotiable instruments, and are thus expressed: 'This Treasury Bill entitles . . . or orders to the payment of, etc.' So long as the blank remains unfilled the bill is an instrument transferable by delivery; so soon as the blank is filled in it becomes an instrument payable to order. In either case it is negotiable. (4 Halsbury's Laws (4th edn) para 514)

TREASURY SOLICITOR

'The office of Treasury Solicitor is derived from the Revenue Solicitors' Act 1828, s 1. He normally acts for Her Majesty or for Ministers of the Crown or other persons in the service of Her Majesty; but he may also, in certain circumstances, be instructed by or on behalf of the Crown to offer his services to a private individual in the course of litigation and, if his services are accepted, may thenceforward act for such private individual. The circumstances which justify such instructions and such a result are that the Crown has an interest in the subject-matter of the litigation.' *Brownsea Haven Properties Ltd v Poole Corpn* [1958] 1 All ER 205 at 209, CA, per Lord Evershed MR; also reported [1958] Ch 574 at 591

TREAT

[The Agricultural Holdings Act 1908, s 42 (repealed; see now the Agricultural Holdings Act 1986, s 79) contained special provisions as to holdings in respect of which it was agreed in writing that the holding should be let or 'treated' as a market garden.] 'The real question is what is the proper meaning of the word "treated" in sub-s 1 of s 42 of the Act of 1908. . . . What is meant by the words "let or treated"? There is no difficulty about "let". With regard to "treated" there may be two views of the meaning of the word. It may mean used and cultivated, that is, physically treated, as a market garden; or it may mean treated as between the parties as a market garden, so that the landlord shall become the landlord of a market garden and the tenant a tenant of a market garden. In my opinion the latter is the true construction.' *Re Masters & Duveen* [1923] 2 KB 729 at 737, CA, per Warrington LJ

Australia [By the Sales Tax Assessment Act (No 1) 1930–1986, s 17 (see now s 17(1)), sales tax is required to 'be levied and paid upon the sale value of goods manufactured . . . by a taxpayer and . . . sold by him or treated by him as stock for sale by retail or applied to his own use'.] 'Treat "is a wide word": *Re Masters and Duveen* [supra]. A number of meanings are given to it in the dictionaries. The most suitable, in the collocation in which it is used in s 17, would appear to be that given in the Shorter Oxford English Dictionary, "To consider or regard in a particular aspect and deal with accordingly".' *Federal Comr of Taxation v York Motors Pty Ltd* (1946) 73 CLR 459 at 468, per Williams J

Australia '"Treat" in the statute covers, I think, any measure taken in the conduct of business with reference to the goods unequivocally referable to a present intention or decision that the goods shall then and there be retail stock.' Ibid at 484, per Dixon J

TREATING *See also* BRIBERY

A person guilty of treating is guilty of a corrupt practice. The following persons are guilty of treating:

(1) Any person who corruptly, by himself or by any other person, either before, during or after an election, directly or indirectly gives or provides, or pays wholly or in part the expense of giving or providing, any meat, drink, entertainment or provision to or for any person (a) for the purpose of corruptly influencing that person or any other person to vote or refrain from voting at the election, or (b) on account of that person or any other person having voted or refrained from voting, or being about to vote or refrain from voting;

(2) every elector or proxy for an elector who corruptly accepts or takes any such meat, drink, entertainment, or provision.

Treating intended to secure general popularity, and so to influence votes, is corrupt treating and a corrupt practice. (15 Halsbury's Laws (4th edn) para 781)

(1) A person shall be guilty of a corrupt practice if he is guilty of treating.
(2) A person shall be guilty of treating if he corruptly, by himself or by any other person, either before, during or after an election, directly or indirectly gives or provides, or pays wholly or in part the expense of giving or providing, any meat, drink, entertainment or provision to or for any person—
(a) for the purpose of corruptly influencing that person or any other person to vote or refrain from voting; or
(b) on account of that person or any other person having voted or refrained from voting, or being about to vote or refrain from voting.

(3) Every elector or his proxy who corruptly accepts or takes any such meat, drink, entertainment or provision shall also be guilty of treating. (Representation of the People Act 1983, s 114)

[Under the Corrupt and Illegal Practices Prevention Act 1883, s 1 (repealed; see now the Representation of the People Act 1983, s 114 (supra)), 'treating' was a corrupt practice.] 'Treating, within the meaning of the Act, does not in my judgment apply to the case where social equals treat each other, being merely one form of hospitality. Treating for the purposes of the Act applies to treating by superiors to secure the goodwill of another, and that would not apply where it was in return for small services, as in case of a railway guard or a man's own servants. It must have a reference to some election, and must be for the purpose of influencing the vote of the person treated.' *Norwich Case, Birbeck v Bullard* (1886) 54 LT 625 at 627, per Cave J

'The practice which was proved in the present case, for the chairman for the time being at smoking concerts and at other social gatherings paying for a glass of beer for those present at the commencement of the concert or meeting is, I think, a very objectionable practice; but I cannot, in the circumstances of the present case, say that the observance of the custom by persons, who from time to time acted as chairman of smoking concerts, was a treating [within the Corrupt and Illegal Practices Prevention Act 1883 (repealed; see supra)] with the intention to influence votes.' *Lancaster (County), Lancaster Division Case, Bradshaw & Kaye v Foster* (1896) 5 O'M & H 39 at 44, per Bruce J

'Treating has been defined as getting at voters through their mouths and through their stomachs, supplying them with food and giving them drink.' *Great Yarmouth Case, White v Fell* (1906) 5 O'M & H 176 at 196, per Channell J

TREATMENT

'Treatment', in relation to disease, includes anything done or provided for alleviating the effects of the disease, whether it is done or provided by way of cure or not. (Medicines Act 1968, s 132(1))

'In my judgment, "treatment" in the definition of "hospital" includes not only medical treatment (I can leave out, for present purposes, dental treatment) in the sense that the patient or subject is looked after and attended by a doctor, but also nursing in the sense that the subject or patient is looked after and attended to by persons professionally trained to look after and attend to the sick.' *Minister of Health v Royal Midland Counties Home for Incurables, Leamington Spa, General Committee*, [1954] 1 All ER 1013 at 1016, 1017, CA, per Evershed MR; see also [1954] Ch 530

Canada [The Canadian Bill of Rights 1960 (Can) c 44, s 2(b), provides that 'no law of Canada shall be construed or applied so as to impose or authorise the imposition of cruel and unusual "treatment" or punishment'.] 'Perhaps historically the word "punishment" in this context means the retributive or exemplary penalty imposed upon a transgressor to deter him and others from repeating or committing a similar offence. . . . The word "treatment" appears as an alternative to "punishment" in the Canadian Bill of Rights. It must be intended to cover a broader aspect of criminal procedure, including measures designed to reform and rehabilitate the offender, such as probation, prison training programs and parole, or to incapacitate him for a long time with the single purpose of denying him an opportunity to inflict further injury or loss upon the public.' *R v Buckler* [1970] 2 OR 614 at 620, Ont Prov Ct, per Carson Prov Ct J

As child of family

[The Matrimonial Proceedings and Property Act 1970, s 27(1) (repealed; see now the Matrimonial Causes Act 1973, s 52(1)) provided that a 'child of the family', in relation to the parties to a marriage, meant (a) a child of both of those parties and (b) any other child . . . who had been 'treated' by both of those parties as a child of their family.] 'The legislature has rejected acceptance as the criterion and has substituted treatment, a concept which, in my judgment, is quite different. Acceptance may involve only the true parent and the acceptor. Treatment of a child involves behaviour towards the child. One can accept a child by behaviour towards the mother, by not discarding her, but treating or continuing to treat her as a wife. One can only behave towards a child if the child is living and capable of being perceived by one or more of the senses. A foetus, or as it is commonly called an unborn child, however viable, cannot be so perceived.' *A v A* [1974] 1 All ER 755 at 763, per Bagnall J

'In the absence of any definition, the construction of the phrase "treated by the deceased as a child of the family in relation to that marriage" in the context of s 1(1)(d) [of the Inheritance (Provision for Family and Dependants) Act 1975] clearly gives rise to certain problems of interpretation. There can be no doubt that the relevant "treatment" is the behaviour of the deceased towards the potential applicant [for family provision]. Furthermore, if at any time during the relevant period treatment of the relevant nature had occurred, the applicant must, I think, qualify, even if such treatment had ceased before the death.' *Re Leach (decd), Leach v Lindeman* [1985] 2 All ER 754 at 759, CA, per Slade LJ

Canada [The Family Law Reform Act 1978

(Ont), c 2, s 1(a), states that 'child' means a child born within or outside marriage and includes a person whom the parent had demonstrated a settled intention to 'treat' as a child of his or her family.] 'The definitions in the Family Law Reform Act, 1978 and the Divorce Act vary in their wording, but the effect of the legislation to me seems the same: "A child . . . whom the parent has demonstrated a settled intention to treat as a child of his or her family", s 1(a) of the Act, seems to me to be the same as a "person is *in loco parentis* towards an infant when he assumes towards the infant the moral obligation to make provision for him as his father would in duty be bound to make": *Powys v Mansfield* [(1836) 6 Sim 637]. The provision of financial support is a common but not conclusive test. In this appeal what money there was for support was provided by the respondent as he was the only one gainfully employed. There was no evidence of any other relationships with the child, whether any interest was in fact taken in the child's well-being. On the contrary, there was evidence that the respondent did not act as a father. To hold the child was a dependant of the respondent would require evidence that he was fulfilling other parental duties and responsibilities as well as financial support. The onus of proving that her child was a dependant of the respondent rests upon the appellant. She has failed to discharge this onus. The use of the words "demonstrated" and "settled" indicate that the intention to treat as a child of the family must be firmly established by acts, the inference from which must lead to the conclusion of settled intention.' *Re Macdonald and Macdonald* (1979) 24 OR (2d) 84 at 86, Ont Co Ct, per Winter Co Ct J

TREATY

Canada 'A treaty is an agreement between states, political in nature even though it may contain provisions of a legislative character which may, by themselves or their subsequent enactment, pass into law. But the essential element is that it produces binding effects between the parties to it.' *A-G for Ontario v Scott* (1956) 1 DLR (2d) 433 at 437, SCC, per Rand J

Canada 'A treaty is primarily an executive act establishing relationships between what are recognised as two or more independent states acting in sovereign capacities; but . . . its implementation may call for both legislative and judicial action.' *Francis v R* (1956) 3 DLR (2d) 641 at 647, SCC, per Rand J

TREES

[A demise of a farm excepted 'trees', woods, coppice, and wood-grounds.] 'The manner in which the words occur shows that they were meant to apply to something of a different nature from these fruit [apple] trees. The exception means trees useful for their wood. It seems to me as if this action had been brought to recover for a supposed mismanagement of these trees; but it seems that you have brought the wrong form of action; for it is impossible to suppose that in Devonshire, when an apple-farm is let, the apple-trees are excepted.' *Wyndham v Way* (1812) 4 Taunt 316 at 318, per Mansfield CJ

TRESPASS

'Whoever is in possession, may maintain an action of trespass, against a wrong-doer to his possession.' *Harker v Birkbeck* (1764) 3 Burr 1556 at 1563, per cur.

'In the judgment of this court, there cannot be a conviction for entering premises "as a trespasser" within the meaning of s 9 of the Theft Act 1968 unless the person entering does so knowing that he is a trespasser and nevertheless deliberately enters, or, at the very least, is reckless whether or not he is entering the premises of another without the other party's consent.' *R v Collins* [1972] 2 All ER 1105 at 1110, CA, per cur.

'Taking the law as expressed in *Hillen and Pettigrew v ICI (Alkali) Ltd* [[1936] AC 65] and in *R v Collins* [supra], it is our view that a person is a trespasser for the purpose of s 9(1)(b) of the Theft Act 1968 if he enters premises of another knowing that he is entering in excess of the permission that has been given to him, or being reckless whether he is entering in excess of the permission that has been given to him to enter, providing the facts are known to the accused which enable him to realise that he is acting in excess of the permission given or that he is acting recklessly as to whether he exceeds that permission, then that is sufficient for the jury to decide that he is in fact a trespasser.' *R v Jones* [1976] 3 All ER 54 at 59, CA, per cur.

Australia 'The word "trespasser" is a basic legal term with an established legal meaning. . . . The essence of trespass by wrongful entry consists in an entry without right or authority by one person on to the land of another who is in possession, using that word in its strict sense so as to include a person entitled to immediate and exclusive possession (*Thompson v Ward* [1953] 2 QB 153 at 158–159). If the right or authority to enter is limited in scope then an entry which is unrelated to the right or authority will amount to a trespass.' *Barker v R* (1983) 153 CLR 338 at 341–342, per Mason J

Trespass ab initio

If a person enters on the land of another under an authority given him by law, and, while there, abuses the authority by an act which amounts to a trespass, he becomes a trespasser ab initio, and may be sued as if his original entry were unlawful. Instances of an entry under the authority of the law are the entry of a customer into a common inn, of a reversioner to see if waste has been done, or of a commoner to see his cattle.

To make a person a trespasser ab initio there must be a wrongful act committed; a mere nonfeasance is not enough. (45 Halsbury's Laws (4th edn) para 1389)

Trespass to goods

Trespass to goods is an unlawful disturbance of the possession of goods by seizure or removal, or by a direct act causing damage to the goods.

The subject matter of trespass to goods must be a personal chattel which is the subject of lawful possession. (45 Halsbury's Laws (4th edn) para 1491)

Trespass to land

Every unlawful entry by one person on land in the possession of another is a trespass for which an action lies, even though no actual damage is done. A person trespasses upon land if he wrongfully sets foot on it, rides or drives over it or takes possession of it, or expels the person in possession, or pulls down or destroys anything permanently fixed to it, or wrongfully takes minerals from it, or places or fixes anything on it or in it, or if he erects or suffers to continue on his own land anything which invades the airspace of another, or if he discharges water upon another's land, or sends filth or any injurious substance which has been collected by him on his own land onto another's land.

Where there is no act of direct intrusion on another person's property, liability in trespass does not arise, although liability may arise in nuisance. If an occupier of land brings onto it anything which is not naturally there, and which is likely to do damage if it escapes, he keeps it at his peril and is liable for all the damage which is the natural consequence of its escape. However, ordinary use of land does not give rise to liability to neighbouring owners or occupiers for such mischief as it may occasion them. (45 Halsbury's Laws (4th edn) paras 1384, 1385)

Trespass to the person

Trespass to the person is a wrong committed against the personal security or personal liberty of one man by another. There are three varieties of trespass to the person, namely assault, battery and wrongful or false imprisonment. The act complained of must be either intentional or negligent. The onus of proof lies on the plaintiff who must plead either that the act was intentional or that the defendant was negligent, stating the facts alleged to constitute the negligence. The act must be done against the will of the person who sues for the wrong. (45 Halsbury's Laws (4th edn) para 1308)

TRIAL *See also* COMMIT

Australia 'The meaning of the word "trial" is described in Jowitt's Dictionary of English Law as "finding out by due examination the truth of the point in issue or question between the parties, whereupon judgment may be given (Co Litt 124b)". In the Oxford English Dictionary the primary meaning given is, "Law. The examination and determination of a cause by a judicial tribunal; determination of the guilt or innocence of an accused person by a court." "The general term for proceedings, civil or criminal, in a court of first instance, frequently involving the hearing of evidence, leading to the Court's determination of the matter in issue." These meanings or definitions perhaps suggest although they do not require that the receiving of a plea of guilty and the passing of judgment thereon do not involve trial. Yet in the Crimes Act 1958 [Vic] it seems that there are some sections, at any rate, where the word "trial" is used to comprehend the receipt of a plea of guilty. For example, s 479(1)(a) begins: "Where upon the trial of any indictable offence a verdict of guilty has been found or a plea of guilty has been received but no judgment or sentence has been given or passed thereon and the judge presiding at the trial ceases for any reason to be such a judge . . ." In that excerpt "the judge presiding at the trial" clearly includes a judge who receives a plea of guilty and the words "when upon the trial of any indictable offence . . . a plea of guilty has been received" are clearly not to be limited to cases where a trial begins with a plea of not guilty and the accused changes his plea during the course of the trial. The remaining paragraphs of s 479 sub-ss (1), (2) and (4) afford further examples of the use of the words "the judge presiding at the trial" as including a judge who receives a plea of guilty.' *R v Symons* [1981] VR 297 at 298, 299, per Young CJ

Canada 'In a general sense, the term "trial" denotes the investigation and determination of a matter in issue between parties before a competent tribunal, advancing through progressive stages from its submission to the court or jury to the pronouncement of judgment. When a trial may be said actually to have commenced is often a difficult question but, generally speaking, this stage is reached when all preliminary questions have been determined and the jury, or a judge in a non-jury trial, enter upon the hearing and examination of the facts for the purpose of determining the questions in controversy in the litigation.' *Catherwood v Thompson* [1958] OR 326 at 331, 332, Ont CA, per Schroeder JA

TRIBUNAL *See also* COURT

'Tribunal' includes the person constituting a tribunal consisting of one person. (Parliamentary Commissioner Act 1967, s 12; Local Government Act 1974, s 34(1))

Statutory tribunal

In this section the expression 'statutory tribunal' means any Government department, authority or person entrusted with the judicial determination as arbitrator or otherwise of questions arising under an Act of Parliament, except that the expression does not include—

(a) any of the ordinary courts of law or a tribunal consisting of one or more judges of any of those courts; or

(b) an arbitrator unless the person to act as arbitrator is designated, or is to be selected from a class or group of persons designated, by the Act or instrument requiring or authorising arbitration.

(Lands Tribunal Act 1949, s 4)

TRIBUTARY

'In ordinary language a "tributary" is a stream running into another stream. The word has no technical meaning, and its popular meaning is not very indefinite, though I should be very sorry to attempt a complete definition. The question as to what is or is not a tributary must depend upon the particular distinguishing circumstances of each case. For instance, where a stream running down a valley was dammed up at various points, so as to form a series of pools by swelling out the current of the stream, which pursued its ordinary course after passing through the pools, I should say that the pools would be tributaries of the stream; or where a stream widens into lakes at no great distance from the sea, with a strong direct stream running through them and out into the sea, it may be that the lakes would be tributaries.' *Harbottle v Terry* (1882) 10 QBD 131 at 137, per Stephen J

'A tributary is a thing which contributes and I cannot understand why a stream should be less a tributary of the River Severn because, before it reaches the Severn, it passes through a stream with another name.' *Evans v Owens* [1895] 1 QB 237 at 238, 239, DC, per Wills J

TRICYCLE

'Tricycle' includes a motor scooter and a tricycle with an attachment for propelling it by mechanical power. (Vehicles (Excise) Act 1971, Sch 1)

'The bicycle or tricycle is a thing which carries. It may carry a man, as a horse does, or a carriage does; it may carry luggage or goods as we know that tradesmen's tricycles do. It is, therefore, in my opinion, a carriage.' *Cannan v Abingdon (Earl)* [1900] 2 QB 66 at 71, DC, per Bigham J

TRINITY HOUSE

'The Trinity House' shall mean the master wardens and assistants of the guild, fraternity, or brotherhood of the most glorious and undivided Trinity and of St Clement in the parish of Deptford Strond in the county of Kent, commonly called the corporation of the Trinity House of Deptford Strond. (Merchant Shipping Act 1894, s 742)

[*See*, generally, 43 Halsbury's Laws (4th edn) para 33]

TRINKETS

[Under the Carriers Act 1830, s 1, a carrier is not liable for the loss of (inter alia 'trinkets' above the value of £10, unless the value and nature of such trinkets is declared by the person sending or delivering them.] 'I am of opinion that this rule should be made absolute to reduce the amount of the damages to £11 17s, the value of the fusee-boxes, which I am of opinion do not properly fall within the definition of trinkets, and therefore are not within the protection of the Carriers Act. As to the other articles, they all, I think, properly come within the denomination given by the Act, and are protected. With respect to the shirt-pins, bracelets, gilt rings, brooches, tortoiseshell port-monnaies and smelling-bottles, there is a distinction between some of these articles, which are used as ornamental to the dress, and others which do not constitute any portion of the dress, and are only occasionally produced, but which when so produced are of an ornamental character. The first of these classes, such as shirt-pins, bracelets, rings and brooches properly come within the definition of trinkets. It is said, their primary object is not merely ornamental, and that they are therefore not trinkets. I do not agree to this. I think that their object is not utility, but essentially ornament; but even supposing their main object to be that of forming some part of the dress, still, if they are intended to be, as these clearly are, ornamental to the apparel, they are, I think, trinkets. There is more difficulty in dealing with the other portion of these articles, which are not always exhibited, but only produced occasionally, that is, when wanted; these are the port-monnaies and glass smelling-bottles. I think that, although these may be articles of use and of necessity, yet, if by superaddition of so much ornament there is given to them such a character as to make their main object ornament, they are trinkets. The intention of this Act is to protect carriers of articles of small bulk but of considerable value; and therefore, if the articles are open to such a construction as to bring them within the Act, we ought to adopt that construction. The fusee-boxes of German silver cannot however, I think, fall within the definition of trinkets. They are made of plain materials, and the main, indeed almost the sole purpose to which they can be applied is, the use for which they were evidently intended: these are clearly articles of use and not ornament, and are not trinkets.' *Bernstein v Baxendale* (1859) 28 LJCP 265 at 267, per Cockburn CJ

'The word "trinkets" [in the Carriers Act 1830, s 1 (see supra)] means articles worn about the person as personal adornments.' *Levi, Jones & Co Ltd v Cheshire Lines Committee* (1901) 17 TLR 443 at 444, per Bruce J

TROLLEY VEHICLE *See* VEHICLE

TROUT

'Trout' means any fish of the salmon family commonly known as trout, including migratory trout and char, and also includes part of a trout. (Salmon and Freshwater Fisheries Act 1975, s 41)

'Migratory trout' means trout which migrate to and from the sea. (Ibid)

TRUE

Australia 'The words "true in substance and in fact" have acquired a settled meaning, and certain consequences in connection with what is commonly called a plea of justification, though of all the ordinary defences to an action for libel that which may be called the plea of truth is the one that with the least propriety can be called a plea of justification.' *Clarke v Norton* [1910] VLR 494 at 499, per Cussen J

Australia [The Income Tax Assessment Act 1936–1986 (Cth), s 170, refers to the full and 'true' disclosure of all material facts by the taxpayer.] '"True" in this phrase appears to me to refer simply to the correctness of the material facts disclosed and to imply nothing as to the taxpayer's knowledge of the erroneous character of any incorrect fact he may state.' *Federal Comr of Taxation v Levy* [1962] ALR 154 at 155, per Dixon CJ

TRUE COPY

'By s 10, sub-s 2, of the Bills of Sale Act 1878, a true copy of the bill must be filed with the Registrar, the object being that if a person borrows money on this class of security, persons who may think of dealing with him shall have an opportunity of seeing the terms on which he is borrowing money, and that the security he has given is valid. There is therefore a provision that a true copy must be filed, otherwise the bill of sale is void. A true copy . . . does not mean an exact copy; for instance, mere mis-spellings, mere failure to fill up blanks which can be filled up from other parts of the deed—matters which do not in any way affect the purpose for which the true copy is required—will not prevent the document registered from being a "true copy" within the meaning of the Act.' *Burchell v Thompson* [1920] 2 KB 80 at 102, CA, per Scrutton LJ

TRUE OWNER

'The words "true owner" must be construed according to their natural meaning. A person may be the true owner of goods, although they may be subject to some lien or equitable charge. He may, as owner, convey goods over which there exist rights of other persons, which qualify his own right and render him something less than absolute owner. There must always be, according to the true meaning of the section [Bills of Sale Act (1878) Amendment Act 1882, s 5] someone who can be spoken of as the true owner of property which is subject to a lien or some such other right. Thus a tenant in common may convey by bill of sale his share in property over which his co-tenant has rights. The existence of such rights do not prevent him from parting with his own property. The position of a partner is the same; if both the partners had joined in this bill of sale, each conveying his own moiety, the bill of sale would have been effectual to pass the whole interest in the chattels assigned; and I think that the elder partner, who is the grantor in this case, was the true owner of his moiety within the meaning of the section.' *Re Tamplin & Son, ex p Barnett* (1890) 59 LJQB 194 at 195, 196, DC, per Cave J

TRUST *See also* INVESTMENT TRUST

Where a person has property or rights which he holds or is bound to exercise for or on behalf of another or others, or for the accomplishment of some particular purpose or particular purposes, he is said to hold the property or rights in trust for that other or those others, or for that purpose or those purposes, and he is called a trustee. A trust is a purely equitable obligation and is enforceable only in a court in which equity is administered.

The trustee holds the property or must exercise his rights of property in a fiduciary capacity, and stands in a fiduciary relationship to the beneficiary.

The property affected by a trust, called the 'trust property' or 'trust estate', must be vested in the trustee, whether the property is a legal estate, a legal right or an equitable interest where the legal title is vested in some other person. . . .

A trust may be created intentionally inter vivos or by will. Essentials of such creation are (1) property or rights capable of being subjected to the trust; (2) a declaration of, or disposition on, trust by a person competent to create a trust, or an obligation for valuable consideration to create a trust; (3) certainty of property and objects so that the trust is administratively workable; and (4) compliance with statutory requirements regarding evidence and the rule against remoteness preventing interests vesting outside the perpetuity period and the rule against inalienability preventing income from being inalienable for longer than the perpetuity period. A trust is void if it is created for an illegal purpose or is otherwise contrary to public policy. Once everything necessary to create a trust has been done, equity will not allow a trust to fail for want of a trustee. . . .

Trusts are either (1) express trusts, which are created expressly or impliedly by the actual terms of some instrument or declaration, or which by some enactment are expressly imposed on persons in relation to some property vested in them, whether or not they are already trustees of that property; or (2) trusts arising by operation of law (other than express trusts imposed by enactments). (48 Halsbury's Laws (4th edn) paras 501, 504, 523)

'Trust' includes an executorship or administratorship. (Public Trustee Act 1906, s 15)

'Trust' does not include the duties incident to an estate conveyed by way of mortgage, but with this exception the expressions 'trust' and 'trustee' extend to implied and constructive trusts, and to cases where the trustee has a beneficial interest in the trust property, and to the duties incident to the office of a personal representative, and 'trustee' where the context admits, includes a personal representative, and 'new trustee' includes an additional trustee. (Trustee Act 1925, s 68)

'Trust' includes an implied or constructive trust. (Settled Land Act 1925, s 117)

'Trust' includes an implied or constructive trust and a trust where the trustee has a beneficial interest in the trust property, and also includes the duties incident to the office of a personal representative, and 'trustee' shall be construed accordingly. (Solicitors Act 1974, s 87(1))

'The Act [Judicial Trustees Act 1896] contains no definition of "trust" and I must therefore give to that word its ordinary meaning. For the purposes of this case I think that I can take the definition in Underhill on Trusts (8th edn), p 3, which reads as follows: "A trust is an equitable obligation, binding a person (who is called a trustee) to deal with property over which he has control (which is called the trust property) for the benefit of persons (who are called the beneficiaries or *cestuis que trust*), of whom he may himself be one, and any one of whom may enforce the obligation". In my opinion, Settled Land Act [1925] trustees are trustees of a trust within that definition.' *Re Marshall's Will Trusts* [1945] Ch 217 at 219, per Cohen J

Australia 'No definition of a "trust" seems to have been accepted as comprehensive and exact. The word is sometimes applied to the trust premises, sometimes to the duties related thereto, sometimes to both. Strictly, it refers, I think, to the duty or the aggregate accumulation of obligations that rest upon a person described as a trustee. The responsibilities are in relation to property held by him, or under his control. That property he will be compelled by a court in its equitable jurisdiction to administer in the manner lawfully prescribed by the trust instrument, or where there be no specific provision written or oral, or to the extent that such provision is invalid or lacking, in accordance with equitable principles.' *Re Scott (decd)* [1948] SASR 193 at 196, per Mayo J

Constructive trust

A constructive trust arises when, although there is no express trust affecting specific property, equity considers that the legal owner should be treated as a trustee of an interest in it for another. This happens, for instance, where one who is already a trustee takes advantage of his position to obtain a new legal interest in the property, as where a trustee of leaseholds takes a new lease in his own name, or acquires the freehold reversion. The rule applies where a person, although not an express trustee, is in a fiduciary position, for example (formerly) a tenant for life in regard to the remaindermen. (16 Halsbury's Laws (4th edn) para 1453)

A constructive trust attaches by law to specific property which is neither expressly subject to any trusts nor subject to a resulting trust but which is held by a person in circumstances where it would be inequitable to allow him to assert full beneficial ownership of the property. Such a person will often hold other property in a fiduciary capacity and it will be by virtue of his ownership of or dealings with that fiduciary property that he acquired the specific property subject to the constructive trust. However, a stranger who receives property in circumstances where he has actual or constructive notice that it is trust property being transferred to him in breach of trust will also be a constructive trustee of that property.

A person who holds property on a constructive trust is a constructive trustee in respect of it. He cannot claim for himself any increase in value of the property or any profits earned by it. If he becomes bankrupt the property is not available for his general creditors but for the beneficiaries in whose favour the constructive trust subsists. (48 Halsbury's Laws (4th edn) para 584)

'The will trustees . . . contend that an implied trust means a trust declared by a party not directly but by implication. That no doubt is a strict and accurate statement, though not exhaustive. . . . They refer to Lewin on Trusts, 12th edn, p 124, n, where the learned author states: ". . . An implied trust is one declared by a party not directly, but only by implication; as where a testator devises an estate to A and his heirs, 'not doubting' that he will thereout pay an annuity of £20 per annum to B for his life, in which case A is a trustee for B to the extent of the annuity". . . . It is true no doubt, as the trustees contend, that a resulting trust in ordinary circumstances is in one sense not really a trust at all. Where property is settled or devised upon limitations that do not exhaust it, a resulting use or trust of the unexhausted part is left in the settlor or devisor. But where, as in the present case, property is devised as a whole to trustees and the trusts declared do not exhaust the income during some particular period, although there is a resulting trust so called to the settlor or her heir at law, it is really a trust construed by the court in the trustees of the income which they so hold, and which they cannot apply in accordance with any express trust in the settlement and which in the present case they hold on trust to pay to the person entitled thereto by reason of this so-called resulting trust. That, I think, is within the general meaning of implied or constructive trust.' *Re Llanover Settled Estates* [1926] Ch 626 at 636–638, per Astbury J

Diocesan trust *See* DIOCESAN TRUST

Discretionary trust

A discretionary trust for a variety of alternative objects or purposes, some legal and some illegal, according as the trustees may select, is valid so far as respects the legal objects or purposes, and the trustees may exercise their discretionary selection in respect of the objects or purposes which are legal, but they cannot validly do so in respect of those which are illegal. (48 Halsbury's Laws (4th edn) para 577)

Executed or executory trust

Express trusts may be either (1) executed, or (2) executory. A trust is executed in the technical sense where the terms of the trust are designated by the instrument or declaration creating it, even though the creator directs a settlement to be executed embodying the designated provisions. A trust is executory in the technical sense where the instrument or declaration by which it is created directs the subsequent execution of an instrument defining the trust and does not itself define with absolute precision the terms of that instrument. (48 Halsbury's Laws (4th edn) para 525)

Express trust

An express trust as regards land is a trust expressly declared by a deed, will or other written instrument; as to personalty (other than leaseholds) the trust can be expressly created orally. To constitute an express trust three matters must be defined: the property subject to the trust, the persons to be benefited, and the interests which they are to take. It is not necessary to use the word 'trust', and the trust is express even if it has to be made out from all the terms of the instrument, although the courts are less ready now than formerly to construe words of recommendation as creating a precatory trust. It is usually sufficient, to establish the relation of trustee and beneficiary, to prove that the legal title is in one person and the equitable title in another. (16 Halsbury's Laws (4th edn) para 1452)

'All trusts are either, first, express trusts, which are raised and created by act of the parties, or implied trusts, which are raised or created by act or construction of law; again, express trusts are declared either by word or writing; and these declarations appear either by direct and manifest proof, or violent and necessary presumption.' *Cook v Fountain* (1676) 3 Swan 585 at 591, per Lord Raynsford CJ

'My notion of an express trust is, that it is a trust which has been expressed; that is to say, expressed either by words in writing or by word of mouth; and that it does not include a trust which arises from the acts of the parties. It does not apply, in my judgment, to a resulting trust, to an implied trust, or to a constructive trust.' *Sands v Thompson* (1883) 48 LT 210 at 211, per Fry J

Imperfect trust

In this Act, 'imperfect trust provision' means any provision declaring the objects for which property is to be held or applied, and so describing those objects that, consistently with the terms of the provision, the property could be used exclusively for charitable purposes, but could nevertheless be used for purposes which are not charitable. (Charitable Trusts (Validation) Act 1954, s 1)

Precatory trust

A precatory trust is a trust established by precatory words, such as expressions of confidence, request or desire that property will be applied for the benefit of a definite person or object, where these words are construed in equity as imperatively constituting a trust. The expression . . . is a roundabout way of saying that the court finds that there is a trust, although the trust is not expressed as such but by words of prayer or suggestion or the like. Nowadays, courts are reluctant to find that precatory words create a trust unless there is little doubt that, looking at the instrument as a whole, a binding trust obligation was intended. (48 Halsbury's Laws (4th edn) para 526)

Private trust

Within the category of private trusts come trusts for the benefit of particular individuals, whether or not immediately ascertainable, or for the benefit of some aggregate of individuals ascertained by reference to some personal relationship, and trusts for the benefit of particular animals and for the maintenance of tombs not forming part of a church, but not trusts for the benefit of the public or a section of the public. (48 Halsbury's Laws (4th edn) para 530)

Public trust

Trusts for public purposes are either (1) charitable, in which case they are governed by the law relating to charitable trusts, or (2) for public objects which are not of a charitable character. With certain exceptions, trusts for public objects which are not of a charitable character are invalid if they infringe the law which restricts the creation of perpetuities; and it seems that, even if they do not infringe the law against perpetuities, such trusts will not in general be recognised by the court except in so far as they are for the benefit of ascertained or ascertainable beneficiaries. (48 Halsbury's Laws (4th edn) para 529)

Resulting trust

A resulting trust may arise solely by operation of law, as where, upon a purchase of land, one person provides the purchase money and the conveyance is taken in the name of another: there is then a resulting trust in favour of the person providing the money, unless from the relation between the two, or from other circumstances, it appears that a gift was intended. There is also another class of resulting trusts, where the creation of the trust is express, although in the events which happen, the beneficial destination of the property is undetermined. This is the case when there is an entire or partial failure of the objects of the trust, and then, to the extent of the failure, the benefit of the trust results to the settlor or his representatives. (16 Halsbury's Laws (4th edn) para 1453)

A resulting trust is a trust arising by operation of law:

(1) where an intention to put property into trust is sufficiently expressed or indicated, but the actual trust either is not declared in whole or in part or fails in whole or in part; or
(2) where property is purchased in the name or placed in the possession of a person ostensibly for his own use, but really in order to effect a particular purpose which fails; or
(3) where property is purchased in the name or placed in the possession of a person without any intimation that he is to hold it in trust, but the retention of the beneficial interest by the purchaser or disposer is presumed to have been intended.

In all these cases, except where the failure of a declared trust arises from the illegality of the object, and the trustee relies on the maxim *in pari delicto potior est conditio possidentis*, the beneficial interest in the property, so far as not applicable to any sufficiently expressed or indicated beneficiary or object, results or reverts to the disposer or purchaser of the property or, in the case of his previous death, to his representatives. (48 Halsbury's Laws (4th edn) para 597)

'If it is intended to have a resulting trust, the ordinary and familiar mode of doing that is by saying so on the face of the instrument; and I cannot get, out of the language of this instrument, a resulting trust except by putting in words which are not there. I must say I for one have always protested against endeavouring to construe an instrument contrary to what the words of the instrument itself convey, by some sort of preconceived idea of what the parties would or might or perhaps ought to have intended when they began to frame their instrument.' *Smith v Cooke, Storey v Cooke* [1891] AC 297 at 299, per Lord Halsbury LC

Secret trust

A secret trust is created where property is in law given to a person either absolutely or upon an indefinite trust, but there has been an undertaking by him or an understanding between him and the donor, not clothed with the requisite formalities for the creation of a legal trust, that it is to be applied for the benefit of some other person or object. (48 Halsbury's Laws (4th edn) para 527)

A secret trust is a trust which a court of equity, proceeding on the ground of fraud, imposes on a person who has obtained title to property, for example by gift by will, obliging him to hold it for the benefit of the persons for whom or purposes for which he knew that it was given or allowed to pass to him. A fully secret trust arises where a testator gives property to a person apparently beneficially, but has communicated to that person during his lifetime certain trusts on which the property is to be held. A half secret trust which will be enforced by the court arises where the fact that the property is given to the legatee upon trust is mentioned in the will but the trusts are not defined by the will. If the will defines the trusts by reference to an earlier document, for example a letter, then the probate doctrine of incorporation by reference applies to treat the trusts of the earlier document as if set out in the will.

In order that there should be a valid fully secret trust, the testator's intention must be communicated to the donee during the testator's lifetime, whereas in the case of a half secret trust the communication must be prior to, or contemporaneous with, the will. Uncommunicated wishes or expectations of the testator, even though written, are not sufficient. A person may accept a secret trust either expressly or by silently acquiescing in it when communicated to him.

If the trustee of a fully secret trust renounces or dies in the testator's lifetime, the trust cannot operate. If such an event occurs in relation to a half secret trust, equity will not allow the trust appearing on the face of the will to fail for want of a trustee, and therefore the personal representatives will hold on the half secret trusts if the terms of such trusts can be ascertained despite the trustee's death. In either sort of secret trust, it seems that disclaimer after the testator's death will not invalidate the trust. (48 Halsbury's Laws (4th edn) para 570)

Voluntary trust

A voluntary trust is a trust made for no valuable consideration, and is not enforceable unless it has been completely constituted.

In general, unless the consideration is plainly illusory, the court does not inquire into its adequacy and treats the trust as made for value. Marriage by itself, without any further consideration, constitutes a valuable consideration. (48 Halsbury's Laws (4th edn) para 528)

TRUST CORPORATION

'Trust corporation' means the Public Trustee or a corporation either appointed by the court in any particular case to be a trustee or authorised by rules made under section 4(3) of the Public Trustee Act 1906 to act as a custodian trustee. (Supreme Court Act 1981, s 128)

TRUST FOR SALE

'Trust for sale' in relation to land means an immediate binding trust for sale, whether or not exercisable at the request or with the consent of any person, and with or without power at discretion to postpone the sale; 'trustee for sale' mean the persons (including a personal representative) holding land on trust for sale. (Trustee Act 1925, s 68; see also Law of Property Act 1925, s 205; Administration of Estates Act 1925, s 55; Land Registration Act 1925, s 3)

[The Settled Land Act 1925, s 1(7), provides that that section does not apply to land held upon 'trust for sale'. Section 3 of the same Act provides that land not held upon 'trust for sale' which has been subject to a settlement is deemed to remain and be settled land. The Law of Property Act 1925, s 2(2), deals with conveyances overreaching equitable interests and powers having priority to the trust for sale, where the legal estate affected is subject to a 'trust for sale'.] 'I come to the following conclusions upon the construction of the Acts: first, that "trust for sale" in the new sub-s of s 1 of the Settled Land Act 1925, and in s 3 of the same Act as now amended [by the Law of Property (Amendment) Act 1926], must be read as meaning an immediate binding trust for sale; secondly, that trust for sale in sub-s 2 of s 2 of the Law of Property Act 1925, as amended is not confined to an immediate binding trust for sale, as otherwise there would be no point in the sub-section; . . . and fourthly, that where there is an approval or appointment of trustees by the court within the sub-section the trust for sale is then capable of operating in relation to the whole subject-matter of the settlement, and (assuming that it is an immediate trust for sale) becomes an immediate binding trust for sale within the definition of that phrase in the Settled Land Act and the Law of Property Act.' *Re Leigh's Settled Estates (No 2)* [1927] 2 Ch 13 at 22, per Tomlin J

'"Trust for sale" is defined [in the Law of Property Act 1925, s 205] as meaning, in relation to land, an immediate binding trust for sale whether or not exercisable at the request or with the consent of any person, and it was contended before me that the land is not held upon an immediate binding trust for sale within the meaning which it was said had been given to those words by Tomlin J in *Re Leigh's Settled Estates* [supra]. In that case the learned judge came to the conclusion that where the subject-matter of a settlement is the whole unincumbered fee-simple, "the land" is not "subject to an immediate binding trust for sale", so long as there is not a trust for sale which is capable of overriding all charges having, under the settlement, priority to the trust for sale. . . . I feel some little doubt as to whether the learned judge held that "the land" in the case before him was not subject to any trust for sale, inasmuch as the subject-matter of the trust was merely the fee simple subject to the incumbrance, or whether he held that no land can ever be subject to a binding trust for sale, unless the trustees have power to overreach prior equitable interests. If the latter be the real reason of his decision, I find myself, with the greatest respect, unable to follow it. . . . The conclusion . . . that I come to as a result of a consideration of all the Acts [Law of Property Act 1925; Trustee Act 1925; Administration of Estates Act 1925; Land Charges

Act 1925] is that the words "trust for sale", when used in reference to land that is subject to a prior equitable interest, are not confined to cases where that equitable interest can be overreached by the trustees.' *Re Parker's Settled Estates, Parker v Parker* [1928] Ch 247 at 257, 258, 261, per Romer J

'The assumed case is . . . that, pursuant to a trust for sale contained in a will, all land has been sold by the will trustees and that the proceeds of sale arising from an exercise of that trust are in the hands of the will trustees. Are those trustees trustees for sale? Certain terms used in the Law of Property Act 1925 are defined in s 205 of the Act. The section, so far as is relevant, runs as follows: "In this Act, unless the context otherwise requires, the following expressions have the meanings hereby assigned to them . . . 'trustees for sale' mean the persons (including a personal representative) holding land on trust for sale." I am of opinion that will trustees, in the assumed circumstances, are not trustees for sale. The trust contained in the definition does not refer to the terms of any trust instrument. Many trusts for sale of land, indeed, arise by operation of law. The test refers to a state of facts and, as a matter of language, to a state of facts subsisting at the time when the question arises for determination. The language of the definition is clear and does not in my view allow one to put on the phrase "persons holding land on trust for sale"—a gloss which would make it include "trustees who have held, but no longer hold, land on trust for sale".' *Re Wakeman, National Provincial Bank Ltd v Wakeman* [1945] Ch 177 at 180, 181, per Uthwatt J

TRUST FUNDS

[The Trust Investment Act 1889, s 3 (repealed; cf now the Trustee Investments Act 1961, s 4), empowered a trustee to invest any 'trust funds' in his hands in certain authorised investments.] 'In my opinion, the expression "trust funds" occurring in the commencement of s 3 of the Act of 1889 signifies funds belonging to the trust, including money invested on security or otherwise, as well as uninvested cash. I do not doubt that such is the ordinary and natural meaning of the words. . . . I do not think that . . . it can be reasonably suggested that the legislature had in view any meaning of the words other than their natural and popular meaning.' *Hume v Lopes* [1892] AC 112 at 115, 116, per Lord Watson

TRUST INSTRUMENT

'Trust instrument' means the instrument whereby the trusts of the settled land are declared, and includes any two or more such instruments and a settlement or instrument which is deemed to be a trust instrument. (Settled Land Act 1925, s 117)

'The words "trust instrument" are defined in s 117, sub-s 1(xxxi) [of the Settled Land Act 1925 (supra)] to this extent, that we are told that a trust instrument means the instrument whereby the trusts of the settled land are declared, and includes any two or more such instruments and a settlement or instrument which is deemed to be a trust instrument . . . I have come to the conclusion that settled land may be held in trust for persons entitled in possession in undivided shares under a trust instrument, although the trust instrument itself does not cause the division, but the division into shares is effected by a subsequent deed or event, and that in such a case the trust instrument should be regarded as the will or other instrument creating the trust.' *Re Hind, Bernstone v Montgomery* [1933] Ch 208 at 222, 223, per Maugham J

TRUSTEE *See also* TRUST

'A trustee is a man who is the owner of the property and deals with it as principal, as owner, and as master, subject only to an equitable obligation to account to some persons to whom he stands in the relation of trustee, and who are his *cestuis que trust*.' *Smith v Anderson* (1880) 15 Ch D 247 at 275, CA, per James LJ

Australia 'A person or body of persons who undertake to administer in the interests of a charity money received by them for that purpose are answerable to a Court of Equity for any diversion of the charitable fund from its purposes on the ground that they occupy in relation to the donors and the beneficiaries the position of trustees. In the broad sense of the term such persons and bodies of persons are trustees.' *Re Padbury, House of Peace for the Dying & Incurable v S-G* (1908) 7 CLR 680 at 695, per O'Connor J

Bare trustee

A bare trustee is a person who holds property in trust for the absolute benefit and at the absolute disposal of other persons who are of full age and sui juris in respect of it, and who has himself no present beneficial interest in it and no duties to perform in respect of it except to convey or transfer it to persons entitled to hold it, and he is bound to convey or transfer the property accordingly when required to do so. (48 Halsbury's Laws (4th edn) para 641)

Charity trustees

'Charity trustees' means the persons having the general control and management of the administration of a charity. (Charities Act 1960, s 46)

Disclaimer by trustee *See* DISCLAIMER

Reasonable acts of trustee *See* REASONABLE

Trustee de son tort

'What constitutes a trustee *de son tort*? It appears to me, if one, not being a trustee and not having authority from a trustee, takes upon himself to intermeddle with trust matters or to do acts characteristic of the office of trustee, he may thereby make himself what is called in law a trustee of his own wrong—i.e., a trustee *de son tort*, or as it is also termed, a constructive trustee.' *Mara v Browne* [1896] 1 Ch 199 at 209, CA, per A L Smith LJ

TRUSTING

[A testator by his will left a sum of money to A, 'trusting' that he would preserve it for any children who should survive him.] 'I am of opinion that there is a trust created. The word used, "trusting" is a word of art, and plainly conveys the intention of the testator.' *Baker v Mosley* (1848) 11 LTOS 372 at 372, per Knight Bruce V-C

TUG

'Tug' means a vessel propelled by mechanical power and used for towing or pushing another vessel or a raft or float of timber. (Port of London Act 1968, s 2)

TUMULTUOUS *See also* RIOT

'I pause to consider what the concepts are which arise in one's mind when the noun, adjective or adverb, "tumult", "tumultuous" or "tumultuously", are applied to an assembly. I would not attempt to give a full definition of any of those words, but it seems to me that all of them bring a certain impression to one's mind. When those words are applied to an assembly of persons, the impression is that the assembly should be of considerable size; that it should be an assembly in which the persons taking part are indulging in agitated movement; an excited, emotionally aroused assembly; excitement or emotion common to the members of the assembly; and generally, though not necessarily, accompanied by noise. I agree with the submissions which have been made, that it is a question of degree whether any assembly of people can properly be said to be acting tumultuously.' *Dwyer (JW) Ltd v Receiver for Metropolitan Police District* [1967] 2 All ER 1051 at 1055, per Lyell J

TUNNEL

'Tunnel' means a tunnel or covered way through which there is a public right of passage and includes the approaches thereto. (London County Council (General Powers) Act 1949, s 31)

TURBARY

Common of turbary is a right of digging turf or peat in another man's ground for fuel in the commoner's house. (6 Halsbury's Laws (4th edn) para 576)

TURF

'The turf is composed of the grass and soil on which it grows, as peat is the vegetable and the soil of which it has become a part.' *Wilkinson v Haygarth* (1847) 12 QB 837 at 845, per Lord Denman CJ

TURNOVER

'The "turnover of the company's annual business" . . . must be taken to include all sums received and receivable in the year as the result of the defendant company's trading, whether normal or abnormal.' *Aris-Bainbridge v Turner Manufacturing Co Ltd* [1950] 2 All ER 1178 n at 1178, per McNair J

TURNPIKE

'A turnpike road is a road across which turnpike gates are erected and tolls taken, and such roads existed previous to the passing of the 13 Geo 3, c 84 [(1773) (repealed)] and independently of that statute altogether. A "turnpike road" means a road having toll-gates or bars on it, which were originally called "turns", and were first constructed about the middle of the last century. Certain individuals, with a view to the repair of particular roads, subscribed amongst themselves for that purpose, and erected gates upon the roads, taking tolls from those who passed through them. These were violently opposed at first, and petitions were presented to Parliament against them; and acts were in consequence passed for their regulation. This was the origin of turnpike roads. The distinctive mark of a turnpike road is, the right of turning back any one who refuses to pay toll.' *Northam Bridge & Roads Co v London & Southampton Rly Co* (1840) 6 M & W 428 at 438, per Lord Abinger CB

TURPITUDE *See* MORAL TURPITUDE

U

UBERRIMA FIDES *See also* GOOD FAITH

'There are some contracts in which our courts of law and equity require what is called "*uberrima fides*" to be shown by the person obtaining them. . . . Of these, ordinary contracts of marine, fire and life insurance are examples, and in each of them the person desiring to be insured must, in setting forth the risk to be insured against, not conceal any material fact affecting the risk known to him. On the other hand, ordinary contracts of guarantee are not amongst those requiring "*uberrima fides*" on the part of the creditor towards the surety; and mere non communication to the surety by the creditor of facts known to him affecting the risk to be undertaken by the surety will not vitiate the contract, unless there be fraud or misrepresentation. . . . But the difference between these two classes of contract does not depend upon any essential difference between the word "insurance" and the word "guarantee". . . . Whether the contract be one requiring "*uberrima fides*" or not must depend upon its substantial character and how it came to be effected.' *Seaton v Heath, Seaton v Burnand* [1899] 1 QB 782 at 792, CA, per Romer LJ

ULTERIOR

[In 1830 A, being desirous of relinquishing his life interest, appointed the estate to his son for life subject to the power expressed in a deed of 1814, 'ulterior to' the limitations therein for the lives of A and his son.] 'The doubt in this case was occasioned by the words, "ulterior to"; one a Latin word used as an English word, and the other, simple, native, old English. Prepositions, such as ultra, and the adjectives derived from them naturally referring to space, are metaphorically applied to time and bear the sense of addition. . . . But the author of the deed of 1830, very properly wishing to avoid expense and prolixity by substituting reference for transcription, has added the word "to", by way of enlarging and fixing the sense of the word, "ulterior", and connecting it with the words "remainders over". And it seems to me that no reasonable interpretation can be given to those words, but that which will describe something that comes after and in addition to, that is, the uses, limitations and powers which, in the deed of 1830, are to be found subsequent and in addition to the limitations to the son for life.' *Morgan v Rutson* (1848) 16 Sim 234 at 249, per Shadwell V-C

ULTIMATE

Australia 'I think "ultimate" and "final" are synonymous.' *Re Wales, Parkinson v Woodfull* [1934] VLR 297 at 302, per Gavan Duffy J

ULTIMATELY

[Under the Conveyancing Act 1881, s 43(2) (see, as to instruments coming into operation since 1925, the Trustee Act 1925, s 31), which deals with the application by trustees of the income or property of an infant for maintenance, it is the duty of such trustees to accumulate the residue of income, and hold those accumulations for the benefit of the person who 'ultimately becomes entitled' to the property from which the same arise.] 'The words of sub-s (2) are, I think to be read thus, "entitled to the property (namely the income) by the accumulation of which the accumulated fund or accumulations arise". If the words be thus read, and for the word "ultimately" there be substituted "in the events which happen", all difficulty disappears. The words will then read thus, "and shall hold those accumulations for the benefit of the person who in the events which happen becomes entitled to the property (namely the income) from the accumulation of which the accumulations arise". I think that is the meaning of the words.' *Re Scott, Scott v Scott* [1902] 1 Ch 918 at 925, per Buckley J

ULTRA VIRES

The term 'ultra vires' in its proper sense denotes some act or transaction on the part of a corporation which, although not unlawful or contrary to public policy if done by an individual, is yet beyond the corporation's legitimate powers as defined by the statute under which is is formed, or the statutes which are applicable to it, or by its charter or memorandum of association; although in favour of a third party dealing with the company in good faith the doctrine no longer applies. The term is misused in applying it to any act or transaction which is beyond the lawful powers of any person. Acts of directors which should not be undertaken by them without the sanction of the members of the company are, however, frequently described as acts ultra vires the directors. (7 Halsbury's Laws (4th edn) para 945)

'In my judgment, much of the confusion that has crept into the law flows from the use of the phrase "ultra vires" in different senses in different contexts. The reconciliation of the authorities can only be achieved if one first defines the sense in which one is using the words "ultra vires". Because the literal translation of the words is "beyond the powers", there are many cases in which the words have been applied to transactions which, although within the capacity of the company, are carried out otherwise than through the correct exercise of the powers of the company by its officers; indeed, that is the sense in which the judge [in the court below] seems to have used the words in this case. . . . In my judgment, the use of the phrase "ultra vires" should be restricted to those cases where the transaction is beyond the capacity of the company and therefore wholly void.' *Rolled Steel Products (Holdings) Ltd v British Steel Corpn* [1985] 2 All ER 52 at 91, CA, per Browne-Wilkinson LJ

UMPIRE *See* ARBITRATOR

UNABLE

Australia 'We think that the word "unable" should not be read as equivalent to impossible.' *Leeder v Ballarat East Corpn* [1908] VLR 214 at 218, per A'Beckett J

Australia 'I am not sure that the word "unable" has not a wider meaning than the words "not able".' Ibid at 224, per Cussen J

UNAVOIDABLE

[The Food and Drugs Act 1955, s 3(3) (repealed; see now the Food Act 1984, s 3(2)) provides that, in a case where food is found to contain extraneous matter, it shall be a defence to prove that the presence of such matter was an 'unavoidable' consequence of the process of collection or preparation.] 'I do not think the words "avoidable" or "unavoidable" are to be construed in any strained metaphysical or absolute sense. I believe they are to be construed with common sense in the way that a jury might construe them. This, in my view, means no more, and no less, than this. If any human agency in any way concerned in a proper process could have avoided the consequence by the exercise of a high standard of reasonable care, then the consequence is avoidable. On the other hand, if no human agency concerned with the process could, by the exercise of a high standard of reasonable care have avoided the contamination, the consequence, if a consequence of the process, is unavoidable within the meaning of s 3(3).' *Smedleys Ltd v Breed* [1974] 2 All ER 21 at 28, HL, per Lord Hailsham of St Marylebone

UNAVOIDABLE CAUSE

A bye-law made under the Elementary Education Act 1870, s 74 (repealed; see now the Education Act 1944, s 39(1)), provided that the parent of every child of a certain age should cause such child to attend school, unless there was a reasonable excuse for non-attendance, and that one of the following reasons should be a reasonable excuse, viz, that the child had been prevented from attending school by any 'unavoidable cause'.] 'If a parent sends a child in such a condition that the child will be refused admission, the fact that the child is refused admission does not amount to the child's being prevented from attending school by an unavoidable cause.' *Walker v Cummings* (1912) 107 LT 304 at 305, DC, per Lord Alverstone CJ

[The Education Act 1944, s 39(1), imposes a duty on parents to secure regular attendance of pupils at school; and s 39(2)(a) provides that a child shall not be deemed to have failed to attend regularly at any time when he was prevented from attending by reason of sickness or any 'unavoidable cause'.] 'We think that the words "unavoidable cause" must be construed in relation to the child. By s 39, sub-s 2(a), it is a defence to a prosecution under that section that the child only failed to attend school "by reason of sickness or any unavoidable cause". In my opinion, "sickness" in that paragraph must mean the sickness of the child. An "unavoidable cause" must be an unavoidable cause which affects the child. The alleged "unavoidable cause" in the present case was one which really affected the mother and not the child. Parliament has not seen fit to provide that . . . "family responsibilities" or "duties" can be relied on as an excuse for a child not attending school. . . . I think "unavoidable cause" must be read as something in the nature of an emergency.' *Jenkins v Howells* [1949] 2 KB 218 at 220, per Lord Goddard CJ

See generally, 15 Halsbury's Laws (4th edn) para 33

UNBORN

[The Trustee Act 1850, s 30 (repealed; see now the Trustee Act 1925, s 45) empowered the court, where a decree was made for specific performance of a contract concerning land, or for the partition or exchange of land, or for the conveyance or assignment of land to declare concerning the interests of 'unborn' persons claiming under any party to the suit.] 'The real question . . . is whether the word "unborn", as used in the 30th section . . . means "non-existent"—that is non-existent in the character to entitle a person to the property in question. I think that is the proper reading of the term. The object was to enable the court to convey a future legal estate devolving upon a person who could not be made a party to the suit. In a sense, the right heirs of a living person are unborn persons. In a sense, the future heir-at-law of a living person, although he may be a living man, is not a living heir. As heir—that is to say strictly in the character of heir—he comes into existence at a future period. Again, the word "person" does not necessarily mean a man at all. It applies by the interpretation clause to a corporation. I think the word "unborn" may be interpreted fairly and properly, looking at the intention and fair spirit of the Act, to mean any person so far not in existence as that he could not be properly made a party to the suit, and the latter words of the section help that view.' *Basnett v Moxon* (1875) LR 20 Eq 182 at 184, 185, per Jessel MR

'No doubt the very expression "unborn persons" which appears in the Act of 1958 [Variation of Trusts Act 1958] itself gives colour to the arguments which have been put; but no authority has been cited to show that a still unembodied spirit can be regarded as a person under our law; and I cannot think that the legislature used that expression otherwise than in the sense of future persons and to connote those future persons who will, if there is no variation, become interested under the trusts of the instrument which it is sought to vary, and without whose consent the proposed variation may not in some event be binding on him. It cannot be that the court is to approve on behalf of all persons who will come into this world but, in my judgment, only those who do in the event by reason of their birth to such and such a person on such and such a day acquire that legal identity which qualifies them as beneficiaries and the approval which is to be given in my judgment so to speak an approval *nunc pro tunc*.' *Re Cohen's Settlement Trusts, Eliot-Cohen v Cohen* [1965] 3 All ER 139 at 142, per Stamp J

UNCERTAIN

[The Law of Property Act 1925; s 184, provides that in all cases where, after the commencement of the Act, two or more persons have died in circumstances rendering it 'uncertain' which of them survived the other or others, such deaths shall (subject to any order of the court) for all purposes affecting the title to property be presumed to have occurred in order of seniority; and accordingly the younger shall be deemed to have survived the elder. But see s 46(3) of the Administration of Estates Act 1925, as added by s 1(4) of the Intestates' Estates Act 1952.] 'Unfortunately the wording of the section is such as to have given rise to controversy. Two views have been advanced as to its meaning and effect. According to one view, which is the view of Lord Greene MR and Goddard LJ [in the court below] the statutory presumption is strictly limited in its application to cases in which: "the court is satisfied as to two things—one that the proper inference from the circumstances is that the deaths took place consecutively, thc other, that the circumstances leave the court in uncertainty as to which death took place first." That is to say, all that the statute does is to fix artificially the order of sequence among consecutive deaths, where that order cannot in fact be ascertained. If the circumstances are such as to justify an inference that all the parties concerned died simultaneously then the circumstances are not such as to render it uncertain which of them survived the other or others, for it is certain that none survived the other or others. This, according to Goddard LJ is the literal construction of the plain words of the enactment. The other view is that when the circumstances are such that it cannot be ascertained that one of the deceased survived the other then the uncertainty which the section postulates exists and the statutory presumption applies. One reason why it cannot be ascertained that one survived the other may well be that the deaths occurred so closely in time that there is a high probability that they were practically simultaneous. . . . Having carefully weighed the arguments in support of each of these rival constructions I pronounce unhesitatingly in favour of the latter. . . . I would only add a few words regarding the term "uncertain" which occurs in the enactment and which was so much canvassed in the course of the argument. The basis of belief may range from mere conjecture through all degrees of probability to absolute demonstration—possibility, probability, certainty. In seeking to arrive at a conclusion in fact in ordinary human affairs the law rejects mere possibility as an insufficient basis of proof, but on the other hand it does not exact absolute or mathematical proof. It is content to proceed upon probability, if it is sufficient, and the test of sufficient probability is that the direct evidence, with all legitimate inferences, is such as ought to satisfy the mind of a person of reasonable intelligence. But the result of a decision on a question of fact by a judge or a jury is not certainty. It is finality, not certainty. Your Lordships in considering a verdict of a jury on a question of fact have often declared that it is not to be disturbed because there was evidence on which a reasonable person could so find but that it is not to be taken that your Lordships would have reached the same conclusion. Can it be said that in such circumstances the fact found by the jury has been ascertained with certainty? It has been determined with finality in law, but not with certainty in fact. In my opinion the legislature in employing the word "uncertain" in the section which the House has to construe was not thinking of the kind of certainty with which the law has to be content but was using the word in its ordinary acceptation as denoting a reasonable element of doubt.' *Hickman v Peacey* [1945] AC 304 at 321–324, HL, per Lord Macmillan

UNCERTAINTY

'In making his submissions, counsel for the appellants used two phrases which have begun to fascinate Chancery lawyers. They are "conceptual uncertainty" and "evidential uncertainty". After a little probing, I began to understand a little about them. "Conceptual uncertainty" arises when a testator or settlor makes a bequest or gift on a condition in which he has not expressed himself clearly enough. He has used words which are too vague and indistinct for a court to apply. They are not sufficiently precise. So the court discards the condition as meaningless. It makes it of no effect, at any rate when it is a condition subsequent. "Evidential uncertainty" arises where the testator or settlor, in making the condition, has expressed himself clearly enough. The words are sufficiently precise. But the court has difficulty in applying them in any given situation because of the uncertainty of the facts. It has to resort to extrinsic evidence to discover the facts, for instance to ascertain those whom the testator or settlor intended to benefit and those whom he did not. Evidential uncertainty never renders the condition meaningless. The court never discards it on that account. It applies the condition as best it can on the evidence available.' *Re Tuck's Settlement Trusts, Public Trustees v Tuck* [1978] 1 All ER 1047 at 1051, CA, per Lord Denning MR

[Lord Denning went on to say that the dichotomy between the two phrases was illogical and to be deplored, merely serving to defeat the intention of the testator or settlor.]

UNCHASTITY

[Under the Slander of Women Act 1891, s 1, words which impute 'unchastity' to a woman or girl do not require special damage to render them actionable.] 'It is contended for the defendant that an imputation of lesbianism is not an imputation of unchastity within the Act of 1891, the argument being that the term "unchastity" in the Act is limited to unchastity between a woman and a man, and excludes immorality between persons of the same sex. . . . The true approach to the construction of "unchastity" seems to me to appear when the question is put: "What imputations on a woman, qua woman, in the sphere of sexual morality, are grave enough to be actionable without proof of pecuniary loss or so likely to cause pecuniary loss as not to call for such proof?" Can any distinction be drawn on this basis between adultery and fornication, on the one hand, and unnatural relations with other women, on the other, except that the imputation of the latter is, if anything, more wounding, more likely to excite abhorrence on the part of average reasonable people, more likely to spoil the victim's prospects of marriage? No such distinction can, in my view, be drawn. Whatever value, high or low, is ascribed to chastity to-day, it does seem to me to be nothing less than fantastic to say of a woman: "She is a notorious lesbian, but she is perfectly chaste." In the absence of any judicial guidance or authority as to the meaning of "unchaste" or "chaste" in this connection, dictionaries can be consulted and their definitions have been cited in this case. Almost all, under the term "unchastity", include "impurity", "lasciviousness", and the like. Can anyone doubt that lesbianism is covered by such terms? In my view, the imputation of lesbianism is an imputation of unchastity within the Act of 1891.' *Kerr v Kennedy* [1942] 1 KB 409 at 411–413, per Asquith J

UNCONDITIONALLY

[An order was made by consent that the respondent should pay to the petitioner a certain sum per annum for maintenance 'unconditionally'.] 'Mr Russell's [counsel's] subsidiary argument was on the word "unconditionally" in the order. He said it means "irrespective of a change of means", and was for the purpose of doing away with the statutory proviso [repealed] of the Judicature (Consolidation) Act 1925, s 190(2). But the natural meaning seems to me to be a consent to pay £300 a year free of tax without imposing any conditions on the other party. For the purposes of the law one must take the natural, first, and usual meaning of the word—that is, without conditions—conditions well known to practitioners which might have been imposed.' *Smith v Smith* (1931) 145 LT 23 at 25, per Langton J

UNCONSCIONABLE BARGAIN

As part of the jurisdiction to grant relief against constructive fraud, courts of equity have acted to protect persons in cases in which it was apparent, from the intrinsic nature and subject of the bargain itself, that it was one which no man in his senses and not under delusion would make on the one hand, and no honest and fair man would accept on the other; in fact, an inequitable and unconscionable bargain.

The principle has now been extended to all cases in which the parties contracting do not meet on equal terms, and is not limited to expectant heirs but applies to all persons under pressure without adequate protection, and the onus of supporting the transaction is thrown on the person benefiting. In determining whether the bargain is a hard one, the whole transaction has to be considered and not only the price. (18 Halsbury's Laws (4th edn) para 344)

UNCONTROLLABLE

Australia 'It is not necessary for us to give an exhaustive definition of "uncontrollable", or one which will fit all cases which may arise. It is sufficient to say that it means not adequately controllable by those entitled to exercise control.' *Skeer v Byrne* [1929] SASR 378 at 384, per Richards J

UNDER

Australia 'In one sense every act of a body which is the creature of statute may be said to be done "under" or by virtue of the statute creating it. In another sense the acts of such a body may be said to be done "under" or by virtue of some provision granting a general jurisdiction to act in relation to a variety of matters. But the expression is also quite commonly used in relation to a particular act, when the general jurisdiction to act is assumed, to designate the more particular power to do that particular act. It is rash to attempt to substitute a different expression for the more simple and usual one used, but in this connection "under" is perhaps more aptly translated by the expression "pursuant to" than by the phrase "by virtue of". It is necessary to have regard to the context to determine in which sense the word is used.' *R v Clyne, ex p Harrap* [1941] VLR 200 at 201, per O'Bryan J

UNDER COMMAND *See* COMMAND

UNDER HAND

'One argument that has been urged on the part of the plaintiff, is, that no document can require a stamp unless it be signed, the words of the Stamp Act [Stat (1815) 55 Geo 3, c 184 (repealed)] imposing a duty upon any "agreement, or any minute or memorandum of an agreement, made in England, under hand only". It appears to me, however, that that is not the meaning of the statute, but that the legislature, in using that expression, merely intended to denote instruments under hand only,—that is, not under seal,—in opposition to instruments under seal.' *Chadwick v Clarke* (1845) 1 CB 700 at 707, 708, per Coltman J

[A testatrix, by her trust-disposition and settlement and codicils, directed, inter alia, that her trustees should give effect to any 'informal writing under my hand'. She left an unsubscribed holograph writing of subsequent date which began 'I (name in full) wish', and concluded 'written by my own hand', followed by the date and place of writing.] 'In this case we are instructed by the testatrix to look for an informal writing "under my hand". We are of opinion that the document before us [the unsubscribed holography writing], being unsigned, does not answer to this description. According to the normal acceptation of the words, a document "under my hand" means a document signed (i.e., subscribed) by me; and an informal document "under my hand" means a document signed by me which is defective either in form or expression, or in solemnities of authentication, or in both. For the purpose of determining whether a document is "under the hand" of the granter, the signature is more than a mere formality or solemnity, and its unique significance as the recognised and indispensable token of deliberate authorisation of a written document, whether formal or informal, has long been accepted by common usage.' *Waterson's Trustees v St Giles Boys Club* 1943 SC 369 at 374, per the Lord Justice-Clerk (Cooper)

New Zealand 'If authority be needed for the view that a requirement in a statute that a notice "under the hand" of the person giving it does not need the actual physical signature of such person it will be found in *Re Diptford Parish Lands* [[1934] Ch 151, 161]. . . . As [counsel] pointed out, there is no prescribed form of notice and the whole object of the demand was to warn the debtor of an impending petition and accordingly whether the notice be signed by the creditor personally or by another on his behalf adds nothing to the value of the notice.' *Bateman Television Ltd v Coleridge Finance Co Ltd* [1969] NZLR 794 at 803, per North P

New Zealand 'For myself I am of the opinion that in the case of a real person who is a creditor it is sufficient if, for instance, his duly appointed attorney executes the notice; and indeed that the words of the subsection are apt to include a notice under the hand of any agent sufficiently shewn to have authority from the creditor company to sign the same.' Ibid at 812, per Turner J

UNDER HAND AND SEAL

Australia 'The requirement, in s 62 [of the Justices Act 1902–1986 (NSW)], that a summons be under the hand and seal of the justice is not to be disregarded. To be under his hand means, I take it, that it must bear his signature. At common law one person may authorise another to sign a document for him. But when a document is required by statute to be under a man's hand or signed by him what is ordinarily meant is that he must personally sign it, with his name or his mark, by a pen or by a stamp. So much for "under his hand". Now for the words "and seal". They mean that the seal must be "his", the seal of the justice affixed to the document. Such a seal may be wax, or a wafer, or a rubber stamp or any other impression put on as a seal. But anything that is to be his seal upon a summons must be put there by the justice, or put there by his authority and adopted by him as his seal when he issues the summons. It must be something affixed or added to the document as an incident of its being issued. Neither it nor the signature can be something already printed on a blank form before it was filled in, signed and issued.' *Electronic Rentals Pty Ltd v Anderson* (1971) 124 CLR 27 at 42, 43, per Windeyer J

UNDER PROTEST

'It is said, that the money was received by the petitioner, and the receipt given "under protest". These words are often used on these occasions, but they have no distinct technical meaning, unless accompanied with a statement of circumstances, showing that they were used by way of notice or protest, reserving to the party, by reason of such circumstances, a right to a taxation, notwithstanding such payment. The words have no distinct meaning by themselves, and amount to nothing, unless explained by the proceedings and circumstances.' *Re Massey* (1845) 8 Beav 458 at 462, per Langdale MR

UNDER WAY

'As every one knows, vessels when fishing are attached to their nets. They are not then under way; that is, they do not enjoy the same liberty of movement as they would when under way. They are then much more like a vessel at anchor than like a vessel under way.' *The Dunelm* (1884) 51 LT 214 at 218, CA, per Brett MR

[Certain navigation rules provided that a sailing vessel 'under way', or being towed, should carry certain side lights.] 'If the *Marian* was at the time of the collision a sailing vessel under way, within the meaning of rule 6, then she ought to have been carrying side lights. But I am clearly of opinion that she was not; her mast had been lowered to enable her to go under the bridges, and it would not have been raised till she had passed through London Bridge.' *The Indian Chief* (1888) 14 PD 24 at 25, per Butt J

'It seems to me that only by a violent construction of the last paragraph of the preliminary article of the Regulations [Sea Regulations 1897 (revoked; but cf the Collision Regulations (Ships and Seaplanes on the Water) and Signals of Distress (Ships) Order 1965)] can the defendants' contention be maintained. That paragraph is: "a vessel is 'under way' within the meaning of these rules when she is not at anchor, or made fast to the shore, or aground". It has been contended that the tug in this case was at anchor because, if the barque was at anchor, as the tug was attached to her, the tug is to be treated as using the barque's anchor as her own anchor, and, therefore, at anchor too, and should have had her anchor lights up; but the tug in this case was not at her own anchor. Was she then under the control of the ship's anchor? I think not. She was in fact moving the ship up to her anchor, and was under way for that purpose just as much as if she had been made fast ahead and was towing her by means of a towing hawser.' *The Romance* [1901] P 15 at 18, 19, per Gorell Barnes J

'I do not think there is any authority which would lead me to the conclusion that a vessel which is still fast by a rope forward to a dredger and controlled by that rope is to be regarded as a vessel under way within the [Port of London] rules.' *The Dagmar* (1929) 141 LT 271 at 273, per Hill J

See, generally, 43 Halsbury's Laws (4th edn) para 884

UNDERGROUND ROOM

In this section 'underground room' means any room which, or any part of which, is so situate that at least half its height, measured from the floor to the ceiling, is below the surface of the footway of the adjoining street or of the ground adjoining or nearest to the room. (Factories Act 1961, s 69)

UNDERGROUND STRATA

'Underground strata' means strata subjacent to the surface of any land, and (subject and without prejudice to s 2(2) of this Act [which deals with water in wells and boreholes]) any reference to water contained in any underground strata is a reference to water so contained otherwise than in a sewer, pipe, reservoir, tank or other underground works constructed in any such strata. (Water Resources Act 1963, s 135)

UNDERLEASE

The expression 'underlease' [in provisions as to forfeiture for non-payment of rent] includes an agreement for an underlease where the underlessee has become entitled to have his underlease granted. (County Courts Act 1984, s 140)

'An underlessee is not an assignee within the statute [(1540)] 32 Hen 8, c 34, s 2 [repealed]. We all know that this is the reason why a mortgage of a lease is usually made by way of underlease in order that the mortgagee may not become liable to perform the lessee's covenants. An assignment of a term differs from an underlease in that the former means parting with the whole and the latter with only a portion of the lessee's interest. An assignment of a lease must necessarily embrace all the estate of the assignor: Preston on Conveyancing, 3rd edn, vol ii, p 124.' *South of England Dairies Ltd v Baker* [1906] 2 Ch 631 at 638, per Joyce J

UNDERSTANDING

'It is difficult to say what an "understanding" means. I do not know a better word than "agreement" or "stipulation".' *Hill v Fox* (1859) 4 H & N 359 at 364, per Wightman J

[A solicitor wrote to a prospective client in the following terms: 'May we please take this opportunity of placing on record the understanding that all the legal work of and incidental to the completion of the development and grant of the leases shall be carried out by us.'] 'If, instead of using the vague word "understanding", he [the plaintiff] had said, "we understand that it is your present intention to instruct us as and when matters arise", and Mr Bilton had accepted that, then clearly a legal claim would not have arisen when the defendants decided to make other arrangements, and in my judgment that was in truth the result of these letters. Mr Lyon deliberately used the word "understanding", which, whatever it may mean, means something quite different from a binding legal contract and I think that, at the most, these letters achieved something in the nature of a gentleman's agreement, or extracted from Mr Bilton confirmation of a present intention on his part to instruct Mr Lyon to do this legal work as and when it arose. To seek to hold the defendants to more than that is, in my view, not legally sound, and it is quite unnecessary to consider whether it would be ethically laudable or desirable to do so.' *Milner (J H) & Son v Percy Bilton Ltd* [1966] 2 All ER 894 at 898, 899, per Fenton Atkinson J

'It was strenuously argued that the use of the word "understood" or "understanding" denoted a transaction binding in honour only. This argument is based on a fallacy. When persons enter into a business arrangement . . . the presumption is that they intend that their business arrangements shall be legally enforceable; but the language that the parties have employed, whether oral or written, may show, either expressly or as a matter of the proper inference to be drawn from their language and of all the relevant circumstances, that they did not intend their arrangements to be legally enforceable. The word "understanding" no more and no less than the word "agreement" is appropriate to express a legally binding agreement. Thus, if A agrees to do something on the understanding (another equally familiar phrase is "on the footing") that another party will do something else that is prima facie evidence of a legally binding agreement unless the rest of the language used or the surrounding circumstances point to a different conclusion.' *Campbell and Another (Trustees of Davies's Educational Trust) v Inland Revenue Comrs* [1968] 3 All ER 588 at 601, HL, per Lord Upjohn

UNDERTAKE

'If a solicitor commences a business on the faith of a general retainer, and in the belief that his client will adopt what he does, he cannot be heard to say that the business was not undertaken [within the Solicitors' Remuneration Order 1883, r 6 (see now the Solicitors' Remuneration Order 1972)] when he first did any work covered by the scale fee.' *Hester v Hester* (1887) 34 Ch D 607 at 617, CA, per Lindley LJ

'"Undertaking any business' I understand to mean not merely accepting the retainer, but rather entering upon the work, i.e. doing something in the matter for which he [a solicitor] would be entitled to make a charge; but if he does anything for which he is entitled to charge, it seems to me impossible to say that he has not undertaken the business, whether that charge is covered by the scale fee or not.' *Re Stewart* (1889) 41 Ch D 494 at 504, per Kay J

'In s 44 of the Act [Cinematograph Films Act 1938 (repealed; see now the Films Act 1985, Sch 1)] the expression "maker" is defined as meaning, in relation to the film, "the person by whom the arrangements necessary for the making of the film are undertaken". This is, perhaps, a strange collocation of words which might in other circumstances give rise to some difficulty of interpretation. "Undertake" means, I think, "be responsible for", especially in the financial sense, but also generally.' *Re F G (Films) Ltd* [1953] 1 All ER 615 at 616, per Vaisey J

Canada 'The word "undertook" or "undertake" has various meanings depending upon the context in which it is used. If it be said that a businessman "undertook" a particular business operation, the word "undertook" indicates only that he embarked upon that operation. If it be said that a solicitor gave an "undertaking" to another solicitor, one does not think primarily in terms of an obligation enforceable by action in the court. Where, however, a statutory provision speaks . . . of an agreement under which a corporation "undertook" to incur expenses, there is no doubt in my mind that the statute is speaking of a legally enforceable agreement to incur those expenses.' *Falconbridge Nickel Mines Ltd v Minister of National Revenue* [1965] CTC 82 at 88, Ex Ct, per Cattanach J

UNDERTAKERS *See* STATUTORY UNDERTAKERS

UNDERTAKERS' WORKS

In this Act the expression 'undertakers' works' means works (including works executed or to be executed on behalf of the Crown) for any purpose other than road purposes, being works of any of the following kinds, that is to say—

(a) Placing apparatus.
Inspecting, maintaining, adjusting, repairing, altering or renewing apparatus.
Changing the position of apparatus or removing it.

(b) Breaking up or opening a street or controlled land for the purposes of works mentioned in paragraph (a) of this subsection, and tunnelling or boring under a street or controlled land for those purposes, breaking up or opening a sewer, drain or tunnel for those purposes, and other works requisite for or incidental to those purposes.

(Public Utilities Street Works Act 1950, s 1)

UNDERTAKING *See also* STATUTORY UNDERTAKERS

(1) In this Act the expression 'undertaking' means any undertaking by way of trade or business, whether or not the trade or business is carried on for profit; and the exercise and performance by a local or other public authority of the powers and duties of that authority shall be treated as a trade or business of that authority.

(2) Where an undertaking is wholly or partly carried on by means of branches situated at several premises, the Board of Trade or other competent authority [now the Secretary of State for Trade and Industry] may agree with the persons carrying on the undertaking that for the purposes of all or any of the provisions of this Act a separate undertaking shall be deemed to be carried on at all or any of those branches by the branch manager or such other person as may be specified in the agreement.

Any such agreement may contain such supplemental provisions as may be expedient for giving effect thereto and shall continue in force for such term and shall be subject to such provisions as to variation and revocation as may be specified in the agreement. (Statistics of Trade Act 1947, s 17(1), (2))

'Undertaking' includes any trade, business or profession, and, in relation to a public or local authority, includes any of the powers or duties of that authority, and, in relation to any other body of persons, whether corporate or unincorporate, includes any of the activities of that body. (Radioactive Substances Act 1960, s 19(1))

[Section 75 of a railway company's Act enabled the company to borrow money on the credit of the 'undertaking'.] 'The question is, whether, in the fair meaning of the 75th sect, the word "undertaking" can be considered as embracing land. I think not; and no rule of law goes the length of saying, that you are to add words to aid such a construction, or give to those employed a meaning which they do not bear.' *Doe d Myatt v St Helen's & Runcorn Gap Rly Co* (1841) 2 Ry & Can Cas 756, at 761, per Williams J

'The form of the instrument is not an assignment, but a charge; the company charge the undertaking, and all sums of money arising therefrom, and all estate, right, title, and interest of the company therein, with payment of the principal sum and interest. . . . I have no hesitation in saying that in this particular case, and having regard to the state of this particular company, the word "undertaking" had reference to all the property of the company, not only which existed at the date of the debenture, but which might afterwards become the property of the company. And I take the object and meaning of the debenture to be this, that the word "undertaking" necessarily infers that the company will go on, and that the debenture holder could not interfere until either the interest which was due was unpaid, or until the period had arrived for the payment of the principal, and the principal was unpaid. . . . I hold that under these debentures they [the debenture holders] have a charge upon all property of the company, past and future, by the term "undertaking", and that they stand in a position superior to that of the general creditors, who can touch nothing until they are paid.' *Re Panama, New Zealand & Australian Royal Mail Co* (1870) 5 Ch App 318 at 322, 323, per Giffard LJ

[The Railway Companies Act 1867, s 4, provides (inter alia) that a person who has recovered judgment against a railway company may obtain the appointment of a receiver of the 'undertaking'.] 'The object of the section was to prevent creditors of the railway company from interfering with the railway, but not to prevent the creditors from obtaining any unpaid calls which they might have a right to get, and therefore a receiver of the "undertaking" means the railway and works as a going concern, and includes the stock and everything else.' *Re Birmingham & Lichfield Junction Rly Co* (1881) 50 LJ Ch 594 at 596, per Jessel MR

'The Railway Companies Act 1867 gives no interpretation of what is meant by the "undertaking of the company", and the natural and proper interpretation appears to me to be that which the company by its constitution, and having regard to all its Acts of Parliament, is authorised to undertake and to do.' *Re East & West India Dock Co* (1888) 38 Ch D 576 at 593, CA, per Cotton LJ

Australia '"Undertaking" is a word of variable meaning. . . . Basically the idea which it conveys is that of a business or enterprise. . . . The word "undertaking", like the word "business" . . . will commonly embrace, when used dispositively, the property or some property which is used in connection with the undertaking, and it may be too, the debts and liabilities, or some debts and liabilities, which have arisen in relation thereto.' *Reference under Electricity Commission (Balmain Electric Light Co Purchase) Act* 1950 [1957] SR(NSW) 100 at 128, per Sugerman J

Australia 'Frequently the word "undertaking" is used in circumstances where it could be interchanged with either the word business or enterprise and with varying shades of meaning. Sometimes it is used alone, sometimes by way of distinction from the assets of the owner and sometimes as a synonym for business. Sometimes it is used to embrace the property which is used in connexion with the undertaking as well as the debts and liabilities which have arisen in relation thereto. For example, in relation to the provision of electrical power or the supply of a public service, it can refer either to the business of the supply or service or to its assets or both. Its meaning to a large extent will depend upon the circumstances and the context in which it is used.' *Top of the Cross Pty Ltd v Federal Comr of Taxation* (1980) 50 FLR 19 at 36, per Woodward J

UNDERWOODS

'It has been said that all wood comes within the description either of timber or underwood, and therefore, that as firs and larches are not timber, they must be considered as underwood. . . . It may, however, be observed, that if all wood which is not timber, be underwood, it would follow, that horse-chestnuts, limes, plane-trees, and aspens would come within that description. Yet, surely, it would be a perversion of language to call such trees underwood. Generally speaking, that term is applied to a species of wood which grows expeditiously and sends up many shoots from one stool, the root remaining perfect from which the shoots are cut, and producing new shoots, and so yielding a succession of profits.' *R v Ferrybridge (Inhabitants)* (1823) 1 B & C 375 at 380–384, per Bayley J

'The firs and larches mentioned in this case are not saleable underwoods within the meaning of those words, as used in the 43 Eliz [Poor Relief Act 1601]. The word "underwood" must be there taken to be used in its popular sense, unless it be shown to have been used differently by the legislature in that or other statutes. After great research upon this subject, Mr Milner has not been able to show that it has been so used by the legislature in any other sense. According to its popular meaning it signifies coppice, as distinguished from hautbois.' Ibid at 385, 386, per Holroyd J

'The first question is, whether this wood is underwood? Small wood, never likely to be used for timber, may be called underwood; so may plantations of timber trees, not intended for permanent growth, but to be cut at stated intervals for use as hop poles, or for other similar purposes. Here the poles were never meant for growth as timber, and may therefore be properly called underwood.' *R v Narberth North (Inhabitants)* (1839) 9 Ad & El 815 at 818, 819, per Littledale J

UNDERWRITING

'Underwriting' usually means agreeing to take the number of shares specified in an underwriting letter or agreement to the extent that the public or other persons do not subscribe for them before a fixed date. (7 Halsbury's Laws (4th edn) para 190)

'Underwriter' includes any person named in a policy or other contract of insurance as liable to pay or contribute towards the payment of the sum secured by the policy or contract. (Insurance Companies Act 1982, s 96(1))

'From the evidence which has been given as to the meaning of the expression "underwriting" as applied to shares, it appears that an "underwriting" agreement means an agreement entered into before the shares are brought before the public, that in the event of the public not taking up the whole of them, or the number mentioned in the agreement, the underwriter will, for an agreed commission, take an allotment of such part of the shares as the public has not applied for. That is what is meant when it is said that a person has agreed to underwrite a certain number of shares in a company.' *Re Licensed Victuallers' Mutual Trading Assocn, ex p Audain* (1889) 42 Ch D 1 at 5, 6, CA, per Cotton LJ

'To underwrite as applied to shares means to take and pay for them if the public do not. . . . The obligation to underwrite shares involves an obligation to take at par so many as others do not take. The option to take at par is an advantage conferred on the underwriter, and entitles him to take at par more than he may be ultimately obliged to take. Effect can only be given to this option by holding that the underwriter is to have the opportunity of exercising it before other people are invited to take shares, which might render it impossible for him to have them.' *Re London-Paris Financial Mining Corpn Ltd* (1897) 13 TLR 569 at 570, 571, CA, per Lindley LJ

United States The term 'underwriter' means any person who has purchased from an issuer with a view to, or offers or sells for an issuer in connection with, the distribution of any security, or participates or has a direct or indirect participation in any such undertaking, or participates or has a participation in the direct or indirect underwriting of any such undertaking; but such term shall not include a person whose interest is limited to a commission from an underwriter or dealer not in excess of the usual and customary distributors' or sellers' commission. As used in this paragraph the term "issuer" shall include, in addition to an issuer, any person directly or indirectly controlling or controlled by the issuer, or any person under direct or indirect common control with the issuer. (Securities Act of 1933, s 2(11))

UNDUE

Undue election

Australia [The Elections Act (Qld) 1915, s 103 (repealed; see now the Elections Act 1983 (Qld), s 135(1) gives a person the right to present a petition complaining of the 'undue election' or return of a member.] 'The Act contains no definition of the expression "undue election" but the words take their meaning from the history of disputed elections. An "undue election" is one in where there has been a departure from the prescribed method of election or one in which there has been misbehaviour or management of a kind which history has shown may result in the selection of a candidate otherwise than by the will of the constituency. The expression does not apply to an election in which the prescribed method of election has been followed but that method is unlawful.' *Re Surfers' Paradise Election Petition* [1975] Qd R 114 at 119, 120, per Dunn J

UNDUE HARDSHIP *See also* HARDSHIP

[The Arbitration Act 1950, s 27, provides that where the terms of an agreement to refer future disputes to arbitration provide for claims to be barred unless the proper steps are taken within a time fixed by the agreement, and a dispute arises, the High Court, if it is of opinion that in the circumstances of the case 'undue hardship' would otherwise be caused, may extend the time for such period as it thinks proper.] 'What, then, is the meaning of "undue hardship"? "Undue", it is said, . . . means something which is not merited by the conduct of the claimant. That may be right. If the result of claimants being perhaps a day late is so oppressive, so burdensome, as to be altogether out of proportion to the fault, I am inclined to think that one may well say that there is undue hardship.' *Watney, Combe, Reid & Co Ltd v E M Dower & Co Ltd* [1956] 2 Lloyd's Rep 325 at 330, CA, per Singleton LJ

'It does appear that in the past the courts have been inclined to emphasise the word "undue", and to say that if a man does not read the contract and is a day or two late, it is a "hardship"; but it is not an "undue hardship", because it is his own fault. I cannot accept this narrow interpretation of the statute. These time-limit clauses used to operate most unjustly. Claimants used to find their claims barred when, by some oversight, they were only a day or two late. In order to avoid that injustice, the legislature intervened so as to enable the courts to extend the time whenever "in the circumstances of the case undue hardship would otherwise be caused". "Undue" there simply means excessive. It means greater hardship than the circumstances warrant. Even though a claimant has been at fault himself, it is an undue hardship on him if the consequences are out of proportion to his fault.' *Liberian Shipping Corporation v A King & Sons Ltd* [1967] 1 All ER 934 at 938, CA, per Lord Denning MR

Australia 'For a hardship to be "undue" it must be shown, in my opinion, that the particular burden to the applicant to have to observe or perform the requirement is out of proportion to the nature of the requirement itself and the benefit which the applicant would derive from compliance with it.' *Re Walsh* [1944] VLR 147 at 153, per O'Bryan J

UNDUE INFLUENCE

A contract may be avoided or set aside at the instance of one of the parties to it on the ground that his consent thereto was obtained by undue influence.

Undue influence may be defined, for this purpose, as the unconscientious use by one person of power possessed by him over another in order to induce the other to enter into a contract. (9 Halsbury's Laws (4th edn) para 298)

A party to a transaction, though consenting to it, may not give a free consent because he is exposed to such influence from the other party as to deprive him of the free use of his judgment. In such a case equity will set the transaction aside, and if property has passed will order restitution, and if necessary follow it into the hands of innocent third parties. The evidence may show that there was actual undue influence in the particular case, but in certain relations the existence of undue influence is presumed and then the party seeking to uphold the transaction must give evidence rebutting the presumption. (16 Halsbury's Laws (4th edn) para 1227)

A will or part of a will may be set aside as having been obtained by undue influence. If the execution of the will is not in dispute the party alleging undue influence has the right to begin, and must discharge the burden of proof by clear evidence that the influence was in fact exercised. To constitute undue influence there must be coercion: pressure of whatever character, whether acting on the fears or the hopes, if so exerted as to overpower the volition without convincing the judgment, is a species of restraint under which no valid will can be made.

A person may exercise an unbounded influence over another, which may be a very bad influence, without its being undue influence in the legal sense of the word. Undue influence may be found against a person who had died before the execution of the will, on the ground that the testatrix was under that person's complete control until his death, and thereby rendered incapable of making a fresh will free from such undue influence. (17 Halsbury's Laws (4th edn) para 911)

Cases in which a gift has been set aside on the ground of undue influence may be divided into two classes. First, there are those cases where the court has been satisfied that the gift was the result of actual influence expressly used for the purpose. Secondly, there are those cases in which the relationship between the donor and donee at the time of or shortly before the making of the gift has been such as to raise a presumption that the donee had influence over the donor. In this second class of case the onus is on the donee to rebut the presumption by showing that the donor made the gift only after full, free and informed thought about it.

The first class of cases may be considered as depending on the principle that no one is allowed to retain any benefit arising from his own fraud or wrongful act. In the second class of cases the court interferes, not on the ground that any wrongful act has in fact been committed by the donee, but on the ground of public policy, and to prevent relations which existed between the parties and the influence arising from them from being abused, in circumstances where proof of the actual exercise of undue influence may be difficult if not impossible to establish. (18 Halsbury's Laws (4th edn) para 330)

(1) A person shall be guilty of a corrupt practice if he is guilty of undue influence.

(2) A person shall be guilty of undue influence—

(a) if he, directly or indirectly, by himself or by any other person on his behalf, makes use of or threatens to make use of any force, violence or restraint, or inflicts or threatens to inflict, by himself or by any other person, any temporal or spiritual injury, damage, harm or loss upon or against any person in order to induce or compel that person to vote or refrain from voting, or on account of that person having voted or refrained from voting; or

(b) if, by abduction, duress or any fraudulent device or contrivance, he impedes or prevents the free exercise of the franchise by an elector or proxy for an elector, or thereby compels, induces or prevails upon an elector or proxy for an elector either to vote or to refrain from voting.

(Representation of the People Act 1983, s 115(2))

'It is said that . . . jurymen, not being men with legal minds, are extremely likely to fall into great error, and might think undue influence was established where a man who was not of strong mind, united to a woman of very strong mind, should be led to devise away large family estates from his own relations to hers, whereas in truth that would not of itself be undue influence according to the construction which the law would put upon that term. Undue influence, in order to render a will void, must be an influence which can justly be described, by a person looking at the matter judicially, to have caused the execution of a paper pretending to express a testator's mind, but which really did not express his mind, but expressed something else, something which he did not really mean. . . . I am prepared to say that influence, in order to be undue within the meaning of any rule of law which would make it sufficient to vitiate a will, must be an influence exercised either by coercion or fraud. . . . In order to come to the conclusion that a will has been obtained by coercion, it is not necessary to establish that actual violence has been used or even threatened. . . . Imaginary terrors may have been created sufficient to deprive him [the testator] of free agency. . . . So as to fraud. If a wife, by falsehood, raises prejudices in the mind of her husband against those who would be the natural objects of his bounty, and by contrivance keeps him from intercourse with his relatives . . . such contrivance may, perhaps, be equivalent to positive fraud. . . . It is, however, extremely difficult to state in the abstract what acts will constitute undue influence. . . . it is sufficient to say, that allowing a fair latitude of construction, they must range themselves under one or other of these heads—coercion or fraud.' *Boyse v Rossborough, Boyse v Colclough* (1857) 6 HL Cas 2 at 33, 34, 48, 49, per Lord Cranworth LC

'It is obvious that when a mob has possession of a town, and beats those who come to the polling booth, or otherwise intimidates them, that is plainly exercising intimidation, and is undue influence, and in my opinion it is the very worst kind of undue influence. It is very bad for a master to threaten and dismiss his men: it is very bad in a landlord to eject his tenant. All these are very bad, improper acts, but they are justifiable acts if it were not for the effect they would produce upon the freedom of election, because they have a right to do so if it were not done to interfere with the freedom of election.' *Stafford (Borough) Case, Chawner v Meller* (1869) 21 LT 210 at 211, per Blackburn J

'We are all familiar with the use of the word "influence"; we say that one person has an unbounded influence over another, and we speak of evil influences and good influences, but it is not because one person has unbounded influence over another that therefore when exercised, even though it may be very bad indeed, it is undue influence in the legal sense of the word. To give you some illustrations of what I mean, a young man may be caught in the toils of a harlot, who makes use of her influence to induce him to make a will in her favour, to the exclusion of his relatives. It is unfortunately quite natural that a man so entangled should yield to that influence and confer large bounties on the person with whom he has been brought into such relation; yet the law does not attempt to guard against those contingencies. A man may be the companion of another, and may encourage him in evil courses, and so obtain what is called an undue influence over him, and the consequence may be a will made in his favour. But that again, shocking as it is, perhaps even worse than the other, will not amount to undue influence. To be undue influence in the eye of the law there must be—to sum it up in a word—coercion.' *Wingrove v Wingrove* (1885) 11 PD 81 at 82, per Hannen P

'The expression "undue influence" is, to my mind, one of ambiguous purport. It is not confined to those cases in which the influence is exerted to secure a benefit for the person exerting it, but extends also to cases in which a person of imperfect judgment is placed or places himself under the direction of one possessing not only greater experience but also such force as that which is inherent in such a relation as that between a father and his own child.' *Bullock v Lloyds Bank Ltd* [1954] 3 All

ER 726 at 729, per Vaisey J; see also [1955] Ch 317

'The doctrine of undue influence . . . merely arises out of the fact that, while equity approves of gifts by a father to a child, and therefore invented the doctrine of presumption of advancement, so on the other hand it dislikes and distrusts gifts by a child to a parent, and therefore invented the presumption of undue influence. Both these presumptions merely mean, in our opinion, that in the absence of evidence, or if the evidence on each side be evenly balanced, in the first case equity will presume that the parent who puts property in a child's name intends to make a gift or give a benefit to the child, while on the other hand money or property passing from the child to the parent cannot be retained by the latter, because it is assumed that so unnatural a transaction would have been brought about by undue use of the natural influence that a parent has over a child, and of the filial obedience which a child owes to his parent. Both presumptions may be rebutted; each is in truth a convenient device in aid of decisions on facts often lost in obscurity, whether owing to the lapse of time or the death of the parties.' *Re Pauling's Settlement Trusts, Younghusband v Coutts & Co* [1963] 3 All ER 1 at 9, CA, per cur.

'What has to be proved to raise the presumption of undue influence is first a gift so substantial (or doubtless otherwise of such a nature) that it cannot prima facie be reasonably accounted for on the ground of the ordinary motives on which ordinary men act; and secondly, a relationship between donor and donee in which the donor has such confidence and trust in the donee as to place the donee in a position to exercise undue influence over the donor in making such a gift. This is just plain common sense to which the ordinary man in the street would readily arrive. In order to provide remedies for abuses of relations of trust and confidence where from the nature of the relationship proof of abuse might be difficult, if not impossible, lawyers established a strong foundation for the presumption of undue influence on public policy. But the courts have refused, rightly in my respectful opinion, to define either undue influence or such relationships of trust and confidence. To do otherwise would be to assume a power of divination more than human, and might exclude from relief for undue influence cases where such relief should readily be available to serve the purpose of the law. Thus both undue influence and those relationships of trust and confidence which raise the presumption are left, unlimited by definition, wide open for identification on the facts and in all the circumstances of each particular case as it arises. As the law has been developed and become established, the presumption seems to me in general at any rate to amount substantially in practice now to no more than the passing of the onus of proof where the amount (or nature) of the gift and the relationship of trust and confidence would, in the ordinary course of a trial, pass, independently of any special formulation of the raising of the presumption.' *Re Craig (decd), Meneces v Middleton* [1970] 2 All ER 390 at 395, 396, per Ungoed-Thomas J

'There is no precisely defined law setting limits to the equitable jurisdiction of a court to relieve against undue influence. This is the world of doctrine, not of neat and tidy rules. The courts of equity have developed a body of learning enabling relief to be granted where the law has to treat the transaction as unimpeachable unless it can be held to have been procured by undue influence. It is the unimpeachability at law of a disadvantageous transaction which is the starting point from which the court advances to consider whether the transaction is the product merely of one's own folly or of the undue influence exercised by another. A court in the exercise of this equitable jurisdiction is a court of conscience. Definition is a poor instrument when used to determine whether a transaction is or is not unconscionable: this is a question which depends on the particular facts of the case.' *National Westminster Bank plc v Morgan* [1985] 1 All ER 821 at 831, HL, per Lord Scarman

Australia 'It cannot be said that there is [in the case under consideration] any direct evidence of the actual exercise of undue influence . . . but like any other matter of fact, this may be established by fair and reasonable inference from the established facts. It is a mistake to treat "undue influence" as being established by the mere proof that the relations of the parties were such that the one naturally relied upon the other for advice and that the other was in a position to dominate the will of the other. In such a case "influence" alone is established. Such influence may be used wisely and judiciously, but to make that influence "undue" it must be established that the dominant party has used that position to obtain some unfair advantage and to so cause injury to the person relying upon him. If confidential relationship be established, and if the transaction impeached be in itself unconscionable or unrighteous then the person in the position to dominate the other has the burden thrown upon him of establishing affirmatively that no domination was practised.' *Parbs v Garrett* [1941] SASR 1 at 2, 3, per Cleland J

UNDULY EMPHASISE

Australia [The Objectionable Literature Act 1954–1986 (Qld), s 5, provides that literature is objectionable if it 'unduly emphasises' matters of sex, horror, crime, etc.] 'The words "unduly emphasise" do not connote a mere failure in artistic construction, about which different minds might well disagree. They connote such a palpable overpresentment either of one such matter or of a combination of such matters that the mind of the susceptible reader is or will tend to be confined to that theme or combination . . . to such an extent that he is likely to be diverted from considering or prevented from appreciating ideas outside that theme or combination or from getting such theme or combination into something approaching a proper perspective of life and human conduct or on to a proper level of values in terms of ordinary good citizenship.' *Literature Board of Review v Invincible Press, ex p Invincible Press & Truth & Sportsman Ltd* [1955] St R Qd 525 at 563, per Townley J

Australia [The Police Offences Act 1958–1986 (Vic), s 164(1) (see now s 164(1)(b)) provides that the word 'obscene' includes 'unduly emphasising matters of sex'.] 'I accept for the purposes of my judgment the view of Martin J, in *Wavish's Case* [[1959] VR 57], that "unduly emphasising matters of sex" means dealing with them in a manner which offends against the standards of the community in which the article is published, distributed etc. It is for the court to ascertain those standards for itself. I agree that it is not to be narrow or puritanical and that it is to recognise that it must allow for many tastes and many degrees and standards of education and of refinement, and for the grave lack of them in some quarters. On the other hand, the court is not called upon to overlook or minimise what is really obscenity, merely in order supposedly to show its own judicial broadmindedness or tolerance or imperturbability or even cynicism.' *Mackay v Gordon and Gotch (Australasia) Ltd* [1959] VR 420 at 426, per Sholl J

UNENCUMBERED

Australia 'In my opinion, these words [unencumbered fee simple] denote an absolute or pure estate in fee simple in the subject land, free of any private conditions, limitations, restrictive covenants, or other inherent restrictions affecting the estate or the land, but subject, of course, to any laws of a general nature that affect the use or alienability of the land.' *CSR Ltd v Valuer-General* (Supreme Court of South Australia) at 55, per Wells J (unreported)

UNFAIR DEALING

'The Sales of Reversions Act 1867 [repealed; see now the Law of Property Act 1925, s 174] . . . provides that "No purchase made bona fide and without fraud and unfair dealing of any reversionary interest in real or personal estate shall hereafter be opened or set aside merely on the ground of undervalue." Now, to come within the meaning of the Act such a purchase must be made bona fide and without fraud or unfair dealing. . . . I rely upon those words "unfair dealing". Now, first of all, I consider that the very fact of an unfair, inadequate price having been given—not of a trifling inadequacy, but of a very substantial inadequacy—necessarily had to be considered on the question, Was the transaction without unfair dealing? I do not say you could always decide upon that fact that there was unfair dealing so as to take it out of the Act altogether, but certainly it is a very material consideration. The courts always treated, and until a plain Act of Parliament is passed reversing the rule they always must treat, the seller of a reversion as being fettered and bound, so it is very difficult to establish that a transaction with him is quite fair. . . . Where a man deals with an expectant heir, assisting him to keep the transaction secret, buying from him the reversion at half-price, allowing him to redeem only on the terms that he should pay somewhere about the real price—to call such a matter unfair is describing it very mildly.' *Brenchley v Higgins* (1900) 83 LT 751 at 751–753, CA, per Rigby LJ

UNFAIR DISMISSAL *See* DISMISSAL

UNFIT

'Unfit' means—

(a) in relation to buildings or works, or to land of which three-quarters or more of the value is attributable to building or works, unfit for the purpose for which those buildings or works were used or adapted for use immediately before the occurrence of the war damage in question, having regard to the class of tenant likely to occupy similar buildings or works which are not unfit for that purpose, to the standard of accommodation available at the material time, and to all other circumstances; and

(b) in relation to other land, unfit for any purpose for which the tenant can be reasonably expected to use the land, having regard to the terms of the lease under which it is held;

and the expression 'fit' shall be construed accordingly. (Landlord and Tenant (War Damage) Act 1939, s 24)

Canada 'A lot is not unfit for building purposes merely because the owner of it chooses to use it for some other purpose. . . . I think that the unfitness of a lot . . . is unsuitability for building purposes for any reason attributable to the land itself such as the nature, condition or situation of it.' *CPR v Scarborough (Township)* (1959) 19 DLR (2d) 393 at 401, 402, Ont CA, per Laidlaw JA

For human habitation

'This appeal raises several points upon the true construction of s 41 of the Manchester Corporation Waterworks and Improvements Act 1867. The section provides that in any case where it is certified to the corporation by the inspector of nuisances, or by any two medical practitioners, that a building or any part of a building is unfit for human habitation, the corporation may by their order, affixed conspicuously on such building or part of the building, declare that the same is not fit for human habitation, and shall not after a date therein to be specified be inhabited. . . . Can a house be, within the meaning of the section, "unfit for human habitation" for a reason extrinsic to itself; for example, because neighbouring buildings preclude the access of air and impair its proper ventilation? It was argued that a building could not be unfit for human habitation within the meaning of the section unless it was in itself, and without reference to surrounding circumstances, so unfit. I agree with the Court of Appeal that this construction cannot be maintained. The sole question in every case is whether the house is as a fact unfit for human habitation, and not in any case the cause of the unfitness.' *Hall v Manchester Corpn* (1915) 84 LJ Ch 732 at 741, 742, per Lord Parker

UNFORESEEN CIRCUMSTANCES

'It seems to me . . . that when one uses the expression "unforeseen circumstances" in relation to the frustration of the performance of a contract, one is really dealing with circumstances which are unprovided for, circumstances for which (and in the case of a written contract one only has to look at the document) the contract makes no provision.' *Tatem Ltd v Gamboa* [1939] 1 KB 132 at 138, per Goddard J

UNFORMED

New Zealand 'In the present case I do not think it can be said that Maungaraki Road was unformed at the relevant time. . . . It may be said that it was only partly formed, but if partly formed it cannot be said to be unformed.' *Jones v Lower Hutt City* [1966] NZLR 879 at 882, per McGregor J

UNFUNDED DEBT *See* NATIONAL DEBT

UNIFORM

[The appellants were arrested and charged with wearing a 'uniform' in a public place, contrary to the Public Order Act 1936, s 1(1).] 'It seems . . . that in deciding whether a person is wearing a uniform different considerations may apply according to whether he is alone or in company with others. If a man is seen walking down Whitehall wearing the uniform of a policeman or a soldier, it is unnecessary to prove that that is uniform of any sort because it is so universally recognised or known as being the clothing worn by a member of the Metropolitan Police or the Army, as the case may be, that it is described as uniform on that account, and judges can take judicial notice of the fact that it is uniform in that sense. If a man was seen walking down Whitehall wearing a black beret, that certainly would not be regarded as uniform unless evidence were called to show that that black beret, in conjunction with any other items appropriate to associate it, had been used and was recognised as the uniform of some body. In other words, the policeman or the soldier is accepted as wearing uniform without more ado, but the isolated man wearing a black beret is not to be regarded as wearing a uniform unless it is proved that the beret in its association has been recognised and is known as the uniform of some particular organisation, proof which would have to be provided by evidence in the usual way. In this case . . . eight men . . . were together. They were not seen in isolation. Where an article such as a beret is used in order to indicate that a group of men are together and in association, it seems to me that that article can be regarded as uniform without any proof that it has been previously used as such. The simple fact that a number of men deliberately adopted an identical article of attire justifies in my judgment the view that that article is uniform if it is adopted in such a way as to show that its adoption is for the purposes of showing association between the men in question. Subject always to the *de minimis* rule, I see no reason why the article or articles should cover the whole of the body or a major part of the body, as was argued at one point, or indeed should go beyond the existence of the beret by itself. In this case . . . the articles did go beyond the beret. They extended to the pullover, the dark glasses and the dark clothing, and I have no doubt at all in my own mind that those men wearing those clothes on that occasion were wearing uniform within the meaning of the Act.' *O'Moran v DPP, Whelan v DPP* [1975] 1 All ER 473 at 480, 481, per Lord Widgery CJ

UNINCORPORATED ASSOCIATION

[The Income and Corporation Taxes Act 1970, s 526(5) (repealed; see now the Income and Corporation Taxes Act 1988, s 832(1)) defined 'company' as any body corporate or 'unincorporated association', excluding partnerships and local authorities.] 'I infer that by "unincorporated association" in this context Parliament meant two or more persons bound together for one or more common purposes, not being business purposes, by mutual undertakings, each having mutual duties and obligations, in an organisation which has rules which identify in whom control of it and its funds rests and on what terms and which can be joined or left at will.' *Conservative and Unionist Central Office v Burrell (Inspector of Taxes)* [1982] 2 All ER 1 at 4, CA, per Lawton LJ

UNISSUED CAPITAL *See* CAPITAL

UNIT

New Zealand 'A "unit" imports . . . something which is a separate thing such as a single manufactured article though, of course, any single article, if accepted for transport as a separate article, would be a "unit".' *New Zealand Railways v Progressive Engineering Co Ltd* [1968] NZLR 1053 at 1056, per Tompkins J

UNIT TRUST

In the Prevention of Fraud (Investments) Act 1958, unless the context otherwise requires, 'unit trust scheme' means any arrangement made for the purpose, or having the effect, of providing facilities for the participation by persons, as beneficiaries under a trust, in profits or income arising from the acquisition, holding, management or disposal of securities or any other property whatsoever.

Normally, a unit trust is constituted by a trust deed made between managers, who are responsible for the selection within the limits prescribed by the trust deed of the portfolio of securities comprised in the trust fund, and trustees, who are responsible mainly for the safe custody of those securities and the collection and distribution of the income from them. Interests in a unit trust are usually known as 'units', and broadly speaking a unit holder has an interest in an undivided proportion of the securities and cash comprised in the trust fund equal to that which the number of units held by him bears to the total number of units in existence. The trust deed will generally provide for some or all of the following matters: investment limits; the creation and issue of further units; the repurchase of units by the managers; the liquidation of units; the collection and distribution to unit holders by the trustees of the income from the trust fund; the transfer of units; the remuneration of the managers and the trustees; and the duration of the trust. (45 Halsbury's Laws (4th edn) para 65)

'Unit' means, in relation to a unit trust scheme, any right or interest (described whether as a unit or otherwise) which may be acquired under the scheme, being a right or interest created or issued for the purpose of raising money for the purposes of the scheme or a right or interest created or issued in substitution (whether directly or indirectly) for any right or interest so created or issued. (Borrowing (Control and Guarantees) Act 1946, s 4)

'Unit trust scheme' means any arrangements made for the purpose, or having the effect, of providing facilities for the participation by persons, as beneficiaries under a trust, in profits or income arising from the acquisition, holding, management or disposal of securities or any other property whatsoever. (Borrowing (Control and Guarantees) Act 1946, s 4; Prevention of Fraud (Investments) Act 1958, s 26(1))

'Unit' means, in relation to a unit trust scheme, a right or interest (whether described as a unit, as a sub-unit, or otherwise) of a beneficiary under the trust instrument. (Finance Act 1946, s 57)

'Unit trust' means any trust established for the purpose, or having the effect, of providing, for persons having funds available for investment, facilities for the participation by them, as beneficiaries under the trust, in any profits or income arising from the acquisition, holding, management or disposal of any property whatsoever. (Charging Orders Act 1979, s 6(1))

UNITED BENEFICE *See* BENEFICE

UNITED KINGDOM *See also* TERRITORIAL WATERS

'United Kingdom' includes the Isle of Man, the Channel Islands, and other adjacent islands. (Foreign Enlistment Act 1870, s 30)

In every Act passed and public document issued after the passing of this Act the expression 'United Kingdom' shall, unless the context otherwise requires, mean Great Britain and Northern Ireland. (Royal and Parliamentary Titles Act 1927, s 2(2))

'United Kingdom' includes the Isle of Man. (Trade Marks Act 1938, s 68)

'United Kingdom' means Great Britain and Northern Ireland. (Interpretation Act 1978, Sch 1)

UNITED KINGDOM NAME OR MARK

'United Kingdom name or mark' means any of the following, that is to say—

(a) the name of any person carrying on a trade or business in the United Kingdom;
(b) the name of any part of, or area, place, or geographical feature in, the United Kingdom;
(c) a trade mark of which a person carrying on a trade or business in the United Kingdom is the proprietor or registered user; and
(d) a certification trade mark of which a person in the United Kingdom is the proprietor.

(Trade Descriptions Act 1972, s 1(6))

UNITED KINGDOM WATERS

'United Kingdom waters' means any part of the sea within the seaward limits of the United Kingdom territorial waters and includes any part of a river within the ebb and flow of ordinary spring tides. (Protection of Wrecks Act 1973, s 3(1))

UNIVERSITY

'In my judgment, the word "university" is not a word of art, and, although for the most part one can identify a university when one sees it, it is, perhaps, not easy to define it in precise and accurate language. There are obviously universities which are such by common consent, the status of which as such no man could deny. That applies not only to the two ancient universities—Oxford and Cambridge—but to others which have since been founded (I think nearly all of them not earlier than the nineteenth century). There is no question that such institutions as the universities of London, Durham, Manchester and so forth, are universities in the fullest and most proper sense. . . . I agree that since the foundation of the University of Wales with its four constituent colleges there has been some confusion. A great many people, I think, might ignorantly be led to believe that St David's College was part of the University of Wales. It is nothing of the kind; it is an entirely separate and older foundation. In a sense it might be regarded as a rival and complement of the University of Wales, but the question which I have to decide is whether or not it stands on the same footing and is of the same character and quality as the University of Wales which was incorporated as a university. It has never called itself a university and, although included with the universities in certain books of reference, I have had no evidence to show that anybody has ever referred to it as a university. It may in certain ways be said to give a university education, that its standards are those of a university, and that its teaching is of the quality which is to be found in a university, but there still remains the gap to be bridged, the doubt whether, however closely it approximates in its aims, character, activities and merits to a university, this college can properly be described as a university. Judging the matter both on broad principles and on the narrow principles of its limited powers and the absence of any express intention of making it a university by the sovereign power, I think that the plaintiffs have not discharged the onus of satisfying me that the college ought to be called and to be considered, in accordance with the proper meaning of the English language, a university.' *St David's College, Lampeter v Ministry of Education* [1951] 1 All ER 559 at 560, 561, per Vaisey J

Australia 'A definition of a university adopted from the Shorter Oxford English Dictionary by Kaye J in *Clark v University of Melbourne* [1978] VR 457 at 467 (which judgment was reversed on another point [1979] VR 66) reads in part: "The whole body of teachers and students pursuing, at a particular place, the higher branches of learning; such persons associated together as a society or corporate body, having the power of conferring degrees and other privileges, and forming an institution for the promotion of education in the higher branches of learning.' The structure of each Australian university varies, but Melbourne University, for example, by s 4(1) of the Melbourne University Act 1958, is a "body politic and corporate" and consists of certain classes of persons, including "the professors", "members of the academic staff" and certain other non-academic staff.' *SSAV Nominees Pty Ltd v Commissioner of Taxation* (1985) 82 FLR 379 at 401, per Ormiston J

UNJUST ENRICHMENT

Canada '[T]here are three requirements to be satisfied before an unjust enrichment can be said to exist: an enrichment, a corresponding deprivation and absence of any juristic reason for the enrichment. This approach, it seems to me, is supported by general principles of equity that have been fashioned by the courts for centuries, though, admittedly, not in the context of matrimonial property controversies.' *Pettkus v Becker* [1980] 2 SCR 834 at 848, SCC, per Dickson J

UNJUSTIFIABLE

Australia 'To be "unjustifiable" the things done will be shown to be lacking in excuse or defence on any reasonable ground, that is to say, inexcusable and indefensible in the relationship of the same to the claimant for relief.' *Cox v Cox* [1949] SASR 117 at 124, 125, per Mayo J

New Zealand 'In my view a person is "unjust" when he does not observe the principles of justice or fair dealing and an act can be said to be "unjust" when it is not in accordance with justice or fairness. That is the ordinary dictionary meaning of the word "unjust", and the word "unjustifiable" . . . has a related meaning. A refusal to sell or supply goods is "unjustifiable" . . . when the party seeking to uphold it is unable to establish that it was done for reasons which accord with justice or fairness.' *Re Kempthorne Prosser & Co's New Zeal Drug Co Ltd* [1964] NZLR 49 at 52, Trade Practices Appeal Authority, per Dalglish J

UNLAWFUL

'There are two senses in which the word "unlawful" is not uncommonly, though, I think, somewhat inaccurately used. There are some contracts to which the law will not give effect; and therefore, although the parties may enter into what, but for the element which the law condemns, would be perfect contracts, the law would not allow them to operate as contracts, notwithstanding that, in point of form, the parties have agreed. Some such contracts may be void on the ground of immorality; some on the ground that they are contrary to public policy; as, for example, in restraint of trade; and contracts so tainted the law will not lend its aid to enforce. It treats them as if they had not been made at all. But the more accurate use of the word "unlawful" . . . namely, as contrary to law, is not applicable to such contracts.' *Mogul SS Co v McGregor, Gow & Co* [1892] AC 25 at 39, per Lord Halsbury LC

[The Sexual Offences Act 1956, s 19(1), makes it an offence for a person to take an unmarried girl under the age of eighteen out of the possession of her parent or guardian for the purpose of having 'unlawful' sexual intercourse.] 'No great assistance is to be derived for present purposes from the language used in . . . earlier statutes, except that it does suggest that the word "unlawfully" in relation to carnal knowledge has not been used with any degree of precision. . . . In our view the word simply means "illicit", i.e., outside the bond of marriage.' *R v Chapman* [1958] 3 All ER 143 at 144, 145, CCA, per cur.; also reported [1959] 1 QB 100 at 105

Australia 'The word "unlawfully" is a word commonly used in statutes creating crimes, misdemeanors and minor offences, and in such Acts it is used in two shades of meaning, one when referring to an act which is wrong or wicked in itself—recognised by everybody as wicked—as for instance, when it is used with reference to certain sexual offences, or with reference to acts which are absolutely prohibited under all circumstances; the other when referring to some prohibition of positive law.' *Lyons v Smart* (1908) 6 CLR 143 at 147, per Griffiths CJ

Canada 'The "unlawful purpose" which is one of the essential ingredients of the crime of criminal conspiracy called for by s 408 of the Code [see now RSC 1970, c C-34, s 423] must in itself be unlawful in the criminal sense, that is to say, a purpose which, if they [the conspirators] carried it out, would render them liable to prosecution for the commission of a criminal act, not something that is unlawful merely because the doing of it is prohibited by a provincial legislature.' *R v Sommervill and Kaylich* (1962) 40 WWR 577 at 587, Sask QB, per Disbery J; affd 43 WWR 87

UNLAWFUL ASSEMBLY *See also* AFFRAY

An unlawful assembly is an assembly of three or more persons with intent to commit a crime by open force or to carry out any common purpose, whether lawful or unlawful, in such a manner as to cause reasonable people to fear a breach of the peace. (11 Halsbury's Laws (4th edn) para 856)

'In Hawkins' Pleas of the Crown, s 9, it is said, "An unlawful assembly according to the common opinion is a disturbance of the peace by persons barely assembling together with the intention to do a thing which if it were executed would make them rioters, but neither actually executing it nor making a motion toward the execution of it." On this definition, standing alone, it is clear that the appellants were guilty of no offence, for it cannot be contended that they had any intention to commit any riotous act. The paragraph, however, continues thus, "But this seems to be much too narrow a definition. For any meeting whatever of great numbers of people, with such circumstances of terror as cannot but endanger the public peace and raise fears and jealousies among the King's subjects, seems properly to be called an unlawful assembly, as where great numbers, complaining of a common grievance, meet together, armed in a warlike manner, in order to consult together—concerning the most proper means for the recovery of their interests; for no man can forsee what may be the event of such an assembly. . . ." What has happened here is that an unlawful organisation has assumed to itself the right to prevent the appellants and others from lawfully assembling together, and the finding of the justices amounts to this, that a man may be convicted for doing a lawful act if he knows that his doing it may cause another to do an unlawful act. There is no authority for such a proposition, and the question of the justices whether the facts stated in the case constituted the offence charged in the information must therefore be answered in the negative.' *Beatty v Gillbanks* (1882) 9 QBD 308 at 314, 315, per Field J

'An unlawful assemblage . . . is an assemblage which attempts to carry out any common purpose, lawful or unlawful, in such a manner as to give other persons reason to fear a disturbance of the peace.' *R v Graham & Burns* (1888) 4 TLR 212 at 226, per Charles J

'There has been canvassed before this court the distinction between unlawful and riotous assemblies. Unlawful assemblies and riotous take many forms. Without, of course, attempting a full definition the difference can be stated in broad terms applicable to occasions of the particular type under consideration. The moment when persons in a crowd, however peaceful their original intention, commence to act for some shared common purpose supporting each other and in such a way that reasonable citizens fear a breach of the peace, the assembly becomes unlawful. In particular that applies when those concerned attempt to trespass, *or* to interrupt *or* disrupt an occasion where others are peacefully and lawfully enjoying themselves, *or* show preparedness to use force to achieve the common purpose. The assembly becomes riotous *at latest* when alarming force or violence begins to be used.' *R v Caird* (1970) 54 Cr App Rep 499, CA, per cur.

'The appellants sought to rely on a number of cases in which unlawful assembly was defined by judicial authority by use of some such phrase as "terror and alarm in the neighbourhood" (cf *R v Stephens* [(1839) 3 Stat Tr NS 1234], per Patteson J; *R v Vincent* [(1839) 9 C & P 91], per Alderson B). I agree with Lawton LJ [in the Court of Appeal] that in those cases "in the neighbourhood" must be read in the context as simply the equivalent of those nearby. I note that in the earliest definition at which I have looked, namely, that contained in the first edition of Hawkins [*Pleas of the Crown* (1716)], the expression "neighbourhood" is not used, but the expression is "such circumstances of terror as cannot but endanger the public peace". I consider that the public peace is in question when either an affray or a riot or unlawful assembly takes place in the presence of innocent third parties. It was accepted on behalf of the appellants that a riot can take place in enclosed premises, e.g. Dartmoor Prison. But an unlawful assembly is only an inchoate riot: see *Russell on Crime* [12th edn (1964), p 256]. When this was pointed out to him, counsel for the appellants was driven to argue that, if rioters in Dartmoor beat the warders inside the prison, they would be rioting, but they would not be guilty of an unlawful assembly unless the noise from inside the prison frightened some of Her Majesty's lieges outside the prison. I find this contention wholly unattractive.' *Kamara v Director of Public Prosecutions* [1973] 2 All ER 1242 at 1248, HL, per Lord Hailsham of St Marylebone

'If . . . obstructors are three or more in number and by conduct show an intention to use violence to achieve their aims or otherwise behave in a tumultuous manner, any police constables present have the duty to disperse them because those present and forming part of the gathering will be committing the offence of unlawful assembly.' *R v Chief Constable of Devon & Cornwall Constabulary, ex p Central Electricity Generating Board* [1981] 3 All ER 826 at 834, CA, per Lawton LJ

UNLESS

[A condition of an insurance policy provided that on the happening of any destruction or damage the insured should forthwith give notice thereof in writing to the corporation, and should within 30 days deliver to the corporation a claim in writing containing as particular an account as might be reasonably practicable of the property destroyed or damaged. The insured was also to give such proofs and information as might reasonably be required. No claim under the policy was to be payable 'unless' the terms of the condition had been complied with.] 'It was . . . argued that in the last sentence of condition 4 "unless" should be construed as meaning "until". I do not think this is sound. I think Branson J was right in saying that the last ten words of that sentence mean no more and no less than "if the terms of this condition have not been complied with".' *Welch v Royal Exchange Assurance* [1939] 1 KB 294 at 312, CA, per MacKinnon LJ

New Zealand '"No one shall be admitted unless he wear a black hat, or unless he wear a white hat." Here it is plain that an alternative is intended. "No one shall be admitted unless he be a barrister of seven years' standing, or unless he be a graduate of some University." Here also it is probable, though not so absolutely clear as in the former case, that an alternative is intended, and that either a barrister or a graduate is admissible. "No one shall be eligible to the County Council unless he be an inhabitant of the County, or unless he own a freehold estate of not less value than £50 per annum." Here it becomes doubtful whether an inhabitant of the County who does not possess a freehold of the value stated is qualified; and whether, on the other hand, a non-resident is qualified who possesses such an estate. . . . In all these sentences it must be observed that the repetition of the word "unless" is clumsy and unnatural where it is really meant to express an alternative. Any one intending to exclude coloured hats would not write as in the first sentence, but would omit the second "unless", would couple with "or" its grammatical companion "either" and would say "unless" he wear either a black hat or a white hat". It is properly pointed out by the Chief Justice that "unless", like its Latin equivalent, includes a negative, and its repetition at once suggests that "or" coupled with it may be read "nor" or "and".' *Re Somerville* (1889) 7 NZLR 400 at 416, 417, CA, per Richmond J

UNLIVERY

'"The place of unlivery of the cargo", "the final port of discharge", and "the final port of destination", are terms which will be found fairly frequently in the various Merchant Shipping Acts, and so far as I can judge are intended to be correlative terms, each pointing to what must be taken to be the end of a voyage; and reading them in this light it seems clear that the end of a voyage is the place where the final or home passage of the whole voyage terminates by reason that it is the place at which the cargo brought home is to be discharged finally.' *The Scarsdale* [1906] P 103 at 115, 116, CA, per Vaughan Williams LJ; affd sub nom *Board of Trade v Baxter, The Scarsdale* [1907] AC 373

UNMARRIED

'In this case the question turns between the children of the marriage and those who would have been the next-of-kin of the wife of Richard Maugham, if she had no children, under the provisions in the articles of the marriage settlement; in which it is provided, that in the event of the wife making no appointment, and dying in the lifetime of the husband, the personal estate should be held for such persons as under the Statute of Distribution [1670] would have been her next-of-kin, in case she had died intestate and unmarried. . . . Is that used in the sense of never having been married? It merely means discoverte.' *Maugham v Vincent* (1840) 9 LJ Ch 329 at 330, 331, per Lord Cottenham LC

'What may be the general construction put upon the word "unmarried" is quite immaterial in the present case. The testator, in the former part of his will, gives to his daughter, during the joint lives of herself and her mother, or until the marriage of his said daughter, an annuity of £300; and if she should survive her mother and be still unmarried, he gave her an annuity of £1,000 from her mother's death till her own death or marriage. Now, what was the meaning of "unmarried" in that place? Clearly the testator meant if she was a single woman; that is, in the same state as she was when he made the bequest.' *Re Thistlethwayte's Trust* (1855) 24 LJ Ch 712 at 713, per Turner LJ

'It is obvious that the term "unmarried" has a different signification, according as it is applied to a person who is married or unmarried at the time. If there be a gift to a woman who is unmarried at the time, with a direction that if she dies unmarried it is to go over, it is quite settled that "unmarried" is to be construed "never having been married". On the other hand, if there be a gift to a woman who is married at the time; "but, if she shall die unmarried, then over", it is obvious that the word "unmarried" may be held to mean "not being in the state of marriage at the time of her death". The word "unmarried", therefore, does not necessarily mean "without having been married", and no fixed meaning can be assigned to it, but it must be determined according to the circumstances of the case.' *Pratt v Mathew* (1856) 22 Beav 328 at 332–334, per Romilly MR

'I do not feel any doubt as to the meaning of this gift. The word "unmarried" is, no doubt, one of flexible meaning. It may mean here either "never having had a husband", or "not having a husband at the time of the death of the tenant for life". The question is, which of these is the true meaning? The words are "upon trust to pay the same into Julia Hannah Hughes, if she be then sole and unmarried, for her own benefit absolutely; but, if she be then married, upon trust for her for her life, with remainder to her children". . . . I think they mean "not having a husband" at the time referred to, whether the legatee had never had a husband, or whether she had lost him by death or by divorce.' *Re Lesingham's Trusts* (1883) 24 Ch D 703 at 705, 706, per North J

'The question is, what is the meaning of the word "unmarried" [in a bequest of certain property to be divided equally amongst the surviving "unmarried" nieces of the testator]? I agree that you must construe the word, which is capable of two meanings, according to the context in which you find it. It may mean either "never having been married", or "not having a husband" at the time in question. In order not to defeat the evident intention of a testator the Courts have in some cases held that the word meant "not having a husband", but I think its primary or natural sense is "never having been married". . . . Why are the unmarried daughters of his wife's sisters selected by the testator as objects of his bounty, and the married daughters left out? The answer, I think is, that in this country when a lady who is a spinster marries some provision is usually made for her . . . by her own relatives or by her husband. This testator was minded to make provision for the "unmarried" daughters of his wife's sisters, and upon the terms of the will, I cannot see any reason for giving to the word "unmarried" any meaning but "never having been married".' *Re Sergeant, Mertens v Walley* (1884) 26 Ch D 575 at 576, 577, per Pearson J

'The document I have to interpret is an informal document made by a lady without legal assistance, and I do not doubt that when she used the word "unmarried" [in the phrase "among all the unmarried daughters"] she meant to include under it only those who had never been married.' *Re Fanshawe's Trusts* (1904) 48 Sol Jo 525 at 525, per Joyce J

'The legacy is subject to a gift over on the death of the legatee unmarried and . . . the expression "unmarried" means "without ever having been married".' *Re Hall-Dare, Le Marchant v Lee Warner* [1916] 1 Ch 272 at 276, per Younger J

'In my opinion the primary meaning of the word "unmarried" is not having been married—that is a spinster.' *Soutar's Trustees v Spence* 1937 SLT 207, per Lord Stevenson

New Zealand [A settlor, by each of two deeds of gift, declared certain trusts for the benefit of his daughter, under which the trust funds would devolve on her surviving brother and sister and the issue of her deceased brother and sister in the event of the death of the daughter 'unmarried'.] 'It has been said in numerous cases that the word "unmarried" is a flexible word and without any violence to the language may mean either "without ever having been married" or "not having a husband living at her death". In the absence of any assistance from the context, the primary meaning is the former "without ever having been married", and the question with which the court must be concerned is as to whether in the deed there is anything in the context to justify the court in placing any other construction upon it: see the decision of Adams J in *Knubley v Collins (No 2)* [[1926] GLR 487, 488, 489] and the cases there cited. . . . According to the authorities, if the words used had been "unmarried and without lawful issue" there could have been no question that such words would have been applicable to death during widowhood as well as death during spinsterhood: *Re Jones, Last v Dobson* [[1915] 1 Ch 246]. I think here that the words were intended to exhaust the beneficial interests and it is not straining the meaning to accept here that of "discoverte", i.e., a spinster or a widow. . . . The meaning of the term "unmarried" as used in the deed of gift is "not in a state of marriage at the relevant time".' *Cameron v Gray* [1954] NZLR 1051 at 1052, 1053, 1054, per McGregor J

Unmarried and without issue

'I am of opinion that, where the word unmarried is applied to a person who is not married at the time, and there is a gift over in the event of that person dying unmarried, it means without ever having been married. . . . There is no doubt great force in the observation that in this view of the case the additional words "and without issue", are merely surplusage, because if a person were to die unmarried he would necessarily die without issue, unless the words are applied to a person who is married at the time of making the gift. If the person is actually married at the time of the gift, it is impossible that the first meaning can prevail, and the second meaning then prevails, and the words "and without issue" have a distinctive and definite meaning. In the other case the words are merely words of surplusage, and are merely used for the purpose of showing the construction which the settlor places on the word "unmarried", which is, that if a child dies without having married, and consequently without having any issue, the gift over takes effect.' *Heywood v Heywood* (1860) 29 Beav 9 at 16, 17, per Romilly MR

'Now, it has been decided by authority which binds me that the word "unmarried", as applied to a man, primarily means, "without ever having been married", i.e., a bachelor, but that although that is the primary meaning of the word, apart from its context, there is a secondary meaning which the words may bear, namely, "not leaving a wife", i.e., being either a bachelor or a widower. . . . If I take the primary meaning, and treat the clause as equivalent to "if he shall die a bachelor and without leaving any child", then the later words are, in one view, wholly useless, for a bachelor cannot have a legitimate child, or, in another view, they are only made sensible by reading "and" as "or", so that the clause would have this meaning, and "if he shall die a bachelor or, not being a bachelor, without having any child". If, on the other hand, I attach the secondary meaning to the word "unmarried", I do not fail to give effect to every word in the clause, which might then be paraphrased, "if he shall die without leaving a wife and without having a child".' *Re Chant, Chant v Lemon* [1900] 2 Ch 345 at 347, 348, per Cozens-Hardy J

'The word "unmarried" in legal documents, whether wills or settlements, prima facie means without having been married, at any rate when used in connection with a reference to the death of the individual. . . . This is also the popular sense of the word. But if the phrase is die "unmarried and without issue", as here, a different question arises: for, since, if a man has never been married he cannot have lawful issue, the latter words add nothing to the meaning, and the event contemplated is one and not two; whereas if "unmarried" were used as equivalent to "not leaving a widow" or "not having a wife then living", effect would be given to all the words.' *Roberts v Kilmore (Bp)* [1902] 1 IR 333 at 338, 339, 341, per Chatterton MR

'The word "unmarried" has been discussed in a number of cases. . . . In its primary sense it means "without ever having been married" and it may be still used in that sense. A secondary meaning has also become attached to it . . . namely, "having no spouse living" at the time with reference to which the word is applied. . . . The context in which the word is used may displace the primary meaning and show that the word has been used in its secondary sense, being also a natural and ordinary meaning of the term. It has been pointed out that the addition of the words "and without issue" will be sufficient to displace the primary meaning, because otherwise these words would be redundant, while, if "unmarried" is read in its secondary meaning, they are not redundant and full force and effect can be given to each of the words used by the testator. We may take it therefore that "unmarried" should be read here in its ordinary secondary sense. Accordingly, the phrase used by the testator should be interpreted, giving full effect to each of the words used in a natural and ordinary sense, to mean "without a spouse and without issue him surviving".' *Re Reilly* [1935] IR 352 at 362, per Kennedy CJ

UNMERCHANTABLE *See* MERCHANTABLE QUALITY

UNMOOR

New Zealand 'It now only remains to consider the alleged improper rejection by the judge of evidence of the harbor regulation No 29, promulgated 1st September 1879. The regulation in question provides that "the master of every vessel shall anchor or moor where the Harbor Master or person deputed by him may direct; and he shall not unmoor or quit the anchorage, nor shall he haul his vessel alongside any public pier, wharf or jetty, without having previously obtained permission from the Harbor Master or his deputy to do so; any master offending against this regulation shall be liable to a penalty not exceeding five pounds". . . . We are of opinion that in merely slacking his lines, and allowing the vessel to move a short distance astern, without quitting hold of the mooring posts, to which she was attached (and no more than this was done) the master did not infringe the regulation. It did not amount to unmooring.' *Williams v R* (1883) 1 NZLR 217 at 229, 230, per cur.

UNOCCUPIED

Australia 'The meaning that should be attached to the word "unoccupied" in relation to dwelling-houses should clearly be that the owner is neither living nor intending at the time to live in the premises himself, and if they are let, that he has not validly re-let them to or authorised some other person to enter them on the departure of the existing tenant for the purpose of residing therein as a home.' *Ex p Jackson, Re Fletcher* (1948) 47 NSWSR 447 at 454, per Davidson J

UNOPPOSED

Australia 'Proceedings are properly described as unopposed when a person entitled to oppose is given the opportunity of doing so and does not do so. It is not sufficient to show merely that no person did oppose the granting of what is being sought thereby.' *CBC (Sydney) v George Hudson Pty Ltd (in liquidation)* [1973] 2 ALR 1

UNPAID SELLER *See* SELLER

UNPROFESSIONAL CONDUCT

Australia '"Unprofessional conduct" is not necessarily limited to conduct which is "disgraceful or dishonourable" in the ordinary sense of those terms. It includes, we think, conduct which may reasonably be held to violate, or fall short of, to a substantial degree, the standard of professional conduct observed or approved of by members of the profession of good repute and competency.' *In the matter of a Practitioner* (1975) 12 SASR 167 at 170, per Gray CJ

UNREASONABLE *See also* REASONABLE; UNFAIR OR UNREASONABLE

'Lawyers familiar with the phraseology commonly used in relation to the exercise of statutory discretions often use the word "unreasonable" in a rather comprehensive sense. It is frequently used as a general description of the things that must not be done. For instance, a person entrusted with a discretion must direct himself properly in law. He must call his own attention to the matters which he is bound to consider. He must exclude from his consideration matters which are irrelevant to the matter that he has to consider. If he does not obey the rules, he may truly be said, and often is said, to be acting "unreasonably".'

Associated Provincial Picture Houses Ltd v Wednesbury Corpn [1947] 2 All ER 680 at 682, 683, CA, per Lord Greene MR

[The Private Street Works Act 1892, s 7 (repealed; see now the Highways Act 1980, s 208(1)(c)) provided that objections to being charged with the expense of executing private street works might be made (inter alia) on the ground that the proposed works were insufficient or 'unreasonable'.] 'I think that "unreasonable" here means unreasonable on any ground other than that of insufficiency, because it might well be said that works which were insufficient were unreasonable because of their insufficiency.' *Southgate Corpn v Park Estates (Southgate) Ltd* [1954] 1 All ER 520 at 525, CA, per Romer LJ

'In my opinion, besides culpability, unreasonableness can include anything which can objectively be adjudged to be unreasonable. It is not confined to culpability or callous indifference. It can include, where carried to excess, sentimentality, romanticism, bigotry, wild prejudice, caprice, fatuousness, or excessive lack of common sense.' *Re W (an Infant)* [1971] 2 All ER 49 at 56, HL, per Lord Hailsham LC

'In public law "unreasonable" as descriptive of the way in which a public authority has purported to exercise a discretion vested in it by statute has become a term of legal art. To fall within this expression it must be conduct which no sensible authority acting with due appreciation of its responsibilities would have decided to adopt.' *Secretary of State for Education and Science v Metropolitan Borough of Thameside* [1976] 3 All ER 679 at 695, HL, per Lord Diplock

Unreasonable delay

'The expression "unreasonable delay" [in the rent review clause of a lease] does, I think, require some definition. It must, I think, mean something more than "prolonged delay" and it may, I suppose, be used to express the notion either of delay for which no acceptable reason can be advanced or delay which no reasonable man would incur acting in his own interest. But if this is its meaning then the absence of reason has no necessary relation to duration. If on the other hand, as I suspect, the phrase is used to describe such delay as it would not in the circumstances be reasonable to expect the other party to put up with, then it seems to me that it contains within it, by necessary implication, the notion of hardship or prejudice, for how otherwise is the other party harmed by it?' *Amherst v James Walker Goldsmith & Silversmith Ltd* [1983] 2 All ER 1067 at 1075, CA, per Oliver LJ

UNROADWORTHY

'If a vehicle be unsafe, it is unroadworthy, and vice versa. . . . If . . . it were found that on leaving, or within quite a short distance of the garage, the brakes refused to act, or some other mechanical defect showed itself, it would, I think, be a fair inference to draw that the car was not roadworthy when it set out.' *Barrett v London General Insurance Co Ltd* [1935] 1 KB 238 at 240, 242, per Goddard J

'In my judgment, the maritime cases decided with reference to the warranty of seaworthiness, though by no means governing the decision in this case by reason of the special features of sea voyages and maritime contracts, are of some assistance. There is a good deal of similarity in the subject-matter. Both ships and road vehicles carry things and people on journeys. A road vehicle does not have to encounter perils of the seas, but does have to encounter perils of the traffic, which are much more numerous and continuous and various for land vehicles than for ships. In the course of an ordinary journey, a driver may well be faced with a situation in which he has to stop suddenly or swerve quickly to avoid an accident, and this may happen to him while he is driving down a hill or round a bend or both down a hill and round a bend. If his car is too heavy for its braking system, or has too much luggage on its roof so that it is top-heavy, or is so badly trimmed as to be seriously unbalanced, the driver, assuming that he is driving his car at a normal speed, will not be able to deal with such a situation. In the maritime cases, it has been held that, in considering whether a vessel is unseaworthy, the loading and stowage should be taken into account. Overloading or bad stowage can render a vessel unseaworthy: *Weir v Aberdeen* [(1819) 2 B & Ald 320]; *Kopitoff v Wilson* [(1876) 1 QBD 377]. That reasoning is based on common sense, and is not attributable to any special features of sea voyages or maritime contracts, and is equally applicable to land vehicles. In my view, it is clear that this vehicle at the material time was, by reason of its overloading, unroadworthy.' *Clarke v National Insurance and Guarantee Corpn Ltd* [1963] 3 All ER 375 at 379, CA, per Pearson LJ; also reported in [1964] 1 QB 199 at 209, 210

UNSATISFIED

'A judgment debt is "still unsatisfied" until it is paid, even though the time has not arrived at which, in accordance with the terms of the judgment, the money has to be paid, that is to say, even though the time has not arrived when execution can be issued. It is therefore, in my opinion, correct to say that a judgment debt which is not paid is "unsatisfied".' *White Son & Pill v Stennings* [1911] 2 KB 418 at 421, CA, per Ridley J

UNSEAWORTHY *See also* SEAWORTHY

[The question was as to the meaning of the word 'unseaworthiness' in a bill of lading]. 'We ought, I think, to hold that the word covers, not only the unseaworthiness of the ship in the sense that it was not fit to meet the perils of the sea, but also in the sense that the ship was not in a fit condition to carry the cargo.' *Rathbone Brothers & Co v MacIver (D), Sons & Co* [1903] 2 KB 378 at 386, CA, per Vaughan Williams LJ

'The ship was unseaworthy when the lemons were shipped on board at Naples. They were carried on the 'tween deck, where they became saturated with the sulphurous fumes used in the process of deratisation. They were not only spoilt in flavour, but were affected in substance also, being to a certain extent rotted. . . . The only view of the evidence that I can take is that there was nothing fortuitous about the injury to the lemons on this particular occasion, and that lemons will not stand being exposed to sulphurous fumes. The defendants therefore received the lemons on board their ship for carriage, the ship being at the time free from sulphurous fumes, but circumstances existing which rendered it inevitable that the ship and cargo would in the course of the voyage be subjected to them. The ship was therefore in my opinion unfit to receive and carry the cargo. That is what is meant by unseaworthiness, quite apart from the fitness of the ship to traverse the ocean.' *Ciampa v British India Steam Navigation Co Ltd* [1915] 2 KB 774 at 779, 780, per Rowlatt J

See, generally, 43 Halsbury's Laws (4th edn) paras 554, 555.

UNSHIP

[The Harbours, Docks and Piers Clauses Act 1847, s 33, provides that a harbour, dock or pier shall be open to all persons for the shipping or 'unshipping' of goods.] 'I do not think that the words "shipping" and "unshipping" are to be confined to the narrow operation of lifting goods from the quay to the ship or from the ship to the quay, nor do I think that the access under the section can be limited to access without any vehicle. It must I think be such access with such vehicle as the party seeking it bona fide deems necessary.' *London & North Eastern Rly Co v British Trawlers Federation Ltd* [1934] AC 279 at 298, per Lord Tomlin

UNSOLICITED

'Unsolicited' means, in relation to goods sent to any person, that they are sent without any prior request made by him or on his behalf. (Unsolicited Goods and Services Act 1971, s 6(1))

UNSOUND MIND *See* MENTAL DISORDER

UNTIL

'It is contended, on the authority of *Nichols v Ramsden* [*Nichols v Ramsel* (1677)] 2 Mod 280 and Owen 50, that in legal proceedings the word until must have an exclusive sense; and it has been argued, from the analogy it bears to the word unto (which word generally bears the same relation to place, which until does to time), that the case of *The King v Gamblingay* [*R v Gamlingay (Inhabitants)* (1790)] 3 Term Rep 513, is to be considered as an authority to the same effect. These words, however, have obtained, in ordinary use, an equivocal sense at least, of which many instances were given at the bar; and I will mention two others. In Sir Mathew Hale's History of the Common Law, p 165, he says, "thus much shall serve for the several periods of growth of the common law until the time of Edward the 1st inclusively". An instance which proves that until *ex vi termini* does not imply exclusion; for if it did, the words above stated "until and inclusively" would involve a contradiction in terms; but that it may, from its context, receive an inclusive sense. . . . If the word until occurred in a contract, and the context or subject-matter evidently showed that it was meant in an inclusive sense, there can be no doubt but that the court, in furtherance of such intention, would so construe it.' *R v Stevens & Agnew* (1804) 5 East 244 at 255–257, per Lord Ellenborough CJ

'The objection is, that the award was made out of time, as it was made on the 1st of July. Whether it was or no, depends on the meaning of the word "until". Now, there is no doubt, that independent of the case of *Pugh v Duke of Leeds* [(1777) 2 Cowp 714] there is no absolute rule as to the meaning to be attached to the word "until", as it may be construed either as inclusive or exclusive, as it may with strict propriety mean either. I think that, in the present case, it was meant to be inclusive of the day on which the award was made. I think, therefore, that construction should be put on it "*ut res magis valeat quam pereat*", and, therefore, that this objection is not sustainable in point of law.' *Kerr v Jeston* (1842) 1 Dowl NS 538 at 539, per Williams J

'The word "until" is ambiguous, and may be construed either inclusive or exclusive of the day mentioned, according to the subject-matter and the true intent of the document in which it is used.' *Bellhouse v Mellor, Proudman v Mellor* (1859) 4 H & N 116 at 123–125, per cur.

'The action is on a time policy of insurance for six months, "from the 14th day of February, 1868, until the 14th day of August, and for so long after as the said assured shall pay the sum of 225 dollars" by way of premium; and the question we have to determine is, whether the policy covers a fire which occurred on the 14th of August. That is all we have to determine, and not whether the 14th of February is excluded, so that no insurance was in force on that day, but whether the 14th of August was included; and I think it was included.' *Isaacs v Royal Insurance Co* (1870) LR 5 Exch 296 at 299, per Kelly CB

'The real question we have to decide is the meaning in this policy [of insurance of goods from the 14th day of February, 1868, "until" the 14th day of August] of the word "until". No doubt the expression is equivocal, but there are many cases in which, where the limit is from one day to another, the last day is included. For example, there is the case of the eight days allowed for pleading. So, where a man insures his premises from the 1st of January in one year to the 1st of January in the next, I think the last day would be covered by the policy.' Ibid at 301, per Martin B

Until further order

'When an interim order is made to extend over a certain day or until further order, it does not mean that it is to go on after that day or until further order, but that it is to stop earlier if the Court shall so order—"until that day or further order", meaning at an earlier date.' *Bolton v London School Board* (1878) 7 Ch D 766 at 771, per Malins V-C

'When an application is made for revision and when the original order has been made "until further order" it seems to me that the Court ought to have regard to all circumstances of the case in the same manner as if those circumstances had existed at the date of the original order.' *Hall v Hall* [1915] P 105 at 109, CA, per Lord Cozens-Hardy MR

Until paid

Canada 'A stipulation for interest at a certain rate on a loan "until paid" is established by a long series of cases . . . to import a contract to pay interest at the specified rate only until the maturity of the loan. To carry the contract for the stipulated rate beyond the maturity of the loan explicit provision to that effect must be made.' *Hossack v Shaw* (1918) 56 SCR 581 at 585, SCC, per Anglin J

Until safely landed

'The question in this case is whether the goods insured have been safely landed within the true intent and meaning of those words in the policy, for to every part of the policy we must give complete effect. Now if we were to hold that the insurers were discharged by the delivery of the goods to the lighter, we should defeat the words "safely landed", and render them altogether nugatory. It is admitted that the business of unloading . . . is carried on by public lighters, and that no private lighters are ever employed by the merchants. Now if that be so, what effect is to be given to the words "until the goods are safely landed", if they do not extend to the goods when on board the public lighter, for in no other manner can they be safely landed. It is true that the master and owners of the ship were discharged when the goods were put on board the lighter; but freight and insurances are not commensurate; the latter is far more extensive than the former. The insurance commences before the freight, for it commences when the goods are put on board the boats at Petersburgh, and it also continues longer than the freight, for it does not determine until the goods are safely landed.'

Hurry v Royal Exchange Assurance Co (1801) 2 Bos & P 430 at 434, 435, per Heath J

'The policy is to cover the goods till they are safely landed, and the underwriter should inquire, therefore, what is the usual mode of landing the goods insured. Here, it appears to have been the usage to trans-ship the goods into shallops. The words "including risk in droghers" have probably been added to policies for greater security; but where it is the usage of the trade, and in the ordinary course of the voyage, to trans-ship into droghers, the underwriters are liable, even though those words are not found in the policy.' *Stewart v Bell* (1821) 5 B & Ald 238 at 239, 240, per cur.

UNUSUAL

[In *Indermaur v Dames* (1866) LR 1 CP 274, Willes J said that an invitee, using reasonable care on his part for his own safety, was entitled to expect that the occupier should on his part use reasonable care to prevent damage from 'unusual danger'.] 'To my mind danger may be unusual though fully recognised and I am not prepared to accept the view that the word "unusual" is to be construed subjectively as meaning unexpected by the particular invitee concerned. . . . I think "unusual" is used in an objective sense and means such danger as is not usually found in carrying out the task or fulfilling the function which the invitee has in hand, though what is unusual will, of course, vary with the reasons for which the invitee enters the premises.' *London Graving Dock Co Ltd v Horton* [1951] AC 737 at 745, per Lord Porter

[See now the Occupier's Liability Act 1957, which abolished the distinction between the duty owed to invitees and that owed to licensees and imposed a common duty of care to all visitors lawfully entering another's premises. The Occupier's Liability Act 1984 extended this duty to trespassers and other persons entering without permission. See 31 Halsbury's Statutes (4th edn) 188, 213]

Canada '"Unusual danger" is a relative term. It is relative to the kind of premises visited and it is also relative to the class of persons doing the visiting. A lady, for example, who comes to a grocery store on a dry summer day to purchase her groceries would not be expected to foresee the presence of water on the floor and the water, to her, could be an unusual danger. To a plumber, on the other hand, who answered an emergency call to that same store, on that same day, to repair a leaking radiator, the water on the floor would not be something unexpected and therefore might not be an unusual danger to him. In the case of a store, an unusual danger would be one which is not usually found by customers when they come to shop in the premises. It is a danger that the particular invitee cannot be expected to foresee and one that he cannot reasonably be expected to guard against so as to avoid being injured.' *Strongman v Oshawa Holdings Ltd* (1979) 23 Nfld & PEIR 457 at 460, PEISC, per MJ McQuaid J

UNVALUED POLICY

An unvalued policy is a policy which does not specify the value of the subject-matter insured, but, subject to the limit of the sum insured, leaves the insurable value to be subsequently ascertained. (Marine Insurance Act 1906, s 28)

UNWALKABLE OUTLET

'Unwalkable outlet' means an outlet which, owing to the gradient thereof or of any part thereof (whether alone or in combination with other circumstances), persons cannot walk up with reasonable convenience. (Mines and Quarries Act 1954, s 182)

UNWHOLESOME

Australia 'The word "unwholesome" [in the Health Act 1958–1986 (Vic), s 236] must mean something more than the words "deleterious to health". The word "unwholesome" in addition to meaning injurious to health also means "not favourable to or promoting good health; not wholesome or healthful".' *Minister v Woolworths (Victoria) Ltd* [1974] VR 514 at 517, per Dunn J

UNWILLING

'The conditions of sale give power to the vendor to annul the contract if the purchaser shall insist upon any objection or requisition which the vendor is unable or unwilling to comply with. I quite agree with the argument that there is a great difference between taking an objection and insisting upon an objection, and that, in order to entitle the vendor to annul the contract, it is necessary for him to show that the purchaser insisted upon the objection. The condition speaks of an objection or requisition which the vendor shall be unable or unwilling to remove or comply with. The question of unwillingness does not arise in the present case, because it is impossible, upon the evidence before us, to say that the vendor ever exhibited any unwillingness whatever to remove the objection. I only refer, therefore, to the question of unwillingness because several cases bearing upon it have been cited before us. Those cases have settled, and, I think, very wisely settled, that the word unwilling, in a condition of sale of this description, is not to be considered as giving an arbitrary power to the vendor to annul the contract. I think that in a case where the vendor annuls the contract on the ground of unwillingness, he must show some reasonable ground for unwillingness; thus, for instance, he may show that if he proceeds to comply with a requisition, he will be involved in expenses far beyond what he ever contemplated, or be involved in litigation and expense which he never contemplated, and for avoiding which he reserved to himself the power of annulling the contract. But to say that a vendor, upon a condition of that description, could annul a contract *brevi manu*, without attempting to answer any of the requisitions which are made on the part of the purchaser, would be opposed both to principle and authority; for that would, in truth, be giving to the vendor the power of saying that that which was intended as a sale, and was a sale, shall, in truth, be no sale at all.' *Duddell v Simpson* (1866) 2 Ch App 102 at 106, 107, per Turner LJ

[A condition of sale provided that in case the purchaser should, within a certain time, make any objection to or requisition on the title which the vendors should be unable or 'unwilling' to remove or comply with, the vendors should be at liberty at any time thereafter, notwithstanding any attempt to remove or comply with such objection or requisition, by notice in writing to be given to the purchaser or his solicitor, to annul the contract, and to return to the purchaser his deposit money without interest, costs, or other compensation.] 'Now I come to the true meaning of the term "unwilling" in a clause of this class. It might have been held that the term is to be taken according to its grammatical import, and that it is for the purchaser to consider, on entering into the contract, whether he would or would not expose himself to the risk of having his contract terminated if the vendor was unwilling to comply with the requisitions made, and the term "unwilling" by itself, of course, refers to the state of mind of the vendor, and prima facie the vendor would only have, according to the literal grammatical meaning, to say "I am unwilling", in other words "I will not, and no other person is to be the judge whether I am exercising my will reasonably or unreasonably". . . . I take it, therefore, that there is some limitation to be put upon the meaning of the term "unwilling", or something has to be added to it, and I take it now to be established sufficiently to bind me, by that case [*Re Glenton & Saunders to Haden* (1885) 53 LT 434, CA] that although the contract is in terms that the vendor may rescind if unwilling to comply with the requisitions, still if it be shown that he is acting capriciously the power is not well exercised, and there is an expression to the effect that if it is not reasonable the power is not validly exercised.' *Re Starr-Bowkett Building Society & Sibun's Contract* (1889) 42 Ch D 375 at 379, 382–384, per Chitty J; affd 42 Ch D 386, CA

'This case raises a question on the authorities relating to conditions of sale, and arises under the 11th condition, which is really common form, and runs: "And if any purchaser shall make any objection or requisition either as to title, the form of the conveyance or other assurance to the purchaser, or any matter appearing in the particulars, conditions, or abstract, or otherwise, which the vendor shall be unable or unwilling to remove or comply with, the vendor shall (notwithstanding any previous negotiations or litigation or attempt to remove or comply with the same) be at liberty to annul the sale." . . . The cases certainly show that some limitation is to be put upon the word "unwilling". It is not to be merely the caprice of the vendor, in the sense that it is enough for him to say, "I will not complete, and there is an end of it". Cotton LJ, in *Re Dames and Wood* [(1885) 29 Ch D 626 at 630] stated that in his opinion "The cases do certainly lay down this, that a vendor cannot avail himself of such a condition arbitrarily, or unless he shows some reasonable ground for his unwillingness to answer the requisitions". . . . It is said that a vendor is not to act capriciously. I rather prefer the word "arbitrarily" . . . which I take to mean "without any reasonable cause".' *Quinion v Horne* [1906] 1 Ch 596 at 600, 602–604, per Farwell J

UNWRITTEN LAW

The . . . unwritten law includes not only general customs, or the common law properly so called; but also the particular customs of certain parts of the kingdom; and likewise those particular laws that are by custom observed only in certain courts and jurisdictions. (1 Bl Com 63)

UP TO

'The expression "up to" is a well known one in accountancy, and when books are said to be written up . . . and accounts to be vouched up to a particular date, no implication arises that any of the operations were completed before or even on the particular date, the true meaning being that the particular date is the one up to which the state of account has been ascertained. So here income tax assessed up to a particular date is not, in my opinion, confined to the tax actually assessed before that date, but includes all assessed tax up to that date, whether the assessment was made before or after the date.' *Gowers v Walker* [1930] 1 Ch 262 at 267, per Eve J

UPKEEP

'The question which is asked is whether upon the true construction of the . . . will, in the events which have happened, the direction in the said will: "that the income be devoted to the upkeep of the King's Heath Baptist Chapel and school and for the provision of prizes for the scholars of both sexes" is (a) a good and valid bequest of the whole of the residuary estate of the testator in favour of the King's Heath (General) Baptist Chapel, Birmingham, or (b) fails either wholly or to any and if so what extent. In my judgment, the direction of the will is a good and valid bequest of the whole of the residuary estate of the testator. . . . It ought to be interpreted, in my judgment, as enabling the trustees to devote the income of the residuary estate of the testator to discharging all those expenses which are necessarily incurred by those who are responsible for providing the services in a Baptist chapel, and maintaining, in a broad sense, a Sunday-school.' *Re Strickland's Will Trusts, National Guarantee & Suretyship Assocn Ltd v Maidment* [1936] 3 All ER 1027 at 1031, per Bennett J

UPON

'The words of the Act [Sacramental Test (1828) (repealed)], "upon his admission", do not, as it appears to us, mean after the admission has taken place, but upon the occasion of, or at the time of his admission: the words of that section show the intention of the legislature to have been that the space of time commencing at the distance of one calendar month next before, and terminating with, the act of admission, should be the limit or period within which the declaration was required to be made; so that, if not made at an earlier time, the latest opportunity of making it would be at the same time and place at which the oath of office was administered, and before the same persons. In effect, the making of the declaration does, by virtue of those words, form a part of the act of admission, and is an essential requisite to the being permitted to exercise the corporate office. And we hold it therefore to be unnecessary to refer to instances of the legal meaning of the word "upon", which, in different cases, may undoubtedly either mean before the act done to which it relates, or simultaneously with the act done, or after the act done, according as reason and good sense require the interpretation, with reference to the context, and the subject matter of the enactment.' *R v Humphery* (1839) 10 Ad & El 335 at 369, 370, per Tindal CJ

[See now, as to the taking of official oaths, the Promissory Oaths Acts 1868 and 1871.]

'Here the Act [Mayor's Court of London Procedure Act 1857, s 8 (repealed)] provides that leave [to move in any superior Court] must be given "upon the trial". That clearly does not mean during the trial, but as it appears to me, it must mean with a reasonable time afterwards.' *Folkard v Metropolitan Rly Co* (1873) LR 8 CP 470 at 471, per Bovill CJ

Australia 'It has been argued that "upon" means substantially at the same time as. There is no substance in this. The word "upon" in different cases may undoubtedly either mean *before* the act done to which it relates, or *simultaneously* with the act done or *after* the act done, according as reason and good sense require the interpretation, with reference to the context, and the subject matter of the enactment (*R v Humphery* [supra]).' *Ex p Lesiputty, Re Murphy* (1948) 48 NSWSR 433 at 436, per Jordan CJ

UPWARDS

Australia 'Desertion under the statute must continue to three years and upwards. The words "and upwards" are in my opinion equivalent to "or more". They indicate that desertion must have continued for a complete and actual period of three years. They are like the words "clear days", "so many days at least", "a month or more", or "not less than"; all of which expressions have been held to indicate that the term is to be computed exclusively of the day from which the period commenced. The cases are collected in Norton on Deeds (2nd edn), at p 185.' *Belfield v Belfield* [1945] VLR 231 at 237, 238, per O'Bryan J

URBAN

[Urban districts ceased to exist when new local authorities were established under the Local Government Act 1972. England is now divided into areas known as counties (metropolitan or non-metropolitan) and districts.]

Australia 'That word [urban] . . . contrasts with a word that could have been chosen in its stead but was not—the word "residential". The word "urban" is not defined, and must, accordingly, be given its ordinary meaning which, as I understand it, conforms to its etymological origins; it means characteristic of, or pertaining to, or situated within the limits of, a city or cities.' *Spic-n-span Corpn Pty Ltd v Fredericks* (1982) 50 LGRA 46 at 50, S Ct of SA, per Wells J

USAGE

Usage may be broadly defined as a particular course of dealing or line of conduct generally adopted by persons engaged in a particular department of business life, or more fully as a particular course of dealing or line of conduct which has acquired such notoriety, that, where persons enter into contractual relationships in matters respecting the particular branch of business life where the usage is alleged to exist, those persons must be taken to have intended to follow that course of dealing or line of conduct, unless they have expressly or impliedly stipulated to the contrary; that is to say that a rule of conduct amounts to a usage if so generally known in the particular department of business life in which the case occurs that, unless expressly or impliedly excluded, it must be considered as forming part of the contract.

The Convention relating to a Uniform Law on the Formation of Contracts for the International Sale of Goods defines usage for its purposes as 'any practice or method of dealing which reasonable persons in the same situation as the parties usually consider to be applicable to the formation of their contract'. Usage in the sense indicated above must be distinguished from user or enjoyment in relation to incorporeal rights, and from the course of conduct of the persons interested under a particular ancient charter or other ancient document. In this last sense it is limited to the conduct of persons actually affected by the document in question, and may be referred to only for the purpose of showing the meaning of expressions which by reason of their antiquity have become obscure. (12 Halsbury's Laws (4th edn) para 445)

'Usage' means any practice or method of dealing with reasonable persons in the same situation as the parties usually consider to be applicable to the formation of their contract. (Uniform Laws on International Sales Act 1967, Sch 2)

'There may be a usage in one place varying from that which prevails in another. Where the usage is general, and prevails to such an extent that a party contracting with a wharfinger must be supposed conusant of it, then he will be bound by the terms of that usage. But then it should be generally known to prevail at that place.' *Holderness v Collinson* (1827) 7 B & C 212 at 216, per Bayley J

Canada 'Usage is defined [in 12 Halsbury's Laws (4th edn) (supra)] as a particular course of dealing or line of conduct generally adopted by persons engaged in a particular department of business life. The requisite characteristics are that the usage be notorious, certain, reasonable, and not offensive to the intention of any legislative enactment. There is no requirement, as there is in the case of custom, that it be shown to have existed from time immemorial. Usage, however recent, may be valid, provided it is generally known. The requirement of notoriety means that any person in the particular market or branch of trade or department of business or amongst the class of persons affected by the usage must be taken to have entered into a contract with the intention that the usage should form part of that contract. The usage must be well known at the place to which it applies, and be capable of ready ascertainment by any person who proposes to enter into a contract of which that usage would form part.' *Frontenac Condominium Corp No 1 v Joe Macciocchi & Sons Ltd* (1974) 3 OR (2d) 331 at 348, Ont SC, per Cromarty J

USE *See also* PERSONAL USE

'The first meaning assigned to the word "use" in Johnson's Dictionary is "to employ to any purpose"; it is, therefore, a word of wide signification. It seems to me that the terms "use" and "make use of" are intended to have a wider application than "exercise" and "put into practice", and, without saying that no limit is to be placed on the two former expressions in the patent, I think, on the best consideration that I can give, that they are not confined to the use of a patented article for the purpose for which it is patented.' *British Motor Syndicate Ltd v Taylor & Son* [1900] 1 Ch 577 at 583, per Stirling J; affd [1901] 1 Ch 122, CA

'We apprehend that a retail tradesman can, with perfect accuracy, be said to be using his stock when he sells it to customers and to have used it up when it is all sold. So here we think that inasmuch as the ratepayer's business consists of the sale and distribution of oil, albeit as agents for others, it is using in its business the oil which it sells and distributes, and the oil is clearly brought to the hereditament with the intention that it should be so used. The word "use" in its natural meaning is a word of wide import. In *British Motor Syndicate Ltd v Taylor & Son Ltd* [supra], Stirling J pointed out that: "The first meaning assigned to the word 'use' in Johnson's Dictionary is 'to employ to any purpose'; it is, therefore, a word of wide significance." In this wide sense it is, we think, apt to cover the commodity in which a merchant trades, be he a petroleum merchant, a timber merchant, or other merchant.' *Shell-Mex & BP Ltd v Clayton* [1955] 3 All ER 102 at 106, 117, CA, per cur.

'"Use" is not a word of precise meaning, but in general it conveys the idea of enjoyment derived by the user from the corpus of the object enjoyed.' *Arbuckle Smith & Co Ltd v Greenock Corpn* [1960] 1 All ER 568 at 574, HL, per Lord Radcliffe

'As occupation is a kind of user, it is difficult to envisage an occupation of land or buildings which is not also a user. The reverse does not apply. Not every use is an occupation, and obviously many things capable of being used are incapable of being occupied. The words are not fully interchangeable but only interchangeable in some contexts.' *Land Reclamation Co Ltd v Basildon District Council* [1978] 2 All ER 1162 at 1166, 1167, per Brightman J

'Where a structure has a roof which covers and protects a separate hereditament on the ground floor as well as other hereditaments above it, it is a realistic and proper use of language to describe the situation as one in which the occupier of the ground floor has the use of the roof and its drainage facility.' *South West Water Authority v Rumble's* [1985] 1 All ER 513 at 518, HL, per Lord Scarman

Canada [On appeal against an order for forfeiture of a rifle, issue arose as to whether the appellant had 'used' the rifle in the commission of an offence within the meaning of the Criminal Code, RSC 1970, c C-34, s 446.1, when he had simply stored it carelessly and had been convicted of that offence.] 'The Ontario Court of Appeal discussed the meaning of the word "use" in *R v Langevin* (1979) 10 CR (3d) 193, 47 CCC (2d) 138, and found that it connotes an active process rather than a passive one. At p 145 Martin JA said: "Being 'armed' with an offensive weapon and 'using' an offensive weapon are not synonymous. A person is 'armed' with an offensive weapon if he is equipped with it: see *R v Sloan* (1974) 19 CCC (2d) 190 at p 192. 'Using' a firearm includes pulling out a firearm which the offender has upon his person and holding it in his hand to intimidate another: see *Rowe v The King* (1951) 100 CCC 97 at p 101, [1951] 4 DLR 238, [1951] SCR 713 at p 717." To invoke s 446.1 [of the Criminal Code, RSC 1970] the judge must find that the accused has used the firearm, that is, done something actively with it. Since this finding was not possible in this situation no order should have been made directing forfeiture of the firearm.' *R v Annas* (1985) 36 Alta LR (2d) 55 at 57, Alberta Court of Queen's Bench, per Wachowich J

In Betting Acts

[Under the Betting Act 1853, s 3 (repealed; but cf now the Betting, Gaming and Lotteries Act 1963, s 1) it was an offence for a person to 'use' premises for the purpose of betting.] 'The words which . . . your lordships have to construe are these: "No house office room or other place shall be opened kept or used for the purpose of the owner occupier or keeper thereof, or any person using the same or any person procured or employed by or acting for or on behalf of such owner occupier or keeper or person using the same or of any person having the care or management, or in any manner conducting the business thereof betting with persons resorting thereto." . . . It is the employment of the words "using the same" which . . . has led to the difference of opinion.

Those words, unless explained by the context, are necessarily ambiguous. In one sense every person who enters the inclosure uses it; but he does not use it in the character of owner, keeper, manager, or conductor of the business thereof. The betting man in his use of the place differs in this respect in no way from any other member of the public who enters it, and who neither does nor intends to bet. . . . Lord Hobhouse, admits the word "use" is ambiguous and limits it by such words as "deliberate, designed and repeated". . . . It is not the repeated and designed, as distinguished from the casual or infrequent, use which the employment of that word imports here, but the character of the use as a use by some person having the dominion and control over the place, and conducting the business of a betting establishment with the persons resorting thereto.' *Powell v Kempton Park Racecourse Co* [1899] AC 143 at 158–160, per Lord Halsbury LC

'It was contended that because the appellant had no interest in the inn or control over the premises he did not "use" the bar in the sense in which that term is employed in the section [Betting Act 1853, s 3 (see supra)]. With that contention I cannot agree. . . . I think that where you find a man habitually frequenting the same room or place for the purpose of carrying on there a regular business of betting with the persons resorting thereto he commits an offence against the Act.' *Tromans v Hodkinson* [1903] 1 KB 30 at 32, DC, per Lord Alverstone CJ

[The Betting Act 1853, s 3 (repealed; see supra), enacted that no premises should be 'used' for the purpose of the owner, occupier, or keeper thereof, or any person 'using' the same, betting with persons resorting thereto.] 'The matter to be determined is not whether the club premises were used for betting—as indeed they were—it is rather whether Payne used them for betting with the members. Apart from authority I should have said that a de facto user of the premises must be proved but that a de jure user is unnecessary. X may commit an offence by using the place for the purpose of X himself using the premises betting with persons resorting thereto or by using it for the purpose of Y using the premises betting with such persons; and in the second case Y also commits an offence under s 1. But Y, who is himself merely a user, may commit an offence, even if the owner or occupier is ignorant of his action, provided that his acts constitute a user of the premises for the purpose of Y betting with persons resorting thereto. In either of the first two cases X must have some sort of control over the premises otherwise he could not use the premises. So likewise in the second and third cases must Y have some measure of control and for the same reason, but neither the one nor the other need be an owner, occupier or keeper. A defined place and sufficient control over it to stay there and bet with persons resorting thereto would seem to be enough. But there must be a place to which people can resort and sufficient occupation of it in fact by some person to enable them to bet with him. So far as Milne is concerned the evidence showed that she was tenant of the premises and carried on the club, and the place was opened, kept or used—any of the three words is appropriate—by her. Moreover, it was used for the purpose of Payne betting with persons resorting thereto—namely the members. Those matters are not in question but are not enough to support a conviction. In order that the conviction may be affirmed Payne must, it is true, bet with persons resorting to the premises, but he must also use the premises for that purpose. What then is meant by "user"? No doubt physical presence might be enough and, though the mere opening of the house for the purpose specified before any actual betting took place would constitute an offence, yet as a rule some evidence of the repetition would be required to show the purpose for which the premises were opened, kept or used. User through a servant or agent including a partner would also, I think, suffice. Some physical control such as a private telephone connecting other premises with those alleged to be used might be enough, and some sharing of profits or payment for the privilege of betting with members might constitute a user of the premises, but I doubt if it is possible to find a formula which would fit all cases. The draughtsman of the Act has adopted the word "user", and though the wording might have been clearer, I doubt whether any more definite word would express the meaning more accurately.' *Milne v Commissioner of Police for City of London, Leonard v Commissioner of Police for City of London, Boundford v Commissioner of Police for City of London* [1940] AC 1 at 43–45, per Lord Porter

Of land

[The Lands Clauses Consolidation Act 1845, s 128, provides that superfluous lands, unless they are (inter alia) lands 'used' for building purposes, shall be first offered to the owner of the lands from whom they were originally taken, or to adjoining owners.] 'It is not because you think that certain land might be applicable for building purposes, and may be very suitable for those purposes, and may be sold for those purposes, that it comes within either the meaning or the spirit of the words "land used for building purposes", by which, I apprehend, is meant land actually used for building purposes; not land contemplated to be used for building purposes, or intended to be used for building purposes, or thoroughly suitable for building purposes.' *London & South Western Rly Co v Blackmore* (1870) LR 4 HL 610 at 617, per Lord Hatherley LC

Australia [A hospital owned a large area of undeveloped land outside its own grounds. It was held not liable to pay rates on this land as it was exempted therefrom under the Local Government Act 1919–1986 (NSW), s 132(1)(d).] 'Counsel for the city council submitted that an owner of land could not be said to use the land by leaving it unused; and that was all that had been done here. Their Lordships cannot accept this view. An owner can use land by keeping it in its virgin state for his own special purposes. An owner of a powder magazine or a rifle range uses the land he has acquired nearby for the purpose of ensuring safety even though he never sets foot on it. The owner of an island uses it for the purposes of a bird sanctuary even though he does nothing on it, except prevent people building there or disturbing the birds. In the same way this hospital gets, and purposely gets, fresh air, peace and quiet, which are no mean advantages to it and its patients.' *Newcastle City Council v Royal Newcastle Hospital* [1959] 1 All ER 734 at 735, PC, per Lord Denning; also reported in [1959] AC 248 at 255

Of trade mark

[The Trade Marks Act 1905, s 3 (repealed; see now the Trade Marks Act 1938, s 68), defined a trade mark as meaning a mark 'used' or proposed to be 'used' upon or in connection with goods for the purpose of indicating that they were the goods of the proprietor of such trade mark.] 'The question really is, what is the meaning of the words "used or proposed to be used upon or in connection with goods" in s 3 of the Trade Marks Act? . . . I think that the word "used" in s 3 of the Act must mean "used in this country".' *Re Neuchatel Asphalte Co's Trade Mark* [1913] 2 Ch 291 at 301, per Sargant J

'I do not think that the fact that a person has improperly said, in a directory or other publication, that AB is the proprietor of a trade mark is a "use" of the trade mark by the person who has made the statement [within the Trade Marks Act 1938]. If he had been authorised by AB to make that statement, it would be a "use" of the trade mark by AB, but not by the person who has made the incorrect statement. The defendants themselves are not applying the trade mark to goods because they are not dealing with goods; and, certainly, they are not "using" the trade mark "in the course of trade" and "in relation to those goods". They are using it in the course of their own trade, which is that of a publisher of a trade directory.' *Ravok (M) (Weatherwear) Ltd v National Trade Press Ltd* [1955] 1 All ER 621 at 623, per Lord Goddard CJ; see also [1955] 1 QB 554

Of vehicle

[The Motor Vehicles (Construction and Use) Regulations 1937, reg 94 (revoked; see now the Motor Vehicles (Construction and Use) Regulations 1978), provided that if any person 'used' or caused or permitted to be used on any road 'a motor vehicle' in contravention of or failed to comply with any regulations contained in Part III of the Regulations, he should for each offence be liable to a fine.] 'In my opinion, giving the ordinary commonsense interpretation to reg 94, I cannot arrive at any other conclusion than that one person using the vehicle in this case was, at any rate, the driver. It may be that the person in charge of the vehicle is a person using the vehicle, but that the person driving the vehicle is using it seems so plain as to make it unnecessary to look at other regulations to see whether they throw light on the question.' *Gifford v Whittaker* [1942] 1 KB 501 at 505, DC, per Lord Caldecote CJ

'The short question in this appeal . . . is what is meant by the word "use . . . a motor vehicle on a road" within the meaning of s 35 of the Road Traffic Act 1930 [repealed; see now the Road Traffic Act 1988, s 143]. Section 35(1) provides: "Subject to the provisions of this Part of this Act, it shall not be lawful for any person to use, or to cause or permit any other person to use, a motor vehicle on a road unless there is in force. . . ." Then the subsection goes on to refer to the necessary insurance cover. One thing seems to be clear, and that is that "use" there is used in contradistinction to the word "drive" which appears in other sections, such as s 11 and s 12, dealing with dangerous and careless driving. Prima facie, "use" is a wider term and includes something more than driving, and certainly it would include moving.' *Elliott v Grey* [1959] 3 All ER 733 at 735, 736, per Lord Parker CJ

'In my judgment, counsel for the second defendant is right in his contention that a person does not "use a motor vehicle on the road" . . . unless there is present, in the person alleged to be the user, an element of controlling, managing or operating the vehicle at the relevant time.' *Brown v Roberts* [1963] 2 All ER 263 at 269, per Megaw J

Australia 'Where a vehicle is authorisedly driven by an employee or owner of the vehicle and there is no relevant permit in existence, it is, in my opinion, the owner who, for the purpose of s 49 [of the State Transport Act 1960–1986 [Qld]], "uses" the vehicle and not the employee who merely drives it under the master's orders. In my opinion, they cannot, in such a case, both be said to have "used" it.' *Jackson v Horne* [1966] ALR 368 at 370, per Barwick CJ

Australia 'I do not think that every act in loading a vehicle for the conveyance of what is loaded upon it is necessarily a use or a part of the use of the motor vehicle [within the Motor Vehicles [Third Party Insurance] Act 1942–1986 (NSW), s 10 (see now s 10(b)(i)). But the act of actually placing the load on the part of the vehicle designed to bear it during transport and for the purpose of its transportation, must, in my opinion, be a use of the motor vehicle in the sense relevant to the Act and to the terms of the policy. In my opinion, the relevant use of the vehicle cannot be confined to the periods it is in motion, or its parts moving in some operation. It may be in use, though stationary.' *Government Insurance Office of New South Wales v Green* [1967] ALR 106 at 108, per Barwick CJ

Canada 'An analogous "use" as distinguished from "operation" is exemplified in the case of a bus. The undertaking in such a case includes the entrance and exit to and from the bus of passengers. If the steps are defective and a passenger is injured, could it be said that injury did not arise out of the "use"? The expression "use or operation" [in an insurance policy] would or should, in my opinion, convey to one reading it all accidents resulting from the ordinary and well-known activities to which automobiles are put, all accidents which the common judgment in ordinary language would attribute to the utilisation of an automobile as a means of different forms of accommodation or service.' *Stevenson v Reliance Petroleum Ltd* (1956) 5 DLR (2d) 673 at 676–677, SCC, per Rand J

New Zealand 'What is required for the concession to apply is that the vehicle must be "personally owned and used . . . for at least one year". Personal ownership is not in question in this case. The important word is therefore "used" which, as any dictionary will shew, has a wide area of meaning. Its meaning must be taken from the context. The thing that is spoken of as being "used" is a vehicle. A vehicle is not a thing that is used continuously, even over a short period. Therefore the word "used" does not connote continuous use. That point gains emphasis from two other features of the context. The use must be by the owner "personally"; and it must extend "for at least one year". Even over a short period of time and in the hands of the keenest owner a vehicle needs to be parked, serviced and garaged. Over a period of a year it might well in addition require extensive repairs. Moreover, its owner would normally require to leave it out of action while he is ill or while he goes away on business. Reading the whole phrase with such considerations in mind, I am of opinion that the word "used" connotes use normal to the kind of vehicle in question, and that normal use does not cease merely because the vehicle is in fact out of action at times and for reasons incidental to normal personal ownership and use. An owner who, choosing deliberately not to use his vehicle, leaves it locked away in a garage for months on end could not be said to be using it. But I do not think that "personal use for at least one year" is broken by the fact that the vehicle is stored in a garage for a period during which the owner is unable for normal reasons to use it. How long that period may be is a question of degree, and that is a question of fact that depends on the circumstances of the case.' *Handiside v A-G* [1969] NZLR 650 at 651, per Wild CJ

USE FOR TRADE

(1) In this Act 'use for trade' means, subject to subsection (3) below, use in Great Britain in connection with, or with a view to, a transaction falling within subsection (2) below where—

(a) the transaction is by reference to quantity or is a transaction for the purposes of which there is made or implied a statement of the quantity of goods to which the transaction relates, and
(b) the use is for the purpose of the determination or statement of that quantity.

(2) A transaction falls within this subsection if it is a transaction for—
(a) the transferring or rendering of money or money's worth in consideration of money or money's worth, or
(b) the making of a payment in respect of any toll or duty.

(3) Use for trade does not include use in a case where—
(a) the determination or statement is a determination or statement of the quantity of goods required for despatch to a destination outside Great Britain and any designated country, and
(b) the transaction is not a sale by retail, and
(c) no transfer or rendering of money or money's worth is involved other than the passing of the title to the goods and the consideration for them.

(4) The following equipment, that is to say—
(a) any weighing or measuring equipment which is made available in Great Britain for use by the public, whether on payment or otherwise, and
(b) any equipment which is used in Great Britain for the grading by reference to their weight, for the purposes of trading transactions by reference to that grading, of hens' eggs in shell which are intended for human consumption,

shall be treated for the purposes of this Part [Part II] of this Act as weighing or measuring equipment in use for trade, whether or not it would apart from this subsection be so treated. (Weights and Measures Act 1985, s 7)

USUAL COVENANTS

'I am clearly of opinion that this case comes within *Hampshire v Wickens* [(1878) 7 Ch D 555] decided in 1878. There the Master of the Rolls (Jessel MR) laid down what were usual and what were unusual covenants. Thus covenants to pay rent; to pay taxes, except such as are expressly payable by the landlord; to keep and deliver up the premises in repair; to allow the lessor to enter and view the state of repair; and the usual qualified covenants by the lessor for quiet enjoyment by the lessee, are usual covenants. On the other hand, a covenant by the lessee that he would not, without the lessor's consent, "assign, underlet, or part with the possession of the said premises, but such consent not to be withheld to a respectable and responsible tenant", is not a usual covenant.' *Bishop v Taylor & Co* (1891) 60 LJQB 556 at 557, 558, DC, per Smith J

'In my view it is a complete mistake to suppose that the usual covenants in regard to a lease, for instance, of a country house are necessarily usual covenants in regard to the lease of a London residence, and I would add that it seems to me that it may very well be that what is usual in Mayfair or Bayswater is not usual at all in some other part of London such as, for instance, Whitechapel. Further, in my opinion, "usual" in this sense means no more than "occurring in ordinary use", and I think that it is an error to suppose that the Court is entitled to hold that a particular covenant is not usual because it may be established that there are some few cases in which that covenant is not used. If it is established that (to put a strong case) in nine cases out of ten the covenant would be found in a lease of premises of that nature for that purpose and in that district, I think that the court is bound to hold that the covenant is usual.' *Flexman v Corbett* [1930] 1 Ch 672 at 678, per Maugham J

Canada [An insurance policy covered personal property 'usual' to occupancy.] 'As to the meaning of "usual", one finds the following definitions in the Oxford English Dictionary, 1961 reprint of the 1933 edition, vol XI, p 477: ". . . Ordinarily used; constantly or customarily employed; in common use; ordinary, customary . . . That ordinarily happens, occurs, or is to be found; such as is commonly met with or observed in ordinary practice or experience . . . Common or habitual *to* a person or thing . . . (as in) Several shapes and effects usual to Fountains of Pleasure." The Random House Dictionary of the English Language, probably the best one-volume dictionary published in North America in recent memory, provides at p 1574 the following suggested meanings: ". . . habitual or customary . . . commonly met with or observed in experience . . . commonplace, everyday . . .". The following are suggested synonyms for "usual" as set out in Random House: "accustomed . . . general, prevailing, prevalent, everyday, familiar, regular, expected, predictable". Stroud's Judicial Dictionary, 4th edn (1974), vol 5, p 2907, has this passage on the matter: "the question of what is a 'usual' clause, condition, or thing, is a fact to be established by proof, having regard to (a) the subject-matter, (b) its locality, (c) its time of arising, and (d), sometimes, its circumstances." Firstly, let me say here that the language employed calls for an objective, rather than subjective approach to the limits of coverage. After all, the phrase in issue directs one to what is "usual or incidental to the occupancy of *the* premises as a dwelling" and not to the *insured's* occupancy. Therefore, bearing in mind the subject-matter of the loss—bee-keeping equipment and materials, processing equipment for honey, and honey—and the locality—a residential dwelling in a city—I cannot see how the personal property in question could be fairly characterised as usually or habitually or commonly related to the user of the premises as a residential dwelling.' *Miller v Gibraltar General Insurance Co* (1979) 104 DLR (3d) 143 at 149, Ont Co Ct, per Killeen Co Ct J

USUAL TERMS

Stay of proceedings

Australia 'Some uncertainty was expressed at the Bar as to what is meant by usual terms, . . . and, in order that there may be no room for misunderstanding or uncertainty in the future, I wish to make plain what it is that is meant by that expression. It is this. Execution on a judgment will be stayed during the period within which under the rules an appeal may be brought, and, if a notice of appeal is filed, and if security for the amount of the verdict and of costs of the action is given to the satisfaction of the Prothonotary, the stay will be continued until the appeal is disposed of or until the Court otherwise orders.' *Goldstein v Craft* (1926) 26 SRNSW 354 at 362, per Street CJ

USUALLY

'I think, when you have got the words "have been usually", referring to the past time, "have been usually" simply means have been as a matter of custom during the years to the passing of which "have been" points.' *Borthwick (Thomas) & Sons Ltd v Nolder* (1926) 11 Tax Cas 261 at 266, per Rowlatt J

USURPED POWER

[A fire policy contained a proviso that the defendants should not be liable if the building insured was burnt by reason of any invasion, foreign enemy or any military or 'usurped power'.] 'The words "usurped power", in the proviso according to the true import thereof and the meaning of the parties, can only mean an invasion of the kingdom by foreign enemies to give laws and usurp the government thereof, or an internal armed force in rebellion assuming the power of government by making laws, and punishing for not obeying those laws.' *Drinkwater v London Assurance Corpn* (1767) 2 Wils 363 at 363, per Bathurst J

UTILITIES

'Utilities' means electricity, gas, water, steam, compressed air and hydraulic power. (Coal Industry Nationalisation Act 1946, s 63)

UTILITY

'I think in law "utility" means an invention better than the preceding knowledge of the trade as to a particular fabric. It does not mean abstract utility. Therefore, even if you are of opinion (I do not know whether I ought to express an opinion that it is foreign to the matter) that stays are very bad things, you must not say this is useless because stays are bad things.' *Young & Neilson v Rosenthal & Co* (1884) 1 RPC 29 at 34, per Grove J

'I may take another test of utility, namely, that an invention is useful, for the purposes of the patent law, when the public are thereby enabled to do something which they could not do before, or to do in a more advantageous manner something which they could do before, or, to express it in another way, that an invention is patentable which offers the public a useful choice.' *Welsbach Incandescent Gas Light Co v New Incandescant (Sunlight Patent) Gas Lighting Co* [1900] 1 Ch 843 at 850, per Buckley J

UTTER

Uttering a counterfeit coin means, prima facie, passing, or trying to pass it, as genuine. Where a person knowingly offers a counterfeit coin in payment there is an uttering although the coin is refused. (11 Halsbury's Laws (4th edn) para 990)

'In order to make it an uttering, we are of opinion that this [a forged note] should be parted with or tendered, or offered, or used in some way to get money or credit upon it.' *R v Skuhard* (1811) Russ & Ry 200 at 202, CCR, per cur.

'"Utter" is, perhaps, not a word which an ordinary man with no legal training would use at all in connection with a counterfeit coin; but a lawyer who had made no special study of coinage law would, I think, suppose that "uttering" a counterfeit coin meant passing it or trying to pass it as genuine. Certainly if I had been told before I sat on this appeal that if I gave or sold to a coin collector, as a curiosity, a bad florin which I had been given in change I was guilty of a criminal offence of uttering a counterfeit coin I would have been surprised. My surprise, I am glad to see, would have been shared by the members of the Court of Appeal of New South Wales who decided the case of *R v McMahon* [(1894) 15 NSWLR 131]. The statutory provision there in question was in similar terms to s 5(3) of the 1936 Act [Coinage Offences Act 1936 (repealed by the Forgery and Counterfeiting Act 1981; see infra)] but the facts of the case were totally different and the actual decision is not inconsistent with the contentions of the Crown on this appeal. But although their language may have been wider than was necessary for the decision it is noteworthy that they said: "After careful consideration we think uttering coin implies using it as current coin for the purpose of currency." . . . To utter a counterfeit coin means, to my mind, prima facie, to pass it or try to pass it as genuine.' *Selby v Director of Public Prosecutions* [1971] 3 All ER 810 at 817, 822, HL per Lord Cross of Chelsea

[The word 'utter' in the Forgery Act 1913 (repealed) has been replaced by the words 'use a false instrument' in the Forgery and Counterfeiting Act 1981, s 3. See the notes to that section in 12 Halsbury's Statutes (4th edn, 1989 Reissue) 755.]

V

VACANCY *See also* CASUAL VACANCY

'The 76th article of association provides for the vacating of the office of director upon the happening of various contingencies, such as bankruptcy or insolvency, or becoming lunatic, or of unsound mind. . . . What is the meaning of the expression [in a subsequent article] "any casual vacancy"? "Any casual vacancy" in my judgment is any vacancy in the office of directors arising otherwise than by the retirement in rotation pointed out by the previous articles. It includes, therefore, the happening of any of the contingencies referred to in the 76th article, and it has been taken, and as I conceive correctly taken, by both sides to include a vacancy occurring by the voluntary retirement of a director.' *Munster v Cammell Co* (1882) 21 Ch D 183 at 186, 187, per Fry J

VACANT POSSESSION

[In a warehouse, sold with 'vacant possession' to the plaintiff, the cellars were so filled with rubbish, e.g. bags of hard cement, as to make then unusuable. The defendant refused to remove the rubbish.] 'It was said that the expression "vacant possession" was merely used in contradistinction to "possession" simpliciter, in order to show that the property was on completion to be transferred free from any claim of right to possession in the vendor or any third person such as a tenant or a licensee: and that the presence on the premises of chattels which had been abandoned by the vendor did not constitute or evidence any such claim or right. . . . Subject to the rule *de minimis* a vendor who leaves property of his own on the premises on completion cannot, in our opinion, be said to give vacant possession, since by doing so he is claiming a right to use the premises for his own purposes, namely, as a place of deposit for his own goods inconsistent with the right which the purchaser has on completion to undisturbed enjoyment. . . . But there is, we think, a quite different ground upon which the judgment under appeal can be supported. The phrase "vacant possession" is no doubt generally used in order to make it clear that what is being sold is not an interest in a reversion. But it is not confined to this. Occupation by a person having no claim of right prevents the giving of "vacant possession", and it is the duty of the vendor to eject such a person before completion. See *Royal Bristol Permanent Society v Bomas* [(1887) 35

Ch D 390, 395] and *Engell v Fitch* [(1869) LR 4 QB 659]. The reason for this, it appears to us, is that the right of actual unimpeded physical enjoyment is comprised in the right to vacant possession. We cannot see why the existence of a physical impediment to such enjoyment to which a purchaser does not expressly or impliedly consent to submit should stand in a different position to an impediment caused by the presence of a trespasser. It is true that in each case the purchaser obtains the right to possession in law, notwithstanding the presence of the impediment. But it appears to us that what he bargains for is not merely the right in law, but the power in fact to exercise the right. When we speak of a physical impediment we do not mean that any physical impediment will do. It must be an impediment which substantially prevents or interferes with the enjoyment of the right of possession of a substantial part of the property.' *Cumberland Consolidated Holdings Ltd v Ireland* [1946] KB 264 at 269–271, CA, per cur.

See generally, 42 Halsbury's Laws (4th edn) para 129

VACATE

New Zealand [Under a contract for the sale of land, the vendor undertook to transfer a certain Maori leasehold if he decided to 'vacate' the property.] 'The word "vacate" will connote, in accordance with the context, either a withdrawal which results in emptiness or vacancy or a mere withdrawal or a departure where no state of vacancy is produced. In the present context, I think the latter is the appropriate meaning.' *McLean v Grace* [1953] NZLR 566 at 569, per F B Adams J

VAGABOND *See* ROGUE AND VAGABOND

VAGUENESS

'As it seems to me, language has been used [in cases cited before the court] which tends to confuse the two distinct ideas, of vagueness in the contract, and vagueness which arises from the difficulty of identifying future property. "Vagueness" is a misleading term. A contract may be so vague in its terms that it cannot be understood, and in that case it is of no effect at law or in equity. There is another kind of vagueness which arises from the property not being ascertained at the date of the contract, but if at the time when the contract is sought to be enforced the property has come *in esse* and is capable of being identified as that to which the contract refers, I cannot see why there is in it any such vagueness as to prevent a Court of Equity from enforcing the contract.' *Re Clarke, Coombe v Carter* (1887) 36 Ch D 348 at 355, CA, per Bowen LJ

VALID

[The Increase of Rent and Mortgage Interest (Restrictions) Act 1920, s 3(2) (repealed) enacted that where the rent of a dwelling-house to which the Act applied was increased, no such increase was due or recoverable until after the landlord has served upon the tenant a 'valid' notice in writing of his intention to increase the rent.] 'In my opinion we must give effect to the requirement of the statute that the notice be a "valid" notice. . . . "Valid" means more than correct in form; it means correct in substance as well as in form.' *Sammon v Byrne* [1926] IR 411 at 420, per Kennedy CJ

Australia [The Commonwealth Electoral Act 1918–1966, s 128A(12) [see now s 245(4)] provides that every elector who fails to vote at an election without a 'valid and sufficient reason' for such failure shall be guilty of an offence.] 'In my opinion a "valid and sufficient reason" means some reason which is not excluded by law, and is, in the circumstances, a reasonable excuse for not voting. If it be, as in this case, an open challenge to the very essence of the enactment, it is, of course, excluded by law and not valid. So also, if there be any express provision of any law with which the alleged reason is in conflict. Again, if a mandatory or prohibitive regulation be contravened, the same result follows. But the reason may be compulsive obedience to law which makes voting practically impossible. Physical obstruction, whether of sickness or outside prevention, or of natural events, or accident of any kind, would certainly be recognised by law in such a case. One might also imagine cases where an intending voter on his way to the poll was diverted to save life, or to prevent crime, or to assist at some great disaster, as a fire; in all of which cases, in my opinion, the law would recognise the competitive claims of public duty. . . . The sufficiency of the reason, in any given instance, is a pure question of fact dependent on the circumstances of the occasion.' *Judd v McKeon* (1926) 38 CLR 380 at 386, 387, per Isaacs J

VALUABLE

'A shop which may only be used for one trade cannot fairly be described as "valuable business premises".' *Charles Hunt Ltd v Palmer* [1931] 2 Ch 287 at 291–293, per Clauson J

VALUABLE CONSIDERATION *See* CONSIDERATION

VALUABLE SECURITY

For purposes of this section [which deals with the suppression, etc, of documents] . . . 'valuable security' means any document creating, transferring, surrendering or releasing any right to, in or over property, or authorising the payment of money or delivery of any property, or evidencing the creation, transfer, surrender or release of any such right, or the payment of money or delivery of any property, or the satisfaction of any obligation. (Theft Act 1968, s 20(3))

VALUABLES

'The *ejusdem generis* rule applies to the words "jewellery or valuables", [in a notice displayed by an innkeeper excluding liability for loss of such goods unless deposited for safe custody] and consequently I cannot hold that a fur coat comes within the meaning of "valuables". I think that the plaintiff would have read that word as applying to small articles of value and not to articles of clothing.' *Cryan v Hotel Rembrandt Ltd* (1925) 133 LT 395 at 397, per Greer J

VALUATION *See also* ARBITRATION

Australia 'The word "valuation" in itself and without more, means merely the estimation of a thing's worth, the price set on a thing; it does not connote that the estimation of the worth of the thing or the price set on the thing is necessarily the estimation or setting of some particular person independent of the owner of the thing and its proposed purchaser and, in my view, it may mean no more than the estimation of the thing's worth in the opinion of reasonable people, the fair value of the thing in the particular circumstances of the case. It seems to me not difficult in the context of this contract to draw the conclusion that when the parties to it agreed that the disposal of this type of stock in a going concern should be effected "at valuation" they meant no more than at a fair valuation, that a fair value should be paid for it. . . . It will follow from what I have said that, in my opinion, when the memorandum of agreement in the present case provided that the stock-in-trade of the subject business was to be sold "at valuation", this constituted an agreement to sell such stock "at a reasonable price" and that such an agreement was a contract enforceable at law.' *Wenning v Robinson* [1964–5] NSWR 614 at 624, per Asprey J

VALUATION LIST

Alteration of *See* ALTERATION

VALUE *See also* FAIR VALUE; MARKET VALUE; MONEY'S WORTH

'Value' means valuable consideration. (Bills of Exchange Act 1882, s 2)

Australia 'In the case of chattels it is often, though not always, easy to ascertain the value. In order that any article may have an exchange value, there must be presupposed a person willing to give the article in exchange for money and another willing to give money in exchange for the article. When there is a large or considerable number of articles of the same kind which are the subject of daily or frequent sale and purchase, the value of the articles is taken to be their current price. . . . In my judgment the test of value of land is to be determined, not by enquiring what price a man desiring to sell could actually have obtained for it on a given day, i.e., whether there was in fact on that day a willing buyer, but by enquiring "What would a man desiring to buy the land have had to pay for it on that day to a vendor willing to sell it for a fair price but not desirous to sell?"' *Spencer v The Commonwealth* (1907) 5 CLR 418 at 431, 432, per Griffith CJ

Australia '"Value" in cases of compulsory acquisition has proved to be a word of very elastic meaning. It is not necessarily the "mere saleable value" (*Spencer's Case* [supra]). It may include compensation for loss of business or goodwill—costs of removal—value of fixtures if taken, or loss if not taken—but these items are, theoretically, considered only as factors or elements affecting what is called the value to the owner.' *Minister for Army v Parbury Henty & Co Pty Ltd* (1945) 70 CLR 459 at 492, per Latham CJ

Australia 'It is established that the value of land which is compulsorily taken is to be estimated at the value to the owner. It is immaterial that the owner is not using the land at the time.' Ibid at 495

Australia 'The ordinary principle applicable to the assessment of compensation for lands compulsorily acquired by statutory authorities is that the owner is entitled to be paid the value to him as it existed at the date of the notice of the taking; and the valuation is to include, as at that time, all advantages present or future which the land may possess: *Cedar Rapids Manufacturing and Power Co v Lacoste* [[1914] AC 569] at p 576. The basic test of value is the amount which a prudent man in the position of the owner would have been willing to give, rather than fail to obtain the land, having regard to those advantages or potentialities: *Pastoral Finance Association Ltd v The Minister* [[1914] AC 1083].' *Grace Bros Pty Ltd v Minister of State for the Army* [1945] NSWSR 206 at 209, per Davidson J

Canada 'Both "worth" and "value" are words of many meanings. Frequently an adjective is used with a view to a more precise definition, and we find "value" described as "actual value" "assessed value", "fair value", "intrinsic value", "market value", "sale value", and in other ways. But in all cases the concept of value is influenced by the purpose of the valuation. Thus, certain property may be "worth" one sum for one particular purpose, e.g., taxation, and have another value for another purpose, e.g., sale, and yet other values for other purposes. Again, the same property might have different values to different persons. "Value of property" means value to some specific person or group of persons and depends upon the capacity of the property to perform service for its owner, or upon the power its ownership may confer to exchange it for money or other property. It is the equivalent in dollars of the loss which an owner of property suffers if he is deprived of it, or, conversely, the advantages possessed by an owner who can exploit it by use or sale.' *White & Co Ltd v The City of Toronto* [1955] OR 320 at 326, Ont CA, per Laidlaw JA

New Zealand 'Differently phrased, "value" means what, with all its advantages and disadvantages, the premises were worth to the owner on the critical date, assuming him to have been, at that date, a man of ordinary prudence and foresight, not anxious to sell for any compelling or private reason, but willing to sell as one business man would to another, both of them being uninfluenced by any consideration of sentiment or need. This language is an adaptation of the words used by Barton J in the course of his judgment in *Spencer v Commonwealth of Australia* [supra]. That was, it is true, a compensation case, but the words, as adapted, seem apposite for all present purposes.' *Re Oriental Hotel, Muir v Niall* [1944] NZLR 512 at 515, 516, 520, per Finlay J; also reported [1944] GLR 202 at 204

United States Except as otherwise provided with respect to negotiable instruments and bank collections (sections 3–303, 4–208 and 4–209) a person gives 'value' for rights if he acquires them

(a) in return for a binding commitment to extend credit or for the extension of immediately available credit whether or not drawn upon and whether or not a charge-back is provided for in the event of difficulties in collection; or
(b) as security for or in total or partial satisfaction of a pre-existing claim; or
(c) by accepting delivery pursuant to a pre-existing contract for purchase; or
(d) generally, in return for any consideration sufficient to support a simple contract.

(Uniform Commercial Code 1978, s 1–201(44))

Annual *See* ANNUAL VALUE

Gross value *See* GROSS VALUE

Of estate

'The question I have . . . to determine arises upon the First Schedule to the Administration of Estates Act 1925, Part II, para 6. The testator has specifically devised certain properties to certain persons, and the question is how as between them the legacies and expenses are to be borne. Part II . . . para 6 says property which is specifically devised or bequeathed is to be applied rateably according to value. The testator had certain property which he devised subject to a mortgage created in his lifetime. It is said with regard to the property so devised that the word "value" in para 6 means the value of the property as unincumbered property and not the value of the property in the hands of the testator. The testator had, in fact, in respect of these particular properties, only an equity of redemption, and that is the value which, in my judgment must be taken for this purpose. The "value" cannot mean the actual price which the property would fetch in the open market free from incumbrances; it must mean the value of the testator, and since all he had was the equity of redemption, that is the value which must be taken.' *Re John, Jones v John* [1933] Ch 370 at 372, per Farwell J

VALUED POLICY *See* POLICY

VALUER

The terms 'valuer' and 'appraiser' have largely the same meaning, namely a person who sets a price upon, or who estimates the worth or the value of, property. However, an appraiser may be not only one who estimates the price or value of property but also one who estimates its quality or excellence. . . .

A valuer is not necessarily an arbitrator because the document appointing him describes him as an arbitrator. It is relevant what functions he is called upon to perform. There must be a matter affecting two parties which is the subject of a defined dispute. An auditor who values shares in a company pursuant to an agreement to sell them at the value determined by him and who, in doing so, is to act as an expert and not as an arbitrator is not an arbitrator. It is not enough that parties who may be affected by the decision have opposed interests; the essential prerequisite is that by the time it is submitted to the valuer for decision there should be a formulated dispute between at least two parties which his decision is required to resolve. Once that is proved, it must be decided whether there are other indicia, such as the reception of rival contentions or of evidence or the giving of a reasoned judgment, which show that the valuer is acting as an arbitrator. (49 Halsbury's Laws (4th edn) paras 1, 6)

VARY

Australia [The Commonwealth Conciliation and Arbitration Act 1904–1950, s 49 (see now the Conciliation and Arbitration Act 1904–1986, s 59), provides that the Court may set aside an award or any of the terms of an award, or 'vary' any of the terms of an award.] 'The word "vary" is one which no doubt in different contexts may have different meanings. In s 49 there is a distinction drawn between setting aside an award or any of the terms of an award and varying any of the terms of an award. But the distinction made, at all events in words, between setting aside and variation, can carry no restriction upon the meaning of "variation" beyond showing that it refers to a change in some part of the award. Probably it is enough to say that to vary the terms of the award is to change them in part whether by addition, by excision, by modification or by substitution or by qualification or otherwise.' *R v Tonkin, ex p Federated Ship Painters' Union* [1954] ALR 777 at 779, per cur.

Australia [The Industrial Conciliation and Arbitration Act 1972–1986 (SA), s 94(2)(a), provides that on the hearing of an appeal the court may confirm, quash or 'vary' the order or decision appealed against.] '[Counsel's] submission was that the learned judge was in error in that he purported to do more than to quash the order of the Industrial Magistrate and that what he did could not come under the power to vary the order contained in s 92(2)(a). He referred to *King (Conway) v Justices of County Tyrone*, a decision of a Divisional Court, in which Andrews J defined the powers of a court to "confirm, vary or reverse, an order" in the following way: "'Confirm' requires no explanation; 'vary' in my opinion, means alter in part, as distinguished from discharging the whole order appealed against and making a wholly different one; and 'reverse' in my opinion imports more than discharge, and means 'change to the contrary'." The Shorter Oxford English Dictionary defines the transitive verb "to vary" as meaning "to cause to change to alter; to introduce changes or alterations into". As an illustration of the verb with that meaning it gives the following—"The court, after such notice, may vary such order in such manner as it may think fit". The dictionary meaning does not accord with that given by Andrews J in that there is no suggestion that the change or alteration must be a change or alteration only in part. In *Scott Pools Pty Ltd v Salisbury Corporation* Jacobs J was of the opinion that the word "varied", appearing in Order 58, Rule 16(1) of the Rules of the Supreme Court [repealed], empowered the Court to discharge an order of the Planning

Appeal Board and substitute a different order for it. I think that the same meaning must be given to the word "vary" appearing in s 94(2)(a) of the Industrial Conciliation and Arbitration Act. In my opinion s 94(2)(a) empowered the learned judge to make the order which he made.' *R v Industrial Court* (1982) 30 SASR 504 at 512, per Mitchell J

VEHICLE *See also* GOODS VEHICLE; MOTOR CAR; MOTOR CYCLE; MOTOR TRACTOR; PUBLIC SERVICE VEHICLE

'Vehicle' does not include a vessel, except any vessel adapted for use on land while it is being so used. (National Parks and Access to the Countryside Act 1949, s 114)

'Vehicle' includes a railway vehicle. (Customs and Excise Management Act 1979, s 1(1))

'Vehicle' includes an aircraft, hovercraft or boat. (Deer Act 1980, s 8)

'The only question for the court is whether a bicycle is a "vehicle" within the meaning of that word in clause 7 [of an insurance policy]. . . . Reading the provisions of the policy together I can not see any reason for putting a limitation on the meaning of the word "vehicle", and I hold that the word includes a bicycle.' *Hansford v London Express Newspaper Ltd* (1928) 44 TLR 349 at 350, per Rowlatt J

[B Ltd transported a heavy load, a cylindrical section, through Leeds. The maximum width of the load was more than nine feet six inches. In order to transport the cylindrical section it was mounted on bogies, one in front and one at the rear. A motor tractor was attached to the front bogies and another at the back was attached to the rear bogies. There were never less than four men, including the drivers of the tractors in direct attendance on the load on the 'vehicle'. Informations were preferred against B Ltd under the Motor Vehicles (Authorisation of Special Types) General Order 1955, art 18(1) (revoked; see now the Motor Vehicles (Authorisation of Special Types) General Order 1979) in that there were not at least three persons in attendance on each tractor.] 'In my opinion it is quite impossible to read the word "vehicle" where it occurs in art 18 as in effect meaning vehicles or a combination of vehicles. Such a construction not only does violence to the language actually used, but also is to be contrasted with other provisions in the order which explicitly provide either for vehicles or for a combination of vehicles. . . . The ordinary meaning so to be given to the words "any vehicle" in this article clearly covers not merely a vehicle that is a motor-propelled vehicle but also a trailer itself.' *Dixon v BRS (Pickfords) Ltd* [1959] 1 All ER 449 at 451, 452, per Lord Parker CJ

[The question was whether a hydrogen trailer assembly not permanently attached to its tractor was itself a 'vehicle' within the meaning of s 13 of the Industrial Development Act 1966, or whether it qualified for an investment grant as machinery or plant. Section 13(1) of the Act of 1966 defines 'machinery or plant' as excluding inter alia any 'vehicle' except (a) a vehicle constructed or adapted for the conveyance of a machine incorporated in or permanently attached to it and of no other load except articles used for the purposes of the machine.] 'I am unable to accept the plaintiff company's contention that "vehicle" here means only such ordinary means of transport as lorries and motor cars. The terms of para (a) of the definition of plant and machinery, in my judgment, make clear that it extends to specialised vehicles and I think that it embraces the large tanker assembly. The hydrogen trailer, on the other hand, seems to me to stand in a different position in this respect. The trailer constitutes a distinct piece of equipment capable of being used, and frequently used, separately from the tractor which moves it. When separate from any tractor it is completely immoveable. Although it is fitted with two wheels at the rear, it cannot be moved until the rear wheels of a tractor unit have been inserted under its front portion to take the weight of that part of the trailer. In my judgment, it is realistic to describe this trailer as a load which is moved by and on its tractor. Although it has some of the characteristics of a vehicle, I do not consider that, when its true nature is appreciated, it can be appropriately described as a vehicle.' *British Oxygen Co Ltd v Board of Trade* [1968] 2 All ER 177 at 183, per Buckley J

[It was held that a certain right of way to a church was for pedestrians only and not for vehicles.] 'While I have held that there is no vehicular right of way, I do not regard a wheelbarrow or other carrying device of small dimensions propelled by man as being a "vehicle" for this purpose.' *St Edmundsbury & Ipswich Diocesan Board of Finance v Clark (No 2)* [1973] 3 All ER 902 at 930, per Megarry J; affd [1975] 1 All ER 772, CA

Canada 'I do not think it has ever been argued that, for instance, a horse-drawn vehicle is not a "vehicle" under the Act [Highway Traffic Act, RSM 1940 (now RSM 1970, c H-60)], and I fail to see any distinction between it and any other vehicle propelled by muscular power—whether that power be human or animal. I would agree with the trial judge that [a] wheel-chair was a "vehicle" within the meaning of the Act.' *Carlson v Chochinov* [1948] 2 WWR 273 at 276, Man CA, per McPherson CJM

Canada 'A "vehicle" as commonly understood may be defined as an instrument of conveyance, and as applied to transportation, as an instrument for transporting either passengers or property.' *R v Thornton* (1949) 96 CCC 323 at 326, NSSC, per Parker J

Canada 'The word "vehicle" in its original sense conveys the meaning of a structure on wheels for carrying persons or goods.' *Sugar City Municipal District No 5 v Bennett & White (Calgary) Ltd* [1950] 3 DLR 81 at 93, SCC, per Rand J

Canada 'I turn . . . to the definition of "vehicle" in the Shorter Oxford Dictionary. The appropriate definition there set out would seem to be as follows: "A means of conveyance provided with wheels or runners and used for the carriage of persons or goods; a carriage, cart, wagon, sledge, etc. A receptacle in which anything is placed in order to be moved." . . . I am of the opinion that each particular apparatus [a mobile home] purchased and installed by each of these appellants was not a "vehicle". It was not a means of conveyance, although it was provided with wheels, and it was not used for the carriage of persons or goods. The purpose of the apparatus, and it is quite apparent from the evidence, was that it should be hauled quite empty to a site and there placed on the site and used, not for the conveyance of persons or goods, but for the installation of goods, to wit, furniture, and the residence of people.' *Farr v Township of Moore* [1978] 2 SCR 504 at 507, 508, SCC, per Spence J

Articulated vehicle

'Articulated vehicle' means a motor vehicle with a trailer so attached to it as to be partially superimposed upon it. (Road Traffic Regulation Act 1984, s 138(3))

Construction and adaptation
See CONSTRUCT

Farmer's goods vehicle

'Farmer's goods vehicle' means . . . a goods vehicle registered under this Act in the name of a person engaged in agriculture and used on public roads solely by him for the purpose of the conveyance of the produce of, or of articles required for the purposes of, the agricultural land which he occupies, and for no other purpose. (Vehicles (Excise) Act 1971, Sch 4, as substituted by the Finance Act 1982, Sch 5, Part A)

Goods vehicle

'Goods vehicle' means a motor vehicle constructed or adapted for use for the carriage or haulage of goods or burden of any description, or a trailer so constructed or adapted. (International Carriage of Perishable Foodstuffs Act 1976, s 19(1))

'Goods vehicle' means a motor vehicle constructed or adapted for use for the carriage of goods or burden of any description or a trailer so constructed or adapted. (Road Traffic Regulation Act 1984, s 138(3))

Heavy commercial vehicle

In this Act 'heavy commercial vehicle' means any goods vehicle which has an operating weight exceeding 7.5 tonnes. (Road Traffic Regulation Act 1984, s 138(1)).

[See sub-ss (4)–(7) as to the Secretary of State's powers to amend sub-s (1) by regulations.]

Motor vehicle

In this Act subject to section 20 of the Clinically Sick and Disabled Persons Act 1970 (which makes special provision with respect to invalid carriages), 'motor vehicle' means a mechanically propelled vehicle intended or adapted for use on roads, and 'trailer' means a vehicle drawn by a motor vehicle. (Road Traffic Regulation Act 1984, s 136(1))

Canada 'A "motor vehicle" as commonly understood may be defined as a vehicle which is capable of being and is ordinarily self-propelled by power generated within itself, as distinct, for example, from a horse-drawn vehicle, or from one which is propelled by the application of externally generated power.' *R v Thornton* (1949) 96 CCC 323 at 326, NSSC, per Parker J

United States The term 'motor vehicle' means any self-propelled four-wheeled vehicle, of less than 6,000 pounds gross vehicle weight, which is designed primarily for use on public streets, roads, and highways. (Petroleum Marketing Practices Act 1978, s 201(7))

Private hire vehicle

'Private hire vehicle' means a motor vehicle constructed or adapted to seat fewer than eight passengers, other than a hackney carriage or public service vehicle, which is provided for hire with the services of a driver for the purposes of carrying passengers. (Local Government (Miscellaneous Provisions) Act 1976, s 80(1))

Road construction vehicle

'Road construction vehicle' means a vehicle constructed or adapted for use for the conveyance of built-in road construction machinery and not constructed or adapted for the conveyance of any other load except articles and material used for the purposes of that machinery. (Vehicles (Excise) Act 1971, s 4(2))

Trolley vehicle

'Trolley vehicle' means a mechanically propelled vehicle adapted for use on roads without rails and moved by power transmitted to it from some external source. (Road Traffic Act 1988, s 192(1))

VEIN

In a legal document, the context may show that the word 'bed' or 'seam', instead of bearing its normal meaning of a layer or member of a series of stratified rocks, is used to designate a deposit consisting of two or more strata of mineral separated by thin layers of other rock, for example shale, as distinguished from any one layer of mineral. In such a case 'vein' is sometimes applied to each of the layers of minerals comprised in the seam. (31 Halsbury's Laws (4th edn) para 12)

VEND

'The granting part of the patent authorises the plaintiff exclusively to "make, use, exercise, and vend" his invention. . . . Then the count alleges that the defendant, without the plaintiff's license, exposed to sale divers chairs intended to imitate and resemble, and which did imitate and resemble, his invention. Do those words necessarily import the vending, spoken of in the granting part of the patent? I certainly think not; because, even assuming that to vend may mean both a selling and an exposing to sale (though I rather think that it means the habit of selling and offering for sale), still those two meanings are not co-extensive; the former may include the latter, but a mere exposure to sale, i.e. with intent to sell, or for the purpose of selling, is not only not equivalent to a sale, but, as regards the patentee may be attended with wholly different consequences.' *Minter v Williams* (1835) 4 Ad & El 251 at 255, per Coleridge J

VENIRE DE NOVO

'The court clearly has jurisdiction to order a *venire de novo* which, of course, means an order on the appellant to attend and take his trial again in respect of the charge that lies against him, to plead to the indictment and be tried thereon duly according to law.' *R v Olivo* [1942] 2 All ER 494 at 495, CCA, per cur.

'*Venire de novo* was a writ issued by the Court of King's Bench when moved by a writ of error (i.e. alleging an error appearing on the face of the record of an inferior court), vacating the verdict and directing the sheriff to summon jurors anew (whence the name of the writ). Writ of error in criminal cases was abolished in England by the Criminal Appeal Act 1907, s 20. *Venire de novo* was and still is available in some other circumstances unnecessary to relate; its scope is highly technical.' *Director of Public Prosecutions of Jamaica v White* [1977] 3 All ER 1003 at 1007, PC, per Lord Simon of Glaisdale

VENISON

'Venison' means the carcase, or any edible part of the carcase, of a deer and includes imported venison, but not canned or cooked venison. (Deer Act 1980, s 8)

VERDICT

Juries in both civil and criminal matters may find general or special verdicts. General verdicts in criminal matters are findings of guilty or not guilty, and in civil causes are statements as to the party for which the juries find, with the amount of damages assessed, if such finding is for the plaintiff, or the sum awarded if the issue is one of assessment solely. Special verdicts are findings of specific facts, on which, in criminal cases, the court must direct the jury to return the general verdict warranted by its special findings. (26 Halsbury's Laws (4th edn) para 642)

'In Coke upon Littleton, 227b, it is stated that "By the law of England a jury, after their evidence given upon the issue, ought to be kept together in some convenient place, without meat or drinke, fire or candle, which some bookes call an imprisonment, and without speech with any, unlesse it be the bailife, and with him onely if they be agreed. After they be agreed they may in causes between party and party give a verdict, and if the Court be risen, give a privy verdict before any of the judges of the Court, and then they may eat and drinke, and the next morning in open Court they may either affirme or alter their privy verdict, and that which is given in Court shall stand. But in criminall cases of life or member, the jury can give no privy verdict, but they must give it openly in Court." It is clear, therefore, that at the time of this work being written there was a distinction to be drawn between civil and criminal cases. In the one case, that is in the civil trial, a privy verdict could be given, and then the jury were allowed to eat and drink, and they could either confirm or alter that verdict, that is that privy verdict, when the verdict was given as a public verdict. In Blackstone's Commentaries, iii, 377, it is stated, dealing with verdicts between party and party, that "A verdict is either privy or public. A privy verdict is when the judge hath left or adjourned the Court: and the jury, being agreed, in order to be delivered from their confinement, obtain leave to give their verdict privily to the judge out of Court: which privy verdict is of no force, unless afterwards affirmed by a public verdict openly in Court; wherein the jury may, if they please, vary from their privy verdict. So that the privy verdict is indeed a mere nullity; and yet it is a dangerous practice, allowing time for the parties to tamper with the jury, and therefore very seldom indulged." It appears, therefore, that the jury when they had once agreed could return an informal verdict called a privy verdict, and that when they had done that they were entitled to eat and drink, as is said in Coke upon Littleton, which was already a relaxation of the rigidity of the old rule; and in Blackstone's time he says that when they were agreed they gave their privy verdict in order to be delivered from their confinement. It seems, therefore, not only were they allowed to eat and drink if they had given their privy verdict, but in Blackstone's time they were no longer confined, and they could on the next morning, when they gave their public verdict, alter the privy verdict or affirm it as they pleased. Now that shows that when Blackstone's Commentaries were written it was clear that in civil trials juries were allowed to give a verdict after they had separated. The progress in the liberty afforded to juries is shown by the allowance of the release from confinement, which is stated in Blackstone, but not in Coke upon Littleton; and even in Coke upon Littleton a reference to the case of *Saunders v Freeman* [(1561) 1 Plowd 209] shows that after there had been a privy verdict the jury were then allowed to eat and drink and lie together. It appears to have been by custom that juries were allowed to do this. The words are "and then the same juries for their ease as is custom to eat and drink together for them aforesaid and to lie together until the morrow aforesaid and then to give their verdict aforesaid openly before the aforesaid justices at Northampton". So that going back to the time of Queen Elizabeth there had already existed some relaxation which is shown by the custom mentioned in Plowden and extended gradually till we get to the date of Blackstone's Commentaries. . . . The conclusion to which I have come upon this point is that in civil trials the separation of the jury does not invalidate the verdict. I think that it is a practice which should be resorted to only in rare instances and where special circumstances demand it.' *Fanshaw v Knowles* [1916] 2 KB 538 at 543–545, 547, CA, per Lord Reading CJ

Majority verdict

[By the Juries Act 1974, s 17, the verdict of a jury in proceedings in the Crown Court or the High Court need not be unanimous if (a) in a case where there are not less than eleven jurors, ten of them agree on the verdict and (b) in a case where there are ten jurors, nine of them agree on the verdict. In the county court, a jury of eight need not be unanimous if seven of them agree on the verdict. See more fully 22 Halsbury's Statutes (4th edn) 418.]

VERMIN

'Vermin', in its application to insects and parasites, includes their eggs, larvæ and pupæ, and the expression 'verminous' shall be construed accordingly. (Public Health Act 1936, s 90)

The expression 'vermin' includes squirrels. (Forestry Act 1967, s 7(5)(b))

VERTU

Objects or articles of

'The will which I have to construe is that of Lord Londesborough, who died in the year 1860. He was a nobleman of very large fortune, a man of great taste and a patron of the arts, and lived in a large house in Carlton House Terrace. After disposing of his collection of armour, autographs and other things, he says, "I bequeath to my wife absolutely all my and her jewels, trinkets, gold and silver plate, ornamental and other china, and all objects of vertu or taste." Then the question arises, whether by this clause he gave to her the pictures which he had in the house. . . . It seems to me very improbable that a man possessed of a collection of very valuable pictures should omit to use the word "pictures" if he intended to give them absolutely. . . . Pictures are undoubtedly articles of taste; but I suppose that this is the first will under which pictures are to pass—if they do pass—by the words "objects of vertu or taste". . . . On the whole, I come to the conclusion that the testator used these words "vertu or taste" as comprehending everything of the same sort—as lawyers say, *ejusdem generis*—with those before enumerated; and I cannot consider that by such words he intended to pass this valuable collection of pictures. I am, therefore, of opinion that Lady Londesborough did not take these pictures absolutely; but that, under the next clause in the will, she is entitled to the enjoyment of them during her life. There is one point which I ought not to pass over. One of the pictures, "a child in a circular frame", is said to be a portrait of Lord Londesborough's daughter; and it was argued that it was very improbable that he could have intended the painting of his daughter to be sold. I quite agree that it is very improbable; but, on the other hand, he may have forgotten all about it. I cannot think that that circumstance sufficiently controls the construction of the will to make these words, "objects of vertu or taste", have an operation which they would not otherwise have.' *Re Londesborough, Bridgeman v Fitzgerald* (1880) 50 LJ Ch 9 at 10, 11, per Malins V-C

'I think an article, in order to be an "article of virtu", must have some artistic merit; there may be articles which are very rare and which are of great interest to men of taste and education which could not be properly described as "articles of virtu". I think the term connotes that there is an artistic element in the article.' *Re Zouche (Baroness), Dugdale v Zouche (Baroness)* [1919] 2 Ch 178 at 185, per Lawrence J

'An article of vertu must be in some sense a product of the fine arts; and the phrase connotes, if not artistic merit, a certain effort on the part of the person who originally produced it, in the direction of what he conceived to be the fine arts.' *Re Tomline's Will Trusts, Pretyman v Pretyman* [1931] 1 Ch 521 at 526, per Maugham J

'It seems to me that the expression "articles of vertu" embraces a very large potential class of articles, and the only common factor possessed by this class is artistic merit of some form or another. Any type of article which a connoisseur or virtuoso might collect for its aristic merit, or the beauty of its workmanship, falls I think within the category.' *Re Coxen, MacCallum v Coxen* [1948] 2 All ER 492 at 495, per Jenkins J

VESSEL *See also* FISHING VESSEL

For the purposes of the Merchant Shipping Acts, a distinction must be drawn between 'vessel' and 'ship'. 'Ship' includes every description of vessel used in navigation not propelled by oars. In the Merchant Shipping Acts, 'vessel' includes any ship or boat or other description of vessel used in navigation. Whether a craft comes within the foregoing meaning of a ship depends on the facts of each case; the statutory definitions are intended to enlarge the meaning of 'ship'. To be a ship, a vessel must be used in navigable waters, either inland or at sea, and although she must be constructed for navigation it is not necessary to the definition that she should be able to navigate under her own power. The presence of a rudder and the manning of the vessel with a crew are important as showing that a vessel is a ship, but the absence of either does not mean that a vessel is not a ship. The purpose for which a vessel has been and is being used is also material when considering whether she is used in navigation. (43 Halsbury's Laws (4th edn) para 91)

The word 'vessel' shall include ship, boat, lighter, and craft of every kind, and whether navigated by steam or otherwise. (Harbours, Docks, and Piers Clauses Act 1847, s 3)

The term 'vessel' includes ship, boat, lighter, and craft of every kind, however, propelled. (Dockyard Ports Regulation Act 1865, s 2)

The expression 'vessel' means every description of vessel used in navigation in whatever way it is propelled; and any reference to a vessel shall include a reference to a boat belonging to such vessel. (Submarine Telegraph Act 1885, s 12)

'Vessel' includes any ship or boat, or any other description of vessel used in navigation. (Merchant Shipping Act 1894, s 742; Sea Fish (Conservation) Act 1967, s 22(1)

'Vessel' means every description of vessel however propelled or moved and includes anything constructed or used to carry persons or goods by water and a seaplane on or in the water a hovercraft and a hydrafoil vessel. (Port of London Act 1968, s 2)

'If the mere question was whether this barge was a "vessel", I think we should be bound to say that it was. The definition given by the Harbours, Docks, and Piers Clauses Act 1847 [supra] which by s 3 of the London & St Katharine Docks Act 1864, is incorporated with that Act, is this—"The word vessel shall include ship, boat, lighter, and craft of every kind, and whether navigated by steam or otherwise', and, if the mere question was whether a [dumb] barge like that described in this case was a "vessel", I think it is clear that the question must be answered in the affirmative. But it is only to be so construed "unless there be something in the subject or context repugnant to such construction". When we come to examine the sections of the Act of 1864, it seems to be clear that it was never contemplated that a barge like this should be considered as a vessel within those enactments; and to hold that it is a vessel would be repugnant to the context and to the whole of the circumstances contemplated by those sections.' *Hedges v London & St Katharine Docks Co* (1885) 16 QBD 597 at 600, 601, DC, per Huddleston B

'The question arises from the fact that the assured's tug, the *Ada*, came into collision with an anchor to which a schooner was riding by about twenty fathoms of chain, the afterpart of the schooner being upon the mud. The question is whether the anchor was part of a vessel. I think that it was, and therefore that the clause in the policy applies which provides for the payment by the insurance company of the amount of any damage caused to the assured's tugs owing to actual collision with any vessel.' *Re Margetts & Ocean Accident & Guarantee Corpn Ltd* [1901] 2 KB 792 at 794, 795, DC, per Ridley J

'To my mind it is clear beyond all question that

this landing-stage is not a vessel. It is a huge floating structure intended to be a permanent structure and stationary, except in one respect, namely, that, for the convenience of passengers, it has the power of rising and falling with the water. Otherwise it is absolutely fixed. It has none of the characteristics of a vessel, and, quite apart from any authority, I am of opinion that it could not possibly be included within the term "vessel".' *The Craighall* [1910] P 207 at 212, CA, per Fletcher Moulton LJ

'According to the enactment [Oil in Navigable Waters Act 1922, s 1(1) (repealed; see now the Prevention of Oil Pollution Act 1971, ss 1–11)] an offence is committed by suffering oil to escape from a vessel into the sea. . . . In the present case HMS *Tiger* (an oil-burning ship whose oil tanks were capable of carrying in bulk 6,500 tons of oil) had been sold to the appellants for the purpose of being broken up, and the process of breaking up had proceeded so far that the vessel at the time of the commission of the alleged offence was (though still afloat) incapable of being navigated as a ship. But her tanks contained a residuum of oil, and those who were engaged in breaking her up, after making some attempts to remove the oil, deliberately allowed the oil to escape into the sea. . . . I do not feel any doubt that HMS *Tiger* was at the time a "vessel" in the sense of the Act of 1922.' *Thomas W Ward Ltd v Waugh* 1933 SLT 619 at 621, 622, per the Lord Justice-General (Lord Clyde)

'Section 742 of the Merchant Shipping Act 1894 . . . is in these terms: "In this Act, unless the context otherwise requires, the following expressions have the meanings hereby assigned to them; (that is to say) 'Vessel' includes any ship or boat, or any other description of vessel used in navigation; 'Ship' includes every description of vessel used in navigation not propelled by oars." I am invited to say that though these craft were in fact propelled by oars, they are not within the definition "ships propelled by oars". The difficulty I have in drawing that conclusion is that the definition, "ship" includes and embraces every description of vessel, which includes in turn, if one refers back to the definition "vessel" "any ship or boat"; but by the definition of "ship" any vessel of any description is only included if it is not propelled by oars. In other words, no vessel which is propelled by oars is within the definition "vessel".' *Edwards v Quickenden & Forester* [1939] P 261 at 268, per Henn Collins J

VESSEL (Receptacle)

'Vessel' includes a receptacle of any kind, whether open or closed. (Food Act 1984, s 132(1))

'The ordinary meaning of the word "vessel" . . . in the non-marine sense . . . is, in my view, confined to receptacles designed to contain substances whose physical character is such as to enable them to conform to the internal shape of the receptacle.' *Haigh v Ireland (Charles W) Ltd* [1973] 3 All ER 1137 at 1148, HL, per Lord Diplock

VEST

The proper legal meaning of 'vest' is vest in interest. Where a testator uses this word, for example by directing that the gift is to vest on a certain event, prima facie it must be given its proper legal meaning, and the gift is then contingent until the happening of the event, whether the gift is of real or personal estate. However, the context may show, by indications that the donee is to take a vested interest before the specified event, that 'vest' is used in another sense, for example in the sense of 'fall into possession', or 'become payable', or 'be indefeasibly vested'. Where 'vested' means 'indefeasibly vested', the gift may be vested before the specified event, subject only to being divested if the event does not happen. A direction with regard to vesting of a gift to a class may, on the construction of a particular will, even introduce a new category of persons to share in the gift. (50 Halsbury's Laws (4th edn) para 588)

'Vesting assent' means the instrument whereby a personal representative, after the death of a tenant for life or statutory owner, or the survivor of two or more tenants for life or statutory owners, vests settled land in a person entitled as tenant for life or statutory owner. (Settled Land Act 1925, s 117)

In relation to settled land 'vesting deed' or 'vesting order' means the instrument whereby settled land is conveyed to or vested or declared to be vested in a tenant for life or statutory owner. (Settled Land Act 1925, s 117)

'The word "vest" is a word, at least, of ambiguous import. Prima facie "vesting" in possession is the more natural meaning. The expressions "investiture"—"clothing"—and whatever else be the explanation as to the origin of the word, point prima facie rather to the enjoyment than to the obtaining of a right. But I am willing to accede to the argument that was pressed at the bar, that by long usage "vesting" ordinarily means the having obtained an absolute and indefeasible right, as contradistinguished from the not having so obtained it. But it cannot be disputed that the word "vesting" may mean, and often does mean, that which is its primary etymological signification, namely, vesting in possession.' *Richardson v Robertson* (1862) 6 LT 75 at 78, per Lord Cranworth

'The only remaining question argued before me is, what is the effect of the devise over, contained in the codicil, in the event of John Arthur Arnold dying without leaving lawful issue before the estates become vested in him. . . . It is argued that the word "vested" must not here receive its ordinary legal acceptation; but that it must mean "vested in possession" and not vested in interest, for the reason that the devises became vested in interest in him immediately on the death of the testator. But I think the word "vested" here, must mean "vested in interest".' *Re Arnold's Estate* (1863) 33 Beav 163 at 172, per Romilly MR

'A will takes effect at the death of the testator, and any gift made by it is void for remoteness if it does not necessarily take effect within twenty-one years from the termination of any life then in being. The question here is, whether the class of objects whom the testator means to benefit are necessarily ascertainable within that time. The class consists of the children and grandchildren, being issue of deceased children of the testator, that is to say, if at the death of the widow there are any sons living, or there are any grandchildren living who are the sons of a deceased child, they are to take vested interests at the age of twenty-four years. In this will it is clear that "vested" means vested. The rule as to the construction of the word "vested" as laid down by Sir W Grant is, that it has its proper legal meaning like every other word, unless you find a context to control it. In this case there is no context to control it, but, on the contrary, in the maintenance clause express mention is made of there being contingent shares. "Vested", therefore, means vested, and, consequently, neither son nor grandson can take a vested interest until he attains the age of twenty-four years.' *Hale v Hale* (1876) 3 Ch D 643 at 645, 646, 649, per Jessel MR

'Their Lordships are of opinion that these interests were at the date of the testator's death vested, though subject in certain events to be divested. In the present case the trustees are directed to hold the fund in trust "for my child (if only one), or for all my children (if more than one), in equal shares". So far the gift is absolute. To what extent is it controlled by what follows? The qualification is thus expressed "and so that the interest of a son or sons shall be absolutely vested at the age of 21 years, and of a daughter or daughters at that age or marriage". The authorities show that the word "vest" may, if the context of the will is in favour of that construction, be read as importing only that the interest previously vested is at a specified time to become absolute and indefeasible. Such a construction was put upon the word not only by Vice-Chancellor Parker, in the case of *Taylor v Frobisher* [(1852) 5 De G & Sm 191] . . . but also by the Lords Commissioners (including Lord Cottenham) in the earlier case of *Berkeley v Swinburne* [(1848) 16 Sim 275] and by Vice-Chancellor Page Wood in the later case of *Poole v Bott* [(1853) 11 Hare 337.' *Armytage v Wilkinson* (1878) 3 App Cas 355 at 372, 373, PC, per cur.

'The word "vested" prima facie means "vested in interest", but by force of a context it may have a different meaning, such as "vested in possession" or "indefeasibly vested" or "payable": *Berkeley v Swinburne* ([1848] 16 Sim 275), *Taylor v Frobisher* ([1852] 5 De G & Sm 191). But to give the word a different meaning from its ordinary one a context is required, and I cannot find any such context here. The whole will is quite intelligible if the word is given its primary and ordinary meaning.' *Re Stevens, Clark v Stevens* (1896) 40 Sol Jo 296 at 296, per Stirling J

Canada '"Vest" and "revest" are words of precise meaning both in ordinary language and in legal use. When land of any natural or legal person is vested in another, the whole estate and interest of the former goes to the latter. Revested, the whole estate and interest is vested back.' *Wardle v Manitoba Farm Loans Association* (1954) 14 WWR 289 at 293, 294, Man CA, per Coyne JA (dissenting); revsd on other grounds [1956] SCR 3

VESTRY

The expression 'vestry' in relation to a parish means the inhabitants of the parish whether in vestry assembled or not, and includes any select vestry either by statute or at common law. (Local Government Act 1894, s 75(2))

VEXATIOUS *See* FRIVOLOUS ACTION

VIADUCT *See* BRIDGE

VICAR

Before the Reformation the rectory, with its emoluments, was frequently appropriated to or by a religious house or collegiate church or some other religious corporation which, as such, could not perform the personal services required in a cure of souls and consequently, put in its place a vicar, hence the name. In such cases provision was made by ecclesiastical constitutions or ordinances and afterwards by statute for his endowment in perpetuity, and where the benefice thus remains annexed to the perpetual use of some spiritual corporation, either sole or aggregate, the benefice is said to be appropriated and the appropriators are recognised as the parson or rector of the parish.

Upon the dissolution of the monastries many of these rectories came into the hands of laymen and are in that case strictly called inappropriate and the lay rectors are said to be the impropriators, but, as before, a vicar was still required for the cure of souls.

The rector, whether spiritual or lay, has the freehold of the church and churchyard, but where the rector is not the incumbent he has no control over the cure of souls or the performance of ministerial duties in the parish, and where there is a lay rector the vicar has the corporal possession of the church and churchyard for the use of the parishioners.

The incumbent of every parish who is not a rector but is authorised to solemnise marriages, churchings and baptisms and who is entitled to receive for his own use the entire fees for the performance of those offices is, for the purpose of style and designation only, deemed and styled the vicar, and his benefice the vicarage, of the parish. 1st April 1969 a person holding a perpetual curacy or any other benefice comprising a parish or parishes with full parochial status, not being a rectory or a vicarage, is in fact a vicar. (14 Halsbury's Laws (4th edn) para 770)

VICARIOUS LIABILITY

'The expression "vicarious liability" or, perhaps, more accurately, vicarious act, is, in my opinion, apt to cover all cases whether the act is in the master's sphere or not—that is to say, whether he is liable directly or liable merely through the servant, he is liable vicariously for the negligent act of the servant done in the course of his employment.' *Broom v Morgan* [1953] 1 All ER 849 at 856, CA, per Hodson LJ (also reported in [1953] 1 QB 597 at 612)

'It is characteristic of commercial contracts, nearly all of which today are entered into not by natural legal persons, but by fictitious ones, i.e. companies, that the parties promise to one another that something will be done, for instance, that property and possession of goods will be transferred, that goods will be carried by ship from one port to another, that a building will be constructed in accordance with agreed plans, that services of a particular kind will be provided. Such a contract is the source of primary legal obligations on each party to it to procure that whatever he has promised will be done is done . . . Where what is promised will be done involves the doing of a physical act, performance of the promise necessitates procuring a natural person to do it; but the legal relationship between the promisor and the natural person by whom the act is done, whether it is that of master and servant, or principal and agent, or of parties to an independent subcontract, is generally irrelevant. If that person fails to do it in the manner in which the promisor has promised to procure it to be done, as, for instance, with reasonable skill and care, the promisor has failed to fulfil his own primary obligation. This is to be distinguished from "vicarious liability", a legal concept which does depend on the existence of a particular legal relationship between the natural person by whom a tortious act was done and the person sought to be made vicariously liable for it. In the interests of clarity the expression should, in my view, be confined to liability for tort.' *Photo Production Ltd v Securicor Transport Ltd* [1980] 1 All ER 556 at 565, 566, HL, per Lord Diplock

VICE *See also* INHERENT VICE

'Whether a railway company are common carriers of animals is a question upon which there has been much conflict of opinion. . . . The question as to their liability may turn on the distinction between accidents which happen by reason of some vice inherent in the animals themselves or disposition producing unruliness or phrensy, and accidents which are not the result of inherent vice or unruliness of the animals themselves. . . . By the expression "vice", I do not, of course, mean moral vice in the thing itself or its owner, but only that sort of vice which by its internal development tends to the destruction or the injury of the animal or thing to be carried, and which is likely to lead to such a result.' *Blower v Great Western Rly Co* (1872) LR 7 CP 655 at 662, 663, per Willes J

VICINAGE *See* COMMON

VICINITY

[The Official Secrets Act 1920, s 3, provided that it shall be a misdemeanour to obstruct, etc, officers or others in the 'vicinity' of any prohibited place.] 'The appellant has referred to the natural meaning of "vicinity", which I take to be quite generally the state of being near in space, and he says that it is inapt and does not cover being in fact on the station [an air force station] in the present case. For my part I am quite satisfied that this is a case where no violence is done to the language by reading the words "in the vicinity" of as meaning "in or in the vicinity of".' *Adler v George* [1964] 1 All ER 628 at 629, per Lord Parker CJ

VICIOUS

'The word "vicious" as applied to animals is well understood and indicates a savage disposition, a propensity to attack people. I think it must also be treated as clear that an animal, though not savage, which is dangerous because of its frolicsome behaviour, must equally be taken to have propensities against which (if he knows of them) the owner has a duty to guard.' *Brock v Richards* [1951] 1 All ER 261 at 266, per Evershed MR; also reported in [1951] 1 KB 529 at 536

'In some of the numerous cases which have been cited to us the words used [of animals] are "vicious or mischievous", an expression which appears to be used in the same sense, i.e., as likely to be mischief, so that both words involve the idea of an attack.' *Fitzgerald v Cooke Zourne (Farms) Ltd* [1963] 3 All ER 36 at 45, CA, per Danckwerts LJ; also reported in [1964] 1 QB 249 at 266

VICTUALS

[Statute (1810) 50 Geo 3, c 41, s 23 (repealed), enacted that nothing in the Act should extend to prohibit persons from selling (inter alia) 'victuals'.] 'I think that the word victuals in the 50 Geo 3, c 41, s 23, comprises everything which constitutes an ingredient in the food of man, and all articles which mixed with others constitute food. Yeast or barm may not perhaps be necessarily used in the making of bread, but it generally is used, and I am therefore of opinion that it is within the exempting clause.' *R v Hodgkinson* (1829) 10 B & C 74 at 76, per Lord Tenterden CJ

VIDEO WORK

(2) 'Video work' means any series of visual images (with or without sound) (a) produced electronically by the use of information contained on any disc or magnetic tape, and (b) shown as a moving picture.

(3) 'Video recording' means any disc or magnetic tape containing information by the use of which the whole or a part of a video work may be produced. (Video Recordings Act 1984, s 1(2), (3))

VIEW

'The circumstances in which a view should be held are the subject of directions in *Goold v Evans & Co* [[1951] 2 TLR 1189], a decision of this court. I refer to the judgment of Denning LJ which is in these terms [at p 1191]: "It is a fundamental principle of our law that a judge must act on the evidence before him and not on outside information; and, further, the evidence on which he acts must be given in the presence of both parties, or, at any rate, each party must be given an opportunity of being present. Speaking for myself, I think that a view is part of the evidence, just as much as an exhibit. It is a real evidence. The tribunal sees the real thing instead of having a drawing or a photograph of it. But, even if a view is not evidence, the same principles apply. The judge must make his view in the presence of both parties, or, at any rate, each party must be given an opportunity of being present. The only exception is when a judge goes by himself to see some public place, such as the site of a road accident, with neither party present." I respectfully adopt those observations as being the correct approach to this question. I would also say in general that a view is something which should be conducted by the judge by appointment, in the presence of representatives of both sides. However, the expression "view" is used indifferently to describe two very different things. Sometimes it refers to what Denning LJ spoke of as a judge going to see some public place, where all that is involved is the presence of the judge using his eyes to see in three dimensions and true colour something which had previously been represented to him in plan and photograph. The other way in which the word "view" is frequently used is to describe some kind of demonstration in which the events of the accident are reconstructed or simulated; and in my judgment it would be exceedingly dangerous for a judge to attend anything which could be described as a demonstration except in strict accordance with the principles laid down by Denning LJ—in the presence of representatives of both sides.' *Salsbury v Woodland* [1969] 3 All ER 863 at 873, CA, per Widgery LJ

[The Town Police Causes Act 1847, s 28, provides that any person who commits certain offences in any street may be taken into custody, without warrant, by any constable within whose 'view' any such offence has been committed.] 'It is common ground that "within his view" in the section means "in his sight" not "in his opinion".' *Wills v Bowley* [1982] 2 All ER 654 at 672, HL, per Lord Bridge of Harwich

VILLAGE

'A vill and a village are the same, and a hamlet is a division of a vill. . . . The whole vill is a constabulary, and a hamlet is commonly a tithing.' *Anon* (1701) 12 Mod Rep 546 at 546, per Holt CJ

'The authorities appear to show, that the word "village" is a word sufficient to pass a district, and that it is not necessarily confined to the small collection of houses to which it is often confined in ordinary parlance. There is certainly no authority for saying that it is to be so confined; and in considering how a word is to be construed, we must always regard the subject matter and context. In a deed of conveyance, the word "village", in the limited sense, would certainly be very indefinite, depending on no known boundary, but one liable to shift as every additional cottage or cabin is erected. And I do not believe it is a word which has been used in the sense now contended for in the description of property in a conveyance, whilst in the other sense, as describing some known district, as vill, town, townslands, etc, it would have an accurate and definite meaning.' *Waterpark (Lord) v Fennell* (1859) 7 HL Cas 650 at 663, 664, per Crompton J

VILLAGE GREEN *See* GREEN

VINTNER

'I am bound to say that in my opinion the word "vintner" means a person who sells wine generally, and the old documents which have been referred to evidently relate to selling wine in gross, that is, wholesale. The words in the old charters and in the rolls of Parliament to which I was referred all point to this—the selling of wine in gross. No doubt the word vintner also implied the selling of wine for immediate consumption.' *Wells v Attenborough* (1871) 24 LT 312 at 313, per Romilly MR

VIOLATION

Canada 'The word "violation" comes from the old French "violacion" or from an adaptation of the Latin "violatio" which is the noun of action formed on "violare" meaning "to violate". Violation implies not only an infringement or breach, but also a flagrant disregard or non-observance of the rule, principle or law. It seems quite clear that if one is to distinguish between "violation" and "contravention" the word violation includes the idea of a "volens" or of wilfulness or of mens rea while "contravention" does not include any notion of wilfulness or of any act of the will.' *Collins v A-G of Ontario* (1969) 6 CRNS 82 at 89, Ont SC, per Addy J

VIOLENCE *See also* CRIME OF VIOLENCE; MOLEST; VIS MAJOR

As used in this connection, 'violent' has been interpreted as connoting the antithesis to 'without any violence at all'. It does not therefore postulate the presence of brutal strength or savage temper, as when the victim is bitten by a dog. Again, an external cause of death, such as the inhalation of gas, may, it seems, be violent in as much as it does violence to the human frame by rendering it incapable of functioning. Similarly, where the cause of injury is some extra exertion or exercise of effort on the part of the assured . . . it is violent in the sense that it does damage impairing the bodily functions, however impaired they may have been before. (25 Halsbury's Laws (4th edn) para 602)

In this section [destroying, damaging or endangering safety of aircraft] 'act of violence' means—

(a) any act done in the United Kingdom which constitutes the offence of murder, attempted murder, manslaughter, culpable homicide or assault or an offence under section 18, 20, 21, 22, 23, 24, 28 or 29 of the Offences against the Person Act 1861 or under section 2 of the Explosive Substances Act 1883, and
(b) any act done outside the United Kingdom which, if done in the United Kingdom, would constitute such an offence as is mentioned in paragraph (a) above.

(Aviation Security Act 1982 s 2(7))

[The offences referred to under the Offences against the Person Act 1861 are those of shooting etc, with intent to do grievous bodily harm or to resist apprehension; inflicting bodily injury, with or without a weapon; attempting to choke, etc, in order to commit an offence; using chloroform to commit an offence; administering poison; causing bodily injury by gunpowder; causing gunpowder to explode, or sending to any person an explosive substance, or throwing corrosive fluid on a person, with intent to do grievous bodily harm. The Explosive Substances Act 1883, s 2, makes it an offence to cause an explosion likely to endanger life or property.]

'I agree that something more . . . is meant by the words [in an insurance policy] "actual forcible and violent entry". At the same time one must remember that this is a business document relating to protection against burglary and housebreaking, and is intended, one would assume, to be a protection against the ordinary methods of burglars and housebreakers. I think that the view taken by the learned judges in *George's Case* [[1899] 1 QB 595] was this: that by the words "actual forcible and violent entry" it was intended to mean an entry effected by the exercise of force in a manner that was not customary in order to overcome the resistance of the usual fastenings and protections in the premises. If a person turns a key he uses force but not violence. If he uses a skeleton key, he uses force but not violence. If on the other hand instead of using a key he uses a pick-lock, or some other instrument, or a piece of wire, by which as a lever he forces back the lock, it appears to me that he uses force and violence, and in the present case both force and violence were used.' *Re an Arbitration between Calf and Sun Insurance Office* [1920] 2 KB 366 at 383, per Atkin LJ

Australia [It was ruled that for the purposes of the Crimes Act 1958 (Vic), s 3A, the act of menacing with a knife was capable of being found by the jury to be an act of 'violence'.] 'In our opinion, the word "violence" where it is used in s 3A is not to be understood to refer only to physical force but rather to include those aspects of intimidation and seeking to intimidate by the exhibition of physical force or menaces as in the past have been considered to constitute violence. When the words "act of violence" and "crime the necessary elements of which include violence" are used in s 3A violence is used in a descriptive sense. "Act of violence" means an act of a violent kind, for there is no legal definition of violence as such inside or outside which any particular act or threats may be said to fall. Nor is there any common law crime in which violence is by definition an element. This view is also consistent with violence as understood during the development of the English language. As a matter of etymology, violence is a word having its origin in the Latin violentia, often connoting vehemence or impetuosity. It is not synonymous with the use of physical force, although physical force falls within its meaning. It is a word of wider significance in the law, as the cases show. Smith and Hall in their English-Latin Dictionary give as their first meaning of violence: "inherent overpowering force, whether physical or mental".

In the Oxford English Dictionary violence is defined as follows: "(Law) unlawful exercise of physical force, intimidation by the exhibition of this".' *R v Butcher* (1986) VR 43 at 53, per cur.

New Zealand 'A threat made . . . with a loaded revolver present (and it might be said presented) in such a way as to lead the person threatened to believe that it would be used may well, in our view, have the effect of rendering the threatened person "incapable of resistance" [within the Crimes Act 1961, s 191] just as effectually as if she were physically incapable, and would be described in ordinary parlance as a "violent means" of producing that effect.' *R v Crossan* [1943] NZLR 454 at 460, CA, per Myers CJ and Callan J; also reported [1943] GLR 301 at 302

VIS MAJOR *See also* ACT OF GOD

'This plea (found to be true) alleges a loss of the moneys by irresistible violence; and the general doctrine is not denied, that, if the subject matter bailed be lost by vis major, which we translate irresistible violence, the bailee is discharged.' *Walker v British Guarantee Assocn* (1852) 18 QB 277 at 286, per cur.

VISCOUNT *See* PEERAGE

VISIBLE

Visible injury

[The plaintiff effected an insurance with the defendants against any bodily injury, caused by violent, accidental, external, and 'visible' means. The policy contained a proviso, excepting among other things, injuries arising from 'natural disease or weakness, or exhaustion consequent upon disease'. In stooping to pick up a marble dropped by a child, the plaintiff dislocated the cartilage of his knee.] 'We have to arrive at the real bargain between the parties by taking the words of the policy and reading them according to their ordinary sense. Reading the words of the clause, it seems to me to be clear that it must be read thus: "Any bodily injury the result of a violent, accidental, external, and visible cause". . . . If the injury had happened by reason of something internal it would not be within the policy; but that is not the case, and I think we must say that because the cause of the injury was not internal it must have been "external", and in that case it was also "visible" within the meaning of the policy.' *Hamlyn v Crown Accidental Insurance Co Ltd* [1893] 1 QB 750 at 753, CA, per Lord Esher MR

Visible means

'A man has not "visible means" if he has only sufficient chattels to pay the costs after a sheriff's sale has swept away all his goods, and turned him out on the world a pauper.' *Watson v M'Cann* (1879) 6 LR Ir 21 at 23, per Dowse B

VISITATION

Visitation, in the common acceptance term, denotes the act of the bishop or of some other Ordinary going to his circuit throughout his diocese or district with a full power of inquiring into such matters as relate to the government and discipline of the church.

The principal object of visitation is that the bishop, archdeacon or other person assigned to visit may get some good knowledge of the state, sufficiency and ability of the clergy and other persons whom he is to visit.

Visitation implies, however, some coercive authority; the bishop has the right to visit his diocese in a more solemn manner at times and places limited by law or custom, and on his visitation to perform all such acts by law or custom are assigned to his charge in that behalf for the edifying and well-governing of Christ's flock, that means may be taken thereby for the supply of such things as are lacking and the correction of such things as are amiss. During the time of the visitation the jurisdiction of all inferior Ordinaries is suspended, save in places which by law or custom are exempt. (14 Halsbury's Laws (4th edn) para 490)

VISITOR *See also* GUEST

'The question is as to the construction of the deed of grant having regard to settled law and principles. Are the pupils at the school "visitors" within the meaning of the grant [made to the defendant, her servants, tenants and "visitors" to use a footpath]? The proper meaning of a visitor is one who comes to see and to stay; but the word is now applied in common parlance to those who stay at a place for either a short or a long time, and who are generally, no doubt, at liberty to leave when they please. I, however, see no reason for restricting the word to those who could come and go as they please. I am bound to look at the circumstances under which the grant was made, namely, that the school was in the occupation of the defendant at the time, and the parties contemplated a grant of a right of way to the lady and her tenants, visitors, and servants, in respect of the use of the school. The fact assists the the court in holding that the word "visitors" must be given a large interpretation, and must include the "pupils" as well as those staying in the house for any length of time, long or short.' *Thornton v Little* [1907] WN 68 at 68, 69, per Kekewich J

'A person is a "visitor" if at common law he would be regarded as an invitee or licensee; or be treated as such, as for instance, a person lawfully using premises provided for the use of the public (e.g., a public park) or a person entering by lawful authority (e.g., a policeman with a search warrant). But a "visitor" does not include a person who crosses land in pursuance of a public or private right of way. Such a person was never regarded as an invitee or licensee, or treated as such.' *Greenhalgh v British Railways Board* [1969] 2 All ER 114 at 117, CA, per Lord Denning MR

[The distinction between the duty owed to invitees and that owed to licensees was abolished, in England, by the Occupiers' Liability Act 1957, which imposed a 'common duty of care' to all visitors. The common law rules continued, however, to determine who was an occupier and to whom the duty of care was owed, and 'visitors' in the Act of 1957 included only those categories who would at common law be treated as invitees or licensees. The Occupiers' Liability Act 1984 extended the duty of care to trespasses and other unauthorised persons.]

Of university

'A visitorial power is an incident of an eleemosynary corporation, that is to say, a corporation founded for the purpose of distributing the founder's bounty. Educational institutions such as the university and the college are classified as eleemosynary corporations. The visitor of the university named in the statutes is Her Majesty in Council. The charter and statutes of the college do not name a visitor and it follows that since the college was incorporated by royal charter the visitor is Her Majesty, exercising her powers through the Lord Chancellor. The visitor is a domestic forum appointed by the founder for the purpose of regulating the foundation's domestic affairs in accordance with its statutes, including the determination of domestic disputes.' *Hines v Birbeck College* [1985] 3 All ER 156 at 161, per Hoffmann J

VOCATION

'The case states the contention of the surveyor that betting systematically and annually carried on came within the provisions of the Income Tax Act [1842] (repealed; see now the Income and Corporation Taxes Act 1988, s 18)] as a vocation. Seeing that the case states enough for us to find here that the appellants are persons who in partnership [as professional bookmakers] attend races and systematically and annually carry on that pursuit so as to make profits, for we must, I think, assume that profits were made—the question is whether the Commissioners were right in holding that those profits were derived from a "vocation" within Schedule D? I think the Commissioners were quite right. The words in 5 & 6 Vict c 35 [Income Tax Act 1842 (repealed; see supra)], s 100, Schedule D, second case, are "professions, employments, or vocations". I am not disposed to put so limited a construction on the word "employment" as that suggested in argument. I do not think that employment means only where one man is set to work by others to earn money; a man may employ himself so as to earn profits in many ways. But the word "vocation" is analogous to "calling", a word of wide signification, meaning the way in which a man passes his life. The appellants attend races, make bets, and earn profits. . . . Can it be said that because bets are made null and void by Act of Parliament the appellants did not carry on a "vocation"? To put such a construction on the Income Tax Act would unduly favour persons not favoured by the legislature. I think the word "vocation" is not limited to a lawful vocation, and that even the fact of a vocation being unlawful could not be set up against the demand for income tax, I think that the case comes within the word "vocation", and therefore the Commissioners were right.' *Partridge v Mallandaine* (1886) 18 QBD 276 at 277, 278, DC, per Denman J

'In this case the appellants [a private backer of horses, as distinguished from a professional bookmaker, as in the previous case] was in the habit of betting on horses at starting prices. He did it on a large and sustained scale, and he did it with such shrewdness that he made an income out of it, and it is found that substantially it was his means of living. Under those circumstances he has been assessed to income tax in respect of those emoluments, and hence this appeal. The question arises under Case 2 and under Case 6 of Sch D [see supra]. . . . It is said that the appellant, by continually betting from his house or from any place where he could get access to the telegraph office, had set up a vocation. That is contended by the respondent on the facts of this case, and certainly the contention is one which, if sound, has very startling results. A loss in a vocation, or a trade, or an adventure can be set off against other profits and we are face to face with this result, that a person earning a profit in some recognised form of industry, but having the bad habit of frequently, persistently and continuously and systematically betting with bookmakers, might for income tax purposes set off the losses by which he had squandered the fruits of his industry against his profits of industry, a very remarkable result indeed and one, I am afraid, which would be of very wide application. Allowances are granted to the income tax payer because of the family he has to support, and we are now threatened with a further allowance in respect of the loss which he makes by habitual betting. It certainly sounds very remarkable, and would entitle a person, when he wastes his earnings by betting, to make the State a partner in his gambling. . . . Now we come to the . . . man who bets with the bookmaker, and that is this case. . . . I think all you can say of that man, in the fair use of the English language, is that he is addicted to betting. It is extremely difficult to express, but it seems to me that people would say he is addicted to betting, and could not say his vocation is betting. The subject is involved in great difficulty of language, which I think represents great difficulty of thought. There is no tax on a habit. I do not think "habitual" or even "systematic" fully describes what is essential in the phrase "trade, adventure, employment, or vocation". All I can say is that in my judgment the income which this gentleman succeeded in making is not profits or gains.' *Graham v Green* [1925] 2 KB 37 at 38–40, 42, per Rowlatt J

VOID

'The title of the Stat [(1788) 28 Geo 3, c 48 [repealed], is general, "For the better regulation of chimney-sweepers and their apprentices", and the recital is, "That the laws in being respecting masters and apprentices are not sufficient to prevent the complicated miseries to which boys employed in climbing and cleansing chimneys are liable." . . . The fourth section begins by enacting, that all indentures, etc for binding any boy under eight years of age as an apprentice to a chimney-sweeper, "than is by this act limited", shall be void in the law to all intents and purposes. The words "than is by this act limited", are not sensible; but it is manifest that the legislature intended to make all indentures void where the child bound to a chimney-sweeper is under eight years of age. . . . But it is said that void is sometimes construed voidable, and where the provision is introduced for the benefit of the parties only, such a construction may be right, but where it is introduced for public purposes, and to protect those who are incapable of protecting themselves, it should receive its full force and effect. Here I think it would be contrary to the spirit of the act to consider the indenture voidable only.' *R v Hipswell (Inhabitants)* (1828) 8 B & C 466 at 470, 471, per Bayley J

'There are cases innumerable to show that "void" may mean "voidable" or "void", at the election of the party contracted with, where otherwise the wrongful act of the other party would put an end to the covenant.' *Hughes v Palmer* (1865) 19 CBNS 393 at 407, 408, per Byles J

VOID AND VOIDABLE CONTRACTS *See* CONTRACT

VOID MARRIAGE *See also* MARRIAGE; NULLITY

'Some confusion has been caused in legal discussion upon the difference between a decree of nullity and a decree of divorce, in regard to their retrospective effects upon the pre-existing marriage, by the use of the words "void" and "voidable". It has been said that in the case of divorce it is good law to speak of the marriage as having been voidable, but not so in the case of nullity; for there the decree pronounces the marriage to have been "void" from the outset. Primarily the use of those two words is a metaphor from the law of contract, and is not truly appropriate to the law of status. But the use of both terms in connection with the status of marriage has received judicial sanction, and is consonant with the ordinary English meaning of the words, although it lends itself to misuse, and may cause confusion.' *Adams v Adams* [1941] 1 KB 536 at 541, CA, per Scott LJ

'It cannot be open to question that a distinction has long been recognised for certain purposes between marriages which are void and those which are merely voidable. The use of the word "voidable" in connection with any marriage which is annulled has, however, been criticised on account of the retrospective form of the decree. As recently as *Adams v Adams* [supra] Scott LJ referred to such criticism and said that primarily the use of the words "void" and "voidable" was a metaphor from the law of contract and was not truly appropriate to the law of status; but, he declared, the use of both terms in connection with the status of marriage has received judicial sanction. I would add that in s 9 of the Matrimonial Causes Act (Northern Ireland) 1939 they also receive legislative sanction. . . . Canonical disabilities, including corporal infirmities, such as impotence, only make the marriage voidable, and not ipso facto void until sentence of nullity be obtained as it must be, if at all, during the lifetime of the parties. Civil disabilities, on the other hand, such as prior marriage, age or idiocy, make the contract void ab initio—not merely voidable. These latter do not dissolve a contract already made; they render the parties incapable of contracting at all. They do not put asunder those who are joined together, but they previously hinder the function. Such a union is a meretricious, not a matrimonial one, and therefore no sentence of avoidance is necessary.' *Mason v Mason (otherwise Pennington)* [1944] NI 134 at 161, 162, per Andrews CJ

[The grounds on which a marriage is void or voidable are codified by the Matrimonial Causes Act 1973, ss 11–16.]

VOLENTI NON FIT INJURIA

Where a plaintiff relies on the breach of a duty to take care owed by the defendant to him it is a good defence that the plaintiff consented to that breach of duty, or, knowing of it, voluntarily incurred the whole risk entailed by it. In such a case the maxim volenti non fit injuria applies. This defence is to be distinguished from the plea of contributory negligence, for a plaintiff may have voluntarily exposed himself to the risk of being injured while himself exercising the utmost care for his own safety and conversely, while knowledge of the risk may show contributory negligence it does not prove voluntary assumption of risk. (34 Halsbury's Laws (4th edn) para 62).

That the plaintiff consented to acts or omissions which amounted to breach of a duty at common law to take reasonable care is a defence to an action of negligence for breach of that duty; the rule is expressed in the maxim volenti non fit injuria and rests on consents to, not merely knowledge of, the risk.

It is not a defence to an action for nuisance that the plaintiff came to the nuisance. (45 Halsbury's Laws (4th edn) para 1262)

'Can . . . a person maintain an action in respect of an injury arising from a defect, of which defect and of the resulting damage he was as well informed as the defendant? I think not. To such a person it appears to me that the maxim volenti non fit injuria applies. . . . If I invite a man who has no knowledge of the locality to walk along a dangerous cliff which is my property, I owe him a duty different to that which I owe to a man who has all his life birdnested on my rocks.' *Thomas v Quartermaine* (1887) 18 QBD 685 at 700, 701, 703, CA, per Fry LJ

'Does the judgment of Bowen LJ in *Thomas v Quartermaine* [supra], . . . mean to say that the mere knowledge of the workman and his continuing in the employ is fatal to him? . . . The learned judge says: "It is not doubt true that the knowledge on the part of the injured person which will prevent him from alleging negligence against the occupier, must be a knowledge under such circumstances as lead necesssarily to the conclusion that the whole risk was voluntarily incurred. The maxim, be it observed, is not 'Scienti non fit injuria', but 'Volenti'. There may be a perception of the existence of the danger without appreciation of the risk; as, where the workman is of imperfect intelligence." So that a dull man may recover damages where a man of intelligence may not! Both know of the danger, but one is imperfectly as to its nature and extent! Taking the whole of that judgment together, it seems to me to amount to this, that mere knowledge of the danger will not do: there must be an assent on the part of the workman to accept the risk, with a full appreciation of its extent, to bring the workman within the maxim Volenti non fit injuria. If so, that is a question of fact.' *Yarmouth v France* (1887) 19 QBD 647 at 656, 657, per Lord Esher MR

'These are two answers to the plaintiff, and I decide against him on both; on one as much as on the other. Volenti non fit injuria, and the plaintiff was volens. I hold that where a man is not physically constrained, where he can at his option do a thing or not, and he does it, the maxim applies. What is volens? willing; and a man is willing when he wills to do a thing and does it.' *Membery v Great Western Rly Co* (1889) 14 App Cas 179 at 187, per Lord Bramwell

'It appears to me that the proposition upon which the defendants must rely must be a far wider one than is involved in the maxim "Volenti non fit injuria". I think they must go to the extent of saying that wherever a person knows there is a risk of injury to himself, he debars himself from any right of complaint if an injury should happen to him in doing anything which involves that risk. For this purpose, and in order to test this proposition, we have nothing to do with the relation of employer and employed. The maxim in its application in the law is not so limited; but where it applies, it applies equally to a stranger as to any one else; and if applicable to the extent that is now insisted on, no one ever ought to have been awarded damages for being run over in London streets; for no one (at all events some years ago, before the admirable police regulations of later years) could have crossed London streets without knowing that there was a risk of being run over. It is, of course, impossible to maintain a proposition so wide as is involved in the example I have just given; and in both *Thomas v Quartermaine* [supra] and in *Yarmouth v France* [supra], it has been taken for granted that mere knowledge of the risk does not necessarily involve consent to the risk. Bowen LJ carefully points out in the earlier case that the maxim is not "Scienti non fit injuria" but "volenti non fit injuria". And Lindley LJ [in the later case] in quoting Bowen LJ's distinction with approval, adds: The question in each case must be, not simply whether the plaintiff knew of the risk, but whether the circumstances are such as necessarily to lead to the conclusion that the whole risk was voluntarily incurred by the plaintiff.' *Smith v Baker & Sons* [1891] AC 325 at 336, 337, per Lord Halsbury LC

'It is, I feel, opposed to principle to say that because a servant knows of the defect or danger he is therefore debarred from damages for injury through his master's negligence. To so suggest seems to me to transpose the maxim "Volenti non fit injuria" which is sound doctrine, into a wholly different maxim, namely, "Scienti non fit injuria" . . . This was clearly pointed out by Lord Esher himself in *Yarmouth v France* [supra] when he said, "The maxim, be it observed, is not 'Scienti non fit injuria', but 'Volenti' ".' *Baker v James* [1921] 2 KB 674 at 683, per McCardie J

'With some qualifications Pollock on Torts, 13th edn at p 172, supports Beven's dictum [4th edn at p 796]: "The whole law of negligence assumes the principle of volenti non fit injuria not to be applicable." He points out, quoting the observations of Lord Halsbury LC in *Smith v Baker* [supra] that any one crossing a London street knows that a substantial percentage of drivers are negligent. If a man crosses deliberately, with this knowledge, and is negligently run down, he is certainly not volens, and is not, therefore, precluded from a remedy. Pollock adds at p 173: "A man is not bound at his peril to fly from a risk from which it is another's duty to protect him, because the risk is known". . . . I find it difficult to believe, although I know of no authority directly in point, that a person who voluntarily travels as a passenger in a vehicle driven by a driver who is known by the passenger to have driven negligently in the past is volens as to future negligent acts of such driving, even though he could have chosen some other form of transport if he had wished.' *Dann v Hamilton* [1939] 1 KB 509 at 517, 518, per Asquith J

'With regard to the doctrine "volenti non fit injuria" I would add one reflection of a general kind. That general maxim has to be applied with specially careful regard to the varying facts of human affairs and human nature in any particular case just because it is concerned with the intangible factors of mind and will. For the purpose of the rule, if it be a rule, a man cannot be said to be truly "willing" unless he is in a position to choose freely, and freedom of choice predicates, not only full knowledge of the circumstances on which the exercise of choice is conditioned, so that he may be able to choose wisely, but the absence from his mind of any feeling of constraint so that nothing shall interfere with the freedom of his will. Without purporting to lay down any rule of universal application, I venture to doubt whether the maxim can very often apply in circumstances of an injury to a servant by the negligence of his master. When the servant is engaged specificially for the performance of a dangerous duty and the presence of the danger is a mutually recognised element in the bargain for remuneration, the servant obviously undertakes the risk for the sake of higher pay. A good illustration is the task of the house-breaker. We have all of us watched its performance during the war on bomb-shattered buildings in the course of demolition and marvelled at its dangers. The task of a horse-breaker is similar, but in contracts of employment where the service is hazardous and for that reason highly paid it is not easy to imagine a circumstance in which the hazard causing the hurt to the servant is also attributable to the negligence of the master, and, unless it is, the servant who is injured suffers no "injuria" in the legal sense of an actionable wrong, which is the condition of the maxim.' *Bowater v Rowley Regis Corpn* [1944] 1 KB 476 at 479, 480, CA, per Scott LJ

'The very substance and foundation of the familiar legal defence of volenti non fit injuria infers a recognition that a man may legitimately and without negligence expose himself to the risks incidental to his employment. If this were not so, and negligence were open to be inferred from every acceptance by the workman of the risks incidental to the locus where his master has set him to work, the plea would neither have been devised nor be required, seeing that in all cases the sufficient defence of contributory negligence would have been open. I hold it to be entirely clear, on the contrary, that there are risks which, as matter of daily occurrence, a workman must accept, and so may accept without negligence. It is clear that much industrial work can only be carried on in dangerous surroundings; and that a workman (unless indeed he is to be encouraged to be obstructive at every turn) must thus be entitled, without incurring a charge of negligence, to leave it to his master, when deciding where to set him to work, to charge himself with the duty of making proper provision for his safety.' *Ward (Thomas) Ltd v Revie & Co* 1945 SLT 49 at 52, 53, per Lord Moncrieff

'This brings me to the defence of volenti non fit injuria . . . In former times this defence was used almost as an alternative defence to contributory negligence. Either defence defeated the action. Now that contributory negligence is not a complete defence, but only a ground for reducing the damages, the defence of volenti non fit injuria has been closely considered, and, in consequence, it has been severely limited. Knowledge of the risk of injury is not enough. Nor is a willingness to take the risk of injury. Nothing will suffice short of an agreement to waive any claim for negligence.' *Nettleship v Weston* [1971] 3 All ER 581 at 587, CA, per Lord Denning MR

Australia 'What the plea really means is this, that the plaintiff, with full knowledge of the very risk which has ultimately led to his injury, has expressly or by implication agreed to take that risk without expecting the defendant to compensate him by way of damages at common law if he is injured as a result of it. The question is thus one of express or implied agreement, and the rule is not limited to the case of master and servant. It extends to many other cases such as participation in athletic sports, boxing and riding with a drunken driver. But in the case of master and servant, the plea is much harder to establish; because the plaintiff must be proved to have been volens as well as sciens, and willingness is not established if the plaintiff is under some constraint, for example, if he objects to the risk but has to undergo it if he is to continue his work.' *Cianciarulo v HP Products Pty Ltd* [1959] VR 170 at 171, 172, per Scholl J

VOLUME

'The first question is whether the publication by the defendants in their paper or periodical is publication of the work "in volume form". I agree with the contention of counsel for the defendants, that this refers to the material form of the work, which is referred to in s 1(2) of the Copyright Act 1911 [repealed; see now the Copyright, Designs and Patents Act 1988], "any substantial part thereof in any material form", but I do not think that that carries the matter very much further. In the Shorter Oxford English Dictionary, under the word "volume", the material part of the definition is, I think, that under "1. 2": "A collection of written or printed sheets bound together so as to form a book . . ." In the same dictionary, under the word "book" I find: "A collection of sheets of paper or other substance, blank, written, or printed, fastened together so as to form a material whole . . ." It seems to me that, whether or not those definitions are to be regarded as really of the highest materiality, the defendants' publication does meet both the definitions which I have read of a "volume" and that of a "book". It is a number of sheets which are fastened together so that they form one volume. Except for certain abridgments, it is the whole work which is published in this way, and it seems to me to be immaterial that it is not published in the form of an object with thick cardboard sides and back, but merely has a paper cover.' *Jonathan Cape Ltd v Consolidated Press Ltd* [1954] 3 All ER 253 at 256, per Danckwerts J

VOLUNTARY *See also* ANNUAL VOLUNTARY CONTRIBUTIONS

'"Voluntarily" means, obviously, the doing of something as the result of the free exercise of the will.' *Re Wilkinson, Page v Public Trustee* [1926] Ch 842 at 848, 850, per Tomlin J

'In the present state of the law an admission of guilt or an admission of facts tending to establish guilt is only receivable in evidence against the party making it if it is shown to be "voluntary". It is clear that the word "voluntary" in this connection is not to be given its widest meaning, but unfortunately the reported cases and the leading text books are not unanimous as to the sense in which the word is to be used. The classic statement of the principle is that of Lord Sumner in *Ibrahim v Regem* [[1914] AC 599 at 609] where he said, "It has long been established as a positive rule of English criminal law that no statement by an accused is admissible in evidence against him unless it is shown by the prosecution to be a voluntary statement, in the sense that it has not been obtained from him either by fear of prejudice or hope of advantage exercised or held out by a person in authority. The principle is as old as Lord Hale." However, in five of the eleven text books cited to us . . . support is to be found for a narrow and rather technical meaning of the word "voluntary". According to this view "voluntary" means merely that the statement has not been made in consequence of (i) some promise of advantage or some threat (ii) of a temporal character (iii) held out or made by a person in authority, and (iv) relating to the charge in the sense that it implies that the accused's position in the contemplated proceedings will or may be better or worse according to whether or not the statement is made.' *R v Harz, R v Power* [1966] 3 All ER 433 at 454, 455, per Cantley V

VOLUNTARY HOME

In this Act, except where otherwise indicated, the expression 'voluntary home' means any home or other institution for the boarding, care and maintenance of poor children, being either—

(a) a home or other institution supported wholly or partly by voluntary contributions, or
(b) a home or other institution supported wholly or partly by endowments, not being a school within the meaning of the Education Act 1944,

but does not in either case include a residential care home, nursing home or mental nursing home within the meaning of Part I of the Registered Homes Act 1984. (Child Care Act 1980, s 56, as amended by the Registered Homes Act 1984, s 57, Sch 1(6))

VOLUNTARY HOSPITAL *See* HOSPITAL

VOLUNTARY SCHOOL *See* SCHOOL

VOLUNTARY TRUST *See* TRUST

VOLUNTEER

'The general servant of A may for a time or on a particular occasion be the servant of B, and a person who is not under any paid contract of service may nevertheless have put himself under the control of an employer to act in the capacity of servant, so as to be regarded as such. This . . . is the position of a volunteer.' *Johnson v Lindsay & Co* [1891] AC 371 at 377, 378, HL, per Lord Herschell

'It is said that anybody who can take under a settlement without being overridden by a subsequent purchaser for value is not a volunteer, and that inasmuch as *Newstead v Searles* (1737) 1 Atk 265, and some other cases show that the children of the first marriage of a lady who makes a settlement upon them, are not volunteers so as to be overridden by subsequent purchasers for value, they are not volunteers at all. We have attended to the numerous authorities cited, and we have considered what effect is to be given to them. . . . Some of the decisions are very difficult to reconcile with each other, some of them, indeed, are to my mind irreconcilable; but there is one feature which appears to me to be common to the whole of them, namely, that the consideration of marriage extends only to the husband and wife and the children of that marriage, and that all other persons whether they are children of a former marriage or children of a subsequent marriage, or whether they are brothers, or whether they are illegitimate children, or whether they are strangers altogether, are volunteers in some sense.' *A-G v Jacobs Smith* [1895] 2 QB 341 at 348, CA, per Lindley LJ

VOTE

'A man may give his vote in divers ways, either in writing, or by hand, or by voice, or by conduct—e.g. by nod. The form in which acquiescence is given matters not if acquiescence be actually indicated.' *Everett v Griffiths* [1924] 1 KB 941 at 953, per McCardie J

VOTER

'Voter' means a person voting at an election and includes a person voting as proxy and, except in the parliamentary elections rules . . . a person voting by proxy, and 'vote' (whether noun or verb) shall be construed accordingly, except that in those rules any reference to an elector voting or in elector's vote shall include a reference to an elector voting by proxy or an elector's vote given by proxy. (Representation of the People Act 1983, s 202(1))

Service voter

'Service voter' means a person who has made a service declaration and is registered or entitled to be registered in pursuance of it. (Representation of the People Act 1983, s 202(1))

VOYAGE

'I see no reason why the word "voyage" in this charterparty should receive an interpretation different from its ordinary acceptation. The charterparty contains a stipulation that the vessel shall sail from Genoa on or before the 30th of July, 1856. When she sails, the voyage commences. Before her departure, no voyage exists to which the penalty could attach.' *Valente v Gibbs* (1859) 6 CBNS 270 at 286, per Willes J

[A ship was insured at and from 'L, to any port or ports in the South and North Pacific in any order backwards and forwards and during thirty days stay in her last port of discharge'. The ship arrived at her last port of discharge on 25th of May at 7 pm and remained anchored there in safety until 24th of June, on which day at 3.45 am she was driven ashore in a gale and lost.] 'According to the practice of insurers and insured in voyage policies, the twenty-four hours after the arrival of the ship in her port of discharge are considered as forming part of the period of the voyage. The other period of thirty days mentioned in this policy is intended to start from the time when the voyage policy ceases.' *Mercantile Marine Insurance Co Ltd v Titherington* (1864) 5 B & S 765 at 768, per Cockburn CJ

'It seems to me that, under this charterparty, the voyage of the "*Smyrna*" commenced when she sailed from the place where she was at the time the charterparty was entered into. She was bound to make that voyage with all convenient speed. The place whence she started was the terminus à quo for the performance of the voyage mentioned in the charterparty.' *Barker v M'Andrew* (1865) 18 CBNS 759 at 775, per Montague Smith J

'I apprehend the voyage is nothing more than the passage of the vessel on the transit. The commencement of the voyage is the commencing to do that for which the shipowner is to be paid freight.' *Harrison v Garthorne* (1872) 26 LT 508 at 509, per Blackburn J

'The question . . . arises whether the shipowners have freed themselves from liability . . . by the clause of the charterparty, which stipulated that they should not be responsible for any act, neglect, or default whatsoever of their servants "during the said voyage". It was contended for the plaintiffs that this only related to the voyage from New Fairwater to Greenock and did not include the period of time during which the vessel was being loaded. . . . I cannot doubt that the exception was not intended to apply only to the time after the vessel left the port of loading, but extended to the whole time during which the vessel was engaged in performing the contract contained in the charter.' *The Carron Park* (1890) 15 PD 203 at 205, 206, per Hannen P

'It must in each case be a question of fact what is a voyage, and in ascertaining what it is a Court may regard the following among other considerations: The duration of the adventure in point of time and its unity; its geographical limits and direction; whether new cargoes are shipped, or new charters made, or ports visited in orderly succession; and in particular whether there has been a sailing from, and afterwards a return to, the United Kingdom.' *Board of Trade v Baxter, The Scarsdale* [1907] AC 373 at 378, per Lord Loreburn LC

'I think that the risk under a port risk policy must cease when the voyage commences and that commences when the vessel, equipped for sea with crew and cargo, has commenced to navigate on her voyage and no longer lies at her moorings.' *Mersey Mutual Underwriting Assocn Ltd v Poland* (1910) 26 TLR 386 at 387, per Hamilton J

'"Voyage", in this context [art III, r 1 of the Hague Rules], means what it has always meant; the contractual voyage from the port of loading to the port of discharge as declared in the appropriate bill of lading. The rule says "voyage" without any qualification such as "any declared stage thereof".' *The Makedonia, Owners of Cargo Laden on Makedonia v Owners of Makedonia* [1962] 2 All ER 614 at 617, per Hewson J; also reported in [1962] P 190 at 194

Change of voyage *See* CHANGE

End of voyage *See* END

In home waters

'Voyage in home waters', in relation to a ship, means a voyage in which the ship is at all times either at sea or within the limits of a port. (Hydrocarbon Oil Duties Act 1979, s 18(6))

International voyage

'International voyage' means a voyage between—

(a) a port in the United Kingdom and a port outside the United Kingdom, or
(b) a port in a Convention country (other than the United Kingdom) and a port in any other country or territory (whether a Convention country or not) which is outside the United Kingdom.

(3) In determining for the purposes of the last preceding subsection, what are the ports between which a voyage is made, no account shall be taken of any deviation by a ship from her intended voyage which is due solely to stress of weather or any other circumstance which neither the master nor the owner nor the charterer (if any) of the ship could have prevented or forestalled; and for the purposes of that subsection any colony, protectorate or other dependency, any territory for whose international relations a Government is separately responsible, and any territory for which the United Nations are the administering authority, shall be taken to be a separate territory. (Merchant Shipping (Load Lines) Act 1967, s 32)

Of fishing boat

The expression 'voyage' shall mean a fishing trip commencing with a departure from a port for the purpose of fishing, and ending with the first return to a port thereafter upon the conclusion of the trip, but a return due to distress only shall not be deemed to be a return, if it is followed by a resumption of the trip. (Merchant Shipping Act 1894, s 370

Voyage policy *See* POLICY OF INSURANCE

W

WAGER *See* GAMING

WAGERING CONTRACT

'A wagering contract is one by which two persons, professing to hold opposite views touching the issue of a future uncertain event, mutually agree that, dependent upon the determination of that event, one shall win from the other, and that other shall pay or hand over to him, a sum of money or other stake; neither of the contracting parties having any other interest in that contract than the sum or stake he will so win or lose, there being no other real consideration for the making of such contract by either of the parties. It is essential to a wagering contract that each party may under it either win or lose, whether he will win or lose being dependent on the issue of the event, and, therefore, remaining uncertain until that issue is known. If either of the parties may win but cannot lose, or may lose but cannot win, it is not a wagering contract. It is also essential that there should be mutuality in the contract. For instance, if the evidence of the contract is such as to make the intentions of the parties material in the consideration of the question whether it is a wagering one or not, and those intentions are at variance, those of one party being such as if agreed in by the other would make the contract a wagering one, whilst those of the other would prevent it from becoming so, this want of mutuality would destroy the wagering element of the contract and leave it enforceable by law as an ordinary one.' *Carlill v Carbolic Smoke Ball Co* [1892] 2 QB 484 at 490, 491, per Hawkins J; affd [1893] 1 QB 256, CA

'The foundation of the rules as to insurable interest is that the contract of marine insurance is essentially a contract of indemnity. Unless the assured is exposed to a risk of real loss by the perils insured against, the contract is not a contract of indemnity, but is a mere wagering contract, and cannot be enforced.' *Moran, Galloway & Co v Uzielli* [1905] 2 KB 555 at 563, per Walton J

WAGES *See also*

EARNINGS; REMUNERATION; SALARY

The term 'wages' includes all earnings by miners arising from any description of piece or other work, or as tributers or otherwise. (Stannaries Act 1887, s 2)

Australia 'In ordinary parlance "wages" is the term used for the remuneration paid for other than "white-collar" jobs.' *Mutual Acceptance Co Ltd v Federal Comr of Taxation* (1944) 69 CLR 389 at 398, per Rich J

WAIFS

Waifs are things stolen and thrown away by the thief in his flight; and they belong to the Crown by prerogative right, as a punishment, it is said, to the owner for not having pursued the thief and retaken the goods. The goods do not belong to the Crown until they have been seized on its behalf, and the property remains in the original owner if he can retake them before they have been so seized. Even when they are in the hands of the Crown, the owner is entitled to restitution if he pursues the thief with due dilgence, or if he afterwards brings him to justice and secures a conviction. (8 Halsbury's Laws (4th edn) para 1516).

[As to restitution, see now the Theft Act 1968, s 28.]

WAIVER

Waiver is the abandonment of a right in such a way that the other party is entitled to plead the abandonment by way of confession and avoidance if the right is thereafter asserted, and is either express or implied from conduct. It may sometimes resemble a form of election, and sometimes be based on ordinary principles of estoppel, although, unlike estoppel, waiver must always be an intentional act with knowledge. A person who is entitled to rely on a stipulation, existing for his benefit alone, in a contract or of a statutory provision may waive it, and allow the contract or transaction to proceed as though the stipulation or provision did not exist. Waiver of this kind depends upon consent, and the fact that the other party has acted upon it is sufficient consideration. Where the waiver is not express it may be implied from conduct which is inconsistent with the continuance of the right, without need for writing or for consideration moving from, or detriment to, the party who benefits by the waiver; but mere acts of indulgence will not amount to waiver; nor can a party benefit from the waiver unless he has altered his position in reliance on it. The waiver may be terminated by reasonable but not necessarily formal notice unless the party who benefits by the waiver cannot resume his position, or termination would cause injustice to him.

It seems that, in general, where one party has, by his words or conduct, made to the other a promise or assurance which was intended to affect the legal relations between them and to be acted on accordingly, then, once the other party has taken him at his word and acted on it, so as to alter his position, the party who gave the promise or assurance cannot afterwards be allowed to revert to the previous legal relationship as if no such promise or assurance had been made by him, but he must accept their legal relations subject to the qualification which he has himself so introduced, even though it is not supported in point of law by any consideration. (16 Halsbury's Laws (4th edn) para 1471)

Waiver is the abandonment of a right, and thus is a defence against its subsequent enforcement. Waiver may be express or, where there is knowledge of the right, may be implied from conduct which is inconsistent with the continuance of the right. A mere statement of an intention not to insist on a right does not suffice in the absence of consideration; but a deliberate election not to insist on full rights, although made without first obtaining full disclosure of material facts, and to come to a settlement on that basis will be binding. (45 Halsbury's Laws (4th edn) para 1269)

'The word "waiver" is a vague term used in many senses. It is always necessary to ascertain in what sense and with what restrictions it is used in any particular case. It is sometimes used in the sense of election as where a person decides between two mutually exclusive rights. Thus, in the old phrase, he claims in assumpsit and waives the tort. It is also used where a party expressly or impliedly gives up a right to enforce a condition or rely on a right to rescind a contract, or prevents performance, or announces that he will refuse performance, or loses an equitable right by laches.' *Smyth (Ross T) & Co Ltd v Bailey, Son & Co* [1940] 3 All ER 60 at 70, per Lord Wright

' "Waiver" is a word which is sometimes used loosely to describe a number of different legal grounds on which a person may be debarred from asserting a substantive right which he once possessed or from raising a particular defence to a claim against him which would otherwise be available to him. We are not concerned in the instant appeal with the first type of waiver. This arises in a situation where a person is entitled to alternative rights inconsistent with one another. If he has knowledge of the facts which gave rise in law to these alternative rights and acts in a manner which is consistent only with his having chosen to rely on one of them, the law holds him to his choice even though he was unaware that this would be the legal consequence of what he did. He is sometimes said to have "waived" the alternative right, as for instance a right to forfeit a lease or to rescind a contract of sale for wrongful repudiation or breach of condition; but this is better categorised as "election" rather than as "waiver". . . . The second type of waiver which debars a person from raising a particular defence to a claim against him, arises when he either agrees with the claimant not to raise that particular defence or so conducts himself as to be stopped from raising it.' *Kammins Ballrooms Co Ltd v Zenith Investments (Torquay) Ltd* [1970] 2 All ER 871 at 894, HL, per Lord Diplock

'The principle of waiver is simply this: if one party, by his conduct, leads another to believe that the strict rights arising under the contract will not be insisted on, intending that the other should act on that belief, and he does act on it, then the first party will not afterwards be allowed to insist on the strict legal rights when it would be inequitable for him to do so. There may be no consideration moving from him who benefits by the waiver. There may be no detriment to him by acting on it. There may be nothing in writing. Nevertheless, the one who waives his strict rights cannot afterwards insist on them. His strict rights are at any rate suspended so long as the waiver lasts. He may on occasion be able to revert to his strict legal rights for the future by giving reasonable notice in that behalf, or otherwise making it plain by his conduct that he will thereafter insist on them. But there are cases where no withdrawal is possible. It may be too late to withdraw; or it cannot be done without injustice to the other party. In that event he is bound by his waiver. He will not be allowed to revert to his strict legal rights. He can only enforce them subject to the waiver he has made.' *W J Alan & Co Ltd v El Nasr Export & Import Co* [1972] 2 All ER 127 at 140, CA, per Lord Denning MR

'In my view, the primary meaning of the word "waiver" in legal parlance is the abandonment of a right in such a way that the other party is entitled to plead the abandonment by way of confession and avoidance if the right is thereafter asserted.' *Banning v Wright (Inspector of Taxes)* [1972] 2 All ER 987 at 998, HL, per Lord Hailsham LC

WAKE

'A "wake" according to English usage is an annual parochial activity, usually on the day (which is treated as a holiday) following some saint's day of special significance to the parish, which takes the form of demonstrations of special skills and athletic prowess.' *Wyld v Silver* [1961] 3 All ER 1014 at 1019, per Lloyd-Jacob J

WALKING POSSESSION

'It was at one time thought that, in order to retain possession, the bailiff, as the sheriff's officer, must actually remain in the house with the goods. He used to sit down in the kitchen and make himself at home; but that has long since been regarded as unnecessary. It is sufficient if he visits the house frequently to make sure that the goods are safely there and not removed. He then still retains possession; but he need not even do as much as that—he need not visit the house—if he gets an agreement by some responsible person in the house to see that the goods are not removed. After getting such an agreement, he is said to take "walking possession".' *National Commercial Bank of Scotland Ltd v Arcam Demolition and Construction Ltd* [1966] 3 All ER 114 at 115, per Lord Denning MR

WALL *See* PARTY FENCE WALL; PARTY-WALL

WANT

[Section 72 of Stat (1825) 6 Geo 4, c 125 (repealed) required any pilot, not having a lawful excuse, to take charge of any ship 'wanting a pilot' when called on by the master or owner so to do.] 'The question is, what is the meaning of these words, any ship wanting a pilot? If they mean any ship being bound by the provisions of the Act to take a pilot, then, inasmuch as the owner or master was certainly not bound, under the circumstances appearing on this record, to take a pilot, the 72nd section would not apply. But we think this is not the true meaning of these words, and that they must be construed to mean any ship the master or owner of which thinks fit to require a pilot.' *Lucey (or Lucy) v Ingram* (1840) 6 M & W 302 at 312, per cur.

WANT OF MUTUALITY

'I am asked to find first of all that a certain contract . . . is void for one of two reasons: First of all because of want of mutuality. . . . I am not, myself, very familiar in this connection with the phrase "want of mutuality"; I am very familiar with it in the other connection, in which it is said that parties have not entered into contract where they have not agreed all the terms one with the other. Here, as I understand the phrase "want of mutuality", in the present position of the cases, it means that there has been no consideration, or no real consideration, for the contract which has been entered into.' *Gaumont-British Picture Corpn Ltd v Alexander* [1936] 2 All ER 1686 at 1690, 1691, per Porter J

WANT OF PROSECUTION

See PROSECUTION

WANTON

'"Wantonly" means, not having a reasonable cause. Here we come to the kernel of the case,—whether one having a lawful right to come to another's house, has a right to stop there at a late hour at night knocking and ringing violently, though he knows that the inmates do not choose to admit him or to receive what he brings. That answers itself. Wantonness consists in the doing that which will annoy another and which the party doing it knows will produce no results to himself.' *Clarke v Hoggins* (1862) 11 CBNS 545 at 551, 552, per Willes J

WAR *See also* LEVY; WARLIKE OPERATION

At common law no state of war exists between the United Kingdom and a foreign state until there has been a formal declaration of war by the Crown or hostilities have been commenced by the authority of the Crown. Similarly a war may be terminated only by the authority of the Crown, and this is usually effected by a treaty of peace and announced to the nation by proclamation or Order in Council. A certificate of the Secretary of State for Foreign and Commonwealth Affairs to the effect that the Crown is still at war with a foreign state is conclusive evidence that the state of war is not at an end. During the course of a war with a foreign state all commerce and intercourse between British subjects resident in British territory and the subjects of that state, or with persons residing there, is prohibited except under licence. Judicial notice will be taken of the existence of a state of war between this country and any other, when that is the fact, even after the termination of hostilities. (48 Halsbury's Laws (4th edn) para 101)

'What is a state of war is well described in Hall on International Law, 4th edn, p 63: "When differences between states reach a point at which both parties resort to force, or one of them does an act of violence, which the other chooses to look upon as a breach of the peace, the relation of war is set up, in which the combatants may use regulated violence against each other, until one of the two has been brought to accept such terms as his enemy is willing to grant".' *Driefontein Consolidated Gold Mines v Janson* [1900] 2 QB 339 at 343, per Mathew J

'We are concerned, and only concerned, with the question whether upon the construction of a particular private document, the owners were entitled to cancel the charterparty, which they are only entitled to do if war breaks out involving Japan. Now it is in my judgment impossible to assert that within the meaning of that clause the words "if war breaks out" mean "if war is recognised to have broken out by His Majesty's Government". War may break out without His Majesty's Government recognising it. If His Majesty's Government had recognised that war had broken out it may be—and I say no more—that a statement to that effect by His Majesty's Government would be a matter which, even when dealing with a document of this kind, the Court would be bound to accept. It is not necessary to decide that question one way or the other, because that is not the question with which we have to deal. . . . I am unable to accept the suggestion that there is any technical meaning of the word "war" for the purpose of the construction of this clause. . . . If there is such a technical meaning, I do not know where it is to be found. . . . But, even if there be such technical meaning, . . . the finding of fact of the arbitrator is unassailable, and I can find no trace on the face of his award that he has misdirected himself in law. That, I think, really concludes the matter. But I must not be taken as in any sense disagreeing with the further view expressed by the learned judge that in the particular context in which the word "war" is found in this charterparty, that word must be construed, having regard to the general tenor and purpose of the document, in what may be called a common sense way. . . . One modern authority, Professor Westlake, so answered it, because he defines "war" as "the state or condition of governments contending by force". . . . It seems to me that to suggest that, within the meaning of this charterparty, war had not broken out involving Japan on the relevant date is to attribute to the parties to it a desire to import into their contract some obscure and uncertain technicalities of international law rather than the common sense of business men.' *Kawasaki Kisen Kobushiki Kaisha of Kobe v Bantham SS Co Ltd (No 2)* [1939] 2 KB 544 at 554, 555, 558, CA, per Greene MR

'I desire to say quite plainly that, in my view, the word "war" in a policy of insurance includes civil war unless the context makes it clear that a different meaning should be given to the word. There is no such context in the policy now under consideration. I can see no good reason for giving to the word "war" a meaning which excludes one type of war.' *Pesquerias y Secaderos de Bacalao de Espana SA v Beer* [1949] 1 All ER 845 n at 847, HL, per Lord Morton of Henryton

WAR BASE

'A war base is evidently a place used for certain purposes of military supply in a time and in an area of war. The term is an administrative one and, whatever it may connote in a text-book on the theory of war, in practice it is simply the place chosen by the competent military authority, on which to base other operations of war. A place is, therefore, not a war base because nature made it so or owing to the fitness of things, but because those directing the war chose it for that purpose.' *Commonwealth Shipping Representative v Peninsular & Oriental Branch Service* [1923] AC 191 at 209, per Lord Sumner

WAR OPERATIONS

'War operations' means action taken by an enemy, or action taken in combating an enemy or in repelling an imagined attack by an enemy. (Compensation (Defence) Act 1939, s 17)

WAR RISKS

'The expression "war risks" means risks arising from action taken by an enemy or from action taken in combating an enemy or in repelling an imagined attack by an enemy. (Restriction of Advertisement (War Risks Insurance) Act 1939, s 6)

'War risks' means risks arising from any of the following events, that is to say, hostilities, rebellion, revolution and civil war, from civil strife consequent on the happening of any of those events, or from action taken (whether before or after the outbreak of any hostilities, rebellion, revolution or civil war) for repelling an imagined attack or preventing or hindering the carrying out of any attack, and includes piracy. (Marine and Aviation Insurance (War Risks) Act 1952, s 10)

'It is well settled that a marine risk does not become a war risk merely because the conditions of war may make it more probable that the marine risk will operate and a loss will be caused. It is for this reason that sailing without lights, or sailing in convoy, are regarded as circumstances which do not in themselves convert marine risks into war risks, but where the facts, as found by the judge, establish that the operation of a war peril is the "proximate" cause of the loss in the above sense, then the conclusion that the loss is due to war risk follows.' *Yorkshire Dale SS Co Ltd v Minister of War Transport* [1942] AC 691 at 698, per Lord Simon LC

WARD OF COURT

The concept of wardship is a facet of the relationship between the Crown (acting through the courts) and its subjects, who owe allegiance to the Crown and to whom the Crown offers its protection, observing a special obligation as parens patriae to minors. In one sense, all British minors are wards of court because they are subject to the parental jurisdiction entrusted to the courts. But the expression 'ward of court' has over the years acquired a more specialised significance, and today an infant can be made a ward of court only upon the making of an application for an order to that effect. The infant becomes a ward on the making of the application, and ceases to be a ward at the expiration of a prescribed period unless within that period an order has been made in accordance with the application. Either upon an application or without an application the court may order that a ward of court is to cease to be a ward. The court's jurisdiction continues even if the ward becomes mentally disordered. (24 Halsbury's Laws (4th edn) para 576)

'If there be a fund in Court under its administration standing to the account of an infant, or to an account under which an infant is entitled, then inasmuch as the Court is bound to administer that fund, the infant will be treated as a ward of Court to the same extent as an infant who is a party to an action for the administration of property belonging to that infant. Undoubtedly, we use the words "ward of Court" in such a case in rather a special sense. In one sense all British subjects who are infants are wards of Court, because they are subject to that sort of parental jurisdiction which is intrusted to the Court in this country, and which has been administered continually by the Courts of the Chancery Division.' *Brown v Collins* (1883) 25 Ch D 56 at 60, per Kay J

WAREHOUSE *See also* STORE

The expression 'warehouse' includes all warehouses, buildings, and premises in which goods, when landed from ships, may be lawfully placed. (Merchant Shipping Act 1894, s 492)

'Building of the warehouse class' means a warehouse manufactory brewery or distillery or any other building exceeding in cubical extent one hundred and fifty thousand cubic feet which is neither a public building nor a domestic building. (London Building Act 1930, s 5)

[Under Stat (1698) 10 Will 3, c 12 (repealed), it was an offence to steal goods in (inter alia) any 'warehouse'.] 'By the word warehouses in the statute are meant, not mere repositories for goods, but such places, where merchants and other traders keep their goods for sale in the nature of shops, and whither customers go to view them.' *R v Howard* (1751) Fost 77 at 78, per cur.

[Under Stat (1827) 7 & 8 Geo 4, c 29 (repealed), it was an offence to break and enter (inter alia) any 'warehouse', and steal therein any chattel, money, or valuable security.] 'A warehouse, in common parlance, certainly means a place where a man stows, or keeps, his goods, which are not immediately wanted for sale; and there is no reason to suppose that the legislature used the term in this statute in a sense repugnant to its ordinary meaning.' *R v Hill* (1843) 2 Mood & R 458 at 459, per Rolfe B

[Under Stat (1827) 7 & 8 Geo 4, c 30 (repealed), it was an offence unlawfully and maliciously to set fire to (inter alia) any 'warehouse'.] 'I am clearly of opinion that this building is neither an outhouse nor a warehouse, within the meaning of this statute. That it is not an outhouse, seems to be admitted, for the cases have certainly laid down a definition of that term, which is quite inconsistent with the facts in this case, seeing that it is not in any manner attached to or connected with a dwelling-house. Neither is it a warehouse, which is, according to the case of *R v Howard* [supra] a place used for the showing and sale of goods and wares by factors and traders, and not one in which they are merely deposited for safe custody. Now this building was not used for the deposit of goods in any capacity whatever; and is not, therefore, a warehouse.' *R v Borley* (1844) 8 JP 263 at 263, 264, per Patterson J

'The word warehouse seems to me to involve the idea of a place where goods are stored for sale, or at least for some other commercial purpose. But it does not prove that a piece of ground where goods are stored for commercial purposes is necessarily a warehouse in law.' *Buckingham v Fulham Corpn* (1905) 53 WR 628 at 629, CA, per Cozens-Hardy LJ

[A local Act provided (inter alia) that a fruiterer should not sell fruit in any private house or 'warehouse', except in his own shop.] 'There may be a warehouse, as *Howard's Case* [*R v Howard* (supra)] shows, which is not a repository only; indeed there may be statutes in which it is clear that the word "warehouse" as there used, is not merely a place in which goods are stored, but a place in which there is also a selling room, but here it seems to me that as you have got "warehouse" in the first part, and "shop" in the second, one would rather, I think, be justified in drawing the inference that in this statute "warehouse" is meant to signify repository or storing place as contrasted with a place in which goods are stored only for the purpose of sale there, as is the case in Mr Ford's business. Looked at as a question of fact, if you have to choose between "warehouse" and "shop" under circumstances not in dispute in this case, I think the true inference is that this building is only, as far as it can be spoken of as a warehouse, a warehouse ancillary and accessory to the main business of the shop; and it seems to follow from that that if you are asked to define the building you would say it is a shop, because the main and principal business is to sell there, and the only storage that takes place there is accessory, ancillary, and incidental to the selling, which is the essential characteristic of the business that there is carried on.' *Haynes v Ford* [1911] 2 Ch 237 at 256, 257, CA, per Kennedy LJ

'A building of the warehouse class is defined [by certain by-laws] as meaning "a warehouse, factory, manufactory, brewery, or distillery". Without taking into account the doctrine of *ejusdem generis*, all these things are, in my opinion, descriptions of buildings where business in the nature of trade is carried on, and I think it would be straining language to say that the common well-known barn, which is nothing more than a store-room for grain, and may be used, when it is empty, for various storage purposes, is a warehouse within that definition.' *R v Preston Rural District Council, ex p Longworth* (1911) 106 LT 37 at 40, DC, per Lord Alverstone CJ

'The ordinary meaning of "warehouse" . . . is supported in cases . . . under the Workmen's Compensation Acts; these all tend to show that where the word "warehouse" is used the main function of the building is intended to be for storage, and, of course, distribution from the building.' *Calcaria Construction Co (York) Ltd v Secretary of State for the Environment* (1974) 27 P & CR 435 at 439, per O'Connor J

Australia 'The predominant, and indeed the sole, purposes of the proposed building are the exposure of goods for sale by wholesale and the storage of large stocks so that buyers may take immediate delivery of the full amount of their purchases. These, in ordinary usage, are the characteristics of a "warehouse" in one of its forms.' *A G Campbell (Properties) Ltd v Parramatta City Council* [1961] NSWR 542 at 543, per Sugerman J

New Zealand 'On a reasonable construction of the definition of "warehouse", sale by wholesale from the premises is permitted, and indeed as a matter of common sense wholesale selling is a necessary element of warehousing, otherwise there would be no difference between a bulk store and a warehouse.' *Rattray & Son Ltd v Christchurch City* (1984) 9 NZTPA 395 at 397, per Roper J

WAREHOUSEMAN

'Warehouseman' includes all persons owning or managing any warehouse, store, wharf, or other premises in which goods are deposited. (Explosives Act 1875, s 108)

WARLIKE OPERATION *See also* CONSEQUENCES; HOSTILITIES

'Part of a warlike operation consists in getting to the proper point for striking at the enemy if actual hostilities of that kind are the object of the expedition, or in proceeding to the point where the duty of undertaking the charge of a convoy is to take effect. Protecting convoys is a form of warlike operation, it is an operation in the course of war necessary to be performed by war vessels for the purpose of protecting the merchantmen. I cannot separate the proceeding under orders to the spot where the duty is to be discharged from the actual discharge of the duty itself; both form part of the warlike operation. It is just as much a part of a warlike operation to get your ships or your troops to the spot where a thing is to be done as it is to do it when you get to the spot. . . . It seems to me perfectly plain that when a war vessel is actually at sea, and is there because she is under orders to go to a particular spot to undertake a warlike operation, whatever its nature may be, she is engaged in that warlike operation, because she is doing that which is necessary to get to the spot where the actual thing is to be done.' *A-G v Ard Coasters Ltd, Liverpool & London War Risks Insurance Assocn Ltd v Marine Underwriters of SS Richard De Larrinaga* [1921] 2 AC 141 at 151, 152, per Lord Finlay

'It will be observed that the words in the present charterparty are "all consequences of hostilities or warlike operations"; but I conceive that since the decision in *Ionides v Universal Marine Insurance Co* in 1863 [(1863) 14 CBNS 259] it is established law that the words "all consequences" must be treated as meaning the "totality of causes" not "their sequence, or their proximity or remoteness". . . . In the first place I think that the *Inkonka* was not herself engaged in a "warlike operation". She was a merchantman. . . . She was not a transport in the ordinary sense. If she had been such a vessel it might be held that she was engaged in warlike operations. In the *Petersham* case [[1921] 1 AC at 100] Lord Atkinson said: "The transfer of the combative forces of a power from one area of war to another . . . for combative purposes would . . . be a warlike operation" . . . an ordinary merchantman is none the less engaged on an operation of peace rather than an operation of war because she is without lights pursuant to imperative

Admiralty directions . . . a merchantman under naval convoy, and bound to obey that convoy, is not thereby engaged in a warlike operation. The convoy may be so engaged, but the merchantman convoyed sails on a different footing . . . the question still remains whether the *Inkonka* was stranded as a "consequence of warlike operations". . . . The arbitrator here has found as a fact that the stranding of the *Inkonka* [a merchantman sailing without lights in a war region under convoy, and ordered to enter Taranto, where she went ashore] was caused by the inefficient lights of the pilot escort, and that if those lights had been adequate there was no reason why the *Inkonka* should not have safely reached Taranto. . . . I support the award of the arbitrator. I hold that although the *Inkonka* was stranded whilst being navigated under war conditions, yet her damage did not arise in consequence of warlike operations.' *Harrisons Ltd v Shipping Controller* [1921] 1 KB 122 at 133–137, per McCardie J

'I think that a Court of law may with propriety, and I hope with substantial conformity to the fact, presume till the contrary is shown, that Government material of war is not idly shifted from war base to war base, or transported at great cost otherwise than for war purposes. If so, it seems to me to be implicit in the facts found, that this transportation of these stores was a warlike operation. This appears to have been the view of Scrutton LJ and, subject to some comment on the language which he used, it was the view of Bailhache J also. The learned judge says [[1922] 1 KB 706 at 710] "if it be a warlike operation to take troops from one place to another, I am unable to see myself that it is not equally a warlike operation to convey munitions of war or ambulance waggons for the use of wounded soldiers from one place to another". I do not think that the learned judge meant to say, at any rate with reference to the transport of chattels, that transport of munitions of war from any place to any other place is necessarily a warlike operation. Possibly there may be some difference in the case of the transport of troops, of which it may be said that any transportation of them in time of war is warlike, but, in the case of chattels, I assume that his remark was intended to be directed to the case in hand as found in the present case.' *Commonwealth Shipping Representative v Peninsular and Oriental Branch Service* [1923] AC 191 at 209, 210, per Lord Sumner

'In para 9 of his award the learned arbitrator says "if and in so far as it is a question of fact, I find, and if and in so far as it is a question of law, I hold (subject to the opinion of the Court) that the *Roanoke* at the time in question, was performing a warlike operation and that the collision was a consequence of hostilities or warlike operations" and your Lordships have to decide on this appeal whether he was right. I think he was. Though the Armistice has been signed, and, having been renewed, was still current, war was not over nor was the renewal of war by any means out of the question. Except in so far as her destination may make the difference, the *Roanoke* was apparently doing what would have been one of her ordinary duties *flagrante bello*, and, if she had been proceeding to her station off the coast of Germany, I do not think it could have been argued, in view of the authorities, that her voyage so made was not a warlike operation. The temporary cessation of hostilities, which is all that an armistice in itself involves, could not deprive the operation of that character.' *Board of Trade v Hain SS Co Ltd* [1929] AC 534 at 539, 540, per Lord Sumner

'The only conceivable connection which the *Alderpool* had with a warlike operation [within the terms of a policy of insurance] when she ran down the *Brendonia* was that the Admiralty then had an uncommunicated intention of using her on a warlike operation at a later stage in her history. It is impossible to say that that fact constitutes that which the *Alderpool* was doing on the night in question the carrying out of a warlike operation.' *Wharton (Shipping) Ltd v Mortleman* [1941] 2 KB 283 at 285, CA, per MacKinnon LJ

'It has been laid down that a vessel like the *Coxwold*, which was carrying munitions of war from one war base to another, is "engaged in a war-like operation", and this was expressly admitted by the respondent in the present case. This, however, is an entirely different thing from saying that any and every accident which happens to such a ship during her voyage is the consequence of a warlike operation. To suggest the contrary would be just as illogical as to say that if a postman, while engaged in the operation of delivering letters, meets with an accident in the street, this is necessarily the proximate consequence of his delivering letters. Authority is hardly needed for the proposition that you do not prove that an accident is "the consequence of" a warlike operation merely by showing that it happened "during" a warlike operation. For example, if a commercial vessel, while proceeding from one war base to another with munitions on board, is destroyed while at sea by accidental fire, the cause of which is quite unconnected with the nature or method of her journey or the nature of the cargo she carries, I should suppose that it could not be said that her destruction was proximately caused by her warlike operation. So with collision. Scrutton LJ is plainly right when he says in *Clan Line Steamers Ltd v Board of Trade* [[1928] 2 KB 557 at 567], that "the question to be decided is: Was the collision a consequence of a warlike operation—not, did it happen in the course of a warlike operation, not, is a warlike operation one of the events which in their totality contributed to the collision, but was the collision a consequence of a warlike operation in the sense in which that expression is understood in insurance matters?" If Lord Dunedin's use of the syllogistic form in *Attorney-General v Ard Coasters Ltd* [supra], were to be understood as stating that anything that happens during a warlike operation is a consequence of it, that passage contains a slip in reasoning and is no essential part of the decision. Lord Sumner, in *Attorney-General v Adelaide Steamship Co Ltd (The Warilda)* [[1923] AC 292 at 305], puts the true test when he asks whether the collision is caused "effectively and proximately" by the warlike operation.' *Yorkshire Dale SS Co Ltd v Minister of War Transport* [1942] AC 691 at 696, 697, per Lord Simon LC

'The conclusion at which I have arrived from a careful examination of the authorities is that a warlike operation is one which forms part of an actual or intended belligerent act or series of acts by combatant forces. It may be performed preparatory to the actual act or acts of belligerency, or it may be performed after such act or acts, but there must be a connection sufficiently close between the act in question and the belligerent act or acts to enable a tribunal to say, with at least some modicum of Lord Dunedin's common sense, that it formed part of acts of belligerency. If military equipment is being taken in a ship to a place behind the fighting front from which the forces engaged, or about to be engaged on that front, may be supplied, that ship may beyond question be said to be taking part in a warlike operation. If a ship is bringing home such equipment after it has been employed on a fighting front or has been lying available for and at the service of a fighting front, again beyond question, she is taking part in a military operation.' *Clan Line Steamers Ltd v Liverpool & London War Risks Insurance Assocn Ltd* [1943] 1 KB 209 at 221, per Atkinson J

'A voyage in ballast to a home port for the purpose of an off-survey is clearly not a warlike operation, and none the more so though the vessel engaged was performing a warlike operation on her voyage out.' *Larrinaga SS Co Ltd v R* [1945] AC 246 at 257, 258, HL, per Lord Porter

[A ship, requisitioned by the British Government and on voyage from Trinidad to Lochalsh and Scapa Flow under a government form of charter was damaged whilst at anchor at Lochalsh prior to discharging her cargo of fuel oil into the receiving ship.] 'The anchoring of this vessel at that point, in those circumstances, at that time, was an essential part of the operation on which she was engaged, namely, the conveyance of war stores from one base to another base. It was impossible for her to discharge her cargo at Lochalsh the moment she arrived, and she was bound to anchor as a necessary step in fulfilling her ultimate object, namely, the discharge of her cargo. It seems to me to violate all one's conceptions of common sense to say that the warlike nature of her occupation ceased when she dropped her anchor and was only resumed when she pulled it up again. The riding at anchor, when she did ride at anchor, was an essential part of the carrying out of the object of her voyage. It seems to me to be completely artificial to treat that period of time when she was riding at anchor as something which can be severed from the totality of the operation which began when the vessel was loaded with petrol at Trinidad and ended when she finally discharged it. . . . The high water mark, I think, of the proposition that, in such a case as this, where the voyage is a warlike operation, there must be, at the moment of injury, some movement of the vessel through the water, is to be found in the words of Lord Porter in the recent case of *Larrinaga Steamship Co Ltd v R* [supra] in which he sums up what he considers to be the result of some of the earlier authorities. He says this: "There is abundance of authority in your Lordships' House that a ship engaged in carrying war stores from one war base to another, or indeed in carrying war stores to a war base, is engaged on the warlike operation of proceeding through the water to her appointed discharging port." We find in earlier cases, where the vessel was in fact proceeding through the water at the relevant time, the same references to "proceeding through the water". Those references, I apprehend, arose because that happened to be the fact in those particular cases. I cannot read these passages as in any way laying down a proposition which was not under discussion at all, namely, that if the vessel has halted—whether because she has stopped her engines and come to rest or because she has cast anchor in addition—that circumstance is really a crucial matter of distinction. . . . But it is perhaps desirable also to add this, that even if the suggested criterion of movement through the water was correct, so that at the precise moment when this vessel, riding, as she was, at anchor, suffered damage, she was not engaged on a warlike operation—I should still be of opinion that the damage that she suffered was a consequence of her warlike operation.' *Athel Line Ltd v Liverpool & London War Risks Insurance Assocn Ltd* [1946] KB 117 at 120–122, CA, per Lord Greene MR

Australia '"Not everything done by a King's ship or a King's officer in time of war is necessarily a warlike operation or the consequence thereof": see *Britain Steamship Co Ltd v R* [[1921] 1 AC 99] at pp 129, 133. And, as already indicated, not every warlike operation, by which I mean an operation of a warlike character as distinguished from an operation or an act of war (see *Britain Steamship Co Ltd v R* at pp 108, 133) excuses a person from the duty of taking care or justifies the suspension of the ordinary law.' *Shaw Savill & Albion Co Ltd v Commonwealth* (1940) 66 CLR 344 at 354, per Starke J

Australia 'In *Attorney-General v Ard Coasters Ltd* [supra], at p 153, he [Lord Sumner] pointed out that operations in war and operations of war are not necessarily the same.' Ibid at 366, per Williams J

WARNING

Australia [The Local Government Act 1919–1986, s 87(2)(f) provides that the president of a shire council may at any meeting of the council remove or cause the removal of any member of the council who, after 'warning', is guilty of disorder.] 'I have come to the conclusion, after a consideration of the subsection as a whole, that the word "warning", when used in this context, means some intimation or statement to the council member concerned of the consequences of his continuing to commit the act or acts of disorder which he has already committed or is committing. I do not think a warning merely that, if he persisted in the line of conduct regarded by the chairman as disorderly, he would be dealt with or that some action would be taken against him is sufficient.' *Ariansen v Bromfield* [1957] SR(NSW) 24 at 31, per Hardie J

New Zealand [The Trespass Act 1980, s 5, requires that a 'warning' shall be given to the individual person concerned before an offence is committed under s 3, of trespassing at a place and refusing to leave after being warned to do so.] 'So the prosecution must show that the defendant was made aware that he was the person or one of the persons being warned to leave. There is no need to read the section as insisting on the idle or sometimes impracticable ritual of uttering the same warning to each member of a group; it is enough if the terms of the warning make it plain to the particular person charged that they are all being warned to leave.' *Skold v Police* [1982] 1 NZLR 197 at 198, per Cooke J

WARRANT

Extradition proceedings

'Warrant', in the case of any foreign state, includes any judicial document authorizing the arrest of a person accused or convicted of crime. (Extradition Act 1870, s 26)

'Now, what is the meaning of the term *foreign warrant* [which is required by the Extradition Act 1870, s 10, to be produced in extradition proceedings]? By the interpretation clause, s 26 [of the Extradition Act 1870 (supra)], the term "warrant" in the case of any foreign state includes any judicial document authorizing the arrest of a person accused or convicted of crime. Therefore, it is upon the production, not of a warrant of a foreign state according to the technical meaning of the term "warrant" in English law, but upon the production of any judicial document authorizing the arrest of a person accused of a crime that the magistrate may commit.' *R v Ganz* (1882) 9 QBD 93 at 103, per Pollock B

See, generally, 18 Halsbury's Laws (4th edn) para 225.

For payment of money

'Any instrument for payment under which, if genuine, the payer may recover the amount against the party signing it, may properly be considered a warrant for the payment of money, and it is equally this, whatever be the state of the account between the parties, and whether the party signing it has, at the time, funds in the hands of the party to whom it is addressed or not.' *R v Vivian* (1844) 1 Car & Kir 719 at 721, per Coleridge J

WARRANTY *See also* GUARANTEE; REPRESENTATION

In the case of some types of contract (e.g. sale, and hire purchase) certain implied terms are classified by statute as conditions or warranties, though the parties are sometimes free to evince a contrary intention. Similarly, common terms in certain types of contracts (e.g. charterparties and contracts of international sale) have, by the process of judicial decision, acquired the status of conditions or warranties and in the absence of clear evidence of a contrary intention will continue to be treated accordingly. In other cases the question whether a term is a condition or a warranty depends upon the intention of the parties as revealed by the construction of the contract, though the fact that a term is called a 'condition' or a 'warranty' is not necessarily decisive as to its status. Where the contract contains no indication on its face of the status of the terms, the court must look at the contract in the light of the surrounding circumstances in order to decide the intention of the parties. (9 Halsbury's Laws (4th edn) para 543)

The term 'warranty' is not defined in the [Food Act 1984], but both at common law and by statute it has been contrasted with the term 'condition' when applied to the law of contract. It may be defined as a provision which is subsidiary or collateral to the main purpose of the contract, a breach of which gives the innocent party a right to damages but not a right to treat the contract as at an end. (18 Halsbury's Laws (4th edn) para 1299 n)

'Warranty is one of the most ill-used expressions in the legal dictionary, but in its essence it is contractual in nature and must be pleaded in terms sufficient to assert that contractual relationship. How a statement in a letter that a valuer has accomplished his task can support an allegation that by that letter a contract came into existence I cannot understand. The document is completely inconsistent with the conception of any contractual intent in writing it. This is one of those cases where the word "warranty" has been used, as it so frequently is, to try to manufacture a cause of action by calling something a warranty which on its face is clearly not contractual. Warranty is something collateral or incidental to some contract, but in this case there is no contract alleged to which it is incidental or collateral.' *Finnegan v Allen* [1943] 1 KB 425 at 430, CA, per Lord Greene MR

'A promise to deliver one pound of first quality beans is just the same as a promise to deliver one pound of beans, warranted first quality only. Likewise an obligation to order a vessel to a safe port on the east coast of Newfoundland is just the same as an obligation to order a vessel to a port on the east coast of Newfoundland, warranted safe. There is no magic in the word "warranted"; every term in a contract is at heart a warranty.' *Compania Naviera Maropan SA v Bowaters Lloyd Pulp & Paper Mills Ltd* [1954] 3 All ER 563 at 568, per Devlin J

'I use the word "warranty" in its ordinary English meaning to denote a binding promise. Everyone knows what a man means when he says, "I guarantee it", or "I warrant it", or "I give you my word on it". He means that he binds himself to it. That is the meaning which it has borne in English law for three hundred years from the leading case of *Chandelor v Lopus* [(1603) Cro Jac 4] onwards. During the last hundred years, however, the lawyers have come to use the word "warranty" in another sense. They use it to denote a subsidiary term in a contract as distinct from a vital term which they call a "condition". In so doing they depart from the ordinary meaning, not only of the word "warranty", but also of the word "condition". There is no harm in their doing this, so long as they confine this technical use to its proper sphere, namely, to distinguish between a vital term, the breach of which gives the right to treat the contract as at an end, and a subsidiary term which does not.' *Oscar Chess Ltd v Williams* [1957] 1 All ER 325 at 327, 328, CA, per Denning LJ

'Looking at the cases once more, as we have done so often, it seems to me that if a representation is made in the course of dealings for a contract for the very purpose of inducing the other party to act on it, and it actually induces him to act on it by entering into the contract, that is prima facie ground for inferring that the representation was intended as a warranty. It is not necessary to speak of it as being collateral. Suffice it that the representation was intended to be acted on and was in fact acted on. But the maker of the representation can rebut this inference if he can show that it really was an innocent misrepresentation, in that he was in fact innocent of fault in making it, and that it would not be reasonable in the circumstances for him to be bound by it.' *Dick Bentley Productions Ltd v Harold Smith (Motors) Ltd* [1965] 2 All ER 65 at 67, CA, per Lord Denning MR

Insurance generally

In most branches of the law of contract, other than insurance law, 'warranty', as distinct from 'condition', is used to describe a provision which is subsidiary or collateral to the main purpose of the contract. However, in relation to insurance 'warranty' is used where the assured undertakes that some particular thing shall or shall not be done or that a particular fact does or does not exist in such circumstances that the undertaking constitutes a fundamental term of the contract so as to confer, in the event of a breach, a right on the insurers' part to repudiate the contract altogether. The contrast between a condition and a warranty in insurance law (so far as any distinction exists) is therefore the distinction between a term which is fundamental to the validity of the contract or the making of a claim under it, but which is one of the ordinary terms of the contract, and a term which, by reason of being specifically superadded to the ordinary terms, has even more importance as a fundamental stipulation of the contract. This use of the word is more frequently met with in marine than in non-marine insurance, but the basic principle is the same. If, for example, in a proposal the proposer signs a form of declaration by which he warrants a truth of the answers he has given, it means that, as a superadded obligation of paramount importance, he accepts that the truth of his answers is fundamental to the whole contract. (25 Halsbury's Laws (4th edn) para 420)

Marine insurance

In the statutory provisions as to marine insurance, a warranty means a promissory warranty, that is a warranty by which the assured undertakes that some particular thing is or is not to be done, or that some condition is to be fulfilled or whereby he affirms or negatives the existence of a particular state of facts. Thus, a warranty may be an undertaking that the thing insured is neutral property, or that the ship insured sailed on a certain day, or that all was well at a given time, or that the ship is to sail on or before a given day, or that she will depart with convoy etc.

A warranty may be expressed or implied. An express warranty does not exclude an implied warranty unless inconsistent with it. Thus, if a policy on cattle provides that the fittings of a ship are to be approved by a Lloyd's surveyor and they are so approved by him, the warranty of seaworthiness is not excluded by the express provision as to the approval of the fittings.

An express warranty must be included in, or written upon, the policy, or must be contained in some document incorporated by reference into the policy.

A warranty is implied if it is a condition implied by law, such as, for example, a warranty in a voyage policy that the ship is seaworthy at the commencement of the voyage. (25 Halsbury's Laws (4th edn) para 52)

(1) A warranty . . . means a promissory warranty, that is to say, a warranty by which the assured undertakes that some particular thing shall or shall not be done, or that some condition shall be fulfilled, or whereby he affirms or negatives the existence of a particular state of facts.

(2) A warranty may be express or implied.

(3) A warranty, as above defined, is a condition whether it be material to the risk or not. If it be not so complied with, then, subject to any express provision in the policy, the insurer is discharged from liability as from the date of the breach of warranty, but without prejudice to any liability incurred by him before that date. (Marine Insurance Act 1906, s 33)

'There is a material distinction between a warranty and a representation. A representation may be equitably and substantially answered: but a warranty must be strictly complied with. Supposing a warranty to sail on the 1st of August, and the ship did not sail till the 2nd, the warranty would not be complied with. A warranty in a policy of insurance is a condition or a contingency, and unless that be performed, there is no contract. It is perfectly inmmaterial for what purpose a warranty is introduced; but, being inserted, the contract does not exist unless it be literally complied with. Now in the present case, the condition was the sailing of the ship with a certain number of men; which not being complied with, the policy is void.' *De Hahn v Hartley* (1786) 1 Term Rep 343 at 345, 346, per Lord Mansfield CJ

'The question in this case is, whether the statement in the charterparty, that the ship is "now in the port of Amsterdam", is a "representation" or a "warranty", using the latter word as synonymous with "condition", in which sense it has been for many years understood with respect to policies of insurance and charterparties.' *Behn v Burness* (1863) 3 B & S 751 at 753, per Williams J

Sale of goods

'Warranty' means an agreement with reference to goods which are the subject of a contract of sale but collateral to the main purpose of such a contract, the breach of which gives rise to a claim for damages but not to a right to reject the goods and treat the contract as repudiated. In order to satisfy the definition, therefore, a warranty must, first, be an agreement, a promise that the representation is or will be true; secondly, the agreement must be collateral to the main purpose of the contract, such purpose being the transfer of the property in and the possession of goods of the description contracted for. A warranty may be given in consideration of an agreement to enter into a contract of sale of the goods to which the warranty relates with a party other than the person giving the warranty.

Whether a stipulation in a contract of sale is a condition, the breach of which may give rise to a right to treat the contract as repudiated, or a warranty, the breach of which may give rise to a claim for damages but not to a right to reject the goods and treat the contract as repudiated, or an intermediate stipulation, the effect of which depends upon the nature of the breach, depends in each case on the construction of the contract. The contract or the Sale of Goods Act 1979 may provide expressly or by implication that a term is one any breach of which will entitle the injured party to terminate the contract, or that it is a term any breach of which will give rise only to a claim for damages. In any other case the injured party will be entitled to terminate the contract if the breach goes to the root of it, but not otherwise. Broadly speaking the test is whether the performance of the stipulation goes to the whole consideration of the other party; if it does, the stipulation is a condition. A stipulation may be a condition even though it is called a warranty in the contract. (41 Halsbury's Laws (4th edn) paras 681, 682)

'Warranty' (as regards England and Wales and Northern Ireland) means an agreement with reference to goods which are the subject of a contract of sale, but collateral to the main purpose of such contract, the breach of which gives rise to a claim for damages, but not to a right to reject the goods and treat the contract as repudiated. (Sale of Goods Act 1979, s 61(1))

'A warranty is an express or implied statement of something which the party undertakes shall be part of a contract; and though part of the contract, yet collateral to the express object of it. But in many of the cases . . . the circumstances of a party selling a particular thing by its proper description has been called a warranty; and the breach of such contract, a breach of warranty: but it would be better to distinguish such cases as a non-compliance with a contract which a party has engaged to fulfil; as, if a man offers to buy peas of another, and he sends him beans, he does not perform his contract; but that is not a warranty; there is no warranty that he should sell him peas; the contract is to sell peas, and if he sends him anything else in their stead, it is a non-performance of it. So if a man were to order copper for sheathing ships—that is a particular copper, prepared in a particular manner; if the seller sends him a different sort, in that case he does not comply with the contract: and though this may have been considered a warranty, and may have been ranged under the class of cases relating to warranties, yet it is not properly so.' *Chanter v Hopkins* (1838) 4 M & W 399 at 404, 405, per Lord Abinger CB

WARREN *See also* BIRD

'The term "warren" is one of those terms which has not always the same precise and definite meaning. It may be the expression of the grant of a franchise only, or it may import a conveyance of the soil. It was insisted, on the part of the appellant, that by a grant of warren *ex vi termini* the soil passes; and that as a franchise cannot be divided the grant of a warren of conies would be bad if it granted merely a franchise, and that to be good it must include within it a grant of the soil. . . . The authorities to support the argument, that the grant of a warren includes within it the soil over which the warren extends, are not very convincing; while on the other hand there are strong grounds for concluding that in general the use of the term would rather import the grant of a liberty or franchise without the soil. There is no doubt that a warren may be claimed by prescription, but land cannot, the title by prescription being applicable only to incorporeal hereditaments.' *Beauchamp (Earl) v Winn* (1873) LR 6 HL 223 at 236–238, per Lord Chelmsford

[Franchises of forest, free chase, park and free warren were abolished by the Wild Creatures and Forest Laws Act 1971, s 1]

WARSHIP

'They [ships] may be armed only for their own defence; as they have no commission to act offensively, they cannot be considered legally as ships of war.' *Re Several Dutch Schuyts* (1805) 6 Ch Rob 48 at 48, per cur.

WAS

'Prima facie I should have thought (i) that the word "was" in its primary meaning refers to something that is past and not to something that is future, and (ii) that, on ordinary principles of construction, where a phrase is used twice in any document it was intended to bear the same interpretation on each occasion; so that, in the expression "was . . . free from rates", the word "was" should be taken to refer to the same point of time (regard being had where necessary to the principle of *mutatis mutandis*), and the quality of "freedom" should be taken to be the same in the one case as in the other.' *Tithe Redemption Commission v Queen Anne's Bounty (Governors)* [1946] 1 All ER 148 at 157, per Romer J

WASTE

Waste consists of any act or omission which causes a lasting alteration to the nature of the land in question to the prejudice of the person who has the remainder or reversion of the land. The obligation not to commit waste is an obligation in tort, and is independent of contract or implied covenant.

Waste is either voluntary or permissive. Voluntary waste implies the doing of some act which tends to the destruction of the premises, as by pulling down houses, or removing fixtures; or to the changing of their nature, as the conversion of pasture land into arable, or pulling down buildings and erecting new buildings, even though of greater value. Permissive waste implies an omission through which damage results to the premises, where, for instance, houses are allowed to fall into decay.

In order to constitute voluntary waste by destruction of the premises, the destruction must be wilful or negligent; the destruction of a building in the course of using it in what was apparently a reasonable and proper manner, having regard to its character and to the purposes for which it was intended to be used, is not waste.

Although changing the nature of the demised premises is technically waste, this is not so if the change has been expressly sanctioned by the landlord. It seems that an act does not constitute waste unless it is in fact injurious to the inheritance, either by diminishing the value of the estate, or by increasing the burden upon it, or by impairing the evidence of title. At any rate, in the case of acts which may be technically waste but in fact improve the inheritance ('meliorating waste'), the court will not interfere to restrain them by injunction, nor will they be a ground for forfeiture under a proviso for re-entry on commission of waste. (27 Halsbury's Laws (4th edn) paras 279, 280)

A tenant for life has the right to the full enjoyment of the land during the continuance of his estate subject to the duty of leaving it unimpaired for the remainderman. This duty is defined by the doctrine of waste. Waste may be legal or equitable, and legal waste may be either voluntary or permissive. (42 Halsbury's Laws (4th edn) para 992)

'The principle upon which waste depends is well stated in the case of *Darcy (Lord) v Askwith* [(1618) Hob 234], thus:—"It is generally true that the lessee hath no power to change the nature of the thing demised; he cannot turn meadow into arable, nor stub a wood to make it pasture, nor dry up an ancient pool or piscary, nor suffer ground to be surrounded, nor destroy the pale of park, for then it ceaseth to be a park; nor he may not destroy the stock or breed of anything, because it disherits and takes away the perpetuity of succession, as villains, fish, deer, young spring of woods, or the like." Thus, the destruction of germens, or young plants destined to become trees, Co Litt 43, which destroys the future timber, is waste; the cutting of apple-trees in a garden or orchard, or the cutting down a hedge of thorns, Co Litt 53,a, which changes the nature of the thing demised; or the eradicating or unseasonable cutting of whitethorns, Vin Abr, Waste, E), which destroys the future growth, are all acts of waste. On the other hand, those acts are not waste which, as Richardson CJ, in *Barrett v Barrett* [(1629) Het 34 at 35] says, are not prejudicial to the inheritance, as, in that case, the cutting of sallows, maples, beeches, and thorns, there alleged to be of the age of thirty-three years, but which were not timber either by general law or particular local custom. So, likewise, cutting even of oaks or ashes, where they are of seasonable wood, i.e. where they are cut usually as underwood, and in due course are to grow up again from the stumps, is not waste.' *Phillips v Smith* (1845) 14 M & W 589 at 593, 594, per cur.

'It is said that if the [demised] building was used in any manner which produced injury, although that user might have been a proper and reasonable user of the class of tenement to which the building belonged, nevertheless, if it produced the destruction of the tenement or a serious injury to its stability, waste was committed. It appears to me that this proposition is a very serious one, and cannot be maintained without great difficulty. It would be a very serious thing to hold that if a man chooses to construct a house in such a flimsy manner as that the moment, for instance, a bedstead is put up in it the timbers give way, and the house comes down, that coming down of the house resulting from the putting into it of the ordinary furniture required for its occupation would be, on the part of the tenant, waste. . . . If it were necessary for me to determine the point, I should be prepared to hold that no user of a tenement which is reasonable and proper, having regard to the class to which it belongs, is waste.' *Saner v Bilton* (1878) 7 Ch D 815 at 821, per Fry J

'I can find no authority for saying that it is ever waste to cultivate land or to cut and dispose of timber according to a prevailing local usage, unless such usage is excluded by the terms of the instrument creating the limited estates which alone give rise to the question.' *Dashwood v Magniac* [1891] 3 Ch 306 at 357, CA, per Lindley LJ

'A man cannot commit waste, even technically, if he is doing that which he is entitled to do by contract—that is to say, he cannot commit waste as against his landlord, if his landlord has entered into a special contract enabling him to do it. . . . The question I have to consider is, is there any damage, any injury to the inheritance? It has been proved to me conclusively, that what the defendant is doing, so far from being an injury to the inheritance, is of the greatest possible advantage; and that the addition of these houses, if they are substantially built, and if they are kept in good order, is a most advantageous addition to a farm of this kind in the neighbourhood of London.' *Meux v Cobley* [1892] 2 Ch 253 at 262–264, per Kekewich J

'Upon his pleadings, the plaintiff based his claim to relief upon the covenants against committing waste or spoil, or ploughing or breaking up any of the pasture lands, and the first question is whether the defendant has ever threatened to do anything which would be a breach of those covenants, or either of them. In my opinion he has not. I think the expression "the pasture lands" in the agreement refers solely to those portions of the farm which were meadow land, or laid down permanently to grass at the date of the agreement, and that it would be straining the language beyond all reasonable limits were I to hold that a field tilled to corn at the date of the agreement and for at least thirteen years previous thereto had become pasture land within the meaning of the covenant because the tenant had in subsequent years left it for a considerable period in grass. Nor do I think that ploughing the field would have been "waste or spoil" on the tenant's part. Some reliance was placed in argument on the use of the two words "waste or spoil", but in my opinion they are synonymous, though possibly the one may be more appropriately used for what is in its nature permissive and the other for what is in its nature destructive.' *Rush v Lucas* [1910] 1 Ch 437 at 441, 442, per Eve J

Equitable waste

Equitable waste is such an unconscionable or unreasonable use of legal powers as goes to the destruction of the subject matter. Unless expressly authorised by the settlement, a tenant for life, although made unimpeachable for waste, is not entitled to commit equitable waste. Thus the courts have restrained a tenant for life unimpeachable for waste from pulling down the mansion house, or other houses, from grubbing up a wood so as to destroy it absolutely, from cutting underwood or saplings of insufficient growth, or at unreasonable times, and from cutting down timber planted or left standing for shelter or ornament of the settled property. (42 Halsbury's Laws (4th edn) para 1003)

Meliorating waste

A tenant for life impeachable for waste is not liable in respect of acts which, although technically voluntary waste, in fact improve the inheritance and are commonly known as meliorating waste. Nevertheless, the opinion has been expressed that such acts are not waste at all. If the acts done in fact constitute an injury to the land, it is no defence to show that there are compensating advantages. (42 Halsbury's Laws (4th edn) para 999)

'If . . . the waste be really ameliorating waste—that is, a proceeding which results in benefit and not in injury—the Court of Equity . . . ought not to interfere to prevent it.' *Doherty v Allman* (1878) 3 App Cas 709 at 724, per Lord O'Hagan

Permissive waste

Permissive waste is an omission by which damage results to premises, such as allowing houses to fall into decay. A tenant for life, whether or not made impeachable for waste, is not liable for permissive waste. If, however, the settlor has imposed a condition that the tenant for life is to keep the premises in repair, there is a personal liability which can be enforced by the court, even in respect of dilapidations existing at the time when the settlement came into force. Damages may be recovered in respect of such a liability from the estate of the tenant for life after his death, the proper measure of such damages being such sum as is reasonably necessary to put the premises in the state of repair in which he ought to have left them. (42 Halsbury's Laws (4th edn) para 1001)

'Since the Statute of Marlbridge and of Gloucester there must have been hundreds of thousands of tenants for life who have died leaving their estates in a condition of great dilapidation. Not once, so far as legal records go, have damages been recovered against the estate of a tenant for life on that ground. To ask me to hold that a tenant for life is liable for permissive waste to a remainderman is to my mind a proposition altogether startling. I should not think of coming to such a decision without direct authority upon the point. Such authority as there is seems to me to be against the contention, and in opposition to the positive decisions in *Gibson v Wells* [(1805) 1 Bos & PNR 209], *Herne v Bembow* [(1813) 4 Taunt 764], and *Jones v Hill* [(1805) 7 Taunt 392], there are only to be found certain dicta of Baron Parke and the late Lord Justice Lush which seem to amount to this, that the words of the Statutes of Marlbridge and Gloucester are sufficient to include the case of permissive waste, at any rate where there is an obligation on the person who has the particular estate not to permit waste, whether that obligation does or does not exist at the common law in the case of a tenant for life. But at the present day it would certainly require either an Act of Parliament or a very deliberate decision of a Court of great authority to establish the law that a tenant for life is liable to a remainderman in case he should have permitted the buildings on the land to fall into a state of dilapidation.' *Re Cartwright, Avis v Newman* (1889) 41 Ch D 532 at 536, per Kay J

Voluntary waste

Voluntary waste is an act which is injurious to the inheritance, either (1) by diminishing the value of the estate, or (2) by increasing the burden upon it, or (3) by impairing the evidence of title. (42 Halsbury's Laws (4th edn) para 993)

WASTE LAND *See also* MANOR

'Waste land of a manor' means and includes any land consisting of waste land of any manor on which the tenants of such manor have rights of common, or of any land subject to any rights of common which may be exercised at any time of the year for cattle levant and couchant, or to any rights of common which may be exercised at all times of the year, and are not limited by number or stints. (Commons Act 1876, s 37)

'The words of the grant are, "all coals under the commons, waste grounds or marishes". It is not necessary here to put a construction on the words "commons" or "marishes", for it appears to me to be clear that the word "waste" is sufficient to pass the foreshore or the coals thereunder. The word "waste" means desolate or uncultivated ground, land unoccupied, or that lies in commons. This is the plain and common acceptation of the word, and undoubtedly land between high and low watermarks falls within this signification.' *A-G v Hanmer* (1858) 27 LJ Ch 837 at 840, per Watson B

'In my judgment the phrase "waste land of a manor", used in relation to a particular piece of land in the context of a statute passed some forty years after copyhold tenure had been abolished, does not as a matter of legal language by any means necessarily import that the ownership of the land still rests with the lord of the relevant manor. The phrase in such a context is equally consistent with the sense that the land is waste land which, as a matter of history, was once waste land of a manor in the days when copyhold tenure still existed.' *Re Chewton Common, Christchurch, Borough of Christchurch v Milligan* [1977] 3 All ER 509 at 514, 515, per Slade J

'Although copyholds were enfranchised by the effect of the Law of Property Act 1922, the lord of the manor retained rights in respect of mines and minerals and franchises and sporting rights. And the waste land of the manor was no less waste land of the manor after the enfranchisement than it was before.' *Box Parish Council v Lacey* [1979] 1 All ER 113 at 115, HL, per Stamp LJ

'Land' is waste if it is open, uncultivated and unoccupied; and it is waste land of a manor if it is open, uncultivated and unoccupied land which forms part of the manor and does not constitute part of the lord's demesne. . . . Land that once was waste may cease to be waste if it is enclosed or cultivated or occupied. Yet as was held in *Re Britford Common* [[1977] 1 All ER 532] land does not cease to be waste merely because the lord takes its produce and cuts the grass for hay or silage; for by merely taking the natural produce of the waste the lord does not turn that waste into demesne land.' *Baxendale v Instow Parish Council* [1981] 2 All ER 620 at 623, per Megarry V-C

WASTE PRODUCT

'Waste' includes any substance which constitutes scrap material or an effluent or other unwanted surplus substance arising from the application of any process, and also includes any substance or article which requires to be disposed of as being broken, worn out, contaminated or otherwise spoilt. (Radioactive Substances Act 1960, s 19(1))

'Waste' includes—

(a) any substance which constitutes a scrap material or an effluent or other unwanted surplus substance arising from the application of any process; and
(b) any substance or article which requires to be disposed of as being broken, worn out, contaminated, or otherwise spoiled, but does not include a substance which is an explosive within the meaning of the Explosives Act 1875

and for the purposes of this Part of this Act [Part I: waste on land] anything which is discarded or otherwise dealt with as if it were waste shall be presumed to be waste until the contrary is proved. (Control of Pollution Act 1974, s 30(1))

[See also ibid, sub-s 30(3), which distinguishes household waste, industrial waste and commercial waste.]

WASTING NATURE

Australia 'Assets and property of a wasting nature are well known to the Courts. We are not going to attempt a comprehensive definition of the phrase, but anything which perishes or becomes worn out, either with use or by lapse of time, is of a wasting nature. . . . We find it impossible to say that buildings and machinery erected for trade purposes, and particularly machinery, are not properties of a wasting nature.' *Worrall v Commercial Banking Co of Sydney* (1917) 17 SRNSW 457 at 463, 464, per Street J

WATCH OR BESET

'The . . . question is whether the case is within sub-s 4 [of the Conspiracy and Protection of Property Act 1875, s 7 (as amended by the Public Order Act 1986)] which prohibits watching or besetting the house, or the place where a person resides, or where he happens to be. It was known or suspected that workmen would arrive at Fleetwood by steamer on February 22. Walker and Wadsworth go there and await the arrival of the steamer, and then enter into communication with the men who land. It seems to me that that is watching a place where the workmen happened to be. There is nothing in the statute which defines the duration of the watching. It may be, it seems to me, for a short time, and as to that I refer to the words of the proviso itself, which speaks of attending at or near a house or place where the person resides, or works, or happens to be. The word "attending" does not necessarily imply any lengthened attendance on the spot; nor is there anything in the statute to limit its operation to a place habitually frequented by the workman, such as the house where he resides or the place where he works. On the contrary, the words "place where he happened to be" seems to me to embrace any place where the workman is found, however casually.' *Charnock v Court* [1899] 2 Ch 35 at 38, 39, per Stirling J

WATER

Canada 'In view of the fact that it is the defendant's contract [of insurance against damage by escaping water], I think that the term "water" should not be construed as meaning only water in a liquid form. I am of the opinion that the term "water" should be held to include water in a gaseous form [i.e. steam] as well as in liquid form.' *Onhauser v Hartford Fire Insce Co* (1952) 6 WWR(NS) 47 at 47, Man CA, per Adamson JA

WATER CLOSET

'Water closet' means a closet that has a separate fixed receptacle connected to a drainage system and separate provision for flushing from a supply of clean water either by the operation of mechanism or by automatic action. (Building Act 1984, s 126)

WATER RATE

'Water rate . . . is a rate paid by persons who use water for the water which they use, and is the same as the price paid for gas. The fact that it is called a rate makes no difference.' *Northampton Corpn v Ellen* (1902) 66 JP 744 at 746, per Bingham J; reversed on other grounds [1904] 1 KB 299, CA

WATER RESOURCES

(1) In this Act 'water resources', in relation to any area, means water for the time being contained in any source of supply in that area, and 'source of supply', in relation to any area, means either of the following, that is to say—

(a) so much of any inland water, other than any inland water falling within subsection (3) of this section, as is situated in that area, and

(b) any underground strata in that area.

(2) For the purposes of this Act water for the time being contained in—

(a) a well, borehole or similar work, including any adit or passage constructed in connection with it for facilitating the collection of water in the well, borehole or work, or

(b) any excavation into underground strata, where the level of water in the excavation depends wholly or mainly on water entering it from those strata,

shall be treated as water contained in the underground strata into which the well, borehole or work was sunk, or the excavation was made, as the case may be.

(3) Except as provided by the last preceding subsection, an inland water which either—

(a) is a lake, pond or reservoir which does not discharge to any other inland water, or

(b) is one of a group of two or more lakes, ponds or reservoirs (whether near to or distant from each other) and of watercourses or mains connecting them, where none of the inland waters in the group discharges to any inland water outside the group,

does not constitute a source of supply for the purposes of this Act. (Water Resources Act 1963, s 2)

WATERCOURSE *See also* DRAIN

Water cannot in general form the subject matter of property. A man cannot bring an action to recover possession of a pool or other piece of water as such, for water is a movable wandering thing which must of necessity continue common by the law of nature. No action can be supported merely for taking water unless the water is contained in a cistern or some other vessel in which the person bringing the action has placed it for his private use. So long, however, as water remains upon the land where it first rises from the earth, the owner of that land alone has a right to appropriate it, for no one else can do so without committing a trespass. When, however, it has left that land the owner has no more power over it or interest in it than a stranger.

It follows from the rules as to ownership of water that the grant of a watercourse does not mean the grant of the water itself. It may mean any one of three things, namely a grant of the easement or the right to the running of water; a grant of the channel-pipe or drain which contains the water; or a grant of the land over which the water flows. The meaning in the case of each particular grant is to be drawn from the context, and if there is no context from which the meaning can be gathered the word 'watercourse' prima facie means an easement. (14 Halsbury's Laws (4th edn) paras 185, 186)

'Watercourse' includes all rivers, streams, ditches, drains, cuts, culverts, dykes, sluices, sewers (other than sewers vested in a local authority or a water authority) and passages, through which water flows. (Water Act 1945, s 59, as amended)

'Watercourse' includes all rivers, streams, ditches, drains, cuts, culverts, dukes, sluices, sewers and passages through which water flows, except—

(a) mains and water fittings within the meaning of Sch 3 to the Water Act 1945;

(b) local authority sewers; and

(c) any such adit or passage as is mentioned in s 2(2)(a) of this Act [constructed in connection with wells, boreholes, etc].

(Water Resources Act 1963, s 135)

'Now, without saying that a watercourse may never mean the channel in which water flows, it certainly may mean also the stream or flow of the water itself; and, whether it means the one or the other in any instrument, will very materially depend on the context.' *Doe d Earl of Egremont v Williams* (1848) 11 QB 688 at 700, per Coleridge J

'I come now to the words of the grant. It is a grant of "all and singular the watercourses . . . in or upon the lands of the said S Taylor, which watercourses, dams, reservoirs, and intended reservoir, are described and laid down in the plan annexed to these presents. . . ." This is a grant of a watercourse. . . . A grant of a watercourse in law, especially when coupled with other words, may mean any one of three things. It may mean the easement or the right to the running of water, it may mean the channel-pipe or drain which contains the water, and it may mean the land over which the water flows. Which it does mean must be shown by the context, and if there is no context I apprehend that it would not mean anything but the easement, a right to the flow of the water. Now . . . I think that in this case the word watercourse means a corporeal heredita-ment, and not merely an easement or right to the running of water, and that it bears the second meaning, that is, the channel through which the water runs, the pipe or drain which, so to say, contains the water. In the present case the channel is an artificial channel made by man, and there was at the time of the grant an actual existing pipe or drain, in some parts covered over and in other parts open. In my opinion, from the context, the word "watercourse" in this document means that, and nothing else. Then what is conveyed by the word "watercourse"? I think that it conveys not merely the pipe or drain, but also the water in it, and that, consequently, if we found nothing else in the deed, we ought to hold that the grantee was entitled to the property of the channel, and to the right to take the water which got into that channel by lawful means.' *Taylor v St Helen's Corpn* (1877) 6 Ch D 264 at 271, 272, CA, per Jessel MR

'It cannot be denied that a "watercourse" may mean, and, perhaps, the more natural meaning of it is, a channel in which water flows, and that the grant of a right to make a watercourse may include the right to fill it with water, and use the water flowing in it when made.' *Remfry v Surveyor-General of Natal* [1896] AC 558 at 560, PC, per Lord Davey

Australia 'Where a stream flows in a defined channel evidently constructed by man, which is of a permanent character, and particularly if it has so flowed for a great time, it is also regarded in law as a watercourse.' *Vinnicombe v MacGregor* (1902) 28 VLR 144 at 173, per Madden CJ

Australia 'Whatever ambiguity might remain in the description "watercourse" when used alone, in my opinion "the whole watercourse" of a river definitely means the area between the extremities of the banks of the river: they, except in times of flood, determine the course of the river. Indeed, even in times of flood, it might well be said that they, even then, determine the course of the river itself.' *R v Ward* (1980) 54 ALJR 271 at 272, per Barwick CJ

Australia 'Natural and ordinary meanings of the word "watercourse" include a stream of water, a river (see Shorter Oxford Dictionary). . . . Where a river has an island or channels in it or some other sort of exposed land between its banks, it is still appropriate to refer to the whole expanse of water from bank to bank as the river. In other words, the combination of channels making up the stream of water of the river still constitute the river. In my view this is the meaning of the term "watercourse" in [a] regulation. It is true that the flow of water, the fairway of water surface or the width of water surface may vary with the rise and fall of the river, but at least some of the boundary cases recognise the legitimacy of such changing boundary.' *Mitchell v Noble* (1981) 58 FLR 418 at 424, per Gallup J

New Zealand 'It has been decided by the Court of Appeal, in *Piripi Te Maari v Matthews* [(1893) 12 NZLR 13], that in New Zealand though a watercourse is dry for a great portion of the year it is nevertheless a watercourse over which a River Board has jurisdiction. The Court in that case said (page 22), "It must be a matter of general knowledge that many rivers and streams in New Zealand are frequently dry for many months at a time, and then by rainfall become raging torrents. No one can question but that they are not the less watercourses when dry. The channel is still there, though blocked up by obstructions which the waters of the lake will shortly remove, when the outlet of the waters of the lake will return." And it has also been held both in England and in America that the bed of a river is not limited to that portion between the banks through which the water flows in dry weather.' *Kingdon v Hutt River Board* (1905) 25 NZLR 145 at 157, per cur.; also reported 7 GLR 634 at 636

[Now defined in the Soil Conservation and Rivers Central Act 1941: 'Watercourse includes every river, stream, passage, and channel, on or under the ground, whether natural or not, through which water flows, whether continuously or intermittently.']

WATERMAN

'Waterman' means a person navigating a passenger boat. (Port of London Act 1968, s 2(1))

WATERWAY

'Inland waterway' includes any such waterway, whether natural or artificial. (Local Government Act 1948, s 144, cf Transport Act 1962, s 92)

'Waterway' means any lake, river, canal or other waters, being (in any case) waters suitable, or which can reasonably be rendered suitable, for sailing, boating, bathing or fishing. (National Parks and Access to the Countryside Act 1949, s 114)

'Inland waterway' includes every such waterway whether natural or artificial. (Transport Act 1962, s 92)

'Independent inland waterway undertaking', means an undertaking not forming part of the undertaking of any of the Boards, being an undertaking engaged in conserving, maintaining, improving or working a canal or other inland navigation or the navigation of a tidal water but does not include—

(a) an undertaking none of the charges of which has been the subject of a Provisional Order made, and confirmed by Parliament, in pursuance of sections twenty-four and thirty-six of the Railway and Canal Traffic Act 1888, or
(b) an undertaking forming part of a harbour undertaking if the inland waterway is situated wholly within the limits of the harbour, or
(c) an undertaking all or any of the charges of which are, under the statutory provisions relating to that undertaking, subject to revision by the Minister and some other Minister acting together.

(Transport Act 1962, s 52)

WATERWORKS

'Waterworks' includes streams, springs, wells, pumps, reservoirs, cisterns, tanks, aqueducts, cuts, sluices, mains, pipes, culverts, engines and all machinery, lands, buildings and things for supplying, or used for supplying, water, or used for protecting sources of water supply. (Public Health Act 1936, s 343)

WAY *See* RIGHT OF WAY; UNDER WAY

WAYLEAVE

Royalties estimated similarly to royalties on demised minerals are often reserved in respect of minerals worked by way of outstroke [the working of an adjoining mine from a demised mine] from and brought through the demised mine or over surface land. Such royalties are known as wayleave rents or wayleaves. If a wayleave is used without authority, the measure of damages is the sum which would properly have been payable in royalty if the right of wayleave had been granted. (31 Halsbury's Laws (4th edn) para 237)

WEAPON *See also* AIR WEAPON; FIREARM; OFFENSIVE WEAPON

'It has been suggested in the case stated that the enforcement of the black-out is the use of a "weapon" for the repulse of enemy action. I do not think that it is. The word "weapon" is used in the section [the Personal Injuries (Emergency Provision) Act 1939, s 8(1)] in its ordinary sense, not in an extended sense.' *Minister of Pensions v Ffrench* [1946] KB 260 at 263, per Denning J

WEAR

[The Public Order Act 1936, s 1(1), provides that any person who 'wears' uniform of a political character shall be guilty of an offence.] '"Wearing" in my judgment implies some article of wearing apparel. I agree . . . that one would not describe a badge pinned to the lapel as being a uniform worn for present purposes. In the present instance however, the various items relied on, such as the beret, dark glasses, the pullovers and the other dark clothing were clearly worn and therefore satisfy the first requirement of the section.' *O'Moran v Director of Public Prosecutions, Whelan v Director of Public Prosecutions* [1975] QB 864 at 873, 874, per Lord Widgery CJ

WEAR AND TEAR

'It only remains to consider whether reasonable wear and tear can include destruction by reasonable use. These words, no doubt, include destruction to some extent, e.g., destruction of surface by ordinary friction, but we do not think they include total destruction by a catastrophe which was never contemplated by either party.' *Manchester Bonded Warehouse Co Ltd v Carr* (1880) 5 CPD 507 at 513, per cur.

'It is a little curious that there is no very satisfactory authority as to the meaning of the words fair or reasonable wear and tear. I cannot agree . . . that no meaning ought to be given to the words at all, nor can I agree that they have no operation in regard to the outside of the premises. The meaning of the covenant in my opinion is that the tenant is bound at the end of the tenancy to deliver up the premises in as good condition as they were in at the beginning subject to the following exceptions, that is to say, dilapidations caused by the friction of the air, dilapidations caused by exposure and dilapidations caused by ordinary use.' *Terrell v Murray* (1901) 17 TLR 570 at 570, per cur.

'The diminished value of an animal or a tree by reason of the effluxion of time is not diminished value by reason of wear and tear; it is simply diminished value because money has been invested in a wasting source of production.' *Derby (Earl) v Aylmer* [1915] 3 KB 374 at 379, 380, per Rowlatt J

'The phrase "wear and tear" is a very old English idiom and the clause "fair" (or "reasonable") "wear and tear excepted", has been common in leases and tenancy agreements for two or three centuries. It is, like many idiomatic expressions, complex in meaning; it implicitly refers to both cause and effect, and in each aspect it covers two classes of disrepair, (a) that brought about by the normal or ordinary operation of natural causes, such as wind and weather, in contradistinction to abnormal or extraordinary events in nature such as lightning, hurricane, flood or earthquake; and (b) that brought about by the tenant, and other persons present in or on the premises with the consent of the tenant, either unintentionally or as a normal incident of a tenant's occupation, in the course of the "fair" (or "reasonable") use of the premises for any of the purposes for which they were let. Sense (a), the first of the two senses covered by the phrase "wear and tear" when used in repairing covenants, is somewhat analogous to the sense of the words when used in marine insurance. There the perils of the sea against which the policy protects are exceptional or abnormal marine events, at least in point of degree, and sufficiently so to constitute them "accidents"; and a line was drawn in old sailing-ship days between the normal damage and cutting away of sails, spars and ropes incidental to ordinary heavy weather on the one hand, which does not constitute a peril insured against, and an abnormal casualty which does; and the old law and even the old idiomatic phrase reappear in statutory guise in s 55, sub-s 2(c), of the Marine Insurance Act 1906. So in the law of landlord and tenant legal interpretation of the phrase as applied to the elements has produced a similar demarcation of degree between the normal and the abnormal, the ordinary and the extraordinary; leaving a penumbral zone where a jury may wander and lawfully come to its own conclusion, a zone of "give and take" decisions, as Willes J said in *Scales v Lawrence* [(1860) 2 F & F 289 at 291]. That the phrase "wear and tear" includes in its scope my sense (b), namely, the tenant's user and its effect, is too plain to need argument, and is well recognised in the decided cases.' *Taylor v Webb* [1937] 2 KB 283 at 302, 303, CA, per Scott LJ

WEATHER PERMITTING

New Zealand 'The words of the advertisement "weather and other circumstances permitting" . . . apply, we think, to the proposed voyage which is advertised to start on a particular day at a particular hour. They would relieve the company from liability where, owing to bad weather or other circumstances beyond the control of the company, the proposed voyage was prevented or delayed.' *Moral v Northern SS Co Ltd* [1922] NZLR 966 at 980, CA, per Sim J; also reported [1922] GLR 284 at 294

WEATHER WORKING DAYS

[A charterparty provided that cargo should be loaded at the rate of 125 fathoms per "weather working day".] 'The question which I am asked to decide in this case really boils down to this: what is the meaning of "weather working day". . . . Mr Pilcher [counsel] says that there is only one case—namely *Bennetts & Co v Brown* [[1908] 1 KB 490]—where the words "weather working day" have ever been interpreted. It is a decision of my great master in the law, Walton J, and therefore I pay unbounded respect to it. He says [at p 496] "I think it has a natural meaning, viz a day on which the work of discharge—it might be of loading, but in the present case it is of discharge—is not prevented by bad weather." . . . Scrutton LJ, in his book on Charterparties, 13th edn, p 365, says that " 'weather working days' means days on which the weather allows working." Personally, I do not see very much difference between what Walton J says and what Scrutton LJ says.' *Dampskibsselskabet Botnia AS v Bell (CP) & Co* [1932] 2 KB 569 at 573, 575, per Bateson J

'In my view, a correct definition of a "weather working day" is a day on which the weather permits the relevant work to be done, whether or not any person avails himself of that permission, in other words, so far as the weather is concerned, it is a working day. In my view, also, the converse proposition must be on the same basis. A day is not a weather working day, it fails to be a weather working day, in so far as the weather on that day does not permit the relevant work to be done, and it is not material to inquire whether any person has intended or planned or prepared to do any relevant work on that day. The status of a day as being a weather working day, wholly or in part or not at all, is determined solely by its own weather, and not by extraneous factors, such as the actions intentions and plans of any person.' *Compania Naviera Azuero SA v British Oil and Cake Mills Ltd* [1957] 2 All ER 241 at 249, per Pearson J also reported in [1957] 2 QB 293 at 303, 304

'The first question is: Is a bore tide that is something in the nature of a tidal wave "weather", so that, if the work on a particular day is prevented by a bore tide, it ceases to be a weather working day? The second question is: If the position is, as it is here, not that the bore tide actually prevented the loading of the ship or, indeed, that it would have prevented the loading of the ship if she remained in the berth . . . but that the threat of the bore tide on the safety of the ship was such as to make it reasonable for her to leave the berth, are the days when she is absent from the berth weather working days? I have had cases cited to me on both sides as to what is the meaning of "weather" for this purpose, whether surf is "weather" and whether ice is "weather"; but I find it simpler to decide this point on the second of the questions which I have set out and I shall assume, without deciding it, that a bore tide is "weather" within the meaning of this clause. No case has been cited to me in which a mere threat of bad weather had been held to make a day not a weather working day, and certainly no case where the threat of bad weather has affected not the operation of the actual work of loading but the safety of the ship in the particular place in which she was. In my judgment, the expression "weather working days" cannot be construed so widely as to cover the circumstances of this case. The expression is used in relation to a berth, that is, it is assumed that the vessel will be in a safe berth and it is contemplated that, notwithstanding the safety of the berth, the weather may interfere with the actual work of loading.' *Compania Crystal de Vapores of Panama v Herman and Mohatta (India) Ltd* [1958] 2 All ER 508 at 511, per Devlin J

'I think that, when the words "working days" are used in relation to lay days, the phrase has a long established and accepted meaning. It describes a type of calendar day which is a day of work as distinguished from a day of play or rest. I cannot believe that by inserting the qualification "weather" before this collocation commercial men intended radically to alter its general meaning and to throw the whole significance of the word "working" into its combination with "weather". "Weather working day", therefore, does not mean any day of the week on which the weather admits working but any working day that is not unavailable to work because of weather. It is, in other words, a fine working day.' *Reardon Smith Line Ltd v Ministry of Agriculture, Fisheries and Food* [1963] 1 All ER 545 at 555, HL, per Viscount Radcliffe; also reported in [1961] AC 691 at 722

WEDDING APPAREL

'Wedding apparel [within the meaning of a contract to pay for "wedding apparel"] is to be taken, accordance to the common parlance, for apparel to be used upon the wedding-day and time of feasting, which is commonly for some days after, according to the dignity of the persons.' *Morris v Fletcher* (1626) Cro Car 53 at 53, per cur.

WEEK

A week is strictly the time between midnight on Saturday and the same hour on the next succeeding Saturday, but the term is also applied to any period of seven successive days. (45 Halsbury's Laws (4th edn) para 1112)

'Week' means the period between midnight on Saturday night and midnight on the succeeding

Saturday night. (Shops Act 1950, s 74; Mines and Quarries Act 1954, s 182; Offices, Shops and Railway Premises Act 1963, s 90)

[A city council, before carrying out certain works were required to insert a notice in a local newspaper for two successive 'weeks'.] 'I take the word "week" in this clause (there being nothing in the context to indicate a different meaning) as signifying a calendar week—i.e. the period beginning with Sunday and ending with Saturday. I do not think it means a period of seven days beginning on any one day and ending on the seventh day thereafter.' *Aberdeen (City) v Watt* (1901) 3 F 787 at 790, per Lord Trayner

Australia 'The word "week". This word is capable of meaning the calendar week commencing on Sunday, any consecutive seven days, the week observed by the particular employer in the calculation of wages, or the five days from Monday to Friday.' *Dunlop Perdrian Rubber Co Ltd v Federated Rubber Workers Union of Australia* (1931) 46 CLR 329 at 341, per Dixon J

Canada [Overtime payments were required for work in excess of 44 hours a week.] 'In a lecture in the Special Lectures of the Law Society of Upper Canada 1976, on "Employment Standards in Ontario", at p 49, Paul Hess QC made the following comments on ss 1(q) and 25(1) [of the Employment Standards Act, RSO 1980, c 137]: "The word 'week' is defined by clause 1(q) as a period of seven consecutive days. The definition may appear to be unnecessary but administrative experience with some employers established its practical necessity to avoid argument that a week meant seven working days as selected by the employer from time to time. The seven consecutive days comprising the week for subsection 25(1) are not the same as the calendar week. It may be any seven consecutive days and is taken to be those days which are established by practice or custom by the employer or in the industry." This accords with the Divisional Court's interpretation of the Act, and with respect, I agree with it. . . . I think it is clear that "week", where a "work week" has been established, means a period of seven consecutive days coinciding with the "work week".' *Re Falconbridge Nickel Mines Ltd and Egan* (1983) 148 DLR (3d) 474 at 491, Ont CA, per Houlden JA; leave to appeal to SCC refused

Week's notice

'In this case the tenancy was what is called a Monday to Monday tenancy, that is, a weekly tenancy from Monday to Monday, and the landlord purported to determine it by a notice given on Monday, 8th of February, to quit on Monday, 15th of February. The simple point whether that is a good notice ought not to be complicated by any reference to yearly, quarterly, or monthly tenancies. I take it that the law is well settled, that in the case of a tenancy from week to week, unless a contrary intention appears, either party can determine it by a week's notice. In this case the only question is, what is a week's notice? The rule in such cases, which is described by Lindley LJ, in *Sidebotham v Holland* [[1895] 1 QB 378, CA], as the usual one, is not to count the day on which the notice is given but to count the day for which it is given. On principle I can see no reason why seven clear days should be required to determine a weekly tenancy, and I think it would be undesirable to establish such a rule, which would only introduce confusion. In the case of a Monday to Monday tenancy to give notice on one Monday for the following Monday is a simple rule; if in such a case it was necessary to give a longer notice, difficulty and uncertainty would be produced. Here the county court judge decided that a notice given on Monday for the following Monday was good, and that a seven clear days' notice was not required. Applying what Lindley LJ called the usual rule of disregarding the day on which the notice is given and including the day for which it is given, it is plain that the recipient of the notice has seven days' notice, but of course it is essential that he should have the whole of the day for which notice is given.' *Newman v Slade* [1926] 2 KB 328 at 329, 330, per Salter J

WEIGHING EQUIPMENT

See EQUIPMENT

WEIGHT

Sale by weight

'Selling by weight is selling under a contract of which weight is a term, selling at a price which by contract between the parties varies with the weight of the article sold.' *Lyons & Co v Houghton* [1915] 1 KB 489 at 498, DC, per Rowlatt J

Weight unknown

'Where in a bill of lading, which is prepared by the shippers for acceptance by the defendants' agent, the agent accepts in the margin a quantity "said to be 937 tons", and in the body of the bill of lading there is a clause "weight, etc, unknown", there is no prima facie evidence that 937 tons have been shipped. . . . I think that the true effect of this bill of lading is that the words "weight unknown" have the effect of a statement by the shipowners' agent that he has received a quantity of ore which the shippers' representative says weighs 937 tons but which he does not accept as being of that weight, the weight being unknown to him, and that he does not accept the weight of 937 tons except for the purpose of calculating freight and for that purpose only. That is the view taken in *Jessel v Bath* [(1867) LR 2 Exch 267 at 273, 274] where Martin B says: "That is a common well-known trade, and it is obvious that goods must be shipped on board hastily, and that goods shipped in bulk at a considerable distance from the shore, as is the case at Genoa, for instance, cannot by possibility be weighed. The person, therefore, signing the bill of lading, by signing for the amount with this qualification 'weight, contents and value unknown' merely means to say that the weight is represented to him to be so much, but that he has himself no knowledge of the matter. The insertion of the weight in the margin, and the calculation of freight upon it, does not carry the matter any further; he calculates the freight, as it is his duty to do, upon the weight as stated to him." . . . I arrive at the conclusion that the statement in the bill of lading that 937 tons had been shipped does not bind the shipowners except for the purpose of estimating freight.' *New Chinese Antimony Co Ltd v Ocean SS Co Ltd* [1917] 2 KB 664 at 669–671, CA, per Lord Reading CJ

'A person who signs for a weight with the qualification "weight unknown" merely means to say that the weight is represented to him to be so much, but that he has himself no knowledge of the matter. A statement so made binds no one.' *Pyman Bell & Co v Ohlson SS Co* (1930) 36 Lloyd LR 57 at 59, per Scrutton LJ

New Zealand 'The words "weight, measurement, contents, quality, and value unknown" exclude any submission as to the contents of the case. By the use of these words the shipowner says in effect: "I accept this case as it appears on the outside; I know nothing about the inside, and will be bound by no statement in reference to it": *Lebeau v General Steam Navigation* [(1872) LR 8 CP 88]; *New Chinese Antimony Co v Ocean Steamship Co* [supra]. In the last-mentioned case Scrutton LJ, in the course of his judgment, put the matter thus: "Suppose a box, described as a 'box of jewels', were deposited for safe custody at a bank, and a receipt were given for it in the words 'received, contents unknown', there would be no evidence of the receipt of any jewellery." The position in the present case, therefore, is that the bill of lading cannot be treated as containing any admission with regard to the contents of the case.' *New Zealand Shipping Co Ltd v Lewis's Ltd* [1920] NZLR 243 at 245, 246, per Sim J; also reported [1920] GLR 143 at 144

WEIR

'With respect to the word "wear" itself . . . we find in the Anglo-Saxon Dictionary that it had anciently a more extensive application than now. At page 243 of Bosworth, the word "waer", or "wer", answering to our "wear", is translated, "1, an enclosure, a place enclosed; 2, a fish-pond, a place or engine for catching and keeping fish, a wear; 3, the sea, a wave." The only reference which we have met in the old books to the use of the word "wear", is the dictum in the Year Book [14 H 8 M fo 2.] from which it seems that a grant or exception of a wear includes the fishery there.' *Malcomson v O'Dea* (1862) 10 HL Cas 593 at 620, per Willes J (delivering the opinion of the judges)

'The question which I propose to investigate on this grant of 1516 and the subsequent deeds, is whether the grant did amount to a grant of a several fishery, with the result that the soil in the river would pass to the owner of the several fishery by the words of the grant describing the fishery; and, inasmuch as the grant was not merely of the fishery, but also of the "wears in and upon the waters and rivers aforesaid", whether those words, "the wears", do of themselves grant the soil, so as to give to the grantee the soil and bed of the river, with the result that he would be entitled to the exclusive right of fishing, because he was owner of the land over which the water flowed. . . . Dealing first with the use of the word "wears", I should . . . come to the conclusion that the grant of the weirs is a grant, not of a mere right of fishing, but of a corporeal hereditament consisting of the soil on which the weir is constructed.' *Hanbury v Jenkins* [1901] 2 Ch 401 at 411–413, per Buckley J

[The Salmon Fishery Act 1873, s 15 (repealed; see now the Salmon and Freshwater Fisheries Act 1975, s 21(1)(b)), enacted that no person should, between certain dates, place upon the apron of any 'weir' any device for taking fish, except wheels or leaps for taking lamperns.] 'The question in the first case arises under s 15 of the Salmon Fishery Act 1873; it is whether the respondent did place upon the apron of the weir in the Test a device for taking fish. . . . In the Standard Dictionary a weir is described as "an artificial obstruction placed in a stream to raise the water, divert it into a mill-race or irrigation ditches, or form a fish pond; a dam". A weir may be simply a dam banking up the water either entirely or partially. It does not cease to be a weir because there may be a natural fall in the river bed. The original condition of things is immaterial. . . . A weir is still a weir notwithstanding some superadded artificial construction, for example, a framework to support hatches. Over some weirs the water flows naturally and continuously. Other weirs are fitted with hatches. Some weirs have hatches extending across the whole breadth of the river so that all the water can be penned back by the hatches. In others the hatches only occupy part of the river's width. Some weirs have hatches in the centre; the water flows over either side, and the hatches are only to allow a more copious flow. But the whole construction with or without hatches is a weir.' *Maw & Holloway* [1914] 3 KB 594 at 601–603, DC, per Avory J

'The summons in this case charged the respondent under s 15 of the Act of 1873 with placing up on the apron of a weir a trap or device for taking fish. . . . I entertain no doubt that para 6 of the case accurately describes a weir. It is true that "weir" is not defined in this Act, but some light is thrown on the matter by the definition of "fishing weir" in s 4 of the Act [repealed; see now the Salmon and Freshwater Fisheries Act 1975, s 41(1)] as "any erection, structure, or obstruction fixed to the soil either temporarily or permanently across, or partly across, a river or branch of a river, and which is used for the exclusive purpose of catching or facilitating the catching of fish". A weir therefore would seem to be "any erection, structure, or obstruction fixed to the soil either temporarily or permanently across, or partly across, a river or branch of a river". This shows that in this Act "weir" is meant to have a wide and not a narrow interpretation. Looking at the plan and at the description in para 6 of the case I think the structure is none the less a weir because it is entirely composed of a number of hatches fixed in a frame work and set upon a sill. This succession of hatches constitutes a weir; each hatch is part of the wier. Then I see no difficulty in drawing the inference that the sloping masonry, which all parties recognise as an apron, is the apron of a weir.' Ibid at 606, 607, per Shearman J

WELFARE *See also* SOCIAL WELFARE

'The duty of the Court [when appointing a guardian] is, in our judgment, to leave the child alone, unless the Court is satisfied that it is for the welfare of the child that some other course should be taken. The dominant matter for the consideration of the Court is the welfare of the child. But the welfare of a child is not to be measured by money only, nor by physical comfort only. The word welfare must be taken in its widest sense. The moral and religious welfare of the child must be considered as well as its physical well-being. Nor can the ties of affection be disregarded.' *Re McGrath (Infants)* [1893] 1 Ch 143 at 148, CA, per Lindley LJ

'The term "welfare" in this connection [custody of a child] must be read in its largest possible sense, that is to say, as meaning that every circumstance must be taken into consideration, and the Court must do what under the circumstances a wise parent acting for the true interests of the child would or ought to do.' *R v Gyngall* [1893] 2 QB 232 at 248, CA, per Kay LJ

'The Guardianship of Infants Act 1925, . . . by s 1 [repealed; see now the Guardianship of Minors Act 1971, s 1] provides that the Court, in deciding any such question as we have here [custody of infant, personal rights], "shall regard the welfare of the infant as the first and paramount consideration". That is no new law, and the welfare referred to there must be taken in its large signification as meaning that the welfare of the child as a whole must be considered. It is not merely a question whether the child would be happier in one place than in another, but of her general well-being. The section merely enacts the rule which had up to that time been acted upon in the Chancery Division.' *Re Thain, Thain v Taylor* [1926] Ch 676 at 689, per Lord Hanworth MR

'It is not necessary for me to say much more than that s 1 of the Guardianship of Infants Act 1925 [repealed; see supra] does not affect what was and is the law, that the first and paramount consideration is the welfare of the child. And it is very much for the child's welfare that she should be in the custody and living in the house of her father rather than with the aunt and uncle, however affectionate and kind they may be, especially in a case such as this, where the father has done nothing worthy of blame.' Ibid at 691, per Sargant LJ

'As has been pointed out again and again the term "welfare" in this connection [custody of a child] must be read in its largest possible sense. And I think that the Court must not only address itself to the child's present comfort and happiness but must also endeavour to look forward and try to consider what is ultimately best in the interest of the child. This will be found stated explicitly in the judgments of the Court of Session in the case of *M v M* [1926] SC 778]. . . . Here I should like to advert for a moment to a point which was raised during argument. Suppose the Court found the considerations on either side to be equally balanced, nothing in the conduct of either parent to lead to any preference between them, and upon the most careful balance nothing to enable the Court to decide that it would be more in the interest of the welfare of the child that he should be entrusted to the custody of the one parent rather than of the other, what view in such circumstances ought the Court to take? There are undoubtedly dicta to be found in the books to the effect that since the Guardianship of Infants Act 1886 [repealed], the parents have been placed on a complete equality but so far as I have been able to discover the precise point has never arisen for actual decision in any reported case either in England or in Ireland. . . . The question, however, . . . was more than once discussed in Scotland by the Court of Sessions [His Lordship then considered *Mackellar v Mackellar* (1898) 25 R 883; *Campbell v Campbell*, [1920] SC 31; and *Stevenson v Stevenson* (1894) 21 R 96, HL]. . . . I think these Scottish decisions afford useful guidance and will have to be given careful consideration if and when a case arises where in seeking to decide what is best from the point of view of the welfare of the child the balance appears to hang evenly between the custody of the father and the custody of the mother.' *Re B, An Infant* [1946] NI 1 at 4–6, per Black J

Australia 'Our primary care must be the welfare of the child, and as pointed out in *Goldsmith v Sands* [(1907) 4 CLR 1648] welfare does not mean merely financial or social or religious welfare, but includes as an important element the happiness of the child.' *Re Alford* [1941] St R Qd 213 at 217, per Philp J

WELL *See* PIT

WELL-BEING

[Land was conveyed to trustees to permit the land to be appropriated and used by the leaders of a mission for the promotion of (inter alia) the religious, social and physical 'well-being' of certain persons.] 'The word "well-being", though qualified by "religious" as well as "social and physical", means primarily, in my opinion, a happy or contented state. Social well-being would be promoted when people were happy together—an important factor in institutional life. Physical well-being is promoted by exercise or recreation, and the health and contentment which normally follow.' *Inland Revenue Comrs v Baddeley* [1955] 1 All ER 525 at 549, HL, per Lord Somervell; see also [1955] AC 572

Canada 'The discretion to encroach is conferred [by a will], to be exercised not merely for the "maintenance and support" simpliciter, but also for the "comfort and well-being" [of the beneficiary]. I agree with the submission of counsel for [the beneficiary] that "well-being" is a broad term, and includes freedom from worry, financial or otherwise.' *Re Mattick's Will* (1967) 60 WWR 503 at 507, BCSC, per Kirke Smith LJSC

WHARF *See also* DOCK; QUAY

'Wharf' includes any quay, landing-place, siding, or other place at which goods are landed, loaded, or unloaded. (Explosives Act 1875, s 108)

The expression 'wharf' includes all wharves, quays, docks, and premises in or upon which any goods, when landed from ships, may be lawfully placed. (Merchant Shipping Act 1894, s 492)

'Wharf' means any wharf, quay, pier, jetty or other place at which sea-going ships can ship or unship goods or embark or disembark passengers. (Harbours Act 1964, s 57)

[A private Act enacted that all 'wharfs'

belonging to a canal company should be rateable.] 'The piece of land comprised in No 1 is not a wharf. That term usually denotes something built or constructed by the art and industry of man; and though it may have been used for some of the purposes for which a wharf is used, it does not therefore follow that it is a wharf. Goods may be, and frequently are, landed upon the sea-beach, but the beach is not therefore a wharf. If this were a wharf it might fairly be expected, that wharfage dues would be payable; but no compensation whatever is paid to the proprietors of the canal for the use of the piece of land specifically, though they do receive wharfage dues for the use of other premises. As this piece of land is not a building constructed by the art of man, and as no wharfage or compensation is paid to the owners for the use of it as a landing-place, I am of opinion that it is not a wharf, within the meaning of this Act of Parliament.' *R v Regent's Canal Co* (1827) 6 B & C 720 at 731, per Littledale J

Australia 'What, then, of the word "wharf"? In its popular signification it seems to mean a place contiguous to water, over which goods pass in the process of loading and unloading, and which serves as a factor in their transference from the water to the land, or from land to water.' *Brooks v South Australian Stevedoring Co Ltd* [1920] SALR 207 at 222, per Poole J

WHARF LABOURER

Australia 'The term "wharf labourer" includes persons labouring in loading and unloading vessels, and . . . it does not include persons who are not labouring in loading and unloading vessels, coaling being regarded as loading, whether the coal be cargo or fuel for the ship's fires.' *Brooks v South Australian Stevedoring Co Ltd* [1920] SALR 207 at 224, per Poole J

WHEN

[A testator gave the sum of £5,000 to all and every the children of X, 'when' and as they should respectively attain the age of twenty-one years.] 'The strong argument in support of maintenance is, that the testator has expressly given it during the mother's life; and it is extremely improbable, therefore, that he intended the children should be without any provision, in case she died leaving them under age. I think, therefore, there is a fair inference from the whole of this will, that the testator's intention was to give maintenance. The words "when" and "as" do not suspend the gift; but only the time of payment.' *Lambert v Parker* (1815) Coop G 143 at 145, per Grant MR

WHENEVER

[A proviso for re-entry in a lease gave the landlord the right to re-enter if and 'whenever' two conditions arose, viz when any one quarter's rent should be in arrear for twenty-one days and no sufficient distress could be had or levied for the same.] 'The language of the proviso is "if and whenever", which I think means that "if and as often as" a quarter's rent is in arrear, and the time arises at which the two conditions co-exist, then, however many causes of forfeiture there may have been before, there is still one existing cause of which the landlord may avail himself.' *Shepherd v Berger* [1891] 1 QB 597 at 600, CA, per Browne LJ

WHEREBY

Australia [The Industrial Arbitration Act 1940–1986 (NSW), s 88F, provides that an order or award may be made declaring void in whole or in part or varying in whole or in part any contract 'whereby' a person performs work in any industry upon certain grounds.] 'The section is concerned with "any contract . . . whereby a person performs work in any industry". As a description of any particular class of contract these words are at first sight far from explicit, but on further examination, with the aid of statutory definitions and context, they may be seen to convey quite a precise meaning. The word "whereby" must, I think, here bear one of its ordinary meanings that of "in consequence of" "as a result of", or "owing to which" (Shorter Oxford Dictionary); the contract must thus be one in consequence or as a result of which a person performs work. The section requires the work to which it refers to be in an "industry", a term defined, so far as presently relevant, as "craft occupation or calling in which persons . . . are employed for hire or reward" (s 5(1)). The contract is then one in consequence of which a person performs work in any occupation etc in which a person is employed for hire or reward.' *Stevenson v Barham* (1977) 12 ALR 175 at 177, per Stephen J

WHICH

'It is clear to me that the words, "such sums of money", occurring in the clause in question in the will, refer to the clause "which I have already advanced", etc, the word "which" being used instead of "as", which would have been more proper, though "which" is often used in this manner in early English writers.' *Whateley v Spooner* (1857) 3 K & J 542 at 546, 547, per Page Wood V-C

WHILE

New Zealand 'The Courts in New Zealand seem to be unique in the Commonwealth in giving to the word "while" a causative [as opposed to a temporal] connotation when used in a context which is not ambiguous or subject to other considerations which may require a Court of construction to depart from the natural meaning of words. No suggestion of a causative overtone is accepted in England. Australia or the United States of America.' *Public Trustee v North Island Motor Union Insurance Co* [1967] NZLR 530 at 533, per Henry J

New Zealand [The Transport Act 1962, s 55(2), provides: that every person commits an offence who, 'while' under the influence of drink or a drug to such an extent as to be incapable of having control of the vehicle, is in charge of a motor vehicle and by an act or omission in relation thereto causes bodily injury to or the death of any person.] 'For the purposes of this section the word "while" is not to be interpreted in its temporal sense but rather in its causative sense.' *R v O'Callaghan* [1985] 1 NZLR 198 at 206, CA

WHILST

[An insurance policy under which compensation was payable for accidental injury while travelling by car contained a proviso that the insurers should not be liable in respect of bodily injury sustained 'whilst' under the influence of drugs or intoxicating liquor.] 'There remains the question of the construction in its context of the word "whilst". In my judgment, it has a temporal meaning, and I am unable to read into the exemption clause any requirement of a causal connection between the bodily injury sustained and the state of being under the influence of intoxicating liquor.' *London v British Merchants Insurance Co Ltd* [1961] 1 All ER 705 at 706, per Lawton J

WHISKY

'Whisky' mean spirits—
(a) which have been produced by the distillation of a mash of cereals which has been—
  (i) saccharified by the diastase of the malt contained therein, with or without other natural enzymes; and
  (ii) fermented by the action of yeast

  to an alcoholic strength of less than 94.8 per cent by volume so that the distillation has an aroma and taste derived from the raw materials used; and
(b) which have matured for at least three years in wooden casks of a capacity not exceeding 700 litres.

(Scotch Whisky Act 1988, s 3(1))

Scotch whisky

'Scotch whisky' means such whisky (distilled and matured in Scotland) as conforms to a definition of Scotch whisky contained in an order made under this subsection by the Ministers [Minister of Agriculture, Fisheries and Food and the Secretary of State]. (Scotch Whisky Act 1988, s 3(1))

'The Sheriff's finding, as I construe it, is substantially this:—That, when whisky is sold as Scotch whisky, the representation that it is Scotch whisky carries the meaning that the entire contents of the container in which it is sold were distilled in Scotland.' *Henderson & Turnbull Ltd v Adair* 1939 SC(J) 83 at 91, per the Lord Justice-General (Lord Normand)

WHOLESALE

'Sale by way of wholesale dealing' means sale to a person who buys for the purpose of selling again. (Radioactive Substances Act 1948, s 12)

(1) In this Act any reference to selling anything by way of wholesale dealing is a reference to selling it to a person who buys it for one or more of the purposes specified in subsection (2) of this section, except that it does not include any such sale by the person who manufactured it.

(2) The purposes referred to in the preceding subsection, in relation to a person to whom anything is sold, are the purposes of—

(a) selling or supplying it, or
(b) administering it or causing it to be administered to one or more human beings,

in the course of a business carried on by that person. (Medicines Act 1968, s 131)

Australia 'One characteristic of the business of a wholesale merchant . . . is that he intervenes as a "middle man" between the producer or manufacturer and the retailer, and it is his function to distribute a particular commodity to the retailer who in turn sells it to members of the public, in reduced quantities but frequently in the same form. This is not, of course, an infallible guide. There are certainly cases in which two or more wholesalers intervene in succession between the producer or manufacturer and the retailer.' *Louie v Willmott*, [1966] SASR 368 at 373, per Walters J

New Zealand 'In England there appears to be some ground for the contention that, in certain circles at all events, a distinction is drawn between a manufacturer and a wholesaler, the latter description applying only to persons who both buy and sell goods in gross or in bulk. In my opinion, whatever the position may be in England, there is no justification for drawing that distinction in New Zealand, where it is a matter of common knowledge that many wholesaler dealers have found it necessary to manufacture the goods they sell in bulk.' *Chemists' Service Guild of New Zealand Inc v Stilwell* [1966] NZLR 654 at 663, CA, per North P

'Having regard, as I may, to such knowledge of affairs as I possess, I would not myself in using the term "wholesaler" exclude from the connotation of this term accepted in New Zealand manufacturers who make their own product and then dispose of it in bulk. Can the word "dealer", then, make any difference? Is it necessary to buy as well as to sell to be a *dealer*? Looking at the definition of this word in the Shorter Oxford Dictionary, I have not found in the definitions there given of "deal", "dealer" and "dealing" anything to compel me to exclude the manufacturer-cum-seller.' Ibid at 668, per Turner J

'Whatever may be the limitations placed on "wholesale" or "dealer" in dictionaries which illustrate their use overseas, and whatever may have been the position in the early days of this Dominion when a more rigid demarcation between manufacturer, wholesaler and retailer was observable, I have no doubt at all that in 1954 a manufacturer selling in quantity direct to the retail trade was covered by the words "wholesaler" or "wholesale dealer" when those words were used in this country.' Ibid at 673, per McCarthy J

WIDOW

'Here the gift is to a named person "during her widowhood". . . . The gift is to commence and finish with widowhood, and, as the lady divorced her husband, she never became a widow, and the period of enjoyment specified has therefore never commenced.' *Re Kettlewell, Jones v Kettlewell* (1907) 98 LT 23 at 24, per Parker J

[A testator, whose wife's former husband was at the time of her marriage to the testator presumed, but not known for certain, to be dead, bequeathed his household effects to his wife 'during her widowhood' with a gift over 'after her decease or second marriage'. After the death of the testator his wife's former husband was found to be alive.] '"Widowhood" means "until she dies or marries again". . . . I think the expression "during her widowhood" was not intended to import a condition but to define the period during which she was to enjoy the gifts. In these circumstances the lady is entitled to the benefits given to her by the will until her death or future marriage.' *Re Hammond, Burniston v White* [1911] 2 Ch 342 at 346, 347, per Parker J

[Under the Widows', Orphans' and Old Age Contributory Pensions Act 1925, s 1(1) (repealed), a pension was payable to the 'widow' of an insured man.] 'It appears to me to be too plain for argument that, when the appellant obtained her divorce from her husband, she ceased to be his wife. If she was not his wife at the date of his death, then I cannot understand how she could become his widow upon his death.' *Colgan v Department of Health for Scotland* 1937 SC 16 at 20, per the Lord Justice Clerk (Lord Aitchison)

'I have been referred to the Oxford English Dictionary for the meaning of the word "widow". It is there defined as "a woman whose husband is dead (and who has not married again); a wife bereaved of her husband". It cannot be said that Mrs Cozens was at any time a woman whose husband was dead. When Mr Cozens died he was not her husband according to the ordinary use of language. It is impossible to say that Mrs Cozens became the widow of a man she had divorced before his death.' *Re Norman's Will Trusts, Mitchell v Cozens* (1940) 84 Sol Jo 186 at 187, per Simonds J

Canada '"Widow" is not defined in the Act [Testator's Family Maintenance Act]. The definition of widow in the compact edition, Complete Oxford English Dictionary, is as follows: "A woman whose husband is dead (and who has not married again); a wife bereaved of her husband." It is defined in Stroud's Judicial Dictionary, 3rd edn, vol 4: "A widow is a woman who has survived a man to whom she was lawfully married, and who was his wife at the time of his death." . . . I find that the applicant, in order to qualify under the statutory provisions of the Testator's Family Maintenance Act [RSNS 1967, c 303], must put herself within the definition of a dependant, as set forth in s 2(1), which definition refers back to s 1(b), and use of the term "widow" implies a lawful marriage. It is common ground by the applicant and the respondent that the applicant, in this instance, was not, nor ever was the lawful wife of the testator.' *Re O'Connell* (1979) 109 DLR (3d) 584 at 584, 585, NSTD, per Grant J

WIDOWER

[Under the Finance Act 1920, s 19 (repealed; see now the Income and Corporation Taxes Act 1988, s 258) a 'widower' was entitled to a deduction in respect of a housekeeper taking charge of his children.] 'I should have thought it was clear beyond any controversy that "widower" meant a person who had lost his wife by death. . . . It would seem clear that the section cannot operate in the case of a gentleman whose wife is not dead but who has had the misfortune to divorce her.' *Kliman v Winckworth* (1933) 17 Tax Cas 569 at 571, per Finlay J

WIFE

[A testator, in a codicil to his will, referred to a woman to whom he was betrothed as his 'wife'. He died before the marriage took place.] 'The legacy given to the plaintiff, is not given on condition of the testator marrying her. The testator made his will under the impression that his intended marriage with the plaintiff would take effect; and he has described the plaintiff with reference to his intention of marrying her.' *Schloss v Stiebel* (1833) 6 Sim 1 at 5, per Shadwell V-C

[The plaintiff therefore took the legacy.]

'The testator devises the premises in question to his "dear wife Caroline". That is a devise to a person by name, and one which appears to be that of the lessor of the plaintiff. There is no competition with any one else of the same name, to whom it can be suggested, that the will intended to refer. The only question is, whether the lessor of the plaintiff, not being the lawful wife of the testator, properly fills the description of his "dear wife Caroline". Formerly, the name was held to be the important thing. This is shown by the 25th maxim of Lord Bacon to which I before adverted, "*Veritas nominis tollit errorem demonstrationis*", and which he illustrates by the following example: "So, if I grant land, *Episcopo nunc Londinensi, qui me erudivit in pueritia*; this is a good grant, although he never instructed me." That rule has, no doubt, been relaxed in modern times, and has given place to another, that the construction of the devise is to be governed by the evident intention of the testator. . . . Here is a person fitly named, and there can be no reasonable doubt that she was the person intended. It being conceded that it was the testator's intention that Caroline should have the property, and he having mentioned her by an apt description, I see no ground for holding, that, because the words "my dear wife" are not strictly applicable to her, the intention of the testator should fail, and the property go to some one to whom he did not mean to give it. Caroline was de facto the testator's wife; and she lived with him, as such, down to the time of his death. . . . Interpreting the language he has used, in its proper and legimate manner, and regard being had to the circumstances existing at the time of the execution of the will, there can be no doubt that the intention of the testator is best effectuated by holding that the lessor of the plaintiff is the person designated, and that apt words have been used to convey the property in question to her.' *Doe d Gains v Rouse* (1848) 5 CB 422 at 426, 427, per Maule J

[A testator made a gift to X, his brother, for life and after his death to X's children. He directed that if X's 'wife' survived X she should take a life interest in the property. After the death of the testator X married a second wife, who survived him.] 'The gift to the wife of the testator's brother applied to the wife who was then living, and . . . the testator did not mean any wife with whom his brother might at any time afterwards intermarry.' *Re Burrow's Trusts* (1864) 10 LT 184 at 184, per Kindersley V-C

'Following *Boreham v Bignall* [(1850) 8 Hare 131] I hold that the gift of the rents [to Nathan Firth for life and after his death, leaving his 'wife' surviving, to pay the rents to such wife for life] is confined to the wife who was alive at the date of the will.' *Firth v Fielden* (1874) 22 WW 622 at 622, per Jessel MR

'As regards the rule of law, the proposition which is admitted in this case is that prima facie where the wife of a person is spoken of by a testator and that person is married at the date of the will, in the absence of any context, the wife existing at the date of the will is the person intended to take.' *Re Drew, Drew v Drew* [1899] 1 Ch 336 at 339, 341, 342, per Stirling J

'This is a case of a policy effected under s 10 of the Married Women's Property Act 1870 [repealed; see now the Married Women's Property Act 1882, s 11]. . . . The policy is expressed to be effected by George Griffiths "for the benefit of his wife, or if she be dead between his children in equal proportions". . . . In this particular case . . . the words are "if she be dead", and those words seem to point to the wife who was living when the policy was effected. . . . In *Re Burrow's Trusts* [supra] there was a gift to the testator's brother, and after his death, to his children, followed by a direction that if the wife of the brother should survive her husband she should receive the rents and profits for her life. Kindersley V-C held that the wife meant was not the second wife. I gather from what Stirling J said in *Re Drew* [supra] that he rather agreed with *Re Burrow's Trusts* than with *Re Lyne's Trust* [(1869) LR 8 Eq 65], and I prefer to follow *Re Burrow's Trusts*. Accordingly, I hold that "wife" here means the wife at the time the policy was effected, and, consequently, that the widow can take nothing.' *Re Griffiths' Policy* [1903] 1 Ch 739 at 741, 742, per Joyce J

'It is settled that if in a will you find a gift by the testator to the "wife" of a person, and that person has at the time a wife living and acknowledged by the testator, the testator prima facie intends to refer to the existing wife, and not to any subsequent wife that person may have; unless, indeed, there may be a sufficient context to enable the Court to say that the testator is referring also to a subsequent wife, and that the prima facie meaning of the gift is displaced.' *Re Coley, Hollinshead v Coley* [1903] 2 Ch 102 at 110, CA, per Romer LJ

'I find that the testatrix, knowing full well that Colonel McClintock's first wife was dead, has directed that this legacy of £5,000 shall be held for the benefit of Colonel McClintock, his wife and children. Now, he had no wife at that time; therefore, if those were the testatrix's wishes at the date of the codicil, the only person who could take under that provision would be, and is, the lady whom Colonel McClintock married after the testatrix's death in 1903. It appears to me, therefore, that I ought to answer the questions . . . by declaring that according to the true construction of the will and codicil, and in the events that have happened, the second wife of Colonel McClintock has an interest for her life or until she shall re-marry in the sum of £5,000.' *Re Hardyman, Teesdale v McClintock* [1925] Ch 287 at 289, 290, 292, 293, per Romer J

'The facts are simple. . . . The words of the will are: "I give, devise and bequeath unto my wife Eliza Ann Smalley all my possessions absolutely." . . . It is contended that the word "wife" prevents one from holding that Eliza Ann Mercer was intended. I do not think so. I think the word "wife" can be used in a secondary sense, and if so the addition of the word "Smalley" really means nothing at all, because obviously Eliza Ann Mercer was living with the testator, and believed to be his wife, and so the word "Smalley" was simply part of the description, linked with the word "wife" to connote the person whom the testator wished to describe as his wife.' *Re Smalley, Smalley v Scotton* [1929] 2 Ch 112 at 116–118, CA, per Lord Hanworth MR

[The Finance Act 1938, s 38 (repealed; see now the Income and Corporation Taxes Act 1988, s 671(1)) enacted that if and so long as the terms of a settlement were such that the settlor or the 'wife' or husband of the settlor might cease to be liable to make any annual payments payable by virtue or in consequence of any provision of the settlement, any sums payable by the settlor or the 'wife' or husband of the settlor by virtue or in consequence of that provision of the settlement in any year of assessment were to be treated as the income of the settlor for that year, and not as the income of any other person.] 'Prima facie . . . one would suppose that the word "wife" means that which is its true natural meaning, a lady who, during the latter part of the joint lives of herself and a man, has been the wife of that man. That is the meaning of the word "wife". It is perfectly true that the word "widow" is used to express the position of a lady when her husband has died. In one sense when a woman has become a widow she is no longer a wife. That is perfectly true. But the description in this section of her as a wife refers to the lady, and has nothing to do with the matter of time. It has nothing to do with whether you are talking of her as being a lady who is living at the same time as her husband or as being a lady who survived her husband. Accordingly, the difference, if difference there be for this purpose, between the words "wife" and "widow" is quite immaterial for the purposes of this section.' *Inland Revenue Comrs v Gaunt* [1941] 1 KB 706 at 713, 714, CA, per Clauson LJ

Canada [Dependants' claim for damages after fatal accident was available for a 'wife'.] 'It is my view that "wife", means lawfully married wife, unless it can be said that "wife" also includes common law wife. . . . Any other construction would not give that word its ordinary meaning. My reasons for this conclusion are that a "wife" is a woman who has acquired that status through a ceremony of marriage with her husband in accordance with the law of an appropriate jurisdiction. "Wife", on the other hand, is a legally unambiguous word which describes a status that can only properly be applied to a woman who has voluntarily taken on an obligation, in accordance with the applicable law, to tie herself in a particularly well-understood relationship with one man during their joint lives. A wife is a woman who also accepts that her union with her husband is dissoluble during their joint lives only in accordance with the law.' *Louis v Esslinger* (1981) 121 DLR (3d) 17 at 32, 33, BCSC, per McEachern CJSC

Wife and children

'Mr George Henry Browne on the 31st of December, 1891, effected a policy of assurance on his own life under the Married Women's Property Act 1882, s 11, "for the benefit of his wife and children". He had at that date a wife living, and there were also living children of his by her. That wife died, and he subsequently married the defendant Florence Brown, by whom also he had children. Florence Browne survived him, and so did children of each marriage. The questions are, first, whether Florence Browne takes any interest under the policy; and secondly, whether the children entitled to take are the children of one marriage exclusive of the children of the other, or whether the children of either marriage all stand on the same footing. . . . Turning to the Act, I find little assistance in the language used, which really throws me back on the proper construction of the policy. The Act says that such a policy "shall create a trust in favour of the objects therein named". No one is in the strict sense "named" in this policy. . . . There is no reason why the trust should not include objects as yet unascertained, and, of course, the ordinary marriage settlement creates a trust of that character. Therefore what the Act means is that there is a trust created by the policy in favour of the persons designated thereby, and for such interests as are there stated according to the true construction of the instrument. I hold that by his wife and children the settlor intended his surviving wife (if any) and his surviving children, whether by his then living or any after-taken wife.' *Re Browne's Policy, Browne v Browne* [1903] 1 Ch 188 at 189–191, per Kekewich J

WILD ANIMAL *See* ANIMAL

WILDFOWL *See* FOWL

WILFUL *See also* NEGLECT

'The rule laid down in *Pickard v Sears* [(1837) 6 Ad & El 474] . . . is "that, where one, by his words or conduct, wilfully causes another to believe in the existence of a certain state of things, and induces him to act on that belief, or to alter his own previous position, the former is concluded from averring against the latter a different state of things as existing at the same time". . . . By the term "wilfully", however, in that rule, we must understand, if not that the party represents that to be true which he knows to be untrue, at least, that he means his representation to be acted upon, and that it is acted upon accordingly; and if, whatever a man's real intention may be, he so conducts himself that a reasonable man would take the representation to be true, and believe that it was meant that he should act upon it, and did act upon it as true, the party making the representation would be equally precluded from contesting its truth; and conduct, by negligence or omission, where there is a duty cast upon a person, by usage of trade or otherwise, to disclose the truth, may often have the same effect.' *Freeman v Cooke* (1848) 2 Exch 654 at 662, 663, per cur.

[The Lands Clauses Consolidation Act 1845, s 89, imposes a penalty on promoters of an undertaking 'wilfully' entering upon lands without consent before payment of the purchase money.] 'I am clearly of opinion that the term "wilfully", as used in the 89th section, means an absence of an honest belief on the part of the company of the existence of the conditions precedent.' *Steele v Midland Rly Co* (1869) 21 LT 387 at 392, per Cockburn CJ

[A local Act imposed a penalty on persons 'wilfully' throwing soil, earth or rubbish into certain rivers, canals, or watercourses.] 'I . . . think that as Sheepscar Beck was a natural stream, and as no injury was caused to the undertakers, the appellant was not liable for discharging refuse into it; in my opinion, a person throwing soil, earth or rubbish into a natural stream flowing into one of the rivers, but at a point beyond the limits of navigation, is not liable to be convicted. . . . Further, I think that the refuse was not "wilfully" thrown in within the meaning of the clause: for it was discharged in the course of carrying on a lawful trade, and, as it appears, in the exercise of a supposed right; "wilfully" appears to me in this section to mean "wantonly" or "causelessly". I, therefore, think that the appellant is entitled to judgment.' *Smith v Burnham* (1876) 1 Ex D 419 at 423, 424, per Bramwell B

'I do not think that "wilful" means wantonly or causelessly, but I think you can be wilful without being wanton, for I think if you permit a thing, not under compulsion, you do it wilfully.' *High Wycombe Corpn v River Thames Conservators* (1898) 78 LT 463 at 465, DC, per Kennedy J

' "Wilfully" means that the act is done deliberately and intentionally, not by accident or inadvertence, but so that the mind of the person who does the act goes with it.' *R v Senior* [1899] 1 QB 283 at 290, 291, per Lord Russell of Killowen CJ

'An act is wilfully done if it is an act of the will done deliberately, as distinct from something done without thought on the spur of the moment.' *Smith v Wemyss Coal Co Ltd* (1927) 21 BWCC 483 at 490–492, per the Lord President (Lord Clyde)

' "Wilful act" is plain English, and I can entertain no doubt that the installing of this machine without guard or fence for use in the factory was a wilful act by some one. . . . "Wilful" is more commonly used in modern speech of bad conduct or actions than of good, though it does not necessarily connote blame.' *Wheeler v New Merton Board Mills Ltd* [1933] 2 KB 669 at 677, CA, per Talbot J

'Wilfully pretending to be a solicitor is treated by the law as a serious offence. Where a man has been on the roll of solicitors and has either been struck off the roll or has had his practising certificate suspended and he deliberately—because that is what "wilfully" means—acts as a solicitor, he has committed a very serious offence.' *Hall v Jordan* [1947] 1 All ER 826 at 827, per Lord Goddard CJ

'If a man permits a thing to be done, it means that he gives permission for it to be done, and if a man gives permission for a thing to be done, he knows what is to be done or is being done, and, if he knows that, it follows that it is wilful.' *Lomas v Peek* [1947] 2 All ER 574 at 575, per Lord Goddard CJ

'The wording of the Landlord and Tenant Act 1730 is: "In case any tenant . . . shall wilfully hold over any . . . tenements . . . after the determination of [his] term." . . . It has been held that "wilfully" means "contumaciously" [*Wright v Smith* (1805) 5 Esp 203], but I can see no reason why the old English word "wilfully" does not exactly express the true meaning of the statute. The statute does not mean that a tenant is a contumacious tenant. It deals only with the moment of time when the tenancy comes to an end. At that moment of time a tenant may say: "I shall stay on. I think I have a right to do so". His staying on is not wilful. On the other hand, a tenant may say: "I will stay on, although I know I have no right to do so". That is wilful, and well illustrates the now sometimes forgotten distinction between "I shall" and the insistent "I will".' *French v Elliott* [1959] 3 All ER 866 at 874, per Paull J

[The Highways Act 1959, s 121(1) (repealed; see now the Highways Act 1980, s 137(1)) provided that if a person, without lawful authority or excuse, in any way 'wilfully' obstructed the free passage along a highway he should be guilty of an offence.] 'Counsel for the appellant has sought to argue that if a person acts in the genuine belief that he or she has lawful authority to do what he or she is doing, then if an obstruction results he or she cannot be said to have wilfully obstructed. Quite frankly, I do not fully understand that submission. . . . I imagine it can be put in this way, that there must be some mens rea in the sense that a person will be guilty only if he knowingly does a wrongful act. For my part, I am quite satisfied that that consideration cannot possibly be imported into the words "wilfully obstructs" in this enactment. If anybody by an exercise of free will does something which causes an obstruction,then I think that an offence is committed.' *Arrowsmith v Jenkins* [1963] 2 All ER 210 at 211, per Lord Parker CJ; also reported in [1963] 2 QB 561 at 567

[The appellant had been arrested and charged with 'wilfully' obstructing a constable in the execution of his duty within the Police Act 1964, s 51(3).] 'The only remaining element of the alleged offence, and the one on which in my judgment this case depends, is whether the obstructing of which the appellant was guilty was a wilful obstruction. "Wilful" in this context in my judgment means not only "intentional" but also connotes something which is done without lawful excuse.' *Rice v Connolly* [1966] 2 All ER 649 at 651, per Lord Parker CJ

Australia [The County Court Act 1958 (Vic), s 54A, provides that where any person 'wilfully' interrupts the proceedings of a court the judge may direct the apprehension of such person and if he thinks fit may commit him to prison.] 'The word "wilfully" means "intentionally", or "deliberately", in the sense that what is said or done is intended as an insult, threat, etc. Its presence does more than negative the notion of "inadvertently" or "unconsciously" (*Bell v Stewart* (1920) 28 CLR 419 at 427). The mere voluntary utterance of words is not enough. "Wilfully" imports the notion of purpose.' *Lewis v Judge Ogden* (1984) 153 CLR 682 at 688, per cur.

Canada 'Standing alone or with the word "wilfully" the word "suffering" deals with a state of mind. "To suffer" means "to allow" or "to permit". "Wilfully" imparts the idea of intention; "wilfully suffering" means "intentionally to allow or permit".' *McDonald v Northern Alberta Rly Co* [1942] 3 WWR 241 at 245, Alta CA, per Ford JA

Canada 'To my mind the word "wilful" in s 168 [of the Criminal Code (now RSC 1970, c C-34, s 118) dealing with obstructing police officers] applies to a state of circumstances where the person charged knows what he is doing and intends to do what he is doing, and is a free agent.' *R v Goodman* (1951) 2 WWR (NS) 127 at 135, BCCA, per Robertson JA

Canada 'Where the evidence establishes that a driver had prior warning of or knew that he was in a drowsy or sleepy condition, his conduct in continuing to drive is "wilful" in the sense that being aware of his disability he consciously and deliberately, and one might add stubbornly and perversely, does so knowing full well as every driver must, that if drowsiness or sleep overcomes him, that his vehicle would continue for all intents and purposes without the benefit of steering or braking controls, to the great jeopardy and peril of himself, his passengers and other persons using the highway; and that the probable, almost inevitable, result would be an accident. His will is a party to such misconduct.' *Muench v Reiter* (1961) 38 WWR 65 at 69, Sask QB, Disbery J

Canada [The accused were charged with wilfully promoting hatred under the Criminal Code, RSC c C-34, s 281.2(2).] 'The word "wilfully" has not been uniformly interpreted and its meaning to some extent depends upon the context in which it is used. Its primary meaning is "intentionally", but it is also used to mean "recklessly". . . . The term "recklessly" is here used to denote the subjective state of mind of a person who foresees that his conduct may cause the prohibited result but, nevertheless, takes a deliberate and unjustifiable risk of bringing it about. . . . The word "wilfully" has, however, also been held to mean no more than that the accused's act is done intentionally and not accidentally. In *R v Senior* [1899] 1 QB 283, Lord Russell of Killowen CJ, in interpreting the meaning of the words "wilfully neglects" in s 1 of the Prevention of Cruelty to Children Act 1894 (UK), c 41, said at pp 290–291: "Wilfully" means that the act is done deliberately and intentionally, not by accident or inadvertence, but so that the mind of the person who does the act goes with it." On the other hand, in *Rice v Connolly* [1966] 2 QB 414, where the accused was charged with wilfully obstructing a constable in the execution of his duty, Lord Parker LCJ said at p 419: " 'Wilful' in this context not only in my judgment means 'intentional' but something which is done without lawful excuse . . .". As previously indicated, the word "wilfully" does not have a fixed meaning, but I am satisfied that in the context of s 281.2(2) it means with the intention of promoting hatred, and does not include recklessness. The arrangement of the legislation proscribing the incitement of hatred, in my view, leads to that conclusion.' *R v Buzzanga* (1979) 101 DLR (3d) 488 at 498, 500, Ont CA, per Martin JA

Wilful default

'The term "wilful default" . . . is not a term of art. . . . Default is a purely relative term, just like negligence. It means nothing more, nothing less, than not doing what is reasonable under the circumstances—not doing something which you ought to do, having regard to the relations which you occupy towards the other persons interested in the transaction. The other word which it is sought to define is "wilful". That is a word of familiar use in every branch of law, and although in some branches of the law it may have a special meaning, it generally, as used in courts of law, implies nothing blameable, but merely that the person of whose action or default the expression is used, is a free agent, and that what has been done arises from the spontaneous action of his will. It amounts to nothing more than this, that he knows what he is doing, and intends to do what he is doing, and is a free agent.' *Re Young & Harston's Contract* (1885) 31 Ch D 168 at 174, 175, CA, per Bowen LJ

[A condition of sale provided that if the purchase should not be completed on the day fixed for completion, the purchaser should pay interest on the balance of purchase money until completion, unless the delay were due to the 'wilful default' of the vendors.] 'The meaning of "wilful default" in a condition such as that which has to be considered was examined with care in *Re Young and Harston's Contract* [supra]. Whatever may be the popular meaning of wilful default, whatever the expression may mean in dealing with other matters, it is now settled that moral delinquency, intentional delay, wilful obstruction on the part of a vendor, may all be absent, and yet there may be wilful default on his part disentitling him to interest under a contract such as that before us. If a vendor knows the material facts—knows that there are difficulties which it is his duty to overcome—knows that he may not be able to overcome them by the time fixed for completion, and he fails to overcome them by that time, although no fresh unforeseen occurrence prevents him from doing so, the delay caused by such failure on his part is attributable to his wilful default in the sense in which that expression is used in contracts of this description; and his right to interest during such delay is excluded.' *Re Hetling & Merton's Contract* [1893] 3 Ch 269 at 281, CA, per cur.

'The words "default" and "wilful" are relative terms. Each case must depend upon its own circumstances. A concise summary of their meaning is given by Stirling LJ in *Bennett v Stone* [[1903 1 Ch 509]: "According to the rule laid down in *Young & Harston's Contract* [supra] a vendor commits a default if he fails to do something which he ought reasonably to do, regard being had to the terms of the contract which he has entered into with the purchaser, and is guilty of wilful default if he so fails when he is a free agent and knows what he is doing and intends to do what he does." To this may be added an obvious corollary—that an honest mistake, the result of oversight or inadvertence, is not wilful unless persisted in after the attention of the vendor has been called to it, mere oversight or inadvertence cannot amount to wilful default. The vendor must have his attention drawn to the matter in question, and exercise his judgment or will on it before his act or default can be considered wilful.' *Re Postmaster-General & Colgan's Contract* [1906] 1 IR 287 at 294, per Barton J

Australia '"Wilful default" is a term which, like most other terms, must depend for its precise connotation on the subject-matter and the context. It does not connote dishonesty. Here [in relation to the director of a company] it means—a course of conduct consciously pursued in circumstances which would indicate to a reasonable man who considered the matter that the duty he has undertaken to the company is not being performed with due care for its interests.' *Gould v Mount Oxide Mines Ltd, Birbeck v Mount Oxide Mines Ltd, Bacon v Mount Oxide Mines Ltd* (1916) 22 CLR 490 at 529, per Isaacs and Rich JJ

Wilful misconduct

'There is such a mass of authorities to show what "wilful misconduct" is, that we should hardly be justified, as a Court of Appeal, in departing from them, even if we thought them to be wrong. Wilful "misconduct" means misconduct to which the will is a party, something opposed to accident or negligence; the misconduct, not the conduct, must be wilful. It has been said, and, I think correctly, that, perhaps, one condition of "wilful misconduct" must be that the person guilty of it should know that mischief will result from it. But to my mind there might be other "wilful misconduct". I think it would be wilful misconduct if a man did an act not knowing whether mischief would or would not result from it. I do not mean when in a state of ignorance, but after being told, "Now this may or may not be a right thing to do". He might say "Well, I do not know which is right, and I do not care. I will do this". I am much inclined to think that that would be "wilful misconduct" because he acted under the supposition that it might be mischievous, and with an indifference to his duty to ascertain whether it was mischievous or not. I think that would be wilful misconduct.' *Lewis v Great Western Rly Co* (1877) 3 QBD 195 at 206, CA, per Bramwell LJ

'I think there was here that degree of negligence which comes under the description of wilful misconduct. Looking at it in that light, I avoid the sort of puzzle . . . which may be thus expressed—"How am I to say that this is wilful misconduct when as a matter of fact the man was negligent in what he did? Negligence is one thing and wilful misconduct another, and therfore, to my mind, if I say that he is negligent I must say that he is not guilty of wilful misconduct." That does not seem to me to be a proper way to look at it. I think he is guilty of negligence, and the question is whether he is guilty of gross negligence, which comes to be wilful misconduct.' *Bastable v North British Rly Co* (1912) 49 SLR 446 at 452, per the Lord President

'In *Norris v Great Central Railway* [(1915) 85 LJKB 285 n], which was heard in this Court a short time ago, Mr Justice Lush and I adopted the definition of "wilful misconduct" given by Mr Justice Johnson in *Graham v Belfast and Northern Counties Railway* [[1901] 2 Ir R 13]—namely, that "wilful misconduct in such a special condition means misconduct to which the will is party as contradistinguished from accident, and is far beyond any negligence, even gross or culpable negligence, and involves that a person wilfully misconducts himself who knows and appreciates that it is wrong conduct on his part in the existing circumstances to do, or to fail, or omit to do (as the case may be), a particular thing, and yet intentionally does, or fails or omits to do, it, or persists in the act, failure, or omission, regardless of consequences". In so doing I drew attention to the fact that in *Forder v Great Western Railway* [[1905] 2 KB 532 at 535] Lord Alverstone made an addition to that definition in these terms, "or acts with reckless carelessness, not caring what the results of his carelessness may be". I ventured to say that I thought that that addition rather tended to introduce confusion into the clear definition which had been given by Mr Justice Johnson. All I meant was that the expression "reckless carelessness" was so indistinguishable from "gross negligence" that I feared it might lead in the future to merely gross negligence or culpable negligence being held to be wilful misconduct. But I now agree with the interpretation Mr Justice Lush applied to this expression—namely, "reckless indifference". I think the words mean that, and nothing more. I adopt that interpretation. In view of it I see no objection to the addition suggested by Lord Alverstone being made to the original definition given by Mr Justice Johnson.' *Sheppard & Son v Midland Railway* (1915) 85 LJKB 283 at 286, DC, per Avory J

'A number of definitions of wilful misconduct have been referred to. In *Lewis v Great Western Railway* [supra] . . . Lord Justice Bramwell says: "'Wilful misconduct' means . . . something opposed to accident or negligence; the misconduct, not the conduct, must be wilful", and Lord Justice Brett in the same case said: "In a contract where the term wilful misconduct is put as something different from and excluding negligence of every kind, it seems to me that it must mean the doing of something, or the omitting to do something, which it is wrong to do or to omit. . .". In the case of *Forder v Great Western Railway* [1905] 2 KB 532 Lord Alverstone cites from *Graham v Belfast and Northern Counties Railway* (1900) ([1901] 2 Ir R 13) the passage in Mr Justice Johnson's judgment to this effect: "Wilful misconduct in such a special condition means misconduct to which the will is party as contradistinguished from accident." Then the learned Lord Chief Justice adds the words, "or acts with reckless carelessness, not caring what the results of his carelessness may be".' *Buckton (Joshua) & Co Ltd v London & North Western Rly* (1916) 87 LJKB 234 at 242, per Astbury J

Wilful obstruction

'It appears to me that directly it is stated that the wall, and the soil which the wall upheld, are the property of the appellant . . . and when it is shown that the wall and soil having fallen across the highway the appellant was required to remove that which belonged to him and obstructed the highway, then there was that which was wilful on his part in leaving them there. It is said there must be some act on his part, and not merely an abstaining from doing some act, to make the word "wilful" apply. There are a number of cases in which an obstruction may not be in the first instance wilful, but yet when it is called to the notice of the owner of the property, and he is required to remove it and does not, it remains there by an exercise of the will; in other words, leaving it there is a wilful act on his part.' *Gully v Smith* (1883) 12 QBD 121 at 124, per Lord Coleridge CJ

'In considering what is meant by the wilful obstruction of a police constable in the execution of his duty within the meaning of the Prevention of Crimes Acts [now largely repealed], it is necessary to bear in mind that the words "wilfully obstructing" are used in association with the words "resisting" and "assault", and the reasonable inference is that wilful obstruction must have the same character as the other matters dealt with in the two relevant sections. In my opinion, to bring a case within these sections it must be proved that the obstruction had some physical aspect.' *Curlett v M'Kechnie* 1938 SC(J) 176 at 179, per Lord Fleming

[The Police Act 1964, s 51(3) makes it an offence 'wilfully' to obstruct a constable in the execution of his duty.] 'The word "wilfully" has been inconsistently interpreted in various Acts which define criminal offences. In some cases it has been held to import a requirement of mens rea. In other Acts it has not. The question in the present case is whether in the relevant section of the Police Act 1964 mens rea is imported by the use of the term "wilfully" or not. I agree . . . that when one looks at *Betts v Stevens* [[1910] 1 KB 1], where [the judge] said: "The gist of the offence to my mind lies in the intention with which the thing is done", it is clear that "wilfully" in this particular Act does import a requirement of mens rea.' *Willmott v Atack* [1976] 3 All ER 794 at 800, per May J

Australia [The respondent was charged with having 'wilfully' obstructed a member of the police force, acting under a warrant, in entering the house that he occupied, contrary to the provisions of the Lottery and Gaming Act 1936–1986 (SA), s 72.] 'It seems to us that we must distinguish between "knowingly" and "wilfully". Both words import *scienter* or intention, but, whilst "knowingly" will generally import knowledge of the attendant circumstances which make the act unlawful, we think that, in this context, the natural meaning of "wilfully" can be satisfied either by knowledge, or by a state of mind which adverts to the possibility of the existence of the attendant circumstances, but forbears to make inquiry, and wills to do the act whether or no [see *Davies v O'Sullivan (No 2)* [1949] SASR 208 at 210].' *O'Sullivan v Harford* [1956] SASR 109 at 115, per Napier CJ

New Zealand 'In determining whether a person was a "wilful" trespasser a distinction must be made between a bona fide belief in legal rights based on a mistaken idea of the relevant facts and a bona fide belief in legal rights which do not exist, no matter what view of the factual situation is held by the trespasser. . . . In the instant case, the appellant believed that he had the legal right to remain [in an office] until he had been given the information that had been denied him. He was under no genuine mistake about the factual situation, only about his legal rights in that situation. His trespass was, therefore, wilful, and he was rightly convicted.' *Police v Shadbolt* [1976] 2 NZLR 409, SC, per Wilson J

Wilful refusal

[The Lands Clauses Consolidation Act 1845, s 80, provides for the payment of costs by the promoters in cases of money deposited in the Bank [of England] under the provisions of the Act, or the special Act, except where such money has been so deposited by reason of the 'wilful refusal' of any party entitled thereto to receive the same, or to convey or release the lands in respect whereof the same is payable.] 'The legislature meant by the words, "wilful refusal", a refusal arising from an exercise of mere will or caprice, and not from an exercise of reason: and . . . as the petitioner's objections to the award had been argued at great length, and the Judges of the Court of Queen's Bench had taken time to deliberate before they pronounced judgment upon them, they could not have been captious or unsubstantial objections; and, therefore, the refusal of the plaintiff to accept the money when the company tendered it to him, was not a wilful refusal.' *Re East India Docks & Birmingham Junction Railway Act, ex p Bradshaw* (1848) 16 Sim 174 at 175, 176, per Shadwell V-C

WILL

A will or testament is the declaration in a prescribed manner of the intention of the person making it with regard to matters which he wishes to take effect upon or after his death. A codicil is of similar nature to a will as regards both its purposes and the formalities relating to it, but in general it is supplemental to and considered as annexed to a will previously made, being executed for the purpose of adding to, varying or revoking the provisions of that will. A codicil is nevertheless capable of independent existence, so that the revocation of a will does not necessarily effect the revocation of a codicil to it. The word 'will', although commonly used to describe one of a series of instruments expressing testamentary intentions, denotes the aggregate formal expression of such intentions of the testator existing at his death. However, although all wills and codicils subsisting at the testator's death are construed together as one testamentary disposition, they are not construed as one document. (50 Halsbury's Laws (4th edn) para 201)

The word 'will' shall extend to a testament, and to a codicil, and to an appointment by will or by writing in the nature of a will in exercise of a power, and also to a disposition by will and testament or devise of the custody and tuition of any child . . . and to any other testamentary disposition. (Wills Act 1837, s 1)

'Will' includes a nuncupative will and any testamentary document of which probate may be granted. (Supreme Court Act 1981, s 128)

'Will' includes any testamentary instrument or act, and "testator" shall be construed accordingly. (Wills Act 1963, s 6)

'A will is to be considered in two lights, as to the testament and the instrument. The testament is the result and effect in point of law, of what is the will; and that consists of all the parts; and a codicil is then a part of the will, all making but one testament: but it may be made at different times and different circumstances, and therefore there may be a different intention at making one and the other. The instrument is that writing in which the will is contained.' *Fuller v Hooper* (1751) 2 Ves Sen 242 at 242, per Lord Hardwicke LC

[A testator bequeathed property to trustees upon trust to pay interest to each of his four daughters for their own private use during their natural lives, the principal to go to their heirs or to any other to whom they might choose to 'will' it.] 'I am of opinion, that the words "to will it" mean to dispose of it by will.' *Paul v Hewetson* (1833) 2 My & K 434 at 436, per Leach MR

'The will of a man is the aggregate of his testamentary intentions, so far as they are manifested in writing, duly executed according to the statute. And as a will, if contained in one document, may be of several sheets, so it may consist of several independent papers, each so executed. Redundancy or repetition in such independent papers, will no more necessarily vitiate any of them, than similar defects if appearing on the face of a single document. Now it was argued that in the case of more than one testamentary paper, each professing in form to be the last will of the deceased, it is necessary for the court, before concluding that they together constitute the will, to be satisfied that the testator intended them to operate together as such. In one sense this is true, for the intention of the testator in the matter is the sole guide and control. But the "intention" to be sought and discovered, relates to the disposition of the testator's property, and not to the form of his will. What dispositions did he intend?—not which, or what number, of papers did he desire or expect to be admitted to probate—is the true question.' *Lemage v Goodban* (1865) LR 1 P & D 57 at 62, per Sir J P Wilde

'It is quite certain that "will" is a word which has, or may have, two meanings. Lord Hardwicke in *Fuller v Hooper* [supra] puts it quite clearly that a will means in one sense all the testamentary documents by which the testator's property is disposed of; and another meaning is not that, but that it is an instrument called a will irrespective of any codicils which may subsequently be made.' *Re Smith, Prada v Vandroy* [1916] 2 Ch 368 at 371, 372, CA, per Cozens-Hardy MR

Alteration in *See* ALTERATION; APPARENT

Appointment under *See* APPOINT

Condition in (Stipulation) *See* CONDITION

Confirmation of *See* CONFIRMATION

Contents of *See* CONTENTS

Informal or nuncupative will

Any form of words, whether written or nuncupative, that is, spoken by the testator in the presence of a credible witness, will suffice to constitute a soldier's or sailor's or airman's will, provided that it is a deliberate expression of his wishes and is intended to have testamentary effect. The will, whether formal or informal, may be revoked by a letter or other informal act expressing an intention to revoke, without any new will, provided that the circumstances of the revocation are the same as are required to give validity to a soldier's or sailor's or airman's will. (50 Halsbury's Laws (4th edn) para 272)

Last will

'With regard to the observation made on the term "last will"; the answer given was the true one; it is a general term, signifying only "a will".' *Walpole (Lord) v Cholmondeley (Earl)* (1797) 7 Term Rep 138 at 150, per Grose J

'As to the expression "last will", it means only the last disposition that a testator intends to make of his property.' Ibid at 151, per Lawrence J

'A person made his will, whereby he bequeathed his personal estate to his mother, and after several intervening limitations, devised the ultimate remainder of his real estate to T Phillipps. He afterwards acquired a new reversionary estate, which he also wished to dispose of; and his mother having in the meantime died, and consequently the bequest of his personal property having lapsed, . . . he makes another will, which he describes as his last will, on which stress is laid. . . . But it is not enough to say, that by making this will in terms large enough to include all his property, he must therefore have meant to revoke the former will; unless it be shown that he has made a disposition of the same property inconsistent with it.' *Thomas* d *Jones v Evans* (1802) 2 East 488 at 494, per Lord Ellenborough CJ

'These words "this is a codicil to the last will and testament of me" . . . apply to the will which at that time had legal existence. . . . I apprehend that when a testator refers in a codicil to a last will, and there is nothing in the contents of the codicil to point to any particular will, it must be construed to refer to the will in legal existence and not to a revoked will.' *Hale v Tokelove* (1850) 2 Rob Eccl 318 at 326, per Dr Lushington

'This instrument is intituled "the last will and testament of me relating to all my real estate whatsoever". This, by several decided cases, has been treated as a strong circumstance to be regarded in the question whether an instrument will operate as a revocation of all previous wills and testamentary instruments. I am confirmed in this view of the case by the circumstance, that, although the testator declares this to be his last will and testament, he limits and confines its effect, in this respect, to his real estate, by which he avoids revoking the testamentary instruments of April, 1838 [previous to the one in question] so far as they relate to personal estate.' *Plenty v West* (1852) 16 Beave 173 at 178, per Romilly MR

'Where there is a will described as the last will by the testator and disposing of the whole of the property, that must be revocatory of any former instrument.' *Richards v Queen's Proctor* (1854) 1 Ecc & Ad 235 at 242, per Sir John Dodson

'In all the cases where revocation has been held to be effected there has been proof of a difference of disposition. . . . The . . . paper contained the words, "This is my last Will and Testament". We are of opinion, that these words do not import that the paper contained a different disposition of the property nor that the mere fact of so calling it could possibly render it as revocatory instrument.' *Cutto v Gilbert* (1854) 9 Moo PCC 131 at 147, PC, per cur.

WILL (Verb)

'The relevant words of the clause [of a charterparty] are: "Should steamer be ordered on a voyage by which the charter period will be exceeded charterers to have the use of the steamer to enable them to complete the voyage, but for any time exceeding termination date charterers to pay market rate, if higher than rate stipulated herein." What is being dealt with is clearly the ordering of a voyage which "will" *ex necessitate*—it is immaterial whether or not the word "will" means "shall"—not which may, exceed the charter period. I have no doubt that the ordinary business man reading cl. 6 would give to it this meaning. It has been contended that I should read the clause as if the words were: "should the steamer be ordered on a voyage which, in fact, or which in the results, exceeds the charter period". If that had been the intention of the parties, it would have been easy to say so in terms in the charterparty. I can see no grounds for reading this clause as if it contained words other than those which, in fact, it contains, and to my mind the words "will be" suggest what is inevitable at the time the voyage is ordered. So construed, the clause has a natural and reasonable meaning. It deals with such a voyage as by the terms of the charterparty should not have been ordered and which inevitably would lead to a failure to redeliver the vessel within the contract period. . . . This clause must be reasonably construed, and a construction which imposes on the charterers the obligation to pay higher freight for a delay for which the owners themselves may be in part responsible, is not reasonable.' *Hector SS Co v Sovfracht (VO) Moscow* [1945] KB 343 at 348, per Atkinson J

[The articles of association of a private limited company which was incorporated in 1941 provided that 'every member who intends to transfer shares shall inform the directors who will take the said shares equally between them at a fair value.'] 'It is admitted that the words "every member . . . shall inform" the directors does create an obligation but it is argued by the defendants that the words "the directors . . . will take the shares" imports in some way the idea of an option or choice or volition on the part of the directors having regard to the inherent difference (not always observed) in the English language between the words "shall" and "will". I appreciate the force of that argument, but I cannot accept it. In this context, while the word "shall" clearly imports compulsion and obligation, the word "will" indicates as it seems to me a resultant prospective eventuality, in which the member has to sell his shares and the directors have to buy them, each being under an obligation to bring that eventuality into effect.' *Rayfield v Hands* [1958] 2 All ER 194 at 196, per Vaisey J

WILLING *See also* ABLE AND WILLING

'This appeal . . . raises an important question under s 25 [repealed] of the Finance [(1909–10)] Act of 1910. That section provides that the "gross value" of land [for the purpose of duties on land values] means the amount which the fee simple of the land if sold at the time in the "open market" by a "willing seller", in its then condition (subject to certain deductions) might be expected to realise. . . . The contest before us has turned mainly upon the words "open market" and "willing seller". . . . I am disposed to think that a willing seller is a person who is a free agent and cannot be required by virtue of compulsory powers to sell.' *Inland Revenue Comrs v Clay, Inland Revenue Comrs v Buchanan* [1914] 3 KB 466 at 471, 473, CA, per Cozens-Hardy MR

'It is well settled that an agreement "subject to contract" is in law of no binding effect and that a person who agrees "subject to contract" can change his mind for any reason. It is, therefore, not clear to me why on several occasions the courts have held that a person who has only agreed "subject to contract" is to be regarded as willing to purchase. I should regard the words "subject to contract" as a condition imposed on their willingness, but the trend of authority is against that view. If that were all, I should follow the trend of those decisions without comment, but no case has dealt with a willingness "subject to satisfactory survey". I feel no doubt that that is an important condition, and, in my judgment, a person is not "willing" who only agrees to purchase if the result of a survey, which has not yet been made, is satisfactory to him, for it is well settled that, if a prospective purchaser agrees to purchase subject to satisfactory survey, he is the arbiter of whether it is satisfactory. He is only willing on a contingency.' *Graham & Scott (Southgate) Ltd v Oxlade* [1950] 1 All ER 91 at 92, per Roxburgh J; affd [1950] 2 KB 257, CA

'A person may not properly be said to be "willing" to purchase, so as to entitle an agent to commission, unless he is irrevocably willing, that is, unless he has given irrevocable proof of his willingness by entering into a binding contract to purchase.' *McCallum v Hicks* [1950] 2 KB 271 at 276, CA, per Denning LJ

Between willing buyer and seller

'The formula "as between a willing buyer and a willing seller" is a common one, and, in our opinion, when applied to a transfer of any shares, imports, according to its ordinary and natural meaning, the conception of a separate bargain of sale by an individual seller to an individual buyer of those shares.' *Short v Treasury Comrs* [1948] 1 KB 116 at 124, CA, per cur.; affd [1948] AC 534

WIN

'I conceive that the coal is won when it is put in a state in which continuous working can go forward in the ordinary way. It is not when you first dig down to a seam of coal and come to water immediately, but when you have got the coal in such a state that you can go on working it, and make provision, if provision is necessary, for sufficient drainage.' *Lewis v Fothergill* (1869) 5 Ch App 103 at 111, per Lord Hatherley LC

'A coal-field is won when full practicable available access is given to the coal hewers so that they may enter on the practical work of getting the coal.' *Rokeby (Lord) v Elliot* (1879) 13 Ch D 277 at 279, per James LJ

WINDING APPARATUS

'Winding apparatus' means, in relation to a mine shaft or staple-pit, apparatus for lowering and raising loads through the shaft or staple-pit. (Mines and Quarries Act 1954, s 182)

WINDOW

'A window is not less a window because it is not capable of being opened, nor is it less a window because it is not fixed in a vertical plane. I think the glazed top [of a conservatory] was just as much a window as the fixed portions of the vertical side.' *Easton v Isted* [1903] 1 Ch 405 at 409, CA, per Joyce J

'I wish to be a little careful in the meaning that I am attaching to the word "windows". . . . We are not concerned with any question of repair to the brick or stone structures containing the actual windows. For the purposes of this case and of the question raised in the originating summons, I take "windows" to mean, and to be confined to, the glass panels and the wooden framework and apparatus in which the glass is placed.' *Holiday Fellowship Ltd v Hereford (Viscount)* [1959] 1 All ER 433 at 434, CA, per Lord Evershed MR

WINDSTORM

Canada 'The words as used in the policy [of insurance] "windstorm", "cyclone" and "tornado" cannot be considered as being synonymous. The ordinarily accepted meaning of the word "windstorm" by the public is a strong wind and not one of unusual vehemence. In default of a definition of windstorm in the policy or by statute, the restricted interpretation of windstorm being a wind of unusual violence or tumultuous force cannot be preferred to one which considers a windstorm as being a wind which practically reached a gale.' *Pollock Bros & Co Ltd v Halifax Ins Co* [1946] 2 DLR 476 at 480, Que SC, per Mackinnon J

WINE

'Wine' means any liquor obtained from the alcoholic fermentation of fresh grapes or of the must of fresh grapes, whether or not the liquor is fortified with spirits or flavoured with aromatic extracts. (Alcoholic Liquor Duties Act 1979, s 1(4))

'Made-wine' means any liquor obtained from the alcoholic fermentation of any substance or by mixing a liquor so obtained or derived from a liquor so obtained with any other liquor or substance but does not include wine, beer, black beer, spirits or cider. (Alcoholic Liquor Duties Act 1979, s 1(5))

'It is difficult to contend that what is generally called and known as "wine" loses that character by the admixture of a little water. Wines differ in alcoholic strength, and their Lordships do not believe that anyone would hesitate to apply the word "wine" to such a mixture, or that it would be an unnatural use of language to do so.' *Read v Lincoln (Bp)* [1892] AC 644 at 656, per cur.

[The question was whether the addition of quinine to wine made the mixture cease to be wine within the meaning of the Licensing (Consolidation) Act 1910, s 65 (repealed; cf now the Licensing Act 1964, s 199(f)).] 'The only question for the Court is whether there were materials for the justices to come to the conclusion they came to—namely, that the liquid was wine. It is contended by counsel for the appellant that it was so unpalatable as to cease to be wine. It is a question of degree, the two extremes being in one case a very small quantity of pleasant medicine in a very large quantity of very good wine, in the other case a very large quantity of nasty medicine in a small quantity of wine. Between these extremes are many degrees which have resulted in the commercial problem of how to put enough medicine in wine to make it cease, for the purpose of argument, to be wine, and yet remain palatable enough to drink. There is abundant evidence to justify the finding.' *Sharp v Sparkes* (1926) 70 Sol Jo 1069 at 1070, per Lord Hewart CJ

WINNINGS

'Winnings' includes winnings of any kind and any reference to the amount or to the payment of winnings shall be construed accordingly. (Betting, Gaming and Lotteries Act 1963, s 55)

'Winnings' includes any prizes or other winnings of any kind and any reference to the amount or to the payment of winnings shall be construed accordingly. (Gaming Act 1968, s 52(1))

'Winnings' includes winnings of any kind, and references to amount and to payment in relation to winnings shall be construed accordingly. (Betting and Gaming Duties Act 1981, s 12(4))

[The Betting, Gaming and Lotteries Act 1963, s 55(1) (as substituted by the Gaming Act 1968, s 53) defines 'gaming' as the playing of a game of chance for 'winnings' in money or money's worth.] 'As I see it the sole question here is whether the introduction of the word "winnings" first in the Act of 1960 and then in the Act of 1963 has altered the law as it previously existed, namely, that gaming took place only when there was not only the chance of winning but also the chance of losing, in other words where some stake had been hazarded. For my part, I cannot think that the addition of the word "winnings" has in any way altered the law as it previously existed. Indeed, it seems to me that, in this context, the context of gaming, winnings does denote the money or money's worth which comes to a player over and above what he has staked.' *McCollom v Wrightson* [1967] 3 All ER 257 at 259, 260, per Lord Parker CJ

WIRELESS TELEGRAPHY

In this Act, except where the context otherwise requires, the expression 'wireless telegraphy' means the emitting or receiving, over paths which are not provided by any material substance constructed or arranged for that purpose, of electromagnetic energy of a frequency not exceeding three million megacycles a second, being energy which either (a) serves for the conveying of messages, sound or visual images (whether the messages, sound or visual images are actually received by any person or not), or for the actuation or control of machinery or apparatus; or (b) is used in connection with the determination of position, bearing, or distance, or for gaining information as to the presence, absence, position or motion of any object or of any objects of any class. (Wireless Telegraphy Act 1949, s 19)

WITH

[The Sexual Offences Act 1956, s 13, makes it an offence for a man to commit an act of gross indecency 'with' another man.] 'This court has come to the conclusion . . . that the word "with" in s 13 of the Sexual Offences Act 1956 does not mean "with the consent of", but has the somewhat looser meaning of merely "against" or "directed towards".' *R v Hall* [1963] 2 All ER 1075 at 1077, CCA, per cur.; also reported in [1964] 1 QB 273 at 277

[By RSC 1965, Ord 6, r 8(1), a writ is valid for the purpose of service for twelve months beginning with the date of its issue.] 'It is no doubt a pity that this inconvenience should arise from the use in the rule of the word "with" instead of the word "from"; but even the shortest single word can affect the whole meaning of any enactment. I do not think that the proposition that a period stated "as beginning with" a certain date does begin on that date depends on any fine distinction, legal subtlety or empty formality. In my view it depends on the plain and natural meaning of ordinary English words.' *Trow v Ind Coope (West Midlands) Ltd* [1967] 2 All ER 900 at 913, per Salmon LJ

WITH REFERENCE TO

[The Theft Act 1968, s 30(3), provides that where a person is charged in proceedings not brought by that person's wife or husband with having committed any offence 'with reference to' that person's wife or husband or to property belonging to the wife or husband, the wife or husband shall be competent to give evidence at every stage of the proceedings.] 'Prima facie it would seem that the words "with reference to" have been intentionally used in preference to "against" in order to widen the category of criminal proceedings against a spouse in which the other spouse shall be competent to give evidence. Whether this be right or not, the words in fact used are ordinary non-technical English words carrying a wider meaning than the word "against" had it appeared in this context in their stead.' *R v Noble* [1974] 2 All ER 811 at 814, CA, per cur.

WITH RESPECT TO

Australia 'In the context of legislation granting power to make regulations, the phrase "with respect to", said Kitto J, in *Herald and Weekly Times v Commonwealth of Australia* [[1967] ALR 300 at 303] "demands", and, as I read his words, demands only, "substantial connection" between the grant of power and the impugned legislation. I accept that the phrase "with respect to" may sweep into the shelter of the grant a wider range of topics than the bare preposition "for".' *Paull v Munday* (1979) 36 LGRA 303 at 306, 307, per Bray CJ

Australia 'The word "for", to my mind, imports the notion of purpose. One must find out what a regulation really does. If its operation reveals that it has a purpose, one must go on and ask whether, if the language of one or more given paragraphs in the subsection is denoting a purpose, the revealed purpose is described by, or comprehended in, that language. . . . The expression "with respect to" imports, in this context, a connexion between a legislative provision and a head of subject matter.' Ibid at 309, 310, per Wells J

WITHDRAW

'What Bennitt by this document agrees to do is "to withdraw from the firm" in consideration of Gray or his executors paying him or his assigns £1,000, by ten yearly instalments, the first instalment to be paid on the 1st of January, 1890. . . . "Withdraw" seems to me to infer plainly two things. First, that the withdrawing partner shall make over to the continuing partners all his interest in the partnership and in the partnership assets, whether there be real or personal estate, whether there be outstanding contracts, or anything of the kind. That seems to me to be clearly the first thing indicated by the term "withdraw". Secondly, it seems to me—applying the ordinary rules of partnership law—that the continuing partners shall indemnify the retiring partner against all the liabilities of the firm from that time forth. They take the assets, they take the benefit of the contracts, they take the chances of success for the future, and they must keep him indemnified. By "indemnify" I do not mean executing any deed or giving any security, but that they must undertake the liabilities that are in abeyance.' *Gray v Smith* (1889) 43 Ch D 208 at 212, 213, CA, per Kekewich J

'I am inclined to think that the expressions "discontinuing" a licence, "withdrawing" a licence, and "withholding" a licence, which for some inscrutable reason the parties to the lease of 1874 chose to use in preference to the simple words of the legislature, may without any strain of language be applied indiscriminately to a case of forfeiture and a case of non-renewal.' *Bryant v Hancock & Co* [1899] AC 442 at 445, per Lord Macnaghten

Australia 'While it may be that, in the context of the law of partnership, the words "withdraw" or "withdrawal" would usually convey the notion of one of a number of partners retiring from the partnership and making over to the other partners all his interest in the partnership and in the partnership assets, the other partners continuing to carry on the partnership business in partnership as between themselves [see *Gray v Smith* (supra)] it is . . . clearly inappropriate, where those words are used in the context of a partnership comprising but two parties, to give to them any meaning beyond "determine", "dissolve" or "put an end to", if only because partnership is a relation which exists between two or more persons carrying on a business in common with a view to profit and, after the withdrawal or retirement taking effect, there will not, in such a case, remain two or more persons continuing in such a relationship.' *Van Der Waal v Goodenough* [1983] 1 NSWLR 81 at 89, per Powell J

WITHHOLD

'The covenant . . . is that the lessee will not assign, underlet, transfer or part with the possession of the flat without the consent of the landlords, such consent not to be withheld in the case of a respectable and responsible person. . . . It appears to me, dealing with the words which I find in this covenant, that, as such consent is not to be withheld in the case of a respectable and responsible person, if the lessee applies for such consent and within a reasonable time that consent is not granted, then within the meaning of the covenant it is withheld.' *Lewis & Allenby* (1909) *Ltd v Pegge* [1914] 1 Ch 782 at 785, 787, per Neville J

Australia [A proposal for fire insurance contained the following declaration: 'I have not withheld any information likely to affect the acceptance of this proposal.'] 'The word "withheld" means more than "omitted to communicate". It means "refrained from disclosing", and would not be satisfied by an omission through failure to advert to the subject.' *Saunders v Queensland Insurance Co Ltd* (1932) 45 CLR 557 at 567, per Dixon J

WITHIN

'According to the common construction of the English language, "within a fortnight before Michaelmas" means, during the period which elapses in the fortnight immediately before Michaelmas. To say that it means, between the time of the expression being used and the commencement of that fortnight, would be inconsistent with the common interpretation of the words.' *Thomas v Lambert* (1835) 3 Ad & El 61 at 62, per Littledale J

'Within any number of days after an act is to be understood exclusive of the day of the act.' *Williams v Burgess* (1840) 10 LJQB 10 at 11, per Littledale J

'According to the true meaning of the Act [Metropolitan Paving Act 1817, s 24 (repealed), which empowered commissioners to rate inhabitants 'within' a street], "houses within the street" are houses to which there is no access except from the street. I do not say that is so in every case; but if a house is only accessible by a gateway from the street, it is prima facie "within the street". Nobody can doubt that Burlington House is in the street called Piccadilly, and that if buildings were erected on both sides of the gateway, it would still be in Piccadilly. The same may be said of Northumberland House, in the Strand. If a space before a house be covered with buildings, the house remains in the street, whether it be approached by an access greater or smaller. The principle will apply *a multo fortiori* when the property to be rated is not merely houses, but also tenements "within the street".' *Baddeley v Gingell* (1847) 1 Exch 319 at 334, per Rolfe B

Australia 'The word "within" in relation to a period of time does not usually mean "during" or "throughout the whole of it"; it is more frequently used to delimit a period "inside which" certain events may happen.' *Reynolds v Reynolds* [1941] VLR 249 at 252, per O'Bryan J

Australia 'The modern rule in relation to a period of time fixed by statute "within" which an act is to be done after a specified event is that the day of the event is to be excluded; the next day is that first day of the stipulated period and the time expires on the last day of the period, counting from and of course including the first day.' *Morton v Hampson* [1962] VR 364 at 365, per cur.

WITHOUT BEING MARRIED *See*

UNMARRIED

WITHOUT CHARGE

Australia 'The first question is whether the testator's daughter . . . is under any obligation to contribute [to certain duties] seeing that the right . . . given to her by the will is a right to reside there [in the testator's residence] "without charge of any kind". I think those are wide enough to exempt her from any such burden.' *Brown v Brown* (1921) 22 NSWSR 106 at 112, 113, per Street CJ in Eq

WITHOUT COLOUR OF RIGHT

New Zealand [The offence, created by the Police Offences Act 1927 (NZ), s 32 (repealed; see now the Crimes Act 1961, s 228) which is commonly called 'unlawful conversion' is defined as (inter alia) unlawfully and "without colour of right', but not so as to be guilty of theft, taking or converting to one's own use a motor car or other vehicle, etc.] 'It would seem that the words "without colour of right" are wide enough to include all acts of taking or converting which in a general sense may be said to be unlawful. If that be so, the word "unlawfully" is surplusage. It is not necessary for the purpose of this appeal to decide that point, so I will do no more than say that "unlawfully" has the effect of preserving such defences, if any, as may exist in law whether taking or converting be with or without colour of right. The Court must therefore look to see if there is any lawful right to use the truck in the manner in which it was used. It must also consider the question of colour of right. The essence of the defence of colour of right is honesty of purpose. Where an accused person really believes he has the right asserted, it is a good defence even if he is mistaken both in fact and in law. Similarly, an honest belief that the owner would authorise the act is a good defence. It is for the prosecution to prove there was no colour of right. If a prisoner put forward, however wrongheadedly, an honest claim of right, he ought to be acquitted.' *Murphy v Gregory* [1959] NZLR 868 at 872, per Henry J

WITHOUT DEDUCTION

'He [a settlor] covenanted to pay his daughter's trustees £25,000 "without any deduction". These words are very important. They show that possible deductions were thought of, and that the settlor clearly intended that his daughter's trustees should be paid £25,000 in full, without any deduction of any sort or kind. It is urged that there is no difference between a covenant to pay £25,000 and a covenant to pay £25,000 without deduction. But the latter form of expression leaves no room for doubt as to the intention of the parties, whilst if the words "without any deduction" are omitted, the intention is by no means equally clear. The language of the covenant in this case is too plain to be got over. It is agreed on all hands that the daughter's trustees are to receive £25,000 free from estate duty. But it is urged that the "settlement estate duty", although called a "further estate duty", and made payable by the executors of the covenantor in respect of the settled fund, ought not to be treated as a deduction from it, but rather as a charge on it when paid over. I cannot accede to this agreement. . . . His covenant is so plainly worded as to preclude any deduction from the

£25,000 in favour of the residuary legatees.' *Re Maryon-Wilson, Wilson v Maryon-Wilson* [1900] 1 Ch 565 at 571, 572, CA, per Lindley MR

'In the present case certain annuities and legacies were given "without deduction", and it is obvious that there is an ambiguity, having regard to the position in which we find the authorities, underlying those words. "Without deduction" has been held to mean without any deduction except that of income tax, and those decisions bind me; but it is quite obvious that a layman may very reasonably, in giving what he believes to be effect to the words which the testator has used in this will, come to the conclusion that when he says "without deduction" he means without deduction, and therefore that you cannot deduct income tax. But that is not so.' *Re Musgrave, Machell v Parry* [1916] 2 Ch 417 at 424, per Neville J

'I cannot regard the direction that the rentcharge was to be payable "without any deduction except for death duties" as imposing any liability on the owner of the rentcharge to contribute to any death duties for which he would not have been liable in the absence of that direction.' *Re Portman (Viscount) (No 2)* [1925] Ch 294 at 301, 302, per Romer J

'The phrase "without deduction of income tax" has the same meaning as free of income tax.' *Re Williams, Williams v Templeton* [1936] Ch 509 at 514, CA, per Greene LJ

'The larger part of income tax is at the present time collected by deduction at the source, and under promised legislation that method of collection is being extended. The association of income tax with "deduction" will no doubt therefore become more direct and more obvious to many people. But that will not alter the meaning to be attributed to the phrase "without deduction" in the gift of an annual sum. If a testator means a specified annuity to be received clear of income tax, he should say so in express terms, and not use a general formula. In so doing, a testator would not, in the general case, be abandoning an accustomed method of stating his ideas, for views on income tax are not usually conveyed under the cover of an amiable general phrase.' *Re Hooper, Phillips v Steel* [1944] Ch 171 at 176, per Uthwatt J

WITHOUT DELAY

Canada 'I emphasize that s 231(3) [of the Income Tax Act 1970–71–72 (Can), c 63] provides that the demand served pursuant to it requires production of the documents "within such reasonable time as may be stipulated therein". The demand in this case required their production "without delay". The words "without delay" are in their ordinary sense the meaning of the word "immediate". See Shorter Oxford Dictionary (1973) vol 1, p 1025, col 1: "Immediate . . . 4. Of time: . . . b. Taking effect *without delay* . . ." (emphasis added).' *Re Joseph and Minister of National Revenue* (1985) 20 DLR (4th) 577 at 580, Ont SC, per Galligan J

WITHOUT ISSUE

'It is now quite settled, that if a gift is made to A, and on failure of issue, or if A die without issue, then B, such a bequest over, whether it be of real estate or of personalty—being taken in the legal signification of the terms to mean after a general failure of issue, a failure of issue at any time—is void for remoteness, and the abolute interest is given to the first taker; unless there appears something in the will indicating a different intention.' *Candy v Campbell* (1834) 2 Cl & Fin 421 at 427, per Lord Brougham & Vaux LC

'By the Wills Act [1837], s 29, a change was made in the law, and it was thereby enacted that "In any devise or bequest of real or personal estate the words, 'die without issue', or 'die without leaving issue', or 'have no issue', or any other words which may import either a want or failure of issue of any person in his lifetime or at the time of his death, or an indefinite failure of his issue, shall be construed to mean a want or failure of issue in the lifetime or at the time of the death of such person, and not an indefinite failure of his issue, unless a contrary intention shall appear by the will." Now, speaking generally, the effect of that I take to be this, that in those cases where before the Wills Act the words "die without issue", and "die without leaving issue", have been read as importing a general and indefinite failure of issue, those words are now to be construed in the same way as in the exceptional cases to which I have referred, namely as importing failure of issue at a particular time. Of course, that is in the absence of any intention to the contrary, and the meaning, which is only a prima facie meaning, must be controlled by the context. Then, if it stood there, I should say that the meaning in this present case was that there was to be an executory gift over in the event of the daughter dying at any time without leaving issue living at that time. But a case of

White v Hight [(1879) 12 Ch D 751] which was cited to me, was very much relied upon, and certainly it approaches very near to the present case, although it is not quite identical with it. . . . So far as I am aware, *White v Hight* has not been followed by any other judge, for in *Re Jackson's Will* [(1879) 13 Ch D 189] it was not cited, and the passage relied on in the judgment of Sir George Jessel has no bearing on the present case. Finding, then, that *White v Hight* had not been followed by North J and finding also that in the present case Kay J, who did not decide the point, expressed a strong opinion that the petitioner had not obtained an absolute vested interest, I think I am at liberty to follow what is my own view, namely, that the words ought to be read "without leaving issue alive at the time of the death of the petitioner".' *Clay v Coles* (1887) 57 LT 682 at 683, 684, per Stirling J

'In every case in which the phrase "without leaving issue" or any similar expression has been read as "without having" etc, the latter phrase has, I think, always been used in the sense of "without having had", that is, without having had in the lifetime of the person whose death is referred to, and not in the more general sense of without having either after his death or his lifetime—in other words without having at any time whether before or after his death.' *Re Davey, Prisk v Mitchell* [1915] 1 Ch 837 at 845, CA, per Joyce J

'It is clear that the words "leaving issue" in their primary significance point to the period of death. It cannot be said that, in the ordinary meaning of the words, Mrs West died leaving issue, since both of her sons predeceased her, but there is a well-known rule of construction which is sometimes referred to as the rule in *Maitland v Chalie* [(1822) 6 Madd 243] and is stated by Romer LJ in *Re Cobbold* [*Re Cobbold, Cobbold v Lawton* (1903) 2 Ch 299, 304]. In reading Romer J's judgment I propose to read it in the form which be undoubtedly intended it to bear. This was pointed out in *Re Davey* [*Re Davey, Prisk v Mitchell* [1915] 1 Ch 847, n]. So amended, the judgment of Romer LJ is as follows: "If you have a gift by will to A for life, and after A's death to his children in terms which would give them an absolute interest in A's lifetime, and then you have a gift over simply in these terms, 'if A dies without leaving children', you are to construe the expression 'leaving' so as not to destroy any prior vested interest. In other words, you construe it as meaning"— now I read the words as altered— "without having had a child who had attained a vested interest. That must now be treated as well settled." In my judgment the rule thus laid down in *Re Cobbold* does not necesarily apply to a case such as the present, where you do not find the two dispositions in a will. Here the disposition in favour of the children of A occurs in a gift in default of appointment, under a settlement, and the subsequent provision in the event of A dying "without leaving children" occurs in a codicil exercising the power of appointment. There is no authority, so far as I am aware, which has extended the rule to such a case. . .. Assuming that the rule of construction stated by Romer LJ does not apply to the present case, I am still of the opinion that I ought to construe the words "without leaving issue" as meaning "without having had a child who has attained a vested interest".' *Re Milling's Settlement, Peake v Thom* [1944] Ch 263 at 268, 269, per Morton J

See, generally, 50 Halsbury's Laws (4th edn) para 619

WITHOUT PREJUDICE

'If a man says his letter is without prejudice, that is tantamount to saying "I make you an offer which you may accept or not, as you like; but if you do not accept it, the having made it is to have no effect at all". It appears to me, not on the ground of bad faith, but on the construction of the document, that when a man says in his letter it is to be without prejudice, he cannot be held to have entered into any contract by it if the offer contained in it is not accepted.' *Re River Steamer Co, Mitchell's Claim* (1871) 6 Ch App 822 at 832, per Mellish LJ

'We must consider the peculiar position of the parties as disclosed by the correspondence. It appears that after the purchaser received the abstract the solicitors examined it with the deeds and made requisitions. These were acts which assumed that a contract existed, and yet the plaintiff now proposes to take proceedings upon the footing that there was no contract at all. It will, no doubt, be said that everything was done "without prejudice to any question which might arise as to the contract of purchase", and that this reservation having been assented to, the defendant is bound by it. But, in my opinion, the words "without prejudice to any question which may arise" mean any question in the execution of the contract, and not to any question as to the existence of the contract.' *Thomas v Brown* (1876) 1 QBD 714 at 723, per Quain J

'I shall not attempt to define the words "without prejudice"—but what I understand by negotiation without prejudice is this: The plaintiff or defendant—a party litigant—may say to his opponent: "Now you and I are likely to be engaged in severe warfare; if that warfare proceeds, you understand I shall take every advantage of you that the game of war permits; you must expect no mercy, and I shall ask for none; but before bloodshed let us discuss the matter, and let us agree that for the purpose of this discussion we will be more or less frank; we will try to come to terms, and that nothing that each of us says shall ever be used against the other so as to interfere with our rights at war, if, unfortunately, war results." That is what I understand to be the meaning, not the definition, of "without prejudice".' *Kurtz & Co v Spence & Sons* (1887) 57 LJ Ch 238 at 241, per Kekewich J

'What is the meaning of the words "without prejudice?" I think they mean without prejudice to the position of the writer of the letter if the terms he proposes are not accepted. If the term proposed in the letter are accepted a complete contract is established, and the letter, although written without prejudice, operates to alter the old state of things and to establish a new one. A contract is constituted in respect of which relief by way of damages or specific performance would be given. Supposing that a letter is written without prejudice then, according both to authority and to good sense, the answer also must be treated as made without prejudice.' *Walker v Wilsher* (1889) 23 QBD 335 at 337, CA, per Lindley LJ

'The meaning of the words "without prejudice to the charterparty" has been settled by decisions which cannot be questioned. The meaning, as settled by the cases of *Shand v Sanderson* [(1859) 28 LJ Ex 278] and *Gledstanes v Allen* [(1852) 12 CB 202], is that it is a term of the contract between the charterers and the shipowners that, notwithstanding any engagements made by the bills of lading, that contract shall remain unaltered. Therefore, in this case the captain was bound to sign the bill of lading presented to him; but his doing so was to be "without prejudice to the charterparty". These words do not limit the obligation under the charterparty to sign the bills of lading presented to him; but when he has done so it does not affect the contract contained in the charterparty.' *Hansen v Harold Brothers* [1894] 1 QB 612 at 618, 619, CA, per Lord Esher MR

'Objection is taken that, where negotiations take place with the parties for the settlement of anticipated litigation, those negotiations whether or not they are expressly stated to be without prejudice, are, and must be treated in this Court as without prejudice in this sense that statements or admissions made by either party at such interviews are not to be admissible as evidence against the maker of the statement or admission. The principle seems to depend upon this, that the Court has always taken the view that every facility is to be given to persons who are in litigation, or anticipate litigation, to come together fully and frankly, to use a popular expression, to place their cards upon the table with a view to coming to some arrangement, and if that is the position, statements and admissions made under those circumstances will not be treated as admissions against the parties.' *Scott Paper Co v Drayton Paper Works Ltd* (1927) 44 RPC 151 at 156, per Clauson J

'The principle to be applied to "without prejudice" negotiations and "without prejudice" correspondence is perfectly clearly set out in the cases to which counsel for the defendants referred us. . . . From those cases it seems to me that the principle which emerges is that the court will protect, and ought to protect so far as it can, in the public interest, "without prejudice" negotiations because they are very helpful to the disposal of claims without the necessity for litigating in court and, therefore, nothing should be done to make more difficult or more hazardous negotiations under the umbrella of "without prejudice". I am well aware . . . that letters get headed "without prejudice" in the most absurd circumstances, but these letters, in my judgment, are not letters headed "without prejudice" unnecessarily or meaninglessly. They are plainly "without prejudice" letters and, therefore, the court, in my judgment, should be very slow to lift the umbrella of "without prejudice" unless the case is absolutely plain.' *Tomlin v Standard Telephone & Cables Ltd* [1969] 3 All ER 201 at 205, per Ormrod J (dissenting)

Australia 'It needs to be recognised that the words "without prejudice" can mean quite different things. Normally they are the formula by which a party invokes privilege against subsequent tender in evidence of a communication. Whether the protection is a part of the law of privilege, or an exclusion on grounds of public policy does not here matter (vide Phipson on Evidence (12 ed), para 623A and para 679). However the phrase is also commonly used (or misused) to convey a reservation of rights. Nowadays it is used in contracts as equivalent to a proviso. A party may say in a perfectly open situation "I am doing this entirely without prejudice to my rights to do that". Sometimes such a statement will be accurate. Other times the law will adjudge it to be a pious but ineffective wish.' *Alleyn v Thurecht* [1983] 2 Qd R 706 at 718, per Thomas J

Canada 'Correspondence without prejudice is one of the exclusionary rules. Contrary to popular belief in some quarters that the shibboleth "without prejudice" written on a letter protects it from subsequent use as an admission is not accurate: see 4 Wigmore (2nd edn), paras 1060–2. That learned authority points out that the basis of the exclusion is a hypothetical admission or concession for the purpose of securing peace or settlement; and since it does not represent the parties' true belief it cannot be taken as a true admission. Therefore, the question to be considered is, what was the view and intention of the party in making the admission; whether it was to concede a fact hypothetically, in order to effect a settlement, or to declare a fact really to exist.' *Kirschbaum v 'Our Voices' Publishing Co* [1971] 1 OR 737 at 738, 739, per Haines J

WITHOUT RESERVE

'When a property is offered for sale without reserve, the meaning, and the only meaning that can be attached to it, is, that, of the bidders—the public—who choose to attend the sale, whoever bids the highest shall be the purchaser; that the biddings shall be left to themselves, and that there shall be no bidding on the part of the vendor. And it is not without reserve, the biddings and not left free from the interference of the vendor, if any means or contrivance, it matters not what, be resorted to for the purpose of preventing the effect of open competition. I consider, therefore, the term "without reserve" to exclude any interference on the part of the vendor (or, which is the same thing, of those who come in under the vendor), which can, under any possible circumstances affect the right of the highest bidder to have the property knocked down to him, and that, without reference to the amount to which that highest bidding shall go.' *Robinson v Wall* (1847) 2 Ph 372 at 375, per Lord Cottenham LC

WITNESS *See also* CREDIBLE WITNESS

In civil proceedings, every person is now a competent witness unless he is (1) a child of such tender years that he has neither sufficient intelligence to testify nor a proper appreciation of the duty of speaking the truth; (2) a person who at the time of being tendered as a witness is mentally incapable of testifying; (3) deaf and dumb, and unable by writing or signs or otherwise to understand questions put to him, or to communicate his answers to others; (4) a person who, from temporary causes, such as illness or drunkenness, is for the time being incapable of understanding questions and of giving a rational account of events; or (5) a person who does not appreciate the nature and obligation of an oath or affirmation.

In criminal cases the rules as to the competence and incompetence of witnesses are the same as in civil matters, subject to special statutory rules governing the unsworn evidence of young children, the right of an accused person to make an unsworn statement instead of giving evidence on oath or affirmation, and the evidence of the accused's wife or husband. (17 Halsbury's Laws (4th edn) para 231)

[The Wills Act 1837, s 9 (as now substituted by the Administration of Justice Act 1982, s 17) provides (inter alia) that the signature to a will shall be made or acknowledged by the testator in the presence of two or more 'witnesses' present at the same time, who shall attest and subscribe the will in the presence of the testator.] 'The normal meaning of "attesting" is testifying or bearing witness to something, and the normal meaning of "witness" is one who is a spectator of an accident or one who is present at an incident. Is mere presence, without the faculty of sight, enough to constitute a person a "witness" for the purposes of s 9 of the Wills Act 1837? Is an act which the witness cannot see done in his presence? The object of the Act is clear. One witness is not enough. The presence of two witnesses is made necessary in order to give certainty and avoid fraud. In the light of common sense, and without any authority, I should be inclined to hold that for the purposes of the Act a "witness" means, in regard to things audible, one who has the faculty of hearing, and in regard to things visible, one who has the faculty of seeing. The signing of a will is a visible matter. Therefore, I think a will is not signed "in the presence of" a blind person, nor is a blind person a witness for the purposes of the section.' *In the Estate of Gibson* [1949] P 434 at 436, 437, per Pearce J

Expert witness

'An expert's opinion is admissible to furnish the court with scientific information which is likely to be outside the experience and knowledge of a judge or jury. If on the proven facts a judge or jury can form their own conclusions without help then the opinion of an expert is unnecessary. In such a case if it is given dressed up in scientific jargon it may make judgment more difficult. The fact that an expert witness has impressive scientific qualifications does not by that fact alone make his opinion on matters of human nature and behaviour within the limits of normality any more helpful than that of the jurors themselves; but there is a danger that they may think it does.' *R v Turner* [1975] 1 All ER 70 at 74, CA, per Lawton LJ

WOMAN

'Woman' means a woman of the age of eighteen years or upwards. (Employment of Women, Young Persons and Children Act 1920, s 4)

'Woman' means a woman who has attained the age of eighteen. (Factories Act 1961, s 176)

'Woman' includes a female of any age. (Sex Discrimination Act 1975, s 5(2))

WOODLAND

'Woodland' includes all land used primarily for the growing of trees. (Agriculture Act 1967, s 57)

WORD

There are few words, if indeed there are any, which bear a meaning so exact that the reader can disregard the surrounding circumstances and the context in ascertaining the sense in which they are employed. Where a word has more than one proper and recognised meaning, the question in which sense it is used in a particular passage must be decided by the context and the surrounding circumstances, and no one meaning can be treated as having a paramount claim to be adopted in preference to any other. (50 Halsbury's Laws (4th edn) para 430)

Any reference in this Act to words shall be construed as including a reference to pictures, visual images, gestures and other methods of signifying meaning. (Defamation Act 1952, s 16)

In this section [which amends the law of defamation by making the publication of words in the course of a performance of a play publication in permanent form] 'words' includes pictures, visual images, gestures and other methods of signifying meaning. (Theatres Act 1968, s 4(3))

In Trade Marks Acts

[The Patents, Designs and Trade Marks Act 1883, s 64 (repealed; see now the Trade Marks Act 1938, s 9), enacted that a trade mark must consist of or contain at least one of certain essential particulars, one of which was a 'word' or words having no reference to the character or quality of the goods and not being a geographical name.] 'Clause (a) of s 10 of the Act of 1888 . . . does not say that the name to be registered need be the name of a living person, nor the name of the applicant or registration. . . . "Irdby" is clearly a "word" within (e), unless it is the name of an "individual" within (a), and I am not prepared to hold it to be within (a). The language of (e) is clear, that of (a) ambiguous, as regards the names of persons who have not, and never had, a real existence. . . . The practice of the office has been to allow the registration of names of imaginary persons, although such names are not printed, impressed, or woven in any particular or distinctive manner. The view taken in the office has been that such names are "words" within clause (e) of s 10, and not names of "individuals" within clause (a). For the reasons I have given, I think this view and the practice founded upon it are correct.' *Re Holt & Co's Trade Mark* [1869] 1 Ch 711 at 719, 720, CA, per Lindley LJ

[The Trade Marks Act 1905, s 9(5) (repealed; see now the Trade Marks Act 1938, s 9(e)), enacted that any other distinctive mark, but a name, signature, or 'word' or words, other than such as fell within the descriptions in paragraphs (1), (2), (3) and (4), should not, except by order of the Board of Trade or the Court, be deemed a distinctive mark.] 'The applicant . . . has contended that no word which is a surname can be "adapted to distinguish" the goods of the person applying to register from the goods of all other persons, as although such word may for a time serve much purpose, if the person registering is the only one of that name in the trade, yet it ceases to be "adapted to distinguish" as soon as another person of the same name enters the trade. In fact the applicant insisted that a word being a surname is incapable of registration under s 9, para 5. . . . By s 9 of the Act, para 1, certain names by para 2 certain signatures, and by paras 3 and 4 certain words may be registered as trade marks, without any preliminary order of the Board of Trade or of the Court. . . . A surname is a word, and therefore is prima facie registrable upon an order of the Board of Trade or the Court being obtained. . . . Every person may still bona fide use his own name although part of his name may be the registered surname.' *Teofani & Co Ltd v Teofani, Re Teofani & Co's Trade Mark* [1913] 2 Ch 545 at 571, 572, CA, per Swinfen Eady LJ

WORK (Noun) *See also* MATERIALS; WORKS

For the purposes of this Part [Part I: health, safety and welfare in connection with work, etc.]—

(a) 'work' means work as an employee or as a self-employed person;
(b) an employee is at work throughout the time when he is in the course of his employment, but not otherwise; and
(c) a self-employed person is at work throughout such time as he devotes to work as a self-employed person.

Health and Safety at Work etc Act 1974, s 52(1))

[A testatrix by her will made a pecuniary gift to a vicar for his 'work'.] 'The question is what she really meant by "for his work", and I have come to the conclusion, without very much doubt about the matter, that by "his work" she meant the work which he carried out and which is referred to and described in the evidence which I have read. She knew of it, and apparently took a considerable interest in it, and she refers to it at the end of the will where she says her clothes are to go to the Rev S G Tinley "for his benevolent work in the parish", showing plainly that there the work she had in mind was work in the parish in regard to which a contribution of clothes would be suitable and apt. I have no doubt that that is the work which she had in mind there, and, having regard to that part of the will and to the fact that it was proved that she knew of, and was interested, in the particular work to which evidence has been directed, I have no doubt that she had a similar intention when making the bequest of £500 for his work in the disposition which I am now considering. It was suggested that I am not really entitled to look at the evidence about the Rev S G Tinley's work because the word "work" is unambiguous and is all-embracing; but if it was a term of ambiguity, then I could look to any evidence which defined the generality of the term, on the authority of *Re Rees* [*Jones v Evans* [1920] 2 Ch 59]. In *Re Rees* it was held that "missionary purposes" is an ambiguous term, and evidence was admissible to show that in that particular will it was intended to be used in a more narrow sense. If the word "work" has a degree of ambiguity about it, then the evidence would be equally admissible. In my view the words "his work" have a sufficient degree of ambiguity to permit the introduction of evidence of this kind just as much as it was admissible in *Re Rees* in relation to the words "missionary purposes". When one finds "his work" referred to in the middle of a clause which is almost entirely devoted to charitable matters, and when one finds that the word "work" at the end is work for which a gift of clothes is considered a suitable donation, there is, I think, some doubt left in one's mind as to what exactly this lady did mean by reference to "his work". In my judgment, evidence was admissible for the purpose of clearing up that doubt, and, in my view, the evidence has cleared up the doubt, and the work to which she was referring was the work to which the evidence has been directed.' *Re Simson, Fowler v Tinley* [1946] 2 All ER 220 at 222, 223, per Romer J

[The British School of Egyptian Archaeology was an unincorporated body founded in 1905 by Sir Flinders Petrie, its objects, as stated in reg 3 of its regulations, being 'A To conduct excavations and to pay all expenses incidental thereto. B To discover and acquire antiquities and to present the same to public museums. To hold exhibitions, when practicable. C To publish works. D To promote the training and assistance of students. All of these objects shall be carried on in relation to Egypt and any part of the former kingdom of Egypt.'] 'Although it is an inelegant phrase and might, in some contexts, be too vague to mean anything in particular, a "work" is something done in relation to whatever the object of study may be. A musical composition is a "work", and one usually hears the word "opus" in that connection. In reg 3C, the word "works" means, in my opinion, works in relation to Egypt and the former kingdom of Egypt, and the phrase "to publish works", when read in connection with excavations, means that the works to be published are works which shall discover to the public the results of the excavations which it is the school's object to carry out.' *Re British School of Egyptian Archaeology, Murray v Public Trustee* [1954] 1 All ER 887 at 890, per Harman J

New Zealand [The plaintiff had hired to the second defendant scaffolding for use by the second defendant in the erection of a building. The employees of the plaintiff were to erect, alter and dismantle the scaffolding as required, the charge being all-inclusive. The question was whether the performance of the contract was 'work' for the purposes of the Wages Protection and Contractors' Liens Act 1939. If so, it would support a lien in favour of the plaintiff.] 'In the present case to supply on hire is the basis of the contract, the labour being ancillary to that. . . . The labour is restricted to making the plant hired usable by others and to removing it when the work is done. For these reasons I do not consider that the supplying of scaffolding on hire is "work" within the meaning of the Act.' *Winstone Ltd v Wellington City & F E Seagar Ltd* [1972] NZLR 399 at 404, per White J

WORK (Verb)

'Worked ironstone land' means land which has been excavated in the course of winning and working ironstone by opencast operations, and includes land on which materials extracted in the course of such operations have been deposited. (Mineral Workings Act 1951, s 41)

For the purposes of this Act—
(a) the working of a mine shall be deemed to include the operation of driving a shaft or outlet therefor;
(b) the working of a quarry shall be deemed to include the operation of removing overburden thereat;
(c) a mine or quarry shall be deemed to be worked notwithstanding that the only operations carried on thereat are operations carried on with a view to abandoning the mine or quarry or for the purpose of preventing the flow therefrom into an adjacent mine or quarry of water or material that flows when wet, but shall not be deemed to be worked by reason only that pumping operations are carried on thereat for the purpose of supplying water to any person.

(Mines and Quarries Act 1954, s 182)

[A local Act provided that no barge should be 'worked' or navigated within a certain area, unless in charge of a licensed waterman or duly qualified person.] 'The question really involves two:—whether each of those barges was being "worked or navigated" within the true meaning of s 66 of the Act, and if it was, whether there was in charge of each craft a licensed waterman or duly qualified person. Looking at the by-laws to see in what sense those who drew them understood it, it is quite clear that a barge being towed is being "worked and navigated", although that is not conclusive. By the words "worked or navigated", I understand a state of moving forward, whether caused by oars, or horses, or steamer. I have no hesitation in holding that these barges being towed were "worked or navigated".' *Elmore v Hunter* (1877) 3 CPD 116 at 120, DC, per Lindley J

[The plaintiff was engaged, after finishing work for the day and clocking-off, in voluntarily helping a fellow workman on a private job in the defendants' machine shop. The question was whether the plaintiff was 'working' on the premises within the meaning of the Factories Act 1937, s 14(1) (repealed; see now the Factories Act 1961, s 14(1)) and regulations thereunder.] 'I do not think that the word "working" is wide enough to cover what the plaintiff was doing at the time. Mr Thomson was really pursuing a hobby of his own, making a table for himself, and all the plaintiff was doing was helping him to pursue his hobby. The plaintiff was a mere volunteer at the time, not employed under any contract of service or for services. He was voluntarily helping Mr Thomson to do a private job of his own. The plaintiff was not at that time "employed" in manual labour, he was voluntarily engaged in manual labour. He was doing it on his own account and not in the course of his employment or for the benefit of his employers. If he could be said to be "working", he has not working under an agreement with the defendant company or under any contract of service.' *Napieralski v Curtis (Contractors) Ltd* [1959] 2 All ER 426 at 432, per Havers J

WORK TO RULE

'"Work to rule" has a perfectly well-known meaning, namely, "give the rules a meaning which no reasonable man could give them and work to that".' *Secretary of State for Employment v Associated Society of Locomotive Engineers and Firemen (No 2)* [1972] 2 All ER 949 at 959, NIRC, per Sir John Donaldson P

WORKER

'Worker' includes a boy, woman and girl. (Agriculture Wages Act 1948, s 17)

'Worker' means a person employed under a contract of service or apprenticeship and 'employer' and 'employed' have corresponding meanings. (Agriculture (Safety, Health and Welfare Provisions) Act 1956, s 24)

'Worker' (subject to the following provisions of this section) means an individual regarded in whichever (if any) of the following capacities is applicable to him, that is to say, as a person who works or normally works or seeks to work—

(a) under a contract of employment; or
(b) under any other contract (whether express or implied, and, if express, whether oral or in writing) whereby he undertakes to do or perform personally any work or services for another party to the contract who is not a professional client of his; or
(c) in employment under or for the purposes of a government department (otherwise than as a member of the naval, military or air forces of the Crown) . . . in so far as any such employment does not fall within paragraph (a) or (b) above,

otherwise than in police service. (Trade Union and Labour Relations Act 1974, s 30(1), as amended by the Armed Forces Act 1981, s 28(2))

[By ibid, sub-s (2), 'worker' includes an individual working as a person providing general medical, pharmaceutical, dental, or ophthalmic services under arrangements made by an Area Health Authority or Family Practitioner Committee.]

'Worker' means any person—

(a) who has entered into or works under a contract with an employer (whether express or implied, and, if express, whether oral or in writing) whether it be a contract of service or of apprenticeship or any other contract whereby he undertakes to do or perform personally any work or services for another party to the contract who is not a professional client of his; or
(b) whether or not he falls within the foregoing provision, who is a homeworker;

but does not include any person who is employed casually and otherwise than for the purpose of the business of the employer or other party to the contract. (Wages Councils Act 1979, s 28)

[As to the meaning of 'homeworker', *see* HOMEWORKER.]

'The fact that a person is self-employed and may thus be said to be in business on his own account and in one sense working for himself does not prevent him from being a "worker". The definition of "worker" [in the Industrial Relations Act 1971, s 167(1) (repealed; see now the Trade Union and Labour Relations Act 1974, s 30(1), supra)] is wide enough to embrace the self-employed'. *Broadbent v Crisp* [1974] 1 All ER 1052 at 1058, per cur.

WORKING CLASSES

'Much has been said in this case as to the meaning of "working classes". . . . These words, "working classes", have appeared in a number of Acts for the last hundred years. I have no doubt that a hundred years ago, the expression had a meaning which was reasonably well understood. "Working classes" fifty years ago denoted a class which included men working in the fields or the factories, in the docks or in the mines, on the railways or on the roads, at a weekly wage. The wages of people of that class were lower than those of the other members of the community, and they were looked upon as a lower class. That has all now disappeared. The social revolution in the last fifty years has made the words "working classes" quite inappropriate today. There is no such separate class as the working classes. The bank clerk or the civil servant, the school teacher or the cashier, the tradesman or the clergyman do not earn wages or salaries higher than the mechanic or the electrician, the fitter or the mineworker, the bricklayer or the dock labourer. Nor is there any social distinction between one or the other. No one of them is of a higher or lower class.' *Green (H E) & Sons v Minister of Health* [1947] 2 All ER 469 at 470, 471, per Denning J; [1948] 1 KB 34

[A testator left a gift for the 'working classes' and their families.] 'The phrase "working class", if it means anything, may mean persons who occupy council houses or houses of that standard. There are now many privately owned houses of that standard, and it may be that "working class" means persons who would occupy such houses if they could obtain them. I cannot think that the description of someone as a man who is anxious to live in a council house connotes that he is poor. Poverty is no part of the qualification for obtaining a house of that type, and, accordingly, I do not see that I can infer poverty from the words used by the testator.' *Re Sanders' Will Trusts, Public Trustee v*

McLaren [1954] 1 All ER 667 at 669, 670, per Harman J

'Some years ago in *Green & Sons v Minister of Health (No 2)* [supra] I said that the phrase "working classes" was quite inappropriate in modern conditions. Fifty years ago the phrase was well understood to mean people who worked with their hands, whether on the land or on the railways or in the mines. Such people in those days earned wages which on the whole were much less than the rest of the community. Nowadays the phrase is quite inapplicable. People who work on the land or in factories often earn more than people who work in offices or shops. Craftsman earn as much as or more than clergymen or teachers. Yet we still have to apply the test whether a house is provided for the working classes. The only way to do it, I think, is to ask whether the house is provided for people in the lower income range, or in other words for people whose circumstances are such that they are deserving of support from a charitable institution in their housing needs. Applying this test, I am quite satisfied that the Guinness Trust does provide houses for such people. The majority of them do fall within the lower income group, and they are deserving of support by this charitable institution. The people in the buildings provided by the trust include dockers from Bermondsey, railway workers at Vauxhall, office cleaners and dustmen in Chelsea, and furniture hands in Shoreditch. There can be no doubt to my mind that this trust in fact provides houses for people who in the old days would have been called of the working class and who today are properly described as falling within the lower income group.' *Guinness Trust (London Fund) Founded* 1890 *Registered* 1902 *v Green* [1955] 2 All ER 871 at 873, per Denning LJ

'I think that the adjectival expression "working men" plainly has some flavour of "lower income" about it, just as "upper class" has some flavour of affluence, and "middle class" some flavour of comfortable means. Of course there are impoverished members of the "upper" and "middle" classes, just as there are some "working men" who are at least of comfortable means, if not affluence: one cannot ignore the impact of such things as football pools. But in construing a will I think that I am concerned with the ordinary or general import of words rather than exceptional cases; and, whichever may be the future meaning of "working men" or "working class", I think that by 1967 such phrases had not lost their general connotation of "lower income".' *Re Niyazi's Will Trusts* [1978] 3 All ER 785 at 788, per Megrarry V-C

WORKING CONDITIONS

Canada 'We are all of the opinion that contracting out as it affects job security of members of the bargaining unit is properly a subject of collective bargaining under that Act and that the term "working conditions" in s 5(1) [Fire Departments Act, RSO 1980, c 164] includes matters relating to job security. It has been held that "working conditions" are words of very broad compass and that the legislature by the use of such general words intended the full-time firefighter to have a reasonable role in determining matters related to his or her employment. . . . In addition to those matters, firefighters must of necessity be concerned about the training and competence of their fellow workmen. Here, the current practice of using volunteer firefighters is clearly a working condition.' *Re City of Welland and Welland Fire Fighters Association, Local 481* (1982) 141 DLR (3d) 425 at 431, 432, Ont Div Ct, per Craig J, dissenting on other grounds

WORKING DAY *See also* DAY; WEATHER WORKING DAYS

'Customary working days' means, in relation to any shop assistant, the daily number of hours during which shop assistants of his class are, while unaffected by any order made under this section, customarily employed in or about the business of the shop in which he is employed. (Shops Act 1950, s 41)

'I think it is wrong to say that a "working day" consists of twenty-four hours—that period comprehends both a day and a night. . . . If the hours of night were to be comprehended in the "working days", I would expect that to be distinctly provided.' *Mein v Ottmann* (1904) 6 F 276 at 281, per Lord Trayner

'In every twenty-four consecutive hours from the commencement of the loading or discharging, 500 tons were to be loaded or discharged if the weather did not hinder it or a holiday or Sunday intervene. And in my opinion the words "working day" in the clause before us are used only in antithesis to the days which were Sundays or holidays.' *Turnbull, Scott & Co v Cruikshank & Co* (1904) 7 F 265 at 273, per Lord Trayner

'A special term is introduced [in a charterparty] by which it is provided that the discharge of cargo shall be not less than thirty "*mille*" per working day. . . . It is not disputed that Sundays and holidays occurring during the discharging of the cargo would not be working days, and they would therefore have to be deducted in calculating the number of working days allowed, and I cannot see any reason in logic or otherwise why the same thing should not be done in regard to days which have been declared to be "surf days" by the captain of the port.' *British & Mexican Shipping Co Ltd v Lockett Brothers & Co Ltd* [1911] 1 KB 264 at 279, 280, CA, per Vaughan Williams LJ

'I . . . think that the words "working day" [in a local Act] . . . mean the days upon which you may work, and not the days on which you do work, and mean, therefore, the six working days of the week, that is, the days of the week other than Sunday.' *Hanbury v Llanfrechfa Upper Urban District Council* (1911) 75 JP 307 at 308, per Neville J

'The first thing to ask in the construction of this clause in the charterparty is: what is meant by "working day"? The word "day" is one thing; a day is a day of twenty-four hours. It may be qualified, however, by the word "working", and if a workman or an employer were asked—"What is your working day? How many hours is your working day?"—he would not say "Twenty-four hours". That is not the working day; one is asleep for a good part of the twenty-four hours. To say a working day is a period of twenty-four hours seems to me to ignore entirely the fact that the word "working" qualifies the word "day" and cuts it down, and, in my opinion, the expression "working day" means the part of a day during which work is carried on. Therefore, to find the working day, one must find what are the customary or ordinary hours worked either at a particular place or in a particular trade.' *Alvion Steamship Corpn of Panama v Galban Lobo Trading Co SA of Havana* [1955] 1 All ER 457 at 459, CA, per Lord Goddard CJ; see also [1955] 1 QB at 442

WORKING HATCH

'The clause as to the time for discharging is this: "The cargo to be taken from alongside by consignees at port of discharge, free of expense and risk to the vessel, at the average rate of 125 tons per working hatch per day, weather permitting." . . . That appears to me to assume that there may be a different number of working hatches on one day than on another. If one considers why there may be a different number of working hatches on one day as compared with another, the answer may be that the hatch is not a working hatch if there is no coal in it to work, but the hatch may be a working hatch though there is coal in it and you do not work it. In the original form in which it came into charterparties, the definition of a working day was a day on which ships in the port ordinarily worked, although a particular ship did not work on that day. A working hatch in the same way, it seems to me, is a hatch with coal in it on that day, and the fact that you do not happen to work it on that day does not prevent it being a working hatch which you ought to have worked, and which must be taken into account on the average.' *The Sandgate* [1930] P 30 at 32–34, CA, per Scrutton LJ

WORKING HOURS

'Working hours' means the time during which the persons employed are at the disposal of the employer, exclusive of any intervals allowed for rest and meals; and 'hours worked' has a corresponding meaning. (Shops Act 1950, s 74)

WORKING PLACE

'The . . . claim is made under the Building Regulations 1926, reg 15 [revoked; see now the Construction (Working Places) Regulations 1966] . . . which reads: "Every working-place and approach thereto shall be efficiently lighted." . . . One thing seems quite clear to my mind, and that is that the regulation is not designed to provide that the whole of the premises should be "efficiently lighted". The regulation says "Every working-place and approach thereto". It contemplates, therefore, a specific working-place where people are doing a specific piece of work. I do not think it can extend to the case of a night-watchman who—leaving out, conceivably, his hut—has no specific working-place at all.' *Field v Perrys (Ealing) Ltd* [1950] 2 All ER 521 at 522, 523, per Devlin J

'I cannot see why I am not to give the words "working place" the ordinary meaning of the English language, that is, a place where work is being done.' *Ball (George & Sons Ltd v Sill* (1954) 52 LGR 508 at 509, per Lord Goddard CJ

' "Working place" means, I think, every place

at which men are working or may be expected to work.' *Gough v National Coal Board* [1959] 2 All ER 164 at 174, per Lord Denning

'Without . . . attempting a more precise definition, by a "working place" within reg 24 [of the Building (Safety, Health and Welfare) Regulations 1948 (repealed; see now the Construction (Working Places) Regulations 1966)] is in my opinion intended a limited and defined area, something at any rate in the nature of a platform and something substantially flat or level, in or on which a workman is set to work for an appreciably continuous period of time.' *Gill v Donald Humberstone & Co Ltd* [1963] 3 All ER 180 at 186, HL, per Lord Evershed

WORKING PLATFORM

'A "working platform" [in the Construction (Working Places) Regulations 1966, reg 28] is a structure erected for the purpose of providing the workman with somewhere from which he can work in a convenient way and at a convenient level to carry out whatever functions he is employed to perform. A "working place" is something having the same character. It is not the *locus in quo* of the demolition, or whatever the work may be, as a whole. It is not the whole of a particular floor of a building or anything of that kind. It is a flat area afforded by some part of the structure of the building, of the same sort of size that a working platform would be and affording facilities for the workman to do whatever is for the time being his particular function in a convenient way and where he will work at that function for some appreciable time.' *Boyton v Willment Bros Ltd* [1971] 3 All ER 624 at 628, CA, per Buckley LJ

'A "working platform", within the meaning of reg 22 of the regulations of 1948 [Building (Safety, Health and Welfare) Regulations 1948 (repealed; see now the Construction (Working Places) Regulations 1966)] is part of what is commonly known as the scaffolding which is commonly known as the scaffolding which is used in building operations.' *Hutchinson v Cocksedge & Co Ltd* [1952] 1 All ER 696, n at 697, per Croom-Johnson J

'"Working platform or stage" would seem to indicate an erected structure and "working place" a part of the existing structure of a building used as a working platform—that is, as a platform from which to work.' *Gill v Donald Humberstone & Co Ltd* [1962] 3 All ER 456 at 458, CA, per cur.

WORKMAN

[Under the Companies Act 1929, s 264 (repealed; see now the Companies Act 1985, Sch 19, para 13] there was paid in a winding-up in priority to all other debts all wages of any 'workman or labourer', not exceeding £25, in respect of services rendered to the company during two months next before the relevant date.] 'I do not propose to attempt to give a general definition of what constitutes a "clerk or servant" within the meaning of head (b) of s 264(1) or what constitutes a "workman or labourer" within the meaning of head (c) of that sub-section. . . . I think that one general broad distinction is that head (c) is primarily directed to persons who are engaged in what is known as manual labour, while head (b) is directed, in the case of businesses, to the black-coated staff and also to persons who would be called servants, although they would not be denominated clerks and who, in the ordinary way, one would not think of as being engaged in manual labour. That, I think, is the broad distinction. Then, of course, you get this class of distinction, that your workman or labourer is usually engaged on some production job, while the clerk or servant is generally not directly engaged on production work. Therefore, to a certain extent, the contrast is between manual labour and service other than manual labour, but one has to look in each particular case at all the circumstances.' *Re London Casino Ltd, National Provincial Bank's Application* (1942) 167 LT 66 at 67, per Uthwatt J

WORKS *See also* EMERGENCY WORKS; UNDERTAKERS' WORKS

The expression 'works' means and includes electric lines, also any buildings, machinery, engines, works, matters, or things of whatever description required to supply electricity and to carry into effect the object of the undertakers under this Act. (Electric Lighting Act 1882, s 32)

'Works' means—

(a) any factory (within the meaning of the Factories Act 1961);
(b) any mine or quarry; or
(c) any premises used by way of trade or business for the purpose of the storage, transport or distribution of any articles or for the supply of electricity or other forms of power; together with any machinery or equipment installed in any factory, mine,

quarry or premises as aforesaid and any land occupied for the purposes thereof, but does not include any factory, mine, quarry, premises or land outside Great Britain.

(Iron and Steel Act 1982, s 37(1))

[A covenant to repair provided that the lessees would from time to time well and sufficiently repair all and singular the furnaces and other 'works'.] 'It is clear that the tramplates and sleepers in question are not part of the demised premises, and, therefore, if they are included at all in the covenant to repair, it must be under the word "works". But that word must be construed in connection with the other words, with which it is immediately joined, "furnaces and other works, houses and other buildings". Upon referring to the other parts of the lease it will be found that this description, in a great degree, runs through the whole of the instrument; and I think that the word "works" was not intended to refer to any such works as mere temporary works of the tenant not affixed to the freehold, and laid down by him only for the purpose of the more convenient transport of the iron ore from the mine to the smelting-house, but that it was intended to refer to permanent and substantial works, similar in their nature to the furnaces, houses and other buildings which are spoken of.' *Beaufort (Duke) v Bates* (1862) 3 De G F & J 381 at 394, per Turner LJ

'The position is shortly this: there was a contract between these parties for the building of a certain number of houses, and the contract provided that the conditions in the schedule thereto should be construed as forming part of the contract. When we come to look at those conditions we find that throughout them the expression "the works" is constantly used as meaning the whole of the works contemplated by the contract, whether executed by the builder, or, in certain events, completed by the building owner through the employment of some other contractor. Thus Condition 1 provides that: "The works shall be carried out in accordance with the directions and to the reasonable satisfaction of the architect"—that is all the works. By Condition 4: "The contractor shall provide everything necessary for the proper execution of the works", meaning the whole of the works. Condition 9 provides that: "The contractor shall, at the request of the architect, immediately dismiss from the works" any person who is incompetent or misconducts himself, clearly referring to the whole of the works. And particularly is this clear in Condition 26, which provides that in the event of the builder being in default "the employer shall take such steps as in the opinion of the architect may be reasonably necessary for completing the works", that is completing the works by other persons after the builder has ceased to have anything to do with them. It is by the light of those earlier conditions that we must read the arbitration clause, Condition 32, on which the present question turns. That condition provides that any dispute or difference arising between the parties is to be referred to arbitration, subject to this, that "such reference, except on the question of certificate"—that is the withholding of a certificate by the architect to which the builder claims to be entitled, and this is not such a question—"shall not be opened until after completion or alleged completion of the works" unless with the written consent of the parties. As it is not in dispute here that the whole of the building contracted for have not been completed, the arbitration was premature.' *Smith v Martin* [1925] 1 KB 745 at 749, 750, CA, per Bankes LJ

WORLDLY ESTATE

[A testator by his will devised such 'worldly estate' as it had pleased God to bestow upon him.] 'My worldly estate comprises as well real, as personal. His worldly estate comprises all he had in the world.' *Beachcroft v Beachcroft* (1715) 2 Vern 690 at 691, per Cowper LC

'The words "My Worldly Estate", unless qualified by other expressions, necessarily comprise both real and personal estate, and there is nothing in this will which amounts to such a qualification.' *Muddle v Fry* (1822) 6 Madd 270 at 274, per Leach V-C

'In the beginning of the will, he [the testator] bequeaths "all his worldly estate and fortune", and he intends by these words to include every thing; and in the residuary clause he makes use of the same expressions; therefore what they would pass in the beginning, they would also pass in this clause.' *Acheson v Fair* (1843) 2 Con & Law 208 at 217, per Sugden LC

WORLDLY GOODS

'The first two clauses in this will are sufficient, in my opinion, to decide this question. The trustees are to hold all the testator's worldly goods upon the trusts under mentioned. If we were to turn "worldly goods" into "personal estate", it would not make the sentence read better. The second "all" must refer to the same property as the first—all (viz) which was given to the trustee, which certainly includes some premises to be quitted. There were no leaseholds, as I am informed. If the premises are to be included in that word "all", then the "all" here referred to must correspond with "all the worldly goods" which were given to the other parties. . . . Declare, therefore, that the words "all my worldly goods, of what nature or kind soever, and wheresoever they may be found", include the whole of the real and personal estate of the testator; and the words, "the rest of all my worldly goods", carry the residuary real and personal estate, which passed to the children named in the will and Richard Wright, born in due time after the testator's decrease.' *Wright v Shelton* (1853) 18 Jur 445 at 446, per Page Wood V-C

Australia 'The words "all my worldly goods" include realty if aided by the context.' *Re Lay* [1934] SASR 196 at 198, per Richards J

Canada 'Two questions are raised for determination, the first of which is: "1 The meaning of the words, 'all my worldly goods and money' that is, does this bequest cover both personalty and realty?" . . . Standing by themselves, the terms "goods" and "money" relate only to personalty. The epithet "worldly" adds nothing to them, because "goods" and "money" are necessarily "worldly things". . . . In the sentence which follows the quoted bequest, the subject-matter of the gift is referred to as "all goods, property and money". The added term "property" indicates that something more than goods and money are being disposed of, because the term "property" includes realty as well as personalty. Inasmuch as the estate in fact includes realty, the words "all . . . property" suggests that the real property was intended to be included in the bequest; especially so because there is no other reference to real estate, and the whole will suggests that the whole estate was intended to be disposed of. . . . This possible view is supported by Jarman on Wills, 7th edn, at p 978, where it is said: "Again, the phrase 'worldly goods', though properly applicable only to personal estate, will include the realty if aided by the context." . . . The answer to the first question must therefore be that the bequest covers both personalty and realty.' *Re Troup Estate* [1945] 1 WWR 364 at 365, 366, Man KB, per Dysart J

WORRY

For the purposes of this Act worrying livestock means—

(a) attacking livestock, or
(b) chasing livestock in such a way as may reasonably be expected to cause injury or suffering to the livestock or, in the case of females, abortion, or loss of or diminution in their livestock.

(Dogs (Protection of Livestock) Act 1953, s 1)

WORSEN

'"Worsening" evidently requires a comparison of some sort. The most natural comparison is between the state of something now and its state at an earlier time. A person's position has worsened if it is worse now than it was last year. The comparison may, of course, be with something else; a man's position may be said to have worsened compared with someone else's or compared with what it would have been if he had been in another job.' *Tuck v National Freight Corpn* [1979] 1 All ER 215 at 233, HL, per Lord Fraser of Tullybelton

WORSHIP

Place of worship

The expression 'place of worship' means any church, chapel, or other building used for public religious worship, and includes a burial ground, Sunday or Sabbath school, caretaker's house or minister's house attached to or used in connection with and held upon the same trusts as a place of worship. (Places of Worship (Enfranchisement) Act 1920, s 5)

In this section 'place of worship' means a building licensed by the bishop for public worship in accordance with the rites and ceremonies of the Church of England, being a building used wholly for the purposes of such worship and purposes ancillary thereto, or partly for those purposes and partly for other ecclesiastical purposes of the parish or purposes ancillary thereto, and includes a building which, pursuant to an agreement under the Sharing of Church Buildings Act 1969, is to be used as a place of worship jointly with another church and is to be owned by the Church of England only or to be jointly owned by that church and any other church. (Pastoral Measure 1983, s 46(10))

'We have had much discussion on the meaning

of the word "religion" and of the word "worship", taken separately, but I think that we should take the combined phrase, "place of meeting for religious worship" as used in the Act of 1855 [Places of Worship Registration Act 1855]. It connotes to my mind a place of which the principal use is as a place where people come together as a congregation or assembly to do reverence to God. It need not be the God which the Christians worship. It may be another God, or an unknown God, but it must be reverence to a deity. There may be exceptions. For instance, Buddhist temples are properly described as places of meeting for religious worship. But, apart from exceptional cases of that kind, it seems to me the governing idea behind the words "place of meeting for religious worship" is that it should be a place for the worship of God. I am sure that would be the meaning attached by those who framed this legislation of 1855.' *R v Registrar General, ex p Segerdal* [1970] 3 All ER 886 at 889, 890, CA, per Lord Denning MR

Australia 'The noun "worship" is defined in the Shorter Oxford Dictionary . . . as follows: "Reverence or veneration paid to a Being or Power regarded as supernatural or divine; the action or practice of displaying this by appropriate acts, rites or ceremony.' This definition rather suggests to my mind the observance of a standard ritual or practice in the nature of divine service, although not necessarily conducted in a church or other fixed place.' *Macrae v Joliffe* [1970] VR 61 at 62, 63, per Starke J

Canada [By the Assessment Act, RSO 1970, c 32, s 3, para 3 (see now RSO 1980, c 31) all real property in Ontario is liable to assessment and taxation, subject to certain exemptions from taxation, including 'places of worship'. The question arose whether a church building which stood vacant and unoccupied came within the exemption.] 'A reading of s 3 reveals that in a number of paragraphs the word "used" is specifically applied so that use is made a condition for exemption. If actual use were also essential to the exemption provided for in para 3, the legislature could easily have so stated just as it had in the others. The words "place of worship" do not have as necessary to their meaning the actual use of the buildings or structures. Rather they name a certain type of building which had as its purpose worship, the legislature has not seen fit to qualify "place of worship" by adding the conditions that it be actually used as a place of worship or that it continue to carry on actively as a place of worship and I am not prepared to read these conditions into the legislation.' *Re Regional Assessment Comr Region No 31 & Corpn Synod of Toronto & Kingston v The Presbyterian Church of Canada* (1974) 4 OR (2d) 773 at 776, Ont HCJ, per Lacourciere

Public worship

'I have come to the conclusion that premises are held upon trust to be used for the purposes of public religious worship none the less because some of the minor or less important parts of those premises are not used for public worship.' *Stradling v Higgins* [1932] 1 Ch 143 at 152, per Maugham J

'There is . . . a strong case for the view that by the phrase "public religious worship" is meant and intended forms or ceremonies of worship distinct from "private religious worship", namely, the religious devotions which a man may offer up in the privacy of his bedroom or which are confined to the members of a family or household. In the latter case the worship is conducted alone or in the intimate presence only of the worshipper's family or household. By contrast in "public worship" the individual worshippers may come from widely different places and may be personally entirely unknown to one another.' *Church of Jesus Christ of Latter-Day Saints v Henning (Valuation Officer)* [1963] 2 All ER 733 at 735, HL, per Lord Evershed; also reported in [1964] AC 420 at 430

'A building on private property must somehow declare itself open to the public if activities which are carried on inside it are to be public, and the nature of those of activities must be brought to the notice of the outside world if they are not to be private activities. As it was variously put from the Bench: the worship must be made public; the doors of the place of worship must be open not merely subjectively in the minds and hearts of the worshipping community but objectively in some manifestation of their intention that it should be open; there must be signs to indicate at least that the place is a place of religious worship, perhaps also that acts of such worship are performed there at particular times, and that the public would not be trespassers if they entered but have permission, express or implied, to go there and to attend worship there.' *Broxtowe Borough Council v Birch* [1983] 1 All ER 641 at 651, CA, per Stephenson LJ

Canada 'Counsel for the appellant cited no decision in support of his proposition that religious services held in a private house cannot be "public worship". In earlier days in this Province it was not uncommon, in lack of a church, to hold public worship in a private house.' *Schmunk v Brook* [1944] 3 DLR 643 at 645, BCCA, per O'Halloran JA

WORTH *See also* VALUE; WILL; WORLDLY ESTATE

'This is the case of a nuncupative will, and I think it clear that the terms "all I am worth", without other words to control them, must pass real as well as personal estate.' *Huxtep v Brooman* (1785) 1 Bro CC 437 at 437, per Lord Thurlow LC

WOUND

In order to constitute a wounding there must be an injury to the person by which the skin is broken; the continuity of the whole skin must be severed, not merely that of the cuticle or upper skin. The skin severed need not, however, be external, but it is not sufficient to prove merely that a flow of blood was caused, unless there is evidence to show where the blood came from. (11 Halsbury's Laws (4th edn) para 1199)

'The words of the statute [(1722) 9 G 1 c 22, s 1 (repealed)], are, "shall unlawfully and maliciously kill, maim, or wound any cattle", etc. It was laid in this case as maliciously "wounding", which word does not import a permanent injury.' *R v Haywood* (1801) Russ & Ry 16 at 17, CCR, per cur.

'It is essential for you to be quite clear that a wound was inflicted. I am inclined to understand, and my learned brothers are of the same opinion, that, if it is necessary to constitute a wound, that the skin should be broken, it must be the whole skin, and it is not sufficient to show a separation of the cuticle only. You will, therefore, have to say on the first three counts, whether there was a wounding in the sense in which I have stated it: viz was there a wound—a separation of the whole skin?' *R v M'Loughlin* (1838) 8 C & P 635 at 638, per Coleridge J

'In my judgment, if one looks as the cases there is a continuous stream of authority (to which I myself can find no exception at all) which does establish that a wound is . . . a break in the continuity of the whole skin. I can see nothing in the authorities which persuades me to think otherwise. This has become such a well-established meaning of the word "wound" that in my judgment it would be very wrong for this court to depart from it." *JJC (a minor) v Eisenhower* [1983] 3 All ER 230 at 233, per Robert Goff LJ

Australia 'A "wounding" . . . is the infliction of an injury which breaks the continuity of the skin.' *R v Newman* [1948] ALR 109 at 110, per Barry J

Australia 'Unlawful wounding means the infliction of a wound under circumstances which the law does not regard as lawful.' Ibid at 111

Australia '[In] *Vallance* (1961) 108 CLR 56, Kitto J was content to use the Oxford English Dictionary definition of wound as meaning "to injure intentionally in such a way as to cut or tear the flesh". Windeyer J said at p 77: "The meaning of 'wounding' is well settled. Lord Lyndhurst in 1834 said that the 'definition of a wound in criminal cases is an injury to the person, by which the skin is broken. If the skin is broken, and there was a bleeding, that is a wound'" (*Moriarty v Brooks* (1834) 6 Car & P 684 at 686).' *Devine v R* (1982) 8 A Crim R 45 at 54–55, per Cosgrove J

New Zealand 'A breaking of the skin would be commonly regarded as a characteristic of a wound. The breaking of the skin will be normally evidenced by a flow of blood and, in its occurrence at the site of a blow or impact, the wound will more often than not be external. But there are those cases where the bleeding which evidences the separation of tissues may be internal. *Harman's* case and *Waltham's* case are illustrations of this. We do not understand the dictionary meaning of the term to exclude them.' *R v Waters* [1979] 1 NZLR 375 at 378, per cur.

WRECK *See also* SHIPWRECK

'Wreck' may be defined as property cast ashore within the ebb and flow of the tide after shipwreck; the property must be a ship, her cargo or a portion thereof. Jetsam, flotsam and lagan are not wreck at common law so long as they remain in or upon the sea, but if they are cast up on the shore they become wreck.

For the purposes of the provisions of the Merchant Shipping Act 1894 relating to wreck and salvage, however, the expression 'wreck' includes jetsam, flotsam, lagan and derelict found in or on the shores of the sea or any tidal water, unless the context otherwise requires. The intention of so extending the meaning of 'wreck' was evidently to bring under one term the rights which pertained to land and those which constituted droits of Admiralty. Fishing boats or fishing gear lost or abandoned at sea, and either found or taken possession of within the territorial waters of the United Kingdom or found or taken possession of beyond those waters and brought within those waters are treated as 'wreck' within the meaning of the above definition.

In relation to certain provisions of the Merchant Shipping Act 1894, the Merchant Shipping Act 1906, the Maritime Conventions Act 1911, the Merchant Shipping (Safety and Load Line Conventions) Act 1932, the Crown Proceedings Act 1947, and to the Merchant Shipping (Navigational Warnings) Rules 1980, and the Merchant Shipping (Signals of Distress) Rules 1977, 'wreck' includes any hovercraft or any part of it or its cargo found sunk, stranded or abandoned in or on any navigable water, or on or over the foreshore , or place where the tide normally ebbs or flows.

In the application of the provisions relating to wreck and salvage to aircraft, 'wreck' includes, subject to certain savings, any aircraft or any part of it or its cargo found derelict in or upon the seas surrounding the United Kingdom or its tidal waters or any ports or harbours of the United Kingdom, or upon or near the shores of those seas and waters, or found or taken possession of outside the United Kingdom and those seas and tidal waters and subsequently brought within those limits. (43 Halsbury's Laws (4th edn) para 1008)

'Wreck' may be defined as property cast ashore within the ebb and flow of the tide after shipwreck; *wreccum maris significat illa bona quae naufragio ad terram appelluntur. (Sir Henry Constable's Case* (1601) 5 Co Rep 106*a*)

'It may here be necessary to refer to some authorities in order to ascertain what is legally meant by "wreck of the sea", or "shipwreck". "It is to be observed," says Blackstone, "that in order to constitute a legal wreck, the goods must come to land; if they continue at sea, the law distinguishes them by the uncouth appellations of jetsam, flotsam, and lagan. These three are, therefore, accounted so far a distinct thing from the former, that by the King's grant to a man of wrecks, things jetsam, flotsam, and lagan will not pass" [Bl Com Vol 1, 290, 292]. In the 2nd Inst [p 167], "wreck, or shipwreck, legally '*wreccum maris*' wreck of the sea, in legal understanding, is applied to such goods as after shipwreck, are by the sea cast upon the land." And Blackstone also says:—"shipwrecks are declared to be the king's property by the Prerogative Stat 17 Ed II; c 13(c), and were so long before at the common law: and in *Sir Henry Constable's Case* [supra] the distinctions between *wreccum maris*, flotsam, jetsam and lagan are explained.' *R v Forty Nine Casks of Brandy* (1836) 3 Hag Adm 257 at 277, 278, per Sir John Nicholl

'The first question is, whether the hogsheads, etc, of tobacco upon the 14th of August were foreign goods derelict, jetsam, flotsam, or wreck, within the meaning of [Stat (1833)] 3 & 4 Will 4, c 52, s 50 (repealed; see now the Merchant Shipping Act 1894, s 510). . . . I admit that there may be a wreck of goods separate from a wreck of the ship; and in an old case, *Sheppard v Gosnold* [(1673) Vaugh 159], it is laid down that goods wrecked pay no custom; but the question is, what is a wreck within the meaning of this statute. The words used in the statute are "derelict", that is, abandoned by the owners; "jetsam", voluntarily cast overboard; "flotsam", goods floating on the waves, and "wreck". Looking at the words which are in conjunction with that word I can only understand by it goods brought on shore by the force of the waves. So far from this having been the case the goods were in the ship whole. The ship remained entire, and the crew only deserted her for about four hours. These goods cannot, therefore, be considered as wreck.' *Legge v Boyd* (1845) 14 LJCP 138 at 141, per Tindal CJ

'We must give to the words found in this Act [Merchant Shipping Act 1854 (repealed; see now the Merchant Shipping Act 1894, s 510)], their ordinary interpretation. Wreck, in many parts of England, belongs to the lords of manors. But in order to constitute a legal wreck the goods must come to land; if they continue at sea the law distinguishes them as jetsam, flotsam or lagan.' *Palmer v Rouse* (1858) 3 H & N 505 at 510, per Watson B

'In this case, whilst ship and cargo were in danger, the plaintiffs saved the lives of fifteen persons, some of whom were of the crew of the ship, and others were passengers on board her. But after such lives were saved, the ship and cargo sunk in deep water, and all who had at any time tried to save ship and cargo abandoned any further attempt to do so. Sometime afterwards, the defendants who were owners of a part of the sunken cargo, which was valuable specie, engaged a staff of divers and workmen, and at great expense raised and recovered four barrels of such specie of the value of £40,000. . . . Let us consider whether this specie was when it was raised from the bottom of the sea "wreck", even within the extended meaning given to the term by the statute 17 & 18 Vict, c 104, s 2 [Merchant Shipping Act 1854 (repealed; see supra)]: "Wreck shall include jetsam, flotsam, lagan and derelict found in or on the shores of the sea or any tidal water." It was not "wreck" in the common law meaning of the word. "Nothing shall be said *wreccum maris* but such goods only which are cast or left on the land by the sea" *Sir Henry Constable's Case* [supra]. The case goes on to say "Flotsam, is when a ship is sunk or otherwise perished, and the goods float on the sea. Jetsam, is when the ship is in danger of being sunk, and to lighten the ship the goods are cast into the sea, and, afterwards, notwithstanding, the ship perish. Lagan (*vel potius* ligan) is when the goods are so cast into the sea, and afterwards the ship perishes, and such goods cast are so heavy that they sink to the bottom, and the mariners, to the intent to have them again, tie to them a buoy or cork, or such other thing that will not sink, so that they may find them again." This specie never was within any of those definitions, and even if it were, would be taken out of them by the fact of its being in the possession of the owner before it was or would be taken possession of by any one else. . . . This specie was once "derelict" but ceased to be so the moment the true owners of it resumed the exercise of their rights of ownership and began to endeavour to recover it, whilst no one else was endeavouring to save it. This specie was, therefore, in my opinion not "wreck" within the meaning of the statute at the time when it was recovered by its owners.' *The Schiller (Cargo Ex)* (1877) 2 PD 145 at 147, 148, CA, per Brett LJ

'The question is, whether this is loss or damage through collision with a sunken wreck or sunken wrecks. It is said on the defendant's side, that it is nothing more than a taking of the ground, and that the ground was unfortunately harder underneath than it ought to be, owing to some submerged wreckage. I do not so regard the facts. The *Munroe* seems to me to have run on to a sunken wreck, and there remained fast until the damage was done by the wreck, and afterwards by the iron ore. . . . The conclusion to which I have come is that this was "loss or damage through collision with sunken wreck", or wrecks within the meaning of the clause which affects this insurance; and that the whole of the damage is covered thereby.' *The Munroe* [1893] P 248 at 253, per Gorrell Barnes J

'In my view "wreck" means such disaster caused by collision with some external object, be it stationary, such as a rock, or moving, as, e.g. another ship or some substance floating in the waves, as destroys her character as a ship, and reduces her practically to the condition, which speaking from memory, I think has been judicially described in the case of a wooden ship as a "congeries of planks". I think that this is what would be ordinarily understood. If one turns to the dictionaries, I find Webster (New International Dictionary) describes "wreck" as "that which has been wrecked or is in a state of ruin; the remains of anything ruined or fatally injured". Johnson describes "wreck" as "destruction by being driven on rocks or shallows at sea; destruction by sea", and the verb "to wreck" as "to destroy by dashing on rocks or sands". Of course neither ordinary parlance nor dictionary is conclusive where we have to construe a word in a particular context.' *The Olympic* [1913] P 92 at 115, 116, CA, per Kennedy LJ

'The word "wreck" is obviously a word of the most vague and general connotation. In the language of the literature of adventure, and possibly also for some legal purposes, it may well be that the wreck of a vessel means, as Kennedy LJ said in his dissenting judgment in *The Olympic* [supra], "such disaster caused by collision with some external object, be it stationary, such as a rock, or moving, as, e.g. another ship or some substance floating in the waves, as destroys her character as a ship, and reduces her practically to the condition which, speaking from memory, I think has been judicially described in the case of a wooden ship as a 'congeries of planks'." . . . It is well to bear in mind what Buckley LJ points out in *The Olympic*, that for the present purpose we have not "to inquire whether the ship was a wreck, that is to say, whether she had become a certain physical thing, but . . . whether she had been so injured and damaged that she ceased to be a ship of service for the purposes of the adventure, the subject of the seaman's contract".' *Barras v Aberdeen Steam Trawling & Fishing Co Ltd* [1933] AC 402 at 443–446, per Lord Macmillan

WRIT

'The main difference between a writ of summons and an originating summons is, that in the one case the proceedings are in Court, and there are or may be pleadings, whereas in the other case the proceedings are in Chambers, and there are no pleadings.' *Re Busfield, Whaley v Busfield* (1886) 32 Ch D 123 at 126, CA, per Chitty J

Australia 'The Service and Execution of Process Act 1901–1986 (Cth), by reason of the definitions of "writ of summons" and "suit" in s 3, authorises, by s 4, the issue out of this Court of an originating summons for service on a defendant in any other State.' *Re Boyd, Woods v Boyd* [1927] VLR 132 at 133, per Mann J

WRIT OF ASSISTANCE *See* ASSISTANCE

WRITING

Writing includes print; and words referring to any instrument, copy, extract, abstract, or other document include any such instrument, copy, extract, abstract, or other document being in writing or in print, or partly in writing and partly in print. (Conveyancing Act 1881, s 2)

'Writing' includes typing, printing, lithography, photography, and other modes of representing or reproducing words in a visible form, and expressions referring to writing are construed accordingly. (Interpretation Act 1978, Sch 1)

'Writing' includes any form of notation or code, whether by hand or otherwise and regardless of the method by which, or medium on which, it is recorded, and 'written' shall be construed accordingly. (Copyright, Designs and Patents Act 1988, s 178)

'The words of the Act of Parliament [Stat (1709) 8 Ann c 21 (repealed)] are very large: "books and other writings". . . . We are of opinion, that a musical composition is a writing within the statute of the 8th of Queen Anne, intitled an act for the encouragement of learning, by vesting the copies of printed books in the authors or purchasers of such copies, during the times therein mentioned.' *Bach v Longman* (1777) 2 Cowp 623 at 624, per Lord Mansfield

WRONG

'In my opinion of the court, there is no doubt that the word "wrong" in the M'Naghten rules means contrary to law and does not have some vague meaning which may vary according to the opinion of the different persons whether a particular act might or might not be justified.' *R v Windle* [1952] 2 All ER 1 at 3, CCA, per cur. (also reported in [1952] 2 QB 826 at 834)

WRONGDOER *See* DEFAULT

WRONGFUL ACT OR DEFAULT

'Section 66 [of the Merchant Shipping Act 1906] clearly contemplates findings of default against persons who are not certified officers, and the power to impose the penalties mentioned on those who are affords no sound ground for restricting the expression "wrongful act or default" to conduct which ought to be punished. The ordinary, natural meaning of the words holds nothing to suggst such a limited interpretation. In my opinion neither the policy nor the text of the legislation calls for any modification of that meaning and I therefore conclude that the proper connotation of "wrongful act or default" is a breach of legal duty of any degree which causes or contributes to the casualty under investigation.' *The Princess Victoria* [1954] NI 178 at 178, per Lord MacDermott LCJ

Australia 'In my opinion, the language of the Act [i.e. Lord Campbell's Act] is capable of being applied to the case of death resulting from breach of contract. The words are very general. "Wrongful act" is a term which in a perfectly natural meaning can be applied to breaches of contract as well as to torts.' *Woolworths Ltd v Crotty* (1942) 66 CLR 603 at 619, per Latham CJ

WRONGFUL EXECUTION *See* EXECUTION

WRONGFUL INTERFERENCE *See* INTERFERENCE

Y

YARD

[The Vagrancy Act 1824, s 4, enacts that every person found in . . . any 'yard', garden or area for any unlawful purpose shall be guilty of an offence.] 'Counsel for the appellants has suggested, in his submissions to us, the essential feature—if that is the right definition—of a yard is that it would be a relatively small area and that it should be contiguous to, or attached to, or used for purposes ancillary to those of a building. In other words, it is an area ancillary to a building and a small area at that. That view of the matter is, I think fully supported by authority.' *Quatromini v Peck* [1972] 3 All ER 521 at 524, per Lord Widgery CJ

YEAR *See also* FINANCIAL YEAR; HALF-YEAR; UNDERWRITER

The term 'year', besides denoting the solar year of the calendar, may also mean any like period time running from a date arbitrarily fixed by statute, contract or otherwise.

'Financial year', when used in any Act of Parliament passed after 1889, with reference to the Consolidated Fund or the National Loans Fund, or money provided by Parliament, or to the Exchequer or to taxes or finance, means, unless the contrary intention appears, the twelve calendar months ending on 31st March. It is with reference to the year so computed that the public accounts are made up, the budget is prepared, and the supplies are voted.

The accounts of local and other authorities which are subject to audit must be made up yearly to 31st March or to such other date as the Secretary of State may direct.

For the purposes of assessment to income tax in England the year is defined as running from 6th April to the following 5th April.

For social security purposes 'benefit year' is accorded a special meaning.

By the terms of a contract any date may be fixed for the beginning of a year, and, in the absence of any express definition of the term, it may appear from the contract that a period beginning or not beginning on 1st January, as the case may be, was intended.

The expressions 'in any one year' or 'in each year' may refer to the calendar year or to any period of twelve calendar months, according to the context in which the expression is used.

The term 'in any one year' may even be used to denote a season or part of a year. (45 Halsbury's Laws (4th edn) paras 1103–1105)

'Year' means any period of twelve months. (Opencast Coal Act 1958, s 51(1))

'The year 1988–89' means the year of assessment beginning on 6th April 1988, and any corresponding expression in which two years are similarly mentioned means the year of assessment beginning on 6th April in the first-mentioned of these two years. (Income and Corporation Taxes Act 1988, s 832(1))

'In those years which consist of 366 days, a hiring and service for a year must be for that same number of days; in like manner as when the year has 365 days, it must have continuance during that number.' *R v Worminghall (Inhabitants)* (1817) 6 M & S 350 at 351, per Lord Ellenborough CJ

'When a leap year occurs a year must be understood to mean 366 days.' *R v Roxley (Inhabitants)* (1829) 5 Man & Ry KB 40 at 43, per Lord Tenterden CJ

'Wherever the words used have, by usage or local custom, a peculiar meaning that meaning may be shown by parol evidence. Here the contract is, that the plaintiff is to be paid, for three years, a salary of £5, £6, and £7, per week in those years. That means, according to the evidence and the finding of the jury, that she is to be paid so much per week during every week that the theatre is open in those years.' *Grant v Maddox* (1846) 15 M & W 737 at 745, per Alderson B

'Article 81 [of the articles of association of a company] does not give remuneration at the rate of £5,000 a year, but only provides that the board shall be entitled to receive by way of remuneration in each year £5,000. I see no ground for extending this language, or for holding that any remuneration can be claimed except for a complete year.' *Salton v New*

Beeston Cycle Co [1899] 1 Ch 775 at 779, 780, per Cozens-Hardy J

New Zealand [A dairyman agreed to take from a farmer 30 gallons of milk a day all the year round.] 'What is the meaning of the phrase "all the year round"? It was contended that there were four possible meanings of the contract—(a) it might mean a supply for one year certain; (b) it might mean for one year at least and until thereafter determined by a reasonable notice; (c) it might mean for one year and so on from year to year; (d) it might mean a contract determinable at will. The contract is, in my opinion, so indefinite that it is impossible to determine with any degree of certainty what it means. . . . In my opinion . . . it was not a contract for a year certain: it was, if it can be construed to have a definite meaning, a continuing contract for a year or more.' *Duff v Kyle* (1901) 20 NZLR 706 at 713, 715, per Stout CJ; also reported 4 GLR 84 at 86, 87

YEAR'S WAGES

'In speaking of a year's wages, the testator plainly used that expression with reference to family servants, usually hired by the year.' *Booth v Dean* (1833) 1 My & K 560 at 560, per Leach MR

'Where a testator gives a year's wages, he must, I think, be understood to mean, that he gives to those whom he has hired at yearly wages. . . . To impute to the testator that he intended, by a year's wages, the aggregate of the wages of fifty-two weeks, would, I think be a most unreasonable and strained construction of the words which he has used.' *Blackwell v Pennant* (1852) 9 Hare 551 at 554, per Turner V-C

YEARLY *See* ANNUAL

YEARLY SUM

Clear *See* CLEAR

YOUNG PERSON

'Young person' means a person who has ceased to be a child and who is under the age of eighteen years. (Employment of Women, Young Persons, and Children Act 1920, s 4)

'Young person' means a person who has attained the age of fourteen years and is under the age of seventeen years. (Children and Young Persons Act 1933, s 107(1))

'Young person' means a person over compulsory school age who has not attained the age of eighteen years. (Education Act 1944, s 114(1))

'Young persons' means a person who is over compulsory school age for the purposes of the Education Act 1944, but has not attained the age of eighteen. (Agriculture (Safety, Health and Welfare Provisions) Act 1956, s 24)

'Young person' means a person who has ceased to be a child but has not attained the age of eighteen. (Factories Act 1961, s 176)

In this section [which prohibits betting transactions, etc, with young persons] the expression, 'young person', means a person—

(a) who is under the age of eighteen years whom the person commmitting an offence in relation to him under this section knows, or ought to know, to be under that age; or
(b) who is apparently under the said age:

Provided that in the case of any proceedings under this section for an offence in respect of a person apparently under the said age, it shall be a defence to prove that at the time of the alleged offence he had in fact attained that age. (Betting, Gaming and Lotteries Act 1963, s 21)

'Young person' means a person has attained the age of fourteen and is under the age of seventeen. (Children and Young Persons Act 1969, s 70(1))

YOUNGER CHILDREN

'The question is whether the gift in favour of the testator's "younger children" naming them, operated to give the son Edward a share. . . . Then come these words, "and so that the share or interest of each of them, my said younger children, shall be absolutely vested at his or her age of twenty-one years". . . . Now, looking at those words, it seems to me impossible to say that Edward did not take an absolute vested interest at the time when he attained twenty-one. At that time, beyond all question, he was a "younger child" in every sense of the words, because he had an elder brother then living.' *Re Prytherch, Prytherch v Williams* (1889) 42 Ch D 590 at 594, per North J

Z

ZINC WORKS

Works in which, by the application of heat, zinc is extracted from the ore, or from any residue containing that metal. (Alkali etc, Works Regulation Act 1906, Sch, para 21)

ZOO

In this Act 'zoo' means an establishment where wild animals . . . are kept for exhibition to the public otherwise than for purposes of a circus . . . and otherwise than in a pet shop. (Zoo Licensing Act 1981, s 1(2))